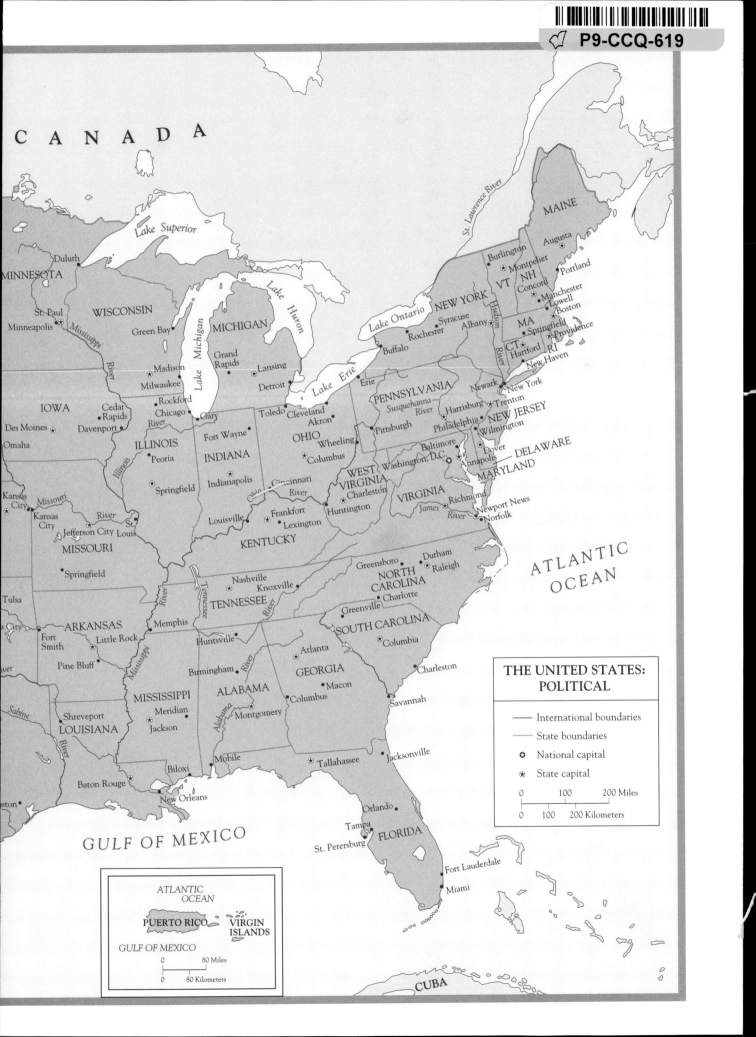

CANADA

Lake Superior

MINNESOTA
Duluth

St-Paul
Minneapolis
Mississippi River

WISCONSIN

Green Bay

Madison
Milwaukee

Lake Michigan

MICHIGAN

Grand Rapids

Lansing

Lake Huron

Detroit

Lake Ontario

Rochester

Buffalo

Lake Erie

Erie

St. Lawrence River

MAINE

Augusta

Burlington
Montpelier
VT NH
Concord

Portland

NEW YORK

Syracuse
Albany

Manchester
Lowell
Boston

MA
Springfield
Providence

Hudson River

CT
Hartford

RI

New Haven

IOWA
Des Moines
Omaha

Cedar Rapids
Davenport

Rockford
Chicago
Gary

ILLINOIS

Peoria

Illinois River

INDIANA

Fort Wayne

Toledo
Cleveland
Akron

OHIO

Wheeling

Columbus

PENNSYLVANIA

Susquehanna River

Pittsburgh

Harrisburg

Philadelphia

Newark
New York

Trenton

NEW JERSEY

Wilmington

DELAWARE

Springfield

Indianapolis

Louisville

Ohio River
Cincinnati
River

Frankfort
Lexington

WEST VIRGINIA

Charleston

Huntington

Baltimore
Washington, D.C.
Annapolis

Dover

MARYLAND

Kansas City
Kansas City

Missouri River

Jefferson City
St. Louis

MISSOURI

Springfield

KENTUCKY

VIRGINIA

Richmond

James River

Newport News
Norfolk

ATLANTIC
OCEAN

Nashville
Knoxville

TENNESSEE

Tennessee River

Greensboro

Durham
Raleigh

NORTH CAROLINA

Charlotte

Tulsa

River

ARKANSAS

Memphis

Greenville

SOUTH CAROLINA

a City
Fort Smith

Little Rock

Pine Bluff

Huntsville

Birmingham

Alabama River

Atlanta

GEORGIA

Macon

Columbus

Columbia

Charleston

Savannah

THE UNITED STATES:
POLITICAL

—— International boundaries

—— State boundaries

⊕ National capital

✳ State capital

0   100   200 Miles

0   100   200 Kilometers

Sabine River

LOUISIANA

Shreveport

MISSISSIPPI

Jackson

Meridian

ALABAMA

Montgomery

Mobile

Biloxi

Baton Rouge

New Orleans

ston

Tallahassee

Jacksonville

GULF OF MEXICO

Orlando

Tampa
St. Petersburg

FLORIDA

Fort Lauderdale

Miami

ATLANTIC
OCEAN

PUERTO RICO

VIRGIN ISLANDS

GULF OF MEXICO

0   80 Miles

0   80 Kilometers

CUBA

www.wadsworth.com

www.wadsworth.com is the World Wide Web site for Wadsworth and is your direct source to dozens of online resources.

At *www.wadsworth.com* you can find out about supplements, demonstration software, and student resources. You can also send email to many of our authors and preview new publications and exciting new technologies.

www.wadsworth.com
Changing the way the world learns.®

Free study resources for your American History course—*available online!*

Primary source documents, video and audio clips, activities, and self-quizzing—all FREE to you when you purchase this text!

American Journey Online

http://ajaccess.wadsworth.com

FREE access with every new copy of the text!

American Journey Online comprises 16 primary source collections that capture the landmark events and major themes of the American experience—through images and the words of those who lived it. Discover hundreds of rare documents, pictures, and archival audio and video, along with essays, headnotes, and captions that set the sources in context. Full-text searchability and extensive hyperlinking make searching and cross-referencing easy.

Also Available:
American Journey Online User's Guide with Activities
This helpful resource is available on the home page of **http://ajaccess.wadsworth.com** and at the Book Companion Web Site (**http://history.wadsworth. com/americanpast7e**).
It is also available as a print resource (ISBN 0-534-17433-7).

Book Companion Web Site

At the Wadsworth American History Resource Center

http://history.wadsworth.com/ americanpast7e

At the Book Companion Web Site for this text, you'll find a wide variety of study aids that will help you make the most of your course! These features include:
Chapter outlines and summaries • Tutorial quizzes • Flashcards • Glossary • Simulations—interactive, detailed accounts paired with critical thinking and multiple choice quizzes • **American Journey Online** activities and video exercises • An *At the Movies* feature that provides descriptions, critical thinking questions, and Web links for major films throughout American history • Crossword puzzles • The U.S. Image Bank, featuring images and maps that can be put into multimedia presentations • Interactive maps with questions • Primary sources • and much more!

To access the Book Companion Web Site, simply visit the URL listed above or click on "Student Book Companion Sites" at the Wadsworth History Resource Center home page (**http://history.wadsworth.com**). Click on your book cover, and you're there!

You can also find your Book Companion Site with the easy-to-use search feature, located in the top right hand corner of the American History Resource Center home page. Simply type in "Conlin," select "Book Companion Web Sites," and click on "Go."

THE AMERICAN PAST

A Survey of American History

SEVENTH EDITION

JOSEPH R. CONLIN

THOMSON

WADSWORTH

Australia • Canada • Mexico • Singapore • Spain • United Kingdom • United States

THOMSON
WADSWORTH

PUBLISHER: Clark Baxter
SENIOR DEVELOPMENT EDITOR: Margaret McAndrew Beasley
ASSISTANT EDITOR: Julie Yardley
EDITORIAL ASSISTANT: Eno Sarris
TECHNOLOGY PROJECT MANAGER: Jennifer Ellis
EXECUTIVE MARKETING MANAGER: Caroline Croley
MARKETING ASSISTANT: Mary Ho
ADVERTISING PROJECT MANAGER: Tami Strang
PROJECT MANAGER, EDITORIAL PRODUCTION: Kimberly Adams
PRINT/MEDIA BUYER: Doreen Suruki
PERMISSIONS EDITOR: Sarah Harkrader

PRODUCTION SERVICE: Orr Book Services
TEXT DESIGNER: Sue Hart
PHOTO RESEARCHER: Lili Weiner
COPY EDITOR: Mark Colucci
ILLUSTRATOR: ElectraGraphics, Inc.
COVER DESIGNER: Lisa Devenish
COVER IMAGE: *New Beginning,* circa 1915. Reprinted with permission from Hulton Archive/Getty Images.
COMPOSITOR: Thompson Type
PRINTER: Quebecor World/Versailles

For more information about our products, contact us at:
Thomson Learning Academic Resource Center
1-800-423-0563
For permission to use material from this text,
contact us by:
Phone: 1-800-730-2214
Fax: 1-800-730-2215
Web: http://www.thomsonrights.com

Library of Congress Control Number: 2003107884

Student Edition: ISBN 0-534-62136-8

Instructor's Edition: ISBN 0-534-62139-2

Wadsworth/Thomson Learning
10 Davis Drive
Belmont, CA 94002-3098
USA

Asia
Thomson Learning
5 Shenton Way #01-01
UIC Building
Singapore 068808

Australia/New Zealand
Thomson Learning
102 Dodds Street
Southbank, Victoria 3006
Australia

Canada
Nelson
1120 Birchmount Road
Toronto, Ontario M1K 5G4
Canada

Europe/Middle East/Africa
Thomson Learning
High Holborn House
50/51 Bedford Row
London WC1R 4LR
United Kingdom

Latin America
Thomson Learning
Seneca, 53
Colonia Polanco
11560 Mexico D.F.
Mexico

Spain/Portugal
Paraninfo
Calle/Magallanes, 25
28015 Madrid, Spain

To the Memory of
J.R.C. (1917–1985)
L.V.C. (1920–2001)

Brief Contents

Table of Contents

List of Maps

Preface

This image captures the joy with which "new immigrants," about 1900, entered New York harbor, dressed in their Sunday best, which they carefully kept neat and clean during their voyage—the men actually tipping their hats at the Statue of Liberty.

The seventh edition of *The American Past* is a newer book than any version since the first: a new publisher, a new look, a more thorough rewrite of the previous edition, and more new material. I doubt that there is a paragraph that has escaped at least a polishing. I have completely rewritten large sections of most of the chapters.

The seventh edition is a lot less hefty than the sixth or, for that matter, the fifth. For about a decade, I have seen survey textbooks, including *The American Past,* grow too big. Some seem more closely related to the unabridged dictionary sitting on a stand in a corner of the library than to the kind of book that students can carry with them in bags slung over their shoulders. An equally painful consequence of textbooks' runaway growth has been the runaway price tags on them. I trust the "streamlined" *American Past* will provide some budgetary as well as physical relief.

I have slimmed down the seventh edition by, first of all, eliminating pure ornament: the bells, whistles, fuss, feathers, and curlicues that are nice enough in a book but add heft and cost to it. We excised 50 pages simply by reducing chapter openers from two-page spreads to a single page. I have forsaken illustrations-for-the-sake-of-a-picture, a few maps that, upon reflection, were superfluous, and chronologies and charts so dense in data that not a student in a hundred is apt to look at them. Expanding the book's trim size has helped reduce the number of pages while maintaining an attractive layout.

I have not dropped a single subject essential to understanding how the United States and the American people got to be the way they are. Nor have I stripped down the treatment of ideas difficult to grasp so that they are inadequately explained. In fact, I have added discussions of topics new to this edition when new research seemed sufficiently basic and convincing to belong in a survey course textbook.

Nevertheless, the total length of the narrative, as well as the size of the book, has been reduced. This was possible because I subjected my prose to a closer and more rigorous editing than I did when revising previous editions. It was an interesting exercise: dismaying when I discovered how verbose I had been just a few years ago; an occasion of jubilation when I realized that while reducing the size of the book, I was also writing a clearer and livelier presentation of American history than I had in six previous tries. Setting aside great literature, there are few passages of prose in the English language that cannot be improved by deleting words. (I believe I have identified four words in the Gettysburg Address that Lincoln might have stricken had the train to Gettysburg been delayed for half an hour.)

My ambition for *The American Past* has, from the first, been to write a book not for research historians, or even for history majors, but for college freshmen and sophomores who intend to become accountants, ecologists, engineers, nurses, psychologists, retailers, webmasters, and zookeepers—students who may be "taking the survey" for reasons other than "history is my favorite subject." I believe that a sense of history—some knowledge of their past—makes such students, if not better accountants, ecologists, and so on, then better citizens and even fuller human beings.

Years at the front of lecture halls, however, taught me that few students can be persuaded that this is so; they must be seduced into it. That, I think, is best accomplished not with flash, dash, and gimmickry. A history textbook attempting to compete with glossy advertisements for SUVs, reality television, and video games is as foolish a venture as the history department softball nine demanding a franchise in the National League. Students have to be wooed to a love of history, or just an appreciation for it, by good lectures, intelligently guided classroom discussion, and a textbook they find enjoyable to read and, therefore, do read.

Narrative is the kind of prose most people find enjoyable to read. Nonspecialists are turned off by turgid explication, compartmentalization, and dissection of minutiae. So narrative is the way I do it. I incorporate into the "story" economic, diplomatic, technological, and other developments when they move the "plot" along, rather than stacking them up in disembodied blocks of information unrelated to the information in the blocks atop or below them. This is particularly important, I think, when working with the relatively recent research of historians of racial and ethnic minorities, gender, and the environment. To treat African Americans, Hispanics, postcontact Indians, women, and children as if they were not part of the flow of American history, but bystanders to be dealt with in another room, is to demean them posthumously—quite as insultingly as they were demeaned in other eras. A textbook is a peculiar sort of book, but a history textbook should be a *book,* not a cluttered collage of snippets.

During the more than two decades that *The American Past* has been in print, I have heard from many professors—perhaps close to 200—who have assigned the text to their classes. It has been gratifying that even some of the annoyed correspondents closed their letters with a comment something like

"My students really like *The American Past*. They actually read it!"

That has been the idea and remains the guiding principle behind the seventh edition.

NEW TO THE SEVENTH EDITION

Streamlined Text and Updated Research

The seventh edition narrative has been tightened, which has reduced the length of the text about 10 percent. And, throughout, I have woven into the story pertinent material from my reading of recent scholarship.

New Map Captions

For the first time, I have written explanatory captions for the maps—"pointers" to help readers locate the significant features of each map. I have added some new maps where they would enhance a point in the text (see, for example, Chapter 20). In Chapter 51, there is a new multi-election electoral vote map that illustrates the significant party shift in presidential elections in the final decades of the twentieth century. I have also eliminated a few maps that seemed to add nothing to the narrative (for example, electoral vote maps of landslide victories when there was no sectional pattern of voting).

Illustrations

Many illustrations are new with this edition. I have written new captions for all of them to make the historical significance clear and so that they serve a pedagogical purpose, rather than simply breaking up the type with a decoration.

"How They Lived" Features

I have written about 15 new "How They Lived" features, placing one in each chapter. In response to reviewer feedback, I have dropped the biographical boxes ("Notable People"), replacing them with new "How They Lived" features, which instructors say they find more useful. These features deal with "slices of life," mostly social history: for example, piracy (Chapter 6), road building (Chapter 14), a ward heeler's day (Chapter 26), smoking (Chapter 32), hobos and tramps (Chapter 35), fads and sensationalism (Chapter 40), drugs (Chapter 48), changing sexual mores (Chapter 49).

Sidebars

There are about a hundred new sidebars highlighting information that is too interesting (or amusing) to pass up but that, if related in the narrative, would interrupt the "conversational" flow of the book.

Revisions to Coverage

Topics that are new with the seventh edition, or those that I have expanded or altered my take on (almost always because of persuasive research I have read since the sixth edition), include fresh material about pre-Columbian Indians in Mesoamerica (Chapter 1) and precontact Indians in what is now the United States (Chapter 5). There is some new material on slave rebellions (Chapters 6 and 18) and rather a lot on family history and the role of gender relations in American development (Chapters 6, 10, 36, and 46). There is new material on Jefferson (Chapters 11 and 12), technology (Chapter 14), crime (Chapter 17), the illegal African slave trade (Chapter 19), and immigration and nativism (Chapters 22, 29, and 51). I have introduced information new to me in just about every chapter dealing with twentieth-century political history, particularly in Chapters 42, 43, 45, and, of course, the final chapters, some of which qualifies as news as well as history.

Evolving Interpretations

One's own historical politics changes over the years. If there existed a person who cared to read the chapters about the Jacksonians and the Whigs in all seven editions of *The American Past* (Chapters 14–16 in this edition), such a drone would discover that I have, albeit slowly, "crossed the aisle" from Andrew Jackson's benches to those of the Whigs. I am sitting there now, in this edition, perhaps closer to Henry Clay and the border state Whigs than to the New Englanders.

There are other eras in which, if my sympathies have not so radically changed, I have come to see both sides of the division with greater balance: colonial governors versus colonial assemblies (Chapters 6 and 7), Federalists versus Jeffersonians (Chapters 11 and 12), and agrarians versus business Republicans (Chapter 32). My assessment of the progressives is still in flux; in any case, I have looked at them differently in this edition (Chapters 34–36 and 38) than I did in the sixth.

A Note on Contemporary History

A comparable mellowing in writing about very recent history—about people and events of which I first read in the newspapers—is due not to a greater certainty, as in the instance of Jackson and the Whigs, but to a rampant uncertainty. I realize that I was dead wrong in some positions I took as a citizen and as a voter, but I am not yet convinced that the other side in those times was quite in the right.

As Margaret Beasley, my editor at Wadsworth Publishing, knows painfully well, I do not much like writing recent history precisely because of this lack of certainty and perspective. Still, in the final chapters, I have resisted the *World Almanac* technique of merely piling up names, facts, and dates—that would mean abandoning the liveliness of the first nine-tenths of the book. So the final few chapters of this edition are rewritten, drawing on previous editions only for phrasings I still like and insights I still think valid. If a reader of these chapters exclaims, "Wrong, wrong, wrong!" I can respond only, "You're probably right, right, right."

ACKNOWLEDGMENTS

I appreciate the comments and suggestions I've received from teaching historians who have read and critiqued chapters of the text:

George Alvergue, Lane Community College
Scott Carter, Shasta College
Richard H. Condon, University of Maine at Farmington
Stacy A. Cordery, Monmouth College
Linda Cross, Tyler Junior College
Barry A. Crouch, Gallaudet University
William Marvin Dulaney, College of Charleston
Carla Falkner, Northeast Mississippi Community College
George E. Frakes, Santa Barbara City College
Thomas M. Gaskin, Everett Community College
Joan E. Gittens, Southwest State University

John E. Hollitz, Community College of Southern Nevada
Robert R. Jones, University of Southwestern Louisiana
Martha Kirchmer, Grand Valley State University
Milton Madden, Lane Community College
Patricia L. Meador, Louisiana State University, Shreveport
Angelo Montante, Glendale Community College
Jack Oden, Enterprise State Junior College
Emmett Panzella, Point Park College
Richard H. Peterson, San Diego State University
Nancy L. Rachels, Hillsborough Community College
Michelle Riley, Del Mar College
William Scofield, Yakima Valley Community College
Richard S. Sorrell, Brookdale Community College
Ronald Story, University of Massachusetts
Daniel C. Vogt, Jackson State University
Loy Glenn Westfall, Hillsborough Brandon Community College
Donald W. Whisenhunt, Western Washington University
Lynn Willoughby, Winthrop University
Larry Wright, Inver Hills Community College

For helping me in the preparation of this revision, I must first name research librarian *ne plus ultra* Marilyn Grande Murphy. She does not answer queries more quickly than a silicon chip does, but she answers them better. Since I have been residing in "the sticks" for several years now, I have realized how important it was to me earlier in life to be able to walk to a good library in 15 minutes and browse the stacks. Now, when the phone lines are working, the Internet is a godsend, but it is not the same thing. I have also learned in recent years to appreciate that it was a very lucky day when I made the acquaintance of Ms. Murphy and she let me have her email address.

Lisa Devenish designed the covers for the three volumes in which *The American Past* is published, and created a first impression on which, indeed, I would not mind the book being judged.

Margaret McAndrew Beasley was the developmental editor for the seventh edition, as she was for the sixth. Once again, she managed me in my most irritable and frustrated moments with a cool, good-humored virtuosity that, when I reflect on it, was dazzling. Perhaps I could have done better; I doubt it.

I am also grateful to Clark Baxter, publisher for history; Kim Adams, production project manager; John Orr, freelance project editor; Lili Weiner, freelance photo researcher; Caroline Croley, executive marketing manager; and the Wadsworth sales team—all for their respective roles in the process of delivering *The American Past* to you.

DISCOVERIES

*Indians, Europeans, and America
15,000 B.C.– A.D. 1550*

*I feel a wonderful exultation of spirits when I converse
with intelligent men who have returned from these
regions. It is like an accession of wealth to a miser. Our
minds, soiled and debased by the common concerns of life
and the vices of society, become elevated and ameliorated
by contemplating such glorious events.*

Peter Martyr

*Broken spears lie in the roads;
We have torn our hair in our grief.
The houses are roofless now,
And their walls are red with blood. . . .
We are crushed to the ground;
We lie in ruins.
There is nothing but grief and suffering
in Mexico and Tlateloco.*

Anonymous Aztec poet

HUMANITY ORIGINATED IN East Africa. From there, people migrated south, west, and north, colonizing Africa, Asia, and Europe—but not the Americas for a geological epoch. Even isolated Australia was populated 20,000 years before a human footprint was impressed in American mud.

The date of the first discovery of America is disputed, but it was likely about 15,000 years ago, when Asian hunters crossed from Siberia to what is now Alaska. They walked, which is impossible today, when 56 miles of frigid sea—the Bering Strait—separate Asia and America. Fifteen thousand years ago, however, the earth was locked in an ice age. Temperatures everywhere were far lower than they are today. Much of the earth's water was frozen in the polar ice caps and in glaciers larger than our nations. Consequently, sea level was about 400 feet lower than it is today. Our beaches were inland, miles from the surf. Vast tracts of sea bottom today were dry, including the floor of the Bering Strait, now 180 feet below the surface. A rather high "land bridge," a hundred miles wide, connected Siberia and Alaska. This was the route traveled by the first discoverers of America.

They did not know they were discovering a "new world." They were nomads checking out the territory, as nomads do, or chasing dinner—herds of caribou?—or fleeing enemies. In as few as a thousand years, however, waves of these immigrants colonized two continents, advancing their frontier, on average, a mile a month. They were the ancestors of the people we call "Indians" or "Native Americans."

THE FIRST COLONIZATION

The Paleo-Indians (*old* Indians) were a *pre*historic people, and so their story is beyond the compass of historians. Historians study the past in the written words the people of the past have left us. They can tell us nothing of human beings who lived, loved, begat, hated, and died before there was writing. To know about *pre*historic (preliterate) people, we must turn to archaeologists, linguists, and folklorists, scholars who sift particles of information, like gold dust, from the gravel of artifacts—things human beings made—from the structure of language, and from tales passed by word of mouth from one generation to the next.

The pictures these men and women sketch are fuzzier than the portraits historians can draw from their written documents. As a Chinese saying has it, "The palest ink is clearer than the best memory." Still, faint is better than blank. Without folklore and analysis of language, oral tradition, and artifacts, the American past would not begin until A.D. 1492, a bit more than 500 years ago. It was then that Europeans, who scribbled endlessly of their achievements, follies, and sins, discovered the Western Hemisphere for themselves, inundating it with their numbers. Thanks to archaeology, linguistics, and folklore, we can pencil in a more ancient heritage.

Diversity

The Paleo-Indians knew no more of agriculture than of alphabets. When they crossed to America, there was not a farmer on the planet. Like all people of their day, the first Americans lived by hunting, fishing, and gathering. They took from nature the makings of their meals and clothing, their shelter, tools, and weapons. They were nomads because there was no alternative to wandering. In all but the lushest environments, even small communities soon exhaust the food that can be hunted and gathered near a fixed abode. Home was where the food was.

By the time the mystery of agriculture was first unlocked in the Middle East about 8,000 B.C., the Paleo-Indians had lost contact with the Eurasian landmass. A global warming 2,000–3,000 years earlier melted the massive glaciers of the Ice Age and reduced the size of the polar ice caps. Sea level rose, drowning the land bridge between Siberia and Alaska.

Paleo-Indian ways of life diversified rapidly. The Americas were uncrowded, and wandering tribes found it easy to split up when their numbers grew too large for the range or when chiefs had a falling out. Soon enough, the vastness of America and the diversity of its climates and land forms isolated the scattered Paleo-Indians from one another, resulting in a dizzying variety of cultures.

Indian languages, for example, once just a handful, multiplied until there were at least 500 of them. Tribes living in harsh environments continued to survive precariously into historic times on what they could hunt, snare, net, gather, and grub. Other Indians learned to farm, producing the surplus of food that, as in the Middle East, India, and China, made the emergence of civilization possible. The Native Americans who learned to *produce* food, rather than depending on nature to provide it, lived in Mesoamerica (meaning "between the Americas": that is, Mexico and Central America) and in Peru.

Some Indians had mastered only primitive tool making when, after 1500, they were dazzled (and crushed) by European technology. Others perfected handcraft to a level of refinement unattained in Africa, Asia, or Europe.

Some Native Americans left no more mark on the land than the remains of campfires and garbage dumps that we need space-age technology in order to identify. By contrast, the labor force of the "Mound Builders" of central North America was sufficiently large and disciplined that they heaped up massive earthen structures that have survived the ages. One great mound, in the shape of a bird, was 70 feet in height, an edifice as impressive and durable as a Mesopotamian ziggurat. In Ohio, two parallel Mound Builder "walls" ran 60 miles from Chillicothe to Newark. Some scholars believe that Cahokia, in Illinois across the Mississippi from St. Louis, had a population of 30,000.

The Indians' closeness to nature made them canny in lore based on observation and on trial and error. For example, the effects of more than 200 natural medicines in use today were known in prehistoric America. Given the isolation of the Indians from the process of cultural diffusion—the ongoing exchange of ideas and techniques—in the "Old

Did Paleo-Indians Wipe Out the Mastodons?
Mastodons, hairy elephants larger than today's, once flourished in North America. They became extinct a few thousand years after the first discovery of America. Did the Paleo-Indians destroy them? They did hunt mastodons; spear points have been found in fossilized mastodon skeletons. Elsewhere in the world, Stone Age people destroyed species: saber-toothed tigers in Europe, any number of brightly plumed birds in New Zealand. Zoologists point out that if hunters kill only slightly more of a species than are born each year, the species will disappear in a few centuries. With single births after a long gestation period, mastodons may well have been one of the earliest species to be wiped out by human beings.

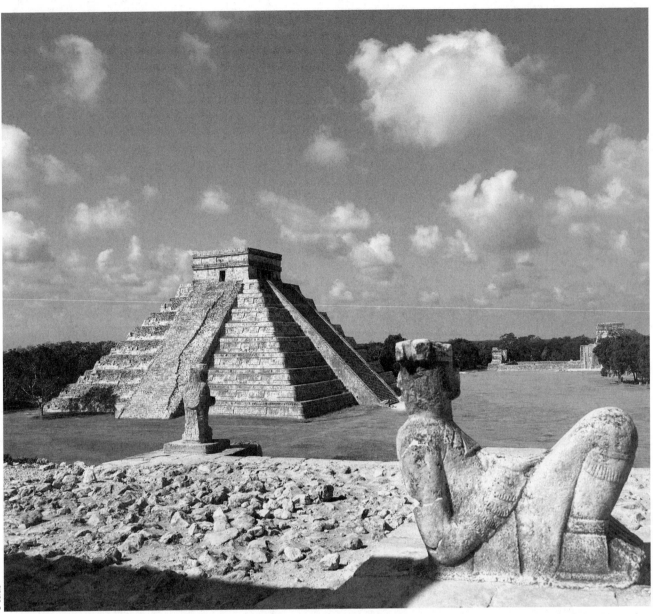

▲ *The Mayans, and the Aztecs after them, built many-storied pyramids of heaped earth faced with stone, quite as formidable as the ziggurats of Mesopotamia. They were symbols of power, and many were used as temples where captives were sacrificed to the gods. Some anthropologists believe that the "Mound Builders" of the American Midwest were recalling Mesoamerican pyramids in building their heaped earth monuments.*

World" of Asia, Africa, and Europe, the first Americans' achievements, in so short a time, are astonishing.

Mesoamerican Civilization

In Guatemala, Belize, and southern Mexico, Indians made the intellectual leap that signals the birth of civilization. Olmecs, Toltecs, and Mayans farmed so productively that they supported a populous and highly organized society in which many individuals could work at tasks other than farming. Just as the ancient civilizations of Asia did, the Mesoamericans developed a system of writing with which they carved records in stone and composed "books" on processed strips of cactus fiber similar to the papyrus of ancient Egypt.

Alas for historians, after 1500 a zealous Spanish bishop condemned these writings as "superstition and lies of the devil." So effective was his command they be burned that only three Mayan literary works survive. But inscribed rock proved too much for censors. Carved writings are abundant in Mesoamerica, and in recent decades, experts have learned to read them. They provide us with a chapter of American history long assumed to be lost.

At one time or another, some 40 cities dotted Mesoamerica. Several were home to 20,000 people. By A.D. 500, Teotihuacán, founded about the time of Christ near present-day Mexico City, was home to 125,000. These cities were governed by an aristocracy of priests and warriors who directed the construction, at the center of each city, of at least one pyramid-shaped earth-and-stone temple. The pyramid at Chichén Itzá rose 18 stories.

The Mayans were superb mathematicians and astronomers. They discovered the use of the zero, a breakthrough achieved in only one other world culture, India. They timed the earth's orbit around the sun as accurately as any other astronomers of their era and applied their findings to an accurate calendar.

War and Religion

The Mesoamerican rulers took little interest in the empire building that obsessed Old World elites. Each city-state was an independent entity with a limited hinterland. Not that the Mesoamericans were peaceable folk. Far from it. They were chronically fighting with their neighbors, for their religion compelled war. Their gods (jaguarlike beings, eagles, serpents, the sun) thirsted for human blood.

In solemn public rituals, noblewomen made symbolic blood sacrifice by drawing strings of thorns through punctures in their tongues. Their brothers and husbands drew the barbs through their foreskins. The blood that fell from their wounds was absorbed into strips of fiber that were burned, dispatching the sacrifice in smoke to the heavens.

But symbolic blood sacrifice was not enough for the Mesoamerican deities. They also demanded that priests throw young women into pits to die and that they drag other victims to the tops of the pyramids, where, using stone knives, the priests tore their hearts, still beating when the operation was correctly performed, from their breasts. Thus the chronic war: The Mesoamericans needed prisoners for sacrifice.

MAP 1:1 Mayan Civilization The Olmecs, among whom Mesoamerican civilization originated, lived in southern Mexico. The Mayans, who succeeded rather than displaced them, were centered to the east in present-day Yucatán, Guatemala, and Belize.

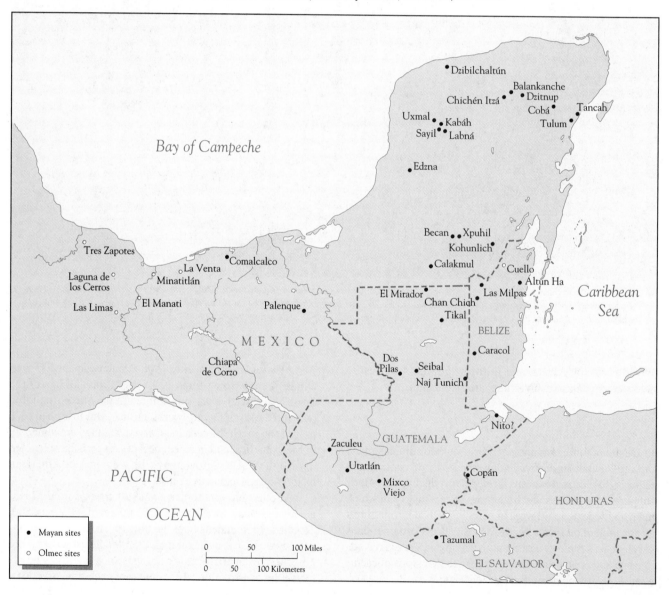

Locked in a Circle of Time

It is impossible to say how Mesoamerican civilization would have evolved had it not been destroyed by technologically superior Europeans. History is what happened, not what might have been. However, there are indications that, about 600 years before Cortés landed at Vera Cruz, Mesoamerican civilization went into a "stall," ceasing to "progress" in the Western sense of the word. One of the Mayans' greatest achievements, their complex system for marking the passing of time, may provide a clue as to why.

Mayan priests were excellent astronomers. Their solar calendar was close to perfect, counting 365 days in a year. Because there are no seasons in the tropics, however, and because even the rainy season in Mesoamerica was erratic and unpredictable, the solar year was of less interest to the Mayans than it was to makers of calendars elsewhere.

So the Mayans devised other calendars, some not yet understood. Two of these were tied into the solar year, and with one another, as the means of dating events. There was a 13-day cycle and another, called *tzolkin*, of 260 days: $20 \times 13 = 260$ (the basis of Mayan mathematics was 20 rather than 10). If one pictures the three cycles as cogs meshing with one another, a 13-cog

© Copyright The British Museum

wheel within a 260-cog wheel within a 365-cog wheel, no single alignment of cogs would be repeated for 18,980 days, or 52 solar years on the button.

The complexity of the calculation shows the sophistication of Mayan mathematics. However, the beauty of their cycles within cycles also locked the Mayan mind into a rigidly circular view of time. The Mayans seem to have believed that each day was a repetition of the day 52 years earlier, and 104 years and 156 years earlier. Each 5,200 years, they believed (introducing the factor of 10?), the universe was destroyed and created anew. Time passed, but there was no "progress"—just a return of things to where they had already been and would be again.

Such a worldview was ill adapted to cope with the unimaginably unexpected. Hurricanes worried the Mayans more because of their unpredictability than because of their destructiveness. How infinitely more troubling must it have been for their cultural heirs, the Aztecs, to learn of the arrival of huge seagoing canoes, white-skinned men with hairy faces, suits of iron, horses, and cannons blasting thunder and death from afar? Mesoamerica's cultural foundations may themselves have been a Spanish ally.

Cultural Cul-de-Sac?

Elsewhere in the world, city-states made war in order to conquer and then exploit their neighbors. Along with the misery they caused, the empires they built—Persia, Rome, China, Islam—advanced the march of civilization. However, the bloodlust of the Mesoamerican gods meant that the Mayans made war not to foster material and, consequently, cultural *progress* (a word unique to Western civilization), but to stand still. Mesoamerican genius and energies were devoted to rounding up people to kill so as to stay on the right side of the gods and avoid a fate worse than that with which they contended when heaven was in a good mood.

Conservatism was not good to the Mayans. By 1500, most of their cities were abandoned. The Spaniards who swooped down on Mesoamerica found the great pyramids smothered in tropical vegetation. Most of those they conquered, including the Mayans, lived in small villages. The Mesoamericans visited the ruins of the once great cities only for religious functions.

What happened? Some scholars think that the Mesoamericans warred themselves into collapse. They point to the massive stone heads the Olmecs sculpted and then buried, as if to hide them from enemies. Others think that the Mesoamerican cities were rendered unlivable by soil depletion. In order to support a large urban population, farmers must produce a large surplus of food. But the soil of the tropical forest is easily exhausted by intense cultivation. Whatever the explanation, by 1500, Mesoamerican civilization was thriving only to the northwest of the Mayan heartland, in the valley of Mexico—the land of the Aztecs.

The Aztecs

The Aztecs (who called themselves the "Mexica") were newcomers in Mesoamerica, emigrating from the north during the 1200s. Their culture then was primitive compared to that of the Toltecs, who had brought civilization to Mexico. However, like the Turks who overran the Arab world and the Manchus who made China their own, the Aztecs recognized

MAP 1:2 Mexico Under the Aztecs, 1519 The sway of the Aztecs–their tributary states–extended to both coasts of Mexico.

a better way of living when they conquered one. Carving out an enclave on the shores of Lake Texcoco about 1325, they embraced Mesoamerican civilization.

Within a century, the Aztecs dominated Mexico. They directly governed few other peoples. By 1500, however, tribute—"protection money," insurance against attack—in the form of grain, cloth, lumber, skins, feathers, and gold, rolled in from as far away as the Pacific and Gulf coasts. The Aztecs put this wealth to work, building one of the world's most splendid cities, Tenochtitlán. By 1500, it covered six square miles and was home to 200,000. One plaza, the site of a market, accommodated 50,000 sellers and buyers. Surrounded by Lake Texcoco, the Aztec capital was superbly defended. Only three narrow causeways, broken here and there by drawbridges, connected Tenochtitlán to the mainland, where other peoples dwelled. Thirty-foot granite walls could not have made a city more secure.

Blood and Gore

The greatest temple in Tenochtitlán was a pyramid with a base 200 feet square. Two dizzyingly steep staircases climbed to altars 200 feet above the street. The steps were stained black with dried blood, for the Aztecs too practiced human sacrifice. Indeed, Huitzilopochtli, a god who accompanied the Aztecs from the north, demanded 10,000 hearts in an ordinary year. In 1478, a year Huitzilopochtli was more agitated than usual, priests in cloaks of human skin and stinking of gore (they were forbidden to wash or to cut their hair) sent 20,000 volunteers and captives to their doom in four days. The emperor Ahuitzotl, so it was said, slaughtered 80,000 to dedicate a new temple. (Such astronomical fig-

ures are difficult to credit; but the point of the Aztec chroniclers who claimed them is clear enough.)

Bad years afflicted the Aztecs all too often during the late 1400s and early 1500s. Their calendar, inherited from the Mayans, implied that a catastrophe was in the works. Omens of all sorts, from natural calamities to female spirits wailing in the streets, had nerves on edge. No one was more anxious than the emperor Moctezuma II, whose reign began in 1502. It has been suggested that, psychologically, he and the Aztecs were ready prey for enemies who devoted their resources not just to staying on the right side of their gods, but to exploiting the new and the strange wherever they found it.

EUROPE: DRIVEN, DYNAMIC, EXPANSIVE

On October 12, 1492, on a beach in the Bahamas, a thousand miles east of the Aztecs, a band of rugged men, mostly Spaniards, waded ashore from three small ships. They named their landfall San Salvador, or "Holy Savior." Their leader was a redheaded Italian about 40 years of age. To his Spanish crew he was Cristóbal Colón, to us Christopher Columbus. To the Arawak, the Bahamians who welcomed Columbus, he represented a bizarre world unlike anything they had imagined.

Christopher Columbus

Falling to his knees, as pious as any Aztec priest, Columbus proclaimed San Salvador the possession of the queen who had financed his voyage, Isabella of Castile, and her husband, Ferdinand of Aragon, the first rulers of unified Spain. Columbus would tell them that the trees were "the most beautiful I have ever seen." He "found no human monstrosities, as many expected." "On the contrary," he said, "among all these peoples good looks are esteemed." Columbus wrote that the Arawak were "very generous," that they did not "know what it is to be wicked, or to kill others, or to steal." He added that it would be easy to enslave them.

Some Spaniards would try to enslave the natives of the New World. For the moment, however, Columbus inquired politely of the Arawak about the location of Japan and China. Those fabulous countries, not the balmy but poor Bahamas, were the places for which he was looking.

The historical development of the America we know, begins with Christopher Columbus and the second significant discovery of America. Our origins as Americans, whatever our genetic inheritance, lay not on the pyramids of Mexico, but in the churches, state chambers, and counting houses of western Europe, in a culture that was to impress itself not only upon the Americas but upon the world.

Motives

To Columbus, San Salvador was an outlying island of "the Indies," the collective name Europeans gave to the mysterious, distant East, which included Cipango (Japan), Cathay (China), the Spice Islands (Indonesia), and India itself. Thus Columbus bestowed upon the inhabitants of the Americas the name that has stuck to their descendants to this day—Indians.

Columbus had sailed from Spain with the idea of finding a feasible sea lane to the Indies. In part, he was driven by religion. A devout Roman Catholic, Columbus believed God had selected him to carry the gospel of Christ to the lost souls of Asia. There were worldly motives too. Columbus longed for personal glory. Like the artists, architects, and scholars of the Renaissance, he craved recognition as a great individual. If obsession with self is tawdry and disagreeable in our own time, individualism was once one of the forces that made the culture of western Europe so dynamic.

Another such force was greed. Columbus wanted money. He meant to get rich doing business with (or conquering and enslaving) the peoples he encountered. Gold and silver were always in season, of course. "Gold is most excellent," Columbus wrote. "He who has it does all he wants in the world, and can even lift souls up to Paradise." Gold and silver paid for the Asian gems and porcelains that rich Europeans coveted, the fine cotton cloth of Syria and the silks of China, and tapestries and carpets that were beyond the craft of European weavers. Then there were the exotic drugs, dyes, perfumes, and especially the spices of the Indies—cinnamon from Ceylon, Indonesian nutmeg and cloves, Chinese ginger, and peppercorns from India—luxuries that made life more pleasant, something more than a struggle for survival on earth and salvation after death. Columbus asked the Arawak about precious metals practically before the Bahamian breezes had dried the surf from his stockings.

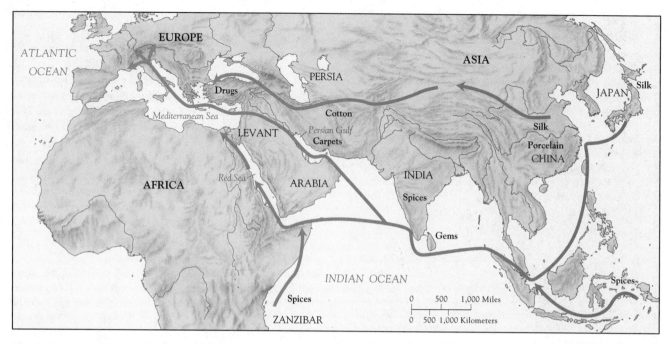

MAP 1:3 European Trade with Asia and Africa   Asian and East African goods—luxuries in Europe—were transported by land and sea as many as 8,000 miles.

High Overhead

The goods of the Indies had trickled into Europe since the days of the Roman Empire. From adventurers who traveled to East Asia, Europeans learned that luxuries expensive to them were abundant and cheap in the East. Crusaders, knights who briefly ruled parts of the Levant (present-day Lebanon, Syria, and Israel), enjoyed firsthand the richer life-style of the Muslims there.

The crusaders were driven back to Europe, but they continued to covet the goods of the East, which the triumphant Muslims were happy to sell them. These textiles, gems, perfumes, and spices were carried by ship through the Indian Ocean and Persian Gulf or Red Sea, or they were brought overland in caravans to the eastern end of the Mediterranean Sea: the Levant, Constantinople (Istanbul), Egypt. They then made their way to Europe in the vessels of powerful Italian city-states, most notably Venice and Genoa. Italian merchants were Europe's middlemen, the wholesale distributors who sold the spices and the rest to retailers all over the continent.

By the time the luxuries of the Indies reached the castles of Spain and the market towns of France, they were expensive indeed. The cost of transport alone was prodigious. The pepper that enlivened an English baron's stew may have traveled as far as 8,000 miles on donkey back. The trade routes passed through the lands of predatory Central Asian tribes or, if the pepper came by sea, through the haunts of East African pirates. Merchants had either to pay for safe passage or hire toughs of their own to battle the locals. Either way, the cost was, as always, passed on to consumers.

The Unpopular Middleman

The Levantines took a handsome profit. They were not in business for the glory of Allah and the service of humanity. The Christian Italians added their markup, shrugging off imprecations that they were gougers. Today, the magnificent Renaissance cathedrals and palaces the Italian merchant princes built are an inspiration to the world. In the time of Columbus, the glories of Italy also aroused resentment among the consumers whose purchases of Asian goods made the construction of these grand buildings possible.

In western Europe, envy of Italian wealth fathered the dream of finding a route to the Indies that bypassed the Mediterranean Sea, which Italian navies controlled. The prince whose sailors could eliminate the Italian middlemen would stop the flow of his country's wealth to Italy. Indeed, such a prince could imagine his subjects displacing the Italians as Europe's wholesalers of Asian products. As for the navigator who found this new route to the Indies, he could expect an opulent reward. Columbus was just one of several Italian sailors who went to Portugal, Spain, England, and France looking for financial backing.

PORTUGAL AND SPAIN: THE VAN OF EXPLORATION

Portugal and Spain were first to search for a new route to the Indies. The map reveals one reason this should have been so. Both countries face the Atlantic, Portugal entirely so. Additionally, Portugal and Spain were Europe's first unified nation-states, shaking off feudalism—a political system in which power was fragmented in many hands—and creating a powerful central government. Such a government, unlike a gaggle of squabbling feudal barons, was capable of accumulating the vast resources needed for world exploration and could find the will to undertake it.

Iberian Nationalism

France and England were well along in the process of national unification at the end of the 1400s. Both countries were to be major players in the overseas expansion of Europe. But Portugal was a unified nation by 1400. Its kings had come to the fore by driving out the Moors, Muslim Arabs and Berbers having roots in what is now Morocco.

Prince Henry, the third son of King John I, turned Portugal's attention to the Atlantic. Leading a life as ascetic as a monk's, he was a stay-at-home (which is ironic, given his nickname, "Henry the Navigator"). He left Portugal only once, on a military expedition across the narrow Strait of Gibraltar. But Henry was obsessed by the sea and far-off lands, both known and imagined. He sent 15 maritime expeditions down the western coast of Africa to buy gold and slaves from black kingdoms west and south of the Sahara. Under his aegis, the Portuguese colonized Madeira, 350 miles off the coast of Africa, in 1418; and the Azores, Atlantic islands 900 miles west of Portugal, in about 1427.

Henry also sponsored an exploration "research and development center" at Sagres in southern Portugal. Mariners were brought there to share their experiences with mapmakers and scholars who studied ancient travel accounts. Together they speculated, sometimes fantastically, sometimes brilliantly, about world geography. When sailors complained of the contrary winds off Cape Bojador that had turned Arab seamen back from "the green sea of darkness," Portuguese shipwrights developed a vessel that bested them—the caravel. Caravels could be rigged with the triangular lateen sails of the Mediterranean, which made it possible to beat against the wind, or with the large square sails of northern Europe, which pushed ships at high speed when the winds were cooperating. Caravels required relatively small crews, so they could be provisioned for longer voyages than other vessels. Caravels were "the best ships in the world and able to sail anywhere," said Luigi da Cadamosto, an Italian in Prince Henry's service.

Portugal's Route to Asia

Henry the Navigator died in 1460, but his legacy lived on. In 1488, a ship commanded by Bartholomeu Dias returned to Portugal after reaching the Cape of Good Hope, at the foot of the African continent. This was the corner to be turned. There would be clear sailing to the Indies by way of rounding Africa.

Not for 10 years would another Portuguese, Vasco da Gama, actually reach the Indian port of Calicut, toting up profits twenty times the investment in his voyage. Portugal then built a commercial empire consisting of small trading posts stretching from West Africa to the Persian Gulf and Macau in China. The single Portuguese holding in the Americas, Brazil, was the consequence of a mishap befalling Pedro Cabral, bound for Asia by da Gama's route, in 1500. Cabral's caravel was blown so far west it touched on the eastern bulge of the South American continent, thus accidentally establishing Portugal's claim to Brazil.

Portugal's African and Asian trade enriched the nation. As early as 1503, peppercorns sold in Lisbon for one-fifth the price the Levantines charged merchants from Venice and Genoa. The Portuguese had bypassed and undercut the Italian middlemen with a vengeance.

Long before 1503, Portugal's success in tracing the African coast had the effect of killing any interest King John II might have had in "the enterprise of the Indies," a

Oceanica Classis

▲ *Columbus commanded three ships on his voyage of 1492. The* Niña *and the* Pinta *were caravels, which Columbus preferred to his flagship, the* Santa Maria, *depicted here in a drawing of 1493. The caravels were nimble sailers; the* Santa Maria, *slow and hard to handle. Its value was that it could carry far more provisions than the* Niña *and* Pinta.

scheme presented to him by Christopher Columbus. Residing in Portugal since 1476, Columbus argued that the best way to get to East Asia was not by hugging the African coast and battling those damnable winds. The best route was due west across the Atlantic. John II entertained this notion for several years but then dismissed Columbus, calling him "a big talker, full of fancy and imagination."

Spain's Decision to Go West

Columbus took his proposition to Spain. He met plenty of ridicule there too. Scholars at the University of Salamanca described his plan as "vain, impracticable, and resting on grounds too weak to merit the support of the government." But Columbus had influential friends as well as mockers. After Dias found the southern tip of Africa for Portugal, Isabella and Ferdinand grew more interested in the Atlantic. They paid Columbus a modest annuity, just to keep him around.

In 1492, when Isabella and Ferdinand captured the last Moorish stronghold in Spain—the preoccupation of their reign—Columbus was making noises about taking his enterprise to France or England. Isabella decided to take a chance, and, suddenly, events moved with remarkable dispatch. Co-

lumbus was commissioned Admiral of the Ocean Sea, quite an exalted title. He was granted extensive authority over any lands he discovered and a generous share of any profits to be made. He was outfitted with two caravels, the *Niña* and the *Pinta,* and a clumsier, larger carrack, the *Santa Maria.* The total cost of the expedition was $14,000 (in today's money), which was small potatoes: Isabella and Ferdinand spent that much entertaining a distinguished visitor for a week.

Frustration

Four times Columbus crossed the Atlantic bearing letters of introduction addressed to the emperors of China and Japan (and letters with blanks in which he could fill in names). Four times he returned after Indians told him no, sorry, they had never heard of such persons. Each time he returned to Spain, Columbus told Isabella and Ferdinand that after one more try, he would surely "give them as much gold" and "all the spices and cotton" they needed.

To the day of his death in 1506, Christopher Columbus insisted that he had reached some of the 7,448 islands Marco Polo said lay off the coast of Asia. Sustained for a lifetime by a dream, he could not admit that his voyages pointed in quite another direction.

Indeed, it dawned only slowly on the Spaniards, who actually settled San Salvador, Cuba, and Hispaniola (present-day Haiti and the Dominican Republic), that they were living not in Asia but in a "new world" previously unknown to Europeans. When they faced this reality, many fell to cursing the lands Columbus discovered as obstacles in the way to Asian riches. Cuba and Hispaniola were notorious for bloody quarrels among the frustrated treasure seekers there.

Why "America"? Why Not "Columbia"?
Columbus cannot complain about the fact that his discovery was not named Columbia after him. He never admitted he had visited anywhere but "the Indies."

America was named for Amerigo Vespucci, another Italian, who twice voyaged to the New World. If Columbus was a medieval man, Vespucci was a modern. Vespucci wrote of his voyages, "Rationally, let it be said in a whisper, experience is worth more than theory," a principle Columbus defied. Marveling at the American animals unknown in Europe, Vespucci noted that "so many species could not have entered Noah's ark," a heresy of which the pious Columbus was incapable.

It was Vespucci who first declared in print that it was a "new world" across the Atlantic. In 1507, a German cartographer, drawing the first map to show the Americas as separate from Asia, named this new world for Amerigo in the Latin of his given name, feminine because the names of the continents of Africa and Asia were of feminine gender.

In the late nineteenth century, a descendant, Signora America Vespucci, petitioned the United States Congress for payment for the 400 year use of her ancestor's name. She did not collect.

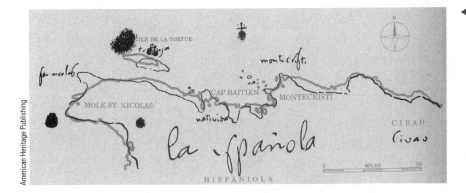

◄ *Columbus's greatness as a navigator is recognized. Not so well known is the fact that he was a superb mapmaker. His sketch of the northwest coast of Hispaniola (present-day Haiti), done by observation aided only by primitive methods of measuring distance, is close to perfect.*

In 1513, an expedition led by Vasco Núñez de Balboa aggravated the disappointment. Balboa crossed the Isthmus of Panama. It was only 40 miles wide at one point, but the isthmus festered with disease. From a mountain, Darien, Balboa looked down on another great ocean, the Pacific. The implication was obvious: Asia might be far indeed from where Balboa stood. In 1519, an expedition commanded by Ferdinand Magellan confirmed the suspicion. A Portuguese sailing for Spain with five ships and 265 men, Magellan found a strait to the Pacific through the southern tip of South America, which now bears his name. He was killed in the Philippines, but one of his vessels, commanded by Juan Sebastián de Elcaño and manned by only 18 wretched survivors, struggled back to Europe.

At hideous cost, it was a magnificent achievement—the first voyage around the world. But the Magellan–de Elcaño route was no trade route. Adverse winds and currents in the Strait of Magellan meant it could take months just to get from the Atlantic to the Pacific. (Columbus crossed the entire Atlantic in just four weeks.) Until almost the end of the age of sail, ship's masters avoided rounding South America from the Atlantic.

Poor Bargain

International politics contributed to Spanish frustration. In 1493, to head off conflict between Spain and Portugal, the pope, in *Inter Caetera,* divided all the world's lands not "in the actual possession of any Christian king or prince" between the two nations. The pope's line of demarcation ran from the North Pole to the South Pole, a hundred leagues (about 300 miles) west of the Azores. The next year, in the Treaty of Tordesillas, the Portuguese persuaded Isabella and Ferdinand to move the line farther west (thus laying the legal grounds for Portuguese settlement of Brazil after 1500). Wherever the line was drawn, Spain was shut out of all Asia but the yet undiscovered Philippines.

Until 1521, the Spanish in the New World thought of Tordesillas as a bad bargain. Their share of the world's non-Christian wealth was nothing like the loot the Portuguese were raking in on their side of the Tordesillas line. The Spanish were stuck with steamy, mosquito-plagued islands where there was no spice, no cotton, no silk, and very little gold.

THE SPANISH EMPIRE

Then, in 1519, pretty much the worst of years in Spanish America, an extraordinary soldier landed on the coast of Mexico with 508 soldiers, 200 Indians, several Africans, seven small cannons, 16 horses, and dozens of war dogs—gigantic mastiffs trained to kill. What this motley party found and did in Mexico brought an end to Spanish grumbling.

Cortés in Mexico

Bearded Hernán Cortés was not the first Spaniard to land in Mexico. Gonzalo Guerrero, shipwrecked in the Yucatán in 1511, became a military leader of the Mayans, helping them to drive out other Spanish adventurers. Like Columbus, however, Cortés was the discoverer who made a difference. He landed at Vera Cruz. After sending word to Cuba of his intention to march to Tenochtitlán, he burned the ships that had brought his army to Mexico. They would conquer or die.

Cortés was attacked by the Tabascans of the coast. The Spaniards, with their cannons, horses, and dogs easily defeated them, losing only two men. The shrewd Cortés then offered the Tabascans an alliance against their tribal enemies inland. He would repeat this procedure—victory in battle, peace, alliance—with every Indian people he confronted on his march to Tenochtitlán. Totomacs, Tlaxcalans, Tolucans, and Cholulans—all joined him to fight the Aztecs, whom everybody detested and no one could defeat. The Mexican battle tactic was to charge the enemy line, trying to break through and turn the flanks. In such a melee, with both sides carrying the same weapons, total victory was difficult. However, when the Spaniards added horses, war dogs, and firearms to the stew, they made decisive victory possible. At the same time, without the numbers his Indian allies provided, ten or more to each Spaniard, Cortés might have ended up as obscure a historical character as Gonzalo Guerrero.

Mexican religion played into Cortés's hands. An Aztec legend held that a fair-skinned deity named Quetzalcoatl would one day emerge from the east to rule Mexico. Moctezuma II feared Cortés to be this god. According to one of his advisers, the emperor "enjoyed no sleep, no food . . . Whatsoever he did, it was as if he were in torment." Reaching

▲ *An Aztec artist drew this picture of Moctezuma II, Cortés, Malinche (Cortés's Mexican mistress and translator), and armored conquistadores proceeding to Tenochtitlán when the Aztecs welcomed the Spaniards. Apparently, a Spaniard altered the painting, depicting Cortés and Malinche in European style.*

Tenochtitlán on November 8, 1519, Cortés was actually welcomed into the city where he promptly made the emperor his hostage.

Aztec nobles soon realized that the Spaniards were less than divine. Cortés ordered a stop to human sacrifice. What god would do such a thing? When soldiers stumbled on a store of jewels, silver, and gold, "as if they were monkeys, the Spanish lifted up the gold banners and gold necklaces. . . . Like hungry pigs they craved that gold." With perverse truth, Cortés told Moctezuma, "I and my companions suffer from a disease of the heart which can be cured only with gold."

Conquest

The Aztecs rebelled, and the Spaniards barely managed to fight their way out of the city. Half of them and perhaps 4,000 Tlaxcalans were killed. With their lives in the balance, the Spaniards nevertheless insisted on carrying eight tons of treasure on their retreat.

But it was the Aztecs, not the Spanish, who were doomed by Mexican gold. Cortés gathered new Indian allies and Spanish reinforcements from Cuba. He returned to Tenochtitlán, besieged the city for 80 days, and conquered it brick by brick. About 15,000 people were killed on the final day of the battle, August 13, 1521.

Hernán Cortés won not just a great battle; he won a ready-made empire. He and his lieutenants inserted themselves at the top of Aztec society in place of the nobility they had exterminated. They lived off the labor of the masses as the Aztec nobles and priests had done. Only rarely has one people been able to set itself up over another with such ease. The already centralized Aztec political structure and the submissiveness of the common people made it possible for the Spaniards to rule with minimal resistance.

The Conquistadores

The conquest of Mexico revived Spanish interest in the New World. There was a rush to the Americas as thousands of all classes packed into ships to search for Mexicos of their own. These young men (and a few not so young) called themselves "conquistadores"—conquerors. In a generation, they subdued an area several times the size of Europe.

Rarely has history shaped a people for conquest as Spanish history shaped the conquistadores. Because much of Spain is mountainous, agriculture never satisfied the ambitious. Because the Christian Spanish associated trade with Moors and Jews, whom they despised, the upper classes shunned commerce. The worldly role of the hidalgo, the Spanish male with pretensions to nobility, was to fight.

He was a caballero, a knight. The bravery and fortitude of the conquistadores under daunting conditions awes us to this day. The other side of their military character, their ruthlessness and cruelty, has also been remembered.

Spain's zealous Roman Catholicism factored into its extraordinary achievement. Because the national enemy had been of another faith, Spanish nationalism and Roman Catholicism were of a piece. Like their Muslim foes, the Spaniards believed that a war for the purpose of spreading true religion was by its very nature a holy war. Death in such a war was a ticket to paradise. It was a belief that made for soldiers nonchalant about death and therefore chillingly formidable.

Such cultural baggage would curse Spain in centuries to come. When the American gold and silver were spent, Spanish disdain for agriculture, trade, and other productive labor contributed to the nation's impoverishment. In the sixteenth century, however, reckless bravery and religious fanaticism were superbly calculated to conquer a whole new world.

Exploration North and South

After the news of Mexico reached Spain, King Charles I (better known as Emperor Charles V) encouraged additional conquests by promising conquistadores the lion's share of the gold and silver they won. (The king got one-fifth.) He also granted land to his subjects, and *encomiendas,* the legal right to force the Indians who lived on the land to work for them. It was not slavery, but, in practice, the distinction was fine.

Only one conquistador's find rivaled that of Cortés. In 1531, an aging illiterate, Francisco Pizarro, led 168 soldiers and 62 horses high into the Andes Mountains of South America. There he found the empire of the Incas, 3,000 miles in extent, tied together by roads Pizarro called unmatched in Christendom, and rich in gold and silver. Bolder than Cortés, for reinforcement was not an option, Pizarro was also an artist of treachery. He captured the Inca emperor Atahualpa, whose person was so sacred to the Incas that 80,000 Inca soldiers were paralyzed. For eight months, they brought Pizarro a ransom of gold that filled a room 22 feet long by 17 feet wide. Then, Pizarro had Atahualpa murdered, and defeated the bewildered Incas.

No other explorer found much gold and silver, least of all those who ventured into what is now the United States. Between 1539 and 1542, Hernando de Soto (who had been with Pizarro) wandered our Southeast in a fruitless search for riches. He was buried by his soldiers in the Mississippi River. Only half the mourners at his funeral got back alive to the West Indies.

During the same years, Francisco Coronado trekked extraordinary distances in the Southwest. His quest was for the "Seven Cities of Cíbola" among which, according to an imaginative priest, Fray Marcos de Niza, was "the greatest city in the world . . . larger than the city of Mexico." Coronado's 1,500 men found only dusty adobe villages. "Such were our curses that some hurled at Fray Marcos," wrote one soldier, "that I pray God may protect him."

Spanish America

No matter. For more than a century, Mexican and Peruvian gold and silver made Spain the richest and most powerful nation of Europe. By 1550, the equivalent of $4.5 million in precious metals was crossing the Atlantic each year; by 1600, $12 million. Not for another century would this river of riches dry to a trickle. American wealth financed the cultural blossoming of Spain as well as huge armies to do the king's bidding. By the end of the 1600s, Spain's empire stretched from Florida to Tierra del Fuego at the foot of South America.

Over so vast an area, economy and society varied immensely. Generally, however, the ownership of land in Spanish America was concentrated in the hands of a small group of *encomenderos* who lived off the labor of Indians in peonage or black Africans in slavery. Government was centralized in the hands of viceroys (vice kings). The Roman Catholic Church exercised great power, mostly for the good, trying to protect those on the bottom from the rapacious upper classes.

The empire flourished. Before more than a handful of other Europeans slept overnight in the New World, Spain boasted 200 towns and cities, and two universities, in the Western Hemisphere. The majority of Spain's American subjects were Indians, whose fate was not pleasant. It has been estimated that there were at least 5 million Mexicans in 1500. In 1600, there were 1 million.

The Black Legend

It can seem a wonder that any Native Americans survived. Indeed, the evils they suffered and the possibility of their extinction was the message of Catholic priests who took up their cause. "I am the voice of Christ," Father Antonio de Montesinos told conquistadores who had come to doze through mass, "saying that you are all in a state of mortal sin for your cruelty and oppression in your treatment of this innocent people."

A conquistador who became a Dominican friar, Bartolomé de Las Casas, devoted his life to lobbying the Spanish king for laws protecting the Indians. The Spaniards treated them, Las Casas said, "not as beasts, for beasts are treated properly at times, but like the excrement in a plaza." His scorching

▲ *This woodcut portrayal of Native Americans was carved in Germany about 1500, almost certainly by someone who never saw an Indian. Note the Indians' European features and the fact that they are rendered as cannibals. Of all the tribes confronted by Europeans by 1500, only the Caribs of the West Indies ate human flesh.*

description of conquistador cruelty, *A Brief Relation of the Destruction of the Indians,* was overblown. Las Casas was a propagandist; propagandists exaggerate. But *A Brief Relation* was not fantasy; the *leyenda nera,* the "black legend" of Spanish cruelty, was not legend in the essence of its message.

The *encomenderos* should not be seen as devils. In the context of the sixteenth century, their atrocities were close to routine. It was an era of indifference to suffering, and callousness was not a European monopoly. The depravity was Asian, African, and Native American too, and it was exercised not only on those of different races. Warfare in Europe meant unmitigated horror for peasants caught in the paths of marauding armies. The bloodiness of Mesoamerican religion has already been noted. Africans devised devilishly ingenious tortures without any tutoring from outsiders.

Many more Indians died of pick and shovel than at sword point. The Arawak of the Caribbean, for example, were a physically delicate people who died off within a few generations under the hard labor they were forced to perform. The Indian population of Hispaniola in 1492 was at least 200,000; in 1508, 60,000; in 1514, 14,000. By 1570, only two small native villages survived on the island.

THE COLUMBIAN EXCHANGE

The collision of worlds occasioned by Columbus's voyage established a biological pipeline between landmasses that had drifted apart 150 million years before human beings appeared on earth. Some species had flourished in both worlds: oaks, dogs, deer, mosquitoes, the virus that causes the common cold. There were, however, a large number of animals and plants in the Americas that were new to the first Europeans to arrive. And they brought with them flora and fauna unknown to the Indians.

Impact on America

Native American mammals were generally smaller and less suited for meat and draft than Old World livestock. The Aztecs had only five domesticated animals: the turkey, Muscovy duck, dog, bee, and another insect. The Incas had only the guinea pig, llama, and alpaca. So the Spaniards were quick to import hogs, cattle, sheep, and chickens along with European grasses to feed them (plus about 70 percent of the plants we know as weeds). Not only did the arrival of these creatures alter the ecology of the New World—profoundly— but the Indians introduced to them soon came to depend on them. Even those native peoples who escaped Spanish conquest were glad to raid the newcomers' flocks and herds. The wool-weaving art that is intimately identified with the Navajo of the American Southwest was refined when the Navajo domesticated European sheep.

The people of Mexico were initially terrified by the sight of a man on horseback. It reinforced their briefly held delusion that the Spaniards were gods. Even after the Indians recognized that horses were ordinary beasts, however, the Spanish equestrian monopoly gave the conquistadores an immense advantage in battle. Within two centuries, runaway, then feral, horses migrated as far as the Great Plains

▲ *An Aztec depiction of victims of the Old World disease that killed more Native Americans than any other—smallpox—which wiped out whole peoples in the Americas. Europeans died of smallpox too, but not in the numbers Indians did. Some Europeans survived epidemics thanks to resistance passed down through millennia of "living with" the disease.*

of North America. There they became the basis of several cultures that never heard of Spain. The Sioux, Comanche, Pawnee, Apache, Nez Percé, Blackfoot, Crow, and other tribes of the plains, previously agricultural peoples, captured the mustangs and became peerless horsemen independent of European example.

Among the valuable "green immigrants" from Europe were grains such as wheat and barley, citrus fruits, and sugar cane. Mexico was exporting wheat to the West Indies by 1535. It is difficult to picture the West Indies without sugar cane. Columbus himself introduced lettuce, cauliflower, citrus fruits, figs, and pomegranates to America. Within a few decades after his death, bananas (from Asia) and watermelons (from West Africa) were being cultivated in the New World.

Impact on the World's Food Supply

If America contributed few food animals to the world's larders, American plant foods revolutionized European, African, and Asian diets. Maize (Indian corn), an American native, astonished Europeans by the height of its stalks and size of its grains. Cultivation of the crop spread to every continent, increasing the food supply and contributing to the rapid increase in population that characterizes the last 500 years of human history.

The sweet potato became a staple in West Africa, where it was introduced by slave traders. (The yam, superficially similar, was already established there.) Beans, squash and pumpkins, peppers, strawberries (there was a European strawberry, but it was inferior to the American), vanilla and chocolate, wild rice, and tomatoes are American foods that were unknown in Europe, Africa, and Asia.

It is estimated that of 640 food crops grown in Africa today, all but 50 originated in the Americas. Manioc (tapioca), also of American origin, is today the staple for 200 million people in the tropics. The white ("Irish") potato, a

native of the Andes, provides basic sustenance for even greater numbers. Curiously, the white potato was slow to make an impact. It took 250 years for its cultivation to spread from Peru to Spain and, from there, across the temperate zone from Ireland to China.

Many national cuisines depend on foods of American origin for their zest, particularly the tomato and the extraordinary variety of chili peppers that have been developed from a Mexican forebear. Think of Hungarian paprika. Think of Italian sauces for pasta. These, as well as tobacco, were contributed to the Old World by the New.

Disease

The most tragic of the intercontinental transactions was in microscopic forms of life. Many diseases for which Europeans, Africans, and Asians had developed resistance were unknown to Native Americans before 1492. Smallpox, measles, influenza, bubonic and pneumonic plague, tuberculosis, typhus, and cholera were as foreign to the Americas as horses and Spaniards. Biologically, the Indians had not learned to "live with" these killer diseases.

Why were they absent? Scholars note that all of these diseases initially spread to human beings from domesticated animals–sheep, goats, cattle, buffalo, pigs, and fowl. The Native Americans had few such domesticates. They hunted herd animals, but they did not, like Europeans, Africans, and Asians, live in close proximity to them. The rarity of large cities in America also explains the absence (so far as we know) of virulent epidemic disease in pre-Columbian America. Smallpox, measles, and the other terrible diseases Europeans brought on their ships are "crowd diseases." Highly infectious, once they were introduced to a dense population, they savaged it. If, before Columbus, similar afflictions appeared in the Americas, they died out for lack of crowds in which to spread.

Old World diseases were catastrophic in America. Transplanted Europeans and Africans suffered badly enough when epidemics swept through the colonies, but the Indians died in heartrending numbers. Bacteria and viruses killed far more Native Americans than did swords or even forced labor.

America's microbic revenge was venereal disease. Europeans first identified syphilis as a new disease in 1493, in Cádiz, Spain, the port to which Columbus returned after his first voyage and released his crew. Syphilis was next noted in Naples, where several of Columbus's crewmen went as soldiers. It spread at terrifying speed throughout the world, following the trade routes. What better agents for spreading a sexually transmitted disease worldwide quickly than seamen and the prostitutes who were their chief sexual partners?

Europeans, Africans, and Asians reacted to syphilis as Indians reacted to measles and smallpox, diseases previously unknown to them. Symptoms were severe, and death came quickly. About 10 million people died of syphilis within 15 years of Columbus's voyage. Only later did the disease take on the slower-acting form in which it is known today and in which American Indians now know smallpox, measles, and the rest.

for FURTHER READING

The most exciting and productive research in American history in recent years has been about pre-Columbian Mesoamericans. Most of this material is in scholarly journals, yet to be synthesized in a book for general readers. However, Brian M. Fagan, *Kingdoms of Gold, Kingdoms of Jade: The Americas Before Columbus,* 1991, presents much of it very well. Also see the relevant sections of Alvin M. Josephy Jr., *America in 1482: The World of the Indian People Before the Arrival of Columbus,* 1991. On Mayan art and religion, see Linda Sechele and Mary Ellen Miller, *The Blood of Kings,* 1986.

Daniel J. Boorstin, *The Discoverers: A History of Man's Search to Know His World and Himself,* 1985, is a fine historian's best work; volume 2 provides a superb narrative and analysis of the adventure of European discovery. Jared Diamond, *Guns, Germs, and Steel: The Fates of Human Societies,* 1997, is a largely persuasive geographical explanation of why, among other things, it was Europeans, and not Indians, Africans, or Asians, who surged into the unknown in the 1400s.

A biography of Columbus by Samuel Eliot Morison, *Admiral of the Ocean Sea,* 1942, is a classic and well worth a read despite many valid revisions of Morison's vision. There was a deluge of books about Columbus published in the early 1990s to coincide with the five hundredth anniversary of his discovery. Almost all of them (and several theatrical films) seem to have been inspired by the belief that the discovery was at best a big mistake and, more likely, one of history's most evil chapters. If one had nothing nasty to say about Columbus in 1992, one said nothing at all.

The most readable of these "politically correct" books is Kirkpatrick Sale, *The Conquest of Paradise,* 1990. Even though Columbus is portrayed as a fool when he is not a fiend, the book is based on exhaustive research and is replete with contemporary accounts of the horrors the discovery meant for the American natives. An exception to the phenomenon of 1992 is William D. Phillips Jr. and Carla Rahn Phillips, *The Worlds of Christopher Columbus,* 1992, a thoughtful and incisive study.

On the conquest of Mexico, see a classic in the grand literary tradition of the nineteenth century, William H. Prescott, *History of the Conquest of Mexico,* 1873. For the story told from an Aztec perspective, see Leon Lopez-Portilla, *The Broken Spears,* 1962. On Spanish America, see James Lockhart and Stuart B. Schwartz, *Early Latin America,* 1983; Mark A. Burkholder and Lyman L. Johnson, *Colonial Latin America,* 1990; and Donald J. Weber, *The Spanish Empire in North America,* 1990.

Alfred E. Crosby, in *The Columbian Exchange: Biological and Cultural Consequences of 1492,* 1972, and in *Ecological Imperialism: The Biological Expansion of Europe,* 1986, was the first to explore discovery and exploration on this elemental level. William Cronon, *Changes on the Land,* 1983, is a superb example of environmental history.

AMERICAN JOURNEY ONLINE AND INFOTRAC® COLLEGE EDITION

Visit the source collections at http://ajaccess.wadsworth.com and http://infotrac.thomsonlearning.com, and use the Search function with the following key terms to explore documents, images, audio and video clips, articles, and commentary related to the material in this chapter:

Aztecs	Hispaniola	Tenochtitlán
Christopher Columbus	Lake Texcoco	
Hernán Cortés	Maya	

Additional resources, exercises, and Internet links related to this chapter are available on *The American Past* Web site: http://history.wadsworth.com/americanpast7e.

HISTORY ONLINE

American Indians of the Pacific Northwest
http://memory.loc.gov/ammem/award98/wauhtml/aipnhome.html
Multi-formatted site dealing with some of North America's most prosperous tribes.

The Columbus Navigation Homepage
www1.minn.net/~keithp/
Excellent look at many aspects of Columbus's achievements.

The Aztecs/Mexicas
www.indians.org/welker/aztec.htm
Thoroughgoing multi-media examination of Aztec culture.

Spanish Exploration and Conquest of Native Americans
www.floridahistory.com
About the explorations of de Soto and Coronado.

SETTLEMENT ACROSS THE SEA

The Idea, the Failures, Success 1550–1624

North Wind Picture Archives

*Where every wind that rises blows perfume,
And every breath of air is like an incense.*

Francis Beaumont and John Fletcher, English poets

The nature of the Country is such that it Causeth much sickness, and the scurvy and the bloody flux, and divers other diseases, which maketh the body very poor, and Weak. . . . We are in great danger, for our Plantation is very weak, by reason of the death, and sickness. . . . I have nothing to Comfort me, nor there is nothing to be gotten here but sickness, and death.

Richard Frethorne, settler in Virginia

ENGLAND'S CLAIM TO a piece of America dated from 1497, when King Henry VII, impressed by Columbus, agreed to fund John Cabot, yet another Italian navigator looking for a backer, to look for the sea route to Asia that eluded Columbus. It eluded Cabot too, but he touched on Newfoundland and Nova Scotia, claiming them and adjacent properties for Henry.

The French monarchy showed little interest in the New World until 1523, when one of King Francis I's privateers (in effect, pirates contracted by the king) captured a Spanish ship carrying Mexican gold. Startled by so pretty a prize, Francis sent his Italian, Giovanni Verrazano, across the Atlantic. Verrazano claimed much of the eastern coast of North America for France.

The pope scolded Francis, reminding him that, in *Inter Caetera,* he had granted the world's non-Christian real estate to Portugal and Spain. Francis dipped his pen in sarcasm and asked to see the provision in Adam's will that entitled the pope to bestow such gifts.

ENGLAND'S SLOW TURN TOWARD AMERICA

Adam's will or not, Spain enjoyed a near monopoly of the Americas for a century. Other nations envied the Aztec and Inca riches that poured into Spain during the 1500s—Spain's *siglo de oro,* or "golden century"—but none was up to challenging Spanish might. Only late in the *siglo de oro,* under Queen Elizabeth I, did England, cautiously, act on John Cabot's claims.

© Corbis

▲ *John Cabot (Giovanni Caboto) of Venice believed, like Columbus, that Asia could be reached by sailing west across the Atlantic. After news of Columbus's crossing reached England, Henry VII came up with the money Cabot had been seeking. In 1497, Cabot reached North America and claimed it for England. The king rewarded Cabot with an income of £20 a year for life, which Cabot collected once. Cabot disappeared during a second voyage in 1498.*

The Protestant Reformation

The sixteenth century was a time of religious turmoil in Europe, the era of the Protestant Reformation. During the years Cortés was shattering the Aztecs, a German monk, Martin Luther, shattered the unity of western Christendom. While Coronado searched for the Seven Cities of Cíbola in the scorching Southwest, a French lawyer in rainy Geneva, John Calvin, was laying the foundations of a dynamic religious faith that would profoundly shape American history.

In 1517, Luther published an attack on several doctrines and practices of the Roman Catholic Church. Called to account by the Holy Roman Emperor, Charles V (King Charles I of Spain, soon to be flooded with Aztec gold), Luther denied the authority of the pope to determine true religion. The only source of God's word, Luther declared, was the Bible.

In a short time, large parts of Germany, Scandinavia, and the Netherlands embraced the new teachings. Many ordinary folk were disgusted by the moral laxity common among Catholic priests. German princes were attracted to Luther's Protestantism because, if they broke with the Roman pope, they could seize church lands, which accounted for a quarter to a third of Europe.

Spain remained Catholic. So did England's Henry VIII, crowned in 1509. He condemned Luther in a scholarly book, *Defense of the Seven Sacraments.* An appreciative reader, Pope Leo X honored Henry as "Defender of the Faith."

The Church of England

The title proved to be high irony, for in 1527, Henry himself broke with Rome. He had no quarrel with Catholic doctrine and ritual. But Henry was determined to dissolve his marriage to a Spanish princess, Catherine of Aragon, who, after a history of babies dead in womb or cradle, was at the end of her childbearing years. There was a daughter, Mary. But these were days when monarchs still joined their soldiers on the battlefield. Henry believed that for his Tudor dynasty to survive, he must have a son, a king. Then there was Cupid. Henry was in love with a comely young flirt of the court, Anne Boleyn, who wanted a wedding ring, not a mistress's pillow.

Popes tended to be supportive when kings had problems of this sort. However, Pope Clement VII feared the wrath of Charles V (who was Catherine of Aragon's nephew) more than he wanted to help out Henry. He refused to annul the king's marriage, whereupon Henry had Parliament declare papal authority invalid in England. The king, according to the Act of Supremacy, was head of the Church of England.

Like the German princes, Henry confiscated the lands of the monasteries and nunneries in England. He sold them to ambitious subjects for whom owning land meant prestige. Thus did a clever king fill his treasury and create a class of well-to-do landowners whose place in society depended on the independence from Rome of the Church of England. History would rank Henry VIII as a jewel of the age of monarchy were it not for a gluttony that transformed him into a grotesque figure and a ruthlessness that carried him through six wives, two of whom he divorced and two of whom he beheaded.

A Changing Church

Henry VIII did not much alter religious practice and church government in England. His reformation had few consequences in the daily lives of common people. But people in power have discovered before and since that tinkering with an established order, however delicately, often liberates a spirit of debate and innovation that becomes tumultuous and revolutionary. That happened in England.

A true Protestantism germinated within the Church of England during the reign of Edward VI, Henry VIII's only son. Alas for the reformers who called the shots for Edward (he was a boy of just 16 when he died in 1553), Edward's successor was his older half sister, Mary Tudor, the daughter of Catherine of Aragon. Mary was a zealous Catholic who had seethed for two decades over her mother's humiliation. Now queen, she married her cousin, Prince Philip of Spain, soon to be known as "His Most Catholic Majesty." Then, Mary alarmed even Philip by the ardor with which she rooted out Protestants in her court. Mary also persecuted Protestants among ordinary people, as well as sixteenth-century methods allowed. Three hundred were executed, earning the queen the unflattering nickname of "Bloody Mary."

Had Mary been a better politician, lived a long life, and borne a child to succeed her, England might have been eased back into the Catholic Church. Like her brother Edward, however, Mary sat on the throne for a very short time. She died in 1558, childless.

English Protestants who had fled to Geneva (home of the most radical of the Protestant reformers, John Calvin) returned to England. They became known as Puritans because they spoke of "purifying" the Church of England of Catholic beliefs and practices such as statues in churches, the burning of incense in religious services, and the authority of bishops. The Puritans found justification for none of these things in the Bible, their only religious authority.

THE ELIZABETHAN AGE: SEEDBED OF COLONIZATION

Mary's successor, Elizabeth I, was one of the shrewdest politicians ever to wear a crown. The daughter of Anne Boleyn, she was a survivor. To have been alive and kicking in 1558, she had to be wily. Her father beheaded her mother as an adulteress and witch when Elizabeth was 3. When Elizabeth was 14, the English church embraced Protestantism under Edward VI, and English foreign policy took an anti-Spanish turn. Elizabeth went along. When she was 20, England returned to Rome under Bloody Mary and became an ally of Spain. Elizabeth went along. Now queen at 25, she was well practiced in the arts of concealing her true sympathies. She knew how to cajole the schemers who crowded the royal court, pushing wildly different views of religious truth and foreign policy. She also knew how to bide her time.

Thus, when Spain's Philip II proposed marriage, Elizabeth waffled. To wed His Most Catholic Majesty would surely set English Protestants to plotting against her. However, to humiliate Philip by rejecting him abruptly might well plunge England into a war with Spain, for which the island nation was not prepared. Flirtatious when circumstances demanded, regally aloof when it served her purposes, Elizabeth seemed to say yes to Philip, then no, then maybe. In fact, she said nothing at all. She wore Philip down and won time to determine the best direction. Elizabeth took her royal duties seriously.

Sea Dogs

Elizabeth's American policy was also devious. During the first two decades of her reign, she tacitly recognized Philip's claim to all the Americas. By the late 1570s, however, Elizabeth first tolerated, then quietly encouraged, a restless, swashbuckling fraternity of Spaniard-hating sea captains who meant to chip away at Philip's empire.

The most daring of these "sea dogs" (the name comes from a shark common in English waters) was a slave trader who aspired to more respectable work, Francis Drake. In 1577, Drake set sail in the *Golden Hind,* rounded South America by the Strait of Magellan, and attacked unfortified Spanish ports on the Pacific. Defenses there were moot—no ship of any nation except Spain had ever plied those waters.

If the pickings were easy, Drake correctly reckoned that Spanish warships awaited him in the Atlantic. Instead of returning the way he had come, Drake sailed north to California, reconditioned the *Golden Hind*, and struck west across the Pacific. His expedition was only the second to circumnavigate the globe.

During the same years, another sea dog, Martin Frobisher, sailed three times to Newfoundland, looking for a likely site to plant a colony and find gold. There was to be no settlement, and the thousand tons of "gold ore" Frobisher proudly brought back to England turned out to be worthless rock. In 1578, Elizabeth quietly licensed two half brothers, Humphrey Gilbert and Walter Raleigh, to establish an English settlement in any land "not in the actual possession of any Christian prince."

In winking at these operations, Elizabeth played her usual game. Officially, she appeared to acquiesce to Spain's New World monopoly. In fact, she was challenging it, discreetly; but by 1580, she abandoned discretion. Drake had returned to England, the *Golden Hind* so stuffed with Spanish treasure that it listed dangerously, a few degrees from capsizing. The profit on the voyage was 4,700 percent. Coveting her royal share of the loot and knowing that Philip II's patience was exhausted anyway, Elizabeth boarded the ship and knighted Drake.

Makeup

Some portraits of Elizabeth I show a clownlike face, as white as paper and overlaid with bright splotches of rouge, with no eyebrows—every hair had been plucked. When older, the queen did indeed wear such unsubtle makeup and dyed her hair a brilliant red. In part, no doubt, her face painting represented the impulse to fiddle with one's appearance, which is found in every culture and must be described as the nature of the species. But the queen also had a political motive for her makeup. With no eyebrows to arch and her face encased in lard encrusted with chalk, she presented her company with an immovable mask. As she wished to do, she betrayed no emotion, neither approval nor anger nor surprise, no matter what a courtier or foreign ambassador said to her.

▲ *For years, Queen Elizabeth pretended that Francis Drake was on his own in his raids on Spanish colonial settlements. (He would have been hanged as a pirate had he been captured.) However, when Drake returned from his voyage around the world, the* Golden Hind *so laden with Spanish gold and silver that it was barely floating, the queen boarded the ship and knighted Drake. There would be no more pretending.*

Lost Colonies

Gilbert and Raleigh tried to be the first English colonizers of America but failed. In 1583, Gilbert built an outpost in Newfoundland, but the descent of the northern winter persuaded him to flee south. Sailing south, his two ships were caught in a nasty storm. A bold old sea dog to the end, Gilbert shouted

Spanish Virginia

The Spanish did not ignore the lands north of St. Augustine. In 1526, about 500 colonists, including 100 slaves, began to build a settlement at the mouth of the Pee Dee River in what is now South Carolina. The slaves rebelled and escaped. Only 150 Spaniards survived to limp back to Hispaniola.

In 1571, a few Jesuit priests established a mission in Virginia, not far from which the English would found their first successful colony 35 years later. They converted several high-ranking Powhatan Indians to Catholicism, or so they thought. The Powhatan killed the missionaries.

his last recorded words across the waves to his second ship: "We are as near to heaven by sea as by land."

The next year, Raleigh's scouts recommended the Chesapeake Bay as a more likely site for a colony. The climate was mild, the soil rich, and the Chesapeake was far enough from Spanish St. Augustine in Florida to seem safe from Spanish attack. Knowing how to flatter the right people, Raleigh named the country Virginia after Elizabeth, the "Virgin Queen" (she never married). In 1587, he shipped 91 men, 17 women, and 9 children there to settle it.

Uncooperative winds blew the expedition to Roanoke Island in what is now North Carolina. The sandy, wooded island was not as well advantaged as any number of other sites on the Chesapeake. Still, Roanoke might have succeeded had it not been three long years before the settlers were resupplied. When Raleigh's agents finally returned in 1590, they found Roanoke's buildings abandoned. The word "CROATOAN" was carved on one of the structures in "fayre Capitall letters."

This was a good sign. Governor John White had instructed the colonists that if they left Roanoke, they were to leave the name of their destination in such a way. If they

▲ *John White, the governor of Roanoke, was an artist who painted the land and its native inhabitants so that Walter Raleigh could use the paintings in his unending quest for financial backers. Here, White depicted a man and woman in the village of Secotan (North Carolina) dining on boiled corn kernels. The Indians boiled food by dropping heated rocks into watertight baskets. Understandably, they coveted the iron pots of the English, which could be set directly on a fire.*

were *forced* to leave, they were to punctuate their message by carving a cross. There was no cross with "CROATOAN," so White concluded that the colony had relocated on Croatan Island near Cape Hatteras. There, White's entourage wandered the woods, discharging muskets and singing English songs to assure any who might be hiding that they were not Spaniards, but to no avail. There was no trace of the Roanoke settlers.

What happened? Some historians believe that the settlers, finding life on Roanoke untenable, joined friendly Lumbee Indians on Croatan. A century later, after the Lumbee had moved to the interior of North Carolina, some members of the tribe were observed to be fair skinned and blue eyed, with a number of English words in their language.

BEGINNINGS OF EMPIRE

Raleigh was slow to resupply Roanoke because of financial problems, for which he had a genius. It was not easy to convince tightfisted Elizabethan investors to pump money into enterprises "without sure, certayne, and present gayne." More important, in 1588 and 1589, England was preoccupied with a threat to the kingdom itself. Philip II, furious with Drake and other sea dogs, had assembled a fleet of 130 ships with which to invade England.

The Spanish Armada

The Spanish Armada (armed fleet) of 1588 was a disaster. Designed to transport 30,000 troops, its ships, built for the Mediterranean, were awkward on the swells of the Atlantic.

The Armada was outmaneuvered in the English Channel by small, quick English pinnaces. Regrouping in the harbor of Calais in France, the Armada was savaged by fire ships, old vessels the English lathered with tar, stuffed with gunpowder, set aflame, and sailed (unmanned) into the midst of the Spanish fleet.

The next year, returning home by rounding the British Isles to the north, the Armada was beset by storms. Only half of the ships, and just a third of Philip's soldiers, made it back to Spain. The Elizabethans may be excused for suggesting that God had lined up on their side. They called the storms that finished off the Armada "the Protestant Wind." They told each other that "God himselfe hath stricken the stroke, and ye have but looked on."

Whatever God's opinion in the matter, the sea dogs had demonstrated that Spain was not invincible. As the *siglo de oro* drew to a close, England, France, the Netherlands, and even Sweden were ready to chance colonies in America.

Promoters

The sea dogs demonstrated that the English could challenge Spain. Some Elizabethan landlubbers promoted the idea that the English *should* establish colonies. The most energetic was Richard Hakluyt, a bookish but by no means parochial, minister of the Church of England. Hakluyt rummaged tirelessly through the libraries of Oxford and London, collecting and publishing hundreds of explorers' accounts of the geography, resources, and attractions of America. His masterwork, *The Principal Navigations, Voyages, Traffiques, and Discoveries of the English Nation,* came out between 1598 and 1600.

In his books and in conversations with moneyed men, Hakluyt argued that investment in American colonies would infallibly produce a profit, add to England's prestige, and "enlarge the glory of the gospel." He lived until 1616, long enough to be a shareholder in the first permanent English settlement in America.

Sir Walter Raleigh continued to promote colonization too. He survived until 1618, but he was not as lucky as Hakluyt. After a lifetime sinking his and others' money in colonial debacles, the dashing soldier, poet, and personal favorite of Queen Elizabeth ran afoul of her successor, James I. Raleigh spent the last 13 years of his life imprisoned in the Tower of London.

Other writers, like advertisers of every era, played down the dangers and risks of investing in colonies, puffed up the attractions, and simply lied through their teeth. Virginia, they said, rivaled "Tyrus for colours, Balsan for woods, Persia for oils, Arabia for spices, Spain for silks, Narcis for shipping, the Netherlands for fish, Pomona for fruit and by tillage, Babylon for corn, besides the abundance of mulberries, minerals, rubies, pearls, gems, grapes, deer."

Hard Economic Facts

Some boosters emphasized the possibility that English conquistadores might stumble on gold and silver mines as the Spanish had or find the water passage to Asia that the Span-

Philip's subjects spent and spent on their luxuries. Philip spent on his endless wars. Their profligacy ensured that one day Spain would be the poorest nation in western Europe.

Easy Come, Easy Go

Instead of devoting American gold and silver to the improvement of agriculture, Spain purchased much of its food abroad, impoverishing its own farmers. Fisheries were neglected in favor of buying fish from others. Philip II's attempt to encourage the manufacture of textiles, leather, and iron goods at home was thwarted by the cheaper costs of imports. Even the majority of Spain's dreaded soldiers were, in fact, German and Italian mercenaries.

The result? Gold and silver dribbled out of Spain as quickly as they were shipped in. American loot ended up in countries with no mines in America but with a class of canny, grasping merchants and hustling manufacturers. Other nations did the final count of the Spanish doubloons. They included enemies of Spain quite glad to make whatever the Spanish would buy and to transport whatever the Spanish wanted shipped. Even the hated Drake easily found Spanish buyers for slaves he had stolen from other Spaniards.

Every transaction left Spain poorer and her enemies richer. England and Holland, Spain's bitterest foes, would fight one another to determine which of them would bleed the Spanish. In the Treaty of Utrecht in 1713, England took as the spoils of victory not territory but the *asiento de negros,* a license to sell 4,000 Africans into slavery in the Spanish colonies each year.

Surplus Population

Another circumstance encouraging interest in colonies was the widespread anxiety that there were just too many people in England. The population of England had soared during the 1500s, largely because of a decline in the incidence of mortal disease. But food production and opportunities for employment had not kept pace with the population explosion.

Some believed that the "enclosure movement" was at fault. That is, raising sheep was more profitable than farming land in small plots. So wealthy landowners, and even villagers who owned land in common, converted separate little fields into large pastures, which they enclosed with hedges as fences. Tending sheep required a fraction of the labor force that tilling the land did. Consequently, villagers who lost their rights to farm the land were sent packing.

Some of these surplus people wandered the countryside in gangs. They worried villagers and gentry alike with their begging, bullying, and theft. The boldest of them waylaid travelers on lonely stretches of highway. Other refugees congregated in cities, forming a half-starved and apparently hopeless underclass that, like the poor of all ages, was a source of disease, crime, and disorder. "Yea many thousands of idle persons," Hakluyt wrote, "having no way to be set on work . . . often fall to pilfering and thieving and other lewdness, whereby all the prisons of the land are daily pestered and stuffed full of them."

▲ *As a young man, Sir Walter Raleigh was a "favorite" of Queen Elizabeth; that is, he was kept around for his conversation and was indulged financially. Artful flattery was a favorite's favorite tool. Raleigh, tirelessly promoting colonization projects, named Virginia for Elizabeth, the "Virgin Queen."*

National Portrait Gallery, London

ish had not. Others pictured American outposts from which sea dogs would sally forth to seize Spanish ships and raid Spanish ports. Hakluyt described dozens of likely harbors and coves suitable to such enterprises.

But an economy could not be built on piracy. Moreover, although it was expensive to protect treasure fleets from raiders—20 warships to defend 20 merchantmen carrying gold and silver—it could be done, and the Spanish did it. More persuasive to sober English capitalists, there were signs by 1600 that Spain's American gold and silver mines were not unmitigated blessings. True, Spain's fabulous wealth enabled grandees at home to purchase whatever they desired, enjoy a style of life that was the envy of Europe's elite, and pay huge armies to terrorize the continent. It was also true, however, that Spain's *hidalgos*, like Miguel Cervantes' fictional Don Quixote, assumed that their inherent nobility and matchless bravery were quite enough on which to build the future.

King Philip II was no Don Quixote. Humorless, hardworking, unimaginative, ascetic, and invariably dressed in black, Philip thought in the longest of terms—eternity. His parents' coffins sat in his living quarters to remind him of his own mortality. Philip understood that the mines of Mexico and Peru had bottoms, that the gold and silver would run out. So he tried to promote industry and trade to provide for his beloved Spain when the easy money was gone. He failed.

Common Seamen

They were small men by our standards; few seamen of the age of discovery and colonization topped five and a half feet. But they were as tough as the oaken ships they sailed. Most were teenagers or men in their early 20s, and reaching maturity did not guarantee a long life. The odds that anyone who survived childhood diseases would die before the age of 35 were overwhelming. They were worse for men who went to sea.

If the sixteenth-century sailor survived shipwreck and battle, he faced hazards on his own vessel. He might be killed by a crewmate in a fight over a triviality. He might die being punished. Discipline on the high seas was immediate and brutal as an object lesson for the crew. Flogging was as regular as rain. Keelhauling (dragging a man underwater the length of the hull, where, if he did not drown, his body was shredded by barnacles—shellfish that clung to the vessel) was not common but was far from unusual. After a mutiny, Magellan beheaded one ringleader, quartered another alive, and marooned a third on a desert island. When he pardoned the other mutineers, they were so grateful that they became Magellan's most loyal followers.

Finally, the common seaman risked not only landlubber diseases; he ran a high risk of contracting scurvy, a vitamin C deficiency. It can be prevented and even reversed by a diet of fruits and vegetables. At sea, however, the menu did not include such foods because they were perishable. Meals consisted of salt beef, rock-hard biscuits, water, and wine. The officers ate slightly better. The onions, garlic, and dried fruit in their larders doubtless explains the lower incidence of scurvy among them.

A sailor's labor was heavy. Seamen hauled heavy canvas up and down masts, with pulleys as their only mechanical aid. Merely holding the ship on course was heavy work. The crude tiller pitted the seaman's strength against the forces of wind and ocean currents. Every ship leaked and had to be pumped by hand constantly—frenziedly during storms.

Ships on long voyages had to be refitted regularly—"serviced." A ship in danger of sinking because of the weight of the barnacles on its hull was sailed to a beach where it was careened (turned on its side). The barnacles were then scraped off, and the hull was recaulked with rope and pitch. If the captain decided that the sails needed to be rearranged, seamen virtually rebuilt the ship above deck. The small crew was kept hopping, repairing sails and lines, and scrubbing the decks with vinegar and salt water. But boredom was more likely than overwork to cause discontent.

Why did men choose such a life? First, *choose* is not quite the right word. Most sailors were born in seaports, literally bred to the life. Their options were few. A portion of the seamen were forced on the ships. Columbus's crew was put together in part by drafting convicts. For several centuries to come, shorthanded captains made up their crews by waylaying ("shanghaiing") hapless young men.

Finally, for all its dangers and discomforts, the sea offered a remote but alluring chance for social and economic advancement. Although some of the great captains of the era were, like Magellan, born into the upper classes, others, like Columbus, worked their way up. Columbus first shipped out as a boy, perhaps only 10 years old, and was illiterate until he was 30. Yet he became an intimate of royalty. Many conquistadores first came to the New World as common seamen and lived to become wealthy landowners. Even the lowliest can dream.

One response to England's population problem was a chilling criminal code. In the seventeenth and eighteenth centuries, a wretch could be hanged for the pettiest of crimes—for the theft of a rabbit from a gentleman's hutch. When the poor were so numerous and desperate, it was easy to believe that only the constant threat of the gallows kept them from running amok.

Or the pestering poor could be sent abroad. To Hakluyt and others, colonies were social safety valves. People who were economically superfluous and socially dangerous at home could, by the alchemy of a sea voyage, become cheerful consumers of English products and suppliers of the raw materials that England needed. "The fry of the wandering beggars of England," Hakluyt said, "that grow up idly, and hurtful and burdenous to this realm, may there be unladen, better bred up, and may people waste countries to the home and foreign benefit, and to their own more happy state."

Indeed, the desperation of the English living in huts of "stickes and turfes" made many glad to go overseas. As for those who found the idea unattractive, the "Bloody Code" served nicely as an incentive. North America was better than the noose. It is estimated that during the first century and a half of English settlement in the New World, one colonist in ten (about 50,000 total) had been convicted of a crime and "transported" as punishment. They were usually minor crimes, but not always. Some of today's country club families claiming ancient American lineage were surely "founded" by rapists, aficionados of mayhem, and murderers.

Private Enterprise

Colonies were financed and organized by private concerns that were forerunners of the modern corporation. These merchant-adventurer companies ("adventurer" refers to the adventuring, or risking, of money) were developed before the colonial era in response to the expense and risks of overseas trade.

It was neither cheap nor a sure thing to send a ship packed with trade goods out to sea. Pirates, warships of hostile nations, and storms and shoals waited to do many vessels in, and they did. Therefore, instead of gambling his entire fortune on a single ship, an investor joined with others in ownership to divide the risks. If a ship owned by such a company was lost, individual shareholders lost money, felt sorry for themselves, and, being human, looked for a way to blame someone else for their misfortune. But they were not ruined. They had not sunk everything they had into the venture. And they likely owned shares of other ships that would return at a profit.

Such capitalists covered themselves at home by securing charters from the Crown granting them special privileges in the business in which they were involved. Thus, the Muscovy Company, founded in 1555, had a chartered monopoly of the importation of furs and forest products from Russia. The most famous and successful of these protocorporations was the East India Company. Founded in 1600, it actually governed large parts of India for a century and a half.

When James I was persuaded that American colonies were a good idea, he chartered similar companies to do the job. In 1606, the king authorized a company in the port of Plymouth to "plant" a colony on the American coast between 38 and 45 degrees north latitude. The London Company was granted the same privilege between 34 and 41 degrees.

The tracts overlapped, but the two companies were forbidden to set up within 100 miles of one another. The buffer zone was designed to avoid rivalries that, in the Spanish West Indies, had sometimes turned violent. The 100-mile no-colony zone also hurried the two companies along: The first to arrive in America had the pick of sites.

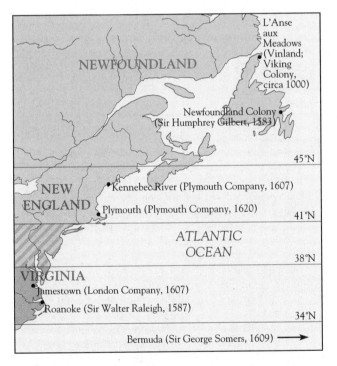

MAP 2:1 The English in America, 1583–1607 Raleigh, Gilbert, and other early colonizers ranged the North American Coast from Newfoundland to just short of Spanish Florida in their efforts to plant a successful English colony. The first successes were in the two regions known as "New England" and "Virginia." Note the zone in which both the London Company and Plymouth Company were authorized to settle, on the condition that their colonies be at least 100 miles apart.

JAMESTOWN

In August 1607, the Plymouth Company established Fort St. George on a bluff above Maine's Kennebec River. Like Humphrey Gilbert's people in Newfoundland a few decades earlier, the 45 colonists found the Maine winter disagreeable. Nevertheless, when Raleigh Gilbert arrived with a re-supply ship the next year, he found "all things in great forwardness." Then, at summer's end, Gilbert learned that he had inherited the family fortune; his childless brother back in England had died. Who needed Fort St. George? The entire contingent returned home with the happy heir.

The First Families of Virginia

The London Company had better luck in Virginia, if 15 years of suffering and wholesale death can be called lucky. In May 1607, Captain Christopher Newport brought three ships into Chesapeake Bay and landed his passengers on a peninsula on the James River (named for the king). Roanoke was on Newport's mind. He would select no island that could be surrounded by Spanish ships. Instead, he picked a peninsula that could be defended against Indians almost as easily as an island. Captain John Smith, a soldier who remained in Jamestown, as the fortified village they built was called, said that Newport's choice was "a verie fit place for the erecting of a great citie."

This was nonsense. Jamestown was surrounded by brackish, malarial swamp, poorly suited to crops. Two centuries later, when the town ceased to serve as a center of government, just about everyone living there gladly moved out.

But Jamestown's limited agricultural prospects were not important to Newport, Smith, or the London Company. The first Virginians were not expected to be self-sufficient. Their assignment was to look for gold and to buy goods from the local Indians that would sell for a profit in England. And, preposterously, several Polish glassmakers (probably refugee Polish Brethren—Protestants fleeing persecution at home) were to set up a workshop in which to practice their craft. The first Virginians arrived with some illusions.

Pocahontas

Not long after landing in Virginia, John Smith was taken prisoner by the Powhatan. According to Smith—and he was more than willing to make a story up—he was seconds away from having his skull crushed by war clubs when Chief Powhatan's 12-year-old daughter, Matoaka, also known as Pocahontas ("the playful one"), begged the chief to spare Smith's life.

Pocahontas was playful. Naked, she visited Jamestown and turned cartwheels in the tracks that passed for streets. In 1614, Pocahontas became a Christian and married John Rolfe. She bore a son, but both his parents died when he was still a lad—Pocahontas in 1617 while visiting England, Rolfe in 1622 when Pocahontas's uncle attacked Jamestown.

Survivors

Mere survival was a struggle. Raw wilderness proved too much for the English. They had no experience as foragers. They could not compete as hunters and gatherers with the Powhatan Indians, for whom extracting a living from nature was at the heart of their culture. In January 1608, a fire destroyed what was left of the provisions the Jamestowners had brought with them. Hunger, as John Smith wrote, "forced many to flee for reliefe to the Savage Enemy."

In the language of the Powhatan, Virginia was called Tsenahkommaka ("densely populated land"). At about 40,000 in 1607, the Native American population of the Chesapeake region may have reached a point at which the Indians themselves were suffering food shortages. The introduction of 200 new residents may have been just too much for Virginia. Once the Jamestowners' numbers declined to a few dozen, they did manage to hang on. If they survived on such things as oysters, snakes, and mushrooms, that is what foraging is all about.

John Smith had a distinguished military record. The Virginians might have lived by raiding Indian farms, and when desperate, they tried. But the Powhatan Confederacy held the preponderance of power. Had they decided to wipe out the interlopers during Virginia's first years, they could have done so in a weekend. Jamestown may have survived destruction because relief ships arrived annually with manufactured goods the Indians learned to covet.

Then there was disease. Malaria, dysentery, typhoid fever, scurvy, and plain enervating apathy took a devastating toll. In 1607, 144 Englishmen landed at Jamestown. The next year, 38 were alive. In 1608 and 1609, 500 new colonists arrived. By 1610, Jamestown's population was 60.

Unpermissive Society

Smith, who rivaled Raleigh as a publicist, credited his military discipline with saving the colony. In fact, Smith's nononsense control—he executed one settler for making a dinner of his wife—probably did avert complete disintegration. But Smith was less than beloved. His successor as governor, George Percy, called him "an Ambitious unworthy and vayneglorious Fellowe."

Thomas West, Baron De La Warr, named governor in 1610, also enforced a rigorous discipline, this time aimed at making the colony self-sufficient in food. Settlers were marched to work in the fields as if they were troops. Troublemakers and the merely idle were dealt with swiftly and harshly. De La Warr and his successors, Thomas Dale and Thomas Gates, prescribed the death penalty for dozens of offenses, including individual trade with the Indians and killing a domestic animal without permission. Virginians were whipped for throwing wash water into the streets or carrying out "the necessities of nature" within a quarter mile of the fort. Under this authoritarian rule, fields were expanded, and "earth-fast" houses (what we call "pole buildings": buildings with no foundations) were erected.

Virginia expanded along the banks of the James, but mortality remained high. Between 1610 and 1618, 3,000 new settlers arrived. In 1619, the population of Virginia was 1,000. Between 1619 and 1623, 4,000 settlers arrived. In 1624, the population of Virginia was 1,300.

The "Stinking Custom"

If the Virginians had found no way to make money, the London Company would surely have written off the colony as a big mistake. But the colonists did find profit growing tobacco, a native American plant that Columbus had brought back to Europe on his first voyage to the New World.

Smoking got off to a bad start in Europe. The first addict, Rodrigo de Jerez, was jailed by the Spanish Inquisition for seven years because of his habit. But Rodrigo was the wave of the future. Slowly, inexorably, the practice of "drinking" tobacco smoke spread. The lure of the exotic—the trendy—is always potent among the leisured classes. And some European physicians seized on tobacco as a miracle drug, prescribing it liberally to their patients and calling it "the holy, healing herb," "a sovereign remedy to all diseases."

When Jamestown was founded, the Spanish West Indies provided just about everyone's weed. The Powhatan grew their own, but John Rolfe, a Virginian with the habit, found the local tobacco "poore and weak and of a byting taste." Securing seed from Trinidad, Rolfe experimented in his garden in 1612. In 1614, he had more than enough for his own pipe and shipped four barrels of the leaf to England. The reception was sensational. In 1617, Virginia exported 10 tons of tobacco at a profit of three shillings a pound! In 1618, the shipment was 25 tons—and by 1628, 250 tons! The price at

Thank You for Not Smoking

Both James I and his son, Charles I, disapproved of tobacco. James called it "a custom loathesome to the eye, harmful to the brain, dangerous to the lungs, and in the black stinking fume thereof, nearest resembling the Stygian smoke of the pit that is bottomless." That was in 1604, before there was a single English colony, let alone a colony flourishing by growing tobacco.

However, as late as 1631, when Virginia was booming thanks to tobacco, Charles I commanded an earl to limit tobacco cultivation on his estate because of "the great abuse of tobacco to the enervation of the body and of courage."

Neither father nor son was willing to take a cut in income in order to stifle the habit. When a giant hike in James I's tax on tobacco resulted in a sharp reduction in imports, and therefore in the tobacco duties he collected (what did he expect?), he slashed the tax to a payable level.

At least two colonies founded later than Virginia enacted antismoking measures. Connecticut tried to license smokers; only those who were prescribed tobacco for reasons of health could apply. Massachusetts briefly forbade smoking *outdoors*—not for moral reasons but to prevent fires.

▲ *When tobacco boomed in Virginia in the 1610s, the inhabitants of Jamestown planted every available square inch of the town with the crop, roadways included.*

which tobacco sold explains this amazing growth. In the early seventeenth century, ordinary tobacco brought the equivalent in today's money of $17 a pound, and the finest grades, $100 a pound.

Who Shall Till the Fields?

Emigrants hurried across the Atlantic. The very streets of Jamestown were planted with tobacco. A colony recently starving now neglected food production in order to cultivate a weed to be burned. Authorities lamented that the settlers' "greediness after great quantities of tobacco causeth them" not to "build good homes, fence their grounds, or plant any orchards." In "An Acte for Tradesmen to Worke on Theire Trades" in 1632, the Virginia Assembly commanded gunsmiths and naylers, brickmakers, carpenters, joyners, sawyers and turners . . . to worke at theire trades and not plant tobacco."

Mostly, it was a losing effort. A carpenter could make a living. A farmer could tend a thousand tobacco plants plus four acres of maize, beans, and squash—enough to support a household of five. It did not require a gift for higher mathematics to calculate what the income from 10,000 or 50,000 tobacco plants would mean.

Land was abundant, rich, seemingly endless, and available for a pittance. The problem was labor. Who would work

for another in a country that offered so extraordinary an opportunity to get rich? The Jamestowners enslaved Indians. However, unlike the Indians of Mexico, the natives of Virginia were alien to intensive, disciplined labor. At the first opportunity, they disappeared into the forest, which to them was not howling wilderness but home.

In 1619, a Dutch ship tied up at Jamestown and paid for the tobacco it took aboard with "20 and odd Negroes," probably seized from a slave trader bound for the Spanish West Indies. Soon, human cargoes from Africa and the West Indies arrived regularly in Virginia. In 1660, there were 900 black Virginians in a population of 25,000. Only after 1700, however, would African Americans be the backbone of the workforce. During the seventeenth century, ambitious Virginians made the transition from toiling farmer to comfortable planter by importing white servants from England.

Under the "headright system" instituted in 1618, each head of household who came to Virginia was granted 50 acres of land for each person whose fare across the Atlantic he paid. Thus, a family of five secured 250 acres upon disembarking. Virginians or Englishmen with cash to spare could amass larger estates by recruiting emigrants from among the masses of England. In return for their transportation to Virginia, these people signed contracts binding themselves to labor for their master without pay for a number of years, usually seven. Thus was Virginia peopled, thus the tobacco grown.

Massacre

For 15 years, the English coexisted with the Powhatan Confederacy. Many held the Indians in contempt, comparing them to the "savage Irish," whom the English detested. Red and white regularly skirmished, although the fights were more brawls than battles. The aged head of the Confederacy, Chief Powhatan, did not view the enclave of pale-skinned outsiders as much of a threat, and he was fascinated by the firearms, woven cloth, pots, pans, and mirrors they offered in trade. In 1614, when John Rolfe married Powhatan's daughter, Pocahontas, something of a détente was inaugurated.

Then Powhatan died, to be succeeded as chief by his brother, Opechancanough, an altogether different character. Opechancanough had nearly been killed by John Smith in 1609, and he recognized what many Indians after him were to learn, always too late: The once tiny, starving white enclaves with interesting things to sell were growing in size, strength, and confidence, and pushing hungrily into the Indians' ancestral lands.

In March 1622, Opechancanough struck. He and his warriors entered Jamestown as if to trade or chat. Suddenly, they attacked, killing the founding father of the tobacco business, John Rolfe, and 346 others. About a third of Vir-

▲ *Visiting England in 1616, Pocahontas sat for this portrait in finery befitting the wife of a prosperous tobacco merchant, which her husband, John Rolfe, was fast becoming.*

▲ *The Jamestown Massacre of 1622 was unexpected, sudden, and terrifying. The start of it probably looked much as this artist rendered it, but the killing continued until 300 Virginians were dead.*

ginia's white population died, a catastrophe. But it was not enough in a place where fortunes were being made. The survivors bandaged their wounds, refused Opechancanough's offer to trade kidnapped women for peace, and retaliated with their superior weapons, sorely punishing the Powhatan. Other Indians were tricked into a peace parley at which as many as 200 were poisoned. Some Virginians called for a kind of genocide, "a perpetuall warre without peace or truce [to] roote out from being any longer a people, so cursed a nation, ungratefull to all benefitte, and incapable of all goodnesse." By 1625, it is estimated, the number of Powhatan was reduced from 40,000 to 5,000.

After one last Indian offensive in 1644, the Powhatan were driven into the interior. In 1669, 2,000 of them were counted. By 1685, apparently, the people and culture were extinct. The pattern of white–Indian relations that would be repeated for more than two and a half centuries had been drawn in the mud of Jamestown.

A Royal Colony

The London Company was also a casualty of the massacre of 1622. Although some planters and merchants were getting rich from tobacco, the company itself never recorded a profit. Citing this failure and the massacre, King James I revoked the company's charter in 1624 and took direct control of Virginia. The House of Burgesses, a legislative assembly of 22 members elected by landowners and established in 1619, continued to function. But the king appointed a governor empowered to veto its actions. Virginia was, thus, the first English colony, the first colony in which there was significant self-government, and the first royal colony directly administered by the Crown.

OTHER BEGINNINGS

By 1622, the English in Virginia were not the only Europeans living in what is now the United States. Before the seventeenth century was 10 years old, both the Spanish and the French had registered their presence in what is now the United States.

French America

In 1562, a French adventurer named Jean Ribault tried to launch Charlesfort, near what is now Port Royal, South Carolina. Like Roanoke, Charlesfort simply evaporated. Two years later, René Goulaine de Ladonnière took 300 colonists to Florida, close by the spot where Ponce de León began his explorations. The settlers were Huguenots, Puritan-like Protestants. They planned to use Fort Caroline as a base from which to raid Spanish treasure ships.

The colony was vexed by Indian troubles and the refusal of the aristocrats there to work with their hands. However, it was destroyed in 1565, when it was attacked by a Spanish expedition led by Pedro Menéndez de Avilés. Florida's history did not have a pretty beginning. When Menéndez discovered that the French he had captured were Protestants, he had them hacked to death.

French interest in America shifted north. In 1608, an extraordinary sailor, Samuel de Champlain (he made 12 voyages to the New World!), founded Quebec on a site on the St. Lawrence River that had been claimed for France in 1535. The next year, in company with Huron Indian allies, Champlain was exploring the lake in New York and Vermont that now bears his name when he stumbled on a party of Iroquois, old enemies of the Huron. At the request of the Huron, the French turned their muskets on the Iroquois. It was their introduction to European military technology and the beginning of long intertribal wars in which the French and English would play major roles.

New France, the St. Lawrence river basin, having no cash crop like tobacco, grew slowly. In 1627, there were but 100 French there; in 1663, only 3,000. In some ways, Quebec was a religious and cultural center: A college was founded there in 1635 (a year before Harvard, the first college of the English) as well as an Ursuline convent school for Indian girls. But mostly, Quebec was a rude, uncomfortable trading post where Indians exchanged hides and furs for decorative trinkets, blankets, textiles, iron tools and implements, guns, and brandy.

Hispanic Beginnings

In 1565, before destroying Fort Caroline, Pedro Menéndez de Avilés established St. Augustine, Florida, between the Matanzas and San Sebastian Rivers. In 1586, Sir Francis Drake sacked the town, but St. Augustine recovered. It is the oldest surviving European settlement (by 42 years) in what is now the United States.

In 1609, two years after the founding of Jamestown, a party of Spaniards hiked the banks of the Rio Grande almost to its source in the Sangre de Cristo Mountains of New Mexico. There they founded Santa Fe, from which traders tapped the numerous Indians of the country for furs, hides, and small quantities of precious metals, while Franciscan missionaries sallied out to win the Indians' souls. By 1630, they claimed to have baptized 86,000 Pueblo, Apache, and Navaho Indians.

Santa Fe is the oldest seat of government in the United States. (St. Augustine was administered from Cuba.) By 1609, however, the Spanish empire had reached the limits of its capacity to expand. Except for England's minuscule trading posts on Hudson Bay, founded much later, Santa Fe remained the remotest European town of any size in North America, isolated by colossal distance from the imperial center of Mexico. Like the French in Canada, the Spanish in Santa Fe would not contribute to American culture as dominant forces but only in their responses to the great English experiment in settlement that had its beginnings in Virginia.

for FURTHER READING

The historical literature dealing with the background of England's colonial era is vast. G. R. Elton, *England Under the Tudors,* 1974, is a good overview. For social and "mental" context, see Peter Laslett, *The World We Have Lost,* 1965. Specifically related to English interest in North America are Carl Bridenbaugh, *Vexed and Troubled Englishmen,* 1968; A. L. Rowse, *Elizabethans and America,* 1959; and Keith Wright, *English Society, 1580–1680,* 1982.

Fixing on important incidents are Thomas E. Roche, *The Golden Hind,* 1973; Garrett Mattingly, *The Armada,* 1959; Karen Ordahl Kupperman, *Roanoke: The Abandoned Colony,* 1984; and David B. Quinn, *Set Fair for Roanoke,* 1985. Relevant biographies include Paul Johnson, *Elizabeth I,* 1974; P. L. Barbour, *The Three Worlds of Captain John Smith,* 1964; Stephen J. Greenblatt, *Sir Walter Raleigh,* 1973; and James A. Williamson, *Sir Francis Drake,* 1975.

On early Virginia, see Carl Bridenbaugh, *Jamestown, 1544–1699,* 1980; Alden Vaughan, *Captain John Smith and the Founding of Virginia,* 1975; and Edmund S. Morgan, *American Slavery, American Freedom,* 1975. On the Indians of the region, see Gary Nash, *Red, White, and Black,* 1982; Thad W. Tate and David W. Ammerman, eds., *The Chesapeake in the Seventeenth Century,* 1979; and Peter Wood et al., *Powhatan's Mantle: Indians in the Colonial Southeast,* 1989. See also the relevant chapters of the following books by James Axtell, our most accomplished and reliable recent historian of Indians: *The European and the Indian,* 1981; *The Invasion Within: The Contest of Cultures in Colonial America,* 1985; and *After Columbus: Essays in the Ethnohistory of Colonial North America,* 1988.

General works (also relevant to subsequent chapters of this book) include Charles M. Andrews, *The Colonial Period of American History,* 1934–1938; Daniel Boorstin, *The Americans: The Colonial Experience,* 1958; Wesley F. Craven, *The Southern Colonies in the Seventeenth Century,* 1949; Jack P. Greene and J. R. Pole, eds., *Colonial British America,* 1984; Curtis E. Nettels, *The Roots of American Civilization,* 1938; John E. Pomfret with Floyd Shumway, *Founding the American Colonies,* 1970; and Clarence Ver Steeg, *The Formative Years,* 1964.

 ## AMERICAN JOURNEY ONLINE AND INFOTRAC COLLEGE EDITION

Visit the source collections at http://ajaccess.wadsworth.com and http://infotrac.thomsonlearning.com, and use the Search function with the following key terms to explore documents, images, audio and video clips, articles, and commentary related to the material in this chapter:

Jamestown
John Smith
Martin Luther
Pocahontas
Powhatan
Richard Hakluyt
Sir Walter Raleigh

Additional resources, exercises, and Internet links related to this chapter are available on *The American Past* Web site: http://history.wadsworth.com/americanpast7e.

HISTORY ONLINE

Discourse of Western Planting
http://odur.let.rug.nl/~usa/D/1501-1600/hakluyt/plant.htm
Extracts from Richard Hakluyt's published promotions of English colonies in North America. These were the arguments with which men like Hakluyt and Raleigh approached investors.

Jamestown
www.gov.colo/Jthanout/JTbriefs.html
Well-selected variety of information about the Jamestown colony.

3

ENGLISH AMERICA

The Thirteen Colonies
1620–1732

We must be knit together in this work as one man; we must entertain each other in brotherly affection . . . we must uphold a familiar commerce together in all meekness, gentleness, patience and liberality; we must delight in each other, make other's conditions our own, rejoice together, mourn together, labor and suffer together.

John Winthrop

They differ from us in the manner of praying, for they winke [close their eyes] when they pray because they thinke themselves so perfect in the highe way to heaven that they can find it blindfold.

Thomas Morton

In 1608, 125 MEN, WOMEN, and children left the English village of Scrooby, made their way to Hull, and took a ship to Holland, where they settled in the "fair and beautifull citie" of Leiden.

They were quiet in their travels because they were breaking the law. Going abroad without royal permission was forbidden. The Scrooby villagers were willing to risk punishment because they were being persecuted for their religious beliefs. They were members of a small sect called "Separatists" because they believed that Christians who were "saved"—elected for salvation by God—should worship only in the company of other such "saints," separate from those who were damned. This belief earned them the hostility of the Church of England, to which all the English were expected to adhere, and of the king, who was the head of the church.

The Separatists are better known to us as the Pilgrims. Their leader for a generation, William Bradford, called them that because they did a good deal of wandering, as if on a pilgrimage, in search of a place they might live godly lives unmolested.

NEW ENGLAND COLONIES

The Pilgrims were not molested in Leiden; the Dutch tolerated most forms of worship. In fact, Leiden was a bit too free and easy for the straitlaced Pilgrims. They fretted that their children were absorbing a casual attitude toward parental authority, "getting the reins off their necks," and embracing the juvenile misbehavior for which the Dutch were notorious. Moreover, like the children of foreigners before and since, the sons and daughters of the Pilgrims were growing up as much Dutch as English. The Pilgrims may have disliked the intolerance of the English crown, but they were also English to the core themselves, as ethnocentric as any Chinese, Ghanaian, or Powhatan Indian.

Plymouth Plantation

Virginia's success, apparent by 1620, helped provide a solution to the Pilgrims' dilemma. The bonanza profits from growing tobacco on the Chesapeake rekindled the enthusiasm of the Plymouth Company, which had failed to develop a colony in Maine in 1607.

The trouble was that Virginia's prosperity lured most would-be emigrants there. The Plymouth Company could not find settlers for an entirely new colony at least a hundred miles north of Jamestown. Then, Sir Edwin Sandys, a major shareholder, had an idea. He won the consent of James I not to persecute the Separatists if they relocated to America.

In 1620, the Leiden exiles returned to England just long enough to board two small America-bound ships, the *Mayflower* and the *Speedwell*. The *Speedwell* leaked so badly it turned back, thus missing the opportunity to enshrine its name in American history books. The *Mayflower* was herself none too seaworthy but survived a rough passage longer than that of Christopher Columbus a century earlier.

A hundred colonists disembarked at the southern end of Massachusetts Bay. They built "Plymouth Plantation" on the site of Pawtuxet, an Indian village that had been wiped out by disease, probably brought by European fishermen, several years earlier. The Pilgrims regarded the fact that their settlement was ready made, with fields ready to plow, as a sign that God approved of their mission. He had "cleared" an already developed land of people so that his saints might dwell on it. He did not send a mild winter, however. Half the settlers died of malnutrition or disease before the spring of 1621.

Then came another positive sign, "a special instrument sent of God": Tisquantum, or Squanto, an Indian who spoke English, wandered into the colony. A native of Pawtuxet, Squanto had been kidnapped in 1605 and taken to England. He made his way to Virginia with John Smith in 1614, was

▲ *A contemporary reconstruction of Plymouth when the settlement was several years old. "Streets" are wide enough for an ox or horse, but not a wagon. Dooryards were fenced not for privacy—there was little—but to keep hogs out of gardens.*

kidnapped by Spaniards but escaped, and, six months before the founding of Plymouth, returned to Pawtuxet to find it abandoned. This well-traveled man, far more cosmopolitan than the Pilgrims, nonetheless adopted them as his tribe. He was an invaluable member of their community. He guided

---

Increasing and Multiplying

Nearly half of Plymouth's settlers died during the colony's first winter. Just two of the survivors more than made up for the loss within their own lifetimes.

John Alden and Priscilla Mullins arrived on the *Mayflower* and married soon thereafter. (The wedding was immortalized two centuries later by Henry Wadsworth Longfellow.) The Aldens both lived into their 80s. They had 12 children, of whom 10 survived to adulthood. Eight of these Aldens married and, together, had at least 68 children—more people than died in Plymouth in 1620–1621. The Aldens' great-grandchildren, a few of whom they lived to know, numbered 400, or four times the original population of the colony.

The "Fun" Colony

"Merrymount," now Quincy, a few miles from Plymouth, is a colony forgotten. In 1623, a curious character named Thomas Morton arrived at Plymouth and persuaded some of his fellow passengers to join in a colony where they would be, in the words of Plymouth governor Bradford, "free from service, and . . . trade, plante, & live togeather as equalls."

According to Bradford, Morton presided over a riotous style of life. The Merrymounters were frequently drunk and "set up a May-pole, drinking and dancing aboute it many days togeather, inviting the Indean women, for their consorts, dancing and frisking together, (like so many fairies, or furies rather,) and worse practices."

Also aggravating, Morton stole Indian trade from Plymouth by offering firearms for furs and hides. This worried Governor Bradford because the Indians were better hunters than the whites "by reason of ther swiftnes of foote, & nimblnes of body" and because the guns could be turned against the colony. He sent Captain Miles Standish and a small force to arrest Morton. There was no battle because, according to Bradford, Morton and his friends were too drunk to resist. The only casualty was a Merrymounter who staggered into a sword and split his nose.

Morton was put on an island to await the next ship bound for England. Indian friends brought him food and liquor and helped him escape; he returned to England on his own and denounced the Pilgrims. Neither he nor the Pilgrim fathers were punished. If authorities then had known the phrase "can of worms," they would surely have applied it to the squabble.

▲ *This rendition of Captain Miles Standish distastefully observing the antics at nearby "Merrymount" was based on the depiction of the settlement by Plymouth governor Bradford. The Merrymounters had to have taken an occasional break from partying; Thomas Morton, the head of the "colony," competed with the Pilgrims in buying furs from the Indians.*

the newcomers about the country, taught them native methods of fishing and cultivation, and, according to Governor William Bradford, asked for prayers so that "he might goe to the Englishmen's God in Heaven."

Self-Government

Squanto was a better citizen than many who arrived on the *Mayflower.* Even before landing, Pilgrim elders like Bradford and William Brewster, and the colony's military officer, Captain Miles Standish, grew nervous that, once ashore, the "strangers" among them—that is, the non-Separatists—would defy their authority. Several had said as much during the voyage. Worse, the grumblers had a legal justification for going their own way. The site of Plymouth lay outside the tract of land assigned to the Pilgrims in the Plymouth Company charter. Therefore, the legal authority the charter vested in the leaders of the expedition was shaky.

To reassert that authority, 41 of the passengers signed the Mayflower Compact while still aboard ship. The document began by asserting the party's enduring loyalty to "our dread Sovereign Lord King James" (whose instructions as to the location of the colony they were flouting). The signers then bound the settlers together in a "Civil Body Politik" for the purpose of enacting and enforcing laws. The Mayflower Compact is memorable because of its implicit principle—that a government's authority derives from the consent of those who are governed. King James got his ceremonial due. However, the signers of the compact, who were a majority of the adult males, also stated that the right to make laws in the colony was based on the fact that the majority consented to be subject to those laws.

Early Plymouth was, in fact, a rather democratic place. Almost every male head of household was a shareholder in the company and could, therefore, vote to elect the governor. (William Bradford held the post for 30 years.) Important questions were resolved by vote. Such broad and active participation of the people in government was found in few places anywhere in the world.

Subsistence Economy

Plymouth was also autonomous of England for most practical purposes. The Crown interfered little in the colony's internal affairs. This was a consequence of the fact that the Pilgrims never came up with a moneymaker like John Rolfe's tobacco plants. Simply put, the colony failed to arouse the interest of influential Englishmen (or much of anyone) back home. Furs purchased from the Indians provided Plymouth some income with which to buy goods from

English merchants. Fishing for cod helped. But Plymouth was just a tiny, distant community of subsistence farmers. The Pilgrims raised enough food to live. Indeed, after the first terrible winter, they thrived. But no one got rich tilling New England's rocky soil or salting codfish for export.

The dearth of profits discouraged the owners of the Plymouth Company. By 1627, they agreed to sell their shares to the settlers. Although it took 15 years to pay them off, the sale had the effect of transferring control of Plymouth Plantation to those who lived there. Plymouth remained a self-governing commonwealth until 1691, when it was absorbed into its younger but much larger neighbor, Massachusetts Bay.

Massachusetts Bay

Virtual self-government was half accidental in Plymouth. Had a Pilgrim plowman turned up a vein of gold ore in his cornfield, the king would have royalized the colony, as he seized Virginia in 1624.

In the most important colony of New England, by way of contrast, self-government was the consequence of well-laid plans meticulously carried out. There were no starving times in Massachusetts Bay, established in 1630 some 40 miles north of Plymouth. The founders of the Massachusetts Bay colony worked out the fine details of their migration long before they weighed anchor. Provisions and supplies were abundant for the thousand people who made up the first wave of settlement. Within a few months, Massachusetts was home to seven towns!

By design, the settlers were a fair cross section of English society. They were of both sexes, more or less balanced in numbers, and of all ages and social classes up to the rank of lady and gentleman. There were skilled artisans and professionals among them, most notably, well-educated ministers of God; there were farmers and laborers. Only nobles were missing from the mix.

The founders of Massachusetts Bay intended to create, quite literally, a *new* England based on the society they knew at home. In just one major particular did the colonists reject old-country ways. Although they called themselves members of the Church of England, they abhorred the church's practices. New England was to be a truly godly commonwealth such as the world had not known since the days of the apostles.

To ensure they were able to create, shape, and control their Zion, the settlers brought with them the charter of the Massachusetts Bay Company, the legal justification of their right to self-government. Shareholders in the company who chose to stay in England sold out to those who went to America. There would be no company directors back home to question decisions made in Massachusetts.

Puritan Beliefs

These cautious, prudent people were the Puritans. Their religion was Calvinist. Like the Separatists, they were disciples of the theologian John Calvin, who believed that human nature was inherently depraved, that all men and women bore the guilt of Adam and Eve's original sin. In the words of a Massachusetts poet, Anne Bradstreet, man was a "lump of wretchedness, of sin and sorrow."

If God were just, and nothing more, all sons and daughters of Eve would be damned to hell for eternity because of their sinful nature. Since God was all good, there was nothing that sin-stained men and women could do to earn salvation. From such corrupt actors, no act of charity, no act of faith, no sacrifice, no performance of a ritual could possibly merit divine approval.

Was there then no hope? In fact there was, and in the Puritans' hope for the next world lies the key to understanding the kind of society they built in this one. For God was not merely just, he was also infinitely loving. He made a gift of grace to some people. These were the "elect," his "saints." No one deserved the gift of grace. No one earned it. Saints were by nature as corrupt as the damned multitudes who surrounded them. God's love, and it alone, was the reason they were predestined to join him in paradise.

In return for the gift of grace, the elect bound themselves to a covenant (contract) with God. They would enforce God's law in the community in which they lived. If they failed to keep their part of the bargain, if they tolerated sin within their community, the Puritans believed, God would punish them as severely as he had punished his chosen people of the Old Testament, the ancient Hebrews.

Errand in the Wilderness

It is not quite correct, therefore, to say that the Puritans came to America in order to worship as they pleased. First of all, the Puritans were a powerful minority in England. Although some were harassed, others worshiped pretty much as they pleased on the fens of Lincolnshire and the Yorkshire moors. One of their most respected ministers, John Cotton, had been the pastor of St. Botolph's in old Boston, said to be the largest parish church in England. Cotton was no wild-eyed

---

Hypocrites?

"We are decendid," wrote humorist Artemus Ward in 1872, "from the Puritans, who nobly fled from a land of despitism to a land of freedim, where they could not only enjoy their own religion, but prevent everybody else from enjoyin' his."

Ward was witty, but mistaken to imply that the Puritans were hypocrites. They did persecute religious practices other than their own; they hanged several Quakers. But they never claimed to have set up in America in the cause of religious toleration. Nineteenth-century Americans saddled them with that reputation. Puritans forthrightly said that other forms of worship were abominations. As Thomas Shephard of Cambridge wrote in 1645, "Toleration of all upon pretence of conscience I think God my soul abhors it." The Puritans were intolerant, but they were not hypocrites.

creature of the fringe, hiding in a hedge from persecutors. He was a man of status and respect.

It is more accurate to say that the Puritans came to America because they were not at all pleased with the way non-Puritans were worshiping in England. They wanted to remove themselves from "the multitude of irreligious, lascivious, and popish persons" in the old country. Their "errand into the wilderness" of Massachusetts was to *purify* the Church of England. Thus their name.

To Puritans, the Church of England was violating the covenant, thus courting divine punishment. "I am verily persuaded," wrote John Winthrop, the soon-to-be governor of Massachusetts, "God will bring some heavy affliction upon this land."

In Massachusetts, the Puritans believed, they would escape God's wrath because there they would honor the covenant. For years, some Puritan leaders harbored the illusion that the English would look across the Atlantic at them, see by their splendid example the errors of their own ways, and invite the Puritan fathers home to escort England into righteousness. "We shall be as a citty on a hill," Winthrop wrote, a beacon of inspiration.

A Commonwealth

The Puritans believed in community, that individuals should support one another in life's spiritual quest and in its material concerns too. In the godly commonwealth, in Winthrop's words, "every man might have need of [every] other, and from hence they might be knit more nearly together in the bond of brotherly affection."

There was little patience in such a community for individualism and none for eccentricity. The Puritans enforced a strict code of moral and social behavior on everyone, saint and sinner alike. Because God punished a community that tolerated sinners, and not just the sinners, the Puritans were swift and harsh with what are today called "victimless crimes," or acts we do not regard as crimes at all. The most ordinary of Puritans understood this principle that can bewilder twenty-first-century Americans. When, in 1656, a simple girl named Tryal Pore confessed that she was guilty of fornication, she said that "by this my sinn I have not only done what I can to Poull Judgement from the Lord on my selve but allso upon the place where I live."

The same sense of community moved Puritans to point out to their neighbors when they were doing wrong. Judge Samuel Sewall of Massachusetts was not thought to be a busybody when he visited a wig-wearing relative to tell him that his hairpiece was sinful. Sewall was seen as looking after his kinsman's soul. The man liked his wig too much to give it up, but he did not tell Sewall to mind his own business. He argued only as to whether wearing a wig really was a sin.

Blue Laws

The law books of Massachusetts and other New England colonies were filled with regulations that, in our day, would be considered outrageous or ridiculous. God commanded that the Sabbath be devoted to him. Therefore, the Puritans forbade on Sundays activities that on Wednesday or Thursday might be perfectly in order: working, sports, "idle chatter," whistling, and even "walking in a garden." Some things appropriate in private were forbidden in public. In 1659, a sea captain named Kemble returned from a voyage of three years. He kissed his wife on the threshold of their home and was sentenced to sit in the stocks for two hours for "lewd and unseemly behaviour."

A woman who was a "scold," guilty of "Exorbitancy of the Tongue in Raling and Scolding," was humiliated on the ducking stool—she was tied to a chair on a seesaw-like lever and dunked repeatedly in a pond to the merriment of onlookers. Unsurprisingly, attendance at church was obligatory. In Maine in 1682, Andrew Searle was fined five shillings "for not frequenting the publique worship of god" and for "wandering from place to place upon the Lords

▲ *A few hours sitting in the stocks—public humiliation—was a fairly common punishment in early New England for minor offenses, especially violations of "Blue Laws." A variation was the pillory, in which the offender stood, head and hands similarly locked in place. Laughter and mockery on such occasions were tolerated; physical abuse of offenders was not.*

Guilt Trip
The early Puritans saw God's working in the most ordinary occurrences. When the Reverend Cotton Mather's small daughter fell into a fire and severely burned herself, Mather in painful anguish wrote in his journal, "Alas, for my sins the just God throws my child into the fire."

days." More serious crimes, such as theft, arson, assault, and wife beating, were punished with a flogging or branding.

As far as capital crimes were concerned, the New England Puritans were far more "liberal" than Old England was. Because the Bible was their guide in crime, as in much else, the Puritans reserved the death penalty for only those offenses that were punished by death in the Bible: murder, treason, witchcraft, incest, sodomy (homosexuality), "buggery" (bestiality), adultery, and blasphemy.

Not that hanging was mandatory for those convicted of these crimes. Between 1630 and 1660, fewer than 20 people were executed in Massachusetts: four murderers, two infanticides, three sexual offenders (including Thomas Granger, who coupled with "a mare, a cow, two goats, five sheep, two calves, and a turkey"), two witches, and four Quakers (members of a religious sect believed to "undermine & ruine" authority). It appears that only one adulterous couple, Mary Latham and James Britton, were hanged. Other adulterers were granted mercy—and a lesser punishment—or acquitted by juries because they did not want the miscreants executed. Connecticut enacted the death penalty for a child who struck or cursed his parents, but it was not enforced. When Joseph Porter was brought to court for calling his father "a thief, liar, and simple ape shittabed," and insulted the judge too, his conviction was thrown out on appeal.

The Puritans believed that social distinctions were divinely decreed. "Some must be rich, some poore," said John Winthrop—not some *are* rich, some poor. It was therefore an offense for people of lesser class to ape the fashions of their betters. In Connecticut in 1675, 38 women were arrested for dressing in silk. Obviously, the offenders could afford their finery, but their social standing in the community did not justify their wearing it. Another law forbade people of modest station to wear silver buckles on their shoes. Such adornments were "fit" only for magistrates and ministers.

A Well-Ordered Society

Between 1630 and 1640, 21,000 English men and women settled in New England. Most were family farmers. Indentured servants, the backbone of Virginia's labor force, were fewer in the North. Slaves of African origin were exotic until after 1700.

New England's authorities retained close control of the expansion of their colonies. Newly arrived groups were allotted land for towns of 50 to 100 families. Each family was granted fields for tillage, a woodlot for fuel, and the right to keep animals on the village common, which was just that—a pasture for common use. Social status in Old England determined just how much land a family was granted.

When newcomers settled too far from the town center to find meetinghouse and common convenient, the township's lands were divided into communities independent of one another. When a township grew overcrowded, some of its people moved west and north, sometimes as individuals but usually as members of a new community with authority from the colony to establish a new town.

Puritan Names

Many Puritans named their children from the Old Testament, not only after the great figures—Adam, Noah, Deborah, Judith—but after obscure characters whose names may have rung as discordantly in most Puritan ears as the names of people today who were named by "hippie" parents: Ahab, Zerubbabel, Abednego, and so on.

Others made a statement with an infant's name. Increase Mather, a prominent minister, was named from the biblical injunction, "Increase, multiply, and subdue the earth." Records have revealed no one named Multiply or Subdue, but there is a Fight the Good Fight of Faith Wilson, a Be Courteous Cole, and a Kill-Sin Pemble. Other notable names include The Lord Is Near, Fear-Not, Flee Fornication, and Job-Raked-Out-of-the-Ashes.

A couple named Cheeseman were told their infant was going to die during childbirth. Not knowing the child's sex, they baptized it "Creature." Creature Cheeseman fooled the midwife and lived a long life with her unusual moniker.

Not too much should be made of these names. Only 4 percent of Puritans were saddled with them. A boy was likelier than today to be named just plain Bill. About half of the girls in records of Puritan baptisms were bestowed only three rock-solid English names: Sarah, Elizabeth, and Mary.

Such firm social control enabled the Puritans to create one of the most literate populations in the world. In 1642, Massachusetts required parents to teach their children how to read. In 1647, townships of 50 families or more were required to support a school; towns of 1,000, a Latin (secondary) school. The Puritans had a college to train ministers, Harvard in Cambridge, Massachusetts, as early as 1636.

THE EXPANSION OF NEW ENGLAND

The rapid growth of population in Massachusetts and Puritan insistence that everyone in the community conform to God's law as the elite defined it prompted the founding of Rhode Island, Connecticut, and New Hampshire within a few years of the founding of Massachusetts itself.

Troublesome Roger Williams

Rhode Island and Providence Plantations, still the long official name of the smallest state, was founded by a brilliant and cranky minister named Roger Williams. In Massachusetts in 1631, he quarreled with Governor John Winthrop (who admired him) and other overseers almost before he was tucked into in his new bed.

Williams was the strictest sort of Puritan, and his demanding conscience, as rigorous with himself as with others, led to his banishment from Massachusetts Bay. He agreed with mainstream Puritans that most people were damned, that only a few were saved. But just who were these

▲ *New England's pioneers did not live in log cabins. That durable American institution was introduced by Swedes and Finns living on the Delaware River. New Englanders built framed houses sided with clapboards like this home constructed in Dedham, Massachusetts, in 1637. Frame construction required a sawmill and skilled artisans, both of which the well-organized Puritans had from the start.*

elect? The establishment had highly refined procedures for determining who were "visible saints" and, therefore, which settlers were eligible for church membership (and the right to vote). Williams disagreed. Nobody, he said, could be sure of anyone's election but his own. To underscore his point, he said that he prayed with his wife but he did not know for certain if she was truly saved. Only she and God knew that.

Williams concluded that religion and government—church and state—should be entirely separate. If no one could know who was truly saved and who not, there must be no religious test, such as in Massachusetts, to determine the right to participate in civil affairs.

Because church members were a minority in Massachusetts, this teaching threatened the Winthrop group's control of the commonwealth, the very reason they had come to America. If the damned majority were to make laws to suit their unregenerate selves, the Lord's covenant would soon lay in tatters, and God would "surely break out in wrath" against the colony.

Rhode Island: "The Sewer of New England"

Williams also offended Massachusetts authorities by challenging the validity of the royal charter on which Puritan control of Massachusetts was legally based. The land had been occupied when the English arrived, Williams pointed out, and the Indians' right to it was as good as anyone's anywhere. The king of England could not give it away; it was not his to give. Only by purchasing land from the natives

could settlers justly take possession of it. The charter was "a solemn public lie."

In fact, the Puritans usually paid the Indians for the land they settled, although their bargaining practices were not always saintly. Nevertheless, when Williams assailed the charter on which the Puritans based their control of Massachusetts, he touched the same tender nerve he had bruised in calling for the separation of church and state. By 1635, Winthrop and his party had had enough. Williams was ordered to return to England. Instead, he escaped into the forest, wintered with the Narragansett Indians, and in 1636, established a farm and township, Providence, on land purchased from that tribe.

If Roger Williams knew in his heart that the king of England had no right to give away Indian land, he was also a realist who knew how to play the political game. In 1644, he sailed to London where he secured a charter for his colony, Rhode Island. The Puritans of Massachusetts, staking so much on the sanctity of their own royal charter, would not dare violate Rhode Island's. Moreover, with Williams and his blasphemous followers dwelling outside the boundaries of Massachusetts, the worst Puritan fears were allayed: The Massachusetts Bay colony would not suffer for the doctrines Williams preached. In an ironic way, Rhode Island was indispensable to Massachusetts. It was a place to which they could banish the dissenters they found obnoxious. They called the colony the "sewer of New England."

Anne Hutchinson

In 1638, another dissenter was banished to the shores of Narragansett Bay. Like Williams, Anne Hutchinson was devout and a member of the elite. (She was John Winthrop's close neighbor.) Taking seriously the admonition that saints should study the word of God, she invited people into her home after Sunday services to discuss the sermon they had just heard. Hutchinson's own observations were often critical and sometimes acidic. When her informal meetings grew in popularity, they raised the hackles of preachers who were wounded by her sharp intelligence and formidable wit.

They shook their heads that a woman should dabble in subtle theology. "You have stept out of your place," Winthrop told Hutchinson. "You have rather bine a Husband than a Wife and a preacher than a Hearer." Her behavior was not "fitting" for her sex. In fact, the governor believed that women jeopardized their mental balance by pondering theological questions.

Still, had Hutchinson's offense been no greater than crowing, she might have gotten off with a scolding. She had influential supporters. But Hutchinson also taught that the Holy Spirit directly inspired some persons, such as herself, to speak out. This tenet, like Williams's, challenged Puritan control of Massachusetts. If the Holy Spirit spoke personally to some people, what they said was not "subject to controll of the rule of the Word or of the State." The doctrine was unacceptable. Puritans shuddered to contemplate—and they could imagine it—a society like our own in which anyone may say just about anything he or she wanted.

▲ *This representation of Anne Hutchinson being questioned in Boston by Governor Winthrop nicely captures the occasion. Records of the confrontation reveal that Hutchinson was confident, unyielding, and witty too. She several times bested Winthrop; but the governor had the power, and Hutchinson was banished.*

Known as antinomianism, Hutchinson's teaching pointed logically, like Williams's, to the separation of church and state. To make sure she was convicted, she was charged with 80 heresies and banished to Rhode Island. She later moved to New York, where, in 1643, she was killed by Indians.

New Hampshire and Connecticut

New Hampshire had been the proprietorship of one Sir Fernando Gorges, but he did nothing with it. The colony was populated beyond coastal Portsmouth only when disciples of Hutchinson, led by her brother-in-law, John Wheelwright, left Massachusetts in 1638. New Hampshire did not, however, have Rhode Island's reputation for eccentricity. Most of its settlers were conventional Puritans looking for land.

The richness of the bottomlands of the Connecticut River valley was the major draw of Connecticut. However, personality conflicts and religious bickering in Massachusetts also played a part. Fed up with Winthrop, Reverend Thomas Hooker and his followers moved there in 1636 and founded Hartford.

The migration so far inland caused a conflict with the Pequot Indians, the most powerful tribe of lower New England. In May 1637, after a Pequot raid on the Connecticut village of Wethersfield, the Massachusetts and Plymouth colonies sent a combined force that, by night, surrounded and set fire to the largest of the tribe's villages. As the Pequot fled the flames, the New Englanders shot and killed more than 400 of them, women and children as well as warriors. After a few smaller actions, the Pequot were for all practical purposes exterminated.

During the Pequot War, Theophilus Eaton and John Davenport, ministers concerned that Massachusetts was too soft on moral offenders, settled at New Haven on Long Island Sound. New Haven was the strictest of the Puritan commonwealths, and its strictures influenced Connecticut, into which New Haven was incorporated in 1662.

ROYAL AND PROPRIETARY COLONIES

Except for New Hampshire, the New England colonies were *corporate* colonies. Their constitutions, patterned on commercial charters of incorporation, provided for broad powers of self-government. Corporate colonies acknowledged the sovereignty of the king, but even this was little more than a symbolic gesture. In practice, the New England colonies were self-governing commonwealths responsible to those having the right to vote.

Virginia was such a corporate colony until 1624, when James I took it over. Then, as a *royal* colony, Virginia was ruled directly by the king through an appointed governor. Royal colonies had elected assemblies with extensive powers over the treasury, but the royal governor could veto any law these assemblies enacted. By the time of the American Revolution in 1776, 9 of the 13 colonies, including New Hampshire from its inception, were royal colonies.

Feudal Lords

Proprietary colonies had yet another structure of government. Ironically for a system that worked quite well in the New World, the principle underlying the proprietary system was antiquated, dating to the Middle Ages. Proprietors of colonies—wealthy gentlemen and nobles who won the king's favor—were, in effect, feudal lords of the American land granted to them. Their rights and privileges were defined as those held by the bishop of Durham in the Middle Ages. The bishop had been the king's vassal in the far north of England and was allowed greater independence than most nobles because he commanded the first line of defense against the Scots.

Moneymaking

Even the proprietors' method of making money was feudal, although, once again, it worked. Like the London Company and later the king in the royal colonies, proprietors encouraged people to settle on their lands by granting headrights: so many acres per head (the amount varied from colony to colony) to each person who came and for each person whose transportation a settler paid.

In return, landowners were required to pay the proprietor an annual "quitrent." This was not rent in our sense of the word. The settlers owned the land; they were not tenants. The quitrent principle dated from the time when the feudal system was breaking up in England (around 1300) and landowners commuted, or changed, their tenants' obligations to work for them into an annual cash payment. People who held land in "free and common socage" were "quit" of (released from) their old obligations, such as serving their lord as a soldier, shearing his sheep, repairing the castle moat, or whatever the lord of the land required.

Colonial quitrents were usually small: the idea was to get people to come to America, not to bleed them for doing so. For example, in Maryland for each acre owned in freehold (that is, owned outright), settlers paid an annual quitrent of two pence' worth of tobacco. The quitrent for 100 acres in New York was a bushel of wheat a year. In Georgia, the quitrent was two shillings per 50 acres.

Not much, but for the proprietor of a vast domain, thousands of such pittances added up to a handsome income, whereas the quitrents the proprietors owed the king were purely symbolic: two Indian arrowheads a year for Maryland, two beaver pelts a year for Pennsylvania.

Maryland: A Catholic Refuge—Briefly

Making money was a major motive of every proprietor, but the two grandest of the breed had other agendas as well. Maryland, chartered in 1631 and formally settled in 1634, was intended by its proprietors, George Calvert and his son Cecilius, the first and second Lords Baltimore, to be a refuge for English Catholics like themselves. The Calverts favored Catholics in making land grants, and they invited priests to the colony.

Catholics took the Calverts up on their offer, but they were a minority in Maryland from the start. By 1689, Catholics were just a quarter of the population. Because they were often the richest planters, Catholics were the targets of social

▲ *Cecilius Calvert, second Lord Baltimore, was the actual founder of Maryland, although the idea of a refuge for English Roman Catholics like the Calverts originated with his father, George Calvert. Originally, the Calverts planned to found their sanctuary in Newfoundland, but two visits there persuaded them to look farther south.*

resentment as well as religious distaste. In 1649, Cecilius Calvert feared for their future and approved the Act of Toleration. It provided that "noe person or persons whatsoever within [Maryland] . . . professing to believe in Jesus Christ, shall from henceforth bee any waies troubled, Molested or discountenanced for or in respect of his or her religion."

It was not complete toleration: Jews were not welcome, as they were in Rhode Island and in the Dutch colony of New Amsterdam. Nevertheless, protecting Catholics as it did, the act was too much for Maryland's Protestant majority. They revolted in 1654 and repealed it, inflicting double taxation and other disabilities on Roman Catholics. In 1689, John Coode led a successful rebellion of Protestants, who, three years later, forbade Catholics to worship publicly. (Oddly, three of Coode's four closest associates were married to Catholics.)

Maryland's Catholics were too well established to be chased out. The colony remained a center of American Catholicism, and in 1808, the first Catholic bishop in the United States was seated in Baltimore.

Politically Correct Maryland

The contemporary university is not unique in forbidding the use of words that might offend someone. Lord Calvert's Act of Toleration called for whipping "Persons reproaching any other within the Province by the Name or Denomination of Heretic, Schismatic, Idolater, Puritan, Independent, Presbyterian, Popish Priest, Jesuit, Jesuited Papist, Lutheran, Calvinist, Anabaptist, Brownist, Antinomian, Barrowist, Round-Head, Separatist, or any other Name or Term, in a reproachful Manner, relating to matters of Religion."

New Netherland and New Sweden

In 1624, a Dutch trading company established New Netherland between the two English settlements of Virginia and Plymouth. The town of New Amsterdam, at the tip of Manhattan Island, defended what the Dutch hoped would be a prosperous farming and fur-trading colony strung along the Hudson River.

Curiously, because the Dutch were a progressive people at home, they tried to populate the Hudson valley by means of a bizarrely archaic plan. The company granted huge "patroonships," vast tracts of land with 18 miles of Hudson River frontage, to any worthy who settled 50 families—people to be beholden to their patroon—on their land. Only one patroonship succeeded, 700,000-acre Van Renssaelerwyck, south of Fort Orange (present-day Albany, New York).

As buyers of furs and deer hides from the Indians, the Dutch were successful, exporting more than 60,000 pelts during New Netherland's first year. Annually, hundreds of Dutch ships tied up at New Amsterdam or anchored in the best harbor (New York harbor) on the Atlantic seaboard. There were problems. Governor Willem Kieft, as incompetent an official who ever breathed American air, slaughtered peaceful Indians who had taken refuge with the Dutch. Several Algonkian tribes retaliated, with results as devastating as the Jamestown Massacre, reducing the population of the colony to 700.

The new governor, Peter Stuyvesant, peg-legged and cantankerous ("his head is troubled," people said, "he has a screw loose") brought the colony back to prosperity, increasing the European and African population to 6,000. Stuyvesant also expanded Dutch holdings. In 1655, ships from New Amsterdam sailed south to the Delaware River, where they took over New Sweden, a string of tiny riverfront settlements of Swedes and Finns. New Sweden had been founded in 1638 by Peter Minuit, a Dutchman who had also been the first director-general of New Netherland. It was Minuit who purchased Manhattan Island from the Manhattan Indians for the equivalent of $24.

New York: An English Conquest

Fair for the Dutch was fair for the English, and easy too, when, after 17 years, Stuyvesant had offended just about everyone in New Amsterdam. In 1664, a British fleet commanded by the Duke of York (the king's brother) threatened to bombard the city but also offered, if there was no resistance, to protect the Dutch language, Dutch religion, and Dutch inheritance laws, which differed significantly from England's. Stuyvesant wanted to fight; no one else did. Without a shot being fired, New Netherland became New York, and New Amsterdam became the city of New York.

New York was a proprietary colony until, in 1685, the Duke of York was crowned King James II, whereupon it was royalized. Unpopular at home because he was a Roman Catholic, the duke was well liked in his colony. Dutch men and women continued to come. Stuyvesant himself stayed and prospered. Tolerance and cosmopolitanism characterized life. There were blacks in the city from the beginning and a small Jewish community. A French Jesuit priest, Isaac Jogues, heard 18 languages on the streets. A Virginian observed that the inhabitants "seem not concerned what religion their neighbor is, or whether hee hath any or none."

> ### Double Dutch
>
> The Dutch of New Netherland coined the word *Yankee*, an anglicized version of the Dutch "Jan Kies (John Cheese)"–their collective personification of New Englanders. Just as World War II soldiers called the Germans "Jerry" and American soldiers in Vietnam called the enemy "Charlie," the Dutch called the English "Jan Kies."
>
> The English retaliated with a host of insulting uses of the word *Dutch*. A one-sided deal was a "Dutch bargain"; a potluck dinner, a "Dutch lunch." Young men and women still speak of "going Dutch" if each pays his or her share of the costs of a date. "Dutch courage" was liquor, a "Dutch nightingale" was a frog, and a "Dutch widow" was a prostitute.

The Quakers

In 1681, Charles II gave a large tract of land, including the present states of Pennsylvania and Delaware, and parts of New Jersey, to William Penn, the son of an admiral to whom the king owed £16,000. Unlike other proprietors, Penn was no conventional courtier. He was a member of a fringe religious sect, the Society of Friends, or, as they were called because they trembled with emotion at their religious services, "Quakers."

The Quakers were figures of scorn, amusement, and some anxiety. They worried authorities because they preached Christian pacifism. Friends were forbidden to take up arms, even in self-defense. Seventeenth-century armies were not made up of draftees, but pacifism was still a challenging doctrine in an age when war was unapologetically considered a normal state of affairs.

The Quakers also disturbed the establishment because they taught that every individual had the light of God within, a teaching similar to Anne Hutchinson's. They said that Christians had no need of priests, ministers, or bishops. Some Quakers challenged the legitimacy of civil authority and social class. When they were haled before magistrats, Quakers refused to remove their hats and to take oaths. Telling the truth was the individual's responsibility to God, they said, and none of the civil authority's business.

The Quakers dramatized their belief in the equality of all people before God by addressing everyone, including nobles and the king himself, in the familiar *thee, thy,* and *thou* forms of the second-person pronoun. This seems quaint today, and it amused Charles II. (He removed his hat when Penn appeared before him because, he said, when the king is present, it was customary that only one man wear a hat.) Nevertheless, for those with less humor than Charles, it was insulting to be called *thee* by a social inferior or even a stranger.

Sunday in Massachusetts

Early Sunday morning, before sunrise in winter, Puritan families bundled up and walked to the meetinghouse. Few skipped services, even during a blizzard. Absence was fined, and, if winter weather could be withering, the distance to be traveled was short. Most New Englanders lived in villages, their homes clustered together near the meetinghouse.

They went to a *meetinghouse,* not to a *church.* To call the simple, unpainted clapboard structure a church would have been "popish"; the Puritans shunned every emblem hinting of the Church of Rome. There were no statues or other decorations such as adorned Catholic and Anglican churches. The meetinghouse was a place of preaching and worship—period. A weathercock rather than a cross crowned the steeple. It reminded the congregation that St. Peter denied to the Romans that he knew Christ before the cock crowed three times. Sinfulness was a theme on which the Puritans constantly harped.

In winter, the meetinghouse was scarcely warmer than the snowy fields surrounding the village. There may have been a fireplace, but the heat had little effect on those sitting more than 10 feet from it. The congregation bundled in fur envelopes—*not* sleeping bags; there was a fine for nodding off! People rested their feet on brass or iron foot warmers that contained coals brought from home. In towns that prohibited the use of foot warmers (they were a fire hazard), worshipers brought a large, well-trained dog to lie on their feet.

In some meetinghouses, women sat on the left side with their daughters. Men sat on the right, but boys, apt to be mischievous, were placed around the pulpit, where a churchwarden could lash out at fidgety ones with a switch. He probably often had his work cut out for him, since the service went on and on, sermons running an hour and a half and sometimes three hours. And, lest anyone wonder how long the sermon was lasting, an hourglass sat conspicuously on the preacher's pulpit; when the sand ran down, the hourglass was turned by the man who kept watch over the boys.

Although the Puritans had no instrumental music in their meetinghouses, they sang psalms, using the *Bay Psalm Book.* It was written with accuracy of translation rather than poetry in mind. Psalms exquisitely beautiful in the King James Version of the Bible (which the Puritans shunned) were awkward and strained. For example, in the Puritan translation, the magnificent and touching Psalm 100 is barely comprehensible:

> The rivers on of Babylon, there when we did sit downe;
> Yes even then we mourned, when we remembered Sion.
> Our harp we did hang it amid upon the willow tree,
> Because there they thus away led in captivitie,
> Required of us a song, thus asks mirth; us waste who laid
> Sing us among a Sion's song unto us then they said.

Services ended about noon. Families returned home for a meal that had been prepared before sundown the previous day. Like observant Jews on the Sabbath, the Puritans took the Lord's Day seriously: no cooking, no work, and certainly no play. Even conversation was spare on Sunday. It was no more proper to talk about workaday tasks than to perform them. At most, a pious family discussed the morning's sermon and other religious subjects. In the afternoon, the family returned to the meetinghouse to hear secular announcements and another sermon and to sing a few more psalms.

Finally, believing that all were equal before God, Quaker women actively preached and testified. This affronted the popular feeling that women should play no role in public life, least of all in religious matters. It is not difficult to imagine Anne Hutchinson, had she survived, becoming a Quaker. In fact, one of her followers, Mary Dyer, was condemned to the gallows in Massachusetts for preaching Quaker doctrine.

Penn's "Holy Experiment"

William Penn was the Quakers' savior. Whereas most Quakers were lower class, he was an educated and wealthy gentleman. Penn used his prestige to moderate some of the Quakers' more extravagant practices, and he gave them a refuge. Like other colonial proprietors, he saw Pennsylvania (which means "Penn's woods") as a way to make money (to which the Friends could think of no objection). But he also envisioned Pennsylvania as a "holy experiment" in toleration. All people who believed in "One Almighty and Eternal God" were welcome.

Pennsylvania thrived from the start. Pietists from the German Rhineland and from Switzerland, whose ideas resembled those of the Quakers, settled there in some numbers. They developed the fertile rolling land of southeastern Pennsylvania into model farms. Their descendants survive as the Pennsylvania Dutch, observing seventeenth-century customs.

Along with Charleston, South Carolina, Philadelphia was a planned city. The streets of the "greene countrie towne" were laid out on a gridiron, making possible a tidiness that even the well-ordered Puritans had been unable to command of Boston. Philadelphia became the largest and most prosperous city in English North America, at least in part because of Quaker liberality. By the mid-1700s, it was "the second city of the British empire," smaller only than London in the English-speaking world.

New Jersey and Delaware developed separately as proprietary colonies. However, they too were heavily populated by Quakers and practiced many of the same policies as Pennsylvania.

The Carolinas: A Feudal Experiment

The proprietor of the Carolina Grant of 1663 (named after King Charles II, *Carolus* in Latin) was a consortium of eight gentlemen and nobles. In 1669, they attempted to enforce on their grant a social structure more fantastic than the patroonship plan for New Netherland. The scheme was outlined in The Fundamental Constitutions of Carolina, the brainchild of Anthony Ashley Cooper, one of the most active of the proprietors. Its 120 detailed articles were written by his secretary, the political philosopher John Locke, whose primary place in history is as a defender of principles of political liberty. In the Fundamental Constitutions, curiously, Locke created a rigidly structured social blueprint.

Carolina was divided into square counties, in each of which the proprietors ("seigneurs") owned 96,000 acres. Other contrived ranks of nobility called "caciques" (an Indian title) and "landgraves" (European) would have smaller but still large tracts. The work would be done by humble "leetmen" and even humbler African slaves, over whom their owners were guaranteed "absolute power and authority."

Some historians think that this fantastic system was simply a promotional device designed to excite English land buyers with the promise of puffed-up titles. Certainly it was unworkable. A city might be laid out in squares, but not a country shaped by rivers, creeks, hills, swamps, and mountains. The mere abundance of land meant that development would be free and open, not a subject of strict regulation. Although the Fundamental Constitutions technically survived for decades, they did not much affect the actual development of the Carolinas.

Two Carolinas

Geography shaped the colony. Differing environments in the northern and southern parts of Carolina determined that settlements there would develop in significantly different ways.

In the north, most settlers were small farmers who drifted down from Virginia and planted tobacco, as they had done at home. Centered on Albemarle Sound, northern Carolina was poor, rather democratic in mood, and independent. It was quite isolated even from Virginia by the Great Dismal Swamp. In 1677, a Virginian named John Culpeper led a rebellion in northern Carolina that briefly defied all outside authority.

In the southern part of the grant, settlers from Barbados (an English sugar-growing island) founded Charleston where the Ashley and Cooper Rivers flowed into the Atlantic. At first, southern Carolina was a trading colony, tapping the interior as far inland as present-day Alabama for furs and hides, and converting the surrounding pine forests into timber and naval stores. By 1700, however, the outline of a plantation system had taken shape.

Probably from African slaves, the planters learned how to grow rice, a lucrative export crop. The easily flooded lowlands along the rivers were ideally suited to its cultivation. Long-staple cotton, used in manufacturing fine textiles, found favorable conditions on the sandy sea islands that fringed the coast. Indigo, a plant that produced a coveted blue dye, was later added to the list of Carolina products that were sold profitably abroad. Indigo was invaluable because it was cultivated and harvested when rice was not in season, thus keeping laborers busy year-round.

All of southern Carolina's crops lent themselves to being worked on large plantations by gangs. By 1700, half of the 5,000 people in the colony were slaves. This was by far the highest proportion of Africans in the population of any mainland colony.

The slaves' owners dominated southern Carolina society to an extent that even the tobacco grandees of Virginia might have envied. The low country that produced their wealth was unhealthy, "in the spring a paradise, in the summer a hell, and in the autumn a hospital." It was actually more like a morgue, thanks to mosquito-borne diseases (malaria, yellow fever) and plague levels of other killers, particularly dysentery. The small elite took to keeping town houses in Charleston, which was open to sea breezes. There they spent at least the summer and fall and, increasingly with the years, the better part of the year.

The result was, at the top, an urban and cosmopolitan society obnoxious to the small farmers of northern Carolina. In 1712, in a recognition of differing social bases rare in the eighteenth century, the proprietors granted the two Carolinas separate assemblies and governors. When they sold their holdings to the king in 1729, he confirmed them as distinct royal colonies: North Carolina and South Carolina.

Georgia: A Philanthropic Experiment

Georgia was the last of the 13 colonies to be founded. It was chartered in 1732, with Savannah established the next year. The Crown wanted a military buffer state protecting valuable South Carolina from the Spanish in Florida. Although Spain had recognized England's right to its colonies in 1676, 10 years later, an armed force destroyed a small English settlement on the Florida side of the boundary. During an English–Spanish war between 1702 and 1713, Charleston was threatened.

In Colonel James Oglethorpe, Parliament found the perfect man to develop a fortress colony. Oglethorpe was an experienced soldier. He was also a philanthropist who was troubled by the misery of the English poor, particularly jailed debtors. At the time (and for a century in America too), a person could be imprisoned for debt and not released until his obligation was paid. Oglethorpe conceived of Georgia (named for the king) as a place to which such unfortunates might go to begin anew.

He and his associates received the colony as a "trust." That is, they were not to profit from the colony, as proprietors did. Landholdings were to be small, only 50 acres, both to discourage speculators and to encourage the formation of a compact, easily mobilized defense force. Slavery was forbidden. Oglethorpe did not want to see the emergence of a slave-owning elite such as dominated South Carolina. He also prohibited alcohol, believing drunkenness to be a major cause of crime and poverty.

As a buffer state, Georgia was successful. In 1742, a Spanish flotilla of 36 ships transported 2,000 soldiers from Cuba to capture Savannah. Oglethorpe could raise only 900 men. But they defeated the Spanish in several skirmishes on St. Simons Island, and the Spanish withdrew. Oglethorpe then destroyed a fortified Spanish town north of St. Augustine.

As a philanthropic enterprise, Georgia was a failure. The trustees sent about 1,800 debtors and paupers to Georgia. Another 1,000 came on their own. Among them were South Carolinians who brought slaves with them. Although Oglethorpe was inclined to be a tyrant, he was unable to enforce the ban on slavery (or on rum). He returned to England disgusted. In 1752, the trustees returned control of the colony to the king, one year earlier than their charter required.

Other English Colonies

With the founding of Georgia, the 13 colonies that were to become the United States were marked on the maps of North America and recorded in the books of the Board of Trade, the agency that administered the colonies for the Crown. It should be noted, however, that England was active elsewhere in the Western Hemisphere. In fact, several English possessions still tied to Great Britain are older than most of the colonies that became part of the United States.

Belize, in Central America, dates from the early 1600s, although, as a haven of pirates, it was hardly an official colony. Bermuda, east of Georgia, was settled in 1609 when a ship bound for Virginia was wrecked there (the inspiration of William Shakespeare's play *The Tempest*). Tobago, a tiny island off the coast of Venezuela, was seized by English adventurers in 1616, four years before Plymouth was founded. Nearby Barbados, where many early South Carolinians originated and through which many of the ancestors of African Americans passed, dates from 1627. Local tradition insists that English settlement in Barbados dates from 1605, two years before Jamestown.

In 1621, Sir William Alexander received a charter to found English colonies in Acadia, present-day Nova Scotia. However, the French controlled most of that rugged land until 1713. In 1655, an English fleet under Admiral William Penn, the father of the founder of Pennsylvania, seized Jamaica from Spain. Several continuously occupied trading posts on Hudson Bay, which was claimed for England by a Dutch navigator, Henry Hudson, were planted in the 1670s. The Bahamas, where Columbus first saw the New World, have been British since about the late seventeenth century.

Tropical islands where sugar cane grew were the most lucrative colonies from the Crown's point of view. To ordinary folk interested in actually settling in the New World, the 13 mainland colonies beckoned more seductively. There, society was remarkably free, and those colonies offered the greatest economic opportunities in the world.

for FURTHER READING

See the appropriate chapters of Charles M. Andrews, *The Colonial Period of American History,* 1934–1938; Curtis E. Nettels, *The Roots of American Civilization,* 1938; Daniel Boorstin, *The Americans: The Colonial Experience,* 1958; Clarence Ver Steeg, *The Formative Years,* 1964; John E. Pomfret with Floyd Shumway, *Founding the American Colonies,* 1970; and Jack P. Greene and J. R. Pole, eds., *Colonial British America,* 1984.

Plymouth colony is one of those rare subjects about which the first book to read is the first that was written: Governor William Bradford's *History of Plimmoth Plantation* (numerous editions). Also see George Langdon, *Pilgrim Colony: A History of New Plymouth, 1620–1691,* 1966.

On Massachusetts Bay, the classic, highly critical of the Puritans, is James Truslow Adams, *The Founding of New England,* 1930. Subsequent appreciation of the Puritans owes largely to the work of two historians, Perry Miller and Edmund S. Morgan. See the following by Perry Miller: *The New England Mind,* 1939, 1953; and *Errand into the Wilderness,* 1964. See these books by Edmund S. Morgan: *Visible Saints,* 1963; *The Puritan Dilemma: The Story of John Winthrop,* 1958; and *The Puritan Family,* 1966. Also see Roger Williams, *The Church and the State,* 1967.

On Anne Hutchinson, see Emery Battis, *Saints and Sectarians: Anne Hutchinson and the Antinomian Controversy in Massachusetts,* 1962. On Rhode Island, see Sydney V. James, *Colonial Rhode Island: A History,* 1975.

In the 1970s, special studies of Puritan society and culture were numerous, and many are of the highest quality. The following are a brief sampling: Sacvan Bercovitch, *The American Jeremiad,* 1978; Andrew Delbanco, *The Puritan Ordeal,* 1989; John Demos, *A Little Commonwealth: Family Life in Plymouth Colony,* 1970; Philip Greven Jr., *Four Generations: Population, Land, and Family in Colonial Andover,* 1970; Kenneth Lockridge, *A New England Town,* 1971; Samuel Powell, *Puritan Village,* 1963; David Stannard, *The Puritan Way of Death,* 1977; Michael Walzer, *The Revolution of the Saints,* 1965; and Larzer Ziff, *Puritanism in Old and New England,* 1973.

For Pennsylvania, see Edwin B. Bronner, *William Penn's "Holy Experiment,"* 1962; Gary Nash, *Quakers and Politics: Pennsylvania, 1681–1726,* 1971; and James T. Lemon, *The Best Poor Man's Country: A Geographical Study of Early Southeastern Pennsylvania,* 1972. On New Netherland/New York, see Michael Kammen, *Colonial New York,* 1975; Robert C. Ritchie, *The Duke's Province,* 1977; and the appropriate chapters of the superb book by Edwin G. Burrows and Mike Wallace, *Gotham: A History of New York City to 1898,* 1999. On New Jersey, see J. E. Pomfret, *The Province of East and West New Jersey,* 1956.

For the later southern colonies, see William S. Powell, *Colonial North Carolina,* 1973; Eugene Sirmans, *Colonial South Carolina,* 1966; and Phinizy Spalding, *Oglethorpe in America,* 1977.

Visit the source collections at http://ajaccess.wadsworth.com and http://infotrac.thomsonlearning.com, and use the Search function with the following key terms to explore documents, images, audio and video clips, articles, and commentary related to the material in this chapter:

Anne Bradstreet
Anne Hutchinson
John Locke
Massachusetts Bay colony
Plymouth colony
Puritans
William Penn

Additional resources, exercises, and Internet links related to this chapter are available on *The American Past* Web site: http://history.wadsworth.com/americanpast7e.

HISTORY ONLINE

Religion in Colonial America
http://lcweb.loc.gov/exhibits/religion/rel01.html
Broad sampling of information about the place of religion in the colonies.

Colonial Slavery
http://cghas.dade.K12.A.us/slavery/british_america/default.htm
Aspects of slavery unique to colonial America.

ENGLISH LEGACIES, AMERICAN FACTS OF LIFE

Colonial Society in the 1600s

And those that came were resolved to be Englishmen,
Gone to the world's end but English every one,
And they ate the white corn kernels parched in the sun
And they knew it not but they'd not be English again.
                                    Stephen Vincent Benét

THE BRITISH LIKED to say that they created their empire in a fit of absentmindedness. There is a bit of truth in that. The Crown's approval, in the form of a charter, was essential if a colony was to be legal. However, neither king nor Parliament took an active part in establishing a single American dominion. Every colony was financed and promoted in what we would call the "private sector," while the Crown generally failed to notice what was going on.

The colonial entrepreneurs were investors or courtiers hoping to make money, religious dissenters seeking sanctuary, and visionaries with images of a better society dancing in their heads. So casual was the Crown concerning its American real estate—in the law, it all began as royal property—that many colonial boundaries were vague and overlapping, breezy strokes of a goose-quill pen on maps in London that caused endless bickering on the actual ground.

Absentmindedly or not, the empire grew. By 1702, when Queen Anne was crowned, 300,000 of her subjects made their homes in English—soon to be British—North America, which stretched, however thinly in many spots, a thousand miles north to south, from above Portsmouth, New Hampshire, to Charleston, South Carolina.

TRADE LAWS

Parliament first tried to frame a coherent colonial policy during the 1650s, when there was no king. Parliament had beheaded Charles I and now (along with a military dictator, Oliver Cromwell) ruled England. When monarchy returned with Charles II in 1660, the colonial policy Parliament had established, the Navigation Acts, was confirmed, and the Crown created a committee (later known as the Board of Trade) to advise the king on colonial affairs. As the board's name indicates, colonial commerce was what interested the English. Charles II said it in 1668: "The thing that is nearest the heart of the nation is trade."

▲ *Ships carrying goods to the colonies and returning with colonial exports tied up at wharves like this one in London, or in other English ports such as Bristol and Plymouth.*

Mercantilism

The economic philosophy that underlay England's trade policy is known as mercantilism. Its principles were first systematized in 1630 in Thomas Mun's *England's Treasure by Foreign Trade,* although the English, French, Dutch, and even the Spanish unsuccessfully had acted in mercantilistic ways for a century.

The object of mercantilism was to increase a nation's wealth in gold and silver—the wealth of all the realm's subjects, not just the royal treasury. The key to doing this was a favorable balance of trade. That is, the people of the nation must sell goods and services abroad that were more costly than the goods and services that they imported from other countries.

Thus the word *mercantilism,* because overseas merchants (*mercator* is Latin for "merchant") were of special value in this philosophy. If a ship out of Bristol carried a cargo of Dutch cloth to the Spanish colony of Cuba and Cuban sugar back to France, the coin he charged the shippers for his services enriched England at the expense of three rival nations. Mercantilist policy was, therefore, to encourage England's merchants in their business in every way possible.

Manufacturing was also dear to the mercantilist heart. Long before 1600, the English learned that it was economic lunacy to send raw wool to Flanders and the Netherlands, as they did, and then to buy it back in the form of cloth. The manufactured cloth cost considerably more than the wool from which it was spun and woven. The difference was coin drained out of England. The Crown, therefore, forbade the export of raw wool and, through subsidies and other favors, encouraged the carders, spinners, dyers, and weavers whose skills and labor added value to the sheep's fleece. Mercantilists urged the Crown to favor all manufacturers with such protections and inducements.

The Colonial Connection

In the best of all possible mercantilistic worlds, England would be totally self-sufficient. The nation would produce everything its people needed and buy nothing abroad. Gold and silver earned from exports and the carrying trade would roll in; none would depart.

In the real world, self-sufficiency was out of the question. An island nation in a northerly latitude, England imported any number of tropical products. The English people produced little wine but drank a good deal of it: Wine was imported from France, Portugal, and the Rhineland. England consumed large quantities of furs for the manufacture of clothing and felt. These came from Muscovy, as Russia was known. As a maritime nation, England needed timber and naval stores (tar, pitch, fiber for rope) in quantities far beyond the productive capacity of the country's depleted forests. Forest products had to be imported from Scandinavia.

In practice, then, the object of mercantilism was to minimize imports, which cost money, and maximize exports and trade, which brought money in. It was at this point that mercantilists became promoters of colonies.

Colonies reduced England's dependence on foreign countries. The forests of North America, seemingly limitless and teeming with beaver, mink, and other fur-bearing animals, meant that England could reduce the flow of gold and silver to Scandinavia and Russia. By occupying islands in the West Indies, the English produced their own sugar and stopped paying Spaniards for it. And by settling dutiful subjects overseas, the Crown created exclusive and dependable markets for English manufacturers. The colonists themselves had to scare up the coin with which to purchase these goods as best they could.

The Navigation Acts

The Navigation Acts of 1660–1663 wrote mercantilism into law. They minced no words in defining the purpose of the American colonies as the enrichment of the mother country. The prosperity of the colonies was a consideration and received attention. However, when the economic interests of colonials clashed with those of the mother country, the latter were what counted. Colonies were tributaries, not partners.

So the Navigation Acts stipulated that all colonial trade be carried in vessels built and owned by English or colonial merchants. These ships were to be manned by crews in which at least three seamen in four were English or colonials. Not even niggardly seamen's wages were to be paid to foreigners, who might take their earnings home with them.

Next, the Navigation Acts required that European goods intended for sale in the colonies be carried first to certain English ports called "entrepôts" (places from which goods are distributed). There they were to be monitored and only then shipped to America. The purpose of this law was to ensure a precise record of colonial trade, to collect taxes on it, and to see to it that English merchants and port laborers benefited from every colonial transaction.

Important and lucrative trade goods fell under this provision. Wealthy colonists had a taste for French claret and the sweet, fortified wines of Spain and Portugal. But they could not import them directly from the source. First, the bottles and casks had to pass through one of the entrepôts in England. Of course, this raised the cost of drinking, but that was the idea. The premium colonials paid for their wines went into English purses.

The Navigation Acts also designated some colonial exports as "enumerated articles." These could be shipped only to English ports, even if they were destined for sale on the continent of Europe. Once again, the object was to guarantee that part of the profit in colonial trade went to English merchants. Moreover, taxes on the enumerated articles were an important source of government revenue. Charles II collected £100,000 a year from the tax on tobacco alone.

The enumerated articles included most colonial products that were readily sold on the world market: molasses, furs and hides, naval stores, rice, cotton, and tobacco. Foodstuffs (grain, livestock, salted fish), and lumber not suited to shipbuilding, were less profitable and not enumerated. Colonials could ship them directly to foreign ports.

MERCANTILISM IN THE SOUTH

The Navigation Acts applied to all colonies. However, the diverse topographies, climates, and social structures of England's far-flung provinces meant that they affected colonials in sharply differing ways.

Well before 1700, the English and American colonials thought in terms of the New England colonies, the Middle Colonies, and the South. New England was New Hampshire, Massachusetts, Rhode Island, and Connecticut. (Maine was a part of Massachusetts; Vermont was Indian territory.) To the south and west lay the Middle Colonies: New York, New Jersey, Pennsylvania, and Delaware. The South included Maryland, Virginia, North Carolina, South Carolina, and, after 1732, Georgia. (Florida was Spanish territory.)

With good reason, English merchants smiled when they thought of the southern colonies. The southern colonies produced tobacco—the most profitable of all the enumerated articles except the sugar that came from the islands of the West Indies. Like the West Indies, the southern colonies were home to a large, bonded labor force of white servants and black slaves for whom cheap clothing, shoes, and tools had to be purchased in England. By 1700, an increasingly rich and extravagant master class, living off the labor of these workers,

The Tobacco God
When Edward Seymour was asked to support the creation of a college in Virginia because the ministers trained there would save souls, he replied, "Souls! Damn your souls! Make tobacco!"

had emerged—an upper class that coveted every luxury any merchant ever thought to load on a sailing ship.

Tobacco: Blessing and Curse

The colonies had a monopoly on tobacco production in the empire. English farmers were forbidden to grow it, a rare instance of a colonial economic privilege. By the 1660s, however, Maryland's and Virginia's advantage was not enough to ensure prosperity. The wholesale price of a pound of tobacco (the price at which the planters sold) collapsed from two pence and a halfpenny to a halfpenny. So much land had been planted in tobacco that the markets for it no longer absorbed production.

To planters, the solution to the problem of falling prices was obvious. The Dutch reached markets the English did not; but because the Navigation Acts forbade the sale of an "enumerated article" to England's chief commercial rival, Dutch buyers were banned from the colonies. Planters complained: "If the Hollanders must not trade to Virginia, how shall the planters dispose of their tobacco? . . . The tobacco will not vend in England, the Hollanders will not fetch it from England. What must become thereof?"

One thing that became thereof was evasion of the Navigation Acts. Smuggling was common and not at all unrespectable. Dutch traders arriving at wharves in Virginia and Maryland did not have to listen to many lectures about English trade law. They had little difficulty persuading planters to sell them tobacco. Such defiance of the Navigation Acts was not difficult, thanks to the topography of the Chesapeake region.

The Tidewater

The Chesapeake is a huge estuary fed by innumerable smaller ones. Along with countless briny creeks and inlets, the rivers that empty into the great bay—the Potomac, the Rappahannock, the James, the Choptank—are broad, slow-moving streams. They were deep enough for the small seagoing vessels of the seventeenth and eighteenth centuries to sail as many miles inland as high tide pushed salt water. The ships—legal and illegal—might careen in river mire when the tide ebbed, but twice a day, the sea dependably returned to float them and their cargoes back to Europe.

The land washed by this salt water, a series of peninsulas called "necks," was known as the Tidewater. It was the first part of the tobacco colonies to be settled, and it became home to an elite that dominated Virginia and Maryland society.

▲ *A tobacco factor (buyer) and planter negotiating the sale of a tobacco crop at the planter's wharf. Tobacco was packed in hogsheads, huge barrels, as most goods transported by ship were. Barrels could be easily rolled, they were watertight, and, properly stacked on their sides, they did not shift in rough seas.*

Although their descendants did not like to admit it, few Tidewater aristocrats were aristocratic when they settled in America. English men and women of high station did not emigrate to a land where the life expectancy was 40 years. Nor, however, were most Tidewater aristocrats descended from the dregs of English society: convicts, beggars, destitute farm laborers. Most of the men and women of the "first families of Virginia" were from the artisan, petty merchant, or yeoman class—the middling sort. They brought enough capital with them to develop plantations, but social pretensions were possible only because of the tobacco boom.

Depression at the End of the World

The chances of going from rags to riches in the tobacco colonies dwindled in the later 1600s. Indeed, making a decent living became a struggle for all but the planters with vast acreage. The collapse in the price of tobacco bankrupted hundreds of small farmers so that larger planters who, like the rich in all times and places, were less vulnerable to the downturn, picked up small holdings in the Tidewater and enhanced their dominance.

After 1660, even ambitious immigrants to Virginia were forced to trek to build an estate. There in the Piedmont, or foothills of the Appalachians, they found hundreds of hardscrabble frontiersmen. Some had been dispossessed in the Tidewater. Others were freed servants without land: unmarried, boisterous young men who got along by hunting, trapping, doing casual work for wages, and less savory things.

In 1676, differences between these Piedmonters and the Tidewater planters erupted in a miniature civil war, ragtag and improvised, but plenty nasty.

East-West Conflict

The royal governor of Virginia in 1676 was Sir William Berkeley. In the colony for more than 30 years—a long time for an English gentleman—he had done quite well for himself. Berkeley was a major landowner, the doyen of Jamestown society, and the political leader of the Tidewater planters.

Berkeley and his friends supplemented their income from tobacco by carrying on a prosperous trade with the Indians. In return for furs and buckskins, they provided manufactured goods, especially woven blankets, iron products ranging from pots to traps and guns, and rum, the cheapest alcohol available. When the bottom dropped out of tobacco prices in the 1660s, this business loomed larger in their accounts. It also provided the Berkeley group with a reason to cultivate a good working relationship with the tribes that supplied the hides and furs.

Settlers in the Piedmont, by contrast, looked on Indians as enemies. As the whites expanded their fields, they encroached on the hunting grounds of the Susquehannock and other peoples, including tribes that had already been forced off their ancestral lands in the Tidewater. Inevitably, there were clashes. The Indians complained to Berkeley of white interlopers. The settlers of the Piedmont complained of hit-and-run raids on their farms. Berkeley and his associates,

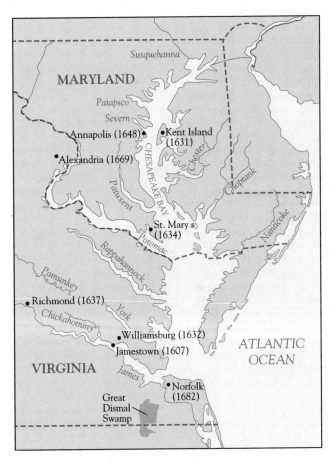

MAP 4:1 The Chesapeake Estuary The Chesapeake Bay region is a land of water. Even seagoing ships could penetrate far up its innumerable tidal rivers and creeks. When Virginians and Marylanders traveled locally, they went by boat. Most important, with the entire early plantation area accessible to ships, there was no need for towns, let alone cities, that were commercial centers.

their trading and political interests caught in the middle, tried to resolve the conflict by building a system of defensive stockades along the line of white settlement.

The plan did not win over the Piedmont whites. The forts were so far apart that Indian marauders, especially the aggressive Susquehannock, easily slipped between them, wreaked havoc, and retreated. More important, like frontier settlers for two centuries to come, Virginia's backcountry pioneers did not think in terms of holding a line against the Indians. Ever increasing in numbers, they were expansive. They meant to clear the land of the natives, not to share it with them.

Bacon's Rebellion

When the death toll of backcountry whites climbed to more than a hundred, and kidnappings of women and children increased, the Piedmont planters took matters into their own hands. Nathaniel Bacon, a recent immigrant of some means, set himself up as the commander of a force that decimated the Oconeechee tribe. The Oconeechee had not attacked whites; indeed, they had expressed interest in an alliance

with the white Virginians against the Susquehannock, who raided them too! No matter—they were Indians. Bacon crushed them and then turned his "army" toward the colonial capital of Jamestown.

Angry words led the governor to arrest Bacon as a rebel, but he was forced to release him when Bacon's supporters made it clear they were quite capable of laying the little town waste. After a spell of uneasy stalemate between the Tidewater and the Piedmont, Bacon returned to Jamestown and blustered that he would hang the governor. Berkeley took him seriously; he fled across the Chesapeake. For several months, Nathaniel Bacon and his frontiersmen governed the colony nearly as extensively as the royal governor and his council had.

We do not know how the Crown would have dealt with the touchy situation. In October 1676, at age 29, Nathaniel Bacon fell ill and died. He must have been a compelling man. With him gone, the rebels lost heart and scattered into the forests. Berkeley returned, rounded up several dozen of the rebels, and hanged them. But the governor was finished too. Charles II was disgusted by Berkeley's vindictiveness, remarking, "The old fool has hanged more men in that naked country than I have done for the murder of my father." Berkeley was recalled to England, where he died within a few months.

The suspicion and ill feeling between the Tidewater and the Piedmont did not die. The Tidewater aristocracy continued to dominate Virginia's economy, government, and culture, and the people of the backcountry continued to resent them.

A Land Without Cities

The great planters' domination of Virginia and Maryland was so thoroughgoing because, in politics, there was no other social group able to compete with them. There was no urban middle class of merchants, bankers, and manufacturers in Virginia and Maryland because there were no centers of commerce, no real cities.

One Marylander attributed this curiosity to the appetite for tobacco lands. "Tobacco," he wrote, "requires us to abhor communities or townships. . . . A planter cannot carry on his affairs without considerable elbow room." Moreover, because the Potomac, James, York, Nanticoke, and Choptank Rivers were navigable so far inland, ships tied up at the private wharves of the great Tidewater plantations. They did not need a central port, a Philadelphia or New York, in which to drop anchor. The planters sold their crop and received the goods that they had ordered the previous year, in their own backyards. Small farmers whose lands did not front on water depended on the great planters' facilities for their trading.

They were exhilarating days in the naked land when the merchantmen arrived. Servants and slaves rolled hogsheads (large barrels) of tobacco to the dock, enjoying the hospitality of the master, which was expansive. Farmers, backcountry planters and their families, and Indians gathered to dance, drink, race on foot and horseback, and shoot targets. For women, who lived a more isolated life than the menfolk, the arrival of a tobacco factor (agent) was a rare opportunity to enjoy company.

▲ *The artist's sympathies in depicting the confrontation between Nathaniel Bacon and Virginia governor Berkeley are not disguised. Bacon is a forthright, handsome cavalier. A pathetic Berkeley is intimidated and cowering. By no means was this opinion of Bacon's Rebellion universal.*

Everyone discussed the news that the shipmasters brought with them about European battles and the machinations of the kings they had left behind. Some received letters from old-country family, friends, and associates. The sailors enlivened the carnival with their giddiness at being ashore after weeks at sea, spending their wages on games and drink and the favors of women.

A People Who Lived on Imports

Central to the headiness of the occasion was the arrival of the manufactured goods on which the colonists depended in order to live in something resembling European style. A single ship might be loaded with spades, shovels, axes, and saws; household items such as kettles, pots, pans, sieves, funnels, pewter tankards, and tableware; odds and ends such as buttons, needles, thread, pins, and ribbons. There were textiles for both the planter families' fine clothing and rough wraps for servants and slaves; shoes and boots; bricks, nails, and paint; goods to trade with the Indians (all of the above plus trinkets, mirrors, and the like); and firearms, shot, and gunpowder. For the very wealthy few, there were luxuries: silver candlesticks, chests and other fine furniture, wine, brandy, spices, books, and even violins and harpsichords with which to grace a parlor and cheer an evening.

Business that was carried out in cities elsewhere in the world, including the northern colonies and Charleston, was transacted at the great plantations of Maryland and Virginia for a few weeks each year. When the ships departed for London, Plymouth, or Bristol, not only did they bring tobacco; they also became Virginia's and Maryland's banks and factory outlets. The commercial middle class of the tobacco colonies lived across the Atlantic. Virginia's and Maryland's shops were afloat.

Even the capitals of the tobacco colonies, Jamestown (Williamsburg after 1699) and Annapolis, were ghost towns when the assemblies were not in session. County seats were mere clusters of buildings at the crossings of trails, nothing more, and nothing at all when court was not in session and there was not an election. Small farmers lived isolated by forest from one another. Churches were few and scattered; public houses—inns and taverns—fewer. Travelers depended on an invitation to a private home, humble or grand, for dinner and shelter from the night.

A Life of Some Elegance

By the end of the seventeenth century, the great planters of Virginia and Maryland were creating a gracious style of life patterned after that of the English country gentry. They copied as best they were able the manners, fashions, and quirks of English squires and their ladies. When tobacco was returning a good price, they built fine houses in the style of English manors and filled them with good furniture. They stocked their cellars with port and Madeira, hock from the Rhineland, and claret from France, which they generously poured for one another at dinners, parties, balls, and simple visits that marked the origins of the famous "southern hospitality."

Finding the Way

Sailors in the African or Asian trade often found their way by the ancient expedient of keeping the coastline in sight. They sailed like the pilot of a small airplane flies, by following landmarks. Deepwater seamen—transatlantic sailors—depended on the compass, the prototype of which Europeans had received from the East in ancient times, and on the astrolabe.

By the seventeenth century, the ship's compass was a brass bowl marked with 32 directions, in the center of which a magnetized needle was delicately balanced. It was positioned within sight of the helmsman and mounted on pivots so that it remained level when the vessel pitched and rolled.

The compass, invented in China, was made into a navigational instrument in medieval Italy. The astrolabe, perfected in Portugal in the 1400s, enabled navigators to measure the angle between the horizon and the sun by day and between the North Star (or below the equator, the Southern Cross) by night. With this information, shipmasters could determine their latitude, that is, the distance of their position from the equator. With an astrolabe, a sailor knew on which east-west line his ship was sailing.

So an English captain seeking to make a landfall at Cape Cod, which he knew was located at about 42 degrees north latitude, sailed in a southerly direction out of England until his ship arrived at 42 degrees. Then, using his compass, he sailed due west. It was simple to the extent winds and currents were cooperative.

What sailors could not determine with any accuracy was longitude—their position on the imaginary arcs that run north-south from pole to pole. On an east-west voyage such as across the Atlantic between the colonies and the mother country, navigators had only an approximate idea of how far they had sailed from their port of departure and, therefore, how far they were from their destination.

There were rude instruments for determining speed, which is what longitude is on an east-west voyage. The log line was a rope knotted every 48 feet with a wood float tied to the end. It was thrown overboard and, measuring minutes with a sandglass, the captain counted the number of knots that passed over the stern in a given period of time. Since the log was not blown as the ship was, the speed of the wind could be roughly ascertained. However, the log line did not take account of the action of ocean currents, which could radically increase or decrease a ship's progress—the log was in the grip of the current just as the ship was.

Not until the mid–eighteenth century was the problem of determining longitude systematically attacked. In 1752, a German astronomer, Tobias Mayer, devised a set of tables and a mathematical formula for determining longitude from the position of the moon, but the method was not practical. Even a skilled mathematician needed four hours to complete the calculation required. In 1767, the Royal Observatory at Greenwich, England (which was to become zero degrees longitude worldwide), issued the *Mariner's Almanac,* a volume of tables that somewhat abbreviated the calculations.

But not until Larcum Kendall invented the chronometer, a highly accurate clock, was longitude mastered. Set to Greenwich mean time at the beginning of a voyage, the chronometer enabled a navigator to know what time it was in Greenwich wherever he was in the world, to compare that with the time aboard his ship (determined from the position of the sun), and thus to establish his position on the globe.

Some Tidewater families educated their sons at Oxford, Cambridge, or the Inns of Court (the law schools of England). Or if they feared the effects of English miasmas on innocent American bodies (smallpox, a deadly scourge in Europe, did not spread so easily in rural America), they schooled their heirs at the College of William and Mary, founded at Williamsburg in 1693.

The grandeur of the great planters' social and cultural life must not be overblown. William Byrd of Westover (one of the richest of them—he owned 179,000 acres when he died in 1744) was well educated and cultured: He preferred living in London. When his first wife, Lucy Park, died, Byrd sailed to England to find the daughter of a wealthy nobleman to replace her. When he found her and proposed, the bride he chose had an annual income equal to Byrd's entire fortune. The lady's father, quite naturally, rejected Byrd as too poor for her. William Byrd looks like a duke in a portrait he commissioned in London. The fact was, even the richest of tobacco planters was a poor relation among the English upper classes.

A Habit of Debt

Like many poor relations with pretensions, the planters were constantly in debt. When the profits from tobacco dropped, Virginians and Marylanders found it difficult to break the pleasant habits of consumption. They continued to order luxuries from England. To pay for them, they mortgaged future crops—at a discount, of course—to the merchants who were to deliver their goods. It was not unusual that, by the time the tobacco went into the ground in spring, the imports it was to pay for had already been purchased and, in the case of wine, consumed.

Planter debt gratified mercantilists. It meant yet more money in the form of interest and discounts flowing from colony to mother country. In time, chronic indebtedness would make anti-British rebels of practically the entire Tidewater aristocracy.

South Carolina

The social structure of South Carolina—with its small, wealthy elite, a struggling class of small farmers, and masses of bonded laborers—was similar to that of Virginia and Maryland. The rhythms of life in South Carolina were, however, quite different. The cash crops there were rice and, by the mid-1700s, indigo, a plant that yielded a precious blue pigment for dying cloth. Indigo was developed as a crop by Eliza Lucas Pinckney on her father's Wappoo plantation.

▲ *Charleston, South Carolina, the only true city south of Philadelphia, was built between the Ashley and Cooper Rivers, which provided this superb harbor. Open to sea breezes, Charleston was home to planters whose wealth was based on crops produced by slave labor in unhealthy, marshy land.*

Rice and indigo nicely complemented one another. They required intensive labor at different seasons, so South Carolina's servants and slaves produced wealth for their masters 12 months a year. However, because the marshy rice lands were breeding grounds for mosquitoes and mosquito-borne diseases—malaria and the dreaded yellow fever—the slaves and hired white overseers were left to be bitten, ail, and die, while South Carolina's planters lived in airy Charleston.

By congregating in a genuine city, South Carolina's elite was all the more conscious of its privileged position, all the more united in its determination to preserve it. No colony (or state) was dominated by so small an aristocracy as ran South Carolina for more than 200 years.

NEW ENGLAND

New England was peopled by immigrants similar in background to the English men and women who went south.

However, the Puritan heritage shaped New England society long after the generation of Winthrop and Cotton died off and their zeal was a memory. Just as important in explaining New England's way of life was geography. The land and the climate decreed an economy and society for Connecticut, Rhode Island, Massachusetts, and New Hampshire quite different from those in the Chesapeake colonies and Carolina.

Geography and Society

The preeminent geographical facts of life in New England were the cold, long winters, short growing season, and the rocky character of the soil.

Winter and summer temperatures in New England were 10 to 30 degrees cooler than in Virginia. The subtropical diseases of the South were unknown. Consequently, New Englanders lived, on average, 10 years longer than southerners. Twice as many children survived infancy in Massachusetts than in Virginia. The result was a large number of

▲ *Clearing land for crops in New England was many times more difficult than elsewhere in the colonies. Not only did the forest have to be cleared—rocks and boulders had to be removed from the soil as well. Felled trees were burned. Stumps were gone in a few years. Removing rocks and boulders went on and on. There was no destroying them; they were piled into stone fences.*

large extended families. In fact, colonial New England was the world's first society in which it was commonplace to have known one's grandparents personally.

In its soil, New England was less fortunate. Geologically, New England is a glacial moraine. It was there that the

How Do You Deal with a Ten-Ton Boulder?

Clearing New England's earth of rocks did not mean just the diverting task of hauling 150-pound stones to the fence line. Boulders of granite heaved to the surface could weigh 500 pounds, a ton, multiple tons. Farmers let the very largest outcroppings go, to become highlights of today's suburban landscape. Others, smaller and definitely in the way, had to be broken up. Sledgehammers were of limited value. There was no dynamite, and gunpowder was too expensive to be used in the quantities needed. The solution was water. Cracks and holes in boulders or outcroppings, natural and created, were filled with water in winter. Falling temperatures froze the water into ice, which is greater in volume than water. The ice split the rocks—preferably into fragments that could be hauled or, at least, hammered with a maul. It was not a one winter's job.

continental glaciers of the Ice Age halted their advance. When they receded, they deposited the boulders and gravel they had scooped from the earth on their trip from the Arctic.

Before the farmers of New England could plow effectively, they had to clear rocks by the thousands from every acre, breaking up the boulders and piling the lot in the endless stone fences of the region that are so picturesque to those of us who did not have to build them. This backbreaking toil went on for generations, for each winter's freeze heaved more rocks to the surface.

The intensive labor required to clear and plant the land reinforced the Puritans' ideological commitment to a society of small family farms. The demanding New England countryside produced a variety of foods for a fairly dense population. But there were no plantations, no big commercial farms. Families grew their own sustenance and a small surplus for sale in towns and cities.

The Need for Coin

Few of New England's products could be sold in Old England. The crops New Englanders produced in no plenitude were much the same as those that flourished in the mother country: grain, squash, beans, orchard nuts, apples, livestock. So English mercantilists looked less approvingly at New England than at the South and the West Indies.

Indeed, England's shipbuilders, merchants, and fishermen found competitors in New England. Boston was sending ships down the ways before 1640. The shipwright's craft flourished in every town with a harbor. Whaling, a calling New Englanders would come to dominate, began as early as 1649. Nantucket and New Bedford, Massachusetts, became synonymous with whalers. New England fishermen sailed out of Portsmouth, Marblehead, New London, and other ports to harvest more than their fair share of the codfish of the North Atlantic. As for commerce, the nickname "Yankee trader" everywhere conjured up a shrewd businessman not quite to be trusted. Newport, Rhode Island, was a center of the African slave trade, another pursuit the English would have preferred to reserve for themselves.

New Englanders had no choice but to compete. It took money—gold and silver coin—to purchase English manufactured goods. With no cash crop, whaling, fishing, and trade were the only solutions to the colonies' balance-of-payments problem.

Yankee Traders

Some New England traders plied routes of three legs. A ship might call in West Africa, purchase captives, and transport them to the West Indies, Barbados, or Jamaica, where they were exchanged for molasses made from sugar cane. The molasses was sailed to New England, where it was distilled into rum. The rum went to West Africa to be exchanged, along with other goods, for slaves. Not only did shippers in this "triangular trade" profit from each exchange of cargoes, but the colonies improved their balance of payments by distilling cheap molasses into higher-priced rum.

There were other so-called triangles. New Englanders carried provisions from the Middle Colonies to the West Indies; sugar and molasses to England; and English manufactured goods back home. Others transported tobacco from Maryland and Virginia to England; manufactured goods to the West Indies; molasses back home or slaves to the southern colonies. (In the 1600s, very few enslaved blacks came to the North American colonies directly from Africa; in fact, almost all were imported from the tiny island of Barbados.)

Not many ships were systematically involved in triangular trading. Most plied a leg or two of these streams of trade when opportunity offered or necessity required. In fact, a majority of New England's merchant vessels were "coasters," small sloops transporting whatever needed to be moved from one colonial port to another: Boston, Newport, New York, Philadelphia, Charleston, and dozens of smaller

MAP 4:2 A Triangular Flow of Trade Very few British and colonial individual ships routinely plied these three-legged routes. Ships' captains were opportunists, taking aboard what was available and taking it where the cargo could be sold. But these triangular routes illustrate the general flow of trade involving seventeenth-century English America.

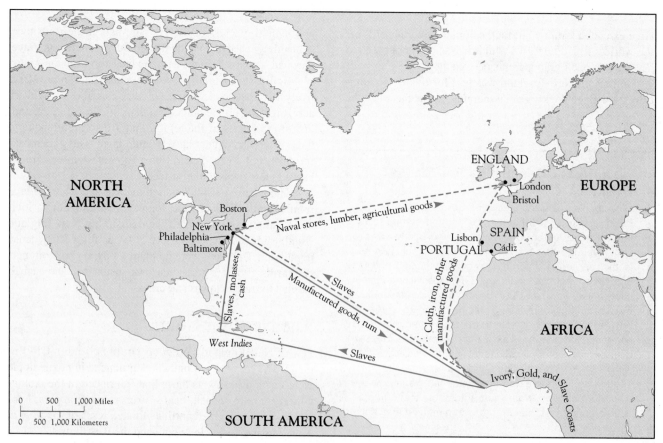

towns. Transatlantic ships did not sail those waters—coastal merchants did; thus the large number of shipwrecks off places like Cape Hatteras and Cape Fear in North Carolina.

An Independent Spirit

To English mercantilists, the Yankees of New England were no better than common smugglers. Indeed, pious Puritan and Quaker shipmasters saw no sin in dodging British trade laws. Because their charters gave them such extensive powers of self-government, the corporate colonies of Massachusetts, Rhode Island, and Connecticut functioned like independent commonwealths. Their leaders—some of them—drank toasts to the king. Some of the grandchildren of the Puritans still entertained the fiction that they were members of the Church of England. But these were little more than the pleasantries of a century when two English kings were dethroned, one of them decapitated, and when it took at least a month, and often two, for a ship to cross the Atlantic connecting the mother country with its colonies.

During the years when Oliver Cromwell ruled England (1649–1658), the New England colonies disregarded almost every directive he and Parliament issued. In 1652, Massachusetts minted its own money, the "pine tree shilling," assuming a right reserved to sovereign rulers since antiquity. Massachusetts did not retreat when Charles II became king in 1660. The colony continued to strike the shilling, to evade royal edicts, and to protect smugglers and even pirates. Charles was forced to sue to have the Massachusetts charter revoked. In 1684, he won his case.

The Dominion of New England

The next year, the new king, James II, combined all the New England colonies into a single unit—the Dominion of New England. (New York and New Jersey were later added.) He abolished local assemblies and endowed his governor, Sir Edmund Andros, with a viceroy's powers. Andros never had a prayer. He was detested in New England from the day he disembarked, and James II's reign proved to be short. In 1688, the king was forced to flee England in the Glorious

And the Award for Incompetence in Colonial Government Goes To . . .

By far the stupidest innovation of the Dominion of New England was a law invalidating all titles to land held under the abrogated Massachusetts charter. *Every* land title in the colony dated earlier than 1685 had been granted under the charter!

James II and Sir Edmund Andros did not intend to evict every Massachusetts family from its land. The idea was to enrich the treasury by collecting fees for the paperwork of revalidating the titles (and to provide opportunities for graft among Sir Edmund's cronies, who, for a consideration, would and could expedite the process).

Revolution. This news was the signal for popular uprisings in several colonies. In Maryland, John Coode seized power from the Catholic proprietors who he assumed had fled with the Catholic James II. In New York, a German named Jacob Leisler gained control, claiming that, in the name of the new sovereigns, William and Mary, he was ridding New York of "Popish Doggs & Divells." In New England, the merchant elite, so briefly out of power, simply resumed acting as it always had—independently. Andros prudently put to sea.

However, the Calverts of Maryland had waffled; they had not committed to James II. When the dust settled, they regained their proprietary rights. In New York, an overconfident Leisler ordered a volley fired at arriving troops, who really did act for William and Mary. He and an aide were sentenced to be "hanged by the Neck and being Alive their bodys be Cutt Downe to the Earth that their Bowells be taken out." On second thought, the judge decided that plain hanging would suffice.

As for New England, William and Mary knew better than to revive the hated Dominion, but they had no intention of allowing Massachusetts to return to its quasi-independent ways. They restored the charters of Connecticut and Rhode Island (there had been little tumult there), but they made Massachusetts, with Plymouth incorporated into it, a royal colony. After 1691, the governor of the Massachusetts Bay colony was no longer elected. He, like the governors of Virginia and the others, was appointed by the Crown.

This was no easy pill for vestigial Puritans to swallow. Their forebears had regarded their mission in America as divinely mandated. That God should allow the Crown to take control of the "citty on a hill" was bitter medicine.

Bully Boy Hysteria

It has been suggested that the loss of the charter and New England's suffering in King Philip's War (see Chapter 5) help to explain the strange hysteria that convulsed Massachusetts in 1692—the Salem witchcraft scare. That is, Puritans believed that God punished the community that tolerated sin within it. The loss of the charter and the devastation wreaked by the Indians led by King Philip could have looked like such punishments. And only the most terrible of sins could account for God's anger at Massachusetts. In 1692, some troubled New Englanders believed they knew what that sin was.

Two pubescent girls of Salem, a village north of Boston, were seized by fits of screaming and crawling about while making odd throaty sounds. Their physician found no earthly affliction. He reckoned that the girls had been bewitched by Satan's servants—witches.

Few were shocked and fewer laughed at the suggestion of witchcraft. A majority of Europeans and Americans of the era believed that individuals struck bargains with Satan. Witchcraft was a capital offense; the Bible said, "Thou shalt not suffer a witch to live." Since the Reformation, thousands had been executed for devil worship, practicing black magic, or for having sexual intercourse with imps called "incubi"

Courtesy Peabody Essex Museum, Salem, Massachusetts

▲ *The woman (or girl) at the left, face covered, accuses a young woman of witchcraft. She has a male defender and lives in a substantial house. In reality, most of the witches hanged at Salem were poor and friendless or nearly so.*

and "succubi." Only a year before the hysteria erupted in Salem, a witch had been hanged in Boston.

The girls who started it all had been agitated by the spooky tales of a West Indian slave in the home of Reverend Samuel Parish named Tituba. Finding themselves the center of attention, the girls began to accuse villagers of bewitching them. Their targets could not have been better chosen for vul-

nerability by a committee of sociologists: Most were women (as were almost all the accusers); some were eccentrics or people unpopular in the community for good reason and bad; several were loners with no friends to defend them; most of the women had no adult sons to speak up on their behalf. Tituba was a slave, easy pickings. Another Salem witch was an impoverished hag who may have been senile; yet another was deaf and probably did not understand the charges against her. There was an 88-year-old man notorious as a crank and, in his younger years, an unabashed open adulterer.

Accusers and accusations multiplied. In time, better-established people were named, most of whom had been on the wrong side of a local squabble involving Reverend Parish. Before it was over—accusation of the wife of the governor was going too far—130 people were accused of witchcraft, 114 were charged, and 19 were hanged. Only one of the 19 was a male of respectable social station.

"Put on More Weight"

The Salem witches were not burned at the stake, as was the fate of many convicted witches in Europe. All were hanged except one man who was "pressed" to death. He was laid prostrate on the ground under a heavy plank. Stones not needed urgently for fence construction were heaped on the plank one by one until he expired, probably of suffocation before his skeleton crumbled.

Why his special treatment? He refused to plead either innocent or guilty when he was accused of being a witch. His reason was mercenary, although not to his own benefit. To plead not guilty and then to be convicted, which he knew was in the cards, meant that he and therefore his heirs would forfeit the property he owned. After each stone was laid on the plank, the magistrates begged him to plead. Even a guilty plea would end the torture.

He refused. His final words were, "Put on more weight."

THE MIDDLE COLONIES

Not everyone believed in witchcraft. At the height of the Salem hysteria, William Penn was asked if there might not also be witches in Pennsylvania. He replied that people were quite free to fly about on broomsticks within the boundaries of his colony. The liberality of the Middle Colonies, particularly policies of religious toleration and easy access to land, ensured that New York, Pennsylvania, New Jersey, and Delaware were generally prosperous and placid.

Balanced Economies

There were great estates in the Middle Colonies, but they were uncommon. As in New England, the agricultural pattern was a patchwork of small family farms (though larger than New England's) tilled by the landowners themselves with some servants and slaves. The climate of the Middle Colonies provided a long growing season, and the soils in the alluvial valleys of the Hudson, Delaware, Schuylkill, and Susquehanna Rivers were deep and rich.

Unlike New England, the Middle Colonies produced a large surplus of grain and livestock. Pennsylvania earned the nickname "breadbasket of the colonies." Because foodstuffs (except rice and molasses) were not enumerated, the products of the Middle Colonies could be sold wherever sellers could find a market. A canny merchant class in Philadelphia and New York soon found an insatiable one. They shipped grain and meat animals on the hoof to the sugar islands of the West Indies, where a small master class forced huge gangs of black slaves to grow cane and little else. The Middle Colonies found a comfortable niche for themselves within the imperial system. They were neither overdependent on the mother country nor sharply in competition with British shippers.

The merchants of Philadelphia and New York governed those cities as though they were personal property. However, because landowning farmers (and therefore voters) were numerous in the Middle Colonies, the merchants never dominated the elected assemblies as planters dominated them in the South; and because their businesses were diverse, they were far more likely than southerners to disagree politically among themselves.

Liberal Institutions

New Jersey and Delaware practiced religious toleration on the same Quaker grounds as Pennsylvania. In New York, the Church of England was established, but laws proscribing other forms of worship were largely ignored. A Roman Catholic, Thomas Dongan, was governor of New York, and a Jewish synagogue established under Dutch rule in 1654 continued to function unmolested under the English.

Indeed, once the Puritan grip on Massachusetts was broken, tacitly accepted religious toleration was the rule in all the colonies. America was a young country in need of people. Whatever the law said, there were few serious attempts to discourage immigration on the basis of religion.

Until 1700, most colonists either had been born in England or had English-born parents or grandparents. There was some ethnic diversity: about 25,000 colonials of African origin, almost all slaves; a handful of Jews in Rhode Island, New York, and South Carolina; a contingent of French Protestants in South Carolina, who had fled persecution at home; and the beginnings of what would become a flood of German emigration in Pennsylvania.

for FURTHER READING

Once again, see the pertinent chapters of Charles M. Andrews, *The Colonial Period of American History,* 1934–1938; Curtis E. Nettels, *The Roots of American Civilization,* 1938; Daniel Boorstin, *The Americans: The Colonial Experience,* 1958; Clarence Ver Steeg, *The Formative Years,* 1964; John E. Pomfret with Floyd Shumway, *Founding the American Colonies,* 1970; and Jack P. Greene and J. R. Pole, eds., *Colonial British America,* 1984. See also Louis B. Wright, *Cultural Life of the American Colonies, 1607–1763,* 1957; and Lewis C. Gray, *History of Agriculture in the United States to 1860,* 1933.

On the southern colonies, see Thomas J. Wertenbaker, *The Planters of Colonial Virginia,* 1927; Louis B. Wright, *The First Gentleman of Virginia,* 1940; and Carl Bridenbaugh, *Myths and Realities: Societies of the Colonial South,* 1963. The standard work on Bacon's Rebellion is Wilcomb E. Washburn, *The Governor and the Rebel,* 1957.

For New England, Bernard Bailyn, *The New England Merchants in the Seventeenth Century,* 1955, is just about old enough to qualify as a classic. See also Stephen Foster, *The Long Argument: English Puritanism and New England Culture, 1570–1700,* 1991; Philip J. Greven Jr., *Four Generations: Population, Land, and Family in Colonial Andover, Massachusetts,* 1970; and Howard S. Russell, *A Long, Deep Furrow: Three Centuries of Farming in New England,* 1976.

Witchcraft in Salem cannot help but be a popular subject. Once the standard explanation, and still provocative, is Marion G. Starkey, *The Devil in Massachusetts,* 1969. Books adding new dimensions to the topic include Paul Boyer and Stephen Nissenbaum, *Salem Possessed,* 1974; John Demos, *Entertaining Satan: Witchcraft and the Culture of Early New England,* 1982; and Carol Karlsen, *The Devil in the Shape of a Woman,* 1987.

AMERICAN JOURNEY ONLINE AND INFOTRAC COLLEGE EDITION

Visit the source collections at http://ajaccess.wadsworth.com and http://infotrac.thomsonlearning.com, and use the Search function with the following key terms to explore documents, images, audio and video clips, articles, and commentary related to the material in this chapter:

Bacon's Rebellion
Glorious Revolution
Salem witch trials

HISTORY ONLINE

An American Time Capsule

http://memory.loc.gov/ammem/rbpehtml/pehome.html

A Library of Congress collection of "broadsides"—single sheet handouts designed to arouse public opinion—from the seventeenth century to the present.

Witchcraft in Salem

http://etext.virginia.edu/salem/witchcraft

Documents, resources, and maps of Salem and Salem Village important in understanding the politics of the witch trials.

OTHER AMERICANS

The Indians, French, and Africans of Colonial North America

Why will you take by force what you may obtain by love? Why will you destroy us who supply you with food? What can you get by war?

Chief Powhatan

This country has twice the population of New France, but the people there are astonishingly cowardly, completely undisciplined, and without any experience in war. . . . It is not at all like that in Canada. The Canadians are brave, much inured to war, and untiring in travel. Two thousand of them will at all times and in all places thrash the people of New England.

Officer, Troupes de la Marine

Is it not enough that we are torn from our country and friends to toil for your luxury and lust of gain? Must every tender feeling be likewise sacrificed to your avarice?

Olaudah Equiano

MOST OF THE English men and women who emigrated to the colonies thought of America as a place where they could improve their lives. Other peoples had other perspectives. To Africans living around the Gulf of Guinea, America was a dread place to which human beings were carried in chains, never to return. To the French, longtime rivals of the English, the colonies were a threat to France's own overseas empire. And then there were those for whom North America was not over any sea, but home, their native land.

THE INDIANS OF NORTH AMERICA

The most striking characteristic of the Native Americans was diversity. Indeed, the story of the Indians is a lesson in just how rapidly and radically cultures diversify when the population is thin and the land is vast, when people of differing beliefs, morals, and ways of doing things are not in constant, intimate contact with one another. Although all North American Indians were descended from culturally similar bands of Asian hunters, they divided and divided again into a patchwork quilt of linguistic and cultural groups, and even distinct physical types.

MAP 5:1 **The Native American Tribes, 1650–1750**   As many Native American peoples as appear on this map, there were many more tribes and autonomous divisions of tribes. By 1700, the English colonies had made contact with most of the Eastern Woodlands and southwestern peoples. The Spanish in Texas and New Mexico were familiar with the Indians of the Southwest and Southern Plains. The French out of Canada had at least confronted the tribes of the Mississippi drainage.

Cultural Diversity

Native American political systems ran the gamut from sophisticated legislative assemblies (such as those of the Iroquois) to the absence of the idea of government among

What's in a Name?

The name most Indian tribes gave themselves translated into English as "the people" or "the human beings." Tribes referred to other Indians in terms that were usually unflattering, like "the other things."

In some cases, like *Kiowa,* we have adopted the name tribal members gave themselves. In others, when whites were introduced to a tribe by a neighboring people, they adopted that people's negative designation, and it stuck. Thus, *Mohawk* is Narragansett for "blood sucker," *Sioux* is Chippewa for "snake," and *Apache* is Zuñi for "enemy."

Then there are names given to tribes by Europeans from their own languages: *Pueblo,* from the Spanish for "village"; *Nez Percé,* from the French for "pierced nose," after a cosmetic practice of that tribe; *Delaware,* from the English for the homeland of the Leni-Lenape, which the English had named after an English investor, Baron De La Warr.

some peoples of the Great Basin. Socially, there were caste systems so complicated that tribes (such as the Natchez) supported genealogists as the only means to keep track of who was who, and there were egalitarian and democratic tribes (such as many of California's dozens of tribes).

There were tribes in which authoritarian men ignored the existence of every woman but their wives and others in which women, among themselves, spoke a language significantly different from that of the men. Yet other tribes were matrilineal, tracing an individual's descent through the female line, endowing almost all property to women, and looking to councils of women to make important tribal decisions. The variety of social relationships among the Indians at the time of European incursion was broader than the social structure was in Europe.

Manners and morals varied too. The Cherokee considered it rude to address another person directly. The Yahi each gave themselves names that they never revealed to another person. Unmarried Natchez girls sold sexual services in order to build up a dowry. The Plains Indians guarded the virginity of their girls as closely as Montagues and Capulets. In the Northeast, rape was the only crime punishable by death, and the warriors of some tribes of that region were bound to strict sexual continence when they were on the warpath. The incest taboo was so strict in some areas that one had to marry outside one's clan, whereas the Tlingit of the Pacific Northwest prized marriages of first cousins. Some tribes of the Great Plains allowed homosexuals special privileges. Others found homosexual practice as abominable as any Puritan did.

Some Indians were warlike and aggressive, renowned for their cruelty toward enemies. There is the site of a village near Crow Creek, South Dakota, where, in the fourteenth century, some 500 men, women, and children were massacred. Every tribe in the Northeast came to fear the Iroquois, a name that meant "terrifying man" in the Algonkian languages. The Pueblo Indians fought only in defense, never taking the initiative against other peoples. Yet other Indians were gentle folk, principled pacifists who survived only by finding secluded nooks of the continent in which to dwell.

Many eastern Indians were functional monotheists who worshiped a single manitou, or Great Spirit. Others were fetishists. They concerned themselves with supernatural powers in stones, trees, bugs, and birds, and consulted magicians to cope with otherworldly powers.

Economy, Ecology, and Language

Indians shaped the environment to the degree their technology allowed. For instance, there was intense irrigated cultivation and a quasi-urban way of life among the Pueblo of New Mexico and Arizona, whereas the Indians of southern New England methodically burned the underbrush in their hunting grounds, creating park-like forests in which grasses and herbaceous plants thrived, luring moose, deer, rabbits, and other game into a created habitat.

In California, by contrast, whole peoples subsisted on little but acorns, roots and berries, and the odd small animal they snared. In the Pacific Northwest, food was so abundant and nutritious (salmon) that some tribes expressed a disdain for material goods, a phenomenon we associate with rich and wasteful economies. Periodically, families that had accumulated great stores of food and other possessions gave them away at festivals called "potlatches," even destroying valuable goods and impoverishing themselves to demonstrate how unimpressed they were with possessions.

There was greater linguistic difference among the Indians than there was among the nationalities of Europe. In one corner of North Carolina, several small tribes living within 10 miles of one another for at least a century could not communicate except by sign language. Some peoples dwelling in comparable proximity were so distinctive physically their ethnicity could be identified from half a mile's distance.

About the only generalization that can confidently be made about the Indians of North America is that, in the end, they were all to be subordinated by the Europeans, whose arrival dated from Ponce de León's search for the Fountain of Youth.

▲ *This watercolor of the village of Secotan in North Carolina was painted by John White about 1585. It shows an orderly society and the fact that the inhabitants planted at least two crops of corn each year in order to extend their food supply.*

PEOPLE OF THE EASTERN WOODLANDS

People speaking Algonkian languages occupied New England and the eastern parts of the Middle Colonies down to North Carolina. Tribes in this language group included Mohegan (or Mohican), Narragansett, Abenaki, Leni-Lenape (Delaware), Pequot, Ojibwa (Chippewa), and, of course, the Powhatan. Algonkians were the first Native Americans with whom English settlers made contact. They were also the first to be victimized by the English, who eventually made enemies of most of them by taking the Algonkians' lands. The colonists adopted quite a few Algonkian words (and more numerous Algonkian place names) that are now an integral part of American English. A few are *hickory, hominy, moccasin, succotash, tomahawk, totem, wigwam, Massachusetts, Connecticut, Susquehanna,* and *Chesapeake.*

The second major language group of the Eastern Woodlands was Iroquoian. This language group extended over a large wedge-shaped territory running from the eastern Great Lakes through New York and into Pennsylvania. The Conestoga and Erie spoke an Iroquoian language, as did the Tuscarora of inland Virginia and North Carolina and the Huron of New France (what is now Canada). But the most important Iroquois as far as the English were concerned were five large tribes that had joined together in a confederation under the legendary figure Hiawatha in about 1570. The Five Nations of the Iroquois Confederacy were the Cayuga, Mohawk, Oneida, Onondaga, and Seneca.

The earliest southern colonials had less contact with the third major linguistic group of the Eastern Woodlands, the Muskogean. The tribes in this language group included the Apalachee, Chickasaw, Choctaw, Creek, Natchez, and Seminole. These socially sophisticated tribes lived in what is now Georgia, Alabama, Mississippi, and Tennessee. Few English settlers penetrated this country until late in the seventeenth century, when South Carolinians developed a slave, fur, and deerskin trade there. In Florida, however, Spanish incursions and the spread of European diseases were already decimating small Muskogean tribes that would, in time, disappear: the Timucuan, Calusa, and Jaega.

Hunters Who Farmed

The economies of the three Eastern Woodlands groups were similar. Agriculture was based on the "three sisters": maize (corn), beans, and squash. They were planted together in small hills heaped up by means of a spade roughed out of stone or wood. (Woodlands Indians had no metallurgy.)

Maize was the easily preserved staple and provided the stalks on which bean vines climbed. Pumpkins and other squash covered the roots of both plants with their foliage, preserving moisture as well as providing food. Here and there, peas, cabbages, melons, and, of course, tobacco were cultivated.

Farmland was cleared by the slash-and-burn method, which was undemanding and therefore suited the Eastern Woodlands Indians, who were primarily hunters and gatherers. Well adapted to an environment in which land was abundant and labor scarce, the slash-and-burn method was adopted by the white pioneers in the densely forested eastern third of the country.

A ring of bark was stripped from around the trunks of the mostly deciduous trees, thus killing them. When the last foliage fell, admitting sunlight to the forest floor, the Indian women (who were the chief farmers in the east) burned the underbrush. In these ghost forests, they planted their crops. There were no plows or beasts of burden among the eastern tribes. Dogs and turkeys were the only domesticated animals.

So casual a mode of cultivation did not itself provide sufficient food. Every tribe looked as much to forest as to field for its survival, depending on hunting, fishing, trapping, and gathering edible plants, fruits, and nuts. Thus each tribe competed with its neighbors for range.

The Eastern Woodlands Indians valued their weapons, tools, and household goods. They thought of them as exclusive personal property, much as Europeans did. But hunting and gathering do not require constant occupation or exclusive control of a specific tract of land. Consequently, the European concept of real estate—private, exclusive ownership of land—was alien to the Indians. Land was God's. People used it and competed to use it, sometimes violently. But no one "owned" it. When a New Englander commented that the Indians "do but run over the grass, as do also the foxes and wild beasts," an Indian might well have shrugged, "Yes. So what?"

Outside of Eden, foraging for food makes for a precarious livelihood. So the Eastern Woodlands Indians' communities were inclined to be small and scattered so that no individual tribe put too much of a strain on the hunting and gathering grounds in the vicinity. The Powhatan, whom the first Virginians encountered, gathered in villages of 500 people during the summer. In winter, however, they split up into smaller groups. European-style agriculture made larger concentrations of population possible. But the Indians benefited from the newcomers' productivity for only a short time.

CONFRONTATION

To the Eastern Woodlands Indians, the world was land, lake, and stream. The Atlantic Ocean was an abyss, the end of the earth. None of them were seafarers. The Indians saw the pale-skinned people as members of a new tribe. Incursion by strangers was not new to them, and the white tribe was soon more numerous than any other they had known. Nonetheless, for many decades, the Indians viewed the English as just another people with whom to fight, to trade, and to compete for the necessities of life. Except as a novelty, skin color meant nothing to Native Americans.

Two Different Worlds

The experience of the Indians who confronted the English was rather different from that of Native Americans who lived in lands the Spanish invaded. First of all, there were not as many of them. Probably about 150,000 Indians lived

Fate Worse Than Death

Colonial women who were captured by Indians, adopted into a tribe, and not rescued within a year or so often decided to remain Indians when they were given the choice of returning. They had formed personal attachments and, if they had borne children, knew that their children would live as equals among the Indians but be outcast half-breeds among whites.

Appalling as such decisions were to colonials, Esther Wheelwright's choices were worse. In 1704, she was kidnapped in Maine by Abenaki and taken to Quebec. There she converted to Roman Catholicism, became a nun, and, in time, mother superior of the Ursuline order. She was the highest-ranking churchwoman in North America.

in the parts of North America the English penetrated during the 1600s. More Aztecs lived in Tenochtitlán alone when Cortés first entered the city.

And yet, the English had a more difficult time dominating the Native Americans than the Spanish had in Mexico and Peru. In large part, this was due to the fact that the English did not wish to conquer the locals, live among them, and govern them, which was precisely the Spanish goal.

The English enslaved captured Indians (which the Spanish were forbidden to do). In 1708, Indian slaves in South Carolina numbered 1,400, accounting for 14 percent of the colony's population. But Indians escaped too easily in a land that was, after all, their home. Imported white servants and black slaves were more dependable. Already by 1708, there were 4,100 black slaves in South Carolina.

The sexual balance of the English colonial population served to keep Indians and Europeans in different spheres. Unlike New Spain, which was conquered by soldiers—all males—New England was settled by families. Even in the plantation South, by the time of Queen Anne, the English population was approaching sexual parity. Only a few colonial men looked to the Indians for wives. One scholar has identified only three Indian-white marriages in Virginia during the colony's first century, including John Rolfe and Pocahontas. With marriage within the race relatively available, it was feasible in English America to define intermarriage as disreputable, the practice of low-life whites. There was plenty of miscegenation, of course, but the colonials consigned "half-breeds" to the Indians, thus creating the first American color line.

In fact, most whites who consorted with Indians eagerly chose to live with their spouse's people, where loyalty to the tribe was what counted, not skin color. So did many of the women and children who were kidnapped by Indians specifically for the purpose of replacing tribal members who had died. A New Yorker commented incredulously in 1699 that he could not "persuade the People that had been taken Prisoners by the French Indians, to leave the Indian Manner of

The "Walking Purchase"

Pennsylvania's "Walking Purchase" of 1683 was once a staple of history textbooks. The story was that canny Quakers agreed with Indians to pay a sum for land as far as a man could walk in a day. The Indians, who knew quite well about how far that was, found they were hornswoggled when, to prepare for the walk, the purchasers cut a path through the forest and stationed young men along it to run in relays as far as they could.

The trouble is, there is no record of such a transaction; it was not William Penn's style; and when the story was first published in 1737, none of the oldest living inhabitants of Pennsylvania had heard of it.

living." White male captives were more likely to view rescue as a liberation.

Land Hunger

The goal of English colonization was to replicate the way of life the settlers knew back home. Indians had no place in this vision. The object was to acquire the Indians' land by purchase or force, pushing the dispossessed survivors outside the pale of white settlement, which almost always meant to the west.

Conscientious colonials devised moral and legal justifications for taking Indian land. The Pilgrims approved their occupation of Plymouth on the grounds that no one was living there when they arrived. Roger Williams, the Pennsylvania Quakers, and, usually, the Dutch in New Netherland bought the land they wanted. Their view of the transactions, however, differed sharply from that of the Indians. To Europeans, purchase meant acquiring exclusive use of the land, as intensive agriculture required. The earliest Indian sellers believed they were agreeing to share the land with the newcomers. Thus Staten Island could be "sold" to the Dutch three times over. To the Dutch, their multiple purchase proved the Indians were dishonest connivers. From the Indian point of view, three different tribes were accepting the Hollanders' presence on Staten Island.

Many Indians must have been bewildered by European real estate deals. Jasper Danckhaerts wrote of a transaction in New York in 1679, "The Indians hate the precipitancy of comprehension and judgement [of the whites], the excited chatterings, . . . the haste and rashness to do something, whereby a mess is often made of one's good intentions."

Many colonials lacked good intentions. They shot, took, and shrugged. Possession by right of conquest was not a universally approved principle in the seventeenth century, but it had a long pedigree and compelling recommendations to the party with the military edge.

Bringers of Baubles

Few Eastern Woodlands Indians were flabbergasted by the appearance of whites as the Arawak and Mexicans had been.

English Legalism

New Englanders were as legalistic as the Spaniards in justifying the taking of land from Indians. The Puritans based the legality of their seizures on the Bible. In 1630, John Cotton spelled out the three ways in which "God makes room for a people." First, in a just war, which God blessed (Psalms 44:2–"Thou didst drive out the heathen before them"), the victors had the right to the land they conquered. Second, newcomers could purchase land or accept land as a gift "as Abraham did obtaine the field of Machpelah" or as the pharaoh gave the land of Goshen "unto the sons of Jacob." Third–and this was major-league legal loophole making–"When Hee [God] makes a Countrey though not altogether void of inhabitants, yet voyd in that place where they [the newcomers] reside . . . there is liberty for the sonne of Adam or Noah to come and inhabite, though they neither buy it, nor aske their leaves."

European explorers and fishermen camped on Atlantic shores for decades before the founding of Jamestown and Plymouth. Gossip among tribes had informed most eastern peoples of the existence of the white tribe before they confronted an Englishman face to face.

The earliest English settlements posed little threat, however, and the colonists offered trade goods that were highly desirable to a Neolithic people. There were the famous baubles, of course: glass beads, ribbons, trinkets, mirrors. New to Indians, they were accorded the high status and price of any novelty. It was with the equivalent of $24 worth of such goods that Peter Minuit purchased Manhattan Island in 1626. A European introduction brimming with tragedy, but coveted nonetheless, was liquor, usually rum (or cheap brandy in New France). Some eastern tribes had made a weak beer from corn but nothing as potent as distilled spirits. From the first, the Indians took with tragic zest to "firewater." It devastated many tribes both physically and morally.

More important to a people who smelted no metals were the European commodities that improved their standard of living: brass and iron vessels; tools (spades, hatchets); woven blankets (which were warmer than hides) and other textiles; and firearms, which allowed the Indians to hunt more efficiently and get a military leg up on old tribal enemies.

In return, the Indians provided foodstuffs to the earliest settlers. When the English became agriculturally self-sufficient, they supplied furs and hides in exchange for goods that had become necessities in a native economy that was no longer self-sufficient.

The Fur and Hide Trade

In the decline of the Eastern Woodlands tribes, furs and hides played a more fundamental role than liquor and the military superiority of the English. The English (and Dutch and French) appetite for animal skins resulted in the destruction of the ecology of which the eastern Indians had comfortably been a part.

Before the whites arrived, the Woodlands tribes killed only the moose, deer, beaver, and other animals that they needed for food and clothing. Why kill more? Because the Indians were few, their needs had minimal impact on the animal population. Indeed, their harvests of game may have had a healthy effect on wildlife by preventing overpopulation and disease.

But Europeans could not get too many skins and pelts. The upper classes back home coveted the lush furs of the beaver, otter, marten, and weasel. Both furs and deerskin were made into felt, which was pressed into hats and dozens of other salable goods. In order to increase production and buy more of what the Europeans offered, the tribes rapidly extirpated the valuable creatures in hunting grounds that had been adequate for centuries.

It does not take long to effectively destroy a species when hunting is relentless and systematic. In only a couple of generations, nineteenth-century Americans would annihilate a population of passenger pigeons that previously

Scalping

In the 1870s, a crusader for Indian causes, Susette LaFlesche, told audiences that whites taught scalping to Indians. Native Americans knew nothing of the practice, she said, until the advent of the English and French.

Her contention, based on the fact that the British army and colonial governments paid Indian allies bounties for the scalps of hostile tribespeople, was revived in the later decades of the twentieth century.

In fact, there is no record of Europeans scalping one another or even a word for the practice in the English, French, and Spanish languages until after 1535, when Jacques Cartier described scalping among some Indians he confronted. It appears that scalping was the peculiar custom of the Mohawk, which only after time was adopted by other tribes of the Northeast and Canada. There seems little doubt, however, that it was white exploration and expansion across the continent that made the gory mutilation the practice of tribes living as distant from the Mohawk as the Dakota and Apache.

darkened the skies. The nearly total destruction of the North American bison after the construction of the transcontinental railroad took only 10 years! Thus it happened in the Eastern Woodlands, as Indians and the odd white hunter and trapper set out greedily after deer and beaver.

Unlike the case of the passenger pigeon, but very much like the case of the bison, the destruction of the animals of the eastern forests meant the destruction of a way of life.

A New Kind of Warfare

The demands of the fur traders introduced a new kind of warfare to the world of the Indians. War was not new to them. Violent conflict with other tribes was an integral part of Iroquois and Algonkian culture. But traditional Indian warfare was largely a ritualistic demonstration of individual bravery. A young man gained as much glory among his people in "counting coups," giving an enemy a sound knock on the head, as in taking his life. Women and children were not typically killed in Indian warfare—where was the glory in that?—although they were kidnapped to be enslaved, married, or adopted.

Once they became suppliers to an intercontinental economy, however, the Indians embraced a different concept of warfare. No longer was the object glory, live captives, and thievery; it became the exploitation of other tribes' hunting grounds and, if necessary, the elimination of the competition. Revenge and retribution had always been a part of Indian culture, but on nothing like the scale the Iroquois practiced once they gained access to English firearms.

In 1649, the Iroquois virtually exterminated their neighbors, the Erie. There were probably 30,000 Huron living north of the Iroquois when the French settled in Huron territory. By 1640, European diseases had reduced the Huron to 12,000. In 10 more years, the Iroquois killed all but several hundred of the survivors. Then, in the quest for furs, they

A Huron warrior. The Huron were the first Indians to befriend the French, a decision that doomed them. They were nearly exterminated during the 1600s by repeated epidemics of diseases contracted from French settlers in Canada and relentless attacks by the mortal enemy of the French, the Iroquois Confederacy.

A HURON—TYPE.

Culver Pictures

drove other tribes out of the Ohio Valley, which did not return until the mid-1700s, when the Iroquois were neutral in the Anglo-French wars.

The colonials—French and English—encouraged intertribal genocide by paying bounties for scalps from enemy tribes. In 1721, Pennsylvania paid the equivalent of $140 for an Algonkian warrior's scalp and $50 for a squaw's. To make the purpose of the bounty unmistakable, a live prisoner was worth a paltry $30.

King Philip's War

Indians battled whites too, of course. In the mid-1640s, having finished off the Huron, the Iroquois Confederacy came very close to driving the French out of North America. In 1675, in King Philip's War, an alliance of New England tribes harbored hopes of at least stemming the advance of the English, if not driving them into the sea.

The war began when Plymouth hanged three Wampanoag for murdering Sassamon, a Christian member of their tribe. The Wampanoag chief, Metacomet, whom New Englanders derisively called "King Philip," was already seething with hatred for the colonials over a personal insult and the obvious dissipation of his tribe's culture.

Metacomet persuaded two other powerful chiefs, Pomham of the Nipmuck and Canonchet of the Narragansett, to join him in a coordinated attack on outlying colonial towns. Through most of 1675, their warriors were unstoppable. Fifty-two of 90 New England towns were attacked;

12 were wiped off the map. A tenth of the New England males of military age were killed or captured.

The next year, the tide turned. Metacomet's armies ran short of provisions and were troubled by internal dissension. Most of the "praying Indians" of New England—Christians, who were about a fourth of the Native American population—allied themselves with the whites. Several tribes of "wild Indians," including the Pequot and Mohican, either joined with the New Englanders or declared neutrality. In an attack on the Narragansett, 2,000 of 3,000 enemy Indians were killed. Metacomet was killed, his head mounted on a stake in best seventeenth-century fashion. Canonchet's head was impaled in Hartford, Connecticut.

Contempt and Respect

The colonials both respected the Indians and held them in contempt. The native peoples were "different." Practices ranging from the trivial (the Indians' toilet habits) to the significant (cruel treatment of some captives) appalled settlers who had less than an anthropologist's appreciation of cultural diversity. The Indians were "savages." Colonials frequently compared them to the Irish, who were despised in the old country for their perceived lack of civilization.

By contrast, some colonials admired and envied aspects of Indian culture. Even Benjamin Franklin, the Pennsylvanian who sanctified hard work and squirreling away money, betrayed a certain wistfulness when he wrote of the Indians: "Having few artificial wants, they have abundance of leisure for improvement by conversation. Our laborious manner of life, compared with theirs, they esteem slavish and base."

Indians regarded the whites with a mix of awe and disdain. Few Native Americans turned their backs on the trade goods the colonials offered. However, as Franklin observed, the nonmaterial benefits of European civilization were lost on them. In 1744, Virginia invited the Iroquois to send six of their boys to the College of William and Mary. The confederacy replied that it had had bad luck with Indian lads educated at New England colleges: "When they came back to us, they were bad runners, ignorant of every means of living in the woods, unable to bear either cold or hunger, knew neither how to build a cabin, take a deer, or kill an enemy; they were totally good for nothing."

However, the Iroquois understood that the whites meant well: "If the gentlemen of Virginia will send us a dozen of their sons, we will take great care of their education, instruct them in all we know, and make men of them."

Tribal Peoples

The concept of "Indian-ness," the idea that all Native Americans had an essence in common with one another that pit them against all whites, is a political conceit of our own times. American Indians, during the colonial period and long thereafter, were tribal to the core. It was tribal identification that gave individuals identity and community and distinguished them from outsiders. Race, racial solidarity, and racism—all meaningful among colonial whites, and a nearly universal obsession today—had little meaning for Indians of the colonial period.

Tribes readily adopted members of other tribes and whites too, a practice rare among English colonials. Intertribal conflicts involving only Indians were common, but conflicts in which one side was entirely white and the other entirely Indian were rare after the very first skirmishes in Virginia and Massachusetts. The Narragansett and Mohican joined the white New Englanders in the massacre of the Pequot in 1634. Almost as many Indians fought against Metacomet as fought for him. The English colonials and Indians, chiefly the Iroquois, made war off and on for more than a century against French colonials (and the Indian allies of the French) in Canada. To the French and English, alliances with Indians were expedient. To the Indians, both sides were alliances of tribes; that two of the inimical tribes were pale of skin was incidental. Indeed, it confirmed the absence of racial categorization among the Indians.

THE FRENCH IN NORTH AMERICA

New France was founded at Quebec and Port Royal, Nova Scotia, in 1608, just a year after Jamestown, by Samuel de Champlain. As in English America, the colony was governed by a commercial company, the Company of the Indies, to be taken over by the French crown in 1663.

Grand Empire, Few People

With the same motives as the English crown, the Bourbon kings of France were determined to keep pace with their national rival in North America. But they were disappointed by the reluctance of French men and women to emigrate across the Atlantic. For farmers, which most of the French were, the disincentive was the climate and soil of New France. The earth was rockier than New England's, and the winters were worse. A high proportion of the immigrants in Canada were people who had been urban laborers in the old country, and about two-thirds of those returned to France to feed the anti-Canadian prejudice with their horror stories.

France might have populated New France with religious dissenters as England populated New England. The Huguenots, Protestants much like Puritans, were a nuisance at home. Many would gladly have emigrated to escape the disabilities, persecution, and uncertainty they knew at home, while remaining French, which was as important to them as remaining English was to Pilgrims and Puritans. But Louis XIV, who reigned more than 70 years, forbade all but Catholics in Canada.

Louis could not, however, with a variety of inducements, build a Catholic population in Canada to rival the numbers in the English colonies. French indentured servants were bound to serve only three years, as opposed to as many as seven years in the English colonies, and the French indentured servants were granted land when their term of service was up. It did little good. The French crown forced emigration on people deemed expendable at home. Entire villages of poor and rugged Brittany were uprooted against their will and shipped to Quebec. Soldiers stationed in North American forts were ordered to remain in Canada when their service was complete. Prostitutes (*filles du roi,* or "the king's daughters") were rounded up and dispatched to be wives of settlers—as were orphan girls and the daughters of peasants who got into trouble with the tax collector.

But New France just would not grow. By 1713, after a century of settlement, the French population in North America was 25,000, about the same number of people as lived in the single English colony of Pennsylvania, which was but 30 years old.

French Expansion

The boldness of the French Canadians almost compensated for the poverty of their numbers. French traders, trappers, and priests fanned out in the north woods surrounding the Great Lakes, whereas the English huddled within a few miles of ocean breakers. Like few English colonials, these coureurs de bois (literally, "runners of the woods") were willing—indeed eager—to adapt more than halfway to the way of life by which the Indians flourished in the wilderness.

Brown Brothers

▲ *In 1673, a French Jesuit missionary stationed in what is now Michigan, Father Jacques Marquette, accompanied a fur trapper, Louis Joliet, on a voyage by canoe down the Mississippi to the mouth of the Arkansas River. The French penetrated the heart of the continent before the English settled the Carolinas and Pennsylvania.*

Champlain encouraged amalgamation with the natives: "Our sons shall wed your daughters and we shall be but one people"—a sentiment unimaginable in the English colonies. In doing so, and in adopting Indian dress with a few of their own affectations added, the coureurs de bois won the friendship and respect of most of the tribes they confronted. When a governor of Virginia reached the crest of the Appalachians, he celebrated by covering a table with pressed linen and setting it with fine china, silver, and crystal. When a Frenchman broke new ground hundreds of miles deeper in the interior, he roasted a slab of venison and ate it with his hands while hunkering in the dust.

Intrepid French explorers charted what is now the central third of the United States. In 1673, Louis Joliet and Father Jacques Marquette, a Jesuit priest, navigated the Mississippi to the mouth of the Arkansas River. They turned back only because Indians told them of other whites to the south, whom Marquette and Joliet correctly reckoned to be Spaniards, hostile to the French.

In 1682, when Pennsylvania was getting started on the hospitable banks of the Delaware, René-Robert Cavelier, Sieur de La Salle, reached the mouth of the Mississippi. In 1699, a generation before the founding of Georgia, Pierre Le Moyne Iberville planted settlements at New Orleans and on the Gulf of Mexico at Mobile. New Orleans became the hub of the second French province in North America, Louisiana.

French America was a flimsy empire by English standards, a string of lonely log forts and trading posts: Kaskaskia and Cahokia in the Illinois country; St. Louis where the Missouri flows into the Mississippi; dots on a map connected by lakes, rivers, creeks, and *portages* (a word that Americans learned from the Canadians, meaning a place canoes had to be *carried* from one waterway to another).

Contrasting Ways of Life

The French had their conflicts with the Indians, most notably with the Iroquois Confederacy, but also, after 1700, with the Fox in Wisconsin and the Natchez of Tennessee, who, in 1729, killed every Frenchman in their territory. Generally, however, the French had better relations with Indians than the English did. There were several reasons for this, none more important than their small numbers. In remaining so few, the French did not threaten the natives with inundation as the ever growing English colonies did.

Second in importance, the English colonial way of life clashed head-on with Indian culture, whereas French interests only benefited the tribes (or so it seemed). Both European peoples offered desirable trade goods in return for furs and hides. However, New France was not much more than a string of trading posts; the English colonies were primarily agricultural. The French waited in their forts for Indians to come to them, or glided through the forests with them. The English insatiably occupied more and more land and chopped the forests down. Each acre of land put to the plow was an acre less where deer could be shot and berries gathered.

▲ *No Protestant denomination in the English colonies was nearly as devoted and industrious in attempting to convert and educate Indians as the Jesuit priests in New France were. They were immensely successful—eventually even among the Iroquois, who martyred six of them in the 1640s and mutilated others.*

Religion

Functional differences between the Roman Catholicism of the French and the Protestant religions of the English, particularly Puritanism, affected Indian-white relations. Both the English and French gave lip service to the goal of winning Indians' souls to Christianity. The establishment of missions was mentioned in every colonial charter. Some pious Englishmen, like Roger Williams and John Eliot, the "Apostle of the Indians," took the task of converting Indians seriously. Dartmouth College in New Hampshire originated as a school for Indians. Virginia's College of William and Mary provided for Indian education. Many Indians in English America accepted baptism.

It was not difficult, however, for English colonials to lose interest in saving savage souls. The Church of England was nationalistic; Puritanism was highly ethnocentric. The religion of the English settlers was intimately wrapped up with their English customs, prejudices, language, manners, and even the cut of the clothes they wore.

The Puritans, moreover, looked upon salvation as a gift of God bestowed on very few of their own kind. They regarded Spanish and French Catholics as near-satanic and saw other Europeans' modestly different customs and manners as evidence of their inferiority. How could such people view Indians—half-naked, with ways of doing things far more exotic to them than the ways of Spaniards and Frenchmen—as "visible saints"? It could be done, but it was not easy to do it.

The French had their own bag of cultural prejudices. (*Huron,* the name they gave their first Indian allies, meant "lout" or "ruffian.") However, it was a basic tenet of their Roman Catholicism that God meant every human being to belong to the church. (*Catholic* means "universal.") So the Roman Catholic Church had been shaped by a history of accommodating a galaxy of different cultures within it. Accepting baptism in the "one true church" was what mattered, not the clothing one wore or the foods one preferred. When French Jesuits preached to Indians, they emphasized the similarities between Indian tradition and Catholic practice. English Protestant preachers seemed always to be talking about the old ways the Indians had to give up.

The priests of New France also had an advantage over Protestant missionaries in the ornate and mystical Roman Catholic ritual. The mystery of the Mass, the welter of ceremonies, and the vividly decorated statues appealed to the Indians' aesthetic sense. The Puritans, by contrast, were a people of the word. Individual study of the Bible and long sermons rooted in European learning and European logic were the foundations of their worship. Indians did not read. European learning was not Indian learning.

The Five Nations

Nonetheless, the English had very valuable Indian allies in the Iroquois, who had long warred with Algonkian tribes and the Huron, who turned to the French. When the Canadians outfitted their allies with firearms, the Iroquois suffered. The hardships and fears their defeats engendered ensured that when they found European contacts—first the Dutch in Fort Orange, then the English, who replaced them in what they called Albany—they embraced the newcomers. They would have embraced devils who brought guns. They had a generation's worth of scores to settle.

Settle them they did. The Iroquois took the offensive against the Algonkians, the Huron, and the French with a terrifying vengeance. Their cruelties shocked both English and French, people who, practicing disembowelment of live convicts, might have been more understanding. The Iroquois slowly burned and chewed the fingers and toes from their captives. They dined on husbands before the eyes of their wives and mothers in front of their children. Canada's coureurs de bois so feared the Iroquois that, in order to avoid them, they detoured as many as a thousand miles when they trekked to the trapping grounds in the Illinois country. Better months of circuitous, laborious travel than crossing the path of Iroquois warriors.

AMERICANS FROM AFRICA

To the English who came to the colonies to farm, the Indians were impediments, like the massive oaks and maples of the forests. They thought in terms of clearing the land of people as well as trees. Colonists came to view America's third great people, however, as essential to economic development. These were people of the black race, mostly from around the Gulf of Guinea in West Africa, who were imported to America against their will in order to solve the commercial farmer's problem of getting things done in a country where land was limitless but backs to bend over it were few.

Slavery and the English

Enslaved Africans and their children had been the backbone of the labor force in the West Indies, in the Spanish mainland colonies, and in Portuguese Brazil long before the founding of Jamestown. So the English, particularly those in the tobacco colonies who needed cheap, dependable labor, had an example to which to look.

The colonists did not, however, turn to Africa or to slavery to bring their crops in—at least not right away. The English lacked a tradition of owning human beings as property. Slavery, even serfdom, had vanished from England centuries before the age of colonies. As for Africa, the English, unlike the Spanish and Portuguese, had little experience of trade and war with its darker-skinned peoples. By the latter 1500s, some English seafarers, notably John Hawkins and Francis Drake, were buying and selling black slaves in the Caribbean. As late as 1618, however, when an African merchant on the Senegal River offered slaves to Richard Jobson in payment for English trade goods, Jobson replied indignantly, "we were a people who did not deal in any such commodities, neither did wee buy or sell one another, or any that had our owne shapes." The African was astonished, saying that other white men who came to his country wanted nothing but slaves. The English captain answered, "They were another kinde of people different from us."

Had this goodly man's principles prevailed, North America would have been spared a great historical wrong, the enslavement of Africans and their descendants. However, just months after the curious incident on the Senegal—and a year before the *Mayflower* anchored at Plymouth, Massachusetts—the history of African Americans began at Jamestown with their enslavement for life.

New Uses for an Old Institution

During the first century of colonization, the English settlers solved their labor problem by adapting to America an institution by which, back home, skills involving long training and practice were passed from generation to generation and by which communities provided for the raising of orphans and illegitimate children.

In England, boys were trained to be blacksmiths, coopers (barrel makers), bakers, and other types of tradesmen by binding them as apprentices to a master of the craft. For a

Enslavement

Unless they were convicts or warriors captured in battle, West Africans taken into slavery were usually seized at night. Whether their captors were Europeans or Africans, darkness provided them with an edge. The clamor of nocturnal raid heightened the terror of the victims and made them more manageable, a fact that twentieth-century secret police forces also understood. Mostly, the traders took men, but teenage girls—healthy and young enough to have a long life of childbearing ahead of them—were also desirable merchandise. The elderly, who could not work or withstand the rigors of the "middle passage," were clubbed to death or, if lucky, left behind.

Captives were marched quickly toward the sea in "coffles"—they were tied or chained together—to discourage the defiant and desperate from making a break for the bush. The practice

North Wind Picture Archives

was adopted by slave traders in America, not to mention prison guards. If the raiders feared a retaliatory attack, there was no delay on behalf of the ill, injured, or exhausted. They were cut out of the coffles and often killed on the spot.

At the mouths of the Niger, Volta, and other rivers, captives were confined in a stockade called a "factory." There they might languish for weeks, fed on yams and millet. If there had not been whites in the capture party, the victims soon made their acquaintance. Well-guarded, white buyers walked through the stockades, kneading muscles and examining teeth as if they were buying horses. They paid (in 1700) about £5 per slave in iron bars, cloth, rum, guns, kettles, and axes. Who can know what thoughts tortured the captives' minds? They had likely heard of others who had been kidnapped but had little idea what happened to them.

The ship on which slaves were transported across the Atlantic was possibly, by the eighteenth century, specially constructed for the trade. In these "slavers," captives were packed side by side on their backs, on shelflike decks, one deck 2 feet above the other. They were chained, wrist to wrist and ankle to ankle. Most vessels in the slave trade, however, were ordinary merchant ships, "multipurpose," on which conditions might be better, or maybe worse.

Scurvy or dysentery commonly swept through the hold. Every morning, the crew's first task was to look for dead, cut

any out, and dump the bodies overboard. If the weather was bad or the captain nervous about mutiny, the Africans would not be allowed a break on deck. The stench and filth in the hold—from sweat, vomit, urine, feces, and death—can hardly be imagined. Some people simply cracked, killing themselves or others in fits of insanity.

Young girls were vulnerable to sexual abuse. It depended largely on the character of the captain. He might be so hardened by the trade that he allowed his men full rein. However—rather more difficult to understand—many slave traders were pious, morally strict Calvinists or Quakers. The business of treating humans like livestock did not challenge their scruples, but they punished rape with whipping.

Comparatively few Africans were taken directly to the continental colonies. Most went first to the West Indies, usually Barbados or Jamaica, both because it shortened the voyage and for "seasoning"—in effect, teaching men and women just what they were: slaves. Arrival in Virginia or South Carolina (or New York or Massachusetts) was practically a deliverance for the captives. There were horrors yet to be undergone—the sale at market, the emotionally devastating experience of settling into a new, altogether foreign way of life, and the lifetime of hard forced labor for which they had been seized and sold. But anything must have seemed for the better after the nightmarish middle passage and seasoning.

---

period of years—commonly seven—the master was entitled to the apprentice's complete obedience and to the use of the boy's labor, in return for housing, board, clothing, and teaching the lad the mysteries of his trade. Ideally, master, apprentice, and society benefited.

Similarly, communities provided for orphans, girls as well as boys, by binding them to householders as servants. In return for the child's labor, the family that took an orphan in assumed the community's financial responsibility to care for him or her until adulthood.

Apprentices and servants were not free. As delineated in the Elizabethan Statute of Artificers of 1562, masters exercised the same broad authority over them that parents exercised over their children, including the legal right to administer corporal punishment that was often nasty. The brutalized servant is a stock character in literature and folklore.

At the same time, apprentices and servants were not slaves. They were not the property of their masters. They retained certain individual rights their masters were legally bound to respect, and the term of their servitude was specified

Before the *Mayflower*

Most indentured servants were British: English, Scots, Welsh, and Irish. As early as 1619, however, a Dutch vessel sailed up the Chesapeake and displayed to the Jamestowners about 20 black Africans whom the Dutch had captured from a slave trader bound for the Spanish West Indies. The Virginians bought them and continued to buy blacks throughout the 1600s.

First- and second-generation African Americans were servants, not slaves. One of the black men who arrived in Jamestown in 1619 took the name Anthony Johnson and became a prosperous farmer with several white servants bound to him. As early as 1650, there was a small, free black population in the Chesapeake colonies. The only plausible origin of this community is the fact that, like white servants, the first blacks in Virginia and Maryland were freed after a specified term of service.

Also by 1650, however, the assemblies of Virginia and Maryland were enacting laws stating that black servants would, in the future, serve *durante vita* ("for life"). This significant turn in law and cruel twist in the fate of African Americans was due to changing economic and social circum-

in a legal document. The day came when the apprentice and the maidservant walked off as free as anyone of their class.

Indentured Servants

Colonial planters and farmers who needed labor, adapted this familiar institution as indentured servitude. For an outlay of £6 to £30 to pay the cost of transatlantic passage and the fee of the contractor who signed up servants in England, a colonist secured the services of a worker bound as a servant for between four and seven years. The price and the length of time served depended upon just how badly American masters needed field hands and how many English men and women were willing to sign an "indenture," as the document was called.

The system worked. Well into the 1700s, indentured servants brought in the bulk of America's cash crops in every colony but South Carolina. The proportion of servants in the population was highest in Virginia and Maryland. Eighty percent were men; by custom, English women were less likely to work in the fields, and that was where a bound laborer was profitable.

A large majority of servants signed their indentures voluntarily. They were more than willing to trade several years of their wretched lives for the chance of a fresh start afterward. However, the practice of filling the hold of a servant ship by kidnapping boys or careless young men in English seaports was common enough. It was unwise to drink too heavily in a tavern near the harbor on the night a servant ship was scheduled to weigh anchor. In addition, English courts sentenced criminals—guilty of petty or vicious crimes—to "transportation" to the colonies, where they joined the ranks of indentured servants.

stances, to problems inherent in the institution of indentured servitude, and to the peculiar vulnerability of an identifiable minority in a society in which the vast majority was white.

Declining Death Rate, Collapsing Prices

A black slave serving *durante vita* cost considerably more than a white servant bound to labor for his master for a few years. The difference in price could amount to several tons of tobacco. Transportation costs from Africa were higher than for servants brought from Britain. And, unlike the agents who signed up white servants at no cost to themselves, slave traders in West Africa had to pay for their human cargoes.

Despite the higher cost, the African slave would seem, on the face of it, to have been a better deal than the white servant. His master could work him for a lifetime; there was no need to replace him after five or seven years. But in fact, the cheaper white servant was the better buy during most of the 1600s. Thanks to malaria, typhoid fever, yellow fever, and other contagious diseases ranging from smallpox to influenza, everyone coming to the Chesapeake colonies faced poor prospects of living a long life. Life expectancy for male immigrants to Maryland was 43. Governor Berkeley of Virginia estimated that, during the 1660s, four out of five indentured servants in that colony died within a few years of arriving.

So it did not matter much that the law gave planters possession of Africans for life. African slave and Irish servant alike were apt to be dead within a few years of purchase. The best buy in such circumstances was the laborer whose purchase price was lower. Term of service was little more than an abstraction. As long as tobacco prices were high, the best business decision was to get your workers as cheaply as you could and squeeze as much tobacco out of them as you could before you wrapped them in a shroud.

In the 1660s, however, the price of tobacco began its decline. By the end of the century, the death rate had noticeably declined too. After 1700, planters were presented with an incentive to save on the *annual* cost of their laborers rather than on the initial outlay. If all Virginians and Marylanders, black and white, were living longer, it made sense to buy workers who served longer. Moreover, blacks seemed more resistant to some of the diseases that toppled whites in the South's semitropical climate, and, as Bacon's Rebellion

illustrated so dramatically, white servants and former servants could be troublesome people—more trouble, planters thought, than black slaves. Finally, by 1700, the law in every colony held that the children of slave parents (or just a slave mother) were also slaves, the property of the master. The children of white servants were free, but still an expense to their mother's master during their infancy.

The Trouble with Servants

Colonial courts were crowded with masters complaining about servants' insolence, negligence, and laziness, about stolen food and drink, rowdy parties, and pregnancy, which exempted women from work for as long as a year. (Servants took their masters to court for mistreatment too, but rarely, and even more rarely did they win their case.)

Then there were runaways. Throughout the colonies, even in the most populated parts of the Tidewater, America was mostly woods. Farms and plantations were gaps in the forest. In Virginia and Maryland, the grandest plantations were separated from one another by belts of virgin hardwood or second-growth "pineys," old fields gone to scrub. In the South, towns were few. Roads were often just tracks, some of them so narrow two horsemen could not pass without jostling.

Determined servants found it a challenge, but far from impossible, to run away, hide, and elude capture. Planters' letters were flecked with annoyance about lost workers and lost investments. The recapture and return of runaways was a major activity of sheriffs, the only law enforcement officers in rural areas, and the source of much of their income. Officials in cities like Baltimore and Philadelphia were flooded with descriptions of runaways. Punishment was harsh—a whipping and extra time in service. Nevertheless, the opportunities of freedom and the odds of success tempted many.

The Badge of Race

The sympathy of many colonials for fugitive servants and the ease with which a white runaway could blend into an urban crowd were two more reasons planters slowly turned from a workforce of white indentured servants to black slaves.

Runaways found help or, at least, passive commiseration. The most famous colonial runaway, Benjamin Franklin, walked out on his master in Boston (his brother) in 1723 and traveled to Philadelphia by sea and land. Any number of people guessed he was a fugitive servant, but no one turned him in.

If a runaway reached a city, Philadelphia, New York, even still little Baltimore, he or she had a good chance of invisibility in the swarms of strangers, newly arrived immigrants, who were always present. An African American's color, however, was a badge, a "red flag." An escaped slave could not lose himself so easily in the throngs. If authorities assumed that blacks were slaves unless they could prove otherwise (free blacks carefully preserved precious documents

An Unusual Verdict

In New York City in 1728, Margaret Anderson, a servant, sued her master for her freedom for "very often Immoderately Correcting her"—beating her badly, in other words. She won her case. Her victory was not unique, but it was unusual. Only a clearly sadistic master could lose such a suit.

establishing their status), black strangers were detained and possible owners informed. Constables and sheriffs collected fees, and for planters, the workforce was that much more controllable.

In 1625, after the Jamestown Massacre, there were 25 black servants in Virginia, 2 percent of the population. In 1660, there were 9,000 blacks in Virginia, less than 4 percent of the population. (It is not clear how many were free or would know freedom.) In 1670, there were 20,000 blacks in Virginia, a majority of them slaves under a law enacted that year. After 1700, the colony's slave population grew rapidly until, by the time of the Revolution, it approached 200,000.

South Carolina was the one colony where, before 1700, slaves formed the bulk of the workforce; African Americans were almost a fifth of the colony's population in 1680. By 1720, 67 percent of South Carolinians were black, all but a few in bondage. A British officer observed, "They sell the servants here as they do their horses, and advertise them as they do their beef and oatmeal."

▲ *A typical advertisement of a slave auction. This one in Charleston in 1769 was unusual in that the people to be sold had been brought directly from Africa. Most African slaves in the colonies made a stop in the West Indies, where they were "seasoned."*

THE SLAVE TRADE

This demand for slave labor transformed attitudes toward trading in African slaves. Ships from England and New England, most famously Newport, Rhode Island, sailed annually to Africa to capture or purchase slaves. The acquisition of slaves in the West Indies, especially Cuba and Jamaica, was an even bigger business.

Collaboration in Atrocity

Some whites ventured up the rivers of West Africa and themselves seized, or "panyared," villagers. A trader of 1787 explained, "In the night we broke into the villages and, rushing into the huts of the inhabitants, seized men, women, and children promiscuously."

Primarily, however, the slave trade was a collaboration between African and white merchants. At first, African kings and lesser chiefs sold their own criminals, unsuccessful rivals, or garden variety troublemakers to the white-skinned strangers. As the demand for slaves grew and profits soared, some aggressive tribes launched raids inland in search of fresh sources of supply among other peoples. The economy of the great Ashanti Confederation of West Africa depended more than casually on the commerce in slaves. By 1750, King Tegbesu of Dahomey was pocketing £250,000 annually by selling slaves to the Americas.

Whites anchored their ships off the coast or fortified themselves in stockades on defensible islands like Gorée off Dakar or at the mouths of rivers. They offered iron bars, steel knives, brass, glass bottles, kettles, bells, cloth, guns, powder, liquor, and tobacco in return for human merchandise. It was not race versus race; it was business. A Dahomeyan felt no more kinship with an Oyo than with a Portuguese or a Quaker.

The vilest part of the slave trade was the sea crossing, called the "middle passage" because it was preceded and followed by overland marches. Rather than providing the most healthful circumstances possible for their valuable, vulnerable cargo and keeping mortality low, the traders crammed the slaves in "like herrings in a barrel."

If only one in 20 captives died, the voyage was considered an extraordinary success. If one in five died, which was by no means unusual, the profits were still considerable. A slave who cost £5 to £10 in Africa in 1700 sold in the New World for a minimum of £25. Only as the eighteenth century progressed did mortality on the middle passage decline. By the late 1700s, shipmasters reported that proportionally more slaves survived than crewmen—of whom, in the Guinea trade, one in five sailors failed to complete a voyage. (Deaths at sea on the North Atlantic routes were one in every 100.)

West African Roots

Most Africans fated to be North Americans were from lands bordering the Gulf of Guinea, the present-day nations of Gambia, Senegal, Guinea, Liberia, Sierra Leone, Ivory

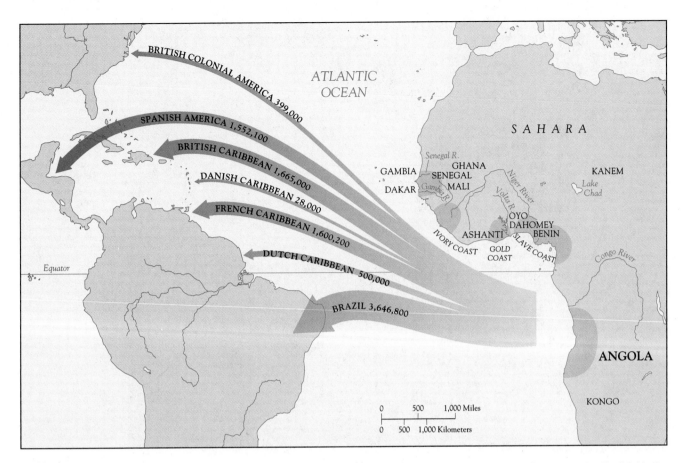

MAP 5:2 **West Africa and the Roots of Slavery, 1500–1810**   Extensive research indicates that enslaved Africans transported to English North America were a tiny fraction of the massive depopulation of West Africa. Most African Americans are descended from ancestors who were taken first to the West Indies, especially Cuba, and only later—a year or two, or a generation or two later—sold in what became the United States.

Coast, Ghana, Togo, Benin, and Nigeria. In ethnic origin, the majority were probably Wolof, Malinke, Oyo, Mandingo, Ashanti, Yoruba, Hausa, and Ibo.

Much of the coastline of West Africa was mangrove swamp, but approximately 100 miles inland the country pitches upward. It provided a living that was rich enough to support a large population and sophisticated cultures. Religiously, most West Africans were polytheists who worshiped a complicated hierarchy of gods and spirits. Many tribes venerated the spirits of dead ancestors, and sacrifice was central to most religions. Islam and Christianity were making headway as Arab slave traders came from the north and Christians from the sea.

West Africa was no Eden. The people who lived there had to be skilled, hardworking agriculturists. Ironically, their range and skills increased as slave traders introduced new crops: maize, cassava, peanuts, and sweet potatoes. The fact that intensive farming was a bulwark of West African culture helps to explain why West Africans were more appealing to American planters than Indians were. In addition to rice cultivation, which Africans probably introduced to the Carolinas, they utilized the heavy hoe, which was the mainstay of chopping weeds in the fertile southern soil.

The Vulnerability of a Disunited People

There was no such person as a typical captive. Male slaves might have been princes, priests, farmers, or murderers. Most commonly, however, they were ordinary people who had the bad luck to catch the eye of raiders. Most female slaves also came from the ordinary classes. Their condition as women in Africa depended on the tribe to which they belonged. In most, women did a major part of the heavy labor. In other tribes, such as the Ashanti, descent was traced in the maternal line, and women were accorded high status, although hardly equality.

Once in the colonies, these diverse peoples adopted English because it was the only feasible means of communication among themselves. In time, they also found in their masters' Protestantism, albeit with a great deal of emphasis on the stories of the ancient Hebrews' captivities and deliverance, a solace in their misery. For the most part, however, they were shut out of the mainstream of American development for more than three centuries after the first African stepped nervously from the gangplank of the Dutch ship anchored at Jamestown in 1619.

The caption on the left side reads vertically: View of Mulberry, House and Street, by Thomas Coram, oil on paper, Gibbes Museum of Art/Carolina Art Association

▲ *The slaves' cabins at South Carolina's Mulberry Plantation were far more substantial than the descriptions of most slave housing of the early 1700s. Mulberry was an outlying development. The handsome "big house" was designed as a fortress in which slaves and neighbors could shelter in case of an Indian attack.*

for FURTHER READING

On Indians, see Alvin M. Josephy, *The Indian Heritage of America,* 1968; Harold E. Driver, *Indians of North America,* 1970; Wilcomb E. Washburn, *The Indian in America,* 1975, and *Cambridge History of the Natives of the World,* vol. 3: *North America,* 1993; and Robert F. Spencer et al., *The Native Americans: Ethnology and Background of the North American Indians,* 1977.

James Axtell is the leading historian of Native Americans in the colonial period. See Axtell's *The European and the Indian,* 1981; and *The Invasion Within: The Contest of Cultures in Colonial America,* 1985. Also see Gary Nash, *Red, White, and Black,* 1982; and Neal Salisbury, *Manitou and Providence: Indians, Europeans, and the Making of New England,* 1982.

A series of books by nineteenth-century literary historian Francis Parkman remain fine reading about the French in North America: *French North America: The Pioneers of France in the New World,* 1865; *The Jesuits in North America,* 1867; *The Old Regime in Canada,* 1874; *Count Frontenac and New France,* 1877; and *LaSalle and the Discovery of the Great West,* 1879. A fine single-volume history of the subject is William J. Eccles, *France in America,* 1972. Also see Eccles's *The Canadian Frontier, 1534–1760,* 1969.

On indentured servitude and the evolution of African slavery in English America, see David W. Galenson, *White Servitude in Colonial America,* 1981; and Edmund S. Morgan, *American Slavery, American Freedom,* 1975. Philip D. Curtin, *The Atlantic Slave Trade,* 1969, is still the definitive work on that subject. An invaluable overview is David B. Davis, *The Problem of Slavery in Western Culture,* 1966. The beginning portion of Kenneth Stampp, *The Peculiar Institution,* 1956, provides important information on early slavery.

Visit the source collections at http://ajaccess.wadsworth.com and http://infotrac.thomsonlearning.com, and use the Search function with the following key terms to explore documents, images, audio and video clips, articles, and commentary related to the material in this chapter:

Algonquian
Atlantic slave trade
Five Nations
Iroquois
King Philip's War (or Metacom's War)

Additional resources, exercises, and Internet links related to this chapter are available on *The American Past* Web site: http://history.wadsworth.com/americanpast7e.

HISTORY ONLINE

The Iroquois
www.tolatsga.org/iro.html
Quick, thoroughgoing essay on the history of the Iroquois, the indispensable Indian allies of the English colonists.

Virtual Museum of New France
www.civilization.ca/vmnf/vmnfe.asp
Comprehensive Canadian site: Text and illustrations on the early years and chief personalities in the development of New France.

African Americans
www.pbs.org/wgbh/aia/home.html
A Public Broadcasting System Web site on African American history beginning in the 1600s.

A MATURING SOCIETY

*Society, Culture, and
War in the 1700s*

North Wind Picture Archives

*God hath sifted a nation that he might send choice grain
into this wilderness.*

William Stoughton

*Sir, they are a race of convicts, and ought to be thankful
for anything we allow them short of hanging.*

Samuel Johnson

IN 1706, A BOY was born into the household of a Boston
tallow maker, an artisan who made candles and soap from
animal fats. There would have been little fuss made over the
arrival of Benjamin Franklin; he was the tenth child in the
family.

Large families were common in the colonies. Typically,
a woman married in her early 20s, several years younger than
women in Britain. She bore 6 to 8 children, a majority of
whom, in the 1700s, survived to be adults, a higher proportion than in Great Britain. Children were economic assets
then, not the costly creatures they are today. Children consumed little but food, which was cheap in the colonies. There
was productive work for them by the time they reached 5 or
6: feeding chickens, gathering eggs, fetching water and firewood. Teenagers (neither the word nor the concept of adoles-
cence as a distinct stage of life was known) put in a full day's
work, thus contributing more to a household's economy than
they took from it. Many families willingly took in teenagers
not their own for this reason.

Benjamin Franklin went to work in his father's workshop at the age of 10. At 12, he was apprenticed to his half
brother, a printer. They did not get along, and, at 17, Ben ran
away to Philadelphia. But he had learned the trade, which,
in the eighteenth century, involved writing as well as setting
the words of others in type. Franklin was good, imitating the
elegant style of the fashionable English essayists Joseph Addison and Richard Steele.

No one faulted him for imitation. Colonials did not say,
as Noah Webster and Ralph Waldo Emerson would say a
century later, that Americans should write distinctively
American literature in a distinctively American language.
Bostonians (and New Yorkers, Philadelphians, and country
folk) were pleased to be colonials. They were proud to be the
overseas subjects of a realm they believed the most beneficent on earth, "a mighty empire in numbers little inferior to
the greatest in Europe, and in felicity to none." They gladly
took their customs and culture, as well as their laws and the

manufactured goods they needed, from the mother country (after 1707, no longer "England" but "Great Britain").

During Franklin's long life (he lived until 1790), British America flowered, then fruited, outgrowing the colonial mentality. Franklin did not miss a turn on the road. He grew rich and became the best-known American of his time, respected at home, lionized in Europe. Founding libraries, learned societies, the first American hospital, and the first trained fire department, he was devoted to social improvement. He was an inventor (the lightning rod, bifocals, and an efficient stove for heat were among his inventions), a scientist, and, as he grew wealthy and famous, a celebrity. He devised a scheme to unite the colonies in 1754, the Albany Plan of Union. (It was rejected.) He signed the Declaration of Independence and the Constitution. Slavery, which during his lifetime quietly evolved from a minor colonial institution into a matter of grave concern, did not escape Franklin's notice. His final public statement called for its abolition.

SOCIETY AND ECONOMY

Between 1700 and 1776, the population of the colonies increased tenfold, from about 250,000 people to 2.5 million. Natural increase accounted for much of this astonishing growth. Both family size and life expectancy were greater in North America than anywhere else in the world. In New England (with the exception of infants, whose first years were dangerous, and women dying in first childbirth), life expectancy was nearly as high as it is today with all of our precautions and medicine. New Englanders were the first people in history to have personally known their grandparents as a matter of routine.

Their grandfathers, anyway—unlike today, when women outlive men by half a dozen years, men were longer-lived in the eighteenth century. The reason was, of course, childbirth, which cut short the lives of young wives. However, a New England male of 20 was apt to die nearer 70 years of age than 60; an inhabitant of the Middle Colonies, more than 60. Life expectancy was less in the South: 45 in Virginia and Maryland, 42 in the Carolinas and Georgia. (Life expectancy for a white person of 20 in the British West Indies was 40; West Indian slaves died in such chilling numbers that there was virtually no natural increase of the black population during the 1700s.)

Large, healthy families were only part of the growth of the colonies. The colonies were also flooded by immigrants, as many as 800,000 between 1700 and the War for Independence. By no means were they all English.

▲ *Benjamin Franklin (1706–1790). Until the War for Independence made George Washington famous, Franklin was the only American widely known in Europe. Rich, an inventor, the founder of numerous institutions in Philadelphia, a lobbyist in London for Pennsylvania and Massachusetts, he was to be a successful diplomat during the Revolution.*

Immigration from Germany

Germans and German-speaking Austrians responded enthusiastically to William Penn's invitation to take up farms in Pennsylvania. By the 1750s, they were so numerous in Philadelphia, Lancaster, and York counties that Benjamin Franklin, who called them "the most stupid of their nation," was alarmed. They will "Germanize us instead of us Anglifying them," he wrote, "and will never adopt our Language or Customs." Germans were a third of Pennsylvania's population in 1776; it was seriously proposed that German, not English, be the official language of the then independent state.

Many German immigrants were members of the plain-living Moravian, Amish, Mennonite, and Hutterite sects. Like the Quakers, they were pacifists and reflexively supported the Quaker party in elections. No doubt, their bloc voting annoyed Franklin, a leader of Pennsylvania's anti-Quaker political faction, as much as the sounds of the German language on Philadelphia's streets.

The Scotch-Irish

More numerous than the Germans (and more widely disliked) were the Scotch-Irish. They were descendants of Protestant Scots whom, a century earlier, James I settled in northern Ireland to displace the rebellious Catholic Irish there. By the 1700s, however, they had lost favor with the Crown and were suffering from steep increases in rent and parliamentary acts undercutting the weaving industry, on which many depended for their livelihood. About 4,000 Scotch-Irish a year gave up on the Emerald Isle and emigrated to the colonies, "huddled together like brutes without regard to age or sex or sense of decency."

They were a combative people in Ireland, ever ready with cudgels to battle Catholics, and they did not mellow in American air. James Logan, the agent of the Penn family in Philadelphia, wrote in consternation, "I must own, from my experience in the land office, that the settlement of five families from Ireland gives me more trouble than fifty of any other people."

The Scotch-Irish wanted land. To get it after 1700, they had to move to the hilly backcountry of western Pennsylvania, Virginia, and the Carolinas. There, with muskets and rifles rather than cudgels, they confronted Indians with whom Quakers like Logan tried to have amicable relations.

The Scotch-Irish frontiersmen made their own Indian policy. Far from the capital of Philadelphia, they attacked their Native American neighbors for good reason and bad. Franklin's anti-Quaker party generally supported them in the colonial assembly and, when Britain and France went to war, so did the Crown, for most of the Indians of the region were at least casual allies of the French in Canada.

The pacifist Quakers were realists during the Anglo-French wars. They accommodated the Crown by such contrivances as voting money "for the king's use," laying on royal shoulders the sin of spending it on guns and soldiers, or for "grain," not specifying whether the grains be of wheat or gunpowder. During periods of peace between Britain and France, however, homegrown Scotch-Irish aggressiveness presented the Quaker establishment with a stickier moral problem. If they stood by their commitment to popular government, they became parties to frontier carnage, a mockery of their pacifism. If they insisted on peace and fair dealings with the Indians, they would defy the demands of the majority of Pennsylvanians, a mockery of their democratic inclinations.

By the end of the 1750s, many Quaker officials gave up, retiring from public life. Thus they preserved their personal

⌦ (No. II.) ⌫

Philadelphische
Z E I T U N G.

SONNABEND, den 24 Jun. 1732.

[German-language newspaper text in two columns, in Fraktur type, largely illegible]

▲ *One of several German-language newspapers published in colonial Philadelphia. Franklin and others worried that their city might become more German than English.*

scruples (and prospered mightily in trade) while the backcountry settlers, Franklin's party, and the Crown had free rein to pursue their Indian wars.

Family, Politics, Property

Whatever the ethnicity or religion of colonials, the family had a standing in law, custom, and sentiment that can be difficult to comprehend today. The family, with broad authority vested in patriarch and matriarch (ultimately in the husband), was the basic social and economic institution, much more than the amorphous, sentimental association it is today. Early Puritan laws requiring all people, including bachelors, spinsters (unmarried women), infants, and the elderly to live within a household were long gone, but the practice survived: The "loner" was looked upon with suspicion.

The family, not the individual, was the political unit. Only the male heads of property-owning families voted. (Women could be heads of household but not voters.) There might be several adult males in a household—grown children, servants, and employees—but they did not vote. Just how much property was required for participation in elections varied from colony to colony, but it was not very much. Whereas about one British male in three could vote, almost threefourths qualified in the colonies. Actual participation was something else: Less than a quarter of male Bostonians actually cast votes; as many as 40 percent of Pennsylvanians and New Yorkers; about half the adult males in Connecticut.

Property laws, adapted from Britain's, were designed to protect the proprietor class and to maintain its families' status in society. For example, Virginia, Maryland, and South Carolina enacted laws of primogeniture and entail. Primogeniture required that a landed estate be bequeathed as a whole to the eldest son of the deceased head of household, or, if there was no male heir, to his first daughter. Entail meant that a property could not be subdivided for sale. To transfer ownership of an estate in any way, one was required to keep it intact.

The purpose of such laws was to preserve the economic power and social privileges of the propertied, particularly the wealthy. If a tobacco planter with a thousand acres and 30 slaves, enough to support his family in grand style, were legally free to divide his estate among four or five children, the result would be four or five households of middling means. If these properties were subdivided by inheritance, the result, from grandparents to grandchildren, would be a gaggle of struggling subsistence farmers where once there had been a grandee. Entail prevented an individual with an opportunity to make a killing in real estate from ripping the social fabric with his greed. Primogeniture kept paternal sentimentality in check.

The colonial rich, especially in the cities, grew richer during the eighteenth century. In 1700, the richest tenth of Philadelphia's population owned about 40 percent of the city's wealth. By 1774, the richest tenth owned 55 percent.

Social Mobility

People of property were not, of course, insensitive to the fate of their daughters and younger sons. They could and did bequeath them money (*personal* as opposed to *real* property) and gave them land not part of an entailed estate. As in Britain, second sons might be educated for a profession: the

---

Dutch Women in New York

Married women in New Netherland (New York plus enclaves in New Jersey and Delaware) had significantly different property rights than married women in the English colonies. They owned family property *jointly* with their husbands, not in *coverture*. When one spouse died, the survivor inherited the whole. If the survivor was a woman and she remarried, her property from her previous marriage remained hers independently of her second husband. When she died, the property from her first marriage was divided equally among the sons *and daughters* from the first marriage.

The English guaranteed these property laws when they accepted the surrender of New Netherland in 1664. In time, English law displaced Dutch. However, ethnically Dutch women in New York stubbornly clung to another Dutch practice at odds with English custom. As late as the nineteenth century, many continued to use their maiden names throughout life, rather than their husbands' surnames. Annetje Krygier, married to Jans van Arsdale, remained Annetje Krygier throughout life.

---

ministry, medicine, law, or the military. A profession maintained their social standing and the possibility of making an advantageous marriage without breaking up the family lands.

George Washington provides a good example. His older brother, Lawrence, inherited the extensive Washington lands. He helped George train as a surveyor (which meant land speculator in the colonies) in the hope George would himself "found a family," that is, acquire property. Washington was also an officer in the Virginia militia, and he kept an eye open toward that other avenue leading to property ownership—an heiress or wealthy widow to court and marry, which he found in Martha Custis.

Daughters of the propertied classes were provided with dowries of money or unentailed land, sometimes quite grand dowries, in order to attract husbands of means or, at least, of the same social class. The woman who came into property as a daughter without brothers, or as a widow, was not surprised to have suitors not many days after she buried her husband. The woman who wished to control her property, which only an unmarried woman could do, required a strong will to resist such pressure to remarry.

In fact, there was a great deal to be said on behalf of marriage for the heiress and younger widow. Few women had the training to supervise an estate or business, and heading a propertied household was, for women, awkward at best. Moreover, a woman could ensure, even enhance, her children's wealth and social position by a shrewd marriage. Mary Horsmanden had two husbands and was far more the founder of several prominent Virginia families, including the Carters and Byrds, than either of the husbands she survived. Frances Culpeper successively married three governors of Virginia, continuing to enjoy a social station she obviously relished.

Woman's Place

The woman of property who married did not, as is often said, lose ownership of it. Her husband had the *use* of it. That is, he managed it and decided how to spend the income it provided; in fact, he could make all decisions regarding his wife's property except the decision to sell it. The legal principle of coverture held that "husband and wife are one, and that one, the husband." However, the property a woman brought to a marriage reverted to her if the marriage was dissolved, which meant, in practice, her husband's death. (Divorce was extremely rare.) And it was hers to bequeath to whom she liked; it was not entailed with her husband's property.

If the colonial woman's status and legal standing were inferior to that of the menfolk, she enjoyed a more favorable situation than women in Europe. In most colonies, husbands were forbidden to beat their wives, which sounds like little but, comparatively, was a great deal. At least one man in Massachusetts was fined because he publicly referred to his wife as "a servant"; that is, he demeaned her. Visitors from Europe unfailingly commented on the deference colonial men paid women and the protections women were provided by custom. In the former Puritan colonies, a woman could sue

> ### The Bright Side of Coverture
> In legally submerging the wife into the husband, coverture had its bright side for women too. If her husband controlled her property, he alone took the fall for a criminal act they performed as a couple *if* the wife could plausibly plead she was submitting to her husband in the doing of the dirty deed: "If through constraint of his will, she carries out her duty of obedience to the excess of doing unlawful acts, she shall not suffer for them criminally." In a few recorded cases, women went scot-free, although they appear to have acted more like Lady Macbeth than like Melanie Wilkes.

for divorce on the grounds of adultery, bigamy, desertion, impotence, incest, or absence for a period of seven years.

The Lower Orders

Laws pertaining to property were of no meaning to people of the lower classes. In the countryside, free workers and poor farmers were, along with servants and sometimes slaves, often at odds with the propertied classes. In the seaports—the only true cities in the colonies—unskilled workers, journeymen, and apprentices, along with a marginal class of servants, ex-servants, slaves, poor free blacks, sailors on leave, roustabouts, and the omnipresent derelicts, found enough work to be done to keep them alive, but not enough compensation to generate a sense of belonging to the community or to have much respect for conventional morals.

Every port, even small ones, had a disreputable quarter where drunkenness and brawling were endemic and the makings of a mob ever ready to combust. The patterns of underclass crime were much as they are today. In New York City, 95 percent of crimes of violence were committed by men, as were 74 percent of thefts. Rape must have been common but was rarely charged among the lower classes and even more rarely prosecuted because convictions were difficult. The victim was unlikely to be a woman of virtue, and her personal morality was of compelling importance to judges and juries. Statutory rape cases were virtually unknown. The traditional English age of consent was 10! Colonial assemblies upped this, but only to 12 and 14. What colonials called statutory rape we call child molestation.

With witchcraft prosecutions disreputable after the Salem hysteria, the only major crime associated with women was infanticide. With high infant mortality a fact of life, it, like rape, was a difficult crime to prove in court. In New York between 1730 and 1780, 20 women were charged with killing their newborns, but only one was convicted. Illegitimate births were common. A third of all colonial births—and not just among the lower classes—occurred outside marriage or in significantly less than nine months after the wedding.

The colonial urban poor were racially mixed, thereby earning the further contempt of their betters. "The crowd" they formed was kept under control by strict laws and erratic but no-nonsense enforcement. Nevertheless, the crowd made its presence and wishes known in occasional "bread riots," and the lower classes were to play a major part in the tumult that preceded the American Revolution. As with submerged classes of people before and since, riot was the most accessible means of political expression.

Slave Rebellions

The lowliest of the lowly were the slaves. Except in New York, they were not numerous north of the Mason-Dixon line, the boundary between Pennsylvania and Maryland—between North and South—surveyed in 1769. Slaves were only 8 percent of the population in Pennsylvania and 3 percent in Massachusetts.

In the southern colonies, by contrast, slavery grew in importance during the eighteenth century. The number of blacks in Virginia, most of whom were slaves, rose to about 40,000 in 1700 to more than 200,000 at the time of the American Revolution. In a few Virginia counties and over much of South Carolina, blacks outnumbered whites.

Now and then, slaves rebelled. In 1712, slaves in New York City staged an uprising, and, in 1741, a series of arsons there was blamed on slaves and poor whites led by a Catholic priest. Eighteen blacks and four whites were hanged; 13 African American slaves were burned alive; 70 slaves were sold to the West Indies.

In 1739, about 20 blacks from the Stono plantation near Charleston seized guns, killed several planter families, and came within an ace of capturing the lieutenant governor. They put out a call for an uprising, and about 150 other slaves joined them. "With Colours displayed, and two Drums beating," they began to march toward Florida, where, they had learned through a remarkable African American grapevine, the governor of the Spanish colony would grant them freedom.

Most were captured within a week, but some managed to reach St. Augustine and settled to the north of the town in the fortified village of Santa Teresa de Mose. They swore to "shed their last drop of blood in defense of the Great Crown of Spain, and to be the most cruel enemies of the English." The threat—or at least the attraction that Santa Teresa held out to other slaves—was great enough that, the next year, General Oglethorpe of Georgia attacked the village.

THE COLONIES AT WAR

The fabulous growth of the 13 mainland colonies during the eighteenth century, coupled with their physical isolation from the mother country, ensured that the expansive and ever more confident Americans could not remain the tail on the British imperial lion. This is not to say that American independence was inevitable. However, some independence of interests and actions surely was. This was evidenced between 1689 and 1763, when the mother country was involved in a series of wars with France. Colonials participated, or withheld participation, according to what they perceived to be their interests, as opposed to the interests of Great Britain.

Another Kind of War

The European wars of 1689–1763 were fought worldwide, for Britain and France both possessed far-flung empires. Battle raged not only in Europe and North America but also in the Caribbean, in South America, in India, and wherever ships flying belligerent flags met on the high seas.

Broad in scope, the wars were not, however, broad in the extent to which they involved ordinary people. In the late seventeenth and the eighteenth centuries, war was considered an extension of diplomacy, the concern of rulers. They fought frankly to win or to defend territory or trade from rivals, or, like medieval barons, to avenge what one prince took as the insult of another. There was no clash of ideologies, no claims that one social, economic, or political system was engaged in a mortal struggle with another.

Armies were made up of professional soldiers, rough men for whom fighting was a means of making a living. Soldiers did not imagine they were defending a nation or furthering an abstract ideal, such as freedom. If they were attached to anything, it was to their fellow soldiers, who were their community, and sometimes to their commander, who saw to it that they were fed, housed, and paid.

Piracy's Golden Age

From the Collections of the Library of Congress

There have been pirates as long as ships have carried cargoes worth stealing. Between about 1660 and 1725, the crime became a major problem for merchants in the colonial trade.

A pirate is a seafaring armed robber and usually a murderer, at least as an accomplice. Pirates were rapists infrequently only because they preyed on merchant ships—where the goods were—and a woman was rare aboard such vessels.

Pirates in American waters were called "buccaneers" because the first of them were riffraff from Hispaniola (present-day Haiti and the Dominican Republic) who lived by hunting before they turned to the sea, cooking their meat by slow-smoking it (*boucaner* in French). The commercial wars of the era contributed to the growth of the profession when, to save money in their naval budgets, France, Holland, Spain, and England commissioned privateers, well-armed privately owned ships, to seize (at a percentage of the take) the ships of the countries they were fighting. Privateering could be lucrative. In 1668, Henry Morgan took a break from seizing Spanish ships, captured Portobelo in Panama, and collected a ransom of 250,000 pesos from Spain.

When peace treaties were signed, some privateers found it difficult to give up the business. They continued to raid ports and steal from ships at sea without regard to the flag their victims were flying. In 1701, Captain William Kidd, a New Yorker, was hanged by the British. Just a few years earlier, they had issued him the privateer's Letters of Marque and Reprisal.

Who were the buccaneers? In the early 1720s, 98 percent of those who were captured had started life as "honest seamen," mostly on the merchant ships upon which they came to prey. A large number said that liquor led them to opt for their life of crime. Indeed, according to the records, life on a pirate vessel can seem to have been one long drunken revel so that, on a given day, a large proportion of the crew was incapacitated.

There were other reasons young men (almost all pirates were in their 20s or younger) became pirates. The honest seaman's life was dull, brutalized, poorly paid, laborious, and likely to terminate in an early death. Piracy was exciting, eternally an attraction to young men vexed by frantic hormones. Pirates might risk their lives during their robberies, and the gallows was their fate if they were caught. But each job filled their purses, and, whether or not they were drunk nonstop between hits, they did not work very much. A merchant sloop (a small vessel with one mast) of 100 tons was sailed by a crew of about a dozen; the same vessel under the black flag of piracy had 80 men aboard to handle the same tasks. Even then, with so little to do, pirates who captured slaves put them to work while they looked for buyers. Captain Kidd spoke of stealing 12 slaves whom his crew "intended to make good use of to do the drudgery of [their] ship."

What did ordinary farmers, artisans, and shopkeepers have to do with such a business? As little as they could. At best, war meant heavier taxation. At worst, people were unlucky enough to make their homes where armies fought or marched. Then they suffered, no matter what flag the fighting men were waving.

Otherwise, ordinary people went on as in peacetime. Because princes neither expected nor sought popular support for their wars, it was not a matter of treason in the modern sense of the word when, as in the world wars of 1689 to 1763, many Americans simply sat out the conflict or even traded with the French enemy.

"Little War"

The wars began when William of Orange, a Dutchman, became king of England in 1689. William's life had been dedicated to preventing the expansion of France, and he meant to throw the resources of the British Isles into the struggle.

In 1689, when Louis XIV of France announced his right to take possession of a minor principality on the Rhine River, William strapped on his sword. Few Americans cared who ruled what in the Rhineland. Unconsciously, but with a certain elegance, they proclaimed their disinterest by calling the War of the League of Augsburg, its official name, "King William's War."

Algonkian allies of the French struck in the winter of 1689–1690 with a series of raids on frontier settlements in New York, New Hampshire, and Maine (then part of Massachusetts). These were hardly great battles in the European pattern. Although often led by French officers, they were Indian-style attacks in which warriors hit without warning at isolated farms, killing or capturing the settlers and burning houses and fields. The French called it *petite guerre* ("little war") and viewed the raids as statements that frontier colonials were trespassing on French lands.

Petite guerre worked. Each successful raid moved the unmarked boundary between New France and New England

Pirate crews were so large because their numbers were one key to their success. They were robbers. They did not want to destroy the ships they attacked with their cannon (which they carried for defense). They wanted to board their victims' vessel with the loot undamaged and take what was worth taking. The captain of a merchant ship with 12 seamen who were not fighting men was a fool to resist when faced with 80 vicious pirates armed with cutlasses, knives, and pistols. Few did. Merchant captains knew that those who gave up without a fight were usually spared the hideous cruelties of which the pirates were capable. The principle was the same as the advice given today to the unlucky soul confronted on a dark street by a thug with a knife: Give him the wallet.

Another key to success in piracy was speed. Pirates needed to catch target vessels in order to exhibit the size of the force they had aboard. So while a few famous pirates like Bartholomew "Black Bart" Roberts and Edward "Blackbeard" Teach had large 40-gun ships, most pirates sailed sloops, large enough to accommodate a hundred drunken cutthroats but fast.

Of course, treasure, such as "pieces of eight" (Spanish currency), was the most desirable booty. Slaves were probably the second favorite; they could be readily sold. When pirates tortured captives who had given up without resisting, it was usually to learn where any money aboard was hidden. Mostly, however, pirates took the food and drink they wanted for their own use and whatever cargo was aboard, even hogsheads of tobacco. Selling the contraband could be a problem. Unlike licensed privateers, pirates could not sail into a port and advertise for buyers. There were a few wide-open pirate towns in the Bahamas and Belize, and in Port Royal in Jamaica, where the governor liked having armed pirate ships in the harbor to discourage Spanish attack. Blackbeard was looking for a site for a new development on Ocracoke Inlet in North Carolina when he was trapped and killed in 1718. But none of the sanctuaries lasted very long. The wildest of them, Port Royal, was destroyed by an earthquake in 1692, to the satisfaction of moralists.

Curiously, pirate vessels were more democratic than New England town meetings. Where to hunt prey, from Newfoundland to the West Indies, was determined by majority vote, as was the decision whether or not to attack a vessel the pirates spotted. The captain (who was elected and could be voted out) claimed a far smaller proportion of booty than the masters of merchant vessels or whalers received, and his allowance of food and drink was equal to that of other crewmen. Only when "fighting, chasing, or being chased" did he have the absolute authority of the commander of a naval vessel.

Pirates in American waters were of a dozen nationalities, although, during the "golden age," most were British or colonials, including blacks. In his last stand, Blackbeard was backed by 13 whites and 6 blacks. In 1722, Black Bart's force of 268 men was captured; 77 of them were African Americans. Observing that the pirate community was entirely male, a few historians have claimed that it was a gay society, but the evidence indicates homosexuality was uncommon among pirates.

The golden age of buccaneering came abruptly to an end during the Long Peace, when the colonial powers could direct their warships against the pirates. In 1720, between 1,500 and 2,000 pirates in about 25 vessels worked the Caribbean and the North American coast. By 1723, their numbers were down to 1,000; by 1726, to 200. There were 50 attacks on merchant vessels in American waters in 1718 but just 6 in 1726. Relentless pursuit of pirates, followed inevitably by hanging, ended the threat. Moreover, men were lured out of the profession by announcements of pardons. Many pirates had, they claimed, been forced into the life when, as "honest seamen," they were captured. The large number of pirates who applied for pardons implies they were telling the truth.

deeper into country the colonials considered their own. More aggravating to the New England commercial elite, quite secure from Indians in Boston, were assaults on their merchant and fishing vessels by French ships out of Port Royal in Acadia (Nova Scotia). In 1690, an expedition from Massachusetts captured Port Royal but in vain. At peace negotiations in 1697, the fortress was returned to France. King William had not fared well in Europe; he gave Port Royal back in order to limit concessions to France in the Rhineland. New Englanders were reminded that their interests were subordinate to England's interests in Europe as interpreted, in this case, by a Dutchman.

Queen Anne's War, 1702–1713

Militarily, the French took North America more seriously. Even before the brief peace of 1697–1702, they constructed a series of forts stretching from the Gulf of Mexico to Canada, sketching the new colony of Louisiana on the map. Then, in 1700, Europe again went to war to decide who would sit on the throne of Spain. This time around, southern colonials, who had ignored King William's War, were in the thick of things. South Carolinians, who competed with both the Spanish and French in the fur and hide trade with the southern Indians, did not care to see their two rivals ruled by the same family. South Carolina's network of Indian contacts extended beyond the Mississippi River, but they also had formidable Indian enemies in what are now Georgia, Alabama, and Mississippi. Slave-catching expeditions among the Creek and Cherokee peoples kept the southwestern frontier in a state of chronic *petite guerre*.

In the north, the French and their Indian allies were more audacious than before, wiping out the substantial town of Deerfield, Massachusetts, in 1704. Once again, New Englanders and the Royal Navy captured Port Royal, and this time, Great Britain kept it and the whole of Acadia. Little, however, changed as far as colonial merchants were concerned. The French retired to Cape Breton Island and built a

▲ *Deerfield, Massachusetts, was no mere cluster of frontier cabins when Indians and French soldiers burned it to the ground in 1704. It was a substantial, comfortable town founded 35 years earlier. The utter destruction of so apparently secure a place set all New England on edge.*

new Atlantic fortress and shelter for commerce raiders, Louisbourg.

In the south, the treaty resolved few difficulties for the simple reason that the European nations did not hold the ultimate power there. The Creek and Cherokee were numerous and confident, less dependent on Europeans than were the Indians of the north. They had buttressed their strength by selectively adopting the ways of the whites, including agricultural techniques and the exploitation of black slave labor, which made them more than self-sufficient in food. The 30 to 40 Cherokee villages began to coordinate their decisions, which was to lead to full confederation in the 1750s.

The Middle Colonies played no notable role in the war, except to profit from it by trading with both sides. "War is declared in England," a New York businessman wrote in his diary, "universal joy among the merchants." The colony of New York actually issued a formal declaration of neutrality.

THE LONG PEACE, 1713–1739

For a quarter of a century, France and Britain were at peace. Tobacco never again sold at bonanza prices, but it returned a handsome enough profit on the Chesapeake. Rice, naval stores, and hides and furs continued to be lucrative, although harder to get. Colonials began to export ginseng (or "sang" as it was called on the frontier), most of which found its way in British ships to China. The colonial merchant marine

grew in size so that there was almost as much tonnage in American ports as in British. In troubled times to come, Americans with a memory would look back on the Long Peace of 1713–1739 as a golden age.

Salutary Neglect

They identified the good times with the policies of the first British prime minister, Robert Walpole. Avuncular and easy-going, fancying his daily outsized bottle of port, Walpole believed that the best way to govern was to govern as little as possible. As far as the colonies were concerned, if they were bustling, prosperous, and content, thus enriching British merchants, then why in the world should Britain do anything to disturb them? Walpole's policy was known as "salutary neglect." Inaction was healthful—salutary—even if it meant ignoring colonial violations of the Navigation Acts, which were common

Alas for history's Walpoles, there are always people who demand government action on behalf of their interests or whims. In 1732, London hatmakers complained that the growth of that industry in the northern colonies was hurting their sales in North America. The prime minister quieted them by forbidding colonials to sell hats outside the boundaries of their own colony and to train African Americans in the craft. London's hatters were mollified. American hatmakers ignored the law. Colonial officials enforced it now and then, but not too often. Walpole dined with friends.

The Molasses Act

The Molasses Act of 1733 was enacted in response to complaints by sugar planters in the British West Indies that Americans were buying molasses from French islands, where it was cheaper. They argued that mercantilism entitled them to a monopoly on the huge molasses market in New England. (Rum, distilled from blackstrap, was the common man's liquor in the colonies and also valuable in the slave trade.) Did not the tobacco growers of Virginia and Maryland have a monopoly on the sale of their product in Great Britain?

What to do? In the Molasses Act, Walpole levied a duty of 6 pence per gallon on French molasses, placating British sugar planters, and then made little effort to collect it, pleasing colonials buying from the French. The colonists either smuggled bootleg French molasses into New England ports or presented customs officers with fraudulent invoices stating that their cargo came from Jamaica or Barbados, British islands. The officials were not often fooled by the phony documents. But they could be bribed, and if a gift of a few pence per barrel pleased them too, that was the idea of salutary neglect. Walpole was not offended by the far grander bribery in which his best friends were involved.

Another law that was ignored in the interests of prosperity and calm was passed in 1750 at the behest of English iron makers, who wanted a monopoly on the colonial market. The act forbade colonists to engage in most forms of iron manufacture. Not only did colonial forges continue to operate with impunity; several colonial governments actually subsidized the iron industry within their borders. Salutary neglect was a wonderful way to run an empire—as long as times were good.

Assemblies and Governors

One consequence of Walpole's easygoing colonial policy was the steady erosion of the mother country's political control of her American daughters. In part, the piecemeal acquisition of governors' powers by colonial assemblies merely reflected what was going on in England at the time. During the eighteenth century, Parliament assumed governmental functions formerly exercised by kings and queens. In the colonies, elected assemblies took powers from the governors, who were appointed by the monarch or, in Maryland and Pennsylvania, proprietors.

▲ *This portrait is believed to be of Lord Cornbury dressed as a woman. Some historians doubt its authenticity. It resembles Lord Cornbury but did not surface until several decades after his death in 1723. If it is the viscount, it may well have been painted as a smear rather than with the governor sitting for the artist.*

And the Governor Wore Organdy

Peers of the realm (nobles) did not accept appointments as royal governors of American colonies. A man with a title enjoyed too good a life at home to trade it for headaches at the end of the world.

The notable exception was Edward Hyde, viscount Cornbury. Between 1701 and 1709, he was royal governor of New York and New Jersey, where he raised some eyebrows. It was said that he dressed in women's clothing, sashaying on the ramparts surrounding the governor's palace; that he was arrested as a prostitute when he dressed up for a walk around town; and that he invited the men at a banquet in his honor to fondle his wife's ears, which he thought beyond compare. (Lady Cornbury was accused of pilfering clothing and jewelry—earrings?—at homes she visited.)

The evidence the governor was a cross-dresser is not reliable. The allegations, although numerous, were made by his political enemies or were hearsay, remarks in letters of what the writer had been told but had not himself seen. And there is a portrait of the viscount in a gown worthy of a queen. (One of Lord Cornbury's alleged explanations of his hobby was that he represented Queen Anne and therefore should appear to be her. In fact, he did resemble the queen, who was his cousin.) Critics of the story have no conclusive evidence to discredit it, but they cast a reasonable doubt, which is all that is asked of defense attorneys.

Whatever his idiosyncrasies, Lord Cornbury was a disaster as governor. He aggravated political cleavages in New York dating from Leisler's Rebellion. He harried the Dutch Reformed Church, which had strongly supported royal government. Lord Cornbury knew he made a mess of things. He lamented that "a Porter in the streets of London is a happier man than a Governor in America." He begged Queen Anne to relieve him. When she finally did, he was promptly thrown into New York's debtor's prison, from which he was released only when he inherited his father's title, earl of Clarendon, and, undoubtedly more important to him at the time, his father's money.

The key to this shift in the structure of government was the British political principle that the people, through their elected representatives, must consent to all tax laws. In Great Britain, Parliament held the power of the purse; all money bills had to be approved by the House of Commons. In the colonies, the elected assemblies—whether called the "House of Burgesses," the "House of Delegates," or whatever—possessed this important prerogative.

Theoretically, the governor of a colony could veto a budget bill that he disliked. But to do so was risky. An assembly determined to have its way could retaliate by denying the governor the funds he needed in order to operate his office and even to maintain his personal household, that is, "starve him into compliance" as a hungry royal governor of New York phrased it.

The power of the purse was a formidable weapon. Few who served as governors in America were excessively wealthy before they took their jobs. Englishmen and Scots rich enough to maintain themselves opulently in London or Edinburgh did not choose to rough it in Portsmouth, Williamsburg, or Charleston. Most royal and proprietary governors were men on the make; that was why they sought positions overseas. To make money in the colonies, however, they had to get along with powerful colonials, the men who sat in their councils or were elected to seats in the assemblies.

Of course, it was possible to get along too well with influential Americans, to yield too much to them. That could excite the displeasure of Crown or proprietor. But during the era of salutary neglect, it came easily for governors to be cooperative: As long as the quitrents flowed back to Great Britain, a governor was doing the important part of his job.

That Old-Time Religion

Even religious developments seemed to reflect British neglect. Although toleration had been the rule in the colonies after the collapse of Puritan power in New England, official religious regimentation almost evaporated in the eighteenth century.

Except in Rhode Island and Pennsylvania, colonials were required to contribute, through a tax, to support the established church, the Congregational Church in Massachusetts and Connecticut, the Church of England elsewhere. In some colonies, members of other denominations were not allowed to vote, serve on juries, or exercise other civil rights. For example, Catholics were penalized in Maryland.

But rarely did authorities interfere with worship. In this atmosphere, one of the peculiarities of American society to this day took root: the bewildering multiplicity of religious denominations. The governor of New York wrote that "of all sorts" of religious opinions "there are some, and the most part none at all." By midcentury, it was not uncommon for modest villages to support two or even three meetinghouses close enough to one another that the congregations might have harmonized their hymns. During the 1740s, religions divided along yet finer lines, and another distinctly American institution, the revival, was born.

The Great Awakening

The first American revival, the Great Awakening, broke out almost simultaneously in several colonies, inspired by numerous preachers. Reverend Jonathan Edwards of Northampton, Massachusetts, was a towering figure. At the age of 17, he was stunned by an emotional conversion experience, "a direct intuitive apprehension of God in all his glory," and it became the theme of his career. In 1734, Edwards began to preach sermons emphasizing the sinfulness of humanity, the torment all deserved to suffer in hell, and the salvation that could be had only through divine grace. Edwards did not honey his message. "The God who holds you over the pit of hell," he said in his most famous sermon, "much as one holds a spider or some loathsome insect over the fire, abhors you, and is dreadfully provoked."

This was good Calvinism, but Edwards might have been suspect in early Massachusetts. In John Winthrop's time, Puritan ministers closely scrutinized the claims of men and

▲ *George Whitefield rarely preached to so small a congregation. His emotional sermons were so popular that news the tireless traveler would speak attracted thousands of colonials.*

women who said they had been saved. Jonathan Edwards was inclined to admit to the fold everyone who displayed the physical, highly emotional signs of being visited by the Holy Spirit.

Revivals were designed to stimulate the trauma of salvation. People broke down weeping, fainting, frothing at the mouth, shrieking, and rolling around on the floors. Many had to be restrained lest they injure themselves. Edwards himself took care not to inspire false conversions with theatrical arm waving and flouncing around. It was said that during all the hysteria, he stared at the bellpull at the entrance to his church.

Other revivalists had fewer scruples. Demagogic preachers tore their clothes and rolled their eyes like lunatics. They pranced and danced around pulpit and platform; they whooped and hollered. They devised a large bag of psychological tricks to arouse their audiences to a state of high excitement.

A Groping for Equality

The Great Awakening affected all social classes, but revivalism appealed most to ordinary people, especially the poorest. Just between 1740 and 1742 (when the population of New England was 300,000), 50,000 people joined a church for the first time in their lives.

The possibility of genuine religious redemption aside, the intense emotion of the revival offered a break from the stress and struggle of surviving on the margins of society. The assurance of happiness in the hereafter compensated for deprivation in the here and now. The emphasis on the equality of all men and women before God rendered society's disdain for the unsuccessful more bearable.

Equality was the message of the farthest ranging of the Great Awakening's ministers, English-born George Whitefield. Traveling tirelessly throughout the colonies—he made seven trips to America—Whitefield often preached 60 hours in a week. During one 78-day period, he delivered more than a hundred *lengthy* sermons. His voice was "an excellent piece of music," Benjamin Franklin said. Far more than those of Edwards, Whitefield's presentations reeked of hell's sulfur.

Many revivalist preachers were without license from a church and even without much education. Their credentials were their claims that the Holy Spirit was in them. In this, they echoed what Anne Hutchinson had claimed a hundred years earlier, but with oratorical and theatrical fireworks that would have disturbed her. The college education of traditional ministers counted for nothing with these "New Lights." What counted was the hand of God on their shoulders. Civil authority had been quick to clamp down on Hutchinson; the freer atmosphere of the eighteenth century permitted the Great Awakening to burn over the colonies.

Curiously, given the anti-intellectual bias of revivalism, the Great Awakening led to the foundation of a number of New Light colleges. In 1747, on the grounds that established institutions of learning like Harvard and Yale were dominated by "dry husks," or passionless intellectuals (in 1722,

the entire faculty of Yale, except Jonathan Edwards, converted to the staid Church of England), the College of New Jersey (Princeton) was founded; Jonathan Edwards was its third president. Other new colleges, such as Brown in Rhode Island, King's College (Columbia) in New York, and Queen's College (Rutgers) in New Jersey, were founded by the "Old Lights" to defend against the new preaching, which they regarded as ignorant and a threat to order.

The Age of Enlightenment

The Old Lights and people of no particular religious inclination, like Benjamin Franklin, embraced to varying degrees the worldview of the European Enlightenment. According to Enlightenment philosophy, human reason by itself, without revelation from the heavens, could unlock the secrets of the universe and guide the improvement, even the perfection, of humanity and society.

The origins of eighteenth-century rationalism lay in the writings of the English scientist Sir Isaac Newton, especially the *Principia Mathematica* (1687) and *Opticks* (1704). In these difficult books, Newton showed that forces as mysterious as those that determined the paths of the planets and the properties of light and color worked according to laws that could be reduced to mathematical equations.

Although Newton was a physicist and mathematician (and his personal religion was rather mystical), the impact of his discoveries was felt in practically every field of human knowledge and art. The order and symmetry that Newton found in the universe were translated into architecture by strict laws of proportion and in literature into inflexible classical rules of style and structure. Baroque music explored the multitudinous variations that could be played on simple combinations of notes.

Enlightenment philosophers likened the universe to a clock—intricate, but understandable when it is dismantled and its parts are examined rationally. According to "deism," as the rationalists called their religious belief, God did not intervene in the natural world. Rather, like a clock maker, he had set nature in motion according to laws that human beings could discover and understand, then he retired to allow his creatures to follow natural law and understand it by means of their precious reason. The educated members of the final generation of colonial Americans were to some degree exponents of this worldview.

THE END OF FRENCH AMERICA

In 1739, Great Britain went to war with Spain in the War of Jenkins' Ear. (Parliament was supposedly enraged when a ship's captain, Robert Jenkins, arrived in London with his ear in a box. It had, he said, been separated from his head by savage Spanish customs officials.) Georgia, South Carolina, and Virginia were involved from the start, not out of sympathy for the disfigured Jenkins but because they were chronically at odds with the Spanish in Florida. It was at this time that Oglethorpe beat back the Spanish assault on Savannah

MAP 6:1 French and British Empires in North America France claimed much more American acreage than Britain. However, beyond narrow strips of fairly dense settlement on the St. Lawrence River and Gulf Coast, French America was largely wilderness, far more under Indian control than French.

and himself attacked the African American fortress town of Santa Teresa de Mose.

King George's War, 1740–1748

In 1740, France joined the war on the side of Spain. The eight-year conflict that began that year is known in world history as the War of the Austrian Succession; in the colonies, it was known as King George's War.

Petite guerre flickered once more on the frontiers of New England, this time extending into New York, but there was nothing on the scale of the Deerfield disaster. Much better prepared than previously, a force of 4,000, mostly from Massachusetts, besieged the French fortress at Louisbourg. On June 17, 1745, the French commander surrendered.

This was a significant victory. Louisbourg was considered impregnable, "the Gibraltar of North America." As the base from which French privateers operated, the fortress was a cloud looming over New England merchants and fishermen. But the American celebration was short-lived. Under the terms of the Treaty of Aix-la-Chapelle, Louisbourg was returned to the French.

Parliament reimbursed Massachusetts for the expense of the campaign, but this did not make up for the 500 men who had lost their lives on Cape Breton Island or for the fact that the French commerce raiders were restored to their sanctuary. The protest was mild. The colonists were loyal British subjects. But the nullification of the greatest military victory Americans had ever won rankled in many breasts.

Struggle for a Continent

The world war that broke out in 1756 differed in several ways from those that preceded it. Most important to Americans, the British regarded North America as a theater at least as important as the battlefields of Europe. This time, Britain would not return North American fortresses in exchange for territory on the Rhine or in India. From the beginning, a large party in Parliament made it clear that their major object was to drive France out of North America.

Despite their usual success at *petite guerre,* the French were in a perilous situation. There were only about 50,000 whites in all of French-claimed territory and fewer than 20,000 Spaniards north of Mexico, compared with 1.2 million white colonists in the 13 English colonies plus Nova Scotia. The French still claimed the goodwill of most Indians in the region, but others were neutral.

For the first time in the Anglo-French wars, the largest colony, Virginia, took a serious interest in the fighting. The Virginians were looking beyond the Appalachian Mountains to the Ohio River valley for lands that were firmly under Indian control. This country was particularly attractive to the wealthy tobacco planters of the Old Dominion because a combination of exhausted soil and a new glut in the international tobacco market was undercutting their income. They saw speculation in Ohio Valley real estate as the likeliest means of maintaining their fortunes.

Humiliations in the Woods

With the heart of New France populated thinly, the French had little hope of effectively occupying the Ohio Valley. But the country was of vital interest to French trappers; French policy was to help the local Indians, friendly to France, retain control of the region. As early as 1753, at Indian urging, the French began to lay out a string of small forts in what is now western Pennsylvania.

Governor Robert Dinwiddie of Virginia responded by sending 22-year-old George Washington to inform the French that they were trespassing on Virginia soil. Accompanied by 150 men, Washington was to construct a fort where the Allegheny and Monongahela Rivers join to form the Ohio (the site of present-day Pittsburgh).

Washington never got that far. Attacked by Indians and French, he built Fort Necessity, little more than a log palisade, and was handily defeated in a battle that he prudently kept almost bloodless. The French occupied the conjunction of rivers and built Fort Duquesne. Washington returned to Virginia, where he accepted a commission under British general Edward Braddock. Again, things went worse than poorly. Braddock, a stubborn, unimaginative soldier, was soundly defeated in 1755 in the Pennsylvania forests; 977 British and colonials were killed, including General Braddock, but only 39 French and Indians. The rout left the frontier vulnerable to raiding fiercer than any since the destruction of Deerfield. The French were also winning the war in Europe and India. For the British Empire, it was a dismal hour.

Germ Warfare and Refugees

Both Braddock and, later, the overall commander of British forces in North America, Sir Jeffrey Amherst, employed a primitive form of germ warfare against the Indians. They saw to it that blankets used by smallpox victims fell into the natives' hands.

In Nova Scotia, the British feared that the French farmers and fishermen who were the majority in the province would rebel, even capture Halifax, a vital naval base. To forestall such a revolt, they launched a mass deportation. Thousands of Acadians—*Acadie* was the French name for Nova Scotia—were forced aboard ship and dispersed throughout the other English colonies from Massachusetts to Georgia and the West Indies. A few managed to make their way back home overland. Others found a haven in the French territory of Louisiana, where their descendants still form a distinct ethnic and cultural group in the state of Louisiana, the Cajuns. (The word *Cajun* is a corruption of the French *Acadien*.)

Pitt and Wolfe

Then, two men appeared on the scene to change the course of North American history. William Pitt became prime minister of Great Britain in 1757. He selected the young General James Wolfe to join Amherst's army in North America. Pitt turned the war around by generously paying Prussia to fight the French and Austrians in Europe while he concentrated British power across the Atlantic. Wolfe engineered one of the most daring attacks on a city in military history.

A nervous, frail-looking young man, brittle in his intensity, perhaps quite insane, Wolfe looked at French Canada as a woodsman eyed a tree. Quebec was the root structure that supported the whole. The St. Lawrence, Ohio, and Mississippi Rivers were but trunks and branches. It was all very well to snip and hack at leaves here and there, as Wolfe saw even the capture of Louisbourg. The secret to a conclusive victory over French Canada was to strike at the source of its life.

The theory was easier than its practical application. Quebec stood atop a steep, rocky cliff. On September 12, 1759, after leading several futile frontal attacks on this natural fortress (which lulled the French commander, Louis de Montcalm, into overconfidence), Wolfe quietly led 4,000 troops up a steep, narrow trail under cover of night. When the sun rose over the Plains of Abraham, a prairie on the minimally defended landward side of Quebec, Montcalm saw a scarlet-coated army in full battle formation.

North Wind Picture Archives

▲ *General James Wolfe died defeating the French outside their fortress at Quebec. A difficult man in life—some thought him mad—the dead Wolfe was immediately immortalized as a national hero. The pensive Indian is a member of the Iroquois, the Native American allies indispensable to British success.*

The Glorious Victory

Wolfe's gambit was risky. He had no supply line or avenue of retreat. If the battle did not end in total triumph (and few military victories were total in the eighteenth century), Wolfe's entire army would have been captured. Montcalm, however, was so unnerved by Wolfe's gamble that, despite his superior position and artillery, he joined battle with little preparation. After a single close-range exchange of musket fire, Montcalm lost his life and with it the French empire in America. Wolfe did not live to savor his triumph. He too died on the battlefield, only 32 years of age.

Bickering over the terms of peace dragged on, but, as far as the colonials were concerned, the war was over when British colors flew over Quebec. Finally, in the Peace of Paris in 1763, the map of North America was officially redrawn. Great Britain took Florida from Spain as well as Canada from France. To compensate Spain for the loss of Florida, France handed over Louisiana (the central third of what is now the United States) to the Spanish. In the Western Hemisphere, France was down to its possessions in the West Indies and two tiny, rocky islands in the North Atlantic. French fishermen could call there, but the islands were useless militarily.

By contrast, the British Empire was in glorious bloom. The mercantile British had elected to make their future not in Europe but as a vast empire overseas, and they had succeeded on every front. Or so it seemed.

for FURTHER READING

Basic works on relations with the mother country include Daniel Boorstin, *The Americans: The Colonial Experience,* 1958; Ian R. Christie, *Crisis of Empire,* 1966; Richard Hofstadter, *America at 1750,* 1971; Leonard W. Labaree, *Royal Government in America,* 1930; James Henretta, *Salutary Neglect,* 1972; and Stephen Webb, *The Governors-General,* 1979. Absolutely essential is Bernard Bailyn, *The Origins of American Politics,* 1968. Also consult the early pages of John C. Miller, *Origins of the American Revolution,* 1957; and Edmund S. Morgan, *The Birth of the Republic,* 1956.

On the Anglo-French wars, the great Francis Parkman is again the classic historian. See Parkman's *A Half Century of Conflict,* 1892, and his *Montcalm and Wolfe,* 1884. See also Howard H. Peckham, *The Colonial Wars, 1689–1762,* 1964; Douglas E. Leach, *Arms for Empire: A Military History of the British Colonies in North America,* 1973; and Fred Anderson, *A People's Army: Massachusetts Soldiers and Society in the Seven Years' War,* 1984. On the Indian role in the conflicts, see two works by Francis Jennings: *Empire of Fortune,* 1990; and *The Ambiguous Iroquois Empire,* 1984. On the same subject, see also James Merrell, *Beyond the Covenant Chain: The Iroquois and Their Neighbors,* 1987.

On cultural developments, see Louis B. Wright, *Cultural Life of the American Colonies,* 1957; Alan Heimert and Perry Miller, eds., *The Great Awakening,* 1967; Perry Miller, *Jonathan Edwards,* 1958; Edwin S. Gaustad, *The Great Awakening in New England,* 1957; and Henry F. May, *The Enlightenment in America,* 1976.

Benjamin Franklin's autobiography, in various editions, will never cease to be a good read. Also see Carl Van Doren, *Benjamin Franklin,* 1938.

 ## AMERICAN JOURNEY ONLINE AND INFOTRAC COLLEGE EDITION

Visit the source collections at http://ajaccess.wadsworth.com and http://infotrac.thomsonlearning.com, and use the Search function with the following key terms to explore documents, images, audio and video clips, articles, and commentary related to the material in this chapter:

Benjamin Franklin
French and Indian War
Great Awakening

Molasses Act
Seven Years' War
Smallpox

Additional resources, exercises, and Internet links related to this chapter are available on *The American Past* Web site: http://history.wadsworth.com/americanpast7e.

HISTORY ONLINE

Primary Sources—Colonial Period
http://personnal.pitnet.net/primarysources/
A broad selection of documents of the colonial period.

Religion in America
http://lcweb.loc.gov/exhibits/religion/rel02
Religion in eighteenth-century America.

7

YEARS OF TUMULT

The Quarrel with Great Britain 1763–1770

Harcourt Picture Collection

Westward the course of empire takes its way;
    The first four acts already past,
A fifth shall close the drama with the day:
    Time's noblest offspring is the last.

George Berkeley

An idea, strange as it is visionary, has entered into the minds of the generality of mankind, that empire is traveling westward; and every one is looking forward with eager and impatient expectation to that destined moment, when America is to give law to the rest of the world. But if ever an idea was illusory and fallacious, I will venture to predict, that this will be so.

Andrew Burnaby

I N 1763, CHURCH BELLS pealed throughout the 13 colonies to celebrate Britain's triumph in the Seven Years' War. In 1775, a dozen years later, these same colonies took up arms against the mother country; after another year, they declared their independence of her. Observing this rush of events, Oliver Wolcott of Connecticut wondered what had gone wrong. "So strong had been the Attachment" of Americans to Great Britain in 1763, he wrote, that "the Abilities of a Child might have governed this Country."

Wolcott blamed the bust-up on British folly, incompetence, and tyranny. He had a point about folly and incompetence. Blunder after stupidity upon miscalculation tells the story of British colonial policy between 1763 and 1776. But it would be a mistake, given the education in tyranny that the twentieth century has provided us, to entertain Wolcott's third explanation of the American Revolution. Far from oppressed by tyrants, colonial Americans may have been the world's freest people.

What made men like Wolcott into rebels was a mismanaged shift in British imperial administration from salutary neglect, with which colonials were happy, to a genuine, although far from oppressive, supervision. What made it possible for colonials to translate their apprehensions into anger, and then into rebellion, was the self-confidence born of the colonies' extraordinary growth.

THE PROBLEMS OF EMPIRE

Wolfe's capture of Quebec put Canada in British hands. Before the peace negotiators gathered in Paris in 1763, however, there was some question as to whether or not the British would retain the vast colony. Influential Britons, like the Duke of Bedford, suggested that it would be wiser to return Canada to France, as Port Royal and Louisbourg had been returned. Better, the duke said, to take as the fruits of victory the French West Indian islands of Martinique and Guadeloupe.

One Side of the Story

A land of endless forest and tundra, mostly unexplored, was not so glorious a trophy, the argument went. What use was Russia's subarctic empire to her? Moreover, the Indians of Canada and the Ohio Valley—former French allies—were numerous, powerful, and suspicious of the British. What could the 50,000 *habitants*—the French Canadian farmers, merchants, trappers, and tradesmen living along the St. Lawrence River—be as British subjects except trouble? Britain had recently deported a much smaller number of French men and women from Nova Scotia for fear they would rebel. The Irish had been periodically rising against English authority for two centuries and showed no sign of calming down. What sense did it make to create yet more unwilling and culturally alien subjects?

The sugar islands, by contrast, were tiny. They could be managed by small military garrisons. The handful of French planters who lived on Guadeloupe and Martinique, exploiting masses of cruelly used black slaves, cared less about the design of the flag flying over their harbors than about the presence of soldiers to keep their laborers in check and about the price for which they sold their crop.

There was yet another consideration. By 1763, the 13 Atlantic colonies, taken together, constituted a substantial country. Was it not possible—even likely—that the colonials had remained loyal to Great Britain only because of their fear of the French and Indian alliance? Remove that threat from their backyard, as the acquisition of Canada would do, and the Americans would have no need of British naval and military protection, and certainly would not be grateful for it. They might well unite, in the words of a Swedish observer, Peter Kalm, and "shake off the yoke of the English monarchy."

All That Red on the Map!

These arguments did not carry the day. British taxpayers were weary of war. They had paid monstrously large sums to fight France. If Canada and Louisiana remained French, another North American conflict was inevitable. Influential colonials like Governor William Shirley of Massachusetts and Benjamin Franklin, who was then in England as agent of Pennsylvania and Massachusetts, warbled lyrically of the potential of the Canadian landmass.

The lobbyists found allies in the sugar planters of the British West Indies. These few but rich and well-connected men—sugar was the British Empire's most valuable product ("white gold")—feared that raising the Union Jack over Martinique and Guadeloupe would glut the imperial sugar mar-

White Gold

By the eighteenth century, sugar had displaced tobacco as the most profitable product of the British colonial empire. Per capita consumption in Britain doubled in just a few decades as the population became addicted to sweet coffee, tea, chocolate, candies, and cakes. Even the poorest British smeared molasses on their bread.

Sugar cane was grown not in the mainland colonies but in the West Indies. French, Dutch, and Spanish islands produced it, but the British dominated the world market from the sugar islands of Barbados, Tobago, Trinidad, Jamaica, and a dozen specks on the map now best known as vacation wonderlands. Thanks to the Navigation Acts, colonial ships hauled almost as much of the "white gold" and molasses (partially processed sugar) as British ships did. Molasses was a vital part of the New England economy because, when distilled into rum, it could be sold anywhere in the world. Rum was also the chief liquor of America below the highest social classes. There was no cheaper drink.

The sugar islands were dominated by an oligarchy of rich planters even smaller than the rice and indigo aristocracy of South Carolina. They were protected by detachments of soldiers such as not even South Carolinians would have tolerated. They needed protection. Sugar required three times as much labor as tobacco, and West Indian slaves were treated with an inhumanity that would have sickened the hardest bitten slave owner on the mainland. Between 1700 and 1775, 1.2 million chained Africans were transported to the West Indies. The black population of the islands was a fraction of that in 1775 because sugar slaves typically died within five years of arriving. Because of their physical condition, slave women were unable to bear children. Infanticide was widespread among slaves; mothers preferred smothering their newborns to raising them to the miseries of the life they knew. Slaves on the mainland, by contrast, worked less arduously, lived longer lives in better health, and increased in numbers naturally at the same rate as free blacks and white colonials.

ket, driving down the price of their commodity just as overproduction of tobacco had shattered the price of that crop.

In the end, the French peacemakers preferred handing over Canada and keeping the sugar islands, and most of Parliament was unreflectively confident of American loyalty. In 1763, it was far more than smug to assume that anyone who had a choice would not choose to be anything but British.

Les Habitants

The Canadians could imagine otherwise. For one thing, they were Roman Catholic, pious communicants of a faith that was disliked and discriminated against in eighteenth-century Britain. Catholics were generally unmolested in the 13 colonies. But there too they were distrusted, and there was a big difference between tolerating a small, quiet, and largely genteel Catholic minority in Maryland and the odd Romanist

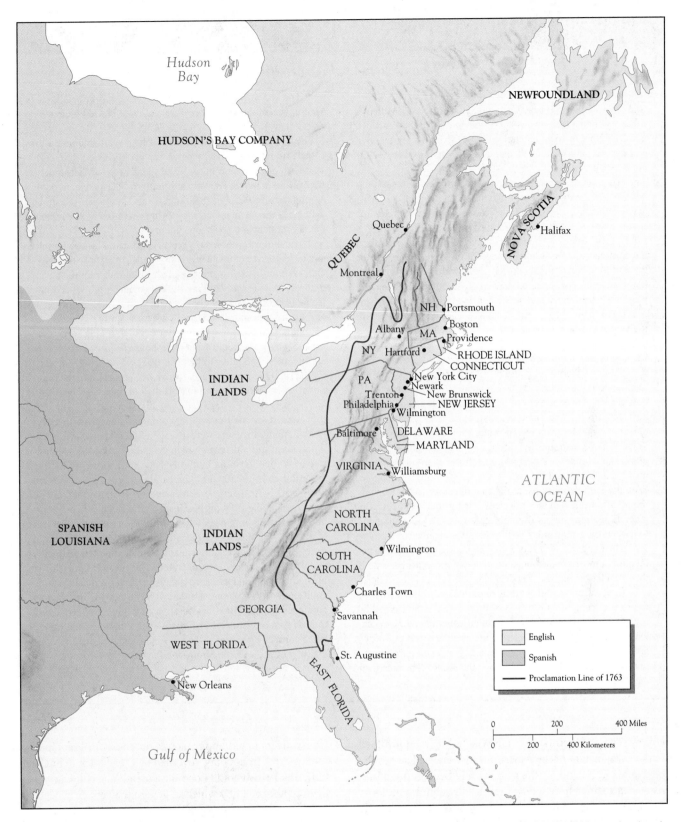

MAP 7:1 The Colonies, 1763–1776 Between 1763 and 1783, Florida was also a British possession. However, Florida was thinly populated, and almost every European there was a Spaniard; Americans did not think of it as a fourteenth colony.

church in Philadelphia and New York and coming to terms with a sprawling province in which almost everyone, Indians included, was Catholic.

The precedent of Englishmen governing foreign Catholics was not encouraging. For two centuries, Catholic Ireland had been a province; in effect, it was England's first

The Matriarchal Iroquois

By the mid–eighteenth century, the Iroquois Confederacy—the Cayuga, Seneca, Onondaga, Oneida, and Mohawk tribes—numbered about 15,000 people and securely controlled much of what is now upstate New York. Iroquois hunters and war parties ranged much farther, to the Mississippi and as far north as Hudson Bay.

Iroquois men, being hunters and warriors, and carrying out the delicate diplomatic negotiations that kept the confederacy together, traveled constantly. Iroquois women stayed home in more or less fixed towns of longhouses in which, semiprivately, families belonging to the same clan lived. Women raised the corn that was the staple of the Iroquois diet. They cared for the children, educating them in Iroquois values. They kept the longhouses in repair and maintained order, governing by social pressure—reputation and social approval were extremely important to the Iroquois—rather than by coercion. Finally, with their husbands and sons absent much of the time, the women effectively decided by whom they would have children or, at least, with whom they would lie.

Descent, therefore, could be reliably traced only through the maternal line. Clans of 50 or 60 people (their animal symbols carved above the door of their longhouse) included the eldest female member and her sisters and daughters, male children, and the sons-in-law when they happened to be in town. When a man married (always outside the clan—the Iroquois had a broad incest taboo), he left the clan into which he was born and joined his wife's, moving into her longhouse. With marital relationships fragile and transitory, many Iroquois men drifted through several clans during their lives. At any given time, however, an Iroquois male was solemnly obligated to defend the honor of his wife's clan. If a member of her clan was killed, injured, or insulted and the matriarch insisted on retaliation, a warrior was obligated to do what was asked, even if the offender belonged to the clan into which he had been born.

In addition to their authority to declare vendettas (they were infrequent, often resolved by discussion, and governed by intricate rules when negotiation failed), the female elders selected the 49 male delegates who met regularly to keep peace among the five tribes of the confederacy. Women participated in these meetings, but quietly, behind the scenes. The men handled the oratory.

The system worked quite well. The Iroquois heartland was secure, peaceful, well governed, and ably defended by the most dreaded warriors in the Northeast. A Quaker wrote of the Seneca, "[They] appear to be naturally as well calculated for social and rational enjoyment, as any people. They frequently visit each other in their houses, and spend much of their time in friendly intercourse. They are also mild and hospitable, not only among themselves, but to strangers, and good-natured in the extreme, except when their natures are perverted by the inflammatory influence of spirituous liquors."

Alcohol was, however, a serious problem. The sale of pelts and hides to the colonials inevitably launched an orgy of drunkenness among men, women, and children that would shock a pirate crew. Nor was drinking the only element introduced into Iroquois culture by their contact with whites, into its fifth generation by the middle of the eighteenth century. Trade with colonials also meant guns and metal tools ranging from scissors, knives, awls, kettles, and other household goods, to hatchets and axes. The latter influenced Iroquois building methods: By the mid-1700s longhouses were made less often in the traditional way—sheets of elm bark lashed to bent saplings—and increasingly of heavy logs and even milled siding.

Indeed, by the time of the colonials' quarrel with Great Britain, many Iroquois were abandoning residence by clan in longhouses and clustering in single-family cabins. The adoption of whites' farming methods made for a more productive agriculture; by 1750, the Seneca alone produced a million bushels of corn. There was little choice in this matter. Game was scarce in the Iroquois heartland after a century of overtrapping. Moreover, both neighboring and distant tribes that the Iroquois had routinely savaged during the 1600s had secured European firearms of their own and were holding the line.

Iroquois appearance changed. European calico shirts, linen loincloths, and woolen blankets characterized the Iroquois eighteenth-century Americans knew. Nevertheless, the Iroquois continued to shun Christian missionaries. Some had converted, to both Catholicism and Protestant denominations. But others "made obscene gestures" when anyone suggested that the colonial way of life was superior to their own.

---

colony. The conquerors of Ireland (including men involved in the early history of the American colonies) had seized the best lands in Ireland for their estates and been guilty of numerous atrocities in reducing the Irish to submission. Their descendants, the Anglo-Irish gentry, looked on the Catholic Irish masses as lazy, superstitious, and barbaric.

As in Ireland, however, the British held the military trump card in Canada. The *habitants* had no experience with representative government (New France had been governed by the military) and no inclination to bombard the Crown with protests and supplications such as the assemblies of the 13 colonies did. To the French Canadians, taking orders

from officers in red uniforms was not much different in day-to-day terms from being governed by Frenchmen in blue and buff. The British could hope for a breathing spell while they devised a formula by which to govern the new province.

Pontiac's Conspiracy

The Indians, former allies of the French, presented a more difficult and more urgent problem. Unlike the French army, the warriors of the Ohio River valley had not been decisively defeated in battle. The Treaty of Paris might proclaim them subjects of King George III. In reality, they were securely in possession of the forests west of the Appalachians and comfortable in a culture that was nearly intact and even strengthened by what they had borrowed from their European neighbors.

Almost immediately, the British blundered in dealing with them. General Sir Jeffrey Amherst, entrusted with this task, looked on Indians as "wretched people" whose proper condition was subjection. He informed the western tribes that they would no longer receive the regular "gifts" of blankets, iron and brass tools and vessels, firearms, and liquor that they were accustomed to getting from the French.

Neolin, a religious leader of the Delaware, a tribe that had been driven west by colonials, preached that "if you suffer the English among you, you are dead men." An Ottawa chieftain, Pontiac, attacked the British fort at Detroit and was soon joined by 18 tribes on a thousand-mile front. Detroit and Fort Pitt (Pittsburgh) held out; but 10 western forts were overrun, and 2,000 people were killed in Virginia and Pennsylvania—more than were lost in any battle of the French and Indian War. Amherst tried germ warfare again. He urged his men to "try to inoculate the Indians by means of Blankets, as well as to try Every other Method that can serve to Extirpate this Execrable Race." The British forces regrouped and defeated Pontiac at Bushy Run near Pittsburgh. But they had only stung the Indians, not "extirpated" them.

The Proclamation of 1763

Amherst restored the gifts and informed the Crown of the problem. In October 1763, in order to let tempers cool, London drew an imaginary line on the Appalachian divide, the crest between the sources of rivers that emptied into the Atlantic and those that flowed into the Ohio–Mississippi River system. The Crown proclaimed, "We do strictly forbid, on pain of our displeasure, all our loving subjects from making any purchases or settlements whatever" west of the line. The frontiersmen who had already settled in the no-go zone were forced to return east; impatient emigrants were urged to head for northern New England, Upper Canada (Ontario), Georgia, and Florida, which was also now British. Land sales west of the Appalachians were frozen.

Colonials considered the Proclamation Line to be what one land speculator, George Washington, called "a temporary expedient to quiet the minds of the Indians." Too many influential colonials dreamed of riches in Ohio Valley real estate to consider the line permanent. Indeed, superintendents of Indian affairs, royal officials, began to purchase western territory from Indians before news of the settlement reached their more remote tribes. In the south, the line of 1763 was redrawn—farther west—within a few months. Regularly over the next decade, trans-Appalachian lands were opened to speculation and settlement.

Nevertheless, by interfering temporarily, even on paper, with the colonials' lust for land, British policy touched a tender nerve. Americans would remember the proclamation of 1763 as an early example of King George III's campaign to throttle their "liberties."

The Redcoats

In the wake of Pontiac's Rebellion, General Amherst asked Parliament for a permanent American garrison of 5,000 to 6,000 troops. The soldiers would be stationed in Canada and in the frontier forts. Parliament responded by voting Amherst 10,000 soldiers, more than double the contingent in North America during the years of the French menace.

Within a few years, when some of these soldiers were billeted in coastal cities in order to police riotous colonial crowds, they became the hated "redcoats" or "lobsters." When they first began to arrive, however, the Americans' biggest concern was the expense of maintaining them—£200,000 a year. The Quartering Act of 1765 charged the cost of the troops' shelter, food, and drink to the colony in which they were posted. Indeed, one of Parliament's motives in doubling Amherst's request for men was to pension off veterans of the French and Indian War at colonial expense. The men had some reward coming to them, but the British traditionally shied away from keeping a large standing army at home. Soldiers looked on duty in America as easy: not much to do, and in a society where the people were friends, not conquered foreigners.

But the "friendly" colonials disliked standing armies too. Soldiers out in the woods watching Indians were one thing; soldiers marching around Boston and New York, quite another.

Reorganization of the Empire

The flurry of changes in the wake of the Seven Years' War signaled that the men who governed Great Britain were taking a new, keener interest in colonial affairs. Some sort of change was in order and easily justified. Counting Canada, the West Indies, and British Honduras, 20 colonies in the Western Hemisphere now flew the British flag. If each were to go merrily its own way, pretty much governing itself as the 13 "ancient provinces" of North America were accustomed to doing, the result would be chaos. Even during the French and Indian War, "the king in Parliament" made it clear that salutary neglect was history. The postwar British Empire was to be supervised more closely from London and integrated into a more rational—more regular—imperial regime.

Money, Money, Money

Before the war, Parliament had been content that the colonies profited British land speculators, manufacturers, and merchants. Since Robert Walpole, ministries had been little concerned that the administration of the colonies was a net cost to the exchequer (the British treasury). The government expected to subsidize mercantilism; administrative costs seemed a most worthwhile expenditure. Before the French and Indian War, governing the colonies cost the Crown, on average, £70,000 a year, whereas colonial trade pumped as much as £2 million a year into the British economy. Who could complain? Who could be bothered?

▲ *Parliament consisted of two houses, the House of Lords, in which seats were inherited or held by appointed bishops of the Church of England, and the House of Commons, pictured here. The Commons was elected by men who owned property. Members were gentlemen from the highest social class below the "lords," as members of the nobility were called.*

By 1764, however, the cost of colonial government had soared to £350,000 a year, and Parliament faced new and serious financial difficulties. Prime Minister William Pitt had levied heavy taxes on the British in order to fight the war. And he had borrowed every penny anyone would lend him. A national debt of £130 million (twice what it had been before the war) had Britain teetering on the edge of bankruptcy. Half of each year's revenues was going to paying interest.

Cost cutting is always an alternative in financially trying times, if never attractive to politicians for whom those costs are personal bread and butter. The British government in the 1760s was top heavy, with officials who slopped at the public trough without doing anything in particular. At every level, it was shot through with graft: padded government contracts, bribes, kickbacks, and pensions were as much a part of the system as they are in the United States today.

Some budgets were slashed. The Royal Navy received £7 million in 1762 (during the last years of the war), £2.8 million in 1766, and £1.5 million in 1769. However, Parliament preferred to look for more revenue rather than inflict similar cuts across the board.

Heavier taxes at home were out of the question. Each year, British landowners paid 20 percent of their income into the exchequer, a crushing burden in an agricultural society. Other taxes were also high. When Parliament tried to increase a small tax on cider, the daily drink of southwestern England, there were riots approaching rebellion.

Grenville: The First Villain

The thankless job of reorganizing government finance fell to George Grenville, who became first lord of the treasury in 1763. Grenville was a talented man, an expert in fiscal matters who thought in terms broader than accounting. If the reforms he introduced had succeeded, history might well have recorded him as the architect of a rationalized British Empire. Instead, he is a walk-on in British history and, to Americans, a villain.

Along with his abilities, Grenville brought a fatal limitation to his task. Like most British politicians of the time, he knew little about Americans and saw no sense in learning more. He had a vision of worldwide British power, but he contemplated it through the half-closed eyes of the complacent British upper crust. To Grenville, Americans were half-civilized louts whose opinions were not worthy of consideration. He would have smiled at Samuel Johnson's famous quip, "I am willing to love all mankind, except an American."

Grenville knew that Americans paid few taxes. He calculated that the average English taxpayer paid an annual tax of 26 shillings, whereas a British subject living in Massachusetts paid one shilling a year, and the average Virginian, only five pence. (One shilling equaled 12 pence.) And yet, the virtually untaxed colonials had gained the most from the French and Indian War, the cause of the national debt that threatened to bankrupt Great Britain. The colonials, therefore, should do more to pay off the debt and, in the future, to shoulder the expenses of governing their colonies.

It is difficult, from a distance, to fault Grenville's reasoning. Indeed, few Americans openly denied that they had a moral obligation to do more financially than they had in the past. Unfortunately, even if the 13 colonial assemblies had been willing to vote Grenville enough money to meet his needs, they did not get the chance to do so. Instead of requesting grants from the colonies, as his predecessors had done, Grenville treated his money problems as part and parcel of his plan to reform imperial administration.

The Sugar Act of 1764

Grenville's first move was to overhaul the ineffective Molasses Act of 1733. Its six-pence-per-gallon tax on molasses

▲ *First Lord of the Treasury George Grenville looked like what he was, a British aristocrat who had climbed to the top of the political heap. His failure to make good on his promise to raise revenue in the colonies contributed to his fall from high office after only two years.*

imported into the colonies from non-British sources was so high that American merchants did not hesitate to evade it. Instead of paying the duty, they bribed customs collectors a penny or so per gallon. If they were arrested as smugglers, they could count on juries of their neighbors to acquit them regardless of the evidence—and then join them at the nearest inn for a drink of rum, the principal by-product of molasses.

The Sugar Act of 1764 struck at both the revenue problem and the problem of law enforcement in the colonies. It enlarged the customs service and transferred the task of enforcing the import duty from local courts to a new system of vice admiralty courts that would try violators without juries. To sweeten the pot, Grenville cut the molasses tax to three pence per gallon. He calculated that American importers would pay the lower rate (not much more than the customary bribe) rather than run the risk of conviction in courts over which they had no control. Also in 1764, Grenville levied duties on imported wines, silks, tropical foods, and other luxury goods. They were modest. Grenville wanted money; he did not want to discourage imports.

The First Protest

In New England, where molasses was a major item of trade, protest was loud and fierce. The Boston town meeting de-clared that the city would import no British goods of any kind until Parliament repealed the obnoxious tax. Other cities, including New York, followed suit. Even "the young Gentlemen of Yale College" announced that they would not "make use of any foreign spirituous liquors" until Grenville backed down from his importunity. This sacrifice, heroic for students, was eased by the fact that limitless quantities of domestic beer and cider were available for after-hours revels.

Grenville was unmoved. He assumed that the Americans simply did not want to pay any taxes, that they wished to enjoy the benefits of being a part of the British Empire at no personal cost. No doubt he was the better part of right. Importers of molasses, sippers of Madeira, and wearers of silk wanted the best bargains they could get. To this extent, the Sugar Act protest was sheer self-pity.

The Rights of British Subjects

And yet, there were principles at stake too. Politically (in the larger sense of that word), colonials were heirs of the British "country party," as opposed to the "court party." They were Whigs, adherents to a political philosophy that considered Parliament to be the foundation of British liberties. In a century, Parliament had beheaded one "tyrannical" king (Charles I); deposed another (James II), creating its own monarch in his place (William III); and, in 1714, chosen as king a German who never learned English (George I) over 40 princes with a better claim to the throne. In other words, Parliament had established its supremacy over the monarchy. The most important of the rights of British subjects that Parliament asserted was the principle that, through Parliament, British subjects consented to the taxes they paid.

Parliament had enacted the Sugar Act, but that parliament sat in Westminster, colonials said. It was not their parliament. They did not elect members to it. Their parliaments were the 13 colonial assemblies, which alone had the right to raise money from the colonies through taxation. On this foundation was built a decade of debate about the nature of representation in government—sometimes hairsplitting, self-serving, and precocious, but at its core, a debate of great seriousness.

Daniel Dulany of Maryland responded to the Sugar Act of 1764 by comparing it to the Molasses Act of 1733, which the colonials had (more or less) accepted. As a tax designed to reduce the importation of French molasses into the empire, Dulany said, the Molasses Act had regulated trade. This was perfectly legitimate. Parliament had the right to regulate the empire's trade. But the Sugar Act of 1764 was not designed to keep foreign molasses out. Indeed, as far as Grenville was concerned, the more foreign molasses the colonies imported legally, the better. His goal was to collect the three pence per gallon. The official title of the Sugar Act was the American Revenue Act.

It was Grenville's goal—revenue—that raised the ticklish constitutional question of the "sacred right" of British subjects to consent to taxes levied on them. The Sugar Act was a tax. The colonials had not consented to it. It was that simple.

Trial by Jury

There was another issue: the right of a British subject accused of a crime to be tried before a jury of his peers. This right, with origins dating to the Magna Carta of 1215, colonials (and British Whigs) believed, set them apart from—made them superior to—the French, Spanish, Poles, Chinese, Hottentots, Shawnee, and everyone else in the world. By denying colonials this ancient right, as the jury-less vice admiralty courts did, George Grenville was tampering with the essence of British liberty.

It is impossible to say what would have happened if Grenville's program had ended with the Sugar Act. The Americans were noisy; some of their language was inflammatory. But there was no violence. The Sugar Act protest began with high-level debate and ended with a legal boycott of imports. To the extent that colonial opposition to the tax on molasses was a manifestation of greed, the protest might well have petered out. The duties of 1764 seriously affected only wealthy consumers and a small number of shippers and distillers, and them not gravely. When, in 1766, the molasses duty was reduced to a penny (the level of the traditional bribe), protest and boycott evaporated, although "the principle of the thing" remained quite intact.

But Grenville did not stop with the Sugar Act. In 1765, he announced a new bill to raise money in America by means of a tax that could not be ducked or stymied by a boycott because those who did not pay it suffered from the very act of noncompliance.

THE STAMP ACT CRISIS

English people had been paying a stamp tax since 1694. In order to be legal, documents such as wills, bills of sale, licenses, deeds, insurance policies, and other contracts had to be inscribed on paper that was embossed with a government stamp. Purchase of the paper, therefore, constituted payment of a tax. Evasion was not feasible. A proof of marriage not inscribed on the stamped paper was not accepted in court when there was a dispute between spouses over property. The transfer of a farm written on ordinary paper was not enforceable.

The Stamp Act of 1765

Grenville's Stamp Act of 1765 went further than the English law. It required that (in addition to colonial legal documents) newspapers, pamphlets, handbills, and even playing cards were to be printed on the embossed government paper. The tax varied from a halfpenny on a handbill announcing the sale of taffeta to one pound for a tavern's license to sell liquor. The sum was significant in both cases.

Enforcement of the law was entrusted to the unpopular vice admiralty courts. However, Grenville tried to gain colonial favor by providing that all money raised under the Stamp Act would be used solely in "defending, protecting, and securing the colonies." Not a farthing would go back to England to retire the debt or for any other purpose.

Stamps

What we call a postage "stamp" is, by eighteenth-century standards, a misnomer. The adhesive-backed evidence that postage has been paid on a letter was invented only in 1834 (the perforations in 1854). When it was, the speakers of no other European language chose *stamp* to name the ingenious device. To them, and to colonial Americans, a stamp was something impressed on or stamped into paper, not something stuck on it. Eighteenth-century stamping was what we call "embossing."

Thus, the stamp that caused all the excitement in 1765 was an embossment, pressed into the paper to be used for licenses, newspapers, and so on. Few Americans ever saw Stamp Act stamps anyway. Except for a few sales in Georgia, none of the embossed paper was ever used.

American sensibilities were not soothed. On the contrary, the stipulation that revenues from the Stamp Act were to be raised and spent entirely within the colonies led a Quaker grandee of Pennsylvania and Delaware, John Dickinson, to devise a detailed constitutional distinction between legitimate *external taxes,* duties on trade between the colonies and other places, and unacceptable *internal taxes,* duties collected within the colonies and spent there.

The Stamp Act was plainly internal, Dickinson said, a direct tax on the people by a body in which they were not represented, Parliament. Only a colonial assembly could enact such a tax within its boundaries. (Massachusetts had, in fact, experimented with a stamp tax in 1755.)

Grenville had no ear for Dickinson's argument. In his administrative scheme, Parliament was the supreme governing authority for the entire empire. Most members of Parliament agreed with him. A dull debate addressed few of the issues that were to explode in the colonies. The House of Commons voted 204 to 49 to enact the Stamp Act. Many prominent Americans also failed to see a problem in the new tax. Richard Henry Lee of Virginia, the man who would introduce the resolution for independence in 1776, applied for a job as a stamp tax collector in 1765.

A Stupid Law

Constitutional niceties aside, the Stamp Act was politically stupid. Its burden fell most heavily on just those colonials who were best able to stir up a fuss. Newspaper editors, with their influence on public opinion, were hard hit. Advertisements, a newspaper's bread and butter, were taxed two shillings, and every edition had to be printed on stamped paper. Printers, who profited by putting out broadsides (posters used for announcing goods for sale and public meetings—including protest meetings), saw their business taxed at every turn of the press.

Lawyers, then as now the single largest group in colonial public office, and persuaders by profession, had to pay a tax on every document with which they dealt. Keepers of taverns, saddled with more expensive licenses by the new

▲ *These stamps, what we call "embossments," pressed into paper, were the cause of the Stamp Act crisis of 1765. Few colonials ever saw them. Except for a few in Georgia, none were sold.*

law, were key figures in every town and neighborhood. Their establishments were the gathering places where, over rum, brandy, coffee, and tea, locals gathered to read newspapers and discuss affairs, such as taxes.

What was worse, most of these groups were concentrated in cities, where they could easily meet with one another, cooperate, organize, and have an impact out of proportion to their numbers. It was one thing to upset such groups one at a time, as the Sugar Act had riled shippers and distillers. The Stamp Act hit all of these key elements of the population at once, and, possibly to everyone's surprise, the protesters won the support of large numbers of working people and even the tumultuous underclass.

Riot

Parliament approved the Stamp Act in February 1765, scheduling it to go into effect in November. As soon as the news reached the colonies, they erupted in anger. Local organizations called Sons of Liberty (a phrase used to describe Americans by one of their parliamentary friends, Isaac Barré) condemned the law and called for a boycott of British goods.

Some of the Sons of Liberty turned to violence. When the stamped paper was delivered to warehouses in port cities, mobs broke in and made bonfires of it. Men appointed stamp masters were shunned if they were lucky, hanged in effigy, or roughed up. A brutal method of punishing stamp tax collectors was to daub them, sometimes naked, with hot tar, roll them in chicken feathers, and carry them, straddling a fence rail, around town.

One official in Maryland was forced to flee for his life to New York. That was a mistake, because the New York Sons of Liberty were the most volatile of all. They located the Marylander and forced him to write a letter of resignation. Led by Isaac Sears, the captain of a merchant vessel, the New Yorkers frightened their own lieutenant governor (a future revolutionary named Cadwallader Colden) so that he went into hiding. When they could not find Colden, they

burned his carriages. In Boston, the crowd looted and burned the homes of several British officials.

Rowdies are seldom popular, but the Stamp Act rioters were. When one governor was asked why he did not call out the militia to restore order, he pointed out that it would mean arming the very people who were wreaking havoc in the streets. The British had expected protests. Isaac Barré had warned of resistance. But everyone was taken by surprise by what seemed to be the whole American people on a rampage.

The Stamp Act Congress

Among those surprised were prominent wealthy colonials who opposed the Stamp Act but shuddered at the sounds of mobs. Mobs are beasts that take on a life of their own, independent of the personalities of those who constitute them. They move easily from one target to another, for the action itself takes the place of a mob's initial goal. The colonial elite knew this and knew that the colonial crowd had as many grievances against them as against Parliament. In October 1765, in an attempt to control the protest, 37 delegates from nine colonies assembled in New York City in the Stamp Act Congress.

Although the congress was the brainchild of one of the most volatile agitators, James Otis of Massachusetts, the 14 resolutions and the "Declaration of Rights and Grievances" that the delegates adopted were largely the work of more cautious and conservative men, like John Dickinson. The Stamp Act Congress criticized the Stamp Act, Sugar Act, and other parliamentary policies while the delegates prominently made it clear they acknowledged "all due subordination" to the Crown.

THE BRITISH CONSTITUTION

What did "all due subordination" mean? Loyalty to the king? Unquestionably. Just about everyone in the eighteenth

Metropolitan Museum of Art

▲ *A New Hampshire man who had applied to be a seller of Stamp Act paper is tortured in effigy, probably just outside his home. He was a lucky one. Mobs like this—riffraff but substantial working men too—beat and tortured other men who had taken the same job.*

century agreed on the importance of the monarch as the symbol that unified the people of a nation or an empire. Lèse-majesté ("injuring the king") was the gravest of political crimes, punishable by hanging, often followed by disembowelment and quartering (harnessing a horse to each of the traitor's four limbs and cracking the whip).

On other basic questions of governance, however, Britons and colonials disagreed. Fundamental disagreement was possible because, whereas the British constitution included a few hallowed written documents, like the Magna Carta of 1215 and the Bill of Rights of 1689, it was largely unwritten. Most of the principles and practices of British governance had won acceptance over the centuries through tradition and usage.

The Question of Representation: The Colonial Case

Colonial protesters said that Parliament had no right to tax them because they were not represented in Parliament; colonials did not elect members of Parliament—it was that simple. Their own assemblies, which they did elect, were their little parliaments. These assemblies alone were empowered to tax them.

The colonial case is easy for us to understand, for it is the governing principle of representation in the United States today. In order for an individual to be represented in government, he or she must be entitled to vote for a city council member, county supervisor, state legislator, representative, or senator. The senators from Kentucky are not held to represent Iowa farmers. Only those senators for whom those farmers vote represent them. Reforms of voting laws throughout United States history—extending the vote to men who did not own property, to African American men, and to women—have been based on the concept that one must be able to vote in order to be represented.

James Otis spoke for this way of thinking at the Stamp Act Congress when he proposed that Parliament end the dispute by allowing colonials to elect members to Parliament. However, Otis's colleagues virtually ignored him. They did not want to send representatives to Parliament. They wanted Parliament to recognize the authority of their own assemblies.

Grenville missed a grand opportunity. He could have confounded and splintered the colonial protest by acting favorably on Otis's proposal. If they voted as a bloc, which was unlikely, given the 13 colonies' disparate interests, colonial members of Parliament would constitute but a tiny party, able to influence policy only when the rest of Parliament was evenly divided, which, in matters of taxing the colonies, it was not. Grenville did not consider this alternative because he and other members of Parliament, including those who sympathized with the colonials, believed that the Americans were already represented in Parliament.

Virtual Representation: The British Case

By the lights of the eighteenth century, Grenville and the members of Parliament were correct. The British concept of representation differed (and differs) from our own. For example, it was not (and is not) necessary that a member of the British parliament reside in the electoral district that sends him or her to the House of Commons. While it is unlikely to happen in our own time, a member of Parliament may never set foot in the district from which he or she is elected. British electoral districts are for the sake of convenience in balloting, but each member of Parliament is regarded as *virtually* representing the entire nation. Edmund Burke, a friend of the Americans, put it this way to his constituents in the city of Bristol during the dispute with the colonies: "You choose a member . . . but when you have chosen him, he is not a member of Bristol, but he is a member of Parliament."

Colonials practiced virtual representation in their own elections. George Washington and other Virginians were elected to the House of Burgesses from counties in which they did not reside. Would-be burgesses stood for seats in more than one county at a time so that they were covered in the event they were defeated in one. Few objected to this practice. It was assumed that those who were elected would act with the interests of all Virginians in mind.

The colonists also practiced virtual representation in their restriction of the suffrage to free, white, adult male heads of household who owned property. The number of actual voters in colonial elections amounted to a small proportion of the inhabitants in every colony. Nevertheless, the colonists considered penniless white men, all women and children, and even, in a strange way, African American slaves, to be virtually represented in their elected assemblies. The assumption was that assemblymen acted on behalf of all, not just on behalf of the freeholders who voted for them.

This was precisely the position Parliament took when the colonials complained that they were not represented in Parliament: The colonists were virtually represented.

BRITISH POLICIES AND POLICY MAKERS

The Stamp Act crisis was not resolved by adding up debaters' points. If the protesters' constitutional argument was flimsy, they formed a powerful and articulate group in every colony with support among all social classes. None of them spoke of independence or, after the riots, of rebellion. But they were adamant that Americans were not represented by Parliament.

Poor Leadership

Some members of Parliament appreciated the colonial position. William Pitt, now earl of Chatham, rejoiced that America had resisted. "Three millions of people so dead to all the feelings of liberty," he said, "so voluntarily to submit to be slaves, would have been fit instruments to make slaves of the rest." Americans returned the compliment. They idolized Pitt.

Edmund Burke, the father of traditional conservatism, saw the colonists as defenders of British tradition and the Grenville group as dangerous innovators. The radical John Wilkes egged on the colonial protesters because he saw them as natural allies in his agitations on behalf of a free press and in opposition to George III. Charles Fox, a future cabinet minister, part opportunist and part man of principle, spoke on behalf of the Americans, as did Isaac Barré.

Unfortunately for the future of the empire, except for a brief interlude in 1766 and 1767, these men were in the opposition. The makers of colonial policy were men unable to see beyond constitutional fine points and their disdain for colonials. This narrow-mindedness was a consequence of the way English politics functioned during the reign of King George III.

Although members of Parliament used the party names "Whig" and "Tory," there was no two-party system resembling the party systems in the United States and Great Britain today. Parliament was a collection of half a dozen—or more—shifting factions. Some, such as Burke's Old Whigs, ever on the watch for violations of traditional liberties, were drawn together by agreement on a principle. So were, ironically, the "High Tories," reflexive supporters of the king because he was a king. Most parliamentary factions, however, were alliances of expediency, cliques of men who cooperated with one another because they were relations by blood or marriage or because, by working together, they could serve their individual, sometimes tawdry, interests.

Colonial Williamsburg Foundation

▲ *When George III was crowned in 1760, he was immensely popular, both at home and in the colonies. Truly an Englishman, unlike his truculently German predecessors, George I and George II, he was personally likable, had the common touch, and was sympathetic to the colonies. Times and opinions change.*

King George III

A new wrinkle was added after 1760, when George III was crowned king at the age of 22. His predecessors, the first two Georges, had used royal favors to reward military heroes, to support musicians and artists, or simply to keep congenial companions hanging around the palace. The first two Georges were German. George I never learned English. George II spoke it but preferred to communicate in French. Coming from the middling German state of Hanover, the Georges were delighted merely to have the large royal income of Britain at their disposal. Neither took much interest in domestic matters, a situation much to the liking of the Whigs.

George III, by contrast, was raised English. His mother had urged him, "Be a king, George"—that is, govern your realm. The days when an English monarch could do much of anything by royal decree were long gone. But George could and did use the patronage he controlled to create a parliamentary faction beholden to him. His party was known as the "King's Friends."

The King's Friends were no more venal than the men of other parliamentary factions. Nor was George III evil, as the Americans would come to paint him. Far from it. He accepted the British constitution; he was conscientious, with a strong sense of duty; he wrote his own letters and speeches. He ate and drank moderately (he feared the obesity that ran in the family). He was a likable person, far more at ease in the company of ordinary folk than any British monarch since. George III could not have been a tyrant had he wished to be. Indeed, several times during his first 10 years as king, he used his influence to support conciliation with the colonies and won American favor for his efforts. There would be plenty of statues of George III to be toppled when American opinion of the king changed.

▲ *An interesting artifact: a "souvenir teapot" celebrating the repeal of the Stamp Act. It was made in Great Britain. The potteries of Staffordshire were multiproduct, mass-production operations. They manufactured everything from cheap everyday tableware to items like this teapot, exploiting a specialty market, much as the people who silk-screen slogans on T-shirts do today. After the Revolution, the potteries shipped statuettes of George Washington to their American outlets.*

Courtesy Peabody Essex Museum, Salem, Massachusetts

Unfortunately, this well-meaning king was stupid, vain, and stubborn. He was uneasy with politicians whose abilities exceeded his own and peevish with those who refused to flatter him. By excluding such men from office, and promoting mediocre men and sycophants to positions of influence, he denied power to those who best understood the American situation. And the king was erratic, dismissing even supporters on slight pretexts. Much later in life, he lost his sanity. It is possible he periodically suffered mild previews of his progressive disease during the quarrel with the colonials.

Mixed Victory

Thus, George III dismissed the able Grenville in July 1765 over a matter unrelated to colonial taxation. Early the next year, during the short ministry of Lord Rockingham, Lord Chatham (William Pitt) moved to repeal the Stamp Act, and it was done. The colonial celebrations were so noisy that few paid attention to the fact that king and Parliament had not yielded on principle. Parliament also passed the Declaratory Act, which stated that Parliament "had, hath, and of right ought to have, full power and authority to make laws and statutes of sufficient force and validity to bind the colonies and people of America, subjects of the Crown of Great Britain, in all cases whatsoever."

Not only did the Declaratory Act deny the Americans' claims for their own assemblies, but the wording was lifted from a law of 1719 that made Ireland completely subject to Great Britain. That should have given colonial protesters pause, for the status of the despised Irish was precisely, and understandably, what they were determined to avoid. But few seemed to notice. Chatham succeeded Rockingham as prime minister and ignored the Declaratory Act with the slickness of Robert Walpole. Chatham also eliminated another aggravation when he reduced the duty on molasses from three pence to a penny per gallon. The colonial protesters were Georgian politicians too. What did a piece of paper matter when a good friend held the reins?

Then, in one of those historical accidents that have grave consequences, Chatham fell seriously ill and ceased to play an active part in government. From the perspective of the colonists, the man who stepped into the vacuum was as bad a stroke of luck as George Grenville had been.

"Champagne Charley" and the Townshend Duties

Charles Townshend was, in fact, no more wicked a fellow than Grenville or King George. He was rather too convivial and charming; he won the nickname "Champagne Charley" because of his habit of arriving at the House of Commons giggling and unsteady on his feet. (In fairness to Townshend, Parliament met in the evening, and, on a given night, any number of members were at less than their best.)

Townshend was chancellor of the exchequer, a post equivalent to our secretary of the treasury, and he hoped to

ㅎㅎㅎㅎㅎㅎㅎㅎㅎㅎㅎㅎㅎㅎㅎㅎㅎㅎㅎㅎㅎㅎㅎㅎㅎㅎㅎㅎ

A LIST of the Names of *thofe*

who AUDACIOUSLY continue to counteract the UNIT-
ED SENTIMENTS of the BODY of Merchants thro'out
NORTH-AMERICA ; by importing Britifh Goods
contrary to the Agreement.

John Bernard,
(In King-Street, almoft oppofite Vernon's Head.

James McMafters,
(On Treat's Wharf.

Patrick McMafters,
(Oppofite the Sign of the Lamb.

John Mein,
(Oppofite the White-Horfe, and in King-Street.

Nathaniel Rogers,
(Oppofite Mr. Henderfon Inches Store lower End
King-Street.

William Jackfon,
At the BrazenHead, Cornhill, near theTown-Houfe.

Theophilus Lillie,
(Near Mr. Pemberton's Meeting-Houfe, North-End.

John Taylor,
(Nearly oppofite the Heart andCrown inCornhill.

Ame & Elizabeth Cummings,
(Oppofite the Old Brick Meeting Houfe, all of Bofton.

Ifrael Williams, Efq; & Son,
(Traders in the Town of Hatfield.

And, *Henry Barnes,*
(Trader in the Town of Marlboro'.

*The following Names fhould have been i ferted in
the Lift of Juftices.*

County of Middlefex.	County of Lincoln.
Samuel Hendley	
John Borland	John Kingfbury
Henry Barnes	
Richard Cary	County of Berkfhire.
County of Briftol.	Mark Hopkins
George Brightman	Elijah Dwight
County of Worcefter.	Ifrael Stoddard
Daniel Blifs	

ㅎㅎㅎㅎㅎㅎㅎㅎㅎㅎㅎㅎㅎㅎㅎㅎㅎㅎㅎㅎㅎㅎㅎㅎㅎㅎ

▲ *By 1770, when protesters called for a boycott of these merchants because they sold goods imported from Britain, the furor over the Townshend Duties was already abating (as, perhaps, the shopkeepers listed here understood).*

be prime minister. To earn that prize, Townshend planned to cut taxes at home and to make up the loss of revenues in the colonies. He studied the Americans' distinctions between external taxes for regulating trade and internal taxes for raising money. He thought them nonsense but nonetheless designed a series of duties that were undeniably external. The Townshend Duties were imposed on paper, paint, lead, glass, and tea—all goods little made in the colonies and, therefore, imported from Britain.

It was an odd combination of goods. If none of them were produced in the colonies in any quantity, all except tea could be manufactured there. Townshend invited a boycott, and he got it. Trade between Britain and America fell off by 25 percent and then by 50 percent. Townshend had predicted that his duties would bring in £40,000 annually. The actual take was £13,000 in 1768 and less than £3,000 in 1769, hardly enough to operate a few frontier forts.

There was little violence. The boycott was organized by well-to-do merchants who were still nervous about the Stamp Act riots. But it worked. English merchants felt the pinch and petitioned Parliament for repeal. They pointed out that if Townshend had answered the colonial distinction between internal and external taxes, he had also penalized goods that English manufacturers and merchants shipped to America. In 1770, with the exception of a three-pence-per-pound tax on tea, Parliament repealed the Townshend Duties. The tea tax was kept in the spirit of the Declaratory Act. It was Parliament's statement that it retained the right to tax the colonies.

for
FURTHER READING

Among the general histories of the events leading to the American Revolution (and differing radically in their explanations) are J. R. Alden, *A History of the American Revolution,* 1969; Bernard Bailyn, *The Ideological Origins of the American Revolution,* 1967, and *British Politics and the American Revolution,* 1965; Lawrence H. Gipson, *The Coming of the Revolution,* 1954; Jack P. Greene, *The Reinterpretation of the American Revolution,* 1968; Merrill Jensen, *The Founding of a Nation,* 1968; Robert Middlekauff, *The Glorious Cause: The American Revolution, 1763–1789,* 1982; Edmund S. Morgan, *The Birth of the Republic,* 1956; Don Higginbotham, *The War of American Independence, 1763–1789,* 1971;

Alfred T. Young, *The American Revolution: A Radical Interpretation,* 1976; and Pauline Maier, *From Resistance to Revolution, 1765–1776,* 1972.

Special studies include John Brook, *King George III,* 1972; Edmund S. Morgan and Helen Morgan, *Prologue to Revolution: The Stamp Act Crisis,* 1953; and Arthur M. Schlesinger Jr., *The Colonial Merchants and the American Revolution, 1763–1776,* 1951. On Pontiac's uprising, see Howard H. Peckham, *Pontiac and the Indian Uprising,* 1947; and Wilbur R. Jacobs, *Wilderness Politics and Indian Gifts,* 1966.

Visit the source collections at http://ajaccess.wadsworth.com and http://infotrac.thomsonlearning.com, and use the Search function with the following key terms to explore documents, images, audio and video clips, articles, and commentary related to the material in this chapter:

George Grenville   Stamp Act
Pontiac   William Pitt
Proclamation of 1763

Additional resources, exercises, and Internet links related to this chapter are available on *The American Past* Web site: http://history.wadsworth.com/americanpast7e.

HISTORY ONLINE

The American Revolution and Its Era
http://memory.loc.gov/ammem/gmdhtml/armhome.html
Period maps of the colonies and the early United States.

Stamps Required by the Stamp Act
www2.gasou.edu/special_collections/artifacts/stamps.html
Examples of Stamp Act embossings in both Great Britain and the colonies; background information.

FROM RIOT TO REBELLION

The Road to Independence 1770–1776

He has dissolved Representative Houses. . . . He has obstructed the Administration of Justice. . . . He has kept among us, in times of peace, Standing Armies. . . . He has plundered our seas, ravaged our Coasts, burnt our towns, and destroyed the lives of our people.

The Declaration of Independence

I can have no other Object but to protect the true Interests of all My Subjects. No People ever enjoyed more Happiness, or lived under a milder Government, than those now revolted Provinces. . . . My Desire is to restore to them the Blessings of Law and Liberty . . . which they have fatally and desperately exchanged for the Calamities of War, and the arbitrary Tyranny of their Chiefs.

King George III

T HE ISSUE OF Parliament's right to tax the colonies was not resolved by the repeal of the Townshend Duties. Neither Parliament nor colonial protesters yielded an inch. Nevertheless, almost everyone involved in the long dispute was relieved to see an end to confrontation and boycott. For three years after 1770, Parliament avoided provocations. In America, anti-British protests were few and muted. In fact, tensions may have been easing before mid-1770, when news of the repeal reached the colonies. A door-to-door survey of New Yorkers revealed that a majority were willing to buy all the Townshend items except tea, which could be had more cheaply from Dutch smugglers. Imports into New England, the most obstreperous colonies, began a steady rise from a low of £330,000 to £1.2 million, more than ever before. As perhaps most people always do, Americans wanted calm—business as usual—a resumption of daily life unaggravated by the folderol of politics.

STORMS WITHIN THE LULL

Nevertheless, several incidents between 1770 and 1773 indicated that not all was harmonious in British North America. On the streets of Boston, a bloody brawl between working-men and British soldiers dramatized a simmering hostility toward the redcoats stationed in the colonies. In North Carolina, frontier settlers took up arms against the elite of the eastern counties who governed the colony. And in Rhode Island, farmers protected smugglers who burned a British patrol boat.

▲ *This engraving of the Boston Massacre, by silversmith and Son of Liberty Paul Revere, was propaganda, not an attempt to portray the incident accurately. The redcoats were actually backed against a wall in genuine danger; the Boston mob was more numerous than the victims here and crowded all around. Revere himself drew an accurate map of the incident for the trial of the soldiers.*

The Boston Massacre

On March 5, 1770, the weather in Boston was frigid. The streets were icy; heaps of gritty snow blocked the gutters. No doubt aggravated by the severity of the winter, which brought unemployment as well as discomfort, some men and boys exchanged words with British soldiers who were patrolling the streets. A handful of hecklers became a crowd cursing and throwing snowballs at the redcoats. A few dared the soldiers to use their muskets.

When the mob pressed close on King Street, backing the redcoats against a wall, they fired. Five, including a boy and an African American named Crispus Attucks, fell dead. Boston, with scarcely more than 15,000 people, was shocked. A few men who had been active in the Stamp Act protest tried to revive anti-British feelings. A silversmith, Paul Revere, engraved a picture of soldiers aggressively attacking innocent people. Samuel Adams, a former brewer, circulated prints of the "Boston Massacre" and tried to rouse tempers. Joseph Warren, a physician, embroidered passionately on the theme. "Take heed, ye orphan babes," he told a public meeting, "lest, whilst your streaming eyes are fixed upon the ghastly corpse, your feet slide on the stones bespattered with your father's brains."

But the agitation failed to bear fruit. Most people seemed to blame the incident on the mob. John Adams, cousin of Samuel and a friend of Warren, represented the soldiers in court. Adams was nobody's stooge, least of all for the British. He was strong-headed to the point of self-righteousness and a critic of British policies. In arguing the redcoats' case, Adams roundly criticized the practice of stationing professional soldiers in cities like Boston. "Soldiers quartered in a populous town will always occasion two mobs where they prevent one," he said. "They are wretched conservators of the peace." Nevertheless, Adams blamed an unsavory mob, not the indicted redcoats, for the tragedy. The jury agreed, acquitting all of the defendants but two and sentencing them only to branding on the thumb, a slap on the wrist by eighteenth-century standards.

The Hated Redcoats

The significance of the Boston Massacre and the Battle of Golden Hill (a soldier-civilian riot in New York in January) was that the vast majority of colonials let them pass. Still, they dramatized a sore spot in colonial city life: Americans did not much like the scarlet-uniformed soldiers in their midst. Property owners resented paying for their keep. Ordinary working people disliked rubbing shoulders with men who commanded little respect. Colonials of the same social class as the soldiers were hostile simply because the redcoats were outsiders.

The eighteenth-century soldier was not the boy next door in uniform, defending the nation and its ideals. He was a rough and lusty young man sieved from the dregs of a rigidly stratified society. Some soldiers were convicted criminals who were in the army because it was offered to them as an alternative to prison. Others, guilty of no crime, were pressed into service simply because they were unable to support themselves.

At best, civilians were wary of them; many despised them. To their officers, *scum* was the word that leapt first to mind when they described soldiers. Redcoats were regularly and brutally punished. If not slaves, they were in bondage, apt to be hanged if they deserted. There was no feeling among them of service to king and country or of commitment to an ideal. In America, they were further alienated by the fact that few colonials enlisted. The "lobsters" were almost all from Great Britain.

A Dangerous Relationship

As long as the soldiers lived in frontier forts or in isolated bases such as Castle Island in Boston Harbor, there was little conflict. However, after the Stamp Act riots, the Crown stationed large detachments within cities and towns. Some 4,000 redcoats were camped on Boston Common at the time of the massacre. Others, under the terms of the Quartering Act of 1765, were billeted in whatever vacant buildings and taverns quartermasters could locate.

This brought the tightly knit redcoats into intimate daily contact with working-class colonials. They were young men, and some found girlfriends—which, naturally, stirred up resentment among colonial men. Others coarsely accosted young women. When off duty, redcoats competed with local men and boys for casual work. There was a fistfight over jobs at a rope factory in Boston just a few days before the Boston Massacre. Redcoats also passed idle hours in the taverns where colonials gathered.

▲ *Most redcoats were rough, crude, even dangerous men. Their intrusion into taverns, the social centers of colonial cities, had more to do with making rebels of ordinary city folk than arguments about taxation and representation.*

Inns and taverns were not just hostels where travelers supped and bedded down. They were a focal point of urban social life—neighborhood meeting places, like contemporary English pubs. Local workingmen popped in throughout the day for a cup of tea or coffee and, in the evening, for a shot of rum, a mug of mulled cider, a pipe of tobacco, and a chat with friends about work and politics. Those with time on their hands, such as the unemployed and seamen between voyages, spent even more time at the "ordinaries," as taverns were called, if only to stand in front of the fire for a bit. The intrusion of uniformed foreigners, laughing loudly and carrying on by themselves, caused resentment even when, as between 1770 and 1773, relations with Great Britain seemed to be good.

Street People

The redcoats had more to do with the anti-British feelings of lower-class colonials than parliamentary taxation did. Poor people worried about the next day's meal, not about the fine points of the British constitution. Such people were central to the protest that boiled over into riot in 1765 and rebellion after 1773. Workingmen, the unemployed, boisterous street boys and apprentices, and the disreputable fringe elements of colonial society did the dirty work in the Stamp Act crisis. They were the ones who taunted soldiers in the streets and who were killed in the Boston Massacre.

They had little to lose as a consequence of rash action. Many of the street people were themselves social outcasts by virtue of their class, their occupation (or lack of one), or their race. Seamen, suspect because they came and went, belonging to no community, were prominent in colonial crowds. (Crispus Attucks was a seaman out of work.) John Adams described the mob on King Street as "Negroes and mulattoes, Irish teagues and outlandish jack-tars." And yet, the revolution he was to join with enthusiasm owed much to the boldness of this motley bunch.

Demon Rum

It is worth noting the curious role of alcohol in the agitation. Soldiers liked their drink. It was standard military practice to pass around rum before battle, and the royal governor of New York dissolved the colonial assembly in 1766 when its members refused to provide the redcoats with their accustomed ration of five pints of beer or four ounces of rum a day.

Colonials were hard-drinking folk too—they drank much more per capita than Americans today—and people at the bottom of the social scale, with more to forget, were the thirstiest of all. Many signal episodes on the road to independence seem to have been carried out by men in their cups. "The minds of the freeholders were inflamed," wrote an observer of the Stamp Act protest in South Carolina, "by many a hearty damn . . . over bottles, bowls, and glasses." The crowd that precipitated the Boston Massacre had come out of the taverns. The Sons of Liberty, who ignited the last phase of the revolutionary movement with the Boston Tea Party of 1773, assembled over a barrel of rum.

Blue Anchor Inn ~ Philadelphia ~ 1776

▲ *Some inns resembled the Blue Anchor in Philadelphia, catering to elegantly well-mannered gentlemen. Workingmen's taverns and ordinaries, however—those into which redcoats were likely to intrude—were ruder, crowded, and far less decorous, even on the slowest days.*

Upper-crust protest leaders had mixed feelings about this kind of agitation. They were more than willing to exploit angry, and perhaps inebriated, crowds by stirring up resentment of the British, then winking at the mobs' mockeries of the law. John Adams, so scornful of the Boston Massacre mob in 1770, called the men at the Boston Tea Party of 1773 "so bold, so daring, so intrepid." But many thoughtful upper-class colonials, and not just those who remained loyal to Great Britain, worried about the "rabble." They knew that mobs do not always fade graciously away after having played their historic role.

The Regulators

Conflict between colonial classes was, as it had been during the seventeenth century, clearer in the countryside. In the backcountry of South Carolina, between 1767 and 1769, frontiersmen rebelled against the refusal of the colonial assembly, which was dominated by Charleston planters, to set up county governments in the west. They created their own counties to which they paid taxes that were legally to go to Charleston. The rebels called themselves "Regulators" because they said they would regulate their own affairs.

In North Carolina, a similar dispute led to actual battle. A band of westerners rode east to demonstrate their resentment of the colony's penny-pinching policies. In May 1771, they were met and defeated by a smaller but better-trained militia at the Battle of Alamance. Only nine men were killed (six were later hanged), but the modesty of the clash did not

sweeten the bitterness in the backcountry. When the Revolution began in 1775, poor, backcountry Carolinians with memories were, more than any other lower-class white colonials, likely to be pro-British.

The *Gaspée*

In June 1772, a British schooner patrolling Narragansett Bay in Rhode Island, the *Gaspée,* spied a vessel suspected of smuggling and sailed after it toward Providence. About seven miles from the port, the *Gaspée* ran aground. That night, men from eight boats boarded the schooner, roughly set the crew ashore, and burned the *Gaspée* to the waterline.

Because the *Gaspée* was a royal vessel, this was an act of rebellion. The authorities were pretty sure the ringleader of the gang was a merchant named John Brown, who had had several run-ins with customs collectors. However, neither a £500 reward nor the fact that Rhode Island's elected governor took part in the investigation persuaded anyone to provide evidence. The commission of inquiry finally disbanded angrily only in June 1773. By that time, the three-year lull in British–American relations was drawing to a close.

THE MARCH TOWARD WAR

The quiet years ended in the spring of 1773, when Parliament once again enacted a law that angered Americans. This time, however, instead of spontaneous protests under the control of

© Bettmann/Corbis

▲ *Rhode Islanders burning the grounded British customs schooner* Gaspée *in Narragansett Bay in 1772.*

no one in particular, resistance to British policy was aroused and organized by a number of able, deliberate men.

They may be described as professional agitators. Some were orators; some, propagandists of the pen. Others were organizers, people willing to devote their time to shaping anger into rebellion. There can be no revolutions without such revolutionaries. Men like James Otis and Samuel Adams of Massachusetts and Patrick Henry of Virginia made the difference between spontaneous incidents like the Boston Massacre and calculated provocations like the Boston Tea Party.

The Troublemakers

James Otis was a Boston attorney, once an effective prosecutor before the unpopular vice admiralty courts. Like celebrated criminal attorneys today, he was a showman, always excitable, an exponent of anything-to-win-a-case litigation, and often vituperative. He described one group of legal adversaries as a "dirty, drinking, drabbing, contaminated knot of thieves," and, what's more, "Turks, Jews, and other infidels, with a few renegade Christians and Catholics." This kind of rhetoric always has its enthusiasts. Otis could fire up the passions of a jury or a town meeting as few of his contemporaries could.

In 1761, Otis led Boston's fight against "writs of assistance." These were broad search warrants empowering customs agents to enter warehouses and homes to search for any evidence of smuggling. Arguing against the writs, Otis

made them an issue of the sacred, basic rights of British subjects, apparently coining the phrase soon to be the slogan of a revolution: "Taxation without representation is tyranny." John Adams would later say of Otis that "then and there the child Independence was born."

For inflammatory rhetoric, Patrick Henry of Virginia was Otis's equal. No deep thinker, Henry was a sharp-tongued, Scotch-Irish shopkeeper who educated himself to become one of the colony's most successful trial lawyers and a member of the House of Burgesses, a station to which few of his class rose. He won notice far beyond Williamsburg when he denounced George III as a tyrant because the king reversed a law passed by the burgesses, something monarchs had been doing since 1624.

During the Stamp Act excitement, Henry caused an even more widespread furor when he was quoted as saying, "Caesar had his Brutus, Charles I his Cromwell, and George III may profit by their example." Naming the king in series with two historical rulers who had died by the knife was pretty heady stuff. Henry was shouted down with cries of "treason." Legend soon had him replying, "If this be treason, make the most of it." Henry would be prominent in the final drive toward independence. He called for the establishment of a colonial army in May 1775 with more words for the quotations books: "Give me liberty or give me death."

Less excitable than Otis and Henry, and no orator (he was nervous at a podium, trembling and stumbling over his words), Samuel Adams of Massachusetts was the most substantial of the three. A brewer as a young man (and a tax collector between 1756 and 1764!), Adams devoted himself to moral censorship and anti-British agitation. Indeed, personal morality and civic virtue were fundamental to his dislike of British rule. He was obsessed by the concept of republican virtue that the educated people of the era attributed to the ancient Greeks and Romans. Adams said that Boston should reconstitute itself as a "Christian Sparta." Humorless, cheerless, bored by socializing, he believed that political power was legitimate only when in the hands of men who lived austerely and were ever vigilant to preserve liberty.

Adams was in the middle of every major protest in Boston: against the Sugar Act, the Stamp Act, the Townshend Duties, the Boston Massacre. He was indispensable, a sober organizer among oratorical prima donnas. He was the man who handled the humdrum but essential tasks that transform protest into politics. He also served as the go-between for the Boston elite (men like the rich merchant John Hancock) and the Sons of Liberty, men of Adams's own artisan class, and through them, the crowd.

Fatal Turn: The Tea Act

Samuel Adams may have daydreamed of the colonies independent of Great Britain by the mid-1760s. If he did, he shared his musings with few other colonials, for they would have seen him as a fantasist. John Adams's opinion aside, the child Independence was born not when James Otis challenged the writs of assistance nor when Patrick Henry threatened George III with executioners. The baby was delivered—that is, responsible colonials began to consider independence as a genuine possibility, in numbers growing steadily like an infant, a child soon to be on its feet—on May 10, 1773, when Parliament's Tea Act became law. After the Tea Act, the colonies' quarrel with the mother country did not, as before, burn out and die. By progressive steps, it intensified into an explosion.

The Tea Act was not designed to tax the colonies. Its purpose was to bail out the East India Company, a corporation invaluable to the Crown. In return for a monopoly on trade with India, the company governed Britain's holdings in India, maintaining an army to defend and expand them: It was empire on the cheap. In 1773, the company was on the edge of bankruptcy. In just a few months, East India shares plummeted in value from £280 to £160 (and many members of Parliament owned shares). Some 17 million pounds of company tea sat in warehouses, and there were no buyers.

To prevent disaster, the company proposed that it be allowed to sell its tea directly in the colonies rather than auction it to middlemen. Because the tea was being dumped—any price was preferable to none—East India tea would be significantly cheaper than the smuggled Dutch tea that had become fashionable in America. To sweeten the cup further, the company asked Parliament to repeal the Townshend tax on tea that had been left in place.

Parliament met the company nine-tenths of the way. The prime minister, Frederick, Lord North, supported by George III, saw a chance to succeed where Grenville and Townshend had failed. Even with the tax, Tea Act tea was a bargain. It would cost colonials money to uphold the cause of no taxation without representation. Like many others, Lord North and the king believed that colonial protest was about greed.

The Tea Parties

They were wrong. When a dozen East India Company ships carrying 1,700 chests of tea sailed into American ports, they were greeted by the angriest defiance of British authority since 1765. The Americans would not be bought. Under the Tea Act, tea may have been cheap, but buying it set the precedent of allowing Parliament to grant monopolies on goods colonials had to import.

The tea was landed in Charleston; it was hastily locked up in a warehouse, where an angry crowd could not get to it. The governors of New York and Pennsylvania ordered the ships to return to England for fear of riots. In Annapolis, Maryland, a tea ship was burned. But it was a milder action in Boston that triggered the crisis.

The American-born governor of Massachusetts, Thomas Hutchinson, would not permit the tea ships to depart Boston. Instead, while sparks flew at public meetings, he hatched a plan to get the cargo under royal (this is, his) control and not that of a private company: He planned to seize the tea for failure to pay port taxes and work from there.

It was a clever idea, but Samuel Adams was cleverer and quicker. On December 16, 1773, the day before Hutchinson could gain custody of the tea, Adams presided over a protest meeting attended by a third of the population of Boston. Some 60 Sons of Liberty slipped out of the meetinghouse, had a few drinks, dressed up as Mohawk Indians, and boarded the East India Company ships. To the cheers of a huge crowd, they dumped 342 chests worth £10,000 into Boston Harbor.

The Indian costumes had a touch of political genius to them. They disguised the perpetrators but also lent the air of a prank to the affair—thus the name "Boston Tea Party." Adams and his colleagues knew that Britain could not let the incident pass; they guessed that Parliament would overreact. Parliament did, grotesquely and foolishly. Instead of

The Morning After

If the men of Boston who dumped the tea into Boston Harbor had been drinking, not all suffered hangovers. One participant remembered what he did the morning after the Boston Tea Party:

The next morning . . . it was discovered that very considerable quantities of [tea] were floating upon the surface of the water, and to prevent the possibility of any of its being saved for use, a number of small boats were manned by sailors and citizens, who rowed them into those parts of the harbor wherever the tea was visible, and by beating it with oars and paddles so thoroughly drenched it as to render its entire destruction inevitable.

flushing out the individuals involved in the party and trying them as garden-variety vandals (the dumped tea had not been under government control), Lord North decided to punish the city of Boston and the colony of Massachusetts.

The Intolerable Acts

A few politicians, like reliable Lord Chatham, feverishly warned that the Coercive Acts of 1774—Americans called them the "Intolerable Acts"—were ill advised, but they sailed through Parliament. First, the port of Boston was to be closed to all trade until the city (not the individual culprits) paid for the spoiled tea. Second, the new governor (a military man, General Thomas Gage) was empowered to transfer out of the colony the trials of soldiers or other British officials accused of killing protesters. It was not unreasonable to see this as an invitation to the redcoats to shoot on the slightest pretext. Third, the structure of the government of Massachusetts was overhauled, with elected bodies losing powers to the king's appointed officials. Fourth, a new Quartering Act further aggravated civilian–soldier relations—this time, to the breaking point. It authorized the army to house redcoats in occupied private homes!

Lord North hoped that by coming down hard on Massachusetts, he would isolate the colony, which had never been popular elsewhere in North America, and thereby issue a warning to protesters elsewhere. Instead, the Coercive Acts proved to be intolerable everywhere. Several cities shipped food to paralyzed Boston. More ominous than charity, when Massachusetts called for a continental congress to meet in Philadelphia to discuss a united response to the Intolerable Acts, every colony except Georgia sent delegates.

Salt in the Wound: The Quebec Act

The Quebec Act of 1774 was not designed as one of the Coercive Acts, but it also agitated many colonials by officially recognizing the French language and giving official status to the Catholic religion in the province of Quebec. Anti-Catholicism was not as rabid in Britain and the colonies as it had been a hundred years earlier, but it was far from dead. (In the Gordon Riots in London in 1780, mobs burned the churches and homes of Catholics for three days.) In 1774, New Englanders shuddered that the Crown was protecting, even promoting, Catholicism in a colony that bordered their own.

Colonials having no particular hostility toward Roman Catholics were agitated by the Quebec Act's second provision, which expanded Quebec's boundary into the Ohio Valley. Had not the French and Indian War been fought to win these lands for the colonies? Speculators with claims to land in the Ohio Valley and farmers eyeing the possibility of moving there were alarmed.

Finally, the Quebec Act did not provide for an elective assembly in the colony. It was true enough that French Canadians had never had an elected assembly. But Canada was British now. Again, the deadly serious issue of the rights of British subjects came to the fore.

THE BEGINNING OF A REVOLUTION

If the Tea Act marks the beginning of a progressive march toward revolution, the Intolerable Acts and the Quebec Act mark the beginning of a coordinated colonial resistance. Before 1774, only the informal "committees of correspondence," groups exchanging news and views among the colonies via the mails, connected one colony's protesters to those of others. Now, while the delegates to the Continental Congress who trickled into Philadelphia during the summer continued to think of themselves as New Hampshiremen and New Yorkers and Carolinians, they were acting in concert—continentally—and with something like formal authority.

The Delegates

The 56 delegates to the Continental Congress began their discussions on September 5. Some of them, such as home-towner Benjamin Franklin, were already famous. Others, like Samuel Adams and Patrick Henry, had recently become notorious. Most, however, were men of only local renown, and, since each of the colonies had closer relations with Britain than with any other American province, few of the delegates had met one another.

They differed in temperament, in their sentiments toward Great Britain, and in their opinions as to what should be done, could be done, and ought not be done. But they got along remarkably well. The heritage they were soon to rebel against gave them much in common. They were all gentlemen in the English mold: merchants, planters, and professionals, particularly lawyers. They prized education and civility. They knew how to keep debates decorous and impersonal. In the evening, they recessed to a round of festive dinners and parties with Philadelphia high society. George Washington of Virginia rarely dined in his own chambers. John Adams gushed in letters to his wife, Abigail, about the lavishness of the meals he was served. Only Samuel Adams, nurturing his ideals of Roman republican frugality, shunned the social whirl and won the reputation of being a killjoy.

The Issues

None of the delegates had an "ideology"; few had an agenda. Most were troubled and uncertain about what to do.

Planter Politicians

William Byrd was born in Virginia in 1674. His father was quite wealthy, so it was Byrd's good fortune to come into his maturity when the Tidewater plantation aristocracy was entering its golden age—no longer struggling to build fortunes, but able to devote its comfortable leisure to sport, "society," scholarship, and politics.

Byrd enjoyed the great planters' unending rounds of entertaining one another at feasts and balls; he loved the chummy men's club atmosphere of Williamsburg, the colonial capital; and he was a social butterfly during two extended periods of residence in London. He seems to have cared less than most planters for hunting with the hounds, one of the planters' many imitations of the British aristocracy, which they admired. Byrd loved books more than most of his peers. Educated in Europe, he began each day reading for several hours in Hebrew, Greek, Latin, French, and Dutch.

What Byrd and the vast majority of eighteenth-century planters had most in common was politics. They regarded holding public office as a social, even sacred, duty and as the responsibility of men whom wealth and breeding provided with leisure, education, and—they liked to say—a selfless disinterestedness. Indeed, the planters were born "governing." As the owners of numerous slaves, they grew up managing the affairs of communities, which large plantations were.

They inherited or bought their slaves. But they had to win election to public offices, the most coveted of which was a seat in Virginia's assembly, the House of Burgesses. (Appointment to the royal governor's council was a step up from that, but open only to the cream of the class, like Byrd.)

Few Virginians who were not planters were eligible for election to the House of Burgesses (or had the time for the job). The property qualification was substantially higher than it was for the right to vote. Middling farmers, including those who owned no slaves, voted but never thought of being a burgess.

These were the "yeomen" whom Thomas Jefferson, born the year before William Byrd died, idealized as the "bone and sinew" of a healthy society and the people whose support the planter had to win in order to be elected to office.

Politics was highly personal. In his own county, the planter candidate knew by name almost every voter who assembled at the courthouse on election day; if he was a candidate in another county (quite legal if he owned property there), the voters knew a lot about him because of his wealth. Elections were intimate. Weather permitting, they were held outdoors. Candidates set out spreads of food and drink, and politely but formally greeted all. There was no gushing; the candidate did not try to act like the same "ordinary fellow" the voters were. Such obvious patronizing would have been a ticket to rejection. The point was this: The candidate was a member of a social class a notch up, the governing class.

Balloting was public. Each voter approached the pollers, who sat at a table, and announced his choice. His candidate stepped forward to thank him, again quite formally. Debate in the House of Burgesses at Williamsburg was equally decorous. There were disturbing moments, as when Patrick Henry savaged the king and was shouted down as a traitor. Mostly, however, since the burgesses were of the same social class, sharing its well-defined code of conduct, and since many were related by blood or marriage, the tiny House of Burgesses was a deliberative assembly with an integrity not always found in state legislatures today.

The leaders of the Revolution from Virginia were educated in this superb political school. Washington, Jefferson, Peyton Randolph (the president of the First Continental Congress), and all of the Virginians who signed the Declaration of Independence were alumni of the House of Burgesses. So was Patrick Henry, although he was no planter, a fact surely remarked upon after his bad behavior at Williamsburg.

They were angry, even those who would later remain loyal to Britain, and they were determined to settle the squabble with Parliament. The congress adopted a defiant set of declarations called the Suffolk Resolves, which were rushed to Philadelphia from Boston (Suffolk County), by the rebellious silversmith who publicized the Boston Massacre, Paul Revere. The resolutions stated that the Intolerable Acts were invalid, and called for a boycott of trade with Britain if the obnoxious laws were not repealed.

But there was no king-bashing in the style of Patrick Henry (although he was present). The delegates toasted themselves tipsy, raising glasses to King George. They agreed to British regulation of colonial trade, and they almost adopted a conciliatory plan designed by Joseph Galloway of Pennsylvania just a few days before they voted for the hard-line Suffolk resolutions. The very notion of rebellion was repugnant.

Unhappily, George III did not share their mood. He was determined to stand firm and, having the military might, more than willing to win the argument with force. "Blows must decide whether they are to be subject to the country or independent," George told Lord North at a time when no colonial leader had publicly mentioned the possibility of independence. Learning of the king's intransigence, the delegates had no alternative but to respond in kind. One of their last actions before adjourning was to call on Americans to organize and train local military units.

Colonial Soldiers

Little encouragement was needed. In the Massachusetts countryside, tempers were already aflame. A British spy, sent out from Boston to get a feel for the people's mood, asked an ancient farmer why, at his age, he was cleaning his gun. The old man replied that "there was a flock of redcoats in Boston, which he expected would be here soon; he meant to try and hit some of them." Did his neighbors feel the same way? Yes, most of them. "There was one Tory house in sight," the old man said, "and he wished it was in flames."

Young men also oiled their guns and collected on village greens to elect officers and drill, as well as they knew how. Practically every adult male in rural America was armed, for guns were tools. Many farm families still hunted for some of their food, and the days when they had to be on guard against Indian raids were not long in the past.

Americans were excellent marksmen, even with smoothbore flintlock muskets, which were not reliable at any distance. Some had adopted the *Jaeger,* the rifle introduced into the colonies by German immigrants. Americans extended the length of its barrel for even greater accuracy at a distance. A British officer observed, "Provided an American rifleman were to get a perfect aim at 300 yards at me, standing still, he most undoubtedly would hit me unless it was a very windy day."

As soldiers, however, colonials had a bad name. Astonishingly few responded to British attempts to recruit them. Militia training was close to a joke. During the French and Indian War, the camps of American militiamen were notoriously filthy; often, the colonials did not dig latrines but made do in the woods. Many more of them died from disease—contaminated water—than did the disciplined redcoats who marched with them. The Americans had been unreliable in battle so often that General John Forbes said, "There is no faith or trust to be put in them." General Wolfe had called his American militia "the dirtiest, most contemptible cowardly dogs you can conceive." Considering the lineaments of eighteenth-century warfare, however, this was almost a compliment.

The Way Battles Were Fought

Eighteenth-century warfare was highly structured. In battle, two armies in close formation maneuvered to face one another in open country from the better position, which usually meant higher ground. After an exchange of artillery, soon to be the key to battle but not yet fully appreciated, the attacking army closed the gap to the oddly cheerful music of fife and drum (or bagpipes if the soldiers were Scots). The armies exchanged musket fire in volleys. The men pointed, rather than aimed, their weapons—muskets were not accurate. The side that stood its ground amidst the horror of smoke, noise, and companions next to them dropping to the sod—in other words, the army that continued to be an army—defeated the one that panicked, broke ranks, and fled the field.

The key to winning battles was long, hard, and tedious training according to manuals written mostly by French and Prussian tacticians. These drills (and a dram of rum or gin before battle) were designed to make a machine of thousands of individual human beings. Marksmanship counted for little. Individual initiative was a curse, to be exorcised by brutal discipline. The goal was nothing less than unnatural behavior on a mass scale: not fleeing from a terrifying experience.

Lexington and Concord

And so, when General Gage decided to seize rebel supplies at Concord, 21 miles from Boston, he did not worry about the "minutemen," farmers pledged to be ready to fight the British at a minute's notice. How could play-soldiers stand up to one of Europe's finest armies? On April 19, 1775, he sent 700 troops to capture the munitions and, if possible, to arrest Samuel Adams and John Hancock, who were thought to be hiding in the area.

The Americans were warned by the midnight ride of Paul Revere (and by William Dawes and Samuel Prescott, who actually got farther than Revere), bringing the news to

John Carter Brown Library

▲ *This depiction of the Battle of Lexington shows the minutemen inflicting casualties on the redcoats in the background. It is patriotic but not accurate. The British sustained no casualties, and their volley scattered the colonials, who may have begun to disperse (accounts of the incident differ) before the redcoats fired.*

crossroads and village commons: "The British are coming!" When Major John Pitcairn arrived at Lexington, a few miles shy of Concord, he found 70 nervous minutemen drawn up in a semblance of battle formation. Their fate seemed to confirm British contempt for American warriors.

In fact, the Americans were sensibly frightened and confused at the sight of the solid ranks of tough, grim men who outnumbered them ten to one. They stood around uncertainly, murmuring among themselves for a few minutes. Pitcairn twice ordered them to disperse. Then a shot was fired.

No one knew who fired it—a colonial hothead determined to force the issue or a British soldier mishandling his musket. Nor did it matter. In London, on the same day as the Battle of Lexington, Parliament was passing another Intolerable Act, which banned Massachusetts fishermen from the Grand Banks of Newfoundland. When Americans heard of that law, which was designed to finish off the already crippled New England economy, it would surely have set off armed rebellion in New England.

Pitcairn's men cleared Lexington Green in minutes and marched on to Concord, where a larger group of Americans met them at a bridge. Surprised by the size of the resistance and the Americans' effectiveness from their superior position, Pitcairn ordered a retreat to Boston. All the way back, minutemen sniped at the British soldiers from behind trees and stone fences; they were in their element, fighting the redcoats as they fought Indians. They inflicted serious casualties. When the British troops reached the city, more than 250 were dead or wounded. The minutemen, elated by their victory, set up camp outside Boston, where others joined them daily.

Bunker Hill

Soon, 16,000 rebels surrounded the city. In London, Edmund Burke pleaded with Parliament to evacuate Boston and allow tempers to cool. As usual, the most thoughtful politician of the age was heard for his eloquence, then ignored. Lord North dispatched another 1,000 troops to Boston, along with three more generals—Henry Clinton, John "Gentleman Johnny" Burgoyne, and William Howe. Curiously, all three, as well as Gage, were personally sympathetic to Americans.

Howe talked Gage into allowing him to occupy high ground on a peninsula across the Charles River. The day before he moved, however, the Americans took the peninsula, including Bunker Hill and, nearer to Boston, Breed's Hill. When Howe's men took to their boats, 1,600 armed colonials were dug in on the summit of Breed's Hill.

Howe sent 2,000 crack troops up the slopes. Puzzlingly, no one returned their fire. Then, when the Americans could "see the whites of their eyes" (in other words, when they could aim rather than volley), they let loose. The redcoats staggered and retreated. They regrouped and again advanced, and again they were thrown back. Now, however, Howe correctly calculated that the Americans were short of powder and shot. Reinforcing his badly mauled front line with fresh men, Howe took Breed's Hill with bayonets.

The British had won. Or had they? Hearing that 200 men had been killed and 1,000 wounded, General Clinton remarked that too many such "victories" would destroy the British ability to fight. Ninety-two officers were lost (one-sixth of the British officers who would be lost over the next six years). Clinton was right. The misnamed Battle of Bunker Hill was an American triumph. Casualties were 370, most of them killed or wounded during the flight from the hilltop. The British gained nothing, for the colonial militias maintained their circle around Boston, while revolutionaries secured their control of the New England countryside.

Ticonderoga

Rebel morale had another boost in the spring of 1775. Soon after Lexington and Concord, the Massachusetts Committee of Safety instructed Benedict Arnold, scion of a wealthy Connecticut family and a proven soldier, to raise an army and attack Fort Ticonderoga on Lake Champlain. Before he started, Arnold learned that backwoodsmen from what is now Vermont, a kind of guerrilla group calling themselves the "Green Mountain Boys," were preparing to march on the same fort, led by an eccentric land speculator named Ethan Allen.

Arnold caught up with the Green Mountain Boys, but he was unable to get the headstrong Allen to recognize his authority. Quarreling all the way to the fort, the two shut up just long enough to capture Ticonderoga on May 10. When the British commander, who had heard nothing of Lexington and Concord, asked in whose name he was being asked to surrender, Allen allegedly replied, "in the name of the great Jehovah and the Continental Congress." Striking and memorable as the words are, Allen was unlikely to have spoken them just that way, since he was an aggressive atheist.

The Arnold–Allen group captured several other British forts. There were no big battles, hardly battles at all. The British garrisons, languishing in the forests, were caught entirely by surprise. But along with Bunker Hill, these actions established that a war had begun, forcing Americans to take sides. Nowhere was the psychological impact greater than in Philadelphia, where the *Second* Continental Congress was already in session.

The Second Continental Congress

The delegates to the Second Continental Congress were less restrained than those of the first congress. Some conservatives, such as Joseph Galloway, were not present. Their places were taken by militants like Thomas Jefferson, a 32-year-old Virginian who had written several scorching anti-British polemics.

The situation had changed radically in a year. Armed rebellion was now a reality: Lexington, Concord, Ticonderoga, Bunker Hill, and an unsuccessful attack by Benedict Arnold on Quebec. Without bloodshed, royal authority was disintegrating everywhere as governors fled to the safety of British warships and self-appointed rebel committees took over the functions of government. If the Continental Con-

MAP 8:1 The First Battles of the Revolution, 1775–1776 The redcoats' march to the villages of Lexington and Concord, which are now suburbs, and their retreat to Boston, was through farmland in 1775. Note that the Battle of Bunker Hill was actually fought on the slopes of Breed's Hill.

gress were to retain the authority ostensibly bestowed upon it by Ethan Allen, the delegates had some catching up to do. They did. They sent George Washington of Virginia, silently voicing his aspirations in the military uniform he wore, to take command of the troops around Boston.

Delegates were discussing independence now, but not officially. In its "Declaration of the Cause and Necessity of Taking Up Arms" in July 1775, the Continental Congress insisted that the rebels sought only their rights as British subjects. But the inconsistency of shooting at George III's soldiers while swearing love for the king was preying on the minds of all. With Lord North refusing to propose any kind of compromise, the Continental Congress held back because of a thread of sentiment—the commitment of virtually all of Western civilization to the necessity of monarchy and a lingering affection for the person of George III, who had once been so popular.

THE FINAL BREAKAWAY

The man who snipped the thread of sentiment was not an American but an Englishman, 38 years of age in 1775, and only recently arrived in the colonies: Thomas Paine. Benjamin Franklin sponsored Paine's emigration. Perhaps because both men were of the artisan class—Paine was a corset maker—Franklin saw beyond Paine's history of failures in business, his "loathesome" personal appearance, and his vainglorious opinion of himself.

Common Sense

Paine's egotism and contentiousness were difficult to take. But his talents as a rouser of protest were formidable. In January 1776, he published a pamphlet that ranks with Luther's 95 Theses and the *Communist Manifesto* as a work of few words that shaped the course of history. In his pamphlet, *Common Sense,* Paine argued that it was foolish for Americans to risk everything for the purpose of British approval. He shredded the Americans' sentimental attachment to King George III, whom he called a "Royal Brute." Indeed, Paine attacked the very idea of hereditary monarchy. Kingship was "an office any child or idiot may fill" that required "only the animal figure of a man."

With a genius for propaganda that would produce many stirring calls on behalf of democracy and liberty over the next 20 years, Paine made converts by the thousands. Within a year, a population of 2.5 million bought 150,000 copies of *Common Sense;* within a decade, 500,000 copies. Every

▲ *This engraving of John Trumbull's classic painting of the signing of the Declaration of Independence depicts an assembly that never existed. By the time the document was ready for signing, most of the delegates had left for home. They signed without ceremony, singly or in twos and threes, later on in the summer or fall of 1776. However, Trumbull went to great lengths to find likenesses of every signer.*

American who could read must have at least skimmed it. Paine boasted that it was "the greatest sale that any performance ever had since the use of letters."

Paine's depiction of the king seemed to come to life with every dispatch from London. George III refused even to listen to American suggestions for peace, and he backed Lord North's proposal to hire German mercenaries to crush the rebels. As the spring of 1776 wore on, colony after colony formally nullified the king's authority within its boundaries. Some instructed their delegates in Philadelphia to vote for independence.

Independence

On June 7, Richard Henry Lee of Virginia introduced a resolution stating that "these United Colonies are, and of right ought to be, free and independent states." For three weeks, the delegates debated the issue. New England and the southern colonies were solidly for independence. The Middle Colonies were divided. New York never did vote for independence, but Pennsylvania, the large, prosperous, strategically located "keystone" of the colonies, gave in when the pacifistic Quaker John Dickinson and the cautious financier Robert Morris agreed to absent themselves so that the deadlock in the delegation could be broken in favor of the resolution. (Both men later supported the patriot cause.)

Delaware, also divided, swung to the side of independence when Caesar Rodney galloped full tilt from Dover to Philadelphia, casting the majority vote in his delegation. On July 2, the maneuvers concluded, and the Continental Congress broke America's legal ties with England. "The second day of July 1776," an excited John Adams wrote to Abigail, "will be the most memorable epoch in the history of Amer-

The Funny *S*

In documents of the revolutionary era, including the Declaration of Independence, the letter *s* is often written f. This is not a lowercase *f*. The character was written with only half a crossbar (and sometimes not that).

The funny *s* originated in German handwriting and was adopted by printers in the old German printed alphabet known as Gothic. It made its way to England because the movable type used by early English printers was imported from Germany, where printing originated.

Use of f was governed by strict rules. It was a lowercase letter, never a capital at the beginning of a proper noun or sentence; the familiar *S* served that purpose then as now. The f appeared only at the beginning or in the middle of a word in lowercase, never at the end. Thus, *business* was *bu∫ine∫s*, and *sassiness* was *fa∫∫ine∫s*. This form of the letter died out during the early nineteenth century.

ica." He was two days off. The "Glorious Fourth" became the national holiday when, on that day, the congress gathered to adopt its official statement to Americans and to the world of why it chose to dissolve the political bands that tied America to Great Britain.

The Declaration of Independence

Officially, the Declaration of Independence was the work of a committee consisting of Thomas Jefferson, Roger Sherman of Connecticut, John Adams, Benjamin Franklin, and Robert Livingston of New York. In fact, appreciating better than we do that a committee cannot write coherently, the work of composition was assigned to Jefferson because of his "peculiar felicity of style." The lanky Virginian, sometimes as careless of his personal appearance as Tom Paine, holed up in his rooms and emerged with a masterpiece.

Franklin and Adams changed a few words, and the congress made some alterations, the most important of which was to eliminate Jefferson's sly, backhanded attack on the institution of slavery. King George, Jefferson had written, "has waged cruel war against human nature itself, violating its most sacred right of life and liberty in the persons of a distant people who never offended him, captivating them into slavery in another hemisphere." Whatever and whomever were to be blamed for slavery, George III was not a culprit. Jefferson knew it, as did fellow southerners in the congress, especially South Carolinians, who were wedded to the institution and who insisted the section be deleted.

King George bore the brunt of all Jefferson's indictments. He was blamed for practically everything that was wrong in the colonies but the weather and worms in apple barrels. The personalization of the attack was nonsense in that the king was beholden to Parliament for every colonial policy. He needed parliamentary support to raise an army. As propaganda, however, Jefferson's device was brilliant. The Declaration of Independence focused anger on a visible and vulnerable scapegoat.

Universal Human Rights

The Declaration of Independence is not remembered for its catalog of George III's high crimes and misdemeanors. It is one of history's great political documents because, in his introductory sentences, Jefferson penned a stirring statement of human rights. For Jefferson did not write solely of the rights of American colonials. He put their case for independence in terms of the rights of all human beings: "We hold these truths to be self-evident, that all men are created equal, that they are endowed by their Creator with certain unalienable Rights, that among these are Life, Liberty and the pursuit of Happiness." And he tersely codified the principles that government drew its authority only from the consent of the people governed and that when the people withdrew that consent, they had the right to rebel.

Wording from the Declaration of Independence would, over the next two centuries, be borrowed by many peoples asserting their right to freedom, from the republics of Central and South America early in the 1800s to the Vietnamese on September 2, 1945. In the United States, groups making demands on society—from African Americans and feminists to labor unions and organizations lobbying against smoking tobacco in bars—have based their demands on their inalienable rights. In the summer of 1776, however, Americans were not thinking of the future of the Declaration of Independence. The rub was to confirm it on the battlefield.

for FURTHER READING

See J. R. Alden, *A History of the American Revolution,* 1969; Bernard Bailyn, *The Ideological Origins of the American Revolution,* 1967; Lawrence H. Gipson, *The Coming of the Revolution,* 1954; Jack P. Greene, *The Reinterpretation of the American Revolution,* 1968; Robert Middlekauf, *The Glorious Cause: The American Revolution, 1763–1789,* 1982; Edmund S. Morgan, *The Birth of the Republic,* 1956; Don Higginbotham, *The War of American Independence, 1763–1789,* 1971; Alfred T. Young, *The American Revolution: A Radical Interpretation,* 1976; and Pauline Maier, *From Resistance to Revolution, 1765–1776,* 1972.

Carl Becker, *The Declaration of Independence,* 1922, is as readable and enlightening today as when it was published. Also see Garry Wills, *Inventing America: Jefferson's Declaration of Independence,* 1978. Special studies include Robert A. Gross, *The Minutemen and Their World,* 1976; Benjamin W. Labaree, *The Boston Tea Party,* 1964; John Shy, *Toward Lexington: The Role of the British Army on the Coming of the Revolution,* 1965; and Hiller B. Zobel, *The Boston Massacre,* 1970.

Relevant biographies include Bernard Bailyn, *The Ordeal of Thomas Hutchinson,* 1974; Richard R. Beeman, *Patrick Henry: A Biography,* 1974; Eric Foner, *Tom Paine and Revolutionary America,* 1976; Noel B. Gerson, *The Grand Incendiary: A Biography of Samuel Adams,* 1973; and Pauline Maier, *The Old Revolutionaries: Political Lives in the Age of Samuel Adams,* 1980.

AMERICAN JOURNEY ONLINE AND INFOTRAC COLLEGE EDITION

Visit the source collections at http://ajaccess.wadsworth.com and http://infotrac.thomsonlearning.com, and use the Search function with the following key terms to explore documents, images, audio and video clips, articles, and commentary related to the material in this chapter:

Battle of Concord	Declaration of Independence
Battle of Lexington	First Continental Congress
Boston Massacre	Paul Revere
Boston Tea Party	Second Continental Congress
Crispus Attucks	

Additional resources, exercises, and Internet links related to this chapter are available on *The American Past* Web site: http://history.wadsworth.com/americanpast7e.

HISTORY ONLINE

The Boston Massacre Trial
www.aw.umkc.edu/faculty/projects/ftrials/bostonmassacre/bostonmassacre.html
Documents of the trial of the British soldiers defended by future patriot, John Adams.

Battle of Bunker Hill
http://masshist.org/bh
A comprehensive look at the Battle of Bunker Hill by the Massachusetts Historical Society.

THE WAR FOR INDEPENDENCE

*Winning the Revolution
1776–1781*

North Wind Picture Archives

*The history of our Revolution will be one continual lie
from one end to the other. The essence of the whole will be
that Dr. Franklin's electrical rod smote the earth and out
sprang George Washington. That Franklin electrified him
with his rod—and thenceforward these two constructed
all the policy, negotiations, legislatures, and war.*

John Adams

*By the rude bridge that arched the flood,
Their flag to April's breeze unfurled,
Here once the embattled farmers stood,
And fired the shot heard round the world*

Ralph Waldo Emerson

THE SIGNERS OF the Declaration of Independence pledged their lives, their fortunes, and their sacred honor to the cause of independence. This was no empty vow. Had George III won the quick victory he expected, the men of the Second Continental Congress would have been punished severely, many probably hanged. The noose had been the fate of Irish rebels and would be again. The Americans called themselves patriots. In the king's eyes, they were traitors, pure and simple.

THE IMBALANCE OF POWER

To an objective observer of 1776, the patriots' chances of success were not bright. Despite the military and moral victories of 1775, the patriots had challenged Europe's premier naval power and one of its finest armies. And they did not even have a majority of Americans behind them.

The Numbers

After the fighting around Boston in 1775, Lord North's military adviser, Lord George Germain, assembled 400 ships and dispatched 32,000 soldiers in them to join the redcoats already in America. It was largest military operation in British history. In addition to British regulars, Germain contracted with several petty German princes, who rented out trained soldiers as their source of revenue, for the services of 18,000 (later 30,000) troops at £7 a head (double the money if the man was killed). Although these mercenaries came from six different principalities, Americans called them "Hessians"—men from Hesse. During much of the war, Britain had 50,000 troops ready for battle.

▲ *George III had been popular in the colonies. Statues of him were erected in several cities. In the giddy days of 1776, they were pulled down by excited patriots and melted for casting into cannons.*

In 1776, the Americans could field only hastily mobilized militia made up of farm boys, apprentices, and city laborers. George Washington thought no more highly of them than British officers did. He observed in the minutemen he took command of around Boston "an unaccountable kind of stupidity." Of other militias he said, "To place any dependence on them is assuredly resting on a broken staff." Terms of enlistment were short, geared to the demands of agriculture. At harvest time every year, whole armies evaporated. Nevertheless, militiamen played a key role in the Revolution. Some, like South Carolina's, fought splendidly and successfully, albeit not according to conventional methods. The shakiest militias asserted patriot authority in areas the British did not occupy.

The Continental Congress created its own force, the Continental Army, but Washington himself was never to command more than 18,500 of these better-trained soldiers at one time. On several occasions, his command dwindled to 5,000. Still, the continental soldiers impressed foreign observers with their commitment to the cause of independence and their willingness to endure setbacks and sometimes terrible hardship. Some 4,400 patriot soldiers were killed in battle, perhaps 20,000 more died of illness. It would have been far worse had Washington not had his troops inoculated against smallpox. A smallpox epidemic raged throughout North America during the war, laying 130,000 people in their graves.

The patriot navy was a joke. Washington had to pay personally for the first American warship, the *Hannah,* a schooner with only four guns. Some merchant vessels carried more. The Continental Congress eventually appropriated funds to build 13 frigates, one for each state, but they fared poorly against the finest navy in the world. Of the eleven frigates actually completed, one was destroyed in battle, seven were captured, two were scuttled in order to avoid capture, and one was accidentally set afire by its own crew. Nor were American seamen much praised: "tinkers, shoe-makers, and horse jockeys," one officer lamented. A high proportion of Continental sailors were pressed into service—drafted.

The Loyalists

The patriots could not always rely on the civilian population. John Adams overshot the mark when he estimated that a third of the white population was Tory, loyal to the king; one-sixth is closer to the mark. Nevertheless, in March 1776, when General Howe evacuated Boston, a city of 15,000 people and notoriously anti-British, a thousand Americans went with him. When Howe established his headquarters in New York in September, he was welcomed more as a liberator than as a conqueror. Some 19,000 Americans joined the British army. At the end of the war, between 60,000 and 100,000 Americans (1 in 30) left their native land for England, the West Indies, or Canada, particularly

Anne S. K. Brown Military Collections, Brown University, Providence, RI

▲ *A watercolor, painted in the field, intended to illustrate different uniforms worn by American soldiers. One of them, an African American, is a reminder that most northern blacks—freemen—supported the patriot cause and enlisted in large numbers. With slavery dying in the North, they looked forward to improved lives with independence. In the South, where most African Americans were slaves, blacks inclined to be pro-British, for the British promised freedom in return for military service.*

Nova Scotia. In 1812, 80 percent of the population of Upper Canada (Ontario) was American-born.

A majority of northern Anglicans were Loyalists. So were some rich merchants with close commercial ties to Britain and, in the South, many farmers from the backcountry Regulator counties. Imperial officials supported the Crown, of course, as did some rich South Carolina and Georgia planters who feared that the social disruptions that accompany war would lead to slave uprisings.

In fact, the British actively sought and won support among southern slaves by offering freedom in return for military service. Some 50,000 African Americans ran away from their masters during the war, many of the men enlisting with the British. After the war, Britain evacuated about 20,000 blacks to Nova Scotia, England, Jamaica, and Sierra Leone in West Africa.

Alexander Hamilton, Washington's aide-de-camp, urged southern patriots to free their slaves if they agreed to take up arms on the American side. "I have no doubt," he wrote, "that the Negroes will make excellent soldiers." He got nowhere. Not even Washington, sacrificing a great deal for the cause, freed any of his slaves for military service. Free northern blacks inclined to be patriots. About 5,000 African Americans donned American uniforms.

Indians were also divided in their choice of sides. After first declaring neutrality, the Iroquois Confederacy split wide open. The Oneida and Tuscarora were patriots. The Seneca, Cayuga, and Mohawk were led to the British side by a high-ranking brother and sister, Joseph Brant and Mary Brant, who believed Iroquois lands would be more secure under British than under American rule.

Patriot Chances

If the odds were unpromising, the patriot cause was far from doomed. The Americans were fighting a defensive war in their homeland, a kind of conflict that bestows a number of advantages on the rebels. Militarily, the patriots did not have to destroy the British army. Rebels on their own ground need only to hold on and hold out until weariness, demoralization, dissent, and a telling defeat here and there take their toll on the enemy.

An army attempting to suppress a rebellion, by contrast, must wipe out the enemy force and then occupy and pacify the entire country. The patriots' loyal friend in Parliament, Edmund Burke, pointed out the immensity of this challenge as early as 1775. "The use of force alone is but temporary," he said. "It may subdue for a moment; but it does not remove the necessity of subduing again; and a nation is not governed which is perpetually to be conquered."

The British never were able to crush the patriot military; they came close only once. Redcoats occupied most port cities through most of the war. As late as 1780, they captured Charleston. But only one American in twenty lived in the seaports. The countryside remained largely under patriot control, a sanctuary for rebel armies. The huge British garrison had to be provisioned from abroad. Even grain for horses was carried by ship from England and Ireland. At one point, British commanders believed they would have to import hay!

The patriots had British friends. Influential politicians like Burke, Charles Fox, John Wilkes, and the Marquis of Rockingham sniped at Lord North's ministry throughout the war. They believed that the Americans were more right than wrong. Even Lord North had his doubts, grave ones; but he was fiercely loyal to the king, who had none.

The patriots also had reason to hope for foreign help. Since 1763, the major powers of Europe had been uneasy with Great Britain's preeminence. In Spanish Louisiana, Governor Bernardo de Gálvez provided arms to the Americans from the start. France, so recently humiliated by the British in North America, India, and Europe, was even more helpful. In May 1776, the French government began to funnel money and arms to the rebels through a not-so-secret agent, Pierre de Beaumarchais, who also provided money to the Americans from his own purse. During the first two years of the war, 80 percent of the patriots' gunpowder came from France.

Business and Pleasure in Paris

In September 1776, the Continental Congress sent Benjamin Franklin, 70 years old but just slightly creaky, to Paris to lobby for a French alliance. Franklin was a social sensation. The French aristocracy was enamored of him. Wigged and powdered ladies and lords were in the throes of a "noble savage" craze. The gist of the fad, based on the writings of Jean-Jacques Rousseau, was that primitives like peasants and the rustic Americans led happy, wholesome lives because of their simplicity and closeness to nature.

Queen Marie Antoinette had a model peasant village built at Versailles, a kind of private theme park. She and her ladies-in-waiting dressed like shepherdesses, milked well-scrubbed cows, and giggled along behind flocks of perfumed geese. Well aware of this nonsense, Franklin (who preferred the high life) made a point of appearing at court and balls wearing homespun wool clothing, no wig on his bald head, and the rimless bifocal spectacles he had invented.

French high society loved it, but the foreign minister, Charles, comte de Vergennes, had his reservations. Quasi-secret arms shipments were one thing. Before Vergennes would commit the French army and navy to open war with Britain, he wanted evidence that the patriots were more than rioters. He insisted on seeing an American victory in a major battle. Through 1776 and most of 1777, the Americans provided little but defeats.

THE TIMES THAT TRY MEN'S SOULS

General Howe, who took command of all British forces despite his comeuppance at Bunker Hill, had learned to be more cautious. He meant to move only when sure of the consequences. Early in 1776, caution dictated that he should evacuate Boston. (Edmund Burke, no soldier, had said the same thing a year earlier.) The citizens of Boston were overwhelmingly anti-British, and, when Massachusetts general Henry Knox arrived outside Boston with 43 cannons and 16 big mortars from Fort Ticonderoga, Washington positioned them on Dorchester Heights, high ground south of the city. If there was a bombardment, Howe's army would be devastated. Washington agreed to allow the redcoats to board ships without firing; after resting in Nova Scotia, Howe decided to relocate his headquarters to New York, where Loyalists were more numerous. Washington would have to fight on ground more favorable to the British.

The Battle for New York

On July 2, 1776, the same day the Continental Congress voted for independence, Howe landed 10,000 men on Staten Island, just south of Manhattan. In New York harbor, he had another 20,000 troops on 400 transport vessels, two men-of-war, and 25 frigates, with 1,200 cannons and 13,000 seamen under the command of his brother, Lord Richard Howe. After a few weeks, Howe invaded Long Island, where Washington's much smaller force had dug in. The American position was untenable, as Washington knew. Control of New York City depended on controlling the waters that surround it. Against Admiral Howe's armada, Washington could call on only a few hundred fishermen from Massachusetts to ferry his soldiers about.

Vision of the Future
Circumstances, John Adams believed, made him a politician and a revolutionary. But he envisioned another kind of future for his country:

I must study politics and war, that my sons may have liberty to study mathematics and philosophy, geography, natural history and naval architecture, navigation, commerce, and agriculture, in order to give their children a right to study painting, poetry, music, architecture, statuary, tapestry and porcelain.

Military Music
Drum, fife, and trumpet were an essential part of armies. Boys of 12 and 13 beat snare drums to set the cadence for soldiers on the march. With his men stepping off 96 paces of 30 inches each in a minute, a commander knew that the army covered 3 miles in 50 minutes, allowing 10 minutes per hour for a breather and a drink.

Fifers played both to entertain the men and to communicate orders: "Pioneers' March" was the signal for road-clearing crews to get started ahead of the infantry. "Roast Beef" meant it was time to eat. Fife and drum were also vital in battle. The men could hear them above the roar of firearms when they might not hear an officer's shouts.

Cavalry also used music for communication, but kettle drums instead of snare drums so as not to be confused with infantry. Cavalry used valveless trumpets (bugles) instead of fifes because, requiring only one hand, bugles could be played on horseback.

On August 27, the Howes almost surrounded Washington at the Battle of Long Island, but the Americans slipped away to fortifications on Brooklyn Heights, just across the East River from Manhattan. Again the redcoats and Hessians punished the 5,000 patriots, but, in a brilliantly executed overnight maneuver, Washington's fishermen managed to spirit the bulk of the army to Manhattan. Howe pursued him, capturing 3,000 at Fort Washington and forcing General Nathaniel Greene to abandon Fort Lee, across the Hudson River in New Jersey. Once again, Washington and his bedraggled troops escaped within hours of capture, north to White Plains and then across the Hudson into New Jersey.

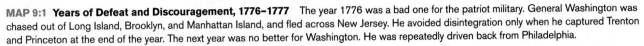

MAP 9:1 Years of Defeat and Discouragement, 1776–1777   The year 1776 was a bad one for the patriot military. General Washington was chased out of Long Island, Brooklyn, and Manhattan Island, and fled across New Jersey. He avoided disintegration only when he captured Trenton and Princeton at the end of the year. The next year was no better for Washington. He was repeatedly driven back from Philadelphia.

The Fox and the Hounds

General Howe was having a good time. The campaign reminded his officers of the gentry's favorite sport, the fox hunt. When the Americans were on the run north of New York, the British infuriated Washington, always supersensitive about his dignity, by sounding the traditional bugle call of the chase.

In truth, Washington's army was as desperate as a fox dodging hounds. Washington had to retreat rapidly across New Jersey to avoid another fight. When he crossed the Delaware River into Pennsylvania, his men were demoralized and ready to desert en masse. In Philadelphia, one day's march to the south, the Continental Congress panicked and fled to Baltimore.

"These are the times that try men's souls," Thomas Paine wrote. "The summer soldier and the sunshine patriot will, in this crisis, shrink from the service of his country." Thousands of captured patriot soldiers in New York and New Jersey took an oath of allegiance to the Crown. The Revolution was close to being snuffed out before all the signatures were affixed to the Declaration of Independence.

But William Howe soldiered by the book, and the book said that an army went into winter quarters when the leaves fell. Howe settled into New York, where his mistress and a lively round of dinners and parties beckoned. He recalled the hounds from Washington's hocks, leaving only small garrisons of Hessians to guard Trenton and Princeton, the front line.

The Crossing of the Delaware

Washington was no more an innovator than Howe was. Had his army not been near disintegration, he too would have followed the book into winter quarters. Instead, on Christmas night, the fishermen rowed the army across the Delaware River into New Jersey, the boats dodging ice floes and, in a thick fog, one another. The troops marched nine miles to Trenton, the most isolated British outpost. At dawn, they caught the Hessians in their bedrolls and none the better for their holiday celebrations. Washington captured almost the entire garrison of 900, while sustaining only five American casualties.

An annoyed Howe sent two forces to stop Washington before the Americans could press close enough to New York to ruin the holidays. Washington wisely avoided a fight with General Charles Cornwallis, but, on January 3, 1777, he defeated a small garrison at Princeton. Cornwallis held the line at New Brunswick, within range of reinforcement from New York. Washington set up winter quarters at Morristown on the Delaware.

Trenton and Princeton were small battles, but in winning them, Washington saved the patriot cause. His sally across the Delaware provided a boost indispensable to patriot morale. Still, Howe's position in New York was snug and dominant. The strategy he hatched with his subordinates between parties was promising.

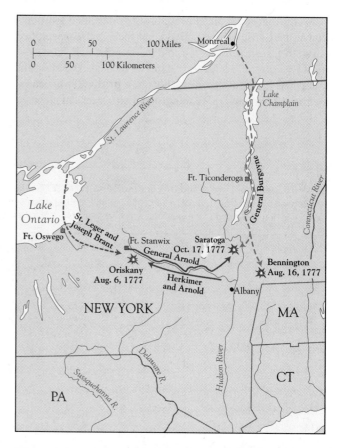

MAP 9:2 **Victory at Saratoga, October 17, 1777** While Washington's army sat outside Philadelphia defeated and demoralized, the British and Hessians suffered a series of defeats in New York at Fort Stanwix, Bennington, and, most important, at Saratoga, where a British army surrendered. Saratoga heartened the French to join the Americans as allies.

The Hudson River Strategy

Howe's plan to win the war in 1777, conveyed by letter to Lord Germain, was to march north up the Hudson, joining forces with Iroquois warriors led east on the Mohawk River by Barry St. Leger and with a larger British army moving south out of Montreal. This pincers movement would isolate New England from the rest of the colonies. With the Royal Navy blockading New England's ports, the British army could easily subdue Massachusetts, Connecticut, and Rhode Island. Thinly populated New Hampshire would fall into line. If the loss of New England was not enough to persuade Washington to ask for terms, the British would move against his army at their leisure.

It was an excellent plan. Germain was persuaded by General John Burgoyne, who had returned to Boston from England and was betting his career on it. A playwright and charming bon vivant popular in London society, Burgoyne would command the army of 8,000 strong, with more than 100 cannons, in Montreal—visions of military glory! Howe, in New York, saw Burgoyne's visions too; Burgoyne was setting things up so that he, not Howe, would get credit for the campaign. Resentment made Howe receptive to the pleas of a prominent Loyalist then in New York, Joseph Galloway of Pennsylvania, to march south rather than north to join Burgoyne. Galloway argued that taking Philadelphia, the colonies' largest city and the de facto capital of the rebellion, would knock the Middle Colonies out of the war and demoralize the rest of the country.

The Watershed Campaign of 1777

In the summer of 1777, leaving just 3,000 men in New York under General Henry Clinton, Howe moved by sea to Pennsylvania. Washington followed overland and, yet again, on September 11, was defeated at Brandywine Creek, southwest of Philadelphia. On September 26, after another victory at Paoli, Howe occupied Philadelphia. On October 4, Washington attacked at the suburb of Germantown. Although he came close to victory this time, he was repulsed again. His army had to fall back to winter quarters at Valley Forge, not even a town like Morristown but rolling farmland. Howe was again ensconced in a comfortable city.

Alas for glory, the success of Howe's campaign was tarnished by news from the forests of New York. In June, Burgoyne had left Montreal, heading south; in August, Loyalists and Iroquois commanded by St. Leger and Mohawk chief Joseph Brant advanced from the west. Their army disintegrated after a series of battles with Nicholas Herkimer and Benedict Arnold around Fort Stanwix, not halfway across the state. Burgoyne's march went well at first. The ancient Indian trail from Montreal to Lake Champlain was now a road. The lake itself provided an even better highway for 125 miles. Fort Ticonderoga, at the foot of Lake Champlain, fell without a fight.

Then the isolation of his position began to take a toll. Burgoyne's artillery and the provisions required by 8,000 troops (and 2,000 camp followers) could be moved only slowly on a trail. Burgoyne's personal baggage was immense, filling 30 carts with a living and dining suite fit for the toast of London. There were heavy beds and tables, linens, china, crystal, silverware, wine, and brandy. Patriots felled trees across the road, creating a far more difficult job of chopping for British axmen. During one three-week spell, Burgoyne's army advanced less than a mile a day.

Bad news fell on Gentleman Johnny like summer rain. He learned there would be no reinforcements under St. Leger and Brant. Hessians Burgoyne sent east on the apparently easy task of seizing supplies in Bennington, Vermont, were wiped out by militia. In a series of skirmishes around Saratoga, another fort, Burgoyne lost more men. By this time, Burgoyne knew that Howe was en route to Philadelphia.

He should have backtracked to Canada. The planned occupation of New England was out of the question. The best Burgoyne could hope for was to save his army. But there was plenty of claret and brandy left. Burgoyne dug in and hoped for help from General Clinton in New York. American General Horatio Gates jumped on Burgoyne's blunder and surrounded him. On October 17, Gates accepted the surrender of 5,700 soldiers. The Battle of Saratoga was the most important event of the year, perhaps of the war. All New England remained under patriot control until, much later, the British took Newport, Rhode Island, from the sea, which, even then, they could hold only by tying down a sizable fleet.

A Turning Point

Saratoga was precisely the news for which Franklin and his colleagues were waiting in Paris. The victory allayed Vergennes's doubts about the patriots' chances. The rout of an army of 8,000 crack redcoats and German mercenaries was no skirmish. When Lord North heard of the defeat, he wrote to Franklin that King George would end the war on the terms demanded by Americans up to July 1776. The Intolerable Acts and other obnoxious laws enacted between 1763 and 1775 would be repealed. Great Britain would cede to the colonies control of their internal affairs in return for swearing loyalty to the king. In effect, Lord North proposed to organize the empire as a commonwealth of autonomous dominions, the status Britain was to accord Canada, Australia, and New Zealand in the nineteenth century.

But victory is a tonic, and American blood was up. By the end of 1777, American animosity toward the mother country had intensified. Patriot propagandists made hay of the murder and scalping of Jane McCrea (a Loyalist, ironically) by Indians under Burgoyne's command, who went unpunished. In New Jersey, British troops had brutally bullied farmers, raping women and girls. The old rallying cry "the rights of British subjects" had lost its magic. The French offered a military alliance that was more attractive than returning, however victoriously, to the British Empire.

War Crimes

Soldiers and Native Americans on both sides were guilty of atrocities. Colonel Henry Hamilton, the British commander of the fort at Detroit, was called the "Hair Buyer" because he paid Indians for patriot scalps, including those from the heads of women and children. In 1776, Cherokee devastated the Virginia and Carolina frontiers, massacring everyone they found. In July 1778, Loyalists and Indians scourged Pennsylvania's Wyoming Valley, and, in November, a similar force swept through Cherry Valley in New York. Two hundred patriots were murdered in Pennsylvania, 40 in Cherry Valley.

At King's Mountain in 1780, American troops fired on redcoats who had surrendered. Virginia and North Carolina militia burned 1,000 Cherokee villages and destroyed 50,000 bushels of corn, not bothering to count the fatalities. In March 1782, Pennsylvania militia murdered 96 Delaware Indians who had tried to stay out of the conflict.

▲ *Burgoyne's march from Montreal to Saratoga was vexed by frustration and defeat at every turn. When he surrendered to General Horatio Gates in October 1777, the news was enough to bring France into the war as a patriot ally. Americans disappointed in Washington, who was being repeatedly defeated outside of Philadelphia, plotted to replace him as overall commander with Gates. They failed, fortunately. Gates was nowhere near Washington's equal and, later in the war, was a rather disappointing general.*

The Continental Insurance Companies

Foreign Friends

In December 1777, Vergennes formally recognized the United States. In February 1778, he signed a treaty of alliance, to go into effect if France and Britain went to war (which they did in June). The agreement provided for close commercial ties between France and the United States and stated that France would assert no claims to Canada after the war. France's reward at the peace table would be in the West Indies.

The war could not have been won without the French alliance. Not only did "America's oldest friend" pour money and men into the conflict; France provided a fleet, which the Americans lacked and could not hope to create. Individual patriot seamen like John Paul Jones (who said, "I have not yet begun to fight") and John Barry (no particularly memorable sayings) won naval victories. But the superiority of the Royal Navy enabled the British to hold Philadelphia and New York for most of the war, and even to capture Savannah and Newport near the end. Without the French navy, the entire coastline might have been blockaded.

In fact, patriot merchant ships had little difficulty moving goods in and out of the many small ports on the Atlantic. Until 1781, when the British occupied the island, Dutch St. Eustatius in the West Indies was, along with French Martinique, the major destination of American merchants. Holland was neutral, but well disposed to the Americans. Ships of all nations brought cargoes destined for America to St. Eu-statius, where American ships collected them for delivery to the continent. When the British fleet finally seized St. Eustatius with a surprise attack, they found 50 American merchant ships in the harbor, and 2,000 American seamen in the port.

Spain had no love for anticolonial rebels but, in her own interests, sent Bernardo de Gálvez into British Florida, where he soon occupied every fort. Vergennes averted a war brewing between Prussia and Austria that would have tied down French troops in Europe, a traditional British objective. He persuaded both countries, as well as Russia, to declare their neutrality. Vergennes denied Britain the allies she sorely needed.

Mercenaries for Liberty

Peace in Europe meant that many military professionals were unhappily unemployed. Aristocratic officers, hungry for commissions with salaries attached, flocked to the United States. There was plenty of deadwood in the bunch; but others were able soldiers, and some were motivated by more than money.

Commodore John Barry was an Irishman; John Paul Jones, a Scot. Marie-Joseph, marquis de Lafayette was a 19-year-old noble (the British called him "the boy") who proved to be an excellent field commander. Also an idealist was Casimir Pulaski, a Pole who had fought Russia for his country's independence. Recruited in Paris by Benjamin Franklin, Pulaski was a romantic figure, a cavalry commander in gaudy uniform and waxed mustache. He was killed

Possibly more valuable than combat officers were specialists like Thaddeus Kosciuszko, a Polish engineer who was an expert in building fortifications, a military field in which few Americans were trained. Friedrich Wilhelm von Steuben, a Prussian who styled himself "Baron" (he was a captain, and there was no *Burke's Peerage* for German baronies), was an expert in drill. He supervised the training at Valley Forge in the winter of 1777–1778 that transformed Washington's continentals into a disciplined army. By 1781, fully one patriot officer in five was a foreigner.

The Continuing War

Steuben in particular arrived in the nick of time. Washington lost 2,500 men to disease and exposure during the winter at Valley Forge, and, by the spring of 1778, it was obvious that the war would go on for years. The Americans did not dare to force the issue in an all-or-nothing battle. Their strategy was to hold on, fighting only under auspicious conditions. Lord Germain and General Clinton (who took over from Howe in May 1778) could hope only to throttle the American economy with a naval blockade and concentrate land operations in the South.

Beginning with the occupation of Savannah, Georgia, in December 1778, the redcoats won a series of victories in the South, but they could not break the stalemate. For each British victory, the Americans won another, or, in losing ground, they cost the British so heavily that the redcoats had to return to the coast, within reach of supply ships.

The war wore heavily on the American side too. Prices of necessities soared. Imports were available only at exorbitant costs. When the Continental Congress failed to pay and provision troops in 1780 and 1781, mutinies erupted on the Connecticut, Pennsylvania, and New Jersey lines. In September 1780, Washington learned that Benedict Arnold, commanding the important fortress at West Point in New York, sold it and his services to the British for £20,000.

The campaign of 1781 opened with American spirits lower than they had been since before Trenton. Washington was idle outside New York. The most active British army, led by Lord Charles Cornwallis, lost a battle at Cowpens,

▲ *Benjamin Franklin, assigned to win an alliance with France, loved Paris and Versailles, and the French aristocracy adored him, titillated by his American simplicity, which Franklin encouraged. John Adams, also in Paris, thought Franklin spent much time partying (and lecherously courting a scandalous widow), but the old reprobate got the job done.*

leading a charge at the Battle of Savannah late in the war. Johann Kalb, a Bavarian who affected the title baron de Kalb, also lost his life during the war, at the Battle of Camden.

Jean-Baptiste, comte de Rochambeau, arrived in Newport, Rhode Island, in 1780 and played a key role in the decisive American victory at Yorktown, Virginia, the next year.

Despair at Valley Forge
The winter of 1777–1778 was extremely difficult for American soldiers. Inadequately fed, clothed, and sheltered at Valley Forge, many fell into deep despair. Albigence Waldo, a surgeon with Connecticut troops, wrote in his journal on December 14, 1777:

Poor food–hard lodging–cold weather–fatigue–nasty cloathes–nasty cookery–vomit half my time–smoked out of my senses–the Devil's in't–I can't endure it–Why are we sent here to starve and freeze?–What sweet felicities have I left at home: A charming wife–pretty children–good beds–good food–good cookery–all agreeable–all harmonious! Here all confusion–smoke and cold–hunger and filthyness–a pox on my bad luck!

▲ *Washington and "the boy," the French general Lafayette, at Valley Forge during the dismal winter (for the patriots) of 1777–1778. Lafayette was 25 years younger than Washington, but they became close friends almost from their first meeting and remained so until Washington's death. Lafayette regarded Washington as the giant of the age.*

South Carolina, but then repeatedly pummeled Nathaniel Greene the breadth of North Carolina. Cornwallis then joined with other commanders (including Benedict Arnold) to amass 7,500 men in Virginia.

An Opportunity for Washington

But Cornwallis had problems. Anywhere away from navigable waters was dangerous ground. On August 1, 1781, he set up what he regarded as a routine encampment at Yorktown, Virginia, on the same neck of land where the first permanent English settlement in America was planted. Cornwallis requested supplies and orders from General Clinton in New York. In mid-August, with Clinton dawdling, Washington learned that a French admiral, Count François de Grasse, was sailing from the West Indies to the Chesapeake Bay with 3,000 French troops aboard 25 warships.

Yorktown was George Washington's backyard. He knew the terrain intimately and realized that, if de Grasse could cut Cornwallis off, Washington had him trapped. He scrapped detailed, almost finalized plans for an assault on New York, maneuvered around the city so that a confused Clinton would sit tight, and raced his best units, from Rhode Island, New Jersey, and New York, across New Jersey. In September, his troops joined with others under Lafayette, Rochambeau, Steuben, and de Grasse. The combined army of 17,000 outnumbered Cornwallis's 8,000, almost the first time in the war that the patriots enjoyed numerical superiority.

Yorktown

Cornwallis did not panic. His men were well dug in, and he expected to move them out by sea, resuming the war of attrition elsewhere. But between September 5 and 10, de Grasse sent the British evacuation fleet sailing off empty to New York. Further defense was futile. On October 17, Cornwallis asked for terms, and on October 19, he surrendered.

Lord Cornwallis was no America basher. He had been only one of four lords in Parliament to oppose the Declaratory Act. But he found his defeat at Yorktown humiliating. Claiming sickness, he sent an aide to the field to surrender his sword. The aide tried to hand it to Rochambeau, but the French general gestured him to Washington. Rather than accept the symbol of capitulation from an inferior officer, Washington delegated the honors to General Benjamin Lincoln, whom the British had similarly humiliated at Charleston. During the ceremonies, the British army band played the hymn "The World Turn'd Upside Down."

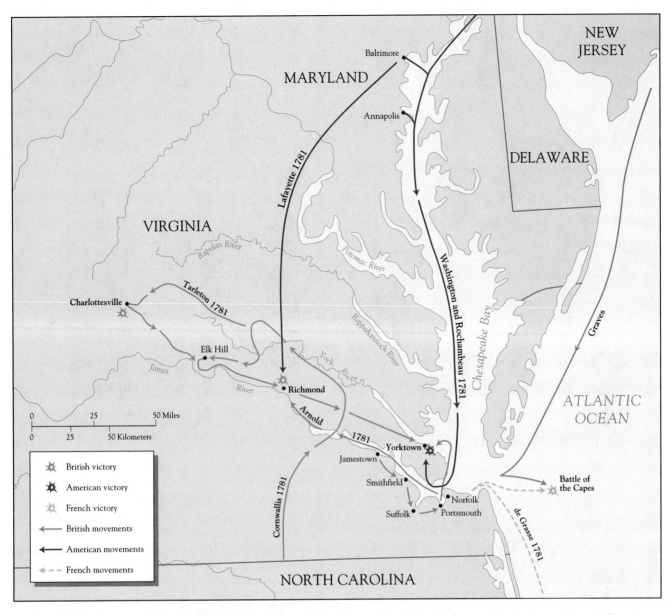

MAP 9:3 **The Battle of Yorktown, May–October 1781**   After wandering around South Carolina, harassed by American militia under Francis Marion, General Cornwallis moved into Virginia, setting up headquarters at Yorktown. There, he assumed, he could be resupplied or evacuated by sea. The coordinated arrival of a large American army and the French fleet resulted in the British defeat that ended the war.

The Treaty of Paris

The British could have fought on. They still had 44,000 troops in North America, far more than the patriots and the French. But eighteenth-century wars were fought with limited, practical objectives, balancing the values of the goals with the costs of reaching them. Rulers did not burrow into bunkers and tell their subjects to fight nobly on until the last of them was dead. In February 1782, the House of Commons voted to end the war. Lord North resigned and was succeeded by the marquis of Rockingham, the Whig who had arranged the repeal of the Stamp Act in 1766.

It took two years to put the Treaty of Paris together. In part, the delay was due to growing suspicions between the Americans and the French. And with good reason: The American delegation in Paris came to terms with the British without French knowledge. The treaty, signed in September 1783, recognized the independence of the United States with the Mississippi River the western boundary. Americans were to have fishing rights off British Newfoundland and Nova Scotia (which New Englander John Adams made his personal project), and the United States promised not to molest Loyalists and to urge the states to compensate them for property that had already been seized.

▲ *There are dozens of artists' depictions of the British surrender of Yorktown, each with its unique focus. This one makes a point more important than the contest of ceremonial one-upmanship between Cornwallis and Washington, emphasizing the critical part played by sea power—de Grasse's French fleet's control of the Chesapeake, which prevented British escape by ship.*

The "Father of His Country"

George Washington, heaped with adulation in Europe as well as America, was, in some ways, an unlikely "father of his country." In most of the particulars by which greatness is measured, Washington comes up short. He lacked originality and boldness. He was no thinker; he seems to have read little and contributed nothing to the literature of colonial protest. Personally, he was reserved, listening far more than speaking. As a field commander, his failures outnumbered his successes. During most of the war, his army was in retreat and more than once on the verge of disintegration.

And yet, it would be difficult to overstate Washington's role in the establishment of the American republic. It was in successful retreat that his military contribution to independence was invaluable. He kept an army in the field in the face of repeated defeats, superior British forces, inadequate provisions, disease, poor shelter, poor support from the Continental Congress, and even a cabal, after the campaign around Philadelphia, to replace him as commander of the army.

In order to explain Washington's achievement, it is necessary to fall back on the intangibles that transfixed his contemporaries. Radicals like Samuel Adams, conservatives like Alexander Hamilton, intellectuals like Thomas Jefferson, warriors like Israel Putnam, and cultivated European aristocrats like Lafayette and Rochambeau all deferred to the Virginian. Washington's deportment, integrity, personal dignity, and disdain for petty squabbles set him head and shoulders above the best of his contemporaries, just as his height of 6 feet 2 inches made him a very tall man in the eighteenth century. He held the Revolution together with that not quite definable quality known as "character." If such a notion rings a little sappy in our time, the dishonor is not to the era of the American Revolution.

Between Yorktown and the Treaty

Between 1781 and 1783, when the Treaty of Paris was signed, British troops remained in and around New York City, so the Continental Congress could not very well send the men of the Continental Army home. They set up quarters in Newburgh, New York. The congress, as always, was negligent in providing for them, and the soldiers were restive. Washington, who sorely wanted to get back to his Virginia plantation, remained with the troops. He lobbied the Continental Congress for pensions and bounties, and, by his own example, discouraged a full-blown mutiny. (A smaller camp of veterans in Lancaster, Pennsylvania, did march on Philadelphia, causing the members of the Continental Congress to flee.)

British soldiers left New York City once the treaty was signed. For decades, New Yorkers celebrated Evacuation Day, November 25, with more gusto than they observed July 4. Independence Day was comparatively decorous; Evacuation Day was party time.

Ignoring the Revolution

John Adams estimated that a third of Americans were patriots, a third were Loyalists, and a third were not particularly interested in who won or lost the war. Francis Hopkinson, a patriot and poet from New Jersey, called the patriots "birds" and the Tories "beasts"; the others were "bats," cozying up to whichever species, haired or winged, seemed to be on top at the moment.

This is unfair; Adams's less acerbic characterization of the "neutrals" is better. However great the issue, whatever the historical era, and whoever the people involved, a large proportion of every population sees no compelling reason to take an interest, let alone to take sides. They "mind their own business."

Such Americans were to be found in every section, but particularly west of the Appalachians. There was combat there, but battles were small and isolated, with mostly Indians involved. The most famous westerner (and Indian fighter) of the era, Daniel Boone, although a major in the Virginia militia, avoided involvement in the great cause, continuing to mind his businesses of hunting, trail blazing, road building, and land speculation. His reputation suffered. He was accused of collaborating with the Shawnee Indians and, through them, with their British allies. Had this been true, and proved, he could have been shot as a traitor.

Born near Reading, Pennsylvania, in 1734, Boone emigrated to western North Carolina. In 1755, driving a wagon, he was part of the disastrous Braddock campaign in western Pennsylvania, but, given his lowly job, did not make the acquaintance of Braddock's young aide, George Washington.

Like Washington, however, Boone survived, spending most of the 1760s and 1770s in the forests of what is now Kentucky. The land there appealed to him as a commodity on which he could get rich by developing and selling, particularly since Kentucky's Native American population was sparse. Both the Cherokee from the south and the Shawnee from the north hunted in Kentucky—Boone had his run-ins with both tribes—but neither lived there in great numbers.

In 1775, when the fighting began back east and the Second Continental Congress assembled, Boone was supervising 30 axmen building the "Wilderness Road" through the Cumberland Gap into Kentucky and connecting it with the Warrior's Path. Just when news of the Declaration of Independence and the full-scale war with the British reached him is not clear, but his only military service was a scouting mission for the Virginia militia, when he was captured by Shawnee and taken to be questioned by British officers north of the Ohio River. Because Boone was gone for a year and returned both unharmed and with nothing to say, he was accused of being a Tory.

Boone denied it and refused to elaborate. He returned to developing Boonesboro and other frontier settlements in Kentucky. His fame as a woodsman and pioneer—Boone engineered a spectacular and well-publicized rescue of his daughter, who had been kidnapped by Indians—made him Kentucky's most effective promoter, but as a land speculator, he was a failure. In part, he was too possessed of a sense of personal honor to succeed in a business in which ethics were a prohibitive burden. He sold thousands of acres to compensate associates for losses in which he shared and felt responsible. He spent thousands on lawyers but had no stomach for going to court himself, whence he lost other huge tracts of Old Kentuck'.

In 1799, Kentucky's most famous resident left the state for Missouri and never returned, despite numerous invitations. He was bitter and broke. When, in 1815, a creditor traveled to Missouri hoping to get Boone to pay him, Boone's son told him, "You have come a great distance to suck a bull and, I reckon, you will have to go home dry." Boone died in 1820, a national hero with a shadow hanging over his patriotism.

for FURTHER READING

See J. R. Alden, *A History of the American Revolution,* 1969; Robert Middlekauff, *The Glorious Cause: The American Revolution, 1763–1789,* 1982; Howard Peckham, *The War for Independence,* 1952; and Christopher Ward, *The War of the Revolution,* 1952.

Focused on special aspects of the war years are Samuel F. Bemis, *The Diplomacy of the American Revolution,* 1935; Don Higginbotham, *The War of American Independence: Military Attitudes, Policies, and Practice,* 1971; J. Franklin Jameson, *The American Revolution Considered as a Social Movement,* 1926; Robert M. Calhoon, *The Loyalists in Revolutionary America,* 1973;

Richard B. Morris, *The Peacemakers,* 1965; Mary Beth Norton, *Liberty's Daughters,* 1980; Charles Royster, *A Revolutionary People at War,* 1979; John Shy, *A People Numerous and Armed,* 1976; and Paul H. Smith, *Loyalists and Redcoats,* 1964. Barbara W. Tuchman, *The First Salute: A View of the American Revolution,* 1988, emphasizes the important role of the French fleet in the war and the role of the Dutch island of St. Eustatius.

Two classic biographies of George Washington are James T. Flexner, *George Washington in the American Revolution,* 1968, and Douglas S. Freeman, *George Washington,* 1948, 1957.

Visit the source collections at http://ajaccess.wadsworth.com and http://infotrac.thomsonlearning.com, and use the Search function with the following key terms to explore documents, images, audio and video clips, articles, and commentary related to the material in this chapter:

Daniel Boone   Saratoga
General William Howe   Yorktown
George Washington

Additional resources, exercises, and Internet links related to this chapter are available on *The American Past* Web site: http://history.wadsworth.com/americanpast7e.

HISTORY ONLINE

The American Revolution
www.multied.com/wars.html
Maps and descriptions of important battles.

Espionage in the Revolution
www.si.umich.edu/spies/index-main2.html
Techniques of spying, accounts of espionage, and the people involved.

INVENTING
A COUNTRY

*American Constitutions
1781–1789*

The National Archives

*Without some alteration in our political creed, the
superstructure we have been seven years raising at the
expense of so much blood and treasure, must fall. We are
fast verging to anarchy and confusion.*

George Washington

*I am uneasy and apprehensive, more so than during the
war. . . . We are going and doing wrong, and therefore I
look forward to evils and calamities.*

John Jay

AMERICANS WERE NOT the first people to fight for independence. The history of empires is the history of uprisings to be free of imperial control. The American Revolution
was, however, singular in the fact that rebels had to invent a
country and a sense of common nationality. They were not
already "a people" as the Dutch were when they fought to
be independent of Spain. Nor had they been subdued by
foreigners, as were the periodically rebellious Irish. Most
Americans were British by descent; those who were not had
emigrated into a British society—all but the Africans, gladly.
Moreover, the 13 colonies—states now—had no political
links with one another before the Revolution. Their only
links were with the mother country.

The political superstructure the patriots forged, the Articles of Confederation, was just a little more than an alliance of independent states with a common foe. Only in
1787, a decade after the Declaration of Independence and
six years after Yorktown, in the Constitution that remains
the basic law of the land today, did "we the people of the
United States" venture to ordain "a more perfect union."

THE REVOLUTION ON PAPER

The constitutions of 11 of the 13 states were drawn up during the Revolutionary War and reflected the patriots' hostility to most things British. (Connecticut and Rhode Island,
quite democratic as colonies, merely rephrased their charters.) The simple fact that they were written and comprehensive, covering every contingency of which the men who
drafted them could think, was itself a break with British practice. The largely unwritten British constitution had served
Britain well and still does. But the debate over the extent of
Parliament's powers was central to the grievances that led to
the Revolution. The patriots believed that Parliament had

violated the unwritten constitution in trying to tax the colonies, but they could not win the point without resorting to force of arms. Written constitutions could be violated too, of course. However, as Thomas Jefferson wrote, "They furnish a text to which those who are watchful may again rally and recall the people."

Limitation of Power, Elimination of Privilege

In Great Britain, Parliament is the government. There is no appeal of what it does, neither to courts nor, by the eighteenth century, to king or queen. The Americans' state constitutions, however, were written not by their little parliaments, the state assemblies, but by conventions elected specifically for the purpose of constitution making. The conventions' work was then ratified by a popular election and could be altered only by a similar procedure, *not* by the legislature. The principle that sovereignty (ultimate government power) rested with the people was thereby institutionalized.

Because the patriots resented the colonial office-holding elite, they guarded against creating their own by requiring that most officials stand for election annually. Many state constitutions (and the Articles of Confederation) limited to a few years the term a person elected to office might serve.

The authors of the first American constitutions feared executive power most of all; the royal governors had been George III's executive officers, agents doing his (and Parliament's) bidding. In order to preclude the emergence of similar centers of power independent of elected assemblies, the new state governors were little more than administrators and ceremonial heads of state. In Pennsylvania, which had the most radical state constitution, there was no governor. Nor was there a chief executive in the government created by the Articles of Confederation.

Other old resentments surfaced in the movement to separate church and state. Except in New England, the Church of England had been the established church, supported by taxes. (The Anglican clergy had been largely Loyalist.) Patriots in the former royal colonies disestablished the Anglican Church—abolished its privileged position and financial support—transforming it into the Protestant Episcopal Church, a private denomination on a par with the Presbyterian and Baptist Churches and, in most states, even the Catholic Church.

And They're Off . . .
Reaction against things British in the wake of the Revolution found form in more than constitution writing. The adoption of the dollar, which was Spanish, rather than the British pound as the American unit of currency was, in part, a patriotic gesture. It was also just after the Revolution that American horse races were run counterclockwise around tracks rather than clockwise, as they were in Britain and had been in the colonies.

Democratic Drift

There were limits to denominational neutrality. In New Hampshire, Connecticut, and Massachusetts, where the pro-patriot Congregationalist Church was established, it remained tax-supported for 40 to 50 years after independence. Eight more state constitutions expressed some preference for Protestant Christianity. Roman Catholics were not permitted to vote in North Carolina until 1835. A Jew or nonbeliever could vote in Pennsylvania but could not hold public office.

Nevertheless, in every new state, the right to vote was extended to more people than had enjoyed it under the Crown. In Georgia, Pennsylvania, and Vermont (a state in fact if not in name), every adult male taxpayer could vote. In most of the others, the property qualification was lowered so that only a few free white males were excluded. Women could vote in New Jersey. In New Jersey, North Carolina, and Massachusetts, free blacks who met other tests were enfranchised. In 1777, New York joined Rhode Island in granting full citizenship to Jews.

Eight states specified rights that were guaranteed to every citizen, beginning with Virginia's constitution in 1776. After the vice admiralty courts, the quartering acts, and arbitrary actions by the British army, the patriots were determined that there would be no vagueness on the subject of government's power over an individual. The rights later listed in the first 10 amendments to the United States Constitution, the Bill of Rights, were found in one or another of the state constitutions written during the Revolution.

Liberty's Limits: Sex and Race

In 1777, when the air was thick with talk of liberties, Abigail Adams wrote to her husband, John, who was engaged in writing the Articles of Confederation, to plead for the rights of "the ladies." But neither Mr. Adams nor many other Americans, male or female, seriously entertained the notion that there was anything amiss in the inferior civil status of women. Only in 1792 would Mary Wollstonecraft publish *Vindication of the Rights of Woman,* and decades passed before noticeable numbers of men and women absorbed her

---

Gradual Emancipation in Pennsylvania
A Pennsylvania law of 1780 proclaimed that no more slaves could be brought into the state and that all children born to slaves in Pennsylvania would be free at age 28. The act was more than obliging to slave owners in the state. Although their claim that they had compensation coming for supporting the children of their slaves when they were children had merit, compensating a slave owner for a child's sustenance with the fruits of his labor until age 28 was clearly excessive. In fact, many Pennsylvania slave owners manumitted their slaves in the decades after the Revolution. Others, however, found a loophole in the gradual emancipation law, selling slaves under age 28 out of state.

▲ *Women (and free blacks) who were heads of household could vote in New Jersey between 1776 and 1807. They were disenfranchised the latter year because, apparently, too many were exercising their right.*

Petition for Freedom

On November 12, 1779, 19 of New Hampshire's African Americans petitioned the state assembly to free slaves on the basis of the ideals of liberty that patriots were asserting. The petition concluded:

Your humble slaves most devoutly pray for the sake of injured liberty, for the sake of justice, humanity and the rights of mankind, for the honor of religion and by all that is dear, that your honors would graciously interpose in our behalf, and enact such laws and regulations, as you in your wisdom think proper, whereby we may regain our liberty and be ranked in the class of free agents, and that the name of slave may not more be heard in a land gloriously contending for the sweets of freedom.

feminist views. New Jersey, still writing "he or she" in reference to voters in 1790, rescinded female enfranchisement (and the enfranchisement of African Americans) in 1807.

In the northern states, slavery was dying out with or without the Revolution. Quasi-independent Vermont abolished the institution in 1777. In Massachusetts in 1780, Elizabeth Freeman (her slave name was "Mumber") sued for her freedom on the grounds that the state constitution stated "all men are born free and equal." The courts agreed, thus ending slavery in the Bay State by court order. New Hampshire followed suit in 1784. Pennsylvania, Connecticut, and Rhode Island adopted formulas that eliminated slavery gradually,

dooming the institution while not financially injuring slave owners. In all, 11 states abolished the slave trade, outlawed the buying and selling of slaves, or prohibitively taxed such transactions, a halfway measure clearly intended as a prelude to further antislavery action.

These 11 states, of course, included most southern states. Southern patriots could hardly ignore the fact that they were fighting for liberty—*they* would not be slaves!—while they held African Americans in bondage. Delaware, Maryland, and Virginia made manumission (freeing individual slaves) easier. By 1810, a fifth of Maryland's slaves were manumitted.

In 1784, Patrick Henry hoped to extend Virginia's liberties to Native Americans when he proposed that the state pay a bounty of £10 to every free white person who married an Indian and £5 for each child born of such unions. Another Virginian, John Marshall, later commented that the bill "would have been advantageous to this country" had it been enacted. He added, "Our prejudices, however, opposed themselves to our interests, and operated too powerfully for them."

AMERICA UNDER THE ARTICLES OF CONFEDERATION

The constitution written to coordinate the affairs of all 13 states—the Articles of Confederation—reflected the same ideals as the state constitutions. Drafted during the heady years 1776 and 1777, the Articles of Confederation created no president or other independent executive. Congress alone was the government. Members were elected annually and could serve only three years out of every six. That is, a man elected to Congress three years in a row was ineligible to serve again until he sat out three years.

Divided Authority

Under the Articles of Confederation, the United States of America was explicitly *not* a nation. It was "a firm league of friendship." Georgia, North Carolina, and the rest retained their "sovereignty, freedom, and independence," each state the equal of every other. Members of Congress, for example, voted not as individuals but as members of their state's delegation. If two of three delegates voted "nay," their state cast a single negative vote.

Congress was authorized to wage war and make peace, to maintain an army and navy, and to supervise diplomatic relations with foreign countries and the Indian nations. Congress was entrusted with maintaining a post office and empowered to establish a system of uniform weights and measures. Congress could mint coins, issue paper money, and borrow money.

Having granted these powers to Congress, however, the Articles of Confederation also permitted the states to issue money and to ignore Congress's standards of measurement. The states could individually negotiate commercial treaties with other countries. A state could even, "with the consent of Congress," declare war as a state on a foreign power. It would be quite "constitutional," in other words, if Delaware went to war with Holland while neighboring New Jersey agreed by treaty to sell gunpowder to the Dutch.

The weakness of the ties binding the states was not the consequence of idiocy, incompetence, or even awkward compromise. Weakness was deliberately written into the Articles of Confederation because of the revolutionary generation's aversion to a powerful central government. Nor was the Confederation government a disaster. On the contrary, it was under the Articles of Confederation that Americans defeated Europe's premier military power. The Confederation Congress created a bureaucracy that adequately administered the day-to-day business of the government. States did contribute, albeit reluctantly sometimes, to the Confederation treasury. And Congress solved a problem that might easily have torn apart a far more powerful government.

The Western Lands

The issue was the land beyond the Appalachians that Great Britain had closed to settlement in 1763 and ceded to the United States in the Treaty of Paris. The question was, who owned it? Colonial charters were responsible for the problem. They had been drafted at different times by different British officials with little knowledge of North American geography and little concern about lands that were then wilderness firmly under the control of Indian tribes.

So the boundaries of the former colonies overlapped in a snarl of conflicting claims. Virginia's colonial charter gave the state boundaries that flared both north and south at the crest of the mountains, encompassing the entire trans-Appalachian region. Connecticut conceded that New York's and Pennsylvania's charters, drafted later than Connecticut's, removed the lands of New York and Pennsylvania from what had been Connecticut's jurisdiction, but the state claimed a "western reserve" beyond those states in what is now Ohio. Massachusetts, New York, North Carolina, South Carolina, and Georgia also had claims in the west.

The snarl was complicated by the fears of six states with no chartered claims to western lands: New Hampshire, Rhode Island, New Jersey, Pennsylvania, Delaware, and Maryland. Reasonably enough, leaders of those states worried that the states with western lands would be able to finance themselves indefinitely by selling trans-Appalachian land, whereas the states without western lands would drive their citizens out because they had to tax them more heavily. On these grounds, Maryland refused to sign the Articles of Confederation until 1781.

There was an obvious solution, suggested by John Dickinson as early as 1776. However, because it called on human beings to give up potential wealth in the interests of an ideal, it was not a solution that promised to be easy. Dickinson proposed that the landed states cede their western territories to the Confederation so that all states shared in the benefits of owning them. Amazingly, cession turned out to be rather easy. Virginia—with the greatest and best western claims—had good reasons to turn its western lands over to Congress. Virginians played prominent roles in the Confederation government, and they did not want to see it fall apart. Moreover, many Virginians believed that free republican institutions could not survive in large states. For the sake of hard-won freedoms, they preferred to see new states, approximately the size of the original states, carved out of the west rather than bickering endlessly in a fight to retain an unmanageable "Great Virginia."

The Northwest Ordinances

In January 1781, Virginia ceded the northern part of its western lands to the Confederation. Within a few years, all the

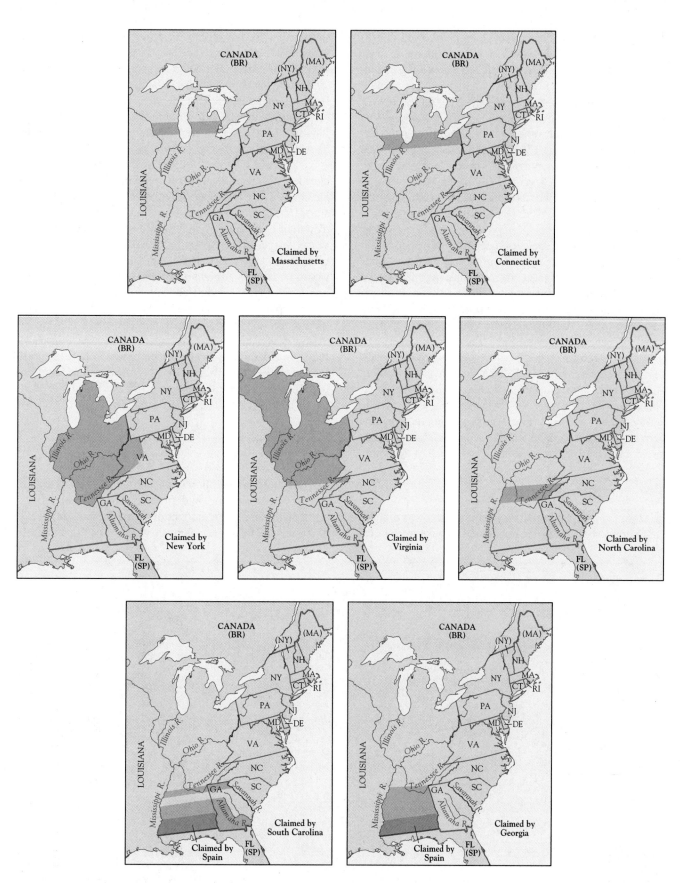

MAP 10:1 The States' Western Claims   British carelessness in drawing colonial boundaries in the west resulted in a tangle of conflicting claims. The crisis did not lead to interstate wars because all the states with western claims ceded those claims (some reluctantly) to the Confederation Congress.

states with western claims except Georgia followed suit. In 1792, Virginia added its southern claims to what was by then a *national* domain. (Georgia held out long after it was realistic to do so, until 1802.)

This remarkable act—European nations went to war over far lesser tracts of real estate—was followed by two congressional acts that were equally novel: the Northwest Ordinances of 1784 and 1787. These ordinances provided a procedure for the creation in the Northwest Territory, the region north of the Ohio River and east of the Mississippi, of five states that would be the equals of the original states. (The five that emerged were Ohio, Indiana, Michigan, Illinois, and Wisconsin.)

The Northwest Ordinances stated that the United States would hold no colonies subordinate to it, as the 13 colonies had been Britain's provinces. As soon as the population in a "territory" in the northwest equaled the population of the smallest state in the Confederation (Delaware in 1787) and met some other reasonable requirements, that territory would be recognized as the equal of the existing states.

Thomas Jefferson was the chief architect of the Northwest Ordinances, and he included an antislavery provision. The act of 1787 forbade slavery in the Northwest Territory. The west would be reserved for the independent yeoman family farmers Jefferson idealized, protecting them by law from an economic competition with slave owners such as had resulted in the aristocracy that dominated much of the South.

The Rectangular Survey

In 1785, Congress adopted a system of survey to prepare the Northwest Territory for public sale. Townships 6 miles square were divided into 36 "sections" of 1 square mile (640 acres) each. Initially, a section was the smallest tract that could be purchased, at a dollar an acre. A square mile was a lot of land, absurdly more than a family needed or could use. It was assumed that well-to-do developers—land speculators—would buy the land from the government and subdivide it for further sale, freeing the government from the massive job of retail sales.

The size and price of the tracts were debated for decades. However, the thinking that underlay the rectangular survey of the west was clearly wise and fruitful from the start. Had purchasers been able to enter public lands and map their own property, they would have carved out oddly shaped parcels of prime agricultural land, making the most of their dollar per acre. Hills, marshes, and rocky ground would remain government property. However, although no one would pay taxes on these scattered plots, settlers would surely exploit them by grazing livestock, cutting wood, digging gravel and stone, and extracting minerals. How, in so vast a domain, could the government monitor such trespassing? The rectangular survey forced buyers to take the poor land with the good. When, in 1791, Alexander Hamilton tried to slip a repeal of rectangular survey through the post-Confederation Congress, he was promptly foiled.

DIFFICULTIES AND FAILURES

Despite the Confederation's achievements, every year that passed convinced more and more prominent Americans—particularly those who thought of themselves as Americans and not as New Yorkers, Pennsylvanians, or Virginians—

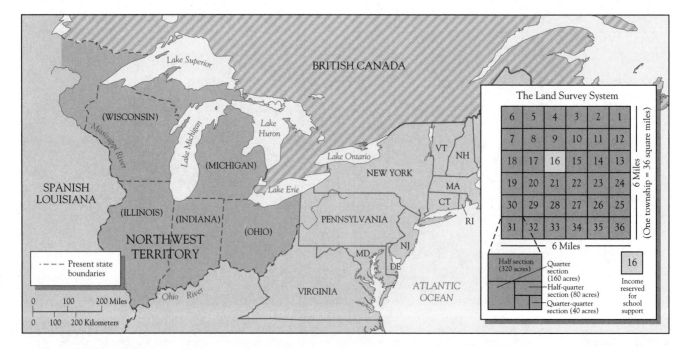

MAP 10:2 The Northwest Territory and the Rectangular Survey   The rectangular survey, an American innovation, avoided chaos and conflict when the Northwest Territory (and lands farther west, later added to the United States) was populated.

▲ *Confederation era money. The "dollar" was borrowed from Spain. However, the Spanish divided their dollar into eighths. The division into sixths illustrated here was a remnant of British practice. Decimalization—100 cents to the dollar—came only in 1791.*

that the government was too weak, that a disaster lay around the corner.

Money Problems

Government finance was a tenacious problem. Even during the war, delegates in Congress bickered and connived, denying or delaying the funds needed to fight. Congress was capable of dithering for hours about whether a man who claimed a mere $222.60 for ferrying troops should be paid. The difficulty was that all 13 states had to approve financial measures. In 1781, of the 13 states, Rhode Island alone refused to approve a tariff of 5 percent on imports. On another occasion, New York alone killed a tax bill.

Because, in effect, Congress could not levy taxes, it resorted to a risky alternative, printing increasingly larger amounts of paper money popularly called "Continentals," which no one would exchange at face value for "hard money"—gold and silver coin. From $6 million in paper money in 1775, Congress printed $63 million in 1778 and $90 million in 1779. By 1781, it required almost 150 paper dollars to purchase what one silver Spanish dollar would buy. "Not worth a Continental" was a catchphrase that long survived the Articles of Confederation.

The states also printed paper money. The assembly of Rhode Island, controlled by farmers in debt, issued it in absurd quantities. Rhode Island's notes were worthless outside the state—no one would accept them—but legal tender within the state, at face value, for payment of debts. Tales were told of creditors fleeing Rhode Island in order to avoid repayment of loans with the wretched paper and of debtors gleefully waving handfuls of the stuff in hot pursuit. Men of property everywhere shuddered to hear such stories. Merchants especially needed a sound paper currency valid in every state and accepted abroad. Such a currency needed a strong central government backing it.

Diplomatic Vulnerability

Squabbles among the states made it difficult for American diplomats to negotiate with other nations and encouraged foreign meddling. In 1784, a Spanish diplomat, Diego de Gardoqui, played on the commercial interests of the northern states in an attempt to split the United States in two. He offered to Congress to open Spanish trade to American ships (which meant northern ships) if Congress gave up the treaty right of Americans to ship goods down the Mississippi River.

New Englanders and New Yorkers cared little about trade on the Mississippi. Their delegations tried to ram de Gardoqui's treaty through Congress. Had they succeeded, the southern states would have been under great pressure to go their own way. The Ohio–Mississippi River system was vital to the tens of thousands who had moved to what are now Kentucky and Tennessee but were then still claimed by Virginia, North Carolina, and Georgia.

Britain schemed to detach Vermont from the United States. Traditionally a part of New York but also claimed by New Hampshire, the isolated Green Mountain country functioned as an independent commonwealth during the 1780s, dominated by Ethan and Levi Allen, two eccentric and cranky Revolutionary War veterans who trusted no one but one another. The Allens actively attempted to make a treaty with the British that would have tied Vermont more closely to Canada than to the Confederation. Congress was powerless to stop them, even militarily; the Continental Army had shrunk to 700 men. Only because the British failed to act quickly did the project fall through.

Wounded Pride

Great Britain also refused to turn over a string of Great Lakes forts that were American under the terms of the Treaty of Paris. Nor did the British send a minister (ambassador) to America. A British diplomat poked fun at American diplomatic impotence, joking that it would be too expensive to outfit 13 men with homes and the other accoutrements of office. In London, the American minister to Great Britain, John Adams, was snubbed and mocked when he acted with the dignity of a national delegate.

There were insults elsewhere. A world-traveling American sea captain said that the United States was regarded "in the same light, by foreign nations, as a well-behaved negro is

Forest to Farm

The Northwest Ordinances looked to the future. During the Confederation era, the Northwest Territory was, in fact, firmly under the control of Indian tribes. During the 1780s, western Pennsylvania, a hilly land of hardwood and conifer forests from which Indians had largely been pushed, was the region that beckoned to young men and women looking to develop frontier farms.

Settlers tried to arrive in April. Winter's snows had melted, but the overarching trees were just beginning to leaf. The pioneers' first tasks were to kill the trees and build a cabin so as to be sheltered by mid-May, when a crop of corn, beans, and squash had to be planted. Pines, spruce, and firs–softwoods with long, straight trunks–were felled for the logs of which cabins and barns were built. The gigantic oaks and maples were girdled, the bark chopped through a couple of feet from the ground. What leaves there were withered and fell, admitting sun to the earth. The "fields" were far from pretty, but the soil was rich, producing even the first year 40 to 50 bushels of corn, wheat, or rye per acre.

Building a log cabin, rude, sometimes windowless, sometimes just a three-sided shelter from the rain, required just one tool, an ax, and little skill—just the muscle power to move the logs into position. If the pioneer had an adze, a squaring tool, he hewed the logs on two sides for a tighter fit when they were stacked. The ends of each log were notched so that, by locking logs perpendicularly, it was possible to construct walls without uprights. The only task of cabin building requiring more than a single man's and woman's labor was raising the roof beam, itself a log. For this task, neighbors were summoned,

Smithsonian Institution

and entertained as thanks for their help. Even the author of an article in the *Columbian* magazine in 1786, who described the Pennsylvania pioneers as the dregs of society, admired the fact that roofs were raised "without any other pay than the pleasures which usually attend a country frolic."

Not only did a log cabin go up quickly; it was a tight, strong house. Its walls, chinked with moss and mud, provided

better insulation from cold than sawed clapboards did. The walls were thick and almost invulnerable to arrowheads, musket balls, and fire. To burn a log cabin, it was necessary to set fire to the roof, which was made of shingles or thatched straw.

A pioneer might keep oxen (the chief beasts of burden), a few horses, and perhaps a milk cow, which were fenced or, just as often, hobbled—that is, their forelegs were bound with a rope or rawhide thong, loosely enough that they could walk but not run. For meat, settlers depended on hogs. They were cheap and, more than a match for any predator, ran loose. They were hunted rather than rounded up for the slaughter, after the October harvest; the settlers salted the meat and packed it into barrels. With deer (still abundant) to supplement the salt pork, meat shortage was less of a problem than keeping animals out of the fields and garden.

For this, pioneers built zigzag fences. Logs split into rails—again, only an ax and wooden wedges were needed—were stacked alternately, at angles a little more than 90 degrees, zigzag. No postholes needed to be dug. They were not very good fences. Deer could leap them while yawning, and the largest hogs could push them over. But they were a first line of defense.

According to the *Columbian* article, "the first settler in the woods" rarely stayed put more than a year or two. He was "generally a man who [had] outlived his credit of fortune in the cultivated parts of the State." Not a very good citizen, he was an anarchic, irreligious, and hard-drinking individual who could not "bear to surrender up a single natural right for all the benefits of government." Soon restless, he sold out to a newcomer who improved the farm, felling and burning the dead hardwoods and adding to the cabin. The people of the second wave were themselves in the business of turning a profit rather than putting down roots. They soon sold to the "the *third* and last species of settler," a solid citizen whose habits were a relief to the article's author. This third settler was, thank goodness, "commonly a man of property and good character."

in a gentleman's family," that is, as an inferior scarcely to be noticed. Even the venal Barbary States of northern Africa looked down on Americans. These little principalities lived

by piracy, collecting tribute (in the name of treaty rights) from nations whose ships traded in the Mediterranean. When Americans lost the protection the British annually purchased for vessels flying the Union Jack, American ships were sunk or captured. The bey (governor) of Algiers sold several American crews into slavery. Congress was unable either to ransom them (money again!) or to launch a punitive expedition. It was a sorry state of affairs for the young men of the Revolution who had dreamed of national greatness.

Calls for Change

A trivial conflict in domestic waters triggered the movement to overhaul the government. In March 1785, a small group of Marylanders and Virginians gathered at Mount Vernon, George Washington's home on the Potomac, to discuss the conflicting claims of Maryland's and Virginia's fishermen in the Chesapeake Bay. They were unable to come up with a boundary acceptable to the two states' fisheries. They did, however, conclude that the problem was only one in a morass of disputes between states and between the states and the Confederation government. They invited all 13 states to send delegates to a meeting the next year in Annapolis, Maryland, to discuss what might be done.

Only five states responded. Decisive action was out of the question. Undiscouraged, Washington's former aide-de-

camp, Alexander Hamilton of New York, persuaded the disappointed few delegates to try again in more centrally located Philadelphia. They should prepare, Hamilton said, to discuss all the "defects in the System of the Federal Government."

Hamilton and others, like James Madison of Virginia, had more than talking in mind. They intended a bloodless coup d'état, peacefully replacing the Articles of Confederation with a completely new frame of government. Rumors of their intentions spread quickly and met less than resounding

© Bettmann/Corbis

▲ *Shays' Rebellion began as bullying and beating up Massachusetts state officials but soon evolved into a genuine, if short-lived, armed insurrection.*

approval. Virginia governor Patrick Henry, Madison's rival in the state's politics, said that he "smelled a rat" and refused to endorse the proposal. Rhode Island officially declared the state would not participate. Hamilton's Philadelphia convention might have fizzled like the Annapolis meeting had it not been for a wave of protests in western Massachusetts that turned into armed rebellion.

Shays' Rebellion

Farmers in western Massachusetts resented the fact that the state's tax laws favored trade at the expense of agriculture. In 1786, hundreds of them held meetings at which they demanded that their property taxes be reduced. To make up for the loss of revenue, they called for the abolition of "aristocratic" public offices in the state government in Boston.

In several towns, angry crowds surrounded courthouses, harassed lawyers and judges, whom they considered parasites, and forcibly prevented the collection of debts. In September, a Revolutionary War veteran, Daniel Shays, led 2,000 armed men against the state arsenal in Springfield.

Shays and his followers did not regard themselves as destructive or dangerous, not even as revolutionaries. They believed they were carrying on the spirit and struggle of the War for Independence against a privileged elite. Then minister in France, Thomas Jefferson agreed with them. "A little rebellion now and then is a good thing," he wrote to a friend.

"The tree of liberty must be refreshed from time to time with the blood of patriots and tyrants." (When he was not on the scene, Jefferson was often titillated by social disorder.)

Shays' Rebellion collapsed in December. But the men who were preparing to gather in Philadelphia the next summer, and some who were considering it, determined not to face another such crisis. To them, it was not Jefferson's pine tree of liberty that needed attention; it was the ailing oak of social stability and order. Washington, Hamilton, and conservatives like them believed that disorders like the uprising in Massachusetts were the inevitable consequence of weak government.

THE CONSTITUTION

The American Constitution has been hailed with a reverence that can be called religious. Politicians, moralists, and historians—Americans and foreigners alike—have bowed before a legal document that could survive for two centuries during which technology, ideology, revolution, imperialism, and war turned the world upside down and then downside up. William E. Gladstone, prime minister of Great Britain in the midst of this tumultuous era, was neither alone nor excessive when he called the American Constitution "the most wonderful work ever struck off at a given time by the brain and purpose of man."

▲ *The "Founding Fathers." George Washington is presiding. Seated second from the left is an idealized Benjamin Franklin. The oldest delegate at 81, Franklin was not as lively as he is shown to be here. He died within three years.*

The National Archives

"Demigods"

The men who struck it off in the summer of 1787—the "Founding Fathers"—have been heaped with praise, as wise, selfless individuals who peered into their nation's future and designed for it a timeless gift. The Constitution was "intended to endure for ages to come," Chief Justice John Marshall proclaimed in 1819. On the floor of the Senate in 1850, a critical year for the union of states the Constitution created, Marshall was echoed by Henry Clay of Kentucky. "The Constitution of the United States," Clay said, "was not made merely for the generation that then existed but for posterity—unlimited, undefined, and endless, perpetual posterity."

The Constitution has in fact been a remarkably successful frame of government, and the generation of political leaders who wrote and debated it was as rich in talent and wisdom as any generation before or since. But the Founding Fathers were not demigods, as Thomas Jefferson feared Americans would make them out to be. They were decidedly human, with prosaic faults and, along with their ideals, very immediate purposes to serve.

The Constitutional Convention

The convention in Philadelphia began on May 25, 1787. The 55 delegates almost immediately agreed that the Articles of Confederation could not, realistically, be revised. Ironically, it was easier to effect a coup d'état, to create a government from scratch, than to amend the Articles of Confederation. Amendment required that all 13 states concur. Rhode Island had already made it quite clear, by sending no delegates to Philadelphia, that it opposed any change of government. The convention was quite willing to form a new union of 12 states in place of the confederation of 13.

The Constitutional Convention met in secret from beginning to end. For four months, the delegates bolted the doors and sealed the windows of the Pennsylvania statehouse (Independence Hall), a demigod-like sacrifice in the hot and humid Philadelphia summer. Every delegate swore not to discuss the proceedings with others. George Washington, who presided, was furious when one misplaced a page of his notes.

The secrecy was not sinister. The goal of the convention—a new frame of government—was common knowledge. The delegates sequestered themselves because they wanted to proceed with caution. As James Wilson of Pennsylvania said, "America now presents the first instance of a people assembled to weigh deliberately and calmly, and to decide leisurely and peaceably, upon the form of government by which they will bind themselves, and their posterity." That was no small matter—never before had a nation been invented. There was an immediate and practical reason for secrecy too: The delegates were politicians; they wanted to voice their frankest opinions without fear that what they said would affect their careers back home.

Moreover, they knew there would be opposition to their new constitution. Wilson said that "the people" were assembled in Independence Hall. The Constitution begins with the words "We the People of the United States." In fact, most of the Founding Fathers represented just one of several American political tendencies. They wanted their platform complete before they had to debate its merits with their critics.

The Delegates

They finished in September 1787. After a bibulous celebration, the delegates scattered north and south to lobby for their states' approval. They were a formidable lot, all of them influential at home by virtue of their wealth, education, and political prominence. Of the 55, only two, Roger Sherman of Connecticut, who had been a cobbler as a young man, and Alexander Hamilton, the bastard son of a merchant in the West Indies, could be said to have been born with anything less glittering in his mouth than a silver spoon.

Lifetimes devoted to justifying independence and creating state governments made many of the delegates keen students of political philosophy. During the years just preceding the convention, James Madison augmented his library with 200 books on the subject. Just as important was the delegates' practical experience: 7 had been state governors; 39 had sat in the Continental Congress.

The Founding Fathers were young. Only nine signers of the Declaration of Independence were among them (and three of them refused to sign the Constitution). Only Benjamin Franklin, at 81, was truly antique. The other Founding Fathers averaged 40 years of age, and the two leading spirits of the movement were only 36 (Madison) and 32 (Hamilton). Ten delegates were less than 35 years of age, and one was 26. Such men had been just old enough in 1776 to play minor roles in the war. They had been children during the Stamp Act crisis. They were heirs of the Revolution, not makers of it.

The youth of the Founding Fathers is of some importance in understanding the nature of the Constitution they wrote. Most of the delegates had never thought of themselves as

Social Butterfly
George Washington was, of course, the "star" of the Constitutional Convention. In 128 days in Philadelphia, he rode every morning at five o'clock, dined out 110 times, attended 69 afternoon teas, went out in the evening on 20 occasions to attend lectures, concerts, and plays, had his portrait painted four times, and went fishing at least once.

And a Partridge in a Pear Tree
Two days before the Founding Fathers signed the Constitution, most of them gathered at the City Tavern for a party in honor of George Washington. They consumed 7 bowls of punch, 8 bottles of cider, 8 bottles of whiskey, 12 bottles of beer, 22 bottles of port wine, 54 bottles of Madeira, and 60 bottles of claret.

colonials. By 1787, most wanted to think of themselves not as New Hampshiremen or South Carolinians, but as Americans. Unlike their more provincial forebears, they had moved freely and often from one state to another. In the Continental Army (a third of the delegates had been soldiers, mostly junior officers) and in the Confederation Congress, they met and formed relationships with men from other states. They thought in terms of a continent rather than of coastal enclaves looking back to a mother country for an identity.

A Conservative Movement

Youth does not, as we are often told to think, equate with radicalism. The men who drew up the Constitution were conservatives in the classic (not the contemporary) meaning of the word. They did not believe with Jefferson (then in France) that human nature was essentially good and eternally malleable, that people and society were perfectible if left free. Most of the Founding Fathers feared the darker side of human nature. They believed that, without strong institutional restraints, selfish individuals were quick to trample on the rights of others. To such conservatives, democracy and liberty did not go hand in hand. On the contrary, if "the people" were untrammeled in their power, they would destroy liberty and a good deal more.

The most pessimistic of the lot was Alexander Hamilton. Sent by friends who recognized his genius to King's College in New York (now Columbia University), Hamilton never returned to the West Indies. He left college to serve Washington as aide-de-camp during the war, impressing the general with his intelligence and, no doubt, with his conservatism, for Washington too viewed democratic ideals with distaste. A few years after the adoption of the Constitution, Hamilton would listen to Thomas Jefferson expound on the wisdom and virtue inherent in "the people" and snap, "Your people, sir, are a great beast."

Had Hamilton been an Englishman, he would have defended those institutions that British conservatives believed helped to control the passions of the masses: the monarchy, the privileged aristocracy, the established church, and the centuries-old accretion of law and custom that is the British constitution. In fact, Hamilton was an admirer of English culture and government. Like Edmund Burke, he thought of the American Revolution as a conservative movement. In rebelling, the Americans had defended tradition against a reckless, innovative Parliament.

▲ *Alexander Hamilton was one of the youngest Founding Fathers. He thought the Constitution allowed the states too much power and the president too little. But he accepted it as a great improvement on the Articles of Confederation.*

In the Constitution, Hamilton wanted to recapture as much of tradition as practicable. He suggested that president and senators be elected for life, thus creating a kind of monarch and aristocracy. Hamilton also wanted governmental power centralized to such a degree that the states became little more than administrative districts.

He was unable to sway his fellow delegates on either count. As much as many of them may have shared Hamilton's apprehensions, they understood better than he that Americans valued their states and would not tolerate backsliding toward hereditary privilege. What the majority of delegates did approve, and Hamilton accepted as preferable to "anarchy and convulsion," was a system of government that had room for democratic yearnings but placed effective checks on them. The government they created was, in the words of John Adams (who, like Jefferson, was not present—he was serving as minister in Britain), a "mixed government": a balance of the "democratical" principle (power in the hands of the many), the "aristocratical" (power in the hands of a few), and the "monocratical" (power in the hands of one).

Checks, Limits, Balances

The House of Representatives was "democratical." Representatives were elected frequently (every two years) by a broad electorate—most free, white, adult males. The Senate and the Supreme Court reflected Adams's "aristocratical" principle.

Hamilton on Democracy

"All communities divide themselves into the few and the many. The first are the rich and the wellborn, the other the mass of the people. . . . The people are turbulent and changing; they seldom judge or determine right. Give therefore to the first class a distinct, permanent share in the government. They will check the unsteadiness of the second, and as they cannot receive any advantage by change, they therefore will ever maintain good government."

Senators were elected infrequently (every six years) and by state legislatures, not by popular vote. They were thus somewhat insulated from the fickleness of the crowd.

The Supreme Court was almost totally insulated from popular opinion. Justices were appointed by the president, but, once confirmed by the Senate, they were immune to his or the Senate's or the people's influence. Justices served for life. They could be removed from the bench only by a difficult impeachment process.

The "monocratical" principle was established in the presidency and was, therefore, the most dramatic break with the Confederation. The president alone represented the whole nation, but he owed his power neither directly to the people nor to Congress. He was put into office by an electoral college that played no other role than selecting the president.

An intricate web of checks and balances tied together the three branches of government. Only Congress could enact a law, and both democratic House and aristocratic Senate had to agree to its last syllable. The president could veto an act of Congress if he judged it adverse to the national interest. However, Congress could override his veto by a two-thirds majority of both houses.

Judging specific cases according to these laws was the job of the judiciary, with the Supreme Court the final court of appeal. In time (it was not written into the Constitution), the Supreme Court claimed a quasi-legislative role of its own in the principle of judicial review; that is, in judging according to the law, the Supreme Court also interpreted the law. Implicit in this process was the power to declare a law unconstitutional and, therefore, void.

Finally, the Constitution can be amended, although the process for doing so was deliberately made difficult. An amendment may be proposed in one of two ways. Two-thirds of the states' legislatures can petition Congress to summon a national constitutional convention for the purpose. Or Congress can submit proposals to the states (this is the only method by which the Constitution has ever been amended). If three-fourths of the states ratify a proposed amendment, it becomes part of the Constitution.

The Federal Relationship

Another network of checks and balances defined the relationship between the central government and the states. Under the Articles of Confederation, the United States was a confederation of independent states, each of which retained virtually all the powers possessed by sovereign nations. Under the Constitution, the balance shifted, with preponderant and decisive powers going to the federal government. The states were not reduced to administrative districts, as Hamilton would have liked. Nationalistic sentiments may have been high in 1787, but local interests and jealousies were far from dead. If the Constitution were to win popular support, the states had to be accommodated.

Small states, like Delaware, New Jersey, and Connecticut (not to mention Rhode Island), were particularly sensitive in this matter. Delegates from the small states insisted that if their states were not to be bullied and even absorbed by larger, wealthier neighbors, they must be accorded fundamental protections. These they received in the decision that states rather than population would be represented in the Senate. That is, each state elected two senators, no matter what its population. Virginia, the largest, was ten times as populous as Delaware but had the same number of senators. Without this "great compromise," which was accomplished only after intense debate in July 1787, the Constitution would not have been completed.

The Constitution and Slavery

The different status of America's 700,000 slaves in the North and the South was reflected in another compromise. By 1787, the institution of slavery was clearly dying in all the states north of Maryland and Delaware. Northern delegates were inclined to hope it would disappear everywhere. Indeed, with the exception of the delegates from South Carolina, few of the southern Founding Fathers looked favorably on slavery. Tellingly, the word "slave" does not appear in the Constitution, as if the framers were embarrassed that such persons existed in a country consecrated to liberty.

Rather, in a provision that prohibited Congress from abolishing the African slave trade for 20 years (Article 1, Section 9), slaves are referred to obliquely as "such Persons as any of the States now existing find proper to admit," a euphemism worthy of a university president. Elsewhere in the document, slaves are designated "all other persons." This expression was also used in the "three-fifths compromise" by which slaves and indentured servants were counted as three-fifths of a person for purposes of both taxation and representation in the House of Representatives.

But that was that. If many white southerners of 1787 hoped that slavery would die out, they did not know how to help the process along. Slaves were a fact of southern life, and "convenient" (embarrassed slave owner Patrick Henry's word) to those who owned them. Few whites could imagine freeing African Americans where they were numerous—in the South—without social turmoil that would make Shays' Rebellion look like minor mischief. Another embarrassed slave owner, Thomas Jefferson, said that living with the institution was holding "a wolf by the ears": One wished to be rid of it but could not let go.

Moreover, the Founding Fathers' first priority was getting the Constitution ratified. Significant action on the matter of slavery would surely have complicated that task, if not doomed it. They dodged the issue.

RATIFICATION OF THE CONSTITUTION

The Constitution provided that it would go into effect when nine states ratified it. Three did so immediately, Delaware and Connecticut almost unanimously, thanks to the "great compromise." Pennsylvania's ratification came quickly, but in a manner that dramatized the widespread opposition to the new government and the determination of the supporters of the Constitution to have their way, by hook and crook if necessary.

Federalist Shenanigans

Those who favored the Constitution called themselves "federalists." This was something of a misnomer, since they proposed to replace a genuinely federated government with a more centralized one. In Pennsylvania, the federalists secured ratification only by physically forcing two anti-federalist members of the state convention to remain in their seats when they tried to leave the hall. This rather irregular maneuver guaranteed a quorum so that the federalist majority could cast a legal pro-Constitution vote.

It was only the first of a series of manipulations that has led some historians to speculate that a majority of Americans probably preferred the Articles of Confederation to the Constitution. In Massachusetts, anti-federalists claimed that scheduling the election of delegates to the ratification convention in midwinter prevented many anti-federalist farmers from getting to the polls because they were snowbound. Even then, ratification was approved by the narrow margin of 187 to 168, and only because several delegates who had pledged to vote against the Constitution voted for it.

In June 1788, Edmund Randolph of Virginia, an announced anti-federalist, changed his vote and took a coterie of followers with him; the federalist victory in Virginia was by a vote of only 89 to 79. A switch of six votes would have reversed the verdict in the largest state, and that, in turn, would have kept New York in the anti-federalist camp.

In New York, a large anti-federalist majority was elected to the ratifying convention. After voting to reject the Constitution, they reversed their decision when news of Virginia's approval reached the state. Still, the vote was closer than in Massachusetts and Virginia, a razor-thin 30 to 27. Moreover, the New Yorkers saddled ratification with the proviso that a convention be called to amend the Constitution in several particulars. It never was. Technically, New York's vote was "nay."

The Anti-Federalists

North Carolina was decisively anti-federalist. Only in November 1789, eight months after the new government began to function, did the state reluctantly vote to ratify. Rhode Island held out longer, until May 1790. Rhode Island became the thirteenth state only when Congress threatened to pass a tariff that would have shut its products out of the other 12 states.

Today, now that the Constitution has worked successfully for 200 years, it can be easy to shrug off the anti-federalists of 1787 and 1788 as cranks. In fact, their reasons for favoring the Articles of Confederation were firmly within the tradition of the Revolution.

Among the anti-federalists were fiery old patriots who feared that centralized power was an invitation to tyranny. Samuel Adams, still padding around Boston shaking his

Unpredictable Critic

Mercy Otis Warren, sister of hell-raiser James Otis and wife of a prominent patriot, would be of a familiar type were she alive today. At the forefront of many radical causes, her blood was the bluest Massachusetts produced, and she knew it. She politely condescended even to those just a notch below her in social status, like John and Abigail Adams, to whom she was a lifelong friend. Her condescension was subtle because her pen was among the deftest of her era, often as precise and eloquent as Jefferson's. She authored several anti-Loyalist plays and a history of the Revolution.

Although a vociferous patriot, Mercy Warren was never, like other rebels, happy with the Articles of Confederation. She called Confederation America a "restless, vigorous youth, prematurely emancipated from the authority of a parent, but without the experience necessary to direct him to act with dignity or discretion."

That sounds like a federalist in the making, but Mercy Warren was no federalist. She regarded the Constitution as a plot, sinister in ways she never quite defined in writing, which was rare for her. Mercy Warren fit into no "type" in the 1780s. There was no other prominent American so critical of both the Articles of Confederation and the Constitution.

head at moral decadence, opposed the Constitution until Massachusetts federalists, needing the old lion's support, agreed to press for a national bill of rights. In Virginia, Patrick Henry battled James Madison around the state. Some of Henry's arguments against the Constitution were rather bizarre. At one point, he concluded that the Constitution was an invitation to the pope to set up court in the United States. Henry had his eccentricities.

But Henry and other anti-federalists also argued that free republican institutions could survive only in small countries such as Switzerland, the city-states of ancient Greece, and, of course, states like a sovereign Virginia. They had the weight of historical evidence on their side. Their favorite example was the Roman republic, which, when it grew into an empire, became despotic. Would the same thing happen to a large, centrally governed United States? Many anti-federalists believed so.

Answering such objections was the federalists' most difficult task. Madison, Hamilton, and John Jay of New York took it upon themselves to do so in 85 essays, the *Federalist Papers,* still a basic textbook of political philosophy. They argued that a powerful United States would guarantee liberty. These ingenious essays, however, were less important to the triumph of the federalists than their agreement, quite unhappy in Hamilton's case, to add a bill of rights to the Constitution.

The Bill of Rights

The Constitutional Convention paid little attention to the rights of citizens. The Founding Fathers were by no means hostile to individual rights, but their preoccupation was strengthening government. Moreover, they assumed that rights were protected in the state constitutions.

Because the Constitution created a national government superior to the states, however, anti-federalists like Samuel Adams and Edmund Randolph agreed to scrap their opposition to ratification only when the rights that had been adopted by the states since 1776 were guaranteed on the federal level. The Bill of Rights, the first 10 amendments to the Constitution, was ratified in 1791, but tacitly agreed upon during the ratification process. The First Amendment guaranteed freedom of religion, speech, the press, and peaceable assembly. The Second Amendment guaranteed the right to bear arms. The Third and Fourth Amendments guaranteed security against the quartering of troops in private homes (then still a sore point with older Americans) and against unreasonable search and seizure.

The famous Fifth Amendment is a guarantee against being tried twice for the same crime and, in effect, against torture. It is the basis of a citizen's right to refuse to testify in a trial in which he or she is a defendant. (British practice did not allow a defendant to testify.) The Sixth Amendment also pertains to criminal trials. It ensures the right to a speedy trial and the right to face accusers: no secret witnesses. The Seventh and Eighth Amendments likewise protect the rights of a person who is accused of committing a crime.

The Ninth and Tenth Amendments are catchalls. They state that the omission of a right from the Constitution does not mean that the right does not exist and that any powers not explicitly granted to the federal government are reserved to the states.

for FURTHER READING

The Confederation era and the Constitutional Convention have been fields of tumultuous controversy for almost a century. The origin of the dispute was Charles A. Beard, *An Economic Interpretation of the Constitution of the United States,* 1913. Beard broke with the general patriotic assumption that the Constitution was the work of selfless demigods striving to save the country from the chaos of the Articles of Confederation (a view best presented in John Fiske, *The Critical Period of American History, 1783–1789,* 1883). Beard instead contended that the Constitution reflected the Founding Fathers' quite immediate political and economic interests. Much of Beard's evidence and analysis have been discredited, but his book remains a "must-read" for students interested in the historians' debate.

Merrill Jensen, *The Articles of Confederation,* 1940, and *The New Nation,* 1950, are "Beardian" histories of the Confederation period. Other milestones in the debate are Jackson T. Main, *The Antifederalists,* 1961, and *Political Parties Before the Constitution,* 1973; Frederick W. Marks, *Independence on Trial,* 1973; Forrest MacDonald, *We the People: Economic Origins of the Constitution,* 1958; Andrew C. McLaughlin, *The Confederation and the Constitution,* 1962; Gordon S. Wood, *The Creation of the American Republic,* 1969; Garry Wills, *Interpreting America: The Federalist,* 1978; and Richard Beeman, Stephen Botein, and Edward C. Carter, *Beyond Confederation: Origins of the Constitution and American National Identity,* 1987.

See also David P. Szatmary, *Shays' Rebellion,* 1980; Lance Banning, *The Sacred Fire of Liberty: James Madison and the Founding of the Federal Republic,* 1995; and Arthur Zilversmit, *The First Emancipation: The Abolition of Slavery in the North,* 1967.

American Journey ONLINE www AMERICAN JOURNEY ONLINE AND INFOTRAC COLLEGE EDITION

Visit the source collections at http://ajaccess.wadsworth.com and http://infotrac.thomsonlearning.com, and use the Search function with the following key terms to explore documents, images, audio and video clips, articles, and commentary related to the material in this chapter:

Abigail Adams
Alexander Hamilton
Bill of Rights
Constitutional Convention
First Amendment

James Madison
Northwest Ordinance
Patrick Henry
Shays' Rebellion

Additional resources, exercises, and Internet links related to this chapter are available on *The American Past* Web site: http://history.wadsworth.com/americanpast7e.

HISTORY ONLINE

Religious Facets of the Confederation Period
http://lcweb.loc.gov/exhibits/religion/rel06.html
Insightful multi-format presentation of the role of religion in the events of the 1770s.

Documents of the Continental Congress
http://memory.loc.gov/ammem/bdsds/bdsdhome.html
A multi-format survey of the Confederation period.

WE THE PEOPLE

Putting the Constitution to Work 1789–1800

The father of his country.

Francis Bailey

First in war, first in peace, first in the hearts of his countrymen.

Henry Lee

America has furnished to the world the character of Washington. And if our American institutions had done nothing else, that alone would have entitled them to the respect of mankind.

Daniel Webster

DURING THE DEBATE over the Constitution, one question never arose: Who would be the first president? In few monarchies has one figure towered over all others as George Washington towered above the United States. The first electoral college voted unanimously to install Washington in what was, at the time, an office unique in the world. He took the presidential oath in New York City on April 30, 1789.

THE FIRST PRESIDENCY

Washington possessed qualities indispensable to the launching of a government designed from scratch. He was committed to the republican ideal. His sense of duty was the foundation of his personality. He knew he had become one of his era's major historical figures. He knew that he would set a precedent with every presidential act, from signing a bill into law to the manner in which he greeted a guest at dinner.

Precedents Set

It is fortunate that Washington was a republican. Lionized as he was in 1789, he could likely have been crowned a king. Some members of the Order of Cincinnatus, a society of Revolutionary War officers, wanted to do just that. It was suggested that Washington be addressed as "Your Elective Majesty," but he settled for "Mr. President."

Not that the president was just one of the boys. Washington toyed with "His High Mightiness" as a possible title, and he was fussy about other trappings of his office. He lived surrounded by servants in livery and powdered wigs, and he drove around New York in a splendid carriage drawn by matched cream-colored horses. He looked and acted like the

▲ *Washington was hurrahed and feted all the way from Mount Vernon to his inauguration in New York City, then the nation's capital. He crossed the Hudson in a splendidly decorated barge and took the presidential oath on a balcony, cheered by thousands in the street below.*

▲ *Military men wear medals. The old soldiers in the Order of Cincinnatus wore this one to identify themselves. The inscription reads, "All sacrificed to serve the republic."*

prince of a small European state, not quite regal but decidedly unique in his surroundings. On a bet that he would not dare do so, New Yorker Gouverneur Morris slapped Washington on the back at a public function. The president stared him down with such iciness that Morris retreated from the room, stammering. They were never quite cordial again. Morris said it was the costliest bet he had ever won.

In being as much a monument as a man, Washington won respect abroad. No European statesmen feared the United States, but neither did any of them mistake George Washington for a head-scratching bumpkin who had had a bit of luck on a battlefield.

The Cabinet

Washington was accustomed to wielding authority as a planter and soldier. A rarer quality among men raised high was his awareness of his personal limitations and need of advice. Far from resenting brighter people (as, for instance, George III did), Washington sought them out and listened to them. Those he saw regularly were five heads of executive departments entrusted with the workaday operations of the government, three of them titled "secretaries." They were soon collectively dubbed the president's "cabinet."

In making his appointments, Washington tried to balance political tendencies and sectional sensitivities. From

The Cincinnati

Lucius Quinctius Cincinnatus was a Roman who was twice made dictator when enemies threatened the republic. Both times, Cincinnatus was quickly victorious; but, instead of using the months remaining of his legal dictatorship to enrich himself and rule as a tyrant, he immediately resigned and retired to his farm. Educated Americans of the revolutionary era, steeped in classical history, thought of George Washington as their Cincinnatus.

In 1784, officers of the Continental Army formed the Order of the Cincinnati. It was controversial from the start. The society's proceedings were secret and membership was hereditary, passed down by charter members to their firstborn sons. In other words, the Cincinnati preserved the aristocratic principle of primogeniture that revolutionary era state governments had abolished in property law.

During the troubled Confederation period, members discussed the possibility of selecting something like a dictator. They were delighted to have Washington as president, but rumors of a military coup by the Cincinnati to increase his power disturbed the followers of Thomas Jefferson, who called the society "a nascent nobility."

Washington discouraged Cincinnati mutterings, and the membership grew long in the tooth without biting. The society abandoned the principle of primogeniture so that all male descendants of Revolutionary War officers might belong, and it evolved into an organization "devoted to the principles of the Revolution, the preservation of history and the diffusion of historical knowledge." As such it exists today.

▲ *The first cabinet, left to right: the president, Secretary of War Henry Knox (depicted at less than his 300 pounds), Attorney General Edmund Randolph, Secretary of State Thomas Jefferson, and Jefferson's rival (and soon to be enemy), Secretary of the Treasury Alexander Hamilton. There is a precedent here: no Vice President John Adams. Adams called his office "useless."*

Virginia came Attorney General Edmund Randolph and Secretary of State Thomas Jefferson. By naming Randolph, an opponent of the Constitution until the last moment, Washington extended a hand of reconciliation to the anti-federalists. Jefferson, by virtue of his agrarian book of 1785, *Notes on the State of Virginia,* was recognized as a spokesman for farmers who were suspicious of the nondemocratic features of the new government.

To balance the southerners, Washington named General Henry Knox of Massachusetts as secretary of war. Knox was a wartime crony of the president, but, more important, as the chief military official under the Confederation, he represented continuity from old government to new. Samuel Osgood of Massachusetts, the postmaster general, was a former anti-federalist like Randolph.

Dynamic Alexander Hamilton of New York was Washington's secretary of the treasury. Partly because his conservative instincts were in tune with the president's, partly because the most urgent challenges facing the new government were financial, Hamilton's power was second only to Washington's.

The First Debate: Funding

To pay the government's operating expenses, Hamilton asked Congress to enact a 5 percent tariff on imports. The duty was low, not enough to impede sales of foreign goods in the United States. Moreover, Hamilton had a penchant for making political statements. Rhode Island's veto of a 5 percent tariff under the Articles of Confederation had been a signal indication of the old government's helplessness in levying taxes.

Revenue from the tariff, Hamilton knew, would be woefully inadequate in a crisis—a war, for example. In fact, the tariff did not usually bring in enough to balance the government's books. The government, like all governments, would have to borrow money. Hamilton, therefore, set out to establish that its credit was sound.

This was no easy chore: The Confederation Congress had been grievously remiss in paying its debts. When it collapsed, it owed $12 million to foreign banks and governments and $44 million to American citizens. Many lenders were wary. Did a new government mean a repudiation of the old

Birthing

A woman who married during the Federalist period could expect to be pregnant about seven times during her life—if she did not die young. One in four women between 15 and 44 gave birth each year. Mothers nursed their infants for about a year. The rich and the very weak hired wet nurses, women already lactating from a recent birth.

There were no maternity hospitals. Children were delivered at home by midwives (*midwife* originally meant "with a woman"), possibly in the company of the mother-to-be's own mother, sisters, neighbors, and older daughters. Childbirth was an exclusively female event except during the early stages of labor, when the husband might be called in to pray with or comfort his wife.

Midwives served an apprenticeship or fell into the profession accidentally after getting "catched" in a number of childbirths and developing a reputation as someone who knew what to do. It brought in some extra money—the sole support of many midwives—and ensured the respect of the community. One Boston woman's tombstone attests that "by the Blessing of God" she had "brought into this world above 3,000 Children."

The presence of several women at a birth was practical. They heated water and washed linens. If the labor was prolonged, they prepared food. Few women gave birth lying on their backs; instead, they squatted or half-stood, supported by their attendants. Moreover, it was common for a new mother to remain in bed for several weeks after childbirth. Her friends and relatives performed her household duties during this final phase of her "confinement."

The attendants also served cultural, social, and psychological purposes. Their presence (and the exclusion of men) emphasized the uniquely feminine character of the suffering childbirth meant. (Liquor was the only anesthetic.) The pains of bearing children were still generally regarded as God's punishment for the sin of Eve. By their presence—because they too had undergone childbirth or expected to do so—the attendants shared in the travail. They also cheered the mother-to-be by distracting her with gossip, comparing her labor with more difficult labors they had suffered, and even making her laugh by telling bawdy jokes.

By 1800, male physicians were taking over the supervision of childbirth. The trend began in Britain during the 1740s when Dr. William Smellie was appalled by the incompetence of many midwives. "We ought to be ashamed of ourselves," he told physicians, "for the little improvement we have made in so many centuries." Smellie invented the forceps used for assisting difficult births.

The development of obstetrics as a branch of medicine also reflected the drift of educated people away from traditional religion. In 1804, Peter Miller of the medical school of the University of Pennsylvania wrote that the dangers of pregnancy and the death of so many newborns were sorrow enough for women. It was absurd to burden them with the message that they were doing penance. Dr. William Dewees, a pioneer of medical obstetrics in the United States, asked, "Why should the female alone incur the penalty of God?"

Among the urban upper and middle classes, male physicians supplanted midwives in a surprisingly short period of time. In Boston and Philadelphia during the Federalist period, physicians were called into childbirth cases only when there were serious difficulties. By the 1820s, doctors virtually monopolized the delivery of children in cities except among the poor.

The survival rate of both mothers and newborns improved, although not dramatically until later in the nineteenth century, when it was discovered that "childbirth fever" (puerperal fever) was caused by the failure of most physicians even to wash their hands before delivery. The triumph of medical obstetrics had other complications. The nineteenth century's demands for sexual modesty obligated doctors to ask questions "of a delicate nature"—just about all questions regarding childbirth—through a woman. It was an unwieldy procedure, to say the least, and in emergencies, dangerous. Moreover, the birth had to be carried out under covers, with the physician working entirely by touch. Even so awkward a procedure offended some. In *Letters to Ladies, Detailing Important Information Concerning Themselves and Infants,* published in 1817, Dr. Thomas Ewell told of a husband who "very solemnly . . . declared to the doctor, he would demolish him if he touched or looked at his wife."

government's obligations? Hamilton reassured them by funding the entire Confederation-era debt at face value. That is, by trading new federal bonds for old Confederation bonds—"restructuring the debt," we would say—the Constitutional government would immediately assert its fiscal reliability.

Few in Congress objected to repaying foreign creditors in full. The United States was cash poor. Big loans could only be had abroad. However, Hamilton's proposal to pay American creditors at par led to a serious debate.

The issue was speculation. Most of the domestic debt dated to the war years, when, moved as much by patriotism as by mercenary motives, thousands of Americans bought government bonds. As the years passed and the Confederation Congress failed to redeem these debts, many lenders lost hope. They sold their bonds to speculators at big discounts; better something than nothing. By 1789, most public bonds were in the strongboxes of financial adventurers.

Nor had they been so very adventurous. As James Madison explained in opposing the funding bill, some speculators, informed in advance of what Hamilton would propose, had scoured rural villages and towns, buying up all the Confederation bonds they could find at as little as a few cents on the dollar. In our parlance, they had traded on "insider information."

Madison said that Congress should not reward such profiteering. Instead, he proposed to pay the face value of the debts plus 4 percent annual interest to original lenders who still held the old bonds. Speculators who bought the bonds at bargain rates, however, were to receive half of the face value.

Madison's argument was morally appealing. It rewarded those who had stepped forward during "the times that tried men's souls." Hamilton replied that morality was beside the point. The issue was the new government's credit. By rewarding capitalists, including the connivers, his funding bill would encourage them to be lenders in the future. Hamilton believed that the moneyed classes were the key to the stability of the new government. He meant to wed them to it.

Hamilton's realism was compelling. And it did not hurt that several dozen members of Congress stood to profit personally from the funding bill. It was enacted.

Assumption and a New Capital

Hamilton next proposed that the federal government assume responsibility for debts contracted by the state governments since independence. By repaying loans that the states had not, the federal government would further strengthen its credit rating. In addition, assumption would enhance the prestige of the federal government vis-à-vis that of the states, an important goal of nationalists like Hamilton.

Money: The Dollar
The word *dollar* derives from the German *Taler,* a silver coin first minted in 1484. The Spanish called the coin *dolar.*

Why, in 1785, did the United States adopt a Spanish monetary unit rather than the British pound that had been the colonial standard? In part, it was another patriotic slap at the former mother country. More important than patriotic symbolism, there were far more Spanish dollars than British pounds circulating in America. The dollar was, as Jefferson said, "a known coin" and "the most familiar of all to the mind of the people."

In practice, Americans continued to trade in any and all gold and silver coins for half a century. Merchants had conversion tables or knew by heart what foreign coins were worth in dollars. As late as the California Gold Rush of 1849, businesses in San Francisco quoted their prices in British pounds, shillings, and pence.

Money: Bucks and Quarters
The word *buck,* slang for dollar, dates to the eighteenth century, when a deer hide, or "buckskin," was commonly used as money (by law in New York). In 1785, when Congress adopted the dollar, a buckskin sold for a Spanish dollar.

Although the American dollar was officially divided into 100 cents in 1793, Americans also divided it into quarters. This custom also reflected the abundance of Spanish coins in the young United States. Spanish dollars were divided into eight reales (the famous "pieces of eight"), which originated in the practice of actually sawing Spanish dollars into eight pieces, as a pie is sliced, to make change. Thus, the now moribund custom of calling a quarter "two bits" and half a dollar "four bits."

Again, James Madison led the opposition. He pointed out that some states, notably his own Virginia, had retired most of their debt. Other states, northern, had let their obligations ride, accruing interest for as many as 15 years. If the federal government now assumed responsibility for the debts of all states, the citizens of some—Virginians!—would, in effect, pay twice. They had dutifully retired their state's debt by paying state taxes. Now, they would pay federal taxes to help pay the debts run up and neglected by others—sometimes, apparently, out of irresponsibility. Was this fair? Just enough congressmen thought not. The assumption bill was defeated in the House of Representatives, 31 to 29.

Assumption was a vital part of Hamilton's financial program, his "primary object" to which "all subordinate points . . . must be sacrificed." He was not going to be foiled by a razor-thin defeat. And Hamilton had a card to play: An emotional issue before Congress was where to locate the permanent capital of the United States. Philadelphia had the best claim to the honor. Home of the Declaration of Independence and the Constitution, it was by far the largest city in the United States, abounding in public buildings and living quarters for government officials, and centrally located. In fact, during the debate over funding, Hamilton had offered to deliver the votes to Philadelphia in return for Pennsylvania's votes for that bill.

The deal proved unnecessary and fell through. In the meantime, some 40 towns and would-be towns had put in bids to be the capital. Virginians, who voted against assumption the first time around, wanted the capital in the South. Hamilton worked out a deal with Jefferson, Madison's political ally. If Jefferson influenced enough southern congressmen to vote for assumption that it was enacted, Hamilton would deliver the votes of enough New Yorkers and New Englanders to locate the capital on the banks of the Potomac. Thus, by means of a masterful political horse trade, Hamilton got assumption. And thus was selected the site of Federal City, later renamed Washington, D.C., in the woods and worn-out tobacco fields of the Tidewater.

Interpretation of the Constitution

The third pillar of Hamilton's fiscal program was the Bank of the United States (BUS), a central financial institution in which all government moneys would be deposited. With such vast resources at its disposal, the BUS would exercise immense power over other banks and the nation's finances in general. Hamilton's BUS was not, however, a government agency. Although the president would appoint 5 of the bank's 25 directors, the remaining 20 were to be elected by private shareholders—Hamilton's men of capital again.

Hamilton had nothing to swap with Jefferson in return for his support, and the secretary of state had had his fill of the marriage between government and capital. When the bank bill passed Congress, Jefferson urged Washington to veto it. He argued that Congress had overstepped its constitutional powers. Nothing in the document gave the government the authority to create such an institution.

▲ *The First Bank of the United States in Philadelphia. Imposing in size, its classical design, borrowed from ancient Greece, was novel and deliberate. While its size conveyed power and stolidity, the classical facade hearkened to the republics of antiquity, with which Americans liked to identify.*

Washington was impressed by Jefferson's reasoning. But Hamilton won the day by arguing that nothing in the Constitution specifically *prohibited* Congress from chartering a national bank. Therefore, the BUS was justified under Article 1, Section 8, which authorized Congress to "make all laws which shall be necessary and proper for" (among other things) regulating commerce, which the BUS would certainly do, and to "provide for . . . the general welfare," which, to Hamilton's way of thinking, the bank would also accomplish. Washington signed the bill.

In the debate over the BUS, Jefferson and Hamilton formulated fundamentally different theories of constitutional interpretation that survive to this day in some disagreements on the Supreme Court. Jefferson's "strict construction" held that if the Constitution did not spell out and properly punctuate a governmental power in black and white, that power did not exist. Hamilton's "broad construction" held that Article 1, Section 8, permitted Congress to exercise any legislative powers that were *not specifically denied* to Congress elsewhere in the Constitution.

Hamilton Rebuffed

Establishing the BUS was Hamilton's last hurrah. Congress rejected the fourth pillar of his financial edifice, a call for a protective tariff, outlined in his "Report on Manufactures" of December 1791. In that report, Hamilton argued, cogently as usual, that the United States already had a solid agricultural and commercial base. He proposed to promote manufacturing by protecting investors in factories from foreign competition. By placing high import duties on, for example, British cloth and shoes, Congress would price them out of the American market. This would encourage American investors to build textile mills and shoe factories in the United States, creating jobs and new founts of wealth.

Farmers were inclined to oppose the protective tariff, particularly southern planters with numerous slaves to clothe and shod. They were consumers of manufactured goods. Hamilton's tariff meant higher prices for them. Agriculturalists also feared that Britain and other European nations stung by high American tariffs on goods they exported would retaliate by enacting high tariffs on American agricultural produce. Some great merchants, otherwise staunch Hamiltonians, opposed the protective tariff. Their business was transporting freight. British mercantilism now excluded them or sharply limited their business in British ports. They did not want their own government shutting down other routes. Hamilton's high tariff was killed. Import duties remained low, providing revenue but not protecting American manufacturers from foreign competition.

Clouds on the Horizon

Washington was reelected without opposition in 1792. He continued to carry out most of his policies and to establish sensible precedents. Most important, he presided over the establishment of a stable government for 4 million people and 900,000 square miles of territory. The United States, so recently a gaggle of ex-colonies, was a going concern of 16 states: Vermont, Kentucky, and Tennessee were admitted to the Union under Washington.

Washington's success story was not unblemished. In effect, the four ongoing and related problems he described in his farewell address of September 1796 were a summation of problems he had been unable to resolve.

First, Washington urged his countrymen not to align themselves in political parties. Washington regarded parties as combinations of selfish men willing to sacrifice the common good in order to benefit their own narrow interests. He saw no good in parties.

Second, he admonished Americans to "discountenance irregular opposition" to the government. That is, they should voice opposition to policies they disliked peacefully through constitutional channels, not by resistance and rebellion.

Third, Washington regretfully identified signs of sectionalism in the United States. He feared that too many Americans pledged allegiance more to the North or to the South than to the federal union. Division along geographical lines was far more dangerous than division on party lines, for it was far more likely to lead to civil war.

Finally, Washington warned against "the insidious wiles of foreign influence"—attempts by European diplomats to entangle the United States in their chronic wars. Honor alliances already in effect, Washington said, but make no new permanent commitments to other countries. Enjoy the Atlantic Ocean as a moat insulating the United States from a corrupt Europe.

TROUBLES ABROAD

The Washington administration's most troubling problems were in the area of foreign policy. This should not be surprising.

As colonials, Americans had entrusted diplomacy to the mother country. In no other arena of statecraft were the Founding Fathers so poorly educated. Moreover, the 1790s were a decade when the cleverest of European diplomats were repeatedly confounded. The old order—old ways of understanding—had been turned upside down.

The French Revolution

They were turned upside down by the revolution in France in 1789. At first a violent rebellion against the extravagance and excesses of the monarchy, the French Revolution soon pushed far beyond what Americans had done in their rebellion.

In 1789, the year of Washington's inauguration, Americans rejoiced at the upheaval in France. Had not the Declaration of Independence spoken of the inalienable rights of all people? Now their ally in the war against Britain was joining them as another land of liberty. It became fashionable for Americans to festoon their hats with cockades of red, white, and blue ribbon—the badge of the French revolutionaries. Lafayette gave Washington the key to the Bastille, the gloomy fortress jail that had symbolized the oppression of the French kings; the president proudly displayed it to guests.

Soon, however, the French Revolution moved beyond liberty to the ideals of equality and fraternity. Conservatives like Washington and Hamilton were not comfortable with palaver of wiping out social distinctions and of the equality of ignorant laborers with men, like themselves, of education and social standing. As for *fraternity*, it meant a national brotherhood, which was inoffensive, but it also smacked of a universal coziness of human affections that was, to conservatives, as fantastic as sea monsters. Even Thomas Jefferson, no conservative and usually keen on everything French, worried privately that the French revolutionaries were moving too far too fast. He doubted that a people accustomed to a powerful monarchy could create overnight a free republic like the United States.

Terror and Reason

Found a republic the French did, and in January 1793, as Washington's first term was ending, King Louis XVI was beheaded. His queen, Marie Antoinette, mounted the scaffold within the year. The Reign of Terror followed—French radicals known as Jacobins guillotined or drowned thousands of nobles and political rivals. The blood that flowed in France was quite as unnerving to Europeans (and many Americans) as the Holocaust was to be in the mid–twentieth century.

Maximilien Robespierre became the virtual dictator of France for a year. In an attempt to wipe out religion, Robespierre converted Paris's Cathedral of Notre Dame into a "temple of reason" where paunchy politicians and perfumed actresses performed rituals that struck many as ridiculous, others as blasphemous.

Few Americans thought warmly of the Catholic Church. However, Robespierre attacked all religion. American preachers shuddered when they heard Americans admiring him. William Cobbett, an Englishman living in the United States, observed with distaste that crowds of city people guillotined dummies of Louis XVI "twenty or thirty times every day during one whole winter and part of the summer." He also reported fistfights between gangs of pro-English "Anglomen" and pro-French "cutthroats."

American Neutrality

Cobbett was observing a point of conflict that contributed to the birth of the political parties that Washington warned against. Americans who supported the French inclined to favor an expanded democracy and the curtailment of social distinctions at home. Working people in the cities, small and middling farmers, and some wealthy southern planters who resented the favors that Hamilton's financial program lavished on northern merchants and capitalists looked increasingly to Thomas Jefferson as their spokesman. They called themselves "Jefferson Republicans." Jefferson (who left Washington's cabinet in 1793) quietly—behind the scenes, really, from his home at Monticello—accepted leadership of the coalescing movement. James Madison was his public spokesman.

Conservatives like Washington, Hamilton, and Vice President John Adams began to call themselves "Federalists." They were neither enamored of democracy, which they equated with mob rule, nor hostile to clear social distinctions, which they regarded as buttresses of stability. Until 1793, they were content to attack the principles of the French Revolution on a philosophical level. Then, Great Britain declared war on France. Under the terms of the treaty of 1778, it appeared that the United States was obligated to join France as an ally.

Washington wanted nothing of it. The Royal Navy was more powerful than ever. The French navy had declined, and the United States had no navy worth noticing. Alexander Hamilton, who was frankly pro-British, found the legal loophole that kept the United States out of the conflict. He argued that the treaty of 1778 was not binding on two counts: It had been contracted with the French monarchy, which no longer existed; and it provided that the United States must help France only if Great Britain was the aggressor, which, with some justification, the British denied.

Washington announced that the United States would be neutral, "impartial toward the belligerent powers." Then, in April 1793, the French minister to the United States, Edmond-Charles Genet, styling himself "Citizen Genet" in the best revolutionary vocabulary, arrived in Charleston.

Citizen Genet

Genet was young and as subtle as flags and fireworks. Soon after stepping ashore, he began to commission American shipmasters as privateers, armed raiders under contract to France to seize British ships. Within a short time, a dozen of these raiders brought 80 British "prizes"—captured merchant vessels—into American ports where Genet presided over trials at which he awarded the loot to the captors. Everything was within the rules of war *except* the fact that Genet was performing a French governmental action on American soil. He spoke to sympathetic audiences as if he were the governor of a French province.

By the time Genet presented his credentials to the president, Washington was livid. Genet's privateers promised to drag the United States into a war with Britain that the president had determined to sit out. Washington received the minister coldly and ordered him to cease bringing captured British vessels into American ports and to subdue his politicking. Genet bowed, retired, and continued to appear at dinners and demonstrations, adding jibes at Washington to his speeches. When he commissioned a captured British vessel, the *Little Sarah,* as a privateer, Washington ordered him to return to France.

This was bad news. Genet's political party back home had been ousted and the Reign of Terror was in full swing. To return to France meant a rendezvous with the guillotine. Suddenly abject, Genet asked Washington for asylum, and the president granted it. Remarkably, Genet actually did quiet down. He married into the wealthy Clinton family of New York and lived a long, contented life as a gentleman farmer.

British Threats

Genet or no Genet, the British kept the threat of war boiling by proclaiming they would fight the war at sea under the Rule of 1756. This British policy asserted that the ships of neutral countries could not trade in ports from which they had been excluded before the war began.

The targets of this proclamation were American merchants who were carrying grain and livestock to the French West Indies—Martinique, Guadeloupe, and Saint-Domingue (present-day Haiti). These ports had previously been closed to Americans, who were now reaping bonanza profits on the sugar and molasses they brought back from the French West

Indies. Shipowners who had recently struggled with hard times were suddenly wealthy, moving their families from apartments in their warehouses on the waterfront, where they had lived amid dirt, clamor, and marginal dockworkers, to elegant "federal period" town houses in neighborhoods somewhat insulated from the lower classes. The elite of New England and Philadelphia, with social lives as elegant as those of southern planters, little resembled their Puritan and Quaker forebears. (New York's great merchants had never been saddled with a gospel of austerity.) The fleets of Philadelphia, New York, and Boston grew until their combined tonnage rivaled that of Great Britain.

The British did not want war with the United States, but they were concerned about the explosive growth of the American merchant marine. Would Britain defeat the French only to discover that their overseas trade had been swiped by upstart Yankees? Enforcing the Rule of 1756 was more an attempt to retard the growth of American maritime commerce than it was retaliation for actions that hindered the British war effort. In any case, it made the news. In 1793 and 1794, British warships and privateers seized 600 American vessels, half of them in West Indian waters, a few within sight of American shores.

American shipowners griped, but not much more. Overseas trade was a high-risk enterprise in the best of times. The wartime business with the West Indies was so lucrative that merchants, great and aspiring, could absorb losses of ships and still end the year in the black. Moreover, the merchant class was generally more sympathetic to Britain than to France. Better to wink at British depredations at sea than to have French atheists victorious.

Impressment

The pro-French party, on the other hand, was hot for a fight with Britain. While Jefferson himself laid low (an unattractive facet of his character), his propagandists, especially the vituperative newspaper editor Philip Freneau, railed against the British seizures of American ships as an affront to national honor. Seamen and their families had a more personal grievance: the Royal Navy's application of the ancient practice of impressment.

Britain (and other seafaring nations) empowered the commanders of warships to replace seamen who died or deserted by means of an impromptu draft. If a ship was in port, press gangs roamed the streets forcing likely young men into service. At sea, warships ordered merchant vessels flying their own flag to heave to—the proverbial shot across the bow— whereupon press gangs boarded them and took their pick. Impressment was unpopular with everyone. Seamen on a signaled merchant vessel feigned crippled legs or idiocy. Serving in the Royal Navy had its advantages over sailing on the merchant ship (there was less heavy labor); but in wartime, naval discipline was brutal, and death in combat was no remote risk.

If British merchant seamen hated impressment, Americans were infuriated when warships flying the Union Jack took crewmen from American ships. Britain claimed the legal right to impress only British subjects, and there were plenty of them on American ships, where conditions and pay were better than in the British merchant marine. But American citizens were also impressed. Whereas the United States naturalized (bestowed citizenship on) British immigrants who applied for it, Great Britain maintained that anyone born British remained British lifelong. Hundreds of seamen were caught in the middle. Impressment aggravated American touchiness about the issue of national independence.

Jay's Treaty: Peace at a Price

In April 1794, faced with a growing clamor for war, Washington sent the chief justice of the Supreme Court, John Jay of New York, to Britain to appeal for peace. This alone was enough to raise the hackles of the knee-jerk anglophobes, especially when the news trickled back that Jay was hobnobbing in London society and had kissed the hand of the queen. But that fuss was nothing compared with the reception given to the treaty Jay brought home. The British made a few concessions. They agreed to evacuate the western forts they should have evacuated in 1783, to compensate American shipowners for vessels seized in the West Indies, and to allow some trade with British possessions. In return, the Americans pledged not to discriminate against British shipping and to pay debts owed to British subjects from before the Revolution.

Nothing was said about impressment, however, the issue most charged with emotion. Like Hamilton's fiscal policy, Jay's Treaty could be interpreted as benefiting only wealthy merchants.

Protest swept the country. When Washington submitted Jay's Treaty to the Senate for ratification, he was attacked personally for the first time, and not gently. Jay resigned from the Supreme Court and joked uneasily that he could travel the length of the country by the light of the effigies of him that were burned by furious Jefferson Republicans. Crowds shouted, "Damn John Jay! Damn everyone that won't put lights in his windows and sit up all night damning John Jay!"

It was, to say the least, an eruption of party spirit, for Washington, Adams, Hamilton, and their supporters did not damn John Jay. However disappointing the terms with which Jay returned, they believed he had done the country a service by preserving peace. They did not yet call themselves a party. With Washington in power, the Federalists dared not organize a formal party apparatus. But the lines between two political parties, already penciled in, were drawn a bit more clearly.

Pinckney's Treaty

The détente between Britain and the United States worried the Spanish too. Spain also had been warring with revolutionary France but, by the end of 1794, wanted out of the conflict. The French were willing to come to terms, but the

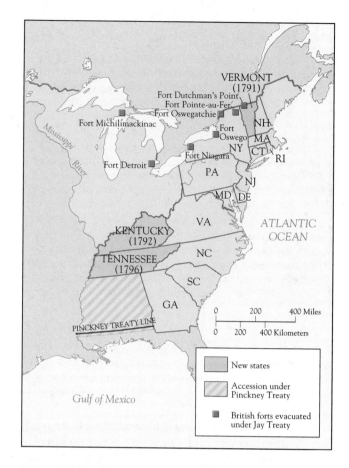

MAP 11:1 The Federalist Treaties Britain's agreement, in Jay's Treaty, to turn over seven frontier forts to the United States was a diplomatic victory but not perceived as such because the British had violated the Treaty of Paris in continuing to occupy them. In giving up, in Pinckney's Treaty, what are now the states of Mississippi and Alabama (except the Gulf Coast), Spain eliminated a dispute that would likely have led to war with the United States.

Spanish worried that, if they ended hostilities, the reconciled British and Americans might make common cause and invade Spanish Louisiana. The fear was not far-fetched.

To head off the possibility, Spanish ministers met with diplomat Thomas Pinckney and acquiesced to practically every demand that the Americans had made on Spain since 1783. In Pinckney's Treaty (officially the Treaty of San Lorenzo), Spain agreed to recognize the American version of the boundary between the United States and Louisiana, to open the Mississippi River to American navigation (the Spanish owned the western bank), and to grant Americans the "right of deposit" in New Orleans. The right of deposit allowed Americans to store their exports (mostly foodstuffs and timber) in New Orleans and to carry on the commercial transactions needed to dispose of them.

These concessions, which somewhat muted the resentment of Jay's Treaty, were invaluable to the more than 100,000 people who, by 1795, had settled in Kentucky, Tennessee, and the Northwest Territory.

THE TUMULTUOUS NORTHWEST

Life west of the Appalachians contrasted sharply with life on the Atlantic coast, settled now for up to seven generations. The killing labor of wrenching a farm out of a forest combined with disease to generate a death rate in the west as high as it had been in seventeenth-century Virginia and Maryland. The mountain barrier to transportation meant that manufactured goods, whether American or European, were expensive—when they were available. Western folkways reflected the hardships. Easterners saw frontier settlers as dangerously violent, "still more depraved than in Virginia," which, apparently, was saying something. "Like dogs and bears," it was said, "they use their teeth and feet, with the most savage ferocity, upon one another." And they used their firearms upon the numerous Indians who lived between the Appalachians and the Mississippi.

We the Marauding People

The federal government sincerely meant to keep the treaties it negotiated with the western tribes. It may have been delusory, but it was not cant when Congress wrote in the Northwest Ordinance of 1787 that "the utmost good faith shall always be observed towards the Indians; their lands and property shall never be taken from them without their Consent; and in their property, rights and liberty they shall never be invaded or disturbed."

Officials did not violate Indian treaties—the people did. New settlers, individually and in groups, crossed treaty lines and skirmished with Indians to whom the lands had been guaranteed. Nothing but "a Chinese Wall or a line of troops" could stop white "encroachment," an exasperated Washington exclaimed.

Nevertheless, when Indians responded violently to white incursions, the government came to the settlers' rescue.

MAP 11:2 Indian Wars in the Northwest Territory By abandoning their claims to southern and eastern Ohio in the Treaty of Greenville, the tribes of the Northwest Territory merely delayed further war with the expansive United States (as dissident Indian leaders protested). American settlers were soon moving north and west of the treaty line.

Dark and Bloody Ground

The most familiar image of Indian wars is set on the Great Plains in the latter nineteenth century. Here were the dramatic battles of pulp novel and film, the Seventh Cavalry in dusty blue battling mounted warriors of Sioux and Comanche in the wide-open spaces. In fact, the confrontations of the late eighteenth century between Americans and the tribes of the Northwest Territory—Miami, Shawnee, Ottawa, Ojibwa (Chippewa), Sauk, Fox—were fiercer and bloodier than the wars on the plains.

For one thing, the tribes of the Eastern Woodlands were more numerous than the Plains Indians. In the 1790s, supplied with firearms by the British in Fort Detroit, they were capable of fighting massive pitched battles. George A. Custer's column at the endlessly celebrated battle of Little Big Horn in 1876 numbered 265 men. In Ohio in 1794, General Anthony Wayne commanded an army 10 times that number. In Kentucky, casualties were so high that both Indians and whites called it "the dark and bloody ground."

In 1790, in retaliation for several Indian attacks on settlers, President Washington sent Josiah Harmer to subdue the Miami and Shawnee under the effective war chieftain Little Turtle. Poorly supplied, wracked by dysentery and malaria, and handicapped by unfamiliarity with the country, Harmer and his men were decimated near the site of present-day Fort Wayne, Indiana. The next year, a better-prepared expedition under Arthur St. Clair met the same fate; 600 soldiers were killed. Washington blamed both defeats on the fact that the soldiers were militiamen, for whom he never had a good word. In 1794, he sent General Anthony Wayne ("Mad Anthony") into Ohio with regular troops who defeated the Miami and Shawnee at the Battle of Fallen Timbers near Toledo. (The trees on the battlefield had been leveled by a tornado.) In the Treaty of Greenville, which followed, the tribes ceded the southern half of Ohio and a sliver of Indiana to the United States. The settlers had their way.

Of Pioneers and Whiskey

The men and women of the frontier were heavy drinkers. They launched their days with an "eye-opener" or "flem-cutter" of whiskey. A jug sat on shop counters; general stores doubled as saloons. Men and women swigged whiskey like wine with their meals and like water with their work. Preachers refreshed themselves with it during sermons. Virginian William Henry Harrison said that he "saw more drunk men in forty-eight hours succeeding my arrival in Cincinnati than I had in my previous life."

Disease played a part in the drinking. Frontier settlers suffered chronically from the alternating chills and fevers of malaria (they called it the "ague"). The medicine for which they reached was alcohol. Isolation contributed. Travelers in the Ohio Valley invariably described conversations with men, and especially women, who commented mournfully on the lack of company. Whiskey was a companion.

Finally, whiskey was cheap. The corn, wheat, and rye from which it was first made were easy to grow. The tech-nology was simple and required little labor: Ferment the mash of grain and water; boil it; condense the steam. Fuel was less than free—the wood from endless land clearing that had to be burned anyway. Many family farmers kept a small still percolating day and night. A market back east for the raw, white whiskey encouraged commercial distillers to set up large operations.

Of Whiskey and Rebellion

Whiskey became a cash crop because, before Pinckney's Treaty, westerners could not ship their grain down the Mississippi River. The cost of transporting such a low-value bulk commodity over the Appalachians was prohibitive. A pack horse could carry a burden of about 200 pounds: 4 bushels of corn, rye, or wheat. Four bushels of grain, in the food-rich United States, sold for pennies.

However, a horse could carry the equivalent of 24 bushels if the grain was converted into liquor. A gallon of whiskey sold for 25 cents or more, which provided just enough profit to make the trek plausible. Hamilton's excise tax of 1791 (7 cents per gallon) wiped the profit out. Like Daniel Shays' followers in Massachusetts, farmers in western Pennsylvania roughed federal tax collectors and rioted in river towns.

The parallels between Shays' Rebellion and the Whiskey Rebellion were not lost on Washington and Hamilton. They recognized an opportunity to demonstrate the contrast between the weakness of the old Confederation and the authority of the Constitutional government. The president himself set out at the head of 15,000 troops to suppress the rebels. He left the column when news reached him that the rebels had scattered. But Hamilton, who had a yen for military glory, pushed on and arrested a few Pennsylvanians who were convicted of treason and sentenced to death. Washington pardoned them, calling them mental defectives. Perhaps they were; perhaps it was just Washington's way of showing his contempt for the rebels and demonstrating that, among his other virtues, he did not thirst for blood.

In one sense, the suppression of the Whiskey Rebellion was a farce. An army as large as the one that had defeated the British—and much larger than the force at Fallen Timbers—was organized to crush a rebellion it could not even find. But the political significance of the episode was profound. The Federalist Hamilton was delighted to assert the national government's right to enforce order within one state with troops raised in other states. The resentment of the westerners, however, ensured that when political parties emerged full blown, they would not vote for Hamilton's party.

FEDERALISTS VERSUS REPUBLICANS

By the summer of 1796, when Washington announced that he would retire, warning Americans against political parties, two parties existed in everything but name. On every controversy that arose during Washington's presidency, Americans divided along the same lines.

▲ *The Whiskey Rebellion began with Pennsylvania frontiersmen assaulting federal tax collectors like this man, stripped, tarred, and feathered. Washington and Hamilton regarded the participants in the Whiskey Rebellion as what we would call "lowlifes," a judgment with which the artist agrees.*

Party Lines

The Federalists supported Hamilton's financial policy, abhorred the French Revolution as a fount of atheism and social disorder, were well disposed toward Great Britain, accepted Jay's Treaty, and believed that the federal government should act decisively and powerfully to maintain internal order. Vice President John Adams and Alexander Hamilton were the Federalists' chief spokesmen (although personally suspicious of one another). The party also included John Jay, the Pinckneys of South Carolina, conservatives like Gouverneur Morris of Pennsylvania, and, whether he liked it or not, George Washington himself. In New England, where money was made in trade and speculation, the urban rich were almost unanimously Federalist. In every state, Federalists were suspicious of "the people." "The many do not think," Massachusetts senator George Cabot put it.

The Jefferson Republicans opposed Hamilton's financial policies. Farmers (and some great planters) believed that they paid the taxes that financed funding and assumption while benefiting little from them. Republicans were friendly to the ideals of the French Revolution, although many of them cautiously. Republicans were generally suspicious of Britain as the former oppressor (Jefferson's anglophobia was lifelong) and as the ally and provisioner of the Indians in the west. Recent exiles from France and, after a rebellion was suppressed in 1797, from Ireland, were vociferously Republican. The Irish were, according to Connecticut senator Uriah Tracy, "the most God-provoking democrats this side of hell." Republicans despised Jay's Treaty. Inclining to democratic values that the Federalists spurned, the Republicans worried about a powerful national government quick to use soldiers against protesters such as those involved in the Whiskey Rebellion.

Washington the Villain

Washington was not universally adored. The invective heaped on him by editor Benjamin Bache (Benjamin Franklin's nephew) rivals anything found in newspapers today. In 1796, Bache wrote, "If ever a nation was debauched by a man, the American nation has been debauched by Washington." When Washington turned over the presidency to John Adams in March 1797, Bache exulted, "If ever there were a period for rejoicing, it is this moment. Every heart, in unison with the freedom and happiness of the people, ought to beat high in exultation, that the name of Washington ceases from this day to give a currency to political iniquity and to legalize corruption."

Election of 1796

Thomas Jefferson was the Republican candidate for president in 1796. Officially, Vice President John Adams of Massachusetts was the Federalists' man, and diplomat Thomas Pinckney of South Carolina, the Federalist vice presidential candidate. They were confident of victory. However, Hamilton, who could not resist a scheme, tried to manipulate the electoral college and put Pinckney in Adams's place. Pinckney dependably did Hamilton's bidding; Adams did not.

Hamilton's plot was possible because, before 1804, presidential electors did not vote separately for president and vice president. Each elector wrote two names on a ballot. The candidate with the most votes (it had to be a majority) became president, the runner-up, vice president. Because, in 1796, electors from nine states were selected by their legislatures—popular elections were held in just six states—Hamilton was able to persuade some Federalist politicians in the South to cast one of their two votes for Pinckney but the other, which should have gone to Adams, to somebody with no chance of winning. The hope was that enough southern Republicans would vote for Pinckney because he was a southerner that Pinckney would finish higher than Adams.

It might have worked. Hamilton's conspiracies were usually well thought out. But Adams's Federalist supporters in New England caught wind of the plot and retaliated by withholding votes from Pinckney. The result was anticipated by no one. Adams won but Pinckney did not finish second. Jefferson did. The president was the titular leader of one political party; the vice president was the actual leader of the other. The vice presidency was not a powerful office. But if the 61-year-old John Adams had died, his political rival, instead of a member of his own party, would have taken his place.

"His Rotundity"

After 200 years, it is easy to admire John Adams. When he was dispassionate, he was a moderate man who acted according to admirable principles. He could be humorous. When scandalmongers said that he had sent Pinckney to London to procure four loose women for his and Adams's use, he responded, "I do declare upon my honor, General Pinckney has cheated me out of my two." His relationship with his wife, Abigail, had a modern ring to it. He sought her advice on everything and often took it. "The President would not dare to make a nomination without her approbation," an opponent said. Adams was "always honest and often great," in Benjamin Franklin's words.

However, it is easier to admire Adams at a distance. He was also, as Franklin added, "sometimes mad." Neurotically insecure, he was vain and peevish. A raging temper often incinerated his judgment, and Adams could be laughably pompous. When wits sniggered at his short, dumpy physique ("His Rotundity," they whispered) and gossiped about his wife, Adams cut himself off, almost becoming a hermit. He spent astonishingly little time in the national capital, Philadelphia, until the last year of his presidency. During his four years as president, he spent one day out of every four at his home in Quincy, Massachusetts. By comparison, Washington was absent from his post fewer than one day in eight. The flaws in Adams's personality and the fact that he kept Washington's cabinet, almost all of them Hamilton's flunkeys, made the second president a president with only half a party behind him.

Another War Scare

Like Washington, Adams was preoccupied with the threat of war, this time with France as the enemy. Angered by Jay's Treaty, the French government ordered its navy and privateers to treat American ships as fair game. By the time Adams was inaugurated in March 1797, the French had seized 300 American vessels. Moreover, the French defined American sailors captured off British ships (many of whom had been pressed involuntarily into service) as pirates, who could legally be hanged. The American minister in Paris,

▲ *President John Adams, "His Rotundity," was able and principled but also "sometimes mad." He kept the United States out of a war with France despite extreme provocation and strident demands for war from his fellow Federalists.*

Charles Cotesworth Pinckney, was threatened with arrest. The French minister in the United States, Pierre Adet, railed against Adams almost as intemperately as Genet had assailed Washington.

Hamilton's supporters, the "High Federalists" who had reacted calmly to British seizures of American ships and sailors, demanded war with France. Determined to keep the peace, Adams dispatched two ministers, John Marshall and Elbridge Gerry, to join Pinckney in Paris, asking for negotiations.

The XYZ Affair

Marshall and Gerry were shunned for weeks, unable to get near the French foreign minister, the charming, devious, and corrupt Charles-Maurice de Talleyrand. Then, Talleyrand sent word through three henchmen—identified in code as "X," "Y," and "Z"—that he would speak with the Americans if they agreed in advance to a loan to France of $12 million and a personal gift to Talleyrand of $250,000.

Bribes were routine in diplomacy; but the sum Talleyrand demanded was excessive, and the tempers of the Americans were worn thin from waiting and humiliation. "Not a sixpence," Pinckney snapped. Back in the United States, Pinckney's reply was dressed up (and changed into the new American currency) as "millions for defense but not one cent for tribute."

The High Federalists were delighted by Talleyrand's insult. Hamilton pressured Adams to mobilize an army of 10,000 men. Washington agreed to become its titular commander on the condition that Hamilton be second in command. Not only did this mean Hamilton would jump rank over a large number of Revolutionary War officers, but it also humiliated Adams and put him in fear of a military coup.

Adams was more comfortable with the navy. He came from a maritime state, and sea power posed no threat to domestic order. (A country cannot be subdued from a ship.) Moreover, although it was difficult to say where France and America might fight on land, an undeclared war already raged on the seas. Adams authorized the construction of 40 frigates and lesser warships, a huge jump from the 3 naval vessels he inherited from Washington's administration.

The Alien and Sedition Acts

Jefferson's Republicans, still pro-French, trumpeted loudly against all preparations for war. The Federalists responded to the protest with a series of laws called the Alien and Sedition Acts of 1798.

The first extended the period of residence required for American citizenship from 5 to 14 years. This was a tacit admission that most newcomers to the United States were Republicans. Another Alien Act allowed the president to deport any foreigner whom he deemed "dangerous to the peace and safety of the United States." To leave no doubt of their political purpose, the Alien Acts would expire shortly after Adams's term ended in 1801.

The Sedition Act provided stiff fines and prison sentences for persons who published statements that held the United States government in "contempt or disrepute." Twenty-five cases were brought to trial; 10 people were convicted. Two Jeffersonians in Newark, New Jersey, were imprisoned because, when Adams was saluted by a volley of gunfire while visiting the city, one said, "There goes the president and they are shooting at his ass." The other responded, "I don't care if they fire through his ass." George Washington's nephew, Judge Bushrod Washington, ruled that these were seditious words exciting resistance to lawful government.

Other prosecutions were not so comical. In an effort to crush the opposition, Federalists convicted four important Republican newspaper editors of sedition.

The Virginia and Kentucky Resolutions

Jefferson and his protégé, James Madison, believed the Alien and Sedition Acts were unconstitutional, a violation of the Bill of Rights. But who was to declare when Congress enacted, and the president signed, a law violating the Constitution? The Constitution did not say. The answer Jefferson and

Madison gave was to haunt American history for half a century and contribute to the Civil War of 1861 to 1865.

In the Virginia and Kentucky Resolutions, adopted in the legislatures of those states in 1798 and 1799, Madison and Jefferson wrote that the federal government was a voluntary compact of sovereign states. Congress, therefore, was the creation of the states. When Congress enacted a law that a state deemed to be unconstitutional, that state had the right to nullify the law within its boundaries. Acting on this principle, the Virginia and Kentucky legislatures declared that the Alien and Sedition Acts could not be enforced in those states.

The logic of the Virginia and Kentucky Resolutions had its merits, but their implications were ominous. They marked a return to the supremacy of states, which, under the Articles of Confederation, no one had denied. In doing so, they challenged the supremacy of the federal government, which, Federalists maintained, the Constitution was written to establish. Nothing came of the challenge in 1799. No other state embraced the resolutions. The death of George Washington in December 1799 briefly calmed political tempers, and, as the election of 1800 drew nearer, it became increasingly obvious that instead of helping the Federalists, the Alien and Sedition Acts were so unpopular that they improved the chances of a Republican victory.

The Bizarre Election of 1800

As it happened, Jefferson's electoral victory over Adams in 1800 was nearly as tight as Adams's victory over Jefferson in 1796, and it was marked by a far more calamitous confusion in the electoral college. Jefferson won 73 electoral votes to Adams's 65. The only significant change in the political alignment of the states was the switch of New York from the Federalist to the Republican column; with 19 electoral votes, New York was the third biggest prize in presidential elections. This neat trick was the handiwork of a man who was Hamilton's rival for control of the state and his equal in political scheming.

Aaron Burr, 44 years old, brilliant and creative, was the Republican vice presidential candidate who swung New York for the Republicans. However, because none of the 73 Republican electors dropped Burr's name from his ballot so that he would finish in second place, the official count had the New Yorker tied with Jefferson.

The Constitution provided (and still provides) that when no candidate wins an absolute majority in the electoral college, the House of Representatives, voting by states, not by individuals, chooses the president. In 1800, this gave the Federalists the balance of power. The votes of nine states were required for election. The Republicans, who dutifully voted for Jefferson, controlled only eight state delegations in the House.

A Vote for Stability

When the first ballot was taken, Jefferson received eight votes to Burr's six; two states were evenly divided. Most Federalists voted for Burr, some because they believed that Jefferson was a dangerous radical, others because they hoped to throw the Republicans into disarray. Burr did not actively lobby Congress on his own behalf. At the same time, he said nothing to help elect Jefferson. He went into seclusion and hoped.

After 35 deadlocked ballots, a Delaware Federalist, James A. Bayard, fearing that the crisis would destroy the national government, announced he would change his vote to Jefferson on the next ballot. In the end, he did not have to do so. Hamilton's agents had contacted Jefferson and extracted vague commitments that he would continue Federalist foreign policy and maintain the Hamiltonian financial apparatus. Just as important, Hamilton loathed Aaron Burr. If Burr became president, Hamilton said, he would form an administration of "the rogues of all parties to overrule the good men." He conceded that Jefferson had at least a "pretension to character."

It was not much of a compliment, but it was enough. Hamilton pressured a few Federalist congressmen from key states to abstain on the thirty-sixth ballot. Jefferson was elected on February 17, 1801, two weeks before inauguration day.

Recognition of Political Parties

The original method of selecting the president was based on the premise that electors dedicated to the health of the republic would select the best man to be president and the second best to be vice president. It worked only as long as George Washington was on the scene. The election of 1796 showed that party politicians were willing to manipulate the electoral process to serve factional ends. The election of 1800 demonstrated that parties were fixtures of the American political process.

The original procedure of electing the president was no longer workable. It promised manipulations ignoring popular elections every four years. In 1804, the Twelfth Amendment provided that, from then on, electors would vote separately for president and vice president—the system that survives today. The amendment tacitly recognized political parties, which made nominations, as part of the constitutional process.

for FURTHER READING

A solid survey of the period is John C. Miller, *The Federalist Era,* 1960. The person of George Washington loomed over the era, so Douglas S. Freeman, *George Washington,* 1948, 1957, remains basic. See also Marcus Cunliffe, *Man and Monument,* 1958; James T. Flexner, *George Washington: Anguish and Farewell,* 1972; Forrest MacDonald, *The Presidency of George Washington,* 1974; Edmund S. Morgan, *The Genius of George Washington,* 1980; and Garry Wills, *Cincinnatus: George Washington and the Enlightenment,* 1984.

On the Adams presidency, see Stephen G. Kurtz, *The Presidency of John Adams,* 1957; and Ralph Brown Adams, *The Presidency of John Adams,* 1975. David McCullough, the finest living American biographer, recently turned his attention to Adams with excellent results. See McCullough's *John Adams,* 2001. John Adams cannot be fully appreciated without reference to his thoughtful wife, whose advice he valued above that of any other person. See Lynne Withey, *Dearest Friend: A Life of Abigail Adams,* 1981.

The emergence of political parties in America is treated (with differing interpretations) in William D. Chambers, *Political Parties in a New Nation,* 1962; Joseph Charles, *The Origins of the American Party System,* 1956; and Richard Hofstadter, *The Idea of a Party System,* 1969. Also see Daniel Boorstin, *The Lost World of Thomas Jefferson,* 1948; and Merrill Peterson, *Thomas Jefferson and the New Nation,* 1970. On Jefferson's great rival, see Jacob E. Cook, *Alexander Hamilton,* 1982.

Sources for episodes of the 1790s include Harry Ammon, *The Genêt Mission,* 1973; Leland D. Baldwin, *Whiskey Rebels: The Story of a Frontier Uprising,* 1939; Gerald A. Combs, *The Jay Treaty,* 1970; Samuel F. Bemis, *Pinckney's Treaty,* 1926; Leonard W. Levy, *Legacy of Suppression: Freedom of Speech in Early America,* 1960; and James M. Smith, *Freedom's Fetters: The Alien and Sedition Laws and American Civil Liberties,* 1956.

 AMERICAN JOURNEY ONLINE AND INFOTRAC COLLEGE EDITION

Visit the source collections at http://ajaccess.wadsworth.com and http://infotrac.thomsonlearning.com, and use the Search function with the following key terms to explore documents, images, audio and video clips, articles, and commentary related to the material in this chapter:

Aaron Burr
Abigail Adams
Alexander Hamilton
George Washington

James Madison
John Adams
Whiskey Rebellion
XYZ Affair

Additional resources, exercises, and Internet links related to this chapter are available on *The American Past* Web site: http://history.wadsworth.com/americanpast7e.

HISTORY ONLINE

The Avalon Project
www.yale.edu/lawweb/avalon/debates/debcont.htm
A superb guide to the debates at the Constitutional Convention prepared by Yale Law School; includes a "Search" function.

White House
www.whitehouse.gov/history/presidents/index.html
An official government resource for presidents from George Washington to the present.

JEFFERSONIAN AMERICA

Expansion and Frustration 1800–1815

Smithsonian Institute, Bureau of American Ethnology

> The immortality of Thomas Jefferson does not lie in any one of his achievements, or in the series of his achievements, but in his attitude toward mankind.
>
> Woodrow Wilson

> Since the days when Jefferson expounded his code of political philosophy, the whole world has become his pupil.
>
> Michael MacWhite

In 1962, President John F. Kennedy invited American winners of the Nobel Prize to the White House. He greeted them by saying, "This is the most extraordinary collection of talent, of human knowledge, that has been gathered at the White House, with the possible exception of when Thomas Jefferson dined here alone."

Kennedy was cleverer than he was precise. Nobelists are honored for profound contributions to knowledge. Jefferson's intellect was not deep; he was not an original thinker. But his intellect ranged more broadly than the combined intellect of a dozen research scientists. Few men and women—certainly no other American president—had so oceanic a breadth of interests and serious studies as the tall, slightly stooped man with graying red hair who took the presidential oath of office in March 1801.

THE SAGE OF MONTICELLO

After writing the nation's birth certificate, the Declaration of Independence, Jefferson was wartime governor of Virginia, then the Confederation's minister to France. He was the first secretary of state, and, from his home at Monticello in Virginia, a political strategist who, in dozens of letters a day, organized the party that elected him president in 1801.

Jack of All Trades

Jefferson was a scholar, constantly in a book, of which there were more than 6,000 in his personal library. He read and spoke several European languages and studied Native American tongues. He wrote better than any other president. His English was precise in vocabulary and mellifluous in its rhythms. He published only one short book, *Notes on Virginia*, but it was superb. His shorter works and letters (18,000 survive) fill bookshelves.

Courtesy of the Thomas Jefferson Memorial Foundation

▲ *Monticello, Jefferson's home in Charlottesville, Virginia. He designed the home and supervised the large plantation and the great number of slaves who supported him. Here, for most of his life, he studied and carried on a correspondence that occupied many hours daily.*

Jefferson founded, and designed the buildings of, the University of Virginia. He designed Monticello and anonymously entered the competition of architects to design the president's mansion—the White House. He invented the dumbwaiter and the swivel chair. He was a gourmet who may have introduced pasta to America. He was a spendthrift. Shopping—frantic, expensive shopping—was a high priority when he lived in Paris and visited London. He spent as much as $2,800 a year on wines and $50 in a day on groceries when a turkey cost 75 cents. He employed French chefs at home and in Washington.

Mixed Reviews

Jefferson was no demigod. His vision of America's future was shallow next to Hamilton's. He could be as peevish as John Adams and more vindictive (perhaps only because he held power longer). He was no orator, partly out of shyness, partly because he was self-conscious of a lisp.

Nor was Jefferson universally admired—not by a long shot. Adams rarely missed an opportunity to snipe at him (although they were reconciled as old men). Hamilton thought him softheaded and frivolous. Other Federalists believed that he was a voluptuary and a dangerous radical. During the presidential campaign of 1800, the *Connecticut Courant* warned that Mad Tom's election would mean "your dwellings in flames, hoary hairs bathed in blood, female chastity violated, children writhing on the pike and the halberd." Not yet exhausted, the editor continued, "Murder, rape, adultery, and incest will be openly taught and practiced" in a

Wine Snob

Jefferson loved his wine and subjected many a guest at dinner to perhaps lengthier discourses on the nuances of the beverage they were sipping than they appreciated. It was a long-standing interest. As early as 1773, Jefferson gave Filippo Mazzei of Florence 200 acres adjoining his own plantation so that he could plant a vineyard from Italian cuttings. Unfortunately, just as it was beginning to produce, Mazzei enlisted to fight the British and never returned.

Jefferson believed that "we could in the United States, make as great a variety of wines as are made in Europe, not exactly of the same kinds, but doubtless as good." He planted several vineyards at Monticello (mostly Italian grapes) but never succeeded in pleasing his palate.

Jeffersonian America. Phlegmatic anti-Jeffersonians contented themselves with the gossip that one of Jefferson's slaves, Sally Hemmings, was his concubine.

JEFFERSON AS PRESIDENT

Jefferson knew he owed his election to Federalists in the House of Representatives. In his inaugural address, he attempted to woo those Federalists who were not "devoted to monarchy" by saying that "every difference of opinion is not a difference in principle. We have called by different names brethren of the same principle. We are all republicans, we are all federalists." Privately, he wrote of "honest and well-intentioned" Federalists.

Continuities

To a degree, the new president acted on his hint of transpartisanship. He quietly abandoned some prepresidential positions and adopted Federalist policies that he had condemned. Nothing more was heard from him or his secretary of state, James Madison, about the doctrine of nullification they had put forward in the Kentucky and Virginia Resolutions. Jefferson allowed Hamilton's financial program to work for him, including the Bank of the United States, which he had called unconstitutional. He appointed as secretary of the treasury the Swiss-born Albert Gallatin of Pennsylvania, who proved to be as responsible a money manager as his Federalist predecessors, without their coziness with northeastern speculators.

Republican Simplicity

Jefferson brought a new style to the presidency. He disliked the pomp and protocol that had been important to Washington and Adams. Instead of exchanging bows, he shook hands. He abolished presidential levees (regularly scheduled, highly formal receptions). Much to the annoyance of some officials and diplomats, he paid scant heed to protocol, the rules that assigned a rank of precedence—a chair at the dinner table, a position in a procession—to every senator, representative, judge, cabinet member, and minister from abroad. Even at state dinners, guests scrambled for the places they believed suited to their dignity. Indeed, Jefferson preferred small dinner parties at which he wore bedroom slippers and served the meal himself.

Jefferson's "republican simplicity" was made easier by the move of the capital, the summer before his inauguration, from sophisticated Philadelphia to Washington. It was no city at all in 1800, but a bizarre hodgepodge of partly completed public buildings and ramshackle boarding houses, isolated from one another by woods and marshes in which strangers often got lost. There were precious few private homes; for years, there would be no place in Washington for congressmen's families. Social life was masculine and on the raw side: smoky card games, heavy drinking, brawls, even the odd gunfight.

Changes

Not all Jefferson's innovations were stylistic. He pardoned the people imprisoned under the Sedition Act, all of whom were his supporters, of course. He restored the five-year residency for citizenship and replaced Federalist officeholders with Republicans. (There were not many jobs to bestow. In 1800, the government employed 3,000 mostly part-time post office workers, 700 clerks, and just 316 people appointed by the president.)

Jefferson and Gallatin slashed government expenditures, reducing the army's budget from $4 million to $2 million and the navy's from $3.5 million to $1 million. Their army consisted of only 3,000 troops; the navy, of just seven ships. Gallatin devised a plan to retire the national debt by 1817.

But these actions hardly constituted the "Revolution of 1800" that Jefferson called his election. The only fundamental innovation in the government during the Age of Jefferson was effected by Jefferson's enemy (although his cousin), the Federalist chief justice of the Supreme Court, John Marshall.

Marbury v. Madison

Shortly before Adams turned the White House over to Jefferson, he appointed 42 Federalists to the bench. Federal judges served for life, so Adams was securing long-term employment for loyal supporters. He also wanted to ensure that the judiciary, which was independent of both presidency and Congress would remain a bastion of Federalist principles.

Adams was setting a precedent. The appointment of "midnight judges" (and issuing last-minute pardons) would become standard operating procedure for outgoing presidents whose party had been defeated at the polls. Like incoming presidents who would follow him, Jefferson could only sit and steam to contemplate the salaries that were lost to his own Republicans.

The case of William Marbury was an exception. Thanks to the inefficiency and oversight that would also become a feature of American government, the document that entitled Marbury to a judgeship was not delivered before March 4, when Jefferson took office. On the face of it, Adams's dereliction was immaterial. According to the Judiciary Act of 1789, the secretary of state—James Madison as of March 4, 1801—was obligated to deliver Marbury's commission. When Madison refused to do so, Marbury sued for a writ of mandamus—a court order that compels a government official to perform his duty (*mandamus* is Latin for "we compel").

By 1803, the case was before the Supreme Court, dominated for three decades by Chief Justice Marshall. The force of his personality was so great, his willingness to do the lion's share of the Court's work so eager, and his legal mind so acute, that Marshall almost always had his way with the other justices. In the case *Marbury v. Madison,* Marshall scolded Madison for unseemly behavior. However, instead of mandating him to deliver Marbury's commission, Marshall ruled that the section of the law under which Marbury had sued was unconstitutional. Congress, Marshall said, had no constitutional right to give the federal courts the powers that the Judiciary Act of 1789 accorded them.

The Doctrine of Judicial Review

Marbury v. Madison was a masterstroke. By sacrificing the paycheck of one Federalist politico and canceling part of one Federalist law, Marshall asserted the Supreme Court's right to decide which acts of Congress were constitutional and which were unconstitutional and therefore void. The Supreme Court not only judged cases *according to* the law; the Court judged the validity of the law itself.

Nothing in the Constitution vested the Court with this substantial power. Jefferson and Madison had claimed it for the state legislatures. And Marshall did not decisively confirm the power for the Supreme Court. Only usage—very cautious usage—established judicial review as unquestioned. (The next time the Supreme Court declared an act of Congress unconstitutional was in 1857.)

Jefferson could not fight Marshall on high ground. Instead, he approved a campaign of machinations against the Federalist judiciary. First, he tried to get rid of Federalist judges by abolishing their jobs. Then, the Republicans impeached and removed from office a Federalist judge in New Hampshire, John Pickering. That was easy; Pickering was given to drunken tirades in court and was probably insane. Jefferson's supporters then inched closer to Marshall by impeaching Supreme Court justice Samuel Chase.

Chase was an inferior jurist, grossly prejudiced, overtly political, sometimes asinine. But the Senate refused to find him guilty of the "high crimes and misdemeanors" that the Constitution sets as grounds for impeachment. Like other presidents unhappy with the Supreme Court, Jefferson had no choice but to wait until seats fell vacant. He was able to name three justices, but they too were captivated by Marshall's mind and will.

THE LOUISIANA PURCHASE

If John Marshall tweaked the Constitution, Jefferson gave it a mighty wrench in the most significant act of his presidency, the purchase of Louisiana from France for $15 million. The Louisiana of 1803 was not the present-day state of that name. As a French (later Spanish) colony, Louisiana included the better part of the 13 states that, today, lie between the Mississippi River and the Rocky Mountains, 828,000 square miles. The United States paid less than three cents an acre, the greatest real estate bargain of all time.

Sugar and Food

Such a deal was possible only because the French emperor, Napoleon Bonaparte, abandoned the notion of creating a new French American empire, an idea he had toyed with. His plan was based on the fact that France's possessions in the West Indies—the islands of Martinique, Guadeloupe, and Saint-Domingue (present-day Haiti)—were valuable producers of sugar and coffee but also vulnerable because their large slave populations depended on food imported from Spanish Louisiana and the United States to survive.

Napoleon's plan was to force Spain, a client state, to return Louisiana to France, after which the West Indian islands would no longer be dependent on American foodstuffs. There were only about 50,000 people of European descent in Louisiana, but the endless lands bordering the Mississippi River invited agricultural development. In 1801, Napoleon regained Louisiana (supposedly in secret, but France's reacquisition of the territory was well known).

A Vital Interest

At Napoleon's request, the Spanish revoked the right of deposit that Pinckney's Treaty had guaranteed—the right of Americans to store and trade their products in New Orleans. The response among the 400,000 Americans who lived in Kentucky, Tennessee, and the Northwest Territory was near panic. They annually shipped 20,000 tons of provisions down the Mississippi to New Orleans on log rafts, which they broke apart and sold in the city for lumber. To westerners, in James Madison's words, the Mississippi was "the Hudson, the Delaware, the Potomac, and all the navigable rivers of the Atlantic formed into one stream." Jefferson added, "There is on the globe one single spot, the possessor of which is our natural and habitual enemy. It is New Orleans."

War with France seemed inevitable. Congress voted funds to call up 80,000 state militiamen. But any attack on New Orleans would require a naval blockade of the port as well as an overland assault, and Jefferson was in the process of eviscerating the American navy. The British, sworn enemies of Napoleon, would be glad to lend a hand, but such an alliance was repugnant to a president who had written the Declaration of Independence.

An Offer Not to Be Refused

Jefferson gambled that there was an alternative to war arm-in-arm with the British. He instructed his minister in France, Robert R. Livingston, to offer Napoleon $2 million (voted him by Congress) for a tract of undeveloped land on the lower Mississippi, where the Americans might build their own port. In January 1803, impatient that no news had arrived from France, Jefferson gambled: He sent James Monroe to Paris to offer up to $10 million (a sum that had appeared in no congressional appropriation) for New Orleans and West Florida—what is now the Mississippi and Alabama coast.

When Monroe arrived, he was stunned to learn that, a few days earlier, the French foreign minister, Talleyrand again, had offered Livingston all of Louisiana for $15 million.

This remarkable turnabout had nothing to do with American wants and needs. Louisiana had become worthless to Napoleon. Black rebels in Haiti, France's most valuable West Indian colony, both slaves and free men, had battered a crack French army. Some 30,000 French troops were killed in battle or incapacitated by tropical fevers. "Damn sugar," Napoleon said on hearing of the debacle. "Damn coffee. Damn colonies! Damn niggers!"

He might have damned Britain too, for he was planning for war with the old enemy, and he knew that the Royal Navy would promptly and easily seize New Orleans and Louisiana.

Constitutional Niceties

The Louisiana Purchase was sealed despite the fact that it was without congressional or even constitutional sanction. The Founding Fathers had made no provision for acquiring territory or, as required by the terms of the sale, conferring United States citizenship on the residents of Louisiana. But it was far too great an opportunity to be rejected.

Some Federalists called Jefferson a hypocrite for abandoning, with a vengeance, his strict constructionist theory of the Constitution. Jefferson—one hopes sheepishly—wrote that "what is practicable must often control what is pure theory." He instructed Republicans in Congress that "the less we say about constitutional difficulties respecting Louisiana the better." Even members of Jefferson's party far more zealous in their legalism than he, like John Randolph and John Taylor of Virginia, held their tongues. What is beneficial and practicable must indeed control what is pure theory.

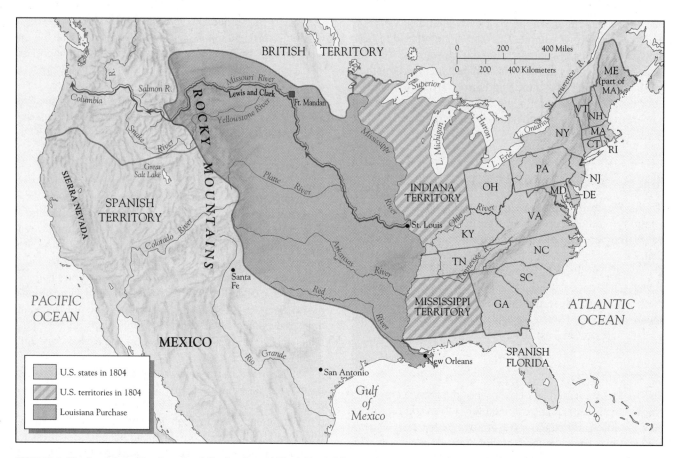

MAP 12:1 The Louisiana Purchase and the Lewis and Clark Expedition, 1804–1805 The Louisiana Purchase virtually doubled the size of the United States. Little was known about the new land and its peoples, however, until a series of explorations that began with the great journey of the Lewis and Clark expedition up the Missouri River and down the Columbia.

The Northwest Passage

The first explorers of North America were looking for a "northwest passage"—a sea route to East Asia through or around the top of the continent. In 1592, Juan de Fuca claimed to have found it from the Pacific and that it was an easy 20-day trip through a land rich in gold. Others looked vainly for de Fuca's "Strait of Anian." Despite their failure, belief in the strait's existence did not completely die until the time of the American Revolution, when explorers James Cook and George Vancouver conjectured, surely correctly, that de Fuca had sailed around Vancouver Island from the north and, reaching open sea, figured it was the Atlantic, then returned the way he had come.

When Jefferson sent Lewis and Clark across the continent, all hoped they would find a workable passage to the Pacific, that is, a *mostly* water route. They found the Rocky Mountains.

Throughout the nineteenth century, intrepid adventurers attempted to sail ships between North America and the Arctic ice cap, no longer in hopes of a trade route but so as to be treated to dinner at the Explorer's Club. A few survived, although their ships were crushed by the ice. Finally, success was attained. In 1958, the first nuclear submarine, *Nautilus,* circled North America by cruising under the ice cap.

The Magnificent Journey

Louisiana aroused Jefferson's lifelong interests in natural science and the still mysterious interior of the continent. He persuaded Congress to appropriate $2,500 to finance an expedition across the continent for the purposes of looking for a feasible overland trade route and to gather scientific data.

African American Explorer

In the informality demanded by wilderness, William Clark's slave, York, participated in the great expedition as an equal. Meriwether Lewis recorded that when many Indians first saw York, they believed he was a white man wearing paint. Only after trying to rub his color from him did they accept York's explanation of himself. Lewis noted that "instead of inspiring any prejudice, his color served to procure him additional advantages from the Indians," a decorous way of saying he had a way with the Indian ladies who wanted a black child. Clark freed York after the expedition, but not gracefully. Despite what he and his human property had accomplished together, Clark wanted to keep York in bondage. York and Clark's friends wore him down only after considerable effort.

▲ *York was one of the most valuable members of the Lewis and Clark expedition, a party of men and one Indian girl who were selected so carefully as to be a perfect complement. He was William Clark's slave and, despite his services, Clark had to be pressured to reward him with his freedom by friends disturbed by Clark's reluctance to do so.*

Jefferson entrusted the mission to a Virginian neighbor, Meriwether Lewis, and William Clark, Lewis's friend and former commanding officer. He must have yearned to go himself, for he attended to the most picayune details of preparation, listing in his own hand the provisions the explorers would need.

The trek exceeded anything ventured by conquistadores or voyagers. Lewis, Clark, and a crew of 40 rowed, poled, and pulled their skiffs up the Missouri to the river's spectacular falls (present-day Great Falls, Montana). After portaging 16 miles, they enlisted the help of the Mandan, Shoshone, Nez Percé, and other tribes of the region to find a tributary of the Columbia River. Following it, they reached the Pacific on November 15, 1805. There they lived four and a half months and returned to St. Louis in September 1806.

Lewis and Clark were among the last Americans to confront Indians untouched by Western civilization. Their experience is instructive. Although there were a few uneasy moments with the Sioux and Shoshone on the trip west, the explorers engaged in nothing resembling a fight with the dozens of tribes they confronted. (They did kill two Blackfoot on their return trip.) Almost all the native peoples of the interior were hospitable. When Lewis needed to show he was not a member of a hated tribe, he exposed his arm to

show his skin was white. York, Clark's slave (freed at the end of the expedition), was a source of endless fascination among the Indians because of his color.

The Shoshone, with whom the expedition could communicate through Sacagawea (a Shoshone teenager who joined the expedition), gave key advice on finding the Pacific, which the Shoshone themselves had never seen. The tribes of the Pacific Coast, however, had traded with American and European seamen, whalers, and fur traders. One woman had the name "Jonathan Bowman" tattooed on her leg. The coastal Indians had adopted as their own the words "misquit, powder, shot, nife, file, damned rascal, son of a bitch."

Jefferson believed that the country Lewis and Clark traversed would provide land for Americans for a thousand generations. His estimate was off by 999. By the 1820s, Americans were trudging through Louisiana to settle in Mexican Texas. There was no frontier line anywhere in the purchase by 1890.

The Further Adventures of Aaron Burr

Louisiana also figured in the bizarre career of Aaron Burr. His fortunes tumbled downhill immediately after his election as vice president in 1801, when Jefferson snubbed him

▲ *Aaron Burr as a young man, painted by Gilbert Stuart. He was a handsome, charming, intelligent, and persuasive man. He was also a rogue grounded in few principles and ruined his political career with his schemes and passions.*

because of Burr's behavior in the election controversy. And Burr, like Adams and Jefferson, found that the vice presidency provided him with little to do.

When men like Burr are bored, they scheme; when Burr schemed, he schemed big. With a few embittered New England Federalists (called the "Essex Junto"), he plotted, apparently, to detach New York and New England from the United States. The plan depended on Burr winning election as governor of New York, but he was defeated, in part because of campaign propaganda authored by Alexander Hamilton. Burr challenged Hamilton to a duel.

Hamilton disapproved of dueling. His son had only recently been killed in a duel. But the feud was beyond shrugging off, and, on July 11, 1804, the two men and their seconds rowed across the Hudson with 0.54 caliber pistols to Weehawken, high on the New Jersey Palisades. They fired at one another from 20 paces. Hamilton's bullet went astray; some said he deliberately shot high, as reluctant duelists often did. Burr aimed; his bullet pierced Hamilton's liver and lodged in his spine. Hamilton died the next day.

The first secretary of the treasury was never beloved, but the death of so eminent a man in a duel shocked the nation. Burr was indicted for murder in New York and New Jersey. He fled to the South while friends ironed out his legal difficulties. Not yet 50 years of age and full of energy, his political career was finished. What next?

The Burr Conspiracy

Like thousands of his contemporaries, Burr went west. He linked up with one Harman Blennerhasset, an Irish exile who lived opulently, on wealth never explained, on an island in the Ohio River. Blennerhasset constructed 13 flatboats, including a barge for Burr outfitted with glass windows, a fireplace, a promenade deck, and a wine cellar. With 60 men, the flotilla meandered down the Ohio and the Mississippi.

Burr met secretly with Andrew Jackson, a prominent politician and soldier in Tennessee, and, in New Orleans, with the head of the Ursuline convent, Louisiana's most powerful woman. He had a number of discussions with James Wilkinson, the territorial governor of Louisiana and a character so devious as to make Burr look like a bumpkin.

What was up? Burr was accused variously of planning to invade Spanish Mexico and of organizing a secession of the western states and Louisiana Territory from the United States. Jefferson was of a mind to believe the worst. When Wilkinson, possibly in a panic over what he had considered, accused Burr of plotting treason, Jefferson had the New Yorker arrested and returned to Richmond, where he was tried before Chief Justice John Marshall.

Marshall was apt to snipe at anything dear to Jefferson, even if it was to the benefit of the likes of Aaron Burr. He insisted on defining treason strictly, as requiring an overt act. No matter: The prosecution's case was sloppy, few accusations were corroborated, and the unsavory Wilkinson was a weak reed on which to support an allegation. Nothing of substance was proved against Burr, and he was acquitted.

Burr moved abroad for a few years, then returned to New York, where one more scandal put him back in the newspapers. His second wife, Eliza Bowen Jumel, formerly a prostitute, claimed to be the only woman in the world to have slept with both George Washington and Napoleon Bonaparte.

FOREIGN WOES

Like Washington and Adams, Jefferson found foreign affairs a frustration. In fact, Jefferson helped to set himself up for trouble by allowing Adams's navy to dwindle to a few ships. He soon learned that a country with vital interests in international trade had to be able to protect its merchant ships.

The Barbary Pirates

One trouble spot was the Mediterranean, where the economy of the Barbary ("Berber") States—Morocco, Algiers, Tunis, and Tripoli—was based on piracy. The Berbers seized

---

Tribute to the Pasha

The annual payment to the pasha of Tripoli, which Jefferson attempted to cancel in 1801, consisted of $40,000 in gold and silver, $12,000 in Spanish money, and an odd assortment of diamond rings, watches, and fine cloth and brocade. The rulers of the Barbary States thought of these as gifts from friends rather than as extortion. For example, in 1806 the bey of Tunis, who also received tribute, sent Jefferson a gift of four Arabian horses.

▲ *Stephen Decatur led several punitive expeditions to the Barbary States. Here he is shown bombarding Tripoli (in present-day Libya). His assaults were effective and popular at home, but it was only when France began to establish imperial control of North Africa that the menace of the pirates was put to rest.*

the vessels of seafaring nations that did not pay annual tribute to their beys and pashas. France, Britain, Spain, Holland, and Venice found paying "protection money" cheaper than maintaining warships to protect their thousands of Mediterranean merchant ships. During the 1790s, the United States paid too, about $2 million.

The indignity of it rankled on Jefferson, who ignored the demands of the pasha of Tripoli for another installment. Tripolitan pirates promptly seized the crew of an American ship and demanded ransom. Jefferson ordered a punitive expedition. After four years of intermittent bombardment and a daring amphibious attack by marines led by Stephen Decatur (commemorated in "to the shores of Tripoli" in the Marine Corps hymn), Jefferson gave up, paying Tripoli $60,000 for the release of captive Americans, a transaction not immortalized in song. Barbary Coast piracy, kidnapping, and slave trading continued for another decade until Decatur returned to North Africa, and France began to establish imperial control over North Africa.

America in the Middle Again

A more serious threat was the war between France and England that began shortly after the purchase of Louisiana. Jefferson declared neutrality, and, at first, American shipowners were delighted to reap profits trading with both sides. Especially lucrative was the reexport trade—West Indian products brought to the United States and then shipped to Europe under the neutral American flag. In two years, this business more than quadrupled in value, from $13 million to $60 million.

Then, in 1805, the Anglo-French conflict reached an impasse with the Royal Navy supreme at sea and Napoleon unchallengeable on the European continent. Both sides dug in for a protracted economic war, each aiming to ruin the other by crippling its trade. The British issued the Orders in Council, forbidding neutrals to trade in Europe unless their ships first called at a British port to purchase a license. New England merchants, who inclined to be pro-British, did not find the Orders in Council intolerable. However, Napoleon retaliated with the Berlin and Milan decrees of 1806 and 1807, enacting what he called the "Continental System": Any neutral vessels that observed the Orders in Council would be seized by the French.

American merchants were caught in the middle. Within a year, the British seized 1,000 American ships, and the French, about 500. Even then, the profits from successful voyages more than compensated for the losses. One Massachusetts senator calculated that if a shipowner sent three vessels out and two were dead losses, the profits from the third made him a richer man than he had been. Statistics bear him out. In 1807, at the height of the seizures, Massachusetts merchants earned $15 million in freight charges alone.

A British press gang boards an American merchant ship and takes a resisting seaman for service in the Royal Navy. If he lived and later proved he was American-born and had never served in the British Navy, he would be released (thousands were)—but not compensated for his impressment.

Impressment Again

Richly paid humiliation is a situation with which a great many human beings have lived and always will. However, the issue in the wars of the 1800s involved more than the balances in American ledgers. Britain's massive naval effort also meant a renewal of the impressment problem of the 1790s. Chronically short of sailors, British captains once again began to board American merchant vessels and draft crewmen who, they insisted, were British subjects. There were plenty of such men on American vessels. Conditions under the American flag were much better than on British ships, the pay sometimes three times as much. As many as a quarter of the 42,000 seamen on American ships were born in Britain.

The trouble was, many of them had become American citizens, a transfer of allegiance British captains did not recognize. Yet others impressed into the Royal Navy were American by birth. About 10,000 bona fide citizens of the United States (by American standards) were forced to serve in the Royal Navy during the Napoleonic Wars. Some 4,000 were released as soon as they reached a British port, but, at sea, arrogant or merely desperate naval officers were grabbing more.

The impressment crisis came to a head in June 1807, when, within swimming distance of the Virginia shore, the HMS *Leopard,* with 50 guns, ordered the lesser American frigate *Chesapeake* to stand by for boarding. The American captain refused, and the *Leopard* fired three broadsides, killing several sailors. A British press gang then boarded the *Chesapeake* and removed four men, including two American-born black men who had once served in the Royal Navy.

The patriotic uproar was deafening. The *Chesapeake* was no merchant ship taking a chance on a commercial expedition but a naval vessel cruising American waters. Jefferson had to act. He chose what he called "peaceable coercion."

The Embargo

Under the Embargo Act of 1807, American ships in port were forbidden to leave. Foreign vessels were sent to sea in ballast (carrying boulders or other worthless bulk in their hulls). All imports and exports were prohibited. The embargo was total economic war, designed to force the British, who also benefited from American trade, to respect American claims.

For Jefferson, who had seen economic boycott bring Parliament around during his youth, the embargo looked like a sure thing. In 1807, however, the British were at odds not with their own colonies but with a national rival sworn to reduce Great Britain to a dependency. The British wanted American trade, but not at any price.

Americans suffered more from the embargo than Great Britain did. Staple farmers lost their foreign markets, the livelihood of many of them. Seaports suffered across the

The Two-Term Tradition

When Washington rejected a third term as president, he made no point of principle about it. He was old and tired, he said. In 1805, beginning his own second term, Jefferson consciously founded the two-term tradition. He wrote of Washington's example, "I shall follow it, and a few more precedents will oppose the obstacle of habit to anyone after a while who shall endeavor to extend his term. Perhaps it may beget a disposition to establish it by an amendment to the Constitution."

Madison, Monroe, and Andrew Jackson all retired after two terms. So did Ulysses S. Grant in 1877; however, in 1880, broke and not yet old, he tried (unsuccessfully) to run again. Theodore Roosevelt retired after nearly eight years in office, although, having been elected only once, he could have run again without violating the tradition. Like Grant, Theodore Roosevelt also tried to return to the White House four years after leaving it. Woodrow Wilson and Calvin Coolidge would both have liked to have a third term but dared not say it, so powerful had the tradition become. Only in 1940, with Europe at war, did Franklin D. Roosevelt seek and win a third term (and four years later, a fourth).

Franklin D. Roosevelt's defiance of the tradition—not the precedents for which Jefferson hoped and got—resulted in the constitutional amendment Jefferson imagined. In 1947, Republicans who had simmered during Roosevelt's long presidency, took a posthumous slap at him by proposing the Twenty-Second Amendment to the Constitution. It forbids a president to serve more than two terms. Ironically, the two presidents since who could probably have won a third term were popular Republicans, Dwight D. Eisenhower and Ronald Reagan.

board. Ships rode at anchor, rotting; tens of thousands of seamen and shore laborers had no work; businesses dependent on their wages struggled if they did not close their doors. The Federalist party, badly maimed when Jefferson was reelected in 1804, began to make a comeback in maritime New England and New York.

By early 1809, the embargo had cost the American economy three times the estimated price of a war. The protests were so loud and widespread that Congress, though overwhelmingly Jeffersonian, was forced to abandon it. Joylessly, Jefferson signed the bill. In just three days, his handpicked successor, the ever dependable James Madison, would be sworn in as president. Jefferson would not burden him with his debacle.

Jemmy Applejohn and the War of 1812

James Madison was a profound student of political philosophy. He is still widely read not out of curiosity but for his wisdom. But Madison was not cut out to be head of a government. He was the butt of gossipy sarcasm, even ridicule, in the highest circles. Short and slight, he encouraged perceptions of him as weak with interminable complaints of aches, pains, and ailments. (Madison's constitution was sound enough—he lived on, sniffling, moaning, and groaning, until he was 85.) His face was pinched by furrows, inspiring the writer Washington Irving to quip that "Little Jemmy" looked like a "withered applejohn," that is, an apple that had been dried so as to be stored. He was "too timid" in the words of a critic, Fisher Ames, and "wholly unfit for the Storms of War" according to his supporter, Henry Clay.

The Non-Intercourse Act and Macon's Bill No. 2

The embargo expired on March 15, 1809, and was superceded by the Non-Intercourse Act. The act reopened trade with all nations *except* England and France and provided that the United States would resume trading with whichever of those two belligerents agreed to respect the rights of neutral American shipping. But all Jefferson and Madison had done (Jefferson signed the Non-Intercourse Act before Madison's

The Emperor of America

President Madison was content to be addressed as "Mr. President." But, in one communiqué, the bey of Algiers called him "His Majesty, the Emperor of America, its adjacent and dependent provinces and coasts and wherever his government may extend, our noble friend, the support of the Kings of the nation of Jesus, the most glorious amongst the princes, elected among many lords and nobles, the happy, the great, the amiable, James Madison, Emperor of America."

inauguration), like chess players of limited skill, was to open the board for a gambit by cleverer players.

The British moved. David Erskine, the British minister to Washington, agreed to American terms, and Madison opened trade with Britain. Then, back in London, the British Foreign Office repudiated Erskine's treaty. Madison was humiliated.

A year later, in May 1810, the Jefferson Republicans replaced the Non-Intercourse Act with Macon's Bill No. 2. It *opened* commerce with both Britain and France, with the proviso that if either of the two ceased to molest American shipping, the United States would cut off trade with the other. In other words, the United States would take its licks at sea for the present but collaborate with the belligerent power that stopped harassing American ships. If the object was to stay out of all-out war, Macon's Bill No. 2 was the worst of the three Jeffersonian trade laws. It effectively proclaimed America's willingness to become an ally of either France or Britain in their economic war.

This time, Napoleon advanced a pawn. With no intention of depriving French privateers of the pleasure of taking American prizes, he revoked the Continental System. Madison, as Macon's Bill No. 2 required, terminated trade with Great Britain. Economically, Americans were allies of France. The British were alarmed. On June 16, 1812, so as to reopen trade with the United States, they canceled the Orders in Council.

It was too late. Only two days later, with the news still aboard a ship just catching the winds out of Britain, Madison bowed to war fever at home and asked Congress for a formal declaration of war against Great Britain. It had been a series of miscalculations, stupidities, and blunders—the history of humanity compressed into five years.

The War Hawks

Madison said that the War of 1812 was fought to defend American shipping and the security of American seamen. However, the mercantile states did not want "Mr. Madison's War." New England, New York, and New Jersey voted 34 to 14 against it. Not a single Federalist congressman voted for war (and the antiwar Federalists increased their contingent in Congress, mostly in the mercantile states, from a low of 24 in 1808 to 68 in 1814).

Who wanted the War of 1812? Jefferson Republicans, almost all of them representing agricultural regions, where, if salt water was needed, people had to dump salt into a cistern. Pennsylvania, the South, and the western states voted 65 to 15 in favor of war.

The prowar party was led by an exuberant claque of congressmen known as the "War Hawks." The Hawks were young—none as old as 40—with the cocky belligerence of youth, and no personal experience of being colonials. To them, the War for Independence was history taught by superpatriotic teachers, authors, and relatives. They were learned anglophobes, the most strident kind. They were ultranationalists who dreamed of conquering Canada and annexing it to the United States.

Socializing on the Frontier

When Europeans traveled through newly opened parts of the United States, they invariably complained about the food of the frontier—greasy fried salt pork and cornmeal mush or fire-roasted corn bread. Many were shocked by the westerners' heavy drinking. But most of all, they shuddered at the isolation of the people building a life in a new country. The Europeans who wrote books about their American experiences were sophisticated and literate; they were accustomed to a full social life. Outside of a few cities, there was nothing like that beyond the Appalachian ridge.

Frances Trollope, an English woman who wrote a celebrated book, *The Domestic Manners of the Americans,* blamed the emotional excesses of western religion on the absence of recreation and of release from daily toil and tedium, even in the large river port of Cincinnati. "It is thus," she wrote, in the shrieking, howling, and rolling around the floor that she witnessed at churches, "that the ladies of Cincinnati amuse themselves; to attend the theatre is forbidden; to play cards is unlawful; but they work hard in their families and must have some relaxation."

Just a few miles outside of Cincinnati, Trollope met a hard-bitten frontier woman who showed off her farm and boasted that it produced everything the household consumed except tea, sugar, and whiskey. When Trollope prepared to depart, her hostess sighed and said, "Tis strange for us to see company; I expect the sun may rise and set a hundred times before I shall see another *human* that does not belong to the family."

Frontier life was lonely, but it was not without social occasions. In the 1820s, William Cooper Howells, a printer who saw northern Ohio develop from wild forest into a populous industrial center, looked back on the parties of his youth with fond nostalgia. Ohio pioneers, Howells wrote, combined amusement with work.

The raising of a cabin or barn was done collectively by neighbors. The host had cut all the logs he needed. They were brought to the building site by means of a community "logroll." The men who best handled an ax notched the logs at each end; others raised them into place. "The men understood handling timber," Howells wrote, "and accidents seldom happened, unless the logs were icy or wet or the whisky had gone around too often." Howells himself, still quite a young man in Ohio's early years, took pride in taking on the job of "cornerman." While others built the walls, he "dressed up" the corners with an ax. "It was a post of honor," he wrote. The job was less laborious

North Wind Picture Archives

than that of raising the walls, but it took a head that "was steady when high up from the ground."

When a gathering of men for such a purpose took place there was commonly some sort of mutual job laid out for women, such as quilting, sewing, or spinning up a lot of thread for some poor neighbor. This would bring together a mixed party, and it was usually arranged that after supper there should be a dance or at least plays which would occupy a good part of the night and wind up with the young fellows seeing the girls home in the short hours or, if they went home early, sitting with them by the fire in that kind of interesting chat known as sparking.

In addition to logrolling and barn raisings, the tedious task of processing flax (for linen and oil) was done in combination with a community party. Other tasks—splitting logs into rails for fences, for example—were spiced up by holding a competition. Abraham Lincoln first ran for political office on his reputation as a virtuoso rail splitter. But by far the most enjoyable kind of work party, remembered wistfully in practically every reminiscence of the frontier, was the husking bee. Not only was the job of husking Indian corn less laborious than other jobs that took place in the autumn, when the harvest was done and the weather was cool. It was also the season when good food was most abundant and spirits were highest.

The ears of corn to be husked were divided into two piles. Two captains chose up sides, selecting their teams alternately from among the young men, boys, young women, and girls. The two teams started husking, standing with the heap in front of them. They threw the husked corn to a clear space over the heap and tossed the husks (for animal fodder) behind them. From the time they began until the corn was all husked, there was no pause except to take a pull at the jug of inspiration (whiskey) that passed along the line.

When one team had finished husking, it let out a great shout (which was the signal to lay a community dinner on the table), briefly exchanged taunts for the excuses of the losers, and then helped the losers finish their husking. Another rule of the game that increased interest was the provision that a boy who husked a red ear could claim a kiss from one of the girls at the party. But Howells concluded, "I never knew it necessary to produce a red ear to secure a kiss when there was a disposition to give or take one."

In 1812, the notion of conquering Canada was not far-fetched. Many Americans, and not just Loyalists, had settled in Upper Canada, the prime lands north of Lake Ontario.

Some were open about their desire to be Americans again. A few Canadians with no American connections preferred the American political system to their colonial status. Militarily, the prospect never looked better. Great Britain, obsessed with defeating Napoleon in Europe, had reduced the professional army in Canada to just 2,200 soldiers. Canadian militias had no better a reputation than American state militias.

The only discouraging factor was the power and effectiveness of the Indians of the Northwest Territory and western New York. They were well supplied by the British, were staunch British allies, and had been reinvigorated by a remarkable religious revival. Then, in November 1811, that formidable impediment to American aggression seemed to crumble.

The Prophet's Revival

For two decades, Canada's defense had depended on the Delaware, Pottawottamie, Miami, some Iroquois, Shawnee, and other peoples living south of the Great Lakes. Defeated and demoralized in 1794, about 10 years later, ever increasing numbers of these tribes were converted to the gospel of a reformed Shawnee drunk, Tenskwatawa, whom the whites called the "Prophet."

Tenskwatawa's religious message was one that would be heard again in Native American history: In order to stop the relentless advance of white settlers—in order, indeed, to rid the Indians' world of them—Indians must forget ancient tribal hostilities and join together. They must abandon the ways of the whites they had embraced—living in American-style houses, wearing clothing made of purchased cloth, using the white man's tools. The Prophet preached that Indians must extinguish their fires, for they had been ignited using the whites' flint and steel, and start new ones by Indian methods. Most important of all, they must give up alcohol, so obvious to all as a major reason for Indian dissipation.

There were other purification ceremonies. Like other founders of new religions, once Tenskwatawa got started, he found it difficult to stop. Despite the gospel of pan-Indian

▲ Tecumseh, a Shawnee chief born about 1768 and killed in battle in 1813, was the most thoughtful and effective of the many Indian leaders who tried to unite formerly hostile tribes in order to stop the advancement of white settlers into their homeland. The blunders of others, rather than his own mistakes, doomed him.

cooperation, his followers killed shamans who opposed the Prophet and drove out Indians who remained Christian.

"Panther Lying in Wait"

The religious revival did not concern white settlers until, after 1808, Tenskwatawa's followers began to concentrate their numbers in Tippecanoe (Prophetstown) in western Indiana and the Prophet's brother, Tecumseh ("Panther Lying in Wait"), made himself, by force of intelligence and personality, chief of a confederation of virtually all the tribes of the Northwest Territory.

Where Tenskwatawa was a cockeyed mystic and no warrior (he was morbidly obese), Tecumseh had both feet on the ground and a reputation for bravery in battle dating back to the victory over St. Clair in 1791, when Tecumseh was only a young brave. Tecumseh understood the whites' culture better than his brother, for he had lived within it for 10 years. In 1798, he formed a friendship with an Ohioan, James Galloway. He studied Galloway's library of 300 books and, in 1808, proposed marriage to his daughter, Rebecca. She consented, but on the condition that Tecumseh abandon Indian ways and live like an American.

Instead, Tecumseh joined his brother at Tippecanoe, becoming the political and military leader of his followers. Tecumseh saw to it that firearms were removed from the

American Hero

Aside from low-life western Indian haters, the kind William Henry Harrison said considered "the murder of the Indians in the highest degree meritorious," Americans admired and respected Tecumseh as much as they feared him. Richard M. Johnson of Kentucky, who claimed to have killed him at the Battle of the Thames, built his political career (he rose to be vice president) on little else. In Lancaster, Ohio, in 1820, where memories of the live Tecumseh were still vivid, a boy was born and named for the great chief. There may have been many others. We know of this one because he was William Tecumseh Sherman, one of the key generals in the winning of the Civil War.

Tecumseh was depicted as a heroic figure in John Dorival's *Battle of the Thames,* painted in 1833, and as godlike in Frederick Pettrick's *The Dying Tecumseh,* begun in 1837. More books have been written about Tecumseh than about William Henry Harrison and Richard Johnson combined.

Prophet's list of taboos and ended persecution of Indians who did not unquestioningly embrace the Prophet's every teaching. He embarked on long journeys to enlist more tribes in his pan-Indian confederation and rarely failed, as western whites soberly noted. Tecumseh was the greatest leader Native Americans ever had. None of his contemporaries sold him short. The British in Canada regarded him as their most important ally. William Henry Harrison, territorial governor of Indiana, called him "one of those uncommon geniuses who spring up occasionally to produce revolutions and overturn the established order of things."

In 1811, Tecumseh embarked on the most important of his journeys, deep into the South, to enlist the powerful Cherokee, Creek, Choctaw, and Chickasaw in his confederacy. Had he succeeded and launched a coordinated attack on the frontier from Lake Michigan to the Gulf of Mexico, the white westerners would have suffered a devastating defeat.

It was not to be. Tecumseh had ordered the Prophet to keep the peace until he returned. However, in November 1811, William Henry Harrison arrived at Tippecanoe, camping about a mile away with 1,000 men. Harrison had come to fight but was alarmed by the size of the Indian force, possibly 3,000 braves. He was considering withdrawing when the Prophet, knowing his superior numbers, ordered an attack. The Indians came within an ace of overrunning the Americans, but the Americans held, won the day, totally leveled Tippecanoe, and made Harrison a hero.

No longer did the War Hawks in Washington have to pause when they were reminded of Tecumseh's confederacy.

Bunglers in Battle

The assault on Canada was, nonetheless, a fiasco. New York militia refused to cross the Niagara River. They delayed their mass desertion only long enough to watch a duel between two American officers (which Canadians across the river also enjoyed). Surprised at American ineffectiveness, the British, Canadians, and Indians counterattacked and captured Detroit. An Indian force destroyed the stockade at Chicago, then called Fort Dearborn.

A Canadian-Indian offense (in five of the seven land battles of the war, Indians formed the bulk of the enemy forces) was stalled when, in September 1813, Captain Oliver Hazard Perry, although outgunned by a Canadian-British flotilla, secured control of Lake Erie for the Americans. Receiving Perry's famous message, "We have met the enemy and they are ours," William Henry Harrison then led 4,500 men toward York (now Toronto), the capital of Upper Canada.

There, the British and Canadians proved as inept as the Americans and, according to Tecumseh, who had returned from the south, cowards. He told the commanding British general, "We must compare our father's conduct to a fat dog that carries its tail upon its back, but when afrightened drops it between its legs and runs off." Harrison defeated the combined British, Canadian, and Indian force at the Battle of the Thames and burned the public buildings in the city. Tecumseh was killed.

In the meantime, the British invaded New York via Burgoyne's route and were stopped at Lake Champlain, again by the navy commanded by Captain Thomas Macdonough. Ironically, although the Americans won few victories on land, American naval forces on both the lakes and the ocean won most of their encounters.

The British revenged the burning of York in August 1814 when they launched a daring amphibious raid on Washington, D.C. The troops burned the Capitol and the White House. British officers claimed that they ate a dinner, still warm, that had been set for James and Dolley Madison. In fact, the president narrowly escaped capture when he drove out to view a battle and the American army fled without fighting.

New Orleans

The British had not wanted war, but, when Napoleon abdicated in the spring of 1814, freeing troops for American service, the British combined the beginning of peace talks at Ghent in Belgium with a plan to seize lower Louisiana from the United States. An army of 8,000 excellent soldiers was dispatched under General Sir Edward Pakenham to attack New Orleans. What augured to be a disaster for the Americans turned out to be an amazing victory and the making of a national hero, Andrew Jackson of Tennessee.

A self-taught lawyer, slave-owning planter, land speculator, Indian fighter, and duelist, Andrew Jackson cobbled together a force of 2,000 Kentucky and Tennessee volunteers, New Orleans businessmen, two battalions of free blacks, some Choctaw Indians, and artillerymen employed by a pirate-businessman, Jean Laffite. Jackson threw up

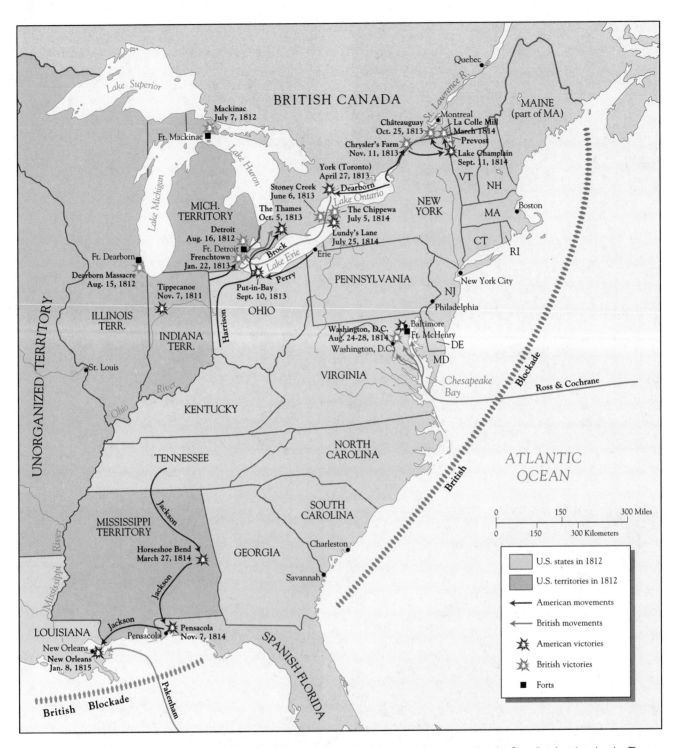

MAP 12:2 The War of 1812 Until the final battle of New Orleans, the War of 1812 was fought at sea and on the Canadian-American border. The war is unique in that the capitals of both combatants were burned by the enemy, York (now Toronto) in April 1813, Washington, D.C., in August 1814.

earthworks 5 miles south of New Orleans, the Mississippi River on his right, an impenetrable swamp on his left. He had created a wide-open battlefield with his army entrenched, textbook perfect.

Disdainful of his motley enemy, Pakenham sent his soldiers through the morning fog on a frontal assault. Laffite's cannoneers raked them with grapeshot, and, when the red-coats were 200 yards from the earthworks, the riflemen opened up with "a leaden torrent no man on earth could face." More than 2,000 redcoats fell dead—1 in 4 on the expedition! Miraculously, only seven Americans were killed, four of them when they mindlessly pursued the fleeing British. (After the battle, Jackson hanged as many American soldiers for desertion as were killed during it.)

▲ *In August 1814, British raiders burned the public buildings of the nation's capital in retaliation for the burning of York (Toronto), the capital of Upper Canada.*

▲ *The Battle of New Orleans. Like many patriotic paintings, this splendid one was more concerned with arousing national pride (and celebrating Andrew Jackson) than with accuracy. The British troops never got closer than a hundred yards from the American position. General Jackson did not direct the battle from a vantage where he could be easily killed by the enemy.*

The Treaty of Ghent, which restored British-American relations to what they had been before the war, was actually signed before the Battle of New Orleans was fought. Nevertheless, the news of the astonishing victory had an electrifying effect on the country. So glorious a conclusion to an ill-advised, unnecessary, and calamitous war seemed a reaffir-mation of the nation's destiny. When, within three years, Jackson crushed the powerful Creek tribe in the southeast and Stephen Decatur returned to the Barbary Coast to sting the Algerians, Americans could imagine they had won respect in a world where armed might was a measure of greatness.

for FURTHER READING

A nineteenth-century classic provides an excellent overview of this period: Henry Adams, *History of the United States During the Administration of Thomas Jefferson and James Madison,* 1889–1891. The most thoroughgoing biography of Jefferson is Dumas Malone, *Jefferson and His Time,* 6 vols., 1948–1981; of Madison, Irving Brant, *James Madison,* 6 vols., 1941–1961. See also Marshall Smelser, *The Democratic Republic, 1801–1815,* 1968; Noble Cunningham, *The Jeffersonian Republicans in Power,* 1973; Merrill Peterson, *Thomas Jefferson and the New Nation,* 1970; and Robert A. Rutland, *The Presidency of James Madison*, 1990. Controversial from the day it was published, but an enjoyable read, is Fawn Brodie, *Thomas Jefferson: An Intimate Biography,* 1974.

Alexander Deconde, *This Affair of Louisiana,* 1976, treats the great purchase in detail. The reigning standard on the Lewis and Clark expedition is Stephen Ambrose, *Undaunted Courage: Meriwether Lewis, Thomas Jefferson, and the Opening of the American West,* 1996. But students should also go to the horses' mouths: Bernard DeVoto, ed., *The Journals of Lewis and Clark,* 1953. Jefferson's problems with John Marshall are treated in Richard Ellis, *The Jeffersonians and the Judiciary,* 1971. On Marshall himself, see Leonard Baker, *John Marshall: A Life in Law,* 1974. For "Mad Tom's" other great nemesis, see Nathan Schachner, *Aaron Burr,* 1984.

On the brief renaissance of the Ohio Valley Indians, see R. David Edmunds, *Tecumseh and the Quest for Indian Leadership,* 1984. On the War of 1812, see Reginald Horsman, *Causes of the War of 1812,* 1962, and *The War of 1812,* 1969; and Donald R. Hickey, *The War of 1812: A Forgotten Conflict,* 1989.

AMERICAN JOURNEY ONLINE AND INFOTRAC COLLEGE EDITION

Visit the source collections at http://ajaccess.wadsworth.com and http://infotrac.thomsonlearning.com, and use the Search function with the following key terms to explore documents, images, audio and video clips, articles, and commentary related to the material in this chapter:

Aaron Burr	Sally Hemmings
James Madison	Tecumseh
Lewis and Clark	Tenskwatawa
Louisiana Purchase	Thomas Jefferson
Marbury v. Madison	

Additional resources, exercises, and Internet links related to this chapter are available on *The American Past* Web site: http://history.wadsworth.com/americanpast7e.

HISTORY ONLINE

Historical Maps of the United States
www.lib.utexas.edu/Libs/PCL/Map_collection/histus.html
Reproductions of period maps tracing the territorial growth of the United States.

The War of 1812
www.multied.com/wars.html
A collection of text, pictures, and maps dealing with the War of 1812.

BEYOND THE APPALACHIANS

The West in the Early Nineteenth Century

When I reflect that all this grand portion of our Union, instead of being in a state of nature, is now more or less covered with villages, farms and towns . . . that hundreds of steamboats are gliding to and fro over the whole length of the majestic river . . . When I remember that these extraordinary changes have all taken place in the short period of twenty years, I pause, wonder, and although I know it all to be fact, can scarcely believe its reality.

John J. Audubon

THE APPALACHIANS ARE not high as mountains go, and there were narrow passes—gaps—through which people, livestock, and, with a little clearing and excavation, vehicles could cross. Western Pennsylvania, the banks of the Ohio River, and much of Kentucky and Tennessee were populated by subsistence farmers, with ambitions to amount to more, before 1800. "Development," however, the creation of a society approximating the society of the original states, with a diversified economy and rich people as well as poor, awaited the new century. Then it was "development" at a rate that exceeded anything that had ever been seen, even in colonial America. The runaway growth of the West, in itself, seemed to justify America's independence of Great Britain.

THE FIRST AMERICAN WEST

By 1830, a quarter of the American population dwelled west of the Appalachians. A majority had been born "back East." The westerners, or their parents, had cut their ties, packed up what they could cart, and struck off to where land was cheap and, therefore, the future lay. Land was synonymous with opportunity in the ordinary American's mind.

The West, which was to loom large in the American imagination for a century, was as much an idea as a place. By 1830, the word *frontier* was defined in the United States rather differently than it was in Europe. In Europe, a frontier was a boundary between principalities. In America, it came to mean exclusively the belt of territory where white civilization phased into wilderness and the domain of the Indians. No one spoke of the Canadian "frontier": That was a *border*. It was the Kentucky "frontier." European frontiers were moved in fits and starts, most commonly after wars. The American frontier was a place of constant motion and chronic conflict.

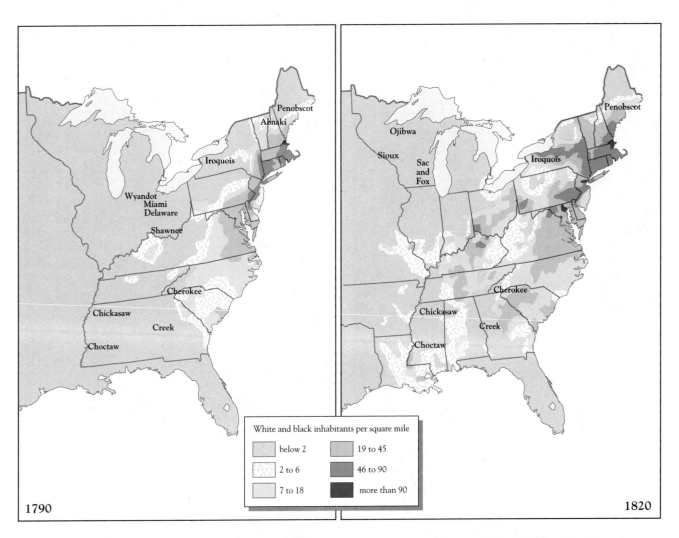

MAP 13:1 **Population Density, 1790–1820** The population of the northeastern states soared between 1790 and 1820, while white settlers (and, in the South, their slaves) displaced Indian tribes throughout the trans-Appalachian West.

Population Explosion

Between 1800 and 1820, the population of present-day Mississippi grew from 8,000 to 75,000. Alabama, with about 1,000 whites and blacks in 1800, was home to 128,000 in 1820.

The states north of the Ohio River grew even more dramatically. In 1800, there were 45,000 white people in Ohio and a very few blacks, all free because of the Northwest Ordinance. Ten years later, the state's population was 230,000. By 1820, Ohio was the fifth largest state in the Union! By 1840, with 1.5 million people, it was fourth. Only New York,

Pennsylvania, and Virginia had larger populations. Ohio, little more than a generation old, was home to more people than Finland, Norway, or Denmark.

Between 1800 and 1840, the white population of Indiana grew from next to nil to 685,856; Illinois, from a few hundred to 476,183. In 1800, American Michigan consisted of one wretched lakefront fort inherited from the French and British. In the 1830s, New Englanders flocked as thickly as passenger pigeons to Michigan's "oak openings," small fertile prairies amidst hardwood forests. Already by that time, the Mississippi itself had ceased to be the frontier. Missouri, on the west bank of the river, had been a state for 10 years.

Ohio, the Forty-Eighth State

Congress could be casual about the proprieties in 1803. On March 1, it seated Ohio's first representatives while neglecting to vote to admit Ohio as a state. The oversight was rectified only 150 years later when Congress voted to admit the forty-eighth state on August 7, 1953.

People on the Move

The abundance of land is not enough to explain this extraordinary influx of people. Russia was blessed with even more land to the east and had a larger and poorer population in its heartland. However, Siberia attracted few Russians until the government dragooned people into moving there. Americans

▲ *The Conestoga wagon was the vehicle of choice for easterners emigrating to the trans-Appalachian West. Dogs were a must—to keep other dogs away from the oxen—but the artist was mistaken to show the driver whipping the oxen. They were prodded and kept moving by constant repetition of voice commands. You could hear an ox team coming.*

as a people seemed inherently restless, as agitated as the "painters" (panthers) they chased deeper into the woods and swamps. To Europeans, and sometimes to themselves, Americans seemed incapable of putting down roots.

The young couple saying their marriage vows and promptly clambering aboard a wagon to head west was as familiar a scene in New England as stone fences between cornfields. During the first decades of the century, white Virginians, some with slaves, headed across the mountains as rapidly as a high birthrate could replace them. In central and western Pennsylvania, the site of a major wagon road west, the economy was closely tied to emigration. Inns and the stables of horse traders dotted the highways. The Conestoga Valley gave its name to the wagon its inhabitants manufactured, a high-slung, heavy-wheeled vehicle designed for travel where there were no roads.

"In the United States," marveled Alexis de Tocqueville, the most observant of foreign tourists, "a man builds a house in which to spend his old age, and he sells it before the roof is on." An Englishman looking over lands in the Ohio Valley reported that if, to be polite, he admired the improvements a settler had made, the man was likely to propose selling everything on the spot so that he could begin again farther west. There was a joke that, in the spring, American chickens crossed their legs so they could be tied up for the next push.

PATTERNS OF SETTLEMENT

Some of these pilgrims were simply antisocial, the "eye gougers" and "frontier scum" of legend and lore. Others were as respectable as the King James Bible and wanted as much company as they could persuade to join them. They meant to re-create the way of life they knew back East, only better, with title to much more land between their house and their neighbor's.

Yet others were developers—a profession still with us and sometimes still honored—dreamers, schemers, and promoters of new Edens, Romes, and Lexingtons. Indeed, the men who, like Abraham Lincoln's father, Tom, made a business of clearing a few acres and building a cabin to sell to a newcomer were developers of a small sort. Rather more important were those who purchased large tracts of land, trumpeted its glories, and sold subdivisions at a profit.

Town boosters named streets before a tree was felled in imagined intersections. Some were merchants or even manufacturers who planned to stay and prosper as the country grew. Others were professional boomers who made their bundle and moved on, as rootless as hunters and trappers, never to invest another thought in the communities they created.

Cities

The military was the cutting edge on some frontiers. Soldiers posted in the West to keep an eye on Indians had to be fed, clothed, and entertained. Shopkeepers, saloon keepers, and log-cabin prostitutes clustered around lonely military installations. The security of the fort encouraged trappers, hunters, and others who tramped the woods to congregate there in winter and during times of Indian trouble. Indians hooked by American goods, alcohol all too often, gathered there. Their wants stimulated the growth of a mercantile economy before there was much tillage in the neighborhood. Vincennes, Detroit, and other towns that were originally French forts developed in this way.

In other areas, cities came first. Only after a fairly advanced (if not refined) urban life had evolved did the hinterland fill in with farmers to provision the town. Cincinnati, Louisville, Lexington, and Nashville were true, if small, cities before agriculture was well developed in the surrounding country. Occupying good locations at which river travelers could tie up their keelboats, canoes, and rafts, they also served as jumping-off points for emigrants. When the cotton lands of the lower Mississippi Valley began to boom, sending out calls for provisions for their slaves, the citizens of the river ports responded with shipments of grain and livestock. Cincinnati, "the Queen City of the West," became famous for its slaughterhouses and packing plants when, not many miles away, the great hardwood forests blocked the sun from the earth and lonely men and women battled malaria.

There were other kinds of manufacturing in the woods. In 1815, when there were no more than 15 steam engines in the whole of France, a nation of 20 million people, half-tamed Kentucky boasted six steam mills that turned out cloth and even paper. Before the War of 1812, St. Louis had a steam mill that was six stories high. Like medieval cities determined to outdo the cathedral of the next nearest city, Cincinnati built a mill nine stories high.

By 1828, in fact, Cincinnati boasted nine factories building steam engines, nine cotton mills, 12 newspapers, 40 schools, two colleges, and a medical school. A metropolis, but unmistakably western: Only one street was paved, and pigs were everywhere.

Speculation as a Way of Life

Such rapid development encouraged heated financial speculation. Many people went to Ohio or Michigan or Alabama neither to farm, run a shop, nor pack pork. They were speculators, men with some capital and plenty of big ideas about growing rich by the timeless, if risky, game of buying land cheap and selling it dear. Some were sharpers by anyone's definition, out to line their pockets and let the buyers beware.

Others were responsible—"builders"—who supervised an orderly development which was, indeed, preferable to the semisavage disorder of the squatter frontier. In a country where growth was the essence of life, just about everyone who could spare (or borrow) a few dollars was attracted, on at least a small scale, to buying land to sell to others.

Daniel Boone is remembered as a hunter, a trailblazer, and an Indian fighter. He thought more about acquiring land in the hope of selling it. He was not very good at speculation; Boone was repeatedly ensnarled in lawsuits he usually lost because he was too disgusted to show up in court. A speculator, shady or ethical, had to spend a lot of time in the company of lawyers and judges. Tom Lincoln had his failures too. When he sold his Indiana farm in 1830, with improvements made over 14 years, he was paid less than the cost of the forest he had purchased. John Crockett, the father of fabled

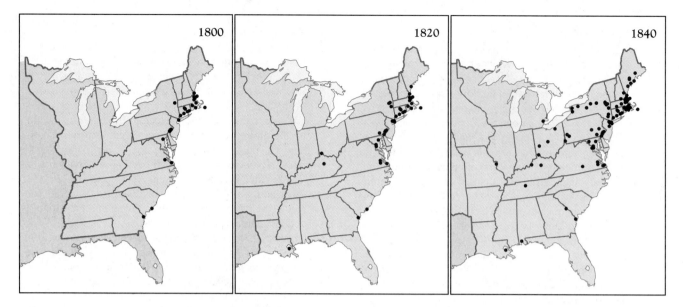

MAP 13:2 Cities of At Least 5,000 Inhabitants, 1800–1840 Eastern cities grew rapidly between 1800 and 1840, but most striking, as shown in these maps, was the emergence of cities in the West where there had been virtually no whites or blacks before the new century.

Davy, managed to move from clearing forest to owning a gristmill and inn, but he was never far from bankruptcy.

Land Policy

The speculative mentality made the price at which the government disposed of its land a matter of considerable interest. (All western land, except for old French grants in the Louisiana Purchase, was government land.) During the 1790s, the federal government offered tracts of 640 acres of western lands at a minimum price of $1 an acre—cash. Settlers protested that 640 acres were more than a family could work, and $640 more than ordinary folks could raise. From the Federalist point of view, the complaint was irrelevant. The land would be developed by the inevitable demand for it by a growing population. Administrative efficiency and the Federalist inclination to favor men of capital dictated that the government be a wholesaler, disposing of the land in large chunks and leaving the retailing of small farms to the private sector.

Jefferson's Republicans, in power after 1800, believed in disposing of land in such a way as to favor the people who actually settled on it with plow and oxen. Jefferson's idealization of the independent, small family farmer mandated a liberal land policy: "The price of land is the thermometer of liberty—men are freest where lands are cheapest." In 1804, a Jeffersonian Congress authorized the sale of tracts as small as 160 acres. The minimum price was $2 an acre, but a buyer needed a down payment of only $80 and could pay the balance of $240 over four years.

The Land Act of 1804 made the government a retailer and a very obliging one. However, it neither shut out sharpers nor satisfied settlers. Sales on credit actually benefited spec-

ulators because, unlike conservative emigrants uneasy about debt, speculators had no compunctions about borrowing heavily and making down payments on as much land as possible. The idea—or at least the hope—was that they would sell at a profit before the second installment came due.

"Wildcat banks," often irresponsible, sprang up all over the West to encourage and—again, it was hoped—to profit from credit speculators. On printing presses carted over the mountains, they churned out paper money with which borrowers made their down payments to the government land office. For a while after the War of 1812, the wildcat banks did quite well. Land sales soared. In 1815, the government sold about 1 million acres; in 1819, more than 5 million.

Much of it went for a higher price than the government minimum: Before land was let go at $2 an acre, it was offered at auction. Auctions also favored speculators. Settlers with families had budgets. They were often unable to bid on the most attractive land against pathological optimists who cared little how much borrowed money they handed across the counter. Some government lands in the cotton belt sold for more than $100 an acre—on paper.

Booms and Busts

The speculative boom in western lands depended, as does all speculation, on greed and the human species' marvelous capacity for self-delusion. Speculation—in land, gold, dotcom stocks, or, as in seventeenth-century Holland, tulip bulbs—is built on the principle of "the greater fool." One person pays an irrationally high price for a commodity on the assumption that there is a greater fool just around the corner chafing to pay him even more. A great deal of money

▲ *Chicago, in 1834, was a collection of rude buildings on a muddy flat on Lake Michigan. Its explosive growth came only later, when it became the northern terminus of the Illinois Central Railroad, the western terminus of several eastern lines, and the eastern end of several transcontinental railroads.*

has been made in speculation. When easy money and greed couple, they beget a great many fools.

A great deal of money has been lost in speculation too. If foolishness is infinite, the supply of potential buyers is not. When it runs dry, and speculators conclude that prices have peaked and it is time to get out and run, the result is a bust, a crash. When big players liquidate their supply of tulip bulbs or land at a modest loss, others follow at a moderate loss, and prices plummet, with the last in line losing everything. When speculators dealt in borrowed money, as the western land speculators of the 1810s did, a significant drop in values was enough to cause a panic to sell so that at least some loans might be repaid. Indeed, if the lenders—the bankers—decide that values are declining, they can trigger a panic by calling in their loans, forcing speculators to sell at whatever prices they can get.

The Panic of 1819

This is what happened in 1819. The directors of the Bank of the United States (BUS), cautious and conservative eastern gentlemen, began to worry about the freewheeling practices of the western banks. They called in the money those banks owed the BUS.

Having loaned their resources to speculators (many times over—the paper money they issued far exceeded what the BUS had loaned them), the wildcat banks called in their loans. When speculators were unable to repay because they could not sell the land on which they had made down payments, the whole paper structure came tumbling down (to use an expression coined the previous century, "the bubble burst"). Speculators as rich in acres as Charlemagne could not meet their obligations to either the banks or the Land Office. Wildcat banks folded by dozens, leaving those thrifty souls who had deposited money in them broke. Worthless banknotes went to the outhouse, the land reverted to government ownership, and the BUS lost money and grew more conservative.

In 1820, chastened by the disaster, Congress abolished credit purchases and tried to dispose of the lands that had reverted to the government by reducing the minimum tract for sale to 80 acres and the minimum price per acre to $1.25. With financial recovery, the speculators were back. In the meantime, western settlers had devised several ways of dealing with speculators and other problems of living beyond the mountains.

PROBLEMS AND PROGRAMS

The word *squatter* has a disagreeable ring to it today, but in the context of the West in the early nineteenth century, it should not. Squatters were settlers who, out of innocence, ignorance, or orneriness, began to develop farms on the public domain before they purchased the land on which their cabins and barns stood. Such improved property was particularly attractive to speculators; buildings and a cleared field substantially increased the land's value. When government surveyors and the Land Office arrived, many squatters saw their claims "jumped." The home they had built on government land was purchased at auction by a newly arrived slicker with a wad of borrowed banknotes in his purse.

In some areas, squatters combated these speculators by vigilante action. Banded together in "land clubs," they promised physical reprisals against anyone who bid on a member's land. Not infrequently, they made good on their threats. But speculators could respond by hiring thugs and cutthroats, never in shortage on the frontier, and more than a match for ordinary farmers. And the law was on the speculators' side.

"Old Bullion" Benton

So it was to the lawmakers that the squatters and other ordinary westerners turned. Their hero was Thomas Hart Benton, called "Old Bullion" because he despised paper money; gold bullion was the only money for him. Born in North Carolina, Benton was among the earliest American settlers in Missouri. Although well read in the classics and supremely eloquent, Benton knew how to turn on the boisterous bluff that appealed to rough-hewn westerners. "I never quarrel, sir," he told an opponent in a debate. "But sometimes I fight, sir; and when I fight, sir, a funeral follows, sir."

Elected senator from Missouri shortly after the Panic of 1819, Benton inveighed at every turn against bankers, paper money, and land speculators. He fought consistently throughout his long career for a land policy that would shut all three out of the West.

Benton's pet project was preemption, or, as it was popularly known, "squatter's rights." Preemption provided that the man who actually settled on and improved land before

---

Western Rhetoric

The following statement was made before a land auction in Missouri by Simeon Cragin, who was not, it would seem, a settler, but himself a speculator:

I own fourteen claims, and if any man jump one of them, I will shoot him down at once, sir. I am a gentleman, sir, and a scholar. I was educated at Bangor, have been in the United States Army, and served my country faithfully. I am the discoverer of the Wopsey, can ride a grizzly bear, or whip any human that ever crossed the Mississippi, and if you dare to jump one of my claims, die you must.

Frontier Violence

The Mississippi Valley frontier's reputation for violence may have been overstated. John J. Audubon, who wandered the region for 25 years, collecting and painting specimens of birds and animals, thought so. He was personally threatened only once, in 1812. As an Indian had warned him, frontier thugs planned to rob and kill him at the cabin where he was lodging. Fortuitously, two more travelers arrived before bedtime, and nothing happened.

"Indeed," Audubon wrote, perhaps in an overstatement of his own, "so little risk do travelers run in the United States that no one born there dreams of any [violence] to be encountered on the road."

---

the government officially offered it for sale would be permitted to purchase it at the minimum price. He would not be required to bid at an auction.

Another Benton program was "graduation." Land that remained unsold after auction would be offered at one-half the government minimum, and after a passage of time, at one-quarter. In a word, the price of the land was graduated downward in order to increase the number of people able to afford it. Eventually, Benton hoped, land that went unsold would be given away to people willing to settle it.

Benton's sentiments were soundly Jeffersonian. He favored those who tilled the soil, "the bone and sinew of the republic" in Jefferson's phrase, over financial interests associated with Alexander Hamilton and, in Benton's era, the Whig party.

Sectional Tensions

Opposition to liberal land policy was strongest in the East. People who lived on the oldest streets of Plymouth and on the James neck of Virginia had no interest in purchasing land in Missouri or Michigan. But they had a stake in how and for how much the federal government sold it. To them, the western lands were a national resource—their wealth as well as that of westerners—a fount from which the government's expenses should be paid. They feared that if the national domain was sold off as quickly and as cheaply as Benton and his allies wished, the old states would lose population. The state and local taxes easterners paid, principally property taxes, would have to increase to make up for the loss.

Northern factory owners feared that, if land was dirt cheap and too inviting, their pool of laborers would shrink. The workers who remained, being in short supply, would demand higher wages.

Well-to-do southern planters, dependent on slave labor, feared that disposing of western lands too cheaply would force the federal government to depend more heavily on the tariff—import duties—to finance its operations. As major consumers of cheap British cloth, shoes, tools, and other products that would be larded with the new duties, they preferred to finance the government through land sales that actually made money.

Land policy, whether it was to generate income or favor western settlers, threatened to set section against section.

Handsome Henry Clay

The man who stepped forward with a plan to avert such a cleavage was himself a westerner, Henry Clay. Perhaps because his home was Kentucky, a state a generation older than Benton's Missouri, Clay was more concerned with welding the West to the old states than with populating it. He wanted to see land in the hands of actual settlers. But he also wanted to see the public domain used in such a way as to integrate the economies of North, South, and West. Clay was a nationalist, with a vision of a future beyond the next election.

Born in Virginia in 1777, Henry Clay trained as a lawyer and settled in Lexington at 21 years of age. He prospered as a planter, a land speculator, and especially in politics. Elected to the House of Representatives in 1810, Clay won notoriety as one of the most bellicose of the War Hawks, who pushed President Madison into war in 1812. When the fighting bogged down in stalemate, Madison named Clay to represent the War Hawk element at the peace talks in Ghent.

In Kentucky, in Europe, and in Washington, Clay had a taste for the high life. Keenly intelligent, famously handsome, graciously mannered, witty, ever sociable, he charmed women and won the friendship and loyalty of men. He was equally comfortable sipping claret with an interested lady and playing faro with the boys until the whiskey was gone. Although he was a poor shot and killed no one, Clay fought several duels, almost a prerequisite of success in western politics at the time.

But Clay's prominence—he hovered near the center of power in the United States for four decades—owed itself only incidentally to his style. Like Benton, he worked to build up the West. Transcending Benton and other westerners, Clay had a vision of a great and united nation that owed much to Alexander Hamilton. Clay, however, lacked Hamilton's contempt for ordinary folk.

The Open Road

Henry Clay's special cause as a young politician was internal improvements, particularly the building of better roads to tie the far-flung sections of the United States together—the costs of construction to be underwritten by the federal government. This was decidedly a western cause. Although the roads and highways of the eastern seaboard were wretched by the standards of western Europe, more than a century of population and development had resulted in a network of sorts. Beginning about 1790, the states and counties of the Northeast had graded and graveled old trails. The Old Post Road between Boston and New York allowed year-round long-distance travel on that important route, albeit an uncomfortable trip.

The Old Post Road was maintained by public moneys. Other eastern highways were privately constructed toll roads known as "turnpikes" because entrances were blocked with

North Wind Picture Archives

▲ *Henry Clay of Kentucky as a young congressman. Handsome, charming, and "one of the boys," his political career was to span four decades. He was beloved by his supporters and disdained by his enemies as devious and obsessed with being president.*

a pole resembling a pike that was turned to allow access when the toll was paid. One of the most successful, the Lancaster Pike, connected the rich farm town of Lancaster, Pennsylvania, to Philadelphia, some 60 miles away.

By 1820, there were 4,000 miles of such toll roads in the United States. Some were surfaced with crushed rock, or macadam, a British import that was the forerunner of blacktop paving. A cheaper surfacing, more likely in the West, was made of planks, or even logs, laid across the roadbed. The latter were called "corduroy roads." The ride they provided was bumpy and shattered many hubs and axles, but they kept narrow wagon wheels out of the mud.

Federal Finance

Few entrepreneurs were willing to invest in roads in the sparsely populated West. There were not enough toll payers. Nor could the young western states afford to do much about the problem. They were caught in the vicious circle of needing good roads in order to attract population and move their products out, while lacking the population and, therefore, the tax base necessary to finance the roads.

Digging the Erie Canal

Thomas Jefferson inscribed his opinions on so many subjects that he may be excused for a gaffe now and then. When he heard of the plan to connect the Hudson River to the Great Lakes by digging a canal, he wrote that "it is little short of madness."

The Erie Canal opened in November 1825, months before Jefferson died. The fabulous excavation climbed (and descended) 500 feet just west of Troy. The hills were scaled by means of 83 locks—fantastic, but not mad. The unnatural waterway cut travel time from Albany to Buffalo from 20 days to 8, and later to 6. The cost of moving a ton of freight across the state was slashed from $100 to $10, and later to $5. The $7 million cost of digging the ditch was repaid with interest in just 12 years.

Then again, Jefferson might not have revised his opinion of the adventure. He had written in *Notes on Virginia,* "Let our workshops remain in Europe." Jefferson believed that "mobs" of workers who do not till the soil "add just so much to the support of pure government, as sores do to the strength of the human body." The 3,000 Irishmen who were lured to upstate New York to do the dirty work and joined by thousands of Americans to expand, maintain, and "navigate" the canal, constituted one of Jefferson's "great cities," albeit one stretched thinly for many miles, like a contemporary "strip city."

They were a rough lot, the "canal boys," fresh off the wretched little potato patches from which the English landlords allowed them to feed themselves. Only a sense of history rare among peasants, a rich oral tradition, and their deep Roman Catholic piety raised them above barbarism. The cash wages they were paid to shovel and heave the dirt of upstate New York threatened to return them to it.

Brothels, gambling dens, and prototypes of the American saloon followed the work crews. The drunken, eye-gouging, ear-biting "ructions" of the canal workers were prodigious. As portions of the canal were opened and work camps became towns and cities built around locks, depots for horses and mules, and junctures for feeder canals, the atmosphere hardly changed. It just moved from tents to clapboard and brick buildings. Canal boats moved around the clock. The canal towns roared around the clock.

The fact that the boisterous, brawling boatmen worked an economic miracle did not often enter into the reflections of the proper New Englanders who traveled the canal. Many authors of accounts of travel on the Erie seem to have trembled for their personal safety when they passed through locks aboard one of the "queer-looking Noah's Ark boats."

Ironically, they were not only quite secure, but they were enjoying a trip that was definitely more bearable than any alternative. Travel on the Erie was rather comfortable for some and elegant for those who could pay the fare on a first-class boat.

The most expensive way to travel on the canal was on the packets. At least 80 feet long and 15 feet wide, they kept to a schedule, whereas other boats moved when they were loaded. The packets were towed around the clock by three trotting horses, which, of course, were changed often. Because the passengers' quarters on a packet were quite comfortable, horses that were resting were not brought aboard, as was done on second- and third-class boats. The companies that ran packets—the Pilot, Telegraph, Merchant's, Washington, Citizen's, and Commercial—maintained large stables at intervals of 10 to 12 miles.

For five cents a mile, a first-class passenger moved at between 4 and 6 miles per hour. The packets overtook slower boats by means of a procedure that was routine but, nonetheless, the occasion of some altercations. The slower boat slackened its tow line and the line of the quicker packet was passed over it. It required even more dexterity when the towpath changed sides: The horses cleared a bridge and galloped up and over it. The best of the canal men took pride in negotiating this maneuver without so much as a tug on boat or horse collar.

On a packet, men and women sat on stuffed sofas in the "saloon," which ran the length of the boat. Meals were served there. Allowing for the era's disinterest in gourmet food, complaints about the cooking on the first-class boats were rare. At locks and stables, or when heavy traffic slowed the pace, passengers could stretch their legs on the towpath ahead of the vessel.

At night, the saloon was divided into separate quarters for men and women. The sofas became beds. Upper bunks folded from the cabin walls. They were not roomy, scarcely more than 5 feet long with just enough room to roll over without unduly disturbing the passenger above.

The solution, in the view of westerners such as Henry Clay, was the federal government. As citizens of states that had been created by the Union, rather than states that were creators of it, westerners were more apt to look to Washington for aid than easterners were. Moreover, the construction of a highway system in the vast West was a massive project. As men like Clay saw it, only the federal government, with its vast resources, could bear the expense.

Clay worked tirelessly on behalf of the first federal construction project in the West—the national road that connected Cumberland, Maryland, on the Potomac River, with Wheeling on the Ohio River. It cost $13,000 per mile to build—an astronomical sum. The terrain was rugged, but the road was completed in 1818. Delighted by what this access to oceangoing commerce meant for Kentucky, Clay worked to have the national road extended to Vandalia, Illinois.

Clay was uncommonly successful as a highway lobbyist, but he had formidable opponents. Many southerners, nationally minded before the War of 1812, began to worry about the cost of internal improvements—and the taxation needed to pay for laying crushed rock and dredging rivers. Some westerners, such as General Andrew Jackson, Clay's archrival for leadership of the section, believed that federal finance of improvements was unconstitutional. Moreover, while Clay was personally blameless, many manipulators made fortunes on unnecessary or wasteful projects, generating opposition to Clay's free spending.

Before the 1820s, congressmen from the New England states inclined to oppose spending federal money on internal improvements. Their own road system was adequate; little federal money would be spent in their backyards. However, the densely populated Northeast would pick up the biggest part of the bill in taxes. Moreover, until the embargo and the War of 1812 disrupted the shipping business, New England's elite thought in terms of the Atlantic as the fount of their economic life. Factory owners feared that an improved West would attract their own people.

The American System

To counter such sectional thinking, Clay revived Alexander Hamilton's gospel of "continentalism." He urged Americans to seek their future, first of all, on the North American continent. He called his program the "American System."

First, Clay argued that northeastern industrialists had no reason to fear the consequences of internal improvements in the West. A populous West, connected to the Northeast by good roads, would provide a massive domestic market for the manufactured goods of New England and the Middle Atlantic states. He confronted the problem of taxes by compromising the Jeffersonian principle that western lands were to be disposed of as cheaply as possible. Although not advocating extremely high prices—Clay supported graduation, for example—he proposed that revenues from land sales pay the greater part of the costs of internal improvements. He also appealed to manufacturing interests by advocating a high tariff that would protect northeastern factories from foreign competition.

To westerners, largely farmers who might otherwise oppose a high tariff, Clay pointed out that a flourishing industry would lead to large urban populations of workers who would buy western food products. Higher prices for manufactured goods—the consequence of the high tariff—were a small price to pay for such a bonanza. To complete the circular flow of products among the regions, the South would supply the mills of New England with cotton.

The capstone of Clay's nationalistic program was the second Bank of the United States. Chartered in 1816, its role in the American System was to regulate the money supply needed to fuel the integrated economy.

The weak link in Clay's program was the South, to which it did not offer very much. Southerners needed no help in finding profitable markets for their cotton and needed to make no concessions to sell it. The mills of Manchester, Leeds, and Bradford in England gobbled up all the fiber that southern planters could grow. With the exception of a few special-interest groups like Louisiana sugar planters, who wanted tariff protection against West Indian competitors, southerners inclined to oppose Clay's program. To them, the American System meant bigger price tags on the manufactured goods that they, as agriculturists, had to buy.

THE TRANSPORTATION REVOLUTION

In the end, Clay had to be content with levering bits and pieces of his comprehensive program through Congress, not at all what he had in mind. Moreover, many of his victories were temporary. His bills were repealed when his enemies captured Congress and the White House. The American economy was to be integrated less by vision and legislation than by a revolution in transportation that conquered seasons, leveled mountains, and diverted the course of rivers.

The Erie Canal

The state of New York led the way in a revolution in transportation. In 1817, after years of promotion by Governor De Witt Clinton, the legislature voted funds to dig a canal from the Hudson River to Lake Erie, from Albany on the Hudson to Buffalo on the lake. The idea was to funnel the produce of the Great Lakes basin through New York City and to make New York "the great depot and warehouse of the western world."

With picks and shovels and little more, for wages of $10 a month, gangs of rough, muscular laborers, many of them immigrants from Ireland, excavated a ditch 4 feet deep, 40 feet wide, and, when it was completed in 1825, 364 miles long. (The canal was later enlarged to 7 feet deep and 70 feet wide.) The Erie Canal was expensive—$7 million, or almost $20,000 per mile. Skeptics waited for the state of New York to buckle under its financial burden. But even before the ditch was finished, the canal was turning a profit.

Travel on the Erie Canal was slow. Mules on towpaths dragged the long, flat-bottomed canal boats carrying up to 50 tons at a lazy 4 miles an hour. Passenger boats accommodated up to 40 people. For a cent a mile, canal travel was none too comfortable, but for five cents a mile, a pilgrim could travel the Erie Canal first class. Far more important, it cost only $8 a ton to move factory goods west or western crops east. That was a 90 percent cut in the cost of overland transport!

The Canal Craze

When the Erie Canal was begun, there were about 100 miles of canal in the United States. They served only small regions; the longest ran only 28 miles. Now, those who had laughed at the Erie Canal's prospects went berserk in their rush to imitate it.

The most ambitious was the Mainline Canal in Pennsylvania. Smarting under the loss of commercial preeminence to New York, Philadelphia merchants pressured the state legislature into pumping millions into the venture. The Mainline was shorter than the Erie. However, whereas the New

MAP 13:3 Rivers, Roads, and Canals, 1825–1860   During the first half of the nineteenth century, the United States boasted two of the world's longest continuous highways, the routes of today's U.S. 1/I-95 and U.S. 40/I-70. American canals, now almost all gone, were even more extensive.

York route rose only 650 feet above sea level at its highest point and required 83 locks to control its water, the Mainline Canal rose 2,200 feet and needed 174 locks. At the Allegheny ridge, the highest in the Pennsylvania Appalachians, boats were hauled out of the canal and over the mountain on fantastic inclined planes. Miraculously, the Mainline Canal was completed—Pennsylvania operated 608 miles of canal—but it was never the gold mine that the Erie was. There were too many bottlenecks crowded with swearing boatmen in the mountains—where no boatman belonged.

All in all, some 4,000 miles of canal were dug in imitation of the Erie. Another 7,000 miles were on the drawing boards when the bubble burst. Although many of the canals were of inestimable local value, only a few made enough money to cover the money invested in them. So many states drained their treasuries to fund poorly advised projects that many politicians, including westerners, swore never again to finance internal improvements. As late as 1848, the constitution of the new state of Wisconsin forbade the expenditure of tax money on such ventures.

▲ *Two locks on the Erie Canal. Long stretches were idyllic, as this artist's depiction shows. Some canal towns were rough-and-tumble places, however, as wild during the construction of the canal as a cow town or mining camp.*

Railroads

The canal craze was also brought to an end by the appearance of a more flexible means of overland transportation, the railroad. As the Mainline Canal showed, canals were plausible only where the terrain was easily passable and the supply of water plentiful and constant. Even the Erie was out of commission during the winter months, when it froze. Railroads never provided transportation as cheaply as canal boats. But railroads could run almost anywhere faster and, except during catastrophic blizzards, every day of the year.

The New York and Erie Railroad

In order to offset the economic advantages that the Erie Canal had brought to the northern counties of New York State, the southern counties proposed to build a railroad between the Hudson River and Lake Erie. Chartered on April 24, 1832, the New York and Erie Railroad (later the Erie) spanned 446 miles between Piermont on the Hudson (26 miles from New York City) and Dunkirk on Lake Erie.

In 1851, trains carried President Millard Fillmore and his cabinet on what was then the longest continuous railroad in the world. Secretary of State Daniel Webster had, it was reported, "on a flat car, at his own request, a big easy rocking-chair provided for him to sit on. He chose this manner of riding so that he could get a better view and enjoy the fine country through which the railroad passed."

The first two railroads in the United States were constructed in 1827, just two years after the first railroad in England proved workable. One line connected the granite quarries of Quincy, Massachusetts, with the Neponset River. The other carried coal from Carbondale, Pennsylvania, to the Lehigh River. Both were only a few miles long and served single business enterprises, supplementing existing routes and means of transportation. In 1833, the Charleston and Hamburg railroad was the longest in the world—at just 136 miles.

The potential of the railroad lay in using it, like the Erie Canal, as the trunk of a transportation system independent of traditional, regional routes. The first entrepreneurs to recognize this were Baltimoreans hoping to put their city back in the race with New York for trade with the West. In 1828, work began on America's first trunk line, the Baltimore and Ohio (B&O).

Construction of the B&O was repeatedly stalled by financial difficulties, but in 1853, the line was finally completed to Wheeling on the Ohio River. In the meantime, dozens of less ambitious railroads were constructed. By 1848, there were more than 6,000 miles of railroad track in the United States. Fewer than 3,000 miles of track existed in the rest of the world.

The railroad conquered time and, eventually, the isolation of the West. At the end of the War of 1812, it took more than seven weeks to ship a cargo from Cincinnati to New York by keelboat, wagon, and riverboat. In 1852, when the two cities were connected by rail, it took six to eight days.

▲ *It cost more to ship by railroad than by canal, but canals could not be dug over mountains. This locomotive was one of the first to cross the Appalachians. The celebrants posing on the "cowcatcher" are probably company officials and their wives. Unless the engine had been scoured for the occasion, they were dirty when they climbed down.*

The cost of constructing a railroad was immense. In addition to securing right of way and hiring armies of laborers, a railroad company had to buy its own rolling stock, freight cars. (Canals and turnpikes collected tolls from users with their own boats and vehicles.) As a result, despite the total mileage of American railroads, few individual lines went very far. Indeed, competitive jealousies among the companies worked against true systems connecting distant points. Railway entrepreneurs deliberately built their lines in different gauges (distances between the tracks) so that the cars of competing lines could not be used on them.

The major canals and the B&O linked the West to the Northeast. However, the West's great natural north-south artery, the Mississippi River, was not neglected during the revolution in transportation.

"Old Man River"

It could not have been otherwise. With its two great tributaries, the Ohio and the Missouri, and dozens of smaller but navigable feeders, the Mississippi (the "Father of Waters") tapped the central third of the continent.

Westerners who lived on the Mississippi system could easily ship their corn or livestock to New Orleans on large log

rafts that, broken up and sawed into lumber, were themselves a source of income. The problem was in bringing goods back upstream. Sailing ships could not do the job. The Mississippi is broad; but its current is mighty, and its channels are narrow and shifting, the playthings of capricious sandbars. High riverbanks periodically stole the wind from sails. Oceangoing vessels could not penetrate much beyond New Orleans, and small sailboats carried too little to be worthwhile.

Some cargo was rowed upriver, some by poling small skiffs. Both methods were arduous and expensive. Savage keelboat men, like the Ohio River's legendary Mike Fink, literally pulled their vessels upstream. The keelboater lashed a heavy line to a tree on the riverbank and, from the deck of the craft, heaved in the ropes, repeating the process with another tree farther on.

It was no job for the languid, nor was it an efficient way to move anything but expensive goods. It took about six weeks for a huge raft to float pleasantly downstream from Pittsburgh, where the Ohio River begins, to New Orleans. It took four to five months to bring a much smaller tonnage back on a keelboat, with even more men drawing wages. It was far more expensive to ship a cargo of English cloth or furniture from New Orleans to Illinois than to sail it from England to New Orleans.

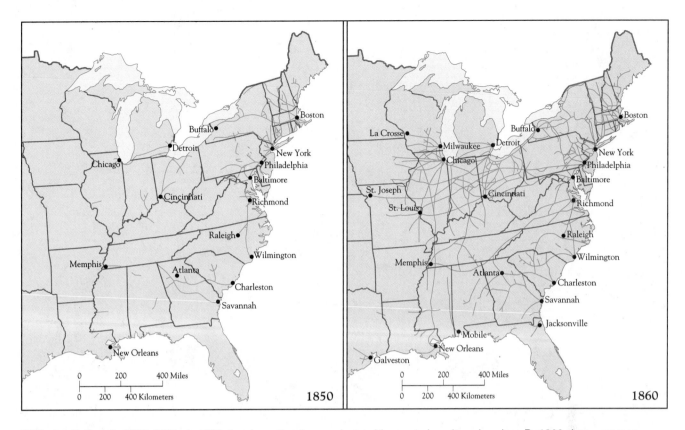

MAP 13:4 Railroads, 1850–1860   In 1850, American railroads were short and fragmented, serving only regions. By 1860, there were more miles of railroad in the United States than in the rest of the world, including several routes running continuously from the Northeast to the West for a thousand miles.

Steamboat A-Coming

The marvel that resolved this dilemma was the flat-bottomed steamboat, which was a long time coming. James Watt, the Scot who first harnessed the power of steam pressure to pump water out of mines, regarded ships as the second most important application of his discovery. However, it was not until 1787 that a Connecticut Yankee named John Fitch ran a 45-foot steamer down *and up* the Delaware River. Several delegates to the Constitutional Convention in Philadelphia witnessed the spectacle.

The "Lord High Admiral of the Delaware," as Fitch commissioned himself, solved most of the problems and briefly provided regular service between Philadelphia and Burlington, New Jersey (not much of a trip). But Fitch was a star-crossed man, obstreperous and obnoxious with his most generous backers. Nor was his humor improved by the indifference of eastern capitalists who still thought in terms of the sea. They could not imagine how a vessel in which a good portion of the hold was committed to carrying fuel could compete with a sleek sailing ship drawing its energy from God's good winds.

In fact, the age of sail was far from over. For more than a century after the perfection of the steamship, clipper ships and great steel-hulled windjammers dominated many world trade routes, particularly the long ones around Cape Horn. Worldwide, the tonnage carried in steamships exceeded that carried in sailing ships only in 1893.

But steamboats conquered the rivers. In 1807, Robert Fulton's *Clermont* wheezed and chugged up the Hudson River from New York City to Albany at five miles per hour. The *Clermont* was three times as long as John Fitch's boat, but the dimension that thoughtful people noticed was that it drew only seven feet of water. The boat was able to clear obstacles that would have upended a sailing ship with less capacity.

Queens of the Mississippi

The steamboat paid its way on eastern rivers like the Hudson. (Fulton's success helped to inspire the campaign to dig the Erie Canal.) But it was in the West that the great vessels found their natural home. In 1817, only 10 years after the *Clermont*'s maiden voyage, there were 17 steamboats on the Mississippi. By 1830, there were 187, with new ones being constructed more quickly than the old ones blew up.

Boiler explosions were no small problem. In order to minimize the weight of the boats, boilers were constructed more flimsily than good sense prescribed. Nevertheless,

▲ *The ingeniously-designed flat bottoms of the river steamboats meant that they could tie up on river banks far from docks. Here a steamboat is taking cotton aboard. More commonly, the boats tied up in remote locations to buy firewood cut by locals, sometimes by slaves working on their own time.*

after the *Tecumseh* set a record of eight days and two hours from New Orleans to Louisville in 1827, Mississippi riverboat captains found it difficult to resist the challenge or just a race. As on the railroad, speed sold tickets and attracted shippers. So, despite the opulence of some riverboats, a trip on one was a bit of a gamble. At the peak of the steamboat age, 500 people died in accidents each year. In the explosion of the *Moselle* in 1838, 150 people were lost.

Designers competed just as frantically to adapt boats to the western rivers. The greatest natural obstacles were the shifting sandbars of the Mississippi and Missouri, and snags—fallen trees that were to the river what icebergs were to the North Atlantic, quiet predators capable of tearing a gaping hole in a wooden hull.

In 1841, the *Orphan Boy* was completed and eased onto the water. It could carry 40 tons of freight plus passengers. Even when fully loaded, however, it skimmed atop water only two feet deep! The *Orphan Boy* was the ultimate, but a good many paddle wheelers needed only three or four feet. Not only was this quality necessary to navigate the Father of Waters and the even trickier Missouri River, but it enabled the boats to tie up at almost any bank in order to take on the cordwood that steamboats burned in prodigious quantities.

Symbols of a New Era

The locomotive and the steamboat knit the far-flung reaches of the United States together. In the words of a Cincinnati booster, they brought "to the remotest villages of our streams, and to the very doors of our cabins, a little Paris, a section of Broadway, or a slice of Philadelphia to ferment in the minds of our young people." The moving machines belching acrid smoke symbolized a sense of nationality as surely as the person of George Washington had symbolized the common cause of independence and constitutional union.

When the steamboat was still in its infancy, however, and the first railroad a decade in the future, Americans were already drawing together in their hearts, or so it seemed. In the wake of the War of 1812, a sense of American nationhood seized on the imaginations of the people of West, North, and even—ever so briefly—the South.

FOR FURTHER READING

On the first American West, see Ray A. Billington, *America's Frontier Heritage,* 1967; R. S. Philbrick, *The Rise of the West, 1754–1830,* 1965; Dale Van Every, *The Final Challenge: The American Frontier, 1804–1845,* 1964; and Malcolm J. Rohrbough, *The Trans-Appalachian Frontier,* 1978. Every inquiry into the American West should look to the "founding father" of western history, Frederick Jackson Turner, in *The Frontier in American History,* 1920.

Important studies dealing with topics treated in this chapter include Richard D. Brown, *Modernization: The Transformation of American Life, 1600–1865,* 1976; W. Elliott Brownlee, *Dynamics of Ascent: A History of the American Economy,* 1979; Thomas C. Cochran, *Frontiers of Change: Early Industrialists in America,* 1981; Eugene S. Ferguson, *The Americanness of American Technology,* 1975; F. W. Gates, *The Farmer's Age: American Agriculture, 1815–1860,* 1960; Walter Havighurst, *Voices on the River: The Story of the Mississippi Waterways,* 1964; L. C. Hunter, *Steamboats on the Western Rivers,* 1949; Philip D. Jordan, *The National Road,* 1948; Douglas C. North, *The Economic Growth of the United States, 1790–1860,* 1951; R. M. Robbins, *Our Landed Heritage: The Public Domain,* 1942; Ronald E. Shaw, *Erie Water West: A History of the Erie Canal, 1792–1854,* 1966; George R. Taylor, *The Transportation Revolution, 1815–1860,* 1951; Richard C. Wade, *The Urban Frontier,* 1964; and Sam B. Warner Jr., *The Urban Wilderness,* 1972.

Pertinent biographies are William Chambers, *Old Bullion Benton: Senator from the New West,* 1970; and Glyndon D. Van Deusen, *The Life of Henry Clay,* 1937.

AMERICAN JOURNEY ONLINE AND INFOTRAC COLLEGE EDITION

Visit the source collections at http://ajaccess.wadsworth.com and http://infotrac.thomsonlearning.com, and use the Search function with the following key terms to explore documents, images, audio and video clips, articles, and commentary related to the material in this chapter:

Erie Canal
Henry Clay
James Monroe

Additional resources, exercises, and Internet links related to this chapter are available on *The American Past* Web site: http://history.wadsworth.com/americanpast7e.

HISTORY ONLINE

The First American West
http://memory.loc.gov/ammem/award99/icuhtm/fawhome.html
Excellent multi-format look at the Ohio River valley frontier.

The Conestoga: A Brief History
www.dvhi.net/wagonworks/history.html
Information and excellent pictures of the wagon on which emigrants headed across the Appalachians (and later across the continent) traveled.

NATION AWAKENING

Political and Economic Development 1815–1824

© Bettmann/Corbis

Our country! In her intercourse with foreign nations, may she always be in the right; but our country, right or wrong.
Stephen Decatur

I can never join with my voice in the toast which I see in the papers attributed to one of our gallant naval heroes. I cannot ask of heaven success, even for my country, in a cause where she should be in the wrong. Let justice be done though the heavens fall. My toast would be, may our country be always successful, but whether successful or otherwise, always right.

John Quincy Adams

HENRY CLAY'S VISION of an integrated national economy, transcending state and sectional loyalties, did not spring full blown from his ruminations. The idea of an "American System" was hatched during an era when a nationalistic spirit permeated American society and culture. The era had its beginnings in 1815 with Andrew Jackson's victory at New Orleans and Stephen Decatur's punishment of insolent Algerians. The news of both events was greeted with the discharging of muskets and pistols, flag waving, sounding church bells, shouting and singing, and patriotic oratory.

THE ERA OF GOOD FEELINGS

In the decade after the divisive War of 1812, Americans in every section of the country embraced an image of themselves as a new chosen people—unique and blessed on the face of the earth, unsullied by the corruption of Europe, nurtured by their comparative closeness to nature, committed in the marrow of their bones to liberty, democracy, and progress.

It was during this period that the Fourth of July became a day of raucous popular celebration. Formerly observed with religious services and decorous promenades of the social elite in city squares, the Glorious Fourth burst into prominence as a day when everyone paid homage to the nation with games, feasting, overdrinking, and boisterous gaiety.

Patriotic Culture

It was an era of patriotism in popular art. Woodcarvers and decorators trimmed canal boats, sailing ships, stagecoaches, and private homes with patriotic motifs: screaming eagles clutching braces of arrows; the idealized, vigilant female pious as Numa; just as Aristides; temperate as Epictetus; patriotic as Regulus; impartial as Severus," and on and on.

Another influential author of the time was Noah Webster, whose *American Spelling Book,* first published in 1783, sold more than 60 million copies in perhaps 300 editions. Webster did not, however, get rich; in 1808, he sold the rights to the book for $2,365. From the "blue-backed speller," schoolchildren learned that the American tongue was superior to British English because Webster had stripped it of Old World affectations. Many of the differences in spelling between American English and British English today (*labor, theater, curb,* and *jail,* as opposed to *labour, theatre, kerb,* and *gaol*) owe to Webster's linguistic tinkering.

Webster was also the father of that great event of the American elementary school, the spelling bee, for Webster believed in uniform spelling. He observed unhappily that even so great a patriotic hero as William Clark, in his journals of the great expedition across the continent, spelled *mosquito* 19 different ways. His *American Dictionary of the English Language,* published in 1828, also distinguished American English by including hundreds of words adopted from Indian tongues.

James Monroe

The gentleman who presided over this outpouring of national pride was, like three of the four presidents who preceded him, a Virginian—James Monroe of Westmoreland County. His is a blurred figure in the history books, a personality with few hard edges.

figure that represented liberty; and the flag, the only national ensign in the world that had progress sewn into it. Between 1816 and 1820, six new stars were added to Old Glory as six new states entered the Union.

The needlepoint samplers that girls made to display their skills began to depict patriotic themes as often as religious themes: the Stars and Stripes or the saying of some national hero, like Nathan Hale's "I regret that I have but one life to give for my country" or Decatur's "Our country right or wrong." Newspapers published exuberant verses that touted the glories of the United States. Songwriters churned out lyrics that celebrated American grandeur.

In 1817, William Wirt wrote a biography of Patrick Henry in which he implied that Virginians led the movement for independence and fought the war more or less singlehandedly. Piqued patriots from other states looked for and dependably found patriotic demigods of their own: Paul Revere of Massachusetts, Nathaniel Greene of Rhode Island, Francis Marion of South Carolina, and so on.

Less controversial because of its singular subject was Mason Locke Weems's *The Life and Memorable Actions of George Washington.* Although originally published in 1800, Weems's unblushing study in hero worship peaked in popularity during the 1810s and 1820s, running through 59 editions. It was Weems who originated the story of the boy Washington chopping down the cherry tree and of an older Washington throwing a silver dollar across the Rappahannock River. So noble was the father of his country that he could not fib; so far was he above other nations' leaders that even in physical strength he was a superman. Weems wrote of Washington, "It is hardly an exaggeration to say that he was as

▲ *The Fourth of July 1818. Twenty years earlier, it was a holiday to which only the genteel paid much attention, promenading in their best clothing. After the War of 1812, Independence Day became somewhat raucous, often lubricated by free-flowing liquor.*

Monroe's achievements can be listed. He was one of Jefferson's most loyal disciples (and the most radical who was close to Jefferson). He was a successful diplomat, a good administrator, and utterly incorruptible. "Turn his soul wrong side outwards," Jefferson said, "and there is not a speck on it." It can be noted that his wife was thought one of the most beautiful women in the country. Portraits of Monroe reveal that his dress was eccentric; he wore the old-fashioned, skintight knee breeches of the revolutionary era while his contemporaries were pulling on the utilitarian trousers of the nineteenth century.

But a two-dimensional oil painting is what James Monroe remains. Perhaps it is because he was so successful as president, faced with problems far less serious than those that vexed his predecessors, calmly dispatching those that did arise, and telling the country what it wanted to hear in pious generalities.

History, like the audience at a play, thrives on conflict. It grows torpid in times of stability. James Monroe had the political good luck, and the historical misfortune, of being president during an interlude of calm between two times of crisis. He could declare in his second inaugural address, and probably believe it, that the United States would "soon attain the highest degree of perfection of which human institutions are capable."

Political Stability

The Founding Fathers' hopes for a government without political parties briefly came to pass under Monroe. The Federalists, revived during the War of 1812, collapsed when the shooting concluded. After Jackson's victory at New Orleans, their opposition to the war seemed more like disloyalty than good sense.

The number of congressmen styling themselves Federalists declined from 68 during the war to 42 in 1817 and 25 in 1821 (compared with 158 Jeffersonian Republicans). By 1821, there were only 4 Federalists in a Senate of 48 members. Old John Adams, in retirement in Quincy, Massachusetts, took scant interest in the evaporation of the party he had helped to found. His son, John Quincy Adams, joined the party of Thomas Jefferson and became Monroe's secretary of state.

During the 1810s, Republican congressmen and senators chose their presidential candidate (and therefore, in effect, the president) in a caucus. Monroe, the choice in 1816, handily defeated Federalist Rufus King. King won only the electoral votes of Delaware, Connecticut, and Massachusetts. The next year, when President Monroe visited Boston, where Jefferson was loathed and Madison despised, he was received as a hero. A Boston newspaper congratulated him for inaugurating an "era of good feelings."

In 1820, Monroe was unopposed in the presidential election. (One member of the electoral college cast his vote for John Quincy Adams so that no president but Washington would have the distinction of being his country's unanimous choice.) With only one political party, the United States had, in effect, no parties at all.

Smooth Sailing

Indeed, voters and even politicians were almost indifferent toward presidential politics. In 1816, William Crawford of

Georgia might have won the Republican presidential nomination over Monroe if he had thought the prize worth a fight. He did not. His supporters did not bother to attend the caucus at which the candidate was named.

Nor was there much popular interest in national elections. In 1816, only 6 of 19 states chose presidential electors by statewide popular vote; in 1820, only 7 of 24 states did. In most of the others, the state legislatures made the choice, and they treated the task as though it were routine, like confirming the governor's proclamation of a Thanksgiving holiday or voting a pension to a retiring doorkeeper. In 1820, the returns from Richmond, Virginia, a city of 12,000 people, revealed that only 17 men had bothered to vote.

There is nothing intrinsically wrong in a subdued presidency and popular indifference to politics, particularly according to the tenets of the Jeffersonian faith. Jefferson said that the government that governed least governed best. The absence of deeply divisive issues during Monroe's presidency reflected the relative prosperity of the times and the American people's concern with westward expansion and economic growth. Moreover, if Monroe was neither mover nor shaker, movers and shakers often do a good deal of mischief. Monroe did none. He was a conscientious, competent, and hardworking executive. His administration was efficient, and, without a popular clamor to distract them, he and his nationalistic secretary of state, John Quincy Adams, had an unbroken string of diplomatic successes.

Reconciliation with the Mother Country

In the Rush-Bagot Agreement of 1817, the United States and Britain agreed to limit the number of armed vessels on the Great Lakes. It was the first major concession that the former mother country made to the Americans since the Revolution. More important, the partial disarmament set the pattern for future policies that established the world's longest unfortified international boundary.

In 1818, Britain and the United States also established the southern boundary of British Canada at 49 degrees north latitude, a line that now runs west from Lake Superior to Puget Sound. Although American claims in the Pacific Northwest were flimsy and American interests there were next to nil, the British conceded Americans equal rights in what was called the "Oregon Country": present-day Oregon, Washington, the Idaho panhandle, and British Columbia.

Florida Secured

With Spain, Monroe-Adams diplomacy reaped even greater rewards. By 1819, the Spanish Empire was quaking. There were rebellions in practically every province, and rebel armies were winning most of the battles. The leaders of the independence movement—Simón Bolívar, José de San Martín, and Bernardo O'Higgins—paid flattering homage to the example set for them by the United States. Their praises of the United States as the beacon of their own freedom provided more fodder for the Americans' bumptious national pride.

The disintegration of the Spanish Empire also gave Florida to the United States. The peninsula never was very valuable. Thinly populated by Europeans and mostly controlled by Indians, Florida was held by the British for 20 years after 1763. In 1818, in pursuit of Indian warriors, Andrew Jackson brazenly crossed the border, ignored Spanish authority, and (on foreign soil) executed two British subjects for treason against the United States!

When the Spanish minister in Washington protested, Secretary of State Adams responded by offering to buy Florida. For $5 million, Spain agreed; it was obvious the Americans were going to take Florida one way or another. Adams had only to confirm Spain's version of the disputed boundary between American Louisiana and Spanish Texas, which was no concession at all. The United States had never seriously contested the Mexican boundary. In the Adams-Oñis Treaty, the United States was guaranteed every acre to which the country had a reasonable claim.

The Monroe Doctrine

John Quincy Adams was also the chief author of the American policy that, almost alone, has earned Monroe's name an entry in the history books. In December 1823, the president wrote in a message to Congress (and to Europe) that the United States was no longer to be considered an appendage of the Old World. With an "essentially different" destiny, the United States pledged not to dabble or intervene in European affairs. In return, Europe was to consider the Western Hemisphere closed to further colonization. Monroe said that any European attempts to establish or reestablish American colonies would be defined in Washington as "an unfriendly disposition." In carefully muted words, he threatened war.

The proclamation of the Monroe Doctrine (a name given it only years later) was prompted by two developments that disturbed the sensitive Quincy Adams. The first was expanded Russian exploration and fur trapping south of Alaska, which had been Russian by right of discovery since 1741. The Russians built an outpost, Fort Ross, provocatively close to Spanish San Francisco, and in February 1821, the czar ordered foreign ships to keep at least a hundred miles clear of Russian America's shores.

Fort Ross was thousands of miles and three mountain ranges from Missouri. Adams was more troubled by rumblings in Austria and France, which had threatened to send troops to the Western Hemisphere to help Spain regain control of its lost colonies.

Assertion of American Identity

Neither worry amounted to anything. The Russians were interested not in settlements but in the plush pelts of the California sea otter. By the early 1820s, trappers had just about wiped out the animals in California's coves. In 1824, the Russians abandoned Fort Ross and withdrew to Alaska. The French and Austrians had other problems more pressing than the fall of the Spanish Empire, and the project, never more than talk, was stillborn. In fact, the United States had no army to send anywhere. If the Adams-Monroe closure of the New World to colonization had any force, it was because the British, now supreme on the Atlantic, wanted Hispanic America to be independent.

In fact, the British foreign minister, George Canning, had proposed that Great Britain and the United States jointly proclaim the Americas closed to further colonization. Previously restricted in the extent of their trade in the rich markets of the old Spanish Empire, the British were the chief beneficiaries of Spanish American independence.

Adams decided to act alone in asserting the different destiny of the Western Hemisphere so that the United States would not look like "a cock-boat in the wake of the British man-of-war." To nationalistic American sensibilities, British friendship was as threatening as British antagonism.

Nationalism in the Courtroom

While Adams and Monroe proclaimed the national dignity of the American republic, Chief Justice John Marshall buttressed the constitutional primacy of the national government in a series of decisions that are still basic American law. Marshall's court never again invalidated a law of Congress, as it had done in *Marbury v. Madison.* But the Court repeatedly asserted its powers in other theaters.

While cultivating a personal reputation for physical laziness and a squalid appearance, Marshall dominated his fellow Supreme Court justices until 1835. In chambers by day and at the boardinghouse (where several justices lived together) by night, over law books and tumblers brimming with whiskey, Marshall whittled away at the power of the states. In *Fletcher v. Peck* (1810), the Marshall court declared a state law unconstitutional, thus establishing the right of the Supreme Court to act in matters that concerned one state alone. In *Martin v. Hunter's Lessee* (1816), Marshall established the Court's authority to reverse the decision of a state court. In *McCulloch v. Maryland* (1819), Marshall forbade the state of Maryland (and all states) from taxing the nationally chartered Bank of the United States. "The power to tax is the power to destroy," the Court declared. No state had the right to interfere with the national government's obligation to legislate on behalf of the common good.

In *McCulloch,* Marshall also propounded his view on the extent of governmental power. If the goal was legitimate and the law did not run counter to the Constitution, Congress and the president had the power to enact whatever legislation they chose to enact. It did not matter that the government in Washington was not specifically authorized by the Constitution to take a certain action, such as the establishment of a national bank—the issue that caused the first split between Hamilton and Jefferson. Now with Hamilton and his party both dead, John Marshall made "broad construction" of the Constitution the prevailing law of the land.

John Marshall served as chief justice during the administrations of six presidents, three of whom served two full terms while he lived. It would be difficult to argue that any of them contributed more to the shaping of American government than Marshall. In 1833, the only Supreme Court justice of the Marshall era whose legal mind rivaled his own, Joseph Story, published *Commentaries on the Constitution of the United States.* Essentially, it was a commentary on fundamental law as John Marshall perceived it.

THE INDUSTRIAL REVOLUTION IN AMERICA

Another of Hamilton's dreams for the United States—and one of Jefferson's nightmares—also headed for fulfillment during the second and third decades of the nineteenth century. To some extent in the West, but particularly in New England and the Middle Atlantic states, manufacturing came to rival agriculture in economic importance, and population began a significant shift from farms and villages to the towns and cities where factories were centered. In this process, the people of the northeastern states were early participants in the Industrial Revolution.

The Implications of Industrialization

Machine technology, the factory system for making goods, and the rapid growth of industrial cities were not revolutionary in the sense that people's lives were changed overnight. But the consequences of machines that made goods quickly and cheaply changed the terms of human existence far more profoundly than any battle or the beheading of any king or queen.

For example, in the United States today, less than 8 percent of the population works in agriculture and no farmers produce more than a tiny fraction of the food they consume and the goods they use. They buy the commodities of life

---

CEO

Women industrialists were rare, but not unknown. Rebecca Pennock Lukens owned and managed the Lukens Steel Company for a quarter of a century. Her father had turned the company over to her husband, Charles Lukens. When Lukens died in 1825, Rebecca was 30, with three children, but she took the factory over and won respect as an iron manufacturer. She retired in 1849, handing the prosperous company over to the husband of one of her daughters.

with money received for performing very specialized jobs. Even the typical farm family raises only one or two crops for market, and purchases the same mass-produced necessities and luxuries that city dwellers buy.

Before industrialization, in colonial and early national America, the situation was reversed. Roughly 90 percent of the population (the proportion was constantly declining) lived on farms or in agricultural villages. They personally produced a sizable proportion of the food they ate and the goods they used. For most people, very little was purchased: shoes; some clothing; tools, such as axes and guns; pottery and tin or pewter wares; some services, such as milling flour, shoeing horses, and so on. As for other necessities, ordinary people improvised them from materials on hand.

The preindustrial farmer or shopkeeper had to be handy. A man with a door to hang made the hinges himself. A woman who kept a tidy house made the broom with which she swept it. In all but the half dozen largest cities, townspeople of some means kept gardens of an acre or so, often a dairy cow, commonly a brood sow. The Industrial Revolution changed that kind of unspecialized, largely self-sufficient life into the specialized, interdependent economy we know today.

Cloth: Where It All Began

The first industrial machines were devised for the manufacture of textiles. This should not be surprising. Cloth is a universal necessity, but making it by hand is tedious, difficult, and time consuming.

In North America, as in much of the Western world, cloth making was largely woman's work, and the process took up much of the spare time of that half of the population. On poor and even middling American farms, cloth was made at home from scratch. Natural fiber from animals (wool) or plants (cotton, and flax for linen) was gathered, cleaned, carded (untangled and combed), spun into thread or yarn, dyed, and then woven or knitted by hand into a fabric that

The Metropolitan Museum of Art, Gift of Mrs. J. Insley Blair, 1948

▲ *A commercially printed fabric of the 1810s. It was probably intended for a wall covering or for drapes in a middle-class home.*

> **Making Mittens**
> In the manufacture of goods that resisted mass production in factories, the "putting out" system continued to flourish and still does, in a small way, today. In fact, Abby Condon of Penobscot, Maine, became a cottage-industry industrialist at just about the same time John D. Rockefeller went into the oil business.
>
> In 1864–wartime, with an attractive government contract in hand–Mrs. Condon collected 25 cents for each pair of soldier's mittens she knitted. After the war, the price collapsed to 6 cents a pair. Instead of quitting, Mrs. Condon became a jobber, recruiting at least 250 knitters–every girl and woman knew how to knit–to make mittens for her, which she resold to civilian retailers. By 1882, knitting machines were replacing nimble fingers. Mrs. Condon purchased 4 of the devices and built a small factory to house them. When she died in 1906, she owned 150 knitting machines. Her business consumed 6 tons of woolen yarn a year, producing 96,000 pairs of mittens.

could warm a body, cover a bed, protect a wagonload, or propel a ship.

Because the process took so much time and required hard-learned skills at every turn, fabric was expensive. The poor dressed in hand-me-downs scarcely better than rags. People of modest means made do with one set of clothing for work and another for attending church on Sunday.

Cottage Industry

Well-to-do people dressed rather more handsomely, of course, and they did not pick, shear, card, spin, and weave. Cloth also had to be made in quantity for plantation slaves, soldiers, and sailors. Before industrialization, the needs of such groups were met by cottage industry, or what was sometimes called the "putting-out system."

It worked like this: Farm wives and daughters contracted with a cloth dealer, sometimes called a "factor," to receive fiber from him and spin it into yarn or thread in their homes. Working in odd, snatched moments, they were paid not by the hour but by the piece. They were, in our terms, independent contractors. The women and children (and sometimes men) in another family might weave cloth under the same arrangements, most of them, again, in their spare time.

This system of production did not significantly disturb traditional social structure and values. Households involved in cottage industry were able to participate in the money economy to the extent of what their women earned. Socially, however, these women remained farmers' wives or daughters, or spinsters (unmarried women in a household). They were not textile workers. Their values and the rhythm of their lives were essentially the same as those of their neighbors who were not part of "putting out."

In England in the middle of the eighteenth century, this system began to change. English inventors devised water-powered machines that spun thread and wove cloth at many

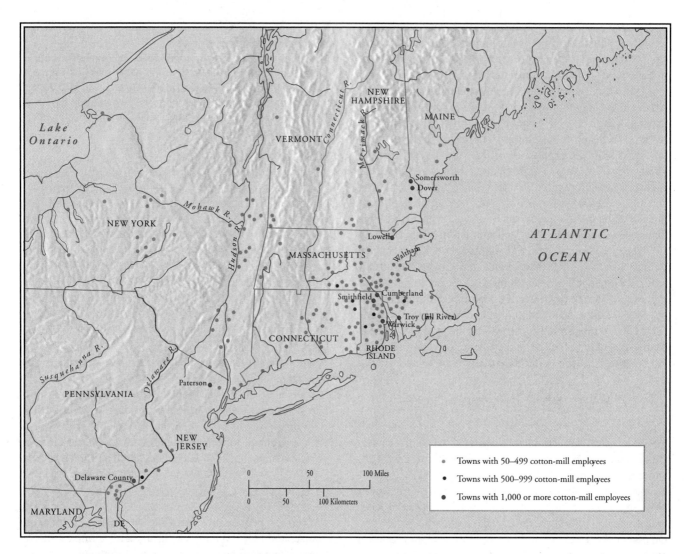

MAP 14:1 Cotton Mills, 1820 Although the mill towns appear to be scattered, they had, in fact, one significant feature in common: All were located next to waterfalls or river rapids where the stream descended many feet within a short span. The mills captured the power of the falling water by running it through a mill race—a ditch—where it turned a waterwheel. Lowell, Massachusetts, was built at the 32-foot falls of the Merrimack River. Paterson, New Jersey, was built where the Passaic River, wandering willy-nilly to the Hudson River, found its route by creating dramatic falls and, therefore, power.

times the speed that hand spinners and weavers could do it and, as a result, at a fraction of the cost. With a monopoly on this technology, Britain prospered, supplying the world with cheap fabric. Not only were most women from Canada to Calcutta delighted to be spared the tedium of spinning and weaving, but the machine-made cloth was cheap enough for almost all to buy, and it was generally of better quality than homemade cloth. England found a market for its cheap cloth everywhere in the world. Comparable machines were developed for other forms of manufacture.

Power

The key to exploiting the new machines was power—a fast-moving river or, somewhat later, the steam engine. A water-wheel or mighty, hissing piston could turn hundreds of machines much faster than any foot-driven spinning wheel. Power is where it is found or made, however. The process of

making cloth had to be centralized, brought under one roof; the machines had to be run for as long as there was light by which to see. Industrialization created the factory and a pace of labor governed by the clock, the tireless machines, and the capitalist's need to use his investment to the utmost.

Industrialization also created a class of workers who did nothing but tend machines. No longer was thread spun by a farmwife in odd, snatched moments. The industrial textile worker spent six days a week, from dawn to dusk, at the factory. Because she worked virtually all the daylight hours, she had to live close to the factory. The mill hand was a town dweller, no longer the farmer's daughter. A new social class emerged—the industrial working class.

Early Factories

The British protected their monopoly on industrial technology as a magician guards his bag of tricks. It was illegal to

The Granger Collection, New York

▲ *The first cotton-spinning mill in America, built by Samuel Slater and Moses Brown at Pawtucket, Rhode Island. Note the falls of the river, which were the power that ran the machines. Also note that neither the scale of the mill nor its design was obtrusive to the small village in which it was constructed.*

export machinery or plans for it. Indeed, engineers and mechanics expert in building or repairing textile machines were forbidden to leave the country.

One such engineer was Samuel Slater, 23 years old in 1790, and quite clever enough to know that the knowledge that provided him a comfortable life in England would make him rich in America. Rather than risk being caught with plans for spinning machines, Slater committed to memory long and intricate lists of specifications. He slipped away from his home and shipped off to the United States, where he struck a bargain with a Rhode Island merchant, Moses Brown, who had tried without success to build spinning machines.

Brown and a partner put up the money; Slater contributed the expertise. In 1790, they opened a small water-powered spinning mill in Pawtucket, Rhode Island. The little factory housed only 72 spindles, a pip-squeak operation compared with what was to come. Still, they were the equivalent of 72 spinning wheels in 72 cottages, and each of the Slater devices turned many times faster and spun much longer than any farmwife could manage.

The capital investment was substantial but operating expenses small. The whole mill could be run by one supervisor and nine children between the ages of 7 and 12. Their labor cost Slater and Brown 33 to 60 cents per worker per week. Within a few years, both men were rich. Slater lived to be one of New England's leading industrialists, owning mills in three states.

There were other such acts of technological piracy. In 1793, two brothers from Yorkshire, John and Arthur Schofield, illegally emigrated to Byfield, Massachusetts, where they established the first American woolens mill.

Francis Cabot Lowell smuggled plans for a power loom out of England. Throughout the nineteenth century, Englishmen would bring valuable technological advances in their sea trunks or heads.

Costly Labor

Once aroused, Americans proved more than able to advance the Industrial Revolution on their own. Alexander Hamilton had observed "a peculiar aptitude for mechanical improvements" in the American people. In the 1820s, a foreign observer marveled that "everything new is quickly introduced here. There is no clinging to old ways; the moment an American hears the word 'invention' he pricks up his ears."

One reason for the American infatuation with the machine was the labor shortage that vexed employers since the earliest colonial days. Land was abundant and cheap in the United States. Opportunities for an independent life were so ample that skilled artisans demanded and generally won premium pay. In the early nineteenth century, an American carpenter made about three times as much in real income as his European counterpart. Even an unskilled worker in the United States lived considerably better than the day laborers of the Old World. What was sauce for the worker, however, was poison to the men who hired help. The machine, which did the job of many handworkers, was inevitably attractive to the hirers.

Inventors Galore

Thus, Oliver Evans of Philadelphia earned a national reputation when he contrived a continuously operating flour mill. One man was needed to dump grain into one end of an ingenious complex of machinery. Without further human attention, the grain was cleaned, ground, weighed, and packed in barrels. Only at this point was a second man required to pound a lid on the keg. Evans saved millers half their payroll.

In 1800, Eli Whitney devised a rotary cutting tool that quickly and cheaply milled small cast iron parts. Whitney's invention promised to make highly skilled gunsmiths and watchmakers obsolete, for, in making new guns and watches and in repairing broken ones, they had to construct each of many moving parts from scratch. Every musket was "custom made," the lock of each individually fashioned by hand; no two guns were the same. Whitney's milling device made it possible to mass-produce parts of muskets that were interchangeable.

He appeared before a congressional committee with 10 functional muskets he had constructed, took them apart, shuffled the components, and reassembled 10 working muskets. His dramatic little show won him a government contract to make 10,000 of the weapons.

Many cultures produce inventors, but the United States was unique in raising the inventor to the status of a hero, quite the equivalent of a conquering general or a great artist. Even bastions of tradition embraced practical science. In 1814, Harvard College instituted a course called "Elements of Technology." In 1825, Rensselaer Polytechnic Institute, a college devoted entirely to the new learning, was founded at Troy, New York. Others followed in quick succession, for Americans found nothing bizarre in teaching engineering side by side with Greek and Latin. Indeed, they were more likely to be suspicious of those who studied the classics.

A COUNTRY MADE FOR INDUSTRY

A cultural predilection to technology was only one of America's advantages in the Industrial Revolution. The United States was also blessed with the other prerequisites of an industrial society: resources (needed to feed the new machines), capital (surplus money to finance the building of factories), and labor (people to work in the factories).

Resources

For a providentially minded people, it was as if the Creator had shaped the northern states with water-driven mills in mind. From New England to New Jersey, the country was traversed with fast-running streams that, dammed and channeled, provided power for factories. When steam power proved superior to water power, there were dense forests and rich deposits of coal to stoke the boilers. America's forests and strong agricultural base produced the raw materials the new industry required, from lumber to leather to hemp for rope. At the same time the textile industry was growing in New England, cotton cultivation expanded throughout the South to provide enough of the snowy fiber for both England and America.

Capital

Money for investment in industry came from the merchants and shippers of the Northeast. Ironically, many of these capitalists were pressured to convert their wealth from ships into mills by the restrictions on trade that they thought would be the ruin of them. In 1800, at the beginning of the Napoleonic Wars, there were only seven mills in New England, with a total of 290 spindles. After Jefferson's embargo, Madison's restrictions on trade, and the War of 1812 had disrupted shipping for 15 years, there were 130,000 spindles in 213 factories in Massachusetts, Connecticut, and Rhode Island alone.

▲ *The Second Bank of the United States in Philadelphia, chartered by Congress in 1816. Alexander Hamilton's First Bank of the United States operated for 20 years, until an indifferent Jeffersonian Congress allowed its charter to expire. Within a few years, the mistake was recognized—the fast-growing country needed to control its currency—and the Second Bank of the United States was created.*

On the Road

The dictionary defines *road* as "an open way, generally public, for the passage of vehicles, persons, and animals." Roads were the first means of overland transportation, of course. But not until the automobile age would Americans invest the massive sums in them that were plunged into canals and railroads. The explanation is not obscure. Roads of any distance were expensive to build and a nuisance, financially and politically, to maintain. And no one could get rich doing either. Even in densely populated New England, with roads connecting each town to its neighbors, voters resisted taxes and labor levies required to keep them repaired. (Connecticut required "every teeme and person fitt for labour" living on a road to devote two days a year of his and his draft animals' labor to maintaining it.)

As long as most Americans lived near water that would float a boat, they preferred to travel, as well as move their goods, by water. From Portsmouth to Savannah, rivers and sheltered coastal inlets were filled with boats sailing or rowed to and fro. George Washington needed four days on horseback to get from Mount Vernon to Williamsburg. On the Chesapeake, he could get there in half the time and without aching muscles. Providence was connected to Hartford and New Haven by the Pequot Trail, early widened to accommodate wagons, but anyone living near Long Island Sound traveled on it. Philadelphia was only a hundred miles from New York, and there was a fairly good road between them by 1700. Nonetheless, better-off travelers rounded New Jersey by schooner or sloop.

Early American roads followed routes blazed centuries earlier by Indians. The Boston Post Road (present-day U.S. Route 1) followed the Pequot Trail. The road British general Braddock built to battle (and be killed by) the French and Indians followed Nemacolin's Path. Daniel Boone renamed the Shawnee and Cherokee Warriors Path through Kentucky the Wilderness Road.

The Granger Collection, New York

Boone did more than rename it. Indians walked, single file at that. Their paths were rarely wider than a foot, too narrow for a horse, let alone a vehicle. They curled and twisted around large trees and outcroppings of rock. Grade was of no interest to hikers traveling light. So, to build even an equestrian road, it was necessary to "underbrush out" the saplings and small trees and to find or build grades that would not injure a horse. To make a road wide and straight enough for wagons—at first, commonly a rod (sixteen and a half feet) wide—the larger trees had to be felled, leaving stumps no higher than 2 feet, so that the wagons could clear them. Even then, low-lying stretches collected water and were impassable mud pits much of the year; when they did dry out, they were rutted deeply enough to break horses' legs and cart wheels.

There was no money to be made in road building, so only government, with interests other than profit, could undertake such projects. Until independence and the adoption of the Constitution, American governments were incapable of financing any roads but post roads (roads over which letters were carried), and they needed to accommodate only horses.

The great breakthroughs in road surfacing and road finance came simultaneously in the wake of the Constitution. A Scot, John McAdam, discovered that it was not necessary to lay roadbeds of large stone blocks, as the Romans had done, to have a roadway that remained firm after heavy rains. His road base (named macadam after him), raised a foot or two above the terrain for drainage, was constructed of small, uniformly sized stones, either broken by hand or mined from gravel deposits. The traffic would continually compact the roadbed.

In 1794, having seen McAdam's success in Britain, Philadelphia capitalists won a charter from the Pennsylvania legislature to build a macadam road 65 miles from Philadelphia to the important farm town of Lancaster. Their reward would be tolls. Locals going a few miles and people going to church drove the Lancaster Turnpike free. Freighters paid tolls to use the road; it was a "limited-access" highway with tollhouses at each entrance and a pole resembling a pike, the obsolete weapon, blocking entrance until money changed hands. The Lancaster Turnpike (present-day U.S. Route 30) was so successful that hundreds of copycat turnpikes were built within 20 years.

The first great free, federally funded highway was the Cumberland Road, approved by Congress in 1811 and completed from Cumberland, Maryland, on the Potomac to the Ohio River in 1818. It was macadamized, 4 rods wide, ditched on both sides, and it crossed streams on sturdy stone bridges.

Canals and, later, railroads stimulated the construction of feeder roads. Not all had macadam beds. A much cheaper surface in forested areas was made by laying 8-foot logs of 6 to 8 inches in diameter across the roadway. (Eight feet of good old dirt road ran alongside so that vehicles could pass, although not always cordially.) Known as "corduroy roads" for obvious reasons, they were built in newly developed areas until late in the nineteenth century. The ride was bumpy and could be dangerous; but corduroy roads kept wagon wheels out of the mud, they were cheap, and they were easy to repair.

Aware of a good thing once they saw it work, industrialists continued to expand. By 1840, there were 2 million spindles in the United States.

Banks and Money

Banks made it easier to channel capital where it was needed, though not everyone was pleased at the multiplication of lending institutions from 30 in 1801 to 88 in 1811. A bank issued more money in paper certificates than it actually had on hand in gold and silver. In 1809, anticipating the obsession of Thomas Hart Benton, John Adams growled that "every dollar of a bank bill that is issued beyond the quantity of gold and silver in the vaults represents nothing and is therefore a cheat upon somebody."

However, as long as the people who built a mill, supplied it with fiber, and worked the machines accepted the paper dollars lent by a bank to the mill owner, and as long as their grocers, landlords, and business associates accepted the paper money from them, it did not matter that the bank owned only $100,000 in gold and issued $1 million in paper. As long as the people who traded in the bills believed that they could present the paper to the bank and receive gold, capital was increased tenfold. As long as confidence and optimism were in rich supply, banks were a source of energy more powerful than the 32-foot falls of the Merrimack River.

The Jeffersonians had allowed the First Bank of the United States to die when its charter expired in 1811. Within five years, they recognized their error and chartered a Second Bank of the United States with much the same powers as the first.

Industry and Politics

With the increasing importance of industrial interests in the Northeast, the section's political interests shifted. Traditionally, New England shipowners were suspicious of high tariffs on imported goods. If taxes on imports were high, fewer Americans bought them, and there was less business carrying manufactured goods across the ocean. Alexander Hamilton failed to get the tariff he wanted partly because New England merchants, Federalists on other issues, joined with farmers (who were consumers of manufactured goods and wanted the lowest prices possible) to defeat him.

As late as 1816, many New England congressmen voted against high tariffs. One of them was Daniel Webster, a 34-year-old representative from New Hampshire who numbered Portsmouth shipmasters among his legal clients. By 1823, when Webster returned to Congress, he had moved to Massachusetts and become counsel and confidant to several manufacturers. Now he was a strong and eloquent supporter of a high tariff. If infant industries were to grow, they had to be protected from competition with the cheaper goods that the older and better-developed British manufacturers could produce.

Labor

Industrialization eventually undercut and almost destroyed handicraft. Many people were needed to tend the machines in the new mills, and the United States lacked England's surplus of "sturdy beggars" roaming the countryside and overcrowding the cities. Few white Americans were desperately poor. Few men who could freely choose among farming profitably, moving west, or working in small independent shops were attracted to low-paying, highly disciplined factory work.

The difficulty of recruiting labor from among traditional groups was reflected in the failure of the "Fall River system." In Fall River, Massachusetts, the mill owners attempted to hire whole families to work in the mills. It was an honest mistake. The family was the unit of production on the traditional farm and in the artisan's shop. But the system did not work very well in factories. In Rhode Island, mill owners put the man of the house on a small farm and put his wife and children to work in the mills.

The Lowell Girls

Rather more successful than both, because it found a niche within the traditional social structure, was the system developed by Francis Cabot Lowell, who built several large mills in Waltham, Massachusetts, in 1813, and in a town he founded and named Lowell in 1826. Lowell dispatched recruiters to roam rural New England. They persuaded farmers to send their young daughters to work in the mills. For 70 hours a week at the machines, the girls and young women earned three dollars, paying half of that for room and board at company-supervised lodging houses. Most—frugal lasses—banked the rest.

The long workweek put off no one. It was a normal enough regimen for a farm girl. The money was attractive too. Farming the stony New England soil never made anyone rich, and Yankee farmers burdened with large families inevitably liked the idea of subtracting one diner from the table, especially if that diner was a daughter who, by going to Lowell for a few years, could save a dowry large enough to attract a suitable husband. The Lowell system was successful precisely because it drew on a body of people for whom there were few other opportunities.

The trick was to persuade straitlaced New Englanders to allow girls of 16 and 17 to leave home. Lowell worked it by providing a closely regulated life for his employees during off hours as well as working hours. The Lowell girls lived in company-run dormitories, attended church services, and were kept busy (as if 70 hours at work were not enough!) with a variety of educational and cultural programs.

Most of the first American industrial workers were women—and children. In 1820, about half the factory hands in Massachusetts mills were under 16 years of age. A society of farmers, in which everyone down to 6 years of age had assigned chores, did not find this inhumane. And the pace of

▲ *New England mill girls, not long off a New England farm. There was no shame in working at a mill. The experience, the new friends, and the cash income (modest though it was) must have been exhilarating to many.*

▲ *Workers at the Lowell Mills and most other factories lived closely supervised lives; attending church (a church of their choice) was a condition of employment. The factory provided after-hours programs of "cultural uplift." As if at college, the workers at Lowell published a literary magazine of their own, the* Lowell Offering. *Supervisors monitored "dating" closely, and there seem to have been few illegitimate pregnancies. But almost all the mill girls found husbands either in the mill towns or back home near the family farm.*

the early factory was far slower than that of a twenty-first-century assembly line. Operatives minding textile machines shut them down when they thought it necessary to do so. In some mills, girls were permitted to entertain visitors while they watched their spindles. English tourists commented that American factories were idyllic compared with England's "dark, satanic mills." Nevertheless, Lowell was no idyll. In 1834 and 1836, angry Lowell Girls shut down the mills until their demands for better compensation were met.

THE SOUTH AT THE CROSSROADS

While westerners tamed land and northeasterners built a society dominated by mills and swelling cities, southerners reaffirmed their agrarian heritage. There were those who would have had it otherwise. In 1816, when Daniel Webster was still speaking for the shipping interests of old New England, John C. Calhoun of South Carolina dreamed of cotton factories in his state.

But Calhoun's flirtation with industrialization, like his War Hawk supernationalism in 1812, was already doomed. His future lay in defending southern sectionalism, the plantation system, and the institution of slavery on which they rested. Ironically, this brilliant political theorist (and somewhat less able politician) was chained to such anachronistic institutions because of a machine that, if its technology was rudimentary, was profound in its dramatic consequences.

Slavery in Decline

When John C. Calhoun was born in 1782, African American slavery appeared to be dying out. The northern states abolished it before Calhoun was an adult. Slavery also declined in the South during the revolutionary era. The world price of tobacco, one of the few crops for which slave labor was profitable, collapsed. On top of that, many of the old Chesapeake and Carolina tobacco fields were exhausted. Other slave-raised crops, such as South Carolina's rice and indigo, lost some luster when British subsidies were lost following independence.

Southerners, as well as northerners, were moved by the ideals of the Declaration of Independence. Thomas Jefferson, its author, agonized throughout his life over the injustice of human bondage. In their wills, Jefferson, George Washington, and many other planters freed at least some of their slaves. Few spoke of slavery as anything better than a tragic social burden, a necessary evil. As late as 1808, only a few southerners objected when Congress (as the Constitution allowed) outlawed further importation of enslaved blacks from abroad. At the peace talks in Ghent in 1815, American and British commissioners discussed the possibility of cooperating in suppressing illegal traders. It is reasonable to suggest that the institution would have been phased out peacefully in the United States (as it was in the British Empire) had it not been for the "absurdly simple contrivance" invented by Eli Whitney.

The Cotton Gin

In 1793, seven years before his demonstration of interchangeable parts, Eli Whitney was living on a plantation near Savannah, Georgia. He saw his first cotton plant and learned that it flourished everywhere in the upland South, where there was plenty of rain and 210 frost-free days spring to fall. Cotton fiber was worth 30 to 40 cents a pound—a fabulous price for the by-product of a plant—but the upland cotton could not be exploited commercially because of the costs of separating the fiber from the plant's sticky green seeds. The job could be done only by hand, and the most nimble-fingered of people could process no more than a pound of fluff a day, hardly enough to justify hiring employees to do it, let alone setting an expensive slave to the job.

On the sandy sea islands off the coast of South Carolina and Georgia, cotton had been cultivated profitably since 1786. But the variety planted there was long-staple cotton with shiny, smooth black seeds that could be popped out of the fiber by running the raw cotton between two rollers. When this method was tried with the cotton of the uplands, the sticky green seeds were crushed, fouling the fiber with oil.

Whitney's device was so simple that a planter who had a decent collection of junk on the grounds could make a

▲ *A lithograph celebrates the revolution in the economy and society of the Deep South wrought by the invention of the cotton gin. The glee of the planters at the left makes sense; the joy of the slaves working the gin does not. The boom in cotton created by the cotton gin increased the demand for slave labor which had been in steady decline everywhere but in the rice growing regions of South Carolina.*

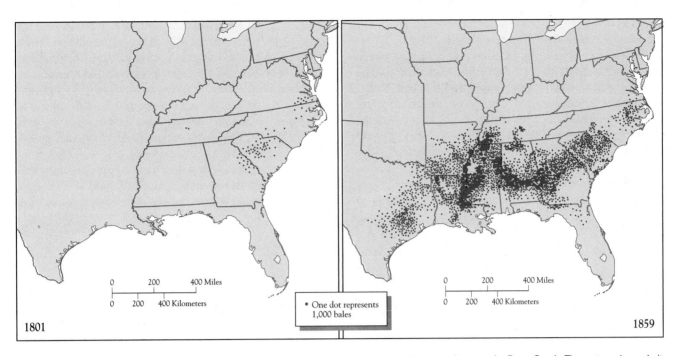

MAP 14:2 **The Spread of Cotton Production**   Short-staple, green-seed cotton grew like a weed across the Deep South. The cotton gin made it possible to grow the fiber as a very lucrative crop.

workable version. In fact, the ease of constructing the cotton "gin" (short for *engine*) denied Whitney the fortune he deserved for inventing it. His patents were ignored, and he was ground down into exhaustion in the courts.

Essentially, Whitney dumped the bolls into a box at the bottom of which were slots too small for the seeds to pass through. A drum studded with wire hooks revolved so that the hooks caught the fibers and pulled them through the slots, leaving behind the seeds without crushing them. Another drum, revolving in the opposite direction, brushed the fiber from the wire hooks.

It was a magnificent device. A single slave cranking a small gin could clean 10 pounds of cotton a day—$3 to $4 worth of cotton at 1790 prices. A larger machine turned by a horse on a windlass could clean 50 pounds a day (worth $15 to $20!). Once steam-powered gins were introduced, the capacity for producing cotton was limited not by the processing problem but by the number of acres that a planter could cultivate.

The Revival of Slavery

Technology had come to the South, but industry had not. The effects of Eli Whitney's machine were the revival of the South's traditional one-crop economy, the domination of southern society by large planters, and the reinvigoration of slavery. Like tobacco, cotton was well adapted to gang cultivation. The crop required plenty of unskilled labor: plowing, planting, chopping (or weeding, an endless process in the hot, fertile South), ditch digging and maintenance, picking, ginning, pressing, baling, and shipping.

Moreover, the fertile belt of uplands that extends from South Carolina and Georgia through eastern Texas was nat-

ural cotton country. Seduced by the same charms of riches that turned western farmers into speculators and doughty New England merchants into industrial capitalists, southerners streamed into the "Old Southwest" (Alabama, Mississippi, and northern Louisiana) and eventually into Arkansas across the Mississippi River. In 1800, excluding Indians, there were about 1,000 people in what is now Alabama. In 1810, there were 9,000; in 1820, 128,000! The growth of Mississippi was less dramatic but not lethargic: in 1800, 8,000; in 1810, 31,000; in 1820, 75,000.

Nor was this an emigration of buckskin-clad frontiersmen with no more baggage than a long rifle and a frying pan. Wealthy planters from the old states made the trek, bringing their slaves with them. In 1800, there were 4,000 blacks in Alabama and Mississippi. In 1810, there were 17,000 blacks, virtually all of them slaves. In 1820, there were 75,000. Almost half the population of Mississippi was African American and in bondage.

The price of slaves soared, doubling between 1795 and 1804. Blacks who were becoming financial burdens in Maryland and Virginia became valuable commodities in the new cotton South. The most humane masters found it difficult to resist the temptation of the high prices offered for their prime field hands, males between 18 and 30 years of age. Slave owners from as far north as New Jersey liquidated their human holdings, selling them to cotton planters.

The Missouri Crisis

There were still a few slaves in the North to be sold in 1819. Most states had adopted a gradualist approach to emancipation, by which no person born or brought into the state after a certain date could be enslaved. (There were a handful of aged slaves in New Jersey as late as the Civil War.)

But there was also, by 1819, a clear-cut line between slave states and free states. North of the Mason-Dixon line (the Maryland-Pennsylvania border) and the Ohio River, slavery was forbidden or in the process of abolition. South of it, the institution remained a vital part of society and the economy. In 1819, quite in the middle of the "Era of Good Feelings," the sectional character of the institution briefly became an explosive issue.

It was ignited by the application of the Missouri Territory to be admitted to the Union as a state. Although west of the Mississippi River, all but a tiny fraction of Missouri lay north of the mouth of the Ohio River. Quite able to read a map and voicing moral objections to slavery, Congressman James Tallmadge of New York proposed that Missouri be admitted only after its proposed state constitution was amended to forbid the further importation of slaves and to free all slaves within the state when they reached 25 years of age. In a word, Missouri would eliminate slavery gradually, as the northern states had done.

Some northern representatives and senators leapt into the breach Tallmadge opened. One described slavery as "a sin which sits heavily on the soul of every one of us." On

---

MAP 14:3 Missouri Compromise, 1820   Note that Missouri, a state in 1820, was largely north of the line demarcating slave and free states. Henry Clay persuaded enough northern congressmen to accept this anomaly on the condition that slavery would be forbidden in all future states so far north. As of 1820, only Arkansas and Florida territories were open to slavery, and it was not guaranteed existence even there.

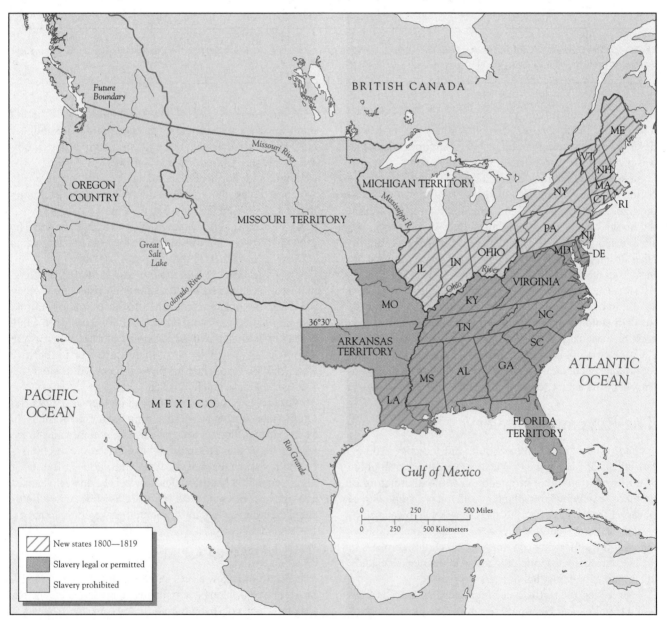

hearing such rhetoric, old Thomas Jefferson wrote from Monticello that he was startled as though he had heard "a firebell in the night." John Quincy Adams expressed concern. What worried both men was that once the morality of the discussants enters a debate, conflicts are not easily resolved by cutting a deal or trading tit for tat. Indeed, southern congressmen, particularly representatives of cotton states like Mississippi and Alabama, replied to their northern censors in fierce and furious language.

The Compromise

Ever unflappable, James Monroe was not unduly disturbed. A Virginian who was ambivalent to the future of slavery, he encouraged compromise in Congress. The deal was actually devised, however, by another southerner who wanted no part of moral imprecations in discussions of slavery, Henry Clay.

Earning the nickname the "Great Compromiser" for his scheme (known as the Missouri Compromise), Clay proposed that Missouri be admitted to the Union as those who wrote its constitution wished, as a slave state. This soothed southern feathers. In order to mollify northerners for whom slavery was an important issue, Clay proposed that the southern boundary of Missouri, 36 degrees, 30 minutes north latitude, be extended through the remainder of American territory—to the crest of the Rocky Mountains. North of that line, slavery was forever prohibited. In territories south of the line, which meant the Arkansas Territory and recently acquired Florida, the citizens living there could decide whether the state would be slave or free.

Passions cooled, tempers eased. Congressmen who had glared at one another shook hands and turned to other business. But Jefferson's "firebell" continued, however muted, to echo in the distance and with a new timbre to its peal. For Clay's compromise implied an equity, even a balance, between free states and slave states. There were 22 states in the Union in 1819, 11 free, 11 slave. When Missouri was admitted, Congress also detached "the Maine District" from Massachusetts and admitted it as a free state.

For 30 years to come, Congress would admit states virtually in pairs, preserving the balance. But because the Missouri Compromise forbade slavery in the major part of the Louisiana Purchase, it was inevitable that, sooner or later, a territory would seek admission to the Union as a free state with no slave state to balance it.

The population of the North was increasing much more quickly than the population of the South. Until 1810, the two sections grew at an uncannily similar rate. In 1820, however, despite the explosive growth of Mississippi and Alabama, there were nearly a million more people in the North than in the South: 5,219,000 versus 4,419,000. As the disparity increased—and all signs said that it would—the good feelings that made James Monroe's presidency such a happy one were bound to be among the casualties.

for FURTHER READING

Comprehensive histories of this era include the appropriate chapters of John R. Howe, *From the Revolution Through the Age of Jackson,* 1973; Robert Heilbroner, *The Economic Transformation of America,* 1977; W. Elliott Brownlee, *Dynamics of Ascent: A History of the American Economy,* 1974; and George Dangerfield, *The Era of Good Feelings,* 1952.

Research subsequent to Dangerfield's work has been incorporated into John Mayfield, *The New Nation, 1800–1845,* 1981. A superb social history, part of which covers these years, is Daniel Boorstin, *The Americans: The National Experience,* 1965.

The standard biography of the president of the Era of Good Feelings is William P. Cresson, *James Monroe,* 1971; the standard biography of Monroe's secretary of state is Samuel F. Bemis, *John Quincy Adams and the Foundation of American Foreign Policy,* 1949. See also Henry F. May, *The Making of the Monroe Doctrine,*

1975; and Dexter Perkins, *The Monroe Doctrine,* 1927. On the major political issue of the Monroe presidency, see Glover Moore, *The Missouri Controversy,* 1953; and Donald L. Robinson, *Slavery in the Structure of American Politics, 1765–1820,* 1979.

Early American industrialization has been a subject of lively inquiry in recent decades. Students should see Thomas Cochran, *Frontiers of Change: Early Industrialism in America,* 1981; Allan Dawley, *Class and Community in Lynn,* 1976; Thomas Dublin, *Women at Work: The Transformation of Work and Community in Lowell, Massachusetts, 1826–1860,* 1979; David J. Jeremy, *Transatlantic Industrial Revolution: The Diffusion of Textile Technologies Between Britain and America,* 1981; Bruce Laurie, *The Working People of Philadelphia, 1800–1850,* 1980; and Leo Marx, *The Machine in the Garden: Technology and the Pastoral Ideal in America,* 1964.

AMERICAN JOURNEY ONLINE AND INFOTRAC COLLEGE EDITION

Visit the source collections at http://ajaccess.wadsworth.com and http://infotrac.thomsonlearning.com, and use the Search function with the following key terms to explore documents, images, audio and video clips, articles, and commentary related to the material in this chapter:

Eli Whitney   Missouri Compromise
John Quincy Adams   Monroe Doctrine

Additional resources, exercises, and Internet links related to this chapter are available on *The American Past* Web site: http://history.wadsworth.com/americanpast7e.

HISTORY ONLINE

Erie Canal Online

www.syracuse.com/features/eriecanal/

Brief history; links to other sites about the Erie Canal.

Mill Girls

www.nps.gov/low/loweweb/Lowell%20History/Millgirls.htm

Treasury of insights on early industrialization in Lowell, Massachusetts, with a focus on the workers, the mill girls.

HERO OF THE PEOPLE

Andrew Jackson and a New Era
1824–1830

Courtesy of the Edward E. Ayer Collection, Newberry Library, Chicago

Thou great democratic God . . . who didst pick up
Andrew Jackson from the pebbles; who didst hurl him
upon a warhorse; who didst thunder him higher than a
throne! Thou who, in all Thy mighty, earthly marchings,
ever cullest Thy selected champions from the kingly
commons.

Herman Melville

Except an enormous fabric of executive power, the
President has built up nothing. . . . He goes for
destruction, universal destruction.

Henry Clay

THE SINGLE-PARTY system of the Monroe years had its virtues. At the top, at least, administration was efficient, and political culture was closer to noble than it would be again until the 1930s. In Congress, debate was candid and eloquent, almost always on a higher plane than in eras when partisanship has reigned. At best, party loyalty is less edifying than loyalty to home, country, or principle. At worst, it rewards tawdry, servile hacks. The Era of Good Feelings was spared the worst that American politics can produce. The era was not, however, spared ambitious men. A single party could not accommodate the hunger of every politician who wanted a better job. There were not enough nominations and appointments to go around.

So, in 1824, as James Monroe packed up in the White House, the Jefferson Republican party flew into pieces—half a dozen pieces attached to men who wanted to be president. Four years later, most of these fragments coalesced into two new parties, the Democratic Republicans (soon simply "Democrats") and the National Republicans (later renamed "Whigs").

THE SKEWED ELECTION OF 1824

During the quarter century the Jefferson Republicans dominated national politics, three traditions had grown up around the presidency: "King Caucus," the "Virginia Dynasty," and succession to the White House by the secretary of state, who was appointed by his predecessor. In 1824, two of these institutions were toppled, and the third was discredited.

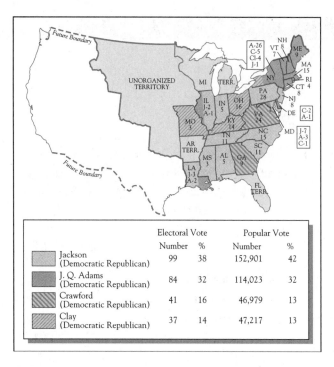

		Electoral Vote		Popular Vote	
		Number	%	Number	%
	Jackson (Democratic Republican)	99	38	152,901	42
	J. Q. Adams (Democratic Republican)	84	32	114,023	32
	Crawford (Democratic Republican)	41	16	46,979	13
	Clay (Democratic Republican)	37	14	47,217	13

MAP 15:1 Presidential Election of 1824 Andrew Jackson was the only one of the four presidential candidates who carried states in the North, the South, and the West.

Caucus, Dynasty, and Succession

The first to be dethroned was King Caucus. This was the name given (by those who did not much like it) to the method by which the Jeffersonians had nominated their presidential and vice presidential candidates. In election years, Jefferson Republican members of Congress met in caucus (that is, as members of the party) and named their nominee for the general election. Until 1824, unsuccessful candidates accepted the decision of King Caucus, as did the party's supporters.

Indeed, fights within the caucus were without much spirit. Monroe challenged Madison in 1808, lost, and three years later became his secretary of state. William Crawford of Georgia ran against Monroe in 1816, lost narrowly, and entered Monroe's cabinet. Partly by chance, but also because of the gentility with which caucus fights were fought, Madison and Monroe both stepped from the office of secretary of state into the White House. An orderly means of succession seemed to be established—presidents, like Roman emperors, "adopting" their heirs.

Americans spoke of a "Virginia Dynasty." All three of the Jefferson Republican presidents—Jefferson, Madison, and Monroe—were Virginians. Until 1824, it was all quite tidy and proper, especially to Virginians.

In 1824, however, the secretary of state was John Quincy Adams, so much a Massachusetts man that southern Jeffersonians regarded him as a Federalist in disguise. They were suspicious of Adams's strident nationalism and disliked his belief that the national government should exercise extensive

powers in shaping both the economy and society. Most southern politicians hoped to make the secretary of the treasury, William Crawford, the party's presidential nominee.

Crawford was from Georgia, but, having been born in Nelson County, Virginia, he could qualify as the Virginia Dynasty's legitimate heir. At odds with Adams, Crawford was an orthodox Jeffersonian who feared a powerful central government and favored strict construction of the Constitution. President Monroe and the party caucus supported him. The trouble was, only Crawford supporters attended the caucus in 1824. Others repaired to their own states, where state legislatures named other candidates.

Candidate Stew

For a while, it appeared that New York governor DeWitt Clinton, the builder of the Erie Canal, and South Carolina senator John C. Calhoun would enter their names in the contest. Clinton dropped out when he attracted little support outside his state. Calhoun found his chances slim and settled for second best, running as vice president with two other candidates.

One of them was John Quincy Adams. Adams's supporters rallied around the tradition that the secretary of state should succeed to the presidency. They also liked Adams because of his assertive and successful foreign policy, his support of a high tariff to protect infant industries, and his belief that the federal government should take an active role in promoting economic prosperity, including a federally financed program of internal improvements. Adams was nominated by the Massachusetts state legislature.

Henry Clay, nominated by the legislature of Kentucky, shared Adams's views. The two men differed in little but their personal aversion to one another's personal habits. When they were negotiators in Ghent, the high-living Clay mocked the hardworking Adams as dull and prudish. Adams, in turn, looked on Clay's drinking, gambling, and womanizing as dissolute. Now, in 1824, they divided the votes of those who favored their nationalistic economic program. Clay's hope was that he would win as the spokesman for the growing West.

Unfortunately, there was another westerner in the contest, General Andrew Jackson of Tennessee. So magical was his name as the conqueror of the British and half a dozen Indian tribes that it did not matter that Jackson's political principles were something of a mystery. Only on the questions of currency and banking was Jackson known to have taken a strong stand. Although rich—the wealthiest man in Tennessee, some said—Jackson detested banks and paper money. He had been ruined in a panic in the 1790s and, as all Americans were soon to learn, Andrew Jackson did not forget a grudge.

In 1824, Jackson's supporters did not allow voters to forget the Battle of New Orleans or the fact that Jackson was a man of action who crossed the Appalachians poor and by hook and crook and wiles and will—the American way—became a hero. "He has slain the Indians and flogged the British," a Jackson man put it, "and therefore is the wisest and greatest man in the nation."

Who Won?

This appeal to sentiment and the support of Calhoun, who was also Jackson's vice presidential candidate, was enough to win Jackson more popular and electoral votes than any of his opponents. He was also the only candidate of the four to win electoral votes in all three sections: Northeast, South, and West. But Jackson fell short of a majority in the electoral college. As in the election of 1800, the task of naming the president fell to the members of the House of Representatives, voting by states.

▲ *John Quincy Adams was one of the ablest individuals ever to be president. He may also have been the most inept politician to live in the White House.*

Under the terms of the Twelfth Amendment, the House selected from among the top three finishers in the electoral college, which eliminated Clay. William Crawford also seemed to be out of the running. He had suffered a stroke that left him bedridden and unable to speak. Crawford's supporters insisted he would recover, and, in time, he did. But they were unable to arouse any enthusiasm outside the southern states.

Jackson's followers were confident of victory. As they saw it, the House of Representatives was morally bound to ratify the election of the man preferred by more voters than any other. It was a good argument—the democratic argument—but it did not carry the day. Instead, because of the political beliefs and personal ambitions of the influential Henry Clay, and perhaps the impulse of Stephen Van Rensselaer, an elderly congressman from New York, the second-place finisher in the election, John Quincy Adams, won the prize.

"Corrupt Bargain!"

Van Rensselaer, who cast the vote that threw the New York delegation and the election to John Quincy Adams, said that he was praying for guidance, glanced at the floor, and saw a piece of paper on which was written "Adams." He took it as a sign from on high. Long before this providential moment, however, Clay had decided to back Adams, and, as Speaker of the House, he was well placed to reward congressmen who were persuaded by his arguments. Clay favored Adams because, despite their personal distaste for one another, they agreed on most political issues. Jackson, on the other hand, was a sworn enemy of one of Clay's favorite projects, the Bank of the United States.

Moreover, Clay wanted to be president—if not in 1824, then later—and Jackson was surrounded by would-be successors: Calhoun of South Carolina (who easily won the vice presidency), John Eaton of Tennessee, and Richard M. Johnson from Clay's own Kentucky. There was no room in the Jackson crowd for Henry Clay. Adams, by contrast, was a cranky, solitary man with few close friends. Because he had spent much of his life abroad as a diplomat, Adams had no circle of political cronies and heirs apparent.

Clay and Adams did not sit down across a table and hammer out a tit-for-tat understanding. Clay was a man for such a deal—how else win the title "Great Compromiser"?—but Adams was too stubborn, proper, and self-righteous to "talk turkey." His distaste for the dirty work of politics would, soon enough, shatter his career as a national politician. Nevertheless, when Clay threw his influence in the House of Representatives behind Adams and Adams later appointed Clay secretary of state, the losers of 1824 were sure they had been cheated by two cynical schemers.

John Randolph of Roanoke, a Crawford supporter, sneered at the union of "the puritan and the blackleg," an insult that led Clay to challenge him to a duel. (No one was hit.) The Jacksonians settled for shouting "corrupt bargain," obstructing the Adams presidency, and planning for revenge.

A New Party

Between 1824 and 1828, Jackson's loose alliance of supporters coalesced into a new political party. It included Jackson's western following and southerners led by John C. Calhoun. Despite this formidable base, the Jacksonians still had to break the grip of the Adams-Clay forces in the populous Northeast. Toward this end, Martin Van Buren of New York called on Jackson at his Tennessee mansion, the Hermitage, and put his influence in his native state at the general's service.

The South, the West, and New York formed the consortium that allowed Jefferson and Aaron Burr to throw the first Adams out of office in 1800. Also, like the Jefferson Republicans of 1800, the Jacksonians appealed to the ordinary fellow—the "common man"—and depicted their opponents as the party of privilege.

This was mostly nonsense. The leaders of the Jackson party were of the same social class as the people close to Adams and Clay, and Andrew Jackson was no common man. He had warned against the "undisciplined rising of the masses." But the Jacksonian appeal to democracy versus a conniving elite came naturally after the "corrupt bargain" controversy. "Let the people rule!" the Jacksonians cried even before Adams was inaugurated. Let them have the president that most of them chose in 1824. Seizing on the theme, the Jacksonians called themselves "Democratic Republicans," soon shortened to "Democrats."

THE AGE OF THE COMMON MAN

Like his father, John Quincy Adams brought impressive credentials to the White House. On paper, no one—surely not the laconic General Jackson—was better qualified for the job. Although Jackson could claim to have been slashed in the face by a British officer at the age of 14, John Quincy Adams at that age was in government service, secretary to an American minister abroad (his father). He had himself been minister in several European countries, senator from Massachusetts, and a secretary of state whose successes still rank him among the most able ever to hold that post.

Another Unhappy Adams

Also like his father, Adams's qualifications ended with his achievements. In temperament, he was out of tune with his times, unable to provide what more and more Americans were demanding of their leaders. In an age of electrifying political personalities—Benton, Clay, Jackson, Calhoun—Quincy Adams excited no one. Among a people beginning to prize equality and easy informality, Adams was standoffish, stuffy, and self-conscious of his abilities, learning, ancestry, and achievements.

In an era when government was becoming more democratic at every level, Adams spoke contemptuously of being "palsied by the will of our constituents."

Worst of all, political horse trading, if far from new, was now open, frank, fast, and furious. Quincy Adams tried to stand above partisan politics. He allowed open enemies to hold office under him. To have removed them and filled their posts with his supporters, Adams felt, would have been to stoop to the level of shabby politics that—unjustly in his opinion—he was accused of in the "corrupt bargain" controversy.

Adams was also thin skinned and short tempered. He took criticism, and sometimes mere suggestions, as affronts to his office and his person. He cut himself off not only from a majority of voters but from allies who had honest, minor disagreements with him. By the end of his term, he had a smaller political base in Washington than any previous president, including his unhappy father.

A Democratic Upheaval

Quincy Adams's view of himself as a member of a "natural aristocracy" of wealth, education, manners, and talent was the view of the previous generation of American politicians, Thomas Jefferson included. During the 1820s, however, politics ceased to be primarily the concern of the leisured, educated classes and came to preoccupy much of the white male population. The foremost foreign commentator on American attitudes, Alexis de Tocqueville, wrote that "almost the

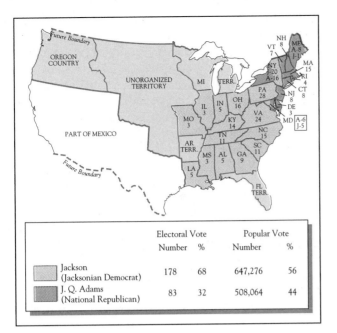

	Electoral Vote		Popular Vote	
	Number	%	Number	%
Jackson (Jacksonian Democrat)	178	68	647,276	56
J. Q. Adams (National Republican)	83	32	508,064	44

MAP 15:2 Presidential Election of 1828 Jackson swept the electoral college, even winning one electoral vote in New England.

only pleasure which an American knows is to take part in government." A less sympathetic visitor to the United States, Mrs. Frances Trollope, was appalled that American men would rather talk politics than mend their fences and tend their crops.

In part, this great democratic upheaval was the fruit of half a century of rhetoric that blatantly flirted with democracy. The Jeffersonians never ceased saying that the people should rule, and, like a slogan in a television commercial endlessly repeated, the idea caught on. The democratic upheaval of the 1820s and 1830s was also the consequence of the extraordinary growth and energy of the young republic. An increasingly prosperous people needed to struggle less in order to survive and had more time to think about public affairs. With issues like the tariff, land policy, and internal improvements bearing heavily on individual fortunes, ordinary folk had good reason to take an interest in politics.

Finally, the wave of democratic spirit that swept Andrew Jackson on its crest had a peculiarly western source. In order to attract population, the young western states extended the right to vote to all free, adult white males. All six states admitted to the Union between 1816 and 1821—Indiana, Mississippi, Illinois, Alabama, Maryland, and, back East, Maine—required no property ownership of voters. Western states enacted other laws designed to appeal to people of modest station. Kentucky abolished imprisonment for debt in 1821. No longer could a man or woman be jailed for financial misfortune.

Democratization spread south and east. Fearful of losing population to the West, most eastern states responded to liberal western voting laws by adopting universal male suffrage. In 1824, about half the states still insisted on some property

qualifications in order to vote. By 1830, only North Carolina, Virginia, Rhode Island, and Louisiana did, and Rhode Island's conservatism in the matter was misleading. Still governed under the state's seventeenth-century colonial charter, which could not be easily amended, Rhode Island was rocked by a brief violent uprising in 1842, Dorr's Rebellion, which resulted in extending the vote to all adult white males.

In 1800, only 2 of 16 states named presidential electors by popular vote. In 1824, 18 of 24 states did. By 1832, only planter-dominated South Carolina clung to selecting electors in the legislature.

Given the right to vote, free adult white males did. In 1824, the first presidential election in which there was widespread participation, about one-quarter of the country's eligible voters cast ballots. In 1828, one-half of the eligible voters voted. In 1840, more than three-quarters of the electorate participated in the national election. If such a proportion of eligible voters voted today, it would be described as a political revolution.

The "Workies"

Some new voters built parties around social issues. During the 1820s, workingmen's parties sprang up in eastern cities. Casually called the "Workies" and supported largely by recently enfranchised "mechanics," as skilled artisans were known, they pushed in city and state elections for a variety of reforms to protect their class: abolition of imprisonment for debt, which hit independent artisans hard; mechanics' lien laws, which prevented creditors from seizing their tools; laws giving wage workers first crack at a bankrupt employer's assets; and free public education for all children. To the workingman of the Northeast, education was the equivalent of the westerner's free land, the key to moving up in the world.

The workingmen's parties had their local victories, especially in New York. But they dwindled when farther-seeing visionaries, most notably Scottish-born Frances "Fanny" Wright, tried to convert the Workies to broader reforms. Wright, for example, was a feminist before feminism's time and advocated "free love," the freedom of all, unmarried and married, to enjoy sexual partners who were not their spouses.

Mechanics had no more interest in modifying the legal status of women than mainstream politicians did, and they were quite as likely as their employers to regard traditional restrictions on sexual activity as right and proper. As inclined to dally as men and women of every social class, mechanics were also conscious of the fact that their social status was superior to that of the urban underclass in part because of the comparatively open promiscuity of the lower classes. When most of the Workies' bread-and-butter reforms were enacted, they drifted into the Democratic party.

The Anti-Masonic Party

The Anti-Masonic party was a curious expression of the democratic upheaval of the 1820s and 1830s. It was founded in upstate New York when a bricklayer named William Morgan

▲ *The Anti-Masons had such astonishing success at the polls because many believed the Society of Freemasons was a conspiracy of the well-to-do that secretly kept the common man down. However, as with many such movements, the Anti-Masonic movement focused on sinister and lurid Masonic rituals (many imagined) in their propaganda.*

published an exposé of the Society of Freemasons and, shortly thereafter, was murdered.

Originally, the Society of Freemasons was a secret association of freethinkers. Many of the Founding Fathers, including Franklin and Washington, had been members; the pyramid with an eye atop it on the back of our dollar bill is a Masonic symbol. After 1800, the Freemasons were largely a club of middling to upper-class gentlemen. Much of Morgan's book dealt with Masonic rituals behind closed doors (hocus-pocus ostensibly hearkening back to ancient Egypt) and the secret handshakes and passwords by which Masons identified themselves to one another in public. For example, Morgan quoted the initiation ceremony during which a new member swore "to keep all Masonic secrets under the penalty of having his throat cut, his tongue torn out, and his body buried in the ocean." When Morgan disappeared and a corpse apparently mutilated according to regulations was dragged out of the Niagara River, outrage swept the state.

Politicians pointed out that Morgan was a workingman whereas most Masons were prosperous farmers, merchants, bankers, and the like. The order, they said, was a conspiracy aimed at keeping Masons on top and the common man down. The handshakes and passwords, they pointed out, quoting from Morgan's book, were to identify fellow Masons so as to do business with them rather than with "any other person in the same circumstances."

Every governor of New York between 1804 and 1828 had been a Mason. What was going on? Secrecy, the Anti-

Masons said, had no place in a free society. Preferential treatment had no place in a free market. The Anti-Masons also benefited from traditional views about the sanctity of the family that Fanny Wright flaunted. By maintaining that some secrets must be shared only with fellow Masons, Anti-Masons pointed out, the order was insinuating itself between husband and wife. If a husband were required to keep secrets from his own spouse, he was violating the marriage contract as surely as a free lover did.

A brace of political leaders who would later play an important part in national politics first came to the fore as Anti-Masons: Thaddeus Stevens, Thurlow Weed, William H. Seward, and Millard Fillmore. In 1832, the party's candidate for president, William Wirt, won 33,000 votes and carried the state of Vermont. In the same year, the party elected 53 candidates to Congress.

President Andrew Jackson was himself an active Mason. Consequently, although democratic to the core, Anti-Masons inclined to join the anti-Jackson Whig party when their single-issue enthusiasm flagged.

In the meantime, the Anti-Masonic party made a lasting contribution to American politics. In Baltimore in 1831, the Anti-Masons were the first party to hold a national party convention. With the caucus system of making presidential nominations dead and nomination by state legislatures not firmly established, the major parties imitated the Anti-Masonic example. The first Democratic convention met in 1832, nominating Andrew Jackson. The Whigs followed suit a few years later.

THE REVOLUTION OF 1828

Thomas Jefferson had called the election of 1800 the "Revolution of 1800." But in 1800, there was not nearly as great a break with what had gone before as there was in Andrew Jackson's victory in the election of 1828. His election ended the era of sedate transfers of power from incumbent president to secretary of state. Jackson was the first chief executive to come from a western state. (He was the first president not from Virginia or Massachusetts.) And the campaign that led to his election was noisier, harder fought, and "dirtier" than any the United States had experienced to date.

Mudslinging

Personally, Jackson followed precedent by taking no part in the campaign of 1828. He sat in the Hermitage while his

---

Don't Vote for That Bastard

Among the campaign mud that found its way into print was this aspersion on Andrew Jackson's lineage:

General Jackson's mother was a COMMON PROSTITUTE, brought to this country by the British soldiers! She afterwards married a Mulatto Man, with whom she had several children, one of which number GENERAL JACKSON IS ONE!

supporters fired insulting salvos at President Adams. They depicted the incumbent as a usurper, an elitist, a man with decadent European tastes who squandered money filling the White House with elegant furniture and its cellar with Euro-pean wines. The Democrats made a great fuss over Adams's purchase of a billiard table; billiards, by virtue of the high cost of the table, was a game of aristocrats. (In fact, Adams paid for his toy out of his own pocket.)

▲ *The "coffin handbill," a widely distributed anti-Jackson advertisement describing in detail the men Jackson had "mur-dered." It was not needed in anti-Jackson New England; it had little effect anywhere else.*

Dueling and Brawling the American Way

The duel—an arranged fight in cold blood between two men in front of witnesses, governed by strict rules—was not concerned with a person's guilt or innocence of a crime. The issue in dueling was a gentleman's honor. A man who believed that he or a woman under his protection was insulted challenged the offender to meet him on the "field of honor." It was not necessary that they fight to the death. Merely observing the intricate code that governed dueling established one's honor. In fact, a majority of duels ended when blood was drawn or, if by pistols, when each party discharged his weapon in the general direction of the other. The point was good manners. Only gentlemen dueled; the vulgar multitude brawled.

Although Edward Doty and Edward Leicester fought something like a duel in Virginia in 1621, the custom was almost unknown in colonial America. Scholars have found records of only a dozen before 1776. Then, during the Revolutionary War, French officers such as Lafayette, Rochambeau, and de Grasse introduced the *Code Duello* to their American friends. A decade later, when some French aristocrats fled the revolution in their country and settled in Louisiana, they made New Orleans the dueling capital of America. On one Sunday in 1839, 10 duels were fought in New Orleans. A woman wrote that the young men of her acquaintance kept score of their duels as young ladies kept count of marriage proposals.

Dueling spread rapidly, as sudden wealth created self-made men who were in a hurry to prove their gentility. Timothy Flint wrote of Mississippi, "Many people without education and character, who were not gentlemen in the circles where they used to move, get accommodated here from the tailor with something of the externals of a gentleman, and at once set up in this newly assumed character. The shortest road to settle their pretensions is to fight a duel." Librarian of Congress Daniel Boorstin has written that "of southern statesmen who rose to prominence after 1790, hardly one can be mentioned who was not involved in a duel."

Button Gwinnet of Georgia, a signer of the Declaration of Independence, was killed in a duel in 1777. James Madison fought a duel in 1797. Maryland-born Commodore Stephen Decatur fought one duel in 1801 and was killed in another in 1820. William H. Crawford, presidential candidate in 1824, fought a duel. John Randolph of Roanoke fought two, the second in 1826 with Henry Clay of Kentucky, who also dueled with other men. Senator Thomas Hart Benton of Missouri fought a number of duels and killed at least one of his opponents. Sam Houston of Texas fought a duel. A great many southerners later prominent in the Confederacy were involved in duels: William L. Yancey, Vice President Alexander H. Stephens, and General John C. Breckinridge. Confederate president Jefferson Davis was challenged to a duel by Judah P. Benjamin, who later became a fast friend and served in three cabinet positions. Romantic legend has it that duels were fought over ladies. In fact, as implied in this list, many were fought over politics.

The most famous American duelist was Andrew Jackson, who did fight over insults to his wife. His enemies said that Jackson was involved in a hundred duels. That is unlikely: Even Old Hickory was not so tough or so lucky as to survive that many tests of honor and marksmanship. In 1806, Jackson faced Charles Dickinson, a Nashville lawyer, in a duel, the written terms of which have survived:

It is agreed that the distance shall be 24 feet, the parties to stand facing each other, with their pistols drawn perpendicularly. When they are ready, the single word fire to be given at which they are to fire as soon as they please. Should either fire before the word is given, we [the seconds of both parties] pledge ourselves to shoot him down instantly. The person to give the word to be determined by lot, as also the choice of position.

Neither Dickinson nor Jackson fired before the word was given, but Dickinson fired first, wounding but not felling Jackson. "Back to the mark, sir," Jackson said when Dickinson staggered in fear of what was to come. Then, according to Jackson's enemies, Jackson's pistol misfired, and in violation of the *Code Duello,* he pulled the hammer back and fired again. This breach of honor haunted Jackson for the rest of his life, for Dickinson died.

Perhaps it was because of this slur on his character that when a man whom Jackson considered no gentleman challenged him some years later, Jackson refused to duel. But he offered to shoot it out in some "sequestered grove" as long as both parties understood that it was not an affair between social equals.

According to *The Code of Honor,* written by a governor of South Carolina, a gentleman who was insulted by a social inferior was to cane him; that is, to flog the impudent lout on the head and shoulders with a walking stick. But Jackson's reaction points up the fact that dueling merged imperceptibly into plain brawling. Fanny Kemble told of a duel in Georgia in which one of the terms was that the winner could behead the loser and impale the loser's head on a stake on the boundary of the land the two were disputing. An Alabama law of 1837 that outlawed dueling also forbade the carrying of the decidedly ungentlemanly weapons "known as Bowie knives or Arkansas Tooth-picks."

Dueling was by no means an exclusively southern and western practice. Alexander Hamilton and Aaron Burr were not southerners. Benedict Arnold was from Connecticut, DeWitt Clinton was from New York, and Nathaniel Greene was from Rhode Island—and they all fought duels. Indeed, the practice was outlawed earlier in the South than in the North. Killing a person in a duel was defined as murder, punishable by death. South Carolina imposed a fine of $2,000 and a year in prison for seconds as well as duelists. Officeholders in Alabama were required to take an oath that they never had dueled or acted as seconds.

The laws were not rigorously enforced. None of the duelists listed here spent a night in jail for defending his honor.

Alarmed by the effectiveness of these tactics, Adams men replied that Jackson was a savage and a murderer. Calling themselves "National-Republicans," they reminded voters that Jackson had executed two British subjects in Spanish Florida in 1818 (conveniently forgetting that Adams had supported Jackson after the fact). They printed broadsides that listed the men whom Jackson had killed in duels and the soldiers whom he had ordered shot.

But the assault that stung Jackson was the claim that he and his beloved wife, Rachel, had lived in sin. "Ought a convicted adulteress and her paramour husband," wrote a Cincinnati editor, "be placed in the highest offices in this free and Christian land?" The circumstances surrounding the Jacksons' marriage were murky. At the least, Rachel's divorce from her first husband was not legally final when she wed Jackson, which required them to go through a mortifying second ceremony. Laxity in observing marriage customs was not rare on the frontier. (When Daniel Boone was absent from his home for two years, he returned to find a son just a few months old, fathered by Boone's brother; Boone shrugged.)

Nevertheless, whatever Rachel Jackson's inclinations as a young woman were, by 1828 she was a prim and proper lady, and she was tortured by the gossip. When she died shortly after the election, Jackson blamed Adams and his supporters for his deeply felt loss.

In the meantime, Jackson's party responded in kind, digging up a tale that, as minister to Russia, Adams had procured the sexual favors of a young American girl for the dissolute czar. Then there were whispers of bizarre perversions in the Adams White House. "Negative campaigning" had come to American politics with a vengeance. Everything was fair game for discussion except important issues.

The Symbol of His Age

It was not mudslinging that won the election of 1828 for Jackson. The Democratic party organization, cobbled together by Jackson, Vice President Calhoun, and Martin Van Buren, turned that trick. Jackson swept to victory with 56 percent of a total vote three times as large as the vote in 1824 and a 178 to 83 victory in the electoral college.

The upswing in popular participation carried over to inauguration day in March 1829, when 10,000 people crowded Washington. They shocked genteel society with their drinking, coarse shouting, and boisterous invasion of the White House. Invited there by the new president, the mob muddied

© Bettmann/Corbis

▲ *Inauguration day, March 1829. Washington, D.C., had never seen such a display. Thousands of Jackson's supporters, many of them common men indeed, poured raucously into the White House. Jackson himself was persuaded to flee for fear he would be injured.*

the carpets, broke crystal stemware, and stood on expensive upholstered sofas and chairs in order to catch a glimpse of their gaunt, white-haired hero.

The adoring mob was so unruly that Jackson's friends feared he might be injured. They spirited the president away through a window; he spent his first night as president in a hotel. Back at the executive mansion, servants lured the mob outside by setting up bowls of lemonade, whiskey punch, and tables heaped with food on the lawn.

The man whom these people worshiped was by no definition a "common man." Jackson's talents were exceptional, his will and integrity extraordinary. Nor was he the vicious desperado whom the Adams forces depicted. Jackson was "erect and dignified in his carriage" in the words of Fanny Kemble, an English woman who met him. He was a gracious gentleman whose manners were on the courtly side.

Jackson thought well enough of himself, but he also believed that his success—he was the first log cabin–born president—was due to the openness of American society. All people were not equally talented, but the good society provided every man the opportunity to exploit his abilities and

---

OK

OK, that curious American expression now heard in almost every language on earth, originated in the days of Andrew Jackson. Where did it come from? The theories are numerous. Some said it was borrowed from the Choctaw *okeh,* which had a similar meaning. Others said it was an abbreviation of *Old Kinderhook* (one of Martin Van Buren's nicknames), *Obadiah Kelly* (an obscure shipping agent), and even *Orrins-Kendall* (a brand of crackers).

A popular theory probably close to the mark was the contention that Jackson, the ignorant old general, marked state papers "o.k." for "oll correct." In fact, Jackson was quite at home with the language. However, it is likely that anti-Jackson Whigs invented the term as a jibe at the president and it caught on. It first appears in print in a Boston Whig newspaper in 1839.

enjoy the fruits of his labor unimpeded by artificial social and economic obstacles. Government's task was to preserve this opportunity by striking down obstacles to it, such as laws that benefited some and, therefore, handicapped others.

Jackson's view of government was, therefore, essentially negative. He believed that government should, as much as possible, leave people, society, and the economy alone so that natural social and economic forces could operate freely. The common term for this point of view is *laissez-faire*, French for (roughly) "leave alone."

Attitudes of a Hero, Attitudes of a People

Jackson's vision of equal opportunity extended only to white males; but in this too, as in his attitudes toward women, children, blacks, and Indians, he embodied the opinion of his era.

Jackson believed that women lived in a different sphere than that of males. While menfolk struggled in a brutal

Thomas Sully, General Andrew Jackson, 1845, 97 × 61¼, oil on canvas. In the Collections of the Corcoran Gallery of Art, Washington, D.C. Gift of William Wilson Corcoran.

▲ *A portrait of Andrew Jackson by Thomas Sully capturing the majesty in which his supporters saw him. No other individual, except perhaps Franklin D. Roosevelt, loomed over his age as Andrew Jackson did. And, like Roosevelt, he was despised by a minority of Americans.*

world, women guarded home and hearth. They were superior to men in religious and moral sensibility. Indeed, it was because of these feminine faculties that men had to shelter women from a public life that was hardening at best and often corrupting. Jackson and most Americans (women certainly included) agreed with the clergymen, increasingly dependent on female congregants, who preached the "gospel of pure womanhood." Woman's "chastity is her tower of strength, her modesty and gentleness are her charm, and her ability to meet the high claims of her family and dependents the noblest power she can exhibit to the world." The Reverend Edward Kirk of Albany, New York, preached that "the hopes of human society are to be found in the character, in the views, and in the conduct of mothers."

The reward due women for accepting their private and submissive role in society was the sacred right to be treated with deference. Jackson was famous for his chivalry. Rough as the old soldier's life had been, he was prim and prudish in mixed company. Even in the absence of the ladies, he habitually referred to them as "the fair." Adding the word *sex* would have violated his sense of delicacy.

Toward children, visitors were appalled to discover, the old soldier was a pussycat. The man who aroused armies to blood lust and slaughtered enemies without a wince, and the president who periodically exploded in rages that left him (and everyone else) trembling, beamed quietly as young children virtually destroyed rooms in the White House before his eyes. The British minister wrote that he could not hear the president's conversation because the two men were surrounded by caterwauling children. Jackson smiled absentmindedly and nodded all the while. At the table, the president fed children first, saying that they had the best appetites and the least patience.

Indulgence of children was not universal in the United States. Many New Englanders raised their families in the old Puritan manner. But Europeans commented in horror that American children generally had the manners of "wild Indians." Some also noticed that American children were more self-reliant than European children because of the freedom that was allowed them. It was this quality—"standing on your own two feet"—that Jackson and his countrymen valued in their heirs.

Democracy and Race

Toward Indians and blacks, Jackson also shared the prejudices of his age. Blacks were doomed to be subject to whites by the Bible or Mother Nature or both. Blacks *were* slaves, and American blacks were fortunate to have such enlightened masters. Jackson did not trouble himself with the implications of the doctrine of equal rights. Having lived with both the Declaration of Independence and human bondage for 50 years, a majority of Americans found them quite compatible.

As a westerner, Jackson had thought a great deal about Indians. He spent much of his life fighting Native Americans and seizing their land. More than any single person, he was responsible for crushing the military power of the great southeastern tribes—the Creek, Choctaw, Cherokee, and Chickasaw.

Although he was ruthless in these wars, Jackson was not the simple "Indian hater" portrayed by his enemies. He found much to admire in Native Americans (as he did not in black people). He admired their closeness to nature, a view promoted during the 1820s by the popular novelist James Fenimore Cooper, and their courage in resisting their conquerors. There was a tinge of tragic regret in Jackson's statement to Congress that the white and red races simply could not live side by side and, therefore, the Indians would simply die out. During the Quincy Adams administration, Commissioner of Indian Affairs Thomas L. McKenney commissioned portraits of Indian leaders who visited Washington, in part because he too believed the culture of a doomed people should be preserved for posterity.

Government by Party

Attitudes are not policies, but President Jackson lost no time in establishing the latter. As the first president to represent a political party frankly and without apologies, he made it clear that he would replace federal officeholders who had opposed his election with his own supporters.

There were about 20,000 federal jobs in 1829, and Jackson eventually dismissed about one-fifth of the people holding them. Even considering the fact that some federal officeholders supported him, that was by no means a clean sweep. John Quincy Adams, who never dismissed anyone, privately admitted that many of those Jackson fired were incompetent.

As for those who were able, when Jackson's critics claimed that the men who were best qualified by education and training should hold government jobs, Jackson answered with quite another theory. He said that every government job should be designed so that any intelligent, freeborn American citizen could perform it adequately. If that were so, it was perfectly legitimate to say, as New York Jacksonian William Marcy said, "To the victor belong the spoils."

Attacks on the spoils system were noisy but short-lived. When the anti-Jackson forces came to power in 1840, they carved up the spoils of office far more lustily than Jackson's men had done. The ruling party's patronage of its members became an established part of American politics.

ISSUES OF JACKSON'S FIRST TERM

When he became president, Jackson did not have particularly strong opinions on the questions of the tariff or internal improvements. In his first address to Congress, he called for a protective tariff, but he later drifted (again without passion) to the southern position of a tariff for revenue only.

Internal Improvements

As a westerner, Jackson understood the need for good roads and rivers free of snags. However, as an advocate of laissez-faire and of strict construction of the Constitution, he worried that it was not constitutional for the federal government to finance them. In 1830, when he vetoed a bill to construct a road between Maysville and Lexington, Kentucky, he told Congress that if the Constitution was amended to authorize such projects, he would approve them.

In the Maysville Road veto, Jackson seems to have been as interested in taking a slap at Henry Clay as in protecting constitutional niceties. The projected road would have been completely within Clay's home state of Kentucky, adding immeasurably to Clay's popularity there. Later, Jackson quietly approved other internal improvement bills when the expenditures promised to win votes for his own party.

On the rising constitutional issue of the day, the division of power between the federal government and the states, Jackson was again inconsistent according to how his personal sensibilities and party interests were involved. When the issue was Georgia's attempt to ignore the treaty rights of Indians, Jackson allowed the state to have its way. But when South Carolina attempted to defy his power as president, he moved quickly and decisively to crush the challenge—coming close to dusting off his old uniform, polishing his sword, and personally leading an army south.

Indian Removal

The rapid settlement of the West brought whites once again into close contact with large Indian tribes. Presidents Monroe and Adams both agreed that warfare was undesirable but living as neighbors impossible. To resolve the dilemma, they devised the policy of "removal," relocation of the tribes to an Indian Territory west of the Mississippi River that would be guaranteed to them "forever."

To implement removal meant scrapping old treaties that had also guaranteed the tribes the land on which they dwelled "as long as the water runs and the grass grows." Nevertheless, burdened by demoralization and faced with a combination of inducements and threats, many trans-Appalachian tribes agreed to "removal" farther west.

Others rebelled. The Sauk and the Fox of Illinois and Wisconsin rose up under Chief Black Hawk. The Seminole of Florida, their numbers augmented by runaway slaves, also fought back. Unlike the Sauk and Fox, the Seminole were never decisively defeated. They escaped into the swamps, from where, between 1835 and 1842, they fought an effective holding action against the army.

Sequoya

Still other tribes, such as the Choctaw, were defrauded. Federal agents bribed renegade chiefs to sign removal treaties that were then enforced on the entire people. Between 1830

Courtesy of the Edward E. Ayer Collection, Newberry Library, Chicago

▲ *Sequoya with the syllabary he created so that the Cherokee language could be written and printed. Sequoya was illiterate. His single-handed achievement, starting from scratch, was the equivalent of what other civilizations had accomplished over generations.*

Appeal of the Cherokee

In 1835, its legal rights ignored, the Cherokee nation appealed to Congress on the basis of the values Americans ostensibly prized, values the Indians had adopted as their own:

In truth, our cause is your own. It is the cause of liberty and of justice. It is based on your own principles, which we have learned from yourselves. . . . On your kindness, on your humanity, on your compassions, on your benevolence, we rest our hopes.

and 1833, the Choctaw were forced to march west under army supervision. A fourth of them died on the way.

Like the Choctaw, the Creek, Chickasaw, and Cherokee were "Civilized Tribes." They had long since given up their traditional seminomadic ways, lived in American-style cabins and houses, and farmed intensively using Euro-American methods. They were part of the market economy, raising cotton for sale using African American slaves.

In 1821, an uneducated linguistic genius and silversmith named Sequoya recognized the power the white men drew from the markings on their books and papers. The Cherokee, he concluded, needed to be able to write and read. Had Sequoya been literate, he would have done what other Indians did—adapted the letters of the Latin alphabet to the tribe's language. But Sequoya could not read English, understanding only that the symbols on a page represented sounds.

He actually reinvented the wheel. Rejecting pictograms as unwieldy, Sequoya borrowed letters from an English spelling book and invented others. He created not a Cherokee alphabet (letters representing single sounds) but a *syllabary:* 86 symbols representing the 86 syllables (combinations consisting of a consonant sound and a vowel sound) that he counted in the Cherokee language. It was the same method that had produced writing in Minoan Crete 3,000 years earlier. Sequoya's syllabary was immediately adopted by the Cherokee, who printed newspapers and books and operated a school system, one of the best in the southern states.

The Cherokee in Court

The Cherokee also saw to it that some tribal members were educated in American professions, particularly law. According to their treaty with the United States government, the Cherokee were entitled to remain where they were. The tribe was recognized as a semisovereign nation within the United States. Therefore, they refused every attempt of the federal government to force them out and made friends in Congress, anti-Jacksonian northerners who agreed that the Cherokee cause was just.

Unlike Congress, Georgia was dominated by people who wanted the rich and developed Cherokee lands for themselves and who were willing to ignore federal treaties to get them. A Georgia court forced the issue by convicting a white missionary of a crime committed in Cherokee territory and, therefore, according to treaty, under tribal jurisdiction. The missionary and the Cherokee nation appealed the case, *Worcester v. Georgia,* to the Supreme Court.

Personally, Chief Justice John Marshall was no more sanguine about the prospect of whites and Indians living side by side than President Jackson was. But Marshall was a staunch defender of the sanctity of contracts, which the treaty with the Cherokee was. "The Cherokee nation is a distinct community," he ruled, "occupying its own territory, with boundaries accurately described . . . which the citizens of Georgia have no right to enter." Georgia could not force the Cherokee to give up their land.

The Trail of Tears

Marshall's decision seemed to settle the matter, and the Cherokee nation celebrated. But Georgia gambled. The state had voted for Jackson in 1828, and the president was a lifelong Indian fighter. Georgia defied the Supreme Court, held on to its prisoner, engineered some fraudulent agreements with Cherokee who could be bought, and began the forcible removal of the tribe.

Georgia won its bet. "John Marshall has made his decision," Jackson was quoted as saying. "Let him enforce it." Congress obliged, with the Indian Removal Act of 1830.

MAP 15:3 Removal of the Southeastern Tribes, 1820–1840 The "Civilized Tribes" had created viable, even prosperous, societies and economies in lands promised them in various treaties. But the tribes were "removed," mostly to present-day Oklahoma, when white southerners coveted their lands. Most Seminole refused to go west but lost their treaty lands.

Thus began the several Trails of Tears, the 1,200-mile trek of the "Civilized Tribes" to what is now Oklahoma. General John E. Wool, sent to supervise one forced march, was disgusted by his assignment. "The whole scene since I have been in this country has been nothing but a heart-rending one," Wool lamented. Indians were forced from ancestral homes under the gaze of, in his words, "vultures ready to pounce on their prey and strip them of everything they have."

Two thousand people died in camps waiting for the migration to begin; another 2,000 died on the trail. About 15,000 Cherokee, and smaller numbers of Choctaw, Chickasaw, and Creek, made it to Oklahoma. It was all over by 1838.

Nullification

If Georgia succeeded in defying the Supreme Court, South Carolina had less luck with Congress and the president. The issue that brought Jackson into conflict with the Palmetto State and with his own vice president, John C. Calhoun, was the tariff.

In 1828, Congress enacted an extremely high protective tariff. Most southern planters hated this "Tariff of Abominations," but South Carolina's cotton planters were enraged.

They believed that their crop was paying the whole country's bills and underwriting industrial investment.

They had a point. Cotton accounted for fully half of the wealth that poured into the United States from abroad. Some of this income was effectively diverted to the North by the tariff that required everyone, including southern cotton planters, to pay higher prices for manufactured goods. Vice President John C. Calhoun, a South Carolinian, saw the problem as constitutional. In 1829, secretly, he wrote *The South Carolina Exposition and Protest,* an ingenious and mischievous interpretation of the relationship of states to the federal union.

The *Exposition* took up where the Virginia and Kentucky Resolutions left off. Calhoun stated that the Union had not been formed by the people of America (as John Marshall and other nationalists said) but by the people acting through the individual states of which they were citizens. This was not mere hairsplitting. It meant that the states were sovereign, not the federal government. That is, the states were the fundamental, indivisible units of government that formed a compact, the Union, for the benefit of the states.

When, Calhoun continued, the Union enacted a law to which a sovereign state objected, as South Carolina objected

▲ *This most famous painting of the Cherokee on the "Trail of Tears," from Georgia to Oklahoma, does not begin to capture the wretchedness of the trek. The accompanying army was not unsympathetic, but fully a fourth of those who set out on the trail died on it.*

to the Tariff of Abominations, that state had the right to nullify the law (prevent its enforcement) within its borders until such time as three-quarters of the other states overruled its decision. (Calhoun was here referring to the amendment process of the Constitution, which requires the ratification of three-fourths of the states.) In such an event, Calhoun concluded, the nullifying state could choose between capitulation to the decision of the other states or secession from the Union.

South Carolina's Declaration and Jackson's Response

Calhoun and his supporters hoped that the Tariff of Abominations would be repealed after Jackson was elected president, thus leaving the *Exposition* in the abstract. However, in 1832, Congress adopted another high protective tariff, and Jackson signed it into law. South Carolinians blew up, electing a convention that declared the Tariff of 1832 "null and void" within the borders of the sovereign state of South Carolina.

Jackson exploded in one of his trademarked rages. South Carolinians would rather rule in hell, he said, than be subordinate in heaven. They could write whatever they chose in expositions, but, Jackson threatened, if "a single drop of blood shall be shed there" in preventing the collection of the tariff, "I will hang the first man I can lay my hand on engaged in such treasonable conduct, upon the first tree I can find."

Congress backed him with a "force bill" authorizing military collection of the tax in South Carolina. Conflict was averted when no other state nullified the tariff, leaving South Carolina in isolation. Calhoun met quietly with Henry Clay to work out a compromise tariff just low enough that South Carolina could save face. In 1833, the state rescinded its nullification of the tariff but expressly did not repudiate the principle of nullification.

Jackson let it ride. It was all on paper, like Marshall's decision in the Cherokee case. He had had his way, and he had identified a new enemy—his own vice president.

for FURTHER READING

Andrew Jackson and what he meant for America have fascinated historians, and they have differed radically in their findings. For an overview of the era, see Glyndon G. Van Deusen, *The Jacksonian Era, 1828–1848,* 1959. Clashing interpretations can be found in Richard Hofstadter, *The American Political Tradition and the Men Who Made It,* 1948; Marvin Meyers, *The Jacksonian Persuasion,* 1957; Edward E. Pessen, *Jacksonian America,* 1978; Robert Remini, *Andrew Jackson,* 1966; Arthur M. Schlesinger Jr., *The Age of Jackson,* 1945; and John W. Ward, *Andrew Jackson: Symbol for an Age,* 1955.

Yet other explanations of the great upheaval of the 1820s can be found in books with a narrower focus, including Lee Benson, *The Concept of Jacksonian Democracy,* 1964; J. C. Curtis, *Andrew Jackson and the Search for Vindication,* 1976; William W. Freehling, *Prelude to Civil War: The Nullification Controversy in South Carolina, 1816–1836,* 1966; Walter E. Hugins, *Jacksonian Democracy and the Working Class,* 1960; Richard P. McCormick, *The Second American Party System: Party Formation in the Jacksonian Era,* 1966; Edward E. Pessen, *Most Uncommon Jacksonians: The Radical Leaders of the Early Labor Movement,* 1967; Robert Remini, *The Election of Andrew Jackson,* 1963; and M. P. Rogin, *Fathers and Children: Andrew Jackson and the Destruction of American Indians,* 1975.

On Indian removal, see John Ehle, *Trail of Tears,* 1988; Michael Green, *The Politics of Indian Removal,* 1982; and Ronald Satz, *American Indian Policy in the Jacksonian Era,* 1974.

AMERICAN JOURNEY ONLINE AND INFOTRAC COLLEGE EDITION

Visit the source collections at http://ajaccess.wadsworth.com and http://infotrac.thomsonlearning.com, and use the Search function with the following key terms to explore documents, images, audio and video clips, articles, and commentary related to the material in this chapter:

Andrew Jackson   Sequoya
Indian Removal Act   Trail of Tears

Additional resources, exercises, and Internet links related to this chapter are available on *The American Past* Web site:
http://history.wadsworth.com/americanpast7e.

HISTORY ONLINE

The History Buff
www.historybuff.com/library/index.html
A collection of newspapers such as became a staple of American political life during the Jacksonian era.

The Trail of Tears
http://ngeorgia.com/history/nghisttt.html
Details, illustrations, maps of the removal of the Cherokee from northern Georgia to Indian Territory.

16

IN THE SHADOW OF OLD HICKORY

Personalities and Politics 1830–1842

He prefers the specious to the solid, and the plausible to the true. . . . I don't like Henry Clay. He is a bad man, an impostor, a creator of wicked schemes. I wouldn't speak to him, but by God, I love him.

John C. Calhoun

[Calhoun is] a smart fellow, one of the first among second-rate men, but of lax political principles and a disordinate ambition not over-delicate in the means of satisfying itself.

Albert Gallatin

Such is human nature in the gigantic intellect, the envious temper, the ravenous ambition, and the rotten heart of Daniel Webster.

John Quincy Adams

Thank God. I—I also—am an American.

Daniel Webster

W HEN ANDREW JACKSON became president in 1829, many who knew him feared he would not live to finish his term. To his supporters around the country, Jackson was "Old Hickory"—a tough and timeless frontiersman as straight as a long rifle. In person, he was a frail, 62-year-old wisp of a man who often looked to be a day away from death.

More than six feet tall, Jackson weighed only 145 pounds. No other president was so frequently ill. He suffered from lead poisoning (he carried two bullets in his body), headaches, diarrhea, kidney disease, and edema, a painful swelling of the legs. He was beleaguered by coughing fits; as president, he suffered two serious hemorrhages of the lungs.

VAN BUREN VERSUS CALHOUN

Jackson's choice of a vice president, therefore, was a matter of some interest. In approving John C. Calhoun in 1828, Jackson was not simply pocketing South Carolina's electoral votes, he was naming his heir apparent as president and leader of the Democratic party.

John C. Calhoun

Like Jackson, Calhoun was of Scotch-Irish background, the descendant of those eighteenth-century emigrants invariably described as hot tempered and pugnacious. Calhoun was—

again like Jackson—a man of passion with a stubborn, steely will. Portrait painters captured a burning gaze just an eyelash short of rage, never the slightest hint of a smile, never a posture to indicate Calhoun knew even odd moments of peace of mind. Photographers, coming along later in his life, confirmed the painters' impressions. He was, in Harriet Martineau's words, "the cast-iron man, who looks as if he had never been born, and never could be extinguished."

By 1828, Calhoun was the captive of an obsession. He feared that the social institutions that were the backbone of his beloved South Carolina—African American slavery and the plantation aristocracy that owed its wealth and privilege to slave ownership—were mortally threatened by the rapid growth of population in the North, the increasing power of industrial capitalists, and what those developments meant for the policies of the national government in the future.

In this fear, Calhoun had broken sharply from the ideals of his youth. The young Calhoun was a nationalist and an proponent of industrialization. In 1815, he wanted to "bind the nation together with a perfect system of roads and canals."

In 1816, he introduced the bill that chartered the Second Bank of the United States (BUS), arguing the desirability of a powerful national financial center. Young man Calhoun urged South Carolinians to build steam-powered mills amid their cotton fields, monopolizing the profits from their coveted crop from seed to bolt of cloth.

But when the South did not industrialize and the North did, and the industrialists then demanded high protective tariffs that raised the prices of the manufactured goods southern agriculturalists bought from others, Calhoun changed his tune. He became a defender of agrarian society and the plantation system. He opposed protective tariffs, was critical of internal improvements because of the taxes required to make them, and even of the BUS he had helped to found. When voices were raised about the morality of slavery, he became a vociferous proponent of the virtues of the institution.

Jackson agreed with most of these sentiments, but the two men differed about the relationship between the federal and state governments. The president believed the national government should be supreme. In *The South Carolina Exposition and Protest,* Calhoun proclaimed the state governments sovereign.

So fundamental a clash was quite enough to sour Jackson on his vice president. However, philosophical differences were exacerbated by a tempest on the Washington social scene that created a rival to Calhoun as Jackson's heir.

Peggy O'Neill Eaton

The center of the storm was Peggy O'Neill, the once fetching daughter of a Washington hotel keeper. Peggy had been married to a sailor who was, as seamen are inclined to be,

▲ *President Jackson never asked Peggy O'Neill to cavort for his cabinet, as in this lampoon of the affair, but he discussed her with them at length. Martin Van Buren, the sole beneficiary of the hubbub, is at the right.*

The New York Historical Society

rarely at home. In her husband's absence, she found solace and several children in the arms of her father's boarder, Tennessee congressman John Eaton, whom Jackson made secretary of war.

The affair was worth a whisper and a giggle, but not much more. Irregular conjunctions were not unheard of in the capital. Washington was no longer the largely male city it had been when Jefferson was president, but there was still a shortage of quarters suitable to families that lived well at home. Many congressmen continued to leave their wives behind and board at hotels. Inevitably, some found lady friends, and, as long as they exercised minimal discretion, little was made of it. Henry Clay was said to have been a roué, an alley cat, and Richard M. Johnson, vice president between 1837 and 1841, cohabited openly with a black woman who was also his slave.

Still, Clay's affairs were discreet, and Johnson left his mistress at home when he attended social functions. When Peggy O'Neill's husband died at sea and Eaton married her, he expected Washington society to receive her. Instead, there ensued a great hullabaloo. It was too much to expect women faithful to the gospel of true womanhood to sip tea with a fallen sister. Peggy O'Neill Eaton was roundly and brusquely snubbed.

The ringleader of the snubbers was Floride Calhoun, the moralistic wife of the vice president. The wives of cabinet members followed her example, and it aggravated Jackson. When his niece, his official hostess, refused to receive Peggy Eaton, Jackson told her to move out of the White House. Still mourning the death of his wife, which he blamed on scandalmongers, Jackson also happened to be charmed by the vivacious Peggy. He actually summoned a cabinet meeting to discuss the subject (as he rarely did on political and economic issues) and pronounced her "as chaste as a virgin." He told his advisers to command their wives to receive her socially.

This was too big an order, even for the "Gin'ral." If women were excluded from public life, morality and the rules of social life were squarely within their sphere. Peggy Eaton continued to find little chitchat at social functions. Only Secretary of State Martin Van Buren, who, as a widower, had no wife to oblige, dared to be seen admiring her gowns and fetching her refreshments.

The Rise of the Sly Fox

Charm and chitchat came naturally to Van Buren. His worst enemies conceded his grace and wit. His portraits, in contrast to Calhoun's, show a twinkle in the eye and a good-natured, intelligent smile.

But Martin Van Buren was much more than a jolly Dutchman. He was a devilishly clever politician, almost always several moves ahead of his rivals, particularly when they were impassioned true believers like Calhoun. Van Buren's wiles earned him the nickname "the Sly Fox of Kinderhook" (his hometown in New York).

He wrote no expositions, but he was the most successful political organizer of his time. He owed his high position in

Jackson's cabinet to delivering most of New York's electoral votes in 1828. He understood that a political party, whatever its ideals, had first and foremost to be a vote-gathering machine; it had to win elections. Therefore, a political party must reward the activists who corralled the votes, by appointing them to government jobs.

Van Buren was ambitious for himself. His sensitivity to the feelings of Peggy Eaton may have been quite sincere, but his courtesy also won Jackson's favor. Then, Van Buren offered the impulsive president a way out of the Eaton mess when the affair threatened to paralyze the administration and shatter the leadership of the Democratic party.

Van Buren proposed to resign as secretary of state, and Eaton would resign as secretary of war. The other members of the cabinet, whose wives were causing the president so much anxiety, would have no choice but to follow their example. Jackson would be rid of the lot, but no particular wing of the Democratic party could claim to have been wronged. Jackson appreciated both the strategy and Van Buren's willingness to sacrifice his prestigious office. He rewarded Van Buren by naming him minister to England—then, as now, the plum of the diplomatic service.

Calhoun: His Own Worst Enemy

The Sly Fox of Kinderhook was lucky too. While he calculated each turning with an eye on a distant destination, Calhoun blundered and bumped into posts like a blind cart horse. While the Eaton business was still rankling Jackson, the

▲ *Martin Van Buren—dapper, good humored, shrewd, and lucky until he became president during a serious depression.*

Courtesy Chicago Historical Society

president discovered in some old cabinet reports that, 10 years earlier, Calhoun (then secretary of war) wanted to punish Jackson for his unauthorized invasion of Florida. Confronted with the evidence, Calhoun tried to explain his way out of his fix in a suspiciously long and convoluted monologue. The president cut him off by writing, "Understanding you now, no further communication with you on this subject is necessary."

Nor, it turned out, was there much further communication between Jackson and his vice president on any subject. In April 1830, Jackson and Calhoun attended a formal dinner during which more than 20 of Calhoun's cronies offered toasts to states' rights and even nullification. When it was the president's turn to lift a glass, he rose, stared at Calhoun, and toasted, "Our Union: It must be preserved." Calhoun got in the last word of the evening. He replied, "The Union, next to our liberty, the most dear." But Jackson took satisfaction from the fact that, as he told the story, Calhoun trembled as he spoke.

The old duelist delighted in such confrontations. Van Buren took pleasure in his enduring good luck, for he was in England during the nastiest squabbling between Jackson and Calhoun, when even the slyest of foxes might have chanced on into a hound.

Then Calhoun blundered again, ensuring that Van Buren would succeed Jackson. Seeking personal revenge, Calhoun cast the deciding vote in the Senate's refusal to confirm Van Buren's diplomatic appointment. This brought the New Yorker back to the United States, but hardly in disgrace. Jackson was yet more deeply obligated to him. Van Buren was named vice presidential candidate in the election of 1832, as he surely would not have been had Calhoun left him in London.

THE WAR WITH THE BANK

Jackson's bid for reelection in 1832 was fought over a serious issue—the future of the Second BUS. The Second BUS was chartered in 1816 for a term of 20 years. After a shaky start (the Panic of 1819), it fell under the control of Nicholas Biddle, a courtly Philadelphian who administered its affairs cautiously, conservatively, profitably, and, so it seemed, to the benefit of the federal government and the national economy. The BUS acted as the government's financial agent, providing vaults for its gold and silver, paying government bills out of its accounts, investing deposits, and selling bonds (borrowing money for the government when it was needed).

The Powers of the Bank

Every cent the government collected from excise taxes, tariffs, and land sales went into the BUS. It was a huge, fabulously rich institution. Its 29 branches controlled about a third of all bank deposits in the United States and did some $70 million in transactions each year.

With such resources, the BUS held immense power over the nation's money supply and, therefore, the economy. In a careless but revealing moment, Nicholas Biddle told congressmen that the BUS was capable of destroying any other bank in the country.

What he meant was that, at any moment, the BUS was likely to have in its possession more paper money issued by a state-chartered bank than the issuing bank had specie (gold and silver) in its vaults. If the BUS presented this paper to be exchanged for specie, the issuing bank would be bankrupt, and all investments in it would be wiped out.

On a day he was more tactful, Biddle said that his bank exercised "a mild and gentle but efficient control" over the economy. That is, simply because the state banks were aware of the sword the BUS held over them, they maintained larger reserves of gold and silver than they might otherwise have kept on hand. Rather than ruining banks, the BUS ensured that they operated more responsibly.

A Private Institution

Biddle was as proud of the public service he rendered as of the BUS's annual profits. Nevertheless, the fact remained that the BUS was powerful because of its control of the money supply—a matter of profound public interest—but was itself a private institution. BUS policies were made not by elected officials, nor by bureaucrats responsible to elected officials, but by a board of directors responsible to shareholders.

This was enough in itself to earn the animosity of a president who abhorred powerful special interests. Biddle therefore attempted to make a friend of the president by readily giving loans to key Jackson supporters. Biddle also designed a plan to retire the national debt—a goal dear to Jackson's heart—timing the final installments to coincide with the anniversary of the Battle of New Orleans. But Biddle's efforts were to no avail. Jackson shook his head and explained to Biddle that it was not a matter of disliking the BUS more than he disliked other banks; Jackson did not trust any of them. Like "Old Bullion" Benton, he was a hard-money man. Faced with a stone wall in the White House, Biddle turned to Congress for friends.

The Enemies of the Bank

Biddle needed friends because the BUS had plenty of enemies. Except for their fear or resentment of the bank, however, those hostile to the bank had little in common.

First, there was the growing financial community of New York City—the bankers and brokers who would soon be known collectively as "Wall Street." Grown wealthy from the Erie Canal and from New York's role as the nation's leading port, they were keen to challenge Philadelphia's last financial powerhouse, the BUS, and its control of the nation's money supply.

Second, the freewheeling bankers of the West disliked Biddle's restraints. Caught up in the optimism of the growing region, these bankers wanted a free hand to take advantage of land values, which were once again soaring. Oddly, the president, who hated all banks, had the support of a good

▲ *A satirical six-cent bill printed by one of Jackson's irresponsible "pet banks," the Humbug Glory. It is covered with Democratic party symbols: Jackson on the penny, a leaf from an old hickory tree, and, curiously, a donkey, which is usually thought to have become a Democratic symbol a generation later.*

many bankers in his hostility toward the BUS, and they were far from the most virtuous of their profession.

A third group that wanted to see the BUS declawed was even more conservative in money matters than Biddle was. Hard-money men (like Jackson and Benton) were opposed to the very idea of an institution that issued paper money in quantities greater than the gold and silver it had on hand. Most eastern workingmen supported the hard-money position. They had too often been paid in banknotes that, when presented to shopkeepers, were worth less than their face value because the banks that issued them were shaky.

BUS notes were "as good as gold." Nevertheless, the working-class wing of the Democratic party, called "Loco-focos" in New York, lumped Biddle with the rest and inveighed against his monopolistic powers.

The First Shot

Jackson did not start the fight that escalated into the "Bank War." Henry Clay fired the first shot when, in January 1832, he was nominated for the presidency by those who had supported John Quincy Adams four years earlier. (They still called themselves National Republicans.) Clay needed an issue. Although the BUS's charter did not expire until 1836, Clay persuaded Biddle to apply for a new charter immediately. A majority of both houses of Congress would support the bid, putting Jackson, as Clay saw it, on the spot.

That is, if Jackson gritted his teeth and signed the bank bill rather than bucking a congressional majority, all well and good. The BUS was one of the pillars of Clay's American System. If Jackson vetoed the bill, Clay would have the issue on which to wage his presidential campaign. Clay believed that, because the bank had proved its value to the economy, he would defeat Jackson by promising to rescue it.

Clay was not the last presidential nominee to believe that, presented with an issue, voters would decide on the basis of it rather than be dazzled by symbols. Congress rechartered the BUS. Jackson vetoed the bill. Clay ran on the issue and went down resoundingly in defeat. Jackson was still a hero, still the reed vibrating in harmony with the popular mood. He won 55 percent of the popular vote and 219 electoral votes to Clay's 49. (Anti-Masonic candidate William Wirt won 7 electoral votes, and South Carolina gave its 11 votes to John Floyd.)

Financial Chaos

In September 1833, six months after his second inauguration, Jackson took the offensive. He ceased to deposit government moneys in the bank, putting them instead into what were called his "pet banks," state-chartered institutions. The BUS, however, continued to pay the government's bills. Within three months, federal deposits in the BUS sank from $10 million to $4 million. Biddle had no choice but to reduce the scope of the bank's operations. He also chose, no doubt in part to sting Jackson, to call in debts owed the bank by other financial institutions. The result was a wave of bank failures that wiped out the savings of thousands of people, just what Jackson had feared BUS power might mean.

Presidential Vetoes

Jackson's veto of the bank bill was just another day's work. No previous president used the power of veto so often. In fact, the first six presidents, between them, vetoed a total of 10 acts of Congress. Jackson, the seventh president, vetoed 12.

Under pressure from the business community, Biddle relented and reversed his policy, increasing the national supply of money by making loans to other banks. This, alas, fed a new speculative boom. To Jackson's chagrin, many of the 89 pet banks to which he had entrusted federal money proved to be among the least responsible in lending money. They fed the speculation.

In 1836, Henry Clay made his contribution to what would be the most serious American depression since Jefferson's embargo. He convinced Congress to pass a distribution bill under the terms of which $37 million was distributed to the states for expenditure on internal improvements. Presented with such a windfall, the politicians reacted as politicians sitting on a bonanza usually do: They spent freely, crazily, backing the least worthy of projects and most questionable of promoters. Land values, both in the undeveloped West and in eastern cities, soared. Federal land sales rose to $25 million in 1836. Seeking to get a share of the freely circulating cash, new banks were chartered at a dizzying rate. There had been 330 state banks in 1830; there were almost 800 in 1837.

And there was no BUS to cool things down gradually, for its national charter had expired in 1836. Instead, the responsibility was Jackson's. In his last year as president, he did the only thing within his powers—he slammed a lid on the sale of federal land, the most volatile commodity in the boom. In July 1836, he issued the Specie Circular, which required that government lands be paid for in gold and silver coin; paper money was no longer acceptable.

Jackson's action stopped the runaway speculation, but with a heavy foot on the brake rather than the tug on the reins that the BUS might have used. In a repeat of 1819, speculators unable to pay what they owed the government for land went bankrupt. Banks that had fueled the speculators collapsed. Gold and silver were drained from the East, contributing to a depression there.

The Giant

Jackson's financial policy was a disaster built on ignorance, prejudice, and pigheadedness. It would have destroyed the career and reputation of a lesser man as, indeed, it destroyed Jackson's successor, Martin Van Buren. By the time the economy hit bottom, however, Jackson had retired to Tennessee. Seventy years old now, the man who many thought would be lucky to live through one term had cut and chopped his way through eight pivotal years in the history of the nation.

Though aching and coughing and refusing to mellow (he said his biggest regret was not shooting Henry Clay and hanging John C. Calhoun), Jackson would live for nine more years, observing from his mansion home an era that unfolded in his shadow. He was never a wise man. His intelligence was limited; his education, spotty; his prejudices, often ugly. He was easily ruled by his passions and confused them with the interests of his country. His vision of America was pocked with more flaws than that of many of his contemporaries, including his enemies.

▲ *Jackson in old age years after leaving the presidency. Until his death in 1845, American politics was played in his shadow.*

But for all that, Andrew Jackson was his era made flesh, the personification of a democratic upheaval that changed the character of American politics. He presided over a time of ferment in nearly every facet of American life. He set new patterns of presidential behavior by aggressively taking the initiative in making policy.

Jackson also impressed his personality on a political party and an era that would end only when African American slavery tore the country apart. Even the Whigs, the party his enemies formed during Jackson's second term, were held together, to a large extent, by hostility toward him and his memory. And the Whigs succeeded only when they imitated the style and methods of the Jacksonian Democrats.

THE SECOND AMERICAN PARTY SYSTEM

By 1834, the realignment of national politics was complete. In the congressional elections that year, the National Republicans joined with former Jacksonians who objected to one or another of Old Hickory's policies—his promiscuous use of the veto, his high-handed treatment of Indians, his blow against South Carolina, and his war against the BUS—and called themselves the Whigs.

Alma Mater

A university student today would have difficulty recognizing the colleges of the early nineteenth century. A student's life then more closely resembled college life in the Middle Ages than in the twenty-first century.

All but a few colleges were private institutions. As late as 1860, only 17 of the 246 colleges and universities in the United States were state funded. Most of the others were maintained by Protestant denominations to train ministers and to indoctrinate other young men in their creeds. This was particularly true of the colleges founded during the Jacksonian era, many of which were inspired by the evangelical commitment to reform society.

Colleges were male institutions. Higher education was regarded as the final polishing of a cultivated man, the foundation for public life and for the practice of the professions. Women, whose social role was domestic and private, had no need for higher learning.

This attitude was beginning to change. In 1833, Ohio's Oberlin College, a hotbed of reform, began to admit women students. A few colleges and universities followed suit, but the real expansion of educational opportunities for women came not with coeducation but with all-female institutions. The first of these were Georgia Female College in Macon (now Wesleyan College) and Mount Holyoke College in South Hadley, Massachusetts, founded by Mary Lyon in 1837.

College was not vocationally oriented, as it is today. That is, students were not taught the specifics involved in the career they planned to pursue. The young man who wanted to become an engineer, an architect, or a businessman apprenticed himself to someone in those callings, learning "on the job." Although some universities had established medical and law schools, apprenticeship was also the most common means of preparing for those professions.

College curriculum remained much as it had been for centuries, a strictly prescribed course of study in the liberal arts and sciences (*liberal* in this case meaning "suitable to a free man"). Students studied Latin, Greek, and sometimes Hebrew; literature; natural science; mathematics; and political and moral philosophy in accordance with the doctrines of the church that supported the institution. There were no electives. Every student took the same courses.

The colleges were small. Except at the very oldest, such as Harvard, William and Mary, and Yale, and some public institutions, such as the University of Virginia, the typical student body rarely numbered more than a few dozen, and the typical faculty, perhaps three or four professors and an equal number of tutors. Although faculty members and students came to know one another by sight and name, relations between them were far from chummy. On the contrary, professors erected a high wall of formality between themselves and those they taught, both because of the belief in the principle of hierarchy and out of the fear that too much friendliness would lead to a breakdown in discipline. The stiff-necked behavior by instructors often also owed to the fact that many of them were little older, and sometimes even younger, than their students. Joseph Caldwell became *president* of the University of North Carolina when he was 24 years old.

Student behavior was regulated by long lists of detailed rules. Students were expected to toe the line not only in class but also in their private lives. Attendance at religious services was mandatory at church institutions. Strict curfews determined when students living in dormitories turned out their lamps. Even impoliteness might be punished by a fine or suspension.

This was the theory, at any rate. In practice, college students were at least as rambunctious as students today. They defied their professors by day—the distinguished political philosopher Francis Lieber had to tackle students he meant to discipline—and taunted them by night. A favorite prank was stealing into the college chapel and ringing the college bell until dawn. They threw snowballs and rocks through their tutors' windows. They led the president's horse to the roof of three- and four-story buildings. Students at Dickinson College in Pennsylvania sent a note to authorities at Staunton, Virginia, where Dickinson's president was visiting, informing them that an escaped lunatic was headed that way, would claim to be a college president, and should be returned under guard.

There were rebellions. Professors were assaulted: stoned, horsewhipped, and fired on with shotguns. At the University of Virginia in 1840, Professor Nathaniel Davis was murdered. Writing to his own son at college in 1843, Princeton professor Samuel Miller warned against sympathizing with potential rebels. Miller lived in fear of student uprisings, perhaps because one rebellion at Princeton was so serious that the faculty had to call in club-wielding townspeople to put it down.

Why the discontent? One reason is that the rules of college life were written at a time when most college students were 14 to 18 years old, whereas, by the Age of Jackson, they were often in their mid-20s. Adults simply were not inclined to conform to behavior appropriate to adolescents, and in a society that took pride in individual freedom, they were quite capable of reacting violently.

Moreover, many college students lived not in dormitories but in private lodgings in town. They fraternized largely with other students and developed a defiant camaraderie directed against outsiders. Enjoying broad freedoms in their off-campus lives, they were unlikely to conform to strict rules of behavior when they were on the campus.

Finally, although the rules were strict, enforcement was inconsistent. "There were too many colleges," writes historian Joseph F. Kett, "and they needed students more than students needed them." Faculty members, ever nervous for their jobs, overlooked minor offenses until they led to greater ones, at which point, suddenly, they drew the line. Inconsistency, as ever, led to contempt for authority.

Colleges might suspend the entire student body for "great rebellion." However, financial pressures usually resulted in readmission of the students for the price of a written apology. Samuel Miller described student rebels as "unworthy, profligate, degraded, and miserable villains," but if they had the tuition, there was a place for them somewhere.

BORN TO COMMAND.

OF VETO MEMORY.

HAD I BEEN CONSULTED.

KING ANDREW THE FIRST.

KING ANDREW
THE FIRST,
" *Born to Command.*"

A KING who, possessing as much power as his Gracious Brother *William IV.*, makes a worse use of it.

A KING who has placed himself above the laws, as he has shown by his contempt of our judges.

A KING who would destroy our currency, and substitute *Old Rags*, payable by no one knows who, and no one knows where, instead of *good Silver Dollars*.

A KING born to command, as he has shown himself by appointing men to office contrary to the will of the People.

A KING who, while he was feeding his favourites out of the public money, denied a pittance to the *Old Soldiers* who fought and <u>bled</u> for our independence.

A KING whose *Prime Minister* and *Heir Apparent*, was thought unfit for the office of ambassador by the people:

Shall he reign over us,
Or shall the PEOPLE RULE!

▲ *The Whigs took their name from the British politicians who steadfastly opposed the monarchy's having any more than figurehead status. The Americans Whigs deftly depicted Jackson as a king and appealed to rule by the people, the slogan on which Jackson had ridden to power.*

The Whigs

The name *Whig* was borrowed from Great Britain. There, the Whigs were the party inclined to reduce the powers of the monarchy and to enhance the sway of Parliament. In the republican United States, the American Whigs said, the monarch that needed reining in was "King Andrew I."

Whiggum

Scholars disagree about the origins of the word *Whig*. One plausible theory is that it derived from the word lowlands Scots and farmers in the north of England used to halt their horses, *whiggum*. In other words, it meant "whoa!" which is what the British Whigs said to the king.

The Whigs were a disparate group, brought together by little more than their abhorrence of Jackson. In the North, the Whig party included most people of education, means, and pretension to social status. Four out of five merchants were Whigs, as were many skilled native-born artisans. There and in the West, supporters of the American System, who believed that the federal government should take the initiative in shaping economic development, were Whigs. Northeastern Whigs tended to support moral legislation: temperance laws, strict observance of the Sabbath, and a welter of moralistic reforms that would become bewildering.

In the South, high-tariff men, like Louisiana sugar planters and Charleston financiers, tended to be Whigs. The party was stronger in the plantation counties (competitive with the Democrats, in fact) than in counties where small farmers owning few or no slaves dominated. Some southern exponents of state supremacy, like John Tyler of Virginia and even the nullifier, John C. Calhoun, allied with the nationalistic Whig party, but that made no sense except as political opportunism.

During the 1830s, Anti-Masons drifted into the Whig party. Traditionalist New Englanders, suspicious of anything attractive to southerners, like Jackson's Democratic party, inclined to Whiggery. So did those few blacks who were permitted to vote, as well as the upper and middle classes of city and town who found the vulgarity of lower-class Democrats and the spoils system offensive. In 1834, this patchwork alliance was enough to win 98 seats in the House of Representatives and almost half the Senate, 25 seats to the Democrats' 27. Until the 1850s, while unlucky in presidential elections, the Whigs fought the Democrats on a basis of equality in the House, Senate, and states.

To the Whigs, "the party of hope," the Democratic party was "the party of fear"—fear of progress. On the state level, following Jackson's example, they hamstrung (and, in seven states, abolished) banks. They opposed government subsidy of railroad construction and took little interest in promoting industry.

The Godlike Daniel

Next to Henry Clay, the best-known Whig was Daniel Webster of Massachusetts. At the peak of his power in the 1830s, he was idolized in New England—a demigod. The adoration owed mostly to Webster's personal presence and his peerless oratorical powers. With a great face that glowered darkly when he spoke, his eyes burned like "anthracite furnaces."

A look from him, it was said, was enough to win most debates. Webster was described as "a steam engine in trousers" and "a small cathedral in himself." An admirer said he was "a living lie because no man on earth could be so great as he looked."

Webster was not a fraction as great as he looked. Although an able administrator and an effective diplomat, Webster possessed less than a shining character. Of humble origin, he took too zestfully to the high life available to the eminent. He dressed grandly, savored good food, and basked in the company of the wealthy. He was also an alcoholic and invested his money—he was never rich—as foolishly as he spent it. He was constantly in debt and periodically broke. This tied him yet more closely to the New England industrialists who regularly sent him money, no strings attached (none that were labeled, anyway). During the Bank War, Webster obliquely threatened to end his services as legal counsel to the BUS unless Biddle paid him off, which Biddle did.

Webster came to expect money in the mail after every speech on behalf of the tariff or even the ideal of the Union. As a result, although he remained popular in New England until the very end of his career, his not-so-secret vices provided an easy target for the Democrats and made him an object of suspicion among fellow Whigs who took personal integrity as seriously as they took public virtue.

Union and Liberty

And yet, it was this flawed man who gave glorious voice to the ideal that was to sustain the indisputably great Abraham Lincoln during the Civil War. In 1830, when Calhoun and Jackson were toasting the relative values of union versus liberty, Webster rose in the Senate to tell the nation that "Liberty and Union, now and for ever," were "one and inseparable."

He was replying to Robert Hayne of South Carolina, himself a fine orator who, when Calhoun was vice president, spoke Calhoun's lines on the floor of the Senate. Hayne identified the doctrine of nullification with American liberty. Webster declared that, on the contrary, the Constitution was the wellspring of liberty in the United States and the indissoluble union of the states was its greatest defense. "It is, Sir," Webster pronounced, "the people's Constitution, the people's government, made for the people, made by the people, and answerable to the people." The liberty and union speech transformed a political abstraction, the Union, into an object for which people were willing to die. (It also provided three generations of schoolchildren with something to memorize.)

1836: Whigs Versus a Democrat

The differences among the Whigs prevented the party convention of 1836 from drafting a platform. The delegates could not even agree on a compromise candidate to oppose Martin Van Buren, the Democratic nominee. Consequently, Whig leaders decided on the curious tactic—unique in American political history—of trying to throw the election into the House of Representatives, as had unintentionally happened in 1800 and 1824.

Courtesy Boston Art Commission

▲ *The Webster-Hayne debate of January 1830, still considered one of the greatest oratorical moments in the history of Congress. It was certainly Daniel Webster's finest hour. He is speaking for the second time. (The speech extended over two days.) Hayne is seated dead center. In an artistic masterstroke, the painter shows John C. Calhoun in shadows at the left. As vice president, Calhoun could not speak, but he was the coauthor of Hayne's defense of the South, sectionalism, and nullification.*

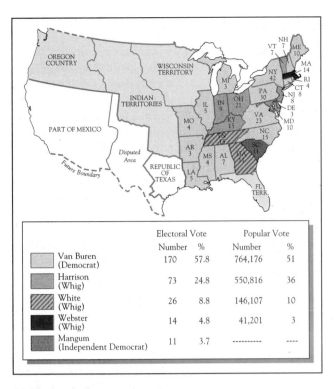

	Electoral Vote		Popular Vote	
	Number	%	Number	%
Van Buren (Democrat)	170	57.8	764,176	51
Harrison (Whig)	73	24.8	550,816	36
White (Whig)	26	8.8	146,107	10
Webster (Whig)	14	4.8	41,201	3
Mangum (Independent Democrat)	11	3.7	----------	----

MAP 16:1 Van Buren's Victory in 1836 The Democrats and Whigs were both national parties. They carried states in the North, South, and West. A Whig carried Jackson's Tennessee, but, otherwise, Democrat Van Buren won on the combination of states he had helped Jackson engineer.

That is, the Whigs named three candidates to run against Van Buren, each in the section where he was most popular. Webster ran in lower New England. Hugh Lawson White of Tennessee was the candidate in the South. In the Northwest and upper New England, the Whigs' man was William Henry Harrison, the hero of the Battle of Tippecanoe. Although the battle was a quarter of a century in the past, the party hoped that the memory of it was still strong among a people ever hungry for new lands.

The strategy failed. Although all three Whigs (and cantankerous South Carolina's favorite-son candidate, Willie P. Mangum) won some electoral votes, Van Buren carried states in every section, with a comfortable 170 to 124 majority in the electoral college. The Whigs held their own in Congress, still a minority but, with South Carolina unpredictable, in a powerful position.

Depression

Election to the presidency was just about the last good thing that happened to Martin Van Buren. When his administration was just a few months old, the country reaped the whirlwind of Jackson's Specie Circular. Drained of their gold and silver, several big New York banks announced in May that they would no longer redeem their notes in specie. Speculators and honest workingmen alike found themselves holding paper money that even the institutions that issued it would not accept.

In 1838, the country sank into depression. In 1841 alone, 28,000 people declared bankruptcy. Factories closed because their products did not sell. Several cities were unsettled by riots of unemployed workers. Eight western state governments defaulted on their debts.

Van Buren tried to meet the fiscal part of the crisis. A good Jacksonian, he attempted to divorce the government from the banks, which he blamed for the disaster. He established the subtreasury system, by which, in effect, the government would keep its funds in its own vaults. The Clay and Webster Whigs replied that what was needed was an infusion of money into the economy, not burying it out of everyone's reach. But they could not carry the issue.

Van Buren also maintained the Jacksonian faith in laissez-faire by refusing to take any measures to alleviate popular suffering. The Founding Fathers, he said (in fact voicing Jackson's sentiments), had "wisely judged that the less government interfered with private pursuits the better for the general prosperity."

Whatever the virtues of Van Buren's position—and whatever the convictions of most Americans on the question of government intervention in the economy—it is difficult for any administration to survive a depression. The president, who reaps the credit for blessings that are none of his doing, gets the blame when things go badly, however nebulous his responsibility for the misfortune. By early 1840, the Whigs were sure that hard times would put their candidate into the White House.

Whig Dilemma

But who was to be the candidate? In that year of likely victory, Henry Clay believed that he deserved the nomination. For 25 years, he had offered a coherent national economic policy that, for the most part, was Whig gospel. For half that time, he led the fight against the Jacksonians. More than any other individual, he personified the Whig party.

Pop Art

In 1834, when the hero of the common man sat in the White House, Nathaniel Currier of New York democratized art in America. He began to sell prints depicting natural wonders, marvels of technology (such as locomotives), battles, prominent people, and scenes of everyday life, both sentimental and comical.

Currier and Ives (the partner arrived in 1852) sold their prints for as little as 25 cents for a small black and white to $4 for a hand-colored engraving 28 by 40 inches. They were cheap enough to be afforded by the poor yet just expensive enough to be acceptable as wall hangings in self-conscious middle-class households.

More than 7,000 different Currier and Ives prints were produced by a process that can only be called industrial. Some artists specialized in backgrounds; others, in machinery or faces; yet others, in crowd scenes. By the late nineteenth century, it was a rare American who could not have identified a "Currier & Ives."

But Clay's great career was also his weakness. In standing at the forefront for so long and being a deal maker by nature, Clay inevitably made mistakes and enemies, some of them bitter. Fellow Whig Edmund Quincy wrote (in purple ink) of "the ineffable meanness of the lion turned spaniel in his fawnings on the masters whose hands he was licking for the sake of the dirty puddings they might have to toss him."

Victory-hungry young Whigs, like Thurlow Weed of New York, argued against nominating Clay because of his baggage. Better, Weed said, to choose a candidate who had little or no political record but who, like Jackson, could be peddled as a symbol. In Weed's view, which echoed that of Martin Van Buren, the first and foremost objective of a political party was to win elections. Only then could it accomplish anything.

"Tippecanoe and Tyler Too"

By Weed's criteria, the ideal Whig candidate was William Henry Harrison. He was the scion of a distinguished Virginia family—his father had signed the Declaration of Independence—and, like Jackson, a victorious western warhorse, the victor of Tippecanoe. Harrison had done better than any other Whig in the peculiar election of 1836, and, best of all, he was associated with no controversial political position. Indeed, in 1836, his handlers admonished one another, "Let him say not one single word about his principles or his creed, let him say nothing, promise nothing. Let no [one] extract from him a single word about what he thinks. . . . Let use of pen and ink be wholly forbidden as if he were a mad poet in Bedlam."

Harrison was nominated in 1840 under pretty much the same conditions. To appeal to southerners, John Tyler of Virginia was nominated vice president—thus the party's slogan "Tippecanoe and Tyler Too!"

Harrison's Invented Image

At first, the Whigs planned to campaign simply by talking about Harrison's military record. Then, a Democratic newspaper editor made a slip that opened up a whole new world in American politics. Meaning to argue that Harrison was incompetent, the journalist sneered that the old man would be happy with an annual pension of $2,000, a jug of hard cider, and a bench on which to sit and doze at the door of his log cabin.

Such snobbery toward the humble life was ill suited to a party that had come to power as the champion of the common man. The Whigs, who suffered Democratic taunts that they were elitists, charged into the breach. They hauled out miniature log cabins at city rallies and country bonfires. They bought and tapped thousands of barrels of hard cider. They sang raucous songs like this little ditty:

> Farewell, dear Van,
> You're not our man,
> To guide our ship,
> We'll try old Tip.

Stealing another leaf from the Jacksonian campaign book of 1828, the Whigs depicted Van Buren as an effeminate fop who sipped champagne, ate fancy French food, perfumed his whiskers, and flounced about in silks and satins. Before he departed for Texas, death, and immortality at the Alamo, the colorful Whig politician Davy Crockett depicted Van Buren as "laced up in corsets such as women in a town wear, and if possible tighter than the best of them. It would be difficult to say from his personal appearance whether he was man or woman, but for his large red and gray whiskers."

It was all nonsense. Harrison lived in no log cabin but in a mansion. He was no simple country bumpkin but, rather, the opposite—a pedant given to tedious academic

A TIPPECANOE PROCESSION.

▲ *The Whigs built mock log cabins for rallies on behalf of William Henry Harrison and also great balls covered with slogans and pushed from town to town on an axle. The phrase "keep the ball rolling," still common parlance, dates from that landmark campaign.*

discourse on subjects of little interest to ordinary, hardworking people. Van Buren, although quite the dandy, was of modest origins (his father had kept a tavern). He was naturally earthy, and he subscribed to much more democratic ideas than did old Tippecanoe.

But nonsense worked, as it often has since. Although Van Buren won 47 percent of the popular vote, he was trounced in the electoral college 60 to 234. Jacksonian chickens had come home to roost. From then on, rarely would a presidential election be contested without great fussing about symbols, images, and irrelevancies.

With their successful appeal to the prejudices of the common man, the Whigs of 1840 demonstrated that the democratic upheaval of the Age of Jackson was complete. Never again would there be political profit in appealing to the superior qualifications of "the better sort" in the egalitarian United States. Finally, what may be most notable about the election of 1840 is that a political candidate was marketed as a commodity—"packaged"—long before the techniques of modern advertising had been conceived.

Fate's Cruel Joke

Wherever William Henry Harrison stood on specific issues, he was fully in accord with one fundamental Whig principle—that Congress should make the laws and the president execute them. He was quite willing to defer to the party professionals, particularly Clay, in making policy. With large Whig majorities in both houses of Congress, the Great Compromiser had every reason to believe that, if not president in name, he would direct the nation's affairs. Old Tip dutifully named four of Clay's lieutenants to the cabinet.

Harrison would have done well to defer to Daniel Webster in his field of expertise—oratory. Webster wrote an inaugural address for Harrison, but the president politely turned it down, having prepared his own. It was the longest, dullest inaugural address in the archives, a turgid treatise on Roman history and its relevance to the United States of America circa March 1841. Not even historians could have enjoyed it, because it was delivered out of doors on a frigid, windy day. Harrison caught a cold that turned into pneumonia. For weeks, he suffered, half the time in bed, half the time receiving Whig office seekers as greedy for jobs as the Democrats of 1828. Then he ceased to rise and dress. On April 4, 1841, exactly one month after lecturing the country on republican virtue, he passed away.

John Tyler

At first, the Whigs did not miss a stride. Clay lectured "Tyler Too" that he was an "acting president," presiding over the formalities of government while a committee of Whigs chaired by Henry Clay made the decisions. John Quincy Adams, now a Whig representative from Massachusetts, concurred. Tyler would have none of it. A nondescript man who had little imagination and a provincial view of national problems, Tyler insisted that the Constitution authorized him

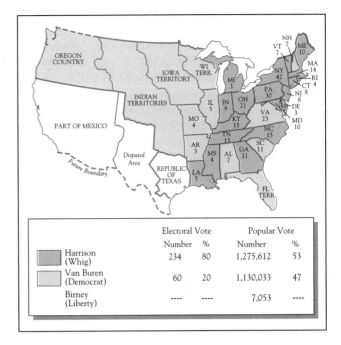

MAP 16:2 The Whig Victory of 1840   Whig William Henry Harrison almost swept the Northeast in 1840 and won three southern states that voted Democratic in 1836.

to exercise the same presidential powers that he would exercise if he had been elected.

Tyler tried hard to get along with Clay. He went along with the abolition of the subtreasury system, and, although a low-tariff man, he agreed to an increase of rates in 1842 as long as the rise was tied to ending federal finance of internal improvements. Tyler also supported Clay's attempt to woo western voters from the Democrats with his Preemption Act of 1841. This law provided that a family who squatted on up to 160 acres of public land could purchase it at the minimum price of $1.25 per acre without having to bid against others.

A President Without a Party

But Tyler was no Whig. He had split with Jackson over "King Andrew's" arrogant use of presidential power. His views on other issues were closer to those of John C. Calhoun than to those of the nationalistic Whigs. Most notably, Tyler wanted no new BUS and warned Clay not to try to force one on him.

Clay tried anyway, and Tyler vetoed one bank bill after another. Furious, the majority Whigs expelled the president from the party, and Tyler's entire cabinet resigned (except Secretary of State Webster, who wanted to complete some touchy negotiations with Great Britain). Clay left the Senate in order to devote full time to winning the presidential election of 1844.

Tyler's new cabinet was made up of nominal southern Whigs who shared Tyler's views. The president's plan was to piece together a new party of states' rights Whigs and some Democrats. Toward this end, he named John C. Calhoun secretary of state. Whig party loyalty was too strong for Tyler's scheme to work. In effect, he was a president without a party.

British-American Friction

The major accomplishment of the Tyler administration was in the area of foreign affairs: solving a series of potentially dangerous disputes with Great Britain and paving the way for the annexation of the Republic of Texas.

The first was a Whiggish goal engineered by Daniel Webster. One of the problems was a boundary dispute between Maine and New Brunswick. According to the Treaty of 1783, the line ran between the watersheds of the Atlantic and the St. Lawrence River. Both sides had agreed to the boundary as drawn on a map in red ink by Benjamin Franklin.

The map had disappeared, however, and in 1838, Canadian lumberjacks began cutting timber in the Aroostook Valley, which the United States claimed. A brief "war" between the Maine and New Brunswick militias ended with no deaths, and Van Buren managed to cool things down. But he could not resolve the boundary dispute.

The Canadian-American line west of Lake Superior was also in question, and there were two more points of friction because of unofficial American assistance to Canadian rebels and the illegal slave trade in which some Americans were involved. The slavery issue waxed hot late in 1841, when blacks on the American brig *Creole* mutinied, killed the crew, and sailed to Nassau in the British Bahamas. The British hanged the leaders of the mutiny but freed the other slaves, enraging sensitive white southerners.

The Webster-Ashburton Treaty

Neither Britain nor the United States wanted war, but old rancor and the Canadians' determination to build a road through the disputed Aroostook country stalled a settlement. Fortuitously, Daniel Webster found a kindred spirit in the high-living British negotiator Lord Ashburton, and, over lots of brandy, they worked out a compromise. Webster made a big concession to the British, too big as far as Maine's loggers were concerned. Never above chicanery, Webster forged Franklin's map to show a red line that gave Maine less territory than he "won" from Ashburton. He warned that the United States had better take what it could get. (The real Franklin map surfaced some years later and showed that the United States was shorted.)

Ashburton was generous too. He ceded a strip of territory in northern New York and Vermont to which the United States had no claim and also about 6,500 square miles at the tip of Lake Superior. Although wilderness at the time, this area, later known as the Mesabi Range, was one of the world's richest iron ore deposits.

When the Senate ratified the Webster-Ashburton Treaty in 1842, every outstanding issue between the United States and Britain was settled except the two nations' joint occupation of the Oregon Country on the Pacific Coast. Webster had good reason to be pleased with himself, and he joined his fellow Whigs in leaving John Tyler's cabinet.

for FURTHER READING

For overviews, see Glyndon G. Van Deusen, *The Jacksonian Era, 1828–1848,* 1959; Edward E. Pessen, *Jacksonian America: Society, Personality, and Politics,* 1978; and Robert Remini, *The Revolutionary Age of Andrew Jackson,* 1985. To appreciate the political and cultural values that informed Jackson's era, see John W. Ward, *Andrew Jackson: Symbol for an Age,* 1955. The appropriate chapters of Richard Hofstadter, *The American Political Tradition and the Men Who Made It,* 1948, are still stimulating. Richard P. McCormick, *The Second American Party System Formation in the Jacksonian Era,* 1966, is essential.

Martin Van Buren, if almost forgotten in popular history, is the subject of three excellent biographical studies: D. B. Cole, *Martin Van Buren and the American Political System,* 1984; John Niven, *Martin Van Buren: The Romantic Age of American Politics,* 1983; and M. L. Wilson, *The Presidency of Martin Van Buren,* 1984. On his hapless nemesis, see Margaret Coit's now classic *John C. Calhoun: American Portrait,* 1950, and the more critical Richard N. Current, *John C. Calhoun,* 1966.

Dealing with the Bank War are Bray Hammond, *Bank and Politics in America from the Revolution to the Civil War,* 1957; Robert Remini, *Andrew Jackson and the Bank War,* 1967; and John McFaul, *The Politics of Jacksonian Finance,* 1972. Sympathetic to Biddle's position is Thomas P. Govan, *Nicholas Biddle: Nationalist and Public Banker,* 1959.

D. W. Howe, *The Political Culture of the American Whigs,* 1979, is a fine survey of a subject long neglected except in biographies. Among the best biographies of the Whigs are Glyndon G. Van Deusen, *The Life of Henry Clay,* 1937; Clement Eaton, *Henry Clay and the Art of American Politics,* 1957; Richard N. Current, *Daniel Webster and the Rise of National Conservatism,* 1955; Sydney Nathan, *Daniel Webster and Jacksonian Democracy,* 1973; and M. G. Baxter, *One and Inseparable: Daniel Webster and the Union,* 1984. On the election of 1840 and its aftermath, see R. G. Gunderson, *The Log Cabin Campaign,* 1957; and O. D. Lambert, *Presidential Politics in the United States, 1841–1844,* 1936.

AMERICAN JOURNEY ONLINE AND INFOTRAC COLLEGE EDITION

Visit the source collections at http://ajaccess.wadsworth.com and http://infotrac.thomsonlearning.com, and use the Search function with the following key terms to explore documents, images, audio and video clips, articles, and commentary related to the material in this chapter:

Andrew Jackson
John C. Calhoun

John Tyler
Martin Van Buren

HISTORY ONLINE

Daniel Webster, Liberty and Union

www.nv.cc.va.us/home/nvsageh/Hist121/Part3/Webster.htm

Text of the speech of 1830 that immortalized Daniel Webster despite his obvious character flaws.

Tippecanoe and Tyler Too

www.multied.com/documents/Tippacanoe.html

Horace Greeley, a prominent Whig editor, writes of the Whig disappointment when William Henry Harrison died after one month in office.

CHAPTER

17

ENTHUSIASM

Evangelicals, Utopians, Reformers

© Bettmann/Corbis

God has found it necessary to take advantage of the excitability there is in mankind, to produce powerful excitements among them, before he can lead them to obey. Men are so spiritually sluggish, there are so many things to lead their minds off from religion, and to oppose the influence of the Gospel, that it is necessary to raise an excitement among them, till the tide rises so high as to sweep away the opposing obstacles.

Charles G. Finney

B Y THE TIME of Andrew Jackson, the established churches of the colonial era were just two denominations among many. Anglicanism (now the Protestant Episcopal Church) was still the faith of the elites of the South, New York City, and, to a lesser extent, Philadelphia (where it was also respectable to be a Quaker). Preserving traditional rituals, valuing restrained preachers, and avoiding political controversy, the Episcopalians provided the comforts of church membership while requiring little more of parishioners than attendance on Sunday and financial support.

The Congregational Church lost its grip on upper-class New Englanders because, in a day where, it seemed, happiness was successfully pursued by individual human effort, the central doctrine of the Puritans, predestination, just did not fit in. New England's self-satisfied merchant elite and professionals quietly put Calvinism away as an old hat is tossed into the corner of the loft. They gravitated to the Anglicans or, more likely, the Unitarians, who coalesced as a denomination in the 1810s by replacing the disturbing doctrine of human depravity with a reassuring belief in human goodness. A newcomer to Boston during Jackson's presidency (a Presbyterian) observed that "all the literary men of Massachusetts were Unitarians; all the trustees and professors of Harvard College were Unitarians; all the elite of wealth and fashion crowded Unitarian churches."

The Congregationalists lost ground among ordinary New Englanders after 1800, when Thomas Jefferson came to power and blood did not run in the gutters of Boston and Hartford, as many Congregationalist ministers had warned. By the 1830s, Democrats could win elections in every New England state. Even Connecticut and Massachusetts abolished the privileges of the Congregationalists.

RELIGIOUS FERMENT

Old-time religion did not disappear. Denominations that had never enjoyed official favor—the Presbyterian Church of the

Scotch-Irish, the Baptists (for whom the separation of church and state was a basic tenet), the Methodists (an offshoot of the Anglicans), *and* hard-shell, old-line Congregationalists—preached the centrality of salvation by means of an emotional conversion experience that evidenced the visitation of the Holy Spirit. But their doctrine had one big, new, democratic, egalitarian difference: Salvation was available not only to a divinely elected few.

Like personal economic improvement, salvation was available to all men and (unlike economic opportunity) to all women. These churches were known as "evangelical" because unlike, for example, the sedate Episcopalians and Unitarians, they aggressively preached the gospel—that is, they "evangelized."

As a force shaping America in the first half of the nineteenth century, the evangelicals were as powerful as Jacksonian Democrats, who were decidedly not evangelicals. The evangelicals were the most durable and constructive part of a spirit of enthusiasm in the original Greek meaning of the word—being possessed by God and assured that God spoke directly to them (no matter how far-fetched the things he said).

Camp Meetings and Circuit Riders

The first signs of the new wave of religious enthusiasm were to be found on the trans-Appalachian frontier. Preachers styling themselves "revivalists" (because, they said, religion needed to be revived) began to organize "camp meetings" during the 1790s. These were multiday, or even weeklong, events held in openings in the forest, where thousands camped in wagons and tents. They listened, morning to midnight, to emotional sermons confirming what they knew all too well: that they were sinful creatures and that they were therefore damned to hell unless they prayed for and won God's grace.

The greatest of the camp meeting preachers was James McGready, who inveighed not only against the garden-variety sins of his listeners but against the greed of the southern elite. The culmination of McGready's career was the camp meeting at Cane Ridge, Kentucky, in 1801. As many as 20,000 people may have gathered there.

Such a concentration of humanity was itself exhilarating on the thinly populated frontier, and the atmosphere of the camp meeting was electrifying. Dozens of preachers—Presbyterians, Methodists, and Baptists—simultaneously harangued the crowd from well-constructed platforms, and freelancers preached from stumps.

Conversions were numerous and passionate. People fell to their hands and knees, weeping uncontrollably. Others scampered about on all fours, barking like dogs. A famous manifestation of God's presence was the "jerks," which caused people to lurch about, their limbs snapping and jerking wildly. At Cane Ridge, the rumor spread that a man who cursed God had been seized by the jerks and had broken his neck. When each day's final exhortations tailed off, the moans of excited people could be heard in every direction.

Plenty of people, especially young men, went to camp meetings for the company, the showmanship, and the chance to exploit the occasion with thieving, heckling, heavy drinking, and the sexual opportunities emotional excitement dependably provides. At first, the scoffers were welcome. Revivalism was, after all, about converting sinners. But violent assaults on preachers and oft-told tales of large numbers of girls conceiving persuaded some churches to abandon the camp meeting for the "circuit rider," a Methodist invention, to minister to scattered westerners. The circuit rider—intensely devoted, poorly paid, usually unmarried—visited, on an unending circuit, 10 or 20 little settlements that were too poor to support a church. They rode through thickets and forded swollen creeks in all weather, often carrying nothing but a Bible. They preached, performed marriages and baptisms, took their rest and meals in the cabins of the faithful, and rode on. For three decades, the most famous of them,

▲ *A camp meeting in the forest. The preacher has some of his listeners writhing in hysteria while others are impassive, there for the show.*

Finis Ewing and Peter Cartwright, were rarely off their horses for more than three days at a time.

The Second Great Awakening

Among the social sins the early evangelicals condemned was slavery. As early as the 1780s, Methodist circuit riders were ordered to free their slaves; all Methodists were pressured to do the same. The Baptist and Presbyterian Churches in the slave states of Kentucky and Tennessee called for the abolition of slavery there. Moral revulsion toward slavery went hand in hand with the "Second Great Awakening" in the eastern states too, as did many other reforms.

The frenzy of McGready-style revivalism was a phenomenon of marginal people. For that reason, it was disdained by the upper and middle classes of the Northeast, who prized propriety. The evangelical spirit was brought to them by a number of preachers who toned down the histrionics of revivalism while retaining the revivalist technique and the message that neither damnation nor social evils were divinely decreed.

The well-tuned revivalist sermon, whether delivered at Cane Ridge in 1801 or Rochester, New York, in 1835, had a form varying only in details. It began with a description, varying in emotion and images, of the capacity of human beings for sin. The second part of the sermon detailed the sufferings of hell, for which sinners were destined. Like good politicians, however, revivalists concluded on an optimistic note. Any person could be saved in the Christianity of equal opportunity if he or she repented and declared faith in Jesus Christ. Religion was voluntary and personal. Salvation was a matter not of God's will but of the individual man and woman. "Don't wait!" said Charles Grandison Finney, the greatest of the Awakening preachers. "Do it! Get saved!" He never failed to make the point that "God has made man a moral free agent."

Finney was a lawyer who, after an emotional personal conversion ("I wept aloud like a child. . . . I could feel the [Holy Spirit] like a wave of electricity going through and through me"), traversed the northeastern states during the Jackson years, preaching to largely middle-class gatherings. Finney emphasized the Christian's duty to fight social wrongs, not just because they were sins but because, by eliminating them, the arrival of the Christian Millennium, a thousand years when Christ would rule the earth, would be hastened. Finney lent support to all sorts of moral reformers, but, curiously, he balked for many years at supporting the greatest evangelical reform of the century, the movement to abolish slavery. It is curious that he should have embraced that cause only late in life because the Great Awakening profoundly influenced the religious beliefs of African Americans, particularly southern slaves, only a minority of whom had previously shown interest in Christianity.

▲ *William Miller's analysis of prophecies and his prediction of the end of the world were illustrated in this Adventist chart tracing the rise and fall of earthly kingdoms from Babylon through the "Mahometans." Like many Protestant groups and the Mormons, the Adventists dwelled on the popes of Rome as the most wicked of earthly rulers.*

The Adventists

The Second Coming of Christ was the core of the teachings of a Baptist, William Miller. About 1831, he began to preach that the world would end between March 21, 1843, and March 21, 1844. Miller convinced thousands in the northeastern states with a complex mathematical formula based on biblical prophecies.

At the beginning of the fateful year, a magnificent omen appeared in the sky, Halley's comet. Converts then flocked to join Miller's Adventists (*advent* means "coming" or "arrival"). Many sold their possessions, contributing the proceeds to the sect, which led critics to accuse Miller and his business manager, Joshua V. Himes, of fraud.

On March 21, 1844, so as to be first to greet the Lord, several thousand people throughout New York and New England climbed hills in "Ascension Robes" sold to them by Himes. When the sun set without incident—the "Great Disappointment"—Miller discovered an error in his computations and set the date of the end at no later than October 22, 1844. Again some towns frothed with anxiety and eager anticipation as the day approached. An even greater disappointment descended when, again, Christ did not appear. Miller

himself was bewildered, a broken man. But a disciple, Hiram Edson, reorganized the remnants of the Millerites around the more serviceable belief that the world would end *soon*. Because Edson observed the Jewish Sabbath, Saturday, rather than the Lord's Day, Sunday, the denomination became known as Seventh-Day Adventists.

The Mormons

Another new religion of the era that was certainly enthusiastic and committed to evangelizing for converts, but was otherwise unique, was the Church of Jesus Christ of Latter-Day Saints, the Mormons. Mormonism also originated in "the burned-over district" of New York State, so called because religious enthusiasts, from camp meetings to Adventism to Finney, had repeatedly scorched the land with their ardor.

The founder of the church was Joseph Smith, a daydreamer who preferred wandering the hills of the region, looking for legendary treasure, to the tedious chores of farm life. When he was 20, Smith told his family and neighbors that, on one of his rambles, an angel, Moroni, showed him gold plates bearing mysterious inscriptions that, using miraculous spectacles, Smith was able to read. He translated these inscriptions in *The Book of Mormon,* a Bible of the New World telling of the descendants of the Hebrews in America, the Nephites, whom Christ had visited.

To many, told from childhood that their country was a new Eden, it was not preposterous that Christ should have visited the New World as well as Judaea. To people unsettled by the frenzied pace of the Age of Jackson, it was not surprising that God should make his truth known in upstate New York. It was a time, as one of Smith's converts, Orson Pratt, wrote, when "wickedness [kept] pace with the hurried revolutions of the age." Poet John Greenleaf Whittier, who was no Mormon, wrote of the Latter-Day Saints, "They speak a language of hope and promise to weak, heavy hearts, tossed and troubled, who have wandered from sect to sect, seeking in vain for the primal manifestation of divine power."

Persecution

To a degree, Joseph Smith was his era's child. He extended the priesthood to all white males, thus appealing to the Jacksonian yearning for equality. And he went west, taking his ever increasing followers to Ohio, Missouri, and, in 1840, to Nauvoo, Illinois. The Mormons prospered. By 1844, Nauvoo was the largest city in the state!

The Mormons' prosperity as a group and their undisguised dislike of outsiders (whom they called the "gentiles") aroused envy and resentment locally. Nevertheless, because the Mormons of Nauvoo voted as a bloc, they were courted by both Whig and Democratic politicians. Joseph Smith could probably have been elected to high office in Illinois by trading Mormon votes for a major party nomination.

Instead, in 1844, he declared that he would be an independent candidate for the presidency. This news, added to fears of the well-armed Mormon militia of 2,000 men,

▲ *Joseph Smith reviews the Mormons' Nauvoo Legion at Nauvoo, Illinois. Although hardly the crack, spit-and-polish troops this painting portrays, and described by Smith as a defense force, the large private militia alarmed "gentiles" in western Illinois and contributed to the panic that resulted in Smith's arrest and murder.*

the Nauvoo Legion, led to Smith's arrest. On June 27, he and his brother were murdered in Carthage, Illinois.

Safe in the Desert

The Mormons might have foundered had not an even more remarkable (and politically wiser) Vermonter, Brigham Young, grappled his way to the top of the church hierarchy. Young also received revelations directly from God. The most important of these was the command that the Latter-Day Saints move beyond the boundaries of the sinful nation that oppressed them to lands that were legally Mexican but, in reality, were governed by no one.

The Mormon migration was organized to the finest detail. Advance parties planted crops that would be ready for harvesting when the multitudes arrived on the trail, and built almost a thousand log huts, where they could shelter during the winter. For his Zion, Young chose the most isolated and inhospitable region known to explorers, the basin of the Great Salt Lake.

"This is the place," he said, looking down from the Wasatch Mountains. There the Mormons laid out a tidy city with broad avenues and irrigation ditches fed by water from the surrounding peaks. Their desert bloomed. Within a few years, more than 10,000 people lived in the Salt Lake basin.

Alas, just as the Mormons were constructing their Zion, American victory in war with Mexico brought them back under the American flag. Young did not fight the troops that arrived in Salt Lake, but he made it clear that controlling Utah, which the Mormons called "Deseret," depended on cooperating with him. Prudently, the authorities named Young territorial governor.

Despite its large population, Utah was not admitted to the Union until 1896. About one in six Mormon men practiced polygamy. The others believed in multiple wives but could not afford them. Young, who could, had 27 wives and 56 children. Congress refused to grant statehood until Young's successor received a revelation that polygamy was to be abandoned.

UTOPIAN COMMUNITIES

The Mormons lived in regulated, authoritarian communities, as insulated from the "gentiles" as was possible. The individualism of the Jacksonians and the widespread American avarice for personal riches were subordinated to the good of the whole. Similar social experiments, without the authoritarian leader, appealed to other Americans distressed by the poverty and moral misery that were, along with material progress, the fruits of a wide-open competitive economy. Some of the communities they founded had religious foundations. Others were based on philosophical ruminations. Most were enthusiastic, broadly defined. There were dozens of such utopias. Most failed, and quickly. A few endured.

Failures

New Harmony, Indiana, was founded in 1825 by Robert Owen, a British manufacturer who believed that if property were held in common, life need not, as it did for most, consist of drudgery; life could instead be morally and intellectually fulfilling. Unfortunately for Owen, New Harmony attracted too many people passionately interested not only in the weekly philosophical discussions but also in the easy life Owen generously financed. They found other fulfilling things to do when it was time to work. Believing deeply in the goodness of human nature, Owen was incapable of throwing the freeloaders out. In 1827, disillusioned and poorer, he returned to Scotland.

Another star-crossed utopia was Fruitlands, Massachusetts, the brainstorm of Bronson Alcott. Alcott was a magnificent and lovable eccentric best remembered as the father of author Louisa May Alcott. Like many intellectuals, he was incapable of coping with workaday life. He could button his own shirt, but he inaugurated Fruitlands by planting several apple trees within two feet of the front door of the community house, dropping his shovel, and returning to his meditations and endless conversations.

It was crackpot heaven. One utopian refused to weed the garden because weeds had as much right to grow as vegetables did. Samuel Larned lived for one year on nothing but crackers (so he said) and the next year on nothing but apples. Another Fruitlander smashed dehumanizing, empty social conventions by greeting people, "Good morning, God damn you!" Everyone at Fruitlands agreed that, somehow, cows were loathsome in all ways, but this insight was not enough to sustain the community. Fruitlands lasted several years only because Mrs. Alcott, who did not take her husband seriously but did know what it took to set a table and raise children, did most of the work.

Success Stories

The Shakers, founded in England by Mother Ann Lee, were celibate. Believing (like the Millerites) that the end of the world was near, there was no need to perpetuate the human

race by the distasteful act by which children were had. Men and women lived separately in, by the 1830s, more than 20 tidy and comfortable Shaker communities. They shared equally the work, which, unlike at New Harmony, got done. Men and women came together for meals, conversation, and religious services.

The Shakers were never persecuted as the Mormons were. Sexual abstinence might strike people as peculiar, but it did not offend, as polygamy did. Moreover, unlike the Mormons, the Shakers were polite, hospitable, cooperative, open, and fair in their dealings with outsiders. Indeed, as a community that needed a constant influx of converts in order to survive, the Shakers, although never overweening, welcomed guests. Their communities served as orphan asylums that were free, always a plus for taxpayers. They took in and raised children unwanted by others, giving them the choice, when they reached adulthood, of remaining or returning to "the world." Shaker-style furniture is still an American standard. The evidence is strong that they invented the flat broom, the wooden clothes pin, the circular saw, and the apple parer. Very small Shaker communities of very old Shakers still exist.

John Humphrey Noyes was not troubled by sexual intercourse, but he disapproved of the institution of marriage. Wedlock, he said, was a form of property: Under American law and customs, the husband effectively "owned" his wife. Hence, Noyes said, both were miserable. Rejecting celibacy as an alternative, Noyes devised the concept of "complex marriage" as an adjunct to collective ownership or property.

▲ *The library at the Oneida Community. Like Robert Owen, Oneida's founder, John Humphrey Noyes believed that by owning property in common and by dividing labor equitably among all, there would be plenty of time for study and other fulfilling and ennobling activities. Owen was inundated by parasites; Oneida did not tolerate them, and it thrived.*

In his utopia at Oneida, New York, every man was married to every woman and vice versa. Couples who chose to have sexual relations for pleasure (the initiative was the lady's) could do so, but not for the purpose of procreation. Noyes was an proponent of what came to be called "eugenics": improving the quality of the human race by allowing only those superior in health, constitution, and intellect to reproduce. (The Oneida method of birth control was male continence.) After long and ardent prayer and study, Noyes concluded that he was an ideal male breeder.

Oneida's free love enraged the community's neighbors. Noyes fled to Canada to escape arrest. Oneida, nevertheless, enjoyed a long life. The community prospered from its manufacture of silverware, silks, and a superior trap for fur-bearing animals. Abandoning complex marriage in 1879, and communal ownership of property in 1881, the Oneidans reorganized as a commercial corporation.

TRANSCENDENTALISM

Noyes was a Perfectionist. That is, he believed that Christ's redemption of humanity was complete. Individuals had it within themselves to be perfect—that is, without sin—and therefore above rules that had been written for the imperfect. People had only to face up to their perfection, and it was so.

Perfectionism was evangelicalism triumphant—for those who were perfect. The evangelicals were determined to rid themselves and society of sin. Noyes had done it, albeit in just one community in upstate New York. Unfortunately, when Noyes put sinlessness into practice at Oneida by approving behaviors defined by his neighbors as quite sinful, he was run out of the country.

Ralph Waldo Emerson of Massachusetts, by contrast, became "America's philosopher" by calling Perfectionism by another name—transcendentalism—and by avoiding its implications in his pronouncements and certainly in the way he led his life.

Pantheism

Ralph Waldo Emerson's pantheism—the belief that nature is divinity—made for beautiful lyric poetry. In "The Rhodora," he reflected on the purple flower of that name that grows only in obscure nooks of the woods:

Rhodora! If the sages ask thee why
This charm is wasted on the earth and sky,
Tell them, dear, that if eyes were made for seeing,
Then beauty is its own excuse for being;
Why thou wert there, O rival of the rose!
I never thought to ask, I never knew:
But, in my simple ignorance, suppose
The self-same power that brought me here,
*   brought you.*

▲ *Ralph Waldo Emerson was a superb writer and lecturer, able to live comfortably on his earnings as a philosopher. He might be considered America's second "celebrity" in our sense of the word. He was "famous for being famous," second in that role only to Benjamin Franklin.*

The Sage of Concord

Emerson was a Unitarian pastor in Boston whose assessment of human nature glowed with warmth. In 1832, he announced that he could no longer accept the Unitarian practice of celebrating the Lord's Supper; he resigned and moved to Concord, Massachusetts. "The profession is antiquated," Emerson said of preaching. But within a few years, he was preaching again, from a lectern rather than a pulpit. He shook his head sadly that people should cling to superstition, yet his own message was a welter of notions far more mystical than the Protestantism of sophisticated Boston.

Transcendentalism defied criticism. Based on feelings rather than reason, transcendentalism exalted a vague concept of nature's superiority to civilization, personal morality over laws, and the individual's capacity within himself to be happy, or sinless. When Emerson was faulted as fuzzy and contradictory, he responded that his critics were not capable of understanding that "consistency is the hobgoblin of little minds," that the enlightened human being could dispose "very easily of the most disagreeable facts."

Transcend means "to go beyond, to rise above." As used by Emerson and his disciples, it meant to go above reason and beyond the material world. God was not a being, but the oversoul, which was within all men and women because it was in nature. "Standing on the bare ground," Emerson wrote, "my head bathed by the blithe air and uplifted into infinite space—all mean egotism vanishes. I become a transparent eyeball; I am nothing; I see all; the currents of the Universal being circulate through me."

Writer Herman Melville, a contemporary, called Emerson's teachings "gibberish" and "self-conceit." But while Melville struggled to eke out a living, Emerson was lionized as the greatest mind of his time. While Melville scrutinized evil in the world, Emerson sniffed gifts of flowers.

Other Transcendentalists

Mostly, Emerson had fans. He supported himself in comfort by packing lecture halls throughout the Northeast and selling collections of his essays. But there were other transcendentalists famous in their own time. Emerson's neighbor in Concord, Henry David Thoreau, was the introspective son of a pencil manufacturer. Unlike the prim and proper Emerson (in Paris, Emerson was stunned into unprecedented speechlessness by the gaiety of Gallic free living), Thoreau flaunted his eccentricity. In 1845, he constructed a cabin in the woods near Walden Pond, just outside Concord. There he wrote *Walden* (1854), an account of his reflections while sitting by the pond.

Although *Walden* is the masterpiece of transcendentalism—possibly the best reflective writing of the century—it is marred by the same dilettantism that robs Emerson's works (also masterpieces of style) of lasting value. Thoreau wrote as if he had seceded from civilization and struck off into the wilderness: "I wanted to live deep and suck out all the marrow of life, to live so sturdily and spartan, like as to put to rout all that was not life, to cut a broad swath and shave close, to drive life into a corner, and reduce it to its lowest terms."

But Walden was no Rocky Mountain fastness. It was a short stroll to Concord, a walk that Thoreau took often when he had a yen for a well-cooked meal. Living deep and sucking the marrow out of life were rather like camping in the backyard.

PHILANTHROPISTS AND REFORMERS

Evangelicals soon moved from personal salvation to saving society by attacking and attempting to kill its sins, as they had done within themselves. They believed that it was their sacred obligation to bear witness against social evils and that it was their Christian duty not only to save the souls of their fellow creatures but also to improve their lives.

Gallaudet, Howe, and Dix

Some evangelicals were specialists. Thomas Gallaudet's concern was deafness and society's indifference to the deaf. Traditionally, Americans regarded deafness, blindness, and other disabilities as punishments for sin, as trials designed

How Others Saw Us

Literate Europeans thought of the United States as a cultural backwater, Americans of no more interest than the Indians whom they dispossessed and the Africans they enslaved. Sidney Smith, a famous British wit, wrote in 1820: "In the four quarters of the globe, who reads an American book? or goes to an American play? or looks at an American picture or statue? What does the world yet owe to American physicians or surgeons? What new substances have their chemists discovered? or what old ones have they analyzed? What new constellations have been discovered by the telescopes of Americans?—What have they done in the mathematics?" Few of Smith's readers would have disagreed, including those few Americans who imported his *Edinburgh Review.*

Times were changing, however. Just the next year, a New Yorker, Washington Irving, published two stories, "Rip Van Winkle" and "The Legend of Sleepy Hollow," that won the British intelligentsia's acclaim. James Fenimore Cooper, another New Yorker, was soon so gratifyingly lionized in England for his *Leatherstocking Tales,* novels about the clash of civilization and nature on the American frontier, that he stayed abroad for seven years.

It was the rise of Jacksonian Democracy, however, that piqued European interest in Americans as people, in their government and politics, and in the curious enthusiasms that seemed to thrive in the United States. Indeed, America became something of a mania among the intelligentsia. Before 1828, the year of Jackson's election, only some 40 books about America were published in Europe. In the decade that followed, hundreds were written in at least a dozen languages. Popular British authors such as Frederick Marryat, Anthony Trollope, Harriett Martineau, and Charles Dickens crossed the Atlantic specifically to describe the scenery, explain the political institutions, and wonder over the manners, morals, and quirks of Americans. The best of the books was *Democracy in America,* a two-volume treatise published in 1835 and 1840 by a French aristocrat, Alexis de Tocqueville, who came to the United States at the behest of the French government to study American innovations in penology.

Tocqueville found much to admire in the United States. Because he was himself a traditionalist, he was surprised to discover that democratic government worked. However, because Tocqueville believed that stability and continuity in human relationships were essential to a healthy society, he was concerned that Americans seemed always on the move. He was disturbed by the Americans' undiscriminating love of the new and disdain for the old and, most of all, by their relentless pursuit of money. He had no trouble liking Americans as individuals but also observed, as many of the literary tourists did, that Americans were chauvinistic and defensive about their country: "A stranger who injures American vanity, no matter how justly, must make up his mind to be a martyr."

Frances Trollope, whose *Domestic Manners of the Americans,* published in 1832, was much more popular than the "American book" of her writer son, Anthony, came to the United States not to write a book but to go into business in Cincinnati. And she did not like Americans a bit: "I do not like their principles. I do not like their manners. I do not like their opinions." With the eye of an eagle and a wit as sharp as talons, Mrs. Trollope swooped through American parlors, kitchens,

---

by God, or simply as an unhappy circumstance visited on some by the roll of life's dice. Whatever the case, handicaps were personal misfortunes. Care of the disabled was the province of the family. The individual who strove to overcome a disability was edifying, but the problem was personal, not society's concern.

Gallaudet believed that the Christian was his brother's keeper, and the unique social isolation of the deaf troubled him. In 1815, he went to England to study new techniques for teaching lipreading and sign language to the deaf. Good evangelical that he was, Gallaudet was disgusted to discover that they were trade secrets, articles of commerce guarded as closely by the people who profited from them as a textile manufacturer guarded the plans for his looms. With a Frenchman who shared his ideals, he returned to the United States and, in 1817, founded the American Asylum, a free school for the deaf in Hartford, Connecticut. Gallaudet taught his techniques to every interested party and encouraged others to establish similar institutions in other cities.

Samuel Gridley Howe organized the Perkins Institute for the Blind in Boston. He also publicized his techniques and toured the country with a young girl named Laura Bridgman, who was both deaf and blind. Howe had established communication with her, laying to rest the widespread assumption that such seriously disabled people were helpless. The most overwhelming impediments to human fulfillment, Howe said, could be overcome if men and women did their moral duty.

The insane aroused less sympathy than did those with physical disabilities. Traditionally, retarded people and harmless idiots were cared for by their families and otherwise ignored or mocked. Dangerous "lunatics" were locked up at home or by legal authorities. The line between violent insanity and criminality was blurred. Many a lunatic was hanged; others were recognized as not morally responsible for their actions but were, nonetheless, confined in prisons or asylums where treatment consisted of little more than restraint.

In 1841, Dorothea Dix, a teacher in Massachusetts, discovered in the Cambridge House of Correction that the insane were locked in an unheated room, even in winter. At 39, Dix had lived a genteel, sheltered personal life. She was pious and shy. Her discovery of evils in the treatment of the insane galvanized her, and she became one of the most effective reformers of the century.

In 1843, she scolded the Massachusetts state legislature because of the "state of insane persons confined within cabins, steamboats, theaters, churches, and houses of business, finding something wrong with everything. Unlike Tocqueville, who wrote in generalities, many of which are eerily relevant today, Mrs. Trollope described the unpleasantness she found with pungent anecdotes. She too was disturbed by the runaway individualism, self-centered vanity, and materialism of Americans. On materialism, she cited an English resident of the United States who told her that "in following, in meeting, or in overtaking, in the street, on the road, or in the field, at the theatre, the coffee house, or at home, he had never overheard Americans conversing without the word DOLLAR being pronounced between them."

Mrs. Trollope observed that Americans rushed through hastily prepared meals. They jogged rather than walked. (Frederick Marryat wrote that a New York businessman "always walks as if he had a good dinner before him and a bailiff after him.") Americans fidgeted when detained by some obligation lest they miss something happening in another part of town. When they did sit down, they whittled, so incapable were they to be still. At least two foreign tourists remembered as the symbol of their American experience the spectacle of a team of horses pulling a house on rollers from one site to another. Nothing in the United States was rooted, neither homes nor the mighty oaks that were mowed like hay; neither customs nor social relationships nor religious beliefs that had served humanity well for centuries.

The great Charles Dickens came to the United States to persuade American publishers, who pirated his books, to pay him royalties. He failed, as Mrs. Trollope failed in business, and this no doubt colored his generally negative reflections in *American Notes* (1842). Fanny Kemble, an actress, came to America in 1832 and was a great success. However, she was swept off her feet, and off the stage, by Pierce Butler. She knew he was rich before they married in 1834 but, curiously, not that his family owned 700 slaves, making the Butlers one of the very largest slave owners in the nation. Fanny Kemble's first book about America, published in 1835, contradicted Mrs. Trollope in finding Americans courteous but agreed with her in other particulars—for example, the difficulty of finding solitude among a people who "take pleasure in droves, and travel by swarms," and the headaches of managing servants in a society in which all were equal. It was "a task quite enough to make a Quaker kick his grandmother."

Those were hired white servants, of course. The slaves who served her at her husband's Georgia plantation she found ignorant and dirty but hardly impudent. When she first arrived, she was mystified that the slaves kissed her dress, hugged her, and showered her with endearments. She later learned that she and her children represented a future less miserable. Her husband had been considering selling the plantation and slaves, which would have meant the breakup of the slaves' families. With Fanny in residence, there was hope.

But Fanny did not remain in residence for long. She left the plantation after less than a year, disgusted by the injustice and cruelties of slavery. She became an abolitionist, divorced her husband, and wrote an account of her life in Georgia that, unlike much antislavery propaganda, was firsthand, forthright, and unexaggerated. Published during the Civil War, Kemble's *Journal* was instrumental in dulling what popular sympathy for the South there was in Britain.

this Commonwealth in *cages, closets, cellars, stalls, pens! Chained, naked, beaten with rods, and lashed* into obedience." Dix's revelations did not square with New Englanders' image of themselves as the nation's most enlightened people. ("O New England," Noah Webster wrote, "how superior are thy inhabitants in morals, literature, civility, and industry!") The Massachusetts legislature promptly passed a bill to enlarge the state asylum and improve conditions elsewhere. Dix then carried her message throughout the nation and the world. She persuaded Congress to establish St. Elizabeth's Hospital for the Insane and 15 states to build humane asylums.

Crime and Punishment

Another institution that attracted the notice of reformers was the penitentiary. Large prisons for convicts serving long terms were new to the United States. Until the late eighteenth century, long prison terms were rare. The most serious crimes were punished by hanging: there were as many as 16 capital offenses in some states. Other felonies merited a flogging or physical mutilation. Thomas Jefferson advocated castration of rapists and homosexuals and boring a half-inch hole through the nose of lesbians. In Massachusetts, in 1805, counterfeiters, arsonists, wife beaters, and thieves were whipped, their ears cropped, or their cheeks branded with a hot iron. Petty offenses—being drunk and disorderly, disturbing the peace—were punished with fines or the humiliation of a dunking, the stocks, or the pillory.

During the 1790s, influenced by an Italian criminologist, Cesare Beccaria, most states reduced the number of capital offenses, abolished mutilation, and restricted the use of whipping. They turned to prison for the punishment of serious crime. The purposes were punishment and the protection of society; everywhere, the conditions of confinement were execrable. Connecticut used an abandoned mine shaft as its penitentiary.

Reformers pointed out that the security of society was not improved if prison transformed every convict into a resentful, hardened criminal. In confining burglars with rapists, penitentiaries acted as schools of the worst crimes. The evangelical alternative was the correctional institution, the prison as a place for moral and social rehabilitation. Theories as to how best to accomplish this worthy goal differed. The Pennsylvania system, for example, kept its convicts in solitary confinement. The idea was that inmates would meditate on their crimes and leave prison determined not to offend again.

▲ *A pillory (top) and the whipping post at New Castle, Delaware. Punishments, including executions, were public in the Age of Jackson. They were thought to deter crime, although many observers had long noted that most of the people who attended did so because they enjoyed the spectacle. Whipping (although not in public) as the penalty for wife beating was legal in Delaware into the 1950s.*

The flaws of the Pennsylvania system, obvious almost immediately, were twofold: individual cells were extremely expensive, and total isolation resulted in numerous cases of mental breakdown.

The Auburn system, named after the town in which New York's state prison was located, addressed the problem of isolation by marching prisoners each day to large workrooms and a common dining hall. Conversation was forbidden, both to prevent education in crime and to keep order. The Auburn system was adopted by other states, including Pennsylvania.

Another innovation of the period was the house of refuge, in which juveniles were kept isolated from adult criminals. By 1830, New York City, Philadelphia, and Boston maintained such facilities.

MORAL UPLIFT

Undesirable behavior among the masses also inspired reforms during the early nineteenth century. While Gallaudet, Howe, Dix, and the prison reformers attended to injustices suffered by a few, other evangelicals addressed social problems that afflicted the entire society.

Do-Gooders

The worthiness of a reform bears no relationship to the agreeableness of the enthusiasts who push it—in the Age of Jackson or in any other era when reform is in the air. The evangelicals whose zeal was essential to demands for change (both change that history has judged beneficial as well as reforms now seen as futile, bigoted, or ridiculous) were often tiresome, bothersome people. Orestes Brownson, who personally knew most of the New England utopians and reformers of the era, wrote:

Matters have come to such a pass, that a peaceable man can hardly venture to eat and drink, to go to bed or to get up, to correct his children or to kiss his wife, without obtaining the permission and the direction of some moral society.

Demon Rum

For example, Americans drank heavily. They always had, but consumption peaked in the 1820s, reaching the level of more than 7.5 gallons of alcohol for each American man, woman, and child! In part, this incredible bibulousness owed to the fact that grain was abundant and cheap. More was grown than was needed as food or could find markets abroad. English-style ales, cider, and rum were the everyday beverages of the East. In the West, the daily tonic was whiskey. Wine and brandy—most of it imported—were fixtures of middle- and upper-class life.

Except among the pathetic dregs of society, drunkenness was universally regarded as sinful and socially disruptive, or at least as disagreeable. Before 1800, Dr. Benjamin Rush of Philadelphia systematically described the physically destructive effects of excessive drinking. With the blossoming of the evangelical spirit during the 1830s, antialcohol reformers added two more arrows to the quiver.

First, they published statistics showing that a substantial number of crimes were committed by people who were drunk. Second, they drew a connection between poverty and drinking. A few said that the miseries of poverty led to drunkenness. Most, steeped in the evangelical sense of individual responsibility, believed that drunkenness was the cause of poverty.

A temperance movement spread rapidly. By 1835, there were 5,000 temperance societies in the United States with a membership of more than a million. In 1840, six reformed sots founded a national organization, the Washington Temperance Society. Two years later, a more militant association, the Sons of Temperance, began to promote sobriety as a basic religious duty.

One of the Sons' most effective lecturers was John B. Gough, an ex-drunk who rallied audiences with the lurid language of the camp meeting revivalist: "Crawl from the slimy ooze, ye drowned drunkards, and with suffocation's blue and livid lips speak out against the drink."

Prohibition

Temperance reformers quarreled and parted ways as promiscuously as drunks. One cleavage ran between the advocates of moderation in the use of alcohol and the complete abstainers. The former argued that drunkenness was the evil, not alcohol itself. They lodged no objection to the occasional sip of wine or the restorative shot. The abstainers, observing that alcohol was addictive, concluded that it was inherently dangerous and sinful. Moderation was asking for trouble. It was necessary to swear off drink "T-totally" (hence their name, teetotalers).

The teetotalers divided between moral suasionists, who regarded abstinence from drink as an individual responsibility, and legal suasionists, who considered the prohibition of the manufacture and sale of liquor as the means of destroying the evil. In 1838, Massachusetts experimented with a law designed to cut down alcohol consumption among the poor. The Fifteen Gallon Law prohibited the sale of whiskey or rum in quantities smaller than 15 gallons. However, the temper of the Age of Jackson ran against any device that provided privileges to the rich, who could afford to buy spirits in bulk. The Fifteen Gallon Law was repealed within two years.

In 1845, New York adopted a more democratic law, which authorized local governments to forbid the sale of alcohol within their jurisdictions. Within a few years, five-sixths of the state was "dry." In 1846, the state of Maine, led by Neal Dow, a Portland businessman, adopted the first statewide prohibition law. By 1860, 13 states had followed suit. But the custom of drinking was too much a part of the culture to be abolished by well-meaning ordinances. Prohibition laws were flagrantly violated; by 1868, they were repealed in every state but Maine.

Temperance and prohibition were largely Protestant movements supported by evangelical reformers and directed at native-born old-stock Americans. In the 1840s, however, the crusade against alcohol took on a new urgency because of the huge influx of immigrants who had (as far as reformers were concerned) an inordinate devotion to beer and whiskey.

The Stresses of Immigration

Only 8,400 Europeans came to the United States in 1820, hardly enough to excite notice. More than 23,000 arrived in 1830, however, and 84,000 in 1840. In 1850, 370,000 people stepped from immigrant ships onto wharves in the eastern seaports and New Orleans. Not only were the immigrants of midcentury numerous, but they were, in large part, adherents of religious faiths little known in the United States before 1840; and many spoke languages other than English.

Thirty-six hundred Irish came to the United States in 1820, most of them Protestant; 164,000 arrived in 1850, most of them Roman Catholic. Immigration authorities counted only 23 Scandinavian immigrants in 1820 and 1,600 in 1850, a number that would nearly triple within two years. In 1820, 968 Germans entered the United States; in 1850, 79,000 arrived.

Scandinavian and German immigrants inclined to cluster in large communities, retaining their languages and preserving Old World customs. Among these was the convivial beer garden, where families gathered to drink lager beer, which was first introduced to the United States in this era. To a teetotaler, the Irish were worse. They were notoriously given to gathering in saloons in cities and on construction sites, and they drank whiskey. Worse, they were Roman Catholic, as were about half of the Germans. Between 1830 and 1860, when the general population slightly more than doubled, the Roman Catholic population of the United States increased tenfold—from 300,000 to more than 3 million.

The "Whore of Babylon"

The growth of Catholicism was difficult for many Protestants to swallow. Since the days of the Puritans, they had been taught that the Church of Rome was not just another Christian denomination but the Bible's Whore of Babylon, a fount of evil.

▲ *In Philadelphia in 1844, militia try to subdue rioters, presumably Protestants because their faces are not in the stereotype used to identify Irish immigrants at the time. Philadelphia did not have a professional police force until 1845; it was, in fact, the murderous riot that persuaded the city it needed one. Note the Catholic church in the background to identify the religious character of the rampage.*

This prejudice took on new life in the second quarter of the nineteenth century because the pope, the spiritual leader of the world's Catholics, was also the political head of a reactionary and repressive principality. In the Papal States in central Italy, dissidents were jailed and, it was believed, tortured. The political principles of Catholicism—monarchy, aristocracy, deference to authority—were the antithesis of American traditions, particularly in the democratizing Age of Jackson. Because the Irish immigrants were intensely devoted to their faith and deferred to the authority of their priests, many Protestants feared that they were the shock troops of political reaction. Many Whigs—and eastern evangelicals were Whigs in their politics—found it worrisome enough that the Irish flocked to the Democratic party.

Finally, the vast majority of the Irish immigrants were destitute. Landless in their native country, they were forced to emigrate because of extreme deprivation and, in the late 1840s, because of the failure of the country's potato crop. Once in the United States, they were willing to accept work at almost any rate of pay, prompting Protestant workingmen to regard them as a threat to the high standard of living that skilled artisans enjoyed. When economic unease combined with religious suspicion and the evangelical crusade against the new immigrants' drinking, the result was a social and political movement.

The famous painter and inventor of the telegraph, Samuel F. B. Morse, wanted to cut off the immigration of Catholics. Street wars between Protestant and Irish Catholic workingmen regularly erupted in northeastern cities. In 1834, aroused by sermons that Catholic priests kept nuns for sexual purposes, murdering the infants born of such unions, a mob burned an Ursuline convent in Charlestown, Massachusetts. In Philadelphia in 1844, 20 people were killed and over a hundred injured in a riot pitting Protestants against Catholics.

Anti-Catholicism took political shape in the Order of the Star-Spangled Banner, a secret organization dedicated to shutting off further immigration. The order's members were called "Know-Nothings" because, when asked by outsiders about the organization, they replied, "I know nothing."

After 1850, the order came above ground as the American party. Capitalizing on the disintegration of the Whigs and anxiety caused by the sectional hostility, the anti-Catholic, anti-immigrant movement swept to power in several states, including Massachusetts, where almost every elected official was a member. At its peak, the American party elected 75 congressmen.

Only a minority of Protestants believed in political action against Roman Catholics. The majority was indifferent to the faith of the newcomers or stood by the guarantees of religious freedom in the First Amendment. Many of these people, however, approved of attempts by various missionary societies to convert Catholics and other peoples to Protestant denominations.

The American Tract Society and the American Bible Society distributed literature among the Catholic population. By 1836, the Tract Society estimated that it had sold or given away more than 3 million publications explaining Protestant beliefs. Another group concentrated on converting the few Jews in the United States.

Blue Hawaii

Most missionary activity, however, was directed overseas. Nothing was more "evangelical" than taking the gospel to the heathen, of course. But the missionary movement received an additional boost because the numerous denominational colleges of the United States turned out many more ministers than there were pulpits to fill. Groups such as the American Board of Foreign Missions raised money to send zealous young men and women to the Indians of the distant West, to Africa, India, and China. No place in the world, however, attracted American missionaries more than the Sandwich Islands, Hawaii.

In 1819, a young Hawaiian Christian told the students of Andover Theological Seminary of the harm done to his homeland by sailors and whalers, Americans prominent among them. The islands' location in the central Pacific made Hawaii an inevitable landfall for whalers from New Bedford and Nantucket, who stopped in Hawaii to refit their vessels, replenish their provisions, and recover from scurvy on island fruits. The diseases they brought devastated the population. Between 1778 and 1804, the Hawaiian population was halved, from about 300,000 to 150,000. The goods the white men brought to trade with a people who had known a simple life irrevocably corrupted the culture of the survivors. Back in New England, evangelicals felt obligated to right these wrongs.

As early as 1820, young ministers and their wives, sisters, and mothers shipped out to Hawaii. Some Hawaiians resisted when the missionaries tried to force proper New England behavior on them. The most celebrated example of the missionaries' incapacity to distinguish religion from custom was their insistence that in the warm, humid climate of the islands, Christian girls and women dress in full-length calico and flannel "Mother Hubbard" dresses.

For the most part, however, the mission to Hawaii was an astonishing success. So disastrous to Hawaiian culture was contact with the West that traditional Hawaiian religious beliefs were discredited before the missionaries arrived; the missionaries brought the Bible into a void. By 1830, their schools enrolled 52,000 Hawaiians (40 percent of the population), teaching the indigenous language and evangelical religion in an alphabet the Americans introduced.

THE WOMEN'S MOVEMENT

Women were the backbone of the missionary movement, in part as a consequence of the migration to the West. Because young men were freer than young women to break old ties and strike off on their own, New England was left with a surplus of women for whom there were not enough spouses. Evangelical activity, being within the realm of morality, was considered an acceptable outlet for their energies. Indeed, preachers of the Great Awakening early recognized that the large majority of their converts were female. Single women were prominent in every reform movement of the era from temperance to abolitionism.

But there was more to the flowering of social activism among American women than demographics. In consecrating their lives to the deaf, the poor, the missions, and other good works, ostensibly privileged and comfortable middle-class women were able to protest, however obliquely, the private, domestic, and dependent status that American society assigned them. This discontent naturally found an outlet in the emergence of feminism as a social movement.

Feminism

In the summer of 1848, a group of women, mostly Quakers, called for a convention to be held at Seneca Falls, New York, to consider the "Declaration of Sentiments and Resolutions" they had drafted. The declaration was a deadly serious parody of the Declaration of Independence:

> When in the course of human events it becomes necessary for one portion of the family of man to assume among the people of the earth a position different from that which they have hitherto occupied, but one to which the laws of nature and nature's God entitle them, a decent respect to the opinions of mankind requires that they should declare the causes that impel them to such a course.

The injustices suffered by women included the denial of the right to vote even when it was extended to "the most ignorant and degraded men"; the forfeiture by a married woman of control over her own property; the nearly absolute power of the husband over a wife's behavior, which "made her, morally, an irresponsible being"—a state utterly reprehensible to an evangelical; and the exclusion of women from the professions and other gainful employment.

Only 68 women and 32 men signed the document, but the Seneca Falls declaration received national attention—sympathetic in reform newspapers, scornful and mocking in more conventional publications. Among the organizers of the conference were Lucretia Coffin Mott and Elizabeth Cady Stanton, who continued to play an important part in the feminist movement for a generation. Among the spectators was Amelia Jenks Bloomer, a temperance reformer who was soon to become famous as the advocate of a new style of dress that bore her name.

The high expectations of 1848—that equal rights for women was a demand whose time had come—were soon dashed to pieces. Americans, including most women, were not ready to think seriously about the civil equality of women. Even the vote, only one of the Seneca Falls demands, lay more than half a century in the future.

Evangelical reformers, although generally sympathetic to women's rights, urged the feminists to set their problems aside until a reform they considered far more important was achieved. This was the abolition of slavery, a cause that was entering its final phase when the Seneca Falls convention was called. "I do not see how anyone can pretend that there is the same urgency," the African American abolitionist (and feminist) Frederick Douglass said, "in giving the ballot to the woman as freedom to the Negro." Stanton and Mott, who were abolitionists before they became feminists, agreed, one of the rare moments in history when a reformer put anything above her or his own prized cause. The feminists never silenced their call for women's rights, but they stepped to the side in the belief that when the slaves were freed, women would have their day.

for FURTHER READING

For background and context, see Perry Miller, *The Life of the Mind in America from the Revolution to the Civil War,* 1966; I. H. Bartlett, *The American Mind in the Mid-Nineteenth Century,* 1967; Russell B. Nye, *Society and Culture in America, 1830–1860,* 1974; and Lewis Perry, *Intellectual Life in America,* 1984. Also valuable are S. E. Ahlstrom, *A Religious History of the American People,* 1972; and Martin E. Marty, *Righteous Empire: The Protestant Experience in America,* 1970, and *Pilgrims in Their Own Land: 500 Years of Religion in America,* 1984.

Basic general studies of nineteenth-century reform include C. S. Griffin, *Thy Brother's Keepers: Moral Stewardship in the United States, 1800–1865,* 1960, and *The Ferment of Reform,* 1967; Arthur M. Schlesinger Jr., *The American as Reformer,* 1960; and R. G. Walters, *American Reformers: 1815–1860,* 1978.

An old but delightful book with a jaundiced view of the American enthusiasms of the era is Gilbert Seldes, *The Stammering Century,* 1928. Also on revivalism, see Bernard R. Weisberger, *They Gathered at the River,* 1958; and C. A. Johnson, *The Frontier Camp Meeting,* 1955. Other titles dealing with religious and utopian sects in the nineteenth century include Leonard J. Arrington, *Great Basin Kingdom,* 1958; A. E. Bestor, *Backwoods Utopias,* 1950; Fawn M. Brodie, *No Man Knows My History: The Life of Joseph Smith,* 1945; Martin Cardin, *Oneida,* 1969; Whitney R. Cross and Henri Destroche, *The American Shakers: From Neo-Christianity to Neo-Socialism,* 1971; and Robert O. Thomas, *The Man Who Would Be Perfect,* 1977.

On specific reforms, see Ray A. Billington, *The Protestant Crusade, 1800–1860,* 1938; F. L. Byme, *Prophet of Prohibition: Neal Dow and His Crusade,* 1961; M. E. Lender and J. K. Martin, *Drinking in America: A History,* 1982; H. E. Marshall, *Dorothea Dix: Forgotten Samaritan,* 1937; Blake McKelvey, *American Prisons: A Study in American Social History Prior to 1915,* 1936; W. G. Rorabaugh, *The Alcoholic Republic: An American Tradition,* 1979; David J. Rothman, *The Discovery of the Asylum,* 1970; and I. R. Tyrrel, *Sobering Up: From Temperance to Prohibition,* 1979.

On feminism, see Lois Banner, *Elizabeth Cady Stanton,* 1980; Carl M. Degler, *At Odds: Women and the Family in America from the Revolution to the Present,* 1980; Eleanor Flexner, *Century of Struggle: The Women's Rights Movement in the United States,* 1975; Aileen S. Kraditor, *Up from the Pedestal: Selected Writings in the History of American Feminism,* 1968; Gerda Lerner, *The Woman in American History,* 1970; Alma Lutz, *Susan B. Anthony,* 1979; William L. O'Neill, *Everyone Was Brave: The Rise and Fall of Feminism in America,* 1970; and Mary P. Ryan, *Womanhood in America,* 1975.

AMERICAN JOURNEY ONLINE AND INFOTRAC COLLEGE EDITION

Visit the source collections at http://ajaccess.wadsworth.com and http://infotrac.thomsonlearning.com, and use the Search function with the following key terms to explore documents, images, audio and video clips, articles, and commentary related to the material in this chapter:

Elizabeth Cady Stanton	Mormons	Seneca Falls Convention	Temperance movement
Henry David Thoreau	Nathaniel Hawthorne	Suffrage	*The Book of Mormon*
Herman Melville	Ralph Waldo Emerson	Temperance	Transcendentalism

Additional resources, exercises, and Internet links related to this chapter are available on *The American Past* Web site: http://history.wadsworth.com/americanpast7e.

HISTORY ONLINE

Religion in America
http://lcweb/loc.gov/exhibits/religion/re101.htm
Documents and photographs about religion in the early nineteenth century.

Shakers and Shakerism
www.nypl.org/research/chss/grd/resguides/shaker.html
A research guide to the most successful of the nineteenth-century communitarians, prepared by the New York Public Library.

A DIFFERENT COUNTRY

The South

There must doubtless be an unhappy influence on the manners of our people produced by the existence of slavery among us. The whole commerce between master and slave is a perpetual exercise of the most boisterous passions, the most unremitting despotism on the one part, and degrading submissions on the other. Our children see this and learn to imitate it. . . . The parent storms, the child looks on, catches the lineaments of wrath, puts on the same airs in the circle of smaller slaves, gives loose to the worst of passions and thus nursed, educated, and daily exercised in tyranny, cannot but be stamped by it with odious peculiarities.

Thomas Jefferson

OODLING AT HIS desk one day, Thomas Jefferson drew up a list of character traits in which, he suggested, northerners and southerners differed. Northerners were cool and sober, he wrote; southerners were fiery and "voluptuary." Northerners were hardworking, self-interested, and devious; southerners were lazy, generous, and candid. Northerners were "jealous of their own liberties, and just to those of others"; southerners were "zealous for their own liberties, but trampling on those of others."

He had a point. Jefferson usually did. And it could not have been easy for a man who called Virginia "my country" to tote up unattractive characteristics in his own people. Still, to fixate on differences between northerners and southerners would be to obscure the reality that they shared a common language and the same religious, cultural, and political heritage. By 1826, the year Jefferson died, they also shared 50 years of history, including the aspiration to relegate the institution of slavery to the dustbin of history.

SOUTHERN ANTISLAVERY

The northern states succeeded in doing so, although, because emancipation was gradual in most states, a few thousand northern blacks remained in bondage in 1826, most of them in New York and New Jersey. (There were legal slaves in New Jersey as late as 1860, all quite elderly.)

The southern states did not, although the same forces that ended slavery in the North made false starts there as well. Just about all southern Quakers freed their slaves by 1780. Wherever the Methodists spread their message, many of their converts freed the slaves they owned, most notably in Maryland and Delaware, where the Methodists converted many whites. (Southern African Americans, free and slave, expressed a preference for the Methodist Church.) Southern delegates to the Constitutional Convention supported the provision that forbade the importation from abroad of slaves after 1807. In fact, most southern states, including South Carolina, outlawed the African slave trade before it was terminated nationally.

Manumission and Race

Until the 1830s, very few of the most powerful southerners, those who owed their wealth, leisure, and status to the labor of their human property, aggressively defended slavery. Like northerners, they worried openly about the undesirable social, economic, and moral consequences of the institution. It was almost common for wealthy planters to manumit—to free—at least some of their slaves in their wills. Robert Carter, who owned more slaves than anyone else in Virginia, freed all of them at his death. George Washington was honored for freeing the 300 slaves he owned. George Wythe, who trained Jefferson, Marshall, and Clay in the law, freed most of his slaves in his will. Jefferson freed a few and has puzzled many of his admirers because he did not free more; Jefferson agonized over the injustice of slavery to the day of his death. In 1833, Virginian John Randolph freed the 400 black people he owned.

The possibility of total abolition arose periodically in the states of the upper South, but, in the end, not even Delaware, where there were only 3,300 slaves in 1830 (3 percent of the population) did so. The decisive factor was the assumption, almost universal among whites, that African Americans were innately inferior in intelligence, initiative, and even moral fiber, that they could not compete with white people in an increasingly competitive America and would, therefore, if free, be the cause of catastrophic social problems.

It was one thing, southerners said, for the northern states to abolish slavery. The black population was numerically insignificant almost everywhere in the North. In 1830, there were 125,000 African Americans in the Northeast in a total population of 5.54 million—African Americans were just 2 percent of the population. There were only 42,000 blacks among the 1.6 million people of the Old Northwest, about the same percentage. So tiny a minority could be ignored,

disdained, and pushed aside to root or die (as, indeed, northern blacks were) without worry of social disturbance.

But blacks were a substantial portion of the population of the South—2.16 million in 1830 alongside 3.54 million whites—and a majority in many areas. African Americans were an overwhelming majority in coastal South Carolina and Georgia and along the Mississippi River in the states of Mississippi and Louisiana. Moreover, they were the backbone of the workforce that brought in every important southern crop: cotton, rice, tobacco, and sugar. If exploiting them as slaves was unjust, immoral, and ultimately dependent on force, thus corrupting slave owners, the alternative of even gradual emancipation was, to most white southerners, hideous to contemplate. As for Delaware, Maryland, Missouri, and large parts of Kentucky, where slaves were a small fraction of the population, the whites who owned slaves dominated politics and, if they profited little from working them, could profit richly by selling them in the cotton states.

Frank confession of such mercenary self-interest is not, of course, one of humanity's strong points, and few slave owners ever confessed it. They did, however, say (many of them quite sincerely) that they were shouldering a burden strapped to them by history and protecting their slaves from the viciousness of poor southern whites, of whom the elite's opinion was not exalted.

Discoverer of Liberia
Paul Cuffee, an African American, was a master mariner who lived on the island of Martha's Vineyard in Massachusetts and was prosperous from coastal and overseas trade. During the 1810s, Cuffee visited Freetown, Sierra Leone, shortly after the British had confirmed their colonial authority there. He explored the coast (mostly mangrove swamp) south of the colony, hoping to locate a site where free American blacks disgusted with their plight in the United States might go. It is not clear if Cuffee pinpointed the future location of Monrovia in Liberia.

Where Is Home?
In 1822, James Forten commented sarcastically on the proposal of the American Colonization Society to pay the way of people like him "back to Africa":

My great-grandfather was brought to this country a slave from Africa. My grandfather obtained his own freedom. My father never wore the yoke. He rendered valuable service to his country in the war of our Revolution; and I, though then a boy, was a drummer in that war. I have since lived and labored in a useful employment, have acquired property, and have paid taxes. . . . Yet some ingenious gentlemen have recently discovered that I am still an African; that a continent, three thousand miles away—and more—from the place where I was born is my native country.

Jefferson's Bequest
Jefferson freed a few slaves in his will. Sally Hemmings, whom Jefferson's enemies claimed was his mistress, was not among them. She was bequeathed to Jefferson's daughter, Patsy. Does this prove the attacks on Jefferson were lies? Some historians think not. They point out that Virginia required manumitted slaves to leave the state. To have freed Sally Hemmings, who was well along in years in 1826, would have forced her to leave her friends and children.

▲ *Monrovia, the capital of Liberia, about the time the nation declared its independence of the American Colonization Society. The town was founded from scratch on empty land in 1822.*

The Colonization Movement

The American Colonization Society, founded in 1817, tried to resolve the dilemma of, on the one hand, an undesirable social institution and, on the other, social chaos. With the active support of distinguished southerners such as Madison, Monroe, John Marshall, and Henry Clay, the society proposed to raise money with which free blacks would be transported to West Africa. By providing a mechanism to eliminate from the South the unwanted population of free blacks, the colonizers hoped to encourage individual slave owners to free their slaves and even prompt state legislatures to adopt abolition laws.

In 1821, the society financed the emigration of a few former slaves to Sierra Leone, a British colony on what was then known as the Guinea Coast, which had been established as a refuge for slaves freed in the British West Indies. The next year, the society, partly with government funds, purchased a stretch of coastline south of Sierra Leone and established Liberia; in 1824, its capital was named Monrovia after President Monroe, who supported the project. About 11,000 African Americans went to Liberia, which functioned rather like an American territory (except that the American Colonization Society appointed the governor) until 1847, when Liberia declared its independence.

Colonization was obviously unrealistic. A few thousand from among a slave population of 1.5 million in 1820 was hardly reducing the black presence in the South, which, in fact, grew to 2 million by 1830—more than could live on a strip of African seacoast. Moreover, the American Colonization Society's antislavery side was something of a fraud, however unconsciously. Few slaves were manumitted so they could emigrate to Liberia. Those who went were blacks who were already free and persuaded, by one argument or another, to go. Indeed, 10,000 or 11,000 was only about 7 per-

cent of the South's free African Americans; there were 37,000 free blacks in Virginia alone in 1820. It is remarkable that so many people were interested in the colonization movement. Free African Americans' assessments of the degraded status in which they were kept may have ranged from misery, through bewilderment, to fury—but they were not Africans. Most were generations removed from their African roots and felt little more attraction to an unknown land than their African ancestors had felt toward America.

As for southern whites, who had been the mainstay of the colonization movement, the longer the price of cotton boomed on the world market, the less was heard about the antislavery side of colonization. When the Mississippi Colonization Society was founded in 1829, its pronounced purpose was to rid the state of all free blacks. Its officers disassociated themselves from the old goal of encouraging planters to free their slaves. Except for one last debate, by 1830, the southern antislavery movement was dead.

The Last Debate

In December 1831, Governor John Floyd of Virginia asked the legislature to consider a plan to phase out slavery gradually. Unlike in the northern states that had done so, slave owners were to be compensated for their losses. For the good of the state, taxpayers would accommodate those who lost property, just as if real estate were taken for the purposes of building a road. For three weeks in January 1832, the legislature discussed the proposal, for the most part moderately and intelligently.

Even the staunchest proslavery men were defensive. Typically, they introduced their speeches by regretting the fact that blacks were ever brought to Virginia and by saying that the state would be a better place if it were developed by free white labor. However, they also concluded that the past

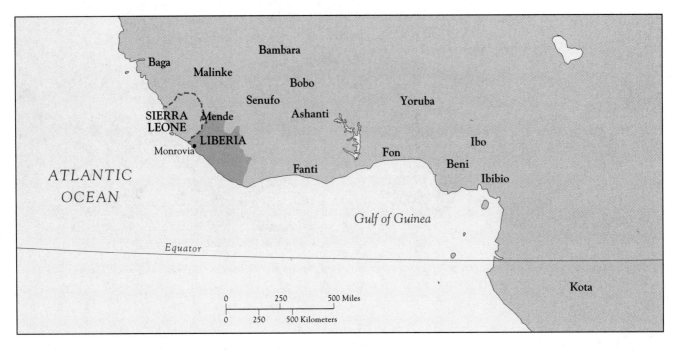

MAP 18:1 Liberia   Liberia, legally the property of the American Colonization Society, was established in 1817. Monrovia was founded in 1822. Liberia declared its independence in 1847. West Africa was a tribal area. The Ashanti, centered east of Liberia, had been rich and powerful as one of the chief suppliers of slaves to European and American buyers, but the tribe had declined with the end of the African slave trade.

was history: Blacks constituted almost half of Virginia's population; so large a population of free blacks was out of the question; and the colonization movement was obviously a failure. However tragic it was for the Old Dominion, Virginia must continue to be a slave state.

The assumption that a biracial society would not work carried the day—but just barely. The legislature rejected Floyd's scheme by 73 to 58. A switch of only eight votes would have altered the course of American history, because the other states of the Upper South—Delaware, Maryland, and Kentucky—could not have ignored abolition in Virginia. Had those states also phased slavery out, the institution would not have split the Union across the middle. It would have been the peculiar institution of a few states in the Deep South, no more able to threaten the Union than the six states of New England. As it was, once Virginia's debate was concluded, no significant body of southern whites ever again considered the possibility of ridding themselves of their "burden."

THREATS TO THE SOUTHERN ORDER

Both Floyd's proposal and the Virginia legislature's rejection of it were profoundly influenced by two events that electrified the South in 1831: the emergence in the North of a new kind of antislavery agitator; and a bloody rebellion of slaves in southern Virginia, the third massive slave insurrection in 30 years and the first in which white people were murdered.

Early Abolitionists

Since the War for Independence, discussions and debates concerning slavery, in the North and South, had revolved around questions of political justice, economic wisdom, and social consequences. However, some voices, even before the evangelicals of the 1780s, spoke of the institution in moral and religious terms. Mostly, they were Quaker voices. French-born Anthony Benezet of Philadelphia, where he taught blacks, began to condemn slavery as immoral around 1750. About the same time, John Woolman of New Jersey, also a Quaker, began to wander the Middle Colonies and Upper South, admonishing Quakers who owned slaves and persuading many to free them. In *A Plea for the Poor,* published in 1763, he outlined the objection to slavery on Christian grounds.

Because Quakers were a small minority and concentrated in New Jersey, Delaware, and Pennsylvania, and because of the self-imposed gentleness of their methods of persuasion, neither Benezet nor Woolman had much impact. During the 1820s, Benjamin Lundy continued the tradition. Slavery was unchristian, he told southerners; but, recognizing economic realities and racial fears, he espoused gradual abolition and advocated colonization of African Americans in Liberia, the black republic of Haiti, Canada, and Texas (then a part of Mexico).

Educated blacks, most notably the mathematician, astronomer, and publisher of a popular almanac, Benjamin Banneker, published moral arguments against slavery. Like the Quakers, Banneker did not rage at slave owners. Indeed, he was as close to being a friend of Thomas Jefferson as Jefferson could imagine an African American as being. Jefferson persuaded Washington to name Banneker the surveyor of the District of Columbia.

The fraternal moral argument against slavery was summed up by the Boston Unitarian preacher William Ellery Channing, who told southerners, "We consider slavery your calamity and not your curse."

David Walker and William Lloyd Garrison

In 1829, language and mood took on new forms. In that year, a black dealer in cloth living in Boston, David Walker, published a pamphlet called *The Appeal*. After reviewing the traditional arguments about the immorality and injustice of slavery, Walker stated that unless whites abolished the institution, blacks had a moral duty to rise up in violent rebellion.

William Lloyd Garrison, a spare, intense young white man of 24, who had been an employee of Benjamin Lundy in Baltimore, did not believe in violent rebellion. Among the many evangelical reform movements he espoused was pacifism—opposition to all wars. However, when Garrison founded an antislavery newspaper in Boston in January 1831, *The Liberator,* his language was incendiary and aimed not only at the institution of slavery (the sin) but at the sinners—slave owners.

"I am aware," Garrison wrote in the first issue, "that many object to the severity of my language; but is there not cause for severity? I will be as harsh as truth, and as uncompromising as justice. On this subject I do not wish to think, or speak, or write, with moderation. No! No! Tell a man whose house is on fire to give a moderate alarm; tell him to moderately rescue his wife from the hands of the ravisher; tell the mother to gradually extricate her babe from the fire into which it has fallen;—but urge me not to use moderation in a cause like the present."

It was a declaration of war. To Garrison, the most extreme of evangelicals, the day of colloquy and persuasion was done. Slavery was evil, pure and simple; slave owners and those who accommodated them were doers of evil. Garrison described the slave owner's life as "one of unbridled lust, of filthy amalgamation, of swaggering braggadocio, of haughty domination, of cowardly ruffianism, of boundless dissipation, of matchless insolence, of infinite self-conceit, of unequaled oppression, of more than savage cruelty."

This sort of thing does not often go down well with those who are the subjects of it. In fact, Garrison was never popular in the North. Even in Boston, a center of evangelical reform and antislavery sentiment, Garrison was hooted and pelted with stones when he spoke in public. On one occasion, a mob threw a noose around his neck and dragged him through the streets. They might well have lynched him had not the aggressiveness of a group of abolitionist women momentarily stunned the mob; the women rescued him. (Garrison was also a supporter of women's rights.)

In the South, Garrison was a monster. Not merely because he was against slavery, at least not at first. Garrison and other extremist abolitionists were hated because they were believed to be inciting slave rebellion. In 1831, the fear of slave rebellion in the South was no abstraction.

The Fear of Rebellion

In 1798, slaves and free blacks in the French colony of Saint-Domingue (now Haiti) rose up in an immense rebellion, murdered hundreds of whites, defeated a crack French army, and forced most of the French who remained to flee the country. Many of them went to Louisiana, then under Spanish control; others, to South Carolina. The horrors they described were news nationally, but, emotionally, hit close to home among southern whites, especially in areas where slaves were numerous. South Carolina and Georgia forbade exiles from Haiti to bring slaves with them for fear they

▲ *William Lloyd Garrison's* The Liberator, *a weekly, was the most extreme and intemperate of abolitionist newspapers but also one of the most popular and effective because of the controversy that swirled around it. Not every writer was as high-strung as Garrison. His newspaper contained many articles on slavery that were based on careful research and included well-reasoned commentary.*

WANTED: Nat Turner

The following is a description of Nat Turner that was posted on a sign advertising for his capture:

Five feet 6 or 8 inches high, weighs between 150 and 160 pounds, rather bright complexion, but not a mulatto. Broad shoulders, large flat nose, large eyes. Broad flat feet, rather knock-kneed, walks brisk and active. Hair on the top of the head very thin, no beard, except on the upper lip and at the top of the chin. A scar on one of his temples, also one at the back of his neck. A large knot on one of the bones of his right arm, near his wrist, produced [by] a blow.

Southern Anxieties

Both antislavery and proslavery southerners feared slave rebellion. The chief difference between them was in the tone in which they spoke of blacks.

Thomas Ritchie, an antislavery Virginian, said, "To attempt to excite discontent and revolt, or publish writings having this tendency, obstinately and perversely, among us, is outrageous—it ought not to be passed over with indifference. Our own safety—the good and happiness of our slaves, requires it."

By contrast, Edward D. Holland, a proslavery South Carolinian, wrote, "Let it never be forgotten that our NEGROES are truly the *Jacobins* of the country; that they are the *anarchists* and the *domestic enemy,* the *common enemy of civilized society,* and the barbarians who would, IF THEY COULD, become the DESTROYERS of our race."

would infect slaves in those states with the Haitian ideals of liberty and revolution.

In 1800, a near calamity in Richmond heightened white fears of slave rebellion. Gabriel (sometimes called Gabriel Prosser), a blacksmith slave, undoubtedly knew something about the events in Haiti. He was literate, and his daily associates were skilled tradesmen, whites and free blacks as well as slaves. Politics was a popular subject of discussion.

Just when Gabriel began to plan his own revolution is not clear, but the uprising was set for August 30, 1800. With a core of about 150, Gabriel expected hundreds more, who had heard the message, to join his army. Instructions were to kill only those who resisted, and to spare Quakers and Methodists, who were antislavery. The plan was to capture the governor (James Monroe) and key sites in the city, then to negotiate a settlement. Gabriel was neither racist nor apocalyptic. He believed poor whites would join his struggle against Virginia's aristocracy, and he was not deluded in thinking he had a chance to destroy Virginia society.

What might have happened? No one knows. Torrential rains on August 30 prevented the rebels from gathering. Individuals clearly up to no good were arrested and questioned, and Gabriel's plan was revealed. Twenty-seven of the leaders were hanged; others were sold outside of the state.

In 1822, a free black carpenter and Methodist preacher in Charleston, South Carolina, Denmark Vesey, hatched a plot to sack the city, seize ships in the harbor, and escape to Haiti, then a black republic. Vesey talked the plot up among slaves in town, including house servants, who, their owners were later shocked to learn, were not so devoted to their masters and mistresses that they did not at least listen and keep their knowledge of the plot to themselves. Vesey's chief

▲ *Nat Turner's conspiracy was not discovered before the rebellion began, as Gabriel's and Vesey's were, because he deliberately informed very few trusted friends about his plans. Turner may well have been familiar with the story of Vesey's foiled uprising. It had been just 10 years, and news of such things hummed along slave grapevines.*

lieutenant, Gullah Jack, an Angolan who attended the African Methodist Church but also practiced Angolan magic, recruited soldiers on nearby plantations. Many were also native Africans; 40,000 enslaved Africans had been rushed into South Carolina in 1807, the last year it was legal to do so.

Again it is difficult to know how many people were involved; some said hundreds, some thousands. The uprising was scheduled for June 16. An informer exposed the conspiracy on June 14, and Vesey called it off. Vesey, Gullah Jack, and 33 others were hanged.

Nat Turner

Gabriel and Vesey were rational men. Neither imagined he could extirpate his enemies. Had Gabriel successfully made captives of Governor Monroe and other prominent Virginians, it is not far-fetched to imagine a negotiated resolution of the crisis, albeit not one that freed all of Virginia's slaves. Vesey was realistic to think that, in a surprise assault, his rebels could have rampaged through Charleston, seized ships, and at least begun to sail toward Haiti.

Nat Turner, whose rebellion in August 1831 was not nipped before it began, was another type altogether. He was apocalyptic; indeed, Turner was on questionable terms with reality. Turner was an ordinary field hand in Southampton County, Virginia, who had been taught to read by his first owner. (His master in 1831 was illiterate.) He was a pious if unorthodox Baptist who pored endlessly over the Bible. He had several visions of Christ, and he heard voices, which he took as God's. When there was a solar eclipse in February 1831, Turner believed it was God's go-ahead to the slaves to rise up and kill their masters. Unlike Gabriel and Vesey, Turner had no idea what he was going to do when his rebels had started killing whites. The trouble with getting military orders from God is that if there is a snag in communications, the soldiers have big problems.

Turner was, however, shrewd enough to divulge his plans to a very few trusted friends. (Did he know of the betrayal of Vesey's Rebellion?) On the night of August 21, 1831, armed with little more than farm tools, Turner and his group swept quickly across the county, killing 60 whites and recruiting supporters from among their slaves. The murders were over in a couple of days, although it was six weeks before the last of 70 rebels were rounded up. Turner and 39 others were hanged. Others, who were acquitted of shedding blood, were sold out of the state. Word of mouth had it that, in the panic of the first days, other blacks were murdered.

Turner's Rebellion terrified slave owners, especially those who lived in the parts of Louisiana, Mississippi, and South Carolina where blacks outnumbered whites. Mary Boykin Chesnut, the wife of a planter, was not offhandedly mentioning a demographic curiosity when she described her home, Mulberry, as "half a dozen whites and sixty or seventy Negroes, miles away from the rest of the world."

White belief in black inferiority meant that some southerners were unwilling to admit that blacks, left to their own devices, were capable of mounting a rebellion like Turner's. It was no coincidence, they said, that the massacre in Southampton County followed the fiery first issue of *The Liberator* by eight months. They took note of the fact that Turner knew how to read, and they blamed white abolitionists like Garrison for the tragedy.

ENTRENCHMENT OF THE SOUTH

Once Virginians decided that the Old Dominion would remain a slave state, the South stood almost alone in the Western world. The northern states had abolished the institution of slavery. The Spanish-speaking republics of the Americas had done so too. Great Britain emancipated slaves in its colonies. In the entire Christian world, slavery survived only in the Spanish colonies of Cuba and Puerto Rico, the tiny French islands of Martinique and Guadeloupe, in a few small Portuguese enclaves, and in Brazil.

After 1832, southerners began to recognize that their slavery was what they called a "peculiar institution," almost unique to them. They moved on three fronts to protect it. They attempted to insulate the South from outside ideas that threatened slavery, and they suppressed criticism of the institution at home. Slave owners ceased to doubt themselves for clinging to slavery and to regret it to outsiders as a historical tragedy or a necessary evil; they devised the argument that slavery was a positive good that benefited slave owner, slave, and southern society as a whole. Finally, they reformed the states' slave codes (the laws that governed the "peculiar institution"), both improving the material conditions under which slaves lived and instituting stricter controls over the black population.

Suppression

Most southern states passed laws forbidding the distribution of abolitionist literature. Officials screened the federal mails and seized copies of *The Liberator*, other antislavery newspapers, and books. Georgia's legislature actually offered a reward of $5,000 to any person who would bring William Lloyd Garrison into the state to stand trial for inciting rebellion.

Even if the resolutions were meant to be symbolic, a state legislature's willingness to sanction kidnapping illustrates the depth of bitterness in the South toward abolitionists. Only in border states like Maryland and Kentucky could native abolitionists like John Gregg Fee and Cassius Marcellus Clay speak their piece without fear of anything worse than heckling and harassment. Elsewhere in the South, the expression of antislavery opinions was no longer acceptable.

Even in Washington, D.C.—where slavery was legal—the expression of abolitionist ideas became unacceptable. Beginning in 1836, southern congressmen annually nagged the House of Representatives to adopt a rule providing that every petition to the House dealing with slavery be tabled (that is, set aside without discussion). Former president John Quincy Adams, now a member of Congress, argued that this gag rule violated the right to free speech. Quincy Adams considered

Pork

Southerners ate beef; so did northerners. But it was by no means the most abundant meat of the early nineteenth century, as it is today, when we consume 2 pounds of it for every pound of our second favorite, pork, including bacon and ham.

Pork was the favorite, by far. Indeed, according to *Godey's Lady's Book*—the combination *Ladies Home Journal, Ms.,* and *Vogue* of the era:

> The United States of America might properly be called the great Hog-eating Confederacy, or the Republic of Porkdom. [In the] South and West . . . it is fat bacon and pork, fat bacon and pork only, and that continually morning, noon, and night, for all classes, sexes, ages, and conditions; and except the boiled bacon and collards at dinner, the meat is generally fried, and thus supersaturated with grease in the form of hog's lard.

Slaves on well-managed plantations were provided half a pound of salt pork a day. All but very poor whites surely consumed more.

Beef was less common—first of all, because it was much more expensive than it is today. Cattle had to be transported on the hoof, which meant that cities could be supplied only from the near hinterland. Farmers of such land could do better cultivating their land than leaving it in pasture. Only with the settlement of the Great Plains after the Civil War did the price of beef decline. Even then, in 1900, Americans ate as much pork as beef.

Unlike cattle, hogs flourished on wasteland—even scavenging on city streets—multiplying their weight 150 times in eight months on nuts and roots, fallen orchard fruit, whatever remained in harvested gardens and grain fields, and garbage. They required next to no attention. Indeed, American razorback hogs, those "bony, snake-headed, hairy wild beasts," needed no protection. (A farmer's fields and the farmer himself needed protection from them!)

Hogs were ideally suited to a nation where land was abundant and labor scarce, and they thrived. As early as 1705, Robert Beverley wrote in his *History of Virginia* that "hogs swarm like Vermine upon the Earth, and are often accounted such . . . [that] When an Inventory of any considerable Man's Estate is taken, the Hogs are left out." In the southern states in 1850, there were two hogs for each human being.

Hogs had another recommendation over steers. They could be slaughtered where they were raised, butchered on the spot, and cheaply preserved in salty brine in barrels, keeping for a year or more. Salt deposits were important to pioneers because of the necessity of preserving pork. Cities on the Ohio and Mississippi Rivers like Cincinnati and St. Louis owed much of their growth to their role as meat packers. The poor, certainly including slaves, owed their survival to salt pork. "I hold a family to be in a desperate way," a character in a James Fenimore Cooper novel put it, "when the mother can see the bottom of the pork barrel."

"Scraping the bottom of the barrel" is not the only catchphrase that survives from the days of the Republic of Porkdom. We still use the term "pork barrel bill" to describe those congressional acts, usually rushed through at the end of a session, that spend federal money in just about every district in which incumbents from the majority party are up for election—a highway improvement here, an agricultural station there, a defense installation somewhere else. The phrase conveys an image once familiar to every American—the none-too-attractive appearance of chunks of pork bobbing about in a barrel of scummy brine.

---

zealots like Walker and Garrison and most other abolitionists irresponsible and destructive. But he insisted on their constitutional right to have their opinions heard. For this, and because he criticized white southerners for quashing the right to petition Congress and be heard, the lifelong nationalist came to be lumped with the abolitionists as an enemy.

A Positive Good

Shortly after Virginia's debate on the future of slavery, a professor of economics at the College of William and Mary, Thomas Roderick Dew, published a systematic defense of slavery. He said that as a means of organizing and controlling labor, it was superior to the system of free wage workers that prevailed in the North and Europe. By 1837, southern preachers and politicians were parroting and expanding on Dew's theories. In the Senate, John C. Calhoun declared that compared with other systems by which racial and class relationships were governed, "The relation now existing in the slave holding states is, instead of an evil, a good—a positive good."

The proslavery argument incorporated religious, historical, cultural, and social proofs of the justice and beneficence of the institution. The Bible, the positive-good propagandists argued, clearly sanctioned slavery. Not only did the ancient Hebrews own slaves with God's blessing, but Christ had told a servant (a slave) who wanted to follow him that he should return to his master. It was his obligation to do so.

Dew and others pointed out that the great, universally admired civilizations of antiquity, Greece and Rome, were slaveholding societies. Hardly barbaric, slavery had served as the foundation of high cultures since the beginning of recorded time. Slavery made possible the existence of a gracious and cultured upper class that, with its leisure, preserved the highest refinements of human achievement.

Southern planters took pride in the fact that, although elementary and secondary education in the South was inferior to that provided by the public school systems of the North, more upper-class southerners were college educated than members of the northern elite were. Even as late as 1860, there were more than 6,000 college students in Geor-

Race in Scripture

Defenders of slavery were hard pressed when abolitionists quoted the Bible on the equality of all men and women before God. A few went so far as to answer that blacks were a different species from whites.

Southerners were more comfortable when they picked the biblical passages. They quoted the story of Noah's son Ham, who had humiliated his father. Noah cursed him: "A servant of servants shall he be unto his brethren." Africans were human beings, proslavery southerners agreed, but their blackness was "the mark of Ham." As Ham's descendants, they were doomed by God to be (borrowing from another source) "hewers of wood and drawers of water."

Consistency

When abolitionists quoted the Declaration of Independence—"all men are created equal"—the southerners were generally forced to make convoluted interpretations of the phrase in order to excuse slavery. John C. Calhoun was consistent. "Taking the proposition literally," he said, "there is not a word of truth in it."

George Fitzhugh, Sociologist

But did all these proofs justify denying personal freedom to human beings? Yes, answered George Fitzhugh, a Virginia lawyer, in two influential books: *A Sociology for the South* (1854) and *Cannibals All!* (1857). Fitzhugh amassed statistics and other evidence with which he argued that the southern slave lived a better life than did the northern wage worker or the European peasant.

Like Dew and Calhoun, Fitzhugh argued that, in every society, someone had to perform the drudgery. In the South, menial work was done by slaves who were cared for from cradle to grave. Not only did the slave owner feed, clothe, and house his workers, but he also supported slave children, the injured and the disabled, and the elderly—all of whom were nonproductive. Fitzhugh delighted to point out that by comparison, the northern wage worker was paid only as long as there was work to be done and the worker was fit to do it. The wage worker who was injured was cut loose to fend for

gia, Alabama, and Mississippi but fewer than 4,000 in the New England states, which were more populous.

As an aristocracy, southerners said, the planters were closer to the tradition of the gentlemanly Founding Fathers than were the vulgar, money-grubbing capitalists of the North. Because gentlemen dominated politics in the South, the section was far better governed than was the North, where demagogues won elections by playing on the whims and passions of the dregs of society. Some planters liked to think of themselves as descended from the cavaliers of seventeenth-century England. The South's favorite author was Sir Walter Scott, who spun tales of knighthood and chivalry.

▲ *Currier & Ives, publishers of prints for home decoration, was a northern company. In depicting a cotton plantation in the Deep South, the publishers presented an idyll of slaves picking cotton (and not working too hard) and a well-dressed white man (the planter) completely at ease as he explains the work to a lady. The dreamland scene would have appealed to "positive-good" southerners, and the print undoubtedly sold well in the North too.*

▲ *The "quarters" of a plantation near the coast in South Carolina. The slaves' cabins are ruder than cabins on some other planta-*
tions, but much better than most, with sound walls, good roofs, and brick chimneys. In the 1840s, magazines catering to slave
owners published plans for slave cabins.

himself. His children, the elderly, and the incompetent were
no responsibility of capitalist employers.

Consequently, Fitzhugh said, the North was plagued by
social problems unknown in the South. The North teemed
with nattering reformers. The lower classes were irreligious
and, in their misery, drunken and tumultuous. The free working class was tempted by socialistic, communistic, and other
doctrines that threatened the social order. By comparison,
Fitzhugh claimed, southern slaves were contented, indeed
happy. "A merrier being does not exist on the face of the
globe," Fitzhugh wrote, "than the Negro slave of the United
States."

Management

Fitzhugh equated happiness with the material conditions of
slave life—housing, clothing, diet—and compared them favorably with the conditions under which the poorest wage
workers of the North lived. By the 1850s, when he wrote,
most southern state legislatures had, in fact, defined minimum living standards as part of their slave codes. Magazines like the *Southern Agriculturalist* featured exchanges
among slave owners about how well they treated their people and what kinds of improvements were desirable.

The most obvious reason for keeping slaves adequately
housed, clothed, and fed was practical: a healthy slave
worked more efficiently and was less likely to rebel or run
away. Also underlying the trend toward improvement in the
conditions of slave life after the 1830s was the South's

determination to show that the abolitionists' depiction of
slavery as a life of unrelenting horror was a lie. Planters who
provided decent accommodations for their slaves took pleasure in showing "the quarters," as slave communities were
called, to northern or foreign visitors. They reassured themselves that they were just the beneficent patriarchs that the
positive-good writers described.

Control

Less likely to be trumpeted were the measures of control
that were devised in the wake of Turner's Rebellion. By
1840, the states of the Deep South had adopted laws that
made it extremely difficult for a slave owner to manumit his
slaves. Even Virginia, where manumission had been honored, required recently freed blacks to leave the state (although this law was impossible to enforce effectively). It
was also a crime in some southern states to teach a slave to
read: Gabriel, Vesey, and Turner had all been literate and, in
fact, voracious readers.

County governments were required to fund and maintain slave patrols. These mounted posses of armed whites
policed the roads and plantations, particularly at night. They
had the legal right to break into slave cabins or demand at
gunpoint that any black (or white) account for himself or
herself. Usually rough, hard-bitten men who were so poor
that they sorely needed the undesirable job, the "paddy-
rollers" (patrollers) were brutal even with unoffending
slaves. Blacks hated and feared them. Their mere presence

and unbridled arrogance cast a cloud of repression over the plantation regions that few outsiders failed to notice.

Blacks who were not under the direct supervision of their masters or overseers were required by law to carry written passes that gave them permission to be abroad, even just a mile or two from their cabins. Free blacks—there were about 250,000 in the South by 1860, 1 to every 15 slaves—had to carefully protect the documentary evidence of their status. Kidnappings of free blacks and sale of them as slaves elsewhere in the South were far from unknown.

The presence of free blacks presented a serious ideological problem for slave owners. One of the most effective means of controlling slaves was to convince them that God and nature intended them to be slaves because of their race and that they should be thankful to be under the care of their masters. But if slaves saw free blacks prospering, the argument disintegrated, and slave owners knew it. Slave owners also believed that free blacks were likely to stir up discontent among slaves, and they were probably right.

Religion, which had inspired the Vesey and Turner rebellions, could also be an effective means of control. Vesey had been a member of a large, independent African Methodist Episcopal Church. After 1830, careful masters paid close attention to the kind of preaching their people heard. Some owners took their slaves to their own churches, where the minister was expected, now and then, to deliver a sermon based on biblical stories such as that of Hagar: "The angel of the Lord said unto her, return to Thy mistress, and submit thyself under her hands." Other masters permitted the blacks, who preferred an emotional Christianity peppered with vestiges of West African religion (Gullah Jack's Methodism plus magic charms), to have preachers of their own race. But these often eloquent men were instructed—specifically or indirectly—to steer clear of topics that might cast doubt on the rightness of slavery. And they were monitored.

Some toed the line. Others conveyed their protest by placing heavy emphasis on the ancient Israelites' bondage in Egypt and Babylon—and their ultimate deliverance. The idealized institution of John C. Calhoun and George Fitzhugh bore only an accidental relationship to slavery as it actually existed.

for FURTHER READING

On the South and its distinctive characteristics, see Avery O. Craven, *The Growth of Southern Nationalism, 1848–1860,* 1953; Clement Eaton, *The Growth of Southern Civilization,* 1961, and *A History of the Old South,* 1975; I. A. Newby, *The American South,* 1979; and Charles S. Sydnor, *The Development of Southern Sectionalism, 1819–1848,* 1948. Few historians today would subscribe to the conclusions in Wilbur Cash, *The Mind of the South,* 1940, and yet it contains many perceptive insights. A contemporary "travel book" about the Old South well worth reading is Frederick Law Olmstead, *The Cotton Kingdom,* 1861.

Of more specific concern but vital to understanding the subject are Edward A. Ayers, *Vengeance and Justice: Crime and Punishment in the Nineteenth-Century American South,* 1984; Dickson D. Bruce, *Violence and Culture in the Antebellum South,* 1979; Victoria E. Bynum, *Unruly Women: The Politics of Social and Sexual Control in the Old South,* 1992; William J. Cooper, *The South and the Politics of Slavery, 1828–1856,* 1978; Elizabeth Fox-Genovese, *Within the Plantation Household,* 1988; John Hope Franklin, *The Militant South,* 1956; Eugene Genovese, *The Political Economy of Slavery,* 1962, and *The World the Slave Holders Made,* 1969; Patrick Gerster and William Cords, eds., *Myth and Image in Southern History,* 1974; Lewis C. Gray, *History of Agriculture in the Southern United States to 1860,* 1933; James Oakes, *The Ruling Race: A History of American Slave Holders,* 1982; Frank Owsley, *Plain Folk of the Old South,* 1949; William R. Taylor, *Cavalier and Yankee: The Old South and American National Character,* 1961; and Gavin Wright, *The Political Economy of the Cotton South,* 1978.

American Journey AMERICAN JOURNEY ONLINE AND INFOTRAC COLLEGE EDITION

Visit the source collections at http://ajaccess.wadsworth.com and http://infotrac.thomsonlearning.com, and use the Search function with the following key terms to explore documents, images, audio and video clips, articles, and commentary related to the material in this chapter:

Abolitionism	Nat Turner
Denmark Vesey	William Lloyd Garrison

Additional resources, exercises, and Internet links related to this chapter are available on *The American Past* Web site:
http://history.wadsworth.com/americanpast7e.

HISTORY ONLINE

Maps of Liberia 1830–1870
http://memory.loc.gov/ammem/gmdhtml/libhtml/libhome.html
Contemporary maps and other information about the early development of the African country planned to be a refuge for freed American slaves.

Turner's Rebellion
www.bigchalk.com/cgibin/WebObjects/WOPortal.woa/
Homework/High_School/History/History_by_Chronology/19th_
Century/Nat_Turner's_Rebellion_64167.html
Documents, sources, and links concerning Nat Turner's uprising.

19

THE PECULIAR INSTITUTION

Slavery as It Was Perceived and as It Was

Oppression has, at one stroke, deprived the descendants of the Africans of almost all the privileges of humanity. The Negro of the United States has lost all remembrance of his country; the language which his forefathers spoke is never heard around him; he abjured their religion and forgot their customs when he ceased to belong to Africa, without acquiring any European privileges. But he remains halfway between the two communities; sold by the one, repulsed by the other; finding not a spot in the universe to call by the name of country, except the faint image of a home which the shelter of his master's roof affords.

Alexis de Tocqueville

I N 1865, THE Thirteenth Amendment to the Constitution, just 43 words, wrought a more fundamental change in America than any other amendment. In stating that "neither slavery nor involuntary servitude . . . shall exist within the United States," the Thirteenth Amendment eliminated "the great exception," an institution that mocked the ideals that Americans endlessly proclaimed, made their nation special in the world: individual freedom, justice for all, and equality of opportunity.

IMAGES OF SLAVERY

Two images of slavery, one reeking of romance, the other rife with horror, contended for possession of the American mind after about 1830, when Garrison's *Liberator* and Turner's Rebellion forced most Americans to come to personal conclusions about the institution. The seeds of the romantic vision of the South were planted by the positive-good theorists and nurtured by the sentimentality that permeated American popular culture. The other image, slavery as horror, was cultivated by abolitionists who drew on their personal experiences and observations, and on information that was sometimes distorted. In a cause commissioned by God, restraint had no place, as Garrison said so vividly.

Minstrel Shows

Entertainers catering to ordinary folk—jugglers, sleight-of-hand artists, musicians, singers, dancers—worked both in cities and on tour, one-night stands in saloons and small-town theaters. Their acts were bawdy, broadly comic, and sentimental. In Louisville in 1830, one of them, Thomas D.

▲ *Publicity for a minstrel show. The players are exuberant, simple, idle, ecstatically happy. So popular were the shows that during the 1850s, there were 100 different minstrel troupes.*

"Daddy" Rice, had a brainstorm. He imitated a dance he had seen a ragged African American perform on the street for pennies.

The dance was called "Jumpin' Jim Crow," and the audience loved it. It became the centerpiece of Daddy's act and had dozens of imitators. By the 1840s, "Ethiopian songs," sung in southern Negro dialect by white men who had blacked their faces, were so popular that a songwriter, Daniel D. Emmett, and an impresario, Edwin P. Christy, organized competing troupes of "minstrels" who put on three-act musical shows following a standardized format. Act 2 was most popular. The minstrels sat in a line across the stage. In the center was the master of ceremonies, "Mr. Interlocutor." He wore no blackface and spoke in a stilted upper-class accent, often an English accent. There were two "end men," "Brother Tambo" (he played a tambourine) and "Brother Bones" (his instrument was "the bones"—two hog ribs). Brother Tambo was a dim-witted plantation slave often called "Jim Crow." The other was a black city slicker, a dandy, called "Zip Coon." Between songs and dances by members of the ensemble, they insulted one another and Mr. Interlocutor with broad comedy.

The makeup and dialect were grotesque and are now seen as racist stereotypes of African Americans. Stereotypes they were, but the minstrel show was not vicious. The characters were good-natured, some lovable. Even Zip Coon, a con man, was comical rather than wicked, his schemes to bilk Mr. Tambo foiled by his own bumbling. At the same time, the blackface characters were stupid, lazy, or childlike, comfortably affirming white convictions that African Americans were their inferiors. Implicitly, there was nothing in the lives of the characters on the plantations, the setting of the minstrel shows, that detracted from their carefree lives.

Stephen Foster and the Sweet Magnolia

The minstrel show depiction of African Americans was not created by proslavery southerners. Emmett and Christy were northerners. Emmett's father was a prominent abolitionist. Christy's minstrels packed a large theater in New York for 2,500 performances. Stephen Foster, who wrote more and better "Ethiopian songs" than Emmett, was from Pittsburgh and had no interest in seeing the South. In fact, Foster disliked the "trashy and really offensive words" of many blackface songs and stopped writing in dialect.

His compositions humanized slaves; there was nothing condescending about the sentiments they expressed; they were the same sentiments in the popular novels of the day. Foster's first hit, "Oh Susannah" (1849), was a nonsense song about two lovers; stripped of racial allusions, it became the anthem of the California Gold Rush. "Old Black Joe" (1860) was an old man's lament appealing to every sentimentalist over the age of 60.

Foster's contribution to the romantic myth of the plantation South lay in the fact that he did not remotely question the legitimacy of slavery and created a relationship between "Ol' Massa" and his slaves that was mutually warm and caring. In "Old Folks at Home" (1851), a slave far from "de old plantation" (a runaway?) wearily wishes he were home. In "Massa's in de Cold, Cold Ground" (1852), all the dead man's slaves are weeping that their master had been kind. The carefree "darky," the grand house, Spanish moss hanging from the oaks, the plunking of the banjo, the sweet scent of magnolia blossoms, and an easy, languid life were the ingredients of Foster's world.

Garrison on the Constitution

William Lloyd Garrison broke few, if any, laws unrelated to slavery. But his thoughts on the Constitution were less than patriotic. He called it "a covenant with death and an agreement with hell" because, however evasively, it sanctioned slavery:

A sacred compact, forsooth! We pronounce it the most heaven-daring arrangement ever made for the continuance and protection of a system of the most atrocious villainy ever exhibited on earth.

Statements like this one explain why many earnest abolitionists gave Garrison a wide berth.

Old Sturbridge Village, photo by Henry E. Peach

▲ *There was nothing romantic about the South the abolitionists pictured: Slavery produced a society of torturers, brawlers, murderers, lynch mobs, drunken gamblers, duelists, and men who whipped children.*

Within a generation after the Civil War, this vision of antebellum southern life was embraced by most white Americans. In the industrial age of the late nineteenth century, paced by the relentless drive of the machine, it was consoling to dream nostalgically of a South that, however imaginary, had been its antithesis. The tradition culminated in Margaret Mitchell's novel of 1936, *Gone with the Wind,* and Hollywood's classic film based on the book.

Theodore Dwight Weld and His Converts

Abolitionists saw another slavery. To zealous black and white lecturers, journalists, and preachers who crisscrossed the northern states, the slave's world was a hell of blacksnake whips, brutal slave catchers and bloodhounds, children torn from their mothers' breasts to be sold, squalor, disease, and near starvation under callous, arrogant masters, the "slavocrats."

William Lloyd Garrison was not alone in presenting this image to northerners. Indeed, because of his rasping self-righteousness, Garrison was probably less effective in the assault on slavery than abolitionists like Theodore Dwight Weld, a white evangelical "as eloquent as an angel and powerful as thunder." No demagogue, Weld concentrated on converting prominent people to the antislavery cause. Two of his proselytes, Arthur and Lewis Tappan, were wealthy New York merchants who generously financed abolitionist institutions like Kenyon and Oberlin Colleges in Ohio, hotbeds of abolition, and the American Anti-Slavery Society, founded in 1833.

Another Weld convert was James G. Birney, an Alabama planter who freed his slaves and ran as the presidential candidate of the antislavery Liberty party in 1840 and 1844. Weld married an abolitionist who had owned slaves, Angelina Grimké of South Carolina. She and her sister Sarah instilled in him a perspective on the problem of slavery that was beyond Garrison, consideration for the moral plight of the conscientious slave owner.

Black Abolitionists

Although the abolitionist movement would have foundered without whites, its most dependable supporters were the North's free blacks. Although generally poor, African Americans contributed a disproportionate part of the money needed to publish antislavery newspapers and send antislavery lecturers on their tours.

Several of the most prominent abolitionists were black. Sojourner Truth was the name adopted by Isabella Van Wagenen, a physical giant of a woman born a slave in New York in 1797. Freed in 1827, she worked as a domestic servant, was briefly a Millerite, then burst on the abolitionist scene as one of the movement's most powerful orators. Sojourner Truth was illiterate to the end—she died in 1893, at 96—but she transfixed audiences, accompanying her speeches with songs she had herself composed.

The most distinguished of the black abolitionists was Frederick Douglass. Born a slave in Maryland, he escaped to Massachusetts, educated himself as well as Harvard educated most of its graduates, and, in 1845, wrote his autobi-

▲ *There was nothing imagined, exaggerated, or contrived in this abolitionist photograph of a slave who had been whipped.*

ography. For a while, because his former master was pursuing him, Douglass lived in England, where he furthered his education and earned enough money to pay his master off. Douglass's effectiveness stemmed from his eloquence, forthright unembellished prose, refinement, and, most of all, firsthand knowledge of life in a slave society.

Mrs. Stowe and Uncle Tom

To people of Douglass's caliber, the decisive antislavery argument was that slavery reduced human beings, God's children, to the status of livestock. That point, however, did not lend itself to emotional appeals. So, black and white abolitionists both focused on the deprivations and cruelties suffered by slaves. Some antislavery lecturers traveled with runaway slaves whose backs had been disfigured by brutal whippings.

The single most effective abolitionist shot was *Uncle Tom's Cabin, or Life Among the Lowly,* written by Harriet Beecher Stowe, the member of a distinguished family. Not only did Stowe's book sell an astonishing 300,000 copies within a year of publication (the equivalent of selling more than 3 million today), but it was adapted into plays performed by professional and amateur troupes in small towns and cities alike. So influential was Stowe's tale of Uncle Tom, a submissive and loyal old slave, that when Abraham Lincoln met her during the Civil War, he remarked, "So you are the little woman who wrote the book that made this great war."

The underlying theme of *Uncle Tom's Cabin* is that no matter how well intentioned an individual slave owner is, he cannot help but do wrong by living with an inherently evil institution. Uncle Tom's owner at the beginning is the epitome of the paternalistic planter beloved of positive-good theorists and minstrels. He genuinely loves Uncle Tom. Nevertheless, when financial troubles require him to raise money, he sells Tom. Heartbroken, he promises that, as soon as he is able, he will find Tom and buy him back. The point is that the noblest of white men sells the best of black men when the law says that he may do so.

It was not this insight that made *Uncle Tom's Cabin* so popular. The book owed its success to the lurid cruelties that Tom witnesses and suffers. Stowe herself thought that this was the book's contribution. When southerners complained that she had distorted the realities of slave life, she responded in 1853 with *A Key to Uncle Tom's Cabin,* which set out the documentary basis of her allegations in quotations from southern newspapers.

WHAT SLAVERY WAS LIKE

Which image is correct? Both and neither. Proslavery and antislavery partisans dealt with the "peculiar institution" as though it were monolithic, the same in Virginia and Texas, on cotton plantations and the New Orleans riverfront, on sprawling plantations and cramped frontier homesteads, for field hand and big-house butler. In the law—the classification of human beings as property—it was one and the same thing. The experience of slavery, however, was as diverse as the South.

Structure of the Institution: White Perspective

The census of 1860, the last taken when slavery was legal, reveals that nearly 4 million people lived in bondage, equally divided between males and females. All but a few lived in the 15 states south of the Mason-Dixon line and the Ohio River. West of the Mississippi River, Missouri, Arkansas, Louisiana, and Texas were slave states. A few Indians in Indian Territory (Oklahoma) owned slaves.

One white southern family in four owned slaves. Even when those whose living depended directly on the existence of the institution—overseers, slave traders, patrollers—are added in, only a minority of white southerners had a material stake in slavery.

The great planter class (the only slave owners in the world of the minstrels) was quite small. In 1860, only 2,200 people, less than 1 percent of the southern population, owned 100 or more slaves. Only 254 owned 200 slaves or more. Nathaniel Heyward of South Carolina was at the top of the pyramid, owning 2,000 slaves on 17 plantations.

Washington the Slave Owner

At the time of his death in 1799, George Washington owned 300 slaves at Mount Vernon and other plantations. The record of the father of his country as a patriarch was mixed. On the one hand, according to a visitor from Poland, the slaves' houses at Washington's River Farm were "more miserable than the most miserable cottages of our peasants." (Washington expressed embarrassment over living conditions at River Farm.)

On the other hand, Washington respected his slaves' family and marriage relationships. Children remained with their mothers until age 14. Slave husbands and wives were separated when one but not the other was needed elsewhere, and some of Washington's slaves were married to the slaves of other planters or to free blacks. However, Washington meticulously recorded who was tied to whom, and he refused to sell surplus slaves "because they could not be disposed of in families" and, he said, "to disperse the families I have an aversion."

Washington's plantations were within four miles of one another and "nightwalking," conjugal visits, were an annoyance of which he complained but about which he did little. In his will, Washington provided that his slaves be freed only after his wife's death because they had intermarried with Martha Washington's "Dower Negroes" and it "would excite the most painful sensations" if they were to be separated.

More typical of the southern slave owner was Jacob Eaton of North Carolina. On his 160-acre farm, he worked side by side with the slave family he owned. Eaton's yeoman class—small independent farmers who owned from none to nine slaves—was the backbone of both the South and the slavery system. About 74 percent of slave owners fell into this category. Another 16 percent of slave owners owned between 10 and 20 people. A mere 10 percent of slave owners owned more than 20 slaves.

Structure of the Institution: Black Perspective

If the big plantation was rare from a white perspective, life in the shadow of the big house was more common in African American lives. By 1860, more than half the South's slaves lived on what we would think of as a plantation rather than a farm. Half a million, one in eight, belonged to members of the great planter class.

There were black slave owners. The census of 1830 revealed 3,775 free African Americans in possession of 12,760 slaves. One curious case was Dilsey Pope, a free black woman of Columbus, Georgia, who owned her husband. The two had a fierce quarrel and Mrs. Pope sold him to a white neighbor. When the couple reconciled, the new owner refused to sell Mrs. Pope's husband back. Their marriage had no standing in Georgia law, so the couple was without recourse.

There were a handful of black great planters, most in Louisiana. Andrew Durnford of New Orleans owned 77 slaves. When questioned, Durnford said that owning slaves was self-interest. It was the only way to wealth in the South. Although he contributed to the American Colonization Society, Durnford freed only four slaves during his lifetime, one other in his will.

First Light to Sundown

Few blacks enjoyed the advantages of living as domestic servants: better food, clothing, and beds. Cooks, maids, butlers, valets, and footmen made life pleasanter for the great planters who could afford them, but they did not make money for their masters. The vast majority of slaves were field hands who raised a cash crop by means of heavy labor from first light to sundown almost year-round. For a slave owner to justify investing capital in a labor force rather than hiring free laborers, it was necessary to keep the property hopping.

Cotton was by far the most important southern product—in fact, the most important American product. During the 1850s, an average annual crop of 4 million bales brought more than $190 million into the American economy from abroad. Cotton represented two-thirds of the nation's total exports and (in 1850) employed fully 1.8 million slaves out of 3.2 million. In 1860, the 12 richest counties in the United States were cotton counties. Other cash crops dependent on slave labor were tobacco (350,000 slaves); sugar (150,000 slaves); rice (125,000 slaves); and hemp (60,000 slaves), from which rope and sacking for cotton bales were made.

Southern farmers and planters strove to be self-sufficient. Therefore, slaves raised corn, vegetables, and hogs for food, and hay for fodder, as well as the cash crop. There was plenty of work to be done on a farm or plantation year-round. Thomas Jefferson heated Monticello with 10 cords of wood a month in winter: a lot of chopping. The calendar of a cotton plantation was packed with jobs, major and odd, except for a short period around Christmas, to which the slaves looked forward as "laying-by time."

King Cotton

Southern politicians repeatedly lectured northerners that the South supported the national economy. That is, the money that cotton brought in from abroad provided most of the surplus capital that paid for the industrialization of the nation. This transaction was direct when protective tariffs on English-made goods forced southerners to buy American-made goods.

The politicians were right. Cotton did industrialize the United States before the Civil War. However, northern antislavery people had another way of considering this economic fact of life. Who, they asked, really produced the cotton? To a large extent, slaves did. And to that extent, the United States was industrialized by the forced labor of the blacks.

▲ *The life a majority of slaves knew: picking cotton. Never was the work harder and the pressure greater; the cotton had to be under cover before the fall rains. Every slave was sent to the fields, including house servants and children barely able to walk. There was no skill involved, just hot, hard labor.*

Because slaves were expensive—by the 1850s, $2,000 for a prime field hand (a healthy male in his 20s or early 30s)—planters preferred to hire free blacks or Irish immigrants for unhealthy and dangerous jobs. Few risked their costly human property on draining swamps or working at the bottom of chutes down which 600-pound bales of cotton came hurtling at high speeds. It was a lot cheaper to give the widow of a dead employee a five-dollar gold piece.

The Rhythms of Labor

By the 1850s, a slave produced from $80 to $120 in wealth each year and cost between $30 and $50 to feed, clothe, and shelter. The margin of profit was not large enough to allow the small-scale slave owner to live without working in the fields along with his slaves.

Planters who owned 10 to 20 slaves were freed of menial tasks; but, because few slaves worked any harder than they were forced to (their share of the fruits of their labor was fixed), they had to be supervised constantly: bribed, cajoled, threatened, or whipped. If a man owned more than 20 slaves, he could afford to hire an overseer or put a slave driver (himself a slave) in charge. On the large plantations, masters had little contact with their field hands.

Slaves on large plantations worked according to the task system or the gang system. Under the task system, a specific job was assigned to each slave each day. When it was done, the slave's time was his or her own. For some planters, this was the most efficient form of organization because, when provided with an incentive, however meager, the slaves worked harder. Other planters complained that the task system resulted in slipshod work, as the slaves rushed so as to get to their own chores or recreation.

Under the gang system, slaves worked from sunrise to sundown in groups under a white overseer or black driver. Who knows how frequently they felt the sting of the whip? The lash was always in evidence, however, whether in a black hand or a white one. Frederick Douglass remarked that

The Health of Slaves

In an age when nothing was known of scientific nutrition, the slaves' diet was comparable to that of poor southern whites and free blacks, and likely better on plantations where slaves were permitted to keep gardens. The life expectancy of slaves was the same as that of free blacks and whites in the South. Statistical surveys done about 1860 showed southern slaves averaging 3 inches more in height than West Africans, 2 inches more than Trinidadians, and an inch more than British marines.

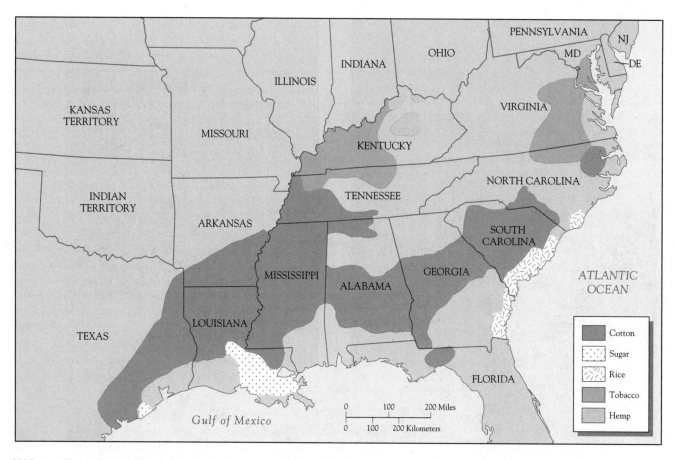

MAP 19:1 **Major Crops of the South, 1860** Cotton was king in the South, but tobacco and rice were still profitable and Louisiana's sugar immensely so. Hemp (for making rope and sacking) was a minor crop, grown mostly in Kentucky and sold mostly in the cotton-growing South.

"everybody in the South wants the privilege of whipping someone else."

Slave Traders

Slaves were defined in law as chattel property—personal possessions legally much the same as cattle, hogs, a necklace, a cotton press, a chair, or a share of stock. They could be bought, sold, bartered, willed, or given away. The commerce in slaves was brisk and profitable.

Even defenders of slavery admitted that the slave trade was ugly. The slave auction was a livestock auction plus coarse sexual joking. Prospective buyers crowded around the auction block, determining the age of the slaves for sale by examining their teeth, as they would do when buying a horse. Slaves were forced to run to test their wind. Buyers wiped their bodies with rags to determine if the auctioneer had dyed gray hair black or rubbed oil into aged dry skin. If adolescent girls were for sale, sexual innuendos amused the crowd. Foreigners, northerners, and many southerners were simultaneously disgusted and fascinated by slave auctions, much as American tourists in Mexico today react to bullfights.

Masters aspiring to be patriarchs disapproved of the slave trade, describing traders as base, crude, unworthy men. Nevertheless, as Harriet Beecher Stowe and others pointed out, with-

out the slave trade, there could be no slavery. If some humans were to be property, owners had to be free to buy and sell them. Where there is trade, there are brokers.

The general flow of the commerce was "down the river"—the Mississippi—from the older, declining tobacco states to the cotton states of the Deep South. Professional slave traders purchased blacks in Virginia, Maryland, and Kentucky, and marched them, like their African ancestors, in coffles to Memphis or New Orleans, where as many as 200 companies were in the business.

LIFE IN THE QUARTERS

The slave codes of most southern states provided that slaves had no civil rights. They could not own property under the law; therefore, they could not legally buy and sell anything. They could not make contracts. They could not marry legally. (If they could, a planter could not sell a woman without her husband.) They could not testify in court against any white person (nor could free blacks in some southern states). They could not leave the plantation without written permission.

It was a crime for a slave to strike a white person under any circumstances, even to save his life. Slaves could not carry firearms. They could not congregate in more than

▲ *A slave auction in St. Louis. There is much more decorum in this depiction than there is in the accounts of northerners and foreign-ers who witnessed auctions. If some buyers were, no doubt, as well dressed as the gentlemen here, not everyone in attendance was.*

small groups except at religious services under white super-vision. They could not be abroad at night. And in most southern states, it was a crime for a white or another black to teach a slave to read.

The slaves' rights were those to life and, under most slave codes, a minimum standard of food, clothing, and shelter.

Humans Without Human Rights

The actual experience of slave life often deviated from the letter of the slave codes. For example, a master could not legally kill his slave, but it was not considered murder when a slave died during "moderate" or "reasonable" correction, words highly debatable in court. Whipping was the most common form of corporal punishment, and 50 lashes—quite enough to kill a man—was not an uncommon punishment. This was hardly "moderate." In the end, the slaves' only guar-antees against brutality at the hands of their masters were the gospel of paternalism, social expectations of the master by his peers, religious scruples, and the slaves' cash value.

There are few better guarantees of a man's good behav-ior than his knowledge that bad behavior will cost him money. But that applies to men who are thinking. Slave own-ers (and surely their overseers) flew into uncontrolled rages

and killed slaves. Because their property rights in their slaves almost always took precedence in court over the slaves' human rights, owners were rarely punished for such crimes. After an incident of hideous torture in Virginia in 1858, with a slave dying after 24 hours of beating and burning, the court punished the sadistic master by imprisoning him. But he did not forfeit ownership of the other blacks he owned.

A Diverse Institution

If the laws protecting slaves were not effective, many slave owners were moved by their religion, their sense of decency, and by their aspiration to be seen as benevolent patriarchs to care generously for their slaves, even in violation of the slave codes.

A family that owned only one or two slaves occasion-ally developed a relationship much like partnership with them. Some white owners and black slaves ate the same food, slept in the same cabin, and worked together inti-mately. However, the slave on a large plantation was likely to be better off than the slave on a small farm because of the poverty of the marginal small farmer.

After about 1840, large-scale slave owners generally pro-vided adequate rations of cornmeal, salt pork, and molasses. It

Slave trader, Sold to Tennessee,

Arise! Arise! and weep no more
dry up your tears, we shall part
no more, come rose we go to
Tennessee,
that happy shore to old virginia
never — never — return. —

the Company going to Tennessee from Staunton Augusta
County, — the law of virginia Suffered them to go on.
I was Astonished at this boldness, the carrier Stopped
a moment, then Ordered the march, I saw the play it is
commonly in this State, with the negro's, in droves Sold,

▲ *A familiar sight in the South: slaves from Virginia marching to the cotton lands of western Tennessee. The unfortunates in this watercolor by an eyewitness are, at least, not hobbled, perhaps because they are family groups. Coffles of young men—"prime field hands"—sold down the river were often chained.*

was common to allow slaves to keep their own vegetable plots of several acres and even chickens. Some masters did not keep their own gardens and coops but purchased vegetables and eggs from their slaves. They concluded, sensibly, that if both master and slave were in the vegetable and chicken businesses, no one could tell from where the slaves' dinners came. For the same reason, very few slave owners allowed slaves to raise hogs for their own use. Pork was one of the staples; the planter needed to control its production and distribution.

Some slaves were permitted to buy and sell beyond the boundaries of the plantation and to keep the money they earned. Along the Mississippi, task-system slaves working on their own time cut wood for the steamboats. Some sold chickens and eggs in towns, and here and there, a slave had a shot-

gun for hunting. One remarkable slave entrepreneur was Simon Gray, a skilled flatboat sailor whose owner paid him $8 a month to haul lumber to New Orleans. Gray commanded crews of up to 20 men, including free whites, and kept detailed accounts. He eventually bought his freedom.

A few masters permitted their slaves to save money in order to purchase their own, their spouse's, or their children's freedom, but the deal depended on the owner's decency. No contract with a slave was enforceable in most southern states (Kentucky was an exception).

A well-known example of wide-open violation of a slave code was the model plantation of Joseph Davis, brother of Jefferson Davis, the future president of the Confederate States of America. Ignoring a Mississippi state law

African Slave Traders: Defying the Law

Congress forbade the importation of slaves from abroad, "the African slave trade" in the parlance of the time, as of January 1, 1808. It was the first day the Constitution permitted Congress to do so.

The Constitution's attention to importing slaves, a specific issue more appropriate to legislation than to a frame of government, reveals several aspects of the status of slavery in America in the late 1700s. All but a few delegates to the Constitutional Convention wanted to put an end to the business. It was ugly, as anyone who saw a ship unloading slaves knew: They were invariably in wretched physical condition and terrified. Moreover, many Americans of the time saw the abolition of the foreign slave trade as a first step toward ridding the United States of the institution of slavery, which they hoped lay in the future. James Madison, the "father of the Constitution," wrote, "Happy would it be for the unfortunate Africans if an equal prospect lay before them of being redeemed from the oppression of their European brethren."

But South Carolina's and Georgia's delegates to the Constitutional Convention balked. Their states were importing a good many slaves from abroad. They made it clear that without temporary protection of the African slave trade, their states would not ratify the Constitution. So the trade was protected. The Constitution prohibited Congress from forbidding the "Importation of such Persons as any of the States now existing shall think proper to admit" for 20 years, until 1808. This provision was specifically exempted from the amendment process. It could not be changed; each state's right to two senators is the only other part of the Constitution future generations were forbidden to amend.

Attitudes toward the African slave trade were unchanged in 1807. Congress easily abolished the trade right on schedule. However, South Carolina imported more slaves during the last year it was legal to do so than in any previous year.

Enforcing the ban was difficult. Major African suppliers of slaves, like the Ashanti king, were mystified. Others were angry, saying that the termination of the business was an insult to Islam. (There were more slaves in Africa in 1807 than in all of the Americas.) The British, who also abolished the African slave trade, bore the major burden of patrolling the West African coast. By the 1840s, more than 30 naval ships were assigned to patrol the African coast, boarding vessels violating the ban and returning captives to Africa. The United States Navy assigned a squadron of up to 8 ships to Caribbean waters to search suspicious merchant vessels. Between May 1818 and November 1821, Americans freed 573 Africans bound for slavery.

From an American perspective, the term *African slave trade* was misleading. In colonial times, and illegally after 1807, very few slave traders carried captives from Africa to North America. It was the terrible nature of the business. So many captives died on the middle passage that profits depended on the voyage being kept as short as possible. The quickest crossing by far was to Brazil, a partial explanation of the fact that 40 percent of Africans sent as slaves to the Western Hemisphere went to Brazil. Slave traders bound farther north did not go to North American ports because it meant bypassing dozens of West Indian islands where their cargoes could be sold. Sailing to North America added weeks to their voyage and more deaths to their balance sheets. American slave buyers purchased their slaves in the West Indies. Almost all Africans who ended up slaves in North America spent some time in Cuba, Jamaica, or elsewhere in the West Indies.

This was even more the case after 1807, when the importation of slaves was illegal. Smugglers still risked British or French capture by buying slaves in Africa, more now from the Fulbe and Mandingo than from the Ashanti. King Gezo of Dahomey (whose bodyguard was a platoon of tall, fierce, strong women) sold 9,000 slaves annually between 1809 and 1850. The major suppliers at Sangha were an American, Paul Faber, and his African wife, Mary, who kept meticulous books, as if they were grocers. But slaves imported illegally into the United States, even those African-born, came mainly from Brazil and Cuba in vessels built for speed so they could outrun naval vessels. In 1839, two British ships brought five Spanish and Portuguese slavers flying the American flag into New York. President Van Buren asked Congress to take action against Brazilians and Cubans using the stars and stripes to evade British patrols.

He was snubbed. By 1839, many southerners and some northerners were sympathetic to the illegal slave trade. There were plenty of willing buyers, particularly in New Orleans and Charleston. The boom in cotton had sent the price of American-born slaves soaring; newly imported Africans were cheaper. Northern shipyards continued to build vessels designed for the slave trade. Of 170 slave trade expeditions identified by the British between 1859 and 1862, 74 had been outfitted in New York. The schooner *Wanderer,* ostensibly a yacht, was built for John Johnston of New Orleans in 1856. The tip-off of its real purpose was its oversized water tanks. Still, the *Wanderer* was not seized until it had successfully landed 325 slaves at Jekyll Island, South Carolina, in December 1858 (between 70 and 80 of the Africans died before arrival).

The penalties for those convicted of slave trading were harsh. The British equated slave traders with pirates. There was also a price to pay if captured by Americans and convicted. By the 1850s, however, it was difficult to get a conviction from a southern jury. In 1859, a United States warship brought the bark *Emily,* obviously a slaver, into port. The case was dismissed. In 1860, the owner of the *Wanderer* was acquitted in Savannah and permitted to buy his ship back for a quarter of its value. In the law, crewmen on a slaver were liable to be prosecuted, but they too rarely suffered more than a slap on the wrist. With such little deterrence, seamen could not ignore the fact that wages on a slave ship running from Cuba were as high as $10 a day, an astronomical sum.

forbidding the education of blacks, Joseph Davis maintained a school and teacher for the children of the quarters.

It is important to recall, however, that for every master like Joseph Davis, there were a dozen masters who kept their slaves just sound enough to work and a dozen more slave owners who, out of stupidity, ignorance, or malevolence, treated their slaves worse than they treated their mules. The editor of a southern magazine made no comment when a subscriber wrote, "Africans are nothing but brutes, and they will love you better for whipping, whether they deserve it or not."

PROTEST

Whether their master was kindly or cruel, their material circumstances adequate or deplorable, the vast majority of slaves hated their lot in life. Although some were sincerely attached to their masters, and although rebellion was rare after Nat Turner, blacks resisted slavery in various ways. When freedom became a realistic possibility during the Civil War, slaves deserted their homes by the thousands to flee to Union lines. A South Carolina planter wrote candidly after the war, "I believed these people were content, happy, and attached to their masters." That, he concluded sadly, had been "a delusion."

Malingering and Thievery

He might have been spared his disappointment had he given deeper consideration to white people's stereotypes of slaves. It was a commonly held belief that blacks were inherently lazy and irresponsible. In fact, free blacks generally worked quite hard, and the same slaves whose "laziness" was an aggravation in the cotton fields often toiled in their own gardens from dawn to dusk on Sundays and by moonlight during the week. The only incentive for a slave to work hard for the master was negative—the threat of punishment. That was often insufficient to cause men and women to ignore the blazing southern sun. When the overseer or driver was over the hill, it was nap time.

Theft was so common on plantations that whites believed blacks to be congenital thieves. Again, the only incentive not to steal a chicken, a suckling pig, or a berry pie was fear of punishment. If a slave was not caught, he had no reason to believe he had done wrong. One chicken thief who was caught in the act of eating his prize explained this point to his master: If the chicken was his master's property and he was his master's property, then the master had not lost anything because the chicken was in his belly instead of scratching around the hen yard. It is not known if his meditation saved the philosopher from a whipping.

Runaways

The clearest evidence of slave discontent was the prevalence of runaways. Only blacks who lived in the states that bordered the free states—Delaware, Maryland, Kentucky, Missouri—had a reasonable chance of escaping to permanent freedom. Some "rode" the "underground railway," rushing at night from hiding places in one abolitionist's home, most often a black abolitionist's, to another.

Harriet Tubman, who escaped from her master in 1849, returned to the South 19 times to lead other blacks to freedom. Tubman, the "Black Moses," was a hands-on and very brave abolitionist. And a shrewd one. Tubman went south only in winter, when the nights were longer and few people were out of doors. She herself never went onto a plantation; she selected a rendezvous several miles away and sent others to tell the slaves where she was.

Departure was always on Saturday night. The runaways, whom Tubman called her "cargo," would be missed Monday morning, but their master would not be alarmed until Monday evening. It was common for slaves, tired or disgusted, to disappear for a few days; the vacation was worth a whipping to many. So Tubman had a two-day head start. She moved only by night, depending on African American families known to her, free and slave, for food and shelter. (Collaborators also helped by tearing down notices of the runaways.) If Tubman had to enter a town for some reason, she approached from the north and left in a southerly direction. She was in appearance and manners "a very respectable Negro, not at all a poor fugitive."

In a dangerous business—if caught she faced serious penalties—Tubman was no sunshine-and-sugar social worker.

Uncle Remus Suggests

Because violent resistance was suicidal, it was unusual among slaves. Elders in the quarters counseled keeping one's wits and acting docile. An Uncle Remus fable recorded after the emancipation of slaves, "Why Br'er Possum Loves Peace," explains the ruse.

Mr. Dog attacks Br'er Coon and Br'er Possum. Br'er Coon fights back and drives Mr. Dog away, but at the price of serious injury. Br'er Possum "plays possum" (plays dead).

Representing blacks who fight back, Br'er Coon berates Br'er Possum for cowardice: "'I ain't runnin' wid cowards deze days,' sez Br'er Coon."

Br'er Possum replies that just because he did not fight does not mean that he is a coward: "I want no mo' skeer'd dan you is right now. . . . but I'm de most ticklish chap w'at you ever laid eyes on, en no sooner did Mr. Dog put his nose down yer 'mong my ribs dan I got ter laffin. . . . I don't mine fightin', Br'er Coon, no mo' dan you duz. . . . but I declar' ter grashus ef I kin stan' ticklin."

Note that it is *Mr.*, not *Br'er* ("Brother"), Dog; the tale is about the races; the Dog was white and no brother.

Daniel Webster's Slave

Daniel Webster, representing a state that abolished slavery before he was born, bought a slave, Paul Jennings, to be his butler in Washington, D.C., where slavery was legal. Webster freed Jennings, but then again, he did not. Jennings had to sign a contract to work off Webster's expenses.

As far as Jennings was concerned, he was still a slave. In 1848, he joined other slaves to charter a sloop in which they planned to escape north. Jennings changed his mind at the last minute and dropped out of the expedition, to his good fortune. The boat was stopped in the Chesapeake, and the passengers were arrested.

▲ *Harriet Tubman (left) with a "cargo" she has led from slavery to safety. She made 19 such trips and, during the Civil War, was a spy behind Confederate lines.*

She refused to accept "cargo" she judged weak: "If he was weak enough to give out, he'd be weak enough to betray us all." She told her runaways she would shoot anyone who gave up and probably would have done so, had she carried a gun. On one occasion, to get a complainer moving, she threatened him so frighteningly that he moved.

"Let My People Go"

The culture of the quarters will never be fully understood because the slaves kept no written records. However, some reliable conjectures can be ventured based on what is known of African American religion and folklore.

By the 1850s, most slaves had embraced an emotional brand of Protestant Christianity, most commonly Baptist or Methodist in temper. Their religious services centered on animated sermons by unlettered but charismatic preachers and exuberant rhythmic singing of both hymns borrowed from the white churches and what became known as Negro spirituals.

Freedom Song

When Israel was in Egypt land
Let my people go
Oppressed so hard they could not stand
Let my people go.
Go down, Moses,
Way down in Egypt land
Tell old Pharaoh
To let my people go.

In both sermons and spirituals, the slaves explicitly identified with the ancient Hebrews. While in bondage in Babylon and Egypt, the Hebrews had been, nevertheless, in their simplicity and misery, God's chosen people. The protest—for God delivered the Hebrews from their captivity—was too obvious to be lost on whites. But as long as the whites were convinced—and the slaves obliged them—that blacks associated freedom with the afterlife, "crossing over Jordan," slave religion was not stifled.

"Bred en Bawn in a Brier Patch"

Another thinly masked form of protest were the folktales for which black storytellers became famous, particularly the Br'er Rabbit stories that were collected after the Civil War as *Uncle Remus: His Songs and Sayings.* In these yarns, elements of which have been traced back to West African folklore, the rabbit, the weakest of animals and unable to defend himself by force, survives and flourishes through wit and complex deceits.

In the most famous of the Uncle Remus stories, "How Mr. Rabbit Was Too Sharp for Mr. Fox," Br'er Fox has the rabbit in his hands and is debating with himself whether to barbecue him, hang him, drown him, or skin him. Br'er Rabbit assures the fox that he will be delighted with any of these fates just as long as the fox does not fling him into a nearby brier patch, which he fears more than anything. Of course, that is exactly what Br'er Fox does, after which Br'er Rabbit is home free. "Bred en bawn in a brier patch, Br'er Fox," Br'er Rabbit shouts back tauntingly, "bred en bawn in a brier patch." The slaves, unable to taunt their masters so bluntly, satisfied themselves with quiet trickery and coded tales about it.

It is worth noting that in the Uncle Remus stories, Br'er Rabbit now and then outsmarts himself and suffers for it. As in all social commentary of substance, the slaves were as sensitive to their own foibles as to those of their masters.

The Slave Community

Like Br'er Rabbit, slaves presented a different face to whites than to their own people. Often, individuals reinforced white beliefs in their inferiority by playing the lazy, dimwitted, comical "Sambo," devoted to "Ol' Marse" and patently incapable of taking care of himself. Observant whites noticed that Sambo was quick witted enough when they surprised him while he was talking to other slaves or that he literally slaved in his garden and slept only when in the fields of cotton.

Recent historical research indicates that the slave family was more vital than the family among poor whites and African Americans today. Both parents were present in two-thirds of slave families, the same proportion as among European peasants at that time. Perhaps the most striking demonstration of the resiliency of African Americans, even when oppressed by slavery, is the fact that, in 1865, when slavery was abolished, there were 10 times as many blacks in the United States as had been imported from Africa and the West Indies between 1619 and 1807. The American slave population was the only slave population in the Western Hemisphere to increase as a result of natural reproduction.

for FURTHER READING

Ulrich B. Phillips, *American Negro Slavery,* 1919, and *Life and Labor in the Old South,* 1929, present romanticized portraits of slavery and yet, despite their bias, contain much valuable information. Kenneth Stampp, *The Peculiar Institution,* 1956, was an explicit response to Phillips, quite unromantic about slavery, and is quite informative.

Since the 1960s, slavery has been studied exhaustively. Just a few of hundreds of titles include Ira Berlin, *Slaves Without Masters,* 1975; John Blassingame, *The Slave Community,* 1972, and *Slave Testimony,* 1977; Carl N. Degler, *Neither Black nor White: Slavery and Race Relations in Brazil and the United States,* 1971; Stanley Elkins, *Slavery,* 1968; Robert Fogel and Stanley Engerman, *Time on the Cross,* 1974 (the findings of which are attacked in Herbert Gutman and Richard Sutch, *Slavery and the Numbers Game,* 1975); and Paul A. David et al., *Reckoning with Slavery,* 1976.

See also George M. Frederickson, *The Black Image in the White Mind,* 1971; Eugene Genovese, *The Political Economy of Slavery,* 1962, and *Roll Jordan Roll,* 1975 (perhaps the best single book about slaves); Herbert G. Gutman, *The Black Family in Slavery and Freedom, 1750–1925,* 1976; Lawrence W. Levine, *Black Culture and Black Consciousness: Afro-American Folk Thought from Slavery to Freedom,* 1977; Gilbert Osofsky, *Puttin' On Ol' Massa,* 1969; Harold Rawick, *From Sundown to Sunup,* 1967; and R. Starobin, *Industrial Slavery in the Old South,* 1970.

On abolitionism, see Ronald Abzug, *Passionate Liberator: Theodore Dwight Weld and the Dilemma of Reform,* 1980; Anna Bontemps, *Free at Last: The Life of Frederick Douglass,* 1971; M. L. Dillon, *The Abolitionists: The Growth of a Dissenting Minority,* 1974; Aileen S. Kraditor, *Means and Ends in American Abolitionism: Garrison and His Critics on Strategy and Tactics, 1834–50,* 1967; Gerda Lerner, *The Grimké Sisters from South Carolina: Rebels Against Slavery,* 1967; Benjamin Quarles, *Black Abolitionists,* 1969; and J. B. Stewart, *Holy Warriors: The Abolitionists and American Slavery,* 1976.

On the proslavery argument, see George M. Frederickson, *The Black Image in the White Mind,* 1971; W. S. Jenkins, *Pro-Slavery Thought in the Old South,* 1935; William Stanton, *The Leopard's Spots: Scientific Attitudes Toward Race in America, 1815–1859,* 1960; and Harvey Wish, *George Fitzhugh: Propagandist of the Old South,* 1943.

AMERICAN JOURNEY ONLINE AND INFOTRAC COLLEGE EDITION

Visit the source collections at http://ajaccess.wadsworth.com and http://infotrac.thomsonlearning.com, and use the Search function with the following key terms to explore documents, images, audio and video clips, articles, and commentary related to the material in this chapter:

Frederick Douglass	Harriet Tubman
fugitive slave	Slave trade
Grimké	Sojourner Truth
Harriet Beecher Stowe	*Uncle Tom's Cabin*

Additional resources, exercises, and Internet links related to this chapter are available on *The American Past* Web site: http://history.wadsworth.com/americanpast7e.

HISTORY ONLINE

Born in Slavery

http://memory.loc.gov/ammem/snhtml/snhome.html

Formers slaves' recollections of slave life as transcribed during the 1930s.

Slaves and the Courts

http://memory.loc.gov/ammem/sthtml/sthome.html

An extensive collection of documents revealing the legal status of slaves between 1740 and 1860.

FROM SEA TO SHINING SEA

American Expansion 1820–1848

Our manifest destiny is to overspread the continent allotted by Providence for the free development of our yearly multiplying millions.

John Louis O'Sullivan

If I were a Mexican, I would tell you, "Have you not room in your own country to bury your dead men? If you come into mine, we will greet you with bloody hands, and welcome you to hospitable graves."

Thomas Corwin

THOMAS JEFFERSON'S GENERATION believed the Louisiana Purchase had established America's boundaries for all time. In the North, the War of 1812 dashed the hopes of all reasonable people that Canada would be joined to the United States. To the west, the Rocky Mountains were as clear and as formidable a natural boundary as any in the world. The Adams-Oñis Treaty of 1819 added Florida, extending the coastline border from the Atlantic to Louisiana.

The treaty also settled on the Sabine River as the boundary between the United States and Spanish Mexico. It was the most dubious of the national frontiers. The land across the Sabine was fertile, well watered, and sparsely populated. But Spain's grip on Mexico was slipping as a popularly supported independence movement neared success. The government of the emerging Estados Unidos de Mexico was cordial to the United States of America. It was difficult to imagine conflict with a new republic that looked to the American Revolution as an inspiration.

Independent Mexico was too cordial to Americans. Within a few decades, President Porfirio Díaz would look back ruefully and lament, "Poor Mexico, so far from God, so close to the United States."

TEXAS

New Spain was the jewel of the Spanish Empire for three centuries. An elite of Spanish-born *gachupines* and Mexican-born white *criollos* monopolized the best lands, living fat off the labor of the Indians. But they were few. Mexico was not only home to the greatest of indigenous New World civilizations; it was an amalgam of Spanish and Indian cultures. The vast majority of Mexicans were, unlike the ethnically diverse Americans, a new people, *la raza* ("the race"), composed of *mestizos,* an amalgam of European and Native American blood.

Mexico's Northward Expansion

The United States expanded to the west. More slowly, for the population of New Spain was much smaller, Mexico expanded to the north. Spanish pioneers and friars planted outposts deep in what is now the American Southwest. The rivers of Texas, especially the Rio Bravo of the north (the Rio Grande), were dotted with presidios (military bases) and missions far more numerous than the old French trading posts along the Mississippi. The northernmost were at Santa Fe in the Sangre de Cristo Mountains, safe at about 75 miles south of the periodically rebellious Indian pueblo at Taos.

During the first years of American independence, a Franciscan priest, Junípero Serra, established a string of missions in California, the northernmost at Sonoma above San Francisco Bay. His plan, eventually fulfilled, made it possible for a foot traveler along the *camino real* (or "royal highway"—present-day California Highway 1 and U.S. Route 101) to shelter every night in a hospitable compound. As in New Mexico, a gracious but simple way of life evolved among the small numbers of *californios* who settled there.

The Santa Fe Trade

The Spanish had banned Americans from California and New Mexico. In 1821, independent Mexico abandoned the Spanish prohibitions on trade with the United States, and William Becknell, an alert entrepreneur in Independence, Missouri, immediately set off cross-country in a wagon packed with American manufactures: cloth, shoes, tools, and some luxury items. Feeling his way by compass and by dead reckoning across what is now Kansas, he blazed an 800-mile-long trail to Santa Fe. The 7,000 inhabitants were so remote from the Mexican heartland that they devoured Becknell's goods, paying him handsomely with furs and gold.

Annually for 14 years, a convoy of wagons rolled down the Santa Fe Trail. A few Missourians, such as Kentucky-born horse handler Christopher "Kit" Carson, settled in New Mexico, happily adapting to the gracious Spanish-Indian culture. Nevertheless, the presence of even a few *sassones* ("Saxons") in New Mexico forged a link between the country and the United States that was—no matter the flag that flew—more substantial than the link between Santa Fe and Mexico City.

The Great American Desert

Americans believed that the land the Santa Fe traders crossed, which was United States territory, was worthless. At about 100 degrees west longitude (central Nebraska and Kansas), the land gradually rises from an elevation of 2,000 feet to, at the base of the Rockies, 5,000 to 7,000 feet. These high plains lie in the rain shadow of the Rockies. Before the winds from the west reach the plains, the moisture in them is scooped out by the great mountains. Except for cottonwoods along the rivers, few trees grew on the plains. The vastness of the landscape unnerved Americans, who were accustomed to dense forests. When they gazed over the windblown buffalo grass, they thought not of farmland but of the ocean. The Santa Fe traders called their wagons

▲ The "Great American Desert" was no desert. It was almost treeless, but once farmers broke the tough sod and dug wells, the eastern parts of the plains supported productive farms.

MAP 20:1 Americans in the Mexican Borderlands, 1819–1848 The Santa Fe Trail, a commercial incursion into the Spanish borderlands, and American settlement of eastern Texas were both welcomed by the infant nation of Mexico. It was the virtual Americanization of eastern Texas that led to conflict and to the independence of Texas.

"prairie schooners." Less romantic military mapmakers labeled the country the "Great American Desert."

It was a mistake, of course, to believe that only land that grew trees naturally would support crops. However, it was true enough that the tough sod of the plains was more than a fire-tempered wood, or even cast iron, plowshare could turn over, and there was not enough rainfall to nourish grain. Travelers observed that the grass that fattened 10 million bison would fatten cattle too. However, it was difficult to imagine how such hypothetical steers might be transported to eastern markets. All agreed that the Indians of the plains, who were satisfied to exchange goods with the Santa Fe traders, were welcome to what they had.

The Texans

The Great Plains extended into Texas, a district of the Mexican state of Coahuila. There, cattle could be grazed within driving distance of the Gulf of Mexico and shipped by water to New Orleans. In 1819, a Connecticut Yankee named Moses Austin was attracted by the possibilities of a grazing economy and the suitability of eastern Texas to cotton cultivation. He proposed to the Mexicans that, in return for grants of lands, American settlers would provide a counterforce to the Comanche, raiders feared throughout the region.

Moses Austin died, but, in 1821, his son Stephen concluded the negotiations. He was licensed to settle

300 American families in Texas, each household to receive 177 acres of farmland and 13,000 acres of pastureland. The settlers would abide by Mexican law, learn the Spanish language, and observe the Roman Catholic religion.

Many of the early settlers were baptized Catholic, but most were not. Austin banned Protestant clergymen but did not force many of them to leave. Texas was far from the centers of Mexican power and culture, and the immigrants were so numerous (20,000 whites and 2,000 black slaves by 1834) that Texas was inevitably American in culture. The Texans never did bridle the Comanche (they remained free agents until the Civil War), but the Texas settlers prospered and paid taxes. Conflict was not inevitable until Mexico abolished slavery in 1829 and, in 1833, General Antonio López de Santa Anna seized power. Slavery was as vital to the economy of Texas as it was in neighboring Louisiana. Santa Anna was a less accommodating Mexican president than his predecessors had been.

Santa Anna wanted to put an end to the squabbling that had plagued Mexican politics since independence by promoting a sense of Mexican nationality. He centralized the government in a new constitution in 1835 and canceled American trading privileges in Santa Fe. Texans feared for the considerable autonomy they had enjoyed and their lucrative economic connections with the United States.

A small number of Anglo and Hispanic Texans rebelled, seizing the only military garrison in Texas, at San Antonio. At first, like the Americans of 1775, the rebels claimed that they were fighting only for the rights they had traditionally exercised. However, they had far less in common with their mother country than the rebels of 1775 had with Great Britain. Some spoke of independence from the start.

The Alamo and San Jacinto

Like George III, Santa Anna had no intention of negotiating with rebels. He welcomed the uprising in Texas as an opportunity to rally the divided Mexican people around a national cause. In 1836, he led an army of 6,000 to San Antonio, calculating he could easily defeat the 200 Texans (and a few newly arrived Americans) who were holed up in the mission compound, the Alamo (which means "cottonwood tree" in Spanish).

Among the defenders were men well known in the United States. The garrison commander was William Travis, a prominent Texan who had taken over from James Bowie, inventor of the famous double-edged knife, who was unable to rise from a sickbed. Best known in the United States was the Whig politician and humorist Davy Crockett of Tennessee, who had left the United States because of Jackson's treatment of the Cherokee.

Santa Anna could have passed the Alamo by, leaving a small detachment to contain the garrison. The real threat lay farther east, where Sam Houston, an old crony of Andrew Jackson, was frantically trying to raise an army. Houston had big problems. By no means did every Texan support the rebellion. Others, just farmers, were uneasy about confronting professional soldiers. By moving quickly, Santa Anna might easily have snuffed out the insurrection.

Instead, he sat in San Antonio for 10 days, daily more infuriated that the defenders of the Alamo, whose cause was hopeless, would not surrender. When, finally, he attacked at tremendous cost to his army, he ordered all prisoners executed. (Only a few women were spared.) Two weeks later, at Goliad, Santa Anna massacred 365 Texans who had surrendered. The atrocities rallied Texans, including many of Mexican culture, to the fight against Santa Anna.

On the banks of the Rio San Jacinto on April 21, Sam Houston's force routed the Mexican army and captured Santa Anna. In order to secure his release, Santa Anna agreed to the independence of Texas with a southern boundary at the Rio Grande rather than at the Rio Nueces, which had been the boundary of the district of Texas. As soon as he was free, Santa Anna repudiated the agreement and refused to recognize the Republic of Texas. But the demoralized Mexican army was in no condition to mount another campaign, and the Texans discreetly remained north of the Nueces.

The Lone Star Republic

In October 1836, Sam Houston was inaugurated president of a republic patterned on the United States. Texas legalized slavery and dispatched a minister to Washington, D.C. Houston hoped that his old friend Andrew Jackson would favor annexation. In his nationalistic heart, Jackson liked the idea of sewing the "lone star" of the Texas republic onto the American flag. However, Congress was embroiled in a nasty debate in which the question of slavery was being bandied about. Jackson did not want to complicate matters by proposing the admission of a new slave state. He recognized Texan independence in order to spare his successor that decision, but only on his last day in office.

President Van Buren opposed the annexation of Texas. He escaped a debate on the question when depression distracted Congress. The Texans, disappointed and worried about Mexico, looked to Europe for an ally.

Santa Anna's Legacy

Santa Anna's first presidency was ruined by Americans in Texas. However, he bore little animosity to the American people. He spent much of his exile between 1841 and 1844 in Staten Island, New York, where he helped inflict an addiction on Americans. Santa Anna chewed chicle, sap from the sapodilla tree. When, in 1844, he hurried back to Mexico, he left some in his home. The chicle fell into the hands of Thomas Adams, who, good American that he was, marketed it as an alternative to chewing tobacco, a ubiquitous habit thought filthy in polite society. Adams made a decent living from "chewing gum." It made William Wrigley Jr. rich when, in 1893, he hit on the idea of sweetening and flavoring the chicle, calling it "Juicy Fruit."

▲ *A fanciful depiction of the final moments of the defense of the Alamo. Commander Travis is at the left. The heroic figure in fringed buckskin and coonskin cap is Davy Crockett, who, if he ever wore a coon tail on his hat, did not at the Alamo. Some accounts have Crockett fighting to the end, as in this picture; some say he was shot from a distance by a sniper; yet others have him surrendering, only to be executed.*

The British were happy to oblige. They coveted Texas cotton and welcomed the opportunity to contain the expansive United States. Had the Texans not been committed to the institution of slavery, which the British had recently abolished in the empire, there might have been more than a commercial connection between the old monarchy and the new republic.

THE OREGON COUNTRY

The American government was uneasy about British influence in Texas. There was also a point of conflict between the two nations on the Pacific coast of North America in what was known as the Oregon Country. This land of mild climate, prosperous Indians, sheltered harbors, spruce and fir forests, and rich valley farmlands was not the property of any single nation. This situation came about when two empires with claims to Oregon voluntarily withdrew.

A Distant Land

Spain's (and therefore Mexico's) claim to Oregon was never more than nominal. Spanish and Mexican influence ended just north of San Francisco, and it was nebulous there. So after 1819, when the northern boundary of Mexico was set at 42 degrees north latitude (the present California-Oregon line), the claim was itself overreaching.

The Russians had founded a string of fur-trapping stations on the Pacific coast as far south as Fort Ross, less than a hundred miles from San Francisco. However, the czars had difficulty populating Siberia. Few Russians were interested

Zorro and the Californios

Alta California—Upper California—was thinly populated when the United States seized it, but it was far from empty. Indians were more numerous in California's mild climate than in any other region except the Eastern Woodlands a century and a half earlier. Thousands of Mexicans had followed the mission fathers in the late eighteenth and early nineteenth centuries. Some of these *californios* clustered around small mercantile towns and presidios: San Diego, Los Angeles, Monterey, Yerba Buena (San Francisco), and Sonoma. Most, however, were ranchers living on vast government land grants. A few Americans and Europeans had taken out Mexican grants too.

The *californios* were rich in acres but not money. The only commodities California produced for the international market were hides and tallow, the fat of cattle and sheep cooked down for use in soap and candle manufacture. Even the richest *californios* lived in plain adobe homes of one or two stories. Furniture, iron products, and most other manufactured goods were made on the scene by Indian craftsmen. Diet was ample (plenty of beef!), but *californio* cuisine was inelegant.

Nevertheless, the *californios* at the top of the social pyramid were proud of their independence and self-sufficiency. They were hidalgos, the rightful rulers but also the benefactors of their lessers, poor Mexicans and Indians.

The *californio* community was divided down the middle by the American invasion. Some, feeling little commitment to distant Mexico, quickly made peace with the gringos and salvaged at least some of their property and social position. Others resisted and won a few small battles before being overcome.

It was less the American victory that inundated the *californios* than the great gold rush of 1849 and 1850. Spanish-speaking ranchers were literally overrun by the tens of thousands of gold seekers. Among those who were ruined was Salomon María Simeón Pico, the son of a soldier who had been granted 11 Spanish leagues (48,829 acres, 19,756 hectares) between the Tuolumne and Stanislaus Rivers. According to legend, Pico not only lost his herds and land, but his wife was raped and beaten, dying soon thereafter.

It is not possible to separate legend from fact in Pico's subsequent career. It is probable he became a masked highwayman on the *camino real* between Santa María and Santa Barbara, and may have cut an ear off each of his mostly gringo victims. (Pico, the story goes, strung his trophies and carried them on his saddle horn like a lariat.) It is less likely that he gave his loot to impoverished *californio* families, but he was a popular hero even during his lifetime. Pico moved around California with impunity for eight years, aided, no doubt, by the fact that his two brothers were the mayors of San Luis Obispo and San Jose.

Pico's most famous scrape with the law came in November 1851, when he shot the hat off the head of Los Angeles judge Benjamin Hayes. Although himself wounded, Pico escaped to Baja California where, in 1854, he was arrested by Mexican authorities and summarily executed.

In the 1920s, Pico became a popular fictional hero in the United States as Zorro ("the Fox"), a name he never used. In 1919, Johnston McCulley collected the many Pico legends, deftly adapted them for an American readership, and published them as *The Curse of Capistrano*. Pico's fictional name was Don Diego Vega, and he lived not in California's American era but earlier, when California was Mexican. His enemies were not gringos but corrupt Mexican authorities.

Don Diego was a gracious hidalgo by day who donned a mask not for the purpose of robbery but to fight for justice and something much like what was called "the American way." So admirable a gentleman could not be amputating ears. McCulley's Zorro left his trademark by cutting a *Z* on his victims' cheeks. Even that was too nasty for television. In the 1950s, when Zorro came into American living rooms on the small screen, he contented himself to cut *Z* into the bark of trees, on the sides of buildings, or (bloodlessly) on the clothing of his adversaries. Rather more remarkable, the television Zorro devoted a good deal of his time to protecting decent and well-meaning gringos from venal Mexicans.

---

in removing to permanent settlements even farther from Europe. By the 1820s, Russian trappers had looted the Pacific coves of the sea otters whose lush, warm furs had brought them there. Rather than get involved in a competition for territory they could not defend, Russia withdrew in 1825 to 54 degrees, 40 minutes north latitude, the present southern boundary of Alaska.

Between 42 degrees (the northern border of Mexico's claim) and 54 degrees, 40 minutes (the southern border of Russia's claim) lay the Oregon Country, into which some Britons and Americans had trickled. Because settlers from their nations were few in the Oregon Country, Britain and the United States easily agreed to what was called "joint occupation," putting other nations on notice that they were not welcome to snoop around.

The Mountain Men

Most of the whites in the Oregon Country were trappers in the chill creeks of the Rockies. Their prey was the beaver, prized in New York, London, and Paris both for the luxury fur and for chopping, steaming, and pressing into the best felt, a versatile fabric with a worldwide market. American and Canadian veterans of the War of 1812, the kind whose interest in home had been killed by their military experience, disappeared into the mountains for 11 months a year. The mountain men probably never numbered more than 500 in a given season. About half took Indian wives and all learned Indian ways of surviving in the ruggedest of wilderness.

At the end of each summer, the trappers brought their furs to prearranged locations on the Platte, Sweetwater, or

Trappers and Indians

In order to survive, the mountain men needed the good-will of at least one of the tribes of the region, another good reason to marry Indian women. With tribal enmities strong, however, identification with one people meant that others were enemies. In confrontations, which were not unusual, the trappers' rifles gave them no edge. The large-bore Hawkens they favored for their stopping power were accurate to 100 yards, 20 or 30 yards more than an Indian archer's arrow. However, it took half a minute to re-load a Hawken. A good bowman could shoot 10 arrows in that time.

The Indians most respected were the Blackfoot. So great was the fear of them that when, by 1840, overtrapping had destroyed the beaver population all over the West, the species remained numerous in Blackfoot country.

Liver-Eatin' Johnson

Mountain man Jeremiah Johnson claimed to have waged a 10-year vendetta with the Crow Indians, killing more than a dozen. He earned his colorful nickname because, in order to inform the Crow that it was he who had killed the dead warriors whose bodies they found, he cut out and ate their livers.

Big Horn Rivers. For a few weeks, buyers from the British Hudson's Bay Company and John Jacob Astor's American Fur Trading Company, mountain men, and Indians traded, drank, enjoyed a riotous orgy, and now and then bit off the ear of an old pal. Of more lasting significance was the knowledge of western geography the mountain men imparted to the folks back home, notably that although it was a long, hard trip, it was possible to cross overland to the Pacific with wagons.

Jedediah Smith opened South Pass in Wyoming, the route that would be followed by most overland emigrants. Jim Beckwourth, the son of a slave woman and a white man, discovered the pass through the Sierra Nevada that rose to the lowest elevation. Jim Bridger was a walking, talking atlas; he explored almost every nook of the Rockies. He was the first non-Indian to lay eyes on the Great Salt Lake.

The Oregon Trail

Among the first to make the six-month journey for the purpose of settling in Oregon were missionaries. In 1834, the Methodists sent Jason Lee to preach the gospel to the Indians. In 1835, four Nez Percé visited the American Board of Foreign Missions and, so the board reported, persuaded them that the gospel they wanted to hear was the Presbyterian. In 1836, Marcus and Narcissa Whitman carried it to them on foot. (The Whitmans converted a Scot, a French Canadian, and a Hawaiian, but not Indians; in 1847, Indians blamed a measles epidemic on the Whitmans and murdered them.)

The Catholic University at St. Louis sent Father Pierre-Jean de Smet to the Oregon Country.

The trek usually began at Independence, Missouri. The first great wagon train was organized there in 1843. A thousand people bound for Oregon outfitted themselves, some packing oddly chosen mementos of home: cumbersome furniture and fragile chinaware. They swore to strict rules of behavior and cooperation for the duration of the crossing and hired mountain men as guides.

The Oregon Trail crossed Kansas to the Platte River and followed that broad, shallow stream to Fort Laramie, the westernmost army outpost. The emigrants crossed the Continental Divide at South Pass and struggled through the Rockies to near the Snake River, which flows into the great Columbia and the Pacific. A wagon train covered up to 20 miles a day (or as few as none at all) depending on the terrain and the weather. At night, exhausted by the tremendous labor of moving a hundred wagons and several hundred head of cattle, horses, and mules, the emigrants drew their prairie schooners into a hollow square or circle.

The Indians of the plains and mountains did not threaten large, well-organized expeditions. Although the Indians were hardly delighted to see hordes of strangers crossing their ancestral lands (3,000 in 1845 alone), the whites were, at least, just passing through. The whites and Indians skirmished constantly with one another, but the tribes had few firearms. The Oregon-bound travelers worried less about Indian attack than about theft. Indians made a game of stealing horses that strayed too far from the caravans. They also traded with the whites and picked up the discarded trinkets that soon littered the trail. Even before the stream of wagons wore ruts into the sod and rock—which can still be seen here and there today—the Oregon Trail was marked with broken furniture, empty barrels, incapacitated wagons, the skeletons of cattle and horses, and simple grave markers. Death from accident or disease, particularly cholera, was common, but it was impossible to lose the way.

MANIFEST DESTINY

By 1845, the American population of the Columbia and Willamette Valleys had grown to 7,000. The British Hudson's Bay Company prudently moved its headquarters from the mouth of the Columbia to Vancouver Island. What is now the state of Washington was a buffer zone between British and American population centers. Still, occasional clashes threatened "joint occupation."

The Americans wanted to annex the Oregon Country to the United States. In July 1843, a group met at Champoeg and established a provisional territorial government under the American flag. A few politicians back East supported them, as much to taunt the British as for any realistic hope of affecting policy. The idea of territorial expansion was taking on a positive dignity—even, to some, the guise of a sacred duty. Increasingly, some Democratic party propagandists claimed that the United States had an obligation to increase the domain in

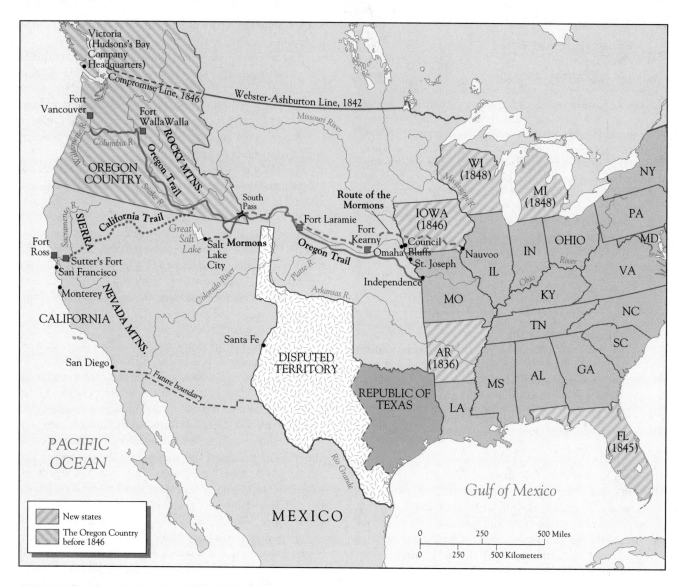

MAP 20:2 Americans in the West, 1819–1848 Britain and the United States split the Oregon Country between them in 1842, pretty much along a line reflecting the presence of the two nations. Present-day California and northern Utah were Mexican territories when Americans began to pour into the region.

which democracy and liberty held sway. It remained for a New York journalist, John O'Sullivan, to coin a phrase. It was, he said, the "manifest destiny" of the United States to expand from sea to sea.

The Texas Debate

Some southerners frankly added slavery to the list of institutions to be carried across the continent. In 1843, Secretary of State John C. Calhoun told Congress that Texas must be annexed lest growing British influence result in the abolition of slavery there. He won the support of many northern Democrats, such as Lewis Cass of Michigan, James Buchanan of Pennsylvania, and Stephen Douglas of Illinois. But, in 1844, the Senate rejected Calhoun's proposal by a two to one vote. Every Whig but one voted nay. In addition

to opposing the admission of a new slave state, most Whigs believed that absorbing Texas would almost certainly lead to a war with Mexico in which the Mexicans, not the Americans, would be in the right.

Both of the likely presidential nominees of 1844 were unhappy to see Texas shaping up as the principal issue of the campaign. Henry Clay knew that his Whig party, already strained by slavery issues, might split in two over Texas. Martin Van Buren, who commanded a majority of delegates to the Democratic nominating convention, had the same problem. The Democrats were torn between proslavery and antislavery factions. If the two old rogues took opposite stances on the question, both parties might be disarrayed. Therefore, the two men quietly met and agreed that both would oppose annexation, competing for votes on other issues.

▲ *Where the overland trail reached the Snake River, it forked—the Oregon Trail continuing along the Snake to the northwest, the California Trail branching southwest into what is now Nevada. This extraordinary photograph, with two wagon trains side by side, indicates how crowded the trail could be.*

Their bargain presented lame-duck President Tyler with an opportunity. He would be a third candidate favoring the annexation. Tyler had no party organization, so his announcement did not unduly disturb Clay and Van Buren. Then occurred one of those unlikely events that unexpectedly change the course of history. Manifest Destiny Democrats revived a neglected party rule that a presidential nominee must win the support of two-thirds of the delegates to the convention, not just a simple majority. Having declared against annexation, Van Buren was stymied. Pro-Texas Democrats numbered far more than a third of the delegates.

After eight ballots, the convention turned to a dark-horse candidate, that is, a man who was not considered a serious contender. He was James Knox Polk of Tennessee, a protégé

Show Time

During the middle years of the nineteenth century, the traveling panorama was a cheap, popular diversion. On sheets of canvas sewn end to end, painters depicted historical events or natural wonders. Paying customers walked along the tableau, sometimes with printed explanations, sometimes listening to narrators. Biblical scenes, Revolutionary War battles, and Indian massacres (and white retribution) were particularly popular.

The largest was John Banvard's "Panorama of the Mississippi," first unfurled in 1846. On canvas 12 feet high and 3 miles long (a walk of a mile and a half), Banvard depicted 1,200 miles of both banks of the Mississippi River from the mouth of the Missouri to New Orleans.

"Dark Horse"

Use of the expression "dark horse" to refer to an unexpected presidential candidate was coined by British novelist (and future prime minister) Benjamin Disraeli in *The Young Duke,* published in 1832. "A dark horse which never had been thought of," he wrote, "and which the careless St. James had never even observed in the list, rushed past the grandstand in sweeping triumph." The phrase entered racetrack lingo in the United States as well as Britain and was first applied in politics to Polk. Other dark horses elected president were James A. Garfield (1880) and Warren G. Harding (1920). Dark-horse candidates who lost were William Jennings Bryan (1896) and Wendell Willkie (1940).

▲ *A family bound overland poses, sunburned, dirty, and weary but still looking plenty tough and determined.*

of Jackson not yet 50 years old (supporters called him "Young Hickory"). Polk was a Van Buren man who personally favored annexation, a perfect compromise candidate.

The Election of 1844

"Who is Polk?" the Whigs asked scornfully when they learned who was running against their hero, Henry Clay. The sarcasm was misplaced. Polk had been governor of Tennessee and served in Congress for 14 years, several years as Speaker. His career and personality, however, were midget set beside those of Henry Clay. A frail, small man with a look of melancholy about him, Polk was priggish, sniffly disapproving of alcohol, dancing, and playing cards.

At first, Henry Clay was pleased to have Polk as his opponent. After three attempts, he would be president at last! The partyless Tyler and the colorless Polk would divide the pro-Texas vote. The anti-Texas vote, including the antislavery Democrats who would have voted for Van Buren, were his.

Then a piece of the sky fell. Tyler withdrew, and every wind brought news that manifest destiny was carrying the day. Clay began to waffle on expansion; on election day, his equivocation alienated enough anti-Texas Whigs to cost him the election. In New York State, which Polk carried (and with it, the election) by a scant 5,000 votes, long dependable Whig districts gave 16,000 votes to James G. Birney's abolitionist Liberty party. Antislavery voters cost Clay his last chance to be president.

Encouraged by the election and egged on by Calhoun, Tyler moved on the Texas question. He could not muster the two-thirds vote in the Senate that ratification of a treaty required, but he had a simple majority of both houses of Congress behind him. Three days before Polk's inauguration,

Congress approved a joint resolution annexing Texas. A few months later, the Texas Congress concurred, and Texas became the twenty-eighth state.

Polk's Promises Kept

Polk was anything but mousy. He proved to be a master politician, a shrewd diplomat, and, in terms of accomplishing what he set out to do, one of the most successful of presidents. When he took his oath of office, Polk announced he would serve only one term. During those four years, he would secure Texas to the Union; acquire New Mexico and California from Mexico; and annex as much of the Oregon Country as circumstances permitted.

Texas statehood was already in the bag. The hardworking president, who was a micromanager ("I prefer to supervise the whole operations of the government myself, rather than entrust the public business to subordinates"), immediately turned to Oregon. He embraced a chauvinistic slogan of the day: "54-40 or fight!" (referring to seizing all of the

Five States of Texas

Texas is not unique among the states because it was an independent nation before it became a state. Hawaii also was. However, by the joint resolution of the American and Texan congresses that brought Texas into the Union, Texas reserved the right to divide into five states without further congressional approval. The advisability of splitting arose periodically in Texas politics because, collectively, the states carved out of Texas would have 10 United States senators instead of 2.

▲ *Amusing in the extravagance of its imagery and symbolism today, this is a splendid representation of the exuberance of American expansion. Indians and bison flee overland emigrants in their wagon, miners, and farmers, followed by the telegraph, the overland stagecoach, and the railroad. The rider to the left of the giantess symbolizing civilization is a pony express rider.*

Oregon Country up to the southern boundary of Russian America, which was at 54 degrees, 40 minutes north latitude). This stance alarmed the British because it threatened a war neither nation wanted. Polk then presented it as a concession to Britain that he would settle for an extension of the Webster-Ashburton line, 49 degrees north latitude, as the northern boundary of American Oregon. The Oregon Country would be cut in half, with Britain retaining all of Vancouver Island. Great Britain accepted. Except for a minor adjustment of the line in the Strait of Juan de Fuca in 1872, the American-Canadian boundary was final in 1846.

Polk was candid about his designs on California and New Mexico. The United States had no legal claim in either Mexican province. Nor could Polk claim, as he could about Texas and Oregon, that California and New Mexico were peopled largely by Americans. Unassimilated gringos were few in New Mexico, and there were only about 700 Americans in California compared with 6,000 *californios*. In 1842, an American naval officer, Thomas ap Catesby Jones, somehow got it into his head that the United States was at war with Mexico and seized Monterey, the provincial capital of California. When he learned that he was mistaken, he had to run down the flag and sail off, rather the fool. But Jones was merely a few years ahead of his time. When Mexico turned down Polk's offer to buy California and New Mexico for $30 million, the president set out to take them by force.

War with Mexico

The luckless Santa Anna was back in power in Mexico City. This time, however, he moved cautiously, ordering Mexican troops not to provoke the Americans. But it was to no avail: Polk was determined to have war. He drew up an address to Congress for a declaration of war because the Mexican government owed $3 million to American banks, pretty weak stuff. Polk ordered General Zachary Taylor of Louisiana to take 1,500 men from the Nueces River in Texas to the Rio Grande. In April 1846, 16 American soldiers were killed in a skirmish with a Mexican patrol.

Affecting moral outrage, Polk rewrote his speech, declaring that because of Mexican aggression, a state of war between the two nations already existed. Constitutionally, this was nonsense; Congress alone has the power to declare war.

Gringos

The origin of the word *gringo,* once a pejorative Mexican term for Americans, now inoffensive, is obscure. One plausible theory is that it originated during the American occupation of Mexico City, when a song popular with American troops began, "Green grows the grass," which to Mexicans was gobbledygook. But they caught the first two syllables and used them to refer to the North Americans.

▲ *Neither James K. Polk nor anyone else thought Polk would ever be president, until the summer of 1844, when he was nominated by the Democratic party as a compromise candidate. Almost immediately, he excited enthusiasm because of his unabashed support for annexing Texas and the Oregon Country.*

But patriotic danders were up; both houses of Congress approved Polk's action. The Mexican army was larger than the American, but most Mexican troops were ill equipped, demoralized by endless civil war, and commanded by officers who owed their commissions to social status rather than merit. In less than two years, the Americans conquered much of the country.

In the summer of 1846, Stephen W. Kearny occupied Santa Fe without resistance. He then marched his troops to California, where he found that the Americans and a few *californio* allies already had won a nearly bloodless revolution and established the Bear Flag Republic. Kearny had only to raise the American flag and defeat a few scattered Mexican garrisons.

In September, Taylor advanced into northern Mexico, defeating Mexican armies at Matamoros and Nuevo León (also known as Monterrey). Although "Old Rough and Ready," as his men called him, showed shrewd tactical judgment, the Nuevo León garrison escaped. Polk, who disliked Taylor, used this mistake as an excuse to divert some of Taylor's troops to a command under General Winfield Scott. Nevertheless, in February 1847, Taylor became a national hero when, with his shrunken army, he was attacked at Buena Vista by Santa Anna himself and won a total victory.

The next month, March 1847, Scott landed at Vera Cruz and fought his way toward Mexico City along the ancient route of Cortés. He won a victory at Cerro Gordo and an even bigger one at Chapultepec, where he captured 3,000 men and eight generals. On September 14, 1847, Scott donned one of the gaudy uniforms he loved (his men called him "Old Fuss and Feathers") and occupied Mexico City, "the Halls of Montezuma."

By the Treaty of Guadalupe Hidalgo, signed in February 1848, Mexico ceded the Rio Grande boundary, California, and New Mexico, which included the present states of Arizona and Nevada (and the Mormon Zion in Utah). The United States paid Mexico $15 million and assumed responsibility for about $3 million that the Mexican government owed Americans. Mexico was dismembered like a carcass of beef. One-third of its territory was detached largely because the United States was strong enough to take it. Although the ineptitude of the Mexican military played a part in the national disaster, the partition of the country could not but leave a bitterness in the historical memory of the Mexican people.

The Opposition

The Mexican War was popular in the United States. The army could accept only a fraction of the young men who volunteered to fight. Most battles were American victories, and only 1,700 soldiers died in battle (11,000 soldiers, however, succumbed to disease). About 50,000 Mexicans lost their lives.

Nevertheless, the war had its critics. Many Whigs, including a young politician from Illinois named Abraham Lincoln, voted against the declaration. In New England, prominent politicians and clergymen condemned the war from platform and pulpit. Ralph Waldo Emerson and much of the Massachusetts intellectual establishment opposed it. Henry David Thoreau went to jail rather than pay a tax

▲ *General John E. Wool and his staff in Saltillo, shortly before or after the Battle of Buena Vista in 1846. This is believed to be the earliest surviving photograph of American soldiers.*

MAP 20:3 The Mexican War, 1846–1847 Mexico lost a third of its territory in the war with the United States, somewhat more if disputed territory is included.

he said would help pay for adding new slave states to the Union.

Not even the army was unanimously keen on the fight. Years later in his autobiography, then Captain Ulysses S. Grant remembered, "I was bitterly opposed to the measure, and to this day regard the war . . . as one of the most unjust ever waged by a stronger against a weaker nation. . . . Even if the annexation itself could be justified, the manner in which the . . . war was forced upon Mexico cannot."

The vote in the Senate ratifying the Treaty of Guadalupe Hidalgo was only 38 to 14. Had four senators changed their votes, the treaty would not have been approved.

Expansion Run Amok

Cynical as the Mexican acquisition was, it was moderate compared to the suggestions of some expansionists. Some southerners wanted Polk to seize even more of Mexico, and he was leaning in that direction when the Treaty of Guadalupe Hidalgo arrived in Washington. When a rebellion broke out in the Yucatán Peninsula in 1848, Polk asked Congress to authorize the army, which was still in Mexico, to take over the tropical province. Curiously, some antislavery northerners were sympathetic. Because slavery was illegal in Mexico, they believed that new American states carved from the country would come into the Union as free states. Thus did slavery obsess and warp the minds of so many Americans.

The president also had designs on Cuba, where 350,000 slaves had long excited the imagination of proslavery southerners. Polk wanted to present the Spanish government there with a choice between selling the rich sugar island or running the risk of a rebellion fomented by the United States, followed by American military intervention.

Even more bizarre was J. D. B. De Bow, an influential southern publisher. He wrote that it was the American destiny to absorb not only all of Mexico but also the West Indies, Canada, and Hawaii. And that was for appetizers. De Bow continued:

> The gates of the Chinese empire must be thrown down by the men from the Sacramento and the Oregon, and the haughty Japanese tramplers upon the cross be enlightened in the doctrines of republicanism and the ballot box. The eagle of the republic shall poise itself over the field of Waterloo, after tracing its flight among the gorges of the Himalaya or the Ural mountains, and a successor of Washington ascend the chair of universal empire.

FURTHER READING

Ray A. Billington was the dean of western historians for many years. See his *The Far Western Frontier, 1830–1860,* 1956, and *Westward Expansion,* 1974. Also essential is Frederick Merk, *History of the Westward Movement,* 1978. More "literary" are Bernard DeVoto, *Across the Wide Missouri,* 1947, and *The Year of Decision, 1846,* 1943.

Other important works on nineteenth-century expansion include John Mack Faragher, *Women and Men on the Oregon Trail,* 1979; Norman A. Graebner, *Empire on the Pacific: A Study in American Continental Expansion,* 1955; Frederick Merk, *Manifest Destiny and Mission in American History: A Reinterpretation,* 1963; D. M. Pletcher, *The Diplomacy of Annexation: Texas, Oregon, and the Mexican War,* 1973; John D. Unruh, *The Plains Across: The Overland Emigrants and the Trans-Mississippi West, 1840–1860,* 1978; and Albert K. Weinberg, *Manifest Destiny,* 1936.

On Oregon, see the contemporary Francis Parkman, *The Oregon Trail,* 1849, as well as Frederick Merk, *The Oregon Question,* 1967, and Malcon Clark Jr., *The Eden-Seekers: The Settlement of Oregon, 1812–1862,* 1981. L. R. Duffus, *The Santa Fe Trail,* 1930, is still the standard work on that subject. On fur trappers and traders, see D. L. Morgan, *Jedediah Smith and the Opening of the West,* 1953; P. C. Phillips, *The Fur Trade,* 1961; and D. J. Wishart, *The Fur Trade of the American West, 1807–1840,* 1979.

On Texas, see E. C. Marker, *Mexico and Texas, 1821–1835,* 1928; W. C. Brinkley, *The Texas Revolution,* 1952; and Frederick Merk, *Slavery and the Annexation of Texas,* 1972. The standard biography of President Polk is Charles Sellers, *James K. Polk: Continentalist,* 1966.

On the Mexican War, see K. Jack Bauer, *The Mexican-American War, 1846–1848,* 1974; Robert W. Johnson, *To the Halls of Montezuma: The Mexican War in the American Imagination,* 1985; and John H. Schroeder, *Mr. Polk's War: American Opposition and Dissent,* 1973.

AMERICAN JOURNEY ONLINE AND INFOTRAC COLLEGE EDITION

Visit the source collections at http://ajaccess.wadsworth.com and http://infotrac.thomsonlearning.com, and use the Search function with the following key terms to explore documents, images, audio and video clips, articles, and commentary related to the material in this chapter:

Battle of the Alamo   Texas Republic
Manifest Destiny   Zachary Taylor

Additional resources, exercises, and Internet links related to this chapter are available on *The American Past* Web site:
http://history.wadsworth.com/americanpast7e.

HISTORY ONLINE

Mountain Men and the Fur Trade
www.xmission.com/~drudy/amm.html
Text, images, sources, and links for the mountain men.

Alamo History
http://drtl.org/History/index.asp
A detailed chronology of the mission compound that became the sacred icon of Texas.

APPLES OF DISCORD

The Poisoned Fruits of Victory 1844–1854

North Wind Picture Archives

The United States will conquer Mexico, but it will be as the man who swallows the arsenic which brings him down in turn.

Ralph Waldo Emerson

T HE VICTORY CELEBRATION was a short one. Even before the Treaty of Guadalupe Hidalgo officially transferred title of California and New Mexico to the United States, the fruits of the Mexican War proved to be apples of discord, setting northerners against southerners as bitterly as the goddesses of Greek mythology scrambled after the prize apple thrown in their midst. That was a golden apple. It was gold that inaugurated the sectional conflict of the 1850s too.

THE SECTIONAL SPLIT

Slavery was, of course, the subject of acrimonious conflict before the Mexican War. Since the 1830s, abolitionists and the defenders of slavery had hurled antagonistic, often vicious, anathemas at one another. Before the Mexican War, the debate had been between zealots and, at best, at the periphery of national politics. Most politicians of the generation of Jackson, Benton, Clay, and Webster recognized the question of slavery's morality as dangerous. They invariably tried to avoid or quash political debates in which the morality of the "peculiar institution" was at the center.

Dead Letter

It was not easy. There were extreme abolitionists in Congress and proslavery fanatics too, as prominent as John C. Calhoun. Thomas Hart Benton was so disgusted by their gratuitous injections of the slavery issue into Senate debates that he likened it to the biblical visitation of plagues on Pharaoh's Egypt:

> You could not look on the table but there were frogs. You could not sit down at the banquet table but there were frogs, you could not go to the bridal couch and lift the sheets but there were frogs! We can see nothing, touch nothing, have no measures proposed, without having this pestilence thrust before us.

Benton was himself a slave owner, although far from hysterical in his justification of the institution. His daughter married a prominent antislavery politician, again not an extremist, John C. Frémont. Benton was disgusted by politicians obsessed by slavery because, a practical man, he knew there were few points at which Congress had the authority to touch the institution of slavery. The Constitution defined slavery as a domestic institution of the states. Short of a constitutional amendment abolishing the institution, slavery was the business of state governments.

An amendment abolishing slavery was out of the question. Three-fourths of the states must agree to any change in the Constitution. During the first half of the nineteenth century, slave states were equal in number to free states. Indeed, when war was declared on Mexico in May 1846, 15 of the 28 states were slave states. Preserving slavery at home, southern state legislatures were, of course, not going to consider abolishing slavery nationally.

Small Steps Toward Abolition

The Constitution did empower Congress "to exercise exclusive legislation in all cases whatsoever" over the District of Columbia. So abolitionist congressmen regularly called for the prohibition of slaveholding in Washington or, at least, a ban on the buying and selling of slaves in the capital. Curiously, some moderate southerners were open to the latter proposal for cosmetic reasons. Slave auctions were ugly. Why put them on view in a city which almost all foreign tourists visited?

Congress also had the power to legislate concerning slaves who ran away from their masters and crossed state lines. The Fugitive Slave Act of 1793 provided that such runaways be returned to their owners. (The law was evaded or obstructed in states where antislavery sentiment was strong, and not vigorously enforced by federal officials there.) Some antislavery northern congressmen wanted to use the Constitution's interstate commerce provisions to prohibit the sale of slaves from one state to another. Southern hotheads proposed reopening the African slave trade, which Congress had the authority to do, as Congress had abolished it. President Polk had so sorely wanted to acquire Cuba because, under the American flag, Cuba would be a treasure house of slaves for sale.

These possibilities aroused the passions of extremists on both sides and vexed the moderates who wanted to keep the slavery issue off center stage. To a large extent, they succeeded—before the Mexican War.

Slavery and the Territories

Congress unambiguously had the power to legislate in regard to slavery in the territories. The Confederation Congress did just that when, in the Northwest Ordinance, it forbade slavery north of the Ohio River. The Constitutional Congress settled the issue of slavery in the Louisiana Purchase lands in the Missouri Compromise.

The Missouri Compromise was the salvation of moderate politicians who wanted to keep the subject of slavery off the floor of Congress. The Missouri bill permitted slavery in territories south of 36 degrees, 30 minutes north latitude, prohibiting it north of that line. After Arkansas was admitted as a slave state in 1836, the only territory in which slaves could legally be owned was Indian Territory (Oklahoma). In the rest of the Louisiana Purchase, slavery was "forever prohibited." There would be no more new slave states.

Then came the annexation of Texas (a slave state), Oregon, and the Mexican territories: The Missouri Compromise line did not apply to those lands. Many antislavery northerners opposed annexing Texas because it added a slave state in violation of the promise of the compromise of 1820. Proslavery southerners were keen on war with Mexico because they looked forward to new territories into which slavery could legally expand.

The Wilmot Proviso and Free Soil Party

Determined to prevent the spread of slavery into newly acquired territory, in 1846, Congressman David Wilmot of Pennsylvania attached a rider, the Wilmot Proviso, to several bills appropriating money to fight the war. The Wilmot Proviso declared that "neither slavery nor involuntary servitude shall ever exist" in any lands taken from Mexico. The House of Representatives approved the proviso in 50 bills between 1846 and 1850. Every northern Whig and all but four northern Democrats voted for it in 1846. Every northern state legislature except New Jersey's officially endorsed it. It was not that so many people were abolitionists. Only a minority of Americans were. However, like Thomas Jefferson in draft-

Riders

In the process of lawmaking, a *rider* is a clause, usually dealing with an unrelated matter, that is attached to a bill already under consideration in Congress or in a state assembly. The strategy of those who propose riders is to turn them into law despite considerable opposition. That is, opponents will so badly want the bill to which the rider is attached that they will pass it even with the objectionable rider. Wilmot tried to attach his antislavery rider to essential appropriations. Only because the anti-Wilmot forces in the Senate were strong enough to strike it did the Wilmot Proviso fail.

The Berrien Proviso

Another rider to a legislative bill of the era, proposed in February 1847 by Senator John M. Berrien, was less successful than David Wilmot's. The Berrien Proviso proposed that "the true intent of Congress in making this appropriation [for the army is] that the war with Mexico ought not to be prosecuted by this Government with any view to the dismemberment of that republic." Even in the northern states, Berrien's anti-expansionism was unacceptable.

ing the Northwest Ordinance, the majority clearly believed that the West should be reserved for family farmers. "Slavocrats" (the planter aristocracy) had to be kept out.

The Wilmot Proviso never became law. John C. Calhoun (naturally) led the fight against it in the Senate. The Constitution, he said, guaranteed to the citizens of all states who emigrated to the territories the same rights they had enjoyed at home. The citizens of some states could own slaves. Therefore, they had the right to take their slaves with them if they went west.

Slave state senators were equal in number (superior in a few Congresses) to free state senators. With the help of a few northern Democrats, the Senate deleted the Wilmot Proviso from every bill to which the House attached it.

When President Polk endorsed Calhoun's reasoning, a large number of northern Democrats bolted from the party and organized the Free Soil party. Some were abolitionists, but by no means all. As a party, the Free Soilers allowed that the people of the South had the constitutional right to preserve slavery at home. Most Free Soilers cared little about the injustice and suffering of African Americans. Some were vociferous racists who wanted to exclude blacks as well as slaves. There was a streak of racism in the rhetoric of many of them; a few wanted to ban free blacks as well as slaves from the western territories. (As late as 1857, Oregon prohibited the emigration of free blacks into the state.)

However, they insisted that the Mexican acquisition must be dedicated to, as their party slogan said, "Free soil! Free speech! Free men!"

The Election of 1848

Polk, as he had promised, did not stand for reelection in 1848. A hard worker, he literally wore himself out and died, at age 54, four months after leaving the White House. The Democrats nominated one of his northern supporters, the competent but gloriously dull Lewis Cass of Michigan. The Whigs, having lost once again with Clay in 1844, returned to the winning formula of 1840—a popular general whose views were unknown. They nominated the hero of Buena Vista, Zachary Taylor of Louisiana. Taylor was a southerner who owned a great many slaves. Whig strategists gambled that he would carry southern states that would otherwise be lost to the Democrats because of northern Whig support of the Wilmot Proviso.

Taylor was a remarkable presidential candidate. "He really is a most simple-minded old man," said Whig educator Horace Mann. "Few men have ever had more contempt for learning," wrote General Winfield Scott. "He doesn't know himself from a side of sole leather in the way of statesmanship," wrote Horace Greeley. A coarse, cranky, and bluntspoken old geezer of 64, Taylor admitted he had never bothered to vote in his life. When the letter from the Whig party announcing his nomination arrived, he refused to pay the postage due on it. When someone else did, he responded diffidently, "I will not say I will not serve if the good people were imprudent enough to elect me."

The Free Soilers put up a more distinguished and able candidate than either major party, former president Martin Van Buren. Along in years, he had announced his opposition to slavery in the territories. Little Van did not have a chance, but his name on the ballot determined the election. He won more votes in New York than Lewis Cass did, thus throwing the state's 36 electoral votes to Taylor. With New York State, as so many times, went the election.

THE CALIFORNIA CRISIS

Moderate Whigs hoped that Taylor's victory would cool southern passions aroused by the Wilmot Proviso and Free Soilers, allowing the party to use the power of government to promote orderly economic development and moral behavior nationally. But Old Rough and Ready was to know little harmony as president. Events in distant California, un-

No-Name City
In the national capital in 1850, California meant sectional crisis. However, when the first California legislature met, the delegates were more interested in making some citizens feel comfortable in the new state. The first law enacted by the legislature reduced the statute of limitations so that Californians with perhaps murky pasts back East could not easily be extradited. The second enactment made it easier for an individual to change his name.

The Gold Rush That Wasn't
In 1844, four years before Marshall's discovery, Pablo Gutiérrez discovered gold in the bed of the Bear River and immediately secured a land grant of 22,000 acres that included what he hoped would be a rich mine. When he went to Sutter's fort in Sacramento to buy mining equipment, Sutter was preoccupied with agitation and revolt near Monterey. He sent Gutiérrez there to learn what was happening, and Gutiérrez was killed by the rebels. The gold fever of 1844 died with him. His Bear River grant was sold to William Johnson, who knew nothing of Gutiérrez's gold. The Bear River was overrun in 1849 and 1850 by miners who ignored Mexican land grants, and the deposit was rediscovered.

Junk Mail
Had the leaders of the Whig party been up-to-date in 1848, they might have spared themselves the embarrassment of having Zachary Taylor refuse to pay the postage due on the letter notifying him of his presidential nomination. The previous year, 1847, the United States Post Office had begun to issue stamps that permitted the sender to pay the postage. Apparently, the idea had not yet caught on.

▲ *Placer miners at Spanish Flat, California. They are using a long tom, shoveling gravel into a box through which a constant stream of water is being sluiced. With luck, there would be several ounces of gold dust in the bottom of the long tom when the sun went down. Note the rocks at the feet of the miner on the right. They were picked out of the gravel by hand.*

folding even as he was nominated and elected, caused a crisis that almost destroyed the Union in 1850.

Gold!

On the evening of January 24, 1848, a carpenter, James Marshall, took a walk along the American River where it tumbles through the foothills of the Sierra Nevada. Marshall worked for John Augustus Sutter, a Swiss adventurer who had turned a vast Mexican land grant into a feudal domain. Sutter's castle was an adobe fort on the Sacramento River, defended by cannon he had purchased from the Russians when they abandoned Fort Ross.

Marshall was building a sawmill for Sutter. Inspecting the tail race—the ditch that returned rushing water to the river after it powered the mill—he picked up a curious metallic stone. "Boys," he told the other workers, "I think I have found a gold mine."

He had, and that was that for the sawmill. Sutter's employees immediately set to shoveling gravel from the river, separating the sand and silt from what proved to be plenty of gold dust and nuggets. Briefly, Marshall's discovery was

the end of San Francisco. A town of 500 souls, it was depopulated when "everyone," including the recently arrived American military garrison, headed for the hills.

The next year—1849—80,000 people descended on California. By the end of the year, the population was about 100,000, more than in the states of Delaware and Florida. These "forty-niners" produced $10 million in gold. Californians said, plausibly enough, that their numbers and value to the nation merited immediate statehood. When Congress convened in December 1849, California's provisional constitution was on the table. In the would-be state of California, slavery was forbidden.

Trauma

The stunning rapidity of these events lay at the heart of the crisis that ensued. Polk and proslavery southerners assumed that California would be peopled slowly by, among others, southern slave owners and their slaves. When, years down the line, it was time to create a state on the Pacific, at least part of California would apply for admission as a slave state.

Now, before the Treaty of Guadalupe Hidalgo was ratified, before California was organized as a territory—work Congress expected to be doing in 1850—proslavery southerners saw their reasonable expectations pulverized by California's application for admission as a free state. The worst of it was that California statehood would mean the South's loss of equality with the northern states in the Senate. There were two more embryonic free states, Oregon and Minnesota, waiting in the wings but not a single potential slave state in sight.

Southerners were already a minority in the House of Representatives, where seats are apportioned according to population. In 1849, there were about 9 million people in the South and 14 million in the North (thus the repeated approval of the Wilmot Proviso in the House). The Senate, therefore, where each state had two members regardless of population, had assumed sacred significance to Calhoun and his like. A majority of southern congressmen immediately declared they would vote against California statehood. The North's toleration of abolitionists, they said, made it impossible for the South to trust in the goodwill of any northern senators. The South must have equality in the Senate.

Henry Clay's Last Stand

To the surprise of some, the southern intransigents discovered that President Taylor was not on their side. He would take up arms to defend his right to his hundred slaves, Taylor said, but he was a nationalist. National pride, prosperity, and security demanded that California be admitted immediately, no strings attached. He further angered southern extremists with his decision that a boundary dispute between slave state Texas and New Mexico Territory be resolved in favor of New Mexico.

How They Mined the Gold

Few American forty-niners knew even the rudiments of gold mining. Only the Mexicans, called "Sonorans" in California after the Mexican state from which most came, and the Cornish from southwestern England had been miners before they came to the gold fields. However, technological innocence was no great handicap because placer mining—recovering pure gold from the sand and gravel of creek beds—called for backbreaking toil but was quite a simple operation.

Placer mining is a mechanical process. To determine whether there was gold in a creek, a miner "panned" it. That is, he scooped up a pound or two of silt, sand, and pebbles in a sturdy, shallow pan; removed the stones by hand; and then agitated the finer contents, constantly replenishing the water in the pan so that the lighter mud and sand washed over the sides while the heavier gold dust remained.

When miners discovered enough "color" to warrant mining of a placer, they staked a claim and built a "rocker" or a "long tom," two easily constructed devices that performed the washing process on a larger scale.

The rocker was a watertight wooden box, three to five feet long and a foot or so across. It was mounted on a base like that of a rocking chair so that it could be tipped from side to side. In the bottom of the box were wooden riffles or a sheet of corrugated metal, and sometimes a fine wire mesh. These simulated the crevices in a creek bed, where the gold naturally collected. Into the rocker, by means of a sluice, also easily built, ran a stream of water. While one partner shoveled gravel and sand into the box, another rocked it and agitated the contents with a spade or a pitchfork. The lighter worthless mineral washed out (stones, again, were manually discarded), and the gold remained at the bottom to be retrieved at the end of the day, weighed, divided, and cached.

The long tom took more time to build, but it was more productive. In effect, the water-bearing sluice was extended into a long, high-sided, watertight box with riffles in the bottom. With a long tom, all the miners in a partnership could shovel gravel: no rocking.

The placer mines were known as the "poor man's diggings" because placer mining neither required much money nor gave the man with capital any advantage. The placer miner needed only a few tools and materials. Because just about everyone in California hoped to strike it rich, few were willing to work for set wages, no matter how high. The lucky discoverer of a valuable gold deposit had to take on partners if he wanted to work it efficiently.

As long as the "poor man's diggings" held out, life in the mining camps was highly democratic and egalitarian. No one was allowed to stake a claim larger than he and his partners could mine within a season or two. Law and order in the earliest mining camps was maintained by the informal common consent of the men who lived in them. Except for small military units that were plagued with desertion, there was no formal legal authority in California until late 1850 and no significant governmental presence in many of the gold fields for several years thereafter.

Not all the fruits of democracy were edifying. A man with the majority of a camp behind him could "get away with murder." Miner democracy did not extend to other than native-born Americans and immigrants from western Europe. Despite the fact that the forty-niners learned what they knew of mining from the Sonorans, they expelled the Sonorans from all but the southernmost gold fields within a year. Chileans, being Spanish speakers, came up against prejudice.

Worst treated of all were the Chinese. Because their culture was so alien and because they worked in large groups, thus spending less to live, the Chinese frightened the forty-niners. They feared that the "Celestials," as the Chinese were called, would drag down the standard of living for all. Chinese miners survived only by working deposits abandoned by white and a few African American miners as too poor. Most of the Chinese who came to the "Golden Mountain" to mine drifted into California's towns and cities and settled for other jobs.

Tempers were boiling. The election of a Speaker of the House, usually a formality, required 63 ballots. In the Senate, Henry Clay, frail and weary at 72, beyond all hope of being president, tried to cap his career as the Great Compromiser by proposing a permanent solution to the question of slavery in the territories.

Clay's Omnibus Bill was a compromise in the old tradition. It required both sides to make significant concessions in the interests of the common good, the Union. California would be admitted as a free state. The rest of the Mexican acquisition would be organized as territories with no reference to the status of slavery there. Clay meant to hold out to proslavery southerners the possibility of future slave states in what is now Utah, Nevada, New Mexico, and Arizona. Texas's border dispute with New Mexico would be resolved

as Taylor had announced (Clay certainly needed the president's blessing) but with face-saving concessions to Texas, including Congress's assumption of the state's large debts.

Clay appealed to the antislavery feelings of many northerners by proposing the abolition of the slave trade in the national capital. To compensate southerners for this symbolic rebuff, Clay included a new, stronger Fugitive Slave Act in the Omnibus Bill.

Failure

Not too many years earlier, the Omnibus Bill would have sailed through Congress amid cheers, tossed hats, and invitations to share a bottle. Texas and California changed all that. Extremists from both sections, and some congressmen

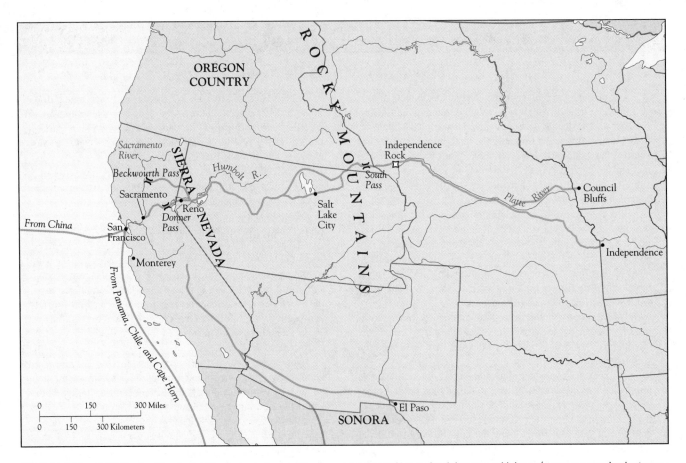

MAP 21:1 The Gold Rush   The route of the forty-niners was long known by mountain men, but it became a highway (some wagon wheel ruts are still visible today) only with the Gold Rush.

regarded as moderates, refused to accept the Omnibus Bill because it included concessions they regarded as morally reprehensible.

Many northerners, not just abolitionists, abhorred the Fugitive Slave Act. By allowing federal officials to arrest people who committed no crime under the laws of their states, it made slavery quasi-legal everywhere. Southern extremists could not vote to abolish the slave trade in Washington, D.C. Slavery was a positive good; they would not apologize for any aspect of it. President Taylor's friends in Congress resented compensating Texas in any way.

The spirit of compromise was dead. New York's William H. Seward called the very idea of compromise "radically wrong and essentially vicious." "Fire-eaters," militantly proslavery young southern congressmen, swore to yield nothing. John C. Calhoun, once master of cool reason and cold logic, was reduced to the sophistry of a cynical lawyer. Obsessed with his goal—the expansion of slavery and southern political power—he devised convoluted, sometimes crazy, schemes to reach it. Calhoun proposed that there should be two presidents, one from the North and one from the South, each with the power of veto over congressional acts and one another. The pathetic old man spent his last

days, dying painfully of throat cancer, surrounded by a gaggle of romantic young disciples who had, among them, half the brain he'd once had in his head.

Henry Clay plugged away among those he thought were moderates, mustering his eloquence one last time. "I have heard something said about allegiance to the South," he told the Senate. "I know no South, no North, no East, no West, to which I owe any allegiance. The Union, sir, is my country."

Because his terminal disease left him almost voiceless, Calhoun's answer had to be read for him. He was equally eloquent and more realistic about the crisis than Clay: "The cry of 'Union, Union, the glorious Union!' can no more prevent disunion than the cry of 'Health, health, glorious health!' . . . can save a patient lying dangerously ill."

Daniel Webster, the last of the Senate's aged triumvirate, had his last word too. It ranked with his greatest orations, and it destroyed him politically. Webster supported the Omnibus Bill. To save the Union, he said, he would vote even for the fugitive slave law in Clay's proposal. Webster was vilified in New England. Nothing better illustrates what the embrace of extremism does to people than the fact that New Englanders who had winked for decades at Webster's personal debauchery and panhandling of bankers now de-

MAP 21:2 Gold Rush California The gold camps (many of them actually sizable towns) were located on the western foothills of the Sierra Nevada. They were supplied through San Francisco and river towns like Marysville, Sacramento, and Stockton.

nounced him to hell for advocating compromise in a crisis that was tearing the Union apart. "The word 'honor' in the mouth of Mr. Webster," wrote Ralph Waldo Emerson, "is like the word 'love' in the mouth of a whore."

THE COMPROMISE OF 1850

The Omnibus Bill was voted down. No matter—President Taylor would have vetoed it. Stubborn and willful, Taylor was set against compensating Texas for land to which, in his view, the state had no claim. It was the most innocuous part of the Omnibus Bill. By gagging on it, Taylor demonstrated that he was no politician.

Clay left Washington, confounded and without hope. In the meantime, however, fate intervened to save his cause and to bring to the fore a resourceful young senator who would be as central in the Senate of his era as Clay was in his own.

Death of a Soldier

Zachary Taylor exited. On July 4, 1850, the president attended a ceremony on the Capitol mall where, for two hours, he sat hatless in the blazing sun listening to long-winded orators. Back at the White House, he wolfed down cherries and cucumbers and several quarts of chilled milk and ice water. A few hours later the old man took to bed with stomach cramps. Instead of leaving him alone, his doctors bled him and administered one powerful medicine after another—ipecac to make him vomit, quinine for his fever, calomel as a laxative, and opium for the pain to which they were adding. Old Rough and Ready was murder on Mexicans and Texans, but he could not handle the pharmacopeia of the nineteenth century. He died on July 9 and was succeeded by Vice President Millard Fillmore.

Fillmore is often ridiculed as the least memorable president. A New Yorker, he had flirted with radical politics early in his career. But in 1850 he was firmly within the moderate Whig camp of Clay and Webster. Although he did not declare publicly for compromise, it was generally thought he favored it.

The "Little Giant"

The senator who broke the impasse was Stephen A. Douglas of Illinois. Barely five feet in height, he was known as the "Little Giant" because of his oratorical powers and his role as tactical mastermind of the Illinois Democratic party. Only three years a senator, Douglas had mobilized contacts among both northern and southern Democrats, and he had an idea.

Instead of presenting the polarized House and Senate with a single compromise bill, parts of which offended everyone, Douglas carved Clay's package into separate bills. These he maneuvered individually through Congress by patching together a different majority for each.

Thus, Douglas could count on northern senators and representatives of both parties to vote for California statehood and the abolition of the slave trade in the District of Columbia. In the House, that was enough. In the Senate, he won the votes of just enough southern moderates from the border states to slip the bills through. He could count on a solid southern bloc for the Fugitive Slave Act and the Texas bills. To this, arguing for the necessity of preserving the Democratic party in both sections, he added enough northern Democratic votes to make a majority.

The "Compromise of 1850" was not a compromise in the sense that both sides gave a little and took a little. A majority of both northern and southern congressmen refused to yield an inch. Only four of 60 senators voted for all of Douglas's bills! Only 11 voted for five of the six bills. (Even Douglas was absent for the vote on the Fugitive Slave Act.) Only 28 of 240 representatives voted for all of the bills.

Douglas's manipulations were brilliant. He made extremely controversial bills into laws when a tiny handful of his colleagues were truly committed to the spirit of compromise. His success was popular in the nation at large, where moderation on sectional questions was probably stronger than it was under the Capitol dome. But Douglas did not extinguish the fires of sectional hostility smoldering in both Congress and the country.

▲ *The great debate of 1850. Henry Clay is making his eloquent plea for compromise in the cause of the Union. John C. Calhoun, accurately depicted as near death, is the third senator from the right. Daniel Webster, seated at the left, head in hand, would soon speak magnificently in support of Clay and be disgraced in Massachusetts.*

The Old Guard

In the Thirty-First Congress of 1849–1851, the nation's second generation of political leaders, those who had governed the country since the passing of the Founding Fathers, rubbed elbows with a third generation, a new breed. Andrew Jackson was already gone, dead in 1845. Henry Clay and Daniel Webster both passed on in 1852. Thomas Hart Benton survived until 1858, but only to discover that the new era had no place for him. Because he refused to defend slavery as a positive good and, like Webster, placed the Union above sectional prejudices, he lost his Senate seat in 1850, was defeated in a race for the House in 1856, and lost when he ran for governor of Missouri.

Calhoun would have won election after election in South Carolina had he lived to be a hundred. Alone of the giants of the Age of Jackson, he made the transition—indeed, led the transition—from commitment to Union to extreme southern sectionalism. But Calhoun did not survive to see the results of his unhappy career. He died before Douglas performed his political wizardry.

Extremists and Moderates

Shortly before his death, Calhoun croaked to one of his disciples that it was up to the young to save "the South, the poor South." With each year of the new decade, such "fire-eaters,"

so called because of the invective with which they spoke of northerners, displaced moderates in southern state legislatures, governorships, the House, and the Senate.

The southern Whig party, the refuge of moderates, dwindled. John Tyler had already led the states' rights Whigs back to the Democratic party. Compromise-minded southern Whigs left politics or, as in the case of Robert Toombs of Georgia, embraced southern extremism. Robert Toombs supported the Compromise of 1850, but within a few years, he was baiting northerners in language as torrid as any Democrat's. A few old southern Whigs were so respected as individuals that they continued to win elections under the party label or while voicing Whig principles as independents. Most of them were from the Upper South, states where the fanatical proslavery spirit burned less brightly.

In the North, abolitionists were proportionally less powerful than the fire-eaters in the South. Abolitionism remained unpopular with the majority of northerners, in part because northern whites shared the racism of southerners, in part because of the self-righteousness of some antislavery crusaders.

Nevertheless, there was a militant antislavery delegation in Congress. Among the ablest was William H. Seward of New York, a former Anti-Mason. Thaddeus Stevens of Pennsylvania was a rare, staunch believer in racial equality whom southerners hated above all other abolitionists. Charles Sumner of Massachusetts succeeded Webster as New England's

PRACTICAL ILLUSTRATION OF THE FUGITIVE SLAVE LAW.

▲ *An antislavery cartoon attacking the Fugitive Slave Act of 1850. Abolitionist William Lloyd Garrison is protecting the runaway slave woman at left (with a gun, which is curious, for Garrison was a pacifist). Daniel Webster, who voted for the law, is the mount for a stereotypical Irishman (most Irish voters were Democrats friendly to slavery) bearing chains for the woman and a noose for Garrison.*

most prominent senator. Some of the antislavery congressmen, like Salmon B. Chase of Ohio, were Free Soilers. Most were Whigs.

With the Free Soilers gone from the party, most northern Democrats were friendly to southern demands and to slavery. A few Democrats preached positive-good propaganda with the best of them. Others, notably Douglas, resembled the northern Democrats of the Age of Jackson. By no means did they look on slavery as a desirable institution. But their sensibilities were not outraged by its existence in the South. For the sake of Democratic party unity, they were willing to tolerate the spread of the institution into the territories. Northern Democrats considered themselves moderates.

THE KANSAS-NEBRASKA ACT

The United States needed a compelling, even charismatic, president committed to preserving the Union. Instead, in 1852, it got Franklin Pierce. Pierce was handsome, amiable, a good speaker, and popular both in New Hampshire and in Congress, where he served between 1833 and 1847. He left the Senate to serve in the Mexican War, then returned to New Hampshire to practice law.

Then, in 1852, the Democratic party, now tightly cinched to the two-thirds rule, deadlocked for 48 ballots. A compromise candidate, acceptable to both northern and southern

Democrats was needed. None could be found in public office. The convention turned to private citizen Pierce.

Pierce won a narrow popular vote victory over Whig candidate General Winfield Scott, but he nearly swept the electoral college. It was all a terrible mistake. As a fellow New Hampshireman commented, "Up here, where everybody knows Frank Pierce, he's a pretty considerable fellow. But come to spread him out over the whole country, I'm afraid he'll be dreadful thin in some places."

Pierce's wife, to whom he was devoted, wanted nothing to do with politics or Washington, D.C. She was an emotionally fragile woman who was completely shattered when, just before Pierce's inauguration, their young son was killed in a railroad accident. Preoccupied with his wife's distraction, Pierce leaned heavily on his personal friend, whom he named secretary of war, Jefferson Davis of Mississippi.

A Railroad to California

Davis was staunchly proslavery but not a fire-eater. With presidential ambitions of his own, he wanted to persuade northern Democrats that he was a nationally minded man, while retaining his southern political base. Of modest background—Davis was born in a log cabin in Kentucky—he looked like an aristocrat. Indeed, his brother, Joseph Davis, was one of Mississippi's richest cotton planters, and a model paternalistic slave owner.

Stephen Douglas, the "Little Giant," was too clever and manipulative a politician for his own good. He masterminded the intricate tactics that enacted the Compromise of 1850 when Henry Clay failed. Douglas also devised and passed the Kansas-Nebraska Act in the face of the opposition of a majority of northerners.

Anthony Burns

Anthony Burns, a slave, fled Virginia for Boston in 1854. He was arrested under the Fugitive Slave Act of 1850, and a furious mob of abolitionists almost freed him. Federal troops had to be brought in to guard him and return him to his owner. In Virginia, Burns was immediately sold for $900, a very low price for a 20-year-old "prime field hand." But Burns was intelligent, self-educated, literate, and obviously determined to be free.

For northerners, the Burns case symbolized the determination of slavocrats to force slavery down their throats in the heart of New England. Bostonians raised the money to buy his freedom and sent him to Oberlin College.

Burns was a symbol for southern fire-eaters too. They rejoiced at his return to slavery. A few southerners had cooler heads. It had cost $100,000 to return one man to slavery. "A few more such victories and the South is undone," wrote the Richmond *Enquirer*.

© Corbis

Already nationally celebrated for his bravery as an officer in the Mexican War, Davis, with the total support of the distracted Pierce, tried to revive the expansionism of the 1840s with unsuccessful attempts to annex Hawaii and Cuba. (Cuba, with its many slaves, figured prominently in southern imaginations.) He tacitly supported American filibusters, freelance adventurers, mostly southerners, who led private armies into unstable Central America in the hopes of creating personal empires.

Davis's most important project was the construction of a transcontinental railroad tying California to the old states. Everyone knew that the railroad would eventually be built. Davis wanted its eastern terminus in the South, knowing that the California trade would enrich the city that was the eastern gateway of the line. From an engineer's point of view, the best route was through Texas and along the southern boundary of the country. There were no mountains of consequence on the route until the projected railroad reached the southern New Mexico Territory, just above the Gila River. There, in order to keep the projected railroad line on the flat, it would be necessary to build in Mexico, which was unacceptable.

To remedy the problem, Davis and Pierce sent James Gadsden, a railroad man, to Mexico City. For $10 million, he purchased a 30,000-square-mile triangle of arid but level land. Davis, it appeared, had plucked a juicy plum for the South that would also be a great national enterprise, big enough, perhaps, to make its chief proponent president.

Douglas's Scheme

Stephen Douglas thought so too, and he wanted the transcontinental railroad for Chicago. However, the so-called Central Route not only crossed several major mountain ranges,

Filibusters

The word *filibuster* is a curious corruption of the Dutch *vrijbuiter,* meaning "freebooter" (that is, "pirate" or "plunderer"). *Filibuster* was used to describe the mostly southern veterans of the Mexican War who saw greater opportunities as warriors in Central America and the Caribbean than back home on a farm or in a shop. The first was actually a Cuban rebel, Narciso López, most of whose soldiers, however, were American. In 1850, with financial support from the South, he tried to overthrow the Spanish in Cuba, the idea being to ask for annexation to the United States. The Spanish executed 50 of his American soldiers. Chastened, the federal government arrested Mississippi governor John A. Quitman before he could lead a filibustering expedition to resume López's fight.

However, Secretary of War Jefferson Davis supported the most famous of the filibusters, William Walker, semi-openly. An extraordinary adventurer, probably more interested in personal glory than in adding slave states to the Union (a highly unlikely outcome had Walker succeeded), Walker invaded Baja California in 1853 but was driven back north within weeks. Better organized, he then went to Nicaragua, which was in an almost anarchic state, and with hundreds of Nicaraguan rebels and American mercenaries, proclaimed himself president. Albeit as a roving warlord, Walker actually ran the country for two years. When things went sour, he was rescued by an American warship but was soon filibustering again, this time in Honduras. He was executed by a firing squad there in 1860.

Slavery in the State of Maine

The Missouri Compromise provided that slavery was "forever forbidden" in the *territories* of the Louisiana Purchase north of 36 degrees, 30 minutes. But did that mean that the *states* that emerged in those lands were forbidden to legalize slavery? In the law, no. Before signing the Missouri act, President Monroe consulted with his advisers. All, including John Quincy Adams, said that once a territory had become a state, its domestic institutions were its own business. In other words, had the state of Maine voted to legalize slavery as late as 1864, it was as constitutionally free to do so as Maryland was constitutionally free to abolish slavery there.

In the real world, forbidding slavery in the territories meant that states developing there would inevitably be free states. There would be no slave owners at the state's constitutional convention.

beyond Missouri's western border, it ran through unorganized territory, parts of the Louisiana Purchase left to the Indians. The only federal presence was a series of forts monitoring the Indians and protecting the overland trail. Southern politicians could kill the Central Route, and win the transcontinental for the South, by refusing to organize territorial governments west of Missouri.

As ingenious as he had been in 1850, Douglas came up with a scheme for seducing the southerners by offering them the possibility of spreading slavery to lands where it was forbidden by the Missouri Compromise.

In May 1854, Douglas introduced a bill to organize two new federal territories, Kansas and Nebraska. The bill explicitly repealed the section of the Missouri Compromise that prohibited slavery there. Instead, the people of the Kansas and Nebraska territories would decide for themselves whether they would allow or prohibit the institution. "Popular sovereignty," Douglas said, was the democratic solution to the problem of slavery in the territories.

Southern congressmen jumped for the bait like trout after a bad winter. None had illusions about Nebraska, through which the Central Route would run. It bordered on the free state of Iowa and would inevitably be populated by antislavery northerners. Kansas, however, abutted on Missouri, where slavery was unimportant economically but an emotionally passionate issue, even with poor whites who owned no slaves.

North Wind Picture Archives

▲ *A poster announcing a rally against the Kansas-Nebraska Act. There were thousands of such meetings all over the North within weeks of Congress's enactment of the law. Rarely has there been so spontaneous a widespread protest.*

Douglas's popularity soared in the South, a bonus, for he hoped to win the Democratic presidential nomination in 1856. He presented himself once again as a broker between the sections. To southerners, he was the man who opened Kansas to slavery. To northerners, he was the man who got the transcontinental railroad.

In fact, although northern Democrats supported him, Douglas was vilified by antislavery northerners as a "dough-face," a Democrat who kneaded his face into one shape in the North, another in the South—in effect, a northern man with southern principles. The epithet was also applied to Pierce and to the Democratic presidential nominee in 1856, not Douglas, but James Buchanan of Pennsylvania.

The Republican Party

The Kansas-Nebraska Act finished off the Whigs. When southern Whigs voted for it, the Whigs of the North bade them farewell. Many northern Whigs were abolitionists. Those who were not, like Abraham Lincoln of Illinois, regarded the Missouri Compromise as their party's greatest achievement. Willing to tolerate slavery in the South, unwilling to accept its expansion, the northern Whigs joined with the Free Soilers to form the new Republican party.

So spontaneous was the explosion of opposition to the Kansas-Nebraska Act that the birthplace of the new party is disputed. (Ripon, Wisconsin, has the best claim.) The fact is, the Republican party combusted and coalesced all over the North. Rather more striking, the Republican demand that the Kansas-Nebraska Act be repealed was so popular that the infant party actually captured the House of Representatives in the midterm election of 1854, months after the Kansas-Nebraska Act became law.

At first, the Republicans were a single-issue party, much like the Free Soilers, who became Republicans. But their leaders were experienced and cagey politicians with varied interests who soon worked out a comprehensive program. The Republicans stole Douglas's thunder by insisting that the transcontinental be built on the Central Route. They appealed to farmers indifferent to the question of slavery in the territories by advocating a homestead act giving western lands free to families who would actually settle and farm it.

From the Whigs, the Republicans inherited the demand for a high protective tariff, thus winning some manufacturing interests to their side. Also appealing to industrial capitalists was the Republican demand for a liberal immigration policy, which would attract cheap European labor to the United States. Also from the Whigs, Republicans inherited a

MAP 21:3 America After the Kansas-Nebraska Act The organization of Nebraska Territory caused no fuss. Proslavery southerners knew that, eventually, states formed there would be free states. Making Kansas safe for slavery, however, became a virtually sacred cause for proslavery zealots.

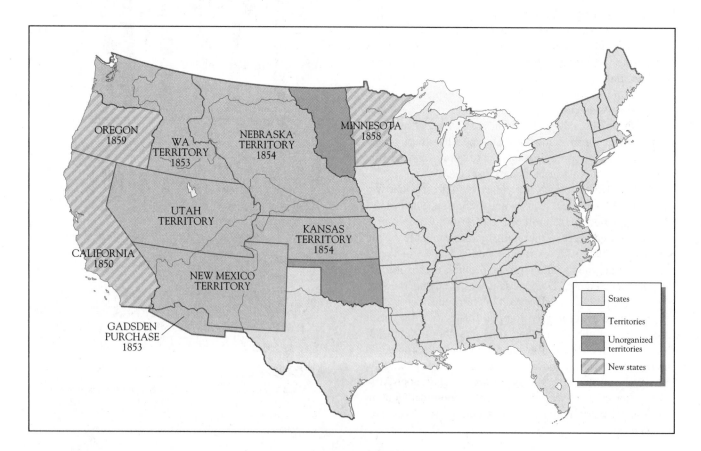

disdain for Democrats as the country's vulgar, self-serving, and ignorant. Poet Walt Whitman put it in a diatribe not to be topped. The Democrats of Washington, D.C., Whitman said, were:

> the meanest kind of bawling and blowing office-holders, office-seekers, pimps, malignants, conspirators, murderers, fancy-men, custom-house clerks, contractors, kept-editors, spaniels well-train'd to carry and fetch, jobbers, infidels, disunionists, terrorists, mail-riflers, slave-catchers, pushers of slavery, creatures of the President, creatures of would-be Presidents, spies, bribers, compromisers, lobbyers, sponges, ruin'd sports, expell'd gamblers, policy-backers, monte-dealers, duellists, carriers of conceal'd weapons, deaf men, pimpled men, scarr'd inside with vile disease, gaudy outside with gold chains made from the people's money and harlot's money twisted together; crawling serpentine men, the lousy combinings and born freedom-settlers of the earth.

The Republicans (the exact opposite on every count, of course) were not a national party, as the Whigs had been. They appealed only to northerners. They did not even put up candidates for office in most slave states. Their hopes of national victory lay in a sweep of the free states, which, indeed, would be quite enough to control the House and win the presidency. In that hope—government by a party frankly representing only one section of the Union—lay a threat to the unity of the country.

for FURTHER READING

Historians have attended to the series of events leading up to the Civil War with great care. Why did extremism triumph in the South and grow into a powerful force in the North? Why did so many Americans abandon the old spirit of compromise? At what point—with what event—did war become inevitable? Why?

See Avery O. Craven, *The Growth of Southern Nationalism, 1848–1860,* 1953 (*southern nationalism* means the sense of the South as a nation), and *The Coming of the Civil War,* 1957; William J. Cooper, *The South and the Politics of Slavery,* 1978; William W. Freehling, *The Road to Disunion,* 1990; Michael Holt, *The Political Crisis of the 1850s,* 1978; Alan Nevins, *Ordeal of the Union,* 1947; David Potter, *The Impending Crisis,* 1976; and Kenneth M. Stampp, *And the War Came,* 1950.

On the Free Soil movement, see C. W. Morrison, *Democratic Politics and Sectionalism: The Wilmot Proviso Controversy,* 1967; Eric Foner, *Free Soil, Free Labor, Free Men,* 1970; Fred J. Blue, *The Free Soilers: Third Party Politics,* 1973; and John Mayfield, *Rehearsal for Republicanism: Free Soil and the Politics of Anti-Slavery,* 1980.

On the prelude to the crisis of 1850, see Joseph G. Rayback, *Free Soil: The Election of 1848,* 1970; K. J. Bauer, *Zachary Taylor:*

Soldier, Planter, Statesman of the Old Southwest, 1985; and Holman Hamilton, *Zachary Taylor: Soldier in the White House,* 1951.

On the Gold Rush, see Rodman Paul, *California Gold: The Beginning of Mining in the Far West,* 1947; and John W. Caughey, *Gold Is the Cornerstone,* 1949. The standard study for the Compromise of 1850 is Holman Hamilton, *Prologue to Conflict: The Crisis and Compromise of 1850,* 1964. See also Richard N. Current, *Daniel Webster and the Rise of National Conservatism,* 1955; Charles M. Wiltse, *John C. Calhoun: Sectionalist,* 1951; and Robert Remini, *Henry Clay: Statesman for the Union,* 1991.

Michael Holt, *The Political Crises of the 1850s,* 1978, carries the story through the Kansas-Nebraska Act. See also James C. Malin, *The Nebraska Question: 1852–1854,* 1953; David Potter, *The South and Sectional Conflict,* 1968; and W. E. Gienapp, *The Origins of the Republican Party,* 1986. On Douglas, see G. M. Capers, *Stephen Douglas: Defender of the Union,* 1959. A sympathetic biography of Franklin Pierce is R. F. Nichols, *Young Hickory of the Granite Hills,* 1931.

AMERICAN JOURNEY ONLINE AND INFOTRAC COLLEGE EDITION

Visit the source collections at http://ajaccess.wadsworth.com and http://infotrac.thomsonlearning.com, and use the Search function with the following key terms to explore documents, images, audio and video clips, articles, and commentary related to the material in this chapter:

Compromise of 1850   Kansas-Nebraska Act
Gold Rush   Stephen Douglas

Additional resources, exercises, and Internet links related to this chapter are available on *The American Past* Web site: http://history.wadsworth.com/americanpast7e.

HISTORY ONLINE

The Mexican War
www.multied.com/wars.html
The battles of the Mexican War: maps, text.

The California Gold Country
http://malakoff.com/goldcountry/images.htm
Photographs from the earliest years of the Gold Rush.

THE COLLAPSE OF THE UNION

The Road to Secession 1854–1861

Shall I tell you what this collision means? They who think it is accidental, unnecessary, the work of interested or fanatical agitators, and therefore ephemeral, mistake the case altogether. It is an irrepressible conflict between opposing and enduring forces.

William H. Seward

"A house divided against itself cannot stand." I believe this government cannot endure permanently half-slave and half-free. I do not expect the Union to be dissolved—I do not expect the house to fall—but I do expect it will cease to be divided.

Abraham Lincoln

T HE KANSAS-NEBRASKA ACT was a tragedy. In devising it, Stephen A. Douglas became the Union's Pandora, the woman of Greek myth who opened a box from which woes and troubles flew. In the myth, Pandora was able to close the lid of the box before hope was lost. The Union had its hopes after 1854, but one by one, they were dashed by events directly traceable to the Kansas-Nebraska Act.

"BLEEDING KANSAS"

The Kansas Territory was a bone of contention from its creation. The southerners who voted to create it assumed that, populated by proslavery Missourians, Kansas would enter the Union as a slave state, and soon. The Republican party was sworn to repeal the Kansas-Nebraska Act and restore the prohibition of slavery in Kansas when it won control of Congress and the presidency. Abolitionists and militant Free Soilers among the Republicans would not wait. Led by New Englanders, they meant to keep slavery out of Kansas under the rules Congress had written—popular sovereignty and majority vote.

Free Soilers and Border Ruffians

Eli Thayer and other abolitionists organized the New England Emigrant Aid Company, which raised money to finance the emigration of antislavery northerners to Kansas. Their success, thanks in part to the continuing decline of New England agriculture, was extraordinary. Within two years of the Kansas-Nebraska Act, Thayer's group alone sent 2,000 people to the Kansas Territory. Undoubtedly, their propaganda—for they praised the land as if they were selling farms there—encouraged many other northerners to go on their own.

By contrast, few southerners seemed interested in emigrating. The fact was, no southern region was so densely populated as New England, and California still exerted more attraction with its gold than Kansas could. Western Missouri, which proslavery southerners believed would populate the new territory, was itself (outside of Independence) a thinly populated frontier. Proslavery politicians were stunned

yet again—this time by the stream of free staters to Kansas. The incipient slave state of Kansas might not be a slave state after all.

If few western Missourians relocated in Kansas, some of the rougher sort, egged on by southern fire-eaters, were willing to take violent action against Kansas free staters. These "border ruffians," as free staters called them, were poor and struggling men who owned few slaves. But they were intensely racist and anti-Yankee. Some of them understood that a free state of Kansas would be an attractive destination for runaway slaves and, perhaps, a place with a large free black population. Others were, no doubt, like so many adolescent males of many places and eras, hormonally excited by the prospect of making trouble. Gangs sometimes numbering in the hundreds periodically rode across the territorial line to harass northern settlers.

Lawrence, Kansas, and John Brown

Kansas was, comparatively, a lawless, anarchic place. But it is not possible to tell how much of the beating, arson, robbery, and murder was prompted by the slavery controversy and how much reflected the disorder common to most American frontiers. However, two celebrated incidents were clearly motivated by the conflict over slavery. Some historians consider them the first battles of the Civil War.

The Granger Collection, New York

▲ *"Border ruffians" in what is obviously a hostile northern depiction. Men living in western Missouri were poor and tough, but not all who harassed free staters in Kansas were frontier scum of this caliber.*

On May 21, 1856, a gang of border ruffians rode into the antislavery town of Lawrence, Kansas, shot it up and set it afire. Only one person was killed, a Missourian crushed by a falling wall, but in other incidents, probably the work of the same gang, several free-state settlers were murdered. Three days later, in an act that he announced was retribution, a Connecticut-born abolitionist named John Brown, accompanied by four of his sons, swooped down on a small settlement on Pottawatomie Creek and hacked five proslavery settlers to pieces.

Southern politicians, who had joked about proslavery violence in Kansas, howled in humanitarian anguish. Northern abolitionists who had wrung their hands over the lesser barbarism of the border ruffians were silent. A few praised John Brown.

The fact that a ritual murder was honored by people who were inclined to parade their moral rectitude indicates the degree to which the hatred between antislavery northerners and proslavery southerners had grown. Extremists on both sides no longer spoke and acted according to rational principles; they were in favor of any act done in the name of "the South, the poor South" or of the godly cause of striking the chains from the bondsmen.

Charles Sumner and Preston Brooks

Congress provided the stage for another debacle in May 1856. Senator Charles Sumner of Massachusetts, an abolitionist who found no contradiction between his pacifism and vituperative oratory, delivered a speech in the Senate called "The Crime Against Kansas."

Sumner described the harassment of free-state settlers and blamed the violence on his southern colleagues. It was pretty standard slavery debate until Sumner added some gratuitous personal insults to an elderly senator from South Carolina, Andrew Butler. Butler suffered from a physical defect that caused him to salivate when he spoke. Sumner coarsely alluded to his slobbering as an indication of the bestiality of slavocrats.

Two days later, Butler's nephew, a congressman named Preston Brooks, walked into the Senate chamber, stood behind Sumner, who was working at his desk, and proceeded to beat the senator senseless with a heavy cane. Brooks said that he was merely putting into practice the *Code Duello* of chivalry, which held that a gentleman must avenge a personal insult from an equal by challenging him to a duel but that one caned a social inferior.

In fact, Brooks's action mocked the "code of honor." He had approached Sumner from behind. (Sumner, a big man, might well have floored Brooks had they met face to face.) Instead of merely humiliating Sumner with a few sharp raps with a cane, Brooks bludgeoned the senator to within an inch of death with a club while Sumner, his legs tangled in his fallen desk, lay helpless on the floor.

Instead of disowning Brooks as a bully and coward, southerners feted him at banquets and made him gifts of dozens of gold-headed canes to replace the one he had broken. The House voted against expelling him; when Brooks resigned, his district reelected him resoundingly. Northerners forgot that Sumner had stepped beyond the bounds of senatorial courtesy and common decency in his description of Senator Butler, and they made Sumner a martyr. While Sumner recovered—it would be several years before he returned to the Senate—Massachusetts reelected him so that his empty desk would stand as a rebuke to the South.

SOUTHERN CHIVALRY — ARGUMENT versus CLUB'S.

▲ *Brooks's clubbing of Charles Sumner readily lent itself to the antislavery movement's depiction of southern whites as barbarous. Note the senators in the background, ignoring or laughing at the incident.*

A HARDENING OF LINES

In normal times, politicians who argue violently in Congress often socialize cordially outside the Capitol. Even Andrew Jackson and Nicholas Biddle were capable of a civil chat at parties and balls. By 1856, this was no longer the case. Both northerners and southerners carried firearms into the congressional chambers and ceased to speak with one another even on informal occasions. Against this foreboding backdrop was held the presidential election of 1856.

The Election of 1856

Inevitably, the Democrats chose a doughface, but he was not Stephen A. Douglas. The Little Giant, a hero in the South in 1854 when he opened the territories to slavery, lost his appeal after events in Kansas indicated that the opening was purely theoretical. Indeed, Douglas told northerners not to worry about the Kansas-Nebraska Act. The concession to slavery, he said, was a symbolic gesture of goodwill to southerners. In the end, Douglas said, Kansas would be a free state because of the greater population of the North and Kansas's unsuitability to plantation agriculture. After the success of the New England Emigrant Aid Society in dispatching antislavery settlers to Kansas, his reasoning rang loudly and unpleasantly in southern ears.

Instead, the Democrats nominated James Buchanan of Pennsylvania, a man of mediocre talent and effeminate manner. (Andrew Jackson called him "Miss Nancy" behind his back.) Politically, Buchanan had been a yes-man, and he was lucky, having been out of the country serving as minister to Great Britain between 1853 and 1856. He was, therefore, not associated with the ugliness in Kansas. He was, however, congenial to southern extremists because he had, with several other diplomats, signed the Ostend Manifesto, a call for the United States to purchase Cuba, which some southerners continued to envision as a sixteenth slave state.

The Republicans chose John C. Frémont, nationally famous as "the Pathfinder," the dashing leader of two exploration parties that helped map the way to Oregon and California. Frémont was no giant of character or intellect. His greatest recommendation was his wife, Jessie Benton, the beautiful, willful, and intelligent daughter of Old Bullion Benton. But in the mood of 1856, Frémont was a logical choice for the Republicans: He was a military hero like the only two successful Whig candidates, and he believed that the western lands should be reserved for family farmers.

The Pathfinder had handicaps. He had abolitionist leanings, and he had been born out of wedlock at a time when illegitimacy carried a stain of shame. But these impediments were minor. Despite the fact he was unlisted on the ballot in every slave state, Frémont won a third of the popular vote and the electoral votes of New England and New York. But Buchanan won every slave state, enough electoral votes to match Frémont's total, plus New Jersey, Pennsylvania, Indiana, and Illinois. A third-party candidate, former president

Millard Fillmore, ran on the anti-Catholic Native American (Know-Nothing) party ticket. Curiously, he did poorly in Massachusetts, a state recently run by the Know-Nothings, but won 44 percent of the popular vote in the slave states, where there were very few Catholics.

Dred Scott

Buchanan's presidency began with a bang. In his inaugural address, he hinted that the issue of slavery in the territories would shortly be settled for all time. Two days later, March 6, 1857, Americans learned what he meant when the Supreme Court handed down its decision in the case of *Dred Scott v. Sandford.*

Dred Scott was a slave in Missouri. Most of his life, he was the valet of an army officer. In 1834, Scott accompanied his master to Illinois, where slavery was prohibited under the Northwest Ordinance. Briefly, he lived in a part of the Louisiana Purchase where slavery was illegal under the Missouri Compromise. For four years, in other words, Scott lived on free soil before returning to Missouri.

▲ *Dred Scott, his wife, and (above them) their daughters. This sympathetic presentation of the beleaguered family indicates how anger in the North toward "the slavocrat conspiracy" had spread far beyond the abolitionists.* Frank Leslie's *was no propaganda sheet but aimed at a broad readership.*

In 1844, Scott's owner died, bequeathing him to his widow, who was opposed to slavery. Rather than manumit him, she was persuaded by abolitionists to cooperate in a test case. Scott sued his owner (eventually a man named Sanford, spelled Sandford in the court records) for his freedom on the grounds that part of his life he was held as a slave in territory where Congress had prohibited slavery.

Missouri courts had released slaves with cases identical to Scott's, but that was before sectional animosity was so bitter. Scott lost his case on the grounds that whatever his status may have been in Illinois in 1834, he became quite legally a slave again when he returned to Missouri. The case slowly made its way to the Supreme Court.

Chief Justice Taney: The Final Solution

Although every Supreme Court justice commented individually on Scott's appeal, Chief Justice Roger B. Taney, an old Jackson henchman from Maryland, spoke for the majority when he declared that because Scott was black, he was not a citizen of Missouri, which restricted citizenship to whites. Therefore, Scott could not sue in Missouri courts.

Taney could have left the decision at that. Several justices did. The decision would have been unpopular among antislavery northerners, but not sensational. But Taney continued. With the highly irregular input of president-elect Buchanan, Taney believed he had discovered the constitutional solution to the question that was tearing the country apart—the status of slavery in the territories. In fact, the doctrine Taney propounded was pure John C. Calhoun, the extreme proslavery position.

Taney declared that the Missouri Compromise had been unconstitutional in prohibiting slavery in the territories because Congress was forbidden to discriminate against the citizens of any of the states. State legislatures could outlaw slavery, to be sure. But territorial legislatures could not do so because they were the creatures of Congress. They were, therefore, subject to the Constitution's restraints on Congress.

The Republican Panic

The Missouri Compromise was already dead, but Republicans were enraged, for their program was to restore a Missouri-type prohibition of slavery in the territories. With the Dred Scott decision, they saw the history of the question of slavery in the territories as a step-by-step whittling away of the power of the federal government to prevent the expansion of slavery.

That is, between 1820 and 1854, under the Missouri Compromise, slavery was illegal in all territories north of 36 degrees, 30 minutes. With the Kansas-Nebraska Act of 1854, slavery could be legalized in territories if the voters there chose to do so. With the Dred Scott decision of 1857, there was no way that, even by unanimous vote of the settlers in a territory, a slave owner could be forbidden to move to

that territory with a hundred slaves in a coffle. *Dred Scott v. Sandford* killed the popular sovereignty of the Kansas-Nebraska Act as dead as the Kansas-Nebraska Act had killed the Missouri Compromise.

Republicans began to speak of a "slavocratic" conspiracy, now involving the Supreme Court, to thwart the will of a majority of the American people. Their fury was fanned in October 1857 when proslavery settlers in Kansas, augmented by a good many illegal voters from Missouri, sent to Congress the Lecompton Constitution, which called for the admission of Kansas as a slave state. Although the Lecompton Constitution was obviously the work of a small group, Buchanan urged Congress to accept it.

Ever increasing arrests of runaway slaves in the North, like the celebrated case of Anthony Burns in 1854, converted more and more northerners to militant antislavery. In Milwaukee, an antislavery mob stormed a jail where a runaway slave was being held and set him free.

The Fugitive Slave Act of 1850 meant that it was no longer possible for a slave to gain freedom by escaping to a free state. Runaways had to get out of the country. Northern abolitionists, particularly free blacks, organized the "underground railroad" to spirit fugitives to Canada. This was a constantly shifting network of households, beginning at the Ohio River and Mason-Dixon line, that hid runaway slaves by day and helped them move to Canada by night.

Lincoln and Douglas: Two Northern Answers

Stephen A. Douglas did not take Taney's rebuke of popular sovereignty lying down. In a series of debates in Illinois in 1858, Douglas and a Springfield Republican who wanted Douglas's seat in the Senate, Abraham Lincoln, proposed two northern solutions to the question of slavery in the territories.

Race

Because few American whites believed in racial equality, it was in the interest of northern Democrats to accuse the Republicans of advocating race mixture. "I am opposed to Negro equality," Stephen A. Douglas said in his debate with Abraham Lincoln in Chicago. "I am in favor of preserving, not only the purity of the blood, but the purity of the government from any mixture or amalgamation with inferior races."

The Democrats' line forced Republicans to reassure their constituents that opposition to slavery did not mean a belief in the equality of the races. Lincoln replied to Douglas, "I protest, now and forever, against that counterfeit logic which presumes that because I do not want a Negro woman for a slave, I necessarily want her for a wife. . . . As God made us separate, we can leave one another alone, and do one another much good thereby."

Lincoln shrewdly took the debate back to the territorial question by saying, "Why, Judge, if we do not let them get together in the Territories, they won't mix there."

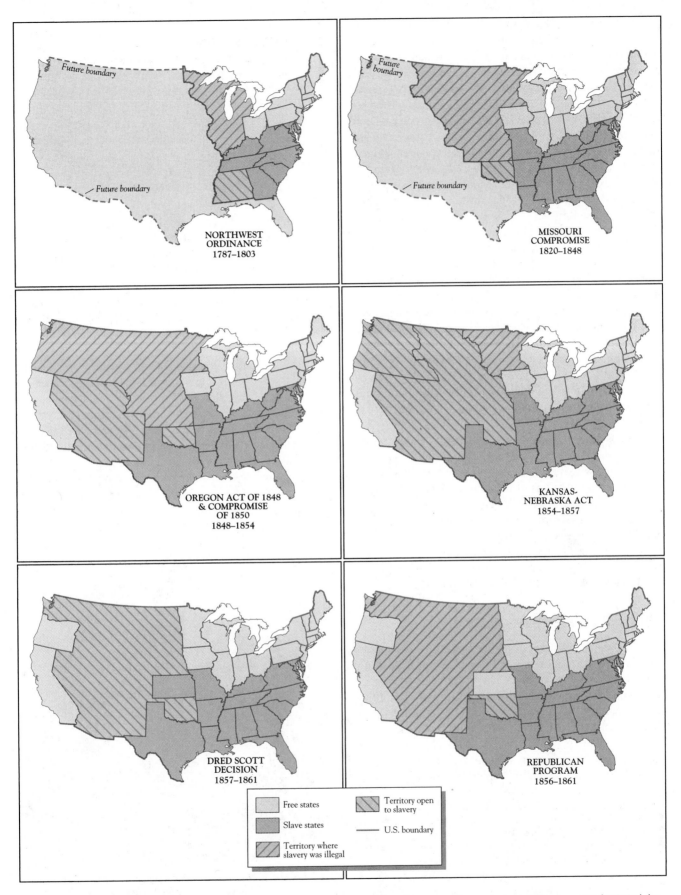

MAP 22:1 The Legal Status of Slavery, 1787–1861   This series of maps explains why ever greater numbers of northerners were frustrated during the 1850s. Even though a majority of Americans clearly wanted no slavery in the territories, the area in which slavery was legal was increased twice within three years.

Map panels

NORTHWEST ORDINANCE 1787–1803

MISSOURI COMPROMISE 1820–1848

OREGON ACT OF 1848 & COMPROMISE OF 1850 1848–1854

KANSAS-NEBRASKA ACT 1854–1857

DRED SCOTT DECISION 1857–1861

REPUBLICAN PROGRAM 1856–1861

Legend:
- Free states
- Slave states
- Territory where slavery was illegal
- Territory open to slavery
- U.S. boundary

"A house divided against itself cannot stand," Lincoln said in June 1858. "I believe this government cannot endure permanently half-slave and half-free." He meant that southerners were clearly not satisfied that slavery was protected where it existed. Nor, with the clear majority of free staters in Kansas, was Douglas's popular sovereignty enough to placate the extremists. With the Fugitive Slave Act and the Dred Scott decision in their pockets, proslavery extremists were forcing the institution on people who did not want it. In their mania, southerners were forcing a showdown that, in the long run, would result in armed sectional conflict.

Douglas insisted that popular sovereignty was still alive and kicking, and was still the best solution to the problem. When Lincoln reminded him that the Supreme Court had ruled popular sovereignty unconstitutional, Douglas replied at Freeport, Illinois, in August 1858, that a territorial legislature could keep slavery out of the territory simply by failing to enact a slave code. No slave owner would dare take his valuable human property to a country where there were no laws to protect his power over his slaves. (Some slave owner forty-niners had discovered in California that their slaves simply walked away from them, even before statehood.) The Supreme Court might be able to overturn a territorial law, Douglas pointed out, but the Court could not force a territorial legislature to enact one it did not choose to enact.

The Freeport Doctrine was ingenious; Douglas was a superb lawyer. And he won reelection to the Senate, although narrowly. But events proved that Lincoln was correct about the intentions of the southern extremists to be stopped by no legal obstacle. When presented with the logic of the Freeport Doctrine, they demanded that Congress enact a national slave code that would affirmatively protect slavery in the territories. That was not in the cards. If Lincoln lost the Illinois Senate race in 1858, Republicans had a comfortable majority in the House of Representatives.

John Brown's Insurrection

John Brown dropped out of sight after the Pottawatomie murders, but he was busy and did not disappear. Moving around New England behind a newly grown beard, incognito at first, Brown persuaded several well-to-do abolitionists that the time had come to strike violently at slavery. With their financial support, he organized a band of 22 insurrectionists, including African Americans and several of his sons, at an isolated farm in Maryland. Just across the Potomac River, at the mouth of the Shenandoah, was Harpers

John Brown's Mountains
In the Appalachians, to which John Brown planned to escape, there were nearly impenetrable places. During the Civil War, gangs of Confederate draft dodgers and deserters roamed the mountains without fear of the authorities. So isolated are some hollows that Elizabethan patterns of speech and folk ballads survived there unchanged into the twentieth century, although they had long since disappeared elsewhere in the English-speaking world.

Ferry, Virginia, site of one of the federal government's two major arsenals. Brown's plan was to seize the arsenal, capture guns and ammunition, and escape into the Appalachians, which rose steeply around Harpers Ferry.

From the mountains, his guerrilla army would swoop down on plantations, free a few slaves at a time, and enlarge the corps. Before long, Brown predicted, slave rebellions would erupt all over the South, decisively destroying the "peculiar institution."

Brown's critics later said that the scheme proved that the old man was out of his mind. Brown may well have been deranged; he was certainly not the sort one would want at a favorite daughter's wedding. But there was nothing crazy about John Brown's military thinking. His plan prefigured in many ways the theory of guerrilla warfare that twentieth-century national-liberation movements put into practice with great success: operate from a remote and shifting base; avoid big battles in which conventional military forces have the overwhelming advantage; fight only small surprise actions when

▲ *A curiously dispassionate nineteenth-century drawing of John Brown and his followers in the final hours in the roundhouse. The man in his arms is his son, who died when marines stormed the ill-chosen fortress. Brown himself was seriously wounded when he was captured. He lay on a stretcher at his trial.*

The Know-Nothing Mind

It is easy today to label the nativists, anti-Catholics, and Know-Nothings of the 1840s and 1850s as bigots and let it go at that. Self-comforting labeling is the genius of our era. It was not so simple.

There was plenty of garden-variety bigotry in the minds of those who made the Know-Nothing party briefly triumphant, but more than that. A political party (officially the American party) that won the mayor's office of New York City, the governorship and all but one seat in the assembly in Massachusetts, and 40 percent of the vote in large parts of the Upper South in 1856, and then disappeared as if a magician had waved a wand, has a more complicated story.

Hostility toward Roman Catholicism was in a corner of the American psyche from the beginning. To the Puritans, the Church of Rome was not merely mistaken; it was evil. The flood of Scotch-Irish Presbyterians who settled and dominated the slopes of the Appalachians brought with them a century of hatred of the Catholics with whom they shared the Emerald Isle.

Outside of Maryland, however, there were few flesh-and-blood targets for anti-Catholics until the 1820s. There were only about 35,000 Catholics in the United States in 1790, when John Carroll was named bishop of Baltimore. And Carroll was all-American. He endorsed separation of church and state, religious tolerance, and even spoke openly of an American church independent of the pope of Rome except as the symbolic father of the church.

Then began the immigration of Catholic Irish, which became a flood with the potato blight of the 1840s. (A million Irish died of hunger and related disease; millions more fled.) The Irish immigrants were poor and uneducated. The men, drawn to heavy labor and saloons, were tumultuous. And the women especially were profoundly deferential to their priests, the only educated people among them. In turn, Irish priests were stolid proponents of the sacred authority of the pope.

During the 1820s, an anti-Catholic tract, *The Awful Disclosures of Maria Monk,* was a sensation because it depicted convents of nuns as the dens of sexual slaves of Catholic priests. Someone has said that anti-Catholic literature was the pornography of the respectable Protestant.

The pope after 1846 was Pius IX, who inveighed against religious toleration, democracy, republican government, and the individual rights and civil liberties that were at the heart of American ideals. Pius IX took little interest in the United States; his devils were liberal Europeans who, however, often pointed to free America as their model. That was enough for American Protestants to worry, some casually, some obsessively, that Catholics, especially the ignorant, slavish Irish, were a threat to America. Calmer proponents of tolerance were not helped by the leading American bishop, John Hughes of New York, who denounced Protestantism and crowed that the Roman Catholic Church would soon displace it as America's majority religion.

In this atmosphere, a number of anti-Catholic, anti-immigrant secret societies were founded among native-born workingmen who saw the Irish as dragging wages downward. The most notable of these groups was the Order of the Star-Spangled Banner, founded in 1849. With the northern Whig party shattered the next year—"cotton Whigs" supporting the Compromise of 1850, "conscience Whigs" opposing it—many of the former drifted into the American party, the secretive Know-Nothings' public political front. In 1854, in fact, a former Whig, James Barker, became head of the party. Many Whigs followed him as their old party disintegrated. A genteel anti-Catholicism had been endemic among Whigs, not the kind that sends men into the streets to brawl (very un-Whiglike behavior!) but a distaste for the drinking and coarseness of the Irish immigrants. (The fact that almost all the Irish voted Democratic did not help their popularity among Whigs.)

The American party advocated temperance (a play for that vote), laws disqualifying Catholics from holding public office, sharp restrictions on immigration (which appealed to native-born workingmen with no particular religious animosities), and an increase in the residency requirement to 20 years for immigrants seeking citizenship. The American party tried to dodge the slavery question, as the Whigs had: New England Know-Nothings inclined to be antislavery, whereas those in the South, where presidential candidate Millard Fillmore ran strongest in 1856, did not.

After the Dred Scott decision of 1857, the slavery controversy killed the Know-Nothings more quickly than they had burst onto the political scene. The threat of slavery in the territories was far more real to northern Know-Nothings than the specter of Bishop Hughes hugging Pope Pius IX as he stepped from a ship to a New York wharf. Most of the Know-Nothings gravitated into the Republican party and voted for Lincoln despite the fact that he had several times denounced the Know-Nothings' bigotry and supported a liberal immigration policy.

In the South, anti-Catholicism and nativism never made much sense. It was a highly theoretical enthusiasm. Outside of Louisiana, Catholics were as rare in the South as polar bears. Few immigrants went South, because slaves did the menial work; Irishmen in the South competed only with free blacks (not a politically powerful group) for jobs too dangerous to be assigned to valuable slaves. Southern Know-Nothings managed to stay clear of the hated Democratic party through 1860, when they voted overwhelmingly for Constitutional Union candidate John Bell, who, like Lincoln, embraced no Know-Nothing principles.

The Know-Nothings, like the Anti-Masons, represented a whirlwind movement—the creation of a unique conjunction of circumstances only some of which, in the case of the Know-Nothings, had to do with Catholics and immigrants. There was, in fact, no Know-Nothing mind but a good many things haunting many minds in troubled times.

the odds favor the freewheeling guerrillas; and win the friendship and support of the ordinary people—in Brown's case, the slaves. The odds were never with him, but his plan was not completely hopeless.

Raid and Reaction

Better evidence of problems in Brown's mental processes was the fact that he abandoned his plan almost as soon as he got started. On October 16, 1859, his band of fighters easily captured the arsenal. Then, however, Brown either lost his nerve or deluded himself into the belief that the slaves in the area were on the verge of joining him. He forgot what Frederick Douglass had told him—what he could see all around him—that Harpers Ferry was "a perfect steel trap." Instead of making for the hills just outside the doors of the arsenal, he holed up in the locomotive roundhouse, where he was promptly surrounded by United States Marines under the command of Colonel Robert E. Lee. In two days, Lee's professional soldiers killed 10 of Brown's followers and captured Brown himself. Brown was promptly tried for treason against the state of Virginia, found guilty, and hanged in December.

Most northerners were shocked by the raid and grimly applauded the speedy trial and execution of the old man. However, most prominent abolitionists were ominously silent. Some of those who had funded Brown fled the country. A few openly praised Brown as a hero and a martyr. Ralph Waldo Emerson said that Brown's death made the gallows as holy as the Christian cross.

There was just enough of this sentiment to arouse the southern fire-eaters to a new pitch of hysteria. Brown's raid revived their deep fears of slave rebellion, and here were northerners praising a lunatic who tried to start one. Southern editors and politicians wondered how they could continue to remain under the same government as people who encouraged their massacre.

It was true that the federal government had moved quickly and efficiently to crush Brown. Southerners had few complaints with Washington. But 1860 was an election year. What was to happen if the "Black Republicans" won the presidency, thus taking control of federal police powers? Could the South still depend on protection against the John Browns, Nat Turners, Harriet Tubmans, and Ralph Waldo Emersons?

THE ELECTION OF 1860

Southern extremists declared that if the Republicans won the presidency in 1860, the southern states would secede from the Union. Then, having threatened northern voters, the same extremists not only failed to work against a Republican victory, but they guaranteed it. They split the Democratic party that had served southern interests so well. John Brown was not the only lunatic walking the streets of America.

The Democratic Split

The Democratic party was almost the last great national institution in the United States. The Methodists had split into northern and southern churches in 1844, the Baptists in 1845, the Presbyterians over the next several years. Fraternal lodges broke in two. The Whig party, the nation's nationalistic party, was a fading memory, buried by the slavery controversy. The young Republican party had an exclusively northern membership. Only within the Democratic party did

men from both sections still come together to try to settle sectional differences.

In April 1860, with the smell of the Brown affair still in the air, the Democratic convention met in Charleston. The majority of the delegates, including many southerners, supported the nomination of Stephen A. Douglas. The candidate must be a northerner, they said realistically, like Buchanan and Pierce. But the southern extremists withheld their votes. The delegations of eight southern states announced that they would support Douglas only if he repudiated the Freeport Doctrine and supported their demand for a federal slave code.

The Douglas men pointed out that to do so would ensure that many northern Democrats would vote Republican. Unmoved, the eight hard-line delegations walked out of the convention. The Douglas forces recessed without nominating their leader, hoping to talk sense into the minority.

The Democrats reassembled in Baltimore in June. The southern extremists refused to budge. Disgusted by what they considered political suicide, the regular Democrats nominated Douglas for president and a southern moderate, Herschel V. Johnson of Georgia, as his running mate. The southern Democrats then nominated John C. Breckinridge of Kentucky to represent them in the election. To give the ticket a semblance of national support, they chose an Oregon doughface, Joseph Lane, as their vice presidential candidate.

The Republican Opportunity

Meanwhile, the Republicans met in Chicago. They were optimistic but cautious. With the Democrats split, they smelled victory. But they also knew that if they ran too extreme an antislavery candidate—as they believed Frémont had been in 1856—many northern voters would back Douglas. Even worse would be winning on too extreme a platform: Southerners would make good on their threat to secede, which none but a few very extreme abolitionists wanted.

So the Republicans backed off from the sometimes radical rhetoric of previous years and rejected party stalwarts William H. Seward of New York and Salmon P. Chase of Ohio. Seward had spoken of "a higher law than the Constitution" in condemning slavery (shades of William Lloyd Garrison) and of an "irrepressible conflict" between North and South. Chase had been a militant abolitionist for more than a decade and had dozens of inflammatory remarks on his record.

Instead, the Republicans picked a somewhat obscure midwesterner, Abraham Lincoln of Illinois. Lincoln was rock solid on the fundamental Republican principle: Slavery must be banned from the territories. But he was no abolitionist; he had steered clear of the Know-Nothings, thus maintaining a good relationship with German voters; and he was moderate, humane, and ingratiating in manner. In his famous debates with Douglas in 1858 and in a speech introducing himself to eastern Republicans in New York City in February 1860, he struck a note of humility, prudence, and caution. Not only was slavery protected by the Constitution in those states where it existed, he said, but northerners ought to sympathize with slave owners rather than attack them. Lincoln himself was born in Kentucky, a slave state. He knew that a quirk of fate would have made him a slave owner; he found it easy to preach the golden rule. By choosing him, the Republicans accommodated southern sensibilities as far as they could without giving up their own principles.

The Republican platform was comprehensive: a high protective tariff, a liberal immigration policy, the construction of a transcontinental railway, and a homestead act. The platform was designed to win the votes of rather disparate economic groups often at odds with one another: eastern industrial capitalists, workers, and midwestern farmers. Moreover, by avoiding a single-issue campaign, the Republicans hoped to signal the South that they were not, as a party, antislavery fanatics. They even named a vice presidential candidate who had been a Democrat as late as 1857, Hannibal Hamlin of Maine.

The Old Man's Party

A fourth party entered the race, drawing its strength in the states of the Upper South: Maryland, Virginia, Kentucky, and Tennessee. Henry Clay's brand of Whiggery—an inclination toward compromise and a deep attachment to the Union—was strong in the border states. The platform of the new Constitutional Union party consisted, in effect, of stalling. It was a mistake, members said, to force any kind of sectional confrontation while tempers were up—better to put off the problem of slavery in the territories to a later, calmer day.

For president, the Constitutional Unionists nominated John Bell of Tennessee, a protégé of Clay. For vice president, they chose the distinguished Whig orator Edward Everett of Massachusetts. But they found little support outside the border states. Republicans and both northern and southern Democrats sneered at them as "the old man's party."

Republican Victory

Abraham Lincoln won 40 percent of the popular vote, but he carried every free state except New Jersey, which he split with Douglas. He won a clear majority in the electoral college. Breckinridge won only 18 percent of the national vote, but he was the overwhelming choice of the South, winning a plurality in 11 of the 15 slave states. Between the two, appealing to sectional feelings, they won a decisive majority of voters.

Douglas won a mere 12 electoral votes (Missouri and New Jersey), but he ran second to Lincoln in some northern states and to Breckinridge in some states in the South. John Bell carried 3 of the border states and was strong almost everywhere. Even if the Douglas and the Bell votes had been combined, however, Lincoln would have won. Nevertheless, inasmuch as many Lincoln, and some Breckinridge, supporters were more interested in making noise than, surely, in a civil war, it seems clear that most Americans wanted some kind of settlement.

The First Secession: South Carolina

They did not get their wish. Having announced that Lincoln's election meant secession, the fire-eaters of South Carolina (where there was no popular vote for presidential electors) called a convention that, on December 20, 1860, unanimously declared that "the union now subsisting between South Carolina and the other States, under the name of the 'United States of America,' is hereby dissolved."

During January 1861, the six other states of the Deep South followed suit, declaring that a Republican administration threatened their domestic institutions. Then came a glimmer of hope. The secession movement stalled when none of the other southern states approved secession ordinances. At the same time they rejected secession, however, conventions in the border states declared their opposition to any attempt by the federal government to use force against the states that had seceded. By rebuffing the big talkers on both sides, the leaders of the border states hoped to force a compromise.

The outgoing president, James Buchanan, was not the man to engineer such a compromise. No one had much respect for Old Buck, including his own advisers, mostly southern, who now betrayed him. His secretary of war, John Floyd of Virginia, transferred tons of war materiel to states that either had left the Union or were on the verge of leaving. Floyd's act skirted close to treason, but Buchanan did nothing.

Other Buchanan allies resigned their offices and left Washington, hardly pausing to remember the president who had worked on their behalf. The first bachelor ever to occupy the White House was quite alone, and he knew it. After a hand-wringing message sent to Congress in which he declared that although secession was illegal, he as president was powerless to do anything about it, Buchanan sat back to wait for the day he could go home.

HOW THE UNION BROKE

As Buchanan slumped, Senator John J. Crittenden stood up. Like many Kentuckians, Crittenden had made a career of mediating between the North and the Deep South. Now he proposed that rather than break up the Union, the territories should be divided. His proposal was to extend the Missouri Compromise line to the California border, guaranteeing slavery to the south of the line and forbidding slavery to the north of it.

Failure of the Compromisers

Because of the Dred Scott decision, Crittenden's plan could not be put into effect by congressional action; the territories could be divided only by constitutional amendment. Crittenden hoped that the specter of civil war, now chillingly real with military companies drilling in both North and South, would prompt both northern and southern state legislatures to act in haste.

With some encouragement, they might have done so. There was a flurry of enthusiasm for Crittenden's compromise

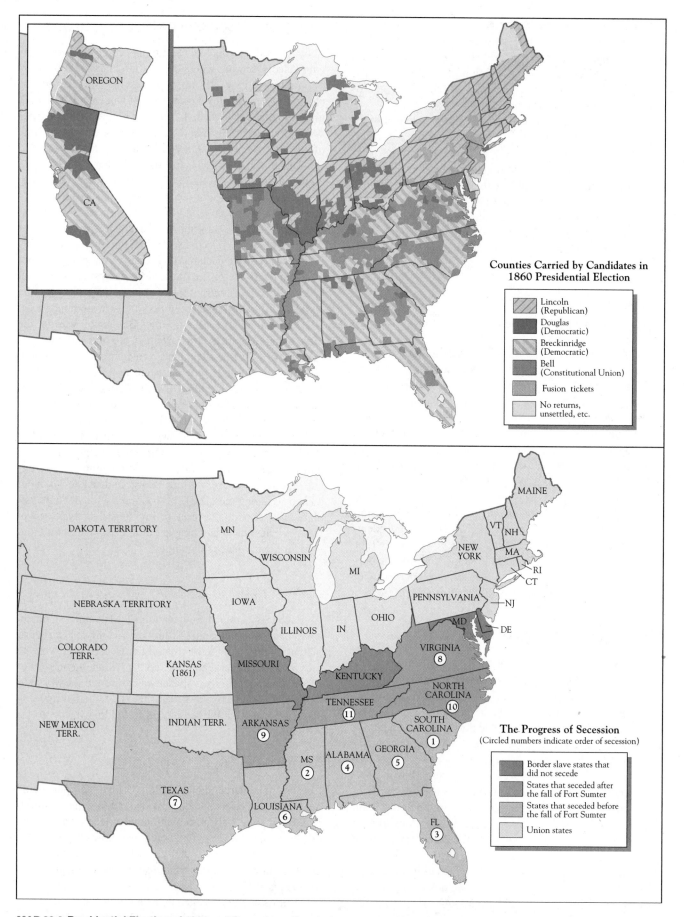

Counties Carried by Candidates in 1860 Presidential Election

- Lincoln (Republican)
- Douglas (Democratic)
- Breckinridge (Democratic)
- Bell (Constitutional Union)
- Fusion tickets
- No returns, unsettled, etc.

The Progress of Secession
(Circled numbers indicate order of secession)

- Border slave states that did not secede
- States that seceded after the fall of Fort Sumter
- States that seceded before the fall of Fort Sumter
- Union states

MAP 22:2 Presidential Election of 1860 and Secession Note, in the upper map, Lincoln's sweep in the North and Breckinridge's in the South. Bell won majorities in the states that bordered the line separating slave and free states. Few counties gave Douglas a majority, but he finished second in many areas in both the North and the South.

▲ *Abraham Lincoln about the time he was elected president. He grew the beard he wore throughout his presidency between election day 1860 and his inauguration because, he said, a girl had written him that he was so homely that a beard would help.*

granted nothing the South did not already possess—and it could be overturned by constitutional amendment at a later date. By February, in fact, the secessionists had lost interest in preserving the Union. They were caught up in the excitement of creating a new nation.

The Confederate States of America

According to secessionist theory, the 7 states that left the Union were now independent republics. However, no southern leader intended his state to go it alone. Although they were disappointed that 8 of the 15 slave states refused to join them, they met in Montgomery, Alabama, shortly before Lincoln's inauguration and established the Confederate States of America.

The government of the Confederacy differed little from the one that they had rejected. All United States laws were to remain in effect until amended or repealed, and they adopted the Constitution of 1787, plus amendments, almost word for word. The changes they made reflected the South's obsession with slavery and with Calhoun's political theories, which resulted in several curious contradictions.

Thus, the Confederates defined the states as sovereign and independent but called their new government permanent. Even more oddly, the Confederates declared that individual states might not interfere with slavery, a restriction on states' rights that no prominent Republican had ever suggested.

The Confederates also modified the presidency. The chief executive was to be elected for a term of six years rather than four, but he was not permitted to run for a second term. Although this seemed to weaken the office, the Confederates allowed the president to veto parts of congressional bills rather than, as in the Union, requiring the president to accept all or nothing.

Jeff Davis

As their first president, the Confederates selected Jefferson Davis. On the face of it, he was a good choice. His bearing was regal, and he was the model slave owner, the sort that southerners liked to pretend was typical of the institution. Davis also seemed to be a wise choice because he was not closely associated with the secessionist movement. Indeed, Davis asked his fellow Mississippians to delay secession until Lincoln had a chance to prove himself. When his state overruled him, Davis delivered a moderate, eloquent, and affectionate farewell speech in the Senate. By choosing such a man, rather than a fire-eater, the Confederates demonstrated their willingness to work with southerners who opposed secession; there were plenty of them. With the respected Davis, the Confederacy could also appeal to the eight slave states that remained within the Union.

In other ways, the choice of Jefferson Davis was ill advised. It was not so much the unattractive coldness of his personality; George Washington had been icier. Davis's weakness was that despite his bearing, he lacked self-confidence and was, consequently, easily irritated and inflexible. He proved incapable of cooperating with critics, even those who differed

on both sides of the Mason-Dixon line. But before the southern extremists were forced to take a stand, Lincoln, now president-elect, quashed the plan. His reasons were political but nonetheless compelling. His Republican party was a diverse alliance of people who disagreed with one another on many issues. The one adhesive that bound them together was the principle that slavery must not expand into the territories. If Lincoln gave in on this point, he would take office with half his party sniping at him.

Lincoln also discouraged a second attempt at compromise, a peace conference held in Washington in February 1861. It was a distinguished assembly, chaired by former president John Tyler. Tyler had been a southern extremist, and, a few months later, he would support the secession of Virginia. But he worked hard for a settlement in February, proposing a series of constitutional amendments along the same lines as Crittenden's.

Once again, Lincoln drew the line on allowing slavery in the southern territories. Instead, he endorsed an amendment, passed by both houses of Congress, that would forever guarantee slavery in the states where it already existed. As he well knew, this was a purely symbolic gesture that

▲ *Jefferson Davis, first and only president of the Confederacy. Davis was zealously proslavery and supported every measure to expand slavery to the territories, but he tried to delay secession in Mississippi, arguing that Lincoln should be given a chance.*

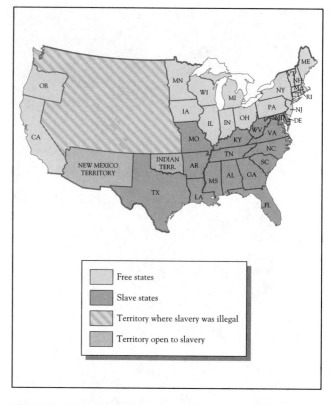

MAP 22:3 Crittenden's Compromise Plan, 1861 Crittenden's plan recognized the justice of northern anger over the Dred Scott decision (see Map 22.1 on p. 313) but provided the South with two territories likely to enter the Union as free states.

with him on minor points. He seemed to need yes-men in order to function, and, as a result, he denied his administration the services of some of the South's ablest statesmen.

Worse, Davis was a dabbler. Instead of delegating authority and presiding over the government, he repeatedly interfered in the pettiest details of administration—peering over his subordinates' shoulders, arousing personal resentments among even those who were devoted to him. He had been a good senator; he was not qualified to be the "father of his country."

Abe Lincoln

By contrast, Abraham Lincoln knew the value of unity and competent help. Rather than shun his rivals within the Republican party, he named them to his cabinet. Seward became secretary of state; Salmon P. Chase was Lincoln's secretary of the treasury. After a brief misadventure with an incompetent secretary of war, Simon Cameron, Lincoln appointed a Democrat, Edwin Stanton, to that post because his talents were obvious. Lincoln wanted able aides, not pals or toadies. Within their departments, Lincoln's cabinet officers were free to do anything that did not conflict with general

policy. As a result, a cantankerous and headstrong group of men never challenged his control of fundamentals.

Lincoln differed from Davis in other ways. Far from regal, he was an awkward, plain, even ugly man. Tall and gangling, with oversized hands and feet, he impressed those who met him for the first time as a frontier oaf. His enemies called him "the baboon." Some of his supporters snickered at his clumsiness and were appalled by his fondness for dirty jokes.

But both friends and enemies soon discovered that the president was no yokel. Lincoln had honed a sharp native intelligence on a stone of lifelong study, and he proved to be one of the three or four most eloquent chief executives. And yet, behind his brilliance was a humility born of modest background that can be found in no other American president.

Lincoln needed all his native resources. On March 4, 1861, when he was sworn in before a glum Washington crowd, the Union was in tatters. During the previous two months, the Stars and Stripes had been hauled down from every flagstaff in the South except for one at Fort Pickens in Pensacola, Florida, and another at Fort Sumter, a rocky island in the harbor of Charleston, South Carolina.

A War of Nerves

Neither of the forts threatened the security of the Confederacy. They were old installations designed for defense and

▲ *Fort Sumter, the day after it was surrendered to the Confederacy. The fort was expected only to make a symbolic resistance—it was at the mercy of the batteries in Charleston—but it took a terrific shelling as this photograph shows.*

were manned by token garrisons. But symbols take on profound importance in edgy times, and the southern fire-eaters, itching for a fight, ranted about the insulting occupation of "their country" by a "foreign power."

Davis was willing to live with the Union forts for the time being. He understood that the Confederacy could not survive as long as it consisted of seven states. His hope was to delay a confrontation with the North until he could make a foreign alliance or induce the eight slave states that remained in the Union to join the Confederacy. He feared that if he fired the first shot, the states of the Upper South might support the Union.

The fire-eaters disagreed. They believed that a battle, no matter who started it, would bring the other slave states to their side. Nevertheless, when the commander at Fort Sumter announced that he would soon have to surrender the fort for lack of provisions, Davis had his way.

Within limits, Lincoln also favored delaying confrontation. He believed that the longer the states of the Upper South did not secede, the less likely they were to go. Moreover, the leaders of Virginia, Kentucky, Tennessee, and Arkansas formally warned him against using force against the Confederacy. If the Union fired the first shot, they would secede.

First Blood

The first blood of the Civil War was not shed at Fort Sumter. No one was killed there. The first deaths of the Civil War occurred in Baltimore a week after the fall of Sumter. A mob attacked soldiers from Massachusetts on the way to Washington as they were marching from one railroad terminal to another. The soldiers fired back. Twelve members of the mob and four soldiers were killed.

Finally, Lincoln did not have the people of the North solidly behind him. Northern Democrats would not support an act of aggression, and Winfield Scott, Lincoln's chief military adviser, told him that the army was not up to a war of conquest. Some abolitionists who were also pacifists, such as Horace Greeley and William Lloyd Garrison, urged the president to "let the wayward sisters depart in peace."

Lincoln had no intention of doing that. He was determined to save the Union by peaceful means if possible, by force if necessary. He reasoned that if the Confederates fired the first shot, the border states might secede anyway, but at least the act of rebellion would unite northerners. If he delayed a confrontation indefinitely, he still might lose the border states and still have a divided, uncertain North.

This was the reasoning behind Lincoln's decision to resupply Fort Sumter. He announced that he would not use force against the state of South Carolina. There would be no arms in the relief ship, only food, medicine, and other nonmilitary supplies. He repeated his wish that the crisis be resolved peacefully. But he insisted on his presidential obligation to maintain the government's authority in Charleston Harbor.

And so the war came. When the relief ship approached the sandbar that guarded Charleston Harbor, the Confederacy attacked. On the morning of April 12, 1861, artillery under the command of General P. G. T. Beauregard opened up. The next day, Sumter surrendered. Davis was reluctant to the end. In a way, he lost control of South Carolina.

Contest for the Border States

In a way, the Battle of Fort Sumter served both Confederate and Union purposes. Although Lincoln was able to call for 75,000 volunteers and to get them, his call for troops pushed four more states into the Confederacy: Virginia, North Carolina, Tennessee, and Arkansas. In deference to Virginia's importance, the capital of the new nation was moved from Montgomery to Richmond.

Secessionist feeling was strong in the slave states of Maryland, Kentucky, and Missouri. Lincoln was able to prevent them from seceding by a combination of shrewd political maneuvers and the tactful deployment of troops. Delaware, the fifteenth slave state, never seriously considered secession.

Then, in the contest for the border states, the North won a bonus. The mountainous western part of Virginia was peopled by farmers who owned few slaves and who traditionally resented the planter aristocracy that dominated Virginia politics and was now in favor of secession. The westerners had no interest in fighting and dying to protect the human property of the rich flatlanders. In effect, the 50 western counties of Virginia seceded from the Old Dominion. By an irregular constitutional process, the Republicans provided the means for West Virginia to become a Union state in June 1863.

For the border states, the Civil War was literally a war between brothers. Henry Clay's grandsons fought on both sides. Several of President Lincoln's brothers-in-law fought for the South, and Jefferson Davis had cousins in the Union army. The most poignant case was that of Senator Crittenden of Kentucky, who had tried to head off war with a com-

promise. One of his sons became a general in the Union army and another a general in the Confederate army.

The Irony of Secession

However much the people of the border states disliked secession, they were not against slavery. In order to reassure them, Lincoln issued several pronouncements that the purpose of the war was to preserve the Union and not to abolish slavery. In emphasizing this war aim, he pointed up the irony of secession. Although southerners claimed that they had gone their own way in order to protect their "peculiar institution," they actually had thrown away the legal and constitutional guarantees that they had enjoyed as United States citizens.

Under the Fugitive Slave Act, slaves who ran away to the northern states were returned to their owners. In order to escape, slaves had to get to Canada, out of the country. With secession, "out of the country" was hundreds of miles closer—over the Tennessee-Kentucky or the Virginia-Maryland line. This fact was dramatized early in the war when several Union generals declared that slaves who fled to Union lines were contraband of war, subject to confiscation and therefore free. At first, Lincoln countermanded these orders so as not to antagonize the loyal slave states, especially Kentucky. But it was obvious that the South had made it easier for slaves to get away than it had been before secession.

In leaving the Union as individual states, the southerners had waived all legal rights to the territories, which were federal property. Their action was the most effective guarantee, short of a constitutional amendment, that slavery would be banned from the territories.

Some southerners had no intention of giving up the territories, of course. The Indians of Oklahoma, for example, were generally pro-Confederate. But to win the Indian lands and, perhaps, New Mexico meant launching the very war that Davis hoped to avoid. Secession was less a rational political act than it was the fruit of passion, suspicion, and sectional hatred blinding the southern extremists to reality.

for FURTHER READING

Most of the books cited here also deal with events treated in Chapter 23, particularly Avery O. Craven, *The Growth of Southern Nationalism, 1848–1860,* 1953, and *The Coming of the Civil War,* 1957; James McPherson, *Battle Cry of Freedom,* 1988; Alan Nevins, *Ordeal of the Union,* 1947; and David Potter, *The Impending Crisis, 1848–1861,* 1976. Also see Eric Foner, *Politics and Ideology in the Age of the Civil War,* 1980.

The events that promoted sectional bitterness in North and South during the 1850s are treated in Stanley W. Campbell, *The Slave-Catchers: Enforcement of the Fugitive Slave Law, 1840–1860,* 1968; James C. Malin, *John Brown and the Legend of Fifty-Six,* 1970; Truman Nelson, *The Old Man John Brown at Harpers Ferry,* 1973; Stephen Oates, *To Purge This Land with Blood: A Biography of John Brown,* 1970; Don E. Fehrenbacher, *The Dred Scott Case: Its Significance in American Law and Politics,* 1978; C. B. Swisher,

Roger B. Taney, 1935; and R. W. Johansen, *The Lincoln-Douglas Debates,* 1965.

On the secession crisis, the standard works are Kenneth M. Stampp, *And the War Came: The North and the Secession Crisis, 1860–1861,* 1950, and W. L. Barney, *The Road to Secession,* 1972. See also Stephen A. Channing, *Crisis of Fear: Secession in South Carolina,* 1970; and R. A. Wooster, *The Secession Conventions of the South,* 1962. Don E. Fehrenbacher, *Prelude to Greatness: Lincoln in the 1850s,* 1962, is essential. Richard N. Current, *Lincoln and the First Shot,* 1963, and *The Lincoln Nobody Knows,* 1958, deal with the president's actions in 1861. For Lincoln's predecessor, see P. S. Klein, *President James Buchanan,* 1962; for his southern counterpart, see Clement Eaton, *Jefferson Davis,* 1977. See also Stephen B. Oates, *With Malice Toward None,* 1979; and Benjamin P. Thomas, *Abraham Lincoln,* 1952.

Visit the source collections at http://ajaccess.wadsworth.com and http://infotrac.thomsonlearning.com, and use the Search function with the following key terms to explore documents, images, audio and video clips, articles, and commentary related to the material in this chapter:

Abraham Lincoln
Dred Scott
Fort Sumter
Harpers Ferry

Jefferson Davis
John Brown
Lincoln-Douglas debates

Additional resources, exercises, and Internet links related to this chapter are available on *The American Past* Web site: http://history.wadsworth.com/americanpast7e.

HISTORY ONLINE

The Dred Scott Case
www.toptags.com/aama/docs/dscott.htm
Text of pleadings in the historic Supreme Court case.

John Brown and the Valley of the Shadow
www.iath.virginia.edu/jbrown/master.html
Comprehensive coverage, with links, of Brown's raid at Harpers Ferry.

TIDY PLANS, UGLY REALITIES

The Civil War Through 1862

The first blast of civil war is the death warrant of your institution.

Benjamin Wade

Had slavery been kept out of the fight, the Union would have gone down. But the enemies of the country were so misguided as to rest their cause upon it, and that was the destruction of it and of them.

Joshua Lawrence Chamberlain

THE BOMBARDMENT OF Fort Sumter answered the big question: There would be a war. When Lincoln called for volunteers to suppress the rebellion and Davis summoned the manhood of the South to defend its honor and independence, both were flooded with recruits. By the summer of 1861, the Union had 186,000 soldiers in uniform; the Confederacy, 112,000.

But what kind of war would it be? What would battle be like? Nowhere had armies of such size clashed since the Napoleonic Wars in Europe half a century earlier. During the Mexican War, the United States had fielded no more than 10,000 men at a time. Now, just 15 years later, two American forces were faced with the challenge of feeding, clothing, sheltering, transporting, training, and controlling a mass of humanity 10 and 20 times that size.

THE ART AND SCIENCE OF WAR

The American Civil War took up where Napoleon and Wellington left off. American officers were educated in a theory of battle devised by a Swiss officer who had served both the French and the Russians, Henri de Jomini. A textbook based on Jomini's *Art of War* was the authority on tactics at West Point, where virtually all the major commanders of the Civil War learned their craft.

Position, Maneuver, and Concentration

Jomini emphasized position and maneuver as the keys to winning battle. The goal of the commanding general was to occupy high ground, ascertain the weakest point in the enemy's lines, and concentrate his power there. The general who prepared more thoroughly, better exploited the terrain, and moved his troops more skillfully than his opponent would break through the opposing line and force the enemy from the field.

The strategic object then was to capture and occupy economically important enemy cities and, best of all, the enemy's capital. The idea was that, losing what we would call a national infrastructure, the enemy had nothing for which to fight. Napoleon defeated his enemies in Europe (except Russia) when he occupied their major cities.

Jomini reduced battle situations to 12 models. Therefore, officers trained in his school (and with a brain in their heads!) knew pretty much what their adversaries had in mind at all times. As long as both sides observed the rules, there would be no long casualty lists. The general who was outfoxed knew that his duty was to disengage so that his men could fight another day under more favorable circumstances. Retreat, far from shameful, was among the most important of maneuvers because it preserved an army as a functioning machine.

The Armies

The armies of the Civil War were divided into cavalry, artillery, and infantry, with support units such as the Corps of Engineers (which constructed fortifications) and the Quartermaster Corps (entrusted with supply).

The cavalry's principal role was in reconnaissance. Horse soldiers were an army's eyes (although there would be some experimentation with anchored balloons in the Civil War). Battle plans were based on the information the cavalry brought back from sometimes spectacular rides that circled the enemy force. Because of their mobility and speed, cavalry units were also used for raids, plunging deep into hostile territory, burning and destroying what they found, sometimes seizing useful booty, and hightailing it out before they were confronted by big guns and masses of infantry.

In a pitched battle, cavalry reinforced weak points in the lines, and, if enemy troops retreated, the horse soldiers pursued, harassed, and scattered them. But cavalrymen were lightly armed by definition; for all the dash and flash, cavalry played a subsidiary role in pitched battle. Nevertheless, it was the glamorous service: the horses, the shades of the days of chivalry!

The artillery was slow to move and, with its toil, noise, and grime, notoriously unglamorous. But, as Napoleon had shown, big guns were critical to both attack and defense. Before an attacking army moved, its artillery slugged away at enemy positions with exploding shells, "softening them up." In defense, the artillery greeted attacking infantry and cavalry with grapeshot (a charge of small iron balls) and canister (projectiles that exploded and filled the air with clouds of metal). Examinations of dead soldiers after Civil War battles revealed that an attacking army suffered far more from cannon fire than from small arms. Indeed, soldiers in the field wryly joked that they fired a man's weight

▲ *Wagons of a Union supply unit in Virginia. The Union's massive resources and efficiency in supplying troops gave it an immense advantage over the Confederacy.*

in lead and iron for each enemy they killed. A Union expert found that calculation conservative; he said that 240 pounds of gunpowder and 900 pounds of lead were expended for every Confederate soldier felled.

As always, the infantry was the backbone of the army. The cavalry might worry the enemy, and the artillery weaken him, but it was the foot soldiers, squander ammunition as they did, who slogged it out face to face, took the casualties, and won and lost the battles.

The Infantry in Battle

The basic infantry unit was the brigade of 2,000 to 3,000 men. Under the command of a brigadier general, the soldiers formed double lines in defense or advanced over a front of about a thousand yards. During the first campaigns of the Civil War, captains in the front lines tried to march the men in step, as had been the practice in the Napoleonic Era. But with the greater firepower of the 1860s, so formal a charge was sensibly abandoned. It was enough that the men continued to run, trot, or simply walk into grapeshot, minié balls (conical bullets), noise like a thunderstorm in hell, and a haze of black, sulfurous smoke. Junior officers led the charge; thus, the ranks of lieutenant and captain suffered high casualties. More senior officers walked behind the lines to discourage stragglers. They carried revolvers and were authorized to shoot men who panicked and broke ranks, and they did.

If the advancing army was not forced to turn back, the final phase of battle was hand-to-hand combat. The attackers clambered over the enemy's fortifications of earth and lumber. Attackers and defenders swung their muskets at one another like the baseball bats they played with in camp until the defenders broke and ran or the attackers were killed or captured. The men had bayonets, but neither side succeeded in training the soldiers to use them very well. The importance of mastering this difficult and deadly skill was one lesson that European military observers took home with them

(as well as the opinion, lasting half a century, that Americans were afraid of cold steel).

There was plenty of shooting but not a great deal of aiming. Except for special units of sharpshooters, foot soldiers were not marksmen. There was little sense in taking on the big and expensive job of training large numbers of men in the skill of hitting small targets at great distances. With a few important exceptions (Shiloh, Antietam, Gettysburg), Civil War battles were not fought in open country. The men confronted one another in dense woods on terrain broken by hills, creeks, stone fences, and ditches. In several battles, attackers had to clamber up Appalachian cliffs on all fours. Often, opposing soldiers could not see one another until they were on the verge of touching.

Even in open country, hundreds of cannons and tens of thousands of muskets filled the air with a dense, acrid smog that, on a windless day, shrouded the battlefield. (Smokeless powder was still in the future.) Even if a soldier could shoot well, there was little he could aim at to prove it.

Billy Yank and Johnny Reb

As in all wars, the men who fought the Civil War were young, most between the ages of 17 and 25, with drummer boys of only 12. They came from every state and social class, although when both sides adopted draft laws (the Confederacy in April 1862, the Union in March 1863), the burden fell more heavily on poorer farmers and working people than on the middle and upper classes.

This was because the draft laws included exemptions favoring the well-to-do. The Confederates exempted men who owned 20 or more slaves. This was sorely resented by "Johnny Reb," the common soldier, who rarely owned one. Both the Confederate and Union draft laws allowed a man who was called to service to pay for a substitute at a price that was beyond the means of the ordinary fellow who did not want to go. In the North, a draftee could hire another to take his place or simply pay the government $300 for an exemption. In July 1863, working-class resentment of the draft led to a weeklong riot in New York City. Mobs of mostly Irish workingmen sacked draft offices, attacked rich men, and harassed and lynched blacks, whom they considered the cause of the war and a threat to their jobs. Some 60,000 people were involved, at least 400 were killed, and some $5 million in property was destroyed.

Bibles, Whiskey, and ID

As the war ground on, veteran soldiers tended to grow quiet and reflective before a battle. Many read their Bibles. The American Bible Society printed 370,000 more Bibles in 1861 than in 1860. Five million Bibles in various formats—most "pocket size"—were given to soldiers during the Civil War. When, in the war's final months, the Confederacy could devote no resources to printing Bibles, Union armies sent Bibles between opposing lines, under a flag of truce.

Some soldiers took a few quick gulps of whiskey. Friends made promises to look for one another when the battle was over and to gather personal belongings to return to family if one of them was killed. During the brutal battles before Richmond, soldiers wrote their names and addresses on pieces of paper pinned to their clothing on the assumption that there would be no friends alive to identify them.

Ads for Substitutes

The following two advertisements ran in the Richmond *Dispatch*:

Wanted—Immediately, a Substitute. A man over 35 years old, or under 18, can get a good price by making immediate application.

Wanted—two substitutes—one for artillery, the other for infantry or cavalry service. Also, to sell, a trained thoroughbred cavalry HORSE.

In the South, resistance to conscription took the form of thousands of draft dodgers heading west or into the Appalachians and the Ozarks, where some organized outlaw gangs, raided farms, and occasionally skirmished with Confederate troops. Most southern opposition to the war centered in the poorer mountain counties of western Virginia and North Carolina and in eastern Tennessee.

Both Union and Confederate armies were plagued by a high desertion rate, about 10 percent through most of the war. A few individuals were professional deserters, the bounty jumpers. Because some units paid cash—bounties—to men who signed up, some made a lucrative, although risky, business of enlisting, skipping out at the first opportunity, and looking for another unit offering bounties. In March 1865, Union military police arrested one John O'Connor, who was surely the champion. He confessed to enlisting, collecting a bounty, and deserting 32 times.

Shirking was not typical of either side, however. Over the course of the war, 1.5 million young men served in the Union army, and more than 1 million, from a much smaller population, with the Confederates. Whatever their resentments, ordinary people thought they had something at stake in the conflict. Despite their exemption, southern slave owners served in proportion to their numbers.

Army Life

The war they knew was not much like the war presented to the folks back home. In drawings in newspapers, masses of men moved in order across open fields amid waving flags and cloudlike puffs of white smoke. In reality, battle was a tiny part of military experience. Mostly, the war involved waiting, digging trenches, building breast works, marching, and being carted from one place to another in crowded trains.

The war meant poor food and shelter. In the South, supply was rarely efficient. Even when the Confederacy had enough uniforms, shoes, and food—which was not always—

there were problems in getting them to the soldiers. In the North, the inevitable profiteers sold the government tainted beef and shoddy blankets that fell apart in the rain. On both sides, physicians were unprepared to cope with so many patients; dysentery, typhoid, influenza, and other epidemic illnesses killed more soldiers than did enemy guns.

A Woman's War Too

A few women, although on no payroll, worked as spies during the war. The most famous Confederate agent was Rose O'Neal Greenhow, a Washington, D.C., widow with access to Washington society. During 1861, she forwarded information learned from Union officers to Richmond but was caught before the end of the year and deported through southern lines. There may have been dozens of less respectable pro-Confederate ladies in Washington, their names unknown for obvious reasons, who wheedled information from officers with whom they slept. There were plenty of Confederate sympathizers of both sexes in the city.

Harriet Tubman continued to penetrate Virginia in her role of harmless "mammy," reporting back to the Union army the disposition of rebel troops and the location of fortifications.

Female nurses were the most numerous and prominent soldiers in the cause. Shortly after Fort Sumter, Elizabeth

Wilhelmina Yank and Joanna Reb

Women fought in the Civil War, posing as men, of course. Official records list 127 female soldiers. One historian suggests the number was 400. Among them was Jennie Hodges, who fought for an Illinois regiment as Albert Cashier. Sarah Lemma Edmonds was Franklin Thompson in the Second Michigan. Passing as Lyons Wake in the 153rd Regiment of the New York State volunteers, Sarah Rosetta Wake rose to the rank of major.

The Cooper Union Museum, New York

▲ *A soldier's sketch of troops on the march. For every day a soldier spent in, preparing for, or regrouping after a battle, he spent dozens in exhausting treks, heavy labor, and training (or languishing) in camp.*

Blackwell, the first American woman to be a medical doctor, organized what became the United States Sanitary Commission, which put 3,000 nurses in army hospitals. At first, the army did not want them. Closeness to the front lines and the gore and male nakedness of the hospitals did not accord with the ideals of the gospel of true womanhood. But spokeswomen like Clara Barton (later founder of the American Red Cross) and Dorothea Dix, both women of impeccable propriety, wore the generals down. The fiercest opponents of women around the army were soon forced to admit that female nurses were infinitely superior to the disabled men who had previously assisted in army hospitals.

Hardly noticed at the time, a shortage of male workers, due to the size of the armies and full employment in industry, opened jobs in the federal bureaucracy for women, at the lowest levels. After the war, the taboo broken, the number of female civil servants steadily increased until they were a majority of federal employees in Washington.

In the South more than the North, because the Confederacy's manpower shortage was far more serious, women took heavy and dirty factory jobs. They took dangerous jobs too: An estimated 100 southern women were killed in explosions in munitions plants.

THE SOBERING CAMPAIGN OF 1861

Army life also meant drilling, day in and day out. But those who rallied to the colors in the spring of 1861 thought of the war as a great adventure, a vacation from the plow and hog trough, that would be over too soon. They trimmed themselves in gaudy uniforms. Some, influenced by pictures of Turkish soldiers in the recently concluded Crimean War, called themselves "Zouaves" (after a type of French infantry soldier) and donned fezzes and baggy pantaloons. Other units adopted names that would have been more appropriate to a boys' club. One Confederate regiment was called "The Lincoln Killers."

Manassas or Bull Run?

Early in the war, the Confederacy generally named battles after the nearest town. So they called the first battle, on July 21, 1861, "Manassas." The Union, although not consistently, named battles after the nearest waterway—thus, the "Battle of Bull Run." The Union's "Antietam" (named for a creek) was the South's "Sharpsburg" (named for a town in Maryland).

The Confederacy named armies after the state (or, in the case of Robert E. Lee's Army of Northern Virginia, part of a state) they were initially assigned to defend. The Union named its armies after rivers—for example, McClellan's Army of the Potomac. There was a Confederate "Army of Tennessee" (named after the state) and a Union "Army of *the* Tennessee" (named after the Tennessee River).

The Attempt to Take Richmond

Abraham Lincoln shared the illusion that the war would be short and painless. He waved off senior general Winfield Scott's warning that it would take three years and 300,000 men to crush the rebellion. Lincoln asked the first volunteers, mostly members of state militias, to enlist for only 90 days. That would be enough. Southerners too spoke of "our battle summer." The soldiers and civilians on the two sides disagreed only as to who would be celebrating when the leaves fell in the autumn of 1861.

These pleasant illusions were blown away on a fine July day about 20 miles outside Washington. Believing that his volunteers could take Richmond before their enlistments expired, Lincoln sent General Irvin McDowell marching directly toward the Confederate capital with 30,000 troops. Laughing and joking as they went, sometimes shooting at targets, the boys from Ohio and Massachusetts were accompanied by a parade of carriages filled with congressmen, socialites, newspaper reporters, and curiosity seekers. The crowd carried picnic lunches and discussed where in Richmond they would enjoy a late supper.

▲ *The Union rout at Manassas (Bull Run). It was a total defeat for the North, but the Confederate army had itself come so close to disintegration that a follow-up march on Washington was out of the question.*

Facing Battle

The Civil War battle experience was much the same whether a soldier wore blue or gray—except that northern troops were almost always better supplied with shelter, clothing, shoes, medicine, food, arms, and ammunition. It is difficult to say how much this meant to the outcome of the war. Cold, wet, tired, and ill soldiers are surely less effective than well-equipped ones. Confederate troops without shoes—not uncommon—were usually, but not always, exempt from charging enemy lines. Nevertheless, "Johnny Reb," the Confederate foot soldier, won the respect of both his officers and his enemies as a fighting man. As early as the second Battle of Bull Run in 1862, the commander of a unit called "Toombs's Georgians" told of leading so many barefoot men against the Yankees that they "left bloody footprints among the thorns and briars."

Johnny Reb and his Union counterpart, "Billy Yank," knew when they were going to fight. In only a few large battles was an army caught by surprise. Preparations for massive attack were so extensive that getting caught napping, as Grant's men were at Shiloh, was rare. In fact, the men who would be *defending* a position were generally prepared for battle with extra rations and ammunition earlier than the attackers, who knew when they would be moving.

Two or three days' rations were distributed before a battle. Historian Bell I. Wiley suggests that in the Confederate ranks:

> this judicious measure generally fell short of its object because of Johnny Reb's own characteristics: he was always hungry, he had a definite prejudice against baggage, and he was the soul of improvidence. Sometimes, the whole of the extra rations would be consumed as soon as it was cooked, and rarely did any part of it last for the full period intended.

Such recklessness could have serious consequences because fighting was heavy labor. Tales of units incapacitated by hunger after a day's battle were common. The men learned immediately to attend to their canteens. Waiting, marching, and running in the heat, cold, and rain, and the grime and dust of battle, made everyone intolerably, constantly thirsty.

As short a time as possible before a battle, each infantryman was given 40 to 60 rounds of ammunition to stash in the cartridge box he wore on a strap slung over a shoulder. (Soldiers rarely carried much ammunition at other times because the powder so easily got damp and useless.) The Springfield repeating rifles took a round that looked like any modern cartridge. The muzzle-loading musket—which was used by all the Confederates and most of the Yankees—took a round that consisted of a ball and a charge of powder wrapped together in a piece of paper that was twisted closed at the powder end. To load the musket, a soldier bit off the twist so that the powder was exposed, pushed the cartridge into the muzzle of his gun, inserted the paper he held in his teeth to keep the ball from rolling out, and rammed a rod (attached to his gun) into the barrel to the breech. Each time he fired, he had to fall to one knee in order to reload. The times when men were reloading or retreating were far more dangerous than when troops were advancing.

On the eve or morning of a battle, the commanding general addressed his troops either personally or in written orations read by line officers. Confederate general Albert Sidney Johnston took the high road in his speech before Shiloh:

> The eyes and the hope of eight millions of people rest upon you. You are expected to show yourselves worthy of your race and lineage; worthy of the women of the South, whose noble devotion in this war has never been exceeded in any time. With such incentives to brave deeds and with the trust that God is with us, your general will lead you confidently to the combat, assured of success.

Others, like General T. C. Hindman in December 1862, were demagogues:

> Remember that the enemy you engage has no feeling of mercy. His ranks are made up of Pin Indians, Free Negroes, Southern Tories, Kansas Jayhawkers, and hired Dutch cutthroats. These bloody ruffians have invaded your country, stolen and destroyed your property, murdered your neighbors, outraged your women, driven your children from their homes, and defiled the graves of your kindred.

They were met by a Confederate force of about 22,000 under the command of General Beauregard, recently arrived from Fort Sumter. The rebels had hastily dug in on high ground behind a creek called Bull Run, near a railroad crossing named Manassas Junction. McDowell attacked immediately, guessing the Confederate left flank to be the weakest point in the line. He was right about that. Although his troops were shocked by the ferocity of the musket fire that greeted them, they almost cracked the southern line.

Had it cracked, the war might have been over in the Upper South. To the rear of Beauregard's line, the road to Richmond was wide open. At the critical moment, however, 9,000 Virginians commanded by Joseph E. Johnston arrived on the field after a frantic train ride from the Shenandoah Valley. A brigade under the command of Thomas J. Jackson,

a 37-year-old mathematics instructor at Virginia Military Academy, shored up the sagging Confederate left. The Union soldiers fell back and then broke in hysteria, fleeing for Washington along with the panicked spectators.

Celebrations and Recriminations

The South had a victory and a hero. At the peak of the battle, a South Carolinian rallied his men by shouting, "There stands Jackson like a stone wall." The name stuck, for it seemed appropriate to more than Thomas J. Jackson's performance on the battlefield. He was introspective and humorless, an object of mockery to his students before the war. He was a stern Scotch-Irish Presbyterian who lacked the human touch.

MAP 23:1 The Battle of Bull Run, July 21, 1861 McDowell's army advanced from Washington along the highway that led to Winchester in the Shenandoah Valley. The battle lines stretched along Bull Run, straddling the Warrenton turnpike. Confederate generals Johnston and Jackson rushed reinforcements to the scene on the Manassas Gap railroad.

The Granger Collection, New York

▲ *Thomas J. "Stonewall" Jackson was the hero of the Confederacy's heady summer after the Battle of Manassas. He was polite at the many celebrations where he was feted but would not have enjoyed himself much. Jackson was the most morally strict and self-controlled of Presbyterians. He liked whiskey but did not drink it, for fear that he might like it too much.*

Jackson awed his soldiers because he came to life when the bullets whistled. He never yielded a line to the enemy, and he was a genius at maneuvering troops. For two years, Jackson would do what the South needed done, inserting his men in critical positions and standing like a stone wall.

By contrast, General Beauregard's reputation collapsed after Bull Run because he failed to follow up his victory by marching on Washington. He was soon replaced as Confederate commander in Virginia by Joseph E. Johnston, who had brought the troops and Stonewall Jackson from the Shenandoah Valley.

Johnston was a far superior field commander, but Beauregard was not to blame for the South's failure to capture Washington. As Johnston himself put it, "The Confederate Army was more disorganized by victory than that of the United States by defeat," and a disorganized army is no army at all. All the better generals at Bull Run, plus desk men like Robert E. Lee, who was President Davis's military adviser, emphasized the need for hard training.

The Summer Lull

Davis, who had been a pretty good junior officer, agreed. He cautioned Richmond society that there was more fighting to come. But few seemed to listen. Casualties had been minor. The soldiers were cocky and overconfident after their victory. Southern politicians spoke as though the war were over. Volunteer officers nagged their tailors to finish sewing gold braid on their dress uniforms so that they could show them off once or twice before the Union capitulated. And they bickered. At an endless round of gala parties in Richmond, old personal jealousies erupted as blustering colonels and generals blamed one another for blunders real and imaginary.

In the North, the defeat at Manassas taught a sorely needed lesson. The spectacle of McDowell's troops throwing down their guns and trotting wild-eyed into Washington, where they lay down to sleep in doorways and on the sidewalks, alarmed Lincoln and brought him around to Winfield Scott's way of thinking. The war would be no summer's pastime but a long, hard fight. Now when Lincoln asked Congress for troops, he wanted 300,000 men under three-year enlistments.

He relieved Irvin McDowell of command of what was now called the "Army of the Potomac," replacing him with George B. McClellan. The former president of the Illinois Central Railroad (for which Lincoln had been a lawyer), McClellan had a reputation as a superb organizer and administrator. In November 1861, Winfield Scott retired, and McClellan also took charge of the Union armies that were being drilled throughout the Midwest.

Northern Strategy

Although Scott was gone, living out the war at West Point, the three-part strategy that he had earlier outlined to Lincoln was effectively adopted. First, it was necessary to defend Washington with the Army of the Potomac and to maintain constant pressure on Richmond in the hope of capturing the city. This was important not only because Richmond, just 100 miles from Washington, was the Confederate capital, but because it was a railroad hub and a major industrial center, home of the Tredregar Iron Works, which was to sustain Virginia's fighting machine throughout the war.

Second—and Lincoln needed no tutoring on this—because the Ohio-Mississippi waterway was vital to the economic life of the midwestern states, Union armies would strike down the great valley. Their object was to gain complete control of the Mississippi as soon as possible in order to permit western farmers to resume the export of foodstuffs, by which they lived, and to split the Confederacy in two. The trans-Mississippi front (Arkansas and Texas) could then be left to small forces while the Union concentrated its power in the East.

Third, the Union would use its overwhelming naval superiority to blockade the South, strangling its export economy. If the Confederates were unable to sell cotton abroad, they could not buy the manufactured goods, particularly the munitions, that were essential in a lengthy war. Scott called the blockade the "Anaconda Plan" after the South American snake that slowly crushes its prey.

On the face of it, an effective blockade was out of the question. The Confederate Atlantic and Gulf coastlines were labyrinths of inlets, sheltered channels, coves, bays, bayous, salt marshes, and lonely broad beaches. It was quite impossible to prevent every vessel from reaching shore or from making a break for the high seas. Nevertheless, a national commerce could not be rowed through the surf or unloaded in swamps; the commanders of the Union navy felt confident that with time and more ships, they could bottle up the Confederate ports.

Dixie's Challenge

Southern strategy had a simpler design but a flimsier foundation. In order to win its independence, the Confederacy needed to conquer nothing. The South had only to turn back Union advances until Britain or France, both of which had expressed sympathy for the southern cause, came to the rescue or until the people of the North grew weary of fighting and forced Lincoln to negotiate. In the broadest sense, the story of the Civil War tells how these hopes were dashed and how, although long frustrated and delayed, the Union strategy succeeded.

The Confederacy's hope of foreign intervention died first. In the case of France, it may have been doomed from the beginning by the personality of the French emperor, Napoleon III. On one day a scheming power politician who recognized that an independent Confederacy might be molded into a valuable French protectorate, Napoleon III was, on the next, a flighty romantic.

At first, while leading the southerners on, he delayed when the more prudent British dithered. (Napoleon did not want to intervene in the war without British approval.) Then, when he was approached by Mexican aristocrats who, in order to defeat a mestizo and Indian revolution, offered to make an emperor of Napoleon's nephew, Maximilian of Austria, Napoleon III saw a far grander opportunity in America's tragedy than helping the South. Whereas the United States at peace might have forcefully resisted French interference in Mexico—it was not so long since some American expansionists spoke of annexing the whole country—the United States tearing itself apart was helpless to act. Anyway, what self-respecting emperor wanted a dependency of quarrelsome, headstrong cotton planters when he could tread in the footsteps of Cortés? Not Napoleon III. By the end of 1862, he was sidestepping the southern diplomats in Paris.

Indians in Gray and Blue

Whereas blacks were a mainstay of the Union army, most Native Americans sat out the war, no doubt somewhat heartened that, for once, the whites were fighting among themselves. Some tribes organized units, however, particularly in Indian Territory, where slavery was legal. About 5,500 Native Americans fought on the Confederate side, and about 4,000 fought for the North. An Iroquois officer served on General Grant's staff.

The pro-Confederate sentiments of the British government were solidly founded. Southern cotton fed the massive British textile industry, and British industrialists generally supported Henry Lord Palmerston's Liberal government. Moreover, many English aristocrats looked upon the southern planters, whose anglophilia and imitation of the British upper classes flattered them, as rough-cut kinsmen. Then, some strategically thinking British politicians saw an opportunity to shatter the growing power of the United States, which, they knew, was destined to eclipse Great Britain's.

The trouble was slavery. British public opinion was staunchly antislavery. In Britain, abolitionists much like America's had won their fight peacefully. British hostility toward slavery had prevented an alliance with Texas. Lord Palmerston was not willing to bear the wrath of antislavery Britons unless the Confederates demonstrated that they had a real chance of winning. Britain would not help the South fight an open-ended war of defense.

A combination of Confederate blunders in export policy, bad luck, Union diplomatic skill, and a Union victory in the Confederacy's brightest hour dashed the Confederate dream of redrawing the map of North America.

King Cotton Dethroned

The blunder was Jefferson Davis's belief he could blackmail Britain into coming to the aid of the South. In the excited solidarity of the Confederacy's first days, he prevailed on cotton shippers to keep the crop of 1860 at home, storing it in warehouses. The idea was to put the pinch on British mill owners so that they would set up a cry for a war to liberate the coveted fiber.

"Cotton diplomacy" did not work. English mill owners had anticipated the war and stockpiled huge reserves. When these supplies ran out in 1862, the price of cotton tripled, inducing farmers in Egypt and the Middle East to expand their cotton cultivation. Within a year, they were filling much of the gap created by the American war. To make matters worse, Union troops captured enough southern cotton in 1861 and 1862 to keep the mills of New England humming and even to sell some to Britain.

As the war dragged on, cotton diplomacy was completely scuttled by two successive poor grain harvests in western Europe. Fearing food shortages, monarchist Britain discovered that Union wheat was more royal than King Cotton. Blessed with bumper crops in those years, northern farmers shipped unprecedented tonnages of grain to Europe at both financial and diplomatic profit.

Diplomacy

In November 1861, a zealous Union naval officer almost ruined the northern effort to keep Britain neutral. The captain of the USS *San Jacinto* boarded a British steamer, the *Trent,* and seized two Confederate diplomats aboard, James M. Mason and John Slidell. Northern public opinion was delighted. It was refreshing to hear for a change of an American warship bullying a British vessel. But Lincoln took a dimmer view of the incident. The British minister in Washington came close to threatening war. For the president, Mason and Slidell were two hot potatoes, and he took advantage of the first lull in the public celebrations to hasten them aboard a British warship. "One war at a time," he remarked to his cabinet.

No harm was done. In France, Slidell was frustrated by Napoleon III's Mexican ambitions, and, in England, Mason proved no match for the Union minister, Charles Francis Adams, in the delicate game of diplomacy. Mason managed to see two commerce raiders, the *Florida* and the *Alabama*, constructed for the Confederacy and put to sea. But Adams cajoled and threatened the British government into preventing a sister ship and several Confederate rams from leaving port. He moved with great skill and energy through the salons of London—it ran in the family—and kept Great Britain out of the war until the North turned the tide in its direction and the possibility of British intervention quietly died.

1862 AND STALEMATE

As hopes of bringing England in dimmed, the South looked increasingly to northern sympathizers and defeatists to aid their cause. Some northerners frankly favored the South. Former president Franklin Pierce openly hoped for a Confederate victory. Prosouthern sentiment was strongest in the Union slave states of Maryland, Kentucky, and Missouri, of course, but also in the lower counties of Ohio, Indiana, and Illinois, a region with a strong southern heritage. However, these northerners who sympathized with the South, called "copperheads" (after a poisonous snake of that name that strikes without warning), were never able to mount a decisive threat to the Union war effort. They were a minority, and Lincoln played free with their civil liberties in order to silence them.

Lincoln and the Copperheads

One of the president's most controversial moves against opponents of the war was his suspension of the ancient legal right of habeas corpus, a protection against arbitrary arrest that is basic to both English and American law. At one time or another, 13,000 people were jailed, almost always briefly, because of alleged antiwar activity. Lincoln also used his control of the post office to harass, and even suppress, anti-administration newspapers.

The noisiest copperhead was Clement L. Vallandigham, a popular Democratic congressman from Ohio. His attacks on the war effort were so unsettling that, after General Ambrose Burnside jailed him, Lincoln feared he would be honored as a martyr. The president solved the problem by handing Vallandigham over to the Confederates as if he were a southern agent. Identifying Vallandigham with treason was unfair but shrewd; in 1863, he was forced to run for governor of Ohio from exile in Canada. At home, or even in prison, he might have won. But in absentia, he was defeated,

Fed Up in Dixie

By no means did all white southerners rally to the "Stars and Bars," as the Confederate flag was nicknamed. In the upland South, the foothills on both sides of the Appalachian ridge, few people owned slaves, and many of them opposed secession as the darling of the great planters, whose political and economic domination they resented. Western Virginia and eastern Tennessee voted against secession and provided thousands of soldiers for the Union army. So did many counties in western North Carolina and northern Alabama. Once the war was under way, the Confederate government's practice of expropriating crops and livestock to feed its armies aggravated the situation. When food became expensive and scarce in cities like Richmond and even in the countryside, southern women rioted to protest the war.

and when he returned to the United States the next year, he was harmless enough that Lincoln could ignore him.

More worrisome than the copperheads was defeatism, the belief that the war was not worth the expense in blood and money. Each time Union armies lost a battle, more and more northerners wondered if it would not be wiser to let the southern states go. Or, they asked, was it really impossible to negotiate? Was Lincoln's Republican administration, rather than the southern states, the obstacle to a compromise peace?

It was, in fact, impossible for Lincoln to secure reunion on any other basis than military victory. Even at the bitter end of the war, when the Confederacy was not only defeated but devastated, Jefferson Davis insisted on southern independence as a condition of peace. As long as the South was winning the battles, negotiation was out of the question.

And the South won most of the battles in 1861 and 1862. The show belonged to Stonewall Jackson and General Robert E. Lee, who succeeded Joseph Johnston as commander of the Army of Northern Virginia when, at the Battle of the Seven Pines on May 31, 1862, Johnston was seriously wounded. Time after time, Lee and Jackson halted or drubbed the Army of the Potomac. Nevertheless, even in his most triumphant hour in the summer of 1862, Lee revealed that his military genius was limited by his supreme virtue, his self-conscious image of himself as a Virginia gentleman, the scion of a distinguished old family.

Lee's cause was not so much the Confederacy as it was the dignity of "Old Virginny." He did not like slavery, the obsession of the southern hotheads. He may never have owned a slave himself and had freed his wife's slaves in 1857, when he was executor of her father's will. He did not much care for the hotheads of the Deep South, regarding them as vulgar parvenus. He had opposed Virginia's secession until it was a fact. Consequently, Lee never fully appreciated the fact that while he was defending the Old Dominion with such mastery, the southern cause was slowly throttled at sea, in the dozens of coastal enclaves Union troops occupied, and in the Mississippi Valley.

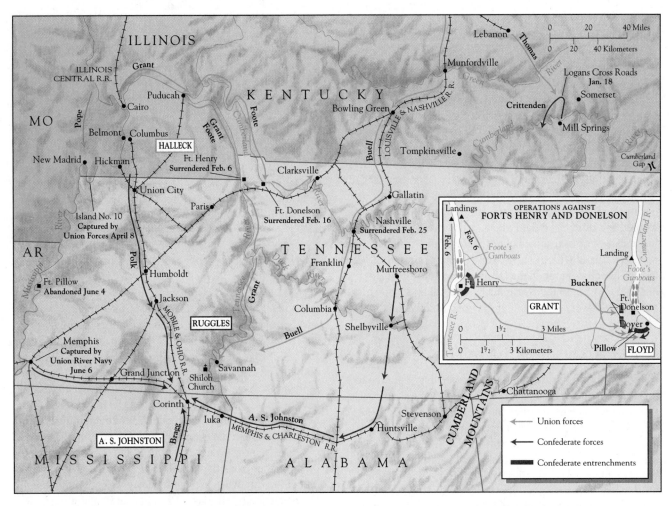

MAP 23:2 The War in the West, 1862 The importance of the Tennessee and Cumberland Rivers for communication and transportation (and thus the importance of their surrender to General Grant in February 1862) can be seen in this map. Grant's advance through Tennessee was without incident. Then came bloody Shiloh on the Mississippi border.

The Campaign in the West

Lincoln, although no military man (and himself the author of several Civil War blunders), understood the importance of the West. "We must have Kentucky," he told his cabinet. Without Kentucky—the southern bank of the Ohio River—he feared the war would be lost. Even before the army recovered from the defeat at Manassas, Lincoln approved moving a large force into the state under the command of Generals Henry Halleck and Ulysses S. Grant. In early 1862, Grant thrust into Tennessee, quickly capturing two important forts, Henry and Donelson. These forts guarded the mouths of the Tennessee and Cumberland Rivers, two waterways of infinitely greater value than muddy Bull Run. Moving on, however, General Grant fought the battle that taught both sides that they were not playing chess.

Moving up (south on) the Tennessee River unopposed, Grant intended to attack Corinth, Mississippi, in the northern part of the state. He knew that Confederate general Albert Sidney Johnston planned to defend the town, but Grant had no idea that Johnston was also prepared to attack. On April 6, 1862, while camped at Shiloh, Tennessee, Grant's soldiers were caught in their bedrolls by 40,000 rebels. Many were killed before they awoke. The others held on, but just barely. Only when Union reinforcements arrived under General Don Carlos Buell that night, did the Confederates withdraw.

Albert Sidney Johnston, regarded by some military historians as one of the Confederacy's best field commanders, was killed at Shiloh. Other southern losses numbered 11,000 of 40,000 troops engaged. The Union lost 13,000 of 60,000 men. Bodies were stacked like cordwood while massive graves were dug. Acres of ground were reddened with blood, and the stench of death sickened the survivors at their grisly job of cleaning up. Compared with the minor casualties at Bull Run—compared with the losses in most battles in any war to that date—Shiloh was a horror.

Grant was disgraced. He was accused of being drunk on the morning of the attack. Soldiers of the two armies ceased to fraternize between battles, as they had done in the woods of Tennessee, where Confederate and Union guards conversed in the night, traded tobacco for coffee, and, on at least one occasion, played a baseball game. Bull Run showed that there would be a long war; Shiloh showed that it would be bloody. Not even the success of naval officer David G. Farragut a short time after Shiloh, which put the Union in control of New Orleans, could cure the sense of melancholy that followed on the terrible battle.

The War at Sea

Confederate seamen on the commerce raiders *Florida, Alabama,* and *Shenandoah* saw quite a bit of the world. These fast, heavily armed ships destroyed or captured more than 250 northern vessels ($15 million in ships and cargo) in every corner of the seas. Sailors on the commerce raiders experienced naval warfare at its most exhilarating.

For the Union sailors assigned to the blockade, by contrast, days were long and boring, spent slowly patrolling the waters outside southern ports in scorching sun and winter winds. In 1861 and 1862, blockade duty was also frustrating. Most blockade runners, Confederate and foreign, outran the navy's ships in and out of southern ports, particularly steamers specially built for the purpose: they were low slung, so as not to be seen until within a few miles, and narrow in the beam. Blockade runners did not sail between the South and Europe. European shippers brought the goods the

Confederates wanted to Bermuda or the West Indies and picked up the cotton with which southerners paid there. Blockade running was ferrying, with quick turnarounds.

The Confederates threatened to break the blockade of the Chesapeake Bay in March 1862. Out steamed an old warship, the *Merrimack,* in brand new clothes. She had been covered over with iron plates in the shape of a tent. The *Merrimack* was a ram, its prow an iron blade like a plowshare that could slice through a wooden hull. Cannonballs glanced off the sloping armor as though they were made of rubber. Within a few hours of her debut, the *Merrimack* sank several Union warships.

Left unopposed for a few weeks, this single ship might have opened the Chesapeake to trade. But the *Merrimack* did not have even a few days. The Union's experimental vessel, the even odder looking *Monitor,* was also ironclad. It resembled a cake tin on a platter skimming the waves. For five hours on March 9, 1862, the two ships had at one another, then disengaged. The battle was technically a draw but effectively a Union victory. The *Merrimack* had to retreat for repairs. In May, the Confederates destroyed the vessel so that it would not fall into Union hands.

Once again, the material disparity between the two nations told in the long run. The South never built another *Merrimack.* The *Monitor* was a prototype for a flotilla of others like it.

Williamson Art Gallery & Museum, Birkenhead, England

▲ *Confederate commerce raiders, which savaged the North's merchant fleet, under construction in Liverpool in Great Britain. Three put to sea, the most famous being the* Alabama. *Union minister Charles Francis Adams was able to persuade the British not to release others after it became clear the Union would win the war.*

▲ *The Union had no better organizer and administrator than General George McClellan. But he was no good in the field—dallying and even avoiding battle either because of an innate timidity, an aversion to exposing his men to high casualties, hopes for negotiation without excessive bloodshed, or all three. Unfortunately, Union military organization did not provide for officers at the top who were "desk men" only.*

Moreover, McClellan was devoted to his soldiers. He could not bring himself to fight a battle in which the dead bodies would pile up as they had at Shiloh. Finally, he was no gambler. If there had to be a battle, he wanted overwhelming superiority. He could never get enough men to suit his conservative nature.

To Lincoln, who did not like McClellan (the feeling was mutual), it was simpler. Lincoln said that McClellan was ill; he had a bad case of "the slows."

The Peninsula Campaign

When McClellan finally moved in April 1862, he did not drive directly on Richmond. Instead, he moved by sea to the peninsula between the York and James Rivers. In a month, he had 110,000 troops poised to take Richmond from the south, bypassing the city's fortifications.

The plan was ingenious; it should have worked. The Confederate Army of Northern Virginia was outnumbered and disrupted by surprise. Having outmaneuvered the southerners, however, McClellan did not throw overwhelming force at the enemy's weakness. He sat, fiddled, and fretted. He overestimated the size of the Confederate force facing him and demanded reinforcements from Lincoln. But Lincoln refused when General Robert E. Lee, who had taken over from the injured Johnston, fooled him into thinking that Washington was in danger.

Lee set one of the traps that flummoxed northern commanders time and again. He sent Stonewall Jackson on a diversionary mission, feigning an assault on Washington that Jackson did not have the strength to bring off. The ruse was successful: Lincoln halted the movement of troops to the peninsula, and Jackson returned to reinforce the Confederates defending Richmond. By the time McClellan gave in to the president's impatient demand for massive action, Lee and Jackson had 85,000 men in position.

Seven days of nearly constant battle followed, between June 26 and July 2, 1862. Again overly cautious and outsmarted on the field, McClellan was fought to a standstill. Even then, he held a favorable position. His supply lines were intact; Confederate morale was badly shaken by the 25 percent casualties the South had suffered; and Richmond was nearly within range of bombardment. A massive Union push in the summer of 1862 might have carried the day.

It was Lincoln's turn to make a mistake. He called off the Peninsula Campaign, ordered the Army of the Potomac back to Washington, and replaced McClellan with General John Pope, who proposed to take the "safe" Manassas route to Richmond.

Pope had won several victories in the West and was a favorite with the abolitionists in Congress because of his opposition to slavery. But he was an unimaginative commander, no match for the wily Lee and Jackson. At the end of August, Lee met him on the same ground as the first Battle of Manassas and beat him back with much more ease than the Confederates had defeated McDowell.

McClellan and "the Slows"

In creating the Army of the Potomac, George McClellan made an invaluable contribution to the Union cause. Not only were his men better trained than most southern troops, but they usually were better armed. Whereas the Confederates had to import or capture most of their guns, McClellan and his successors had a limitless supply of munitions and constantly improved firearms. The Springfield repeating rifle, introduced toward the end of the war, allowed Union soldiers to fire six times a minute instead of once or twice.

The problem with McClellan was that he did not exploit the tremendous edge he created. He was a man of contradictions. On the one hand, he posed, strutted, and issued bombastic proclamations in the style of Napoleon. On the other, when it came time to fight, he froze as though he were one of Napoleon's statues. It was not entirely a matter of personality. McClellan was a Democrat. He did not want to crush the South. He believed that by creating a terrifying military machine, he could persuade the Confederates to give in and negotiate a peace.

MAP 23:3 McClellan's Peninsula Campaign and the Seven Days' Battles, March 17–July 2, 1862 The Peninsula Campaign was brilliant in conception. By approaching Richmond from the southeast, virtually all the fortifications built to defend the city to the north were rendered irrelevant. But McClellan dawdled. Although his numerical advantage was overwhelming, he wanted more troops. Brilliant maneuvers by Johnston, Jackson, and Lee brought McClellan to a standstill practically within sight of the Confederate capital.

Antietam

Lincoln recalled McClellan, and the eastern theater bogged down into a stalemate that began to worry Jefferson Davis as much as it did Lincoln. Davis's critics were not satisfied with Lee's brilliant defenses; they wanted the war carried into the North. With the chances of British intervention rapidly fading, a major victory on Union soil seemed to be the only way that Britain might be brought into the war.

Unfortunately, although Lee worked defensive miracles with inferior numbers, his army of 40,000 was not up to an advance when the enemy was 70,000 strong. Moreover, he suffered a fatal stroke of bad luck when his battle plans, wrapped around a pack of cigars, fell into McClellan's hands. The Union commander caught Lee when he was least prepared to fight, at Sharpsburg, Maryland, near Antietam Creek.

The fighting was as vicious and gory as at Shiloh. Lee lost a quarter of his army, and he was in no condition to retreat in order into Virginia. Stoically, with no lines of supply, he waited for the counterattack that would destroy his army. To Lee's amazement, McClellan did not move. He was down with "the slows" again. On the second night after the battle, hardly believing his luck, Lee slipped back to the safety of Virginia.

Emancipation: A Political Masterstroke

During the first year of the war, Lincoln insisted that his aim was not the destruction of slavery but the preservation of the Union. Not only did he constantly reassure uneasy political

▲ *An unlikely subject for a landscape artist: the heaps of Confederate dead at "Bloody Lane" after the Battle of Antietam, the worst single day of the war. Their position was a road long since sunken by wagon traffic. Union troops overran the makeshift position.*

leaders from the loyal slave states, but he twice counter-manded orders of generals in the field that slaves within their departments—in the Confederacy itself—were freed as acts of war. Nevertheless, Congress chipped away at the pecular institution by declaring that those slaves employed in pro-ducing arms in the South and the slaves of people who had committed treason were free.

Antislavery feeling was growing. In August 1862, when abolitionist newspaper editor Horace Greeley publicly de-manded that Lincoln move against the hated institution, the president replied, "If I could save the Union without freeing any slave, I would do it; and if I could save it by freeing all the slaves, I would do it; and if I could do it by freeing some and leaving others alone, I would also do it."

In fact, Lincoln had already decided to free some slaves. In the summer of 1862, he read the Emancipation Procla-mation to his cabinet. The proclamation declared that, as of a date yet to be decided, all slaves held in territory still under the control of rebel forces were henceforth free. Secretary of State William Seward persuaded Lincoln to keep the Emancipation Proclamation in his pocket until the North could win a major victory. Otherwise, Seward argued, Lin-coln's proclamation would look like an act of desperation. That major victory was Antietam. On September 22, 1862, five days after the battle, Lincoln issued his proclamation, to go into effect January 1, 1863.

A few abolitionists pointed out that Lincoln's blow against slavery did not free a single person. (It did not apply to the loyal slave states or to parts of the Confederacy occupied by Union troops.) They were unfair. The Emancipation Procla-mation was a political masterstroke. It reassured loyal slave owners by allowing them to keep their slaves. Lincoln hoped it would be an inducement to Confederate slave owners to make peace before January in order to save their property.

The Emancipation Proclamation also permitted northern commanders to make use of African Americans who, once Union armies were nearby, fled to freedom by the thousands. Many young black men wanted to join the army but, so long as they were legally slaves, they could not be enlisted. Thanks to the Emancipation Proclamation, fully 150,000 blacks served in Union blue. One Billy Yank in eight was black.

African American units were usually assigned the dirti-est and most dangerous duty, heavy labor in the rear, for ex-ample, and mining tunnels under Confederate fortifications. They were paid only half a white soldier's wages, about seven dollars a month. And yet, because they were fighting for freedom rather than for an abstraction, black soldiers were said to bicker and gripe far less than whites did.

A Fight to Make Men Free

The Emancipation Proclamation served Lincoln as a trial balloon. Without committing himself either way, he was able to test northern opinion on the subject of abolition. When Union soldiers adopted Julia Ward Howe's abolitionist "Bat-tle Hymn of the Republic" as their anthem—"let us fight to make men free"—Lincoln learned that by striking at slav-ery, he had improved morale. He had also ensured British neutrality. Dismayed by the Confederate defeat at Antietam, the pro-Confederates were almost completely silenced by the popularity of the Emancipation Proclamation among or-dinary people.

Finally, Lincoln mollified his chief critics within the Republican party. Called the Radicals because they wanted an all-out conquest of the South and a radical remaking of its social institutions, this group controlled the Joint Committee on the Conduct of the War. The Radical leaders, Thaddeus Stevens in the House and Charles Sumner in the Senate, were not satisfied with the Emancipation Proclamation. They wanted a constitutional amendment that would abolish slavery in the Union as well as in the Confederacy. But Lincoln's action subdued them. Lincoln also played for Radical support by once again dismissing the Democrat McClellan and appointing another antislavery general, Ambrose E. Burnside, as commander of Union forces in the East.

Stalemate

Burnside did not want the job. An able corps commander, as McDowell and Pope were, he knew that he was not up to the complexities and responsibilities of directing an entire army. But he was too good a soldier to turn Lincoln down and, on December 13, led a tragic assault on an impregnable southern position on high ground near Fredericksburg, Virginia. The slaughter of 1,300 Union soldiers (10,000 wounded) shocked the hardest of men. Union general Darius Crouch exclaimed, "Oh, great God! See how our men, our poor fellows are falling!" Robert E. Lee remarked to an aide that "it is well that war is so terrible or we would grow too fond of it." Burnside retreated, in tears and broken. And the Union and Confederate armies settled down to winter quarters on either side of the Rappahannock River.

The war also bogged down in the West. After Shiloh, a Confederate force under General Braxton Bragg moved across eastern Tennessee into Kentucky in an attempt to capture that state. At Perryville on October 8, he fought to a draw against General Don Carlos Buell, decided his supply lines were overextended, and moved back into Tennessee. On the last day of 1862, Bragg fought another standoff with the Union army at Murfreesboro. Both sides went into winter quarters—neither beaten, neither within sight of victory.

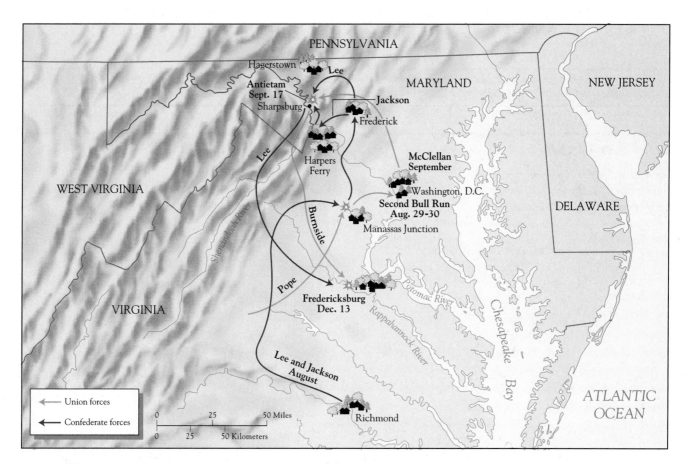

MAP 23:4 Stalemate in the East, 1862   Lee and Jackson displayed their mastery at the second Battle of Bull Run in August 1862 but were almost destroyed at Antietam, on the Maryland side of the Potomac, in September, in part because Lee's plans had fallen into McClellan's hands. Lee's reputation was restored when Union troops made an ill-advised attempt to cross the Rappahannock River at Fredericksburg at the end of 1862.

for FURTHER READING

On the Civil War, see James McPherson, *Ordeal by Fire: The Civil War and Reconstruction,* 1988. Larger, longer works are Bruce Catton, *Centennial History of the Civil War,* 3 vols., 1961–1965; Shelby Foote, *The Civil War: A Narrative,* 3 vols., 1958–1974; and Alan Nevins, *The War for the Union,* 4 vols., 1959–1971. Also see Bruce Catton, *Mr. Lincoln's Army,* 1951, and *Glory Road,* 1952.

More specialized works on the military history of the war include R. Beringer, *Why the South Lost the Civil War,* 1986; Robert Durden, *The Gray and the Black,* 1972; Herman Hattaway and Archer Jones, *How the North Won,* 1983; Frank Van Diver, *Their Tattered Flags,* 1965; and Bell I. Wiley, *The Life of Johnny Reb,* 1943, and *The Life of Billy Yank,* 1952. On black soldiers, see Dudley T. Comish, *The Sable Arm,* 1966.

On politics in the war era, see Eric Foner, *Politics and Ideology in the Age of the Civil War,* 1980; Frank L. Klement, *The Copperheads in the Middle West,* 1960; Emory Thomas, *The Confederate Nation,* 1979; and Frank Van Diver, *Jefferson Davis and the Confederate State,* 1964.

Valuable biographical studies include T. L. Connelly, *The Marble Man,* 1977 (on Lee); Clement Eaton, *Jefferson Davis,* 1977; Douglas S. Freeman, *Lee: A Biography,* 1934–1935; W. W. Hassley, *General George McClellan,* 1957; William S. McFeeley, *Grant: A Biography,* 1981; Stephen B. Oates, *With Malice Toward None,* 1979 (on Lincoln); Benjamin P. Thomas, *Abraham Lincoln,* 1952; and Frank Van Diver, *Mighty Stonewall,* 1957 (on Jackson).

Two reference works are essential: M. M. Boatner, *The Civil War Dictionary,* 1959; and E. B. Long, *The Civil War Day by Day,* 1971, a comprehensive chronicle of events.

AMERICAN JOURNEY ONLINE AND INFOTRAC COLLEGE EDITION

Visit the source collections at http://ajaccess.wadsworth.com and http://infotrac.thomsonlearning.com, and use the Search function with the following key terms to explore documents, images, audio and video clips, articles, and commentary related to the material in this chapter:

African American soldiers
Antietam
Civil War women
Emancipation Proclamation

George B. McClellan
Robert E. Lee
Stonewall Jackson

Additional resources, exercises, and Internet links related to this chapter are available on *The American Past* Web site: http://history.wadsworth.com/americanpast7e.

HISTORY ONLINE

American Civil War Homepage
http://sunsite.utk.edu/civil-war/warweb.html
Many links to Civil War Web sites.

Index of the Civil War
Informationhttp://www.cwc.lsu.edu/cwc/civlink.htm
Another compilation of Civil War resources on the Internet.

The Valley of the Shadow
http://valley.vodh.virginia,edu
An ingenious in-depth comparison of life during the war in a northern and southern community.

DRIVING OLD DIXIE DOWN

*General Grant's War of Attrition
1863–1865*

The rebels now have in their ranks their last man. The little boys and old men are guarding prisoners and railroad bridges, and forming a good part of their forces, manning forts and positions, and any man lost by them cannot be replaced. They have robbed the cradle and the grave.

Ulysses S. Grant

National Park Service, Harpers Ferry Center

BY THE SPRING of 1863, the Confederacy was suffering severe shortages and an inflation of the currency just short of runaway. In the Union, the problem was frustration. Lincoln had men and money, but he could not find a general who would both fight and win. In the East, Robert E. Lee had defeated or confounded four commanders. In the West, the situation was little more encouraging. Southern Louisiana and western Tennessee were occupied, but not even Kentucky was secure from Confederate cavalry raids. In the West too, the war was at a standstill.

THE CAMPAIGNS OF 1863

The third campaign of the war began with more bad news for the Union. By the end of the year, however, the tide had unmistakably turned against the South. Lee's second invasion of the Union ended in a Confederate disaster worse than Antietam. In the West, Union armies broke the stalemate, and Lincoln found there a general who knew how to win the war.

Chancellorsville

After Burnside's debacle at Fredericksburg, his most outspoken critic was General Joseph Hooker, called "Fighting Joe" because of his aggressiveness in the Peninsula Campaign. Hooker was regularly indiscreet. He had left the military in 1853 when his bad-mouthing of fellow officers angered Winfield Scott. After Fredericksburg, he assailed even Lincoln, saying that what the country needed for the duration of the war was a dictator. In one of the most unusual commissions ever given a military officer, Lincoln told Hooker that only victorious generals could set up dictatorships. If Hooker could win the victory that the North badly needed, Lincoln would run the risk that Hooker was a Napoleon.

Hooker was no more capable than Burnside. In early May, he crossed the Rappahannock River with more than twice as many soldiers as Lee's 60,000. Lee took Hooker's measure and calculated he could gamble. He divided his army—forbidden by the rules—left his fortifications, and hit Hooker from two directions near the town of Chancellorsville.

Lee should have lost his bet, but at the moment that a Union attack would have given the battle to Hooker, Fighting Joe ordered a withdrawal. His commanders on the field were incredulous. One told the courier who delivered the order, "You are a damned liar. Nobody but a crazy man would give such an order when we have victory in sight!" General Henry Slocum rode to Hooker's headquarters to confirm the message.

▲ *Every inch an aristocrat, always impeccably tailored, and soberly dignified, Lee was "the marble man" even during his lifetime. He was a brilliant tactician but far from flawless, as would be learned at Gettysburg.*

Once again, Lee had won. The Army of the Potomac suffered 11,000 casualties. Hooker was humiliated and soon relieved of command. However, the Battle of Chancellorsville also exposed a weakness in the South's fighting capacity that could only grow more serious. Lee's losses were larger than Hooker's, with a population base less than half that of the Union. If the war continued indefinitely as it had been going, with Lee winning almost all the battles, the Confederacy would run out of soldiers.

The casualty Lee noticed was his "strong right arm," Stonewall Jackson. Returning from a reconnaissance mission, Jackson was shot by his own troops and died. Lee said he could never replace Jackson and never placed the same degree of confidence that he had had in Jackson in the advice of any other general.

The Fortress of Vicksburg

In the West, the Union's object remained the control of the Mississippi River. By holding fast to a 150-mile stretch of the river between Vicksburg, Mississippi, and Port Hudson, Louisiana, the rebels were able to shuttle goods and men from one end of the Confederacy to the other. The farmers of the Midwest were unable to export their crops down the Mississippi and had to depend on railroads, which were more expensive and added to their costs.

The key to the impasse was Vicksburg. The city sat on high cliffs at a sweeping bend in the river. A Confederate force commanded by a renegade Pennsylvania Quaker, John C. Pemberton, manned heavy artillery on the top of the bluffs. Vessels passing below ran the risk of destruction. Infantry could not easily approach the city from the north, for Vicksburg was protected by rugged woodland laced by creeks and bayous—a tangle of earth, brush, and water. When Union forces approached, the Confederate garrison sallied out and repelled every assault. Vicksburg was as near and as far from the Union's western armies as Richmond was from the Army of the Potomac.

U. S. Grant

Then, within a few weeks, an unlikely candidate for the laurels of heroism broke the western stalemate. He was young General Ulysses S. Grant, just 41 years old, but with, it seemed, a century's worth of failures behind him. A West Point graduate, Grant was cited for bravery in the Mexican War but was then shunted off to duty at a lonely desert fort and then to a cold, wet, and lonelier outpost on the northern California coast. Grant took to the whiskey bottle and, after a dressing down by his superior, resigned from the army. In business and trying to farm back in Illinois, he failed. When the Civil War began, he was a clerk in a relative's store.

The Civil War was a godsend for men like Grant. Critically short of officers, the army did not quibble that Joe Hooker had been disruptive and Grant a drunk. Grant was given the command that won the first notable Union victory of the war, the capture of Forts Henry and Donelson. Then,

▲ *To say Grant's appearance was unprepossessing is an understatement. He was not slovenly, but he was careless of the state of his uniform and lacked a "soldierly bearing." But he knew what he was doing and was decisive.*

however, came Shiloh and a revived suspicion of Grant's friendship with the bottle.

Everyone who met Grant commented on his unimpressive presence. He was a dumpy man with a carelessly trimmed beard. His uniform was perpetually rumpled and often stained. From a distance, he could be mistaken for an aging corporal in danger of demotion. Up close, he struck some as listless, even stupid. But he was neither; nor was he a drunk. Grant was capable of boldness equal to that of Stonewall Jackson, and he had Lee's easy confidence with large commands. His written instructions alone should have allayed the worries of those who doubted him. Dashed off on his knee, they were superbly clear and precise.

The Siege

At Vicksburg, Grant scored a feat of old-fashioned military derring do and then sat down to an exercise in total war, not maneuvering with an army but assaulting the society that supported the enemy. First, he transferred most of his army to the western bank of the Mississippi, marched them swiftly to a few miles below Vicksburg, and then recrossed the river, ferried by gunboats that raced by night under the Confederate guns.

Having bypassed the rugged country where Pemberton had been unbeatable, Grant abandoned his lines of supply, a risky maneuver but one that confused the Confederates. He charged to the east and forced a small Confederate force under Joseph Johnston to withdraw from the area. Grant feigned a full assault on Jackson, the capital of Mississippi, and, when its defenders were holed up there, he reversed direction, turning back west to Vicksburg. The befuddled Pemberton was trounced in a series of brief battles. In a little more than two weeks, Grant won half a dozen confrontations and captured 8,000 southern troops. On May 19, with Pemberton penned up in Vicksburg, Grant sat his men down to besiege the city. Nothing was settled. Vicksburg was a natural fortress and still commanded the river below. But Union forces had broken through where they had been helpless for a year. Richmond was alarmed.

The Gettysburg Campaign

Some of Lee's advisers urged him to send part of the Army of Northern Virginia to attack Grant from the rear and lift the siege. Lee decided instead to invade Pennsylvania and threaten Washington from the north. Lincoln, he calculated reasonably enough, would be forced to call Grant's troops east. Indeed, Lee might even take the Union capital.

Had Lee succeeded, his reputation as a strategist would equal his reputation as a battlefield tactician. But he failed because, ironically, in the most famous battle of the Civil War, Lee made the most serious tactical mistake of his career.

At first, all went well. Lee's thrust into Pennsylvania (no plans wrapped around lost cigars this time) surprised the Army of the Potomac, put under the command of General George Meade when Lee's whereabouts were a mystery. An unglamorous but methodical general, Meade drifted northwest, able only to hope he would find Lee on ground favorable to his army. Forward units of both armies bumped into each other near Gettysburg, Pennsylvania, on July 1, 1863. The Confederates were looking for shoes.

Both armies descended on rolling farmland south of Gettysburg. The Confederates occupied the battlefield from the north; the Yankees, from the south. Both established strong positions on parallel ridges about half a mile apart:

Loaded Guns

Some 24,000 of 37,000 muskets and rifles that were collected from the battlefield at Gettysburg were still loaded, never fired that day. About 6,000 had between 3 and 10 charges in them. The soldiers were so excited that they continued to reload without discharging their weapons.

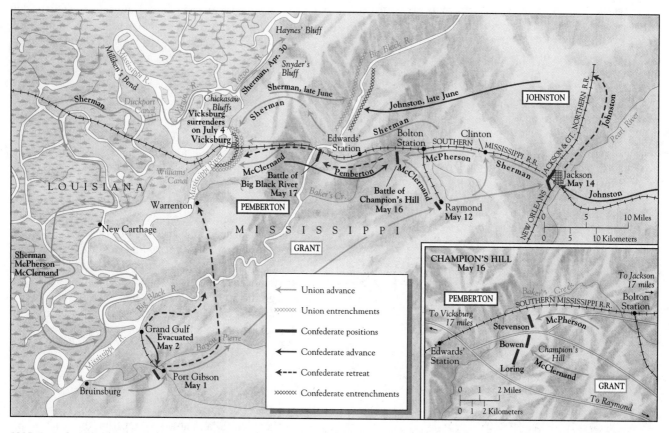

MAP 24:1 Grant's Vicksburg Campaign, May–July 1863 The boldness of Grant's Vicksburg campaign lay in taking a large army south of Vicksburg and into the heart of Mississippi with no line of supply to either the north or the south. Once Grant had penned up Confederate forces in Jackson and Vicksburg, his troops could be supplied via the Mississippi River.

the rebels on Seminary Ridge and the Union troops on Cemetery Ridge.

Deciding to move before the enemy's entrenchments were complete, Lee attacked with his left and almost won the battle on the first day. His men pushed Meade's line back until it was curled into the shape of a fishhook. Then, however, the Union soldiers held, and Lee did not have the resources with which to flank the line without exposing the rest of his army to an attack that would cut his supply lines.

On July 2, Lee attacked on his right, at the other end of the Union line, at the eye of the fishhook. Once again, the rebels came within a few yards and a few hundred men of breaking through. But when the sun set on the second day, Union troops under Joshua Lawrence Chamberlain of Maine had survived horrendous casualties to hold a bulbous knoll called Little Round Top. It was a valuable position—indeed, decisive. The troops that occupied Little Round Top—and Chamberlain was flooded with reinforcements overnight—could "enfilade" the open fields that separated the two armies. That is, they could shoot into an advancing army from the side, vastly increasing the odds of finding targets.

That night, Lee's imagination failed him. Although badly outnumbered now, he decided on a massive frontal assault on the Union center. One of his generals, James Longstreet, argued long, loudly, and late into the night

against a movement that reminded Longstreet of Burnside's charge into a powerful Confederate position at Fredericksburg. Longstreet pointed out that with two days in which to dig, the Union troops would be well entrenched on Cemetery Ridge. Better, he said, that the Confederates sit tight, improve their entrenchments, and force Meade to attack. In the war to that date, the advantage always rested with the defensive position.

Pickett's Charge

Stonewall Jackson might have persuaded Lee to dig in or, alternatively, to try to turn the Union's right again. James Longstreet could not, but he was dead right. Just a few miles

"Dixie" and "The Battle Hymn"

The unofficial anthems of the Confederate and Union soldiers, "Dixie" and "The Battle Hymn of the Republic," were both stolen from the other side. "Dixie" was written for a minstrel show by Dan Emmett, the son of an abolitionist. The music to "The Battle Hymn of the Republic" (and its predecessor, "John Brown's Body") was an anonymous southern gospel song, first heard in Charleston during the 1850s.

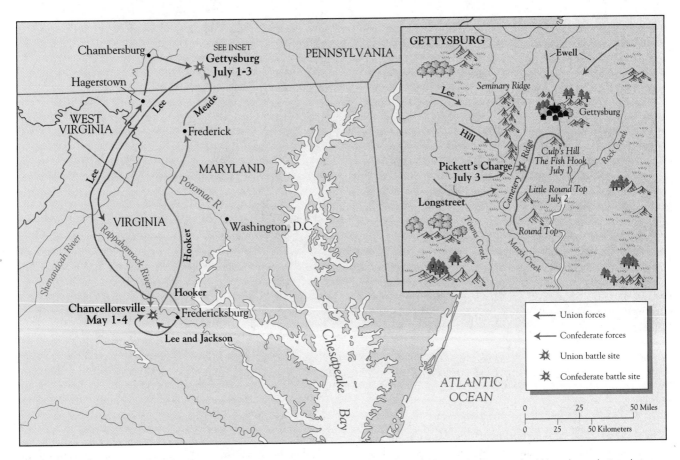

MAP 24:2 Chancellorsville and Gettysburg, May–July 1863 Almost all experts agree that General Lee's army should have been shattered at Chancellorsville. Whether he won the battle because of his brilliance or Union general Hooker's bizarre withdrawal from the field, Lee was able to make his bold foray into Pennsylvania and gain two near victories at Gettysburg before the disastrous final Confederate assault known as Pickett's Charge.

away, General Meade was betting on an assault on his center and he was ready for it. He concentrated his forces there and, on the afternoon of July 3, had the satisfaction of seeing his decision pay off. Between one and two o'clock, howling the eerie rebel yell, 15,000 men in gray began to trot across the no-man's-land. This was Pickett's Charge, somewhat of a misnomer because the angry Longstreet was in command of it. The attack was a nightmare. The men were slaughtered, first by artillery and then by minié balls. The most destructive fire came from Little Round Top.

About a hundred Virginians and North Carolinians actually reached the Union lines. There was a split second of glory, but there were too few rebels. They were surrounded by a thousand Union soldiers and killed or captured.

Pickett's Charge lasted less than an hour. When the survivors dragged themselves back to Seminary Ridge, 10,000 men were dead, wounded, or missing. Five of 20 regimental commanders were wounded; the other 15 were dead. So were two brigadier generals. Robert E. Lee rode among the survivors, restraining his tears, apologizing over and over.

On July 4, with 28,000 fewer rebels than he had led into Pennsylvania, Lee waited for the Union counterattack. It never came. Meade was still ruminating over Pickett's Charge. He would not expose his men to the horrors of cross-

ing an open field into the mouths of cannon. By nightfall, a drizzle became a downpour, making the Potomac impassable and setting up Lee's army for plucking. Defeated and huddled together, the Confederates were in a worse position than they had been in after Antietam. But the rain discouraged Meade too. He did not attack. "We had them within our grasp," Lincoln fumed in a rare display of temper. "We had only to stretch forth our hands and they were ours. And nothing I could say or do could make the Army move."

High Tide

For all Lincoln's disappointment, Gettysburg was an important victory. It ravaged southern morale. Intelligent Confederates understood that their armies would never again be capable of an offensive campaign. Lincoln was still without the decisive, relentless general who would exploit the Union's advantages. Meade was obviously not that man. But that was to change. Not long after the news of Gettysburg arrived in Washington, a spate of telegrams from the West informed the president that the siege of Vicksburg had also ended on July 4, 1863.

Literally starving, after having stripped the streets of pets and the cellars of rats, the people of Vicksburg had

▲ *The high water mark of the Confederacy: the culmination of Pickett's Charge. Miraculously, about a hundred rebels made it through the terrifying gunfire and leaped over Union fortifications. They were too few and quickly overcome. Most of the men who made the charge and were still alive were already trudging back to the Confederate line.*

surrendered. Five days later, Port Hudson, Louisiana, the last Confederate outpost on the Mississippi, gave up without a fight; Union general Nathaniel Banks took 30,000 prisoners. Within a week, the Confederacy lost several times more men than the rebels had put into the field at the first Battle of Bull Run.

The Tennessee Campaign

Worse followed bad. In September, a previously cautious Union general, William S. Rosecrans, attacked the remaining Confederate army in the West. Rosecrans pushed Braxton Bragg out of Tennessee and into northern Georgia. Union troops occupied Chattanooga, an important railroad center on the Tennessee River.

Like Grant at Shiloh, however, Rosecrans was surprised by a counterattack. On September 19, reinforced by grim Confederate veterans of Gettysburg, Bragg hit him at Chickamauga Creek. It was one of the few battles of the war in which the Confederates had the larger army, 70,000 to Rosecrans's 56,000, and the numbers made a difference. The rebels smashed through the Union right, scattering the defenders and making Chickamauga one of the bloodiest battles of the war. It would have been a total rout but for the stand on the Union left flank led by a Virginian who remained loyal to the Union, George H. Thomas, the "Rock of Chickamauga." Thanks to Thomas, the Union troops were able to retire in good order to behind the fortifications of Chattanooga.

Wisely, Bragg decided to besiege the city rather than attack it. But unlike Grant at Vicksburg, Bragg had enemies other than the army trapped inside the town. Grant himself marched his men to Chattanooga and brought 23,000 troops

from the east, also Gettysburg veterans, by rail. Late in November, he drove Bragg's Confederates from strongholds on Missionary Ridge and Lookout Mountain and back into Georgia.

The long campaign for Tennessee was over. It took two years longer than Lincoln had anticipated, but at last the Confederacy was severed in two; and the stage was set for what was hoped to be the final Union offensive. After Vicksburg and Chattanooga, there was no doubt about the man who was to lead it. Early in 1864, Lincoln promoted U. S. Grant to the rank of lieutenant general and gave him command of all Union forces. Grant turned his western command over to his "strong right arm," William Tecumseh Sherman.

TOTAL WAR

Grant had proved that he was a daring tactician of the old school. At Vicksburg, with dash and flash, he outsmarted and outmaneuvered the enemy. Now he informed Lincoln that his primary object was not the capture of Confederate flags, commanders, cities, and territory, but the total destruction of the enemy's ability to fight. Even Richmond

Lincoln on Grant
General Grant was on the receiving end of torrid criticism throughout his command, but Lincoln always defended him. When the president was told that Grant was a drinker, he replied, "Give me the brand, and I'll send a barrel to my other generals."

mattered to Grant because of its industry, not the Confederate government ensconced there.

The Union's numerical superiority was now overwhelming, and Grant intended to put it to work. He would force the Confederates to fight constant battles on all fronts, trading casualties that the North could bear and the South could not. At the same time, he would destroy the Confederacy's capacity to feed, shod, and arm its soldiers. He would complete on land what the naval blockade had begun: the strangulation of the South.

Grant's brand of fighting was not chivalrous. It involved making war not only on soldiers but on a society. It was left to William Tecumseh Sherman to give it a name. "War is hell," Sherman said. He was a no-nonsense man, even unpleasant in his refusal to dress up dirty work with fuss, feathers, and pretty words.

Sherman's assignment was to move from his base in Chattanooga toward Atlanta, the railroad center of the Deep South and the heart of the rich agricultural production of the black belt. Grant, with General Meade as his field commander, would personally direct the onslaught against Richmond.

Grant Before Richmond

The war of attrition—grinding down the Confederacy—began in May 1864. With 100,000 men, Grant marched into the "Wilderness," wooded country near Fredericksburg where Burnside had been defeated. There, he discovered that Lee was several cuts above any commander he had yet faced. Although outnumbered, Lee outmaneuvered Grant and actually attacked. Although Grant's men suffered almost twice as many casualties as the southerners did, replacements rushed to the Union front. On the southern side, Lee counted his dead and sent his wounded men home.

Now it was Lee's turn to discover that he too was up against a new kind of adversary. Instead of withdrawing to Washington where his men could lick their wounds and regroup as all Union commanders had done, Grant shifted his army to the south and attacked again, at Spotsylvania Courthouse. For five days, spearheaded in places by African American troops, the Army of the Potomac assaulted the southern trenches. Grant lost 12,000 men, again almost twice Lee's casualties. Northern congressmen and editors howled. The man was a butcher! But Grant was unmoved. He sent a curt message to Washington that he intended "to fight it out on this line if it takes all summer."

It took longer. Time after time, Lee rallied his shrinking army and somehow managed to scratch together enough munitions and provisions to keep his men in the field. Time after time, he threw Grant back. At Cold Harbor, south of Spotsylvania, the two fought another gory battle. Before they charged, Union troops wrote their names on scraps of paper and pinned the tags to their uniforms. They expected to die.

Petersburg and the Shenandoah

Grant again swung south. On June 18, he attempted to capture Petersburg, a rail center that was the key to Richmond's survival. He might have succeeded immediately but for the

▲ *A Union depot in Virginia. Grant's soldiers before Richmond were abundantly supplied. The troops at Petersburg were treated to a grand dinner on Thanksgiving 1864. The Confederates facing them had cornmeal mush; by the end of winter, thousands were shoeless.*

© Bettmann/Corbis

The Battle of the Crater

Early in the siege of Petersburg occurred one of the war's most bizarre battles. It was Ambrose Burnside's idea, and it was a good one. Miners from Pennsylvania dug a tunnel under a salient in the Confederate lines and planted 4 tons of gunpowder beneath a critical point in the fortifications. The plan was to detonate the charge and send a massive assault force led by a crack unit of African American troops.

At the last moment, the blacks were replaced by a less experienced white unit, with the African Americans in support. Some said the reason for the change was the Union officer's fears they would be accused of using black troops as cannon fodder. (The charge had been levied before.)

In fact, Union officers were responsible for the disaster resulting in the deaths of both white and black soldiers. The explosion blasted a crater 170 feet long, 60 feet wide, and 30 feet deep—larger than expected. Confederate troops a hundreds yards on either side of the hole were killed or fled. The gap in the lines was wide enough for a brigade to crash through.

Incomprehensibly (unless he was drunk as it was said he was), the incompetent general in command waited fully an hour before ordering the troops to advance. Then he sent them not around the crater but into it! The Confederates had long since regrouped and slaughtered the Union soldiers in the trap they had created. Black soldiers who tried to surrender were murdered.

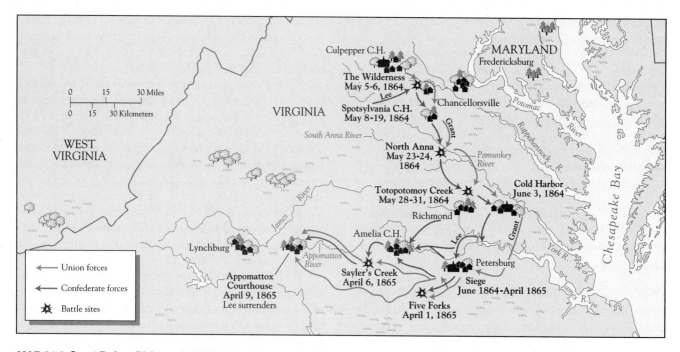

MAP 24:3 **Grant Before Richmond, 1864–1865** Grant was a different kind of Union commander. Five times, Lee's Army of Northern Virginia repelled him after hideously bloody battles. Each time, instead of withdrawing, he attacked further south until he reached Petersburg. Lee won the battles at the cost of the reduction of his army to a near starving fraction of its size in May 1864.

failure of General Benjamin Butler, a political general in charge of 30,000 reinforcements, to join him in time. By now, Grant was as shaken by the casualties as his critics were. Some 55,000 had been lost in the campaign, more men than Lee had under arms. One unit from Maine attacked with 850 soldiers and returned to the lines with 218. Grant sat down to besiege Petersburg. The siege would last nine months, seven months longer than Vicksburg, through the harshest winter of the war.

In July, Lee tried a trick that, with Stonewall Jackson in charge, had worked in 1862. He sent General Jubal Early on a cavalry raid toward Washington designed to force Grant into weakening his army. Early was remarkably successful.

His men actually rode to within sight of the Capitol dome and some tough-talking politicians began to stutter. But Early's raid was the Confederacy's last hurrah. Grant did not panic, and, this time, neither did Lincoln. (In fact, Lincoln nearly got himself shot by a sniper when he rode out to witness the battle and did not take cover.) Grant's infantry stayed outside Petersburg, and Grant confounded Lee by sending Union cavalry under General Philip Sheridan to intercept Early, preventing him from rejoining Lee.

Sheridan chased Early into the Shenandoah Valley, the fertile country to the west of Richmond that had been an untouched Confederate sanctuary and Richmond's breadbasket for three years. Sheridan defeated Early three times. More important, he laid waste to the valley that fed the Army of Northern Virginia, burning houses, barns, and crops, and slaughtering what livestock his men did not eat. He reported that when he was done, a crow flying over the Shenandoah Valley would have to carry its own provisions.

Sherman in Georgia

General Sherman was equally destructive in scouring Georgia. He moved into the state at the same time Grant entered the Wilderness. At first, he met brilliant harassing action by Joseph E. Johnston. Then an impatient Jefferson Davis, unaware that Johnston's army was not up to a major battle, replaced him with courageous, reckless John B. Hood, whom Sherman defeated. On September 2, 1864, with Grant beginning his third month outside Petersburg, Union troops occupied Atlanta. The loss of the city was a devastating blow to the economy of the Deep South and to Confederate morale.

▲ *Trenches at Petersburg. Both armies dug in for nine months, Union troops over more than 50 miles. The static front was a glimpse into the future, to World War I, although no one could know it.*

Marching Through Georgia

In the fall of 1864, General William Tecumseh Sherman, with a battle-tempered army of 60,000, occupied Atlanta, Georgia, the most important Confederate city aside from Richmond. In order to win the prize, Sherman's men had fought a series of ugly actions, including victories that had been close calls.

But Atlanta was an insecure prize. The civilian population was fiercely hostile. A strong Confederate army, its whereabouts not precisely known, menaced Sherman. The Yankee line of supply, a jugular vein for so large an army, was fragile, 100 miles of easily raided railroad to Chattanooga, Tennessee. Sherman had reason to be apprehensive of a massive battle.

Instead, he proposed to Washington that he would evacuate Atlanta, burning it so that the city would be useless to the Confederates. "Let us . . . make it a desolation," he urged on August 10. Sherman would then "astonish" the Confederates by marching without supply lines across Georgia, "smashing things generally," and rendezvous with a naval relief force at Savannah. His men would "eat out" the country.

Sherman had more in mind than the delicacy of his isolation. He meant to savage southern society and the economy of rural Georgia, punishing the staunch Confederates of the region for sustaining four years of costly rebellion. President Lincoln was under powerful pressure to decline Sherman's proposal, but he agreed when Grant expressed confidence in Sherman's judgment and explained that Sherman's defeat in battle would mean the loss of his entire army.

On November 11, Sherman's men evacuated the burning city. So as to move quickly, lest they be caught by the Confederates, the men marched in four parallel columns, cutting a swath 30 miles, sometimes 60 miles wide, through the rich Georgia countryside. Each column usually stretched out for 5 miles when, after 15 miles of marching, it paused for the night's rest.

Sherman charged his men to "discriminate" against the rich in seizing the food, mules, horses, oxen, and hogs the army needed in order to keep moving. He told his officers to leave enough at every farm for the people who lived there to survive. They were to punish soldiers guilty of rape, and soldiers were not to "enter the dwellings of the inhabitants, or trespass."

How strict Sherman meant to be in enforcing these orders cannot be known. However, they were immediately and widely ignored, and the general shrugged off accusations of brutal behavior with the observation that his men had suffered brutality at the hands of the rebels.

In fact, crime against persons was not wholesale. Only six rapes were documented, a remarkably low figure with 60,000 young men on the loose. Georgians in Sherman's path knew that women were safe. Frequently, when Sherman's army approached, the men of plantations and farms hid, leaving their women behind to plead for mercy or glower with hatred at the Yankees. One Confederate soldier wrote that "the Federal army generally behaved very well. . . . I don't think there was ever an army in the world that would have behaved better, on a similar expedition. . . . Our army certainly wouldn't."

This was a rare southern voice. Almost every other witness of the March, Union as well as Confederate, trembled in describing the damage Sherman's army did. The typical farm or village was not hit just once but several times, first by foraging parties ("pioneers") seizing food and livestock, then by the column itself, the first comers looting, the rear guard burning or shooting the animals that were still alive. An estimated 15,000 horses, 20,000 cattle, and 100,000 hogs were seized, eaten, or simply destroyed. Half a million bushels of corn disappeared, and 100,000 bushels of just-harvested sweet potatoes.

There was little armed conflict. The Confederate army under bold but ineffective General John Hood never caught up with Sherman. The 60,000 Union soldiers were confronted only by tiny bands of guerrillas able, at most, to snipe and run.

For a century, Sherman's march across Georgia was burned into the southern psyche. Even at the time, many northerners protested. For the most part, however, Sherman's vengeance filled a deep-felt need in the hearts of northerners. They believed the war should have been ended before Sherman's men left Atlanta. General Robert E. Lee, in Virginia, was finished by the fall of 1864. By preparing for another campaign in the spring, he seemed ready to cause tens of thousands more casualties—but for what? The Confederacy was dead. Sherman's terrible rampage was emotional compensation for frustration in the Union. Indeed, Sherman's partisans said it was his march through Georgia, more than any other factor, that compelled Lee to give up in the spring of 1865 before the "campaign of 1865" began.

Sherman knew that holding the city was problematical. With a military imagination the Union had not known before the emergence of Grant, Sherman asked for approval of a march to the sea, living off the land, and "making Georgia howl" by destroying everything his army did not need. After some hesitation, Lincoln approved the daring plan.

Sherman ordered the people of Atlanta to evacuate the city and put it to the torch. He then set out in four columns to the southeast, moving quickly in order to avoid a battle that, without supplies, he could not risk. His men were instructed to destroy everything of use to the Confederacy in a swath 60 miles wide. They not only tore up the railroad between Atlanta and Savannah, but they burned the ties and twisted the iron rails around telegraph poles. "Sherman bow ties" they called them. Sherman's purpose in laying Georgia waste was to punish the people of Georgia. Those who caused and supported the war (and profited grandly from it, as Georgia had) would suffer for the suffering they had abetted. This was total war.

Sherman reached Savannah on December 10 and captured it two weeks later. Resupplied from the sea, he turned north, continuing to scorch the earth in South Carolina. He intended to join forces with Grant and fight the war's final battle.

▲ *Wounded soldiers waiting to be taken into a hospital. Many, even with less serious wounds, would die of infection.*

The Sudden End

That battle was never fought. In February 1865, Jefferson Davis sent Confederate vice president Alexander H. Stephens and two others to meet Lincoln and Secretary of State Seward on a ship off Hampton Roads, Virginia, and try to make peace with them. Absurdly, their instructions were to insist on Confederate independence as a condition of peace. Davis was out of touch with reality.

Late in March, Lee tried to draw Grant into a battle in open country. He had 54,000 men to Grant's 115,000 and was easily pushed back to Richmond. On April 2, knowing that his 37-mile-long lines were too much to man (Union lines were 53 miles long), Lee abandoned Petersburg and therefore Richmond. He plan was to make a dash west, turn south, resupply in untouched North Carolina, and link up with Johnston for a last stand. Jefferson Davis, fleeing Richmond, was able to put a happy face on the loss of the capital. "Relieved of our obligation to defend cities, we . . ."

Grant cut Lee off. Desertions had reduced the Army of Northern Virginia to 30,000 men, some of whom were shoeless. On April 9, Lee met Grant at Appomattox Courthouse in Virginia in, ironically, the home of a man who had moved there from Manassas after the first Battle of Bull Run.

Grant's terms were simple and generous. The Confederates surrendered all equipment and arms except for the officers' revolvers and swords. Grant permitted both officers and enlisted men to keep their horses for plowing. After taking an oath of loyalty to the Union, the southern troops could go home. At Lee's request, Grant provided rations for the starving southerners.

Jefferson Davis ordered Joseph Johnston to fight on. The veteran soldier, who had not fared well by Davis's whims, knew better. On April 18, he surrendered to Sherman at Durham, North Carolina. The ragged remnants of two other Confederate armies gave up over the next several weeks.

THE AMERICAN TRAGEDY

More than a third of the men who served in the two armies died in action or of disease or were wounded, maimed permanently, or captured. In some southern states, more than one-quarter of all the men of military age lay in cemeteries. The depth of the gore can best be understood by comparing the 620,000 dead (360,000 Union, 260,000 Confederate) with the population of the United States in 1860, about 30 million. Considering that half the population was female

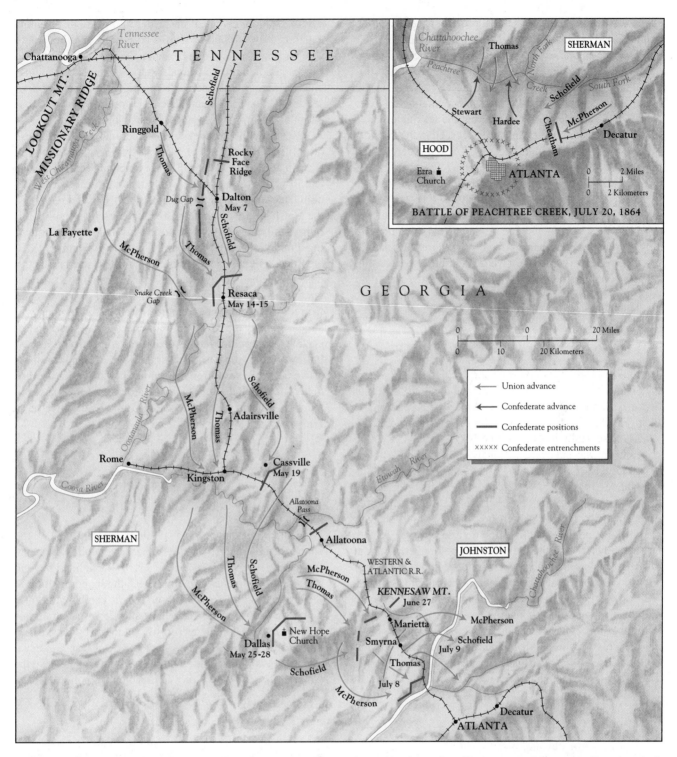

MAP 24:4 The Campaign for Atlanta, May–September 1864 Sherman began his advance from Chattanooga to Atlanta when Grant launched his assault on Richmond. Sherman captured his objective but, with an effective Confederate army outside Atlanta, abandoned the city after burning it to the ground.

and 7 or 8 million males were either too old or too young for military service, more than 1 out of every 25 men who were "eligible" to die in the war did. Until the Vietnam War of the 1960s and 1970s added its dead to the total, more Americans were killed in the Civil War than in all other American wars combined.

Assassination

There was one more casualty to be counted. On April 14, a few days after the fall of Richmond, President Lincoln and his wife attended a play at Ford's Theater in Washington. Shortly after 10 o'clock, Lincoln was shot in the head at point-blank range by a zealous pro-Confederate, John Wilkes Booth. Lincoln died early the next morning.

Booth was one of those disturbed characters who pop up periodically to remind us of the significance of the irrational in history. An actor with delusions of grandeur, Booth organized a cabal including at least one mental defective to avenge the Confederacy by wiping out the leading officials of the Union government. Only he succeeded in the mission, although one of his gang seriously wounded Secretary of State Seward with a knife.

As he escaped the theater, Booth shouted, *"Sic semper tyrannis!"* (which means "Thus always to tyrants!")—the motto of the state of Virginia. Booth fled into Virginia; on April 26, he was cornered and killed at Bowling Green. In July, four others were hanged for Lincoln's murder, including a woman, Mary Surratt, in whose boardinghouse the plot was hatched. But vengeance did not bring the president back, and his loss proved to be inestimable, perhaps more for the South than for the North.

Father Abraham

To this day, Lincoln remains a central figure of American history. More books have been written about him than about any other American. He was the American Dream made flesh. He rose from modest frontier origins to become the leader of the nation in its greatest crisis.

Lincoln was not overwhelmingly popular as a president. The Radicals of his own party assailed him because of his reluctance to make war on slavery early in the war and his opposition to punishing the South when the war neared its end. Northern Democrats vilified him because the war dragged on and the casualties mounted to no avail. As late as September 1864, with the casualties before Petersburg at horrible levels, Lincoln expected to lose his bid for reelection to the Democratic party candidate, his old nemesis, General George McClellan. Several advisers said he should call the election off. With his religious devotion to the Constitution, Lincoln never considered it.

Lincoln weathered McClellan's threat thanks in part to political machinations; he made Nevada a state, gaining three electoral votes, although Nevada consisted of little more than a dozen mining camps of uncertain future. He directed his generals to put Republican units on furlough so they could vote on election day while he kept units thought favorable to McClellan on duty. Lincoln also appealed to prowar Democrats by dropping the name "Republican" and calling himself the "Union party" candidate. For vice president, he chose a Democrat from Tennessee, Andrew Johnson.

But Lincoln did not win the election of 1864 because of political ploys. He won because Sherman had captured Atlanta and it was obvious to everyone but Jefferson Davis and Robert E. Lee that the Confederacy was doomed. Lincoln had won the respect of the majority of the people in the North by the example of his dogged will, personal humility, and eloquent humanitarianism. In a speech dedicating a national cemetery at Gettysburg in November 1863, he stated American ideals more beautifully (and succinctly) than anyone had done since Jefferson's preamble to the Declaration of Independence. His second inaugural address, delivered in Washington a month before Lee's surrender, was simultaneously a literary masterpiece, a signal to southerners that they could lay down their arms without fear of retribution, and a plea to northerners for a compassionate settlement of the national trauma. "With malice toward none," he concluded, "with charity for all; with firmness in the right, as God gives us to see the right, let us strive on to finish the work we are in."

CONSEQUENCES OF THE CIVIL WAR

The triumph of the Union guaranteed several fundamental changes in the nature of the American republic. Once and for all, the inseparability of the states was defined beyond argument. The theories of John C. Calhoun, compelling in the abstract, were buried without honor. The United States was not a federation of sovereign states. It was a nation, one and indivisible. Politicians (mostly southerners) have called themselves "states' righters" since the Civil War. But never after 1865 would anyone suggest that a state could leave the Union if its people disapproved of a national policy.

Don't Swap Horses

Until the end of the nineteenth century, candidates for the presidency did not actively campaign. They did, however, urge on their supporters. In the wartime election of 1864, Lincoln provided his party's slogan by telling the story of the Dutch farmer who said he never swapped horses in the middle of a stream. Indeed, Americans never have changed presidents voluntarily during a war. Even during the unpopular war in Vietnam, it took the retirement of Lyndon B. Johnson in 1968 to put Republican Richard M. Nixon in the White House. With the war still on in 1972, Nixon won reelection by a landslide.

Union and *Nation*

Before 1861, *United States* was grammatically plural; since 1865, it has been singular. That is, before the Civil War, one said, "The United States *are* . . ." Since, we have said, "The United States *is* . . ."

Lincoln quietly charted the transformation in his speeches. In his first inaugural address (March 1861), he used the word *Union* 20 times but *nation* not once. In his first message to Congress (July 1861), he said *Union* 49 times and *nation* 3 times. In the Gettysburg Address, Lincoln never said *Union* but referred to *nation* 5 times.

A New Political Majority

The political dominance of the South was dead. Since the founding of the republic, southerners played a role in the government of the country out of all proportion to their numbers. Eight of the 15 presidents who preceded Lincoln came from slave states. At least two of the seven northerners who held the office—Pierce and Buchanan—were blatantly prosouthern in their policies. After Lincoln and Andrew Johnson, no citizen of a former Confederate state would occupy the White House until Lyndon B. Johnson in 1963, and he was more westerner than southerner. Only in 1976, with the election of Jimmy Carter of Georgia, was an unambivalent southerner accepted by the American people as their leader.

Since the Age of Jackson, southerners had dominated Congress through a combination of political skill and agrarian alliance with western farmers. In making good on the threat to secede, the southern bloc destroyed this alliance. The Democratic party remained a major force in New York and the agricultural Midwest. But the Republicans held the edge above the Mason-Dixon line; never again would an agricultural coalition dominate the federal government.

In its place, northeastern industrial and financial interests came to the fore. Businessmen had been late in joining the antislavery coalition. To bankers, great merchants, and factory owners, the Republican party was of interest more because of its economic policies than because of its hostility to slavery. With the war concluded, however, these forces held a strong position and exploited the emotional attachment of most northern voters to the "Grand Old Party."

New Economic Policies

During the war, the Republican Congress enacted a number of laws that would have been defeated had southerners been in their seats and voting. In July 1862, about the time of Antietam, both houses approved the Pacific Railways Act. As modified later in the war, this act gave 6,400 square miles of the public domain to two private companies, the Union Pacific and the Central Pacific Railroads. These corporations were authorized to sell the land and use the proceeds to construct a transcontinental railway, the ultimate internal improvement. In 1864, while Grant slogged it out with Lee before Richmond, Congress gave the Northern Pacific Railroad an even more generous subsidy. These acts revolutionized the traditional relationship between private enterprise and the federal government.

The tariff was another issue on which southern agricultural interests had repeatedly frustrated the manufacturers of the Northeast. Since 1832, with few exceptions, the Democratic party drove the taxes on imported goods ever downward. The last tariff before the war, passed in 1857 with the support of southern congressmen, set rates lower than they had been since the War of 1812.

In March 1861, even before secession was complete, the Republican Congress rushed through the Morrill Tariff, which pushed up import duties. In 1862 and 1864, rates went even higher. By 1867, the average tax on imported goods stood at 47 percent, about the same as it was under the act of 1828 that the southerners had called the "Tariff of Abominations" and that Calhoun called fit grounds for secession.

The South had long frustrated the desire of northern financial interests for a centralized banking system. Opposition to a national bank was one of the foundation stones of the old Democratic party. During the war, with no southern congressmen in Washington and with the necessity of financing the Union army looming over Congress, New York's bankers had their way.

Financing the War

The Union financed the war in three ways: by heavy taxation, by printing paper money, and by borrowing—that is, selling bonds both abroad and in the United States. The principal taxes were the tariff, an excise tax on luxury goods, and an income tax. By the end of the war, the income tax provided about 20 percent of the government's revenue.

The government authorized the printing of $450 million in paper money. These bills were not redeemable in gold. Popularly known as "greenbacks" because (like our money) they were printed on one side in green ink, they had value (again like our own money) because the federal government declared they must be accepted in the payment of debts. When the fighting went badly for the North, the greenbacks were traded at a discount. By 1865, a greenback with a face value of $1 was worth only 67 cents in gold. This inflation was minuscule compared with that in the Confederacy, where government printing presses ran amok. By 1864, a citizen of Richmond paid $25 for a pound of butter and $50 for a breakfast. By 1865, prices were even higher; many southern merchants accepted only gold or Union currency, including greenbacks!

The banking interests of the North were uncomfortable with the greenbacks. However, they profited nicely from the government's large-scale borrowing. By the end of the war, the federal government owed its own citizens and some foreigners almost $3 billion, about $75 for every person in the country. Much of this debt was held by the banks. Moreover, big financial houses, like Jay Cooke's in Philadelphia, reaped huge profits in commissions for their part in selling the bonds.

Free Land

Another momentous innovation of the Civil War years was the Homestead Act. Before the war, southern fear of new free states in the territories paralyzed every attempt to liberalize the means by which the federal government disposed of its western lands. In May 1862, the system was overhauled. The Homestead Act provided that every head of family who was a citizen or who intended to become a citizen could receive 160 acres of the public domain. There was a small filing fee, and homesteaders were required to live for five years on the land that the government gave them. Or, after six months on the land, they could buy it outright for $1.25 per acre.

A few months after approving the Homestead Act, Congress passed the Morrill Act. This law granted each loyal state 30,000 acres for each representative and senator that state sent to Congress. The states were to use the money they made from the sale of these lands to found agricultural and mechanical colleges. In subsequent years, the founding of 69 land-grant colleges greatly expanded educational opportunities, particularly in the West.

Again, it was a free-spending policy of which parsimonious southern politicians would never have approved, and the revolutionary infusion of government wealth into the economy spawned an age of unduplicated expansion—and corruption.

Free People

No consequence of the Civil War was so basic as the abolition of slavery in the United States. In a sense, the "peculiar institution" was doomed when the first shell exploded over Fort Sumter. As Congressman Ben Wade of Ohio told southerners in 1861, "The first blast of civil war is the death warrant of your institution." Slavery was not only an immoral institution; by the middle of the nineteenth century, it was

hopelessly archaic. It is the ultimate irony of wars that are fought to preserve outdated institutions that war itself is the most powerful of revolutionary forces. Precariously balanced institutions such as slavery rarely survive the disruptions of armed conflict.

Once hundreds of thousands of blacks had left their masters to flee to Union lines, once virtually all the slaves had learned of the war, it was ridiculous to imagine returning to the old ways. Even if the South had eked out a negotiated peace, even if the North had not elected to make emancipation one of its war aims, slavery would have been dead within a decade.

▲ *By the end of the war, 150,000 African Americans had donned Union uniforms, serving both in units doing menial labor (where some officers wanted to keep them) and in some of the fiercest assaults of 1864. In several instances, Confederate soldiers murdered black prisoners.*

And yet, many southerners refused to recognize this reality until the end. Several times, the Confederate Congress turned down suggestions, including one from General Lee, that slaves be granted their freedom if they enlisted in the Confederate army. Only during the last two months of the conflict did any blacks don Confederate uniforms, and those few never saw action.

On the other side of the lines, 150,000 African Americans, some free northerners, most of them runaway slaves, served in the Union army. They were less interested in preserving the Union than in freeing slaves. Their bravery won the admiration of many northerners. Lincoln confessed his surprise that blacks made such excellent soldiers, and he seems to have been revising the racist views that he shared with most white Americans.

For a time, at least, so did many Union soldiers. Fighting to free human beings, a positive goal, was better for morale than fighting to prevent secession, a negative aim at best. By 1864, as they marched into battle, Union regiments sang "John Brown's Body," an abolitionist hymn, and Julia Ward Howe's more poetic "Battle Hymn of the Republic":

> As He died to make men holy,
> Let us die to make men free.

Because the Emancipation Proclamation did not free all slaves, in February 1865, Radical Republicans in Congress proposed, with Lincoln's support, the Thirteenth Amendment to the Constitution. It provided that "neither slavery nor involuntary servitude, except as a punishment for crime . . . shall exist within the United States." Most of the northern states ratified it within a few months. Once the institution of slavery was destroyed in the United States, only Brazil, Cuba, Puerto Rico, Muslim lands, and undeveloped parts of the world continued to condone the holding of human beings in bondage.

for FURTHER READING

The works listed in "For Further Reading" in Chapter 23 are relevant to this chapter as well. See also E. D. Fite, *Social and Industrial Conditions in the North During the Civil War,* 1976; J. F. C. Fuller, *Grant and Lee,* 1957; Paul D. Gates, *Agriculture and the Civil War,* 1965; Leon F. Litwack, *Been in the Storm So Long,* 1979; Robert P. Sharkey, *Money, Class, and Party,* 1959; Hans A. Trefousse, *The Radical Republicans,* 1969; and Bell Wiley, *Southern Negroes, 1861–1865,* 1938, and *The Plain People of the Confederacy,* 1943.

American Journey Online www AMERICAN JOURNEY ONLINE AND INFOTRAC COLLEGE EDITION

Visit the source collections at http://ajaccess.wadsworth.com and http://infotrac.thomsonlearning.com, and use the Search function with the following key terms to explore documents, images, audio and video clips, articles, and commentary related to the material in this chapter:

African American soldiers
Appomattox
Gettysburg Address
Ulysses S. Grant
Vicksburg

Additional resources, exercises, and Internet links related to this chapter are available on *The American Past* Web site:
http://history.wadsworth.com/americanpast7e.

HISTORY ONLINE

Civil War Treasures
http://memory.loc.gov/ammem/ndlpcoop/nhihtml/cwnyhshome.html
Documents and photographs from the New York Historical Society.

Civil War Maps
http://memory.loc.gov/ammem/gmdhtml/cwmhtml/cwmhome.html
Collection of maps used by the armies during the Civil War.

The U.S. Sanitary Commission
www.netwalk.com/~jpr/index.htm
A treasure of information on how the Union army dealt with health problems.

AFTERMATH

The Reconstruction of the Union 1865–1877

National Archives

Republicans gave the ballot to men without homes, money, education, or security, and then told them to use it to protect themselves. It was cheap patriotism, cheap philanthropy, cheap success.

Albion W. Tourgée

Oh, I'm a good old rebel, that's what I am,
And for this land of freedom, I don't give a damn,
I'm glad I fought ag'in her, I only wish we'd won,
And I don't axe any pardon for anything I've done.

Reconstruction Era doggerel

WHEN THE GUNS fell silent in 1865, some southern cities—Vicksburg, Atlanta, Columbia, Richmond—were flattened, eerie wastelands of charred timbers, rubble, and freestanding chimneys. Few of the South's railroads could be operated for more than a few miles. Bridges were gone. River-borne commerce had dwindled to a trickle. Old commercial ties with Europe and the North had been snapped. All the South's banks were ruined.

Even the cultivation of the soil had been disrupted. The small farms of the men who served in the ranks lay fallow by the thousands. Great planters who abandoned their fields to advancing Union armies discovered that weeds and scrub pine were more destructive conquerors than Yankees. The former slaves who had toiled in the fields were likely to be gone. If they remained in the only home they had ever known, they wondered who owned the land they had toiled over.

THE RECONSTRUCTION DEBATE

In view of the desolation and social dislocation, *reconstruction* seems to be an appropriate description of the 12-year period following the Civil War. But the word does not refer to the literal rebuilding of the South, the laying of bricks, the spanning of streams, the reclaiming of the land, and only secondarily to the rebuilding of a society.

Reconstruction refers to the political process by which the 11 rebel states were restored to a normal constitutional relationship with the national government. It was the Union, that great abstraction over which so many had died, that was to be built anew.

Blood was shed during Reconstruction too, but little glory was won. Few political reputations—northern or southern, white or black, Republican or Democratic—emerged

▲ *Richmond in ruins. Atlanta was worse. The Shenandoah Valley and northeastern Georgia were laid waste. Even areas of the South untouched by war were impoverished, dwellings and fields neglected. This was the region that had to be "reconstructed" and reintegrated into the victorious Union.*

from the era unstained. Abraham Lincoln may come down to us as a sainted figure only because he did not survive the war. Indeed, the Reconstruction policy Lincoln proposed in 1863 was repudiated by members of his own party, who would surely have fought him as they fought his successor, Andrew Johnson. Lincoln foresaw the problems that he did not live to face. He described as "pernicious" the constitutional hair-splitting with which both sides in the Reconstruction debate masked their motives and goals.

Lincoln Versus Congress

By December 1863, Union armies occupied large parts of the Confederacy. Ultimate victory, although not yet in the bag, was reasonable to assume. To provide for a rapid reconciliation after victory, Lincoln declared that as soon as 10 percent of the voters in a former Confederate state took an oath of allegiance to the Union, the people could organize a state government and elect representatives to Congress. Moving quickly, occupied Tennessee, Arkansas, and Louisiana complied.

Congress refused to recognize the new governments, returning the three states to military command. Almost all Republican congressmen were alarmed by the broad expansion of presidential powers during the war. No previous president, not even Andrew Jackson, had assumed so much authority as Lincoln had—at the expense of Congress. During a war that threatened to destroy the Union, one could swallow his anxieties. But Reconstruction was a postwar issue, and Lincoln's proposal did not involve Congress in any way.

The Radical Republicans, a minority of the party but vociferous, had another reason to reject Lincoln's proposal. Most of them were former abolitionists who hated the southern "slavocracy" and, for reasons that varied, insisted on full civil and political rights for the freedmen, as the former slaves were called. The Radicals framed the Wade-Davis Bill of July 1864, which provided that only after *50 percent* of the white male citizens of a state swore an oath of loyalty could the Reconstruction process begin. Then, in the Wade-Davis plan, Congress—not the president—would decide when former Confederate states were readmitted to the Union. Wade-Davis meant to slow down a process Lincoln wanted to speed along, and the bill aimed to put the power over approval of reconstruction of each rebel state in the hands of Congress.

Lincoln killed the Wade-Davis Bill with a pocket veto. Congress was about to adjourn and he simply did not sign it. Thus, he did not have to explain his rejection of the plan. During the final months of his life, he hinted that he was ready to compromise with Congress, even reaching out to the Radicals (whom he had never much liked) by saying he had no objection to giving the right to vote to blacks who were "very intelligent and those who have fought gallantly in our ranks." He urged the military governor of Louisiana to extend suffrage to some blacks.

Stubborn Andy Johnson

Lincoln's lifelong assumption that blacks were different from whites—inferior, in general—and his determination to reconcile southern whites to the Union quickly, made it difficult for him to accept Radical demands for the full citizenship of all African Americans. However, he let it be known he was flexible. "Saying that reconstruction will be accepted if presented in a specified way," he said, "it is not said that it will never be accepted in any other way." Andrew Johnson, his successor, was not a man of flexible positions.

Andrew Johnson of Tennessee grew up in stultifying frontier poverty. Unlike Lincoln, who taught himself to read as a boy, Johnson grew to adulthood illiterate, working as a tailor. Only then did he ask a schoolteacher in Greenville, Tennessee, to teach him to read and write. She did, later mar-

▲ *President Andrew Johnson. He was a man of integrity but inflexible and, despite his hatred of secessionists, hostile to every suggestion that the freedmen be granted civil equality.*

ried him, and encouraged Johnson to go into politics. He was a resounding success, winning elective office on every level from town councilman to congressman to senator. During the war, he was appointed governor of occupied Tennessee. No other president had so much political experience.

Experience, alas, is not the same thing as aptitude. Where Lincoln was an instinctively coy politician, sensitive to the realities of what he could and could not accomplish, Johnson was unsubtle, insensitive, willful, and stubborn— bullying when his goals were blocked. Personally, he got off to an unlucky start as Lincoln's vice president. Almost collapsing with a bad cold on inauguration day, he bolted several glasses of brandy for a pick-me-up, and took the oath of office obviously drunk. Fortunately, the ceremony was private, and Lincoln quietly told aides that Johnson was not to speak at the ceremony outside the Capitol.

The minor scandal was suppressed because Johnson had the goodwill of Lincoln's chief Republican critics, the Radicals. He had several times called for the harsh punishment of high-ranking Confederates (he wanted to hang Jefferson Davis), which was right up the Radicals' alley. But they misread him. Johnson had owned slaves as late as 1862 and considered every suggestion that the freed slaves be accorded citizenship an abomination. The Radicals' delight that he was president was short-lived. Like Lincoln, he insisted that it was the president's prerogative, and not Congress's, to decide when the rebel states were reconstructed.

Johnson: They Are Already States

Johnson based his case for presidential supervision of Reconstruction on the assumption that the southern states had never left the Union because it was constitutionally impossible to do so. The Union was one and inviolable, as Daniel Webster had said. It could not be dissolved. Johnson, the entire Republican party, and most northern Democrats held to that principle in 1861. Johnson stuck by it in 1865.

There had indeed been a war and an entity known as the Confederate States of America. But individuals fought the war and created the Confederacy. Punish individual rebels, indeed, Johnson said. He approved several confiscations of rebel-owned lands, but not the states of Virginia, Alabama, and the rest. They were still states, constitutional components of the United States of America. Seating their duly elected representatives in Congress was a purely administrative matter. Therefore, the president, the nation's chief administrator, would decide how and when to do it.

Logic Versus Horse Sense

There was nothing wrong with Johnson's logic; he was an excellent constitutionalist. The president's problem was his refusal to see beyond constitutional tidiness to the messy world of human feelings, hatreds, resentments, and flesh and blood—especially blood.

The fact was, virtually every senator and representative from the rebel states left his seat in the winter and spring of

1861. Johnson was the only senator of 22 who remained loyal. Although a rump by Johnson's reasoning, Congress had functioned constitutionally through four years of war. (Johnson's embarrassing presence in the Senate was resolved by naming him governor of Tennessee.) More than half a million people had been killed, and most northerners blamed the calamity on arrogant, destructive slave owners who, when Johnson announced he would adopt Lincoln's plan of Reconstruction (with some changes), assumed the leadership in their states that, as slavocrats, they had always held.

Nor did Johnson's reputation as a scourge of rebels hold up. By the end of 1865, he had pardoned 13,000 Confederate leaders, making them eligible to hold public office under his Reconstruction program. In elections held in the fall under Johnson's plan, southern voters sent many of these rebels to Congress: four Confederate generals, six members of Jefferson Davis's cabinet, and, as senator from Georgia, former Confederate vice president Alexander H. Stephens. It did not go down well for Americans who, for example, were buying tombstones for the menfolk they had lost.

The Radicals: They Have Forfeited Their Rights

Thaddeus Stevens, Radical leader in the House of Representatives, replied to Johnson's argument. The Confederate states had committed state suicide when they seceded, he said. They were not states. Therefore, it was within the power of Congress, and Congress alone, to admit them. Senator Charles Sumner argued that the southern states were "conquered provinces" and therefore had the same political status as the federal territories in the West.

These theories were worthy of John C. Calhoun in their ingenuity but also as contrived as Calhoun's logic-chopping. A lesser known Republican, Samuel Shellabarger of Ohio, came up with a formula that made sense constitutionally and appealed to angry, war-weary northerners, as Stevens's and Sumner's theories did: The rebel states had forfeited their identity as states.

Old Thad Stevens

Few Radical Republicans were so sincerely committed to racial equality as Thaddeus Stevens of Pennsylvania was. In his will, he insisted on being buried in a black cemetery because blacks were banned from the one where he normally would have been interred.

Nevertheless, even Stevens came to terms with the racism of northern whites who refused the vote to blacks in their own states. In order to win their support for black suffrage in the South, Stevens argued that the situation was different in the South because blacks made up the majority of loyal Union men there. "I am for negro suffrage in every rebel state," he said. "If it be just, it should not be denied; if it be necessary, it should be adopted; if it be a punishment to traitors, they deserve it."

Congress's Joint Committee on Reconstruction found that "the States lately in rebellion were, at the close of the war, disorganized communities, without civil government, and without constitutions or other forms, by virtue of which political relations could legally exist between them and the federal government." This state of affairs meant that only Congress could decide when the 11 disorganized communities might function as states of the Union.

The Radicals

Congress refused to seat the senators and representatives who came to Washington under the Johnson plan. The Radical Republicans meant to crush the southern planter class they had hated for so long and, with varying degrees of idealism, to help the freedmen who, for so long, had been victimized by their owners.

Some Radicals, like Stevens, Sumner, and Benjamin "Bluff Ben" Wade of Ohio, believed in racial equality. George W. Julian of Indiana proposed to confiscate the land of the planters and divide it, in 40-acre farms, among the freedmen. With economic independence, they could guarantee their civil freedom and political rights. Other Radicals wanted to grant the freedmen citizenship and the vote for frankly partisan purposes. Black voters would provide the core of a Republican party in the South, which did not exist before the war and was unlikely to be more than a splinter group if only southern whites voted.

The Radicals were a minority within the Republican party. However, they were able to win the support of party moderates because of Johnson's repeated blunders and a series of events in the conquered South that persuaded most northern voters that Lincolnian generosity would mean squandering the Union's hard-won military victory.

THE CRITICAL YEAR

Most southern blacks reacted to the news of their freedom by testing it. They left the plantations and farms where they had been slaves, many flocking to the cities that they associated with free blacks. Others, after a period of wandering, gathered in ramshackle camps in the countryside, eagerly discussing the rumor that each freedman's household would soon be allotted 40 acres and a mule for plowing. With no means of making a living in the stricken land, these congregations of freedmen were potentially, and in many cases in fact, dens of hunger, disease, disorder, and crime.

The Freedmen's Bureau

In order to prevent chaos in the liberated South, Congress created the Bureau of Refugees, Freedmen, and Abandoned Lands, popularly known as the Freedmen's Bureau. Administered by the army under the command of General O. O. Howard, the bureau provided relief for impoverished freedmen (and some whites) in the form of food, clothing, and

▲ *The Freedmen's Bureau was an effective federal agency, one of the few concerned with social problems before the twentieth century. Among the services it provided to African American southerners during Reconstruction, none was more important than its schools. Most of the teachers at bureau schools were idealistic white women from the North.*

shelter. The bureau attempted less successfully to find jobs for the freedmen. It set up hospitals and schools run by idealistic black and white women from the northern states, sometimes at the risk of their lives, and otherwise tried to ease the transition from slavery to freedom. When the Freedmen's Bureau Bill was first enacted, Congress assumed that properly established state governments would take over its responsibilities within a year after the end of the hostilities, a reasonable conjecture. The bureau was scheduled to expire in March 1866.

In February 1866, however, Reconstruction was at a standstill. Congress refused to recognize Johnson's state governments but had created none to its own liking. The former Confederacy was, in effect, still under military occupation. So Congress passed a bill extending the life of the Freedmen's Bureau.

Johnson vetoed it and, a month later, vetoed another act that granted citizenship to the freedmen. Once again, his constitutional reasoning was sound. The Constitution gave the states the power to rule on the terms of citizenship within their borders, and Johnson continued to insist that the state governments he had set up were legitimate and able to provide for the freedmen's needs.

He might have won his argument. Americans of the time took their constitutional fine points seriously, and Radical demands for black civil equality ran against the grain of white feelings about race. However, the refusal of many southern whites to acknowledge the simple fact that they had lost an ugly war nullified every point Johnson scored.

The Black Codes

Blacks as slaves had been the backbone of the southern economy. The Johnson southern state legislatures expected blacks to continue to bring in the crops. The freedmen certainly wanted the work. Far from providing farms for them, however, the Johnson state governments established a system of employment that scarcely acknowledged the Thirteenth Amendment. The so-called black codes defined a second-class form of citizenship for the freedmen that appeared to be more like slavery than freedom.

In some states, blacks were permitted to work only as domestic servants or in agriculture, just what they had done as slaves. Other states made it illegal for blacks to live in towns and cities, a backhanded way of keeping them in the fields. In no state were blacks allowed to vote or to bear arms. In fact, few of the civil liberties listed in the Bill of Rights were accorded them.

South Carolina said that African Americans could not sell goods. Mississippi required freedmen to sign 12-month labor contracts before January 10 of each year. Those who did not could be arrested, and their labor sold to the highest bidder in a manner that (to say the least) was strongly reminiscent of the slave auction. Dependent children could be forced to work. Blacks who reneged on their contracts were not to be paid for the work that they already had performed.

The extremism of the black codes angered many northerners who would have accepted a milder form of second-class citizenship for the freedmen. Only a few northern states allowed African Americans full civil equality. Northerners were also disturbed when whites in Memphis, New Orleans, and several smaller southern towns rioted, killing and injuring blacks, while the Johnson state governments sat passively by.

The Fourteenth Amendment

In June 1866, perceiving the shift in mood in their favor, the Radicals and moderate Republicans drew up a constitutional amendment on which to base congressional Reconstruction policy. The long and complex (and later controversial) Fourteenth Amendment banned from high federal or state office all high-ranking Confederates unless they were pardoned *by Congress*. This struck directly at many of the leaders of the Johnson governments in the South. The amendment also guaranteed that *all* "citizens of the United States and of the State wherein they reside" were to be treated equally under the laws of the states.

If ratified, the Fourteenth Amendment would preclude southern states from passing any more laws like the black codes. However, it also promised to cancel northern state laws that forbade blacks to vote, and in that aspect of the amendment Johnson saw a political opportunity. Calculating that many northerners, particularly in the Midwest, would rather have Confederates in Washington than grant full civil equality to African Americans, Johnson decided to campaign personally in the 1866 congressional election against the Radicals.

The Radicals' Triumph

The first step was to organize a political party. Johnson, conservative Republicans such as Secretary of State Seward and a few senators, and some Democrats called a convention of the "National Union party" in Philadelphia. The message of the convention was sectional reconciliation. To symbolize it, the meeting opened with a procession of northern and southern Johnson men in which couples made up of one southerner and one northerner marched arm in arm down the center aisle of the hall.

Unhappily for Johnson, the first couple on the floor was South Carolina Governor James L. Orr, a huge, fleshy man, and Massachusetts Governor John A. Andrew, a little fellow with a way of looking intimidated. When Orr seemed to drag the mousy Andrew down the length of the hall, Radical politicians and cartoonists had a field day. Johnson's National Union movement, they said, was dominated by rebels and preached in the North by their stooges.

In the fall, Johnson made things worse. He toured the Midwest seeking support—he called it his "swing around the circle"—and from the start discredited himself. Johnson had learned his oratorical skills in the rough-and-tumble, stump-speaking tradition of eastern Tennessee. There, voters liked a red-hot debate between politicians who scorched each other and ridiculed the hecklers that challenged them.

Midwesterners liked that kind of ruckus well enough, but not from their president. When Radical hecklers taunted Johnson and he responded in kind, Radicals shook their heads sadly that a man of so little dignity should be sitting in the seat of Washington and Lincoln. He was drunk again, they supposed.

The result was a landslide. Most of Johnson's candidates were defeated. The Republican party, now led by the Radicals, controlled more than two-thirds of the seats in both houses of Congress, enough to override every veto Johnson handed them.

RECONSTRUCTION REALITIES AND MYTHS

The Radical Reconstruction program was adopted in a series of laws passed by the Fortieth Congress in 1867. They dissolved the southern state governments that were organized under Johnson and partitioned the Confederacy into five military provinces, each commanded by a major general. The army would maintain order while voters were registered: blacks and those whites not specifically disenfranchised by the Fourteenth Amendment. The constitutional conventions that these voters elected were required to ratify the Thirteenth and Fourteenth Amendments and give the vote to adult black males. After Congress approved their work, the reconstructed states were admitted to the

---

Discouraging Rebellion

Among other provisions of the Fourteenth Amendment, the former Confederate states were forbidden to repay "any debt or obligation incurred in aid of insurrection or rebellion against the United States." By stinging individuals and banks that had lent money to the rebel states, the amendment was putting supporters of future rebellions on notice that there were consequences.

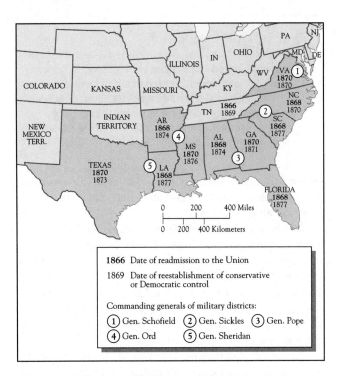

MAP 25:1 **Radical Reconstruction** The Radicals divided the defeated Confederacy into five military districts. The Union army supervised the establishment of state governments guaranteeing equal rights for the freedmen. Tennessee was not part of the program. The state had been occupied for much of the war by Union forces. Ironically, Tennessee had a viable state government by 1866 because of its wartime Union governor, Andrew Johnson, who, as president, opposed Radical Reconstruction.

Union, and their senators and representatives were admitted to Congress. The Radicals assumed that at least some of these congressmen would be Republicans.

Readmission

Tennessee complied immediately and was never really affected by the Radicals' plans to remake the South. Ironically, the groundwork for a stable government in Tennessee had been built by Andrew Johnson when he was military governor of Tennessee during the war.

In 1868, largely as a result of a large vote by freedmen, six more states were readmitted. Alabama, Arkansas, Florida, Louisiana, North Carolina, and South Carolina all sent Republican delegations, including some black congressmen, to Washington. In the remaining four states—Georgia, Mississippi, Texas, and Virginia—some whites obstructed every attempt to set up a government in which blacks participated. The military continued to govern them until 1870.

In the meantime, with Congress more firmly under Radical control, the Radicals attempted to establish the supremacy of the legislative over the judicial and executive branches of the government. With the Supreme Court, they were immediately successful. By threatening to reduce the size of the Court, the Radicals intimidated the justices. Chief

Justice Salmon P. Chase decided to ride out the difficult era by ignoring all cases that dealt with Reconstruction issues, exactly what the Radicals wanted.

Congress took partial control of the army away from Johnson and then struck at his right to choose his own cabinet. The Tenure of Office Act forbade the president to remove any appointed official who had been confirmed by the Senate without the Senate's approval of his dismissal. It was a step in a plot obvious to all. The Radicals wanted Johnson to violate the Tenure of Office Act so they could impeach him.

The Impeachment of Andrew Johnson

Johnson had delayed Radical Reconstruction with vetoes, which were overridden. He tried to obstruct it by urging southern whites not to cooperate, thus the late readmission of Georgia, Mississippi, Texas, and Virginia. But the strict constitutionalist in him had come to terms with the fact of the Radicals' control of Congress. He executed the duties assigned him under the Reconstruction acts. However, also because of his constitutional scruples, he defied the Tenure of Office Act. To allow Congress to decide if a president could fire a member of his own cabinet was a clear infringement of the independence of the executive branch. In February 1868, Johnson dismissed the single Radical in his cabinet, Secretary of War Edwin Stanton.

Courts may have ruled that the Tenure of Office Act did not apply to Stanton's dismissal because he had been appointed by Lincoln, not by Johnson. Nevertheless, the House of Representatives passed articles of impeachment and appointed Johnson's prosecutors, as the Constitution provides. The Senate was the jury in the trial; the chief justice presided.

A President on Trial

All but two of the 11 articles dealt with the Tenure of Office Act. As expected, Johnson's defenders in the Senate argued that it did not apply to the Stanton case and, in any event, its constitutionality was highly dubious. The other two articles condemned Johnson for disrespect of Congress. This was

▲ *A ticket to the impeachment trial, the high point of Washington's social season. The president did not attend.*

undeniably true; Johnson had spared few pungent words in describing Radicals of both houses. The president's defenders responded that sharp and vulgar language did not approach being the "high crimes and misdemeanors" the Constitution stipulates as grounds for impeachment.

Conviction of an impeached federal official—removal from office—requires a two-thirds majority of the Senate. In 1868, that meant 36 senators had to vote to convict, no more than 18 to acquit. The vote in Johnson's case was 35 to 19. He remained president by a single vote.

Actually, it was not that close. About six moderate Republican senators agreed privately that if their votes were needed to acquit, they would vote for acquittal. They did not believe that the president should be removed from office simply because he was at odds with Congress. Moreover, if Johnson were removed, his successor would be Ben Wade of Ohio, a Radical of such dubious deportment—he was notorious as a foulmouth—that by comparison, Johnson was a statesman. Finally, 1868 was an election year, and Andy Johnson's days were numbered. The immensely popular Ulysses S. Grant would be the Republican nominee. Victory in November was a sure thing. They wanted to wait for that.

But they were practical politicians. Johnson had very little support among Republican voters. If possible, the six did not want to go on record as favoring the president. It was possible, barely, and the fence-sitters were right. A Republican senator from Kansas who was thought to have cast the vote that acquitted Johnson lost his bid for reelection.

The Fifteenth Amendment

In 1868, Grant easily defeated New York governor Horatio Seymour in the electoral college, by 214 to 80. However, the popular vote was much closer, a hair's breadth in some states. Nationwide, Grant won by 300,000 votes. Some rudimentary arithmetic showed that he got 500,000 black votes in the southern states; Seymour may have been the choice of a majority of whites. Grant lost New York, the largest state, by a very thin margin. Had blacks been able to vote in New York, Grant would have carried the state easily. In Indiana, Grant won by a razor-thin margin. Had blacks been able to vote in that northern state, it would not have been close.

In a word, the future of the Republican party seemed to depend on the black man's right to vote in the northern as well as the southern states. Consequently, the Republicans, including moderates, drafted the Fifteenth Amendment. It forbade states to deny the vote to any person on the basis of "race, color, or previous condition of servitude." Because Republican governments favorable to blacks still controlled most of the southern states, the amendment was easily ratified.

Legend

By the end of the nineteenth century, a legend of Reconstruction took form in American popular consciousness. Most white people came to believe that Reconstruction was a time of degradation and humiliation for white southerners. Soldiers bullied them, and they languished under the political domination of ignorant former slaves who were incapable of good citizenship, carpetbaggers (northerners who went south in order to exploit the tragedy of defeat), and scalawags (low-class white southerners who collaborated with blacks and Yankees).

The "Black Reconstruction" governments were hopelessly corrupt. The blacks, carpetbaggers, and scalawags looted the southern state treasuries and demeaned the honor of the South. Only by heroic efforts did decent white people, through the Democratic party, redeem the southern states when they took control of them. Some versions of the legend glamorized the role of secret organizations, such as the Ku Klux Klan, in redeeming the South.

As in most legends, there was a kernel of truth in this picture of Reconstruction. The Radical governments did spend freely. There was plenty of corruption; for example, the Republican governor of Louisiana, Henry C. Warmoth, banked $100,000 during a year when his salary was $8,000. In 1869, the state of Florida spent as much on its printing bill as was spent on every function of the state's government in 1860. Sometimes theft was open and ludicrous. Former slaves in South Carolina's lower house voted a payment of $1,000 to one of their number who lost that amount in a bet on a horse race.

The Legend in Perspective

Large governmental expenditures were unavoidable in the postwar South. The southern society and economy were being built from desolation in many areas—an expensive proposition. It was the lot of the Radical state governments to provide social services—for whites as well as blacks—that had simply been ignored in the South before the Civil War. Statewide public school systems were not founded in the South until Reconstruction. Programs for relief of the destitute and handicapped were nearly unknown before the Republicans came to power.

Corrupt politicians are inevitable in times of massive government spending, no matter who is in charge. Shady deals were not peculiar to southern Republican governments during the 1860s and 1870s. The most flagrant theft of public treasuries during the period was the work of Democrats in New York, supporters of white southerners who wanted to reduce the blacks to peonage. In fact, the champion southern thieves of the era were not Radicals but white Democrats hostile to black participation in government. After a Republican administration in Mississippi ran a nearly corruption-free regime for six years, the first Democratic treasurer of the state absconded with $415,000. This paled compared to the looting done by E. A. Burke, the first post-Reconstruction treasurer of Louisiana, who took $1,777,000 with him to Honduras in 1890.

As for the carpetbaggers, the portrayal of them as low-class parasites was false. Many of them brought much-needed capital to the South. They were hot to make money, to be sure, but in the process of developing the South, not as mere exploiters. Some scalawags were "poor white trash," but the majority were respectable whites who had been opposed to secession—onetime Whigs—and some had been prominent, well-to-do Confederates.

Blacks in Government

Few of the African Americans who rose to high office in the Reconstruction governments were ignorant former field hands. Most were well-educated, refined, even rather conservative men. Moreover, whatever the misdeeds of Reconstruction, black voters could not be blamed. African Americans never ran the government of any southern state. Eighty percent of Republican voters, blacks held only a fifth of public offices. For a short time, African Americans were the majority in the legislature of South Carolina (where blacks were a large majority of the population) and filled half the seats in the legislature of Louisiana. Only two African Americans served as senators, Blanche K. Bruce and Hiram Revels, both cultivated men from Mississippi. No black ever served as a governor, although Lieutenant Governor P. B. S. Pinchback of Louisiana briefly acted in that capacity when the white governor was out of the state. Whatever Reconstruction was, its color was not black.

The crime of Reconstruction in the eyes of most southern whites was that it allowed blacks to participate in government. The experiment failed because black voters lacked the economic independence with which to guarantee their civil equality and because northerners soon lost interest in the ideals of the Civil War.

The Klan and the Redeemers

In 1866, General Nathan Bedford Forrest of Tennessee, whom Sherman thought the South's military genius, founded the Ku Klux Klan as a social club for Confederate veterans. Like other men's lodges, the Klan was replete with hocus-pocus, including white robes and titles like Kleagle and Grand Wizard. In 1868, with the triumph of the Radical Republicans in Congress, the Klan was politicized, and similar organizations, like the Knights of the White Camellia, were born.

Determined to prevent black participation in government with harassment and terrorism, Klan night riders threatened, roughed up, whipped, and killed African Americans who were politically active, who were merely deemed "impudent," or who simply refused to work for whites. They hit the South like a tornado. The federal government estimated that the Klan murdered 700 blacks in 1868. The next year was worse.

Because the Klansmen were masked, it was impossible to bring the murderers to trial. So, in 1870 and 1871, Congress passed two Ku Klux Acts, making it illegal "to go in disguise upon the public highway . . . with intent to . . . injure, oppress, threaten, or intimidate [citizens] and to prevent them from enjoying their constitutional rights."

Providing authorities and the army carte blanche to harass the Klansmen proved effective in some states. Between 1870 and 1872, Texas arrested 6,000 Klansmen and broke the organization there. It took years elsewhere in the South to end the terror. The single greatest Klan atrocity, the "Colfax Massacre," occurred in April 1873, when 100 blacks were killed.

▲ *Representative Robert Elliott of South Carolina in the House of Representatives. More African Americans were elected to the House from South Carolina during Reconstruction than from any other state.*

By then, many southern blacks had concluded that staying home on election day was a small price to pay for their families' freedom from terror. (The Klan killed women too.) Moreover, few southern blacks owned land. In order to make a living, they found that a major condition of employment was to stay away from the polls.

One by one, the Republicans lost the southern states to the Redeemers, as Democrats running frankly on a platform of "white supremacy" called themselves. Year by year, the interest of northerners in preserving the rights of southern blacks deteriorated. Never had more than a minority of northern whites been convinced that blacks were their equals. When an era of unprecedented economic expansion unfolded during the presidential administration of Ulysses S. Grant, support for Reconstruction dwindled. Albion W. Tourgée, a white northerner who fought for black civil equality in North Carolina, wrote that trying to enforce the Fourteenth and Fifteenth Amendments without federal support was "a fool's errand."

THE GRANT ADMINISTRATION

Ulysses S. Grant, only 46 years old when he took the oath of office in 1869, was the youngest man to be president up to his time. In some ways, his presence was as unimpressive as when reporters caught him whittling sticks on the battlefield. In some photographs, Grant has an odd cast to his eye as though he suspected he had risen above his capabilities. In fact, Grant disliked the duties of the presidency—the job; but he delighted in its perquisites. He took with relish to eating caviar and tournedos sauce béarnaise, and sipping the best French wines and cognac. The general whose uniform was always rumpled developed a fondness for expensive, finely tailored clothing.

Indeed, the elegant broadcloth on his back was the emblem of Grant's failure as president. Money and fame came too suddenly to a man who had struggled to pay the bills for

▲ *Ku Klux Klan night riders shoot up the house of an African American who voted or, possibly, just insisted on his dignity as a free man. In 1868 and 1869, two or three blacks were murdered each day by Klanlike terrorists.*

40 years. He and his wife were overwhelmed by the adulation heaped on them after Appomattox. When towns and counties took his name, and cities made gifts of valuable property and even cash—$100,000 from New York City—Grant accepted with a few mumbled words of thanks. He never grasped the fact that the gift givers might actually be paying in advance for future favors. Or, he saw nothing wrong in returning kindness with the resources at his disposal. Among the least of his mistakes, he gave federal jobs to any of his and his wife's relatives who asked, and they were not bashful. Worse, Grant remained as loyal to them, even after they betrayed him, as he had been loyal to junior officers in the army. In the military, backing up subordinates when they slip up is a virtue, essential to morale. Grant never learned that, in politics, backing up subordinates who consciously steal is quite another thing.

Black Friday

Grant's friends, old and new, wasted no time in stealing. Unlucky in business himself, the president luxuriated in the flattery lavished on him by wealthy men. In 1869, two unscrupulous speculators, Jay Gould and Jim Fisk, made it a point to be seen in public with the president while they schemed secretly with Grant's brother-in-law, Abel R. Corbin. The stakes were high: Gould and Fisk planned to corner the nation's gold supply.

With Corbin's assurance he would keep Grant from selling government gold, Gould and Fisk bought up as much gold and gold futures (commitments to buy gold at a future date at a set price) as they could find on the market. The immediate sale of so much gold sent its price soaring. By September 1869, gold was bringing $162 an ounce. Gould and Fisk's plan was to push the price a bit higher, dump their holdings, and pocket a fortune.

Finally grasping that he was an accomplice to the scheme, on Friday, September 24, Grant put $4 million in government gold on the market. The price collapsed, but Gould and Fisk suffered little. Jim Fisk simply refused to honor his futures commitments and hired thugs to threaten sellers who insisted. (High finance could be highly exercising during the Grant years.) But businessmen who needed gold to pay debts and wages were ruined by the hundreds; thousands of workingmen lost their jobs. The luster of a great general's reputation was tarnished before he was president for a year.

Other Scandals

During the construction of the Union Pacific Railway, the directors of the UP set up a dummy construction corporation called the "Crédit Mobilier." It charged the Union Pacific some $5 million for work that the Crédit Mobilier paid subcontractors $3 million to perform. The difference went into the pockets of Union Pacific executives. Because the Union Pacific was heavily subsidized by the federal government, and therefore under scrutiny, key members of Congress were cut in on the loot. Among the beneficiaries was

Black Politicos

Better a white crook than a black crook; better a white grafter than a black of stature and probity. Such was the view of the "Redeemers," white Democrats who wrested control of southern state governments from the Republican party during Reconstruction. They depicted black officials as incompetent, corrupt, and uninterested in the welfare of the South as a whole. With most southern whites contemptuous of the freedmen, it was an effective appeal. Other issues paled nearly into invisibility in what seemed the blinding urgency of asserting "white supremacy."

At low levels, some black officials were incompetent and self-serving. A few high officials were venal grafters. That their Redeemer challengers were no better and often worse did not, however, lead to reflection among southern Democrats. Race was all.

As a group, the African Americans who sat in Congress during Reconstruction and, in a few cases, beyond, were as able and worthy as any other identifiable category of congressmen of any era. Between 1869 and 1901, 20 blacks served in the House, two in the Senate. South Carolina sent eight; North Carolina, four; Alabama, three; and Virginia, Georgia, Florida, Louisiana, and Mississippi, one each. Both black senators, Hiram K. Revels and Blanche K. Bruce, represented Mississippi, where potential black voters outnumbered whites.

Thirteen of the 22 African Americans in Congress had been slaves; the others were lifelong free blacks. Their educational attainment compared well with that of Congress as a whole. Ten of the black congressmen had gone to college, and five had graduated. Six were lawyers; three were preachers; four were farmers. Most of the others were skilled artisans.

Hiram Revels was a Methodist pastor. He was born in North Carolina in 1822 but, as a free black, prudently moved to Indiana and Ohio, where, during the Civil War, he organized a black regiment. The end of the war found him in Natchez, Mississippi where his cultivated and conservative demeanor (and a willingness to defer to white Republicans) made him an attractive candidate for the Senate.

Blanche K. Bruce was born a slave in 1841, but he was well educated: His owner leased him to a printer. In 1861, he escaped from his apparently lackadaisical master and, in the wake of the Union army, moved to Mississippi. His record in the Senate was conservative.

The most durable of the black congressmen was J. H. Rainey of South Carolina. He sat in Congress between 1869 and 1879, winning his last election in the year of the Hayes-Tilden debacle. In most of his district, blacks outnumbered whites by six to one. He was retired in the election of 1878 only as a consequence of widespread economic reprisals against black voters and some Klan-type violence.

Rainey's parents had bought their freedom long before the Civil War, but, in 1862, he was drafted to work on the fortifications in Charleston Harbor, a condition tantamount to enslavement. He escaped to the West Indies and worked his way to the North, returning to his home state during the early part of Reconstruction. Rainey was vindictive toward the white South. He exploited racial hostilities as nastily as any Redeemer. He was, unsurprisingly, preoccupied with civil rights issues. However, Rainey was not oblivious to other political problems. By the end of the 1870s, he used his seniority to work for southern economic interests that transcended the color line. He defended the rights of Chinese in California on "probusiness" Republican, as well as racial, grounds and attempted to improve relations with the black republic of Haiti.

George H. White was the last African American from a southern state to sit in Congress before the passage of the Civil Rights Act of 1964. Born a slave in 1852, after the war, he attended Howard University in Washington and practiced law in North Carolina. In 1896, he won election to the House of Representatives by adding white Populist votes to the black Republican bloc still enfranchised in North Carolina. Some southern Populists, like Thomas Watson of Georgia, preached interracial political cooperation in an attempt to build a solid agrarian front against the "Bourbons" into which the Redeemers had been transformed.

Populist support put White in an impossible situation, for the national Republican party was staunchly anti-Populist. If he were not to be shut out of the party in Washington, he had to support the policies of the McKinley administration, such as a high protective tariff, the Spanish-American War, and imperialism. Inevitably, his positions alienated those whites who had helped elect him. Moreover, southern Populism was undergoing a momentous transformation during the late 1890s. Democratic party politicians like Benjamin "Pitchfork Ben" Tillman of neighboring South Carolina combined populist appeals to poor whites with an incendiary hatred of blacks.

Conservative party-line Republicans like White were easy targets. In 1898, the North Carolina Populists switched sides, supporting the Democratic candidate and almost ousting White after only one term. He knew his political future was doomed and spoke out loudly about what was happening to African Americans in the South. The only black in Congress, he described himself as "the representative on this floor of 9,000,000 of the population of these United States."

By 1900, black voters in White's district had been reduced to a fragment. He did not even bother to stand for reelection. Instead, in his farewell speech in Washington in 1901, he delivered his finest oration, an eloquent speech that served as the coda to Reconstruction's failure to integrate blacks into American society:

> These parting words are in behalf of an outraged, heartbroken, bruised and bleeding, but God-fearing people, faithful, industrial, loyal people, rising people, full of potential force. The only apology that I have to make for the earnestness with which I have spoken is that I am pleading for the life, the liberty, the future happiness, and manhood suffrage for one-eighth of the entire population of the United States.

Schuyler Colfax, Grant's vice president. Speaker of the House James A. Garfield also accepted a "stipend."

Three of Grant's cabinet were involved in corruption. Carriers under contract to the Post Office Department paid kickbacks in return for exorbitant payments for their services. The secretary of war, William W. Belknap, took bribes from companies that operated trading posts in Indian reservations under his authority. He and his subordinates shut their eyes while the traders defrauded the tribes of goods they were due under the terms of federal treaties. Grant insisted that Belknap resign but refused to bring charges against him.

Nor did Grant punish his secretary of the treasury, Benjamin Bristow, or his personal secretary, Orville E. Babcock, when he learned that they sold excise stamps to whiskey distillers in St. Louis. Whenever the president came close to losing his patience (which was considerable), Roscoe Conkling or another stalwart Republican reminded him of the importance of party loyalty. Better a few scoundrels escape than party morale be damaged and the Democrats take over.

The Liberal Republicans

Although the full story of the Grant scandals was known only later, enough was suspected in 1872 that a number of prominent Republicans broke with the president. Charles Sumner of Massachusetts, a senator since 1851 and chairman of the Senate Foreign Relations Committee, fought the president fiercely over Grant's determination to annex Santo Domingo (now the Dominican Republic).

Senator Carl Schurz of Missouri and the editor of *The Nation* magazine, E. L. Godkin, were appalled by the atmosphere of corruption in Washington and the treatment of public office as a way of making a living rather than as a public service. Schurz and Godkin (although not Sumner) had also given up on Radical Reconstruction, which Grant enforced. Although not necessarily convinced that blacks were inferior to whites, they concluded that the protection of African Americans' civil rights was not worth the instability chronic in the South or the continued presence of troops in several southern states. Better to allow the white Redeemers to return to power.

The Election of 1872

This was also the position of the man whom the Liberal Republicans named to run for president in 1872, the editor of the *New York Tribune,* Horace Greeley. He described southern blacks as "simple, credulous, ignorant men," and the carpetbaggers he had once encouraged "as stealing and plucking, many of them with both arms around negroes, and their hands in their rear pockets." The freedmen, Greeley and others thought, needed the guidance of selfless gentlemen like himself or even responsible southern whites.

Greeley was a terrible choice as a presidential nominee, for he was a lifelong eccentric. Throughout his 61 years, Greeley clambered aboard almost every reform or fad from abolitionism and women's rights to vegetarianism, spiritualism (communicating with the dead), and phrenology (reading a person's character in the bumps on his or her head).

His appearance invited ridicule. He looked like a crackpot, with his round, pink face exaggerated by close-set, beady eyes and a wispy white fringe of chin whiskers. He wore an ankle-length overcoat on the hottest days and carried a brightly colored umbrella on the driest. Republican cartoonists like Thomas Nast had an easy time making fun of Greeley.

To make matters worse, Greeley needed the support of the Democrats to make a race of it. He proposed to "clasp hands across the bloody chasm" between North and South. This was asking too much of Republican party regulars. Many who disapproved of Grant disapproved much more of southern Democrats.

Moreover, throughout his editorial career, Greeley had printed just about every printable vilification of the Democrats—particularly southerners—that the English language offered. The Democrats did give him their nomination, but southern whites found it difficult to support him. A large African American vote for Grant in seven southern states helped give the president a 286 to 66 victory in the electoral college.

▲ *Horace Greeley, a celebrated newspaperman but a hopeless eccentric. Even if all the Grant administration scandals had been known in 1872, it is unlikely that the easily mocked Greeley could have defeated Grant.*

Culver Pictures, Inc.

THE TWILIGHT OF RECONSTRUCTION

The liberals returned to the Republican party. For all their loathing of President Grant, the liberals found their fling with the Democrats humiliating. Of the bunch, only Charles Sumner remained true to the cause of the southern blacks. His Civil Rights Act of 1875 (passed a year after his death) guaranteed equal accommodations for blacks in public facilities such as hotels and theaters and forbade the exclusion of blacks from juries. Congress quietly dropped another provision forbidding schools segregated by race.

The Civil Rights Act of 1875 was the last significant federal attempt to enforce equal rights for 80 years. Not only had northerners lost interest in Civil War idealism, but southern white Democrats had "redeemed" most of the former Confederacy. By the end of 1875, only three states remained Republican: South Carolina, Florida, and Louisiana.

The Disputed Election

The Democratic candidate in 1876, New York governor Samuel J. Tilden, said he would remove the troops from these three states, which would mean a decline in black voting, bringing the white supremacy Democrats to power. The Republican candidate, Governor Rutherford B. Hayes of Ohio, ran on a platform that guaranteed African Americans rights in the South, but Hayes, personally, was known to be skeptical of black capabilities and a personal friend of several white southern politicians.

When the votes were counted, Hayes's opinions seemed beside the point. Tilden won a close popular vote and appeared to have won the electoral college 204 to 165. However, Tilden's margin of victory included the electoral votes of South Carolina, Florida, and Louisiana, where Republicans still controlled the state governments. On instructions from Republican leaders in New York, officials there declared that Hayes had carried their states. According to this set of returns, Hayes eked out a 185 to 184 electoral vote victory.

It was not that easy. When the returns reached Washington, there were two sets from each of the three disputed states—one set for Tilden and one set for Hayes. Because the Constitution did not provide for such an occurrence, a special commission was established to decide which returns were valid. Five members of each house of Congress and five members of the Supreme Court sat on the panel. Seven of them were Republicans; seven were Democrats; one, David Davis of Illinois, a Supreme Court justice and once Abraham Lincoln's law partner, was known as an independent. No one was interested in determining the case on its merits; each commissioner intended to vote for his party's candidate no matter what documents were set before him. The burden of naming the next president of the United States fell on David Davis.

He did not like it. No matter how conscientious and honest he was, half the nation's voters would call for his scalp. Davis prevailed on friends in Illinois to get him off the hook by naming him to a vacant Senate seat. He resigned from the Court and, therefore, from the commission. His replacement was a Republican justice, and the stage was set for the Republicans to steal the election.

The Compromise of 1877

The commission voted on strict party lines, eight to seven, to accept the Hayes returns from Louisiana, Florida, and South Carolina—giving Rutherford B. Hayes the presidency by a single electoral vote. Had that been all there was to it, there might well have been violence. At a series of meetings, however, a group of prominent northern and southern politicians and businessmen came to an informal agreement that was satisfactory to the political leaders of both sections.

The "Compromise of 1877" involved several commitments, not all of them honored, for northern investments in the South. Also not honored was a vague agreement on the part of conservative southerners to build a white Republican party in the South based on the economic and social views that they shared with northern conservatives.

As to the disputed election, Hayes would move into the White House without resistance by either northern or southern Democrats. In return, he would withdraw the troops from South Carolina, Florida, and Louisiana, thus allowing the Democratic party in these states to oust the Republicans and eliminate African American political power.

---

for FURTHER READING

James McPherson, *Ordeal by Fire: The Civil War and Reconstruction,* 1982, is the best recent account of Reconstruction. Also see Eric Foner, *Reconstruction: America's Unfinished Revolution,* 1988. See William A. Dunning, *Reconstruction: Political and Economic,* 1907, for the old, harshly critical view of the era's policies that dominated American historical thinking for half a century. For a rejoinder, see W. E. B. Du Bois, *Black Reconstruction,* 1935. John Hope Franklin, *Reconstruction After the Civil War,* 1961, provides a more brief, objective account, as does Herman Belz, *Reconstructing the Union,* 1969. A splendid account of the reaction of blacks to freedom is Leon F. Liwack, *Been in the Storm So Long,* 1979.

Valuable studies of special topics include Richard N. Current, *Three Carpetbag Governors,* 1967; Stanley Kutler, *Judicial Power and Reconstruction Politics,* 1968; Eric McKitrick, *Andrew Johnson and Reconstruction,* 1960; Robert C. Morris, *Reading, 'Riting, and Reconstruction: The Education of Freedmen in the South, 1861–1870,* 1981; Willie Lee Rose, *Rehearsal for Reconstruction,* 1964; Hans A. Trefousse, *The Radical Republicans,* 1969; A. W. Trelease, *KKK: The Ku Klux Klan Conspiracy and Southern Reconstruction,* 1971; and C. Vann Woodward, *Reunion and Reaction: The Compromise of 1877 and the End of Reconstruction,* 1951.

Visit the source collections at http://ajaccess.wadsworth.com and http://infotrac.thomsonlearning.com, and use the Search function with the following key terms to explore documents, images, audio and video clips, articles, and commentary related to the material in this chapter:

Andrew Johnson
Freedmen's Bureau
Reconstruction

Additional resources, exercises, and Internet links related to this chapter are available on *The American Past* Web site: http://history.wadsworth.com/americanpast7e.

HISTORY ONLINE

The Andrew Johnson Impeachment Trial

http://law.umkc.edu/faculty/projects/ftrials/impeach/impreachmt.htm

A thoroughgoing analysis of America's first presidential impeachment trial.

African American Perspectives

http://memory.loc.gov/ammem/aap/aaphome.html

African American pamphlets from the abolitionist period through 1907.

KKK

http://blackhistorypages.com/reconstruction

Freedmen's Bureau reports about Ku Klux Klan activities in North Carolina and Alabama.

PARTIES, PATRONAGE, AND PORK

Politics in the Late Nineteenth Century

University of Hartford Collection

That . . . a man like Grant should be called—and should actually and truly be—the highest product of the most advanced society, made evolution ludicrous. One must be as commonplace as Grant's own commonplaces to maintain such an absurdity. The progress of evolution from President Washington to President Grant, was alone evidence to upset Darwin.

Henry Adams

THE PRESIDENTS OF the late nineteenth century are not inspiring. Their portraits lined up on a gallery wall—Grant, Hayes, Garfield, Arthur, Cleveland, Harrison, McKinley—would resemble a line of mourners at a midwestern funeral. They were dignified and grave. They were drab (except Arthur, who was a bit of a dandy) and grandly bewhiskered (except McKinley). Their honesty was beyond reproach (except for a slip by Garfield), as were their morals (except for a slip by Cleveland). They competently performed their executive duties. But it is difficult to imagine the child who, looking at the row of portraits, would say, "I want to be like them when I grow up."

The presidents' lack of charisma is one reason that Americans today find them uninteresting. In our age of ceaseless commercial amusement, it is the natural entertainer—Ronald Reagan, Bill Clinton—who has the edge in the race for the great American prize. Moreover, Americans have gotten used to vigorous chief executives who seize the initiative (John F. Kennedy, George W. Bush). The presidents from Grant to William McKinley were of a different breed. They *assumed* that Congress, the maker of laws, should take the initiative. The president's task was to represent the nation in his person (thus the importance of gravity), to enforce the laws Congress enacted, and, when necessary, to apply a brake on an erring Congress.

Another explanation of why there are no giants in this gallery of presidents is the fact that what was most vital in America in the late nineteenth century—what attracted the most energetic men, those with "greatness" in them—was not politics. It was the growth of the economy, the emergence of businesses of unbelievable size, and the development of the "Wild West." A historian might be tempted to rush through the era's politics in a few paragraphs—except for two striking facts.

First, politics was itself a business in the late nineteenth century, from the White House down to brick-and-board city halls. Politicians too expressed the nation's preoccupation with getting ahead. Second, Americans of the era loved politics as a sport. In no other period of American history did a higher percentage of eligible voters actually vote. Fully 80 percent of those eligible to vote in the 1870s, 1880s, and 1890s did vote. In the early twenty-first century, by comparison, less than half the eligible voters turn out.

THE WAY THE SYSTEM WORKED

Presidential elections brought out the most voters. In part, this was because, nationally, the two major parties were evenly matched. A man (and in a few western states after 1890, a woman) found plenty of evidence that a few votes really did make a difference. Between 1872, when Grant won reelection by a smashing 750,000 votes, and 1896, when William McKinley ushered in an era of Republican dominance with an 850,000 vote plurality, two presidential elections (1880 and 1884) were decided by fewer than 40,000 votes in a total of 9 to 10 million. In two elections (1876 and 1888), the winning candidates had fewer popular votes than the losers: The winners won in the electoral college.

In fact, the only presidential candidate between 1872 and 1896 to win more than half of the popular vote was Samuel J. Tilden, who lost the "stolen election" of 1876.

Harcourt Picture Collection

▲ *Uncle Sam weighs the Republican and Democratic parties and finds them evenly matched. President Grant is in the background. His ally, Republican "Stalwart" Roscoe Conkling (who was mocked for having a "turkey gobbler strut"), is perched at the upper right. The man at the left is holding a pathetic Liberal Republican party, which opposed Grant in 1872.*

Solid South and Republican Respectability

The parties were not so evenly matched within regions or among identifiable social groups. Except for Connecticut, which was evenly divided between Republicans and Democrats, New England was dependably Republican, as was Pennsylvania. The upper and middle classes of the Northeast and Midwest were largely Republican. They thought of the "Grand Old Party" (GOP) as a bastion of morality and respectability. Ironically, most big cities, run by cynical and often corrupt political machines, voted Republican. (The important exception was Democratic New York City.) Finally, the few African Americans who retained the right to vote once the South was "redeemed" were staunch Republicans. The GOP paid little more than symbolic attention to their rights after 1877, but the Republican party was still the party of Lincoln and emancipation.

The Democrats built their national totals upon the foundation of the "Solid South." Blacks and the white people of Appalachia who had opposed secession formed Republican minorities in Virginia, North Carolina, and Tennessee. But not a single former slave state, Union or Confederate, voted Republican in a presidential election during the late nineteenth century. The Democrats also invariably won New York City by appealing to immigrants, and they commanded a majority of the immigrant and white ethnic vote elsewhere.

Swing States

Because most states were in the bag for each of the two parties, national elections turned on the returns of a handful of "swing states," particularly Illinois, Indiana, Ohio, and New York. Hard-core Republicans and Democrats were about equal in number in those states, so winning their large blocs of electoral votes depended on appealing to soft-core partisans and independents, who could jump either way, depending on local issues, party organization, and the personalities of the candidates. Several presidential elections were decided in New York State, where the result depended on how big a majority New York City's Democrats could turn in to counterbalance the Republican edge upstate.

Party leaders believed that the personal popularity of a candidate could make the difference in the swing states. Consequently, a disproportionate number of late-nineteenth-century presidential and vice presidential nominees came from Indiana, Ohio, and New York. In the elections held between 1876 and 1892, the major parties filled 20 presidential and vice presidential slots. Eighteen of the 20 (90 percent) were filled by men from the swing states. Eight (40 percent) were from New York and 5 from Indiana. Neither party was particularly interested in finding "the best man for the job." The idea was to win the election; that meant carrying the swing states.

Bosses at Conventions

National conventions, which met every four years, were much more important to the parties than they are today. The difference was communications. Today, political bosses from every part of the country can discuss affairs with every other by picking up the phone, sending a fax or email, or hopping on a plane. In the late nineteenth century, congressmen saw one another in Washington on a regular basis. However, governors and state and city political bosses, who were sometimes the real powers in party politics, did not meet regularly with their counterparts elsewhere.

At the quadrennial conventions, however, they wheeled and dealed, bargained and traded, made and broke political careers. There was no army of television reporters to shove microphones and cameras into the midst of every circle of politicos who gathered on the floor of the barnlike convention halls. Newspaper reporters were kept away by strong-arm bodyguards, often ex-boxers, when the discussion promised to be interesting.

Today, primary elections ensure that a party's presidential candidate will be known long before the delegates answer the roll call at the conventions. In the late nineteenth century, nominations were usually decided at the convention, perhaps on the floor, but just as likely by bosses meeting in hotel rooms over oysters, beefsteak, whiskey, and Vichy water. Delegates, whose livelihoods depended on party bosses, did as they were told.

In the Democratic party, the most important bosses were the head of New York's Tammany Hall, who reliably delivered that city's vote, and the "Bourbon" leaders of the Solid South. (The latter, because of their extreme conservatism, were named after the Bourbon kings of France—not after Kentucky's famous liquor.) In the Republican party, men like Boss Matthew Quay of Pennsylvania and Boss Thomas C. Platt of New York traded the support of their delegations for the promise of a prestigious cabinet post or a healthy share of the lucrative government offices and contracts that a victorious party had at its disposal. Curiously, Republican delegations from the South, which could deliver no electoral votes in November, were courted assiduously by rival candidates for their votes at conventions. Republican conventions were the only sector of American politics in which African Americans played a significant part.

Patronage

The spoils system had come a long way. Andrew Jackson had 5,000 federal jobs to give to the party faithful. There were 50,000 federal jobs in 1871, three-quarters of them postmasterships. Most of them involved real work and meager compensation. Postmasters earned their salaries. So did Indian agents, who administered the government's treaty obligations. In the Customs Service, there was enough paperwork to bury several thousand clerks wearing green visors and celluloid cuffs to protect their white shirts from smudges of ink and graphite. (There was state patronage too. Republican Pennsylvania had 20,000 jobs to hand out.)

Most of these positions were filled by party activists who worked to get the vote out (or, sometimes, their widows if the party's local patronage agent had a heart). In election years, political appointees were assessed a modest percentage of their income to finance the party's campaign. This was politics for its own sake. The party scratched the jobholder's back; the jobholder reciprocated.

The higher ranking the party worker, the more rewarding the job. Setting corruption aside (it was rife in the Indian Bureau), it was possible to get rich legally in a government job. The post of collector of customs in large ports was particularly lucrative. In addition to a handsome salary, the collector was paid a share of import duties on goods reclaimed from smugglers who were caught. This curious incentive system made for a remarkably uncorrupt Customs Service; there was more to be made in catching violators than in taking bribes from them.

Thus, Collector of the Port of New York Chester A. Arthur earned an average of $40,000 a year between 1871 and 1874, and in one big case, he shared a bounty of $135,000 with two other officials. He was the best-paid government official in the country that year, earning more than the president. And he was assessed a handsome sum for the privilege by the Republican party. On a more modest level, southern blacks benefited from the patronage when the Republicans were in power. Some federal appointments in the South went to African American Republicans, including plums like postmaster of Atlanta and customs collector in New Orleans.

Pork

Private contributors to party campaign chests were thanked with contracts for government work in "pork-barrel" bills. At the end of each congressional session, coalitions, often bipartisan, pieced together bills to finance government construction projects in each member's district—a new post office here, a government pier there, the dredging of a river channel. The idea was not so much to get needed work done but to reward businessmen who supported the party.

The River and Harbor Bill of August 1886 provided for an expenditure of $15 million to begin work on more than a hundred new projects, although 58 government projects remained unfinished and unfunded.

Of course, there was not a job or contract for every voter. In order to turn out the vast numbers of voters they did, the parties exploited the emotional politics of memory and, for the Republicans, the less sentimental politics of pensions.

Memories, Memories

If the Republican party forgot its commitments to African Americans, it remembered the Civil War. Party orators "waved the bloody shirt," reminding northern voters that Democrats had caused the Civil War. Lucius Fairchild, a Wisconsin politician who lost an arm in battle, literally flailed the air with his empty sleeve during campaign speeches. With armless and legless veterans hobbling around every sizable town to remind voters of the bloodletting, it was an effective technique.

The Civil War loomed over the era. Between 1868 and 1901, every president but the Democrat Grover Cleveland had been a Union officer. When Cleveland, believing that sectional bitterness was fading, returned captured Confederate battle flags to their states for display at museums and war monuments, an angry protest in the North forced him to back down and contributed to his failure to win reelection the next year.

The Republican who defeated Cleveland in 1888, Benjamin Harrison, was still waving the bloody shirt after 20 years. "I would a thousand times rather march under the bloody shirt, stained with the lifeblood of a Union soldier," Harrison told voters, "than march under the black flag of treason or the white flag of cowardly compromise." Dwelling on the past could not possibly be constructive, but it won elections, for the Democrats in the South too. They waved the Confederate Stars and Bars, reminding voters of the nobility of the lost cause and of the white supremacy that the Redeemer Democrats had salvaged from that cause and from the "Black Republicans."

Pensions

In their pension policy, the Republicans converted the bloody shirt into dollars and cents. Soon after the war ended, Congress provided for pensions to Union veterans who were disabled from wartime wounds and disease. The law was strictly worded, excessively so, in fact. Many genuinely disabled veterans could not qualify under its terms. Rather than change the basic law, northern congressmen introduced "special pension" bills that provided monthly stipends to specifically named constituents.

By the 1880s, the procedure for awarding special pensions was grossly abused. Congressmen took little interest in the truthfulness of the petitioner or the worthiness of his grievance. (One applicant for a pension had not served in the army because, he said, he had fallen off a horse on the way to enlist.) They simply introduced every bill that any constituent requested. When almost all Republicans and many northern Democrats had special pension bills in the hopper, bunches of them were rushed through by voice vote. Instead of declining as old soldiers died off, the cost of the pension program climbed to $56 million in 1885 and $80

Civil War Pensions

Between 1890, when pensions for Union veterans and their dependents were granted practically for the asking, and 1905, when the practice was prohibited, it was not uncommon for very young ladies to marry very old veterans in order to collect widows' pensions after their not-so-lusty bridegrooms died. As late as 1983, 41 Civil War widows were still receiving a monthly check of about $70 from the federal government.

The Surplus

Many late-nineteenth-century congressmen voted for dubious veterans' pensions and pork-barrel bills because spending won votes. However, there was also a profoundly good economic reason to get rid of the government's money during the 1880s. The United States Treasury collected about $100 million more in taxes each year than it spent. Each dollar that rested in the treasury was a dollar less feeding the economy. Allowing the surplus to grow meant risking a depression.

Reducing revenue was out of the question. More than half the government's collections came from the tariff, which was backed by powerful interests. So the government spent on pensions, often dubious internal improvements, and, during the 1890s, on the construction of a large modern navy.

Even then, it took a major depression and war to wipe out the surplus. In 1899, after a war with Spain, the government had a deficit of $90 million.

The Bloody Shirt in Indiana

Indiana politician Oliver Morton said:

Every unregenerate rebel . . . every man who labored for the rebellion in the field, who murdered Union prisoners by cruelty and starvation calls himself a Democrat. Every wolf in sheep's clothing who pretends to preach the gospel but proclaims the righteousness of man-selling and slavery; every one who shoots down negroes in the streets, burns up negro school-houses and meeting-houses, and murders women and children by the light of their own flaming dwellings, calls himself a Democrat. . . . In short, the Democratic party may be described as a common sewer and loathsome receptacle, into which is emptied every element of treason North and South, every element of inhumanity and barbarism which has dishonored the age.

▲ *Members of the Grand Army of the Republic (GAR), an organization of Union veterans, parade in 1902. The GAR held annual encampments—huge gatherings—in the late nineteenth century. It was, in effect, an auxiliary of the Republican party because of the party's generous pension policy.*

PRESIDENTS AND PERSONALITIES

After the Grant scandals, a presidential candidate's reputation for honesty became a popular campaign cry. In 1876, the Republicans turned to Rutherford B. Hayes, and the Democrats to Samuel J. Tilden, largely because, as governors, they had not stolen a cent. Hayes and his running mate, *The Nation* editorialized, were "eminently respectable men—the most respectable men, in the strict sense of the word, the Republican party has ever nominated." When Hayes was named the victor in the "stolen election," Democrats took particular delight in calling him "His Fraudulency" or "Rutherfraud" B. Hayes.

Hayes, Integrity, and Oblivion

Hayes was a Civil War hero who was twice seriously wounded and the first president who traveled for pleasure. His White House was dry. Mrs. Hayes, "Lemonade Lucy," was an inflexible advocate of temperance.

As president, Hayes pleased Lucy but not a great many others. Old Radical Republicans were irked by his abandonment of southern blacks to the Redeemers. (In fact, Hayes

million in 1888. Pensions were one of the biggest line items in the federal budget, and a veterans' lobby, the Grand Army of the Republic (GAR), came to serve, in effect, as a Republican political action committee.

In 1888, Congress enacted a new general pension law granting an income to every veteran who served at least 90 days in the wartime army and was disabled for any reason whatsoever. An old soldier who fell off a stepladder in 1888 was eligible.

President Cleveland vetoed the law and was sustained. The Republicans ran against him that year with the slogan "Vote Yourself a Pension" and won the election. The next year, the new president, Benjamin Harrison, signed the even more generous Dependent Pensions Act and appointed the head of the GAR, James "Corporal" Tanner, to distribute the loot. "God help the surplus," Tanner said, referring to the money in the treasury. He meant it. By the end of Harrison's term, Tanner had increased the annual expenditure on pensions to $160 million! Local wits took notice of young women marrying doddering old Billy Yanks who had a gleam in their eyes and a check in the mail.

Northern Democrats posed as the party of principle in the bloody shirt and pensions controversies. In the South, however, Democrats played the Civil War game in reverse. State governments provided benefits for Confederate veterans.

▲ *A balloon lamp ("Chinese lantern") hung at a night rally for presidential candidate Benjamin Harrison. There would have been hundreds of them. Harrison was the grandson of President William Henry Harrison; thus the reference to Tippecanoe.*

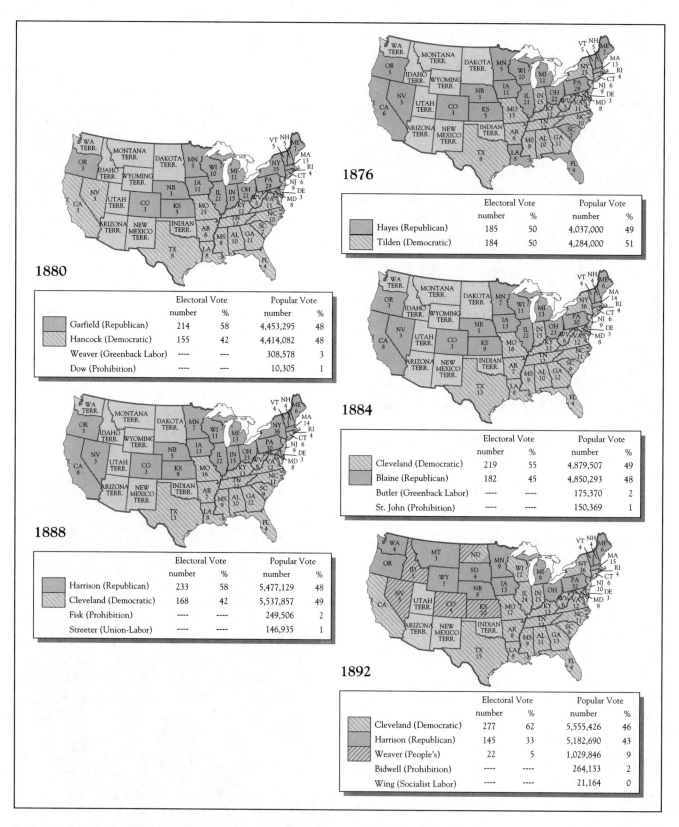

1876

	Electoral Vote		Popular Vote	
	number	%	number	%
Hayes (Republican)	185	50	4,037,000	49
Tilden (Democratic)	184	50	4,284,000	51

1880

	Electoral Vote		Popular Vote	
	number	%	number	%
Garfield (Republican)	214	58	4,453,295	48
Hancock (Democratic)	155	42	4,414,082	48
Weaver (Greenback Labor)	----	---	308,578	3
Dow (Prohibition)	----	---	10,305	1

1884

	Electoral Vote		Popular Vote	
	number	%	number	%
Cleveland (Democratic)	219	55	4,879,507	49
Blaine (Republican)	182	45	4,850,293	48
Butler (Greenback Labor)	----	----	175,370	2
St. John (Prohibition)	----	----	150,369	1

1888

	Electoral Vote		Popular Vote	
	number	%	number	%
Harrison (Republican)	233	58	5,477,129	48
Cleveland (Democratic)	168	42	5,537,857	49
Fisk (Prohibition)	----	----	249,506	2
Streeter (Union-Labor)	----	----	146,935	1

1892

	Electoral Vote		Popular Vote	
	number	%	number	%
Cleveland (Democratic)	277	62	5,555,426	46
Harrison (Republican)	145	33	5,182,690	43
Weaver (People's)	22	5	1,029,846	9
Bidwell (Prohibition)	----	----	264,133	2
Wing (Socialist Labor)	----	----	21,164	0

MAP 26:1 Presidential Elections, 1876–1892 Except for Connecticut, New England was dependably Republican, as was Pennsylvania. Ohio voted Republican in all of these elections, but the Democrats were competitive there. After the end of Reconstruction in 1877, the former slave states were dependably Democratic. Illinois, Indiana, and especially New York were the states where electoral college victories were won.

was bound to do so by the Compromise of 1877.) Neither of the Republican party's two major factions, the "Stalwarts" (Grant supporters) and the "Half-Breeds" (critics of Grant), believed that Hayes allotted them as much patronage as they deserved. There never was a question of renominating him; even Hayes yearned to hit the tourist trail.

Long before Hayes's term ended, two prominent Republicans announced their intention of succeeding him: Senator James G. Blaine of Maine, leader of the Half-Breeds, and Ulysses S. Grant, out of office four years and nearly broke. Grant needed the salary; when he became president, he was obligated to give up his lifetime pay as a general.

Garfield: A Dark Horse

Neither Blaine nor Grant was able to win a majority of the delegates to the Republican convention. They were frustrated by several sanguine favorite-son candidates, men who came to Chicago backed only by their own states. The hope of the favorite son is that there will be a deadlock between the front-runners, forcing the delegates to turn to him as a compromise candidate.

After 34 ballots, there was certainly a deadlock in 1880. Blaine's supporters recognized that their cause was lost. However, instead of turning to one of the favorite sons, who were responsible for the deadlock, they switched their votes to a man whose name was not in nomination, James A. Garfield of Ohio. On the thirty-sixth ballot, he became the Republican candidate.

Garfield was a Half-Breed, a Blaine man, but he courted New York senator Roscoe Conkling, the head of the pro-Grant Stalwarts. Garfield traveled to New York to assure Conkling a fair share of the patronage, and Conkling made peace. Garfield went to the polls with a nominally united party behind him.

The Democrats, having failed to win with an antiwar Democrat in 1868 (Seymour), a Republican maverick in 1872 (Greeley), and a rich reformer in 1876 (Tilden), tried their luck with one of their few Civil War generals, Winfield Scott Hancock. An attractive but uninspiring man, Hancock made the election extremely close. Garfield drew only 39,000 more votes, just 48.3 percent of the total.

Another President Murdered

Garfield was a more intelligent and substantial man than his opportunistic career indicates. Whether or not he would have blossomed as president cannot be known, for he spent his four short active months in the White House sorting out claims to government jobs made by Republican party workers, who were "lying in wait for [him] like vultures for a wounded bison." He exclaimed to Secretary of State Blaine, "My God! What is there in this place that a man should ever want to get into it!"

Garfield tried to placate both wings of his party. But when he handed the choicest plum of all, the post of collector of customs of the Port of New York, to a Blaine man, Roscoe Conkling broke with the president. He and his protégé in the New York Republican machine, Thomas Platt, resigned their seats in the Senate. Their intention was to remind Garfield of their political power by having the state legislature reelect them.

By the summer of 1881, it appeared that Conkling and Platt had lost their battle. The Half-Breeds succeeded in blocking their reelection. But the conflict was finally resolved by two gunshots in a Washington train station. Charles Guiteau was a ne'er-do-well preacher and bill collector who worked for the Stalwarts but was not rewarded with a government job. On July 2, 1881, he approached Garfield as the president was about to depart on a holiday and shot him twice in the small of the back. After living in excruciating pain for 11 weeks, the second president to be murdered died on September 19.

"I am a Stalwart! Arthur is president!" Guiteau shouted after firing the fatal shots. He meant that the new president was none other than Conkling's longtime ally, Vice President Chester A. Arthur. The deranged Guiteau actually expected Arthur to free him from prison and reward him for his patriotism. He was hanged, shouting, "Bound for glory! I'm bound for glory!" He should have been committed to an insane asylum.

Civil Service Reform

Arthur had been known as the "prince of spoilsmen." As president, however, he was able and statesmanlike. He signed the first law limiting the political parties' use of government jobs for political purposes. The Pendleton Act of 1883 established the Civil Service Commission, a bureau empowered to draw up and administer examinations for applicants for some low-level government jobs. Once in these civil service jobs, employees could not be fired simply because the political party to which they belonged lost the presidency.

▲ *President Garfield, who did little during his first four months in office but receive Republicans wanting government jobs, is shot in the back in a railroad station in Washington. The man assisting him is Secretary of State James G. Blaine. At the left, the assassin, Charles Guiteau, has been seized.*

At first, only 10 percent of 131,000 government workers were protected by civil service. However, the Pendleton Act empowered the president to add job classifications to the civil service list at his discretion. Because the presidency changed party every four years between 1880 and 1896, each incumbent's partisan impulse to protect his own appointees in their jobs led, by the end of the century, to a fairly comprehensive civil service system.

Thus, after the Democrat Grover Cleveland was elected in November 1884, but before he took office in March 1885, outgoing president Arthur protected a number of Republican employees by adding their jobs to the civil service list. Cleveland did the same thing for Democratic government workers in 1888, Benjamin Harrison for Republicans in 1892, and Cleveland again for Democrats in 1896. By 1900, 40 percent of the federal government's 256,000 employees held civil service positions. About 30 percent of government clerks were women.

The Pendleton Act also abolished assessments. The parties were forbidden to require that members who held government jobs donate a percentage of their salaries to political campaign chests. Until the presidency of Benjamin Harrison (1889–1893), the professional politicians were at a loss as to how to replace these revenues. Harrison's postmaster general, John Wanamaker, came up with the solution. He levied contributions on big businessmen who had

an interest in Republican victory at the polls. This method remained the chief means of financing national political campaigns until the 1970s.

Chet Arthur

Chester A. Arthur may have been president illegally. The Constitution says that only a native-born American citizen may be president; Arthur's enemies said he was born not in Fairfield, Vermont, as he claimed, but in a cabin a few miles north—in Canada. However that may have been, the urbane and elegant Arthur, resplendent in his New York wardrobe compared to the gray look favored by Republican politicians, did a good job as president and wanted a second term. He tried to mend fences with the Stalwarts by twice offering Roscoe Conkling (a superb lawyer) a seat on the Supreme Court. He tried to woo the Half-Breeds by deferring to Sec-

Turkey
Roscoe Conkling was a physical-culture enthusiast. He exercised daily and was extremely proud of his physique. This provided his enemy, James G. Blaine, with an easy target when he described Conkling's "haughty disdain, his grandiloquent swell, his majestic, over-powering, turkey-gobbler strut."

retary of State James G. Blaine's judgment in foreign affairs. But Blaine rebuffed him and resigned from the cabinet. With Conkling's political career in eclipse, Blaine easily won the Republican nomination in the summer of 1884.

1884: Blaine Versus Cleveland

Blaine expected to win the election as well. New York, as so often, was the key to victory, and Blaine expected to win the state despite the fact that some old Liberal Republicans known as mugwumps (an Algonkian word for "big chief," a reference to their often pompous self-righteousness) had deserted the party because Blaine had been involved in some dubious financial transactions.

Blaine expected to make up this defection and more by winning much of the Irish vote, which was usually solidly Democratic. He was popular in the Irish American community because, in an era when Republican leaders frequently bad-mouthed the Catholic Church, Blaine had a few Catholic relatives. Moreover, Blaine liked to "twist the lion's tail"—taunt the British, the ancestral enemy in many unsmiling Irish eyes. Then the news broke that Blaine's Democratic opponent, Grover Cleveland, while he was a lawyer in Buffalo, had fathered an illegitimate child. Republicans chanted:

Ma, Ma, Where's my Pa?
Gone to the White House,
Ha, ha, ha.

Cleveland nimbly neutralized the morality issue by admitting the folly of his youth and explaining that he tried to make amends by financially supporting the child. Indeed, the Democrats turned the scandal to their advantage when they argued that if Cleveland had been indiscreet in private life, he had an exemplary record in public office, whereas Blaine, admirable as a husband and family man, engaged in several dubious stock deals as a congressman from Maine. Put Cleveland into public office where he shined, they said, and return Blaine to the private life that he richly adorned.

Little Things That Decide Great Elections

A few days before the election, disaster struck the Blaine campaign. The confident candidate made the mistake of dining with a group of millionaires in Delmonico's, the most regal restaurant in New York City. It was not a good idea when he was courting the votes of hardworking Irishmen. Before another group, he ignored the statement of a Presbyterian

▲ *A political toy: Republican candidate Benjamin Harrison (left) and Democrat Grover Cleveland weighed in the balance. It is a Republican toy, with Harrison coming in more substantial. In fact, he was a small man, and Cleveland was tall and fat.*

minister, Samuel Burchard, who denounced the Democrats as the party of "rum, romanism, and rebellion"—that is, the party of the saloon, the Roman Catholic Church, and southern secession.

It would have been pretty ordinary stuff at a Republican rally in Portland, Maine. But it was New York City, and Blaine was wooing Irish Americans, the biggest ethnic bloc in the city and sensitive, to put it mildly, about their Catholic religion. When Democratic newspapers plastered the insult across their front pages, Blaine rushed to express his sincere distaste for this kind of bigotry and to explain that had he heard Burchard's words, he would have called him down. But the damage was done. Irish voters trundled back into the Democratic column, and blizzards upstate snowed many Republican voters in. New York State and the presidency went to Grover Cleveland.

In 1888, four years later, Cleveland was undone in his bid for reelection by a similarly trivial incident. A Republican newspaperman posing as an English-born naturalized American wrote to the British ambassador in Washington asking which of the two candidates, Cleveland or Benjamin Harrison of Indiana, would be the better president from the

A District Leader's Day

2 A.M.: Aroused from sleep by the ringing of his doorbell; went to the door and found a bartender, who asked him to go to the police station and bail out a saloon-keeper who had been arrested for violating the excise law. Furnished bail and returned to bed at three o'clock.

Thus began a working day, about 1900, in the life of George Washington Plunkitt, "sachem" (chief) of Tammany Hall, the Democratic party machine in New York City, and leader of District 15. Plunkitt was born in 1842 in an Irish neighborhood that was later razed to build Central Park. He worked for a butcher as a teenager; but before he was old enough to vote, he was running errands for Tammany Hall—a "statesman" in the making, as he put it.

As a sachem, he was one of the dozen political bosses who ran New York's Democratic party, which usually meant they ran New York City. Like other Tammany men, Plunkitt believed that "politics is as much a regular business as the grocery or the dry-goods . . . business. You've got to be trained up to it or you're sure to fail." Before he was 30, when Boss Tweed ran the city, Plunkitt made money in business by collecting three city salaries at once. Later, he went into real estate speculation, not really "on the side." In "Honest Graft," the most famous of the talks on practical politics he gave to a newspaper reporter, Plunkitt explained:

My party's in power in the city, and it's goin' to undertake a lot of public improvements. Well, I'm tipped off, say, that they're going to lay out a new park at a certain place.

I see my opportunity and I take it. I go to that place and I buy up all the land I can in the neighborhood. Then the board of this or that makes its plan public, and there is a rush to get my land, which nobody cared particular for before.

Ain't it perfectly honest to charge a good price and make a profit on my investment and foresight? Of course, it is. Well, that's honest graft.

Like other Tammany leaders, "as a matter of policy, if nothing else," he stayed away from "dirty business" because there was "so much honest graft lyin' around."

6 A.M.: Awakened by fire engines passing his house. Hastened to the scene of the fire, according to the custom of the Tammany district leaders, to give assistance to the fire sufferers, if needed. Met several of his election district captains who are always under orders to look out for fires, which are considered great vote-getters. Found several tenants who had been burned out, took them to a hotel, supplied them with clothes, fed them, and arranged temporary quarters for them until they could rent and furnish new apartments.

8:30 A.M.: Went to the police court to look after his constituents. Found six "drunks." Secured the discharge of four by a timely word with the judge, and paid the fines of two.

9 A.M.: Appeared in the Municipal District Court. Directed one of his district captains to act as counsel for a widow against whom dispossess proceedings had been instituted and obtained an extension of time. Paid the rent of a poor family about to be dispossessed and gave them a dollar for food.

11 A.M.: At home again. Found four men waiting for him. One had been discharged by the Metropolitan Railway Company for neglect of duty, and wanted the district leader to fix things. Another wanted a job on the road. The third sought a place on the Subway and the fourth, a plumber, was looking for work with the Consolidated Gas Company. The district leader spent nearly three hours fixing things for the four men, and succeeded in each case.

Although he was 60, Plunkitt worked long, exhausting days, providing personal, practical services to voters with problems. He took little interest in "issues" because he knew that ordinary New Yorkers, struggling to stay afloat, took no interest in them. But he did take an interest in the residents of his district:

British point of view. Foolishly, the ambassador replied that Cleveland seemed to be better disposed toward British interests. The Republican press immediately labeled Cleveland the British candidate. Thousands of Irish Democrats in New York, who were reflexively hostile to anything or anyone the British favored, voted Republican and helped give the state to Harrison.

This sort of folderol, and the color and excitement of political rallies, could make the difference when the two parties were so evenly balanced. Unlike twenty-first-century Americans, who are flooded with entertainment from a dozen media and to whom elections are just one show among many, late-nineteenth-century Americans enjoyed politics as a major diversion. They flocked to rallies in num-

bers almost unknown today in order to hear brass bands, swig lemonade or beer, and listen to speeches that were more show than statement of principle.

ISSUES

Principles and issues did play a part in politics. Within the Republican party, a shrinking minority of leaders tried to revive the party's commitment to protecting the welfare of southern blacks until as late as 1890. When President Grant tried to seize Santo Domingo in 1870, he was frustrated by the resistance of senators from his own party who were impelled by antiexpansionist prejudices.

I know every man, woman, and child in the Fifteenth District, except them that's been born this summer and I know some of them, too. I know what they like and what they don't like, what they are strong at and what they are weak in. . . .

For instance, here's how I gather in the young men. I hear of a young feller that's proud of his voice, thinks that he can sing fine. I ask him to come around to Washington Hall and join our Glee Club. He comes and sings, and he's a follower of Plunkitt for life. Another young feller gains a reputation as a baseball player in a vacant lot. I bring him into our baseball club. That fixes him. You'll find him workin' for my ticket at the polls next election day. . . . I don't trouble them with political arguments. I just study human nature and act accordin'.

3 P.M.: Attended the funeral of an Italian as far as the ferry. Hurried back to make his appearance at the funeral of a Hebrew constituent. Went conspicuously to the front both in the Catholic church and the synagogue, and later attended the Hebrew confirmation ceremonies in the synagogue.

7 P.M.: Went to district headquarters and presided over a meeting of election district captains. Each captain submitted a list of all the voters in his district, reported on their attitude toward Tammany, suggested who might be won over and how they could be won, told who were in need, and who were in trouble of any kind and the best way to reach them. District leader took notes and gave orders.

8 P.M.: Went to a church fair. Took chances on everything, bought ice cream for the young girls and the children. Kissed the little ones, flattered their mother: and took their fathers out for something down at the corner.

9 P.M.: At the clubhouse again. Spent $10 on tickets for a church excursion and promised a subscription for a new church bell.

Bought tickets for a baseball game to be played by two nines from his district. Listened to the complaints of a dozen push-cart peddlers who said they were persecuted by the police and assured them he would go to Police Headquarters in the morning and see about it.

10:30 P.M.: Attended a Hebrew wedding reception and dance. Had previously sent a handsome wedding present to the bride.

12 P.M.: In bed.

Plunkitt got started in politics by bringing "marketable goods"—votes—to the party:

Let me tell you: I had a cousin, a young man who didn't take any particular interest in politics. I went to him and said: "Tommy, I'm goin' to be a politician, and I want to get a followin'; can I count on you?" He said: "Sure, George." That's how I started in business. I got a marketable commodity—one vote. Then I went to the district leader and told him I could command two votes on election day, Tommy's and my own. He smiled on me and told me to go ahead. If I had offered him a speech or a bookful of learnin', he would have said, "Oh, forget it!"

Soon, he had three votes in his following and, before long, 60 in the George Washington Plunkitt Association. As Plunkitt told it:

What did the district leader say then when I called at headquarters? I didn't have to call at headquarters. He came after me and said: "George, what do you want? If you don't see what you want, ask for it. Wouldn't you like to have a job or two in the departments for your friends?"

That was how the political machine worked, and how George Washington Plunkitt became a statesman.

However, both episodes illustrate the fact that differences of principle and opinion were as likely to lie within the parties as between them. The political party's business was to win power. Having cooperated in that effort, politicians lined up on issues with only casual or self-serving nods toward the organization to which they belonged.

Even the question of the tariff, the nearest thing to an issue dividing Republicans and Democrats, found members of both parties on both sides. The level at which import duties were set could inspire orators to sweating, thumping, and prancing. But their position on the issue, low tariff or high protective tariff, depended on the place their constituents occupied in the economy, not on the party to which they belonged.

The Tariff

With the exception of the growers of a few crops that needed protection from foreign producers—Louisiana's sugar cane planters, for example—farmers inclined to favor a low tariff. Corn, wheat, cotton, and livestock were so cheaply produced in the United States that American farmers were able to undersell local growers of the same crops in large parts of Europe and Asia—*if* other countries did not levy tariffs on American crops in retaliation for high American duties on their exports. Moreover, low duties on imported manufactured goods meant lower prices on the commodities that consumers of manufactured goods, such as farmers, had to buy.

The interest of agriculturalists in keeping import duties down meant that the Democratic party, with its powerful southern agrarian contingent, was generally the low-tariff party. However, Republican congressmen representing rural areas also voted for low rates.

Whereas industrialists, who wanted to protect their factories from foreign competition, were generally Republican and set the high-tariff tone of the party, equally rich and powerful railroad owners and bankers often supported lower duties. Some remained within the Republican party in the company of other capitalists. Others, such as the grand financier August Belmont, were Democrats. As far as bankers like Belmont were concerned, the more goods being circulated around the country, the better—no matter whether they were foreign or domestic in origin. Railroaders had an another incentive to support a low tariff. They were huge consumers of steel for rails, which was one of the commodities that received the most protection.

In the late nineteenth century, high-tariff interests had their way. After bobbing up and down from a low of 40 percent (by no means a low tariff) to a high of 47 percent, rates were increased to 50 percent in the McKinley Tariff of 1890. That is, on average, an imported item was slapped with a tax equivalent to half of its value.

When a depression followed quickly on the act, Grover Cleveland and the Democrats campaigned against the McKinley rates and won the election of 1892. But the tariff that Congress prepared, the Wilson-Gorman Bill, lowered duties by only about 11 percent—to a level of 39 percent of the value of imports. This rate was good enough for Cleveland's supporters in commerce and finance but too high for the farmers who voted for him. The president's rather wishy-washy way out of his quandary highlights the fact that tough issues were intraparty problems, not questions that divided the two parties. Cleveland did not sign the Wilson-Gorman Bill; he did not veto it; he let it become law by ignoring it. He tried to play to both sides.

Money

The issue that would, in the 1890s, shatter the political equilibrium of the 1870s and 1880s was money. The question was, what should be the basis of the circulating currency in America's rapidly expanding economy? Should it be gold, and paper money redeemable in gold from the bank that issued the paper money? Or should the supply of money be regulated by the government in such a way as to adjust to changing economic needs?

The controversy had its roots in the Civil War greenbacks, the value of which, in gold, fluctuated. When the war was going badly, the greenbacks were discounted, redeemed in gold at something less than their face value. Even after the war was won, bankers remained suspicious of a paper money that was not redeemable in gold at face value. Therefore, several secretaries of the treasury, who shared the conservative views of the bankers, determined to retire the greenbacks. When the notes flowed into the treasury in pay-

ment of taxes, they were destroyed and not replaced by new greenbacks.

The result was deflation, a contraction of the amount of money in circulation. Prices dipped, and so did wages. It took less to buy a sack of flour or a side of bacon than it had when the greenbacks flowed in profusion. That meant that the farmer who grew the wheat and slopped the hogs received less for his efforts.

This would not have mattered so much if the farmers had not been debtors. They were. They had borrowed heavily to increase their acreage and to purchase machinery when the greenbacks were plentiful and prices and their incomes high. Now they had to repay the bank in deflated currency—currency that was harder to get. In dollars, agricultural income was down. Farmers were, they believed, being gouged. For example, a $1,000 mortgage on a farm taken out during the 1860s represented 1,200 bushels of grain. By the 1880s, when a farmer might still be paying off his debt, $1,000 represented 2,300 bushels. He had to produce twice as much to pay back each dollar he had borrowed, not to mention the interest he owed.

The Greenback Labor Party

Protesting the retirement of the greenbacks as a policy that enriched banker-creditors at the expense of producer-debtors, farmers formed the Greenback Labor party in 1876. In an effort to convince industrial wage workers that their interests also lay in an abundant money supply, the party chose as its presidential candidate Peter Cooper, a New York philanthropist and an exemplary, popular employer.

Cooper made a poor showing, but in the congressional race of 1878, the Greenbackers elected a dozen congressmen, and some Republicans and Democrats backed their calls for inflation. However, President Hayes's monetary policy was as conservative as Grant's, and in 1879, retirement of the greenbacks proceeded apace. In 1880, the Greenback Labor ticket, led by a Civil War general from Iowa, James B. Weaver, won 309,000 votes, denying Garfield a popular majority but, once again, failing to affect national policy.

In 1884, Benjamin J. Butler of Massachusetts led the Greenbackers one more time but received only one-third of the votes Weaver had won in 1880. The demand to inflate the currency was not dead. Within a decade, American politics was turned upside down and inside out because of it. But the greenbacks were gone. Just as industrialists had their way on the tariff, banking interests got the money policy they wanted.

POLITICS IN THE CITIES

By 1896, silver coinage had replaced the greenbacks as the talisman of Americans who wanted to inflate the nation's money supply. Both the Republican and Democratic parties were shaken by a fierce debate in which gold and silver became sacred symbols (see Chapter 32). The political atmosphere was religious, evangelical, even fanatical. "Gold bugs" and "free silverites" both believed they were engaged in a holy war in which there could be no compromise. The political equilibrium of the 1870s and 1880s was shattered.

The Democratic party convention of 1896 was the most tumultuous since the party destroyed itself in 1860. Richard Croker, then the leader of New York City's Democrats, was bewildered by the fury. He listened to an agitated gold-versus-silver debate and shook his head. He could not understand what the fuss was about. As far as he was concerned, gold and silver were both money, and he was all for both kinds.

The Political Machine

Urban politics in the late nineteenth century resembled national politics in some ways. Issues were of secondary importance. What counted was winning elections. The big-city political party existed, like a business, for the benefit of those who "owned" it. The technique of election victory, therefore, was the politician's profession. His skill and willingness to work for "the company," and his productivity in delivering votes, determined how high he rose in an organization as finely tuned as any corporation.

The chairman of the board of the urban political company was the "boss." He was by no means necessarily the mayor, who was often a respectable front man. The boss coordinated the complex activities of the machine. Voters had to be aroused by the same sort of emotional appeals and hoopla that sustained national political campaigns. The ma-

chine was expected to provide material incentives comparable to the GOP's pensions program. The party activists who worked to get the voters out to the polls (the company's "employees") and kept them happy between elections were "paid" with patronage and pork, courtesy of the city treasury. Control of the municipal treasury, not the service of

The Granger Collection, New York

▲ *William Marcy Tweed ("Boss Tweed"), the head of the Democratic party machine in New York City during the 1860s. The Tweed ring may have stolen more public money than any other urban political machine.*

principles or the implementation of a program, was the purpose of politics.

"You are always working for your pocket, are you not?" an investigator into government corruption asked Richard Croker, thinking to embarrass him. Croker snapped back, "All the time, the same as you." On another occasion, Croker told writer Lincoln Steffens, "Politics is business, and reporting—journalism, doctoring—all professions, arts, sports—everything is business." Candor as blunt as the prow of a ferryboat was one quality that distinguished municipal politicians from national politicians. Another was that the control of cities that many political machines exercised was so nearly absolute that political profiteering sometimes took the form of blatant thievery.

The Profit Column

The political machine in power controlled law enforcement. In return for regular cash payments, politicians winked at the operations of illegal businesses: unlicensed saloons, gambling houses, opium dens, brothels, even strong-arm gangs. "Bathhouse" John Coughlan and "Hinky-Dink" Kenna, Chicago's "Gray Wolves," openly collected tribute from the kings and queens of Chicago vice at an annual ball.

The political machine in power peddled influence to anyone willing to make a purchase. Although he was no lawyer, William Marcy Tweed of New York, the first of the great city bosses, was on Cornelius Vanderbilt's payroll as a legal adviser. What the commodore was hiring was the rulings of judges who belonged to Tweed's organization. In San Francisco, after the turn of the century, Boss Abe Ruef would hold office hours on designated nights at an elegant French restaurant; would-be purchasers of influence filed in between appetizer and entrée, and entrée and roast, and negotiated their deals.

Kickbacks and Sandbagging

The rapid growth of cities in the late nineteenth century provided rich opportunities for kickbacks on contracts awarded by city governments. In New York, Central Park was a gold mine of padded contracts. The most notorious swindle of all was the New York County courthouse, a $600,000 building that cost taxpayers $13 million to erect. Plasterers, carpenters, and plumbers who worked on the building had standing orders to bill the city two and three times what they needed to make a reasonable profit, kicking back half or more of the padding to Tammany Hall, the men's club that controlled the Democratic party. Forty chairs and three tables cost the city $179,000. "Brooms, etc." cost $41,190.95.

Another technique for getting rich in public office was called "sandbagging." It worked particularly well in dealing with traction companies, the streetcar lines that needed city permission to lay tracks on public thoroughfares. It goes without saying that it took bribes to get such contracts in machine-run cities. The most corrupt aldermen, such as Coughlan and Kenna in Chicago, would grant a line the rights to lay tracks on only a few blocks at a time; thus, the Chicago "Traction King," Charles T. Yerkes, would be back for a further franchise at an additional cost.

Another variety of sandbagging involved threatening an existing trolley line with competition on a nearby parallel street. Rather than have their traffic decline by half, traction companies coughed up the money to prevent new construction.

It was not necessary to break the law to profit from public office. A well-established member of a political machine could expect to be on the city payroll for jobs that did not really exist. In one district of New York City where there were four water pumps for fighting fires, the city paid the salaries of 20 pump inspectors. Probably, none of them ever looked at a pump. Their real job was to keep the political machine in power at taxpayers' expense.

It was possible to hold several meaningless city jobs simultaneously. Cornelius Corson, who kept his ward safe for the New York Democratic party from an office in his saloon, was on the books as a court clerk at $10,000 a year, as chief of the board of elections at $5,000 a year, and as an employee of four other municipal agencies at $2,500 a year per job.

This was a munificent income in the late nineteenth century, but the bosses at the top of the machine did even better. Altogether, the Tweed ring, which controlled New York City for only a few years after the Civil War, looted the city treasury of as much as $200 million. Tweed went to jail, but his chief henchman, Controller "Slippery" Dick Connolly, fled abroad with several million dollars.

Richard Croker, head of Tammany Hall at the end of the century, retired to Ireland a millionaire. Timothy "Big Tim" Sullivan also rose from poverty to riches as well as adulation; when he died as the result of a streetcar accident, 25,000 people attended his funeral.

The Way Bosses Stayed in Business

Big Tim's send-off illustrates the fact that despite their obvious profiteering, machine politicians stayed in office. Although few of them were above stuffing ballot boxes or marching gangs of "repeaters" from one polling place to the next, they won most elections fairly; the majority of city voters freely chose them over candidates pledged to govern honestly.

The machines acted as very personalized social services among hard-pressed people. During the bitter winter of 1870, Boss Tweed spent $50,000 on coal that was dumped by the dozens of tons at street corners in the poorest parts of the city. Tim Sullivan gave away 5,000 turkeys every Christmas. It was the duty of every block captain to report when someone died, was born, was taking first holy communion in the Catholic Church, or was celebrating a bar mitzvah in a Jewish synagogue. The ward boss had a gift delivered.

Ward bosses brought light into dismal lives by throwing parties. In 1871, Mike Norton treated his constituents to 100 kegs of beer, 50 cases of champagne, 20 gallons of brandy, 10 gallons of gin, 200 gallons of chowder, 50 gal-

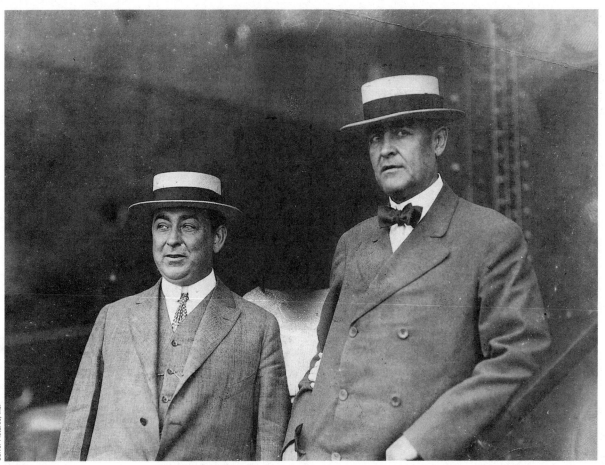

▲ *Tim Sullivan (right), an immensely popular ward boss in New York. His nickname was "Dry Dollar" Sullivan because, it was said, as a young man, he was found drying out the excise stamp from a barrel of whiskey, thinking it was a dollar bill.*

lons of turtle soup, 36 hams, 4,000 pounds of corned beef, and 5,000 cigars.

Ward bosses fixed up minor (and sometimes major) scrapes with the law. In control of the municipal government, the machines had jobs at their disposal, not only the phony high-paying sinecures that the bosses carved up among themselves but jobs that required real work and that unemployed men and women were grateful to have. Boss James McManes of Philadelphia had more than 5,000 positions at his disposal; the New York machine controlled four times that number. It is estimated that 20 percent of New York's voters had a direct financial interest in the outcome of municipal elections. When the votes of appreciative relatives and friends were added in, the machine had a very nice political base with which to fight an election.

The Failure of the Goo-Goos

Not everyone brimmed with gratitude. The middle classes, which paid property taxes, periodically raised campaigns for good government and sometimes won elections; the bosses called them "Goo-Goos." The Tweed ring's fall led to the election of a reform administration; in 1894, even the powerful Richard Croker was displaced. Chicago's "Gray Wolves" were thrown out of city hall, and a major wave of

indignation swept Abe Ruef and Mayor Eugene Schmitz out of power in San Francisco in 1906. But until the turn of the century, reform governments were generally short-lived. The machines came back.

One political weakness of the Goo-Goos was that they offered no alternative to the informal social services the machine provided. They believed that honest government was synonymous with very inexpensive government. Faced with material problems and inclined from their European backgrounds to think of government as an institution that one used or was used by, the immigrants preferred the machines.

Erin Go Bragh

"The natural function of the Irishman," said a wit of the period, "is to administer the affairs of the American city." In fact, a few bosses had other lineages: Cox of Cincinnati and Crump of Memphis were white Anglo-Saxon Protestants; Tweed was of Scottish descent; Ruef was Jewish; and Schmitz was German. But a list of nineteenth-century machine politicians reads like a roll call of marchers in a St. Patrick's Day parade: Richard Connolly, "Honest" John Kelley, Richard Croker, George Plunkitt, Charles Murphy, and Tim Sullivan of New York; James McManes (unlike the New Yorkers, a Republican) of Philadelphia; Christopher

Magee and William Finn of Pittsburgh; and Martin Lomasney of Boston.

The Irish were so successful in politics in part because they were the first of the large ethnic groups in the cities and in part because they were highly political in their homeland as a consequence of rule by Great Britain. Moreover, the Irish placed a high premium on oratory, which led naturally to politics. Most important of all, the Irish spoke English, a head start in the race to succeed over the other major immigrant groups of the late nineteenth century.

Ethnic Brokers

The primacy of the Irish did not mean that later immigrants were shut out of politics. The political machine lacked ethnic prejudice. If a ward became Italian and an Italian ward boss delivered the votes, he was welcomed into the organization and granted a share of the spoils commensurate with his contribution on election day. In many cities, although the police forces retained an Irish complexion, sanitation departments and fire departments often were predominantly Italian.

In the twentieth century, it was unwritten law among New York Democrats that nominations for the three top elective offices in the city (mayor, president of the city council, and controller) be divided among New York's three largest ethnic groups—Irish, Italians, and Jews. Later, with the arrival of Puerto Ricans and of blacks from the South, certain public offices were assigned to their leaders—for example, president of the Borough of Manhattan to a black and political leadership of the Borough of the Bronx to a Puerto Rican.

for FURTHER READING

The best survey of politics during the "Gilded Age," the late nineteenth century, is H. Wayne Morgan, *From Hayes to McKinley: National Party Politics, 1877–1896,* 1969. For a more jaundiced view, see Matthew Josephson, *The Politicos, 1865–1896,* 1938. Also valuable are John A. Garraty, *The New Commonwealth, 1877–1890,* 1968; Ray Ginger, *Age of Excess,* 1965; Vincent P. DeSantis, *The Shaping of Modern America, 1877–1916,* 1973; and Robert H. Wiebe, *The Search for Order,* 1967.

On prominent politicians and individual administrations, see Harry Barnard, *Rutherford B. Hayes and His America,* 1954; R. G. Caldwell, *Gentleman Boss: The Life of Chester A. Arthur,* 1975; D. B. Chidsey, *The Gentleman from New York: A Life of Roscoe Conkling,* 1935; Justus T. Doenecke, *The Presidencies of James A. Garfield and Chester A. Arthur,* 1981; Allan Nevins, *Grover Cleveland: A Study in Courage,* 1932; Allan Peskin, *Garfield: A Biography,* 1978; and Harry J. Sievers, *Benjamin Harrison: Hoosier Statesman,* 1959.

On specific political issues and institutions, see A. B. Callow Jr., *The Tweed Ring,* 1966; M. R. Dering, *Veterans in Politics: The Story of the G.A.R.,* 1952; Ari Hoogenboom, *Outlawing the Spoils: A History of the Civil Service Reform Movement, 1865–1883,* 1961; Morton Keller, *Affairs of State: Public Life in Late Nineteenth-Century America,* 1977; Paul Kleppner, *The Third Electoral System, 1852–1892,* 1979; J. Morgan Kousser, *The Shaping of Southern Politics,* 1974; Seymour Mandelbaum, *Boss Tweed's New York,* 1965; R. O. Marcus, *Grand Old Party: Political Structure in the Gilded Age, 1880–1896,* 1971; Walter T. K. Nugent, *Money and American Society, 1865–1880,* 1968; D. J. Rothman, *Politics and Power: The United States Senate, 1869–1901,* 1966; John G. Sproat, *The Best Men: Liberal Reformers in the Gilded Age,* 1968; and Tom E. Terrill, *The Tariff, Politics, and American Foreign Policy, 1874–1901,* 1973.

AMERICAN JOURNEY ONLINE AND INFOTRAC COLLEGE EDITION

Visit the source collections at http://ajaccess.wadsworth.com and http://infotrac.thomsonlearning.com, and use the Search function with the following key terms to explore documents, images, audio and video clips, articles, and commentary related to the material in this chapter:

Benjamin Harrison	Pendleton Act
Chester A. Arthur	Rutherford B. Hayes
Grover Cleveland	William Marcy Tweed (or Boss Tweed)

Additional resources, exercises, and Internet links related to this chapter are available on *The American Past* Web site: http://history.wadsworth.com/americanpast7e.

HISTORY ONLINE

Political Cartoons of Thomas Nast
www.boondocksnet.com/gallery/nast_intro.html
The cartoons of Republican Thomas Nast whom Boss Tweed blamed for his downfall.

Plunkitt of Tammany Hall
www.lib.umd.edu/ETC/ReadingRoom/Nonfiction/Plunkitt/
The entire text of the ruminations of the James Madison of the big-city political machine from the University of Maryland's Gutenberg Project.

BIG INDUSTRY, BIG BUSINESS

Economic Development in the Late Nineteenth Century

Southern Pacific Transportation Company

This movement was the origin of the whole system of modern economic administration. It has revolutionized the way of doing business all over the world. The time was ripe for it. It had to come, though all we saw at the moment was the need to save ourselves from wasteful conditions. . . . The day of the combination is here to stay. Individualism has gone, never to return.

John D. Rockefeller

The growth of a large business is merely the survival of the fittest. The American Beauty Rose can be produced in the splendor and fragrance which bring joy to its beholder only by sacrificing the early buds which grow up around it. This is not an evil tendency in business. It is merely the working out of a law of nature and a law of God.

John D. Rockefeller Jr.

I N 1876, AMERICANS celebrated the nation's centennial. The birthday party, the Centennial Exposition, was held in Philadelphia, where the Declaration of Independence was signed. It was a roaring success. Sprawling over the hills of Fairmount Park, housed in more than 200 structures, the great show dazzled 10 million visitors with its displays of American history, ways of life, and products.

The emphasis was on the products. The center of the fair was not the hallowed Declaration of Independence but a building that covered 20 acres and housed the latest inventions and technological improvements: from typewriters and the telephone through new kinds of looms and lathes and a dizzying variety of agricultural machines.

Towering above all the pulleys and belts, five times the height of a man, was the largest steam engine ever built, the giant Corliss. Hissing, rumbling, chugging, and gleaming in enamel, nickel plate, brass, and copper, the monster powered every machine in the building through 75 miles of shafts and belts. It was literally the heart of the exposition. When President Grant opened the fair by throwing the switch that set Machinery Hall in motion, he proclaimed that Americans were not just free and independent, but they were hitching their future to machines that made and moved things quickly, cheaply, and in astonishing quantities. "It is in these things of iron and steel that the national genius most freely speaks."

From the Collections of the Library of Congress

▲ *American industrialization rested upon a rich agricultural base, both because productive farmers produced cheap foodstuffs for factory workers and because agricultural exports provided capital for investment. Cotton was the king of exports before the Civil War. Wheat was the money maker in the final decades of the century. The "wheat belt" stretched from Minnesota to eastern Washington and Oregon.*

A LAND MADE FOR INDUSTRY

Between 1865 and 1900, the population of the United States more than doubled, from 36 million to 76 million. Wealth grew even more rapidly. At the end of the Civil War, the annual production of goods was valued at $2 billion. It increased to $13 billion in 1900.

Even in 1860, the United States was the fourth largest industrial nation in the world, with more than 100,000 factories capitalized at $1 billion. Nevertheless, the United States was primarily a farmer's country. More than 70 percent of the population lived on farms or in farm towns. In 1860, scarcely more than a million people worked in industrial jobs. Because many of them were women and children who did not vote, factory workers were inconsequential in politics.

By 1877, change was everywhere. Railroads had become so central to the national economy that a strike by railway workers shook the country to its foundations. By 1900, $10 billion was invested in American factories, and 5 million people worked in industrial jobs. Early in the 1890s, American industrial production surpassed that of Great Britain, making the United States the world's premier industrial nation. By 1914, fully 46 percent of the world's industrial and mining economy was American, more than the combined shares of Germany and Great Britain, the second and third industrial powers.

An Embarrassment of Riches

Viewed from the twenty-first century, the success story seems to have been as predestined as John Winthrop's throne in paradise. The ingredients of industrial transformation were heaped upon the United States in an abundance no other country has enjoyed.

In contrast to the plight of undeveloped countries today, America was rich in capital and able to welcome money from abroad without losing control of its destiny. Once the Union victory in 1865 assured foreign investors that American government was stable, the pounds, guilders, and francs poured in. By 1900, more than $3.4 billion in foreign investment fueled the American economy. Americans had to divert only 11 to 14 percent of their national income into industrial growth, compared with 20 percent in Great Britain half a century earlier and in the Soviet Union decades later. Consequently, the experience of industrialization was far less painful in the New World than in the Old. Americans sacrificed less for the sake of the future than other industrial peoples.

The United States was blessed in both the size and character of its labor force. The fecund and adaptable farm population provided a pool of literate and mechanically inclined people to fill the skilled jobs the new industry created. Unlike Asian and European peasants attached to an ancestral plot of ground and suspicious of unfamiliar ways, American farmers were quick to move on at opportunity's call. In the late nineteenth century, not only did new industries beckon seductively, but the labor-saving farm machinery that factories sent back to the farm made it possible for farmers to increase production while their sons and daughters packed themselves off to the city.

During these same years, Europe's population underwent a spurt of growth with which the European economy could not keep pace. Cheap American food products undersold crops grown at home, helping to displace European peasants. They emigrated to the United States, filling low-paying, unskilled jobs. At every level in the process of industrialization, the United States enjoyed a plenitude of clever hands and strong backs.

A Land of Plenty

The United States was blessed with vast and rich agricultural land producing cheap food; seemingly inexhaustible forests supplying lumber; deposits of gold, silver, semiprecious metals; and plenty of dross: phosphates and gravel. Most important in the industrial age, there were also huge stores of coal, iron, and petroleum.

The gray green mountains of Pennsylvania, West Virginia, and Kentucky seemed made of coal, the indispensable fuel of the age of steam. In the Marquette range of Michigan was a mountain of iron ore 150 feet high. The Mesabi range of Minnesota, just west of Lake Superior, was opened in the 1890s to yield iron ore richer and in greater quantity than could be found in any other area in the world.

The United States had a huge, ready-made market for mass-produced goods in its constantly growing population. And with the growth of industry (and the political influence of industrial capitalists), federal and state governments were quick to oblige the needs of manufacturers.

"Yankee Ingenuity"

Abraham Lincoln (who himself owned a patent) observed that Americans have "a perfect rage for the new." An English visitor to the Centennial Exposition wrote, "As the Greek sculpted, as the Venetian painted, the American mechanizes." Actually, the invention that turned the most heads at the great fair, the telephone, was the brainchild of a Scot who came to the United States via Canada, Alexander Graham Bell. Visitors to the exposition picked up the odd-looking devices he had set up and, alternately amused and amazed, chatted with companions elsewhere in the room. Young men at the fair dropped a hint of what was to come by "ringing up" young ladies standing across from them, casually striking up conversations that would have been unacceptable face to face.

Only in the United States could Bell have parlayed his idea into the gigantic enterprise it became, the American Telephone and Telegraph Company. As a writer in the *Saturday Evening Post* at the end of the century put it:

> The United States is the only country in the world in which inventors form a distinct profession. . . . With us, inventors have grown into a large class. Laboratories . . . have sprung up almost everywhere, and today there is no great manufacturing concern that has not in its employ one or more men of whom nothing is expected except the bringing out of improvements in machinery and methods.

The Telephone

Bell was a teacher of the deaf who, while working on a mechanical hearing aid, realized that if he linked two of the devices by wire, he could transmit voice over distance. He set up a pilot company in New York, and the telephone seized the American imagination. President Hayes put a telephone in the White House in 1878. By 1880, only four years after they first heard of the thing, 50,000 Americans were paying monthly fees to hear it jangle on their walls. By 1890, there

University of Oregon Library

▲ *The first telephone operators were teenage boys. Bell soon fired all of them because, to amuse one another, a major aspiration of adolescent boys, they were sarcastic with callers. Thus was born an employment opportunity for young working-class women whom Mark Twain called "Hello Girls." They were instructed to say "thank you" no matter what customers said. They worked 12-hour shifts.*

U.S. Dept. of the Interior, National Park Service, Edison National Historic Site. Photo taken by Matthew Brady, 1878

▲ *Thomas Edison was worshiped for his inventions when still a young man. He founded the first "R&D" laboratory but was not half as good a businessman as an inventor. His numerous business blunders allowed others, who invented nothing, to reap most of the profits of Edison's inspiration and perspiration.*

were 800,000 phones in the United States; by 1900, 1.5 million people in the tiniest hamlets knew all about exchanges, party lines, and bored, nasal-voiced "operators."

Most systems were local. But as early as 1892, eastern and midwestern cities were connected by a long-distance network, and rambunctious little western desert communities noted in their directories, "You can now talk to San Francisco with ease from our downtown office." Instantaneous communication was an invaluable aid to business. Just as important to some entrepreneurs, it left no written records of dubious transactions as letters and telegrams did.

The Wizard of Menlo Park

More celebrated than Bell was Thomas Alva Edison. Written off in boyhood as a dunce, Edison was, in fact, befuddled throughout life by people who pursued knowledge for its own sake. He was the ultimate, practical American tinkerer who looked for a need—and an opportunity to make money from it—and went to work. Abrupt, even obnoxious personally, Edison became a folk hero because of the way in which, he said, he approached invention. He said that genius

was 1 percent inspiration and 99 percent perspiration. With a large corps of assistants toiling in his research and development laboratory in Menlo Park, New Jersey, he took out more than a thousand patents between 1876 and 1900.

Most of these patents were for improvements in existing processes. (He perfected a transmitter for the telephone.) However, other Edison inventions were seedbeds for wholly new industries: the storage battery, the motion picture projector, and the phonograph. The most important of his inventions was the incandescent lightbulb, a means of converting electricity into stable, safe, controllable light.

Electric Light

Edison solved the theoretical principle of the electric bulb—the 1 percent inspiration—almost immediately. Within a vacuum in a translucent glass ball, an electrically charged filament would burn (that is, glow) indefinitely. The perspiration part was discovering the fiber that would work. In 1879, after testing 6,000 materials, Edison came up with one that burned for 40 hours, enough to make it practical. Before he patented the incandescent lightbulb early the next year, Edison improved the filament so that it glowed for 170 hours.

The financier J. P. Morgan, who loathed the telephone, was fascinated by electric light. His home and bank were among the first electrically illuminated structures in the United States. Morgan realized that many people disliked gas, the principal source of illumination in cities. Gas was clean, unlike kerosene, the illuminant of the countryside. But it could be dangerous. Thousands of fires were caused when, in a moment of ignorance, forgetfulness, or drunkenness, people blew out the flame instead of turning off the gas. Hotel managers nervously plastered the walls of rooms with reminders that the lights were gas.

The incandescent bulb succeeded as dramatically as the telephone. From a modest start in New York in 1882 (about 80 customers), Edison's invention spread so quickly that by 1900, more than 3,000 towns and cities were electrically illuminated. Within a few more years, the gaslight disappeared, and the kerosene lantern survived only on farms.

No single electric company dominated the industry, as American Telephone and Telegraph controlled Bell's patents. Nevertheless, like the railroads, regional companies were loosely associated by interlocking directorates and the influence of the investment banks.

The Problem of Wide-Open Spaces

George Westinghouse became a millionaire by inventing the air brake for railroad trains. By equipping every car in a train with brakes, operated from the locomotive by pneumatic hoses, Westinghouse solved the problem of stopping long strings of railroad cars. The air brake saved thousands of lives. It also meant bigger profits for railroads by making longer trains possible.

Westinghouse then turned his inventiveness to electricity and capitalized on Edison's stubborn resistance to alternating current. Edison's direct current served very well over small areas, but it could not be transmitted over long distances. By perfecting a means to transmit alternating current, Westinghouse leaped ahead of his competitor by fully utilizing massive natural sources of power at isolated places such as Niagara Falls.

Like Bell's, Westinghouse's invention confronted the single great impediment Americans faced in their drive toward massive industrial development: the very vastness of the country. The United States spanned a continent dissected by rivers, mountains, and deserts into regions as large as the industrial nations of Europe. Had geography had the last word, the United States would have remained a patchwork of distinct manufacturing regions in which small factories produced goods for the people of the vicinity. Indeed, this is a fair description of manufacturing in the United States before the Civil War.

THE RAILROAD REVOLUTION

The railroad conquered American geography. The steam-powered locomotive, belching acrid smoke, its whistle piercing the air of city and wilderness, tied the country together on its "two streaks of rust and a right of way." Railroads made it possible for Pittsburgh steelmakers to bring together the coal of Scranton and the iron of Michigan. Thanks to the railroad, great flour mills in Minneapolis could scoop up the cheap spring wheat of the distant Northwest, grind it into flour, and put their trademarked sacks into every cupboard in the country.

Because most western railroads made their way into Chicago, the Windy City quickly eclipsed river-based Cincinnati as "hog butcher to the world" and the nation's dresser of beef. Livestock fattened on range land a thousand miles away rolled bawling into Chicago in rickety trains and then rolled out—packed in cans, barrels, and refrigerator cars—to the East Coast and, from there, around the world.

With the possible exception of the telegraph line, the railroad was the physical manifestation of industry that most people knew. Rails and the noisy locomotives that sailed along them penetrated to the very centers of cities and reached into the most remote deserts and mountains. Where the railroad ran, the landscape was forever changed by massive excavations, embankments, bridges, and tunnels.

Inefficiency and Chaos

By 1865, the United States was already the world's premier railway country, with about 35,000 miles of track. With a few exceptions, however, individual lines were short, serving only the hinterlands of the cities in which they terminated. In the former Confederacy, there were 400 railroad companies, with an average track length of only 40 miles each. It was possible to ship a cargo between St. Louis and Atlanta by any of 20 routes. Competing for business in cutthroat rate wars, not a single southern line was financially secure.

Few lines linked up with one another. Goods shipped over long distances, and therefore on several lines, had to be unloaded (hand labor added to costs), carted across terminal towns by horse and wagon (another bottleneck), and reloaded on another train. No two of the six railroads that ran into Richmond shared a depot. Before the Civil War, Chicago and New York were linked by rail on the map, but a cargo going the entire distance had to be unloaded and reloaded six times.

Some railroaders encouraged this inefficiency in order to discourage takeovers by companies interested in consolidation. They deliberately built in odd gauges (the distance

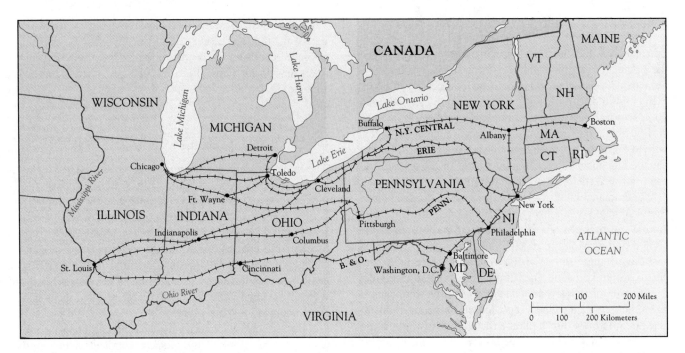

MAP 27:1 The Great Eastern Trunk Lines, 1850s–1870s   Four huge railroads, trunk lines, connected the four largest Atlantic seaports with Chicago or St. Louis and soon, through those cities, with the developing West.

between rails) so that only their own locomotives and rolling stock could run on their tracks. As narrow as two feet apart in mountainous areas, the distance between rails ran to five feet in the South. Until 1880, the important Erie Railroad clung to a monstrous six-foot gauge. The Illinois Central, the nation's third largest railroad, employed two different gauges.

Lack of coordination among railroads presented shippers and passengers with another headache. Each railway company scheduled its trains according to the official time in its headquarters city. But local time was different in cities a few miles apart. When it was noon in Chicago, it was 11:27 in Omaha, 11:56 in St. Louis, 12:09 in Louisville, and 12:17 in Toledo. When it was noon in Washington, D.C., it was 12:24 in Baltimore, 70 miles away, and 11:43 in Savannah. The Baltimorean in Washington who tried to catch a noon train home might discover that his watch was quite right for Baltimore but that he was nearly half an hour late for the train in Washington. In Buffalo's station, which served the New York Central and the Michigan Southern, three clocks were necessary: one for each railroad and one

for local time. In the Pittsburgh station, there were six clocks. Traveling from Maine to California on the railroad, one passed through 20 time zones. There were 80 such zones in the United States.

Consolidators

Charles F. Dowd introduced the idea of four official time zones in 1870; his plan was enacted into law at the behest of the railroads in 1883. (In 1884, 25 nations convened in Washington and adopted the "universal day": worldwide time zones based on the Greenwich Observatory outside London as 0 degrees longitude.)

Long before that, men like J. Edgar Thomson of the Pennsylvania Railroad and Cornelius Vanderbilt of the New York Central labored outside the law, and often in conflict with it, to bring order out of the chaos of independently owned short lines. They secretly purchased stock in small railroad companies until they had control, then drove other competitors out of business with ruthless rate wars. They built the "Pennsy" and the New York Central ever westward

Standard Gauge

The standard American railroad gauge is 4 feet, 8 and 1/2 inches. Why this odd figure? Because the English builders of trams and trains used the same jigs they used to make wagons, and 4 feet, 8 inches was the width of wagon wheel ruts in English roads. Why? Because the oldest roads in England were Roman roads. The Romans spaced their chariot wheels 4 feet, 8 inches apart because that was just enough to accommodate the behinds of two horses, harnessed side to side.

Narrow Gauge

The narrow-gauge feeder railroads that snaked into canyons and around mountains to bring out ore or logs were not as colossal as the trunk lines, but the engineering required to build them could be more demanding. The California Western, which brought redwood logs down to the port of Fort Bragg, was only 40 miles long but never ran on a straightaway for even a mile. It crossed 115 bridges and went through one tunnel 1,122 feet long.

from New York to Chicago and, thus, connected with lines that ran to the Pacific. All along their main lines, feeders tapped the surrounding country.

Thomson was all business, a no-nonsense efficiency expert with little celebrity outside railroad circles. Vanderbilt, who began life as a ferryman in New York's harbor, was colorful and often in the news. Ferrying was a rough business, no place for a milquetoast. The "Commodore," as Vanderbilt styled himself, dressing in a mock naval uniform, fired more than one cannon at a competitor's harbor barge.

Vanderbilt gave up brawling as his shipping empire grew, but he was as tough and unscrupulous behind a broad desk as he had been at the tiller of a ferry. Once, when a reporter suggested that Vanderbilt had broken the law in a conflict with a rival, he snapped, "What do I care about the law? Hain't I got the power?"

He had, and he used it masterfully to crush competition. By the time of the Civil War, Vanderbilt had a near monopoly on New York Harbor commerce. He even controlled the business that hauled New York City's monumental daily production of horse manure to farms on Staten Island. Vanderbilt's waterborne transportation empire led him naturally into moving the commerce of America's greatest city overland.

The Commodore was never quite respectable. His rough-and-tumble origins resonated in his speech. He befriended Victoria Woodhull and Tennessee Claflin, two sisters who outraged society by preaching free love and not shunning its practice. He set them up as stockbrokers, and they made a good deal of money until ruined by their sexual high jinks. The mention of Vanderbilt's name caused ladies and gentlemen of genteel New York society to shudder—for a while. Because he said out loud what other businessmen did qui-

etly—that ethics and social responsibility did not always make good business—he was an easy target for moralists. Vanderbilt could not have cared less. Like many of the great capitalists of the era, he regarded his fortune—$100 million when he died—as justification for what he did.

Pirates of the Rails

Thomson and Vanderbilt can be justified because they built transportation systems of inestimable social value. The Pennsy was famous for safe roadbeds in an age of frequent, horrendous railroad accidents. The New York Central pioneered the use of steel rails and was equipped with the life-saving Westinghouse air brake while other lines halted (or failed to halt) their trains mechanically. The Commodore's son and heir, William Vanderbilt, was best known for saying "The public be damned!" but he also played a major part in standardizing the American railroad gauges.

Other early railroad magnates simply took, making their fortunes by destroying what others had built. The most famous of these pirates was a trio that owned the Erie Railroad. The senior member of the "Erie ring" was Daniel Drew, a pious Methodist who knew much of the Bible by heart but

The Granger Collection, New York

▲ *Jay Gould. He was undoubtedly a scoundrel during the Erie War, but Gould's business methods were probably close to the norm throughout most of his long career. Nonetheless, he was used by critics and cartoonists to personify the "bad businessman." Reclusive anyway, Gould was happy to be persona non grata in the high society that attracted other millionaires of the era.*

Social Mobility

"Rags to riches" was a popular catchphrase in the nineteenth century, the idea being that the thousands of new industrial millionaires had risen from the dregs of society, "born in a log cabin," in effect. Actually, very few American magnates had such lowly origins. Andrew Carnegie is the only major industrial figure who started out at the very bottom; his family was utterly impoverished. A few of the era's giants were born rich: J. P. Morgan is the obvious example.

Most of the great millionaires of the era and the high corporate executives whose names do not make the history books had middle-class backgrounds or were, at least, several notches above rags. Rockefeller's family knew bad years, although that was largely due to the fact that the head of the household, Rockefeller's father, was a scoundrel, a con man who was home only erratically. (He boasted that he prepared John D. for business by cheating him in any arrangement between them involving money.)

If the starting line was not in the pit of poverty, the social mobility of the era was dramatic. The Field family of Connecticut was of *Mayflower* vintage. For 250 years, they were farmers and shopkeepers. The highest to which any Field aspired or rose was to fill a pulpit at a Congregationalist church. Reverend David Field, born in 1781, was social-climbing when, in midlife, he exchanged his pulpit in tiny Haddam, Connecticut, for one in Stockbridge, Massachusetts, a slightly larger town.

Field had six sons. In the dynamic nineteenth century, four of them became national figures in law, business, technology, and popular culture. The eldest, David Dudley Field (1805–1894), was America's foremost legal reformer. As a lawyer in New York, he observed that the century-old tangle of ordinances that had worked well enough in a small commercial city were inadequate in a burgeoning metropolis and commercial empire. He labored, much of the time drawing on his own resources, to sift, reform, and codify city and state law. New York State adopted David Dudley's codification of criminal law in 1881, although not the civil code he proposed. His influence had been somewhat tarnished by his political and business associations. Field had defended "Boss" William Marcy Tweed, the head of the corrupt political machine that governed New York City during the 1860s, as well as Jim Fisk and Jay Gould.

David Dudley Field had the curious experience of arguing cases before the Supreme Court when his younger brother was an associate justice. Stephen Johnson Field (1816–1899), also an attorney, was a forty-niner, rushing off to California in search

of gold or, perhaps, litigants. He settled in the supply town of Marysville, was elected mayor, and, in 1857, was named justice of the California supreme court. Stephen Field was a Democrat but also a staunch supporter of the Civil War. In 1863, Abraham Lincoln named him to the United States Supreme Court. He was a probusiness justice but also a defender of civil liberties. His defense of the rights of Chinese immigrants in California probably cost him further advancement in public life. He was several times considered as a favorite-son candidate for the presidency but was denied the prize because he had offended white workingmen with his "pro-Chinese" judicial decisions.

Cyrus Field (1819–1892) was a technological visionary of extraordinary persistence. A successful paper manufacturer before he was 30, in 1854, he turned to promoting the idea of a cable between Europe and North America over which telegraphic messages could be sent. Such a device would be of inestimable value to business, but the difficulties of laying such a cable seemed overwhelming. Indeed, Field's first attempt at laying a cable between Ireland and Newfoundland in 1857 failed, and a second, in 1858, lasted just three weeks.

In 1865, Cyrus Field tried again, this time using the largest ship in the world, the British-built *Great Eastern.* Almost 700 feet long and 120 feet across, the "great iron ship" was an engineering marvel that was never used properly. Able to power itself by sail, paddle wheel, or screw, it could carry 4,000 passengers and 2,000 crew. Instead of exploiting its size in long voyages, such as between Britain and Australia, the *Great Eastern*'s owners put it on the Atlantic run, where it did not compete well with smaller ships. Repeatedly, its owners went bankrupt.

Cyrus Field saw the *Great Eastern* as a massive cable factory. He outfitted the ship to reel out the continuous, fragile wire that would tie together Old World and New. In 1865, he lost a cable once again, but, on July 27, 1866, the connection was made. Despite his achievement, Cyrus Field did not die wealthy. Too trusting of his business associates, notably Jay Gould, he saw his fortune evaporate before he died.

The youngest Field brother, Henry Martyn Field (1822–1907), was not quite big-time. He was a Presbyterian minister who wrote adulatory biographies of David Dudley and Cyrus (but, oddly, not Stephen). However, he too made his mark as a communicator. During the 1890s, with the American middle class large, energetic, and curious, he wrote best-selling travel books for vicarious sojourners.

put a liberal interpretation on the verse in Exodus that said "Thou shalt not steal."

James Fisk, only 33 years old in 1867, was another sort altogether. No Bible for "Jubilee Jim"; he was a stout, jolly extrovert who fancied garish clothing, tossed silver dollars at street urchins, and caroused in New York's gaslit restaurants and cabarets with showgirls from the vaudeville stage, who, at the time, were considered little better than prostitutes.

(One of them, Josie Mansfield, was his undoing; in 1872, Fisk was murdered by another one of her suitors.)

Jay Gould was a man of the shadows. When Drew went to church and Fisk slapped on cologne, Gould slipped home to his respectable Victorian family. Furtive in appearance, tightfisted, and closemouthed, Gould was the brains of the Erie ring. Certainly, he lasted the longest, marrying his daughter to a French count. He had his defenders: John D. Rockefeller said Gould was the greatest businessman he knew; Henry Flagler said he was the "fairest, squarest" railroad man in the country. In fact, Gould retreated to apparently legitimate business practices after the famous "Erie War." His behavior during the episode, however, lends credence to the rather different eulogy of a onetime partner, who described Gould as "the worst man on earth since the beginning of the Christian era . . . treacherous, false, cowardly and a despicable worm incapable of generous nature."

The Erie War

In control of the Erie Railroad, the Erie ring knew that Vanderbilt was quietly making large purchases of Erie stock. In order to separate him from as much of his money as possible, they watered Erie's stock; that is, they sold shares in the dilapidated railroad far in excess of the Erie's real assets. Erie's value on the stock market rose from $24 million to $78 million in a few years when nothing was done to improve the line. Gould said, privately, of course, "There is no intrinsic value to it, probably."

As Vanderbilt bought and bought, Drew, Fisk, and Gould pocketed the money. The Commodore came to his senses and went to the judges, whom he regularly bribed, to indict the trio. Forewarned, Drew, Fisk, and Gould escaped to New Jersey, where they owned a few judges. A settlement was pieced together. In the meantime, the Erie amassed the worst accident record among world railroads, and the company was devastated as a business. The Erie did not pay a dividend to its stockholders until the 1940s. For 70 years, what profits there were went to make up for the thievery of three men over six years.

THE TRANSCONTINENTAL LINES

In the East, the creation of railroad systems—trunk lines—was largely a matter of consolidating short lines that already existed. During the 1880s, the names of 540 independent railway companies disappeared from the registers. In the West, railroad lines were extensive, integrated transportation systems from the start, constructed from scratch.

Land for Sale

In order to promote land it owned in Nebraska, the Burlington and Missouri River Railroad offered a number of come-ons. A would-be purchaser had to pay his own fare to go out to look at the land, but the railroad would refund his fare if he bought. Once a landowner, he would receive a free railroad pass, as well as "long credit, low interest, and a twenty percent rebate for improvements." Prices were not extravagant. The Union Pacific disposed of pretty good Nebraska land at $3 to $5 an acre.

Public Finance

The transcontinental railroads were built and owned by private companies but financed by the public (with one exception, James J. Hill's Great Northern). The sparseness of population between the Mississippi Valley and California and Oregon (Washington State after 1889) made it impossible to attract private investors to railroads connecting the East and West. Construction was too expensive. Building a mile of track meant bedding 3,000 ties in gravel and attaching 400 rails to them by driving 12,000 spikes. Having built that mile in Utah or Nevada, a railroader had nothing to look forward to but hundreds more miles of scarcely inhabited desert mountains.

With no customers along the way, there would be no profits; without profits, no investors. The federal government had political and military interests in binding the Pacific Coast to the rest of the Union, and, in its land, the public domain, it had the means with which to subsidize railroad construction.

The Pacific Railway Act of 1862 granted to two companies, the Union Pacific (UP) and the Central Pacific (CP), a right of way 200 feet wide between Omaha, Nebraska, and Sacramento, California. For each mile of track that the companies built, they were to receive, on either side of the tracks, 10 alternate sections (square miles) of the public domain. The result was a belt of land 40 miles wide, laid out like a checkerboard on which the UP and the CP owned half the squares.

The railroads sold the land to provide the money for construction and created customers in the buyers. Or they used their vast real estate as collateral against which to borrow cash from banks. In addition, depending on the terrain, the government lent the two companies between $16,000 and $48,000 per mile of track at bargain interest rates.

The Romance of the Rails

The business operations of the transcontinentals were sometimes shady—as in the case of the Crédit Mobilier. The actual construction of the line, however, was heroic. The UP, employing thousands of Civil War veterans and immigrant Irish pick-and-shovel men, the "Paddies," laid over 1,000 miles of track. The workers lived in shifting cities of tents and freight cars built like dormitories. They toiled by day, and bickered and brawled with gamblers, saloon keepers, and prostitutes by night. Until the company realized that it was more efficient to hire professional gunmen as guards, the workers kept firearms with their tools in order to fight off any Indians who sensed that the iron horse meant the end of their way of life.

The builders of the CP had no trouble with Indians, but a great deal with terrain. Just outside Sacramento rose the majestic Sierra Nevadas. There were passes in the mountains through which the line could snake, but they were narrow and steep. Under the direction of a resourceful engineer, Theodore D. Judah, 10,000 Chinese chipped ledges into the slopes, built roadbeds of rubble in deep canyons, and bolted together trestles of timbers two feet square.

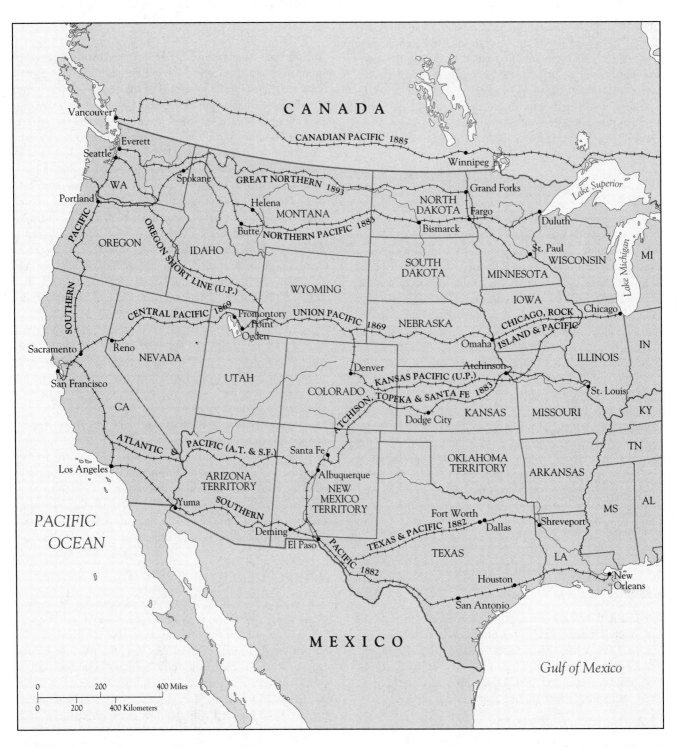

MAP 27:2 Transcontinental Railroads, 1862–1900 There were five transcontinental railroads across the West by 1900 (and another, followed by two more, in Canada). Two of the lines, the Santa Fe and the Southern Pacific, had eastern terminuses in the South, and both of those also had much busier connections to St. Louis.

The heavy Sierra snows presented a difficult problem, not only for the builders but for the operation of the line. To solve it, the workers constructed snow sheds miles long. In effect, the transcontinental railroad crossed part of the Sierra Nevadas indoors. Once on the Nevada plateau, the experienced CP crews built at a rate of a mile a day for an entire year.

The UP and CP joined at Promontory Point, Utah, on May 10, 1869. The final days were hectic. Because the mileage each company constructed determined the extent of its land grants, the two companies raced around the clock. The record was set by the crews of the CP. They built 10.6 miles of more or less functional railroad in one day (just about the

▲ *Most of the laborers who built the Central Pacific, from Sacramento to Utah, were Chinese immigrants. For a few years, they enjoyed employment opportunities otherwise denied them for racial reasons in the Gold Rush and after the massive construction projects in the West were finished.*

MAP 27:3 Northern Pacific Land Grant, 1864   The Great Northern was the only one of the five transcontinental railroads built without a federal land grant. (The Northern Pacific had the greatest grant.) James J. Hill financed the Great Northern by promoting settlement (customers) along completed sections of the line, then pushing farther west.

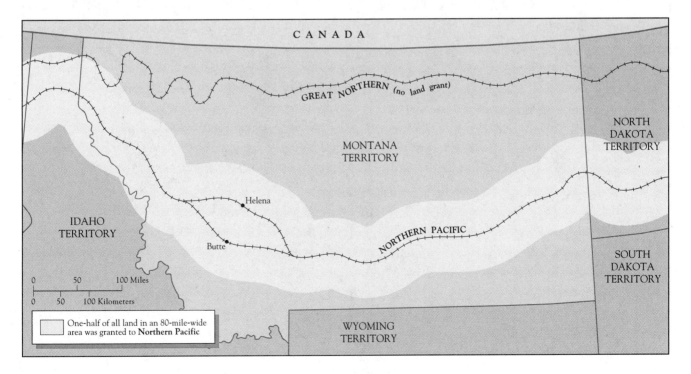

same length of track the company laid down during the whole of 1864). That involved bedding 31,000 ties and pounding 120,000 spikes!

Railroad Mania

Seeing that the owners of the UP and CP became instant millionaires, other ambitious men descended on Washington in search of subsidies. In the euphoria of the times, Congress in 1864 was doubly generous to the Northern Pacific, which planned to build from Lake Superior to Puget Sound. In the territories, the Northern Pacific received 40 alternate sections of land for every mile of railway built! The Atchison, Topeka, and Santa Fe ran from Kansas to Los Angeles. The Texas Pacific and Southern Pacific linked New Orleans and San Francisco at El Paso, Texas. In 1884, the Canadians (who were even more generous with government land) completed the Canadian Pacific.

The costs were considerable. The federal government gave the railroads 131 million acres. To this, state governments added 45 million acres. Totaled up, an area larger than France and Belgium was given to a handful of capitalists. In addition, towns along the proposed routes enticed the builders to choose them as sites for depots by offering town lots, cash bounties, and exemption from taxes.

These gifts were not always offered with a glad hand. If a railroad bypassed a town, the town might die. Railroaders did not hesitate to set communities against one another like roosters in a cock fight. The original Atchison, Topeka, and Santa Fe, popularly known as "the Santa Fe," did not enter the city of that name. Nearby Albuquerque offered the better deal and got the tracks.

The Panic of 1873

Western railroaders made money by building railroads with public and borrowed money, not by actually operating them. Consequently, they built too much railroad too soon. When the time came to shoulder high operating costs and to pay off loans out of fees paid by shippers and passengers, many of the new companies found that there were not enough customers to go around. In 1872, only one railroad in three made a profit.

On September 18, 1873, a Friday, the chickens came home to roost. Jay Cooke and Company, a bank that loaned heavily to western railroads, announced that the firm was

MAP 27:4 Railroad Expansion, 1870–1890 Between 1870 and 1890, much railroad expansion was in the construction of "feeder lines" tying productive parts of the West into one or another of the transcontinentals.

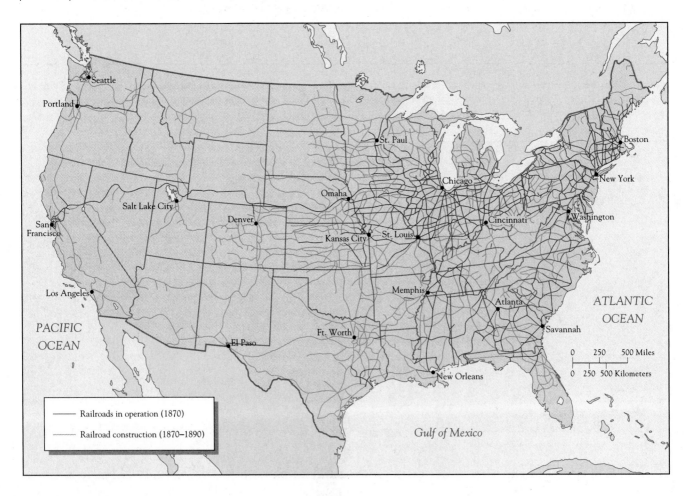

bankrupt. Jay Cooke was not an ordinary bank. It was the most prestigious house of finance in the United States; Cooke had been the government's chief financial agent during the Civil War. Its failure caused a panic as speculators rushed to sell their stocks. The market crashed. By the end of 1873, 5,000 businesses had declared bankruptcy and a half million workers were jobless. The depression of the 1870s was the worst in American history to that time.

It would not be the last. A by-product of fabulous economic growth was a wildly erratic business cycle, the "unprecedented disturbance and depression of trade," in the words of a contemporary. For a time, the industrial capitalist economy boomed, luring investment and speculation, encouraging expansion and production. Sooner or later, the capacity of railroads to carry freight, or factories to produce goods, outpaced the capacity of the market to absorb their services and products. When that happened, banks closed, investments and savings were wiped out, factories locked their gates, workers lost their jobs, and the shops they frequented went broke.

THE ORGANIZERS

In a free, unregulated economy, the cycle of boom and bust was inevitable, and Americans were committed to the ideal of a free and unregulated economy. They believed that their country's peculiar virtue lay in the fact that competition was open to everyone having the will and wherewithal to have a go at it.

Once a businessman reached the top of the economic pyramid, however, he was apt to become disenchanted with the competitive ideal. To the entrepreneur who was no longer scrambling but in charge of a commercial or industrial empire worth millions of dollars and employing thousands of people, freewheeling competitors threatened stability and order, like so many yapping spaniels. In the late nineteenth century, Andrew Carnegie in steel, John D. Rockefeller in oil, and other canny businessmen in dozens of industries devoted their careers to minimizing the threat of competition. Carnegie organized his company so efficiently that he could determine the price structure of the entire steel industry without regard to what other steelmakers did. Rockefeller destroyed his competitors by fair means and foul, and simply gobbled them up.

Steel: The Bones of the Economy

Steel is the element iron from which carbon and other impurities are burned out at high temperatures. Nineteenth-century engineers were well aware of its potential in construction. Steel is much stronger than iron per unit of weight. Produced in quantity, steel could be used in buildings, bridges, and, of particular interest at the time, superior rails. Until the mid–nineteenth century, however, the costs involved in producing the super iron restricted steel's use to small, expensive items: blades, firearms, precision instruments, bearings for machinery, and the like.

By the time of the Civil War, working independently of each other, two iron makers, Henry Bessemer of England and William Kelly of the United States, developed a method by which steel could be made in quantity at a reasonable price. No one grasped the significance of their discovery more quickly than Andrew Carnegie, an immigrant from Scotland who, beginning as a telegrapher, had become an executive of the Pennsylvania Railroad. Already a rich man by the end of the Civil War from the manufacture of iron bridges (his company built the first span across the Mississippi), he decided to sell everything and concentrate on steel, "putting all his eggs in one basket, and then watching that basket." In 1873, he began construction of a huge Bessemer plant in Braddock, Pennsylvania, outside Pittsburgh.

A Head for Business

Carnegie knew apples as well as eggs—how to polish them. He named his factory after J. Edgar Thomson, the president of the Pennsy, which would be a major customer of Carnegie Steel. But Carnegie also knew to locate the great works outside of Pittsburgh, which was served by the Pennsylvania Railroad alone. In Braddock, Carnegie could play several railroads against one another, winning the most favorable shipping rates. Nor was it luck that Carnegie built his mill during the depression of 1873. For the next 25 years, he took advantage of hard times, when the price of everything was down, to expand his factories, abandon old methods, and introduce new technology.

Carnegie also prided himself on spotting talent, putting it to work for him, and rewarding it. Charles Schwab, later the president of United States Steel and the founder of Bethlehem Steel, was an engineer's helper at Carnegie Steel whom Carnegie promoted and made a partner. Henry Clay Frick, a coal and coke magnate, brought to Carnegie's company not only mines and factories but an interest in day-to-day operations of which Carnegie knew nothing.

Vertical Integration

Carnegie's contribution to business organization was his exploitation of the principle of "vertical integration." That is, in order to get a leg up on his competitors, he expanded his operation from a base of steel manufacture to include ownership of the raw materials from which steel was made and the means of assembling those raw materials at the factory. For example, Bessemer furnaces were fueled by coke, which is to coal what charcoal is to wood, a hotter-burning distillation of the mineral. Rather than buy coke from independent operators, Carnegie absorbed the 5,000 acres of coalfields and 1,000 coke ovens owned by Henry Clay Frick, who became a junior partner in Carnegie Steel. Carnegie and Frick then added iron mines to their holdings.

Although never completely independent of trunk-line railroads, Carnegie controlled as much of his own shipping as he could. He owned barges that carried iron ore from Michigan and the Mesabi to his own port facilities in Erie, Pennsylvania. He owned a short-line railroad that brought the ore from Erie to his greatest factory, Homestead. By eliminating from his final product price the profits of independent suppliers, distributors, and carriers, Carnegie was able to undersell competing companies that were not vertically integrated and, therefore, had to include the profits of independent suppliers in their price.

Vertical integration served Andrew Carnegie very well. His personal income rose to $25 million a year. He lived much of the time in a castle in Scotland not far from where his father had worked as a weaver, while his company steadily assumed a more dominant role in the steel business. In 1870, there were 167 iron and steel firms around Pittsburgh. By the end of the century, there were 47.

In 1901, 66 years old and bored with business, Carnegie threatened to combine most of these into a behemoth that would threaten companies organized by the banker J. P. Morgan with an all-out price war. Morgan was persuaded to buy Carnegie out for $500 million, the largest personal commercial transaction ever made. Morgan then created the first billion-dollar corporation, United States Steel. From its birth, the company controlled "the destinies of a population nearly as large as that of Maryland or Nebraska" and spent more money and carried a larger debt than most of the world's nations.

The Corporation's Edge

Carnegie was progressive in many ways. But he organized his company as a partnership, disdaining the business structure that was the chief means of consolidation in the late nineteenth century, the corporation. Corporate structure—selling small shares in a company on the open market—was advantageous to both investors and business organizers. Dispersed ownership meant dispersed risk. The investor who owned shares in a number of companies did not lose everything if one of those companies failed. American law also provided investors with the privilege of limited liability. That is, the corporation's legal liability was limited to the assets of the corporation. It did not extend to the assets of shareholders. If an individually owned business or partnership went bust, creditors could seize the other assets of the owners, including home and personal property.

These inducements made it possible for entrepreneurs to raise the huge amounts of capital needed to finance expensive industrial enterprises. However, by reserving controlling interest to themselves, they did not have to share decision making with small investors. Abuses were common enough. Pirates like the Erie ring could drain a corporation of its assets, enrich themselves personally through their control of corporate policy, allow the company to go under, and walk away with their ill-gotten personal fortunes. But such crookery was far less common and catastrophic in the late nineteenth century than it was in the 1990s.

The Fourteenth Amendment to the Constitution, securing equality under the law to all persons, proved more valuable to corporations than to the African Americans for whom it was written. In 1886, the Supreme Court ruled in *Santa Clara County v. Southern Pacific Railroad* that a corporation was a "person" under the meaning of the Fourteenth Amendment. The states were forbidden to pass laws that applied specifically to corporations and not also to flesh-and-blood persons because such laws denied corporate persons civil equality. However, unlike a man or woman flouting the law, a corporation could not be sent to jail.

John D. Rockefeller

There were many corporations, but none so great as the one created by the solemn, muscular, and deeply religious John Davison Rockefeller. An accountant, Rockefeller avoided service in the Civil War by hiring a substitute. He made a small fortune selling provisions to the Union army, but that was only an appetizer. Outside of home and Sunday school, which he taught, he talked of little but business. After swinging a lucrative deal as a young man, he danced a two-step jig and exclaimed, "Bound to be rich! I'm bound to be rich!"

Rockefeller disapproved of smoking and drinking, in part because of his Baptist faith, but in part because cigars and whiskey cost money that could be invested to make more money. He carefully recorded how he spent every dime; he spent few frivolously. He would remove his stovepipe hat and bend down to pick up a penny on the street. John D. Rockefeller would have succeeded no matter

The Granger Collection, New York

▲ *John Davison Rockefeller at the time he was creating Standard Oil. He wanted to be rich. He became the richest man in the world. Generous throughout life to the Baptist Church he loved, he became the nation's greatest philanthropist.*

what his business. The one he chose proved to be as basic in the modern world as steel.

Black Gold

Crude oil has seeped to the surface of the earth since before there were human beings to step into it and growl. Ancient Mesopotamians wrote of it. Europeans used it as a lubricant. Jesuit priests in western New York in the seventeenth century reported of "a stagnant thick water that ignites like brandy, burning with bubbles of flame when fire is tossed into it." The Seneca ate it for a laxative. That classical American huckster, the snake oil salesman, bottled the stuff, flavored it with sugar and spices, added in a shot of alcohol, and claimed it cured everything from "female weakness" to rainy days. The farmers who lived around Titusville in western Pennsylvania hated it. It fouled the soil, polluted streams, and caught fire.

In 1855, a chemist, Benjamin Silliman, discovered that one of the components into which crude oil could be broken down was kerosene, a liquid that could be burned to heat a house or cookstove, or illuminate the night. It was a timely discovery. By the 1850s, overharvesting had decimated the world's population of whales. Whale oil, used to illuminate middle- and upper-class homes (the poor used candles or went to bed) had soared in price. Kerosene was cheap; even the poor could afford it. In 1859, seeing the opportunity, a former army officer named Edwin Drake went to Titusville and devised a drill-and-pump system by which crude oil could be extracted in commercial quantities.

The Pennsylvania oil rush that followed was as wild as the Gold Rush of 1849. Drilling for oil, like panning for gold, required only modest capital, so thousands of men dreaming of instant riches descended on western Pennsylvania. John D. Rockefeller, living in nearby Cleveland, Ohio, came and looked. But he did not like the social disorder and moral laxity, or the fact that the independent drillers, competing fiercely to stay afloat, repeatedly declared price wars on one another. In 1861, the price of crude oil swung crazily from $10 to 10 cents a barrel; in 1864, it bobbed up and down from $4 to $12. Drilling for oil was not accountant Rockefeller's kind of business.

Horizontal Integration

Oil refining was fragmented too; there were 250 refining companies as late as 1870. However, operating a refinery called for rather more capital than sinking a drill into the ground and saying a prayer. Rockefeller recognized that, unlike drilling, which would always attract "wildcatters" who might get lucky and become competitors overnight, the refining end of the business was manageable. It was a narrows on the river of oil that flowed from well to consumers. Like the robber barons of medieval Europe, who built castles at narrows on the Rhine and Danube, from which they decided which boat might pass and which might not, the company that controlled refining would be able to determine production and prices. It did not matter how many wild-eyed visionaries roamed the countryside with a drilling rig. If there was one great refiner, they would sell their crude to him at the price the refiner was willing to pay.

Controlling an entire industry by controlling a key phase of its process is known as "horizontal integration." Instead of setting the standards for an industry by integrating a portion of the business from top to bottom, from source of raw materials to market (as Carnegie did in steel), horizontal integration meant establishing an effective stranglehold on an industry at its key point.

With several associates (his brother William, Samuel Andrews, and Maurice Clark), this is what Rockefeller did. In 1870, their Standard Oil Company of Ohio refined 3 or 4 percent of the nation's oil. Within 20 years, Standard Oil controlled 90 percent of American refining. They worked this magic by persuading cooperative competitors to throw in with them and by driving weak and uncooperative refiners out of the business.

Rebates

Rockefeller ground some refineries down in cutthroat rate wars. With generally superior facilities, Standard Oil was able to take losses over the short term that less efficient competitors could not bear. On one occasion, Rockefeller bought up every barrel, stave, and hoop in the oil region. Competitors could not ship their products for lack of containers.

Much more effective was the "drawback," or rebate. Because Standard Oil could promise railroads a fixed, large amount of oil to carry east each day, Rockefeller demanded of the railroads a refund of part of their published rate—under the table. With smaller competitors paying the published rates, Rockefeller had a huge advantage when it was time to sell. For a short period, Rockefeller got a rebate from the Erie Railroad for each carload of kerosene his competitors shipped! This was his price to the Erie for continuing to use the line. The rebate was particularly effective in fighting

the refiners of Pittsburgh, who were served by only one railroad, which, therefore, did not have to bargain.

The Standard Oil Trust

In order to win these wars, Rockefeller had to occupy a commanding position in the refining industry. At the beginning, however, he and his associates lacked the vast capital resources necessary to buy out other large producers. The solution, designed by Rockefeller's lawyers, Samuel C. T. Dodd and John Newlon Camden, was to adapt the ancient legal device of the trust to the running of a business.

Traditionally, the trust was the means by which the property of a minor or an incompetent was managed on his or her behalf. That property was put into the care of a trustee whose obligation it was to see to it that the property was well administered. Rockefeller, Andrews, Clark, and Henry Flagler explained to their major competitors that if they surrendered control of their refineries to the Standard Oil Trust, for which they would receive trust certificates (stock, in effect), they would be spared the duties of management and the risks of competition while, because the trustees would coordinate the use of the combined facilities, their income would soar. The wiser refiners saw the point and agreed (and became very wealthy). Rockefeller, once in control of a near monopoly, was able to mop up refiners who resisted him.

The goal of the trust was not to drive retail prices up to extortionate levels. Rockefeller enjoyed telling hostile interrogators that with each step toward monopoly, Standard had reduced the retail price of a gallon of kerosene. The goal of the trust, he said, was economic order, not rapacious profiteering.

Rockefeller had no apologies for what he did. He remained a scathing critic of the gospel of competition to the end of his days. However, the fact that a handful of men could dictate the doings of an entire, vital industry—Standard Oil was run by only nine trustees—aroused a storm of fear and resentment in the land.

for FURTHER READING

For overviews of American economic development, see Elliott Brownlee, *Dynamics of Ascent: A History of the American Economy,* 1974; Thomas C. Cochran and William Miller, *The Age of Enterprise,* 1942; Vincent P. DeSantis, *The Shaping of Modern America, 1877–1916,* 1973; John A. Garraty, *The New Commonwealth, 1877–1890,* 1968; Samuel P. Hays, *The Response to Industrialism, 1885–1914,* 1957; Robert Higgs, *The Transformation of the American Economy,* 1971; Matthew Josephson, *The Robber Barons,* 1934; Glenn Porter, *The Rise of Big Business, 1860–1910,* 1973; Robert H. Wiebe, *The Search for Order,* 1967; and Daniel Boorstin, *The Americans: The Democratic Experience,* 1973.

Valuable special studies include Roger Burlingame, *Engines and Democracy: Inventions and Society in Mature America,* 1940; A. F. Chandler, *Strategy and Structure: Chapters in the History of the American Industrial Enterprise,* 1962, and *The Visible Hand: The Managerial Revolution in American Business,* 1977; Thomas C. Cochran, *Railroad Leaders, 1845–1890,* 1953; Robert W. Fogel,

Railroads and American Economic Growth, 1964; Edward C. Kirkland, *Dream and Thought in the Business Community, 1860–1900,* 1956, and *Men, Cities, and Transportation,* 1948; Gabriel Kolko, *Railroads and Regulation,* 1965; James McCague, *Moguls and Iron Men,* 1964; Elting E. Morison, *From Know-How to Nowhere: The Development of American Technology,* 1974; David F. Noble, *America by Design: Science, Technology, and the Rise of Corporate Capitalism,* 1977; Walter T. K. Nugent, *Money and American Society, 1865–1880,* 1968; George R. Taylor and R. D. Neu, *The American Railroad Network, 1861–1900,* 1956; and John F. Stover, *The Life and Decline of the American Railroad,* 1970.

Robert V. Bruce, *Alexander Graham Bell and the Conquest of Solitude,* 1973, is a magnificent biography, as is Ron Chernow, *Titan: The Life of John D. Rockefeller, Sr.,* 1998. For other personages prominent in this chapter, see Matthew Josephson, *Edison,* 1959; Harold C. Livesay, *Andrew Carnegie and the Rise of Big Business,* 1975; and J. F. Wall, *Andrew Carnegie,* 1971.

Visit the source collections at http://ajaccess.wadsworth.com and http://infotrac.thomsonlearning.com, and use the Search function with the following key terms to explore documents, images, audio and video clips, articles, and commentary related to the material in this chapter:

Alexander Graham Bell
Andrew Carnegie
Cornelius Vanderbilt
Jay Gould

John D. Rockefeller
Panic of 1873
Thomas Edison

Additional resources, exercises, and Internet links related to this chapter are available on *The American Past* Web site:
http://history.wadsworth.com/americanpast7e.

HISTORY ONLINE

Central Pacific Railroad
http://cprr.org/
Text and superb photographs from the Central Pacific Photographic Museum.

Alexander Graham Bell's Path to the Telephone
www.iath.virginia.edu/albell/homepage.html
Text and images explaining Bell's concept and invention of the telephone.

LIVING WITH LEVIATHAN

Reactions to Big Business and Great Wealth

Success is counted sweetest
By those who ne'er succeed.

Emily Dickinson

A successful man can not realize how hard an unsuccessful
man finds life.

Edgar Watson Howe

The moral flabbiness of the exclusive worship of the
bitch-goddess SUCCESS. That—with the squalid cash
interpretation put on the word success—is our national
disease.

William James

IN *DEMOCRACY IN America,* Alexis de Tocqueville admired the equity with which wealth was distributed in the United States. In Jacksonian America, except for slaves, few Americans were so poor that they could not hope to improve their situation; few families were so rich that they had coalesced into an aristocracy. Consequently, ordinary Americans seemed confident that their country was indeed the land of opportunity, where their fates lay in their own hands. At the same time, wealthy Americans Tocqueville met seemed haunted by the fear that one stroke of ill fortune would send them tumbling down into the world of hard work, sore backs, and callused hands.

Jacksonian America probably did not apportion its wealth so equitably as Tocqueville believed. Nevertheless, the gap between dirt poor and filthy rich was not nearly so yawning as it became in the late nineteenth century. Industrialization and big business created a class of multimillionaires whose fortunes were so great that it was absurd to imagine them slipping back into the unwashed masses. Cornelius Vanderbilt amassed $100 million. His son, William, doubled it in a few years. In 1901, Andrew Carnegie pocketed $500 million in a single transaction. John D. Rockefeller gave away that much every several years all the while his family grew richer.

The industrial and financial aristocracy's control of technology, transportation, industry, and money seemed to mock the American dream of equality of opportunity. How could an ordinary fellow succeed against such entrenched power and privilege?

REGULATION OF THE RAILROADS AND TRUSTS

Railroads were the first big business and drew criticism from the beginning. Romantic poets, painters, and philosophers saw "the machine in the garden," the noisy, dirty locomotive, defiling the pastoral and the natural, the good in American life. In cities, the issue was grittier: People were killed by trains running on city streets, 330 in Chicago one year, almost one per day. Residents banded together to demand they be insulated from the tracks.

But the naysayers were few. Most Americans welcomed the iron horse, especially those who lived in isolated rural areas. To them, the railroad provided the opportunity to ship their produce to market and thereby earn money with which to escape a life of mere subsistence.

A Short Honeymoon

The honeymoon was brief. Episodes like the Erie War cast doubt on the probity of the men who ran the railroads. Along trunk lines like the Pennsy and Baltimore and Ohio, and particularly along the transcontinental railroads, important business of all kinds had to be cleared with the local railway manager. Western farmers learned that the railroads were

less their servants, carting their produce to market, than their masters.

California's "Big Four"—Collis P. Huntington, Leland Stanford, Mark Hopkins, and Charles Crocker—it was said, "owned" the state, thanks to their control of the Southern Pacific Railroad (SP), which absorbed the Central Pacific and ran the length of California too. The SP was, next to the federal government, California's biggest landowner. The SP held tight to much of its holdings in California's fertile central valley and the forested slopes of the state's mountains, further enriching the Big Four as land prices in California rose to 10 times what railroad land cost elsewhere in the West.

By the end of the century, the SP actually used its tremendous leverage to drive small farmers and ranchers out of business. The line's political officer, William F. Herrin, was widely considered to be the boss of the state legislature,

▲ *The Union Pacific, the pride of the nation when it was completed in 1869, was the subject of this cartoon depicting it as a bandit and oppressor just a few years later. The thug astride the locomotive is William Vanderbilt, son of Cornelius Vanderbilt.*

Courtesy of the New York Historical Society, New York City

monitoring every law that was passed in the interests of the SP. Novelist Frank Norris summed up the SP for many Californians in the title of his novel of 1901, *The Octopus*. The SP's tentacles reached into every corner of the state.

The Farmers' Grievances

Some grain belt farmers discovered that a railroad did not necessarily usher in a golden age. The problem was monopoly. Almost everywhere in the West, one line handled all the traffic. Consequently, the rates at which farmers shipped their wheat, corn, or livestock to markets in the East were dictated by the railroads. Too often for goodwill to prevail, farmers saw their margin of profit consumed by transportation costs.

Most bothersome was the railroads' control of storage facilities, the grain elevators that stood close to the depot in most railway towns. Farmers had to pay the railroad storage fees until a train was sent to haul the grain away. It was often in the railroad's interests to delay shipment and let the storage fees pile up.

Attempts to Regulate

In the early 1870s, the Patrons of Husbandry, founded as a social and cultural organization, became the focus of farmer protest in the Midwest. The Grangers, as members called themselves, transformed the society into a political pressure group, and the Patrons of Husbandry proceeded to grow like sunflowers. In 1869, there were 39 Granges (local chapters); by the mid-1870s, there were 20,000, with 800,000 dues-paying members.

Pro-Granger politicians won control of the state legislature of Illinois and exercised considerable influence in adjoining states. Allied with small businessmen, who also felt squeezed by railroads, they passed a series of Granger laws that set maximum rates that railroad companies could charge both for hauling and storing grain. Several other state governments imitated the Illinois laws.

The railroad barons launched a legal counterattack, hiring high-powered corporate lawyers like Richard B. Olney and Roscoe Conkling to challenge state regulatory legislation. At first, the Grangers prevailed. In *Munn v. Illinois* in 1877, a Supreme Court dominated by old-fashioned Lincoln Republicans declared that when a private company's business affected the public interest, the public had the right to regulate that business for the common good.

Nine years later, the personnel of the Supreme Court had changed. In 1886, justices on cordial terms with the new order wrote several prorailroad doctrines into the law of the land. The most important was handed down in the Wabash case (*Wabash, St. Louis, and Pacific Railway Co. v. Illinois*) in 1886. In this decision, the Court reinterpreted the interstate commerce clause of the Constitution in such a way as to protect large railroad companies. That is, the Constitution provides that only Congress can regulate commerce between and among states. In the Wabash case, the Court ruled that because the Wabash Railroad ran through several states, the Illinois legislature could not regulate freight rates even be-

tween two points within the state. The Wabash decision left state governments with authority over only short, generally insignificant local lines that were rarely exploitative anyway.

The Interstate Commerce Commission

The Wabash decision was unpopular. Rural politicians and urban reformers condemned the Court as the tool of the railway barons. If Congress can bridle the iron horse, they shouted from Grange halls and from the stages of city auditoriums, let Congress do so. In 1887, Congress did, by enacting the Interstate Commerce Act.

On the face of it, the law brought the national railroads under control. It required railroads to publish their rates and to charge them; under-the-table rebates were forbidden. Railroads were forbidden to charge less for long hauls along routes where there was competition than for short hauls in areas where a company had a monopoly. The act also outlawed the pooling of business by railroads, a practice by which, many shippers believed, they were controlled and fleeced. To enforce the act and to regulate rates, Congress created a permanent independent federal commission, the Interstate Commerce Commission (ICC).

The Interstate Commerce Act calmed antirailroad protest, but it did not have much effect on railroad policy. The ICC had little real power. When commissioners wished to compel a railroad to comply with their regulations, they had to take the company to the same courts that had favored the railroads over the state legislatures. Commissioner Charles A. Prouty commented, "If the ICC was worth buying, the railroads would try to buy it. The only reason they have not is that the body is valueless in its ability to correct railroad abuses."

In fact, the railroads did not have to buy the ICC; it was given to them. The Harrison, Cleveland, and McKinley administrations (1889–1901) were sympathetic to big business and staffed the commission with railroaders and lawyers friendly to them.

The Money Power

By the early 1890s, the trunk lines of the country were consolidated into five great systems. By 1900, these had effectively fallen under the control of two New York investment banks, J. P. Morgan and Company and Kuhn, Loeb, and Company, the latter in league with Union Pacific president Edward H. Harriman.

The bankers took over because, when the government ceased to subsidize construction, the railroads had to look elsewhere for the capital needed to lay second tracks, modernize equipment, and buy up competitors. Freight charges were rarely enough to meet such costs. Nor were stock issues. No railroads were so overvalued as the tortured Erie, but many were overvalued.

Enter the investment banks. These institutions served both as sales agents, finding moneyed buyers for railway

▲ *The Patrons of Husbandry, the Grange, idealized farmers and farm life in this lithograph of 1873. Originally a social and cultural organization, by 1873 the Grange was actively mobilizing votes for politicians, Republicans and Democrats, who supported its demands for regulation of railroads.*

stock at a commission, and as buyers themselves. In return for these services, bankers like John Pierpont Morgan insisted on a say in making railroad policy by placing representatives of the bank on the client's board of directors.

Because every large railroad needed financial help at one time or another—every transcontinental but the Great Northern went under during the depression of 1893 to 1897—Morgan's and Kuhn Loeb's men soon sat on every major board of directors, creating a complex interlocking directorate. Like all bankers, their goal was a steady, dependable flow of profit, and they intended to achieve that end by eliminating wasteful competition. They called a halt to the periodic rate wars among the New York Central, Pennsylvania, and Baltimore and Ohio in the eastern states. In 1903, J. P. Morgan tried to merge the Northern Pacific and the Great Northern, two systems with parallel lines between the Great Lakes and the Pacific Northwest. Competing for traffic, he believed, hurt them both.

Banker control had many benefits. No more did unscrupulous pirates like the Erie gang ruin great transportation systems for the sake of making a killing in the short term. The integration of the nation's railways also resulted in a gradual but significant lowering of fares and freight rates. Between 1866 and 1897, the cost of shipping a hundred pounds of grain from Chicago to New York dropped from 65 cents to 20 cents, and the rate for shipping a hundred pounds of beef, from 90 cents to 40 cents. J. P. Morgan's self-justification was identical to John D. Rockefeller's. Competition was wasteful and destructive; consolidation better served the nation as a whole, as well as its capitalists.

J. P. Morgan

The control of so important a part of the economy by a few men on Wall Street called into question some very basic American ideals. Where was individual freedom and opportunity, people asked, when a secretive, sinister money power could decide on a whim the fate of millions of farmers and working people? The anxiety was sometimes anti-Semitic, targeting not just "the bankers" but "Jewish bankers." This was ironic because, although three investment houses owned by Jews had been major powers in New York's financial circles a generation earlier—J. and W. Seligman, Kuhn Loeb, and August Belmont—New York banking itself had taken an anti-Semitic turn. The old Jewish houses were declining, and the son of the founder of Seligman was denied membership in an exclusive club his father had helped found.

There was nothing Jewish about the prince of investment banking, J. P. Morgan, a resplendent, cultivated man who owned yachts larger than the flagships in most countries' navies and an art collection superior to most countries' national museums. Morgan never attempted to disguise his power or his contempt for ordinary mortals. In return, he was feared, held in awe, and hated.

Morgan shook it all off. In the end, he was vulnerable only to ridicule. An affliction of the skin had given him a large, bulbous nose that swelled and glowed like a circus clown's when he was angry. Making fun of it, however, was the only foolproof way to make it light up, and Morgan did not rub elbows with the kind of people who would notice his single human weakness.

An Age of Trusts

In addition to railroaders, Morgan found plenty of company among the industrialists whose trusts and other devices for doing business he organized for fees of a million dollars and more. The trust was most useful in industries in which, like oil, there was a single critical stage of manufacture that

▲ *John Pierpont Morgan, the single most powerful man in the United States in the 1890s and 1900s by virtue of his bank's reorganization of railroads and other major industries. Morgan created United States Steel in 1901, the first billion-dollar corporation.*

involved relatively few companies. Some of John D. Rockefeller's most successful imitators were in sugar refining (the sugar trust controlled about 95 percent of the nation's facilities) and whiskey distilling. In 1890, James Buchanan Duke of Durham, North Carolina, founded the American Tobacco Company, a trust that coordinated the activities of practically every cigarette manufacturer in the United States. In effect, he dictated the terms by which tens of thousands of tobacco growers did business.

By 1890, many Americans were convinced that when a few men could control an entire industry, the principle of economic opportunity and the foundations of American democracy were in jeopardy.

The Sherman Antitrust Act

Responding to public pressure, Congress passed the Sherman Antitrust Act, which stated, "Every contract, combination, in the form of trust or otherwise, or conspiracy, in restraint of trade or commerce among the several states, or with foreign nations, is hereby declared to be illegal." The Sherman Act authorized the attorney general to move against such combinations and force them to dissolve, reestablishing the independence of the companies that formed them.

The Sherman Act was no more successful in halting the consolidation movement than the Interstate Commerce Act was in controlling the railroads. Critics said that the Sherman

Act was a sham from the beginning, designed to quiet unease but not to hurt big business. In fact, the weakness of the law lay in the inability of congressmen to comprehend this new economic phenomenon. Real monopoly was so unfamiliar to the lawmakers that they were unable to draft a law that was worded well enough to be effective. The language of the Sherman Act was so ambivalent that a shrewd lawyer—and the trusts had the best—usually found loopholes.

Moreover, although congressmen took fright at popular uproars, the courts were immune to them. The Wabash case was only one of a series of decisions by the Supreme Court that ensured the survival of the biggest of businesses. In the first major case tried under the Sherman Act, *U.S. v. E. C. Knight Company* in 1895, the Court found that a nearly complete monopoly of sugar refining in the United States did not violate the law because manufacture, which the sugar trust monopolized, was not a part of trade or commerce, even though its sugar was sold in every state.

Nor was the executive branch keen to attack big business. President Grover Cleveland's attorney general, Richard B. Olney, was a corporate lawyer. Under Benjamin Harrison and William McKinley, the other presidents of the 1890s, the Justice Department was similarly probusiness. During the first 10 years of the Sherman Act, only 18 cases were instituted, and four of those were aimed not at businesses but at labor unions, which were also "conspiracies in restraint of trade."

Between 1890 and 1901, big business actually got bigger. The number of state-chartered trusts grew from 251 to 290. The amount of money invested in trusts rose from $192 million to $326 million. By the end of the century, there was no doubt that the demands of modern manufacturing meant that mammoth organizations were here to stay.

RADICAL CRITICS OF THE NEW ORDER

The Interstate Commerce and Sherman Antitrust Acts were enacted by mainstream politicians who believed that the individual pursuit of wealth was a virtue. They wished only to restore competition and the opportunity to succeed that big business threatened to destroy. Outside the mainstream, sometimes radical critics of the new industrial capitalism raised their voices and wielded their pens in opposition to the new order itself. At least briefly, some of them won large followings.

Henry George and the Single Tax

A lively writing style and a knack for simplifying difficult economic ideas made journalist Henry George and his "single tax" the center of a short-lived but momentous social movement. In *Progress and Poverty,* published in 1879, George observed what was obvious, but also bewildering to many people. Instead of freedom from onerous labor, as the machine once seemed to promise, the machine had put millions to work under stultifying conditions for long hours. Instead of making life easier and fuller for all, the mass production of goods had enriched the few in the "House of Have" and impoverished the millions in the "House of Want."

George blamed neither industrialization nor capitalism as such for the misery he saw around him. Like most Americans, he believed that the competition for wealth was a wellspring of the nation's energy. The trouble began only when those who were successful in the race grew so wealthy that they ceased to be entrepreneurs, and became parasites who lived off the income their property generated, or rent.

George called income derived from mere ownership of property "unearned increment" because it required no work or ingenuity of its possessors. Property grew more valuable, and its owners richer, only because other people needed access to it in order to survive. Such value was spurious, George said, even heinous. Government had every right to confiscate unearned increment by levying a 100 percent tax on it. Because the revenues from this tax would be quite enough to pay all the expenses of government, all other taxes could be abolished. "Single tax" became the rallying cry of George's movement. It would destroy the idle and parasitic rich as a social class. The entrepreneurship and competition that made the country great would flourish without the handicaps of taxation.

George's gospel was popular enough that in 1886 he narrowly missed being elected mayor of New York, a city where unearned increment from real estate was higher than anywhere in the world.

Edward Bellamy's Socialistic Vision

Another book that became the Bible of a protest movement was Edward Bellamy's novel of 1888, *Looking Backward, 2000–1887.* Within two years of its publication, the book sold 200,000 copies and led to the founding of 150 Nationalist clubs, made up of people who shared Bellamy's vision of the future.

The story that moved them was simple; its gimmick, conventional. A proper young Bostonian of the 1880s succumbs to a mysterious sleep and awakes in the United States of the twenty-first century. There, he discovers that technology has produced not a world of sharp class divisions and widespread misery (as in 1887) but a utopia that provides abundance for all. Like George, Bellamy was not opposed to industrial development in itself.

Capitalism no longer exists in the world of *Looking Backward.* Through a peaceful democratic revolution—won at the polls—the American people have abolished competitive greed and idle, unproductive living because they were at odds with American ideals. Instead of private ownership of land and industry, the state owns the means of production and administers them for the good of all. Everyone contributes to the common wealth. Everyone lives decently, none miserably or wastefully.

Bellamy's vision was socialistic. However, because he rooted it in American values rather than in Marxism, he called it "Nationalism." The patriotic facet of his message made his gospel palatable to middle-class Americans who, although troubled by the growth of fantastic fortunes and of wretched poverty, found foreign ideologies and talk of class warfare frightening.

Socialists and Anarchists

Marxism, including the doctrine of class conflict, had some appeal in the United States. A few old-stock Americans were converted to Marxist socialism. Mostly, however, Marxism found its adherents among immigrants and the children of immigrants. Briefly after 1872, the General Council of the First International, the official administration of world socialism, made its headquarters in New York, where Karl Marx had sent it to prevent the followers of his anarchist rival, Mikhail Bakunin, from winning control of it.

Marxists taught that the capitalist system of "wage slavery"—workers laboring for wages in the employ of a capitalist class that owned the means of production (the factories and machines)—would fall under its own weight to socialism and then communism, under which, respectively, the state and the workers themselves would own the factories and machines.

Some Marxist socialists (the "revisionists") held that in democratic countries like the United States, this social revolution would be voted in peacefully. Social democratic movements flourished in a number of cities, most notably in Milwaukee, where an Austrian immigrant, Victor L. Berger, built a party that, after 1900, would govern the city (and very well) for decades.

Other Marxist socialists held that the overthrow of capitalism would inevitably be violent. The most extreme of these revolutionaries were the anarchists, some of whom held that individuals could hasten the great day through "the propaganda of the deed"—acts of terrorism against the ruling class. Anarchists figured prominently in an incident in Chicago in 1886 that led to a passionate reaction against them.

Haymarket

In May 1886, workers at the McCormick International Harvester Company, the world's largest manufacturer of farm machinery, were on strike. The Chicago police were blatantly on the side of the employers, and over several days, they killed four workers. On May 4, a group of anarchists, mostly German but including a Confederate army veteran of some social standing, Albert Parsons, held a rally in support of the strikers at Haymarket Square, just south of the city center.

The oratory was red-hot; but the speakers broke no laws, and the crowd was orderly. Indeed, the rally was about to break up under the threat of a downpour when a platoon of police entered the square and demanded that the assembly disperse. At that instant, someone threw a bomb into their midst, killing seven policemen and wounding 67. The police fired a volley, and four workers fell dead.

News of the incident fed an antianarchist hysteria in Chicago. Authorities rounded up several dozen individuals

© Bettmann/Corbis

▲ *There was no need for Chicago police to march into Haymarket Square in May 1886; the demonstration there was peaceful and about to disband. When the police did arrive, an unknown assassin threw a bomb into their midst, killing seven and wounding 67. Chicago's outrage was so great that the public accepted the railroading of eight anarchists for the crime (four were hanged) despite the lack of evidence any were involved.*

who were known to have attended anarchist meetings, and authorities brought eight to trial for the murder of the officers. Among them were Parsons and a prominent German agitator, August Spies.

The trial was a farce. No one on the prosecution team knew or even claimed to know who threw the bomb. (His or her identity remains unknown.) Nor did the prosecution present evidence to tie any of the eight to the bombing. One, a deranged young German named Louis Lingg, was a bomb maker, although even he had a plausible alibi. Several of the defendants had not been at the rally. Parsons was sick in bed; indeed, he had been ill since before the rally was called.

All these facts proved to be irrelevant. Chicago was determined to have scapegoats, and, although the charge was murder, the Haymarket anarchists were tried for their ideas and associations. Four were hanged. Lingg committed suicide in his cell. The remaining three were sentenced to long prison terms.

The Social Gospel

Some influential Protestant clergymen took a moral approach to the social tensions of the late nineteenth century. Troubled by the callousness of big business, preachers of the "social gospel" emphasized the Christian's social obligations, his duty to be his brother's keeper.

Walter Rauschenbusch began his ministerial career in Hell's Kitchen, one of New York City's worst slums. "One could hear human virtue cracking and crushing all around," he wrote. To Rauschenbusch, poverty was the cause of crime and sin, and mass poverty was the result of allowing great capitalists a free hand in enriching themselves. Later, as a professor at Rochester Theological Seminary, Rauschenbusch taught the obligation of the churches to work for both the relief of the poor and a more equitable distribution of wealth.

Washington Gladden, a Congregationalist, called unrestricted competition "antisocial and anti-Christian." He did not propose the abolition of capitalism, but he did call for regulation of its grossest immoralities. He was highly moralistic. Late in life, Gladden described John D. Rockefeller's fortune as "tainted money" and urged his church not to accept contributions from the millionaire. (Rockefeller found plenty of untroubled clergymen to whom to write checks.)

The social gospel appealed to middle-class people, often modestly well-to-do themselves. They did not suffer directly from the power of the very wealthy but were offended by the extravagance and idleness of the lives of the superrich. William Dean Howells, editor of the *Atlantic Monthly,* wrote a novel about a successful paint manufacturer (*The Rise of Silas Lapham,* 1885) who finds the idleness of wealth discomfiting. He "rises," and finds purpose and happiness again, only when he loses his fortune and is forced to return to productive work. Howells even convinced an old friend from Ohio, former president Rutherford B. Hayes, to go on record as an advocate of the peaceful abolition of capitalism.

DEFENDERS OF THE FAITH

Such a barrage of criticism did not, of course, go unanswered. At the same time that great wealth was taking its knocks, it was reaping the praise of defenders. In part, like the critics, they drew on traditional American values to justify the new social system. In part, also like the critics, the defenders created new philosophies, original to the era of industrial capitalism.

Social Darwinism

Intellectuals at peace with their era found a justification for great wealth and even dubious business ethics in a series of books, essays, and lectures by the British philosopher Herbert Spencer. Because Spencer seemed to apply Charles Darwin's celebrated theory of biological evolution to human society, his philosophy is known as social Darwinism.

According to Spencer, as in the world of animals and plants, where species compete and those best adapted sur-

---

A Survival of the Fittest Sampler

We have unmistakable proof that throughout all past time, there has been a ceaseless devouring of the weak by the strong.

Herbert Spencer

The ultimate result of shielding men from the effects of folly is to fill the world with fools.

Herbert Spencer

Whatever capital you divert to the support of a shiftless and good-for-nothing person is so much diverted from some other employment, and that means from somebody else.

William Graham Sumner

The price which society pays for the law of competition . . . is . . . great; but the advantages of this law are . . . greater still, for it is to this law that we owe our wonderful material development, which brings improved conditions in its train. But whether the law be benign or not, we must say of it . . . : It is here; we cannot evade it; no substitutes for it have been found; and while the law may be sometimes hard for the individual, it is best for the race, because it ensures the survival of the fittest in every department.

Andrew Carnegie

---

vive, the fittest people rise to the top in the social competition for riches. Eventually, in the dog-eat-dog world, they alone survive. "If they are sufficiently complete to live," Spencer wrote, "they do live, and it is well that they should live. If they are not sufficiently complete to live, they die and it is best they should die."

The tough-mindedness of social Darwinism made Spencer immensely popular among American businessmen who were as proud of their practicality as of their success. An Englishman, Spencer was never as celebrated in his own country as he was in the United States. Although a vain man, he was mortified by the adulation heaped on him at banquets sponsored by American academics and rich businessmen. Social Darwinism accounted for brutal business practices and underhanded methods with a shrug, justifying them as "natural," the law of the jungle.

The language of social Darwinism crept into the vocabulary of businessmen and politicians who represented business interests. John D. Rockefeller Jr. described the growth of a large business as "the survival of the fittest." But neither he nor many other American millionaires were true social Darwinists. The very ruthlessness of the theory—"Nature, red in tooth and claw"—made it unpalatable to men and women like the Rockefellers, who, in their personal lives, were deeply committed to traditional religious values. Moreover, businessmen are rarely intellectuals, and Spencer's philosophy and writing style were as murky as crude oil. Understanding him demanded careful study, for which businessmen rarely had time. Spencer's explanation of the new society was most influential among intellectuals who wanted to snuggle up to the rich.

William Graham Sumner

The most important American social Darwinist, William Graham Sumner, was too consistent to snuggle up to the industrial elite. He was uncompromising in his opposition to aiding the poor, putting government restrictions on business practices, and interfering in any way whatsoever with the law of the jungle. "The men who are competent to organize great enterprises and to handle great amounts of capital," he wrote, "must be found by natural selection, not political election."

However, Sumner also opposed government actions on behalf of capitalists. He opposed protective tariffs; to subsidize American manufacturers by taxing imports was just as unnatural as regulating the growth of trusts. If American manufacturers were not fit to compete with European manufacturers in a free market, Sumner said, they were not fit to survive. Likewise, Sumner opposed government intervention in strikes on behalf of employers. He believed that the strike was a natural test of the fitness of the employers' and the workers' causes. The outcome of a strike determined which side was right.

To businessmen who used government trade policy and courts to their own purposes, Sumner's impartial applications of "natural law" were going too far. They had no objection to the right kind of government action.

After the turn of the century, the principles of social Darwinism were turned on their head by the sociologist Lester Frank Ward of Brown University. Whereas Sumner argued that nature in society must be allowed to operate without restraint, Ward suggested that human society had evolved to a point where natural evolution could be guided by government policy. Just as farmers improved fruit trees and ranchers improved livestock through selective breeding, government could improve society by intervening in the naturally slow evolutionary process. Ward's "reform Darwinism" influenced two generations of twentieth-century liberals.

The Gospel of Success

The "gospel of success" had far more influence among nineteenth-century capitalists than social Darwinism did. The United States was built on the desire to prosper, believers in the gospel of success said. Therefore, if competition for riches was a virtue, what was wrong with winning? Far from a reason for anxiety or evidence of social immorality, the fabulous fortunes of America's wealthy families were an index of their virtue. The Carnegies and Morgans deserved their money. John D. Rockefeller was quoted as saying of his money, "God gave it to me."

Success manuals, books purporting to show how anyone could become a millionaire, were read as avidly as the works of George and Bellamy, and by far more people. All much the same, the manuals drew on the assumptions that hard work, honesty, frugality, loyalty to employers and part-

ners, and other bourgeois virtues inevitably led to success. Having succeeded, America's millionaires deserved not resentment but admiration and imitation.

A Baptist minister from Philadelphia, Russell B. Conwell, made a fortune delivering a lecture on the same theme. In "Acres of Diamonds," which the eloquent preacher delivered to paying audiences more than 6,000 times, Conwell said that great wealth was a great blessing. Not only could every American be rich, but every American *should* be rich. If a man failed, the fault lay within himself, not with society. "There is not a poor person in the United States," Conwell said, "who was not made poor by his own shortcomings." The opportunities, the acres of diamonds, were everywhere, waiting to be collected. Those who already were rich were by definition virtuous. "Ninety-eight out of one hundred of the rich men of America are honest. That is why they are rich." Conwell was a popular man in honest circles.

Horatio Alger and Ragged Dick

Through the 130 boys' novels written by another minister, Horatio Alger, the gospel of success was conveyed to the younger generation. Alger's books sold 20 million copies between 1867 and 1899, and a battalion of imitators accounted for millions more.

Alger was a terrible writer. His prose was wooden, his characters were snipped from cardboard, and his plots were

▲ Horatio Alger's "Ragged Dick" books for boys preached that living a virtuous life would lead to material success.

variations on two or three simple themes. All assumed as a given that one of the paramount goals of life was to get money. All taught that wealth was within the grasp of all. Most of Alger's heroes are lads grappling with destitution. They are also honest, hardworking, loyal to their employers, and clean living. Ragged Dick, Alger's first hero and the prototype for Tattered Tom, Lucky Luke Larkin, and dozens of others, is insufferably courteous and never misses church.

Curiously, Ragged Dick and Alger's other characters rarely, if ever, got rich slowly through hard work. At the beginning of the final chapter, the hero is often as bad off as he was on page 1. Then, however, he is presented with what amounts to a visitation of grace, a divine gift as a reward for his virtues. The child of an industrialist falls off the Staten Island Ferry; or a rich girl stumbles into the path of a runaway brewery wagon drawn by panicked horses; or she slips into the Niagara River just above the falls. Because the Alger hero acts quickly, rescuing her, the heroic lad is rewarded with a job, marriage to the daughter, and, eventually, the grateful father's fortune. While appealing to the adolescent boy's yen for adventure, the novels also touched the American evangelical belief in divine grace. Just as he did with Rockefeller, God gave Ragged Dick his money as a reward for his virtues.

Philanthropy

The flaw in the gospel of success as a justification of great fortunes was the obvious fact that many rich men got their money by practicing the opposite of the touted virtues—dishonesty, betrayal of partners and employers, reckless speculation—and they grew richer while living a life of sumptuous, even decadent, leisure. John D. Rockefeller's business practices were not nearly as unethical as his many enemies said, but there was no question that he cut ethical corners. Similar suspicions surrounded practically every rich family in the country.

Perhaps in part to compensate for the negative marks on their reputations, many wealthy businessmen turned to philanthropy as a kind of retroactive justification of their fortunes. Horatio Alger supported institutions that housed homeless boys in New York City. Russell B. Conwell founded Temple University, where poor young men could study very cheaply and improve their prospects. Leland Stanford built a wholly new "Harvard of the West" in California—Stanford University. Rockefeller and other industrial millionaires gave huge sums to their churches and to universities. In retirement, Rockefeller took particular interest in helping American blacks to break out of the prison that racial discrimination had built around them. Spelman College in Georgia existed only because of Rockefeller's gifts.

Andrew Carnegie devised a coherent theory that justified fabulous fortunes on the basis of stewardship. In a celebrated essay titled "Wealth," he argued that the unrestricted pursuit of riches made American society vital and strong, but it also made the man who succeeded a steward, or trustee. He had an obligation to distribute his money where

▲ *Andrew Carnegie, second from the right, with other businessmen-philanthropists at Tuskegee Institute, the most famous African American college in the United States. Tuskegee president Booker T. Washington is front and center. John D. Rockefeller was friendly to African American charities too. Spelman College in Georgia was named for his wife.*

it would provide opportunities for poor people to join the competition of the next generation. Carnegie said that the rich man who died rich, died a failure.

Carnegie retired from business in 1901 and devoted the rest of his life to granting money to libraries, schools, and useful social institutions. Despite his extraordinary generosity, he died a multimillionaire.

THE LIFESTYLE OF THE VERY RICH

Probably nothing reconciled ordinary Americans to the existence of multimillionaires more than the fascination of the multitudes with the splendor amid which the very rich lived. As Thorstein Veblen, an eccentric sociologist, observed in several books written at the end of the century, the very wealthy literally lived to spend money for the sake of proving that they had money. Veblen called this showy extravagance "conspicuous consumption," and the propensity to throw it away, "conspicuous waste."

Conspicuous Consumption

Having much more money than they could possibly put to good use, the very rich competed in spending it by hosting lavish parties, building extravagant palaces, purchasing

The Last Dance of the Idle Rich

In the winter of 1896–1897, Americans were wrestling with a depression worse than the depression of the 1870s. Businesses had failed by the thousands. Several million people were out of work. Perhaps a hundred thousand people had been evicted from farms and homes. The treasuries of charitable organizations were drained; some had closed their doors. Jobless people had marched on Washington; others had rioted; yet others plodded on day by day—gathering coal along railroad tracks or picking through the garbage pails behind expensive restaurants.

At breakfast in his Fifth Avenue mansion, Bradley Martin, one of high society's grandest adornments, had an idea. "I think it would be a good thing if we got up something," he told his wife and his brother, Frederick. "There seems to be a great deal of depression in trade; suppose we send out invitations to a concert."

Mrs. Martin observed that a concert would benefit only foreigners. Most professional musicians were German or Italian; she wanted to do something for Americans. "I've got a far better idea," she said. "Let us give a costume ball at so short notice that our guests won't have time to get their dresses from Paris. That will give an impetus to trade that nothing else will."

The conversation was recorded by Frederick Townshend Martin with no intention of making his brother and sister-in-law look ridiculous. In fact, he justified their economic theories, explaining that "many New York shops sold out brocades and silks which had been lying in their stockrooms for years."

The ball was held on February 10, 1897, in the ballroom of the Waldorf-Astoria Hotel, which had been decorated to resemble the palace of the French kings at Versailles. To the Martins' set, it was a glorious success. According to experts, there was never such a display of jewels in New York. August Belmont came in gold-inlaid armor that cost him $10,000. The costumes of others were inferior only by comparison. One woman said that in order to help the particularly hard-pressed Indians, she had had Native Americans make her Pocahontas costume. Bradley Martin made a curious selection. As the host at Versailles, he had first claim to be Louis XIV, the Sun King, who had built the great palace and was universally conceded to be the most glorious of the French monarchs. But Bradley chose to be his great-grandson, Louis XV. He would not have wanted to be Louis XVI, who had been beheaded because of his and his predecessors' extravagance in a country where the poor suffered wretched misery.

"Everyone said it was the most brilliant of the kind ever seen in America."

Not quite everyone. Even before the first waltz, Martin and his friends were being vilified from pulpit, editorial desk, and political platform for their callous decadence in a difficult time. Much more significant, the ball was criticized by more than one business leader. If idle heirs such as the vapid Martin did not know that such affairs caused resentment, class hatred, and (in more than one instance in the past) social revolution, hardheaded businessmen did. Two years after the ball, in his book *The Theory of the Leisure Class,* sociologist Thorstein Veblen would give a name to Bradley Martin's lifestyle, "conspicuous consumption." However, already by that time, America's wealthy were learning to enjoy their riches more quietly. Indeed, looking back after several decades, two distinguished historians, Charles and Mary Beard, called the Bradley Martin ball of 1897 the "climax of lavish expenditure" in the United States. "This grand ball of the plutocrats astounded the country, then in the grip of a prolonged business depression with its attendant unemployment, misery, and starvation."

It was not only the fear of social upheaval that wrote an end to conspicuous consumption on a grand scale. To a large extent, high-society affairs like the ball were the doings of women, the wives and daughters of rich businessmen. After the turn of the century, many of them rebelled against their enforced idleness and frivolity and began to take an interest, sometimes a leading role, in social and political causes: votes for women, of course, but also Prohibition, suppression of the "white slave racket" (prostitution), amelioration of lower-class suffering, and other social programs of the Progressive Era.

Not Mrs. Bradley Martin and her husband, however. Unreconstructable denizens of the ballroom, they carried on as before, but not in New York. The ball was so unpopular there that city hall slapped a large tax increase on the Martin mansion on Fifth Avenue. In a huff, the Martins moved to London. Brother Frederick Townshend Martin wrote of this relocation with an air of despondency; the United States had lost two valuable citizens.

---

huge yachts that were good for little but show, adorning themselves with costly clothing and jewelry, and buying European titles for their daughters.

High-society parties lasting but a few hours cost more than $100,000. At one, hosted by the self-proclaimed "prince of spenders," Harry Lehr, a hundred dogs dined on "fricassee of bones" and gulped down shredded dog biscuit prepared by a French chef. The guests at one New York banquet ate their meal while mounted on horses (trays balanced on the animals' shoulders). The horses munched oats out of sterling silver feedbags, possibly making more noise than their riders. At a costume affair, guests boasted that they had spent more than $10,000 each on their fancy dress.

It was the golden age of yachting. Cornelius Vanderbilt's *North Star* was 250 feet long. Albert C. Burrage's *Aztec* carried 270 tons of coal; it could steam 5,500 miles without calling at a port for fuel. As on land, J. P. Morgan was champion at sea. He owned three successively larger, faster, and more opulent yachts called *Corsair.* Morgan had a sense of humor; a corsair is a pirate.

Nowhere was consumption more conspicuous than at upper-class resorts like Newport, Rhode Island. A summer "cottage" of 30 rooms, used only three months a year, cost $1 million. Coal baron E. J. Berwind spent $1.5 million to build his vacation house, the Elms. William K. Vanderbilt outdid everyone with Marble House, which cost $2 million; the furniture inside it cost $9 million.

Those places were for vacations. At home in the cities, the millionaires created neighborhoods of mansions, such as New York's Fifth Avenue, a thoroughfare given over to grand houses for 20 blocks; Chicago's Gold Coast, which loomed over the city's lakeshore; and San Francisco's Nob Hill, from which palaces looked down on the city like the castles of medieval barons.

A Lord in the Family

Another fad of the very rich was the rush during the 1880s and 1890s to marry daughters of magnates to titled Europeans. Nothing better dramatized the aristocratic pretensions of the new elite. Wealthy families took pride in the price they paid to have an earl or a duke as a son-in-law. They were win-win arrangements: The American daughter got a title to wear to Newport; the impoverished European aristocrat got money with which to maintain himself in fine wines, horses, and hounds.

Thus, heiress Alice Thaw was embarrassed on her honeymoon as countess of Yarmouth when creditors seized her husband's luggage. She had to wire her father for money to get it out of hock. Helena Zimmerman, the daughter of a coal and iron millionaire from Cincinnati, married the duke of Manchester. For 20 years, their bills were paid by the duchess's father out of the labor of workers living on subsistence wages.

The most famous American aristocrats were the heiresses of two of the original robber barons, Jay Gould and Cornelius Vanderbilt. Anna Gould became the Countess Boni de Castellane. Before Anna divorced him in order to marry his cousin, the higher-ranking Prince de Sagan, the count extracted more than $5 million from Jay Gould's purse, more than any American businessman ever had. Consuelo Vanderbilt was married against her wishes into one of the proudest families in England, the Churchills. Both when Consuelo married the duke of Marlborough and when she divorced him, the payoff ran to several million.

Women as Decor

The role of young heiresses in the game of conspicuous waste helps illustrate the curious role of the women of the new social class. They were idler than their menfolk. A role in business or public life was denied them, and they had none of the homemaking duties of middle-class women to occupy their time.

What, then, to do? In effect, the women of the wealthiest classes became their families' chief conspicuous consumers. The rich woman's role was to reflect her husband's accomplishment in amassing wealth; she was a glittering mannequin for costly clothing and jewelry. Mrs. George Gould, daughter-in-law of Jay, went through life known for little more than the fact that she owned a pearl necklace worth $500,000. No one ever mentioned Mrs. Gould in any other context. Her life revolved around the moments when she entered ballrooms, all eyes on her pearls.

Women's fashions were designed to emphasize their wearers' idleness. Indeed, fashion, by its very nature, is conspicuously wasteful. In keeping up with changes, the whole point of fashion, the wealthy woman demonstrated that it made no dent in her husband's fortune if she annually discarded last year's expensive clothing to make room in her closet for the latest from Paris.

Fashion reflected social status in other ways. When wealthy women laced themselves up in crippling steel and bone corsets, which made it difficult for them to move, let alone perform any physical work, they were making it clear that they did not have to do such work; they were purely decorative.

Photograph by Byron. The Byron Collection, Museum of the City of New York

▲ *A banquet of wealthy gentlemen in a New York restaurant, probably Delmonico's. Women were beginning to dine at elegant restaurants by the end of the century, but they were still largely masculine institutions.*

Men's clothing reflected social status, too. The tall silk hat, the badge of the capitalist, was a completely useless headgear. It offered neither protection nor warmth. But wearing one did prevent a man from so much as bending down to dust his patent leather shoes. "White collar," displaying clean linen at wrist and neck, made it clear that the wearer did nothing that might soil his clothing.

Unlikely Neighbors

For the most part, ordinary Americans knew of the shenanigans of the very rich only through hearsay and the popular press. Farmers and factory workers did not vacation at Newport or attend costume balls or ducal weddings at Blenheim Palace. The nature of urban life in the late nineteenth century was such, however, that the idle rich could not conceal their extravagance from the middle and lower classes.

You Can Take It with You

At the Vanderbilt family tomb on Staten Island, watchmen punched a time clock every hour on the hour around the clock. William Vanderbilt, son of Cornelius Vanderbilt, had a deathly fear of grave robbers.

The rich employed legions of servants to maintain their mansions. The grandeur and waste of upper-class life were well known to these poorly paid people. (Two million women worked in domestic service at the end of the century.) More important, because it was impossible to commute long distances in the congested cities, whether for business or social life, the wealthy lived not in isolated suburbs but close to the centers of New York, Boston, Philadelphia, Chicago, and other great cities.

The tradesmen who made daily deliveries of groceries, meat, vegetables and fruit, ice, coal (for heating), and other necessities, not to mention repairmen and those who delivered durable goods, became familiar with the luxury their customers enjoyed. Marginal workers who were employed in the service or light manufacturing industries of the city center walked daily past palaces and saw the rich come and go in lacquered carriages tended by flunkies in livery.

Popular Culture

In newspapers aimed at a mass readership, in popular songs, and in the melodramas favored by working people, the idleness and extravagance of the filthy rich were favorite themes. The wealthy were depicted with a mixture of envy and resentment. New York's Tin Pan Alley, the center of the

▲ *Beautiful Consuelo Vanderbilt did not want to marry the duke of Marlborough, but such a prize—few other dukes ranked as high as he—was too much for her parents to resist. Consuelo was miserable and later divorced the dissolute duke, costing the Vanderbilts yet more money.*

In the popular melodramas of the day, simple plays with little subtlety of character and a completely predictable plot, right-living poor people were pitted against an unscrupulous rich villain. "You are only a shopgirl," said the high-society lady in a typical play. "An honest shopgirl," replied the heroine in stilted language, "as far above a fashionable idler as heaven is above earth!" (The poor but virtuous shopgirl was often rewarded in the final act by marriage to a rich young man; presumably, when the curtain fell, she embraced the life of idleness that she had condemned through two and a half acts.)

Juicy Scandals

Ordinary people studiously followed the scandals that periodically rocked high society. In 1872, "Jubilee Jim" Fisk was shot to death by a rival for the affections of his showgirl mistress, Josie Mansfield. Newspaper readers could find a moral in the fact that Fisk's great wealth and power could not save him from a violent death at the age of 38. Nevertheless, a good part of the story's appeal were the details of Fisk's sumptuous personal life, on which the newspapers lovingly dwelled.

Even more sensational was the 1906 murder of architect Stanford White by millionaire Harry Thaw. During his trial, Thaw accused White of having seduced his beautiful fiancée, Evelyn Nesbit. Her testimony concerning the famous White's peculiarities behind closed doors simultaneously titillated the public and served as a moral justification for the murder. (Thaw went free.)

Such scandals were the stock in trade of nationally circulated periodicals appealing to working people, such as the *Police Gazette* and *Frank Leslie's Illustrated Newspaper*. By the end of the century, many large daily papers also took to bumping conventional news to back pages when an upper-class scandal came up in the courts.

sheet music industry, preached a combination of pity for the "bird in a gilded cage," the wealthy woman, and the traditional moral that because poor people worked, they were more virtuous.

for FURTHER READING

Most of the works cited in "For Further Reading" in Chapter 27 are relevant here, particularly Vincent P. DeSantis, *The Shaping of Modern America, 1877–1916,* 1973; John A. Garraty, *The New Commonwealth, 1877–1890,* 1968; Samuel P. Hays, *The Response to Industrialism, 1885–1914,* 1957; Glenn Porter, *The Rise of Big Business, 1860–1910,* 1973; and Robert H. Wiebe, *The Search for Order,* 1967. Also see Sigmund Diamond, *The Reputation of American Businessmen,* 1959; and L. Galambos, *The Public Image of Big Business in America,* 1975.

Justifications and defenses of the new order are studied in John G. Cawelti, *Apostles of the Self-Made Man in America,* 1966; Sidney Fine, *Laissez-Faire and the Welfare State: A Study of Conflict in American Thought, 1865–1901,* 1956; Richard Hofstadter, *Social Darwinism in American Thought,* 1944; Edward C. Kirkland, *Dream and Thought in the Business Community,* 1956; and Irwin Wyllie, *The Self-Made Man in America,* 1954.

Criticisms of the new commonwealth are the focus in C. A. Barker, *Henry George,* 1955; Gabriel Kolko, *Railroads and Regulation,* 1965; Samuel T. McSeveney, *The Politics of Depression: Political Behavior in the Northeast, 1893–1896,* 1972; Andrew Sinclair, *Corsair: The Life of J. Pierpont Morgan,* 1981; John L. Thomas, *Alternative America: Henry George, Edward Bellamy, Henry Demarest Lloyd,* 1983; and Thorstein Veblen, *The Theory of the Leisure Class,* 1899.

The Granger Collection, New York

Visit the source collections at http://ajaccess.wadsworth.com and http://infotrac.thomsonlearning.com, and use the Search function with the following key terms to explore documents, images, audio and video clips, articles, and commentary related to the material in this chapter:

Edward Bellamy   J. P. Morgan

Haymarket riot   Sherman Antitrust Act

Additional resources, exercises, and Internet links related to this chapter are available on *The American Past* Web site: http://history.wadsworth.com/americanpast7e.

HISTORY ONLINE

Horatio Alger

www.washburn.edu/sobu/broach/algerres.html

The man who preached the gospel of success to boys, including parodies of Alger heroes.

Evelyn Nesbit

http://evelynnesbit.com/players.html

Multi-media presentation of the Harry Thaw trial, done in the sensationalist style with which Americans devoured the sex and murder scandal among New York's wealthy.

WE WHO BUILT AMERICA

Factories and Immigrants

So at last I was going to America! Really, really going at last! The boundaries burst! The arch of heaven soared! A million suns shone out for every star. The winds rushed in from outer space, roaring in my ear, "America! America!"

Mary Antin

L ELAND STANFORD AND James J. Hill thought of themselves as the men who built the railroads. Journalists referred to Andrew Carnegie as the nation's greatest steelmaker. In the popular mind, industries were associated with individuals, just as battles were identified with generals: Sherman marched across Georgia, and Grant took Richmond. Vanderbilt ran the New York Central; Philip D. Armour and Gustavus Swift put cheap fresh meat on the dining-room table. J. P. Morgan even spoke of his hobby, yachting, in personal terms. "You can do business with anyone," he huffed, "but you can only sail a boat with a gentleman."

In reality, Morgan merely decided when and where the boat was to go. It took 85 grimy stokers and hardhanded sailors to get the *Corsair* out of New York Harbor and safely into Newport or Venice. Stanford, Hill, Rockefeller, Carnegie, Swift, Armour, and other great businessmen oversaw the creation of industrial America, but the edifice was built by anonymous millions of men and women who wielded the shovels and tended the machines that whirred and whined in the factories and mills.

A NEW WAY OF LIFE

America's working people could not be kept below decks like the crew of the *Corsair*. While the population of the United States more than doubled between 1860 and 1900, the size of the working class quadrupled. In 1860, 1.5 million Americans made their living in workshops and mills, and another 700,000, in mining and construction. By 1900, 6 million people worked in manufacturing, and 2.3 million, in mining and construction. Industrial workers, once negligible in numbers, constituted a large and distinct social class.

Bigger Factories, Better Technology

The size of the workplace also grew, a fact of profound importance to the quality of working people's lives. In 1870, the average workshop in the United States employed eight workers. It was owned by an individual or by partners who

Culver Pictures, Inc.

▲ *Andrew Carnegie's Homestead Mill, the capital of his steelmaking empire. It was by far the largest factory in the world for decades and wracked in 1892 by a violent strike.*

lived nearby and personally supervised the business, often working at the bench with their employees. Like it or not, kind, callous, or cruel as individuals might be, such bosses were personally involved in the lives of their workers. They heard of births of children and deaths of parents. They discussed wages, hours, and conditions in the shop face to face with their employees. Even Pittsburgh's iron and steel mills, the largest factories in the country, employed on average just 90 workers.

By 1900, industrial workers labored in shops averaging 25 employees. Plants employing 1,000 men and women were common. The average number of employees in Pittsburgh steel plants was 1,600, and a few companies listed 10,000 on the payroll; Carnegie Steel employed 23,000. The men who directed such firms might never step on the factory floor. They were interested in wages, hours, and conditions only as entries in the ledgers that lined the walls of their offices.

The increased application of steam power and improved machinery affected workers in other ways. The highly skilled craftsman, trained for years in the use of hand tools, ceased to be the backbone of manufacturing. Not many crafts disappeared (as they would in the twentieth century). A few, like the machinist's trade, increased in importance. But in most industries, machines took over from artisans, performing their jobs more quickly and often better.

Many machines were tended by unskilled or semiskilled men, women, and children who merely guided the device at its task. Unlike craftsmen, these workers were interchangeable, easily replaced because the jobs they did required little training. Consequently, they could be poorly paid, and they commanded scant respect from employers, small businessmen, professionals, politicians, and skilled workers. "If I wanted boiler iron," said one industrialist, "I would go out on the market and buy it where I could get it cheapest; and if I wanted to employ men I would do the same."

Wages

In numbers of dollars in the pay envelope, wages declined during the final decades of the century. However, "real wages"—purchasing power—rose as the cost of food, clothing, and housing dropped more radically than hourly pay did. Taken as a whole, the industrial working class enjoyed almost 50 percent more purchasing power in 1900 than it had in 1860.

But this statistic can be misleading: The skilled "aristocracy of labor"—locomotive engineers, machinists, master carpenters, printers, and other highly trained artisans—improved their situation much more than did the unskilled workers at the bottom of the pile. The average annual wage for all manufacturing workers in 1900 was only $435, or $8.37 a week. Unskilled workers were paid about 10 cents an hour on average, about $5.50 a week. A girl of 13, tending a loom in a textile mill, might take home as little as $2 a week after various fines (for being late to work, for example) were deducted from her pay. In 1904, sociologist Robert Hunter estimated that one American in eight lived in poverty.

Hours

Hours on the job varied. Most government employees enjoyed an 8-hour day. Skilled workers, especially in the building trades (bricklayers, carpenters, plumbers), generally worked 10. Elsewhere, a factory worker was counted lucky if he or she worked a 12-hour day, as telephone operators did. During the summer months, many mills ran from sunup to sundown, as long as 16 hours—with only one shift.

The average workweek was 66 hours long in 1860, and 55 hours in 1910. People were on the job five and a half or six days a week; a half-day Saturday was considered a holiday. In industries that had to run around the clock, such as steel (the furnaces could not be shut down), the workforce was divided into two shifts on seven-day schedules. Each shift worked 12 hours. At the end of two weeks, the day workers switched shifts with the night workers. This meant a vacation of 24 hours once a month. The price of the break was working 24 hours straight two weeks later.

True holidays were few. However, because of the swings in the business cycle, factory workers had plenty of unwanted time off. Some industries were seasonal. Coal miners could expect to be without wages for weeks or even months during the summer, when people did not heat their homes.

Conditions

Although some employers were safety conscious, the number of injuries and deaths on the job are chilling by today's standards. Between 1870 and 1910, there were 10,000 major boiler explosions in American factories—almost one per workday. Between 1880 and 1900, 35,000 American workers were killed on the job, one every two days. Railroads were particularly dangerous. Every year, one railroad worker in 26 was seriously injured, and one in 400 was killed. In 1910, 3,383 railway workers were killed, 95,671 injured.

In many cases, injured workers and the survivors of those who were killed on the job received no compensation. In others, compensation amounted to little more than burial expenses. In the coalfields, mine owners were thought generous to a family if they allowed a dead miner's son younger than the regulation age to take his father's job in the pit.

Employer liability law was stacked against workers. Courts held that employers were not liable for an injury on the job unless the employee could prove he in no way contributed to his accident. Short of the collapse of a factory roof or the boss's son running amok with a revolver, total lack of responsibility for a mishap was difficult to prove. Courts ruled that if an employee was hurt because his machine was dangerous but he was aware of the danger, the employer was not liable.

Occupational diseases—the coal miner's "black lung," the cotton mill worker's "white lung," and the hard-rock miner's silicosis—were not recognized as the employer's responsibility. Poisoning resulting from work with chemicals was rarely identified as job related.

COMPOSITION OF THE WORKFORCE

Skilled workers were usually native-born white males. Unskilled jobs were filled by children, women, and recent immigrants. In many industrial towns, half to three-quarters of the workforce was foreign-born.

Children

In 1900, the socialist writer John Spargo estimated that 1.8 million children under 16 years of age were employed full time. They did all but the heaviest jobs. Girls as young as 12 tended spinning machines in textile mills. "Bobbin boys" of 10 hauled wooden boxes filled with spindles from spinning rooms to weaving rooms and back again. Children swept filings in machine shops. Boys of 8 were found working the "breakers" at coal mines, handpicking slate from anthracite in filthy, frigid wooden sheds.

In sweatshops in city tenements, whole families sewed clothing, rolled cigars, or made small items by hand; children worked as soon as they were able to master the simplest tasks. In cities, children practically monopolized messenger service work, light delivery, and some kinds of huckstering.

▲ *An oyster cannery in Louisiana. Women are shucking the oysters, a job paying precious little. They have brought their daughters to work, one not more than four years old. Shucking oysters was her most likely future.*

In part, child labor was the fruit of greed. On the grounds that children had no dependents to support, employers paid them less than they paid adults, even when the jobs were identical. In southern textile towns, the "mill daddy" became a stock figure. Unable to find work because his own children could be hired for less, the mill daddy was reduced to carrying lunches to the factory and tossing them over the fence each noon.

But child labor is also an example of cultural lag. Children had always worked. It took time for society to recognize that the nature of labor in the world of the dynamo and factory was different from chores on a family farm. Relations on the farm or in the small shop were personal. The limited capacity of children, particularly their fatigue when set to tedious, repetitive tasks, was easy to recognize and take into account. Placed in a niche in a massive factory, the child laborer was a number on the payroll.

Women

The first industrial workers were female, partly because the first modern industry was textiles and women had been the mainstay of cloth making in western culture, partly because the founders of the first American textile mills—like the Lowells—could not imagine factory work as a suitable lifetime career for a male head of household. In time, the heavy nature of much factory work resulted in an industrial workforce that was predominantly male. Nevertheless, the difficulty of supporting a family on one income forced many working-class women to continue to labor for wages even after they married. In 1900, almost 20 percent of the total workforce was female. About half the workers in textiles were women, and the percentage in the needle trades was much higher.

With few exceptions, women were paid less than men for performing the same tasks for the same number of hours. Abysmally low pay was particularly characteristic of the largest female occupation. In 1900, 2 million women were employed for subsistence wages or less in domestic service: cooking, cleaning, and tending the vanities and children of the better-off. In an age before household appliances and other mechanical conveniences, even middle-class families had a maid.

Women in the Workforce

There was at least one woman in each occupation listed by the Census Bureau in 1890. More than 225,000 were running farms, and 1,143 listed their occupation as clergyman. Women outnumbered men as teachers and as waiters (by 5 to 1). There were 28 female lumberjacks. In all the United States, however, out of 12,856 wheelwrights (makers and repairers of wagon wheels), there was only one woman.

No Blacks Need Apply

Although blacks found work in southern turpentine mills and coal mines, and factory jobs in the most menial positions—sweepers, for example—most industrial work went to whites. African Americans remained concentrated in agriculture and in low-paying service occupations, working as domestic servants, waiters, porters, and the like. In 1900, more than 80 percent of the black population lived in the South, most of them on the land.

The industrial color line, drawn everywhere, was inflexible in the South. When the cotton textile industry moved south at the end of the century, mill owners drew on the poor white population for its workforce. Implicitly, and sometimes explicitly, employees were informed that if they were troublesome (that is, if they complained about wages, hours, and conditions), the companies would replace them with blacks. Their own racism kept southern mill workers the poorest industrial laborers in the country. Rather than risk the loss of their jobs to the hated blacks, they accepted their low wages and standard of living with little resistance.

THE ORGANIZATION OF LABOR

However poorly industrial work paid, it was preferable to the alternatives. The majority of workers, most of the time, tacitly accepted inadequate wages, hours, and conditions of labor. They expressed their discontent (or desperation) in ways as ancient as civilization. Absenteeism was high, particularly on "blue Monday" after a beery Sunday. In good times, when getting another job was not difficult, workers needing a vacation for health, sanity, or just plain relaxation quit on a minute's notice.

Sabotage was a word yet to be invented, but the practice was well understood. When the pace of work reached the breaking point, or a foreman stepped beyond the bounds of tolerable behavior, it was easy enough to jam or damage a machine so that it appeared to be an accident—and take a break while it was fixed. An angry worker who made up his mind to quit might decide literally to throw a monkey wrench into the works or to slash the leather belts that turned the factory's looms, drills, stampers, or lathes. For obvious reasons, the incidence of this kind of labor protest is impossible to quantify.

A Heritage of Violence

Violence was common. During the nationwide railroad strike of 1877, an unorganized, spontaneous outbreak that had its roots in the depression, workers did not merely walk off the job; they stormed in mobs into railroad yards and set trains and buildings afire. In a few places, they fought pitched gun battles with company guards and, toward the end of the unsuccessful strike, with troops called out to put them down.

At Andrew Carnegie's Homestead Works in 1892, a strike led by the Amalgamated Association of Iron and Steel

▲ *A woman and a teenage girl in a southern cotton mill. The girl was by no means the youngest employee in the factory. Younger girls and "bobbin boys" would have been kept out of sight when this posed photograph was taken.*

Workers besieged the giant factory and forced the retreat of a barge bringing 300 armed guards into the town. Then, in 1894, came another nationwide labor crisis when a strike at the Pullman Palace Car works in Illinois led to a widespread railroad strike and the massive intervention of the federal government.

George Pullman's employees, who built bunk-bed sleeping cars for railroads—"pullmans"—as well as elegant private cars, were required to live in a company-owned town, Pullman, Illinois. The town of Pullman was considered a model of paternalistic employer goodwill. Workers lived in well-built cottages, and the town provided a full range of services. However, when a decline in business prompted George Pullman to cut wages by 25 percent, he did not cut rents and utility bills in the town. Some 4,000 employees responded by joining the American Railway Union; a majority of them struck the Pullman plant in May.

A few weeks later, American Railway Union members on several of the nation's major railroads voted to support the strikers by boycotting pullman cars. That is, they refused to hook pullmans to trains. A federal judge ordered the boycott to cease, saying that the boycotters were interfering with the United States mail. (Sometimes, mail cars had to be dis-connected and reconnected in order to cut out the pullmans.) Over the protests of Illinois governor John Peter Altgeld, President Grover Cleveland ordered federal troops into Chicago. This enraged railroad workers from California to the East Coast. They destroyed millions in railroad property. Not until mid-July did the trains begin to run again. The American Railway Union was destroyed, and its leader, Eugene V. Debs, was jailed for disobeying the court's order.

The Molly Maguires

During the early 1870s, many Irish coal miners in northeastern Pennsylvania gave up on the possibility of peaceably improving the conditions of their unhealthy and dangerous work. Within a fraternal lodge, the Ancient Order of Hibernians, they formed a secret society called the Molly Maguires. The Mollys launched a campaign of terrorism against the mine owners and supervisors. They systematically destroyed mine property and murdered loyal company men.

Because of the ethnic aspect of the conflict—almost all the miners were Irish, and almost all the bosses were American or Cornish—the Molly Maguires were able to maintain an effective secrecy. Employers did not know who they were, how numerous they were, or how much support they had in the community. But the mine owners had the last word. They brought in an Irish American undercover detective, James McParland, an employee of the Pinkerton Agency, which specialized in breaking up unions. McParland infiltrated the Mollys and gathered evidence that led to the hanging of 19 men.

The Union Makes Us Strong

Violence comes naturally to human beings, but it is the longest of shots, even immoral, as a mode of protest in a stable, open society. At the very least, it wins few friends. Sensible advocates of working people called for organization—union—as working people's answer to their material needs and, in some cases, called for reforming America's social order. Workingmen's associations had been buttresses of Jacksonian democracy in New York. By the 1870s, skilled workers, such as machinists, iron molders, carpenters, locomotive engineers, and firemen, had formed effective local associations to improve their working lives.

For the most part, these scattered unions had little to do with one another. Developing at a time when industry was decentralized, the unions inevitably lagged behind employers in recognizing the need for national organization. By the end of the Civil War, however, the outlines of the new industrial order were sketched in. In 1866, William Sylvis, a visionary iron puddler (a man who made castings from molds), founded the National Labor Union (NLU) and devoted the last three years of his life to traveling by foot around the northeastern states, rallying workers of many occupations in churches and fraternal lodges.

Sylvis believed that the workers' future depended on political action. He formed alliances with a number of reform groups, including the women's suffrage movement and farmers' organizations lobbying for a cheap currency. The National Labor party put up candidates in the presidential election of 1872 but with so poor a showing that the party and the union folded. In 1872, the NLU had a membership of 400,000 but disappeared within two years.

The Knights of Labor

A different kind of national labor union had already emerged. Organized in 1869 by tailors led by Uriah P. Stephens, the Noble and Holy Order of the Knights of Labor

▲ *Delegates to the Knights of Labor national convention in 1886. Women (and African Americans) not only were admitted to the Knights as equals of white males but were an important component of the membership. Neither women nor blacks were welcome in the American Federation of Labor.*

spread its message much more quietly than Sylvis had. Indeed, the Knights were a secret society. Knowing that employers fired union organizers, the Knights, when they announced meetings in newspapers, did not reveal their meeting place (which was known to members) or even their name; they identified the group as "******". The Knights of Labor also differed from the National Labor Union in their disinterest in political action as an organization. Members were urged to vote, but Stephens believed that the interests of working people were served by solidarity in the workplace, not at the ballot box.

Some Knights believed in class conflict, irreconcilable differences between producers and parasites: workers and farmers on the one hand, capitalists on the other. But their concept of class lines was far less precise than that of the Marxists; the Knights barred from membership only saloon keepers, lawyers, and gamblers (hardly the professions that ran industrial America). Stephens himself disliked the idea of class conflict; he looked forward to a day when all men and women of goodwill would abolish the wage system and establish a cooperative commonwealth.

Women were welcome in the Knights; so were African Americans and unskilled workers, who were usually overlooked as union material. However, the Knights failed to appeal to one group that was essential to the success of any American labor organization: Roman Catholics, particularly Irish Americans.

Stephens, a lifelong Mason, had encrusted the Knights of Labor with the mystery, symbolism, ritual, secret handshakes, and other rigmarole of the Masons. The trouble was that, in Europe, the Masons were anti-Catholic, and the pope forbade members of the church to join them or any secret societies resembling the Masons. So long as Irish Catholics, an important component of the working class, were suspicious of the Knights, their prospects were limited.

Terence Powderly

In 1879, Stephens was succeeded as Grand Master Workman by Terence V. Powderly. Himself a Roman Catholic, Powderly brought the Knights into the open and toned down the Masonic flavor of their rituals. He persuaded an influential

Catholic bishop, James Gibbons, to prevail on the pope to remove his prohibition of Catholic membership in the union.

Gibbons succeeded, and the Knights grew at a dazzling rate. With 110,000 members in 1885, the organization claimed 700,000 the next year. Ironically, for Powderly opposed strikes, the major impetus of this growth was a victory by the Knights in a strike among employees of Jay Gould's Missouri Pacific Railroad. Gould had vowed to destroy the union. "I can hire half the working class to kill the other half," he growled. But the Knights closed down the Missouri Pacific, forcing him to meet with their leaders and agree to their terms.

The dramatic victory and explosive growth of the union proved to be more curse than blessing. Powderly and the union's general assembly were unable to control the new members. Instead of coordinating their activities nationally—the rationale of a national labor organization—local leaders went at it alone in a dozen unrelated directions. Powderly fumed and sputtered and refused to back the rash of strikes in 1885 and 1886. But he could not stop them. Then, in 1886, the Haymarket tragedy was unfairly but effectively attributed to the Knights. Membership plummeted.

▲ *Samuel Gompers dominated the American Federation of Labor for four decades. Considered a reactionary conservative by visionary labor leaders because of his hostility toward socialism and refusal to organize unskilled workers, he built a solid and successful federation of craft unions.*

Samuel Gompers and the AFL

In the same year as Haymarket, a national labor organization dedicated to union and stability for *some* workers, the American Federation of Labor (AFL), was put together by a few dozen existing associations of skilled workers. The AFL's guiding spirit was a cigar maker born in London of Dutch Jewish parents, an emigrant to the United States as a boy.

Samuel Gompers astonished his fellow workers (and their employers) with his intelligence, learning, toughness in bargaining, and eloquence on the soapbox. He was a homely, even ugly, man, squat and thick of body with a broad, coarse-featured face. But this uncomely character had very definite ideas about how labor organizations in the United States could not only survive but become one of the interlocking forces that governed the country.

First, Gompers believed that only skilled workers could effectively force employers to negotiate with them. When bricklayers refused to work, and they stuck together, the employer who wanted bricks laid had no choice but to talk. When unskilled hod carriers (men who carried the bricks to the bricklayers) went out on strike, employers had no difficulty in finding other men with strong backs and growling

stomachs to take their place. Therefore, Gompers concluded, the AFL would admit only skilled workers.

Second, the goal of the AFL unions was "bread and butter"—period—higher wages, shorter hours, and better working conditions. Gompers had no patience with utopian dreamers, particularly socialists. What counted was the here and now, not "pie in the sky." Unions with utopian programs of reform and revolution not only distracted workers from the concrete issues that counted but were easy targets for suppression by the bosses who were able (as in the Haymarket episode) to convince Americans that labor organizations threatened the very foundations of their society.

Third, although Gompers believed that the strike, as peaceful coercion, was the union's best weapon, he made it clear that AFL unions would cooperate with employers who recognized and bargained with them. Make unions partners in industry, he told employers, meaning AFL unions that supported the capitalist system. Their industry would be peaceful and stable; radical anticapitalist organizations would wither and die.

Friends of Friends

Gompers, who lived until 1924, served as president of the AFL every year but one. With his carrot-and-stick approach to dealing with employers—striking against those who refused to deal with the AFL, cooperating with those who accepted unions—he saw the AFL grow from 150,000 members in 1888 to more than a million shortly after the turn of the century.

Most employers, however, continued to hate him and the AFL as dearly as they hated socialists and revolutionary labor unions. "Can't I do what I want with my own?" Cornelius Vanderbilt had said. The majority of American industrialists believed with him that the wages they paid and the hours their employees worked were no one's business but their own. The worker who did not like his job was free to quit. In 1893, such hard-nosed antilabor employers formed the National Association of Manufacturers to fight unions wherever they appeared.

In 1900, more-enlightened manufacturers, led by Frank Easley and Senator Mark Hanna of Ohio, a former Rockefeller associate, came to the conclusion that labor unions were a permanent part of American industry. The choice was not between unions and no unions. The choice was (as Gompers had preached for more than a decade) between conservative, procapitalist unions willing to cooperate with employers and desperate, revolutionary unions determined to destroy capitalism. Easley and his associates joined with Gompers in 1900 to form the National Civic Federation. Its purpose was to work for industrial peace through employer-union cooperation.

A NATION OF IMMIGRANTS

Increasingly, as the century drew to a close, recent immigrants filled the less-skilled jobs in construction, factories, mines, and sweatshops in urban tenements. By 1900, immigrants and their children were half the population in Philadelphia, Pittsburgh, and Seattle; 60 percent in Buffalo, Detroit, and Minneapolis; 70 percent in New York, Chicago, and Milwaukee.

The Flood

Immigration had been a conspicuous American phenomenon from the beginning, of course. The word *immigration* itself, meaning migration *to* a place, was coined by an American, as more appropriate in the United States than *emigration*, movement *from* a place. From 10,000 newcomers in 1825, immigration topped 100,000 in 1845. Except for the first two years of the Civil War, the annual total never dipped below that figure. In 1854, a record 428,000 foreigners stepped ashore. That record was beaten in 1880, when 457,000 immigrants made landfalls in Boston, New York, Philadelphia, Baltimore, New Orleans, and smaller ports. Only the crippling depression of the 1890s pushed the annual total below 300,000. For each of six years after the turn of the twentieth century, more than a million people arrived in the United States. On one day in 1907, 11,747 immigrants

were processed at a single point of entry, New York's famous Ellis Island. Always a stream, sometimes swollen, immigration had become a flood.

Immigration after 1880 differed in character from what had gone before. Before 1880, a large majority of immigrants listed the British Isles, Germany, or Scandinavia as their place of birth. Although these northern and western Europeans continued to arrive in large numbers after 1880, an annually increasing proportion of newcomers originated in southern Italy, the Turkish Empire (Turks, Armenians, Bulgarians), Greece, and the Austro-Hungarian Empire (Hungarians, Romanians, Serbs, Croatians, Slovenes). From Russia, which then included most of Poland, came both Christian and Jewish Russians, Poles, Lithuanians, Latvians, Estonians, and Finns. From Asia came Japanese.

Before 1880, only about 200,000 people of southern and eastern European origin resided in the United States. Between 1880 and 1910, about 8.4 million arrived. In 1896, this new immigration exceeded the old for the first time. By 1907, new immigrants were almost the whole of the influx. Of 1.3 million legal immigrants registered that year, 1 million began their long journey in southern and eastern Europe.

MAP 29:1 European Immigration, 1815–1914 Overwhelmingly, the "old immigrants" originated in northern and western Europe. Only after 1880 did "new immigrants" from southern and eastern Europe begin to emigrate in large numbers, eventually constituting a large majority of newcomers.

The Emigration Experience

The immigrant's trek began with a walk. Most of the people who came to the United States after 1880 were from rural areas far from a seaport or even, for many, a railroad. So they walked, a circumstance that put a stricter limit on the baggage they could carry than did the rules of the steamship companies. Most left with a cheap suitcase or a bundle stuffed with clothing; a blanket or down-filled comforter; a treasured keepsake; and sometimes a vial of the soil of the native land that they would never see again.

In Italy, they usually walked all the way to the sea, to Genoa in the north, Naples in the south. In Greece, all peninsulas and islands, there would usually be a ferry ride to Piraeus, the port of Athens. From deep within Russia, Lithuania, Poland, and Germany, there would be a train ride. Russians and Poles usually headed for a German port, Bremen or Hamburg. While the czarist government provided both Christians and Jews with excellent reasons to leave, it did not help emigrants; German steamship lines built "villages" where emigrants could live while they decided on a ship.

Tickets were cheap. By the 1890s, heated competition among steamship companies for passengers in steerage (the lowest class of accommodation)—steerage was where the profits were,

AP/Wide World Photos

▲ *The dining hall at Ellis Island. The immigrants, of many ethnic groups, would have found the food unfamiliar and, perhaps, disagreeable, but it was better than what they had been served aboard ship.*

not first class—pushed the price of transatlantic passage below $20. There were humiliating but important ceremonies on departure day: a rude bath and fumigation for lice, and a close examination by company doctors for contagious diseases (especially tuberculosis), insanity, feeblemindedness, and trachoma, an inflammation of the eye that leads to blindness and was endemic in Italy and Greece. The United States refused entry to anyone with those diseases, and the ship that brought them over was required to take them back. With paying passengers waiting in America for passage to Europe, captains took care to minimize rejects who would take up space without paying.

The immigrants were crowded into steerage. "It is a congestion so intense, so injurious to the health and morals," said one commentator, "that there is nothing on land to equal it!" although it was probably not as bad as in the age of sail. Large steamships carried as many as a thousand steerage passengers. There were no cabins until after 1905, but large dormitories formed by bulkheads in the hull. Men and women slept in separate compartments; families were united only during the day. Bickering and fistfights were common, although there was not much sexual depredation, unless by crewmen. Except when the weather was bad, almost

Birth Pains of a World Economy

Only parts of Europe, North America, and Japan may be described as "industrialized" in the nineteenth century. However, the effects of the economic and social revolution were felt everywhere but the remotest corners of the earth. A decline in infant mortality and an increase in life expectancy, side effects of technology, resulted in a giant leap in population in agricultural as well as in industrial countries.

World production of foodstuffs soared too, but not uniformly. The biggest gains were made where agriculture was mechanized, such as in the United States and Canada. In those parts of the world where peasants with hand tools remained the agricultural workforce, food production lagged behind the increase of population there. Peasants growing grain on small parcels of land were undersold in their own backyards by grain from the broad American and Canadian prairies. Even a Pole living in Warsaw, at the center of "the

granary of eastern Europe," could buy American flour cheaper than flour milled 25 miles away.

The bottom fell out of the standard of living in these economic hinterlands. During the latter decades of the nineteenth century, southern Italian and Polish farmworkers made between $40 and $60 a year. The cash income of peasants in southern China was too small to be worth calculating. When large landowners in Europe attempted to consolidate and modernize their holdings so they could mechanize American-style, they pushed people off the land more efficiently than declining incomes were doing.

The Jews of Russia felt the effects of the worldwide Industrial Revolution in their own way. Forbidden by law to own land, most of them were old-fashioned artisans who handcrafted shoes, clothing, cabinetry, and furniture, anything that might make a kopeck. Others were retailers, shopkeepers fixed in one place or peddlers wandering around. Both craftsmen and peddlers found their way of life under-everyone preferred sitting on the open deck to huddling in the hold.

Cooking was prohibited, except the brewing of tea on the open deck. Meals, included in the price of passage (another change from sailing ships), were, unsurprisingly, cheap, simple, and not very good. (The German and Italian governments tried to regulate the quality of food and cookery.) Meals were taken in shifts: The final breakfast shift was followed immediately by the first dinner shift. Even when meals were decent and prepared in sanitary galleys, the ship's galley could not please every ethnic group's preferences. Immigrant manuals recommended smuggling familiar sausages or the like on board, even though that was forbidden by the steamship companies.

Between meals, the immigrants chatted, sewed, played games, sang, danced, studied English, read and reread manuals and letters from friends and relatives who were already in the United States. Days could be interminable, but the voyage was not long. Depending on the port of embarkation and the size of the ship, it took from eight days to two weeks to arrive in New York or Philadelphia, the chief ports of entry.

Indeed, a steamer arriving at the same time as others might lie at anchor for almost as long as it had taken to cross the Atlantic. In 1892, the United States Immigration Service opened a facility on Ellis Island (a landfill site in New York Harbor that had served as an arsenal) designed specifically for the rapid "processing" of newcomers. Laid out so that a stream of immigrants would flow in controlled lines through corridors and examination rooms to be inspected by physicians, nurses, and officials, Ellis Island, its architects boasted, could handle 8,000 people a day. Fifteen thousand immigrants passed through on some days.

Ellis Island was an experience few immigrants forgot. Crowds milled about and shoved for position before they entered the maze of pipe railings that took them from station to station. Instructions were boomed over loudspeakers in half a dozen languages; children wailed, and anxious parents called for their lost children. The first person to examine the immigrants was a doctor expected to make an instant diagnosis of afflictions for which the newcomers might be denied entry. If he saw a facial rash, he marked a large *F* on the immigrant's clothing with a piece of soft white chalk. People so marked were cut out of the queue and examined more closely. *H* meant suspected heart disease; *L* meant limp and examination for rickets (children were made to do a little dance); and a circle around a cross meant feeblemindedness and immediate return to the ship.

Those who were not chalked were more closely examined for trachoma and brusquely interviewed by an immigration officer. Everyone was prepared for the trick question "Do you have a job waiting for you?" Immigrant manuals cautioned in capital letters *not* to reply in the affirmative. The Foran Contract Labor Law of 1885 forbade making agreements to work before arriving. Previously—and surreptitiously after 1885—labor contractors had impressed immigrants into jobs under virtually slavelike conditions.

About 80 percent of those who entered Ellis Island were given landing cards that enabled them to board ferries to the Battery, the southern tip of Manhattan Island. The United States government was through with them; a horde of agents who made their living by offering "services" took charge. Again in a babel of languages, previously arrived countrymen shouted that they could offer jobs, provide train tickets, change currency, recommend an excellent boardinghouse. Some, not many, were honest. Every large ethnic group in the United States eventually founded aid societies to provide newcomers with such services, protecting them from being swindled within hours of their arrival in the land of opportunity.

---

cut by modernization. The shoes made by a Warsaw cobbler could not compete with cheap, machine-made shoes from England or the United States. The peddler who wandered around Russian Poland trying to sell hats and trousers learned the same lesson.

Industrialism and Immigration

American industrialists encouraged immigration. Until the Foran Act of 1885 made it illegal to do so, some companies

Divide and Conquer
A western lumber magnate explained that in order to have an easily manageable workforce, an employer should hire from several ethnic groups: "Don't get too great a percentage of any one nationality. Mix them up and obliterate clannishness and selfish social prejudices."

paid immigrants' fares if they signed contracts in Europe agreeing to work for their patrons when they arrived in the United States. James J. Hill plastered every sizable town in Sweden with posters describing the richness of the soil along his Great Northern Railroad. (South Dakota got its nickname the "Sunshine State" in a promotional campaign; some advertisements had palm trees swaying in the balmy Dakota breezes.) The American Woolens Company circulated handbills in southern Italy showing a well-dressed immigrant worker with a sleek handlebar moustache carrying a heavy sack of money from the mill to a bank across the street. In the West, before 1884, railroaders paid Cantonese labor recruiters to import gangs of Chinese "coolies" to do heavy construction work at minuscule wages.

Employers liked immigrant labor because it was invariably cheaper than American labor, because immigrants gladly took the menial, dirty jobs that Americans shunned, and because the newcomers were more docile employees than old-stock Americans. So far from familiar surroundings and customs, they hesitated to complain. Many intended to work in America only temporarily, a few months or a few years, and then return to their homelands. They were more likely to accept very low wages, live on next to nothing, and save. Such immigrants had no interest in joining a union or going on strike, sacrificing in the short run to improve their situation in the long run. For them, the long run was back home.

From a national perspective, immigrant labor was pure asset. More than 60 percent of arrivals on late-nineteenth-century immigrant ships were able-bodied males; the percentage was higher among Italians and Greeks. The "old country" had borne the expense of supporting these people during their unproductive childhood years and was still supporting their womenfolk and children. In the United States, immigrants were producers, pure and simple. It was a very profitable arrangement.

ETHNIC AMERICA

In addition to the general push and pull that affected all immigrants, each ethnic group had unique reasons to leave its ancestral homeland and make a new home in a country known only from hearsay based on differing experiences in the United States.

The British and the Irish

Immigrants from England, Scotland, Wales, and the Protestant north of Ireland continued to be numerous in the late nineteenth century. Between the Civil War and the turn of the century, 1.9 million of them came to the United States. They were more at home than other immigrants: In appearance they were indistinguishable from the majority of white Americans; they practiced the religious faiths that were most common in the United States; they were familiar with the basic culture and folkways; and they spoke the language.

The story was a little different for the Catholic Irish, who constituted almost all of the 3.4 million Irish who came to the United States between 1845 and 1900. Almost all spoke English, and they too were familiar with Anglo-American culture, but somewhat from the outside.

First, they were Catholics, arousing the suspicion and sometimes the hatred of American Protestants. The Know-Nothings were long gone, but, in 1887, organized anti-Catholic prejudice was revived with the formation of the American Protective Association (APA), which was especially strong in the Midwest. Members of the APA took an oath to "strike the shackles and chains of blind obedience" to the Roman Catholic Church from the minds of its communicants, but, in practice, their chief activity was to discriminate against those still in bondage to the pope. Idealistic Republicans who disapproved of demeaning stereotypes of African Americans were not disturbed by the chimpanzee faces newspaper cartoonists used to identify Irish thugs, maids, and respectable workingmen alike. APA employers hung the sign "NINA" ("No Irish Need Apply") on their gates and in their shop windows.

And yet, Irish Americans took with zest to their adopted home. Numerous enough that they could insulate their personal lives from anti-Catholicism, the Irish parlayed their cohesive sociability and bent for eloquence into becoming a formidable political force. By the time of the Civil War, the Democratic party organizations in heavily Irish cities like Boston and New York were catering to the interests of the Irish community and reaping the reward of an almost unanimous Irish vote. By the 1880s, Irish immigrants and Irish Americans dominated urban politics in much of the East, Midwest, and in San Francisco. Ironically, it was their considerable power on the West Coast that led to the first American anti-immigrant legislation since the Alien Acts of 1797.

Guests of the Golden Mountain

In 1849, seamen brought the news to the Chinese port of Canton that a "mountain of gold" had been discovered in California. In a country plagued by overpopulation, flood, famine, epidemic disease, and tyrants, the southern Chinese listened avidly to the usual distortions of life across the ocean. "Americans are a very rich people," one promoter explained. "They want the Chinaman to come and will make him welcome."

By the time the Chinese arrived in any numbers, the rich mines were already exhausted. Accustomed to working communally, they made a living in diggings Caucasians had abandoned and found employment in menial jobs that whites disdained: cook, laundry man, gardener, farmworker, domestic servant. By 1860, there were 35,000 Chinese living in California. Most of them were young men who hoped to return home after they made their fortune. There were only 1,800 Chinese women in the state, a good many of them prostitutes. In San Francisco, Sacramento, and Marysville, lively Chinatowns flourished.

Race and a radically different culture kept the Chinese separate. "When I got to San Francisco," wrote Lee Chew, later a wealthy businessman, "I was half-starved because I was afraid to eat the provisions of the barbarians. But a few days living in the Chinese Quarter and I was happy again." Leaders of the Gum Shan Hok—the Guests of the Golden Mountain—encouraged the immigrants to stick to themselves. "We are accustomed to an orderly society," explained a leader of San Francisco's Chinatown, "but it seems as if the Americans are not bound by rules of conduct. It is best, if possible, to avoid any contact with them."

When the construction of the transcontinental railroad began in 1864, Chinese immigration increased. Previously about 3,000 to 6,000 a year entered California; after 1868, the annual number jumped to 23,000.

Keeping John Chinaman Out

As long as there was plenty of work, hostility toward the Chinese was restrained. In 1873, however, the West sunk into depression with the rest of the country. In 1877, when the Chinese were 17 percent of California's population, a San Francisco teamster named Denis Kearney began to speak to white workingmen at open-air rallies in empty sandlots. He blamed their joblessness on the willingness of the Chinese to work for less than an American could survive on. Kearney led several rampages through Chinatown. The violence spread. Once-large Chinatowns disappeared in Oroville and Marysville, California, because of mob violence. As late as 1885, an anti-Chinese rampage in Rock Springs, Wyoming, left 28 Chinese dead.

The violence begat political action. In 1882, led by Californians, Congress choked off Chinese immigration in the Chinese Exclusion Act. There were a few tiny loopholes. A few hundred Chinese women entered the country legally each year to become wives of Gum Shan Hok already here. There was a trickle of illegal immigration via Canada and Mexico. Otherwise, the Chinese American community was isolated from China as well as from others within the United States.

In smaller numbers, Japanese replaced the Chinese on the West Coast. They began to trickle in, often via Hawaii, where Japanese were the backbone of the agricultural labor force. Paradoxically, Caucasians resented them not because they were so docile in accepting substandard wages but because the Japanese were ambitious and many of them prospered, becoming landowners. Race, as ever, obliterated in the white mind the fact that Chinese and Japanese immigrants were quite unlike one another.

Germans

Today, more Americans have German ancestors than have English ancestors. The immigration of Germans was constant

The Granger Collection, New York

▲ *Irish American women, readily identifiable by their chimpanzee-like upturned noses and weak chins, look scornfully on Chinese in San Francisco. The objects of scorn here are the ladies. The Chinese are depicted as orderly and industrious. Middle- and upper-class Californians, many of them employers wanting cheap labor, favored the Chinese over the Irish, who were trade unionists as well as anti-Chinese.*

for 200 years, beginning in the early 1700s. After 1848, however, there was a political dimension to the German influx. The failure of a series of liberal revolutions in several German states—revolutions aimed at establishing American-style democracy and individual rights—forced many leading German liberals into exile. The most famous of them to come to the United States was Carl Schurz, who became a senator from Missouri, a leading liberal Republican, and a member of Rutherford B. Hayes's cabinet.

Many of the 4.4 million anonymous Germans who came to the United States in the second half of the nineteenth century, an average of about 100,000 a year, were impelled by fears that their lives were deteriorating under the German Empire, which was established in 1871. German Catholics, in particular, fled the *Kulturkampf,* the anti-Catholic campaign of the German chancellor, Otto von Bismarck.

Because many had owned land in Germany, German immigrants often had enough money when they reached the United States to move west and develop free or cheap land into farms. Wisconsin became heavily German in the late nineteenth century. By 1900, more Milwaukeeans spoke German as their first language than spoke English. Nationally, about 800 German-language newspapers were being published.

Scandinavians

Like the Germans, Scandinavians inclined to become farmers in the United States. Norwegians predominated in many counties in Wisconsin and Minnesota. Swedes were numerous in Minnesota and in the Pacific Northwest. Finns, who speak a different language than Swedes but were historically tied to them, were conspicuous in Swedish regions and elsewhere, such as the logging country areas of the Midwest and Northwest and in the iron mines of the Mesabi Range.

Ethnic groups that predominated over large areas found adaptation to the New World comparatively easy because they could approximate familiar Old World ways. They founded schools that taught in their native languages, newspapers and other periodicals, and European-style fraternal organizations (such as the Germans' athletically oriented *Turnverein* and the Norwegians' musical Grieg societies). They continued to eat familiar foods and raise their children by traditional rules. They were numerous enough to deal with Americans from a position of strength.

The problems that these immigrants faced were common to all settlers of new lands in the West. Ole Rölvaag, a gloomy Norwegian American writer, focused on the loneliness of life on the northern prairies, an experience shared by all pioneers. He did not write much about cultural alienation, for Norwegian Americans did not feel it.

Sephardic and German Jews

Other immigrant groups had a comparatively easy time adapting because they were so few and, therefore, threatened no one. Sephardic Jews (descended from the Jews expelled from Spain and Portugal in the 1490s) came in small numbers to the United States. Generally educated, sophisticated, and often well fixed, they eased into middle- and even upper-class society before the Civil War, particularly in Rhode Island, New York, Charleston, and New Orleans. Considering the fewness of their numbers, they contributed a remarkable number of prominent citizens. Jefferson Davis's strongest political ally in the Confederacy was Judah P. Benjamin, a Sephardic Jew. Supreme Court justice Benjamin Cardozo had a Sephardic background, as did twentieth-century financier and presidential adviser Bernard Baruch of South Carolina.

By 1880, there was a small German Jewish community in the United States, perhaps 150,000 strong. Most were small-scale tradesmen or businessmen; rare was the southern town without its Jewish-owned dry-goods store. Some German Jews, such as Levi Strauss, pioneered in the founding of the American ready-made clothing industry. In New York, Jews dominated the business, Germans running it, Jews from eastern Europe working in it. The Guggenheim syndicate, mostly Jewish at the top, was one of the nation's leading owners of metal mines by the turn of the century. Three of the nation's most important banks in the middle of the century were owned by German Jews, but all were in decline by 1900.

The German Jews clung to their religious heritage but quickly adopted American mores and customs. Led by Rabbi Isaac Mayer Wise of Cincinnati, German Jews founded Reform Judaism, which abandoned ancient dietary laws and other observances they regarded as archaic, creating instead communities dedicated to moderate social reform.

The Trauma of Immigration

Adapting to their new homeland was not so easy for the new immigrants who arrived after 1880. Very few of the newcomers from southern and eastern Europe had much money when they arrived. Most were illiterate, and their Old World experience in peasant village and shtetl (a Jewish village in Russia) did not prepare them for life in the world's greatest industrial nation during its era of frenzied development.

However serious the immigrants' reasons for leaving ancestral homes, those homes were still ancestral, the rhythms of life familiar, and the customs second nature. Wherever their origins, the new immigrants were accustomed to a traditional way of life that was the antithesis of

Hold Fast!
Some immigrants may have believed that the streets of the United States were paved with gold, but there is no sign of that fantasy in an immigrants' manual of 1891 that advised:

Hold fast, this is most necessary in America. Forget your past, your customs, and your ideals. Select a goal and pursue it with all your might. No matter what happens to you, hold on. You will experience a bad time, but sooner or later you will achieve your goal.

life in the United States. In the United States, they were members of a minority.

Strangest of all for people who came from traditional, preindustrial cultures where life was regulated and slowed by the seasons, the weather, and the use of hand tools, American life was regulated and rushed by the tyrannical clock and powered by the relentless churning of the dynamo. In the industrial society of the late nineteenth century, Americans were even more driven than they had been when Alexis de Tocqueville's head was set spinning by the American pace of life. This was particularly true in the big cities, where a majority of the new immigrants settled and which, in the minds of other Americans, were intimately associated with the newcomers.

for FURTHER READING

The general histories listed in "For Further Reading" in Chapters 26 through 28 are pertinent to this chapter as well. Specifically dealing with immigrants are Rowland T. Berthoff, *British Immigrants in Industrial America*, 1953; Leonard Dinnerstein and David Reimers, *Ethnic Americans: A History of Immigration and Assimilation*, 1975; Nathan Glazer and Daniel P. Moynihan, *Beyond the Melting Pot*, 1970; Oscar Handlin, *The Uprooted*, 1951; Marcus L. Hansen, *The Immigrant in American History*, 1940; John Higham, *Send These to Me: Jews and Other Immigrants in Urban America*, 1975; Maldwyn A. Jones, *American Immigration*, 1960; Dale Steiner, *Of Thee We Sing*, 1986; and Philip A. M. Taylor, *The Distant Magnet*, 1970.

Books with a focus on working people include David Brody, *Workers in Industrial America*, 1979; Robert V. Bruce, *1877: Year of Violence*, 1959; Melvyn Dubofsky, *Industrialism and the American Worker, 1865–1920*, 1975; Foster R. Dulles and Melvyn Dubofsky, *Labor in America*, 1984; Herbert G. Gutman, *Work, Culture, and Society in Industrializing America*, 1976; Harold C. Livesay, *Samuel Gompers and the Origins of the American Federation of Labor*, 1978; David Montgomery, *Workers' Control in America: Studies in the History of Work, Technology, and Labor Struggle*, 1979; Daniel Nelson, *Managers and Workers: Origins of the New Factory System in the United States, 1880–1920*, 1975; Henry Pelling, *American Labor*, 1960; Daniel T. Rogers, *The Work Ethic in Industrial America, 1850–1920*, 1974; and Philip Taft, *The A.F. of L. in the Time of Gompers*, 1929.

American Journey ONLINE *www* AMERICAN JOURNEY ONLINE AND INFOTRAC COLLEGE EDITION

Visit the source collections at http://ajaccess.wadsworth.com and http://infotrac.thomsonlearning.com, and use the Search function with the following key terms to explore documents, images, audio and video clips, articles, and commentary related to the material in this chapter:

Ellis Island
Homestead Strike
Knights of Labor
Pullman Strike
Samuel Gompers

Additional resources, exercises, and Internet links related to this chapter are available on *The American Past* Web site:
http://history.wadsworth.com/americanpast7e.

HISTORY ONLINE

Angel Island
www.sandiego-online.com/forums/chinese/htmls/angel.htm
Multimedia portrait of Angel Island, the Ellis Island for Chinese immigrants.

The Samuel Gompers Papers
www.inform.umd.edu/EdRes/Colleges/ARHU/Depts/
History/Gompers/web1.html
Selections from Gompers's public and private writings providing an insight into his abilities, philosophy, and practices.

30

BRIGHT LIGHTS AND SLUMS

The Growth of Big Cities

The mobs of great cities add just so much to the support of pure government as sores do to the strength of the human body.

Thomas Jefferson

I have an affection for a great city. I feel safe in the neighborhood of man, and enjoy the sweet security of streets.

Henry Wadsworth Longfellow

ONCE IN THE United States, the new immigrants discovered that, to Americans of older stock, they were exotic. Even those Protestants who had grown accustomed to the restrained Roman Catholic worship of the Irish and Germans were troubled by the mystical Catholicism of the Poles and the public ceremonies of the Italians. Indeed, Irish bishops worried about the "paganism" implied in the magnificently bedecked statues of the Madonna and the gory, surrealistic depictions of the crucified Christ that peasants from Sicily and the Campania carried through the streets of "Little Italy" accompanied by the music of brass bands. The Orthodox religion of the Greeks, Russians, some Ukrainians, and Balkan immigrants was even more alien. The Jews and the Chinese, of course, were not even Christian and, therefore, stood out all the more.

The newcomers looked different. The Greeks, Armenians, Assyrians, Lebanese, and Italians were often swarthy, a formidable handicap in a nation that drew a sharp color line. Polish women arrived clad in the colorful babushkas, aprons, and billowing ground-length skirts of the eastern European peasant. The impoverished Russian Jews dressed drably enough, but the men, if religious, never removed their hats. Their Saturday Sabbath attracted attention because the Jews turned Sunday into a combination holiday and market day, which offended the sensibilities of some Protestants.

Americans who visited immigrant neighborhoods were unsettled because even the smells in the air were alien. Clinging to traditional cuisines, many of which employed more onion and garlic than old-stock Americans deemed decent, the immigrants seemed determined to resist becoming American, all the while living on American soil and sharing in the national bounty.

CITIES AS ALIEN ENCLAVES

In his novel of 1890, *A Hazard of New Fortunes,* William Dean Howells sent Basil March, a genteel middle-class

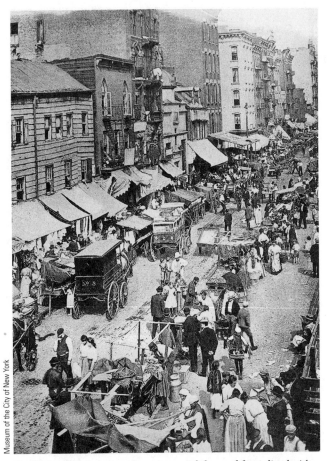

▲ *Hester Street was a major commercial thoroughfare—lined with shops—in New York City's largest Jewish neighborhood, on the Lower East Side of Manhattan Island. Streets serving the same function were found in every ethnic ghetto in all the major cities.*

American, on a ride on an elevated train in New York City. March "found the variety of people in the car as unfailingly entertaining as ever," but he felt like a foreigner in his own country. Even the Irish, who ran the city, were outnumbered by "the people of Germanic, Slavonic, of Pelagic [Mediterranean], of Mongolian stock." March noted "the small eyes, the high cheeks, the broad noses, the puff lips, the bare, cue-filleted skulls, of Russians, Poles, Czechs, Chinese, the furtive glitter of Italians, the blonde dullness of Germans; the cold quiet of Scandinavians—fire under ice—were aspects that he identified, and that gave him abundant suggestion for the . . . reveries in which he dealt with the future economy of our heterogeneous commonwealth."

A Patchwork Quilt

The cities, particularly in the Northeast and Midwest, where 80 percent of the new immigrants settled, seemed to be the strongholds of invading armies. By 1890, one-third of the population of Boston and Chicago, and one-quarter of Philadelphia's people, had been born abroad. When the children of immigrants, who seemed to old-stock Americans as obstinately foreign as their parents, are added to this total, the anxiety of "American" residents and visitors to the cities is easy to understand.

In fact, the immigrants threatened no one. Members of each ethnic group clustered together into ghettos that were exclusively their own. A map of New York, wrote journalist Jacob Riis, himself a Danish immigrant, "colored to designate nationalities, would show more stripes than the skin of a zebra and more colors than the rainbow." Jane Addams sketched a similar patchwork in the poor part of Chicago, where she established Hull House, a settlement house—that is, a privately funded institution providing social services to immigrants. The same was true of most large eastern and midwestern cities and of many smaller industrial towns. In Lawrence, Massachusetts, a woolens-manufacturing town, more than 20 languages, and probably twice that many dialects, were spoken.

There were ghettos within ghettos. In New York City's Greenwich Village, an Italian community, people from the Italian region of Calabria monopolized housing on some streets, as immigrants from Sicily did on others. On such regional blocks, Italians from a specific village would sometimes be the sole occupants of an "Agrigento tenement," and so on. Grocery stores and restaurants advertised themselves not as Italian but as purveyors of Campanian or Apulian food. Italian priests frequently ministered to the same people whom they had known back in Italy; Italian lawyers represented the same clients.

The same held true for Jewish neighborhoods, where Galician Jews (Galicia was in what is now southern Poland) looked with suspicion on Jews from Russia. Romanian Jews fastidiously set up their own communities, and the assimilated and better-established German Jews wondered what the world was coming to. Christian Germans divided along Lutheran and Catholic lines. Serbs and Croatians separated from one another on the basis of religion and alphabets— the Croatians were Catholics who wrote their language in the Latin alphabet; the Orthodox Serbs, in the Cyrillic alphabet of Russia.

The Impulse to Assimilate

The desire to assimilate, to become "American," varied in intensity from group to group. Some immigrants found solace in the familiar language, customs, foods, and fellowship of a "Little Italy," "Jewville," or "Pollack Town" and clung tenaciously to the old ways. The ethnic ghetto was a buffer against the prejudices of old-stock Americans and the hostility of other ethnic groups with which its inhabitants competed for low-level jobs. Even an educated immigrant from the Austro-Hungarian Empire found himself disoriented in his attempts to shift from old to new ways of thinking and reacting:

> I never knew if my reactions would be in line with the new code of conduct and had to think and reflect. Whenever I decided on the spur of the moment I found myself out of sympathy with my environment. I did not feel as they felt and therefore I felt wrongly according to their standards. To act instinctively in an American fashion and manner was impossible, and I appeared slow and clumsy. The proverbial slowness of foreigners is largely due to this cause.

Others seized on American ways with an extraordinary enthusiasm. This was perhaps best illustrated in the large Jewish community of New York's Lower East Side, which in its earliest years was sharply divided between those who clung to the medieval customs of the Russian and Polish shtetls and the city-wise and sophisticated younger immigrants and children of immigrants who embraced America as the "Promised Land" and scorned their elders' "greenhorn" customs.

Hard work at menial jobs was the lot of most immigrants. The urban political machine, which had room near the top for anyone who could deliver votes, provided an avenue of advancement for a few who recognized the opportunities the machine provided. Others joined the American quest for material success by pursuing careers in areas that were not quite respectable and, therefore, less attractive to members of established social groups—show business, professional sports, and organized crime, that is, illegal business. A roster of surnames of leading entertainers, boxers, baseball players, and gangsters over a period of decades resembles the strata of a canyon, each layer dominated by members of a new, aspiring ethnic group.

Immigrant Aid Institutions

Ethnic groups established institutions to assist their countrymen in adjusting to the new life. Some encouraged assimilation, some clannishness. Sephardic and German Jewish families that were comfortably established in the United States were often, at first, dismayed by the customs of eastern European Jews, which they too found disagreeable. But they soon founded the Hebrew Immigrant Aid Society to minister to the needs of the poor among them. The Young Men's and Young Women's Hebrew Associations, dating back to 1854, expanded several times over during the final decade of the century.

Among the Catholic population, which grew from 6 million in 1880 to 10 million in 1900 (making Roman Catholicism the country's largest single denomination), traditionally charitable religious orders, such as the Franciscans and the Sisters of Mercy, established hospitals and houses of refuge in the slums. The St. Vincent de Paul Society functioned much like the Protestant Salvation Army, without the military trappings, providing food, clothing, and shelter for the desperate.

The American Catholic Church was torn between serving as an agency of assimilation and maintaining its high standing among Catholic immigrants—who often clung to their religion with more piety than they had in Europe—by encouraging a "fortress mentality" toward the dominant Protestant culture. The church approved of parishes organized along ethnic rather than geographical lines, both to reinforce the religious loyalty of Catholic immigrants and to assuage the prejudices of Irish and German Catholics toward the newcomers. In places like Detroit and New Orleans, there might be an Italian, a Polish, a Lithuanian, and a geographical parish church—that is, an Irish-German church—within a few blocks of one another.

Settlement Houses

Old-stock Americans created the settlement house, patterned after Toynbee Hall (which had been established in a notorious London slum), to assist immigrants in coming to terms with their new country.

During the 1880s, a number of middle-class Americans imbued with the New England evangelical conscience, which dictated concern for others, traveled to England to learn how Toynbee worked. They found that Toynbee provided food and drink to the destitute, as traditional charities had, but also child care for employed mothers, recreational facilities, and courses of study in everything from household arts and the English language to social skills needed for advancement in society. The mostly young men and women who worked at Toynbee Hall also told the Americans that they had been morally elevated by their sacrifices and exposure to a misery they had not known in their own lives.

The first American settlement house was the Neighborhood Guild, set up in New York City in 1886. More famous, however, because of the powerful personalities of their founders, were Jane Addams's Hull House in Chicago (1889), Robert A. Woods's South End House in Boston (1892), and Lillian Wald's Henry Street Settlement in New York (1893). From comfortable middle-class backgrounds, well educated, and finely mannered, Addams, Woods, and Wald were exemplars of the middle class morally discomfited by the selfish materialism of their culture. Alleviating the deprivations of poor city dwellers was a way to alleviate their own spiritual distress. Hull House and several other settlements were devoutly patriotic but also rejoiced in the cultural diversity the immigrants brought to the country. They promoted programs at which different ethnic groups showed off their native costumes and cookery.

THE GROWTH OF GREAT CITIES

Many Americans (although certainly not all) had an ingrained prejudice against cities, dating back to Thomas Jefferson, who was pathological on the subject. Nevertheless, by the end of the nineteenth century, the United States was one of the world's most urbanized countries. The proportion of city dwellers in the total population, the number of cities, and the size of cities all increased at a faster rate in the United States than in any other country.

In 1790, when the first national census was taken, only 3.4 percent of Americans lived in towns of 8,000 people or more. By 1860, the eve of the Civil War, 16 percent of the population was urban, and by 1900, 33 percent. Even more

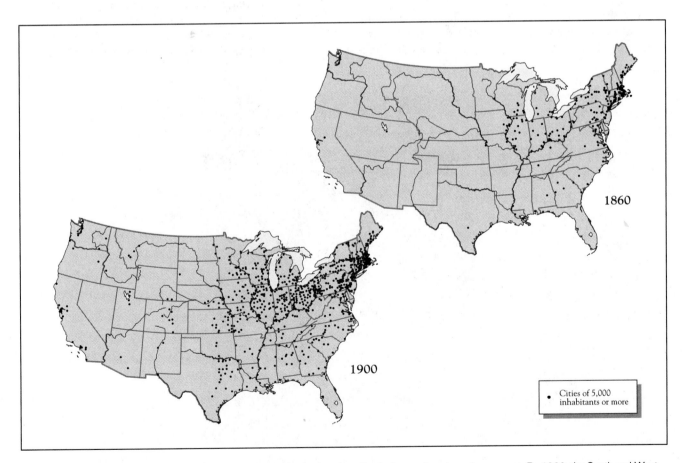

MAP 30:1 Growth of Cities, 1860 and 1900 In 1860, urbanization was effectively a northeastern phenomenon. By 1900, the South and West were also home to a large number of cities, several of them quite populous.

striking was the increase in the number of cities. In 1790, only 6 American cities boasted populations of 8,000 or more. The largest of them, Philadelphia, was home to 42,000 people. In 1860, 141 municipalities had at least 8,000 people within their limits; by 1890, 448 did; and by 1910, the number was 778! Fully 26 cities had a population larger than 100,000 in 1900, and 6 of them topped 500,000. Philadelphia counted 1.3 million people at the turn of the century and, even with so large a population, was only third in size—behind New York and Chicago.

From Country to City

The immigrant flood was largely responsible for the runaway growth of cities at the end of the century. However, native-born Americans also moved to the cities from the country in great numbers. Unhappy with the isolation of farm life, ground down by the heavy labor, and, by the 1880s, discouraged by a slow but steady decline in farm income, rural Americans were lured to cities by jobs for the literate and mechanically inclined that paid well; some had visited a big city and were dazzled by the bright lights, the abundance of company, the stimulation of a world in constant motion, and the tales of the fortunes that might be made in business.

Parents, rural ministers, and editors of farm magazines begged, threatened, and cajoled in an effort to keep the children of the soil at home, but their efforts met with limited success. A former farm girl told Frederick Law Olmstead,

"If I were offered a deed to the best farm on condition of going back to the country to live, I would not take it. I would rather face starvation in town."

Although the total number of farm families grew during the late nineteenth century, the proportion of farmers in the total population declined, and in some regions, even the numbers of farm people dropped. During the 1880s, more than half the rural townships of Iowa and Illinois declined in population, while Chicago underwent its miraculous growth. In New England, while the overall population of the region increased by 20 percent, three rural townships in five lost people to the dozens of bustling mill towns that lined the region's rivers and to Boston and New York.

For the most part, the American migration from farm to city was a white migration. Only 12 percent of the 5 million blacks in the United States in 1890 lived in cities, most in the South. Nevertheless, about 500,000 blacks moved from the rural South to the urban North during the final decade of the century, foreshadowing one of the most significant population movements of the twentieth century.

Metropolis

Although rapid growth was the rule in cities large and small, the most dramatic phenomenon of American urbanization in the late nineteenth century was the emergence of the metropolises, the six cities of more than 500,000 people that dominated the regions in which they sat, like imperial capitals. Philadelphia doubled in size between 1860 and 1900.

W. Louis Sonntag, Jr., The Bowery at Night, 1895. Museum of the City of New York.

▲ *Louis Sonntag's* The Bowery at Night *captured the excitement of the gaslit city for ordinary people. The wealthy had once strolled the broad avenue but had moved to Broadway for shopping by the 1890s, when this picture was painted. The Bowery was a shopping and entertainment center for middle-class and even working-class New Yorkers.*

New York, with 33,000 people in 1790, and over 1 million in 1860, quadrupled its numbers until, in 1900, after combining with Brooklyn, 4.8 million lived within its five boroughs. New York was the second largest city in the world, smaller only than London.

Chicago's crazy rate of growth as the hub of the nation's railroad system amazed Americans and foreigners alike. With only a little more than 100,000 souls in 1860, Chicago increased its size 20 times in a generation, numbering 2.2 million inhabitants in 1900.

The "Walking" City

Before the 1870s, cities so populous were unimaginable. When the mass of a city's people moved around by foot or in horse-drawn conveyances, city growth was limited in area to a radius of a mile or two, as far as workers could walk to their jobs, bosses to their offices, and housekeepers to market.

To be sure, the well-to-do owned horses and carriages, but a working horse moved only a little faster than a pedestrian and rather more slowly when the streets were choked with people wending to and fro or other horses and wagons were lined up ahead. With transportation so major a consideration, in the walking city, the most desirable neighborhood was centrally located. Lots were small, 20 feet wide typically, even where the well-to-do lived. Streets were narrow. Parks were few. With a 12-hour day to work, there was little time for commuting. With a few exceptions, space was not wasted on broad avenues or places to breathe fresh air.

Except for those on the very bottom, the social classes of the walking city lived in close proximity. The wealthy needed to have their maids and butlers in their homes, and, nearby, the small businessmen who provided services: keepers of stables, retailers of all kinds, coal and ice dealers, artisans needed to be within easy reach. Small businessmen lived behind or above their offices and warehouses, and the people who worked for them lived nearby.

The line between city and country was vividly clear. Where built-up neighborhoods, paved streets, water and gas lines, and sewers ended, farmland began. Often, the edge of a large city was a belt of ramshackle shantytowns inhabited by people who had not found a role to play in the city's life or who were discarded by a competitive society. Unlike today, when homeless people cluster in the central cores of cities, the walking city relegated the marginal to the suburbs.

Not that city-center living was delightful. In fact, the congestion, pace, turmoil, noise, and dirt of urban life were such that, when the opportunity to flee presented itself, the wealthy and middle classes were quick to seize it, leaving the city center to the businesses that were the source of their prosperity.

Transportation

The first device making it possible for people of means to put distance between their residences and the city center was the horsecar line. With charters from city hall, entrepreneurs installed light rails down major thoroughfares on which they ran horse-drawn streetcars with seats open to the public. Fares were cheap, usually five cents, but that was still too much for working people to pay twice daily. They continued to walk to their jobs, which meant living close to the docks, warehouses, and factories. However, well-paid skilled workers, upper-level white-collar workers, and small businessmen took advantage of the quick, cheap transportation to move away from the congestion: north on the island of Manhattan, west across the Schuylkill River in Philadelphia, north and west out of Chicago and Boston, into the hills above Cincinnati.

Making possible even more-distant residential neighborhoods were the steam-powered elevated train, or "El," which ran at high speeds above the crowded streets on ponderous and ugly steel scaffolding, and (in cities on large bodies of water) ferryboats catering to passengers.

In 1870, New York completed the first El on Ninth Avenue, and the range of the trains, soon up to the northern tip of Manhattan, encouraged the middle classes to move even farther away from Wall Street and the once leafy, now crowded and bawdy, Bowery. In making the suburbs more accessible and desirable, the Els also served to begin the process of pushing the residents of the shantytowns into inner-city housing abandoned by the middle classes.

The steam ferry had the same effect. As early as 1850, fast ferryboats were shuttling across the East River between Manhattan and Brooklyn every few minutes. By 1860, 100,000 people made the six-minute crossing daily. Camden, New Jersey, was Philadelphia's ferry suburb, across the Delaware River. San Francisco Bay, spacious as the great harbor is, was vexed by ferryboat traffic jams as early as 1900.

Electric Trolleys

The utility of elevated trains was limited by the high cost of constructing them. Only the richest and largest cities (and the most corrupt) were able and willing to shoulder the expense of the massive iron support structure. Moreover, no sooner did the Els stimulate residential construction along their routes, where they ran at ground level, than the noisy, dirty, and dangerous locomotives roused the ire of the very people who rode them to work and recreation.

It was the electric trolley car, pioneered by inventor-businessman Frank J. Sprague, that transformed most walking cities into sprawling conurbations. Cheap to build, faster than horsecars, easy to stop, clean, quiet, even pleasantly rhythmic in their click-clack and melodious in their bells, the trolleys were key to the growth of both metropolises and smaller cities. Richmond, Virginia, in 1887, was the first to build an electric trolley system. By 1895, 850 lines crisscrossed American cities on 10,000 miles of track. They were as important to the urbanization of the United States as the railroads were to the settlement of the West.

Building Up

In fostering the construction of residential neighborhoods miles from city business districts, the trolleys made it possible

▲ *Electric trolleys on San Francisco's main thoroughfare, Market Street. They ran to every part of the city except the steepest hills, where the famous cable cars provided quick transportation from residences to downtown. The "cow catchers" on the trolleys were, of course, to prevent pedestrians from being run over.*

for many more people to congregate in city centers for work, business, and entertainment. The moneymaking potential of real estate in town caused property values in the city center to soar.

The theoretical solution to the problem was obvious: Multiply the square footage of midtown properties by building ever taller structures, more stories. But there were practical limits to building upward. Masonry construction—piling stone on stone, laying brick on brick—meant that on the lower floors of an 8- or 10-story building, the weight-bearing walls had to be so thick as to defeat the whole purpose of building upward,

Safety Record

Few manufacturers can take the pride in their products the Otis Elevator Company can. In 150 years, only one Otis elevator has fallen to the bottom of the elevator shaft, in 1943, when a plane crashed into the eighty-ninth floor of New York's Empire State Building and one elevator at the seventeenth floor plummeted to the ground. Even then, the operator survived.

which was to provide more room. Moreover, the lower levels of any building were more desirable: The more stairs a businessman (and his customers) had to climb to his office, or the hotel guest to his room, the less valuable the floor space.

Elisha Graves Otis's safety hoist, or elevator, solved the problem of access to upper floors. Mechanical hoists had been around since the days of the pharaohs; a steam-powered lift was put into service in England in 1835. Until Otis, however, hoisting cables and ropes snapped so often as to make a ride on an elevator a dangerous adventure. Beginning in 1852, Otis and his equally imaginative sons developed safety systems based on ratchets; if the hoisting cable broke, the elevator stayed where it was. No longer were the upper stories of a building the least desirable because of the effort required to reach them. Indeed, they were more desirable because, in the words of an Otis promotional brochure, "Monsieur [makes] the transit in half a minute of repose and quiet, and arriving there, [enjoys] a purity and coolness of atmosphere and an exemption from noise, dust, and exhalations." By 1878, hydraulically hoisted elevators climbed at 600 to 800 feet per second.

▲ *New York's Flatiron Building, built in 1905, was one of the first skyscrapers, double the height of architect Louis Sullivan's Wainswright Building in St. Louis. Its height was doubled by the Singer Building, at 41 stories, in 1908.*

William L. Jenney solved the problem of massive weight-bearing walls. In 1885, he perfected the I-beam girder, a steel support with little mass that was so strong that it became possible to build towering skeletons of steel on which, in effect, builders hung decorative siding of cast iron or stone. The potential height of structural steel buildings seemed limitless; they could rise so high as to scrape the sky. Indeed, once the method was perfected, corporations competed to erect the tallest tower, as medieval cities had competed to build the tallest cathedral spire.

New York was to become the most dramatic of the skyscraper cities; but Chicago architects pioneered in the design of "tall office buildings," as Louis H. Sullivan, the most thoughtful of architects, rather prosaically described his graceful structures. In an article in *Lippincott's Magazine* in 1896, Sullivan explained how through the use of "proud and soaring" vertical sweeps, "a unit without a single dissenting line," the artistic form of the skyscraper reflected the essence of its construction. In the twentieth century, Sullivan's protégé, Frank Lloyd Wright, was to apply the principle of form following function to a wide variety of structures.

Building Over

Another technological innovation that contributed to the expansion of cities was the suspension bridge, which erased broad rivers as barriers to urban growth. Its pioneer was a German immigrant, John A. Roebling, who came to the United States in 1831 as a canal engineer and set up the first American factory for twisting steel wire into cable. Roebling's associates scoffed at his contention that if a bridge were hung from strong cables instead of built up on massive pillars, much broader rivers could be spanned. Obsessed with the concept of the suspension bridge, Roebling devoted his life to perfecting a design. Before the Civil War, he had several to his credit, including an international bridge over the Niagara River near the falls.

Roebling planned his masterpiece for the East River, separating downtown New York, which was bursting at the seams, from the roomy seaport of Brooklyn on Long Island. While working on the site in 1869, he was injured, contracted a tetanus infection, and died. Without delay, his son, Washington A. Roebling, carried on the work. He too suffered serious injuries, crippled by "the bends," later associated with deep-sea divers, as a result of working too long below sea level on the foundations of the bridge's towers. Nevertheless, from a chair in a room overlooking the great span, now called the Brooklyn Bridge, he saw it completed in 1883, his wife carrying his instructions to the site and acting as general foreman. The Brooklyn Bridge was (and is) admired for its beauty as well as its engineering.

In providing easy access to Manhattan—33 million people crossed the bridge each year—the bridge ignited a residential real estate boom in Brooklyn; within a few years, Brooklyn was the fourth largest city in the United States. But the bridge also spelled the end of Brooklyn's independence. A satellite of Manhattan in fact, Brooklyn was incorporated into the City of New York with Queens, Staten Island, and the Bronx by popular vote in 1898.

The Great Symbol

The Brooklyn Bridge was dedicated with a mammoth celebration. President Chester A. Arthur proclaimed it "a monument to democracy"; sides of beef were roasted in the streets; oceans of beer and whiskey disappeared; brass bands competed in raising a din; races were run; prizes were awarded; dances were danced; and noses were punched. A fireworks display of unprecedented splendor topped off the festivities, illuminating the fantastic silhouette from both sides of the East River. The Brooklyn Bridge was America's celebration of the city.

It was also an indictment of the city. On the morning of the gala, one dissenting newspaper editor groused that the Brooklyn Bridge had "begun in fraud" and "continued in corruption." It was no secret that much of the $15 million the project cost had gone not into concrete, steel, and Roebling cable but into the pockets of crooked politicians.

The glories of the bridge were also tarnished by its cost in lives. At least 20 workers were killed building it, and others who just vanished probably fell into the river unnoticed. Many more workers were maimed by the bends and badly broken bones. Then, just a few days after the dedication, a woman stumbled while descending the stairs that led from

Sweatshops

The wealthy took their wants in clothing to small shops where tailors and seamstresses made fine garments by hand from fabric to suit or gown. They worked not from patterns, as someone who sews today would do, but from "fashion plates"—carefully drawn pictures in magazines of people dressed in the latest styles. In the nineteenth century, Paris was considered the authority in such matters. At the beginning of the century, the middle classes depended on their womenfolk for their garb. That is why needlecraft learned at a mother's knee was such an important part of a young girl's education; clothing her family would be one of her most important duties as a wife and mother.

As for the poor, they made do with castoffs either scavenged or purchased from merchants who bought, reconditioned, and sold used clothing. The fact that such garments had been made to fit an individual did not matter when the point was warmth and the rudiments of modesty. Only sailors, slaves, and—after 1849—miners in the West were likely to wear clothing such as nearly everyone does today, "ready made" in quantity to standard sizes and sold "off the rack." Sailors were not in port long enough to be fitted, and they had other uses for their money than tailoring. (The first ready-made clothing stores were called "sailors' shops.") Slaves had no choice in the matter of what they put on their backs; their owners were an attractive market for enterprising tailors who abandoned the custom trade and took to producing rough, cheap garments in quantity. Miners, like sailors, were in a hurry, and they lived in an almost entirely masculine society. Their demand for sturdy, ready-made clothing provided the impetus for the founding in 1850 of the Levi Strauss Company of San Francisco, today perhaps the best-known manufacturer of clothing in the world.

By 1900, things had changed. Nine Americans in 10 were wearing ready-made clothes. A "clothing revolution" had taken place as a consequence of technology, with a boost from the American Civil War. Among the technological inventions were the sewing machine, patented by Elias Howe in 1846, and powered scissors that could cut through 18 pieces of fabric at once, thus making pieces for 18 pairs of trousers or coats of the same size. Standardized sizes were provided by the United States government when the Civil War made it necessary to buy uniforms for hundreds of thousands of men. The army's Quartermaster Corps measured hundreds of recruits and arrived at sets of proportions that provided a fit for almost all. It was a simple step for clothing manufacturers to do the same for women's sizes after the war ended, and ready-made clothing shops began to compete with tailors and seamstresses.

How were the new ready-made clothes manufactured? Not in factories. No oversized machinery was involved in the making of garments, no central source of power. (Sewing machines were treadle powered.) It made no sense to bring workers to one location as it did in textile mills. Once the garment was assembled by sewing machine, the rest was handwork, such as finishing buttonholes, attaching buttons, installing linings, prettying up a dress with ribbons and flounces. This work was farmed out to people working in their homes, just as, before the spinning jenny and power loom, cloth making had been.

The old putting-out system had involved the wives and daughters of farmers, leaving people on the land. Putting out needlework engaged poor people in cities for whom the work was their entire livelihood.

The system was called "sweating," and the places in which the garment makers worked were called "sweatshops," because of the peculiarly exploitative nature of the system. A clothing manufacturer kept a small headquarters; at most, the material was cut to pattern in his "factory." The pieces of garments were handed over on a weekly or daily basis to people, usually Jewish or Italian immigrants, who took them home to their tenements. There, the whole family—and perhaps some boarders and neighbors—sat down in the daylight hours to make up the garments. Some households saw a coat (called a "cloak" in the nineteenth century) or a gown through from components to completion. Others specialized in roughing the garment in, making buttonholes, attaching pockets, and so on.

Everyone involved was paid by the piece—so much per jacket, so much per lining. An intricate hierarchy of subcontractors and sub-subcontractors paid those below them in the chain as little as possible. The man who provided finished cloaks to the company received so much for each garment he delivered. In order to make a profit, he had to pay less than that to the households to which he farmed out the work. If the head of a household sweatshop had boarders or neighbors sewing, he had to pay them less than he was getting per piece. Everybody was "sweating" somebody else.

When a jobber's or a worker's productivity increased, the sweater above him was often inclined to cut the piece rate. Everyone down the chain got less for their work. The operator of a Chicago sweatshop explained the results to a congressional committee in 1893:

Q. In what condition do you get the garments?
A. They come here already cut and I make them up.
Q. What is the average wage of the men per week?
A. About $15 a week.
Q. How much do the women get?
A. About $6. They get paid for extra hours. . . .
Q. Are wages higher or lower than they were two years ago?
A. Lower. There are so many who want to work.
Q. How much do you get for making this garment?
A. Eighty cents.
Q. How much did you get for making it two years ago?
A. About $1.25.
Q. Is the help paid less now?
A. Yes, sir.

A cloak maker told the same panel that he had earned about $20 a week in 1885 for completing fewer garments than he had sewn in 1890, when he had made $13 to $14 a week. In 1893, he was making $11 a week for even greater productivity.

▲ *The Brooklyn Bridge not long after it was completed in 1883. It was (and is) as stunning in its beauty as in its size. The bridge made Brooklyn, the fourth largest city in the nation, an appendage of Manhattan and, in 1898, part of greater New York City.*

the causeway to the ground, and someone shouted, "The bridge is sinking!" In the stampede that followed, 12 people were trampled to death.

THE EVILS OF CITY LIFE

City people died at a rate not known in the United States since the seventeenth century. At a time when the national death rate was 20 per 1,000 annually, the death rate in New York City was 25. In the slums, it was 38 per 1,000, and for children under 5 years of age, 136 per 1,000. The figures were only slightly lower in the other big cities, and in parts of Chicago, they were higher. In one Chicago slum as late as 1900, the infant mortality rate was 200 per 1,000; 1 child in 5 died within a year of birth. By comparison, the infant mortality rate in the United States today is less than 20 per 1,000, and the total death rate is less than 9.

Too Many People, Too Little Room

City people died at high rates largely because of the crowded living conditions of the poor. Statistically, Philadelphia was the healthiest city, because, with a great deal of land on which to build, it was a city of inexpensive two-story brick "row houses." The number of residents per square foot of living space was far lower than in any other metropolis.

In Boston and Chicago, typical housing for working people was in old wooden structures that had been comfortable homes for one family; in the late nineteenth century, half a dozen families, plus boarders, crowded into them.

In New York, the narrow confines of Manhattan Island made the crowding even worse. Former single-family residences were carved into tenements that housed a hundred and more people. In 1866, the board of health found 400,000 people living in tenements with no windows and 20,000 living in cellars below the water table. An investigator said that cellar dwellers "exhibited the same lethargic habits as animals burrowing in the ground." At high tide, their homes filled with water, and they sheltered where they could. The board closed the cellars and ordered 46,000 windows cut in airless rooms; but in 1900, people whose memories dated back to the 1860s said that they preferred conditions then.

Jacob Riis, a newspaper reporter who exposed squalid urban living conditions in a book of 1890, *How the Other Half Lives,* estimated that 330,000 people lived in a square mile of slum—almost 1,000 people per acre. New York was more than twice as congested as the London that turned Charles Dickens's stomach, and parts of it were more populous than Bombay, Americans' image of hell on earth. On one tenement block in the Jewish section of the Lower East Side, just a little larger than an acre, 2,800 people lived. In an apartment of two tiny rooms there, Riis found a married couple, their twelve children, and six adult boarders.

When architect James E. Ware designed a new kind of building to improve housing for the poor, he was accused of making the situation worse. His "dumbbell" tenement, named for its shape, ostensibly provided 24 to 32 apartments, all with ventilation, on a standard New York building lot of 25 by 100 feet. However, when two dumbbells were constructed side by side, the windows of two-thirds of the living units opened on an air shaft, sometimes only two feet wide, that was soon filled with garbage, creating a threat to health worse than airlessness. Nevertheless, the dumbbells met city building standards; by 1894, there were 39,000 of them in Manhattan, housing almost half the population.

Health

Crowding led to epidemic outbreaks of serious diseases like smallpox, cholera, measles, typhus, scarlet fever, and diphtheria. In Philadelphia's row houses, it was possible and effective to quarantine afflicted families. In other cities, quarantine did little good: Where were unafflicted people to go? Even less-dangerous illnesses like chicken pox, mumps, whooping cough, croup, and the various influenzas were killers in the crowded cities. Common colds were feared as the first step to pneumonia.

In his famous book, Jacob Riis took readers on a tour of a tenement: "Be a little careful, please! The hall is dark and you might stumble. You can feel your way, if you cannot see it. Close? Yes! What would you have? All the fresh air that enters these stairs comes from the hall-door that is forever

▲ *Traffic jams long predated the automobile. Here, trolleys, horse-drawn wagons, and a sea of pedestrians have created what seems a hopeless gridlock.*

slamming." He paused at the entrance to a windowless apartment. "Listen! That short, hacking cough, that tiny, helpless wail. . . . The child is dying of measles. With half a chance it might have lived; but it had none. That dark bedroom killed it."

With New York still a city of heavy industry, the air was polluted, according to the board of health, by sulfur, ammonia, kerosene, acids, and phosphates, not to mention the odors of slaughterhouses and horse manure.

Sanitation

Sanitation was a serious problem in big cities. Whereas free-roaming scavengers—chickens, hogs, dogs, and birds—handily cleaned up the garbage in small towns, and backyard latrines were adequate in disposing of human wastes, neither worked when a hundred people lived in a building and shared a single toilet. City governments provided for waste collection, but even when honestly administered (which was the exception), sanitation departments simply could not keep up.

Horses compounded the problem. They deposited tons of manure on city streets daily, and special squads could not begin to keep pace. Moreover, on extremely hot and cold days, old and poorly kept horses keeled over by the hundreds;

in New York, the daily total could top 1,000. Although, by law, the owner of the dead beast was required to dispose of the carcass, this meant he dumped it into the river. More often, because the task was so formidable, owners of faltering horses cut them out of harness and disappeared. In summer, the corpses bloated and began to putrefy within hours.

In the poorest tenements, piped water was available only in shared sinks in the hallways, which were typically filthy. Safe water was so heavily dosed with chemicals that it was barely palatable. The well-to-do bought bottled spring water

Horse-and-Buggy Days

A horse dead was a sanitation problem in big cities, but so was a horse alive. Each horse produced as much as 25 to 40 pounds of manure each day. In New York City in 1900, there were about 150,000 horses. The potential litter problem, therefore, weighed between 1,500 and 3000 tons daily, not to mention 60,000 gallons of equine urine. Most manure merely dried and crumbled where it dropped, blowing or washing away in time. Some was scooped up by the city or by private entrepreneurs and sold to farmers on the outskirts as fertilizer.

that was trucked into the cities. Other people depended on wells in the streets that were inevitably fouled by runoff.

Tenement apartments did not have bathrooms. Children washed by romping in the water of open fire hydrants or by taking a swim in polluted waterways. If you did not come home tinged gray or brown, one survivor of New York's Lower East Side remembered, you had not washed. When a bath was necessary, adults went to public bathhouses, where there was hot, clean water at a reasonable price. Many of these establishments were quite respectable. Others were known as dens of immorality.

Vice and Crime

As they always are, slums were breeding grounds of vice and crime. With 14,000 homeless people in New York in 1890, many of them children—"street Arabs," they were called— and work difficult to get and unsteady in the best of times, many found the temptations of sneak thievery, pocket picking, purse snatching, and, for the bolder, violent robbery, too much to resist. As early as the 1850s, police in New York were vying with (or taking bribes from) strong-arm gangs who were named after the neighborhoods where they held sway. Among them were the Five Points, Mulberry Bend, Hell's Kitchen, Poverty Gap, and Whyo Gangs.

They occasionally struck outside their areas, robbing warehouses and the like, and preying on middle- or upper-class fops who were slumming. (The best residential neighborhoods were well policed.) But the gangs' typical victims were slum dwellers struggling to survive and escape—the workingman who paused for a beer before he took his pay envelope home—and small businessmen who were forced to make regular payments or risk physical violence. Whereas the rate of homicide and other serious crimes declined in German and British cities as they grew larger, it tripled in American cities during the 1880s. An Italian visitor to the United States, Cesare Lombroso, exclaimed, "Lawlessness is an American phenomenon with no equal in the rest of the world." The prison population of the nation doubled in the last years of the century, but plenty of thugs remained at large.

By the end of the century, the more-sophisticated gangs moved into vice, running illegal gambling operations, opium dens, and brothels. Prostitution flourished at every level in a society where domestic sexual activity was repressed by middle-class prudery or working-class pregnancy. There was a plentiful supply of impoverished girls and women who had no other way to survive. The lucky few set themselves up as mistresses or in fancy houses that catered to the well-to-do. More common was the wretched prostitute who plied her

© Bettmann/Corbis

▲ *A slum in New York City about 1900. Every big city had them: the Flats in Cleveland, Cross Keys in St. Louis, the North End in Boston, the Stockyards in Chicago.*

trade on the streets, under the costly protection of a gang if she did not want to be beaten.

An Urban Culture

And yet, for all the horror stories (which no one savored more than the people who lived in the cities) and lurid accounts of urban life in books, newspapers, magazines, sermons, lectures, plays, and scandalized reports by people who visited New York, Chicago, Kansas City, or other "dens of pestilence," a vital, exciting, and excited urban culture developed in American cities. City people compared rural "yokels" and "hayseeds" unfavorably to themselves. Once established, city people were unlikely to move to the country or even to be attracted by jobs beyond the municipal limits.

The cities continued to grow at an extraordinary rate after 1900. Indeed, had it not been for the existence of a more traditional American frontier larger than any that had gone before, it is likely that the rural population would have declined in the late nineteenth century, as it was to do in the twentieth.

for FURTHER READING

See Vincent P. DeSantis, *The Shaping of Modern America, 1877–1916,* 1973; John A. Garraty, *The New Commonwealth, 1877–1890,* 1968; and Samuel P. Hays, *The Response to Industrialism, 1885–1914,* 1957. Arthur M. Schlesinger, *The Rise of the City, 1878–1898,* 1933, is still a valuable source.

To augment and correct Schlesinger in particulars, see Robert H. Bremner, *From the Depths: The Discovery of Poverty in America,* 1956; Howard Chudakov, *The Evolution of American Urban Society,* 1975; John Higham, *Send These to Me: Jews and Other Immigrants in Urban America,* 1975; Blake McKelvey, *The Ur-* *banization of America, 1860–1915,* 1962; Zane Miller and Patricia Melvin, *The Urbanization of Modern America,* 1987; Thomas L. Philpott, *The Slum and the Ghetto,* 1978; Barbara Rosenkrantz, *Public Health and the State,* 1972; Stephan Thernstrom, *The Other Bostonians: Poverty and Progress in the American Metropolis,* 1973; Sam B. Warner, *Streetcar Suburbs: The Process of Growth in Boston, 1870–1900,* 1971, and *The Urban Wilderness: A History of the American City,* 1972; and Morton White, *The Intellectual Versus the City,* 1962.

AMERICAN JOURNEY ONLINE AND INFOTRAC COLLEGE EDITION

Visit the source collections at http://ajaccess.wadsworth.com and http://infotrac.thomsonlearning.com, and use the Search function with the following key terms to explore documents, images, audio and video clips, articles, and commentary related to the material in this chapter:

Hull House
Jacob Riis
Jane Addams
Sweatshops

Additional resources, exercises, and Internet links related to this chapter are available on *The American Past* Web site: http://history.wadsworth.com/americanpast7e.

HISTORY ONLINE

The Life of a City
http://memory.loc.gov/ammem/papr/nychome.html
Early films of New York City.

The Great Chicago Fire
www.chicagohs.org/fire/
"Virtual" exhibit of the greatest American urban disaster of the later nineteenth century.

CHAPTER

31

THE LAST FRONTIER

Winning the Last of the West 1865–1900

To the frontier the American intellect owes its striking characteristics. That coarseness and strength combined with acuteness and inquisitiveness; that practical, inventive turn of mind, quick to find expedients; that masterful grasp of material things, lacking in the artistic but powerful to effect great ends; that restless, nervous energy; that dominant individualism, working for good and for evil; and withal that buoyancy and exuberance which comes with freedom—these are traits of the frontier, or traits called out elsewhere because of the frontier.

Frederick Jackson Turner

AFTER COUNTING THE American people in 1890, the Census Bureau announced that there was no longer a frontier. No line could be drawn on the map marking where settled land ended and wild lands began. The bureau's definition of "settled" land was not rigorous: just 2.5 people per square mile, a population density that, to us, seems appropriate to howling wilderness. Even by the bureau's standards, at the time of the Civil War, the unsettled part of the United States comprised roughly half the nation's area. Twenty-five years later, it was gone—settled. In a quarter of a century, Americans tamed as much country as they had in the first 250 years after the founding of Jamestown.

THE LAST FRONTIER

In 1865, with the exception of California, Oregon, and Washington Territory on the west coast (where 440,000 people lived), the Great Salt Lake Basin (where the Mormon Zion was home to a population of 40,000), and New Mexico (which a few Anglos made home), the frontier ran north to south about 150 to 200 miles west of the Mississippi River. Settlers had barely spilled over the far boundaries of Minnesota, Iowa, Missouri, and Arkansas. Half of the state of Texas was beyond the frontier.

An Unusable Land

Most believed that this last West would never be settled. Americans thought agriculturally. Pioneering meant bringing land under tillage. Except for a few pockets of fertile, well-watered soil, none of the three geographical regions of the West was suitable to agriculture.

In the middle of the last West lay the majestic Rocky Mountains. The snowy peaks of the Rockies were known to easterners from landscape paintings by artists who accompanied military expeditions and the transcontinental wagon trains or who, having learned of the natural glories of the West, had ventured there on their own, easel, oils, and canvases packed in their lumbering wagons. The very grandeur of the Rockies, however, told Americans that the mountains could not support a population living as people did back East.

West of the Rockies and east of California's Sierra Nevada lay the high desert and the Great Basin—the rugged, arid home of birds, snakes, rodents, comical armadillos, cactus, creosote bush, sagebrush, and tumbleweed. In the basin, the soil was rocky, thin, and usually alkaline. It is called a "basin" because its rivers lose heart in their search for an outlet and pool up in the desert, evaporating in the sun. With irrigation, the Mormons worked miracles in one of those sinks, the Great Salt Lake Basin, but no part of the West seemed less inviting to Americans than this genuine desert.

East of the Rockies were the Great Plains, rainier than the Great Basin but still dry and almost treeless. Short grasses carpeted the plains, and rivers like the Missouri and the Platte meandered through them. Nevertheless, where trees did not grow, Americans believed, agriculture was impossible as, indeed, were the kinds of farming they knew.

The Native Peoples of the West

People did live in the "unsettled" United States, of course. In addition to the Mormons and the *nuevos mexicanos,* perhaps 350,000 Indians preserved traditional ways of life influenced to varying degrees by their contact with Americans. Even the most forbidding parts of the Great Basin supported the Ute, Paiute, and Shoshone, who coped with the torrid, dry summers by dividing into small foraging bands and seeking higher elevations.

To the south, in the marginally less forbidding environment of present-day Arizona and New Mexico, the Pima, Zuni, and Hopi had been farming intensively for centuries before the explorations of Francisco de Coronado in the 1530s. Their pueblos (a Spanish term) were communal houses or groups of apartments, sometimes perched high on sheer cliffs, where a delicately integrated village culture evolved. The Navajo, more numerous than any other people in the desert south of the Grand Canyon (and comparative newcomers there), lived in family groups spread out over the country. The Navajo were skilled weavers of cotton when the introduction of Spanish sheep provided them with the opportunity to raise their craft into a more durable art. Both the Navajo and the Pueblo Indians feared the warlike Apache raiders who, before the Civil War, dwelled mostly in Mexico, but ranged widely in search of booty. Just between 1862 and 1867, Apache killed 400 Mexicans and Anglo settlers in the borderlands, and Indians no one bothered to count.

In Oklahoma, then called Indian Territory, the "civilized tribes" native to Georgia and Alabama, and remnants of tribes of the old Northwest, had rebuilt their amalgam of indigenous and American cultures. They farmed intensively, lived in American-style dwellings (many in towns), maintained a school system, and published newspapers in Cherokee and English.

But the Indians who most fascinated easterners were, curiously, those who were most determined to resist the whites and their ways—the tribes of the Great Plains. From the writings of intrepid travelers like historian Francis Parkman and painters Karl Bodmer and George Catlin, the Comanche, Cheyenne, and Arapaho peoples of the southern plains, and the Mandan, Crow, Sioux, Nez Percé, and Blackfoot of the northern grasslands, awed easterners and, to a degree, won their admiration.

Plains Culture

The lives of the Plains Indians—economy, social structure, religion, diet, dress—revolved around two animals: the native bison and the immigrant horse. The bison, as many as 30 million of them in 1800, provided food and hides that were made into clothing, footwear, blankets, portable shelters (the conical teepees), bowstrings, and canvases on which

▲ *One of the last frontiers in the lower 48 states: Arizona near the Verde River, 1885.*

artists recorded heroic legends, tribal histories, and genealogies. The bison's manure made a tolerable fuel for cooking and warmth in a treeless land where winters were harsh.

The Plains Indians were nomadic. Except for the Mandan, they grew no crops; they trailed after the bison herds on their horses. It was not an ancient culture, like that of the Pueblo Indians. Horses descended from Spanish herds in New Mexico, liberated by the thousands in an Indian revolt in 1680, reached the Snake River by about 1700, the central Great Plains about 1720, and the Columbia Plateau, home of the Nez Percé, about 1730. The Plains Indians learned to capture the feral "spirit dogs" and developed their mode of horsemanship—no stirrup, saddle, or bit—independent of Mexican example. The Comanche were generally regarded as the most skilled riders. "Almost as awkward as a monkey on the ground," painter George Catlin wrote of a Comanche in 1834, "the moment he lays his hand upon a horse, his face even becomes handsome, and he gracefully flies away like a different being." (Catlin's paintings show that some Comanche had, by the 1830s, taken to using iron stirrups, but that was a recent development.) One Comanche band of 2,000 had a herd of 15,000 horses.

The wandering ways of the plains tribes brought them frequently in contact with one another and with tribes that farmed to the east. Although they traded and could communicate with remarkable subtlety through a common sign language, the Plains Indians were just as likely to fight one another. Their wars were fought not for the purpose of territorial conquest—as nomads, they thought in terms of dominating ranges, not owning land—but to capture horses and women, and to demonstrate courage, the noblest quality of which a Great Plains male could boast.

With only about 225,000 Indians roaming the Great Plains in 1865, warfare was not massive, but it was chronic. Permanent peace was as foreign to the Plains Indians' worldview as the notion that an individual could claim sole ownership of 160 acres of grassland (and a thousand people 160,000 acres).

By 1865, every plains tribe knew about the "palefaces" or "white-eyes." They did not like the wagon trains that had traversed their homeland for two decades, and they occasionally skirmished with the white wayfarers. (Only 350 of 100,000 overlanders were killed by Indians.) But the outsiders were welcome to the extent that they traded, abandoned, or neglected to secure their horses, clothing, iron tools, and rifles, all of which improved the Indians' standard of living.

The Destruction of the Buffalo

This wary coexistence began to change when Congress authorized the construction of the transcontinental railroad. The crews that laid the tracks of the Union Pacific and Kansas Pacific across the plains were not interested in staying. But, unlike the California and Oregon emigrants, their presence led directly to the destruction of the bison.

A Mandan village in 1832, just about the high point of the tribe's history. They hunted buffalo like other Plains Indians but were unique in that they also farmed. Their crops made them a tempting target for the Sioux, who, along with smallpox contracted from whites, destroyed the Mandan within a generation.

In order to help feed the construction crews, railroads hired hunters like William F. "Buffalo Bill" Cody, an army scout and stagecoach driver, to harvest the herds. Using a 0.50 caliber Springfield rifle, Buffalo Bill alone killed more than 4,000 bison in 18 months in 1867 and 1868. That made no dent in the buffalo population, estimated to have been 15 million. However, when some hides were shipped back East, they caused a sensation as fashionable buffalo robes, and the leather proved to be excellent for the belts used to drive machinery. Methodical, wholesale slaughter of the animals began at Dodge City, Kansas, in 1872. In three months, 700 tons of hides (43,000 animals) were shipped from the rail-head town.

As many as 2,000 hunters jumped into the business. A team of marksmen, reloaders, and skinners could down and skin a thousand bison a day. Buffalo were easy pickings. Living in huge herds, they were not bothered by loud noises; they stood grazing, pathetically easy targets, as long as they did not smell or see the hunters. By 1875, the southern herd was effectively wiped out. By 1883, the northern herd was gone.

The railroads encouraged the slaughter because a herd of bison could obliterate the flimsy iron railroad tracks merely by crossing over them. Settlers on the edge of the plains were glad for the hunters because they (correctly) linked their "Indian problem" to the abundance of bison. "So long as there are millions of buffaloes in the West," a Texan told Congress, "so long the Indians cannot be controlled." The army concurred. General Philip Sheridan, commander of western troops and an unabashed Indian hater, said that Congress should strike a medal with "a dead buffalo on one side and a discouraged Indian on the other."

To apply the finishing touches, wealthy eastern and European sportsmen chartered special trains and, sometimes without stepping to the ground, shot trophies for their mansions and clubs. Their services were not really needed and, in the case of Russian grand duke Alexis Alexandrovich, not very efficient. With Buffalo Bill in attendance, he fired 12 revolver shots at two buffalo and did not hit either. He then took a rifle and killed one from about 10 feet.

In 1874, Congress tried to end the slaughter, prohibiting the shooting of bison except for food. President Grant, obliging his old comrade, General Sheridan, vetoed it. By 1889, when preservationists stepped in to save the species, fewer than a thousand American buffalo were alive. (Most of the 200,000 bison today are descended from just 77 animals.) It was probably the most rapid extinction of a species in history.

The Cavalry

The United States Cavalry accompanied the railroads, ostensibly to enforce the Indians' treaty rights as well as to protect the workmen. Some of these troops were captured Confederate soldiers who elected to take an oath of loyalty to the Union and serve in the West as preferable to languishing in prisoner-of-war camps. After the war, they were joined by northern whites and by blacks in the Ninth and Tenth Cavalries, two of just four African American regiments in the peacetime army.

Some officers respected the tribes and tried to deal fairly with them. General George Crook, remembered as one of the ablest of the army's Indian fighters, prided himself on

▲ *The transcontinental railroad meant the destruction of the great herds of bison. The animals blocked, even destroyed, roadbeds, and their meat provided a cheap means of feeding construction workers. Once the value of buffalo hides and leather was discovered back East, some 15 million were reduced to 2 or 3 million in just a few years. By 1890, only hundreds survived.*

dealing justly with the tribes. Others shared the values of General Sheridan, who was reputed to have told a Comanche chief at Fort Cobb in 1869, "The only good Indian is a dead Indian."

Overall, of course, the sympathies of the army were with the railroaders, miners, cattlemen, and, eventually, farmers who intruded on Indian lands. Whites assumed that because the Indians, like the Mexicans, used the land inefficiently, their claims to it were not equal to their own, let alone superior. Beginning in 1862, when the final wave of Indian wars began with a Sioux uprising in Minnesota, to 1890, when the military power of the Sioux was shattered at Wounded Knee, South Dakota, the United States Cavalry finished the job the buffalo hunters began: the destruction of the western tribes.

The Last Indian Wars

To the end, Indian war remained a war of few pitched battles and innumerable small skirmishes. Between 1869 and 1876, the peak years of the fighting, the army recorded 200 incidents, a number that did not include many unopposed Indian raids and confrontations between civilians and the tribes. Still, the total casualties on the army's side (and possibly that of the Indians) were less than in any of several Indian-white battles in the 1790s.

Moving amid the Hostiles

A cavalry unit, unlike its movie versions, was accompanied by long wagon trains, sometimes 150 vehicles. In addition to a soldier, each horse carried 80 to 90 pounds of equipment. With such a load, a horse needed to be rested frequently. This was accomplished without arresting progress by dividing the soldiers on the march into two troops. One troop rode until it was half a mile ahead of the plodding wagon train. The soldiers then dismounted to rest and graze their horses until the wagons were half a mile ahead. As they caught up, the other troop moved on ahead and repeated the maneuver. In this way, there was always a troop, in two columns, at either side of the precious supplies.

Buffalo Soldiers

The Indians called the African Americans of the Ninth and Tenth Cavalry Regiments "buffalo soldiers" because, to the Indians, the soldiers' hair resembled buffalo hides. The black regiments' record in the West was excellent. They had a high enlistment rate, the lowest desertion rate, and the fewest court-martialed soldiers of any western regiments; individual soldiers from the Ninth and Tenth Cavalry Regiments won 18 Congressional Medals of Honor in the Indian wars.

The army wanted to fight decisive battles, which favored the soldiers' training and superior technology. But the Indians clung to traditional hit-and-run attacks that exploited their advantage—mobility—and allowed them to avoid fights in which, with their inferior arms and numbers, they had little chance of prevailing. One consequence was frustration among the soldiers and a cruelty toward the enemy such as had been seen in the Civil War only in Confederate treatment of African American prisoners. In 1871, Commissioner of Indian Affairs Francis Walker explained that "when dealing with savage men, as with savage beasts, no question of national honor can arise. Whether to fight, to run away, or to employ a ruse, is solely a question of expediency."

By 1876, the year of the centennial, the army's final victory seemed near. Little by little, the soldiers in their dusty blue uniforms hemmed in the wandering tribes and whittled away at their ability to subsist. The typical state of a surrendering tribe was near starvation, with a large proportion of the young men dead. But Indian resistance was not quite at an end.

Custer's Last Stand

In June 1876, an audacious colonel of the Seventh Cavalry, famous as a hero of the Civil War, George Armstrong Custer, led 265 men into a battle with the Sioux and

Cheyenne on Montana's Little Bighorn River. In a rare total victory for the Indians, every one of Custer's men was killed. Although a completely unexpected defeat, "Custer's Last Stand" thrilled Americans. Denied in life the advancement he believed his record and talents merited, "Yellow Hair" (as the Sioux called him) became a romantic hero in death. A brewery commissioned an imaginative painting of the Battle of the Little Bighorn and within a few years distributed 150,000 reproductions of it.

Senior officers who disapproved of the flamboyant and impetuous Custer, and thought him to blame for the disaster, kept their mouths shut. Only in the next century would the episode be fully appreciated from the Indians' point of view, as a final great military victory brilliantly engineered by Sioux and Cheyenne war chiefs. At the time, however, the tribes' joy was short-lived. Most of the victors were under federal control within the year.

Good Intentions, Tragic Results

In 1881, a Coloradan, Helen Hunt Jackson, published *A Century of Dishonor,* one of the decade's best-sellers. In meticulous detail and with few errors of fact, she traced the cynicism with which the United States government had dealt with the Indians since independence. The list of Indian treaties was a list of broken treaties. Time and again, "Christian" whites had cheated "savage" Indians of their land, herding them onto reservations on lands judged to be next to worthless and then chipping away at those.

▲ *"Custer's Last Stand" so thrilled Americans that, within a few years, dozens of artists painted renditions of the battle. None saw it, of course, or knew eyewitnesses who might have described it to them—every man with Custer was killed. Red Horse did fight in the Battle of the Little Bighorn and recorded this painting of it.*

By 1876, the government was not making treaties with the Indians. Those tribes that did not resist American control were defined as wards of the federal government; they were not citizens but were under Washington's protection and enjoyed a few privileges. After the publication of *A Century of Dishonor,* many easterners demanded that the government use this wardship in a just manner.

In 1887, Congress approved the Dawes Severalty Act. Intentions were the best. Assuming that the traditional Indian way of life was no longer feasible, which was obvious, the sponsors of the Dawes Act argued that the Indian peoples must be Americanized. That is, they must become self-sustaining citizens through adoption of the ways of the larger culture. Therefore, under the Dawes Act, the tribes were dissolved, and the treaty lands were distributed homestead-style, 160 acres to each head of the family, with an additional 80 acres to each adult member of the household. Lands left over were sold to whites. In order to avoid further ravaging, remaining Indian land could not be sold or otherwise disposed of for 25 years.

The supporters of the Dawes Act overlooked a number of vital facts. First, few of the western Indians were farmers; traditionally, they were hunters, gatherers, traders, and raiders. Second, the reservation lands were rarely suited to agriculture; they were allotted to the Indians precisely because they were unattractive to white farmers. Third, tracts of a few hundred acres in the arid West were rarely enough

to support efficient farmers, let alone novices at tillage. Finally, no western Indians thought in terms of private ownership of land. The tribe, which the Dawes Act aimed to relegate to the dustheap, not the nuclear family, was the basic social unit of the Native Americans. The defeated Indians were demoralized by the forced and rapid disintegration of their culture, and individuals too often fell prey to idleness and alcohol.

Geronimo

The Apache Geronimo, who fought on after his tribe made peace with the United States, was a resourceful leader. For eight years his ever dwindling band (at the end, 17 warriors, 14 women, and 6 children) evaded capture by hundreds of troops assigned to no other task, by slipping back and forth across the Mexican border. He finally gave up to the Americans because he knew the Mexican army would treat his people brutally.

Geronimo, like Sitting Bull, became a pop culture hero during a long imprisonment in Florida. Dozens of journalists interviewed him. Hundreds of people paid him to pose with them for photographs. He was, however, not a man to be lionized. Resourceful he might have been, but he was also a murderer, fighting soldiers less than he raided Mexican and American farms, often gratuitously killing the unoffending people who lived on them.

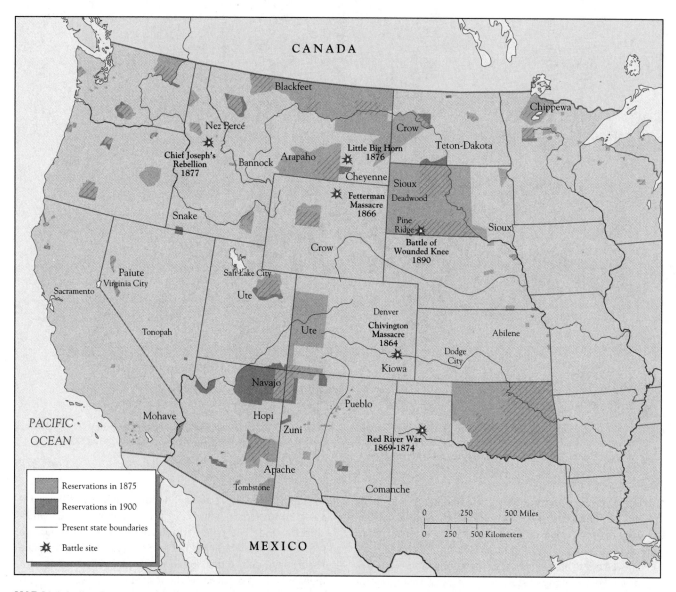

CANADA

Blackfeet

Chippewa

Nez Percé

Crow

Teton-Dakota

Chief Joseph's
Rebellion
1877

Arapaho

Little Big Horn
1876

Bannock

Cheyenne

Sioux

Snake

Fetterman
Massacre
1866

Deadwood

Pine
Ridge

Sioux

Crow

Battle of
Wounded Knee
1890

Paiute

Virginia City

Salt Lake City

Sacramento

Ute

Sioux

Tonopah

Ute

Denver

Abilene

Chivington
Massacre
1864

Dodge
City

Kiowa

Navajo

Mohave

Hopi

Pueblo

PACIFIC
OCEAN

Zuni

Red River War
1869-1874

Tombstone

Apache

Comanche

MEXICO

Reservations in 1875

Reservations in 1900

Present state boundaries

Battle site

0   250   500 Miles

0   250   500 Kilometers

MAP 31:1 Indian Reservations, 1875 and 1900   Before the destruction of the bison in the early 1870s, the Plains Indians were almost unimpeded in ranging from above the Canadian border to northern Texas, between the Rockies and the cow towns of Kansas. After 1875, they were herded onto reservations that shrunk in size steadily and sharply in just 25 years, by both legal purchases and white settlers' pressure on the federal government.

Wounded Knee

Among these desperate and demoralized people appeared a religious teacher in the tradition of the Prophet. Jack Wilson, or Wovoka, was a Paiute who was fascinated by the Christian doctrine of redemption. Calling on Christianity and Native American practices and aspirations, he created a religion promising redemption for Indians on this earth. Preached throughout the West by Wovoka's disciples, the Ghost Dance religion appealed to thousands.

According to Wovoka, by performing a ritual dance, the Indians, who were God's chosen people, could prevail on the Great Spirit to make the white man disappear. The Ghost Dance would also bring back to life the buffalo herds and

Indians who had been killed in the wars. The old way of life, which in the 1880s adult Indians vividly remembered, would be restored.

This sort of belief, simultaneously edifying and heart-rending, is common among peoples who have seen their world turned upside down. In parts of the Southwest that were untouched by Wovoka's religion, defeated Indians turned to peyote, a natural hallucinogenic drug, as a way to escape a bewildering, intolerable reality.

To understand the appeal of the Ghost Dance religion, it is necessary to recall just how rapidly the culture of the Plains Indians was destroyed. The Dakota Sioux, for example, did not go to war with the whites until the end of the 1860s. Within another decade, the survivors were herded

▲ *A Sioux village on the reservation at Pine Ridge, South Dakota, in 1891. In a village much like this, late in 1890, Sitting Bull, one of the most influential Sioux chiefs, was shot during an attempt to arrest him.*

onto the Pine Ridge Reservation in South Dakota, where Wovoka's message was preached by Kicking Bear. There, on Wounded Knee Creek in December 1890, when the Dakotas took avidly to the Ghost Dance religion and the soldiers guarding them tried to take their guns away, a shoving incident led to a one-sided fight in which about 200 people, half of them women and children, were killed. For the Indians of the Great Plains, there was no escape, not even in mysticism.

THE CATTLE KINGDOM

In 1870, American forests yielded about 12.8 billion board feet of lumber. By 1900, this output had almost tripled to 36 billion. Although the increase reflects in part the development of forest industries in the southern states, the region of greatest expansion was a new one, the Pacific Northwest.

In 1870, Americans were raising 23.8 million cattle. In 1900, 67.7 million head were fattening on grasslands, mostly in the West, and in western feedlots.

Annual gold production continued at the fabulous levels of the gold-rush era; until the end of the century, it was nearly double the totals of 1850. Annual silver production, only 2.4 million troy ounces in 1870, stood at 57.7 million in 1900.

The First Buckaroos

Acre for acre, cattlemen won more of the West than any other kind of pioneers. They were motivated by the appetite of the burgeoning cities of the East (and Europe) for cheap meat. They were encouraged in their venture by the disinterest in the rolling grasslands of anyone except the Indians. Their story thrills Americans (and other peoples) to this day partly because it was romanticized and partly because the cattle kingdom was established so quickly and just as quickly destroyed.

The cowboy rode into American legend just before the Civil War. In the late 1850s, enterprising Texans began to round up herds of half-wild longhorns that ranged freely

▲ *Authentic Texas cowboys. The photograph was posed: They, their sombreros, and their clothing are too clean and unrumpled for them to have been on an exhausting long drive. The picture was probably taken shortly before they began the trek across Texas and Oklahoma to a railhead town in Kansas.*

between the Nueces River and the Rio Grande. They drove them north over an old Shawnee trail to Sedalia, Missouri, a railroad town with connections to Chicago. Although the bosses were English-speaking, many of the actual workers were Mexicans, who called themselves *vaqueros,* or "cowboys." *Vaquero* entered the English language as "buckaroo."

Although Anglo-Americans were the majority of this mobile workforce, numerous former slaves were cowboys, and much of what became part of American folklore and parlance about the buckaroos was of Mexican derivation. The cowboy's colorful costume was an adaptation of Mexican work dress. The bandana was a washcloth that, when tied over the cowboy's mouth, served as a dust screen, no small matter when a thousand cattle were kicking up grit. The broad-brimmed hat was not selected for its picturesque qualities but because it was a sun and rain shield. Extremely durable when manufactured from first-quality beaver felt, the sombrero also served as a drinking pot and washbasin.

The pointed, high-heeled boots, awkward and even painful when a man was walking, were designed for riding in the stirrups, where a *vaquero* spent his workday. The western saddle was an adaptation of Spanish design and quite unlike the English tack that easterners used. Chaps, leather leg coverings, got their name from chaparral, the ubiquitous woody brush against which they were designed to protect the cowboy.

Meat for Millions

The Civil War and Missouri laws excluding Texas cattle (because of hoof-and-mouth disease) stifled the cattle-driving business almost before it began. However, in 1866, when the transcontinental railroad reached Abilene, Kansas, a wheeler-dealer from Illinois, Joseph G. McCoy, saw the possibilities of underselling steers raised on private pasture back East with Texas longhorns. McCoy built holding pens

> ### Cattlemen and Sheepherders
> A common theme in the folklore of the West is the conflict between cattlemen and sheepherders. Cattlemen disliked sheep because, they said, sheep destroyed the range. In fact, because cattle stroll as they graze and sheep continue to eat the grass at their feet until they have devoured it to the ground, sheep that were not forced to move were more destructive than cattle were. Many ranchers nevertheless preferred sheep because the labor costs involved were lower and easier to control (a single herder and a dog could supervise several thousand sheep) and wool, unlike meat on the hoof, could be stored indefinitely.

on the outskirts of the tiny Kansas town, arranged to ship cattle he did not then have with the Kansas Pacific Railroad, and dispatched agents to southern Texas to induce cowboys to round up and drive cattle north to Abilene on a trading route called the Chisholm Trail.

In 1867, McCoy shipped 35,000 "tall, bony, coarse headed, flat-sided, thin-flanked" cattle to Chicago. In 1868, 75,000 of the beasts, next to worthless in Texas, passed through Abilene, and Chicago meat packers cried for more. In 1871, 600,000 "critters" passed through the pens of several Kansas railroad towns on their way to American dinner tables.

The profits were immense. A steer that cost about $5 to raise on public lands could be driven to Kansas at the cost of a cent a mile ($5 to $8) and sold for $25 or, occasionally, as much as $50. Such a business attracted investors from back East and England. They built ranches that were as comfortable as the gentlemen's clubs of New York and London. The typical cattleman at Wyoming's Cheyenne Club never touched a gun, and he sat on a horse only for a photographer. His mount was a plush easy chair, his range a fine carpet, and he puffed on Havana cigars when he discussed accounts with his fellow buckaroos.

The railhead continued to move westward, and with it went the destination of the cowboys, who were soon arriving from the North as well as the South. Nor did most of the citizens of old cow towns like Abilene object to the migration of the railhead. They concluded after a few seasons that the money to be made as a cattle-trading center was not worth the damage done to their own ranches and farms by hundreds of thousands of cattle. The wild atmosphere given their towns by the rambunctious cowboys, many of them bent on a blowout after months on the trail, was even less conducive to respectable civic life. As a cow town grew, its "better element" demanded churches and schools in place of saloons, casinos, and whorehouses. The stage was set for the taming of a town, which is the theme of so much folklore.

Never, though, did the cowboys lack for someplace to take their herds. There were always newer, smaller towns to the west to welcome them and their wages. In Kansas alone, Abilene, Ellsworth, Newton, Wichita, Dodge City, and Hays had their wide-open period.

Disaster

The cattle kingdom lasted only a generation, ending suddenly as a result of a collaboration between human greed and natural disaster.

The short-term profits to be made in cattle were so great that exploiters ignored the long-term damage that their huge herds were doing to the grasslands. Vast as the plains were, they were overstocked and overgrazed by the mid-1880s. Unlike the bison, which migrated constantly in search of the lushest grass, leaving the land they grazed to recover, cattle's wanderings were limited. They fouled clear-running springs, even trampled them into mud pits. Weeds never noticed in the West replaced the native grasses that had been overgrazed. Hills and buttes were scarred by cattle trails. Some species of migratory birds that once darkened the skies twice a year simply disappeared; the beefsteaks on the hoof had beaten them to their provisions.

Then, on January 1, 1886, a great blizzard buried the eastern and southern plains. Within three days, 3 feet of snow drifting into 20- and 30-foot banks suffocated the range. Between 50 and 85 percent of the livestock froze to death or died of hunger. About 300 cowboys could not reach shelter and died; the casualties among the Indians never were counted. When spring arrived, half the American plains reeked of the smell of death.

Drought in the summer of 1886 ruined the cattlemen who survived the snows. Grasses that had weathered summer droughts for millennia were unable to do so after the blizzards; they withered and died, and cattle already weakened by winter starved. Then, the next winter, the states that escaped the worst of the blizzard of 1886 got 16 inches of snow in 16 hours, followed by weeks more of intermittent snowfall.

The cattle industry recovered, but only when more prudent and methodical businessmen took over the holdings of the speculators of the glory days. Cattle barons like Richard King of southern Texas forswore risking all on the open range. Through clever manipulation of land laws, King built a ranch that was as large as the state of Rhode Island. If their success was not quite as spectacular as King's, others imitated his example in Texas, Wyoming, Montana, and eastern Colorado.

Even more important in ending the days of the long drive and the romantic image of the cowboy as a knight-errant was the expansion of the railroad network. When new lines snaked into Texas and the states on the Canadian border, and the Union Pacific and Kansas Pacific sent feeder lines north and south into cow country, the cowboy became a ranch hand, a not so freewheeling employee of large commercial operations.

Oh, Give Me a Home

Even in the days of the long drive, the world of the cowboy bore scant resemblance to the legends that came to permeate American popular culture. Despite the white complexion of the cowboys in popular literature and in western films of the twentieth century, a large proportion of cowboys were Mexican or black. In some cases, all acted and mixed as equals. Just as often, the cowboys split along racial lines when they reached the end of the trail, frequenting segregated restaurants, barbershops, hotels, saloons, and brothels.

Black, white, or Hispanic, they were indeed little more than boys. Photographs that the buckaroos had taken in cow towns like Abilene and Dodge City (as well as arrest records, mostly for drunk and disorderly conduct) show a group of very young men, few apparently older than 25. The life was too arduous for anyone but youths—days in the saddle, nights sleeping on bare ground in all weather. Moreover, the cowboy who married could not afford to be absent from his own ranch or farm for as long as the cattle drives required.

The real buckaroos were not constantly engaged in shooting scrapes such as have made western novels and movies so exciting. Their skills lay in horsemanship and with a rope, not with the less-than-accurate Colt revolver that they carried mostly to signal distant coworkers. Indeed, toting guns was forbidden in railhead towns. With a drunken binge on every cowboy's itinerary, the law officer in charge of keeping the peace did not tolerate shooting irons on every hip. Those who did not leave their revolvers in camp outside town checked them at the police station before they hit the saloons.

THE WILD WEST IN AMERICAN CULTURE

The legend of the cowboy as a romantic, dashing, and quick-drawing knight of the wide-open spaces was not a creation of a later era. The western themes familiar today were fully formed when cold reality was still alive on the plains. Oddly, the myths of the "Wild West" were embraced not only by easterners but by the cowboys themselves.

Punching Cows

It took three or four months to drive a herd of cattle from the vicinity of San Antonio to a railhead town in Kansas. To be asked to join a trail crew was a coveted honor among the young men of the country. The wages were low, only $1 a day plus board and as good a bed as the sod of the plains provided. But because a lot of money and many lives rested on every member of a crew, only those who had impressed a trail boss with their skills and reliability were invited to go.

A crew consisted of the trail boss, usually the owner of the cattle; his *segundo,* or assistant; a cook; a wrangler, who was in charge of the *remuda,* or herd of horses that accompanied the expedition; and a hand for every 250 to 300 cattle. Most herds numbered 2,000 cattle, so 10 to 12 cowpunchers was typical. (The "cows" were actually steers—castrated males; the name *cowpuncher* derived from the job of punching the cows with poles into corrals and loading chutes.)

A herd moved about 10 to 15 miles a day, the animals grazing as they got the chance. Two men rode "lead" or "point," one on either side of the milling steers; two rode "swing" and "flank," in pairs alongside the herd; and two or three rode "drag," behind the herd to hurry up stragglers.

Each position had its peculiarities and was assigned in rotation or with an eye to a particular cowpuncher's abilities or his standing at the moment in the trail boss's graces. Riding point was the most dangerous in the event of a stampede, but it was also the most prestigious and most pleasant in terms of dust and odor. Conversely, riding drag was the safest but also the least desirable job, not only because of the quality of the air but also because there was not a moment in which some independent-minded "dogies" were not determined to set off on their own.

The day's drive started at first light and ended as late toward dusk as the trail boss could find satisfactory grass and water, but the cowboy's work was not done. After a big dinner at the chuck wagon, the hands had to "ride night." In two-hour shifts, pairs of riders circled the herd in opposite directions, looking out for predators and soothing the nervous steers. The western singing tradition developed as a means of keeping a herd calm; music soothed the generally docile, if not the savage, beast. Night riding was dangerous and detested work. Almost all stampedes started at night, tripped by a bolt of lightning, a steer dodging a coyote, or, in human reckoning, no reason whatsoever. Except for river crossings—there were four major watercourses between Texas and Kansas—the stampede was the most frequent cause of death written on the wooden markers that dotted the Shawnee, Chisholm, and Goodnight-Loving trails.

There was little singing in the pouring rain that came often enough. When it rained, the night riders donned yellow oilskin slickers that covered them and their saddle, and cursed or slept. It was said that a cowpuncher who had a good night horse could sleep in the saddle, since his mount knew to wake him at the end of the two-hour shift.

Cowboys on the long drive might bring a horse of their own, but the boss supplied the tough, wiry work ponies. They were geldings, about 7 to 10 for each hand. There were morning horses, afternoon horses, and night horses. A highly specialized mount was the water horse, a good swimmer on which a cowboy could count to get him across as much as a mile of strong current. The most talented mount was the cutting horse, which knew exactly how a steer would act without the rider's instructions. The best were as agile as sheepdogs.

At the end of the drive, the horses were sold along with the cattle. Few hands returned to Texas overland. After they had spent most of their money on liquor, women, and cards, cowboys climbed aboard an eastbound train, rode it to the Mississippi, and struck south by riverboat.

Pulp Fiction

The most important creator of the Wild West was a none-too-savory character named E. Z. C. Judson. A former Know-Nothing who was dishonorably discharged from the Union army, Judson took the pen name Ned Buntline. Between 1865 and 1886, he churned out more than 400 romantic, blood-and-guts, and chivalric novels about western heroes. Some of his characters he invented; others were real people highly fictionalized. Called "pulps" after the cheap paper on which they were printed, or "dime novels" after their price, the books by Judson and his many competitors were devoured chiefly, but not exclusively, by boys.

Buntline's mythical world enamored even those who should have known better. During the 1880s, while living as a rancher in North Dakota, future president Theodore Roosevelt helped capture two young cowboys who robbed a grocery store. In their saddlebags, Roosevelt found several Ned Buntline novels that no doubt featured outlaws who were unjustly accused of crimes. The tiny town of Palisade, Nevada, on the Central Pacific railroad line, won the reputation in eastern newspapers as a den of cutthroats because brawls and gunfights broke out so regularly when passengers left the train for refreshment. In fact, Palisade was the first theme park: The fights were staged by locals, in part to twit eastern fantasies, in part because the locals were just plain bored with the Wild West in which they lived.

American Heroes

In pulp fiction and later in films, Americans discovered that the bank and train robbers Jesse and Frank James were really modern-day Robin Hoods who gave the money they took to the poor. When Jesse was murdered, his mother, Zerelda (who had lost an arm in a scuffle with Pinkerton detectives), made a tourist attraction of his grave, charging admission and explaining that her son had been a Christian who read the Bible in his spare time. Jesse, according to Zerelda, examined all train passengers and did not rob those whose hands were callused because they, like him, were workingmen.

Belle Starr, the moniker of one Myra Belle Shirley, was immortalized as "the bandit queen," as pure in heart as Jesse James's social consciousness. Billy the Kid (William Bonney), a Brooklyn-born hired gun in New Mexico, was romanticized as a tragic hero who had been forced into a life of crime by an uncaring society. James Butler "Wild Bill" Hickok, a gambler and dandy who killed perhaps six people before he was shot down in Deadwood Gulch, South Dakota, in 1876, was credited with dozens of killings, all in the cause of making the West safe for women, children, and psalm books. Calamity Jane (Martha Cannary), later said to have been Wild Bill's paramour, wrote her own romantic autobiography in order to support a drinking problem.

Calamity Jane and other living legends of the West personally contributed to the mythmaking by appearing in Wild West shows that traveled to the East and Europe, where they dramatized great gun battles. The most famous of the shows was the creation of "Buffalo Bill" Cody, who easily made the transition from hunter to impresario. Among his featured performers was Sitting Bull, the Hunkpapa Sioux chief who had overseen the defeat of George Custer. Reality and myth were cruelly confused in Sitting Bull's life. After a short, successful career in show business, he returned to the Rosebud Reservation, where, during the Ghost Dance excitement, he was accidentally killed by two Indian policemen who were arresting him.

A few creators of the legendary West were conscientious realists; Frederic Remington, whose paintings and bronze statues of cowboys and Indians are studiously representative, is an example. Others, although romantics, were talented artists; Owen Wister, an aristocratic easterner, created the finest prototype of the western knight without armor in *The Virginian,* published in 1902. If the cowboy gave you his word, Wister wrote, "he kept it; Wall Street would have found him behind the times. Nor did he talk lewdly to women; Newport would have thought him old-fashioned."

THE MINING FRONTIER

The folklore of the precious-metal mining frontier is second only to the legend of the cowboy in the American imagination. Deadwood, for example, where Wild Bill Hickok was gunned down and Calamity Jane spent much of her life, was a gold-mining center.

Gold and Silver Rushes

After the richest of the California gold fields played out, prospectors in search of "glory holes" fanned out over the mountains and deserts of the West. For more than a generation, they discovered new deposits almost annually and very rich ones every few years. In 1859, there were two great strikes. A find in the Pike's Peak area of Colorado led to a rush reminiscent of that of 1849. About the same time, gold miners in northern Nevada discovered that a "blue mud" that was frustrating their operations was one of the richest silver ores ever discovered. This was the beginning of Virginia City and the Comstock lode. Before the Comstock pinched out in the twentieth century, it yielded more than $400 million in silver and gold.

In 1862, Tombstone, Arizona, was founded on the site of a gold mine; in 1864, Helena, Montana, rose atop another. In 1876, rich placer deposits were discovered in the Black Hills of South Dakota (then forbidden to whites by treaty with the Sioux). The next year, silver was found at Leadville, Colorado, almost two miles above sea level in the Rockies.

During the 1880s, the Coeur d'Alene in the Idaho panhandle drew thousands of miners, as did the copper deposits across the mountains in Butte. In 1891, the Cripple Creek district in Colorado began to outproduce every other mining town. In 1898, miners rushed north to Canada's Klondike, Alaska's Yukon, and then to Nome, where the gold was on the beach. As late as 1901, there was an old-fashioned rush when Jim Butler, the classic grizzled old prospector in a slouch hat, "his view obscured by the rear end of a donkey," drove his pick into a desolate mountain in southern Nevada and found it "practically made of silver." From the town of Tonopah, founded on its site, prospectors discovered rich deposits in Goldfield, a few miles away.

Mining Camps and Cities

Readers of the dime novels of the time, and film viewers since, have savored the vision of boisterous, wide-open mining towns, complete with saloons rocking with the music of tinny pianos and the shouts of bearded men. The live-for-today miner, the gambler, and the prostitute with a heart of gold are permanent inhabitants of American folklore. Nor is the picture altogether imaginary. The speculative mining economy fostered a risk-all attitude toward life and work.

However, efficient exploitation of underground (hardrock) mining required a great deal of capital and technical expertise. Consequently, the mining camps that were home to 5,000 to 10,000 people and even more, within a short time of their founding were also cities with a variety of services and a social structure more like that of old industrial towns than that of the towns of the cattleman's frontier.

In 1877, only six years after it was founded on a vein of gold, Leadville, Colorado, boasted several miles of paved streets, gas lighting, a modern water system, 13 schools, five churches, and three hospitals. "Camps" like Virginia City, Nevada, Deadwood, South Dakota, and Tombstone, Arizona,

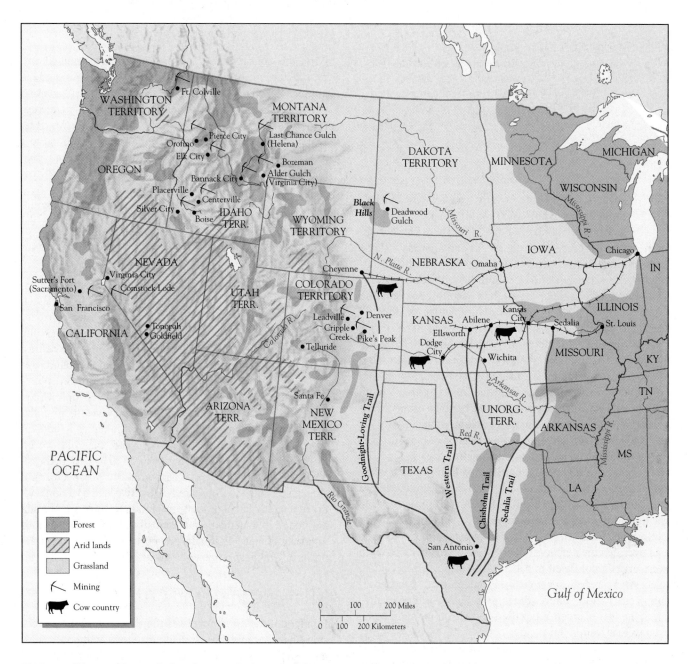

MAP 31:2 Western Economic Development in the 1870s The cattle kingdom ran from the Canadian line to Texas, between the Rockies and the farmlands in eastern Kansas and Nebraska. There were six major centers of precious-metal mining (and many that were founded and evaporated in a year): California and northwestern Nevada; southern Nevada; Idaho and western Montana; the Black Hills of South Dakota centered at Deadwood; the Rockies centered around Denver; and southern Arizona. Lumbering was centered on the Washington, Oregon, and California coasts.

are best remembered as places where legendary characters like Wild Bill Hickok and Wyatt Earp discharged their revolvers; but they were also the sites of huge stamping mills (to crush the ores) and of busy exchanges where mining stocks were traded by agents of San Francisco, New York, and London bankers.

In Goldfield, the last of the wide-open mining towns, one of the most important men in the camp was the urbane Wall Street financier Bernard Baruch. The Anaconda Copper Company of Butte, Montana, was one of the nation's ranking corporate giants. The Guggenheim mining syndi-

cate was supreme in the Colorado gold fields. Rockefeller's Standard Oil was a major owner of mines in the Coeur d'Alene. If it was sometimes wild, the mining West was no mere colorful diversion for readers of dime novels but an integral part of the national economy. In fact, the gold and silver that the hard-rock miners tore from the earth stood at the very center of a question that divided Americans more seriously than any other after the end of Reconstruction: What was to serve as the nation's money?

The miners and mine owners alone could not make an issue of the precious metals from which coins were minted,

▲ *Deadwood, South Dakota, in 1876. The gold camp was all bustle and movement. The already famous Wild Bill Hickok was killed and buried in Deadwood in 1876, but it was not the dangerous place easterners liked to picture. There were only four homicides in Deadwood in 1876, not many more than in a Pennsylvania city of the same size.*

with which goods were bought and sold, and in which debts were incurred and paid off (or not paid off). There were too few of them. However, as the century wound to a close, the money question became of great interest to a group of people who formed a major part of the American population and who had once been its most important segment—the farmers on the land.

for FURTHER READING

Three fine books deal with the West in general from rather different perspectives: Ray A. Billington, *Westward Expansion: A History of the American Frontier,* 1967; Thomas D. Clark, *Frontier America: The Story of the Westward Movement,* 1969; and Frederick Merk, *History of the Westward Movement,* 1978. Also see Robert W. Wiebe, *The Search for Order,* 1968. An essential book by the "founding father" of frontier history is Frederick Jackson Turner, *The Frontier in American History,* 1920. Also see Ray A. Billington, *Frederick Jackson Turner,* 1973, and *America's Frontier Heritage,* 1967.

Useful special studies include Ralph K. Andrist, *Long Death: The Last Days of the Plains Indians,* 1964; Allan C. Bogue, *From Prairie to Corn Belt,* 1963; E. Dick, *The Sod-House Frontier,* 1937; Dee Brown, *Bury My Heart at Wounded Knee,* 1970; E. E. Dale, *The Range Cattle Industry,* 1930; David Day, *Cowboy Culture: A Saga of Five Centuries,* 1981; Richard Drinnon, *Facing West: The Metaphysics of Indian Hating,* 1980; Robert R. Dystra, *The Cattle Towns,* 1968; Gilbert C. Fite, *The Farmer's Frontier, 1865–1900,* 1966; Joe B. Frantz and J. E. Choate, *The American Cowboy: The Myth and the Reality,* 1955; William S. Greever, *The Bonanza West: The Story of the Western Mining Rushes,* 1963; William T. Hagan, *American Indians,* 1961; Howard L. Harrod, *Renewing the World: Plains Indians Religion and Morality,* 1987; E. S. Osgood, *The Day of the Cattleman,* 1929; Rodman W. Paul, *Mining Frontiers of the Far West, 1848–1880,* 1963; J. M. Shagg, *The Cattle Trading Industry,* 1973; Fred A. Shannon, *The Farmer's Last Frontier,* 1967; Duane A. Smith, *Rocky Mountain Mining Camps,* 1967; Henry Nash Smith, *Virgin Land: The American West as Symbol and Myth,* 1950; J. R. Swanson, *The Indian Tribes of North America,* 1953; Robert M. Utley, *Last Days of the Sioux Nation,* 1963; Wilcomb E. Washburn, *The Indian in America,* 1975; Thomas H. Watkins, *Gold and Silver in the West,* 1960; and Walter P. Webb, *The Great Plains,* 1931.

A recent development in the historiography of the West (exemplified in some of the titles listed above) is the "new western history," to which two principal contributors are Patricia Nelson Limerick, *Legacy of Conquest: The Unbroken Past of the American West,* 1987, and Richard White, *"It's Your Misfortune and None of My Own": A History of the American West,* 1991.

Visit the source collections at http://ajaccess.wadsworth.com and http://infotrac.thomsonlearning.com, and use the Search function with the following key terms to explore documents, images, audio and video clips, articles, and commentary related to the material in this chapter:

Bison	Sitting Bull
George Armstrong Custer	Transcontinental Railroad
Geronimo	Wounded Knee
Ghost Dance	

Additional resources, exercises, and Internet links related to this chapter are available on *The American Past* Web site: http://history.wadsworth.com/americanpast7e.

HISTORY ONLINE

The Northern Great Plains

http://memory.loc.gov/ammem/award97/nndfahtml/ngphome.html

Photographs of the Great Plains during the era of settlement, 1860–1920.

Prairie Settlement

http://memory.loc.gov/ammem/award98/nbhihtml/pshome.html

Photographs and letters of Nebraska's pioneers.

History of the American West

http://memory.loc.gov/ammem/award97/codhtml/hawphome.html

Photographs of the last West of the late nineteenth century.

32

STRESSFUL TIMES DOWN HOME

Agriculture, 1865–1896

When the lawyer hangs around and the butcher cuts a
*   pound,*
Oh the farmer is the man who feeds them all.
And the preacher and the cook go a-strolling by the brook
And the farmer is the man who feeds them all.

Oh the farmer is the man, the farmer is the man,
Lives on credit 'til the fall.
Then they take him by the hand and they lead him from
*   the land*
And the middle man's the one that gets them all.

Farmers' song of the 1890s

EVER SINCE THE world's first farmer poked a hole in the ground and covered a seed with dirt, tillers of the soil have gambled with nature, betting a year's living on uncertainties such as the date of winter's final frost and summer's yield of sunshine and rain. But farmers have also known that their work was the bedrock on which civilization is based. They produced the third necessity of life after air and water.

American farmers were particularly conscious of their place in society. They were the nation's most valuable citizens, the "bone and sinew" of the republic. So they had been told by Thomas Jefferson and succeeding generations of politicians fishing for their votes. William Jennings Bryan, the hero of American farmers in the 1890s, told his constituents that if their farms were destroyed, the grass would grow in every city in the nation, but destroy the cities and leave the farms, and the cities would spring up again as if by magic.

The staple farmers of the West and South needed reassurance, for the grand old truisms looked to be wearing. In the new America of gigantic railroads, multimillion-dollar corporations, mighty investment banks, and a marketplace that included the entire earth, even nature seemed to be a minor threat to farm prosperity. In the 1890s, long-welling resentments down on the farm culminated in a radical political movement that shook the confidence of the conservative men who governed the United States.

BEST OF TIMES, WORST OF TIMES

Farmers rarely led the way on the last frontier. Miners and cattlemen and soldiers were the pioneers. Subsistence farming appealed to few Americans, and commercial agriculture was feasible in the West only after the railroad arrived to connect field and corral to the eastern and foreign cities. Once the railroad made its appearance, however, settlers with a plow and a couple of oxen inundated the last frontier.

Success Story

Never in the history of the world have people put so much new land to the plow so quickly as Americans and immigrants did in the final three decades of the nineteenth century. Up until 1870, Americans had brought a total of 408 million acres of land under cultivation, an average of 1.6 million acres of new farmland a year. Between 1870 and 1900, a single generation of farmers brought 431 million acres of virgin soil into production, an average of 14.4 million acres annually.

Crop production increased even more sharply. By 1900, American farmers were producing up to 150 percent more of the staple grains—corn and wheat—than they had in 1870. Hogs, a by-product of corn, numbered 25 million in 1870, 63 million in 1900.

The ravenous appetites of American and foreign city dwellers encouraged this amazing growth. The expansion of the railroads made it possible for crops raised by a Great Plains farmer to feed the inhabitants of Chicago and New York, even London and Warsaw.

Cool, Clear Water

There were natural problems for farmers in the plains. Americans and immigrants from northern Europe were accustomed to summer rains nourishing their crops. Between the Atlantic seaboard and eastern Kansas, 32 to 48 inches of rain fell each year; it was wetter in the Deep South.

West of about Wichita, however, annual precipitation declined to 16 to 32 inches a year, with much of the year's rain falling during the winter. Farther west, in the "rain shadow" of the Rockies, at about the eastern boundary of Colorado, rainfall dropped to 16 inches and less. This was the "Great American Desert," which an early explorer called "almost totally unfit for cultivation." The central valley of California was rainless during the summer.

The Californians solved their problem with large-scale irrigation. They formed cooperative "ditch companies" that tapped the water of the San Joaquin, Sacramento, and other rivers, channeling it to their crops. Irrigation brought them into conflict with hydraulic miners who, in washing down mountainsides to win their grains of gold, clogged the rivers and irrigation ditches with mud. The more numerous farmers won the contest in California's legislature and courts, shutting down the hydraulic operations.

California-style ditch companies were out of the question on most of the Great Plains. The level of the largest rivers dropped too low by midsummer to be productively tapped; smaller streams dried up completely. Some farmers individually irrigated their fields from wells on which they mounted prefabricated windmills. However, the cost of the windmills and of drilling a well, between $1 and $2 a foot,

---

Lady Homesteaders

About one in five homesteaders was a woman. Some were heads of household, widows, or bold spinsters. Some were women living together, who, with no legal relationship to one another, were each eligible for 160 acres. Most were the wives or the wives-to-be of male homesteaders. On the arid plains, 160 acres was often insufficient to support a family. Before she married, a woman could double the size of her family's homestead by filing a claim. It was easy enough to throw up a dwelling and, if local officials winked at what was going on, which they usually did, easy to evade the residency requirement.

---

was too much for many settlers to risk when they had no idea whether they would hit water at 25 feet or 200.

So, to some extent, Great Plains farmers deluded themselves. The summers of the 1870s and early 1880s, when cultivators arrived in the region, were abnormally rainy. This convinced even some experts such as Charles Dana Wilber that "rain follows the plow." That is, when farmers broke the primeval sod, they permanently altered the climate by liberating long imprisoned moisture from the earth that would return indefinitely in the form of heavier rains.

The theory was nonsense, as a devastating drought in 1887 was to show. However, Great Plains farmers realistically made the most of what moisture was in the ground by plowing more deeply than eastern farmers did. The thick layer of dust that settled in the foot-deep furrows acted as a mulch.

A Treeless Land

Except for cottonwoods along the rivers, there were no trees on the Great Plains and, therefore, no wood with which to build. Importing lumber for a respectable frame house had to be delayed until after a family harvested a few crops and squirreled away a little money. In the meantime, pioneers lived in sod houses, which were constructed of blocks cut from the tangled turf of the plains. Sod houses were not pretty; they dripped mud in the spring rains and were dusty during the long summers. They were, however, snug in winter, the season that could kill you.

Fences could not be built of sod; but crops needed protection from open-range cattle, and the settler's own livestock needed to be kept under control. The cost of ringing 160 acres with wooden posts and rails was prohibitive. The solution was long known—in theory: a wire fence that could restrain cattle. In 1873, after many had failed with sometimes bizarre inventions, Joseph Glidden of DeKalb, Illinois, perfected a machine that mass-produced cheap, effective barbed wire. With the flimsiest of scavenged fence posts, a Great Plains farmer could erect a steel hedge so efficient that a starving cow would lie down and die rather than push through it. (In the blizzard of 1886, tens of thousand of cattle fleeing ahead of the storm piled up at barbed-wire fences and froze.)

Barbed wire was a fabulous success. The company that bought Glidden's patent produced 2.84 million pounds of barbed wire in 1876. By 1880, 80.5 million pounds had been sold.

Barbed wire caused numerous clashes between settlers who used it (sometimes called "nesters") and open-range cattlemen accustomed to running their animals freely on the plains. When fences blocked the stock from streams and

MAP 32:1 Expansion of Cultivation Between 1860 and 1890, acreage under cultivation in the United States almost doubled. By 1900, it had doubled.

1860

1890

Improved land

▲ *The grandeur and isolation of a farm on the Great Plains are captured in this roving photographer's picture. Photographers crossed the country in their buggies, taking portraits and occasional masterpieces, like this candid shot of a little girl and her home.*

water holes, cattlemen retaliated by damming streams above nester land, cutting fence wire into shreds, and, in Johnson County, Wyoming, hiring gunfighters to terrorize them.

Machines on the Land

Barbed wire was but the simplest of technology's contributions to the expansion of American agriculture. A chilled-steel plow perfected by Oliver Evans in 1877 sliced through sod and heavy soils that broke cast-iron plowshares. Disc harrows cultivated wide swaths with each pass, allowing "dry farmers" to tend the larger acreage they needed. Manufacturers like John Deere and International Harvester developed machines that planted seeds, shucked corn, threshed wheat, bound shocks, and shredded fodder for livestock. The value of farm machinery in use in the United States increased from $271 million in 1870 to $750 million in 1900.

Machinery made the American farmer the most productive farmer in the world. He was able to cultivate six times as much land as his father had farmed back East before the Civil War. That is, plowing and seeding wheat by hand, harvesting it with a sickle, and threshing it with a flail, a farmer in pre–Civil War times worked between 50 and 60 hours to harvest about 20 bushels of wheat per acre. With a gang plow and a horse-drawn seeder, harrow, reaper, and

thresher—all in widespread use by 1890—a farmer produced a much larger crop with only 8 to 10 hours of work per acre.

Hard Times

Machinery, however, cost money that few farmers on new land had. Already short-term debtors, borrowing each year for seed and their provisions during the growing season and paying back after the harvest, the typical farmer of the late nineteenth century was also a long-term debtor. He owed money for his machines. Many farmers were up to their necks in obligations, even if they had gotten their land free under the Homestead Act.

Then, beginning about 1872, the western growers of wheat and corn, and keepers of livestock, watched their incomes slowly sag and, after 1890, collapse. Crops that in 1872 brought a farmer $1,000 in real income (actual purchasing power) brought only $500 in 1896. A farmer 48 years of age in 1896, still actively working, had to turn out twice as many hogs, or bushels of corn or wheat, as he had produced as a young man of 24, just to enjoy the same standard of living he had known in 1872. It was not comforting to look back on a quarter-century of toil and to realize it had yielded nothing but the prospect of more struggle. By the 1890s, the price of corn was so low (eight cents a bushel) that some farmers, instead of buying coal, burned their corn for warmth and cooking.

Those unable to pay their debts went under. Between 1889 and 1893, some 11,000 Kansas farm families lost their homes when they failed to make their mortgage payments. In several western counties of Kansas and Nebraska, 9 out of every 10 farms changed hands. The number of farm tenant families—those that did not own the land they worked—doubled, from 1 to 2 million, between 1880 and 1900, most of the increase coming after 1890. For every three landowning farm families in the North and West, there was one tenant family. For them, farming was no longer the basis of independence and hope for the future but was grinding toil for the sake of putting a meal on the table and keeping the banker from the door.

Nebraska State Historical Society Photograph Collections

▲ *A sod house and sod stable in Custer County, Nebraska, 1887. With luck—which did not flow freely on the plains in the 1890s—the family would have a frame house within a few years but would still use the sod house for animals or storage until the rains destroyed it.*

The South: Tenants and Sharecroppers

Tenancy was more common in the South, particularly in the cotton belt. Below the Ohio River, there were as many tenant farmers as there were families working land they owned. Among African Americans, tenants and sharecroppers outnumbered landowners by almost five to one.

The problem originated in Reconstruction. Having freed blacks from bondage, the Republican party failed to provide the freedmen the means to survive on their own. After some consideration, the Republicans rejected radical proposals to confiscate large plantations and divide them into 40-acre farms for the blacks who worked them as slaves. With a few exceptions, such as on the sea islands of South Carolina, land was left in the hands of those who had owned it before the war.

But how, without slavery, were the crops to be got in? Even with pay, former slaves resisted working in gangs; it was too reminiscent of life under slavery. They wanted a family life such as whites and free blacks enjoyed, and for farmers, family life meant a family farm. Moreover, few southern landowners (even those who had been great planters) had money with which to pay wages. Slaves had been their capital; the Confederacy destroyed what other money had been in the South. As late as in 1880, there was more money in the banks of Massachusetts than in all the banks in the former Confederacy.

The solution was a system of cultivation that, on the face of it, seemed fair to both landowner and worker: sharing the crop and its proceeds. Landowners partitioned their acreage into family farm–size plots on which cabins were constructed. In return for the use of the dwelling and the land, share tenants, who provided their own mule, plow, and seed, turned over to the landlord one-quarter to one-third of each year's crop. Sharecroppers were tenants who were too poor to rustle up a mule, plow, and seed. The landlord provided them in return for one-half of the crop.

As a means of production, the system worked. Southern cotton production reached its 1860 level in 1870 and exceeded the prewar record (1859) a few years later. As in the West, however, greater production was accompanied by a decline in wholesale prices. The price of a pound of cotton fell to six cents by the 1890s, and briefly in 1893 to a nickel: $30 for a 600-pound bale!

Debt Bondage

One result of declining prices was a physically and morally debilitating poverty. Pellagra, a fatal disease caused by niacin deficiency, unknown in slavery times, became a problem of epidemic proportions in the South. Another consequence was a form of debt bondage that, wrote Charles Oken in 1894, "crushed out all independence and reduced its victims to a coarse species of servile labor."

The victims were white as well as black. Many white farmers with modest holdings before the war lost their land to creditors, usually local merchants. The ledgers of one southern merchant, T. G. Patrick, show that during one season he provided about $900 worth of seed, food, tools, and other necessities to a farm owner named S. R. Simonton. When, in the fall, the price of cotton dropped well below Simonton's expectations, he was able to repay only $300, leaving Patrick with a lien against his property of $600. Simonton cut his costs drastically the following year, to just $400, but the accumulated debt of $1,000 was more than Patrick would carry. He took Simonton's land, and Simonton became his tenant.

Once a farmer became a tenant or sharecropper, the farmer's debts bound him to the land almost as irrevocably as if he were a serf. Tenants and sharecroppers bought their necessities on credit from a general merchandiser, often their landlord, putting up as collateral their share of the crop. If the income from their share did not cover the year's debt, the merchandiser put a lien on the next year's harvest, effectively binding the cropper to work for him indefinitely. There was no quitting and moving out. In several states, to try to flee such a debt was a criminal offense punishable by imprisonment on a state-owned plantation or on a farm to which the convicted was hired out. To be a convict in the South was a horror. Between 1877 and 1880, the Greenwood and Augusta Railroad contracted with the state of Georgia for 285 convict laborers. Almost half of them died. Those who got back to the prison must have thought themselves blessed.

Hayseeds

Southern black farmers needed no tutoring to know that they were excluded from full participation in mainstream American life. The color line was drawn ever more sharply in the South as the century waned. White farmers of the South and West experienced a more subtle deterioration in their political power and status. Not only did the proportion of agriculturalists in the population decline annually, but the

▲ *A sharecropper's cabin in North Carolina. Many croppers were so deeply in debt to the owner of the local general store, who often owned the land on which they farmed, that being free and clear was impossible to imagine. There was a kind of security in debt bondage: Landlords did not evict croppers who owed them money—a kind of security similar to slavery.*

legislators whom farmers sent to Washington and the state capitals seemed all too often to forget their constituents once they made the acquaintance of back-slapping lobbyists for railroads, industry, and banks.

The ebullient urban culture depicted the man of the soil in popular fiction, songs, and melodramas as a thick-skulled yokel in a tattered straw hat with a length of straw clenched between his teeth—a "hayseed" who put traveling salesmen into bed with his daughters. Rather more serious chroniclers of rural life, such as Hamlin Garland, commiserated with farmers but wanted no part of their lives. In his popular book of 1891, *Main-Travelled Roads,* Garland depicted rural life as dreary and stultifying.

Tens of thousands of farmers' sons and daughters followed Garland in his flight to the city. "Who wants to smell new-mown hay," playwright Clyde Fitch wrote in 1909, "if he can breathe gasoline on Fifth Avenue instead?" With each son and daughter who opted for urban fumes, farmers who clung to the Jeffersonian image of themselves became further dejected, agitated, and demoralized.

PROTEST AND ORGANIZATION

To counter jokes and jeers, farmers could repair to the good old gospel of agrarianism, the assurance that they were peculiarly valuable to society. They could and did disdain the cities as sinks of iniquity and sin. In speech and sermon, and in the pages of magazines catering to country people, politicians, preachers, and journalists repeated the old clichés. In sturdy pillars of American popular culture, like the *McGuffey's Reader,* in which, for half a century, schoolchildren learned their ABCs and their values too, the ennoblement of farm life was alive and well.

Rural Renaissance

And yet, life on the western American farm was undeniably isolated, arduous, and often dreary. The winds on the Great Plains dispatched men and women to state asylums in numbers high enough to catch the attention of the doughtiest Jeffersonian. Aside from church—which was not for everyone—and moments snatched on shopping trips to town, there was little to relieve the tedium and monotony, especially for farm women, who were far more isolated from company than were their menfolk. Writing of farm life, Hamlin Garland said that "even [his] youthful zeal" was inadequate when he tried to describe the hardships that women endured. "Before the tragic futility of their suffering," wrote Garland, "my pen refused to shed its ink."

In the 1870s, farm women and their husbands joined the Patrons of Husbandry (the Grange), which sponsored dances, fairs, and lecturers who spoke on everything from the date of

Thank You for Smoking

During Reconstruction, some white southerners argued that the South needed industry. If the South remained an agricultural region, said people like Henry W. Grady, the wisecracking editor of the Atlanta *Constitution,* it would remain a weak, dependent appendage of the North.

By the end of the century, the South wooed the cotton industry to the land of cotton by providing workers who would accept much lower wages than New Englanders. Similar inducements, plus local coal and iron deposits, made Birmingham, Alabama, the "Pittsburgh of the South"—the center of a booming steel industry. By 1890, Birmingham produced more pig iron than Pittsburgh.

The single most successful southern industrialist was the pioneer and practically single-handed creator of an entirely new business: the manufacture, promotion, and sale of cigarettes. Americans had always been big consumers of tobacco in the form of cigars, pipe tobacco, and plugs for chewing. (In 1890, the national consumption of "chaw" was 3 pounds per capita!) Cigarettes were known. Invented by a Turkish soldier in 1832, they had the advantage of chewing tobacco in that you could get your nicotine fix unobtrusively almost everywhere. (Cigar smoking among upper- and middle-class men was highly ritualized, done, for example, when the ladies left the table after dinner.)

Cigarettes had advantages chaw did not: Smokers did not create the sickening mess chewers did with their incessant spitting (which made the habit unacceptable in polite society). The smoke they created was less offensive to nonsmokers than cigar and pipe smoke were, and a cigarette could be smoked in minutes, unlike cigars and pipes. Another boost was the invention of "safety matches" in 1855. They could be struck only on a special surface attached to each box, thus eliminating the problem of the older "lucifers," which often ignited in a man's pocket.

For these reasons, many soldiers took to cigarettes during the Civil War. They rolled their own, or they bought commercial cigarettes rolled by hand in a simple machine. The business was centered in Great Britain (Philip Morris was the giant of the industry), but there were American companies too. About 1880, James Buchanan "Buck" Duke of Durham, North Carolina, persuaded 125 Russian Jewish cigarette makers to emigrate there. The most desirable cigarette tobacco was the mild "bright leaf," cured by a method newly developed in Virginia and North Carolina.

Still, cigarette smoking lagged distantly behind pipes, cigars, and chaw. They were associated with "sissies" (a term coined in the 1890s), "bohemians," men and women living lives considered unconventional, and big-city "street Arabs"—the hordes of homeless boys living in gangs in abandoned buildings in slums or on the streets, the kind of lads who picked your pocket.

Buck Duke, the son of an antislavery tobacco grower, envisioned a huge future for the "coffin nails," so big he needed a way to produce them in quantity. In 1883, he bought the rights to a little known cigarette-making device, the Bonsack machine, which had been patented only three years earlier. In 1884, Duke churned out more "Dukes of Durham" than the entire industry had produced the previous year. Now the problem was finding—creating—enough customers to smoke them. A brilliant businessman, Duke enticed boys by printing pictures of boxers and comely actresses on the cardboard inserts that were put in cigarette packs to stiffen them. They were a "premium," an extra, "trading cards," collectibles—might as well smoke the cigarettes one had to buy to get them. In 1886, Duke fished for women with a "feminine" brand, "Cameos." (Duke was also a pioneer in hiring women as sales representatives.) Able to outproduce his competitors to an extent Rockefeller could only dream about, Duke launched a price war that drove most of them out of business, Buck picking up the pieces at bargain prices. In 1889, he spent $800,000 on advertising. Only the ready-to-eat cereal makers, Post and Kellogg, staked so much on publicizing their products. Shortly after the turn of the century, Duke had a near monopoly of the cigarette business with his American Tobacco Company; he owned or controlled 150 factories.

Cigarettes had enemies from the start. The Women's Christian Temperance Union propagandized and lobbied against them almost as actively as they fought alcohol. They were effective. By 1890, 26 states had some sort of anticigarette legislation on the books, most of the laws forbidding their sale to young people under a particular age (from 14 to 24, depending on the state). By 1901, 43 of 46 states had such laws, even North Carolina. They were, of course, impossible to enforce. However, beginning with Washington, several states completely outlawed cigarettes. In 1898, the Tennessee supreme court approved that state's prohibition of them when it defined cigarettes as "not legitimate articles of commerce, because wholly noxious and deleterious to health."

Still, the habit spread. When, in 1904, a woman was jailed in New York for smoking in front of her children, even nonsmokers joined the criticism of the anticigarette zealots. Although Duke remained on the defensive until World War I, he continued to sell more cigarettes each year than the year before. Perhaps the anticigarette crusade's last gasping celebration was in 1912, when Topsy, an elephant at Coney Island, killed her keeper when he put a lighted cigarette in Topsy's mouth.

World War I was Buck Duke's victory too. Millions of packs of cigarettes were given free to American soldiers. When the war was over, America was hooked, including a substantial proportion of women, few of whom had touched tobacco in the age of the pipe, cigars, and chaws.

---

creation to the habits of the people of Borneo. In the 1880s, new organizations—the Agricultural Wheel, the Texas State Alliance, the Southern Alliance, and the Colored Farmers' National Alliance—mushroomed all over the countryside to take over many of the same functions. Their value was ines-

timable, particularly for women. A leader of the Southern Alliance, the largest of the regional organizations, declared that it "redeemed woman from her enslaved condition, and placed her in her proper sphere." Indeed, women were to play an active role in the agrarian movement at every level.

Like the Grange, the alliances were originally nonpolitical. In the increasingly harder times, however, farmers getting together asked themselves what—or who—was to blame for their woes. The Grangers blamed the railroads and successfully regulated railroads' rates by electing sympathetic politicians to state legislatures. The alliances taught that the truculent individualism of the farmers in a highly organized society contributed to their distress; the alliances encouraged members to form cooperatives and other economic combinations.

The Co-op Movement

In consumer cooperatives, farmers pooled resources to purchase essential machinery in quantity and therefore more cheaply. Money pools, associations much like contemporary credit unions, sprouted all over the Midwest. Through these associations, which were capitalized by members and operated on a nonprofit basis, farmers hoped to eliminate their dependence on banks. Although some survived to serve the credit needs of members for generations, money pools suffered from the hostility of bankers and the inexperience of often amateur administrators. Farmers too often put friends rather than professionals in charge of the money pools, and the rate of mismanagement and embezzlement was high.

Producer cooperatives were designed to counter the power of the railroads over farmers' lives after the Wabash Case of 1886 struck down the Granger laws that regulated charges for storing grain. Corn belt farmers pooled funds and built their own grain elevators in the expectation they could keep their crop off the market until they liked the selling price.

But co-ops could not remedy the problem that was at the root of agricultural distress: American staple farmers were too many and too productive for their own good. Too much land was opened to settlement by too many railroads too quickly. Improvements in farm machinery and new methods produced far more grain, livestock, and fiber than the market could absorb.

Sinister Forces

Some agrarian leaders recognized overproduction as the problem. Canadian-born "Sockless Jerry" Simpson of Kansas called on the federal government to carve out new markets for American farm goods abroad. Mary Elizabeth Lease of Kansas, one of the nation's first female lawyers and an orator of withering intensity, told farmers to "raise less corn and more hell." But that was a slogan, not a program. To the individual farmer, the only solution to declining prices was to plant not less corn but more, thus worsening the situation.

Moreover, few farmers believed that overproduction was the sole or even the chief cause of agrarian distress. Mother Lease herself pointed out that the streets of American cities teemed with hungry, ill-clad people while foodstuffs rotted in Kansas and cotton went unsold in Alabama. She and other agrarian leaders—Simpson, Ignatius Donnelly of Minnesota, William Peffer of Kansas, and Thomas Watson of Georgia—said that sinister, parasitical forces were at work like thieves in the night to enrich themselves at the expense of the men and women who actually produced wealth. Their villains included the railroaders, the politicians and judges compliantly in the railroads' employ, and, most of all, the "money power"—a conspiracy of bankers and lawyers who manipulated the nation's currency.

THE MONEY QUESTION

Money is a token that the people of a society agree represents value. It makes the exchange of goods and services more workable than simple barter. The value of money can change. At the time of the first European incursions in North

The Granger Collection, New York

▲ *"Mother" Mary Elizabeth Lease was one of the fieriest and most popular orators of the agrarian movement and later a leading Populist. She affected "down-home" manners and language but was, in fact, well educated, one of the first women lawyers in the United States.*

Southern Funeral

Henry Grady promoted southern industrialization in a speech he delivered to hundreds of southern audiences. He began with a story of a funeral he had attended in rural Georgia. "They buried him," Grady told listeners, "in a New York coat and a Boston pair of shoes, and a pair of breeches from Chicago and a shirt from Cincinnati." The coffin, Grady continued, was made from northern lumber and hammered together with northern-forged nails. "The South," he said, "didn't furnish a thing on earth for that funeral but the corpse and the hole in the ground."

America, the eastern tribes' money was wampum—strings and belts of beads made of shell or stone. Because wampum was difficult to make, its quantities were limited, an essential characteristic of money. But when Europeans introduced cheap glass beads into this economy, giving them to Indians in exchange for pelts but refusing to accept the beads as payment for iron tools and other European products, wampum was soon worthless to everyone.

Gold, Silver, and Greenbacks

The economically sophisticated nations of the world used precious metals—gold and silver—as their medium of exchange. Gold and silver were durable and limited in supply. There was little danger the world would be flooded with them or that some would refuse to accept them as money. Their value was stable. The farmer who received gold coins in payment for his crop knew that the suppliers of the goods his family needed would accept the gold, and at a predictable value. In the United States, gold was minted in coins of $5, $10 (called "eagles"), and $20 (called "double eagles").

Coins of smaller denomination (dimes, quarters, and dollars) were silver, which was more common than gold and therefore less valuable. Because the supply of both metals appeared to be so stable, in 1837, Congress determined that the value of silver as money would be pegged to that of gold at a ratio of 16 to 1. That is, 16 ounces of silver was worth 1 ounce of gold.

Large commercial transactions were carried out in paper money issued by banks that pledged to exchange it for silver and gold. The value of this paper money depended, of course, upon people's confidence in the ability of the bank that issued it to hand coin over the counter when presented with its notes.

During the Civil War, finding itself with too little gold and silver to pay for the army, the Lincoln administration issued a new kind of paper money, some $433 million in bills called "greenbacks." The greenbacks were not redeemable in gold or silver. Their value rested entirely upon the fact that the government accepted them as payment and defined the greenbacks as legal tender.

The greenbacks were not "as good as gold" (or silver). Their worth fluctuated, depending on the success or failure of the Union army or a new twist in federal financial policy. At the end of the Civil War, a person needed $157 in greenbacks in order to buy what $100 in gold or silver would purchase.

Inflation and Deflation

Discounted as they were, the greenbacks nevertheless circulated. The Union did, after all, survive and continue to accept them. Indeed, the greenbacks won many friends because, by increasing the amount of money in circulation, they inflated wages and prices, including prices at which farmers sold their crops. The Civil War was a prosperous time down on the farm. Looking back on it in bleaker days, many farmers associated the good times with the greenbacks. They argued

that the federal government should continue to use them to regulate the amount of money in circulation so as to accommodate the shifting needs of a dynamic people, for the supply of gold and silver remained static or expanded too slowly to keep up with the explosive economy.

Bankers thought otherwise. They dealt in large sums of money and feared having the value of their property—and the money others owed to them—reduced in value by politicians currying favor with voters. These monetary conservatives insisted that money had absolute "natural" value, determined by the amount of gold in existence and, until the 1870s, by the amount of silver.

With their close ties to the executive branch of the government after the Civil War, such conservatives generally had their way. By February 1868, $45 million in greenbacks had been retired from circulation. When paid to the government in taxes, they were simply burned. The total money in circulation shrank; the value of gold and silver—the amount they would buy—increased. This was called "deflation" because, in cash, wages and prices both dropped. A dollar bought more than it used to buy, and it was harder to earn.

Debtors, notably farmers, were the victims of deflation. The $1,000 a man borrowed in "cheap" money, he had to pay back in deflated money. Protest was so widespread that, in October 1868, Congress ordered the Treasury Department to stop retiring the greenbacks.

But the victory for inflation was short-lived. In 1875, ascendant conservatives ordered that for every new $100 issued by banks (money backed by gold), $80 in greenbacks be retired. In 1879, Secretary of the Treasury John Sherman ordered that all payments to the government be made in specie (that is, gold or silver coin). This spelled the greenbacks' doom: If the government would not accept them, who would? Between 1865 and 1878, the amount of all kinds of money in circulation in the United States shrank from $1.08 billion to $773 million. Whereas in 1865 there had been $31.18 in circulation for every American, in 1878 there was but $16.25.

In an attempt to stem this deflation, many farmers, working people, and some small businessmen joined together to form the Greenback Labor party, which was dedicated to the single issue of inflating the currency. Like most third parties in American history, the Greenbackers attracted few voters. In 1880, former Civil War general James B. Weaver of Iowa won 308,578 votes. In 1884, Benjamin F. Butler won just 175,370 votes, not much more than the Prohibitionist party candidate. By 1884, people who wanted the currency inflated had turned to another form of money for their salvation—silver coin.

Silver to the Fore

Between 1837 and 1873, the price of silver in the United States was legally pegged to the price of gold at a ratio of 16 to 1. During the 1860s, however, American mines produced considerably less than 16 ounces of silver for each ounce of gold produced. Consequently, silver mine owners preferred to sell their product not to the United States Mint, which

▲ *A "gold bug" cartoonist lampoons bimetalism by depicting a currency based on both gold and silver as a bicycle with two unequally sized wheels. The bicycle was a newfangled invention and a sensation of the era.*

paid the official price, but to private or foreign buyers, who were willing to pay more: an ounce of gold for just 14 ounces of silver.

In 1873, with little silver being presented to the mint for sale, Congress enacted the Demonetization Act, ceasing government purchases of silver. The silver dollar was dropped from the list of coins the government minted. Rather than money with a value set by law, silver became a commodity like wheat, hogs, lumber, or petticoats. Its money value (in gold) was set not by Congress but by the laws of supply and demand. President Grant signed the Demonetization Act without ado.

Already as the ink from his pen was drying, however, the relative production of silver and gold was changing again. New silver strikes throughout the West and better methods of smelting it resulted in a vast increase in production of the white metal. In 1861, only $2 million worth of silver had been mined in the United States, compared to $43 million worth of gold. In 1873, the value of silver and gold mined was about equal, $36 million each. During the rest of the 1870s, silver production increased so rapidly that its price on the private market, the only market for it, collapsed.

Politician friends of mining interests, like Democrat Richard "Silver Dick" Bland of Missouri and Senator Henry W. Teller of Colorado, began to denounce the Demonetization Act as the "Crime of '73." They accused the govern-

ment of conspiring with bankers to punish silver miners for their success. There was no crime of 1873; no one but a fantasizing western prospector could have anticipated the tremendous increase in silver production when Congress passed the Demonetization Act.

Nevertheless, when silver production did rise, monetary conservatives were relieved that the government was no longer buying and minting it (which would have inflated the currency and reduced the value of their wealth). The "gold bugs," as Bland and Teller called them, began to look upon abundant silver as a threat to the value of their money as serious as the greenbacks.

By themselves, mine owners and miners did not have the political power to force the government to resume the purchase and minting of silver. Even after the admission of mineral-rich Colorado in 1876, mining interests were significant in few states. However, inflationist congressmen from agricultural states—mostly southern and western Democrats but also some Republicans—seized on silver coinage as a way to get more money into circulation. In the depression year of 1878, they forced the conservatives to agree to a compromise. The Bland-Allison Bill of that year required the secretary of the treasury to purchase between $2 million and $4 million worth of silver each month for minting into coin. The silver dollar was back.

The Sherman Silver Purchase Act

The silver dollar was back, but the principle of "bimetalism" (both gold and silver as money, the value of each pegged by law to the other) was not. In both Republican and Democratic administrations, the treasury department was safely in the hands of gold bugs dedicated to keeping gold the sole standard of value. The government almost invariably bought the minimum $2 million worth of silver required by law. Silver dollars were, in effect, tokens—like copper cents and paper money. They had value only in that they represented gold.

The national production of silver continued to grow during the 1880s, and the market price of the metal continued to decline. By 1890, an ounce of gold bought nearly 20 ounces of silver. To silver producers and agrarian inflationists, the old legal ratio of 16 to 1 took on a sacred significance.

In 1889 and 1890, the balance of power tipped to the side of the inflationists. Two states in which silver was an important commodity (Montana and Idaho), and four in which inflationist farmers were a majority (the two Dakotas, Washington, and Wyoming), entered the Union, bringing 12 new "silver senators" to Washington.

The result was the Sherman Silver Purchase Act of 1890. Like the Bland-Allison Act, it was a compromise. The Sherman law required the secretary of the treasury to purchase 4.5 million ounces of silver each month, in effect the entire monthly production of the nation's silver mines. However, the government bought silver at the market price, which continued to decline, from 20 to 1 in 1890, to 26.5 to 1 in 1893. Consequently, the Sherman Silver Purchase Act failed to relieve discontent in the mining regions and led to violent strikes as mine owners attempted to cut costs by forcing down wages.

Farmers, who wanted silver "monetized" (its value pegged to that of gold by law) in order to inflate the currency and raise prices, were also disappointed. Although he signed the Sherman Silver Purchase Act, President Benjamin Harrison was a gold-standard man. He instructed the secretary of the treasury to pay all the government's bills in gold. To distressed farmers already inclined to look for sinister forces at work in the night, the presidency itself seemed in the employ of the money power.

THE POPULISTS

By 1890, the alliance movement was at flood tide. The Southern Alliance had 1.5 million members; the Colored Farmers' National Alliance, a million; other groups combined, about the same. Feeling their oats, the leaders of the various regional organizations gathered in Ocala, Florida, in December to draw up a list of grievances and consider the possibility of organizing a third party.

Hesitation

In December 1890, Kansas farmers had organized a statewide people's party. Calling themselves "Populists" after the Latin word for "the people," *populus,* they won control of the state legislature. At Ocala, however, Republican and Democratic loyalties were too strong, and racial anxieties too tense, for the delegates to take the same leap.

Southern white farmers hesitated because they had made inroads in the Democratic party and feared that if they split the white vote in the South by forming a new party, blacks would regain the political equality they had held during Reconstruction. The leaders of the Colored Farmers' National Alliance were reluctant to give up their allegiance to the Republican party, which had, however uncertainly, defended the civil rights of African Americans.

But events were already under way to undermine old loyalties. In July 1890, the same month the Silver Purchase Act was passed, the Republican majority in the United States Senate failed to enact the Force Bill, a law to protect the right of southern blacks to vote. In effect, in 1890, the Republican party abandoned southern black voters to the mercies of southern whites. Some African American southerners called for a new party. Some southern whites, like Tom Watson of Georgia, a hot-tempered lawyer who had been cheated out of elective office by the Democratic party machine, called for an alliance between black and white farmers. In a magazine article published in 1892, he told white and black farmers:

You are kept apart that you may be separately fleeced of your earnings. You are made to hate each other because upon that hatred is rested the keystone of the arch of financial despotism which enslaves you both. You are deceived and blinded that you may not see how this race antagonism perpetuates a monetary system which beggars both.

The Omaha Convention

In February 1892, delegates from the various farmers' alliances, and more than a few self-appointed spokesmen for farmers and silver miners, met in Omaha, Nebraska, to launch a new party. They adopted the name Populist from the Kansas party that had already sent several congressmen and Senator William Peffer to Washington.

To symbolize the fact that farmers of the North and South had bridged the sectional chasm, the Populists nominated former Union general and Greenbacker James B. Weaver for president and former Confederate general James

▲ *Populists in the Kansas legislature in January 1893. The elections had been contested, and these Populists meant to install their candidates by guns if necessary. For several years, the Populist party was the dominant party in Kansas.*

G. Field for vice president. No one expected them to win, and they did not. Grover Cleveland, the Democratic candidate, won a comfortable victory in the electoral college. But Weaver did well enough, winning more than a million votes and carrying Kansas. All along, the Populists at Omaha had their eyes on 1896, when they expected to restore democracy and justice to a corrupted country.

Observers of the Omaha convention were taken aback by the religious fervor of the Populists, who acted as if they were embarked not on a political campaign but on a crusade against satanic evil. We are "a nation brought to the verge of moral, political, and material ruin," Ignatius Donnelly of Minnesota wrote in the preamble to the party platform. "Corruption dominates the ballot box, the legislatures, the Congress, and touches even the ermine of the bench." William Peffer, looking like a biblical prophet with his waist-length beard, railed about the inequities of the land. "Conspiracy" was a word on everyone's lips: the conspiracy of the great railroads to defraud the shipper, the conspiracy of politicians to destroy democracy, the conspiracy of the money power, even the conspiracy of Jews.

"The people are at bay," Mother Lease said. "Let the bloodhounds of money beware." When the platform was approved, according to one not too sympathetic reporter, "Cheers and yells . . . rose like a tornado . . . and raged without cessation for thirty-four minutes, during which time women shrieked and wept, men embraced and kissed their neighbors, locked arms, marched back and forth, and leaped upon tables and chairs in the ecstasy of their delirium."

A Far-Reaching Program

The atmosphere was, no doubt, disarming. And yet, the platform the Populists wrote was far from lunatic. It was a comprehensive program for reform that, if enacted, would have transformed American development, and not necessarily for the worse.

Indeed, the Populists' political reforms were (in years to come) to become the law of the land. The Populists called for the election of United States senators by popular vote rather than by state legislatures, a reform instituted in the Seventeenth Amendment to the Constitution in 1913. They demanded the universal use of the Australian, or secret, ballot to prevent landlords and employers from intimidating their tenants and workers into voting as they said. By the early twentieth century, public balloting was abolished everywhere but in town meetings.

The Populists introduced the concepts of the initiative, recall, and referendum to American government. The initiative allows voters, through petition, to put measures on the ballot independent of action by legislatures and thus, in theory, free of manipulation by professional lobbyists and their accomplices. The recall allows voters, also through petition, to force a public official to stand for election before his or her term is up. The Populists hoped that the recall would discourage politicians from backing down on campaign pledges. The referendum allows voters to vote directly on laws rather than indirectly through their representatives; it is the means by which initiative measures and recall petitions are decided. All three are accepted procedures in most states today.

The most controversial Populist demand was for the abolition of national banks and for government ownership of railroads and the telegraph. Their enemies pointed to this plank as evidence that the Populists were socialists. They were not; they were landowners or tenants who aspired to own land. However, they believed that natural monopolies—huge enterprises that could be run efficiently only under a single management—should not be in private hands. To the Populist mind, decisions that affected the interests of all should be made democratically, not by private parties interested only in their own enrichment.

The Populists also called for a postal savings system so that ordinary people might avoid depositing their money in privately owned banks and for a graduated income tax. In 1894, the federal income tax was 2 percent for all; the Populists wanted the wealthy to pay a higher percentage of their income than the modest farmer or wage worker paid.

Finally—as only one plank of many—the Populists addressed the silver question. They called for an increase in the money in circulation to $50 per capita. This inflation was to be accomplished through the free and unlimited coinage of silver, its value pegged to that of gold. In 1892, this was perhaps the mildest of the Populist demands. It represented only an adjustment of the Sherman Silver Purchase Act. In just over a year, however, "free silver" was to become the Populists' obsession, nearly destroying their ardor for the rest of the Omaha platform.

A Most Unpopular Man

In February 1893, the Reading Railroad, a major eastern trunk line, announced it was bankrupt. For two months, the stock market was jittery; then it collapsed. Hundreds of banks and thousands of businesses joined the Reading in bankruptcy. By November, the country was sunk in a depression worse than that of the 1870s.

Fearing for the safety of their government bonds, American and British financiers rushed to redeem them. President Cleveland, as committed to the gold standard as Harrison, redeemed all demands in gold alone. By fall, the government's gold reserve—the actual metal in its vaults—sunk to below $100 million, the level regarded as the absolute minimum for maintaining the government's credit.

Cleveland blamed the crisis on the Sherman Silver Purchase Act. "To put beyond all doubt or mistake" the commitment of the United States to the gold standard, the president called for the repeal of the Sherman Act, and a frightened Congress obliged him. That lost him the support of Democrats from the mining states. Then the news leaked that, at the height of the crisis, Cleveland had called on J. P. Morgan for help in increasing the government's gold reserve. Throughout the South and Midwest, more Democrats denounced him as Wall Street's flunky.

Then, in 1894, Cleveland's attorney general, Richard B. Olney, crushed the Pullman strike, alienating industrial workers. When Jacob S. Coxey, an eccentric millionaire from Ohio, led an almost entirely orderly march of unemployed men to Washington to ask for relief—"a petition with its boots on"—Olney ridiculed the protesters by having Coxey arrested for walking on the grass.

Few presidents have been as unpopular as Grover Cleveland was in his second term. When his supporters, dwindling in numbers, reminded voters of the president's unquestioned integrity, William Jennings Bryan of Nebraska replied, "Cleveland may be honest, but so were the mothers who threw their children in the Ganges."

With every blow to Cleveland's reputation, the Populists celebrated. In their eyes, Cleveland's Democrats and the Republicans were indistinguishable. Both parties were the puppets of the money power. The people did indeed seem to be at bay. The word *revolution* was voiced in many a gathering of "the bone and sinew of the republic."

for FURTHER READING

For background and context, see Vincent P. DeSantis, *The Shaping of Modern America, 1877–1916,* 1973, and Robert H. Wiebe, *The Search for Order, 1880–1920,* 1967. The classic studies of the agrarian problem are Gilbert C. Fite, *The Farmer's Frontier, 1865–1900,* 1966, and Fred A. Shannon, *The Farmers' Last Frontier: Agriculture 1860–1897,* 1945. Also see Allan C. Bogue, *From Prairie to Corn Belt,* 1963; E. Dick, *The Sod-House Frontier,* 1937; and Walter P. Webb, *The Great Plains,* 1931.

On farmers' movements, see Solon J. Buck, *The Granger Movement,* 1913; R. F. Durden, *The Climax of Populism,* 1965; Lawrence Goodwyn, *Democratic Promise: The Populist Movement in America,* 1976; John D. Hicks, *The Populist Revolt,* 1931; the appropriate chapters of Richard Hofstadter, *Age of Reform,* 1955; J. Morgan Kousser, *The Shaping of Southern Politics: Suffrage Restriction and the Establishment of the One-Party South, 1880–1910,* 1974; Walter T. K. Nugent, *Money and American Society, 1865–1880,* 1968, and *The Tolerant Populists: Kansas Populism and Nativism,* 1963; Norman Pollock, *The Populist Response to Industrial America,* 1966; Theodore Saloutos, *Farmer Movements in the South, 1865–1933,* 1960; Irwin Unger, *The Greenback Era: A Social and Political History of American Finance, 1865–1879,* 1964; Allen Weinstein, *Prelude to Populism: Origins of the Silver Issue, 1867–1878,* 1970; and C. Vann Woodward, *The Strange Career of Jim Crow,* 1974.

P. E. Coletta, *William Jennings Bryan: Political Evangelist, 1860–1908,* 1964, and Louis W. Koenig, *Bryan: A Political Biography of William Jennings Bryan,* 1971, present somewhat different views of the man who came to personify agrarian aspirations. The model biography of the leading southern populist is C. Vann Woodward, *Tom Watson: Agrarian Rebel,* 1938.

AMERICAN JOURNEY ONLINE AND INFOTRAC COLLEGE EDITION

Visit the source collections at http://ajaccess.wadsworth.com and http://infotrac.thomsonlearning.com, and use the Search function with the following key terms to explore documents, images, audio and video clips, articles, and commentary related to the material in this chapter:

Greenback party
Mary Elizabeth Lease
Populist party
Sod House
William Jennings Bryan

Additional resources, exercises, and Internet links related to this chapter are available on *The American Past* Web site: http://history.wadsworth.com/americanpast7e.

HISTORY ONLINE

First Person Narratives of the American South
http://memory.loc.gov/ammem/award97/neuhtml/fpnashome.html
Life in the nation's poorest agricultural region.

Scenes from the 1893 World's Fair
http://65.54.246.250:80/cgibin/linkrd?_lang=EN&lah=cd63fe2d152
a61ffdea13c05ade7439b&lat=1045588104&hm___action=http%
3a%2f%2fwww%2eku%2eedu%2fhistory%2fVL%2fUSA%2f
Photographs of the Columbian Exposition that opened just as the depression of the 1890s was descending.

IN THE DAYS
OF McKINLEY

The United States as a World Power
1896–1903

> *God has not been preparing the English-speaking and Teutonic peoples for a thousand years for nothing but vain and idle self-contemplation. No. He made us the master organizers of the world to establish system where chaos reigned. He has given us the spirit of progress to overwhelm the forces of reaction throughout the earth. He has made us adept in government that we may administer government among savage and senile peoples. Were it not for such a force as this the world would relapse into barbarism and night. And of all our race, He has marked the American people as His chosen nation to finally lead in the redemption of the world.*
>
> Albert J. Beveridge

FEW PRESIDENTIAL ELECTIONS have been held amid such anxiety as swirled around the election of 1896. Like the election of 1860, which pitted North against South, the contest of 1896 seemed to pit class against class. The election was, in fact, a political watershed. When it was decided, the political era that had begun with the end of Reconstruction was dead. No one knew what the new era would be like when the campaign began. That depended upon which party won the electoral college in November.

A POLITICAL WATERSHED

The Republican convention came first, in St. Louis in June. It was deceptively placid on the surface. Most Republican agrarians had long since left the Grand Old Party and signed on with the Populists. However, some free silverites from the mining states were there. A small contingent led by Senator Teller of Colorado tried to win concessions from the party, but the "gold bugs" were in charge and inflexible. When they quashed Teller, albeit gently, he and his followers walked out.

Mark Hanna and Bill McKinley

With little folderol, the delegates then chose as their candidate a man who was a model of conservatism, prudence, respectability, and sobriety—William McKinley of Ohio. Or, as the Populists and Democrats soon claimed, the Republicans sat back and allowed a beefy Cleveland industrialist, Marcus Alonzo Hanna, to choose their candidate for them.

Bald, scowling Mark Hanna was nearly 60 years of age in 1896, six years older than McKinley. An associate of the

▲ *William McKinley was the personification of middle-class sobriety, integrity, and dignity—the perfect foil for the energetic and bombastic Bryan. He is seated on the front porch of his modest home, from which he campaigned for the presidency.*

applaud. He was a bit of a stiff. Journalist William Allen White quipped that McKinley "was destined for a statue in the park and he was practicing the pose for it." McKinley refused to smoke his beloved cigars in public lest he be accused of setting a bad example for America's youth. He needed a Mark Hanna behind him, a wheeler-dealer who marched into an office, cigar blazing, and planted a hefty haunch on the desk of the man he wanted to see.

The Frightening Boy Bryan

The partnership of energy and solemnity proved just right for the Republicans in 1896 because the Democratic party candidate, nominated at a frenzied convention in July, was a tornado with a singular lack of dignity. William Jennings Bryan, scarcely beyond the 35 years of age the Constitution requires a president to be, was a two-term congressman from Nebraska, a newspaperman, and a celebrity in the farm belt because of his talents as a platform orator. Bryan's subject for four years had been the free coinage of silver, and he had polished a single speech, the "Cross of Gold," to perfection in phrasing, timing, and theatrical gesture. Deeply religious, Bryan enlisted God in the cause of silver coinage. He identified the gold standard with the crucifiers of Christ, silver with democracy and Christianity.

To many, Bryan was a blasphemer. But if the evangelical intensity of his oratory were set aside, he was a rather conservative man. Bryan did not approve of much of the

Rockefellers, he had made a fortune in coal and iron, and was known in business circles as a spokesman for flexibility in dealing with labor unions. Socialists were the chief villains in Hanna's book, but he also railed against exploitative capitalists because their pigheaded lack of vision made working people receptive to radical preachers.

Only with the depression of the 1890s did Hanna take an interest in national politics. He had personal ambitions but also the sense to know that a man could not leap from the corporate boardroom to high office in a month. Putting his aspirations on hold, Hanna devoted his considerable talents and energies to promoting the presidential qualifications of fellow Ohioan, former congressman and governor William McKinley.

McKinley was the Republican party's chief expert on the tariff, and he was himself ambitious. Theodore Roosevelt later remarked that McKinley approached every introduction with an eye on the advantage it might mean to him. And yet, without Hanna, it is unlikely that McKinley would have won the Republican presidential nomination in 1896. The issue dominating—indeed, obsessing—political discourse that year was not the tariff but the gold standard versus the free coinage of silver, a question that had never interested McKinley.

Moreover, although McKinley's dignity commanded respect, he lacked the charisma that made people stand up and

▲ *William Jennings Bryan on the platform. He was probably the best orator of his day, but in 1896, when this photograph was taken, he had only one campaign issue: silver.*

comprehensive reform program the Populists had put together, just free silver. Nevertheless, his manner (and his youth) alarmed Republicans. They called him "Boy Bryan" and "the boy orator of the Platte," scornfully but also with trepidation. The Democrats, committed as a party to the cause of silver when the Chicago convention was planned, felt differently. They scheduled Bryan and his "Cross of Gold" speech to close the debate on currency.

Later, it would be said that Bryan's speech transformed him from an unknown into a presidential candidate by acclamation. In fact, Bryan and his supporters had paved the way for his nomination as carefully as Mark Hanna had engineered McKinley's. It is true, however, that Bryan's speech was so electrifying that many western farmers began to celebrate a November victory in July. And the enthusiasm for "Boy Bryan" blew from Chicago to St. Louis, where, a few weeks later, the Populists convened.

The Populist-Democratic Fusion

No less apocalyptic than they had been in Omaha, the Populists faced a difficult practical decision. If they nominated one of their leaders for president, they would split the free-silver vote with Bryan, putting William McKinley and the gold standard in the White House. If they nominated Bryan—and just about everyone except Mark Hanna agreed on this in July 1896—they would easily elect a man whose style suited the Populists and whose position on free silver could not be improved on.

The trouble was, Bryan opposed just about everything in the Populist reform program. For the sake of a free-silver president, the Populists would have to discard their grand plan to remake America in the interests of the common man.

Moreover, fusing their party with the larger Democratic party meant destroying the identity they had created and with which they had alarmed the nation.

Urban Populists like Henry Demarest Lloyd urged the party to think long term. Lloyd told the Populists to maintain their independence and the integrity of their program, accept defeat in 1896, and wait until 1900, when the Democrats would join them. Some southern Populists, like Tom Watson of Georgia, had another reason for opposing fusion. In the South, the political enemy was not the Republican party but the Democrats whom the fusionists now wanted to marry. To join with the Democrats in the South meant party suicide and destroying the alliance that Watson and others had been forging between poor white and poor black farmers. Southern blacks would not vote for the white supremacist Democrats. They would return to the Republican party that, at least, had taken some interest in their rights.

Midwestern Populists like Jerry Simpson were unmoved. They wanted fusion because fusion meant victory. "I care not for party names," Simpson said. "It is substance we are after, and we have it in William J. Bryan." The Populists from the mining states agreed. Free silver was the all of their rebellion. The rest of the Populist program was of minor interest to miners and mine owners, and businessmen opposed it. What they wanted was a market for the silver they produced—the United States Mint.

The fusionists won. The Populist party nominated Bryan, and, to placate the antifusionists, nominated Tom Watson for vice president, asking the Democrats to make a show of goodwill by accepting Watson as their candidate too. It was a modest, reasonable request. Bryan ignored it.

Waves Against a Rock

Rallying voters was Bryan's forte. Handsome, tireless, and completely at ease among ordinary, hardworking farm people, whether exhorting them to a crusade or gobbling up potato salad after a speech, Bryan revolutionized presidential campaigning in the United States.

With a few exceptions, presidential nominees had remained at home. It insulted the dignity of the office to hustle votes like a candidate for sheriff in an Appalachian hollow. President Johnson's enemies successfully berated him when he took to the campaign trail in 1866. Bryan was not deterred. His speaking tour in 1896 took him 13,000 miles by train. He delivered 600 speeches in 29 states in 14 weeks, more than six speeches a day. The enthusiasm of the crowds that greeted him in the West and South confirmed his zeal and threw bankers and industrialists into a panic.

Panic was exactly what Mark Hanna wanted to see. He tapped wealthy Republicans (and more than a few conservative Democrats) for large contributions to McKinley's campaign. Hanna spent more on posters, buttons, rallies, picnics, advertisements, and a corps of speakers who dogged Bryan than had been spent by both parties in every election since the Civil War. The Republicans printed five pamphlets for every American voter. Hanna was so successful a fund-raiser that, before election day, he began to return contributions. (Imagine a politician today doing such a thing!)

Knowing that the phlegmatic McKinley could not rival Bryan on the stump, Hanna kept his candidate at his modest home in Canton, Ohio. Republican speakers compared McKinley's self-respect with Bryan's huckstering. In fact, McKinley's campaign was as frantic as Bryan's and nearly as tiring. Delegations of the party faithful streamed daily to Canton, where they marched through the town behind a brass band, gathering on McKinley's front lawn. McKinley delivered a short speech from the porch and invited "all his friends" to join him for lemonade or beer, depending on the delegation's attitude toward alcohol. (This had been discreetly ascertained by party workers when the visitors arrived at the depot.) About 750,000 friends visited McKinley's home, trampling his lawn "as if a herd of buffalo had passed through."

Momentous Results

More people voted for Bryan, 6.5 million, than had voted for anyone ever elected president. But he lost. McKinley won 7 million votes and, in the electoral college, 271 votes to Bryan's 176. It was the first time in a quarter of a century that a presidential candidate had won an absolute majority. What happened? As late as September, professional politicians believed that Bryan was well ahead.

First, although Bryan's supporters were noisy and numerous, his appeal was limited to Democrats from the Solid South, to hard-pressed western staple farmers, and to classes of people significant in only a few states, like western metal miners. McKinley swept the Northeast, including the swing states, and also the largely agricultural states of North Dakota, Minnesota, Wisconsin, Iowa, Michigan, and Illinois. Farmers whose conditions were not desperate accepted the Republican contention that Boy Bryan was a dangerous radical.

Nor did Bryan have much support among factory workers and city people generally. He hardly tried to win them over. Imbued with rural prejudices against big cities and the "foreigners" who lived there, he made only one visit to vital New York State and was quoted as calling New York City "the enemy's country," as though the metropolis were inhabited solely by bankers and grain speculators. Fourteen of the 15 biggest cities were controlled by Republican machines, and they delivered the urban vote to William McKinley.

Some industrialists tried to intimidate their employees into voting Republican. The Baldwin Piano Works posted notices on election eve to the effect that if Bryan won, the plant would close for good the day following. But Bryan's weakness in the industrial districts was not due to such tactics. His single-issue free-silver campaign offered little to factory workers. They found more convincing the Republican argument that inflation would hurt them by increasing prices and that McKinley's high tariff protected their jobs against cheaper foreign competitors.

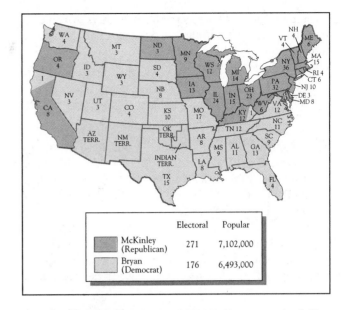

MAP 33:1 Presidential Election of 1896 Note, except for California and Oregon, the sharp sectional split in the election. McKinley carried the populous northeast quarter of the country, including several border states. Bryan carried the South and West.

Finally, Mark Hanna shrewdly judged the instincts of a newly important element in American politics, the growing middle class of small businessmen, professional people, salaried town dwellers, and highly skilled, well-paid workingmen: railroad engineers and firemen, factory foremen, and workers in the building trades. Conscious of their respectability and the social gap between them and the unskilled, they were frightened by Bryan and the ragged, restive farmers whom he represented. To them, the Republican party was "the party of decency." For 40 years after 1896, they were to make the Republican party the nation's majority party.

The Death of Populism

As Tom Watson feared, fusion with the Democrats meant the end of the Populist party. Having sacrificed their comprehensive reform program for the chance of winning free silver with Bryan, the Populists had nothing left when Bryan lost. In the West, the party withered away, in part because of the rebuke at the polls, in part because farm income slowly but steadily rose. Newly discovered gold deposits in Canada and Alaska gently inflated the currency, making free silver irrelevant. Several poor harvests in Europe increased the demand for American foodstuffs.

In the South, fusion with the Democrats finished what Klan violence and Redeemer economic pressure on blacks had started: the nearly total exclusion of African Americans from politics. In the 1880s, despite the Redeemers' efforts, southern blacks generally improved their economic lot. In Virginia in 1890, thanks in part to Buck Duke's demand for cigarette tobacco, 43 percent of black farmers owned their own land. In North Carolina, an African American held on to his seat in Congress with the help of white Populist voters. But African Americans who had held on to their voting rights could not, when the Populists fused with the Democrats, vote for a party that was explicitly committed to white political supremacy.

Even before 1896, Benjamin R. "Pitchfork Ben" Tillman of South Carolina devised the formula for political success in the South. His demands for agrarian reform and condemnation of the "Bourbon" Redeemers were as radical as any Populist's, but he remained within the Democratic party and viciously, where the Redeemers had been genteel, demanded that blacks be kept down. Others imitated him, including Tom Watson, once a proponent of interracial cooperation. Watson was elected senator from Georgia when he perfected the technique of vilifying African Americans.

Disenfranchisement and Lynching

Beginning with Florida and Tennessee in 1889, the former Confederate states found legal devices to keep blacks out of polling booths that did not conflict head-on with the Fifteenth Amendment. The poll tax, a Bourbon idea, set a fee for the right to vote just high enough that the vast majority of southern blacks could not afford it. Poll taxes disenfranchised poor whites too, which was fine from the Bourbon point of view. But race-baiting populistic Democrats like Tillman reenfranchised the poor whites who were their chief supporters, by introducing literacy and "understanding" tests, and the "grandfather clause," into state law.

The grandfather clause (enacted in Alabama, Louisiana, North Carolina, and Georgia) provided that if a man's grandfather had been eligible to vote prior to Radical Reconstruction, that man could vote without paying the poll tax. No African American's grandfather had been eligible to vote before 1867, of course. With 50 percent of southern blacks illiterate in 1900 (the percentage was higher among adults) but just 12 percent of whites, a huge block of African Americans were excluded from the polls by the requirement that a voter be able to read. Seven southern states employed literacy tests. Illiterate whites could be enfranchised if they demonstrated they "understood" questions asked to them about the state constitution by local officials. Records reveal semiliterate sheriffs passing obviously retarded whites but not passing any blacks with the temerity to take the "understanding" test, even educated men.

By the late 1890s, it took a good deal of temerity for a black man to present himself at the courthouse to take a test. The lynching of blacks accused or merely suspected of having committed a violent crime against a white (most commonly rape) became an epidemic. During the 1890s, 150 men were taken from jails or their homes and hanged by southern white mobs each year. No one feared prosecution. Law officers, sympathetic or merely concerned about keeping their jobs, made themselves scarce. Many lynchings were photographed, clearly showing the faces of the people

in the mob. They were souvenirs, printed on postcards and pasted in family albums. A few lynchings were announced in advance. In one case in Georgia, a train was chartered to transport spectators to a hanging. In Oklahoma in 1911, a woman was lynched when she tried to protect her teenage son from a mob.

Most respectable southern whites were disgusted by lynching. But not all: Rebecca Felton of Atlanta, a feminist and antialcohol crusader who worked for compulsory public education and child-care facilities for the poor—a true progressive—said she would be glad to see a lynching "a thousand times a week" to protect white women.

The Atlanta Compromise

In this atmosphere in 1895, the head of Alabama's Tuskegee Institute, Booker T. Washington, who was born in slavery, addressed a convention in Atlanta aimed at promoting investment in the South. He proposed to blacks and promised whites that "in all things . . . purely social we can be as separate as the fingers, yet as one as the hand in all things essential to mutual progress." In other words, blacks would cease demanding the vote, accept racial segregation, and be content with manual jobs (the training for which was Tuskegee's specialty) in return for economic assistance and (unspoken) relief from lynching and terrorism.

Washington was widely respected among African Americans as their most prominent spokesman. He was highly successful in winning financial support for Tuskegee and other black educational institutions from millionaires, mostly northerners. Even the southern states obliged him in founding all-black public colleges. He had his African American critics, the most famous being the urbane northerner W. E. B. DuBois, who insisted that civil equality of the races was indispensable, more important than handouts, no matter how generous. Most southern blacks, living daily with forced segregation and the threat of lynch mobs, favored Washington. They kept their part of the Atlanta Compromise, but their exclusion from southern life and politics grew even sharper after 1900, and lynching continued at only a slightly reduced rate than in the 1890s.

IMPERIALISM

McKinley hoped for a quiet presidency, watching over the retrenchment of the nation after the years of depression and agitation. His confidence in the resilience of American business convinced him that prosperity was just around the corner.

McKinley got his prosperity. Even before he was inaugurated in March 1897, the economic indicators began to improve. Peace and quiet, however, were more elusive. As little as the role suited him, President McKinley led the American people into a series of overseas adventures that transformed a nation born in an anticolonial revolution into something of an empire, with colonies in both hemispheres.

American Isolationism: A Myth

Not that the United States was isolated from world affairs before McKinley. Far from it. The American government maintained missions in all important capitals. The United States fought a war with Mexico in order to take land the Mexicans owned—the oldest kind of interaction between peoples in history—and several times came close to war in defense of American prestige. In 1889, only a typhoon that sank German and American warships near Samoa prevented a full-scale naval encounter with a major European power.

The United States was a major international trader. American ships and sailors were common sights in the world's most exotic ports. As early as 1844, the United States had signed a trade treaty with the Chinese Empire. In 1854, a naval squadron under Commodore Matthew Perry anchored off Yokohama, Japan, and threatened to bombard the city unless the Japanese agreed to abandon their country's genuine isolation and begin to purchase American goods.

By 1870, American exports totaled $320 million, mostly agricultural produce bound for Europe. By 1890, $857 million in goods were sold abroad, and American manufacturers competed with European industrialists in peddling steel, textiles, kerosene, and other products in Pacific countries, Latin America, and Europe. Even Populists like Jerry Simpson wanted the United States to pursue markets abroad—aggressively: "American factories are making more than the American people can consume; American soil is producing more than they can consume. . . . The trade of the world must and shall be ours."

Anticolonialism

If Americans were not isolationists, neither were they colonialists. Neither the people nor most statesmen wanted anything to do with the scramble for colonies that engrossed Europe and Japan in the late nineteenth century. To most Americans, there was a difference between taking the West from a handful of Mexicans and Indians, and establishing suzerainty over distant and densely settled countries. Periodic attempts to annex Cuba and the Dominican Republic were squelched in Congress. With the exceptions of Alaska and the tiny Pacific island of Midway, both acquired in 1867 and neither with much population, the United States possessed no territory that was not contiguous to the states.

Two deep convictions worked against the occasional proposal that the United States take colonies. First, the country was founded in a war against an empire. Could the heirs of the first great anticolonial rebellion take over the lands of others? Second, the vastness of the American continent provided a more than adequate outlet for American energies; there was plenty of work to be done at home. William McKinley shared these assumptions. In all sincerity, he said in his inaugural address that the United States "must avoid the temptation of territorial expansion."

The Nature of Imperialism

But times were changing. By 1897, the United States was the single most important industrial power in the world. Conscious of their national wealth, some politicians, intellectuals, and moralists believed that the United States should assume its "rightful" place among the great nations, which, in the 1890s, were imperialist nations. India was British; Indonesia was Dutch; Indochina and most of northern Africa were French. Korea and Taiwan were falling under Japanese control. Half a dozen nations were scrambling to carve up Africa.

The initial impulse to empire was economic. Colonies provided raw materials and a market for the products of the mother country. Colonies were also a measure of national pride. British imperialists took pleasure in seeing "all that red on the map." (Mapmakers colored British possessions in red.) Germany seized parts of Africa that had little economic value, just for the sake of having them.

In Britain, and later in the United States, this bumptious chauvinism was known as "jingoism," from a British song of 1877: "We do not want to fight, but by jingo, if we do . . ." To the jingoes, being strong enough to overcome less advanced peoples was reason enough to do so.

Some young American politicians, such as Henry Cabot Lodge of Massachusetts and Theodore Roosevelt of New York, itched to join the scramble for colonies. They worried publicly that, in their wealth and prosperity, Americans were becoming soft and flabby. The country needed war now and then in order to toughen up. Roosevelt, a bodybuilding enthusiast, often drew analogies between individuals and nations, between boxing matches and battles.

Anglo-Saxons

Lodge, Roosevelt, and other expansionists were influenced by a theory of race that evolved in part out of social Darwinism. Whereas Herbert Spencer applied his doctrine of "survival of the fittest" to relationships within a society, disciples such as Harvard historian John Fiske and Congregationalist minister Josiah Strong applied it to relationships among different races and cultures. In separate publications of 1885, Fiske and Strong wrote that the Anglo-Saxons (British and Americans) were obviously more fit to govern than were most other peoples. They had done a better job of it. According to Strong's *Our Country,* the Anglo-Saxons were "divinely commissioned" to spread their institutions. It was not a betrayal of American ideals to take over other lands. There was a racial and religious duty to do so.

Strong believed that inferior races would eventually die out. An influential political scientist at Columbia University, John W. Burgess, stated flatly in 1890 that the right of self-determination did not apply to dark-skinned peoples. He wrote that "there is no human right to the status of barbarism."

Alfred Thayer Mahan

In 1890, expansionists found a highly calculating spokesman in naval captain Alfred Thayer Mahan. In an international bestseller, *The Influence of Sea Power upon History,* Mahan argued that the great nations were always seafaring nations possessing powerful navies. He chided Americans for having allowed their own fleet to fall into decay. (In 1891, jingoes who wanted war with Chile had to quiet down when they learned the Chilean navy would make short work of the American fleet.) Mahan urged a massive program of ship construction. Congress responded with large appropriations.

A modern steam-powered navy needed coaling stations scattered throughout the world. That in itself required taking colonies, even if they were mere dots on the globe like little Midway, or building bases in ostensibly independent countries like Hawaii, where, in 1887, the United States cleared a harbor at the mouth of the Pearl River.

America Without a Frontier

Another theory of history that fired up the expansionists was based on the announcement of the Census Bureau that, as of 1890, there was no more frontier. At the 1893 meeting of the American Historical Association, a young historian named Frederick Jackson Turner propounded a theory that the frontier was the key to the vitality of American democracy, social stability, and prosperity. Turner was a scholar of the past, but the implication of his theory for the future was unmistakable. With the frontier gone, was the United States doomed to stagnation and social upheaval? To some who found Turner convincing, the solution was to find new frontiers abroad. Throughout the 1890s, American financiers pumped millions of dollars into China and Latin America because they felt that investment opportunities within the United States were shrinking.

By 1898, Americans' attitude toward the world was delicately balanced. Pulling in one direction was the tradition of anticolonialism. Tugging the other way were jingoism, Anglo-Saxonism, and apprehensions for the future. All it took to decide the direction of the leap was a sudden shove—which was provided by a war for independence just 90 miles from American shores.

THE SPANISH-AMERICAN WAR

On a map, Cuba looks like an appendage of Florida, a geographical curiosity that has excited the notice of many American expansionists. In 1895, along with Puerto Rico and the Philippines, Cuba was all that was left of the once mighty Spanish Empire. Not that Cubans were better colonials than Mexicans or Argentines. Rebellion was chronic on the island. But with less empire to control, even a weak Spain had held fast.

The uprising of 1895 was serious. Cuban exiles in the United States smuggled in arms from Florida, and the rebels had widespread support. Unintentionally, the Wilson-Gorman Tariff of 1894 aggravated the discontent by taxing Cuban sugar so highly that little could be sold in the American market.

The Cuban rebellion was a classic guerrilla war. The Spanish army and navy controlled the cities of Havana and Santiago and most large towns. By day, Spanish soldiers moved with little trouble among a seemingly peaceful peasantry. By night, however, docile field-workers turned into rebels and sorely punished the Spanish troops. As in most guerrilla wars, fighting was bitter and cruel. Both sides were guilty of atrocities.

Americans would have been sympathetic toward the rebels in any event. Their sympathy was whipped into near hysteria when two competing newspaper chains decided that Cuba could be used to sell papers.

The Yellow Press

William Randolph Hearst's New York *Journal* and Joseph Pulitzer's New York *World,* and affiliates of each in a dozen large cities, competed not only in gathering news but in outdoing one another by exploiting sensations and contriving gimmicks with which to woo readers. The Hearst and Pulitzer chains invented the daily comic strip. The first was called "The Yellow Kid," from which came the term *yellow press* to describe newspapers employing such undignified antics to increase circulation. Colorful writers squeezed the most lurid details out of celebrated murder and sex cases, and pioneered the "invented" news story. In 1889, Pulitzer's *World* sent Elizabeth S. "Nellie Bly" Cochrane around the world in an attempt to break the record of the fictional hero of Jules Verne's novel *Around the World in Eighty Days.* (She did it, in 72 days, 6 hours, and 11 minutes.)

It was no great leap from promotions like Nellie Bly to making hay out of Spanish atrocities. The yellow press dubbed the Spanish military commander in Cuba (Valeriano Weyler) "the Butcher" for his repressive policies, which included the establishment of concentration camps. Warring against a whole population, Weyler tried to stifle the uprising by herding whole villages into camps; everyone who was found outside the camps could be defined as enemies, to be shot on sight. This strategy was inevitably brutal, and Cubans died in the camps from malnutrition and disease.

Real suffering was not enough for Hearst and Pulitzer. They transformed innocuous incidents into horror stories and invented others. When Hearst artist Frederic Remington wired Hearst from Havana that everything was peaceful and he wanted to come home, Hearst ordered him to stay: "You furnish the pictures. I'll furnish the war." One sensational drawing showed Spanish soldiers and customs officials leering at a naked American woman. It was based on a real incident—except that the woman, suspected of smuggling, had been searched quite properly in private by female officers.

McKinley's Dark Hour

McKinley wanted calm. Influential American businessmen had substantial investments in Cuba, about $50 million in railroads, mines, and sugar cane plantations. They feared the revolutionaries more than the Spanish. McKinley only hoped Spain would abandon its harshest policies and pla-

▲ *The destruction of the battleship* Maine *in Havana Harbor, as reported by Joseph Pulitzer's New York* World. *Even if Pulitzer had not been promoting war with Spain, so great a disaster would have received such sensational front-page coverage.*

cate both Cubans and bellicose Americans by liberalizing government on the island. The Spanish responded to American pressure. In 1898, a new government in Madrid withdrew Weyler and proposed autonomy for Cuba within the Spanish Empire. McKinley was satisfied. But the war came anyway, largely because of two unforeseeable events.

On February 9, Hearst's New York *Journal* published a letter written by the Spanish ambassador in Washington, Enrique Dupuy de Lome. In it, Dupuy said that McKinley was

"weak, a bidder for the admiration of the crowd." It was by no means an inaccurate assessment of the president, but it was rough and insulting.

Six days later, on February 15, 1898, the battleship USS *Maine* exploded in Havana Harbor with a loss of 260 sailors. To this day, the cause of the disaster is debated. The explosion may have been caused by a coal fire that spread to the magazine. A bomb may have been planted by Cuban rebels hoping to provoke the United States into declaring war on Spain. Or the tragedy may have been the work of Spanish diehards who opposed the new liberal policy in Cuba. So charged was the atmosphere that some suggested William Randolph Hearst himself planted the bomb for the sake of a headline!

There were plenty of headlines and outrage, and most Americans seemed to accept the least credible explanation: The Spanish government, which was trying to avoid war at all costs, had destroyed the *Maine*.

McKinley continued to vacillate for a month and a half, while flooding Spain with demands for a change of policy. As late as March 26, Mark Hanna urged him to keep the peace, and on April 9, the Spanish government gave in to every demand McKinley made on it. In the meantime, however, fearing that to continue resisting the war fever would cost the Republicans control of Congress in the elections of 1898, McKinley caved in. On April 11, practically ignoring the Spanish capitulation, the president asked Congress for a declaration of war and got it.

"Splendid Little War"

The United States Army numbered 28,000 men, most of them stationed in the West. Such a force, less than half the size of the army of tiny Belgium, was not up to launching an invasion even just a short sail from Florida.

The spanking new navy was ready, however. It struck first not in Cuba but halfway around the world in Spain's last Pacific colony, the Philippines. On May 1, acting on the instructions of Undersecretary of the Navy Theodore Roosevelt (the secretary of the navy was ill), Commodore George

Dewey steamed a flotilla into Manila Bay and completely surprised the Spanish garrison. He destroyed most of the Spanish ships before they could weigh anchor.

But Dewey had no soldiers with which to attack on land. For more than three months, he and his men sat outside Manila Harbor, baking in their steel ships, while Filipino rebels struggled with the Spanish garrison in the city. Finally, in August, troops arrived and took the capital. Although they did not know it, a peace treaty had been signed the previous day: shades of the Battle of New Orleans.

By that time, American troops had conquered Cuba and Puerto Rico. Secretary of State John Hay called their campaign a "splendid little war" because so few Americans died in battle. In order to celebrate so gaily, however, it was necessary that Hay overlook the more than 5,000 soldiers who died from typhoid, tropical diseases, and poisonous "embalmed beef," tainted meat that was fed to the soldiers because of corruption or simple inefficiency.

Although the Spanish army in Cuba outnumbered the Americans until the last, both Spanish commanders and men were paralyzed by defeatism. Despite shortages of food, clothing, transport vehicles, medical supplies, ammunition, and horses, an American army of 17,000 was landed in Cuba in June and defeated the Spanish outside Santiago at the battles of El Caney and San Juan Hill. (With 200,000 soldiers in Cuba, the Spanish had stationed only 19,000 in Santiago.)

The victory gave Americans a popular hero. Theodore Roosevelt had resigned from the Navy Department to accept the post of colonel in a volunteer cavalry unit called the Rough Riders. It was a highly unmilitary group, made up of cowboys

▲ *Men of the Tenth Cavalry Regiment atop San Juan Hill after the battle. No one faulted the bravery of Teddy Roosevelt's Rough Riders, who fought to the right of the Tenth, but a number of observers said quietly that the professional and experienced Tenth was the key unit on that sector of the battle line.*

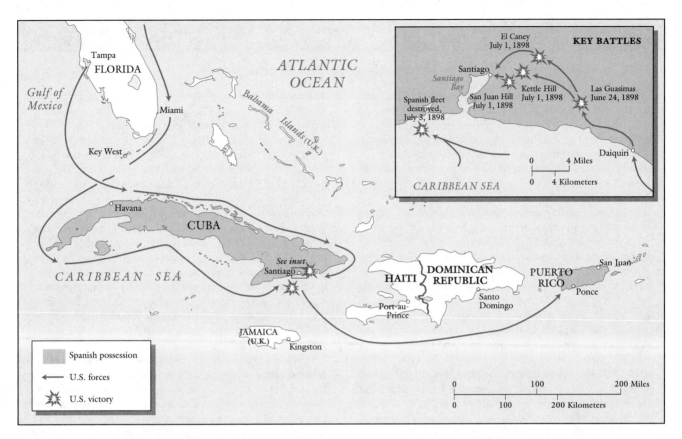

MAP 33:2 **The Fighting in Cuba**   After the destruction of the Spanish fleet and a few small battles west of Santiago, Spanish resistance collapsed. Puerto Rico was taken virtually without a fight.

from Roosevelt's North Dakota ranch, show business fops, and upper-class polo players and other athletes. The Rough Riders had to fight on foot because the army was unable to get their horses out of Tampa, Florida. They fought bravely in the hottest action on San Juan Hill but, luckily for them, were side by side with the Ninth and Tenth United States Cavalry Regiments, African American units hardened by service in the West. As usual, the white Rough Riders got complete credit for a victory in which they had played only a small part.

EMPIRE CONFIRMED

When the Spanish gave up, American troops occupied not only Manila in the Philippines and much of Cuba but also the island of Puerto Rico. But what to do with these prizes? The colonialism controversy was no longer an academic debate. It involved three far-flung island countries inhabited by millions of people who spoke Spanish or Malayan languages and adhered to traditions very different from those of Americans. The Cubans and Puerto Ricans were of familiar European and African ancestry, but the Filipinos were not. Only a small minority of the three populations wanted to become colonial subjects of the United States.

To the dismay of the imperialists, the independence of Cuba had been guaranteed before the war had begun. In order

to get money from Congress to fight Spain, the administration accepted a rider drafted by Senator Teller of Colorado. The Teller Amendment forbade the United States to take over the sugar island. Therefore, the great debate over imperialism centered on Puerto Rico and the Philippine Islands.

The Debate

The anti-imperialists were a disparate group; their arguments were sometimes contradictory. In Congress, they included old radical Republicans like George Frisbie Hoar of Massachusetts, onetime liberal Republicans like Carl Schurz, and much of the old mugwump wing of the party. Some Republican regulars opposed taking colonies, including the witty and dictatorial Speaker of the House of Representatives, Thomas B. Reed of Maine. A substantial part of the Democratic party, led by William Jennings Bryan, opposed annexation of any former Spanish lands. Henry Teller became a Democrat in 1900 because of his opposition to imperial expansion.

The anti-imperialists reminded Americans of their anti-colonial heritage. "We insist," declared the American Anti-Imperialist League in October 1899, "that the subjugation of any people is 'criminal aggression' and open disloyalty to the distinctive principles of our government. We hold, with Abraham Lincoln, that no man is good enough to govern another man without that man's consent."

Remembering the Maine

Secretary of State John Hay called it "a splendid little war." Undersecretary of the Navy Theodore Roosevelt resigned in order to fight in it. William Allen White remembered the glad excitement that greeted the declaration of war in the Midwest: "Everywhere over this good, fair land, flags were flying. . . . crowds gathered to hurrah for the soldiers and to throw hats into the air."

The celebrants' favorite cry was "Remember the *Maine;* to hell with Spain." Americans looked on the war as an opportunity to prove the arrival of the United States as a world power and, at home, as a chance to seal the reunion of North and South by having northern and southern boys join together to fight Spain. Although McKinley would not allow William Jennings Bryan to go abroad and make a military reputation, he was delighted to appoint old Confederate officers like Fitzhugh Lee and General Joseph Wheeler to active commands.

But, for the soldiers in the ranks, the war was grim and dirty. Only the poor morale of Spanish soldiers and the ineptitude of Spanish commanders made the war short and "splendid." The army was not ready. In 1898, it was only 28,000 strong. Congress authorized increasing this force to 65,700 for the duration of the war, but, despite an initial rush of enlistments, the army never grew this large. The young men who rallied to arms in every state preferred to join the state militias or volunteer units, in which enlistments were for two years unless discharged earlier (as almost all would be).

In 1898, the militias numbered 140,000 men, but regular army officers justly doubted the effectiveness of their training and equipment. Indeed, training was inadequate across the board because of the rush to get into action, and supplies were never well handled. Companies mustering, mostly in the southern states, were issued heavy woolen winter uniforms and Civil War–vintage Springfield rifles. Much meat provided to the soldiers was tainted, and sanitary conditions in the crowded camps were such that filth-related diseases like typhoid and dysentery ravaged the recruits. When the dead were counted at the end of 1898, 379 men were listed as killed in combat; 5,083 men were dead of disease.

About 274,000 served in the war; an equal number of volunteers were turned down. Among the rejects were Bryan; Frank James, brother of the fabled train robber Jesse James; and Buffalo Bill Cody, who annoyed the War Department by writing a magazine article titled "How I Could Drive the Spaniards out of Cuba with Thirty Thousand Indian Braves." Martha A. Chute of Colorado was discouraged in her offer to raise a troop of women, as was William Randolph Hearst in his suggestion of a regiment of professional boxers and baseball players. "Think of a regiment composed of magnificent men of this ilk," the editor of the *Journal* wrote. "They would overawe any Spanish regiment by their mere appearance." Nevertheless, the Rough Riders, a motley collection of cowboys, athletes, and gentlemen, were accepted and shipped to Cuba, albeit without their horses.

In fact, there were few battlegrounds in Cuba or in the Philippines that were suited to cavalry. Both are tropical countries, and most of the fighting was done in summer and in jungle. The army tried to prepare for jungle warfare by authorizing the recruitment of up to 10,000 "immunes," young men who were thought to be immune to tropical diseases. However, medicine's comparative ignorance of the nature of tropical diseases combined with racism to make the immune regiments no more serviceable than any others. Whereas the original idea had been to fill these units with men who had grown up in marshy areas of the Deep South, within months, recruiters were turning away white Louisianians from the bayous and accepting blacks from the upland South and even urban New Jersey. African Americans were believed to possess a genetic immunity to malaria, yellow fever, and other tropical afflictions.

Blacks played a large part in both the Cuban and the Philippine campaigns. When the war broke out, there were four black regiments in the regular army: two infantry and two cavalry, the Ninth and the Tenth Horse Regiments. All four saw action. In fact, although Theodore Roosevelt described the capture of San Juan Hill as an accomplishment of the Rough Riders, other witnesses believed that the Rough Riders would have been devastated had it not been for the black Tenth Cavalry, which was immediately to the left of the Rough Riders at the beginning of the charge and entirely integrated with them at the end (except for celebratory photographs). In the words of the restrained report of their commander, later to be a general, John J. "Black Jack" Pershing, "The 10th Cavalry charged up the hill, scarcely firing a shot, and being nearest the Rough Riders, opened a disastrous enfilading fire upon the Spanish right, thus relieving the Rough Riders from the volleys that were being poured into them from that part of the Spanish line." About 10,000 African Americans served in the war, 4,000 of them in the "immunes."

A study of white regiments indicated that the Spanish-American War was a poor man's fight and, rather more surprising, a city man's fight. From largely rural Indiana, for example, of those volunteers who listed their occupation, only 296 were farmers. There were 322 common laborers, 413 skilled laborers, and 118 white-collar workers (clerks). Only 47 in the regiment were professional men, and 25 were merchants. The army was far less representative of the general population than were the American armies of the two world wars. In age, however, it was typical: The average age of the soldiers was 24. Their average height was 5 feet, 8 inches, and their average weight was 149 pounds.

Some of the anti-imperialists appealed to racist feelings. With many people uncomfortable with the nation's large black population, did it make sense to bring millions more nonwhite people under the flag? When Congress finally decided to take the Philippines and pay Spain $20 million in compensation, House Speaker Thomas B. Reed resigned in disgust, grumbling, "We have bought ten million Malays at two dollars a head unpicked, and nobody knows what it will cost to pick them."

However, feelings of white racial superiority worked mostly in favor of the imperialists. Shrewd propagandists like Roosevelt, who was now governor of New York, Henry

Cabot Lodge, and the eloquent Albert J. Beveridge, senator from Indiana, preached that the white race had a duty and a right to govern inferior peoples. "God has not been preparing the English-speaking and Teutonic peoples for a thousand years for nothing but vain and idle self-contemplation and self-admiration," Beveridge told the Senate. He had made them "the master organizers of the world."

Well-grounded fears that, if the United States evacuated the Philippines, Japan or Germany would occupy them, motivated other politicians to support annexation. But most of all, the American people were in an emotional, expansive mood. Coming at the end of the troubled, depressed, and divided 1890s, annexation of colonies seemed a way to unite the country.

Hawaii

McKinley found it easier to call for annexation of the Philippines and Puerto Rico because the United States had already taken its first real overseas colony. In July 1898, shortly after the Spanish-American War began, Congress annexed the seven main islands and 1,400 minor islands of the mid-Pacific nation of Hawaii. Shortly thereafter, Wake and Baker Islands and Guam were added to the empire as coaling stations for the navy.

The annexation of Hawaii was long in the making. The descendants of American missionaries on the islands had grown rich by exporting sugar to the United States, and they had won the confidence of the Hawaiian king, David Kalakaua. Until 1890, they were content with the independent island paradise they virtually ran.

Then, the McKinley tariff of 1890 introduced a two-cent-per-pound bounty on American-grown sugar. This encouraged enough mainland farmers to produce cane or sugar beets that Hawaiian imports declined sharply. Unable to affect American tariff policy from outside, the haole (white) oligarchy concluded that it must join the islands to the United States and benefit from the subsidy.

Their first attempt was squelched. In 1891, Kalakaua's sister, Liliuokalani, replaced him on the throne and moved to preserve Hawaiian independence by withdrawing some of the privileges the wealthy haoles enjoyed. "Hawaii for the Hawaiians" was her slogan, and she was popular among native Hawaiians who were pressured not only by haoles but by increasing numbers of Japanese plantation workers.

Alarmed, the oligarchy acted quickly with help from the American ambassador in Honolulu. He landed 150 marines from the USS *Boston,* who quickly took control. "The Hawaiian pear is now fully ripe . . . for the United States to pluck it," he informed Washington. The Senate had

Hawaii State Archives

▲ *Liliuokalani ("Queen Lil"), last monarch of Hawaii, bore no racial animosity toward whites. Her husband, behind her, was Italian. She did try to arrest and reduce the nearly complete economic domination of the islands by a haole oligarchy including Sanford Dole of pineapple fame, who is seated at the left.*

a treaty of annexation on the table when Grover Cleveland was inaugurated in March 1893; but, after investigating Hawaiian public opinion, he withdrew the treaty and ordered the marines to return to their ships and to the naval base at Pearl Harbor.

The haole oligarchy had gone too far to chance restoring Queen Liliuokalani. They declared Hawaii a republic. As long as Cleveland was president, they bided their time. In the excitement of the imperialist expansion of 1898, Hawaii was annexed by means of a joint resolution of the American Congress and Hawaiian legislature, the same device under which Texas had joined the Union.

Many Hawaiians continued to resent the takeover. Liliuokalani spent much time in the United States trying to win financial concessions for herself and the islands' natives. But, as the white population grew and the islands attracted Japanese, Chinese, and Filipino immigrants, the native Hawaiians declined into a small minority. Like the Indians, they became foreigners in their own homeland. The famous islands' anthem, "Aloha Oe," which was written by Liliuokalani, translates as "Farewell to Thee." It has more than one meaning.

The Philippine Insurrection

Taking over the Philippines was neither easy nor cheap, as Thomas B. Reed had predicted. If the war with Spain had been something like splendid, the war that followed it was a great deal like ugly. The Filipinos were experienced in guerrilla warfare. Led by Emilio Aguinaldo, a well-educated pa-

triot who was as comfortable in the jungle as he was in the library, the rebels withdrew from the American-occupied cities and fought only when the odds favored them.

In response, the American army of occupation was expanded to 65,000 men by early 1900, but, even then, the troops could make little progress outside the cities. The American commanders were unable to draw the *insurrectos* into a conventional battle in which superior firepower told the tale.

The fighting took a vicious turn. The Filipinos frequently decapitated their captives. The Americans, frustrated by failures, the tropical heat, insects, and diseases, retaliated by slaughtering whole villages thought to support the rebels. The army never did defeat the *insurrectos*. The rebellion

▲ *Emilio Aguinaldo (on the horse) was in exile in Hong Kong when Admiral Dewey asked him to return to the Philippines to lead the Filipinos in the war against Spain. Aguinaldo assumed the goal was Philippine independence. When the United States absorbed the country as a colony, he mounted a well-executed but failed insurrection against American rule.*

ended only when, in March 1901, troops under General Arthur MacArthur succeeded in capturing Aguinaldo by a clever trick. Weary of the bloodshed, Aguinaldo took an oath of allegiance to the United States and ordered his followers to do the same. (He lived quietly and long enough to see Philippine independence in 1946.) More than 5,000 Americans died in the cause of suppressing a popular revolution, a queer twist in a conflict that had begun, three years earlier, in support of a popular revolution.

The Open Door in China

The Philippines provided a superb base for Americans engaged in the China trade. On the face of it, China too was a pear ripe for plucking. The emperor had little power outside Beijing; powerful regional warlords battled one another in the provinces; and most of the imperialist nations of Europe, plus Japan, had carved out spheres of influence. There, their own troops maintained order, and their own laws governed their resident citizens.

However, the most powerful of the nations in China, Great Britain, opposed partitioning China in the way Africa was being partitioned. Longer in the empire business and therefore more conscious than Japan, Russia, Germany, and Italy of the headaches and expense that attended imperial glory, the British believed that, with their efficient industrial complex, they could dominate the market of a weak but independent China. American businessmen believed they would win the lion's share of the prodigious purchases 160 million Chinese were capable of making. So they supported the British policy of preventing the other imperialist nations from turning their spheres of influence into full-fledged colonies.

Indeed, McKinley's secretary of state, John Hay, rushed ahead of Great Britain to circulate a series of memorandums called the "Open Door Notes." These declarations pledged the imperial powers to respect the territorial integrity of China and to grant equal trading rights in their spheres of influence to all other countries.

Anticolonialist as it was, the Open Door policy by no means established the self-determination of the Chinese people or ended military intervention by outsiders. In 1900, when antiforeign rebels known as Boxers (the Chinese name of their religious movement was "Righteous Harmonious Fist") besieged 900 foreigners in the British legation in Beijing, American troops joined the soldiers of six other nations in defeating them. The victory encouraged beliefs in white superiority (despite the Japanese contribution to the victory) and convinced other nations that cooperation in maintaining the Open Door policy in China was the best approach.

McKinley Murdered

In 1900, the Democrats again nominated William Jennings Bryan to run against McKinley. Bryan tried to make imperialism the issue, but the campaign fizzled out. Americans were either happy with their overseas possessions or simply uninterested in the issue. McKinley sidestepped the debate

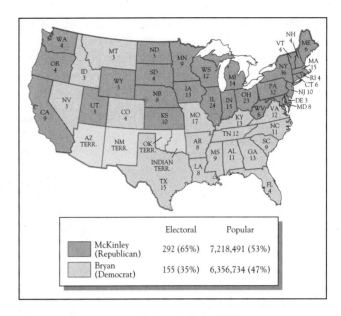

MAP 33:3 **Presidential Election of 1900** McKinley's popularity as president can be seen by comparing the results of his reelection in 1900 with his first victory in 1896 (see Map 33.1 on p. 481). Bryan's command of the West in 1896 was gone. Prosperity and the Spanish-American War turned six states that had been Bryan's four years earlier.

and crowed about prosperity; the Republican slogan was "Four More Years of the Full Dinner Pail." Dinner pails carried the day. Several states that voted Democratic-Populist in 1896 went Republican in 1900, including Bryan's own state of Nebraska and the once revolutionary Kansas.

There was a new vice president. Theodore Roosevelt moved quickly from his exploits in Cuba to the governorship of New York. There, however, he alienated the Republican party boss, Thomas C. Platt, by refusing to take orders and even attacking some corrupt members of Platt's organization. When McKinley's first vice president died in 1899, Platt saw a chance to get rid of the troublesome Rough Rider. He would inter him in the political burial ground of the vice presidency.

Mark Hanna, whose vision was broader than Platt's, opposed the nomination. What would happen to the country, Hanna asked McKinley, if something happened to him, and

Dewey's Blunder

Commodore George Dewey was a national hero after his victory at Manila Bay. He was a Democrat and could likely have had the party's presidential nomination in 1900. At first, Dewey rebuffed the feelers put out by conservative Democrats because he did not think he was qualified for the office. Then he changed his mind: "Since studying the subject, I am convinced that the office of the president is not such a very difficult one to fill." His candor, seen by others as arrogance, alienated almost all of his early supporters. One could not run for president saying that the job was a piece of cake.

the manic Roosevelt became president? McKinley was almost 60, a ripe old age in 1900. Two presidents had been assassinated in his lifetime. "It is your duty to your country to live another four years," Hanna told the president.

McKinley's obligations were in another man's hands. On September 6, 1901, the president paid a ceremonial visit to the Pan-American Exposition in Buffalo. Greeting a long line of guests, he found himself faced by a man extending a bandaged hand, the gauze concealing a pistol of large bore. Leon Czolgosz, a pathetic figure, uneducated, unsophisticated, a lifelong sucker for panaceas, was an anarchist who "didn't believe one man should have so much service and another man should have none." He shot the president several times in the chest and abdomen. Eight days later, McKinley died. "Now look," Hanna shook his head at the funeral. "That damned cowboy is president."

A Flexible Imperialist

Unlike every accidental president who preceded him, Teddy Roosevelt was to leave an indelible mark on the nation. The young New Yorker (42 when he was sworn in) knew only one way to do anything: rush into the lead and stay there. Nowhere was his assertive personality more pronounced than in his foreign policy, an extension of the zest that took him bellowing up San Juan Hill.

Roosevelt's actions varied according to the part of the world with which he was dealing. With the European nations, he insisted that the United States be accepted as an equal, active imperial power. Although friendship between Great Britain and the United States had long been growing, Roosevelt hastened it by responding cordially to every British request for cooperation. Toward Latin America, Roosevelt was arrogant. Privately, he called Latin Americans "dagoes." Officially, he told both Latin Americans and Europeans that the whole Western Hemisphere was America's "sphere of influence." In regard to Asia, Roosevelt supported the Open Door policy.

During Roosevelt's presidency, American capital poured into China. International consortia developed mines, built railways, and set up other profitable enterprises. In 1905, the president applied his policy of equilibrium in China by working through diplomatic channels to end a war between Russia and Japan. Much to the surprise of most Europeans, Japan handily defeated Russia and threatened to seize complete control of Manchuria and other parts of northern China. Through a mixture of threats and cajolery, Roosevelt got both sides to meet at Portsmouth, New Hampshire, to work out a treaty that maintained a balance of power in the area and guaranteed Chinese independence.

High-Handedness in Latin America

In Latin America, Roosevelt was not so accommodating. He made it clear to the European nations that the United States held a special, preeminent position in the Western Hemisphere. In 1904, when several European nations threatened to invade the Dominican Republic to collect debts owed to their citizens, Roosevelt proclaimed the "Roosevelt Corollary" to the Monroe Doctrine: When necessary to preserve the independence of American states, the United States would exercise an international police power. In other words, although European nations still had to keep out of the Americas, the United States would intervene south of the border if circumstances called for such action.

Roosevelt wasted no time in putting his corollary to work. Marines landed in the Dominican Republic and took over the collection of customs, seeing to it that European creditors were paid off. From 1904 until the 1930s, the United States intervened in a number of Latin American countries as (according to General Smedley Butler, who was involved in several interventions) "a glorified bill collecting

Send in the Marines
Among the early United States interventions in the Caribbean region were interventions in Panama in 1903; Cuba in 1906; Honduras in 1907; Nicaragua in 1910 and 1912; Mexico in 1914; Haiti in 1915; and the Dominican Republic in 1916.

Old Boys
Most of Theodore Roosevelt's advisers were drawn from his own social class. They were gentlemen of old family who automatically assumed that they were the people intended to govern the United States. They took their duties lightly. Cabinet meetings could seem like a club room full of joking old boys at a Harvard reunion.

When Teddy Roosevelt asked Attorney General Philander C. Knox to prepare a legal justification of his actions in detaching Panama from Colombia, Knox replied, "Oh Mr. President, do not let so great an achievement suffer from any taint of legality." After a long, blustering explanation of his actions to the cabinet, Roosevelt asked, "Well, have I defended myself?" Secretary of War Elihu Root replied, "You certainly have, Mr. President. You have shown that you were accused of seduction and you have conclusively proved that you were guilty of rape."

Haiti
The high-handedness of American policy in the Caribbean should not obscure the fact that the problems there were often very serious. The history of Haiti, for example, was the history of a mess. In the 72 years preceding American intervention in Haiti in 1915, there had been 102 coups, revolts, and all-out civil wars. Of 22 presidents, only 1 served a complete term, and only 4 died of natural causes. At the time of the American intervention, 80 percent of the Haitian government's budget went to paying *interest* on the national debt. Many Americans opposed in principle to intervention found it easy to wink at intervention in countries with such concrete problems.

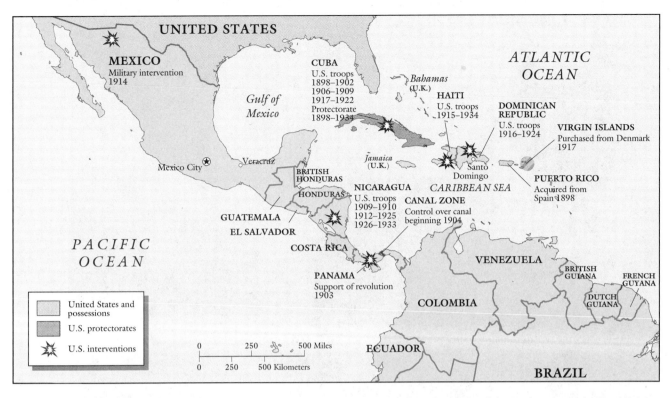

MAP 33:4 The United States in the Caribbean Region, 1898–1934 For more than three decades, until the proclamation of the Good Neighbor policy in 1934, the United States intervened at will in the internal affairs of Caribbean and Central American nations.

agency." These interventions pleased European and American investors, but they created a reservoir of ill will in Latin America that is far from drained today. No action offended Latin Americans more than Roosevelt's high-handed seizure of the Panama Canal Zone, which the president considered his greatest achievement.

In 1911, when the construction of the canal was nearly complete, Roosevelt reflected (quite accurately) that only his decisiveness had moved the project along. "If I had followed traditional, conservative methods," he said, "the debates on it would have been going on yet. But I took the Canal Zone and let Congress debate; and while the debate goes on the Canal does also."

A Path Between the Seas

Naval officers had long recognized the value of a quick route between the Atlantic and the Pacific. During the Spanish-American War, the battleship *Oregon,* stationed in San Francisco, took 67 days to steam the 12,000 miles to Cuba via Cape Horn. Had there been an isthmian canal, the voyage would have been but 4,000 miles.

A French company had started to dig a canal across Panama, then part of Colombia, in the 1880s. But the project was abandoned because of financial and engineering difficulties and the ravages of malaria and yellow fever. Three out of five French men and women in Panama died, and they were the supervisors, living under the best conditions. The mortality was undoubtedly higher among the laborers,

mostly blacks from Jamaica. The horrors of the French experience convinced most American experts that the path between the seas should be dug not in Panama, but in Nicaragua, which was more healthful and provided a lower crossing of the American landmass than Panama did.

It was a Nicaraguan canal that Secretary of State Hay had in mind when he negotiated a treaty with Britain promising the United States full control of the project. Congress also favored the Nicaragua route. Then, however, two of the most effective lobbyists of all time, an agent of the French company that held rights to the Panama route, Philippe Bunau-Varilla, and an American wheeler-dealer, William Nelson Cromwell, went to work in Washington's restaurants, the cloakrooms of Congress, and in the White House itself.

Their goal was to win approval of the Panama route, then sell the assets of the French company in Panama, including an American-built railroad, to the United States. There was no good reason why their proposal should have been accepted. Even if the United States opted for the Panama route, the French company's rights on the isthmus were due to expire shortly, and most of its equipment was useless. Nevertheless, Bunau-Varilla and Cromwell won over President Roosevelt and key members of Congress.

The Taking of Panama

Then the project stalled in Bogotá. The Colombian government turned down the American offer to pay Colombia $10 million and an annual rent of $250,000. (The Colombians

▲ *America's means of acquiring the Panama Canal Zone has rightly been faulted, but the construction of the canal was a triumph of engineering and organization. To a large extent, construction was the gigantic job of removing blasted earth from the scene at top speed. The parallel railroads at this cut indicate how it was done. The railroads were repeatedly built, torn up, and relocated.*

wanted $25 million.) Rather than take a step backward, Roosevelt conspired with Bunau-Varilla to start a revolution in Panama. On November 2, 1903, the president moved several warships to the vicinity, and the next day, the province erupted in riots and declared its independence. On November 6, the United States recognized the new Republic of Panama. On November 18, the first foreign minister of Panama, none other than the Frenchman Bunau-Varilla, signed a treaty with the United States that granted perpetual use of a 10-mile-wide canal zone across the isthmus on the terms that Colombia had refused.

None of Roosevelt's successors in the presidency were quite so arrogant in dealing with Latin America. Roosevelt's handpicked successor, William Howard Taft, tried to replace gunboat diplomacy with dollar diplomacy: to influence Latin America (and China) through investment rather than armed force. In 1921, over the protests of Roosevelt's old ally Henry Cabot Lodge, the United States attempted to make amends to Colombia for Roosevelt's high-handed actions by paying the $25 million that the Colombians originally demanded for the right to dig the Panama Canal.

But such gestures could not change America's "big brother" behavior or the simmering resentment of many Latin Americans. The plunge into imperialism established intervention as an essential part of American diplomacy. Every president from Theodore Roosevelt to Herbert Hoover used troops to enforce American wishes in Latin America. After 30 years of the "Good Neighbor" policy—no interventions—Lyndon B. Johnson and Ronald Reagan revived the practice in the Dominican Republic and tiny Grenada.

for FURTHER READING

The essential background of the political upheaval at the end of the nineteenth century can be found in Vincent P. DeSantis, *The Shaping of Modern America, 1877–1916,* 1973; H. Wayne Morgan, *From Hayes to McKinley: National Party Politics, 1877–1896,* 1971; and Robert H. Wiebe, *The Search for Order, 1880–1920,* 1967.

Valuable special studies include Howard K. Beale, *Theodore Roosevelt and the Rise of America to World Power,* 1956; Robert L. Beisner, *From the Old Diplomacy to the New, 1865–1900,* 1975; C. S. Campbell, *The Transformation of American Foreign Relations, 1865–1900,* 1976; John Dobson, *America's Ascent: The United States Becomes a Great Power, 1880–1914,* 1978; Robert F. Durden, *The Climax of Populism: The Election of 1896,* 1965; Frank Freidel, *The Splendid Little War,* 1958; Lloyd Gardner, Walter R. Le Feber, and Thomas McCormick, *The Creation of the American Empire,* 1973; Ray Ginger, *Altgeld's America: The Lincoln Ideal and Changing Realities,* 1958; Paul F. Glad, *The Trumpet Soundeth,* 1960, and *McKinley, Bryan, and the People,* 1964; S. L. Jones, *The Presidential Election of 1896,* 1964; Walter R. Le

Feber, *The New Empire: An Interpretation of American Expansion, 1860–1898,* 1963; Ernest R. May, *Imperial Democracy: The Emergence of America as a Great Power,* 1961; David McCullough, *The Path Between the Seas,* 1977; Dwight C. Miner, *Fight for the Panama Canal,* 1966; Thomas J. Osborne, *American Opposition to Hawaiian Annexation, 1893–1898,* 1981; J. W. Pratt, *Expansionists of 1898: The Acquisition of Hawaii and the Spanish Islands,* 1936, and *America's Colonial Experiment,* 1950; Emily S. Rosenberg, *Spreading the American Dream: American Economic and Cultural Expansion, 1890–1945,* 1982; William A. Russ Jr., *The Hawaiian Republic, 1894–98,* 1961; and William A. Williams, *The Tragedy of American Diplomacy,* 1959.

Biographies of major figures of the era include P. E. Coletta, *William Jennings Bryan: Political Evangelist, 1860–1908,* 1964; Louis W. Koenig, *Bryan: A Political Biography of William Jennings Bryan,* 1971; Margaret Leech, *In the Days of McKinley,* 1959; H. Wayne Morgan, *William McKinley and His America,* 1963; and Edmund Morris, *The Rise of Theodore Roosevelt,* 1979.

 ## AMERICAN JOURNEY ONLINE AND INFOTRAC COLLEGE EDITION

Visit the source collections at http://ajaccess.wadsworth.com and http://infotrac.thomsonlearning.com, and use the Search function with the following key terms to explore documents, images, audio and video clips, articles, and commentary related to the material in this chapter:

Henry Cabot Lodge   Theodore Roosevelt
Panama Canal   William Jennings Bryan
Social Darwinism   William McKinley
Spanish-American War   William Randolph Hearst

Additional resources, exercises, and Internet links related to this chapter are available on *The American Past* Web site: http://history.wadsworth.com/americanpast7e.

HISTORY ONLINE

1896: The Grand Alignment
www.jefferson.village.virginia.edu/seminar/unit8/home.htm
A very good portrait of the most important election of the generation.

Racial Stereotypes
www.ferris.edu/jimcrow/menu.htm
A superb collection of images, plus good essays, about the era when America's colored line hardened.

The Spanish-American War
http://memory.loc.gov/ammem/sawhtml/sawhome.html
Films of the war from the infancy of motion pictures.

The Last Days of a President
http://memory.loc.gov/ammem/papr/mckhome.html
McKinley at the Pan-American Exposition, where he was assassinated; includes a motion picture.

34

TEDDY ROOSEVELT AND THE GOOD OLD DAYS

American Society in Transition 1890–1917

Reproduced from the Collections of the Library of Congress

He played all his cards—if not more.

> Oliver Wendell Holmes Jr.

The universe seemed to be spinning round, and Theodore was the spinner.

> Rudyard Kipling

And never did a President before so reflect the quality of his time.

> H. G. Wells

TO AN AFRICAN American, to an Indian of the plains or a Hispanic of the Southwest, to workingmen in marginal jobs, and to most of the 12 million immigrants who arrived between 1890 and 1910, the decades that spanned the turn of the century were less than rosy. During most of the 1890s, the country languished in an economic depression. Most Mexican Americans lived no better than Mexicans south of the border. It was the decade of Wounded Knee, the Pullman strike, and bloody labor battles in the mountain states. The 1890s saw lynching, particularly of African Americans in the South, become epidemic.

Life expectancy at birth for native-born white Americans was about 45 years; it was lower for blacks and immigrants, and much lower for Indians. Infant mortality in New York City was worse than it had been since the seventeenth century. Nationwide, people were 6 times more likely to die of influenza than they are today, 60 times more likely to die of syphilis, and more than 80 times more likely to die of tuberculosis. Diseases that are minor health problems in the twentieth-first century—typhoid, scarlet fever, strep throat, diphtheria, whooping cough, and measles—were common killers in the 1890s and 1900s.

SYMBOL OF AN AGE

But these were not the people who were shaping America. Those who were, a large and newly conspicuous middle class and well-paid working people, later looked back on the final decade of the century as the "Gay Nineties," a time of nickelodeon music and Coney Island, of a night of vaudeville and a week at the seaside, of family-friendly beer gardens and ice cream parlors, of the bicycle craze and winsome Gibson girls.

The first years of the twentieth century have lived on in the popular consciousness as the original "good old days." The long decade preceding World War I is the era to which popular novelists and filmmakers repair when they want to portray an America that is recognizable to us but a better place. Life was less complex. The summer sun was warmer, the hot dogs tastier, the baseball more exciting, the newfangled automobiles downright adventurous, the boys more gallant, the girls prettier, and the songs lilting and cheerful.

A Recognizable Culture

The turn of the century has shed so alluring a glow over time because middle-class values and aspirations have dominated American popular culture ever since. In the 1890s and early 1900s, the middle class as we define it—urban or suburban, well-educated, and financially comfortable, made up of professionals, white-collar employees, and well-paid skilled workers—came into its own. The troubles of poor farmers, factory workers, blacks, Indians, Mexicans, and recent immigrants were real, but they were not at the center of the culture. When many of the children born into turn-of-the-century working-class families climbed the social ladder in the twentieth century, they too looked back on the era with nostalgia.

The new middle class was numerous enough to create and sustain a distinctive lifestyle, to support a bustling consumer economy, and to embrace technology devoted to physical comfort, convenience, individual self-improvement, and the enjoyment of leisure time. The middle class quietly shelved the zealous religious piety of parents and grandparents. The people of the "good old days" were by no means oblivious to social evils. Far from it; they were also the citizens of the Progressive Era, a time of rampant reform. But progressivism was itself the manifestation of a confident people. War and revolution were not yet constant companions, brusquely reminding everyone of the darker side of human nature.

Teddy Roosevelt

The buoyant temper of the period was personified in the man who, in September 1901, succeeded William McKinley as president—Theodore Roosevelt. Roosevelt was climbing a

Reproduced from the Collections of the Library of Congress

▲ *Teddy Roosevelt, "the bride at every wedding and the corpse at every funeral." If any other president enjoyed being president as much as Teddy did, none did so as boisterously and obviously.*

mountain in the Adirondacks when he got the news of McKinley's death. He rushed to Buffalo, took the oath of office, and confided to a friend, "It is a dreadful thing to come into the presidency in this way. But it would be a far worse thing to be morbid about it." Roosevelt intended to enjoy the presidency, as his fellow Americans were "making the most of life." No other chief executive before or since has had such a "bully" time living at 1600 Pennsylvania Avenue.

Both critics and friends of the president poked fun at his personal motto: "Speak softly and carry a big stick." They observed Roosevelt wildly waving clubs around often enough but rarely knew him to speak softly. Everything Roosevelt did was accompanied by fanfares. He swaggered and strutted like an exuberant adolescent, hogging center stage and good-naturedly drowning out anyone who dared compete for the spotlight. He insisted on being, as one of his children put it, "the bride at every wedding and the corpse at every funeral." "You must remember," the British ambassador said, "that the president is about six years old."

Roosevelt shattered the image of statue-like dignity that had been successfully conveyed by every president since Rutherford B. Hayes. He stormed about the country far more than any predecessor had, delivering dramatic speeches, happily mixing with crowds of all descriptions, camping out, climbing mountains, and clambering astride horses and atop farm and industrial machines. When a motion picture photographer asked Roosevelt to move for the ingenious new camera, Roosevelt picked up an ax and furiously chopped down a tree.

Pop Tunes

Two musical classics, one now international, were written in 1893. "Happy Birthday to You" began as "Good Morning to You" and was written by Patty Smith Hill, a pioneer of the kindergarten movement who taught at the Teacher's College of Columbia University. Irving Berlin tried to steal it from Hill in 1921, but she sued and won.

The lyrics of "America the Beautiful" were put to the music of a hymn by Katherine Lee Bates, a professor of English at Wellesley College. Congress annually receives petitions demanding that the song, which celebrates American beauty and natural grandeur, replace the militaristic (and unsingable) "Star-Spangled Banner" as the national anthem.

The Strenuous Life

From an old Dutch family, Roosevelt was sickly as a youth, hopelessly nearsighted and asthmatic. As a teenager, however, he took up bodybuilding and revealed his tremendous inner energy. He fought on the Harvard boxing team and rode with cowboys on his North Dakota ranch. As police commissioner of New York City, he accompanied patrolmen on night beats as dangerous as any in the world. When the war with Spain broke out, he volunteered. In dozens of articles and books—for he was a prolific writer—he wrote of the glories of "the strenuous life."

Roosevelt liked to show off his large, handsome, and affectionate family, with himself center stage, the stern but generous patriarch. He sported a modest paunch (a desirable attribute in that sensible era), a close-snipped moustache, and thick pince-nez that dropped from his nose when he was excited, which was often. His teeth were odd, all seemingly incisors of the same size and about twice as many as normal. He displayed them often in a broad grin that he shed only when he took off after enemies whom middle-class Americans also found it easy to dislike: Wall Street bankers, socialists, and impudent Latin Americans.

Unlike the prim and proper William McKinley, Roosevelt had no compunctions about smoking cigars in public. What was the harm in a minor vice that brought a man pleasure? More than any other individual, he taught Americans to believe that their president must be a good fellow and a showman.

America Personified

Roosevelt had critics. But most Americans, especially those of the vibrant new middle class, found him a grand fellow. They called him "Teddy" and named the lovable animal doll they bought for their children, the teddy bear, after him. He was the first president to be routinely identified in newspapers by his initials, *T. R.* Even Elihu Root, a stodgy eastern aristocrat who served as both secretary of war and secretary of state, waxed playful when he congratulated the president on his forty-sixth birthday in 1904. "You have made a very good start in life," Root said, "and your friends have great hopes for you when you grow up."

Kansas journalist William Allen White, the archetype of the middle-class townsman, wrote that "Roosevelt bit me and I went mad." White remained a lifelong devotee of "the Colonel," as did Finley Peter Dunne, the urbane Chicagoan who captured the salty, cynical humor of the big-city Irish in his fictional commentator on current events, Mr. Dooley. Radicals hated Roosevelt (who hated them back with interest), but they were at a loss as to how to counter his vast popularity. Labor leaders and socialists stuck to the issues when they disagreed with him. There was no advantage in attacking Teddy Roosevelt personally.

Although Roosevelt was a staunch believer in Anglo-Saxon superiority, he won the affection of African Americans when he waved off the squeals of southern white supremacists and invited Booker T. Washington to the White House. Women's suffragists, gearing up for the last phase of their long battle for votes, petitioned rather than attacked him. Elizabeth Cady Stanton addressed him from her deathbed in 1901 as "already celebrated for so many deeds and honorable utterances."

Much mischief was done during Theodore Roosevelt's nearly eight years in office. He committed the United States to a role as international policeman that damaged the nation's reputation in many small countries. He was inclined to define his opponents in moral terms, a recurring and unfortunate characteristic of American politics since his time.

THE NEW MIDDLE CLASS

The symbiosis between the boyish president and the worldly middle class is one of the most striking historical facts of the years spanning the turn of the century. Like their president between 1901 and 1909, the worldly middle class of the Gay Nineties and good old days was confident, optimistic, and glad to be alive.

An Educated People

The foundation of middle-class vigor was wealth. America as a whole had grown so rich that despite the disproportionate fortunes of the great multimillionaires, millions of people in the middle could afford to indulge interests and pleasures that had always been the exclusive property of tiny elites. Among these was education beyond "the three Rs"— "readin', 'ritin', and 'rithmetic." During the final third of the nineteenth century, and especially after 1890, the American educational system expanded and changed in character to accommodate the numbers and aspirations of the new class.

There were only about 300 secondary schools in the United States in 1860 (in a population of 31.4 million people). Only about 100 of them were free! Although girls were admitted to most public elementary schools, girls of modest means rarely attended for more than a few grades, just enough to learn the three Rs.

There were actually more colleges and universities— about 560 in 1870—mostly very small and catering to the wealthy and young men who wanted to be ministers. They offered the traditional course in the liberal arts (Latin, philosophy, mathematics, and history) that was designed to polish young gentlemen rather than train people for a career. The handful of "female seminaries" and colleges that admitted women before the Civil War also taught the ancient curriculum, usually laced with evangelical religion.

After about 1880, educational institutions rapidly multiplied, and the courses they offered became far more diverse. By 1900, there were 6,000 free public secondary schools in the United States, and by 1915, there were 12,000, with 1.3 million pupils. Educational expenditures per pupil increased from about $9 a year in 1870 to $48 in 1920. Secondary schools no longer specialized in preparing a few for the university; they now offered courses leading to jobs in industry and business, from engineering and accounting to agriculture and typing.

A New Kind of University

The Morrill Land Grant Act of 1862 and the philanthropy of millionaires expanded Americans' opportunities for higher education. The Morrill Act provided federal land to the states for the purpose of serving the educational needs of "the industrial classes," particularly in "such branches of learning as are related to agriculture and mechanical arts." It not only fostered the founding of technical schools in which middle-class youth might learn a profession but put the liberal arts curriculum within the financial reach of all but the very poor. Many of the great state universities of the West we know today owe their origins to the Morrill Act.

Late-nineteenth-century millionaires competed for esteem as patrons of learning by constructing buildings and by endowing scholarships and professorial chairs at older institutions. Some founded completely new universities. The story was told that railroad king Leland Stanford and his wife traveled to Harvard with the notion of erecting a building in memory of their son, who had died young. As President Charles W. Eliot was explaining how much it had cost to construct each of Harvard's buildings, Mrs. Stanford exclaimed, "Why, Leland, we can build our own university!" And they did: Stanford University in Palo Alto, California, was founded in 1885.

Cornell (1865), Drew (1866), Johns Hopkins (1876), Vanderbilt (1872), and Carnegie Institute of Technology (1905) were universities that bear the names of the moguls who financed them. In Philadelphia, preacher of the gospel of success Russell B. Conwell established Temple University in 1884 explicitly to educate poor boys ambitious to rise in social station. John D. Rockefeller pumped millions into the University of Chicago (1890), making it within a decade one of America's most distinguished centers of learning. George Eastman, who made his money from Kodak cameras, gave to the University of Rochester.

The midwestern and western state universities, beginning with Iowa in 1858, admitted women to at least some programs. In the East, however, separate women's colleges were founded, again with the support of wealthy benefactors. Georgia Female College (Wesleyan) and Mount Holyoke dated from before the Civil War. In the later decades of the century, they were joined by Vassar (1861), Wellesley (1870), Smith (1871), Radcliffe (1879), Bryn

▲ *Commencement day at Mt. Holyoke College, one of the elite "Seven Sisters" women's colleges in the northeastern states. The curriculum was demanding at some, little more than "finishing" for the daughters of the upper classes at others.*

Mawr (1880), and Barnard (1889). Vassar's educational standards rivaled those of the best men's colleges, but it was necessary to maintain a kind of "head start" program in order to remedy deficiencies in the secondary education provided to even well-to-do girls.

Career-Based Education

Although some institutions, most notably Yale, clung tenaciously to the traditional liberal arts curriculum, the majority of American universities quickly adopted the elective system that was pioneered by the College of William and Mary, Washington College (now Washington and Lee) in Virginia, and the University of Michigan. The elective system was most effectively promoted by President Eliot of Harvard. Beginning in 1869, Eliot abandoned the rule that every student follow precisely the same sequence of courses. Instead, he allowed individuals to choose their field of study. "Majors" included traditional subjects but also new disciplines in the social sciences, engineering, and business administration.

From Germany, educators borrowed the concept of the professional postgraduate school. Before the 1870s, young

people who wished to learn a profession attached themselves to an established practitioner. They were very much apprentices, although far from bound servants. A would-be lawyer agreed with an established attorney to do routine work in his office, from sweeping floors to helping with deeds and wills, in return for the privilege of reading law in the office and observing and questioning his teacher. After a few years, the apprentice lawyer hung out his own shingle. Physicians and pharmacists were trained the same way. Civil and mechanical engineers learned their professions on the job in factories. All too often, elementary school teachers received no training. Often, they were unmarried young women with little more schooling than their most advanced pupils. They were miserably paid, about $200 a year in rural

▲ *Tuskegee Institute emphasized practical, vocational courses of study, but President Booker T. Washington also insisted on a liberal arts curriculum so that graduates would be cultivated and well rounded. This is a class in United States history, which, as in white colleges, would have been highly patriotic in tone.*

Reproduced from the Collections of the Library of Congress

states, and were required to board with a local family, their behavior watched by everyone.

Women, Minorities, and the New Education

Women dauntless enough to put up with the ridicule of male classmates could be found in small numbers at every level of education. By the mid-1880s, the word *coeducational* and its breezy abbreviation, *coed,* had become part of the American language. The first female physician in the United States, Elizabeth Blackwell, was accredited in 1849. In 1868, she established a medical school for women in New York City. By that date, the Woman's Medical College of Pennsylvania was already in operation and recognized, however grudgingly, as offering one of the nation's best programs of medical education.

Female lawyers were unusual at a time when women were not considered equal to men in several legal categories. In 1873, the Supreme Court approved the refusal of the University of Illinois law school to admit women, on the grounds that "the paramount mission and destiny of women are to fulfill the noble and benign offices of wife and mother." By the end of the century, several dozen women were practicing law, including the Populist "Mother" Mary Lease. Antoinette Blackwell, sister-in-law of Elizabeth, paved the way for the ordination of women ministers, and by the turn of the century, the more liberal Protestant denominations, such as the Unitarians, had ordained a few women.

Also in small numbers, well-to-do Jews and Catholics began to take advantage of the new educational opportunities. The Sephardic and German Jews were secular people who preferred to send their sons to established institutions rather than to found Jewish colleges. The Catholic Church, by contrast, the largest religious denomination in the United States by 1900 but mainly a church of the lower classes, founded numerous colleges. Church policy was to prepare the sons and daughters of the Catholic middle class for active careers in business and the professions while simultaneously shoring up their loyalty to their faith by means of rigorous courses in church doctrine, history, and observance.

The most famous Catholic colleges dated from before the Civil War. Notre Dame was founded in 1842. Holy Cross (1843) and Boston College (1863) were explicitly created as foils to aristocratic Protestant Harvard, which admitted few Catholics. John Quincy Adams's dream of a "national university" was, curiously, most nearly fulfilled by the Roman Catholic Church with the founding in 1889 of the Catholic University of America in Washington. It is difficult to imagine Adams quite happy about the sponsor.

On a smaller scale, educational opportunities for blacks expanded. The old colleges and universities in New England and many of the sectarian colleges of the Ohio Valley continued to admit a small number of African Americans. W. E. B. DuBois, later a founder of the National Association for the Advancement of Colored People, earned a Ph.D. at Harvard.

Hamilton S. Smith earned a law degree from Boston University in 1879 (the first black to do so), and when he could not make a living as an attorney, attended the Howard University School of Dentistry. Howard was a private university educating the children of the small black middle class.

In the South—as well as the North—philanthropists and state governments founded institutions for blacks only. Beginning with Lincoln University in Pennsylvania (founded as the Ashmun Institute in 1854), idealistic benefactors supported schools such as Howard in Washington (1867) and Fisk in Nashville (1866). After Booker T. Washington's Atlanta Compromise speech of 1895 and the Supreme Court's decision in *Plessy v. Ferguson* (1896) gave the go-ahead to segregation at all levels of education, southern state governments founded "agricultural and mechanical" schools patterned after Alabama's Tuskegee Institute (1881), at which blacks could train for manual occupations.

The accomplishments of these institutions should not be underestimated. Few scientific researchers of the time were more productive than Tuskegee's botanist, George Washington Carver. Nevertheless, the educational level of blacks lagged so far behind that of whites that in 1910, when only 7.7 percent of the American population was illiterate (the figure includes the millions of recent immigrants), one black in three above the age of 10 could neither read nor write.

A LIVELY CULTURE

Americans continued to buy the books of European authors and the works of the older generation of American poets—Emerson, Longfellow, Whitman, and Whittier. Emily Dickinson of Amherst, Massachusetts, a recluse all but unknown until after her death in 1886, was immediately recognized as one of the country's finest writers. But it was first of all an age when novelists flourished, some growing quite rich from the demand for their books.

Twain and James

Samuel Langhorne Clemens, or Mark Twain, was quintessentially and comprehensively American. A Missourian, he deserted a ramshackle Confederate militia before it could be described as organized, went west to Nevada, and eventually settled in Hartford, Connecticut, when he was rich enough to choose his style of life. He brilliantly captured both the hardships and ribald humor of western life in *Roughing It* (1872); he earned an international reputation with *The Adventures of Tom Sawyer* (1876) and *The Adventures of Huckleberry Finn* (1885). Readers sometimes missed the profound and subtle social criticism in Twain's work (as an old man, he grew melancholy and cynical), but they read him with pleasure for his wit and mastery of the American language.

Twain's favorite settings and themes were western. The other great novelist of the period, Henry James, settled in England because he found American culture stultifying. James set most of his novels in the Old World and peopled them with well-to-do Americans in Europe. Like Twain, his goal was to come to grips with the meaning of being American. In *The Americans* (1877), *The Europeans* (1878), and *Daisy Miller* (1879), James explored the relationship of enthusiastic and sometimes pretentious American characters with sophisticated, often jaded and decadent Europeans.

Realism and Naturalism

An able novelist in his own right, William Dean Howells presided over the American literary scene as editor of the *Atlantic Monthly.* Like *Harper's, Forum,* and the *Arena,* the *Atlantic* published a mix of poetry, stories, and elegant essays that sometimes dealt with contemporary issues but usually at a fastidious distance.

Howells was a realist. He had no patience with the high-flown, preposterous motives and beliefs that sentimental writers gave their characters. In *The Rise of Silas Lapham* (1885), a novel about a successful industrialist, when one sister loses a suitor to another, she does not react selflessly, nor does the sister who gets her man think seriously of sacrificing herself—dependable themes in the popular sentimental novels by what Nathaniel Hawthorne called "a damned mob of scribbling women." Nevertheless, neither Howells nor the *Atlantic* would have considered dealing explicitly, let alone graphically, with sexual matters or the degradation that poverty and squalor created. Because the proper upper and middle classes themselves considered such discussions unacceptable in mixed company, the writings of realists like Howells have sometimes been lumped with romanticism as part of the genteel tradition.

Naturalistic writers defied some of the taboos, a few enjoying commercial success. In *Maggie: A Girl of the Streets* (1893), Stephen Crane depicted the poor not as noble and selfless but as miserable and helpless. In *The Red Badge of Courage* (1895), the Civil War is described as something other than glory, bugles, bravery, and flying colors. (If anything, with the members of the Grand Army of the Republic still numerous and influential, it was more daring a venture than a book about a prostitute.) In *McTeague* (1899) and *The Octopus* (1901), Frank Norris dealt with people driven almost mechanically by animalistic motives.

The most popular of the naturalists was Jack London. His *Call of the Wild* (1903) is comparable to *Huckleberry Finn* in that it is simultaneously a grand story of adventure (about a dog) and, at a deeper level, a profound commentary on the human condition. Theodore Dreiser broke with a moralistic literary convention by allowing characters such as the protagonist in *Sister Carrie* (1900) to enjoy rich lives despite sinful pasts. Dreiser's success was doubly remarkable because, from a midwestern German-speaking household, his treatment of the English language was adversarial at best, and sometimes sadistic. But his mind was profound, and he delved into corners of American society where others feared to tread.

A Hunger for Words

The genteel tradition was also challenged by a new type of magazine that made its appearance in the 1880s and 1890s.

Nellie Bly

Elizabeth Cochrane, forced to go to work at menial jobs when her father died, got into newspaper work when she criticized an editor in Pittsburgh who said that women who did not marry were useless. Cochrane said that girls should have employment opportunities because they were "just as smart" as boys and "a great deal quicker to learn." Using the pen name Nellie Bly (from a Stephen Foster song), she wrote exposés of working and living conditions in Pittsburgh, then moved to New York to write for Joseph Pulitzer's booming *World.* She was an immediate sensation when she had herself committed to an asylum for insane women and penned a blistering account of conditions there.

Then Nellie had an idea for what may have been the first "manufactured news story." As a girl, she had read Jules Verne's *Around the World in Eighty Days,* in which a British dandy circled the globe with unbelievable speed. Several adventurers had tried to beat the fictional record and failed. Nellie locked herself up with train and steamship timetables and told the *World* that she could make the trip in 75 days. The editors liked the idea but said only a man could do it. Nellie replied, "Very well. Start the man and I'll start the same day for some other newspaper and beat him."

She left Jersey City on November 14, 1889, and, after a trip that sometimes seemed leisurely as she waited for steamships to depart, returned to her point of departure via a special transcontinental train on January 25, 1890. Her trip took 72 days.

Catering to the not so intellectual middle classes, these periodicals illustrate the interaction of industrial technology, the larger reading public, and the modern advertising that was first exploited in 1883 by Cyrus H. K. Curtis and his *Ladies' Home Journal.*

Improved methods of manufacturing paper, printing, and photoengraving, as well as cheap mailing privileges established by Congress in 1879, inspired Curtis to found a magazine for women who were hungry for a world beyond the kitchen and parlor. The *Ladies' Home Journal* sold for only 10 cents (compared with the 35-cent *Atlantic* and *Harper's*) and emphasized women's interests. It was not a feminist publication. On the contrary, editor Edward Bok preached a domesticity that reassured homemakers that their conventional prejudices were proper. He honored the middle class as a steadying influence between "unrest among the lower classes and rottenness among the upper classes."

More daring were the new general-interest magazines of the 1890s: *McClure's, Munsey's,* and *Cosmopolitan.* They too cost a dime, putting them within reach of a mass readership. (The *Saturday Evening Post,* which Curtis bought in 1897, sold for only a nickel.) Without stooping to sensationalism, they presented readers with a livelier writing style than the older journals and were lavish with photographs and illustrations.

McClure's and *Munsey's* pioneered the novel economics of selling their publications for less than it cost to print and mail them. They made their profit from building up subscription lists so long they dazzled manufacturers of consumer goods wanting to reach people with their advertising. Subscriptions to *McClure's* increased from 8,000 in 1893 to 250,000 in 1895. (There was $60,000 worth of advertising per issue.) *Munsey's* grew from 40,000 to 500,000 during the same two years. By 1900, the combined circulation of the four largest magazines totaled 2.5 million per month, more than all American magazines combined only 20 years earlier.

Libraries and Lyceums

The cultural hunger of the middle class was also expressed in the construction of free public libraries. Again, men suddenly grown rich gave millions to build them. Enoch Pratt donated $1 million to Baltimore for its municipal library. Wealthy lawyer and presidential candidate Samuel J. Tilden gave New York City $2 million, and William Newberry founded one of the nation's greatest collections of books and valuable manuscripts in Chicago with a munificent bequest of $4 million. Beginning in 1881, the self-taught Andrew Carnegie made libraries his principal philanthropy. Before his death in 1919, Carnegie helped found 2,800 free public libraries.

The old lyceum idea of sending lecturers on tour to speak to people who lived far from big cities was revived in 1868 by James Redpath. Offering large fees, Redpath persuaded the most distinguished statesmen, ministers, and professors of the day to deliver highly moral and usually informative addresses in auditoriums and specially erected tents in hundreds of small cities and towns.

Chautauqua

The lyceum movement was a throwback to the pre–Civil War period, when only the very wealthy traveled away from home and the middle class still held fast to Calvinistic assumptions that constant work was the human fate and idleness, like travel for pleasure, was sinful. The lyceum scheduled programs in the evening, when the day's toil was done.

The phenomenon that was born in 1874 at Lake Chautauqua in New York was more characteristic of the new age. The original "Chautauquas" were eight-week summer training programs for Sunday school teachers. During the 1890s, however, cheap excursion fares on the trains made it feasible for people who might have little interest in church work to make the trip for the sake of the cool mountain air and relaxation. To accommodate them, the Chautauqua organizers broadened their program to include lectures on secular subjects.

By the turn of the century, a middle-class family spending a few weeks at Lake Chautauqua could expect to hear talks by individuals as prominent as William Jennings Bryan and to watch "magic-lantern" (slide) shows about the Holy Land, Persia, or China presented by professional world travelers. Distinguished professors expounded on their theories about human character, happy marriage, or child rearing. German oompah bands, Hawaiian dancers, trained dogs, Italian acrobats, and Indian fire-eaters provided lighter entertainment.

AMERICANS AT PLAY

Promoters founded more than 200 Chautauqua-type resorts, some in the mountains, some at the seaside. Enough people could afford a vacation from work that a tourist industry was soon flourishing. Nevertheless, old biases died hard. Resort promoters found it advisable to provide at least the appearance of usefulness for the vacations they offered. If the middle class trekked to Lake Chautauqua or Lake George in New York and to Long Beach, Atlantic City, or Cape May in New Jersey primarily for rest and relaxation, they could tell others and try to persuade themselves that the cultural and educational aspects of their holiday meant they were not just wasting time.

Health Resorts

A similar conjunction of relaxation and constructive use of time underlay the resorts that were devoted to good health. Owners of mineral springs claimed miraculous powers for their waters. Baths in naturally heated mineral waters or in hot mud were prescribed as cures for dozens of afflictions. Hydropathy, a nineteenth-century medical fad, taught that virtually constant bathing and drinking of water improved health. For decades, the wealthy made prosperous summer resorts of places like Saratoga Springs in New York and White Sulphur Springs in West Virginia, where "taking the cure" could be done in pleasant surroundings among congenial people. Now thousands of middle-class people followed them, again rationalizing their desire for relaxation by extolling the health benefits of their holiday.

Leisure and the Working Class

Working people could not afford to take a week in the mountains or at the seashore. However, leisure became a part of their lives too. Great urban greens, beginning with New

Hot Dog

The hot dog is second only to the hamburger as an emblem of American cuisine, but its origins are hotly disputed. Not the origins of the mild sausage itself: It was being made commercially in Frankfurt, Germany, and Vienna, Austria, in the early nineteenth century. (Thus the names "frankfurter" and "wiener"–Vienna in German is *Wien*.) The disputed point is who first put one of the things in a soft roll and provided the classic condiments of yellow mustard, chopped onion, and sweet pickle relish.

Some claim Coney Island; hot dogs were once called "coneys" too. Others credit Anton Feuchtwanger, who sold the sausages so quickly at the St. Louis World's Fair in 1904 that he had to add the roll so that his customers did not burn their hands. Yet others say the roll was first added at a New York Giants baseball game in April 1900, where the wieners were called "dachshund sausages." A popular cartoonist of the time who liked his baseball, Tad Dorgan, provided the more durable name "hot dog."

Coney Island: Democratic Amusement

The coneys—rabbits—were just about wiped out when, in the mid–nineteenth century, Coney Island's broad beaches and ocean breezes began to attract vacationers. And it was not an island. It was separated from the city of Brooklyn by a smallish creek. George Cornelius Tilyou was born there in 1862 and grew up, as the local slang had it, "with sand in his shoes." When he was three, his father leased a lot on the beach for $35 a year and opened a hotel catering to the middling sort, especially (since Tilyou Sr. was a Democrat) Democratic political bosses from Manhattan and Brooklyn.

As a teenager, George was looking for ways to pocket the vacationers' pocket change. In 1876, with the Centennial Exposition in Philadelphia attracting people from all over the nation, he filled old medicine bottles with seawater, and cigar boxes with Coney beach sand, selling them for 25 cents each. He made enough from these dubious but classic souvenirs to be able to dabble in beachfront real estate. The township did not sell land on the beach but, instead, leased it to people to whom the political machine was friendly. These people then sublet choice business locations to others, sometimes at extraordinary profits. Because of his contacts, Tilyou was able to open a theater that featured vaudeville acts.

Then he made what appeared to be a fatal mistake. He broke with the local political boss, John Y. McKane, who protected brothels and illegal gambling dens. Tilyou organized a party devoted to the idea that Coney Island's future lay in becoming a wholesome family resort. When McKane won the battle, Tilyou found himself shut out of the profitable leasing deals.

In 1893, however, McKane was jailed for stuffing ballot boxes, and Tilyou was back in business. Just in time: In the same year, he went to the Chicago World's Fair and, like everyone, was awed by its centerpiece, the Ferris wheel. It was 250 feet in diameter. Suspended on the gigantic circle were 36 "cars," each of which held 60 people. When the fair closed, 1.5 million people had taken a whirl on it.

Tilyou contracted with George Ferris to build a wheel half its size at Coney Island; Tilyou advertised the ride as "the world's largest Ferris wheel." (Only within the last decade has a Ferris wheel bigger than Chicago's been built.) He began to make money before it was done, selling concessions around the wheel to vendors. Then Tilyou constructed other "amusements,"

Museum of the City of New York

▲ *Coney Island about 1900, still bucolic beyond the competing amusement parks. (Note there are no automobiles.) The photograph was taken early in the morning before the trolley lines delivered thousands of New Yorkers and Brooklynites ready to spend a few dollars each.*

at first simple gravity devices, such as giant sliding boards and seesaws, but soon enough, electrically powered forerunners of devices still active on boardwalks and at fairs today.

From another Coney Island entrepreneur, Paul Boyton, Tilyou copied the idea of fencing in a large "amusement park" and charging a single admission fee. Coney's clientele, working-class people, did not have the means for extravagant spending; better to commit their entire day to Steeplechase Park, where they would have to buy their food and other extras rather than having them wander over to Tilyou's competitors, Luna Park and Dreamland.

Steeplechase Park opened in 1897. A favorite ride was a gravity-driven "horse race" imported from England. People mounted wooden horses—a beau and his belle could ride together, a big attraction—that rolled on tracks over a series of "hills" and entered the central pavilion. Upon exiting, the customers were mildly abused by a clown and costumed dwarf. The biggest hit at Steeplechase was the jet of compressed air, which shot out of the floor, blowing young ladies' skirts into the air amid great shrieks and guffaws.

Innocent sexual horseplay was the idea in many of the mechanical amusements Tilyou constructed. Air jets were everywhere. Other amusements were designed to throw young ladies in such a position that their ankles were exposed or they landed in the laps of their escorts or, perhaps, someone whom they were interested in meeting. Tilyou's formula worked. For a time after the turn of the century, Steeplechase Park lost ground to newer amusement parks—Luna Park, which featured "a trip to the moon," and Dreamland, where patrons could stroll through the streets of an Egyptian city and among Philippine headhunters or see the eruption of Mount Pelée, the Johnstown flood, the Galveston tidal wave, or other natural disasters.

But Tilyou was irrepressible. When Steeplechase Park burned to the ground in 1907—every wooden Coney Island attraction burned at one time or another—he hung up a sign:

I have troubles today that I didn't have yesterday.
I had troubles yesterday that I have not today.
On this site will be erected shortly a better, bigger, greater Steeplechase Park.

Admission to the Burning Ruins—10 cents.

York's magnificent Central Park, provided free relief on weekends for the masses of the city's slums. Working people in large cities were also able to enjoy themselves at commercial amusement parks that sprang up as a means by which trolley car companies could exploit their investments to the fullest.

That is, traction companies made a profit only from those parts of their lines that traversed the crowded parts of cities, and then only on weekdays. However, the high cost of city-center real estate required them to build their sprawling car barns (storage and repair facilities) outside the city. If they were not required by their franchise to run trolleys on Saturday and Sunday, they still wanted to make use of their equipment on weekends.

How to encourage people to ride the trolleys beyond the city centers? The trolley companies encouraged the construction of amusement parks at the end of the line or, in some cases, built playlands themselves. The most famous was New York's Coney Island, located on the ocean in Brooklyn. The fare from downtown Manhattan was five cents, children riding free. Once there, for a dollar or two, a large family could ride the mechanical amusements such as George C. Tilyou's Bounding Billows, Barrel of Love, and the Human Roulette Wheel. They could imitate Buffalo Bill at shooting galleries, visit sideshows and exotic Somali villages, or simply loll on the beach with a picnic lunch or a sausage muffled in two halves of a roll.

These homey pleasures were as exciting to working people as a trip to Saratoga was to the middle class. Coney Island, Philadelphia's Willow Grove, Boston's Paragon Park, and Chicago's Cheltenham Beach represented an organized industry—manufacturing, packaging, and merchandising leisure time.

Working-class leisure was more frankly devoted to simple fun than were the middle-class Chautauquas. Nevertheless, even Coney Island's promoters said that their resort was educational and good for health. Sordid sideshows were touted with moralistic spiels. Knocking over weighted bottles for a prize of a Kewpie doll was defined as honing a valuable skill. Even suggestive dancing by "hoochie-koochie girls" like Fatima, the sensation of the Chicago World's Fair of 1893, was described as glimpses into the culture of the Turkish Empire. A writer in prim *Harper's Weekly* approved of the trolley parks because they were "great breathing-places for millions of people in the city who get little fresh air at home."

The First Fitness Craze

Good health was the rationale for a series of sporting manias that swept the United States at the turn of the century. To some extent, the concern for bodily health was introduced by German immigrants, whose Turnvereins (clubs devoted to calisthenics) were old-country carryovers like democratic socialism and beer gardens. However, it was obvious by the mid–nineteenth century that the urban population walked less and got less exercise generally than had its

Cocaine

The Western world learned of the invigorating effects of chewing the coca leaf when the Spanish conquered the Inca empire in the sixteenth century. Over the next three centuries, the odd European (and American) experimented with the drug; but only after 1860, when the plant was crystallized into "cocaine," a hundred times more powerful than the leaves, did its use spread. Parke-Davis, a drug manufacturer, called it "the most important therapeutic discovery of the age, the benefit of which to humanity will be incalculable." The American Hay Fever Association praised it. Nor were the drug's social "benefits" neglected. In 1878, a magazine touted it as "the cure for young people afflicted with timidity in society." Cocaine was added to patent medicines and soft drinks.

By the end of the century, cocaine's addictive qualities were well documented. Reformers crusaded against it, and use by the middle class sharply declined. Cocaine came to be associated with blacks, as a 1903 release by the American Pharmacological Association indicates: "The state of Indiana reports that a good many of its Negroes and a few white women are addicted to cocaine." In 1914, the police chief of Atlanta blamed 70 percent of the city's crime on cocaine. What had come close to being fashionable became the vice of a despised underclass within a generation.

farmer forebears. In the first issue of the *Atlantic Monthly* in 1858, Thomas Wentworth Higginson asked, "Who in this community really takes exercise? Even the mechanic confines himself to one set of muscles; the blacksmith acquires strength in his right arm, and the dancing teacher in his left leg. But the professional or businessman, what muscles has he at all?" Only a society with plenty of spare time could take Higginson's question to heart.

Croquet, archery, and tennis, all imported from England, enjoyed a vogue in the 1870s. Roller-skating, because cheaper, was more popular. Great rinks like San Francisco's Olympian Club, with 5,000 pairs of skates to rent and a 69,000-square-foot floor, charged fees that were within reach of all but the poorest people. But no sporting fad was as widespread as bicycling.

Bicycles

Briefly during the 1860s, French "dandy horses" were seen on American city streets. These crude wooden vehicles were powered by pushing along the ground. About 1876, the "bone crusher," with its 6-foot-high front wheel, made its appearance. By 1881, when the League of American Wheelmen was founded, more than 20,000 intrepid young Americans were devoting their idle hours to pedaling furiously around parks and city streets.

Some praised bicycling as a health-giving outdoor exercise, but moralists condemned the sport for promoting casual relations between young people of the opposite sex. Although

▲ *The "bone crusher" was difficult to mount and balance, and very hard to pedal; with no sprockets and chain, there was only one "high gear." A spill from 6 feet all too often meant a serious injury. And yet, the "new woman" of the 1890s took to the bone crushers as avidly as men did. During the decade, the "safety bicycle," essentially the same as bikes today, was introduced and soon displaced the big wheelers.*

young men and ladies might leave home for a Sunday ride in proper groups of their own sex, they found it easy to strike up acquaintanceships in parks far from the eyes of parents and chaperone aunts. More than one worried preacher thought that the bicycle was a first step toward moral chaos.

Indeed, it was on the pneumatic tires of the bicycle that many emancipated young women of the 1890s escaped into a refreshing new freedom. The safety bicycle, which had much the same design as bicycles today, took the risk of broken bones out of the sport. On fair Sundays, the streets were full of them, and a good number carried young women in candy-striped blouses with billowing sleeves, sporty broad-brimmed hats, and full free-flowing skirts.

The Gibson Girl

The new-look woman of the 1890s took the name of "Gibson girl" after the magazine illustrator Charles Dana Gibson, who created the style. Gibson's vision of ideal American womanhood charmed the nation from Newport high society to working-class suburbs. The Gibson girl was not a feminist or, at least, not a suffragette. She took no interest in political

issues. Essentially, she remained an object of adoration—fine featured, trim, coy, flirtatious, even seductive—but an object of adoration who knew what she was about.

The Gibson girl was novel. She was no shrinking violet. She did not faint after the exertion of climbing a staircase. She played croquet, golf, and tennis. She rode a bicycle without chaperones. She was quite able to take care of herself. One of Gibson's favorite themes was the helplessness of young men in the hands of his self-assured young ladies.

Theodore Roosevelt's daughter, Alice, who became a national sweetheart when the popular waltz "Alice Blue Gown" was named for her, might have been sculpted by Gibson, and middle-class women adopted her style. Photographs of mill girls leaving textile factories in Massachusetts and of stenographers in offices in New York reveal an air of Gibson girl self-assurance. The new independence of women was also indicated by the fact that they were marrying later. In 1890, the average age for a woman on her wedding day was 22, two or three years older than it had been in 1860.

The Changing Office

The telephone created jobs for women and, with the jobs, a taste of independence. So did the typewriter. Because handwriting was often illegible and potentially costly in business, dozens of inventors had taken a stab at creating a "writing machine." The first practical typewriter was perfected in 1867 by Christopher Latham Sholes and first marketed in 1874 by the Remington Company, a firearms manufacturer in search of a product with which to diversify its interests.

Before the use of the typewriter became standard in business, almost all secretaries were men. They not only wrote letters for their employers, but they ran various errands and sometimes represented the boss. The typewriter made it possible for businessmen to split the secretarial profession into assistant and typist. Men continued to hold the more responsible and better-paid job, rising to a status that would be described as junior executive today. The mechanical task of transcribing letters and business records into type went to women.

QWERTY

Sholes's typewriter printed only capital letters; the "Shift" key came later. The arrangement of the letters on his keyboard, however, is the same as the arrangement on your computer. It is called "QWERTY" after the first six letters at the upper left. This layout was dictated by the fact that the typewriters were entirely mechanical: The typist pushed a key (hard), and a striker stamped the letter on the paper. Sholes spread out the most common letters on the keyboard so that a fast typist was not constantly jamming the machine. Critics of QWERTY have proved that there are much better and faster layouts of the alphabet now that the problem that produced QWERTY no longer exists. But no manufacturer has dared to put a new arrangement on the market.

▲ *The typewriter, like the telephone, created a new occupation that was almost exclusively female in personnel. It was clean "white-collar" work, appropriate to a respectable young lady and also poorly paid.*

Like telephone operators, typists did not require a level of education that was available only to determined women willing to raise eyebrows. It was not heavy labor, an important consideration in an age that defined respectable young women as "delicate." And the job did not usually involve much responsibility, which nineteenth-century men were disinclined to allot to women. By 1890, 15 percent of clerical workers were female; by 1900, almost 25 percent.

The Big Game

Football was a college boy's game at the turn of the twentieth century but was taken quite seriously both by players (18 were killed in 1905) and by spectators. Thanksgiving Day, still largely a religious observance up to the time of the Civil War, became the day of the big game in a more secular, more fun-seeking United States. Harvard and Yale, the nation's two most venerable institutions of higher learning, mauled one another in New York City on Thanksgiving until Harvard's president tired of the players' off-field behavior and opted out of the rivalry. Yale had to settle for Princeton or, later, Rutgers for a Turkey Day match. In the twentieth century, other great Thanksgiving rivalries developed: Penn-Cornell, Case–Western Reserve, Kansas-Missouri, Tulane-LSU, and Texas–Texas A&M.

SPORTS

The turn of the century was a golden age of organized sport. Although football (with somewhat different rules from today) was a game played exclusively by university students, people of all social classes avidly followed the fortunes of the nearest Ivy League team. Basketball, invented in Springfield, Massachusetts, in 1891 by Dr. James Naismith, who was looking for a sport that his students could play during the rigorous New England winter, was in its infancy. The spectator sports that obsessed Americans were baseball and boxing. Both evolved from traditional folk recreations, but by the end of the nineteenth century, both were well-organized as money-making enterprises.

The National Pastime

Baseball developed out of two ancient children's games, rounders and town ball, which were brought to the United States by English immigrants. According to Albert G. Spalding, a professional pitcher for baseball clubs in Boston and Chicago, the rules of the sport were first drafted by Abner Doubleday of Cooperstown, New York, in 1839. This was poppycock. There is no evidence Doubleday invested a minute thinking about the game. Spalding circulated the tale

Boston Public Library

▲ *Michael "King" Kelly, who played for a number of professional teams between 1878 and 1893, was one of the heroes of baseball's first era. In this painting,* Slide, Kelly, Slide, *he has successfully stolen second base. Kelly batted .307 over 14 seasons and hit 69 home runs, more impressive than it sounds. Most games were played with the same ball; after a few innings, it was soft—"dead."*

to promote the sporting goods manufacturing company that made him a millionaire. In reality, baseball "just growed." The first recognizable baseball game to be recorded was played in New York City in 1847, but there was little agreement on even some basic rules until after the Civil War.

Towns organized "pickup" teams to play neighboring towns on special occasions like Independence Day. However, the professional sport emerged from upper-class baseball clubs, such as the New York Knickerbockers. Soon concerned more with defeating rivals than with enjoying an afternoon of exercise and fellowship, the clubs began to hire (at first surreptitiously) long-hitting and fast-pitching working-class "ringers" to wear their colors. In 1869, the first openly professional team, the Cincinnati Red Stockings, went on tour and defeated all comers.

Teams were focal points of civic pride. Important games got more attention in the newspapers than did foreign wars. After Brooklyn became a borough of New York City in 1898, its baseball team, the Trolley Dodgers, became the former city's sole symbol of an independent identity.

At first, professional baseball was open to African Americans. The catcher on an "all-star" team that toured Europe was black. In 1894, however, when lynch law was at its peak in the South, white players led by the foremost hitter of the era, Adrian "Cap" Anson (himself a northerner) demanded that, at the top, professional baseball be a game for whites only. When, after the turn of the century, John McGraw, manager of the New York Giants, recruited several African Americans, claiming they were Indians, he was forced to back down and not play them.

Boxing and Society

Watching a fight between two strong men may be humanity's oldest diversion. In 1867, as boxing was becoming a "manly art" practiced by the upper class, an English sportsman, the marquis of Queensberry, devised a code of rules

that was adopted in the United States. The Queensberry rules hardly made for a gentle sport. One of them read that "all attempts to inflict injury by gouging or tearing the flesh with the fingers or nails and biting shall be deemed foul."

As with baseball, the opportunities to make money from paid admissions encouraged promoters to search out popular heroes. The first to win a national reputation was a burly Boston Irishman named John L. Sullivan, who started out by traveling the country and offering $50, and later $1,000, to anyone who could last four rounds with him. Between 1882 and 1892, the "Boston Strong Boy" bloodied one challenger after another, personally collecting as much as $20,000 a fight and making much more for the entrepreneurs who organized his bouts.

The crowds that watched great championship bouts and most baseball games included comparatively few working people. However, they followed their heroes in the new sports pages of the newspapers, which devoted column after column to important fights. Because Sullivan and his successor as heavyweight champion, Gentleman Jim Corbett, were Irish, they became objects of ethnic pride. So entangled in the culture did the sport become that when a black boxer rose to the top, he caused a stir that reached into the halls of Congress.

Jack Johnson

John Arthur "Jack" Johnson, an African American from Galveston, Texas, had a national reputation by 1902, but three consecutive heavyweight champions, Jim Jeffries, Robert Fitzsimmons, and Tommy Burns, refused to fight him. Finally, in 1908, Burns gave in (in Australia) and was badly defeated. Johnson battered every challenger, rankling many whites. Johnson aggravated the hatred for him by gleefully insulting every "great white hope" he fought. Tragically indiscreet, he flaunted his white mistresses at a time when the color line was being drawn across practically every American institution.

Southern states, which had been the most hospitable to professional prize fights, forbade Johnson to box within victory over former champion Jim Jeffries in Reno in 1910. Finally, in 1912, racists defeated him not in the ring but through an indictment under the Mann Act, which forbade transporting women across state lines "for immoral purposes." (Johnson had taken his common-law wife to another state for a holiday.)

Johnson fled to Europe but was homesick. In 1915, he fought white boxer Jess Willard in Havana and lost. It was widely believed, especially by African Americans, that Johnson threw the match as part of a deal with the Justice Department by which he could reenter the United States and receive a light sentence. A photograph of the knockout in Havana shows Johnson on his back, looking unhurt, even relaxed, shielding his eyes from the Caribbean sun. In fact, Johnson did not return to the United States for five years and was imprisoned for eight months.

their borders. Politicians raved at every Johnson victory and gaudy public appearance. Congress actually passed a law that prohibited the interstate shipment of a film of Johnson's

for FURTHER READING

Overviews of the era are Vincent P. DeSantis, *The Shaping of Modern America, 1877–1916,* 1973; Ray Ginger, *The Age of Excess,* 1965; William L. O'Neill, *The Progressive Years: America Comes of Age,* 1975; and Robert H. Wiebe, *The Search for Order, 1880–1920,* 1967. On general social and cultural history, see Frederick Lewis Allen, *The Big Change,* 1952; Van Wyck Brooks, *The Confident Years, 1885–1915,* 1952; and the classic Mark Sullivan, *Our Times,* 1926–1935.

Studies of special topics include G. W. Chessman, *Governor Theodore Roosevelt,* 1965; Carl M. Degler, *At Odds: Women in the Family in America from the Revolution to the Present,* 1980; Ann Douglas, *The Feminization of American Culture,* 1977; Foster R. Dulles, *America Learns to Play,* 1940; Ray Ginger, *Altgeld's America: The Lincoln Ideal and Changing Realities,* 1958; Otis L. Gra-

ham Jr., *The Great Campaigns: Reform and War in America, 1900–1928,* 1971; Jack D. Kirby, *Darkness at the Dawning: Race and Reform in the Progressive South,* 1972; J. R. Krout, *Annals of American Sport,* 1924; Margaret Leech, *In the Days of McKinley,* 1959; Henry F. May, *The End of American Innocence,* 1959; H. Wayne Morgan, *William McKinley and His America,* 1963; George E. Mowry, *The Era of Theodore Roosevelt,* 1958; and Steven A. Reiss, *Touching Base: Professional Baseball and American Culture in the Progressive Era,* 1980.

Three fine books about "Teddy" are John M. Blum, *The Republican Roosevelt,* 1954; W. H. Harbaugh, *Power and Responsibility: The Life and Times of Theodore Roosevelt,* 1961; and, best of all, Henry F. Pringle, *Theodore Roosevelt,* 1931.

American Journey ONLINE AND INFOTRAC COLLEGE EDITION

Visit the source collections at http://ajaccess.wadsworth.com and http://infotrac.thomsonlearning.com, and use the Search function with the following key terms to explore documents, images, audio and video clips, articles, and commentary related to the material in this chapter:

Booker T. Washington	NAACP
Carrie Chapman Catt	*Plessy v. Ferguson*
Elizabeth Cady Stanton	Theodore Roosevelt
Emily Dickinson	W. E. B. DuBois
Mark Twain	Woman Suffrage
Morrill Land Grant	

Additional resources, exercises, and Internet links related to this chapter are available on *The American Past* Web site: http://history.wadsworth.com/americanpast7e.

HISTORY ONLINE

Agricultural Laborers in California
http://findaid.oac.odlib.org/findaid/ark/13030/+f20000/qw
Photographs of Chinese, Japanese, and Mexican farm laborers.

Images of Advertising
http://memory/loc.gov/ammem/award98/nodhtml/eeahome.html
Pictorial history of advertising: 1850–1921.

35

AGE OF REFORM

The Progressives

'Tis not too late to build our young land right,
Cleaner than Holland, courtlier than Japan,
Devout like early Rome with hearths like hers,
Hearths that will recreate the breed called man.

Vachel Lindsay

A man that'd expect to thrain lobsters to fly in a year is
called a loonytic; but a man that thinks men can be
tu-rrned into angels be an illiction is called a rayformer
an' remains at large.

Finley Peter Dunne

IN 1787, THOMAS Jefferson wrote to James Madison, "A little rebellion, now and then, is a good thing, as necessary in the political world as storms in the physical." To another friend he said, "The tree of liberty must be refreshed from time to time with the blood of patriots and tyrants."

Jefferson was saying that political progress depended upon violent uprising. Was he right? The history of the United States seems to say not. During more than two centuries that, worldwide, have been marked by social convulsions and bloody carnage beyond Jefferson's imagination, the United States has been an island of stability. The nation has been shaken by revolution only once, the secession of the southern states in 1861, and that uprising was neither progressive nor successful. Reform has been fitful in the United States, but it has been largely peaceful. One of the most significant and, by its own terms, successful upwellings of the reform spirit was the Progressive Era that spanned the first two decades of the twentieth century.

THE PROGRESSIVES

Few of the reforms of the early 1900s were original to the new century. The progressive movement inherited the spirit of the evangelical reformers, as well as impulses and ideas from the mugwumps, the social gospel, the half-century-old feminist movement, urban social workers, populism, and even the sundry varieties of socialism expounded in the late nineteenth century. However, none of these eruptions rallied the better part of their generation as the progressives did.

Middle America

The progressives were drawn from, and chiefly appealed to, the middle class. They were small businessmen, professionals (such as lawyers, physicians, ministers, teachers, journalists, and social workers), and, notably, women—wives and daughters of businessmen and professionals whose first reform was personal, breaking free of nursery, parlor, and chapel. The industrial and financial elite produced few progressive leaders. Few progressives rose from the masses of laboring people and poor farmers. The movement was middle class in its heart and head.

The progressives were acutely aware that they were in between. Knocking about in the back of the progressive mind was the assumption that what was best about America was the people who were not so rich as to endanger the republic and not so poor as to have no stake in it. Like Thomas Jefferson and his disciples a century earlier, most progressives felt that the people in the middle were threatened by plutocrats from above and by the potentially dangerous mob from below.

Thus, virtually all progressives were committed to bridling the immense power of the great corporations and banks. They intended that the Rockefellers and the Morgans behave in ways that were compatible with the good of society, as the progressives defined it.

Most progressives were concerned with the material and moral welfare of those below them on the social ladder. However, they also feared the masses. In the cities, progressive reformers often voiced concern that the slums were tinderboxes of anger, ready to explode in destructive anarchy. In the Midwest and West, most progressive leaders had been staunch anti-Populists because they saw the farmers' rebellion as an upheaval of the impoverished, uneducated, and unwashed. William Allen White, a leading midwestern progressive, first made his name as the author of a scathing anti-Populist manifesto called "What's the Matter with Kansas?" Years later, a little sheepishly, White explained that he wrote the piece not because an idea occurred to him in his office, but because he had been jostled on a street corner in Emporia by "lazy, greasy fizzles" whose vulgarity offended him.

Many progressives saw clearly the relationship between the power of great wealth and dangerous restiveness among the exploited poor. Early in the century, Woodrow Wilson of New Jersey put the thought in a curious way when he blamed the automobile, then a plaything of the rich, for the spread of socialism. Driving their cars around recklessly, frightening horses, killing chickens, and disturbing ordinary folk, Wilson wrote, the rich were displaying their arrogance on every country road in the nation.

Righteous, Optimistic, and WASP

Louis Brandeis, a lawyer from Louisville, Kentucky, who helped design the Democratic party's progressive program,

was Jewish. Alfred E. Smith and Robert F. Wagner, progressive politicians in New York State, were Irish and German, respectively, and Roman Catholic in religion. W. E. B. DuBois, who helped to found the National Association for the Advancement of Colored People, was an African American. But they were exceptions. Most progressive leaders were "WASPs" (white Anglo-Saxon Protestants) from old stock; they were people whose American roots ran through several generations.

Most were urban people, brought up in cities or towns. Even the progressive politicians who represented farm states, like Robert M. La Follette of Wisconsin and George Norris of Nebraska, had grown up in towns. As boys, they rubbed elbows with farmers, but they had not plodded behind plows or milled about anxiously next to their wagons as railroad agents weighed, graded, and put a price on the year's crop. Indeed, like William Allen White, La Follette was an anti-Populist during the 1890s.

Progressive political leaders inclined to be moralistic to the point of self-righteousness, ever searching for the absolute right and absolute wrong in every political disagreement. California's Hiram Johnson irked even his aides with his clenched-teeth sanctimony. La Follette did not know what a sense of humor was. To "Fighting Bob," as La Follette was called, life was one long crusade for what was right. Theodore Roosevelt described the beginning of an election campaign in biblical terms: "We stand at Armageddon and do battle for the Lord." Woodrow Wilson, stern looking in wing collar and spectacles, eventually destroyed himself because he would not compromise with critics, even when doing so was the only way to save the most important cause of his life.

And yet, although their noses were ever to the wind for a hint of foul odors, the progressives believed that progress was possible because human nature was intrinsically good. "Our shamelessness is superficial," wrote Lincoln Steffens. "Beneath it lies a pride which, being real, may save us yet." They were optimists.

The Answer: Government

Almost all progressives believed that a powerful government, active in taking the initiative and holding it, was the key to improving America. In their faith in the state, they were rather unlike earlier reformers who were more apt to consider government a part of the problem. Jane Addams, whose main work was helping the urban poor and who had herself been suspicious of government, said that private institutions like her Hull House were "today inadequate to deal with the vast numbers of the city's disinherited."

As for the corporations that threatened American ideals, the progressives believed that a powerful state was the only agency that could bring them to heel. The goals were still Jeffersonian, Herbert Croly wrote in *The Promise of American Life* (1909): the welfare of the many as determined by the will of the many. But, to Croly and most progressives, the old Jeffersonian principle of "the less government the better" had been rendered obsolete by the magnitude of twentieth-century social problems and the vast power of the plutocrats. Croly would have Jeffersonian ends achieved through the use of Hamiltonian means, the power of the state. His most important convert, Theodore Roosevelt, said in 1910, "The betterment which we seek must be accomplished, I believe, mainly through the national government."

This is the single most important novelty of progressivism as a reform movement: Government action was the key to social and even moral improvement. It is a dogma very much alive in the twenty-first century.

Coat of Many Colors

Beyond a commitment to government action, progressivism was variety, a frame of mind rather than a single coherent movement. There were Democratic progressives and Republican progressives. In 1912, breakaway Republicans formed the Progressive party, whereas some progressives considered democratic socialists—those who rejected violent revolution as an agent of change—to be their kin.

On some specific issues, progressives differed among themselves as radically as they differed from the old guard against whom they all battled. For example, many progressives believed that labor unions had the right to exist and fight for the betterment of their members. Others, however, opposed unions for the same reason that they disliked powerful corporations: Organized special-interest groups were at odds with the ideal of serving the good of the whole. On one occasion, leaders of the National American Woman Suffrage Association said that women should work as strikebreakers if, by doing so, they could win jobs currently held by men.

Some progressives were ultranationalists. Others clung to a humanism that embraced all people of all countries. Some progressives were expansionists. Senator Albert J. Beveridge of Indiana saw no conflict in calling for broadening democracy at home while urging the United States to rule colonies abroad without regard to the will of their inhabitants. Others were anti-imperialists, even isolationists, who looked on Europe as a fount of corruption.

Progressives disagreed among themselves about laws regulating child labor. By 1907, about two-thirds of the states governed or influenced by progressives forbade the employment of children under 14 years of age. However, when progressives in Congress passed a federal child labor law in 1916, the progressive President Woodrow Wilson expressed grave doubts before signing it. Wilson worried that to forbid children to work infringed on their rights as citi-

The Smithsonian Institution

▲ *There were no photographs when President Roosevelt entertained Booker T. Washington at the White House. This composite was created by an African American to express black pride in Washington's stature. Despite the fact that Washington acquiesced on the color line and on the exclusion of blacks from politics in the South, Roosevelt's invitation caused widespread howls of protest among southerners.*

zens. This was essentially the same reasoning stated by the conservative Supreme Court in *Hammer v. Dagenhart* (1918), which struck down the federal child labor law.

Race

Many, and probably most, progressives could not imagine blacks as citizens equal to whites, participating fully and actively in American society. Some were frank racists, especially the southern progressives: Governor James K. Vardaman of Mississippi, Governor Jeff Davis of Arkansas, and Senator Benjamin "Pitchfork Ben" Tillman of South Carolina. As president of Princeton University, Woodrow Wilson helped to segregate the town of Princeton on racial lines, including even separate "white" and "colored" water fountains. As president of the United States, he approved the introduction of "Jim Crow" practices in the federal government. Other progressives tolerated discrimination against blacks out of habit or because they feared the consequences of racial equality with a high percentage of the African American population illiterate.

Other progressives ranked racial prejudice and discrimination among the worst evils afflicting America. Journalist Ray Stannard Baker wrote a scathing and moving exposé of racial segregation in a series of magazine articles titled "Following the Color Line." In 1910, white progressives, including Jane Addams, joined with the African American Niagara Movement to form the National Association for the Advancement of Colored People. Except for his color, W. E. B. DuBois, the guiding spirit of the Niagara Movement, was the progressive par excellence. Genteel, middle class, and university educated, he was devoted to the idea that an intellectual elite should guide government and that the "talented tenth" of the black population would lead the race to civil equality in the United States.

Brownsville

The limitations of progressives on matters involving race were displayed by the federal government's actions after black soldiers of the Twenty-Fifth Infantry Regiment were accused of shooting up Brownsville, Texas, in August 1906. Although no individual was found guilty of the crime, or even tried for it, progressive President Theodore Roosevelt dishonorably discharged all 167 black soldiers stationed at the fort, including six winners of the Medal of Honor.

Circumstantial evidence indicated that a few of the men were guilty of the shooting; other evidence seemed to exonerate all of the others. But Roosevelt was more interested in calming the tempers of those whites who assumed the worst of the blacks than in acting on principles of justice. The only prominent white politician to take up the cause of the African American soldiers was a rock-ribbed Republican conservative, Senator Joseph B. Foraker of Ohio.

Forebears

So diverse a movement had a mixed ancestry. From the Populists' Omaha platform, the progressives took a good deal. As William Allen White remarked, the progressives "caught the Populists in swimming and stole all of their clothing except the frayed underdrawers of free silver." Like the Populists, progressives called for the direct election of senators and a graduated income tax that would hit the wealthy harder than it hit the middle classes. Both reforms were enacted by constitutional amendment in 1913. Progressives favored the initiative, referendum, and recall—also Populist projects. Some progressives, though not all, wanted to nationalize the railways and banks. Many more believed that local public utilities such as water, gas, and electric companies, being natural monopolies, should be government owned.

The progressives also harked back to the "good government" idealism of the mugwumps. Indeed, in the progressives' intense moralism, and their compulsion to stamp out personal sin as well as social and political evils, they could sound like the evangelicals of the early nineteenth century.

In exalting expertise and efficiency, and in their belief that a new order must be devised to replace the social and economic chaos of the late nineteenth century, the progressives owed a debt to people whom they considered their enemies. Marcus A. Hanna, certainly no progressive in any way when he died in 1904, preached collaboration between capital and organized labor as an alternative to class conflict.

Frederick W. Taylor, the inventor of "scientific management," was rarely described as a progressive and personally took little interest in politics. Nevertheless, in his conviction that the engineer's approach to solving problems could be fruitfully applied to human behavior, he was a forebear of the progressive movement. The progressives believed that society could be engineered as readily as Taylor engineered the shape of the shovel a workingman used to perform his job and the motions with which he used his tool.

PROGRESSIVISM DOWN HOME

Progressivism originated in the cities. In the last years of the nineteenth century, capitalizing on widespread disgust with the corruption endemic to municipal government, a number of reform mayors swept into office and won national reputations. They were not, like their predecessors in the 1870s and 1880s, easily ousted after a year or two.

Good Government

One of the first of the city reformers was Hazen S. Pingree, a shoe manufacturer who was elected mayor of Detroit in 1890. Pingree spent seven years battling the corrupt alliance between the owners of the city's public utilities and Detroit city councilmen. In nearby Toledo, Ohio, another businessman, Samuel M. Jones, ran for mayor as a reformer in 1897. Professional politicians mocked him as an addle-headed eccentric because he plastered the walls of his factory with the golden rule and other homilies. But his employees, whom Jones treated fairly by sharing profits with them, were devoted to him, and workers in other companies admired him. As "Golden Rule" Jones, he took control of Toledo and proved to be a no-nonsense administrator. Within two years, he rid Toledo's city hall of graft.

Another progressive mayor was Cleveland's Thomas L. Johnson, elected in 1901. Not only did he clean up a dirty government, but he actively supported women's suffrage, reformed the juvenile courts, took over public utilities from avaricious owners, and put democracy to work by presiding over open town meetings at which citizens could air their grievances and suggestions.

Lincoln Steffens, a staff writer for *McClure's,* called Cleveland "the best-governed city in the United States." Steffens was the expert; in 1903, he authored a sensational series of articles for *McClure's* called "The Shame of the Cities." Researching his subject carefully in the country's major cities, he named grafters, exposed corrupt connections between elected officials and dishonest businessmen, and demonstrated how ordinary people suffered from corrupt government in the quality of their daily lives.

Steffens's exposés accelerated the movement for municipal reform. Joseph W. Folk of St. Louis, whose tips put Steffens on his story, was able to indict more than 30 politicians and prominent Missouri businessmen for bribery and perjury as a result of the outcry that greeted "The Shame of the Cities." Hundreds of reform mayors elected after 1904 owed their success to the solemn, bearded journalist.

The Muckrakers

No medium was more effective in spreading the gospel of progressivism than the mass-circulation magazines. Already well established by the turn of the century thanks to their cheap price and lively style, periodicals like *McClure's,* the

▲ *Ida M. Tarbell, one of the most conscientious researchers and best writers among the muckrakers. Her most famous work was a highly critical study of John D. Rockefeller and the Standard Oil Trust.*

Arena, Collier's, Cosmopolitan, and *Everybody's* became even more successful when their editors discovered the popular appetite for the journalism of exposure.

The discovery was almost accidental. Samuel S. McClure himself had no particular interest in reform. Selling magazines and advertising in them was his business, hobby, and obsession. When he hired Ida M. Tarbell and Lincoln Steffens at generous salaries, he did so because they wrote well, not because they were reformers. Indeed, Tarbell began the "History of the Standard Oil Company," exposing John D. Rockefeller's dubious business practices, because of a personal grudge: Rockefeller had ruined her father, himself an oil man. Steffens was looking for a story, any story, when he stumbled upon the shame of the cities.

But when Tarbell's and Steffens's sensational exposés caused circulation to soar, McClure and other editors were hooked. The mass-circulation magazines soon brimmed with sensational revelations about corruption in government, chicanery in business, social evils like child labor and prostitution, and other subjects that lent themselves to indignant, excited treatment. In addition to his series on racial segregation, Ray Stannard Baker dissected the operations of the great railroads. John Spargo, an English-born socialist, discussed child labor in "The Bitter Cry of the Children." David

Nothing But the Facts, Ma'am

The muckrakers were keenly aware that part of the revolution they worked in American journalism was to sensationalize it. Lincoln Steffens chafed under the regime in which "reporters were to report the news as it happened, like machines, without prejudice, color, and without style; all alike." Ray Stannard Baker wrote impatiently that "facts, facts piled up to the point of dry certitude, was what the American people really wanted." Both remained true to high standards of journalistic integrity, but many other muckrakers did not.

William Randolph Hearst, who sponsored a good deal of muckraking in his newspapers, said that "the modern editor of the popular journal does not care for facts. The editor wants novelty. The editor has no objections to facts if they are also novel. But he would prefer novelty that is not fact, to a fact that is not a novelty."

Graham Phillips, later a successful novelist dealing with social themes, described the United States Senate, elected by state legislatures, as a kind of millionaires' club.

President Roosevelt called the journalists "muckrakers" after an unattractive character in John Bunyan's religious classic of 1678, *Pilgrim's Progress.* The writers were so busy raking through the muck of American society, he said, that they failed to look up and see the glories in the stars.

He had a point, especially when, after a few years, the quality of the journalism of exposure deteriorated into sloppy research and wild, ill-founded accusations made for the sake of filling pages with type and attracting attention. During the first decade of the century, no fewer than 2,000 articles and books of exposure were published. Inevitably, like so many other similar crusaders, the muckrakers ran out of solid material. As a profession, muckraking became the province of hacks and sensation mongers.

But the dirt could be real enough, and the early reform journalists were as determined to stick to the facts as to arouse their readers' indignation. Their work served to disseminate the reform impulse from one end of the country to the other. The 10 leading muckraking journals had a combined circulation of 3 million. Because the magazines were also read in public libraries and barbershops, and just passed around, the actual readership was many times larger.

In the Jungle with Upton Sinclair

Upton Sinclair was the most influential muckraker of all. In 1906, he wrote a novel, *The Jungle,* about how ethnic prejudice and economic exploitation in Chicago turned an industrious and optimistic Lithuanian immigrant into a revolutionary determined to smash the capitalist system. This message did not particularly appeal to the editors of the mass-circulation magazines, and Sinclair turned to a Socialist party weekly newspaper, the *Appeal to Reason,* to run it as a serial. Even the *Appeal* had a big readership; one issue sold over 1 million copies. *The Jungle* was a mighty success. Published as a book, it sold 100,000 copies, reaching even the desk of President Theodore Roosevelt.

Sinclair's book converted few Americans to socialism. In fact, its literary quality decays rapidly in the final chapters when the protagonist takes up the red flag. However, millions were moved by the passages in the book that luridly described the conditions under which meat was processed in Chicago slaughterhouses. *The Jungle* publicized documented tales of rats ground up into sausage, workers with tuberculosis coughing on the meat they packed, and filth at every point along the production line.

"I aimed at the nation's heart," Sinclair later said, "and hit it in the stomach." He meant that within months of the publication of *The Jungle,* a federal meat-inspection bill that had been languishing in Congress was rushed through under public pressure and promptly signed by President Roosevelt. It, and a second Pure Food and Drug Act, which forbade food processors to use dangerous adulterants (the pet proj-

White Primary

Mississippi instituted a primary in 1902 (the same year as Oregon's, which is usually considered the nation's first). However, Mississippi's primary, like those in other southern states, was designed not only to take the nomination of candidates for office away from political bosses but even further to deny African Americans a say in politics.

That is, Mississippi and most other southern states were, effectively, one-party states. The only Republicans in the Deep South were the few blacks who held on to the right to vote and the even fewer whites who got federal jobs when the Republican party held the presidency. In the Democratic party primary (or "white primary," as it was soon known), Republicans, of course, did not vote. With the winner of the Democratic primary a shoo-in in the general election, the "white primary" was the election that counted. In it, Democratic party rivals could compete against one another without having to worry that, in a close contest, the few African American voters might hold the key to victory, forcing Democrats to promise concessions. The general election was safe for white supremacy.

ect of a chemist in the Agriculture Department, Dr. Harvey W. Wiley), expanded the power of government in a way that was inconceivable a few years earlier.

Efficiency and Democracy

In 1908, Staunton, Virginia, introduced a favorite progressive municipal reform, the city manager system of government. The office of mayor was abolished. Instead, voters elected a city council, which then hired a nonpolitical, professionally trained administrator to manage the city's affairs. Proponents of the city manager system reasoned that democracy was protected by the people's control of the council. However, because the daily operations of the city were supervised by an executive who was free of political influence, they would be carried out without regard to special interests. By 1915, over 400 mostly medium-sized cities followed Staunton's example.

The "Oregon system" was the brainchild of William S. U'ren, one of the first progressives to make an impact at the state level. U'ren believed that the remedy for corruption in government was simple: more democracy. The trouble lay in the ability of efficient, well-organized, and wealthy special interests to thwart the good intentions of the people. Time after time, U'ren pointed out, elected officials handily forgot their campaign promises and worked closely with the corporations to pass bad laws or defeat good ones.

Between 1902 and 1904, U'ren persuaded the Oregon legislature to adopt reforms pioneered in South Dakota in 1898—the initiative, recall, and referendum. The Oregon system also included the first primary law. It took the power to nominate candidates for public office away from the bosses and gave it to the voters. Finally, U'ren led the national movement to choose United States senators by popular vote rather than in the state legislatures. U'ren lived to the ripe old age of 90, long enough to see 20 states adopt the initiative and 30 adopt the referendum.

"Fighting Bob"

The career of Wisconsin's "Fighting Bob" La Follette is almost a history of progressivism in itself. Born in 1855, he studied law and served three terms in Congress as a Republican during the 1880s. As a young man, he showed few signs of the crusader's itch. Then, a senator offered him a bribe to fix the verdict in a trial. La Follette flew into a rage at the shameless audacity of the suggestion, and he never quite calmed down for the rest of his life.

In 1900, he ran for governor in defiance of the Republican organization, attacking the railroad and lumber interests that dominated the state. He promised to devote the resources of the state government to the service of the people, and his timing was perfect; La Follette was elected. As governor, he pushed through a comprehensive system of regulatory laws that required every business touching the public interest to conform to clear-cut rules and submit to close inspection of its operations.

▲ *"Fighting Bob" La Follette, uncharacteristically calm and affable. He was the leading progressive in the Senate for more than 20 years.*

Attempted Murder?
In late May 1908, Robert La Follette led a filibuster against a financial bill. He spoke for nearly 17 hours before giving up. Through much of this time, La Follette sipped a tonic of milk and raw eggs prepared in the Senate dining room. After he had been taken violently ill on the floor, it was discovered that there was enough ptomaine in the mixture to kill a man. Because no one else suffered from eating in the Senate dining room that day, many assumed that La Follette's enemies had tried to kill him.

The "Wisconsin Idea"

La Follette went beyond the negative, or regulatory, powers of government to create agencies that provided positive services for the people. La Follette's "Wisconsin idea" held that in the complex modern world, people and government needed experts to work on their behalf. A railroad baron could not be kept on a leash unless the government could draw on the knowledge of specialists who were as canny as the railroaders. Insurance premiums could not be held at reasonable levels unless the state was able to determine when the insurance company's profit was just and when it was rapacious. The government could not intervene to determine what was fair in a labor dispute unless it had the counsel of economists.

La Follette formed a close and mutually beneficial relationship with the University of Wisconsin. In control of the state government, he generously supported the institution, making it one of the nation's best universities at a time when most tax-supported schools were poorly funded. In return, distinguished professors like Richard Ely, Selig Perlman, and John Rogers Commons put their expertise at La Follette's disposal. The Wisconsin law school helped build up the first legislative reference library in the United States so that assemblymen would no longer have to rely on lobbyists in order to draft complex laws.

The university's school of agriculture not only taught future farmers but carried out research programs that addressed problems faced daily in Wisconsin's fields and barns. La Follette even made use of the football team. When enemies hinted there would be trouble if he spoke at a rally, he showed up in the company of Wisconsin's burly linemen, who folded their arms and surrounded the platform. There was no trouble.

La Follette's unique contribution to progressivism was his application of machine methods to the cause of reform. He was idealistic, but he was no innocent. In order to ensure that his reforms would not be reversed, he built an organization as finely integrated as Tammany Hall. Party workers in every precinct got out the vote, and if they did not violate La Follette's exacting demands for honesty in public office, they were rewarded with patronage.

In 1906, La Follette took his crusade to Washington as a United States senator and held his seat until his death in 1925. In Wisconsin and elsewhere, he was loved as few politicians have been. He was "Fighting Bob," incorruptible and unyielding in what he regarded as right. La Follette's mane of brown hair, combed straight back, which turned snow white (some said overnight), waved wildly during his passionate speeches. He looked like an Old Testament prophet, and, in a way, La Follette devoted his life to saving the soul of American society as Jeremiah had done for Israel.

Prominent Progressives

In New York State, Charles Evans Hughes came to prominence as a result of his investigation into public utilities and insurance companies. Tall, erect, dignified, with a smartly trimmed beard such as was going out of fashion at the turn of the century, he lacked the charisma of La Follette. Hughes was "a cold-blooded creature" in the words of the hot-blooded Theodore Roosevelt. But he was unshakably honest as governor of New York between 1906 and 1910.

William E. Borah was not elected to the Senate from Idaho in 1906 as a progressive. On the contrary, his career in politics was characterized by a close and compliant relationship with the mining and ranching interests that ran the state. In the Senate, however, Borah usually voted with the progressive bloc. This record and his isolationism—like many westerners, Borah believed that the United States would be corrupted by close association with foreign powers—guaranteed his reelection until he died in office in 1940. Only decades later was it discovered that, unlike most progressives, Borah was not above accepting quietly given gifts of cash.

George Norris of Nebraska was elected to Congress in 1902 and to the Senate in 1912. He was a Teddy Roosevelt Republican, supporting the president when Roosevelt was at odds with the party's business establishment. Like Borah, he was an isolationist and would be one of a handful of senators who opposed American intervention in World War I.

Progressivism in California

Hiram Johnson of California came to progressivism by much the same path as La Follette. A prim, tight-lipped trial lawyer from Sacramento, Johnson won fame by taking over the prosecution of the corrupt political machine of Boss Abe Ruef in San Francisco.

At first it appeared to be a garden-variety graft case. Ruef, Mayor Eugene E. Schmitz, and a majority of the board of aldermen won office by appealing to ethnic voters, then collected payoffs from brothels, gambling dens, and thieves in return for running a wide-open city. In the wake of the great San Francisco earthquake and fire of 1906, Ruef set up a system by which those who wished to profit from the rebuilding had to clear their plans with him. Scarcely a street could be paved or a cable car line laid out until money changed hands. On one occasion, Ruef pocketed $250,000, of which he kept one-quarter, gave one-quarter to Schmitz, and distributed the remainder among the aldermen. Like other city bosses, Ruef bought and sold judges in lawsuits.

But Johnson discovered that Ruef not only was associated with vice and petty graft but was intimately allied with the most powerful corporation in the state, the Southern Pacific Railroad. The distinguished and ostensibly upright directors of the Southern Pacific, men whom Johnson had admired, were tangled in a web that stretched to include profiting from the misfortune of the wretched syphilitic prostitutes on San Francisco's notorious Barbary Coast.

Never a model of equanimity, Johnson was transformed into "a volcano in perpetual eruption, belching fire and smoke." In 1910, he won the governorship on the slogan "Kick the Southern Pacific out of Politics." No longer would he assume that great wealth and a varnish of propriety indicated a decent man. Indeed, his sense of personal rectitude was so great that it cost him a chance to be president. In 1920, Republican party bosses (such as Johnson loathed) asked him to run as vice presidential candidate in order to balance the conservative presidential nominee, Warren G. Harding. Johnson turned them down in a huff. As a result, when Harding died in office in 1923, he was succeeded by the conservative Calvin Coolidge instead of the volcano from California.

THE FRINGE

Most progressives advocated municipal ownership of public utilities, but they were staunchly antisocialist. Progressives like La Follette and Johnson warned that the reforms they proposed were necessary to preserve the institution of private property from a rising red tide in American politics.

This message had a special urgency in the early years of the twentieth century because the Socialist Party of America, founded in 1900, came close to establishing itself as a permanent fixture in American politics. Pieced together by local socialist organizations and frustrated former Populists, the Socialist party nominated the leader of the Pullman strike, Eugene V. Debs, for president in 1900; he won 94,768 votes. In 1904, running again, Debs threw a scare into progressives and conservatives alike by polling 402,460 votes. All told, he would run for president five times.

Debs and Berger

In many ways, Debs resembled a progressive politician. He was a fiery, flamboyant orator, a master of the theatrical and gymnastic style of public speaking favored by Americans in their preachers and politicians. He was more a moralist than an intellectual or, certainly, a politico. Debs freely admitted that he had little patience with the endless ideological hair-splitting of which other socialists, especially those with European ties, were enamored. Personally, he was most at home in the company of ordinary working people; he shared their prejudices and foibles, and their lack of pretension. Unsurprisingly, Debs's followers worshiped him as progressives worshiped La Follette, Borah, and Roosevelt.

▲ *The "Red Special." In 1908, the socialists were so confident presidential candidate Eugene V. Debs would make a strong showing ("socialism is coming like a prairie fire and nothing can stop it," crowed* The Appeal to Reason*) that the party strained its resources to charter a train so that Debs could make a nationwide whistle-stop tour.*

But Debs's resemblance to the progressives must not be overdrawn. He did not seek to smooth over the conflict between classes; he meant it when he exhorted working people to take charge. If he was not an ideologue, he agreed with the Marxists that the class that produced wealth should decide how that wealth was to be distributed.

Victor Berger of Milwaukee more clearly linked socialism and progressivism. An Austrian immigrant, middle class in background, and the calculating politician that Debs was not, Berger forged an alliance among Milwaukee's large German-speaking population, the city's labor movement, and many from the reform-minded middle class. His Social Democratic party (a part of the Socialist party) refrained from revolutionary rhetoric, downplayed its ultimate goals, and promised Milwaukee honest government and efficient city-owned public utilities. Once, when he and Debs were being interviewed by a journalist, Debs said that capitalists would not be compensated when their factories were taken from them; their property was stolen from working people, and theft would not be rewarded. Berger interrupted: No, capitalists would be compensated for their losses. Property might very well be theft, but Berger would not alienate his middle-class supporters with loose talk about confiscating it.

To radical members of the party, Berger's "sewer socialism," a reference to his emphasis on city ownership of utili-

ties, was nothing more than progressivism. Berger thought otherwise. He insisted that by demonstrating to the American people the socialists' ability to govern a large city, the Socialist party would win their attention to the revolutionary part of its program. In 1910, he got what seemed his chance to do just that. Berger was elected to the House of Representatives, and socialist candidates for mayor and city council were swept into power in Milwaukee.

Labor's Quest for Respectability

Berger also hoped to advance the fortunes of socialism by capturing the American Federation of Labor (AFL). Socialists were a large minority in the union movement, actually a majority among members who were not Roman Catholic. At the AFL's annual conventions, the socialists challenged the antisocialist leadership of Samuel Gompers and several times came close to ousting him from the presidency.

In the end, they failed. Presenting a moderate face to the American people was central to Gompers's strategy for establishing the legitimacy of the labor movement, and his version of moderation included support of progressive capitalism. His glad willingness to cooperate with employers won him many friends among progressives (and some conservatives such as Mark Hanna). In 1905, President Theodore Roosevelt intervened in the coal miners' strike, effectively on behalf of the miners. During the William Howard Taft administration (1909–1913), progressives established the Commission on Industrial Violence, with a membership that was skewed in a prounion direction. Progressive Democratic president Woodrow Wilson named Samuel Gompers to several prestigious government posts and appointed a former leader of the AFL's United Mine Workers, William B. Wilson, to be the first secretary of labor.

The union movement grew in the favorable climate of the Progressive Era. Membership in the AFL rose from about 500,000 in 1900 to 1.5 million in 1910, with some 500,000 workers holding cards in independent organizations. Nevertheless, this was a pittance in a nonagricultural labor force of almost 20 million.

Wobblies

Members of the IWW were called "Wobblies" by both friends and enemies. There are several explanations of the origin of their name. According to one, members of the IWW were so strike prone that they were "wobbly" workers. The story the IWW favored told of a Chinese restaurant operator in the Pacific Northwest who gave credit only to Wobblies because he could depend on them to pay. When someone asked for a meal on credit, the restaurant owner, unable to pronounce the name of the letter *W* in *IWW,* asked "I-Wobbly-Wobbly?"

Bindle Stiffs, Tramps, and Bums

We associate "the homeless" with big cities. The utterly penniless, derelicts, and the mentally ill congregate where they find some security and society in numbers, and where at least minimal social services are available.

From about 1880 to 1920, homelessness was associated with young males who crisscrossed the country on the railroads in empty boxcars or walked the roads and highways. When they congregated, it was in the "hobo jungles" (camps near the tracks) or in "skid roads," which were just as likely to be found in small cities like Spokane, Fresno, and Helena, Montana, as in New York, Chicago, or Seattle (where the term *skid road* originated—it was a street where logs were skidded down a hill to the waterfront).

Migrant "casual workers" were essential to the economies of the wheat belt (from the Dakotas to eastern Oregon and Washington), the vegetable- and fruit-growing regions (from Washington's apple country south through the entire length of California's Central Valley), and even the potato-growing regions of Long Island and Maine. All were crops that required comparatively little labor until it was time to harvest them. Then, for a few weeks—different weeks according to the crop or latitude—as many workers as possible, laboring hard all day every day, were needed before rains ruined the wheat, or fruits and vegetables rotted. Small family farms made do with local teenagers. Big commercial operations (and there was hardly any other kind in the wheat belt, where expensive machinery required a grower to be well capitalized) needed armies of workers to descend on them and, when the crop was in, to disappear. There was nothing for the pickers and harvest hands to do after the crop was picked and even less local interest in having large numbers of jobless, unattached young men in the vicinity.

The wheat, fruit, and vegetable belts could not have existed without migrant workers. But they were scorned. They were dirty, unshaven, and always dressed in rough work clothing; riding the rails, their only baggage was a "bindle"—a bedroll with very little wrapped inside. They were often rambunctious when not working and, inevitably, there were unsavory sorts who were a source of crime. Mostly, that crime was theft, and it was opportunistic rather than methodical: picking up something salable one stumbled across. There were also assaults, armed robberies, and rape. Such crimes against persons were not common, but the occasional lurid incident was enough to arouse wariness, fear, and hostility toward every hobo who walked into town for a meal or knocked at a kitchen door offering to chop firewood in return for a night's shelter in the barn.

In fact, casual workers said they did not steal, and, in general, they were telling the truth. There was a hierarchy among the homeless men of the Progressive Era. The "bindle stiffs"

(their name for themselves) were at the top of the pyramid. They prided themselves on being workingmen who earned their living honestly. They differed from factory workers, they said, only in that they had no homes and families, and moved constantly from one short-term job to another. They prided themselves on being free and independent—good old American values. If a boss offended them, they did not grovel; they rolled up their blankets and moved on.

The "tramps," as the bindle stiffs called them, were homeless too, rode the rails, and camped in the same hobo jungles. But they did not work. They survived by panhandling, stealing, and sometimes more serious crime. The working hobos looked down on them as parasites.

There was a "class" of homeless men even lower than the tramps—the "home guard," bums who neither worked nor traveled. They lived more or less permanently in the run-down skid roads found in most towns of any size. The bindle stiffs came to the skid roads when they were looking for work at exploitative employment agencies, which they hated, and to live through the winter. Lodging, meals, and drink were cheap on skid road and a casual worker could pass the days with others like him. The home guard, with whom they rubbed elbows and despised, was more pathetic than sinister, people reduced to bare survival by alcoholism and mental deficiency.

These distinctions were lost on the farmers and townspeople for whom the denizens of skid road and dusty, wandering men were virtually a daily sight. When, beginning about 1908, the Wobblies began to have some success organizing bindle stiffs, conventional people began to see the masses of homeless men as part of a dangerous conspiracy. Unexplained fires and damaged machinery were blamed on them. There was a myth that mysterious markings on gateposts and buildings were a code with which hobos informed one another that the police were brutal in a town or that a particular woman was a soft touch for a sandwich.

After World War I, the age of the hobo came to an end. Tramps still wandered into towns, but fewer working bindle stiffs did. The increasing hostility of the railroads to nonpaying passengers on the freight trains played a part. Where they had once been ignored or, at worst, thrown off the train, tough railroad security men, the "bulls," beat up the riders without fear of the law. Cheap second-hand automobiles, abundant by 1920, made it possible for four or five bindle stiffs to migrate from job to job inconspicuously. In time, cheap cars meant that families, including children, replaced single men as the agricultural workforce, mostly poor whites in the South, blacks in the East, Mexican Americans in the West.

The Wobblies

The most important unions outside the AFL were the cautious and conservative Railway Brotherhoods of Locomotive Engineers, Firemen, Conductors and Brakemen (the Pullman car porters, African Americans, did not organize a

Brotherhood until 1925), and the revolutionary Industrial Workers of the World (IWW), whose members were called "Wobblies."

Founded in 1905 by socialists and labor radicals disgusted by Gompers's conservatism and his refusal to recruit unskilled workers, the IWW found some friends among progressives but, more often, sent chills racing down their spines.

Some western progressives supported the Wobblies when, between 1909 and 1913, they sponsored a series of free-speech fights to protect their campaign to recruit farmworkers by speaking on street-corner soapboxes in towns where the transient workers congregated. Progressive sensitivity to traditions of personal liberty was agitated when policemen assigned to destroy the union arrested Wobblies for reading publicly from the Declaration of Independence and the Constitution. In 1912, progressive organizations, particularly women's clubs, helped the IWW win its greatest strike victory among immigrant textile mill workers in Lawrence, Massachusetts. They publicized the horrendous living conditions in Lawrence, lobbied congressmen, and took the children of strikers into their homes, a masterful public-relations ploy.

The capacity of middle-class progressives to back the Wobblies could not, however, go much beyond well-wishing. The Wobblies called loudly and gaily for revolution, precisely what progressives were determined to avoid. Although the IWW officially denied employing violent methods, including sabotage, individual members spoke of driving spikes into logs bound for sawmills and throwing hammers into the works of harvesters, threshers, and balers. And, although the first blow was more often thrown by employers than workers, fistfights, riots, and even murders characterized enough Wobbly strikes to besmirch the union's reputation.

Nor were middle-class progressives alone in considering the IWW beyond the pale. No one used fiercer language in denouncing the organization than Samuel Gompers. In 1913, Victor Berger and a prominent New York socialist, Morris Hillquit, led a movement within the Socialist party that successfully expelled the leader of the IWW, William D. "Big Bill" Haywood, from the party's National Executive Committee.

Feminism and Progressivism

Another "ism" with an ambivalent relationship to the progressive movement was feminism. In 1900, the struggle on behalf of equal rights for women was more than 50 years old. Despite the tireless, lifelong labors of now ancient leaders like Elizabeth Cady Stanton and Susan B. Anthony, the victories were few. In their twilight years at the beginning of the Progressive Era, Stanton and Anthony could look back on liberalized divorce laws, women voters in six western states, a movement unified for the moment in the National American Woman Suffrage Association, and the initiation of a new generation of leaders including Carrie Chapman Catt and Anna Howard Shaw, a British-born physician.

But the coveted prize, a constitutional amendment guaranteeing women the right to vote, seemed as remote as it had at Seneca Falls in 1848. Most articulate Americans, women as well as men, continued to believe that women's finer moral sense made it best that they remain in a sphere separate from men, a private, domestic sphere. If women

---

Teddy Roosevelt on Votes for Women

Theodore Roosevelt said:

Personally, I believe in woman's suffrage, but I am not an enthusiastic advocate of it, because I do not regard it as a very important matter. I am unable to see that there has been any special improvement in the position of women in those states in the West that have adopted woman's suffrage, as compared to those states adjoining them that have not adopted it. I do not think that giving the women suffrage will produce any marked improvement in the condition of women. I do not believe that it will produce any of the evils feared, and I am very certain that when women as a whole take any special interest in the matter they will have suffrage if they desire it.

Helen Keller on Votes for Women

In 1911, Helen Keller told a British suffragist: "You ask for votes for women. What good can votes do when ten-elevenths of the land in Great Britain belongs to 200,000 and only one-eleventh to the rest of the 40,000,000 population? Have your men with their millions of votes freed themselves from this injustice?"

---

participated in public life, they would be sullied as men were and lose their vital moral influence in the home.

In fact, when Anthony died in 1906, success was fewer than 15 years away. The democratic inclinations of the progressives made it increasingly difficult for them to deny the franchise to half the American people. Even progressive leaders who had little personal enthusiasm for the idea of female voters publicly supported the cause.

Changed Strategies

The key to the victory of the women's suffrage movement was a fundamental shift in its strategy. Under the leadership of Carrie Chapman Catt, the National American Woman Suffrage Association came to terms with popular prejudices as Stanton and Anthony never quite could. Catt's movement quietly shelved the comprehensive critique of women's status in American society that the early feminists developed, which had sometimes included doubts about the institution of marriage. The new suffragists downplayed, even jettisoned, the traditional argument that women should have the right to vote because they were equal to men in every way.

A few "social feminists" clung to the old principles. Charlotte Perkins Gilman, an independently minded New Englander, argued in *Women and Economics* (1898) that marriage was itself the cause of women's inequality. Alice Paul, a Quaker like many feminists before her, insisted that suffrage alone was not enough to resolve "the woman question."

But most of the middle-class suffragists argued that women should have the right to vote precisely because they

MAP 35:1 Woman Suffrage Before the Nineteenth Amendment
Women's suffrage became part of the Constitution in 1919. By that
date, however, as this map indicates, hard-core and absolute opposition to women's voting was restricted largely to white males in New
England and the South—strange bedfellows, indeed.

Legend:
- No voting by women
- Women voting in presidential election
- Women voting in primaries
- Complete voting rights for women

were more moral than men. Their votes would purge society
of its evils. Not only did the suffragists ingeniously turn in
their favor the most compelling antisuffragist argument—
the belief that women were the morally superior sex—but

they told progressives that, in allowing women to vote, they
would be gaining huge numbers of allies. In fact, women
were in the forefront of two of the era's most conspicuous
moral crusades, the struggle against prostitution and the prohibition movement.

White Slavery

To earlier generations, prostitution was an inevitable evil
that could be controlled or ignored by decent people, but not
abolished. By 1900, most states, counties, and cities had
laws against solicitation on the grounds that streetwalking
"hookers" were a public nuisance. Somewhat fewer declared
the quiet, private sale of sex to be a crime. Even where prostitution was nominally illegal, it was common to tolerate
"houses of ill repute" that were discreetly operated (and usually made contributions to worthy causes such as the welfare of the police).

Communities in which men vastly outnumbered
women—cow towns, mining camps, seaports, migrant farmworker and logging centers—tolerated red-light districts in
a corner of town. A stock figure of small-town folklore was
the woman on the wrong side of the tracks who sold favors
to those sly or bold enough to knock on her door.

In the large cities, prostitution ran the gamut from
lushly furnished and expensive brothels for high-society
swells, such as Sally Stanford's in San Francisco, to the

▲ *Under Carrie Chapman Catt, the National American Woman Suffrage Association shunned the confrontational tactics of British
suffragists (who chained themselves to palace gates and one of whom threw herself in front of racehorses and was killed). The
Americans emphasized their respectability, femininity, and even domesticity, as in this parade.*

Birth Control

Margaret Sanger was a nurse in New York City who ministered to poor women giving birth to children they could not afford, and to girls and women who came to the hospital after botched abortions and often died. In 1912, she began to devote all her time and the rest of her life to publicizing and providing women with condoms, diaphragms, and spermicidal jellies. Two years later, she coined the term *birth control,* mainly to avoid offending middle-class progressive women she recruited to support her cause. Despite the euphemism, she was jailed when she opened a birth control clinic in 1916. Her enemies equated the advocacy of birth control with promoting sexual promiscuity.

Nevertheless, Sanger's insistence that "a woman's body belongs to herself alone" and that women "cannot be on an equal footing with men until they have full and complete control over their reproductive function" appealed to many progressives, particularly women, of course. Ironically (because Sanger's concern was poor women), her American Birth Control League (later Planned Parenthood) had its greatest influence on educated middle-class women.

▲ *A prostitute in a Colorado mining town. In such largely male enclaves, brothels were openly tolerated even when, sometimes, illegal, and many prostitutes married and lived conventional lives. On the streets of cities, prostitutes could look forward to little more than venereal disease and poverty.*

"cribs," tiny cubicles rented by prostitutes who serviced workingmen for a dollar or less. Because their pay was so low, thousands of New York working women moonlighted as prostitutes part time. Novelists Stephen Crane (*Maggie: A Girl of the Streets,* 1893) and Upton Sinclair *(The Jungle)* both dealt with tacitly forced prostitution.

The world's oldest profession had affronted proper people long before the Progressive Era. In most places, the middle class was content to declare the trade illegal and then tolerate it out of their sight. Some cities restricted prostitution to neighborhoods far from middle-class residential areas, such as New Orleans's Storyville, San Francisco's Barbary Coast, and Chicago's South of the Loop.

The progressives, spearheaded by women's organizations, determined to wipe out the institution. During the first decade of the twentieth century, most states and innumerable communities passed strict laws against all prostitution and enforced them rigorously. In 1917, prodded by the army when it established a big training camp nearby, even wide-open Storyville, the birthplace of jazz, was officially closed. By 1920, all but a few states had antiprostitution laws on the books. Within a few more years, only Nevada, with its stubborn mining frontier outlook, continued to tolerate the institution within the law.

The Limits of Progressive Moralism

Action on the federal level was more complicated. Prostitution was clearly a matter for the police powers of the states and localities. However, progressives were so convinced that government held the key to social reform and must act at every level that, in 1910, they joined with some conservatives to put the interstate commerce clause of the Constitu-

tion to work in the cause. Senator James R. Mann of Illinois sponsored a bill that struck against the exaggerated practice of procurers luring poor girls from one part of the country to become prostitutes elsewhere; it was called the "white slave trade." The Mann Act forbade transporting women across state lines "for immoral purposes." Because the white slave trade was not nearly as extensive and systematic as the reformers believed, the Mann Act was soon best known as a means to selectively "get" unpopular men like the boxer Jack Johnson.

Neither local and state laws nor the Mann Act eliminated prostitution. The campaign may be the best example of the progressives' excessive faith in the powers of the government. Brothels continued to operate, albeit less openly and probably with more police graft than before. Streetwalkers, previously the most despised and degraded of prostitutes, became the norm because they were less easily arrested. Wealthy men continued to maintain paid mistresses and created the "call girl," a prostitute who stayed at home until "called" by a hotel employee or pimp who worked the streets and hotel lobbies.

Daddy's in There---

And Our Shoes and Stockings and Clothes and Food Are in There, Too, and They'll Never Come Out.
—*Chicago American.*

▲ *A handout published by the Anti-Saloon League. Drinking as the cause of poverty and of neglect and abuse of mothers and children was an effective theme exploited in pamphlets and newspaper advertisements.*

Prohibitionists

The evangelicals' impulse to combat the evils of drink never quite died. Temperance advocates and outright prohibitionists battled back and forth with distillers and with ordinary people who simply enjoyed a cup of cheer. By 1900, however, antialcohol crusaders were emphasizing social arguments over their moral distaste for drunkenness and, in so doing, won widespread progressive support.

The prohibitionists pointed out that the city saloon was often the local headquarters of the corrupt political machines. Close the saloons, the reasoning went, and the bosses would be crippled. The prohibitionists also argued that the misery of the working classes was the consequence of husbands and fathers spending their wages on demon rum. Because the public bar was then an all-male institution, the temperance movement formed a close alliance with feminists.

Carry Nation of Kansas was a woman who suffered in poverty for many years because of a drunken husband. Beginning in 1900, she launched a campaign of direct action, leading hatchet-wielding women into saloons, where, before the bewildered eyes of saloon keepers and customers, they methodically chopped the place to pieces.

Frances Willard, head of the Woman's Christian Temperance Union, opposed such tactics. She and her followers also entered saloons, but instead of breaking them up, they attempted to shame drinkers by kneeling to pray quietly in their midst. In addition, the Woman's Christian Temperance Union turned to politics, supporting women's suffrage for its own sake as well as for the purpose of winning the final victory over liquor.

Increasing numbers of progressives adopted the reform. Only in the big cities, mostly in the eastern states, did socially minded politicians like Alfred E. Smith and Robert Wagner of New York actively fight the prohibitionists. The large Roman Catholic and Jewish populations of the cities had no religious tradition against alcohol; on the contrary, they used wine as a part of religious observance. Elsewhere, libertarian progressives argued that the government had no right to interfere with the individual decision of whether or not to drink.

Nevertheless, the possibilities of moral improvement, of striking a blow against poverty, and of joining battle against the political manipulations of the big distillers and brewers converted many progressives to prohibition. In the waning days of the movement (though they were not thought to be waning at the time), the prohibitionists had their way.

for FURTHER READING

For general background on the Progressive Era, see Vincent P. De-Santis, *The Shaping of Modern America, 1877–1916,* 1973; Robert H. Wiebe, *The Search for Order, 1880–1920,* 1967; and William L. O'Neill, *The Progressive Years: America Comes of Age,* 1975, which is perhaps the most readable survey of the era. The following general interpretations are valuable or, at least, stimulating: Arthur Ekirch, *Progressivism in Practice,* 1974; Lewis L. Gould, *Reform and Regulation: American Politics, 1900–1916,* 1978; the appropriate chapters of Richard Hofstadter, *The Age of Reform,* 1955; Gabriel Kolko, *The Triumph of Conservatism,* 1963; Christopher Lasch, *The New Radicalism in America,* 1965; and George E. Mowry, *The Era of Theodore Roosevelt,* 1958.

More narrowly focused books with excellent insights about progressives are John D. Buenker, *Urban Liberalism and Progressive Reform,* 1973; D. M. Chalmers, *The Social and Political Ideas of the Muckrakers,* 1964; Carl M. Degler, *At Odds: Women in the Family in America from the Revolution to the Present,* 1980; Louis

Filler, *Crusaders for American Liberalism,* 1939; David M. Kennedy, *Birth Control in America: The Career of Margaret Sanger,* 1970; Jack D. Kirby, *Darkness at the Dawning: Race and Reform in the Progressive South,* 1972; Roy Lubove, *The Progressives and the Slums,* 1962; George E. Mowry, *The California Progressives,* 1951; William L. O'Neill, *Everyone Was Brave: The Rise and Fall of Feminism,* 1969; J. T. Patterson, *America's Struggle Against Poverty,* 1981; James H. Timberlake, *Prohibition and the Progressive Movement, 1900–1920,* 1963; James Weinstein, *The Corporate Ideal in the Liberal State, 1900–1918,* 1968; and Robert H. Wiebe, *Businessmen and Reform,* 1962.

Biographical studies include John M. Blum, *The Republican Roosevelt,* 1954; David McCullough, *Mornings on Horseback,* 1981; W. H. Harbaugh, *Power and Responsibility: The Life and Times of Theodore Roosevelt,* 1931; and David P. Thelen, *Robert M. La Follette and the Insurgent Movement,* 1976.

Visit the source collections at http://ajaccess.wadsworth.com and http://infotrac.thomsonlearning.com, and use the Search function with the following key terms to explore documents, images, audio and video clips, articles, and commentary related to the material in this chapter:

Carrie Chapman Catt
Charlotte Perkins Gilman
Eugene V. Debs
Hull House
Ida Tarbell
Jane Addams

Muckraking
Robert La Follette
Theodore Roosevelt
Upton Sinclair
Woodrow Wilson

Additional resources, exercises, and Internet links related to this chapter are available on *The American Past* Web site: http://history.wadsworth.com/americanpast7e.

HISTORY ONLINE

Touring Turn of the Century America
http://65.54.246.250:80/cgibin/linkrd?_lang=EN&lah=cd63fe2d1
52a61ffdea13c05ade7439b&lat=1045588104&hm___action=http
%3a%2f%2fwww%2eku%2eedu%2fhistory%2fVL%2fUSA%2f
Vast collection of photographs from a Detroit newspaper file.

Eugene V. Debs
www.eugenevdebs.com/
Web site of a foundation dedicated to the memory of America's greatest socialist; comprehensive, illustrated.

36

STANDING AT ARMAGEDDON

The Progressives in Power 1901–1916

Big business is not dangerous because it is big, but because its bigness is an unwholesome inflation created by privileges and exemptions which it ought not to enjoy.
Woodrow Wilson

We demand that big business give the people a square deal; in return we must insist that when anyone engaged in big business endeavors to do right he shall himself be given a square deal.

Theodore Roosevelt

B Y 1904, PROGRESSIVE reform commanded the allegiance of congressmen from both parties and of President Theodore Roosevelt himself. The irony that he, the scion of an old and privileged family, should be the titular leader of a popular protest movement was not lost on Roosevelt. In a letter to the decidedly unprogressive Senator Chauncey Depew of New York, Roosevelt wrote in mock weariness, "How I wish I wasn't a reformer, Oh Senator! But I suppose I must live up to my part, like the Negro minstrel who blackened himself all over!"

Was Roosevelt mocking his own sincerity? Perhaps in part, but it was not so bizarre that he chastised and disciplined powerful industrial capitalists he considered to be "malefactors of great wealth." His family's fortune and status were preindustrial; he was a member of an older American elite that was elbowed aside by the industrial new rich of the late nineteenth century. Mrs. Astor reacted to the slight by creating the "Four Hundred," a short list of old-money New Yorkers whom she found acceptable. Theodore Roosevelt reacted by going into politics and refusing, like so many of his peers, to play the grinning flunky for big businessmen.

Moreover, despite the sigh of resignation to duty in his letter to Depew, Roosevelt loved to be in the thick of things. When he was in the White House, reform was where the action was.

THEODORE ROOSEVELT'S GROWING LEADERSHIP

At first, accidental president Roosevelt moved cautiously. He knew that the Republican party's old guard distrusted him as a "damned cowboy." Mark Hanna openly discussed opposing T.R. for the 1904 Republican presidential nomination with party bosses Tom Platt of New York and Matthew

Quay of Pennsylvania. Roosevelt knew that far more Republican professionals were beholden to them than to him.

But no one was to contest Roosevelt's leadership of the party. Mark Hanna died suddenly in February 1904, Matt Quay a little later. Had they lived and been hale and hearty, it would have made no difference; they would have had to tip their hats to the cowboy. In a little more than two years, Roosevelt built up an immense personal following in the country. Within the party, he quietly replaced mediocrities McKinley had appointed, replaced them with his own supporters, and won the loyalty of McKinley men he kept by giving them an autonomy they had not enjoyed under McKinley.

He kept the ablest men from the McKinley cabinet: Secretary of State John Hay, Secretary of War Elihu Root (who succeeded Hay in the State Department in 1905), Attorney General Philander C. Knox, Secretary of the Interior E. A. Hitchcock, and Secretary of Agriculture James Wilson. Roosevelt did not fear competence in his subordinates, as some leaders do. He was happy to delegate responsibility because there was no doubt in anyone's mind as to who was in charge.

Attack on Taboos and Trusts

In April 1902, T.R. directed Attorney General Knox, a former corporate lawyer, to have a go at the most powerful corporate organizers in the United States. His target, the Northern Securities Company, was designed by J. P. Morgan and railroaders Edward H. Harriman and James J. Hill to put an end to destructive railroad competition in the northwestern quarter of the country. Funded by the nation's two richest banks, Northern Securities was a holding company patterned after Morgan's United States Steel Corporation.

Morgan was stunned by Roosevelt's antitrust prosecution. Under McKinley, the Sherman Antitrust Act had languished, almost unused. In a revealing moment, Morgan wrote to the president, "If we have done anything wrong, send your man to my man and we can fix it up." That, indeed, was how things had been done, but the suggestion was not apt to appeal to Teddy Roosevelt. He read it as an invitation to sit in Morgan's waiting room, holding his hat.

Knox pushed on in the courts and, in 1904, won the case. The Supreme Court ordered the Northern Securities Company to dissolve. Progressives cheered. When Roosevelt instituted several more antitrust suits, 40 in all (25 were won), progressives nicknamed him the "trustbuster."

Roosevelt continued to socialize among the millionaires with whom Knox was contending in court. Indeed, in 1907 he allowed Morgan's United States Steel Company to gobble up a major regional competitor, Tennessee Coal and Iron, without comment. The trustbuster's criteria for determining what made one business combination acceptable and another not were vague. In a way, Roosevelt's antitrust campaign was drama and symbol. He wanted to show big business and the American people that he and the United States government were in charge. In the Tennessee Coal and Iron case, Morgan had to send his man to Roosevelt's man, and not vice versa.

The Workingman's Friend

More startling than trust-busting was Roosevelt's personal intervention in the autumn of 1902 in a long, bitter strike by 140,000 anthracite miners. The men's demands were moderate. They wanted a 20 percent increase in pay—not excessive given the abysmally low wages the miners were paid—an eight-hour day, and their employers' agreement to recognize and negotiate with their union, the United Mine Workers (UMW). The mine owners refused to yield on a single point. Theirs was a competitive, unstable business. With so many companies engaged in mining coal, the price of the commodity fluctuated radically and unpredictably. Coal mine operators traditionally avoided long-term commitments to anyone—buyers, shippers, or employees.

Most of the operators were entrepreneurs of the old hard-nosed school. Their property was their property, and that was that; they would tolerate no interference in how they used it, least of all by grimy employees. George F. Baer, the spokesman for the operators and more pious than prudent, stirred up a furious public reaction when he told a journalist that he would never deal with the UMW because God had entrusted him with his mines.

By contrast, union leader John Mitchell was depicted in the progressive press as a moderate, modest, and likable man. Roosevelt, keenly sensitive to public opinion, knew where the applause was to be had. Moreover, Mitchell was an antisocialist and constantly engaged in a fight with the union's large socialist minority for control of the UMW. Roosevelt did not mind giving Mitchell a boost in his factional battle by helping him in the strike. In October, the president let it be known that if the strike dragged on into the winter, he might use federal troops to open the mines. Knowing that the Rough Rider was capable of so drastic (and dramatic) an action and knowing it would be popular among people with no heat in their homes, the ubiquitous

---

Church and State

Beginning in 1864, the motto "In God We Trust," from the "Star-Spangled Banner," was inscribed on most American coins. In 1907, thinking that this represented an unconstitutional entanglement of religion and government and that money was a tawdry place for a religious sentiment, Theodore Roosevelt ordered the motto removed. After a rare public outcry against the popular president, Congress reversed his order, and, in his final year in office, Roosevelt let the issue die.

In 1955, "In God We Trust" was added to American paper currency and declared the national motto. During the 1970s, a series of protests akin to Roosevelt's in 1907 took the issue to the Supreme Court. In 1983, Justice William Brennan, who usually took the broadest view in opposing the mixing of religion and government, approved the motto on the grounds that the words "have lost any true religious significance."

▲ *During the miners' strike of 1902, coal was so scarce and expensive in some areas that people scavenged for enough to cook their meals. Here they are fishing it from waters near docks where coal barges were moored. Roosevelt rightly anticipated a major crisis if the strike continued into the winter.*

Morgan pressured the mine owners to go to Washington and work out a settlement. Coal mine owners did not buck J. P. Morgan. They went.

The result was a compromise that rather favored the owners. The miners got a 10 percent raise and a nine-hour day. The operators were not required to recognize the UMW as the agent of the workers. (Baer refused even to meet face to face with Mitchell.) Nonetheless, the miners were elated, not to mention people who needed coal to ward off winter's cold. The big winner, as in most of his chosen battles, was Theodore Roosevelt. He had forced powerful businessmen to accommodate him so that workers had a "square deal."

Teddy's Great Victory

By 1904, T.R. was basking in adulation. He was unanimously nominated and presented with a large campaign chest. The Democrats, hoping to capitalize on the grumbling of some conservative Republicans, did an about-face from the party's populist agrarianism of 1896 and 1900. They nominated a Wall Street lawyer and judge with impeccable social credentials but also a record of sympathy for labor, Alton B. Parker. The urbane, colorless Parker was the antithesis of William Jennings Bryan and, Democratic bosses hoped, a foil to the histrionic Roosevelt.

Parker was stodgy, but even the second most colorful politician in the country would have looked like a cardboard cutout next to Roosevelt. Not even Parker's Wall Street friends

voted for him. If they disliked T.R.'s antitrust adventures, they recognized that Roosevelt espoused an anti-inflationary money policy and did not molest the high tariff, both of which were of more importance to big business than courtroom spats. J. P. Morgan, although recently stung in the Northern Securities case, donated $150,000 to Roosevelt's campaign.

The president won a lopsided 57.4 percent of the vote. His 336 to 140 electoral sweep was the largest since Grant's in 1872. Building on the coalition of money and respectability that was put together by McKinley and Hanna in 1896, Roosevelt enlarged the Republican majority by appealing to middle-class progressives who would have been uncomfortable with any candidate the party bosses selected.

THE PRESIDENT AS REFORMER

There was one disturbing figure in the election returns: a remarkable showing of the Socialist party candidate, Eugene V. Debs. His 400,000 votes amounted to only 3 percent of the total but represented a fourfold increase over his vote in 1900. Roosevelt did not like it. Increasingly after 1904, he seized every opportunity—and created a few—to denounce anticapitalist radicals.

His most gratuitous attack followed on the arrest and illegal extradition late in 1905 of Charles Moyer and Big Bill Haywood, the socialist leaders of the militant Western Federation of Miners. Charged with murder in Idaho of a former governor of the state, the two were, in effect, kidnapped by authorities in Denver, Colorado, and taken across state lines. It was, therefore, a federal matter, but Roosevelt shrugged it off because, he said, the two were "undesirable citizens." Haywood's lawyer, Clarence Darrow, justifiably complained that with the president of the United States making such statements, a fair trial was not likely. (Nevertheless, both men were acquitted.)

At the same time he assailed the socialists, Roosevelt set out to co-opt them by unleashing a whirlwind of reform.

The Railroads Derailed

As they had been for 30 years, the railroads were a focus of popular resentment. The arrogance of their directors and the vital role of transportation in the national economy preoccupied progressives at every level of government. Prodded by regional leaders, most notably Senator La Follette, Roosevelt plunged into a long, nasty struggle with the railroad companies. In 1906, he won passage of the Hepburn Act. This law authorized the Interstate Commerce Commission to set maximum rates that railroads might charge their customers and forbade railroads to pay rebates to big shippers.

Rebates were already forbidden, but the prohibition had not been effectively enforced. The Hepburn Act gave the Interstate Commerce Commission some teeth. More than any of Roosevelt's previous actions, the Hepburn Act blasted the railroads' traditional immunity from government interference.

Also in 1906, Congress passed an act that held railroads liable to employees who suffered injuries on the job. By European standards, it was a mild compensation law, but in the United States, it marked a sharp break with precedent, which held employees responsible for most of their injuries.

Purer Food

Affecting more people were the Pure Food and Drug Act and the Meat Inspection Act, both signed in 1906. The former forbade adulteration of foods (by large processors), enforced stringent sanitary standards, and put the lid on the

---

American Essence

Coca-Cola, which William Allen White called "the sublimated essence of all that America stands for," had its beginning as a kind of health food. An Atlanta druggist concocted it in 1886 as an alternative to alcohol. Within a year, a pious Methodist named Asa G. Candler purchased all rights to "Coke" for $2,300 and sold it as a "brain tonic," promoting its kick. Indeed, until 1902, Coke was made with coca leaves and may have been slightly addictive; southerners called it "dope" for decades. Candler's advertising was certainly addictive. By 1908, the Coca-Cola Company had plastered 2.5 million square feet of billboard and walls with posters. By 1911, more than a million dollars a year was spent on promoting the elixir.

---

patent medicine business, a freewheeling industry of hucksters who marketed addictive and sometimes dangerous drugs as "feel-good" cure-alls.

By requiring food processors to label their products with all ingredients used in making them and by providing hefty penalties for violators, the Pure Food and Drug Act eliminated sometimes toxic preservatives and fillers from canned and bottled foodstuffs, which were an ever increasing part of the American diet. The Meat Inspection Act provided for federal inspection of meatpacking plants to eliminate the abuses that Upton Sinclair detailed gruesomely in *The Jungle*.

Big meat packers like Armour, Swift, Wilson, and Cudahy grumbled about the federal inspectors, who, notebooks in hand, puttered around their factories. But, in time, they realized that meat inspection worked in their favor and to the detriment of the smaller regional slaughterhouses with which they competed. With their greater resources, the big meat packers were easily able to comply with the federal standards. Many smaller companies, able to stay in business only by slashing costs at every turn, found the expense of sanitation in an inherently dirty business to be beyond their means.

The big packers made advertising hay of the inspection stamps on their products—the government endorsed them! Small companies closed their doors or restricted their sales to the states in which they were located. (Like all federal programs, meat inspection applied only to firms involved in interstate commerce.)

War on Drugs

Proportionately, there may have been more drug addicts in the United States at the beginning of the twentieth century than there are today. Some were frankly hooked on opium or morphine and had minimal difficulty meeting their needs at unregulated pharmacies. Others—perhaps 300,000 people—were unknowingly (or unadmittedly) addicted to various patent medicines advertising themselves as cure-alls. Concoctions with names such as Vin Mariani and Mrs. Winslow's Soothing Syrup were laced with cocaine. Even Lydia Pinkham's Vegetable Compound, decorously packaged and aimed in fine print at ladies suffering from "female complaints," was a strong alcoholic elixir laced liberally with opiates. All over the country, thousands of nice middle-aged ladies sat in stuffed chairs in a stupor, some, no doubt, reading pamphlets from the Women's Christian Temperance Union.

The Pure Food and Drug Act of 1906, which restricted the use of cocaine, cannabis, opiates, and alcohol in over-the-counter medicines, and required labeling of ingredients, undercut this dubious business. Soft drink companies were also affected. Some, including the gigantic Coca-Cola Company of Atlanta, used a by-product of cocaine processing in their beverages to give it a "kick." Coca-Cola had introduced caffeine as its stimulant as early as 1902 but, with the passage of federal drug legislation in 1906, was able to advertise its "purity."

Natural Resources in Jeopardy

Theodore Roosevelt and his progressive allies were not always far seeing. Many of their reforms were the fruit of passionate impulse or of playing to the whims of their constituents. In their campaign to conserve natural resources, however, they looked to the distant future and created monuments for which they are rightfully honored.

A lifelong outdoorsman, Roosevelt loved camping, riding, hiking, climbing, and hunting. As a historian, he was more sensitive than most of his contemporaries to the role of the wilderness in forging the American character. He actively sought and gained the friendship of John Muir, the adopted Californian who founded the Sierra Club in 1892. Muir's interest in nature was aesthetic, cultural, and spiritual. He wanted to protect from development such magnificent natural wonders as Yosemite Valley, which he helped to establish as a national park in 1890. Roosevelt shared his sentiments, to a degree. As president, he created a number of national parks and national monuments.

Muir was, properly speaking, a preservationist. The motives of conservationists like T.R.'s tennis partner and America's first trained forester, Gifford Pinchot of Pennsylvania,

▲ *Theodore Roosevelt and America's leading preservationist, John Muir, in Yosemite National Park. Roosevelt wanted to preserve both natural wonders and resources from rapacious exploitation.*

Progressive Legacy

The halt that the progressives called to the unmonitored, unregulated exploitation of natural resources has borne fruit of unmistakable measure. In terms of wildlife population, for example, in 1900, Virginia, or white-tailed, deer numbered about 500,000; in 1992, 18.5 million. About 650,000 wild turkeys survived in 1900; in 1992, there were 4 million. In 1907, the government counted some 41,000 elk, or wapiti, in the United States; in 1992, there were 772,000.

were different from those of the Sierra Club. "Wilderness is a waste," Pinchot said. His concern was the protection of forests and other natural resources from rapacious exploiters interested only in short-term profits. He wanted to ensure that future generations of Americans would have nonrenewable natural resources such as minerals, coal, and oil to draw on, and the continued enjoyment of renewable but destructible resources like forests, grasslands, and water for drinking and generating power. In December 1907, Roosevelt told Congress, "To waste, to destroy, our natural resources, to skin and exhaust the land instead of using it so as to increase its usefulness, will result in undermining in the days of our children the very prosperity which we ought by right to hand down to them amplified and developed."

Pinchot and Roosevelt had good reason to worry about the nation's natural resources. Lumbermen in the Great Lakes states had already mowed down forests once thought endless, moved on, and left the land behind them to go to scrub. Western ranchers put too many cattle on grasslands, turning them into deserts. Coal and phosphate mining companies and drillers for oil thought in terms of next year's profit sheet and never of the fact that, in a century, the United States might run out of these vital resources because of their greed. Virtually no one in extractive industries worried that they were destroying watersheds vital to urban water supplies, polluting rivers, and sending good soil into the sea.

Americans had always been reckless with the land, none more so than the pioneers of legend. But there was a big difference between what a few frontiersmen could do to it with axes and oxen-drawn plows, and the potential for destruction of irresponsible million-dollar corporations.

Conservation

The National Forest Reserve, today's National Forests, dates from 1891, when Congress empowered the president to withhold forests in the public domain from private ownership, then licensing and monitoring logging there. Over the first 10 years of the law, Presidents Harrison, Cleveland, and McKinley declared 46 million acres of virgin woodland off limits to loggers without government permission.

Enforcement was lax until, prodded by Pinchot, Roosevelt began to prosecute timber pirates who raided public lands and cattlemen who abused government-owned

Changing Sexual Mores

"No tendency is quite so strong in human nature," William Howard Taft observed, "as the desire to lay down rules of conduct for other people." He may have been thinking of the type of progressive who believed that government could eliminate morally undesirable behavior by passing laws against it. Prohibitionists were a mixed lot, but, in the end, they all desired that no one should be able to sit down and have a drink.

The "purity movement" was contemporary with the prohibition movement. Its targeted evil was sexual immorality. Like prohibitionism, its origins were religious and suasionist. Purity societies combated illicit sex, from fornication to prostitution, by brother's-keeper-type persuasion of sinners (and potential sinners) to live cleanly. They discussed sex openly (which was taboo in polite society) and condemned the "double standard" that held women to strict chastity while overlooking, within limits, illicit male sexual activity. Some purity organizations "rescued" and reformed prostitutes, whom they saw as the principal, sexual outlet for men who lacked restraint.

When they were discouraged by the ineffectiveness of persuasion, purity crusaders, like the prohibitionists, turned to legislation to win their battle. In the Progressive Era, government seemed to be the answer to every social problem. The prohibitionists got their constitutional amendment in 1919. The purity movement got the Mann Act in 1911.

Fornication and adultery were obviously not federal business. Nor was prostitution, which the purity people regarded as the institutional heart of sexual immorality. States and cities had antiprostitution laws, but most authorities left brothels, and even streetwalkers, alone unless they were a "public nuisance." Spotty local enforcement of antiprostitution laws turned the purity crusaders, like prohibitionists and progressives generally, to the federal government. They found the grounds to strike at prostitution nationally in the Constitution's interstate commerce clause. The Mann Act (or "White Slave Traffic Act") of 1911 made it a federal crime to "transport, or cause to be transported, or aid or assist in obtaining transportation for . . . in interstate or foreign commerce . . . any woman or girl for the purpose of prostitution or debauchery, or for any other immoral purpose."

The bill sailed through Congress because the nation was in the midst of a minor hysteria (a progressive specialty) over "white slavery." "White slaves" were girls and women who were lured into prostitution by being seduced or raped while drunk or drugged (and therefore "ruined"), after which they were held captive—enslaved—in brothels. No doubt, such things happened. By 1910, however, muckrakers and politicians desperate to find a new evil to battle had created the image of white slavery as a pervasive national phenomenon. Dozens of "white slave narratives," patterned on the old slave and captive nun narratives, were published. At least six movies had white slavery as their theme. In the four years after 1910, the *Reader's Guide* listed 156 magazine articles on the subject compared to 36 during the 20 years preceding 1910. A United States attorney who was a friend of Congressman James R. Mann, wrote that "the white slave traffic is a system operated by a syndicate . . . with 'clearing houses' or 'distributing centers' in nearly all the big cities."

It was all nonsense, and when no sinister syndicate could be located, federal authorities began using the Mann Act to arrest men who had crossed a state line with willing women, their girlfriends, having sexual relations with no commercial aspect. In *Caminetti v. the U.S.* (1917), the Supreme Court approved the prosecution of interstate noncommercial sex because the Mann Act had criminalized not just prostitution, but also "other immoral purposes," when a state line was crossed. The Prohibition Era was also a boom time for convictions and imprisonment of men caught, in effect, going with their sexual partners from Philadelphia to Atlantic City for the weekend.

If the Mann Act was not about white slavery or even, primarily, about prostitution, what was it about?

It was a reflection of the same social anxieties that gave the country Prohibition, the red scare, immigration restriction, and the anti-Catholic, anti-Semitic Ku Klux Klan: the perception that undesirable new immigrants and big cities were destroying old American values, in this case, sexual morals. There was a powerful anti-immigrant, particularly anti-Semitic component in the white slavery scare. Destitute and ignorant immigrant girls were a major target of the white slavers; once decent and God-fearing young American women, working and living in the cities without parental supervision, were another. Living an "unnatural" life, they were susceptible to "ruination," which led to prostitution. Jane Addams wrote, "Many a working girl at the end of a day is so hysterical and overwrought that her mental balance is plainly disturbed." The girls "dated" rather than "courted," as they would have done back home. "The danger begins," wrote Florence Dedrick in 1909, "the moment a girl leaves the protection of Home and Mother."

Progressive Era Americans believed that casual unmarried sex, however voluntary on the lady's part, was a step toward prostitution, just as a glass of beer was a step toward falling-down drunkenness. In fact, the definition of *prostitution* as the sale of sexual services ("promiscuous inchastity for gain" in the language of the day) had not been universally accepted. Iowa defined a prostitute as a woman who "indiscriminately" practiced sexual intercourse that she "invites or solicits by word or act"— what we would call "flirtation." Alabama defined the word as "a woman given to indiscriminate lewdness." A widely used *Webster's* defined prostitution as "the act or practice of offering the body to an indiscriminate intercourse with men."

The common thread was not money changing hands—that was not even there—but the fact that the woman's sexual activity was "indiscriminate," casual. Any "loose" woman was a prostitute. Women defined today as prostitutes were specified "professional prostitutes." The slang for a working girl who went out to dinner or a few drinks with a date and had sex was "charity girl," a prostitute who was free. The notion that a woman had sex more or less casually because she herself enjoyed it was impossible to digest. The Mann Act boyfriend-girlfriend prosecutions of the 1910s and 1920s were yet another reflection of values in flux and the anxieties the changes caused.

grasslands. Within a few years, Roosevelt added 125 million acres to the national forests and reserved for future use 68 million acres of coal deposits, almost 5 million acres of phosphate beds (vital to production of munitions), a number of oil fields, and 2,565 sites suitable for the construction of dams for irrigation and generation of electrical power.

Progressives cheered. Some of the multiple uses to which the national forests were dedicated—recreation and preservation—won the praise of preservationists. Others—flood control, irrigation, and development of hydroelectric power—pleased social planners. The principle of sustained yield, managing forests to ensure an adequate supply of lumber indefinitely, even won over the big lumber companies with their huge capital investments and encouraged them to employ foresters on the lands they owned.

In the West, however, an angry opposition developed. Cattlemen, clear-cut loggers, and private power companies banded together in an anticonservation movement that, in 1907, succeeded in attaching a rider to an agricultural appropriations bill that passed Congress. It forbade the president to create any additional national forests in six western states. Roosevelt had no choice but to sign the bill; the Department of Agriculture could not have functioned otherwise. But he had one last go at what he called the "predatory interests." Before he wrote his name on the bill, he reserved 17 million acres of forest land in the interdicted states.

The Reformer's Retirement

In 1908, Roosevelt called for a comprehensive program that included federal investigation of major labor disputes and close regulation of the stock market and businesses engaged in interstate commerce. Congress sidestepped virtually all of his proposals because he was a "lame duck." It was a presidential election year, and, four years earlier, celebrating the victory of 1904, Roosevelt impulsively declared that "a wise custom which limits the President to two terms regards the substance and not the form, and under no circumstances will I be a candidate for or accept another nomination." Having served three and a half years of McKinley's term, Roosevelt had defined himself as a two-term president.

In 1908, he almost certainly regretted his pledge. Except perhaps for Coolidge and Reagan, Theodore Roosevelt relished being president, and flourished in the job, more than anyone before or since. Unlike Coolidge and Reagan, who treated the office as a personal homage, Roosevelt was a worker. He was not yet 50 years of age in 1908 and was as popular as ever. He would undoubtedly have won reelection had he been willing to forget his promise not to run. Politicians have forgotten much more important statements.

But he kept his word and settled for handpicking his successor, which no president had been able to do since Andrew Jackson. That William Howard Taft, then secretary of war, was not the man whom either conservative or progressive Republicans would have chosen indicates just how high Roosevelt was flying.

A CONSERVATIVE PRESIDENT IN A PROGRESSIVE ERA

Taft would not have been nominated without Roosevelt's blessing. He would not have dreamed of running for president. Regularly in his correspondence, he dashed off the exclamation, "I hate politics!" and he meant it. He was a lifelong functionary, not a politician. He disliked public speaking. He was utterly unable to remember names. His only elective post was as a judge in Ohio. Taft remembered that job as the most congenial he ever held, for his temperament was judicial. Slow thinking, sober, cautious, and reflective, Taft worked well in a study, but he was no showman.

Amid a people who savored Roosevelt's gymnastic style, Taft's very body militated against him. He weighed over 300 pounds and was truly at ease only when he settled into a specially reinforced swivel chair behind a desk or sank into an overstuffed couch with other easygoing men. He slept a lot. So did Coolidge, but only in bed. Taft once fell asleep in an open car in a motorcade in his honor. His single form of exercise, golf, did not help his image: batting a little white ball around an oversized lawn was considered a sissy's game in the early twentieth century. Taft's fondness for the game identified him with plutocrats like John D. Rockefeller, another avid golfer.

Taft was no reactionary. He had loyally supported Roosevelt's reforms, and Roosevelt calculated that he, more than anyone else, would carry out the "square deal" policy. So did other progressives. They supported him, as did the conservative wing of the Republican party. Anyone was preferable to the man whom they had begun to refer to privately as the "mad messiah."

The Election of 1908

The election was an anticlimax. The Democrats returned to William Jennings Bryan as their candidate, but the thrill was long gone. The "Boy Orator of the Platte" was worn beyond his years. He had grown jowls and a paunch as penance for his lifelong vulnerability to the deadly sin of gluttony, and he was rapidly losing his hair.

Moreover, his once worshipful followers, the staple farmers of the Midwest, were no longer struggling to survive. They were prospering, beginning to dress like the townsmen they had jostled in 1896 and to build substantial homes. Even the issue of 1900, imperialism, was dead. Taft, who served as American governor of the Philippines, could claim credit for having transformed the anti-American Filipinos, whom he called his "little brown brothers," into a placid and apparently content colonial population. Puerto Rico was quieter. Hawaiians did the hula for increasing numbers of American tourists. Central America simmered, but the specter of American power kept the lid on it. Thousands of West Indians were digging their way across Panama under American direction—thrilling.

The Smithsonian Institution

▲ *William Howard Taft. Taft did not want to be president. He detested much of what he had to do as president. And yet, not only did he agree to run in 1908 at Teddy Roosevelt's behest, but he ran for reelection against Roosevelt in 1912.*

The upshot was that a lethargic Bryan won a smaller percentage of the popular vote than in either of his previous tries. The Socialist party was also disappointed in the results. Bubbling with optimism at the start of the campaign, they chartered a private train, the "Red Special," on which candidate Debs crisscrossed the country. The crowds were big and enthusiastic. But Debs's vote was only 16,000 higher than in 1904 and represented a smaller percentage of the total. It appeared that Roosevelt's tactic of undercutting the socialist threat with a comprehensive reform program had worked.

Taft's Blunders

Taft lacked both the political savvy and the inclination to exploit progressive zeal. For example, even though he initiated 90 antitrust suits during his four years as president, twice as many as Roosevelt launched in seven and a half years, no one complimented him as a trustbuster. Indeed, Taft managed to alienate the progressives immediately after taking office when he stumbled over an obstacle that Roosevelt had danced nimbly around: the tariff.

In 1909, duties on imports were high, set at an average 46.5 percent of their value by the Dingley tariff of 1897. Republican conservatives insisted that the rate was necessary in order to protect the jobs of American factory workers and to encourage investment in industry. Midwestern progressive Republicans and Democrats disagreed. They believed that American industry was strong enough to stand up to European manufacturers in a fair competition. To maintain the Dingley rates was to subsidize excessive corporate profits by allowing manufacturers to set their prices inordinately high. Farmers were twice stung because the European nations, except Great Britain, retaliated against the Dingley tariff by levying high duties on American agricultural products.

Roosevelt had let the Republican old guard have their way on the tariff, placating (or distracting) progressives by pounding other tubs. By 1909, evasion was no longer possible, and Taft called Congress into special session for the purpose of tariff revision. The House of Representatives drafted a reasonable reduction of rates in the Payne Bill. In the Senate, however, Nelson Aldrich of Rhode Island, a trusty ally of industrial capitalists, engineered 800 amendments to what became the Payne-Aldrich Act. On most important commodities, the final rate was higher than under the Dingley tariff.

Taft was in a bit of a bind. Politically, he was committed to a lower tariff. Personally, however, he was more comfortable with the likes of Aldrich and the five corporate lawyers in his cabinet than with low-tariff congressmen, who were Democrats or excitable Republican progressives like La Follette and Jonathan Dolliver of Iowa. After equivocating, Taft worked out what he thought was a compromise in the Roosevelt tradition. The conservatives got their high tariff but agreed to a 2 percent corporate income tax and a constitutional amendment that legalized a personal income tax (which was ratified in 1913 as the Sixteenth Amendment). Instead of emphasizing the progressive aspects of the arrangement, as Roosevelt would have done, Taft described the Payne-Aldrich Act as "the best tariff that the Republican party ever passed."

The Insurgents

This angered the midwestern Republican progressives, especially after Taft came out in favor of a trade treaty with Canada that threatened to dump Canadian crops on the American market. But they broke openly with the new president only when he sided with the reactionary Speaker of the House of Representatives, Joseph G. Cannon of Illinois, against them.

"Uncle Joe" Cannon offended the progressive Republicans on several counts. He was so inflexibly conservative as to be a stereotype. As Speaker of the House and chairman of the House Rules Committee, he put progressives on unimportant committees and loaded the meaningful ones with old-guard friends. Finally, whereas the progressives inclined to be highly moralistic, even prudish, Uncle Joe was a crusty old tobacco chewer, a hard drinker who was not infrequently drunk, and a champion foul mouth.

Taft also found Cannon's company unpleasant. However, the president believed in party loyalty, and when a number of midwestern Republican progressives, calling themselves "Insurgents," voted with Democrats to strip Cannon of his near-dictatorial power, Taft joined with the

Speaker to deny the Insurgents access to party money in the midterm election of 1910. The result was a Democratic victory; Cannon was out of the speakership, never to return.

The Conquering Hero

It is impossible to say how Theodore Roosevelt would have handled the quarrel between Cannon and the Insurgents. But he surely would not have done what Taft did in a dispute between Secretary of the Interior Richard A. Ballinger and Chief Forester Gifford Pinchot.

When Ballinger released to developers a number of hydroelectric sites that Pinchot had persuaded Roosevelt to reserve, Pinchot protested to Taft and won the president's grudging support. However, when Pinchot leaked his evidence against Ballinger to *Collier's* magazine, which was still in the muckraking business, Taft fired him. This may have been exactly what Pinchot wanted. He acted as if he were prepared, almost immediately booking passage to Italy, where his friend and patron, former president Roosevelt, was vacationing. Pinchot brought with him an indictment of "Big Bill" Taft as a traitor to the cause of reform.

Roosevelt was having a great time on his extended world tour. He left the country shortly after Taft's inauguration to give his successor an opportunity to function outside his aura. First, Roosevelt traveled to East Africa, where he shot a bloody swath through the still abundant big game of Kenya and Tanganyika (Tanzania). He bagged over 3,000 animals, many of which he had stuffed to give his home at Oyster Bay, Long Island, that certain something.

Then he went to Europe to bask in an adulation that was scarcely less fierce than he enjoyed at home. He hobnobbed with aristocrats and politicians, who thought of him as the ultimate American, a twentieth-century Ben Franklin. Roosevelt topped off his yearlong junket by representing the United States at the funeral of King Edward VII, strutting and shining in the largest collection of royalty ever assembled in one place.

And yet, something was missing. Roosevelt longed for the hurly-burly of politics, and he was all too willing to believe Pinchot. When he returned to the United States in June 1910, he exchanged only the curtest greetings with the president. He spoke widely on behalf of Republican congressional candidates, at first playing down the split between regulars and Insurgents. Then, at Osawatomie, Kansas, in September 1910, Roosevelt proclaimed what he called the "New Nationalism," a comprehensive program for further reform. To the Republican old guard, it was frighteningly radical.

Roosevelt called for women's suffrage, a federal minimum wage for women workers, abolition of child labor, strict limitations on the power of courts to issue injunctions in labor disputes, and a national social insurance scheme much like the Social Security system of today. He struck directly at Taft's policies by demanding a commission that would set tariff rates "scientifically" rather than according to political pressures. He supported the progressive initiative, recall, and referendum, including a new twist—a referendum on some judges' decisions. This was enough in itself to aggravate the juridical Taft, but in demanding a national presidential primary law under which the people, and not professional politicians, would make party nominations, Roosevelt also hinted that he was interested in running for the presidency again.

Challengers of Taft

Taft was not the only politician concerned about Roosevelt's presidential plans. Robert La Follette was preparing to seek the Republican presidential nomination in 1912 and believed he had a chance to defeat Taft (that is, if Roosevelt did not also run). As little as he liked doing it, La Follette sent mutual friends to ask Roosevelt his intentions, implying that he would drop out if Roosevelt was running. Roosevelt responded that he was not interested in the White House. In January, La Follette organized the Progressive Republican League to promote his candidacy.

Most progressive Republicans supported La Follette, including Roosevelt backers who not so secretly hoped that their real hero would change his mind. In fact, Roosevelt was itching to run. When, in March 1912, La Follette collapsed from exhaustion while making a speech, Roosevelt announced with unseemly haste, "My hat is in the ring."

La Follette was not seriously ill, and he never forgave T.R. for having, as he believed, used him as a stalking-horse. But Fighting Bob was no match for the old master when it came to stirring up party activists, and his campaign fell apart. Roosevelt swept most of the 13 state primary elections, winning 278 convention delegates to Taft's 48 and La Follette's 36. If La Follette was beaten, however, the suddenly aroused Taft was not, and he had a powerful weapon in his arsenal.

Taft controlled the party organization. As president, he appointed people to thousands of government jobs, wedding

▲ *Known as the "trustbuster" when he was president, as a presidential candidate in 1912, Theodore Roosevelt distinguished between good (regulated) trusts and bad trusts. His shooting rampage in East Africa was well known; thus the cartoonist's image.*

The Granger Collection, New York

their careers to his own success. In the Republican party, the power of patronage was particularly important in the southern states, where the party consisted of little more than professional officeholders, including blacks, who made their living as postmasters, customs collectors, agricultural agents, and the like. Although the Republicans won few congressional seats and fewer electoral votes in the South, a substantial bloc of delegates to Republican conventions spoke with a Dixie drawl. They were in Taft's pocket. Along with northern and western party regulars, they outnumbered the delegates Roosevelt won in the primaries.

When the convention voted on whether Taft or Roosevelt would be awarded 254 disputed seats, Taft delegates won 235 of them. Roosevelt's supporters shouted "Fraud!" and walked out. They formed the Progressive party, or, as it was nicknamed for the battle with the Republican elephant and the Democratic donkey, the Bull Moose party. (In a backhanded reference to La Follette's allegedly poor health and Taft's obesity, Roosevelt had said that he was "as strong as a bull moose.")

DEMOCRATIC PARTY PROGRESSIVISM

In one piece, the Republican party was unambivalently the nation's majority party, as four successive presidential elections had demonstrated. Split in two, however, the GOP was vulnerable; the Democrats smelled victory. When the Dem-

ocratic convention assembled in Baltimore, there was an abundance of would-be nominees ready to serve their party. As at the Republican convention, but for a rather different reason, the key to winning the party's presidential nomination lay in the southern state delegations.

Because the South was solid in delivering electoral votes to the Democratic column, it held a virtual veto power over the nomination. The old two-thirds rule, so important in shaping the Democratic party before the Civil War, was reinstituted after it. In order to be nominated, a Democrat needed the vote of two-thirds of the delegates. No one could approach that total if the southern delegates opposed him as a bloc. A candidate with the southern delegates solidly behind him had a handsome head start on the nomination.

Democratic Hopefuls

In 1912, none of the leading candidates was offensive to the South, and each had southern supporters. William Jennings Bryan was still popular with southerners and, incredibly, he was interested. As a three-time loser, however, Bryan was not very attractive. His only hope was a deadlocked convention when he might be selected as a compromise candidate.

Oscar Underwood of Alabama was another minor hopeful; he commanded the support of the southern Bourbon conservatives, but for that reason, he was unacceptable to southern progressives, who might more accurately be described as racist populists. Some progressives supported Judson Harmon of Ohio. Others backed Champ Clark, the "Old Hound Dawg" of Missouri, which was as much a southern as a western state. In fact, Clark went into the convention confident of winning. The man who left it a winner, however, was New Jersey governor Woodrow Wilson, nominated on the forty-sixth ballot.

A Moral, Unbending Man

Wilson was a southerner; he was born in Virginia and practiced law in Georgia as a young man. He abandoned the law, however, earned a Ph.D. degree, and ended up as a professor of political science at Princeton University. In 1902, he was named president of Princeton, the first nonminister to hold that post at the Presbyterian school.

Horseplay

Stern and ministerial in his public persona, Woodrow Wilson the private man was rather the opposite. On the morning after marrying his second wife in 1915, he was seen in a White House corridor doing a dance and singing, "Oh, you beautiful doll." His daughters by his first wife, Margaret, Jessie, and Eleanor, showed no signs of moralistic browbeating. One of their amusements in the White House was to join tourists who were being shown around by guides and make loud remarks about the homeliness and vulgarity of the president's daughters (themselves).

Wilson had a lot of the Presbyterian clergyman in him. His father and both grandfathers had been ministers, as was his wife's father. He was raised to observe an unbending Calvinist morality and to have a sensitivity to the struggle between good and evil in the world. With his family and a few friends, Wilson was fun-loving and playful, a fan of the cinema, and liable to erupt in horseplay with his daughters, who adored him. Publicly, he was formal, sometimes icy.

Wilson's meteoric rise in politics was almost accidental. In 1910, he was merely an honored educator. He had indeed transformed Princeton from an intellectually lazy finishing school where rich young men made social contacts, into an institution that commanded respect. But Wilson's stubbornness caught up with him in the most trivial of matters. He tried to close down Princeton's eating clubs, exclusive student associations much like fraternities, and clashed with trustees and alumni, "old boys" dedicated to preserving the clubs.

When he was offered the Democratic nomination for governor of New Jersey, he quit academic life. To everyone's surprise except, perhaps, Wilson's (he attributed election victories to God's will), he won the governorship; the upset made him a national figure overnight. He was less social reformer than honest-government progressive, and he set about cleaning up the state bureaucracy and Democratic party. Like Teddy Roosevelt in New York a decade earlier, Wilson was soon at odds with the state party bosses. They were delighted when he decided to seek the presidency. Ironically—given what was to follow—he offered himself as a safe and sane middle-of-the road alternative to Bryan and Champ Clark, a conservative.

The Campaign of 1912

In fact, Wilson's "New Freedom," as he called his program, was a decidedly less ambitious blueprint for reform than Roosevelt's New Nationalism was. Wilson emphasized states' rights to the extent that he opposed the Progressive party's comprehensive social program as strongly as Taft did. He considered Roosevelt's proposals to augur a dangerous expansion of government powers.

Wilson and Roosevelt differed even more sharply on the question of trusts. Roosevelt had concluded that consolidation, even monopoly, was inevitable in a modern industrial society and that the federal government should supervise, or even direct, the operations of big corporations in the public interest. Wilson condemned this vision as "a partnership between the government and the trusts." Wilson believed that competition in business was still possible. In his view, the government's task was to play watchdog over business, ensuring and restoring free competition by breaking up the trusts. In 1912, he opposed the huge, permanent government apparatus that Roosevelt endorsed.

With the Republican organization in tatters and Taft practically dropping out of the campaign, it would have been difficult for Wilson to lose the election. Nevertheless, he campaigned tirelessly and skillfully. Articulate, as a college professor is supposed to be, Wilson was also exciting, as not all professors are. Lifelong dreams of winning public office

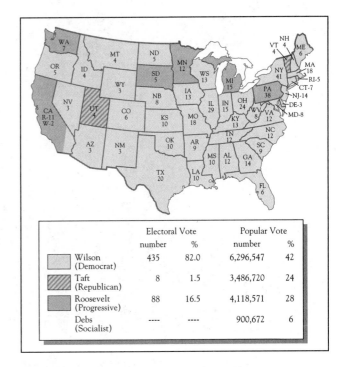

MAP 36:1 Presidential Election, 1912 Only 4 of 10 voters chose the Democrat Wilson, but the Republican party split down the middle, giving Wilson a sweep of the electoral college.

flowered in eloquent speeches that left no doubt that the schoolmaster was a leader.

Wilson won only 41.9 percent of the popular vote but a landslide in the electoral college: 435 votes to Roosevelt's 88 and Taft's 8. Eugene V. Debs, making his fourth race as the Socialist party nominee, won 900,000 votes, 6 percent of the total. The big jump after four years of a conservative president seemed to indicate that it was necessary to reform in order to stifle the socialist challenge. Taft, the only conservative candidate, won but 23.2 percent of the total vote.

Tariffs and Taxes

Roosevelt had usually gotten his way by outflanking Congress, interpreting the president's constitutional powers in the broadest possible terms. Taft deferred to congressional leaders, ultimately collapsing before the pushiest of them. Wilson's style was to act as a kind of prime minister. He was not a member of Congress as the Canadian prime minister is a member of Parliament, but he could and did address Congress personally as though he were. He was the first president to appear personally before Congress since John Adams.

Wilson's brief address was aimed less at persuading congressmen than at inspiring their constituents to put the heat on them, and it worked. A number of Democratic senators who were dragging their feet on tariff revision fell into line. The Underwood-Simmons tariff reduced the Payne-Aldrich rates by 15 percent and put on the free list several commodities that were controlled by trusts—iron, steel, woolens, and farm machinery—thus lowering prices on them.

▲ *That Wilson was more an honest-government progressive than a reformer was well understood by this admiring cartoonist.*

The lower tariff reduced revenue for the government. To make up the losses, Wilson sponsored both a corporate and a personal income tax. It was not high by present standards. People who earned less than $4,000 a year paid no tax. On annual incomes between $4,000 and $20,000, a tidy sum in 1913, the rate was only 1 percent. People in the highest bracket, $500,000 and up, paid only 7 percent, a fraction of the low brackets today. Nevertheless, by forcing the rich to pay proportionately more toward supporting the government, Wilson's income tax represented a triumph of progressive principles.

Wilson's Cabinet

Wilson designed his cabinet in order to unite the Democratic party. The president never liked William Jennings Bryan, but he named him secretary of state because Bryan still owned the affection of southern and western Democrats.

Other appointments rewarded key components of the party, including the labor movement. The president chose William B. Wilson, a leader in the American Federation of Labor, as secretary of labor. The most valuable member of the cabinet was William G. McAdoo. As secretary of the treasury, he provided the president with excellent advice on banking policy. When McAdoo married Wilson's daughter, he became a kind of heir apparent.

Three confidants did not sit in the cabinet. Joseph Tumulty, a canny Irish politician, served as Wilson's private secretary and reminded the president of the sometimes sordid realities involved in running a political party. Colonel

Edward M. House, a Texas businessman, was a shadowy but not sinister figure. Self-effacing and utterly devoted to the president, House neither desired nor accepted any official position. Instead, he traveled discreetly throughout the United States and abroad, informally conveying the president's views and wants to businessmen and heads of state.

Louis D. Brandeis, a corporate-lawyer-turned-antitrust-progressive, provided Wilson with both economic principles and a social conscience. The father of the New Freedom, Brandeis turned Wilson away from the limitations of the program after 1914 and toward a broader progressivism. In 1916, Wilson rewarded him by naming him to the Supreme Court, on which Brandeis served as one of the best liberal justices of the twentieth century. He was the first justice to consider sociological information along with legal precedent in adjudging the constitutionality of laws.

The New Freedom in Action

Two laws that reflected Brandeis's influence were the Federal Reserve Act of 1913 and the Clayton Antitrust Act of 1914. The first was designed both to bring order to the national banking system and to hobble the power of Wall Street. The law established 12 regional Federal Reserve Banks, which dealt not directly with people but with other banks. The Federal Reserve system was owned by private bankers who were required to deposit 6 percent of their capital in it. However, the president appointed the majority of the directors, who sat in Washington, theoretically putting the government in control of the money supply.

▲ *Washington and Adams addressed Congress in person. The third president, Jefferson, did not. He sent his messages in writing, and every president followed his precedent until Woodrow Wilson in 1913. Since then, every president has followed Wilson's example.*

The greatest power of the Federal Reserve system was (and is) its control of the discount rate—the rate of interest at which the Federal Reserve lends money to other banks for lending to private investors and buyers. By lowering the discount rate, the Federal Reserve could stimulate investment and economic expansion in slow times. By raising the rate, the Federal Reserve could cool down an overactive economy that threatened to blow up in inflation, financial panic, and depression.

The Federal Reserve Act did bring some order to the national banking system. But it did not, as many progressives hoped, tame the great bankers. Indeed, because representatives of the private banks sat on the Federal Reserve Board, the long-term effects of the law were to provide Wall Street with an even more efficient, albeit more accountable, control of national finance.

In 1914, Wilson pushed his antitrust policy through Congress. The Clayton Antitrust Act stipulated that corporations would be fined for unfair practices that threatened competition, forbade interlocking directorates (the same men sitting on the boards of competing companies, thereby allowing competitors to coordinate policies), and declared that officers of corporations would be held personally responsible for offenses committed by their companies. Another bill passed at the same time created the Federal Trade Commission to supervise the activities of trusts. This agency looked more like Roosevelt's New Nationalism than the New Freedom Wilson had called for in 1912.

A Change in Direction

After the congressional elections of 1914, Wilson shifted far more sharply toward the reforms that Teddy Roosevelt promoted. Although the Democrats retained control of both houses, many Bull Moosers returned to their Republican voting habits in 1914 and cut the Democratic margin in the House. It was obvious to both the president and Democratic congressmen that if they were to survive the election of 1916 against a reunified Republican party, they would have to woo these progressive voters.

Consequently, Wilson agreed to support social legislation that he had opposed as late as 1914. He did not like laws that favored any special interest, farmers any more than bankers, but in order to shore up support in the West, he agreed to the Federal Farm Loan Act of 1916, which provided low-cost credit to farmers. Early in his administration, Wilson opposed a child-labor law on constitutional grounds. In 1916, he supported the Keating-Owen Act, which severely restricted the employment of children in most jobs.

The Adamson Act required the interstate railroads to put their workers on an eight-hour day without a reduction in pay. Wilson even moderated his antiblack sentiments, although Washington definitely took on the character of a segregated southern city during his tenure. Despite a lifelong opposition to women's suffrage, the president began to encourage states to enfranchise women and to hint that he supported a constitutional amendment that would guarantee the right nationwide.

By the summer of 1916, Wilson could say with considerable justification that he had pushed progressive reform further than had any of his predecessors. He enacted or supported much of Theodore Roosevelt's program of 1912, as well as his own. By 1916, however, Americans' votes reflected more than their views on domestic issues. They were troubled about their nation's place in a suddenly more complicated world. Simultaneous with the enactment of Wilson's New Freedom and more than a little of Roosevelt's New Nationalism, Europe had tumbled into the bloodiest war in history.

for FURTHER READING

Overviews of the era are Vincent P. DeSantis, *The Shaping of Modern America, 1877–1916,* 1973; Arthur S. Link, *Woodrow Wilson and the Progressive Era,* 1954; George E. Mowry, *The Era of Theodore Roosevelt,* 1958; William L. O'Neill, *The Progressive Years: America Comes of Age,* 1975; and Robert H. Wiebe, *The Search for Order, 1880–1920,* 1967.

Virtually all the books cited in the "For Further Reading" section in Chapter 35 are relevant to this chapter as well. In addition, see D. F. Anderson, *William Howard Taft: A Conservative's Conception of the Presidency,* 1973; John Morton Blum, *Woodrow Wilson and the Politics of Morality,* 1956; P. E. Coletta, *The Presidency of William Howard Taft,* 1973; John A. Garraty, *Woodrow Wilson,* 1956; Lewis L. Gould, *Reform and Regulation: American Politics, 1900–1916,* 1978; Otis L. Graham Jr., *The Great Campaigns: Reform and War in America, 1900–1928,* 1971; Samuel T. Hays, *Conservation and the Gospel of Efficiency: The Progressive Conservation Movement, 1890–1920,* 1959; and the multivolume Arthur S. Link, *Woodrow Wilson,* 1947–1965.

AMERICAN JOURNEY ONLINE AND INFOTRAC COLLEGE EDITION

Visit the source collections at http://ajaccess.wadsworth.com and http://infotrac.thomsonlearning.com, and use the Search function with the following key terms to explore documents, images, audio and video clips, articles, and commentary related to the material in this chapter:

Big Bill Haywood
Clayton Antitrust Act
Eugene V. Debs
John Muir
Meat Inspection Act

Progressivism
Sherman Antitrust Act
Theodore Roosevelt
William Howard Taft

Additional resources, exercises, and Internet links related to this chapter are available on *The American Past* Web site: http://history.wadsworth.com/americanpast7e.

HISTORY ONLINE

Theodore Roosevelt: American Icon
www.npg.si.edu/exh/roosevelt/
Images of the first president to exploit his physical image systematically.

The Evolution of the Conservation Movement
http://memory/loc.gov/ammem/amrrhtml/conshume.html
TR's conservation reforms; multimedia history of conservation between 1850 and 1921.

OVER THERE

The United States and the First World War 1914–1918

The world must be made safe for democracy. Its peace must be planted upon the tested foundations of political liberty. We have no selfish ends to serve. We desire no conquest, no dominion. We seek no indemnities for ourselves, no material compensation for the sacrifices we shall freely make.

President Woodrow Wilson

Good Lord! You're not going to send soldiers over there, are you?

Senator Thomas S. Martin

A FEW DAYS before his inauguration in 1913, Woodrow Wilson was reminded of a difficulty in American relations with Mexico. He thought for a moment and remarked, "It would be the irony of fate if my administration had to deal chiefly with foreign affairs."

Wilson did not fear the challenge. His self-confidence was as sturdy as Theodore Roosevelt's. He once said, "I am sorry for those who disagree with me, because I know they are wrong." But his academic and political interests had been domestic; he had paid little attention to the snarls of international relations. When Woodrow Wilson thought about the rest of the world, he did so more on the basis of assumptions and sentiments than in the context of a coherent vision.

WILSON, THE WORLD, AND MEXICO

Like most Americans, the president was proud that in population and industrial might, the United States ranked with a handful of countries as a great nation. Also like others, he believed that the United States was unique: Insulated by broad oceans, the United States needed no large standing army. Spared that expense, America expended its resources in constructive ways. Founded on an idea rather than because of an accidental inheritance of a common culture and territory, the United States could act toward other countries in accordance with principles rather than out of narrow self-interest.

Moral Diplomacy

Because of his Presbyterian moralism, Wilson had criticized Teddy Roosevelt's gunboat diplomacy as bullying. He pointedly announced that his administration would deal with the weak and turbulent Latin American countries "upon terms of equality and honor." As a progressive who was suspicious of Wall Street, Wilson disapproved of Taft's dollar diplomacy. Shortly after taking office, Wilson canceled government backing of an investment scheme in China because it implied the United States had an obligation to intervene if the investors' profits were threatened. If Wall Street wanted to risk money in China, fine; but they would have to risk it, not expect the government to guarantee it against losses.

Wilson was influenced by the same inclinations to Christian pacifism to which Secretary of State Bryan was strongly committed. Bryan believed that war was justified only in self-defense; if nations seriously discussed their conflicts, they could avoid spilling blood. With Wilson's approval, Bryan negotiated conciliation treaties with 30 nations. The signatories pledged that in the event of a dispute, they would talk for one year before considering war. Bryan believed that during such a "cooling-off" period, virtually every conflict between nations could be resolved without using force.

The Missionary

High ideals. Once in the cockpit, however, Wilson found that applying them was more difficult than flying the recently invented airplane. In part, this was because of the eternal untidiness of reality. In part, it was because Wilson was also the creature of assumptions and prejudices that conflicted with his moral and political principles.

A southerner, Wilson reflexively assumed that the white race was superior to others. He was no redneck apt to join a lynch mob. Wilson was of the southern social class that abhorred the brutality of "white trash." Wilson's attitudes toward African Americans were those of the southern gentleman: kindly and generous but patronizing. He was confident that social segregation and the exclusion of blacks from government were the only ways of maintaining racial peace. The academic world in which he had spent his adult life was permeated with theories and pseudosciences that taught Caucasian superiority. As president, Wilson found it easy to be cordial with nonwhite nations such as Japan and the racially mixed Latin Americans but difficult to think of them as his equals.

His commitment to diplomacy by good example was complicated by a missionary's impulse to prescribe proper behavior. When weaker nations did not willingly emulate American ways of doing things, Wilson could wax arrogant. If other peoples did not recognize what was best for them, the teacher Wilson could reach for the hickory stick. He was not as vulgar as Theodore Roosevelt, but he was not as unlike Roosevelt as both men thought.

So Wilson acquiesced in a California state law that insulted racially sensitive Japan by denying Japanese immigrants the right to own land. In 1915, Wilson ordered the marines into black Haiti when chaotic conditions threatened American investments. The next year, he sent troops to the Dominican Republic. He and Teddy Roosevelt were not so different.

¡Viva Madero! ¡Viva Huerta! ¡Viva Carranza!

In 1911, Porfirio Díaz, who had been the dictator of Mexico for 35 years, was overthrown. British and American investors, whom Díaz had favored, were worried. The leader of the revolution, Francisco Madero, had spoken of returning control of Mexican resources to Mexicans. Americans owned $2 billion in property in Mexico: most of the country's railroads, 60 percent of the oil wells, and more mines than Mexicans owned. About 50,000 Americans lived in Mexico.

Madero and Wilson might have been able to talk. Both were well educated and classic nineteenth-century liberals. But they never had the chance. Quietly encouraged by American diplomats appointed by Taft, a group of generals led by the hard-drinking, no-nonsense Victoriano Huerta staged a coup shortly before Wilson was inaugurated. Madero was murdered.

Wilson said that he would not deal with "a government of butchers" and pressured Britain to withdraw its hasty recognition of the Huerta regime. When peasants rebelled in several parts of Mexico and a constitutionalist army took shape behind a somber, long-bearded aristocrat, Venustiano Carranza, Wilson openly approved.

In April 1914, the United States intervened directly in the Mexican civil war when seven American sailors on shore leave in Tampico were arrested by one of Huerta's colonels. He freed them almost immediately—Huerta, an old Díaz man, wanted no trouble with gringos—but he refused the rather excessive demand of Admiral Henry T. Mayo for a 21-gun salute as the appropriate apology. Claiming that American honor was insulted (and heading off a German ship carrying arms to Huerta), Wilson ordered troops into the gulf port of Vera Cruz.

To Wilson's surprise, ordinary Mexicans joined Huerta's soldiers to fight the Americans; 400 people were killed. Wilson had failed to understand that, although Huerta was less than beloved, the humiliation of the Mexican War was fresh in the Mexican memory. Even Carranza, firmly in control of northeastern Mexico, condemned the American landing. Alarmed by the fix into which he had gotten himself, Wilson quickly agreed to an offer by Argentina, Brazil, and Chile to mediate the crisis.

Pancho Villa

Before anything could be resolved, Carranza ousted Huerta. However, he immediately quarreled with one of his own generals, a bizarre, charismatic character who was born Doroteo Arango but was universally known as Pancho Villa. Alternately jovial and sadistic, part-time bandit and part-time social revolutionary, Villa was romanticized in the American press by a young journalist, John Reed, as the "Robin Hood of Mexico." Villa enjoyed the fame and played for American approval. For a time, Wilson believed that Villa represented democracy in Mexico.

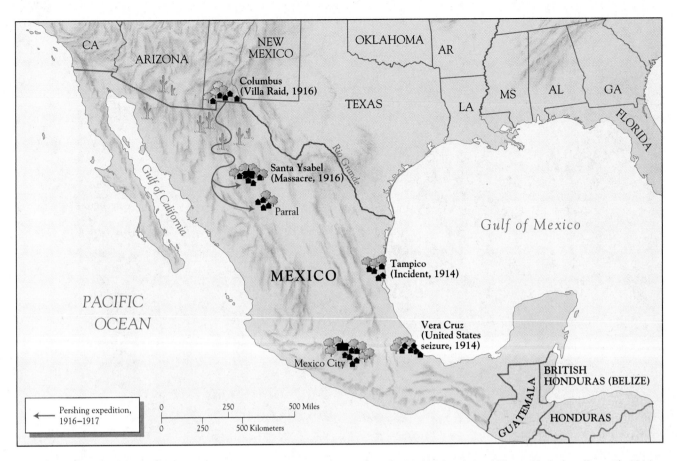

MAP 37:1 **The Mexican Expedition**   The United States was frustrated both in the navy's high-handed activities on Mexico's gulf coast in 1914 and in a justified but humiliating pursuit of the Mexican state of Chihuahua's warlord, Pancho Villa, in 1916.

But Wilson wanted stability most of all. When Carranza took Mexico City in October 1915, Wilson recognized his de facto control of the government. This stung Villa, and he displayed his seamier side. Calculating that American intervention would cause chaos in Mexico, creating an opportunity for him to seize power, Villa stopped a train carrying American engineers who had been invited by Carranza to reopen abandoned mines and shot all but one of them. Early in 1916, he sent raiders across the border into the dusty little desert town of Columbus, New Mexico, where they killed 17 people.

Instead of allowing Carranza to run Villa down, which he wanted to do, Wilson ordered General John J. Pershing and 6,000 troops, including the African American Tenth Cavalry, to capture the bandit general. Another humiliation: In the arid mountainous state of Chihuahua that was his home, Villa easily evaded the American expedition, leading the soldiers 300 miles over a zigzag route during which time they never caught sight of Villa's army. Pershing's men did, however, worsen the situation by exchanging fire with Carranza's troops, and, in one skirmish, 40 died. Wilson had alienated every political faction in Mexico.

In January 1917, he ordered "Black Jack" Pershing home. It was not so much Pershing's failure in Mexico; the United States was now facing a more formidable enemy than Pancho Villa—the German Empire.

THE GREAT WAR

By 1917, Europe had been at war for two and a half years. In June 1914, a Serbian nationalist had assassinated Archduke Franz Ferdinand of the Austro-Hungarian Empire,

Pancho in Retirement

In 1920, no more able to capture Pancho Villa in Chihuahua than Pershing had been, the Mexican government made peace with him. Villa and about 400 soldiers and their families—the *villistas*—were promised they would not be molested if they contained themselves on several haciendas at La Purísima Concepción de El Canutillo. Villa was ready to retire; he was too rich to be hiding in the desert. The *villistas* mechanized their farms and founded schools. Pancho himself became something of a health nut, a jogger. The *villistas* still worshiped him, but many people on whom he had preyed did not. He could not leave the hacienda without an armed escort of 50 men, which, however, did not prevent his being assassinated just a few years after he retired.

▲ *Pancho Villa (Doroteo Arango), center, was charismatic and a superb guerrilla commander. His numerous villistas were devoted to him, and he was popular in Chihuahua. Villa was not universally loved, however, for he preyed on Mexican villagers when not at war. His murder of American engineers and raid on Columbus, New Mexico, led to a futile intervention by American troops.*

which included two provinces, Bosnia and Herzegovina, that Serbia claimed. At first, it appeared the incident would pass with protestations of grief and wrath. Europe had seen an epidemic of sensational assassinations over the previous decades. Or, at worst, it was thought, there would be a localized war between little Serbia and a less than overwhelming Austria-Hungary.

Those hopes were dashed by the obligations to one another that the real military powers of Europe had written into secret treaties, the weak character of the Russian czar, the irresponsibility of Germany's Kaiser Wilhelm II, and a frenzied arms race in which Russia, Germany, and France had been engaged for a generation.

Then as now, Slavic Serbia looked to the greatest Slavic country, Russia, as its protector, and the czar backed the little country in its defiance of Austria. A decaying Austria-Hungary looked to Germany for encouragement and got it. France, its leaders sworn to revenge a German victory in 1870–1871, was involved because of secret agreements promising support to Russia. Even Britain, traditionally aloof from European entanglements, had been so frightened by Germany's construction of a worldwide navy (second in size only to Britain's) that the nation had signed agreements with both France and Russia.

Many smaller European nations were associated with the "Central Powers" (Germany, Austria-Hungary, Italy,

Bulgaria, and Turkey) or the "Allied Powers" (England, France, Russia, and eventually Italy, which switched sides). By August 1914, most of Europe was at war. Eventually, 33 nations would fight.

The American Reaction

Americans reacted to the explosion with a mixture of disbelief and disgust. "This dreadful conflict of the nations came to most of us as lightning out of a clear day," a congressman said. For a generation, Americans had shrugged off European saber rattling; their popular Teddy Roosevelt was himself a blusterer with a military strut. But Roosevelt, it seemed, had understood the difference between a bully dis-

What's in a Name?
The British called it the "European War." Americans were inclined to use that term until the United States intervened in April 1917. Then, a few elegant but awkward tags were floated: "War for the Freedom of Europe," "War for the Overthrow of Militarism," "War for Civilization," and, best known, "Wilson's War to Make the World Safe for Democracy." Only after 1918 did "the Great War" and "the World War" become standard—until 1939, when the outbreak of another worldwide war made it "World War I."

play and a catastrophe. Until 1914, so had the Europeans. Even Kaiser Wilhelm II of Germany, a somewhat absurd and broadly ridiculed figure with his extravagant uniforms, gold and silver spiked helmets, and a comic-opera waxed moustache, had acted prudently in the crunch. Americans concluded that constant talk about war without going to war would continue indefinitely. They did not really believe that powerful, civilized countries would turn the twentieth century's terrifying technology for killing on one another.

Once the European nations did just that, Americans consoled themselves that the United States, at least, was above the savagery. Politicians, preachers, and editors quoted and praised the wisdom of George Washington's warning against entangling alliances. They blamed Europe's tragedy on Old World corruption, kings and princes, nationalistic hysteria, and insane stockpiling of armaments that were superfluous if they were not used and suicidal if they were.

Never did American political and social institutions look so superior. Never had Americans been more grateful to have an ocean between themselves and Europe. As reports of hideous carnage on the battlefield began to hum over the Atlantic cables, Americans shuddered and counted their blessings. No prominent person raised an objection when President Wilson proclaimed absolute American neutrality. However, when the president also called on Americans to be "neutral in fact as well as in name . . . impartial in thought as well as in action," he was, as he was apt to do, demanding too much of human nature, even the nature of what Wilson called "this great peaceful people."

Sympathy for the Allies

A large proportion of Americans looked to Great Britain as an ancestral motherland or identified with England's cultural legacy and were, therefore, sympathetic to the Allies. Wilson was an unblushing anglophile. Before becoming president, he vacationed regularly in Great Britain, and he wrote a book in which he praised the British parliamentary form of government virtually as superior to America's. In his first year in office, he resolved the last outstanding points of conflict with Great Britain: a minor border dispute in British Columbia, a quarrel between Canadian and American fishermen off Newfoundland, and British objections to discriminatory tolls on the Panama Canal.

Hardly noted at first, American and British capitalists were closely allied. British investments in the United States were vast, and when the cost of purchasing everything from wheat to munitions required that these holdings be liquidated, they were sold to Americans at bargain rates. Banking houses like the House of Morgan lent money to the British, at first with Wilson's disapproval, and acted as agents for Allied bond sales. By 1917, Great Britain owed Americans $2.3 billion. That was a strong tie when compared to the meager $27 million that the Germans managed to borrow in the United States. Wall Street had good reason to favor a British victory or, at least, to pale at the thought of a British defeat.

Some Americans were sympathetic toward France. Francophilia had been fashionable among the wealthy in the late nineteenth century. The historically minded remembered France as America's "oldest friend," the indispensable ally of the Revolution. And France was, except for the United States, the only republic among the world's major powers.

Sympathy for the Central Powers

One American in three was either foreign-born or a first-generation citizen, many with Old World attachments that made them sympathetic toward Germany or unfriendly toward Britain. Millions of Americans traced their roots to Germany or Austria-Hungary. Most had come to the United States for economic reasons; they bore no grudges toward their motherlands. No sensible German, Austrian, or Hungarian Americans suggested that the United States take the side of the Central Powers. But they did expect neutrality, and in heavily German areas like Wisconsin, they said so loudly. The National German League numbered 3 million members and actively propagandized on behalf of Germany.

Some German Americans joined with Irish Americans in the German-Irish Legislative Committee for the Furtherance of United States Neutrality. Many of the nation's 4.5 million Irish Americans hated Great Britain. When the British crushed a rebellion in Ireland in 1916, a few prominent Irish Americans declared for the German cause.

Similarly, many Russian and Polish Jews, who had suffered brutal persecution under the czars, inclined to favor Germany. Germany and Austria were countries where Jews enjoyed near civil equality with Christians, whereas Jews were chronically harassed in the Russian Empire. Socialists, an important minority in both the Jewish and German American communities, hated Russia above all other countries because of the cruelty of the czar's secret police.

With such a tangle of conflicting loyalties, Wilson's policy of neutrality was not only admirable, but it was his only plausible option. The Democratic party depended on ethnic voters in the industrial states. And Wilsonian neutrality might have worked if Europe's "Great War" (as it was then called) had been fought for clearly stated and limited goals, and had been concluded quickly, with a decisive victory by one side or the other.

The Deadly Stalemate

Quick, decisive victory was what Germany had in mind. The Schlieffen Plan, developed in 1905 and updated just a year before the war began, was designed to resolve Germany's expectation of a two-front war: France in the west, Russia in the east. The plan was to knock the modern French army out of the war in six weeks by concentrating seven-eighths of Germany's army there, flanking France's defensive fortifications. This meant invading France through neutral Belgium. But once in control of the channel coast, the general staff believed, German troops could delay British intervention and sweep down on Paris, as they had done in 1870.

▲ *The trenches, where European and (after 1917) American troops lived if they were stationed at the front. The American unit that spent the most time in the trenches was the African American 369th Infantry, which, as a unit, was awarded the French Croix de Guerre.*

In the meantime, Von Schlieffen warned, the weak German forces on the eastern front would take a battering from the Russians. All that was expected of the army there was that it hinder the Russian advance in what is now Poland. Once France was defeated, troops from the western front would be sped eastward to meet the large but unrespected Russian army on railroads laid out for just that purpose.

The Schlieffen Plan failed in 1914 because, instead of providing an avenue into France, the Belgians resisted heroically. Capturing the single fortress city of Liège took the Germans 12 days, longer than they expected to be in Belgium. Frustrated, the invaders treated captured Belgian soldiers ferociously and civilians scarcely better. German soldiers earned a reputation as savage "Huns." The image was to influence American public opinion profoundly.

During the fighting in Belgium, the Russians advanced deeply into German Poland. However, instead of hunkering down and absorbing the losses, as the Schlieffen Plan prescribed, the German general staff lost its nerve. At a critical moment, the army on the western front was weakened in order to divert troops to stop the Russians.

The Russians were stopped cold; the German army won a tremendous victory at the Battle of Tannenberg, capturing a million soldiers. But, on the western front, the war bogged down into a stalemate. The opposing armies dug entrenchments and heaped up earthworks 475 miles long. The opposing trenches faced one another across a no-man's-land of moonscape craters, spools of barbed wire, and the smell of death. Periodically for three years, men on both sides hurled themselves "over the top" and died by the tens of thousands to advance their line a few miles.

The Technology of Killing

A revolution in military technology (and the slowness with which the generals comprehended it) made the war unspeakably bloody. Although the airplane captured the imagination of romantics, it was of minor importance in the war. (Ordinary soldiers considered pilots playboys; in fact, the life expectancy of British pilots at the front was two weeks.) Nor was poisonous mustard gas, used by both sides, decisive. Its results were devastating, incapacitating entire divisions, but a shift in the wind blew the toxic fumes back on the army that had loosed it. Moreover, reasonably effective gas masks were soon issued to troops on both sides.

THE ROAD TO WAR
SUMMER 1914

1 **June 28**
Assassination at Sarajevo

2 **July 28**
Austria-Hungary declares
war on Serbia

3 **July 30**
Russia begins mobilization

4 **August 1**
Germany declares war
on Russia

5 **August 3**
Germany declares war
on France

6 **August 4**
Great Britain declares war
on Germany

7 **August 6**
Russia and
Austria-Hungary at war

8 **August 12**
Great Britain declares war
on Austria-Hungary

Allied Powers and possessions, 1916	⬛⬛⬛ British naval blockade
Central Powers, 1916	----- Trench line, western front, 1915
Neutral countries	----- Eastern front, 1915

MAP 37:2 European Alliances and the Road to War, 1914 The Central Powers and the Allies. Italy was a fourth major Central Power in 1914 but blamed the war on Austria-Hungary and refused to declare war on the Allies. Later, Italy entered the war on the Allied side.

The machine gun, by contrast, was the hallmark of the war. It made the old-fashioned charge, such as had characterized battle in the American Civil War, an exercise in mass suicide. When one army charged out of its trenches, enemy machine guns filled the air with a hurricane of lead that mowed men down by the thousands in minutes. On the first day of the Battle of the Somme in July 1916, 60,000 Britons were slaughtered or wounded, the majority of them within a half hour after they went over the top. By the time the Somme campaign sputtered to an indecisive end, British losses were 400,000, and French casualties were 200,000. The Germans lost 500,000 men.

The British developed the tank as a means of neutralizing German machine guns. The armored vehicles could be driven unharmed directly into gun emplacements. But the British generals rarely used their edge to advantage. They attached the tanks to infantry units, slowing them to a walk, rather than sending groups of the steel monsters rapidly in advance of the foot soldiers to knock out the machine guns. Incompetence at the top of every army contributed substantially to the bloodshed.

The War at Sea

Americans were sickened by the news from Europe, but it was the war at sea that directly touched national interests. As in the past, naval war was economic war; it was aimed at destroying the enemy's commerce and, therefore, the enemy's capacity to carry on the fight. Naval superiority allowed Great Britain to strike first at sea, proclaiming a blockade of Germany.

According to the rules of war, all enemy merchant ships were fair game for seizing or sinking, although tradition required that crews and passengers be rescued. The ships of neutral nations retained the right to trade with any nation as long as they were not carrying contraband (at first defined as war materiel).

The laws of blockade were more complicated, and, in 1914, Great Britain introduced several new wrinkles. The British blockaded Germany by mining parts of the North Sea. Ships, including those of neutrals, risked destruction by entering minefields. Britain also redefined contraband to mean almost all trade goods, including some foodstuffs. When neutral Holland, Denmark, and Sweden began to import goods for secret resale to Germany (pastoral Denmark, which never before had purchased American lard, imported 11,000 tons of it in the first months of the war), the British slapped strict regulations on trade with those countries.

American objections were mild. The German market was never important to the United States, and wartime sales to England and France rose so dramatically that few exporters needed extra business. American trade with the Allies climbed from $825 million in 1914 to $3.2 billion in 1916, a fourfold increase in two years.

As long as they expected a quick victory on land, the Germans were indifferent to the British blockade. When the war stalemated, however, the German general staff recognized the necessity of throttling England's import economy. Germany's tool was another recent creation of military technology, the "U-boat" (from the German *Unterseeboot,* or "undersea boat")—that is, the submarine.

Submarine Warfare

Ironically, for it was to play a key role in dragging the United States into war, the modern submarine was the invention of two Americans, John Holland and Simon Lake. When the United States Navy rejected their device as frivolous, they took their plans to Europe. The Germans recognized the submarine's potential and launched a large-scale construction program. By February 1915, Germany had a large enough flotilla of U-boats, each armed with 19 torpedoes, to declare the waters surrounding the British Isles a war zone. All enemy merchant ships within those waters were to be sunk, and the safety of neutral ships could not be absolutely guar-

▲ *U-Boat 15, one of Germany's first. When the fleet numbered a hundred submarines at the end of 1916, the German general staff believed that Britain could be starved out of the war before the United States could send enough soldiers to Europe to make a difference.*

anteed. Within days, several British vessels went to the bottom. President Wilson warned the kaiser that he would hold Germany to "strict accountability" for American lives and property lost to U-boats.

Submarine warfare was immediately described as peculiarly inhumane. On the surface, the U-boat, with no armor, was helpless. A light 6-inch gun mounted on the bow of a freighter was enough to sink it. Moreover, early submarines were slow in diving; British merchant vessels could ram them. Therefore, German submarine commanders had no choice but to strike without warning, giving crew and passengers of target vessels no opportunity to evacuate the ship, as an enemy warship could. Since submarines were tiny, their small crews cramped, there was no room to take aboard people who abandoned a ship when it began to sink. Survivors of torpedoed vessels were on their own in the midst of the ocean.

Many Americans grumbled that if the British blockade was illegal, the German submarine campaign was immoral. The British were thieves, but the Germans were murderers, drowning seamen by the hundreds. And not only seamen. On May 7, 1915, the English luxury liner *Lusitania* was torpedoed off the coast of Ireland; 1,198 people of the 1,959 aboard were killed, including 139 Americans. What kind of war was this, Americans asked, that killed innocent travelers? The *New York Times* described the Germans as "savages drenched with blood."

A Victory for Wilson

The Germans replied that they had specifically warned Americans against traveling on the *Lusitania* in advertisements in New York and Washington newspapers. They pointed out that the *Lusitania* was carrying 4,200 cases of small arms purchased in the United States and some high explosives. So many people were lost because the *Lusitania* went down in a mere 18 minutes, blown wide open not by the torpedo but by a secondary explosion. The British, the Germans said, had used innocent passengers as hostages in order to import war materiel.

Wilson knew the Germans were right; he did not hold the British blameless in the tragedy. Nevertheless, he sent several strongly worded memorandums to Germany. The second was so antagonistic that the pacifistic Bryan feared it would mean war. He resigned rather than sign it. Wilson (somewhat relieved) replaced him in the State Department with Robert Lansing, an international lawyer.

Although making no formal promises to Wilson, the Germans stopped attacking passenger vessels, and the *Lusitania* uproar faded. Then, early in 1916, the Allies announced that they were arming all merchant ships, and Germany responded that the U-boats would sink all enemy vessels without warning: unrestricted submarine warfare. On March 24, 1916, a French channel steamer on a scheduled run between

Dieppe and Folkestone, the *Sussex,* a sitting duck, went down with an American among the casualties. Wilson threatened to break diplomatic relations with Germany—which, at the time, was considered a prelude to a declaration of war—if unrestricted submarine warfare were continued.

The German general staff did not want the United States in the war. Plans for a major offensive were afoot, and the German navy did not have enough U-boats to sustain a full-scale attack on British shipping. In the Sussex Pledge of May 4, 1916, the Germans promised to observe the rules of visit and search before attacking enemy ships. This meant abandoning the submarine's effectiveness, but it kept the United States at home, which was the idea.

AMERICA ON THE WAY TO WAR

Wilson had won a spectacular diplomatic victory at the beginning of his campaign for reelection. He was enthusiastically renominated at the Democratic convention, and his campaign was given a theme that did not entirely please him. The keynote speaker, New York governor Martin Glynn, built his speech around the slogan "He Kept Us out of War."

Preparations for War

Wilson did not like the slogan. He confided to an aide, "I can't keep the country out of war. Any little German lieutenant can put us into war at any time by some calculated outrage." He meant that a submarine commander, acting on his own, could bark out the order that would torpedo the Sussex Pledge. Like many national leaders before and since, Wilson had trapped himself in a position where control over a momentous decision was out of his hands.

Wilson had begun to prepare for the possibility of war as early as November 1915, when he asked Congress to beef up the army to 400,000 men and to fund a huge expansion of the navy. To some extent, he was pushed into "preparedness" by his political enemy, Theodore Roosevelt, who jabbed and poked at the fact that the army totaled 108,000 men, ranking it seventeenth in the world; that the Quartermaster Corps (the military supply corps) had only recently begun using trucks; and that, at one point in 1915, the American artillery had enough ammunition for only two days'

fighting—with cannon that were a generation obsolete.

On the other side, Wilson had to contend with pacifists. Henry Ford chartered an entire ship to sail to Europe to seek peace. Feminists Jane Addams, Carrie Chapman Catt, and Charlotte Perkins Gilman formed the Women's Peace Party and attended a pacifist conference in the Netherlands. There were dozens of similar groups.

Much more worrying was an antipreparedness faction in Congress led by Representative Claude Kitchin of North Carolina. With widespread backing among western progressives, on whom Wilson generally depended for support, Kitchin pointed out that it had been Europe's preparedness that plunged the continent into war in the first place. If the United States had the means to fight in the war, it was all the more likely that the United States would enter the war. Wilson had to settle for a compromise, less of a military buildup than the interventionists wanted but more than Kitchin and his supporters liked.

The Election of 1916

The progressives nominated Roosevelt, who wanted the Republican nomination too. When he realized that it was beyond his grasp, he announced his support for his personal friend, Henry Cabot Lodge, for the Republican nomination. Lodge was warlike enough, but he was no progressive. In trying to force a virtual reactionary on the Bull Moosers, Roosevelt demonstrated how shallow his commitment to progressive ideals was when there was a chance for military glory. When the Republicans nominated Supreme Court justice Charles Evans Hughes, a progressive in the past, Roosevelt dropped out of the race. William Allen White wrote that the progressives were "all dressed up with nowhere to go." In fact, progressive voters were to go to both the Republicans and the Democrats, depending on their position on intervention.

Hughes's integrity was unimpeachable. In dignity and presidential bearing, he was Wilson's match. He spoke in high-sounding phrases. But Hughes lacked Wilson's toughness, and his views on the war differed little from the president's. He too wanted to avoid war but knew the United States was likely to be forced into it. Nevertheless, thanks to Theodore Roosevelt, who stormed around the country calling for Hughes's election, the judge was regarded as the war candidate, and Wilson, as the president who "kept us out of war."

These perceptions probably cost Hughes the presidency. It was a very close race. Hughes carried every northeastern state but New Hampshire and every midwestern state but Ohio. He went to bed on election night confident he had won. Then, one antipreparedness western state after another turned in majorities for Wilson. His electoral vote grew in three- and four-point increments, whittling Hughes's lead down. When Wilson carried California by a paper-thin margin, it made the difference. He was reelected, 277 electoral votes to 254. The election was on Tuesday. Not until Friday was it known for certain who would lead the country for the next four years.

Henry Ford's Peace Mission

Henry Ford hoped that the American celebrities on his ocean liner in December 1915 would, with their collective prestige, persuade the belligerents to make peace. Ford's scheme was viewed as crack-brained from the start, and he recruited more quacks and freeloading reporters than he recruited dignitaries.

So disastrous was the adventure that Ford jumped ship before it had completed its rounds. On returning to the United States, he said, "I didn't get much peace but I heard in Norway that Russia might well become a huge market for tractors soon."

▲ *The* American *announces the news to New York City. Every newspaper in the country reported the declaration in banner headlines.*

Failure to Keep the Peace

Elated but still nervous about the "little German lieutenant" in a U-boat somewhere, Wilson tried to mediate between the Allies and Central Powers. He had concluded that only by ending the fighting in Europe could he keep the United States out of it. During the winter of 1916–1917, he seemed to be making progress, at least with the Germans. For a short time, Wilson considered the British the major obstacle to peace.

On January 22, 1917, Wilson outlined his mediation plan to Congress. Only a "peace without victory," a "peace among equals" with neither winners nor losers, could end the slaughter. But Wilson did not call for a mere cessation of hostilities. He meant to pledge the warring powers to uphold the principles of national self-determination and absolute freedom of the seas, and to establish some kind of international mechanism for resolving future disputes.

It was all illusion. Wilson and the American people were in for a rude awakening. The president's proposal was not even half digested when, a week later, the German ambassador informed Wilson that, as of February 1, German submarines would resume unrestricted submarine warfare.

What had happened?

First, 1916 had been devastating for both the Allies and Central Powers. A German offensive against the fortress city of Verdun cost each side more than 300,000 men. A British offensive along the Somme River killed more than a million. The war could not be won on the ground, but the German general staff believed that it would be won at sea in just a few months.

The submarine fleet was up to a hundred vessels, with more under construction. With an all-out assault on shipping bound for Britain, the German generals and admirals calculated that the British should literally be starved into capitulation. Breaking the Sussex Pledge meant American intervention. However, because the United States was far from ready for action, the Germans believed the war would be over before more than a token American army could be landed in Europe. "They will not even come," the secretary of the navy informed the general staff, "because our submarines will sink them. Thus, America from a military point of view means nothing, and again nothing, and for a third time nothing."

Wilson broke diplomatic relations with Germany and asked Congress for authority to arm American merchant ships. When progressive Republicans La Follette, Norris, and Borah filibustered against the bill, Wilson denounced them as "a little group of willful men, representing no opinion but their own."

The president, not Theodore Roosevelt, was now the leader of the "war party." On the evening of April 2, after submarines sent three American freighters to the bottom, a solemn Wilson asked Congress for a formal declaration. "The right is more precious than peace," he said, "and we shall fight for the things which we have always carried nearest our hearts."

For four days, a bitter debate shook the Capitol. Six senators and about 50 representatives held out against war to the end. They blamed Wilson for failing to be truly neutral; some claimed that the United States was going to spill its young men's blood in order to bail out Wall Street's loans to England and to enrich the munitions manufacturers, the "merchants of death." In the most eloquent speech, Senator George Norris of Nebraska said, "We are going into war upon the command of gold. . . . We are about to put the dollar sign on the American flag."

Reasons Why America Went to War

In years to come, historians called "revisionists" would say that Norris had been right. With varying emphasis, they agreed that special interests wanted war and methodically maneuvered the United States into it. To the extent that Wall Street favored a British victory for the sake of its investments and that munitions makers profit from war, they were correct.

But to say that certain interest groups wanted war is not to say that they had their way with Woodrow Wilson and Congress. Wilson was as unlikely to take a cue from Wall Street and the DuPont munitions works as he was to seek opinion on a point of theology from Theodore Roosevelt. To Wilson, freedom of the seas was sacred, a right on which Americans had insisted since the 1790s. Moreover, the president shared in the profound shift in public sentiment from 1914, when virtually no American dreamed of going to war, to the spring of 1917, when the majority favored entering the conflict. The reasons for the about-face lay in the growing belief that Germany represented an evil force in the world.

The Hun and His *Kultur*

The image of Germans as barbaric "Huns" practicing a diabolical *Kultur* (merely German for "culture" but having a sinister ring to it in American ears) had its origins in the German violation of Belgian neutrality. Figuratively at first, the British and French called the invasion the "rape" of Belgium

▲ The "Hun." This poster is aimed at recruiting enlistees after the United States declared war on Germany. However, pro-intervention propaganda groups had been disseminating the same subhuman image of Germans for more than a year.

▲ *The Zimmerman telegram. It was transmitted, in code, through the same channels used for ordinary telegrams.*

and soon discovered the propaganda value of that ugly word. In fact, the German occupation of Belgium, although high-handed and harsh, as the German military was known to be, was not much harsher than the wartime controls the British slapped on the rebellious Irish. But wall posters representing the broken body of a young girl being dragged away by a bloated, beastlike German soldier in a spiked helmet elicited the revulsion they were intended to inspire.

German insistence that their troops observed all due proprieties toward civilians was undermined in October 1915, when the occupation forces executed Edith Cavell, the British head of the Berkendael Medical Institute in Brussels. Cavell was guilty of acts defined as espionage in international law (she helped British prisoners escape), but the execution of a nurse was profoundly stupid in an era when women were only rarely executed for committing murder.

German saboteurs were probably not as active in the United States as prowar propagandists claimed. Nevertheless, several German diplomats were caught red-handed in 1915 when a bumbling agent left incriminating papers on a train, and, in 1916, the huge Black Tom munitions stores in New Jersey were completely destroyed in a suspicious explosion.

However, the propaganda blockbuster was a telegram. On February 25, 1917, the British gave Wilson a message that the German foreign minister, Arthur Zimmerman, had telegraphed to the Mexican government. It said that in the event that the United States declared war on Germany, Germany would finance a Mexican attack on the United States,

which would keep the American army home. When Germany won the war, Mexico would be rewarded with the return of the "lost provinces" of New Mexico and Arizona, taken by the United States after the Mexican War 70 years earlier.

It was a foolish proposal. Mexico was wracked by civil turmoil, in no condition to make war on Guatemala, let alone the United States. Nevertheless, with American danders already up, and waiting for news of a U-boat attack on an American ship, the Zimmerman telegram persuaded many people that the Hun was indeed a worldwide threat.

The American Contribution

The Germans provoked American intervention on a gamble. They bet that their U-boat assault would defeat Britain before the United States could contribute to the war effort. For three months, it appeared they bet right. In February and March 1917, German submarines sank 570,000 tons of shipping around Great Britain. In April, the total ran to almost 900,000 tons. A quarter of the British merchant fleet lay at the bottom of the sea. (All told, 203 U-boats sank 5,408 ships during the war.) At one point in April 1917, the British had enough food on hand to feed the island nation for only three weeks.

But the worst passed, and the Germans lost their wager. At the insistence of American admiral William S. Sims, merchant ships ceased to travel alone. Guarded by naval vessels, particularly the small, fast, and heavily armed destroyers (designed to be the nemesis of the U-boats), merchant ships crossed the Atlantic in huge convoys. Over the objections of the Royal Navy (but with the support of Prime Minister David Lloyd George), Sims succeeded in building a "bridge of ships." In May 1917, U-boat kills dropped drastically, far below what the German navy expected. By July, the American navy took over defense operations in the Western Hemisphere and sent 34 destroyers to Queenstown (present-day Cobh) in Ireland to assist the British. So successful was the convoy system that only 200 out of 2 million American soldiers sent to France in 1917 and 1918 were drowned on the way. In the meantime, by commandeering more than a hundred German ships that were in American ports (including the huge *Vaterland*, renamed the *Leviathan*) and by launching a massive shipbuilding program, the Americans

The Doughboys

Sergeant York (actually a corporal when he performed his amazing feat) was simple and uneducated, and all the more lionized because he was ordinary. Except for his bravery, marksmanship, and luck, he was representative of the men of the American Expeditionary Force. The majority of the doughboys had less than seven years of schooling; one in four was illiterate. According to primitive IQ tests administered to all recruits (which should not be taken too seriously) half fell into the category of "moron."

Ten percent of the soldiers were African American. Almost one doughboy in five was an immigrant.

The Tin Lizzie

No sooner was the railroad perfected than inventors began experimenting with a self-powered vehicle that would run on the ground. In fact, George Stephenson put the first locomotive on rails because running on a road required more power than his engine could generate and steam boilers were so heavy that a steam carriage would have been tipped over by the holes with which the best roads were pocked. A Frenchman built a functioning but impractical steam tractor as early as 1858. An American, Richard Dudgeon, built a steam carriage to run on city streets in 1867. But it was dirty, noisy, and hot. It had no future competing with horsecar lines.

The mania over bicycles in the late nineteenth century provided the inspiration for dozens of tinkerers to develop small self-powered vehicles. Bicyclists also contributed to the emergence of the automobile by successfully lobbying for the paving of both city streets and roads in the country. And, in 1888, the pneumatic tire was perfected in Ireland to provide bikes with a safer and more comfortable ride. Pneumatic tires on spoked wheels were light and strong. Mechanics were able to experiment with engines, necessarily heavy, that were powerful enough to move a "horseless carriage." Rather good steam-powered cars were developed and sold by the Locomobile and Stanley companies. After the perfection of the storage battery in 1892, electric cars hit the streets. Both steam and electric cars were produced into the 1920s, but they never seriously competed with automobiles powered by internal combustion engines—using gasoline.

From the Collections of Henry Ford Museum & Greenfield Village

The Model T Ford. From a distance, the 1927 Model T looked much the same as one manufactured in 1910.

In 1900, there were 8,000 cars manufactured by 30 competing companies in the United States. They were quite expensive, affordable only to the very wealthy and fanatics willing to spend more than they could afford to race around noisily, making nuisances of themselves, frightening horses, running down animals and people. Carmakers competed for attention in popular races on tracks and endurance drives over hundreds of miles, happily reported by the yellow press.

The central figure in the revolution the automobile caused in the American economy, society, and culture was Henry Ford, an engineer who worked for Thomas Edison in Detroit. Ford had "wheels in his head": He was a genius mechanic, building his first car in 1896 and moving on to develop several commercial models.

But Ford was more than a manufacturer. He had an idea at which everyone else in the industry scoffed. He wanted to "build a car for the great multitude," a basic, easy-to-drive vehicle assembled by mass-production techniques in quantities so large that the selling price would be within the reach of almost everyone—the "universal car." That car was the Model T. It made its debut in 1908. It had a four-cylinder, 20 horsepower engine and a two-speed (plus reverse) planetary transmission operated by pedals (so there was no gear grinding); it sat high off the ground originally on wheels 3 feet in diameter. It cleared obstacles that brought other cars to a halt with a dismaying crunch of metal.

It cost $825. That was not peanuts in 1908, but Ford sold 10,000 Model T's that year. Although the car was soon dubbed the "tin lizzie" and the "flivver" because it looked flimsy, the Model T was, in fact, the toughest American car. Its body was made of a vanadium steel alloy with a tensile strength of 170,000 pounds compared to the 60,000-pound strength of the steel in other American cars. (It took other manufacturers five years to realize the superiority of Ford's alloy and adopt it themselves.) In 1909, in a race from New York to Seattle, only two cars finished, both Model T's.

Ford made comparatively few changes in the Model T each year. However, with his eye on increasing production and lowering the price, he constantly perfected the assembly line on which the cars were made, reducing each of the many operations required to build so complex a machine to just as many quick, simple, repetitive tasks performed by workers standing in one place. The parts the workers attached were brought to them in a finely orchestrated conveyor operation. In 1910, Ford made and sold 19,000 Model T's; in 1912, 78,440. In 1914, 260,720 Model T's rolled off the assembly line—half of all the cars made in the United States that year. There was a new Model T every couple of minutes. The price of the car dropped almost annually, bottoming out at $290, which *was* peanuts. When, after 19 years, the Model T was discontinued (only the Volkswagen Beetle had a longer run), 15 million had been built.

Not only was Ford very rich; he was a folk hero, and deservedly so. As he said he would do, he "democratized" the automobile. If not "everybody" could afford a Model T—Ford was hardly alone in ignoring the poor—millions of ordinary people could, most significantly farmers, whose social isolation the Model T destroyed. Not many technological devices have so profoundly changed the way ordinary Americans lived in so short a time. Perhaps only the television and computer are in a class with the tin lizzie.

▲ *General John J. Pershing leads the first contingent of the American Expeditionary Force on parade through Paris in July 1917. American soldiers did not play a major role in the fighting until 1918.*

were soon producing two ships for every one that the Germans sank.

The Fighting over There

As soon as the United States declared war, the British asked Wilson to send them 500,000 raw recruits, whom they would train and incorporate into the British Expeditionary Force. Wilson refused; the Americans would be trained at home and go "over there," in the words of a popular song, under American command. General Pershing arrived in Paris in July 1917 with the first units of the American Expeditionary Force, the First Infantry Division. It was a symbolic gesture. Pershing refused to send the inadequately trained men to the front. The first Americans to see action, near Verdun in October, were used only to beef up French, British, and Canadian units decimated by the fighting the previous year.

The autumn went poorly for the Allies. The Germans and Austrians defeated the Italian army in Italy and, in November, knocked Russia out of the war. A liberal democratic government that had deposed the czar in March 1917 proved unable to keep the mutinous Russian army supplied, and revolutionary Communists, the Bolsheviks, led by Vladimir Ilyich Lenin, seized power, promising "peace and bread." The Treaty of Brest-Litovsk, which the Germans forced on the Russians, was vindictive and harsh. News of its terms convinced even more Americans that the country did right in going to war to stop the Hun. By closing down the eastern front, however, the Germans were able to throw a bigger army into France.

In May 1918, Germany launched a do-or-die offensive. The Allies fell back to the Marne River, close enough to Paris that the shelling could be heard on the Champs Elysées. But, by this time, there were 250,000 fresh American troops in France, including 27,000 at Château-Thierry, near the hottest part of the fighting. By the middle of June, when the Germans attempted one last drive toward the capital, about 85,000 Americans helped hurl them back at Belleau Wood.

The supreme Allied commander, Field Marshal Ferdinand Foch, wanted to incorporate American troops into exhausted British and French units. Pershing stubbornly insisted that the Yanks fight as a unit. This was important to him not only for reasons of morale but because Wilson made it clear that the United States was not an ally of Britain and France—only their "associate." In order to ensure his "peace without victory," Wilson was determined to play the role of impartial independent at the peace conference.

By the summer of 1918, the Americans in France represented the margin of victory over the Germans. The best of the German generals, Erich von Ludendorff, attributed the crash in German morale to "the sheer number of Americans arriving daily at the front." In July, the Americans took over

MAP 37:3 American Operations in World War I For American troops, 1918 was the year of war. Most of the significant American battles with the Germans were fought on the Allies' southern flank.

the attack on a bulge in the German lines called the Saint-Mihiel Salient and succeeded in clearing it out. The final American battle was along a 24-mile line in the Argonne Forest, a rugged country just short of the border between France and Germany that had been transformed into a ghostly wasteland by four years of digging and shelling. It was in that position that over a million "doughboys" (as the American soldiers were called) were sitting when, on November 11, 1918, the Germans surrendered.

Armistice

In the trenches and back home, Americans celebrated deliriously. Millions of people gathered in city centers throughout the country, dancing and whooping. The Yanks had won the war! Had not the Germans stalemated the French and

British until our boys went "over there"? Then, just a year after the Americans began to fight, it was over. Pershing was a hero. An even greater hero was Alvin C. York, Sergeant York, a simple Tennessee mountain boy who, a few weeks before the armistice, attacked a German machine gun nest alone, killed 17 men with 17 bullets, and single-handedly marched 132 prisoners and 35 machine guns back to American lines.

Never Such a War
At the end of the war, the trenches on the western front ran from the English Channel to the border of Switzerland. There were so many soldiers massed along and behind this line that there was one man for every 4 inches of front.

World War I Casualties	Total Mobilized Forces	Killed or Died	Wounded	Prisoners and Missing	Total Casualties
United States	4,791,000	117,000	204,000	5,000	326,000
Russia	12,000,000	1,700,000	4,950,000	2,500,000	9,150,000
France	8,410,000	1,358,000	4,266,000	537,000	6,161,000
British Commonwealth	8,904,000	908,000	2,090,000	192,000	3,190,000
Italy	5,615,000	650,000	947,000	600,000	2,197,000
Germany	11,000,000	1,774,000	4,216,000	1,153,000	7,143,000
Austria-Hungary	7,800,000	1,200,000	3,620,000	2,200,000	7,020,000
Total	58,520,000	7,707,000	20,293,000	7,187,000	35,187,000

The American intervention was invaluable to the Allied victory. Three million boys were drafted; 2 million went to France. But the unmitigated joy in the United States was possible only because the American sacrifice was comparatively minor. Over 100,000 American soldiers died, more than half of them from disease. By comparison, 1.4 million French and almost a million British soldiers died. Three-quarters of all the Frenchmen who served in the armed forces were casualties. Both France and Britain were badly maimed. Germany and Russia were defeated. If it was not true that Americans won the war, it was certainly true that the United States was the only belligerent nation where people could feel as if they were victors.

for FURTHER READING

See E. H. Buehrig, *Woodrow Wilson and the Balance of Power*, 1955; Foster R. Dulles, *America's Rise to World Power, 1898–1954*, 1955; Otis L. Graham Jr., *The Great Campaigns: Reform and War in America, 1900–1928*, 1971; P. Edward Haley, *Revolution and Intervention: The Diplomacy of Taft and Wilson with Mexico, 1910–1917*, 1970; George F. Kennan, *American Diplomacy, 1900–1950*, 1951; N. G. Levin Jr., *Woodrow Wilson and World Politics: America's Response to War and Revolution*, 1968; A. S. Link, *Wilson the Diplomatist*, 1957, and *Woodrow Wilson: War, Revolution, and Peace*, 1979; Ernest R. May, *The World War and American Isolation, 1914–1917*, 1959; and Walter Millis, *The Road to War*, 1935.

Probably the best single book about the war is John Keegan, *The First World War*, 1999. Other good books are Lawrence Stallings, *The Doughboys*, 1963, and Russell Weigley, *The American Way of War: History of United States Military Policy and Strategy*, 1973.

 AMERICAN JOURNEY ONLINE AND INFOTRAC COLLEGE EDITION

Visit the source collections at http://ajaccess.wadsworth.com and http://infotrac.thomsonlearning.com, and use the Search function with the following key terms to explore documents, images, audio and video clips, articles, and commentary related to the material in this chapter:

Lusitania
Model T
Pancho Villa (and Doroteo Arango)
Woodrow Wilson
World War I

Additional resources, exercises, and Internet links related to this chapter are available on *The American Past* Web site: http://history.wadsworth.com/americanpast7e.

HISTORY ONLINE

The Great War
http://users.tibus.com/the-great-war
This site has a British emphasis but includes links to dozens of sites relating to World War I.

World War I
www.multied.com/wars.html
Text and maps focus on battles involving American soldiers.

38

OVER HERE

*World War I at Home
1917–1920*

The National Archives

*Once lead this people into war, and they'll forget there
ever was such a thing as tolerance. To fight you must be
ruthless and brutal, and the spirit of ruthless brutality
will enter into the very fiber of our national life.*

Woodrow Wilson

*When I think of the many voices that were heard before the
war and are still heard, interpreting America from a class
or sectional or selfish standpoint, I am not sure that, if the
war had to come, it did not come at the right time for
the preservation and reinterpretation of American ideals.*

George Creel

WOODROW WILSON CALLED the Great War "a war to make the world safe for democracy." He sent the doughboys to Europe and threw the industrial might of the United States behind the Allies in the belief there would be no victors in the traditional sense of the word. Instead, the peacemakers would create a new world order dedicated to settling disputes between nations justly and peaceably. Wilson also called the war "a war to end all wars."

THE PROGRESSIVE WAR

The First World War was simultaneously the apogee of progressivism, when reformers turned their ideas into policy, and the undoing of the progressive movement. For two years, progressive moralists and social planners had free rein in Washington. Within two years of the armistice, however, there was no progressive movement, only a few voices crying in the wilderness in Congress and hearing only echoes.

Split

The question of intervention split the progressives. A few itched to fight from the start, most notably Theodore Roosevelt (a pathetic shrill figure in his final years). When the United States declared war, he asked for a command in Europe. Wilson ignored him.

Other Republican progressives, mostly westerners like La Follette, Norris, Borah, and Hiram Johnson, fought the declaration of war. When they lost, they moderated their antiwar rhetoric but not their opinion that intervention was foisted on the country by munitions makers and bankers. The "willful men" prolonged the debate on the Conscription Act of 1917 for six weeks until Congress exempted boys under 21 from the draft. Any affinity the isolationist progressives felt with Wilson before April 1917 dissipated thereafter.

Democratic party progressives wholeheartedly supported the war. Like Wilson, they came to believe that Germany was a serious threat to free institutions everywhere. Moreover, in the task of mobilizing resources in order to fight the war, and in the wave of patriotic commitment that swept the country, progressives saw a golden opportunity to put their ideas for economic and social reform to work.

They were right on one count. It was impossible to wage a modern war while clinging to a vision of a free, unregulated economy. Armies numbering millions of men could not be supplied with food, clothing, shelter, medicine, and arms by private companies free to do entirely as their owners chose to do. France and Britain had clamped tight controls on their factories and farms in 1914. (Germany already had them.) When America went to war, progressives knew that their government had to do the same.

They were not disappointed. Proposals for regulation of business that were rejected as "radical" in peacetime proved, in the urgency of wartime, to be less than was necessary. Although generally with a soft touch, the federal government virtually took over the direction of the economy.

Planned Economy

The federal government grew like a mushroom. Government spending increased tenfold. The federal bureaucracy doubled in size. Employees of the executive branch, 400,000 in 1916, numbered 950,000 in 1918.

All sorts of government agencies were set up during the 20 months that the United States was at war. Some were useless and wasteful, established without thought; they served little purpose beyond providing desks, chairs, inkwells, and salaries for the functionaries who ran them. A few agencies were just plain failures. The Aircraft Production Board was commissioned to construct 22,000 airplanes in a year. That figure was unrealistic. But the 1,200 craft and 5,400 replace-ment motors that the board actually delivered were far fewer than the right hustler with a bank loan could have supplied.

Other agencies were successful. The Shipping Board, founded in 1916 before the declaration of war, produced vessels twice as fast as German submarines could sink them. Privately run shipbuilding companies, loaded with deadwood in management, were not up to that achievement.

The United States Railway Administration, headed by Wilson's son-in-law and secretary of the treasury, William G. McAdoo, was created early in 1918 when the owners of the nation's railroads proved incapable of moving the volume of freight the war created. The government paid the stockholders a rent equal to their earnings in the prewar years and simply took over. McAdoo untangled a colossal snafu in management within a few weeks; he reorganized the railroads into an efficient system such as the nation had never known. About 150,000 freight cars short of the number needed to do the job in 1917, American railroads had a surplus of 300,000 cars by the end of the war.

The war production boards were coordinated by a superagency, the War Industries Board, headed by Wall Street financier Bernard Baruch. His presence at the top of the planning pyramid indicated that the progressives had not won their campaign for a directed economy without paying a price. American industry and agriculture were regulated as never before. But elected officials and public-spirited experts with no stake in the profits were not always in the driver's seat.

Herbert Hoover: The Administrator as War Hero

The task given to Food Administrator Herbert C. Hoover was even more difficult than McAdoo's, and he was daily in the public eye. Hoover's job was to organize food production, distribution, and consumption so that America's farms could feed the United States, supply the Allied armies, and help many European civilians to survive.

Only 43 years old when he took the job, Hoover was already known as a "boy wonder." An orphan, Hoover grew up in California with relatives. He worked his way through Stanford, graduated as a mining engineer, and decided to work abroad on new strikes rather than work for established mining companies at home. Hoover had his share of adventure; he and his wife were besieged in China during the Boxer Re-

Profiteering

If Woodrow Wilson was America's most prominent movie fan (producers sent him prints of whatever films he requested), he was far from alone. Perhaps as well as any statistic, the income earned by Mary Pickford, "America's Sweetheart," the nation's favorite leading lady, gauges the storm with which movies took the United States. A minor Broadway actress before 1910, Mary Pickford made $25 a week. In 1910, moviemaker Carl Laemmle lured her to Hollywood with the astronomical weekly salary of $175. In 1914, Adolph Zukor of Famous Players paid Pickford $20,000, then $52,000, a year. In 1915, she demanded and got $104,000 per movie, plus one-half the profits it earned. In June 1916, her price was $1 million guaranteed against half the profits.

Hooverizing

Herbert Hoover encouraged city dwellers to plant "victory gardens" in their tiny yards. Every tomato that was raised at home, he said, freed commercially produced food for the front. He promoted classes for homemakers in economizing in the kitchen and distributed cookbooks on how to prepare leftovers. The impact of his programs was so great that, half-seriously, Americans coined the verb *hooverize* to mean "economize," and they used it. Chicago proudly reported that the city's housekeepers had "hooverized" the monthly output of garbage down by a third.

bellion. Mostly, however, Hoover developed mines, made shrewd personal investments, and was so soon a millionaire that he was bored by moneymaking when still a young man.

Hoover's interests and ambitions were in public service. He believed that able, wealthy men like himself had special responsibilities to society. He got his chance when he happened to be in London at the outbreak of the war. He was asked to take over the problem of getting food to the people of devastated Belgium, and he jumped at the challenge. Hoover liquidated his business interests, mastered the complex and ticklish task of feeding people in a war zone, and undoubtedly saved hundreds of thousands of lives.

He did it without charm or personal flash. Hoover was intense and humorless. He was all business. His method was to apply engineering principles to the solution of human problems. Progressives admired just such expertise, and the cool, methodical Hoover was a refreshing contrast to humanitarians who moved around in a perfumed cloud of pious self-congratulation. It is an insight into the spirit of the times that he became a war hero in the same rank as Pershing, Alvin York, and America's ace pilot, Eddie Rickenbacker.

In one significant matter, Hoover was not a typical progressive. He preferred voluntary cooperation to government coercion. Consequently, food was never rationed in the United States as it was in Europe. Instead, Hoover engineered colorful publicity campaigns urging Americans, in the spirit of patriotism and cooperation, to observe wheatless Mondays, meatless Tuesdays, porkless Thursdays, and so on. The program worked because compliance was easy yet psychologically gratifying. Making do without a vital commodity one day a week was no real sacrifice, but it made civilians feel as though they were part of the fighting machine. Nor was it just hype. When a meatless Tuesday was observed by tens of millions, the savings were enormous.

Hoover increased farm production through a combination of patriotic boosting and cash incentives. He helped increase the acreage planted in wheat from 45 million in 1917 to 75 million in 1919. American exports of foodstuffs to the Allies tripled over high prewar levels. Hoover added "Miracle Man" to his list of flattering nicknames. Another young Washington administrator, Undersecretary of the Navy Franklin D. Roosevelt, wanted the Democratic party to nominate Hoover for president in 1920.

Managing People

People were mobilized along with railway cars and potatoes, workers and housewives as well as soldiers. In May 1917, Congress passed the Selective Service Act, the first draft law since the Civil War. Registration was compulsory for all men between the ages of 21 and 45. (In 1918, the minimum age was lowered to 18.) From the 10 million who registered within a month of passage (24 million by the end of the war), local draft boards selected able-bodied recruits according to quotas assigned by the federal government. Some occupational groups were deferred as vital to the war effort, but no

one was allowed to buy his way out, as was possible during the Civil War. Indeed, authority to make final selections was given to local draft boards in order to silence critics who said that conscription had no place in a democracy. The draft contributed about 3 million young men to the armed forces, in addition to 2 million who volunteered.

About 21,000 draftees claimed to be conscientious objectors on religious grounds, although, in the end, only 4,000 insisted on assignment to noncombatant duty, as medics or in the Quartermaster Corps. Approximately 500 men refused to cooperate with the military in any way, some for political rather than religious reasons. They were imprisoned and, in general, treated poorly. Camp Leonard Wood in Missouri had an especially bad reputation. In Washington State, a man who claimed that Jesus had forbidden him to take up arms was sentenced to death. He was not executed, but the last conscientious objector was not freed from prison until 1933, long after most Americans had come to agree with him that the war had been a mistake.

SOCIAL CHANGES

War is a revolutionary or, at least, an agitator. The changes impressed on American society from the top in the interests of victory inevitably affected social relationships. Some groups consciously took advantage of the government's wants, needs, and preoccupations to achieve old goals. Others were merely caught up by the different rhythms of a society at war.

Victories for Labor

In order to keep the factories humming, Wilson made concessions to the labor movement that would have been unthinkable a few years earlier. He appointed Samuel Gompers, the patriotic president of the American Federation of Labor (AFL), to sit on Baruch's War Industries Board. The postmaster general refused to deliver an issue of a socialist magazine in which Gompers was criticized. In return for recognition and favors, Gompers pledged the AFL unions to a no-strike policy for the duration of the conflict.

Because wages rose during the war, there were comparatively few work stoppages. Business boomed, and employers dizzy with bonanza profits did not care to jeopardize them by resisting moderate demands by their employees. Most important, the National War Labor Board, on which five AFL men sat, mediated industrial disputes before they disrupted production.

The quiet incorporation of organized labor into the federal decision-making process made the AFL respectable as it never had been before; this was Samuel Gompers's dream come true. From 2.7 million members in 1914, the union movement (including independent unions) grew to 4.2 million in 1919.

Blacks in Wartime

Like Gompers, leaders of black organizations hoped that by proving their patriotism in wartime, African Americans would win improved civil and social status. About 400,000 young black men enlisted or responded to the draft. Proportionately, more blacks than whites donned khaki in World War I.

It was difficult to ignore the contradiction between, on the one hand, Wilson's declaration that the purpose of the war was to defend democracy and liberty and, on the other, the second-class status of African Americans. W. E. B. DuBois, the leader of the National Association for the Advancement of Colored People, pointedly reminded the president of the dichotomy, and Wilson went as far as to issue a stronger condemnation of lynching than he had done before the war. Nevertheless, mere war could not destroy deeply rooted racist sentiments. Black soldiers were assigned to segregated units and usually put to menial tasks such as digging trenches and loading trucks behind the lines. Only a few black units saw combat.

Military segregation paid dividends to a few blacks. In order to command black units, the army trained and commissioned 1,200 African American officers. This was gratifying to DuBois, whose hopes for the future rested on the creation of an African American elite.

Race Riots at Home

More important than African American officers was the massive emigration of blacks from the rural and strictly segregated South to the industrial cities of the North. Before 1914, only about 10,000 blacks a year drifted from the South to New York, Philadelphia, Detroit, and Chicago. After 1914, while the risks of ocean travel choked off foreign immigration just as factories filling war orders needed more employees, 100,000 blacks made the trek north each year. It was not as great a leap in miles as the European immigration but just as wrenching socially and culturally. Moving from a Mississippi delta cabin to a Detroit factory and urban home meant a massive change in a family's way of life.

Most of the African Americans who moved north were young people, less conditioned than their elders to accept the daily humiliations that came with being black in America. This was particularly true of the men in uniform, who assumed that

▲ *Members of the 369th Infantry. The army was segregated racially; the 369th was entirely African American. In fact, whereas General Pershing insisted that white units serve under American officers, he "loaned" the 369th to the French. As a unit, these soldiers (note their medals) won the French Croix de Guerre for gallantry.*

▲ *Three generations of an African American family arrive in Chicago from the Deep South, part of a massive shift in the black population to northern cities. They appear to be as apprehensive as immigrants from Italy or Poland. Indeed, they too had moved between sharply different cultures, and if they knew the language, they labored in the face of racial prejudice much more powerful than European immigrants faced.*

their service entitled them to respect. In France, moreover, African American soldiers discovered a white society in which the color line was insignificant and crossable. Black soldiers wrote home that they were treated like persons in France.

Back home, 1917 was a year of violent racial conflict. There was a frightening race riot in industrial East St. Louis, Illinois. In Houston, white civilians fought a pitched battle with black soldiers, and 12 people were killed. Although both sides shared the blame for that riot, 13 black soldiers were hanged, and 14 were imprisoned for life. No whites were punished. DuBois and the National Association for the Advancement of Colored People were only partly correct in their analysis of how the war would affect blacks. Society made economic concessions to African Americans in the interests of winning the war, but it did not move even inches toward social equality or, in the South, political rights.

A Woman's War

The women's suffrage movement, by contrast, parlayed wartime idealism and fears into final victory for the long-sought cause. Imitating British and French examples, the armed forces inducted female volunteers, mostly as nurses

and clerical workers. More important was the same labor shortage that created opportunities in northern factories for blacks. Working-class women began doing factory work and other jobs that had been closed to them in peacetime. Women operated trolley cars, drove delivery trucks, cleaned streets, directed traffic, and filled jobs in every industry from aircraft construction to zinc galvanization.

Middle-class women organized support groups. They rolled bandages, held patriotic rallies, and filled the holds of ships with knitted sweaters, socks, and home-baked cookies for the boys in France. With women's contributions to waging the war so conspicuous, it was increasingly difficult for politicians to oppose suffrage with the argument that women belonged in the nursery, kitchen, and church.

Suffrage at Last

By 1917, the feminist movement had a radical and a conservative wing. Curiously, although the two groups exchanged harsh words, their different approaches both contributed to the victory of the suffrage movement. Thus, when the aggressive Women's Party led by Alice Paul demonstrated noisily in Washington, burning a copy of Wilson's Fourteen

▲ *A woman welder. Although in nothing like the numbers during World War II, women took manual factory jobs during World War I that, before the war, it was unthinkable for women to do.*

nently. In 1914, only one-quarter of the states had some sort of Prohibition law on the books, and it was, in many cases, only casually enforced. By the end of 1917, when a constitutional amendment prohibiting alcohol nationally was proposed, only 13 states were completely dry. And yet, within a year and a half, Prohibition was the law of the land.

With American participation in the war, the antialcohol forces added several new arguments to their armory: for example, the distilling of liquor consumed grain that was needed as food. Shortly after the declaration of war, Congress passed the Lever Act, which forbade the sale of grain to distilleries.

Breweries, which had always distanced themselves from distillers, contrasting the wholesome beer garden with the disreputable saloon, suddenly found themselves vulnerable because many were run by German Americans, their Teutonic names emblazoned proudly on bottle and barrel. They were easy targets for flag-waving prohibitionists, who associated beer with the hated Hun. The war put Prohibition over the top. The Eighteenth Amendment prohibited "the manufacture, sale, or transportation of intoxicating liquors" in the United States.

Efforts to End Prostitution

War usually means a relaxation of sexual morality as young men are removed from the social restraints of family and community, and so it was in the First World War. The doughboys in France discovered that, with more than two years of military presence preceding their arrival, brothels were everywhere, even in tiny French villages. Moralistic progressives in Wilson's administration tried to combat the menace of casual sex. Every recruit was warned of the dangers of venereal disease—"A German bullet is cleaner than a French whore"—and American soldiers on leave were forbidden to spend their time in wide-open Paris. (The order was widely defied; American deserters invariably headed for Paris, where they could lose themselves in the city's seamier quarters.)

Josephus Daniels, the deeply religious secretary of the navy, actually thought that having so many young men under his control was an opportunity to *improve* their sex morals. He called his ships "floating universities" of moral reform. Daniels gave orders to the navy to clear out the red-light districts that had been a fixture in every port; the army did the same in cities near its bases, most notably in New Orleans, with its fabled Storyville.

Prostitution no more disappeared than people stopped drinking booze. But the flush of excitement in the reformers' short-term victories confirmed their belief that, along with its horrors, the First World War was a blessing on those who would shape society for the better.

Points and chaining themselves to the fence in front of the White House, many politicians went scurrying for reassurance to the more genteel National American Woman Suffrage Association.

Led by Carrie Chapman Catt, the association obliged them. Not only did most American women oppose such irresponsible behavior, Catt argued, but social stability and conservative government could be ensured only by granting women the vote. Their numbers would counterbalance the increasing influence of radicals, immigrants, and machine voters at the polls.

The suffrage movement was too long in the field and too large to be denied. Even Wilson, who instinctively disliked the idea of women voting, announced his support. On June 4, 1919, a few months after the armistice, Congress sent the Nineteenth Amendment to the states. On August 18, 1920, ratification by Tennessee put it into the Constitution. "The right of citizens . . . to vote," it read, "shall not be denied or abridged by the United States or by any State on account of sex." Carrie Chapman Catt had no doubt about what put it over. It was the war, the former pacifist said, that enfranchised American women.

The Moral War

Another long progressive campaign had already been brought to a victorious end. Like the suffragists, on the eve of the war, the prohibitionists appeared to be stalled perma-

CONFORMITY AND REPRESSION

It was no blessing for civil liberties. As Wilson privately predicted, white-hot patriotism scorched traditions of free political expression and toleration of disparate ways of life.

Drawn by CALVERT SMITH

THE POISON AND THE ANTIDOTE

▲ *The earliest feminists (and the feminists of the 1970s and 1980s) argued that women should have rights equal to men's because they had the same intelligence, abilities, and character. During the Progressive Era, suffragists argued that women should be able to vote because of a sensitivity and morality superior to those of males. This cartoon reflects that line: The proper middle-class woman follows the sleazy Irish machine voter to the ballot box.*

There was, of course, plenty of intolerance in the United States before the First World War. But never had violation of the Bill of Rights been so widespread as it was during the war. Never before had the federal government so openly tolerated and even initiated repression.

The Campaign Against the Socialists

The Socialist Party of America was the most important national political organization to oppose intervention. In April 1917, as war was being declared in Washington, the party met in emergency convention in St. Louis and proclaimed "unalterable opposition" to a conflict that killed working people while paying dividends to capitalists. Rather than hurting the party at the polls, this stance earned the Socialist party an increase in votes; many nonsocialists cast ballots for Socialist party candidates as the only way to express their opposition to the war.

Governments moved quickly to head off the possibility of a socialist antiwar bandwagon. The legislature of New York expelled seven socialist assemblymen simply because they objected to the war. Not until after the war did courts overrule the expulsion as unconstitutional. Socialist Victor Berger was elected to Congress from Milwaukee but was denied his seat by the House. When, in the special election to fill the vacancy, he defeated an opponent supported by both the Democratic and Republican parties, Congress again refused to seat him. Berger's district remained unrepresented until 1923, when, finally, he was allowed the place he had been elected to fill five years earlier. In the meantime, the Milwaukee socialists' *Social Democratic Herald* and many other socialist papers were denied cheap mailing privileges by Postmaster General Albert S. Burleson. Most of them never recovered from the blow. The golden age of the American socialist press was over.

The most celebrated attack on the socialists was the indictment and trial of the party's longtime and much beloved leader, Eugene V. Debs, for a speech opposing conscription. In sending Debs to an Atlanta penitentiary, the Wilson administration was taking a chance. The four-time presidential candidate was admired by many nonsocialists. At his trial in September 1918, Debs was at his most eloquent. "While there is a lower class I am in it; while there is a criminal element I am of it; while there is a soul in prison, I am not free," he told the jury. But in prosecuting and jailing him and other prominent socialists, such as Kate Richards O'Hare, the government made it clear that dissent on the war issue would not be tolerated.

Destruction of the IWW

The suppression of the Industrial Workers of the World (IWW) was heavier handed. This was ironic because, although the radical union officially opposed the war, Secretary-Treasurer William D. "Big Bill" Haywood tried to play down the issue. The IWW was enrolling new members by the thousands every month. Haywood hoped to ride out the patriotic hysteria of wartime and emerge from the war with a powerful labor organization.

In fact, the federal government decided to destroy the IWW less because of its nominal opposition to the war but precisely because it was an increasingly large and effective labor union. Unlike the Socialist party, which numbered many articulate and politically active middle-class people among its supporters, the IWW's constituency was working people on the very bottom, people with little influence on public opinion and widely regarded as undesirables. By 1917, moreover, the Wobblies were concentrated in three sectors of the economy that were central to the war effort:

among the migrant harvest hands who brought in the nation's wheat; among loggers in the Pacific Northwest; and among copper miners in western towns like Globe and Bisbee in Arizona, and Butte, Montana. And these workers refused to abide by the no-strike pledge that Samuel Gompers made on behalf of the AFL.

The IWW was crushed by a combination of vigilante terrorism and government action. In July 1917, 1,000 "deputies" wearing white armbands so as to recognize one another rounded up 1,200 IWW strikers in Bisbee, loaded them on a specially chartered train, and dumped them in the Hermanas Desert of New Mexico, where they were without food for 36 hours. The next month, IWW organizer Frank Little was lynched in Butte, possibly by police officers in disguise. In neither case was there any serious attempt to identify the vigilantes.

In the grain belt, sheriffs and farmers had a free hand in dealing with suspected Wobblies. In the Sitka spruce forests of Washington and Oregon (Sitka spruce was the principal wood used in aircraft construction), the army organized the Loyal Legion of Loggers and Lumbermen to counter the popularity of the IWW. There, at least, conditions were improved as the union was repressed, but attacks on the IWW were consistently vicious. Local police and federal agents winked at, and even participated in, everyday violations of civil rights and violence against Wobblies and their sympathizers.

Civil Liberties Suspended

The fatal blow fell in the fall of 1917 when the Justice Department raided IWW headquarters in several cities, rounded up the union's leaders, and indicted about 200 of them under the Espionage Act of 1917. Later enhanced by the Sedition Act of 1918, the Espionage Act not only outlawed overt treasonable acts but made it a crime to "utter, print, write, or publish any disloyal, profane, scurrilous, or abusive language" about the government, the flag, or the uniform of a soldier or sailor. A casual snide remark was enough to warrant bringing charges, and a few cases were based on little more than wisecracks.

In *Schenck v. the United States* (1919), the Supreme Court unanimously upheld this broad, vague legislation. As if to leave no doubt as to the Court's resolve, Oliver Wendell Holmes Jr., the most liberal-minded justice on the Court, was assigned to write the opinion establishing the principle that when "a clear and present danger" existed, such as the war, Congress had the power to pass laws that would not be acceptable in normal times.

Even at that, the government never proved that the IWW was guilty of sedition. In effect, the individuals who were sentenced to up to 20 years in prison were punished because of their membership in an organization the government wanted dead. Liberals who had no taste for IWW doctrine were shocked at the government's cynicism and fought the prosecutions. In 1920, led by Roger Baldwin, they organized the American Civil Liberties Union to guard against a repetition of the repression of the Great War.

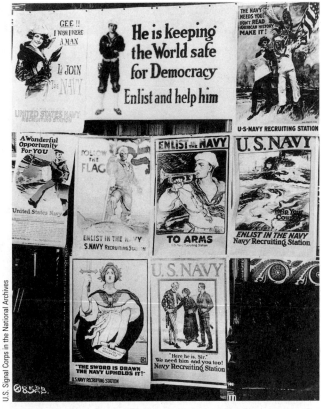

▲ *The Committee on Public Information plastered the country with patriotic posters in the first intensive modern government propaganda program in American history. Fortuitously, poster art reached an unprecedented level of distinction and effectiveness during World War I that has, in fact, never been reached again.*

Manipulation of Public Opinion

The attack on the socialists and the Wobblies was only one fulfillment of Wilson's prediction that war would bring a spirit of ruthless intolerance to American life. Many otherwise ordinary people were stirred by patriotism to believe that they were part of a holy crusade against a foe with the wiles and dark powers of the devil.

Violent acts against individual German Americans were common. Most incidents were spontaneous; for example, a midwestern mob dragged a German American shopkeeper from his home, threw him to his knees, forced him to kiss the American flag, and made him spend his life savings on war bonds. But intolerance and vigilante activity were also abetted, and even instigated, by the national government.

The agency entrusted with mobilizing public opinion was the Committee on Public Information (CPI). It was headed by George Creel, a progressive newspaperman who had devoted his career to fighting the very sort of intolerance he now found himself encouraging. Creel's task was twofold. First, in order to avoid demoralization, the CPI censored the news from Europe. CPI dispatches emphasized victories and suppressed or played down stories of setbacks and the misery of life in the trenches. With most editors and publishers solidly behind the war, Creel had little difficulty convincing them to censor their own correspondents.

"They Dropped Like Flies": The Great Flu Epidemic

About 10 million died in battle between 1914 and 1918. Small wonder the war staggered the confidence of Western civilization.

But the war was an amateur killer compared with the "Spanish flu." During only four months late in 1918 and early in 1919, a worldwide flu epidemic killed 21 million. The American army in Europe lost 49,000 men in battle and 64,000 to disease, the majority to the flu. At home, 548,452 American civilians died, 10 times as many as soldiers felled in battle.

The disease first appeared in the United States in March 1918 at Fort Riley, Kansas. After a dust storm, 107 soldiers checked into the infirmary complaining of headaches, fever and chills, difficulty breathing, and various aches and pains. The illness had hit them in an instant; one moment they were feeling fit, the next they could barely stand. Within a week, Fort Riley had 522 cases, and in a little more than a month,

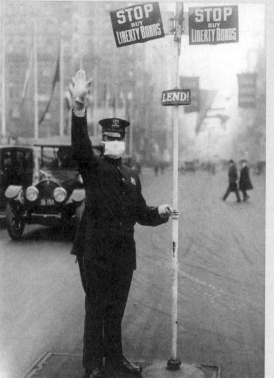

National Archives

when the affliction abruptly disappeared, 8,000 cases. About 50 of the sick men died, not too disturbing a rate in a time when a number of common contagious diseases were deadly. Some doctors noted the curiosity that the victims were in the prime of life and, after basic training, in excellent condition.

The soldiers from Fort Riley were shipped to Europe in May. The flu made a brief appearance in the cities of the eastern seaboard, but it did not rival any of a number of flu epidemics,

including a serious one in the United States in 1889 and 1890. In Europe in 1918, the disease was far more deadly. In neutral Switzerland alone, 58,000 died of it in July. Deaths in the trenches from the flu were so numerous that German general Erich von Ludendorff curtailed a major campaign. By June, the flu was sweeping Africa and India, where the mortality was "without parallel in the history of disease." The catastrophe in India could be attributed to the wretched poverty of the subcontinent. But what of Western Samoa, where 7,500 of the island's 38,000 people died?

The totals had not been calculated when the flu began a second world tour. The war had created ideal conditions for a pandemic. People moved about in unprecedented numbers; 200,000 to 300,000 crossed the Atlantic to Europe each month, and almost as many crowded westbound steamships. Moreover, war crowded people together on land as well as sea. Conditions were perfect for both the spread and the successful mutation of viruses. With so many hosts handy, the emergence of new viral strains was all the more likely.

That is apparently what happened in August, either in western Africa, France, or Spain (which got the blame—Americans called it the "Spanish flu"). A much deadlier mutation of the flu at Fort Riley swept over the world, and this time the effects in the United States were cataclysmic.

Second, the CPI took up the task of molding public opinion so that even minor deviations from full support of the war were branded as disloyal. Obviously, all German Americans could not be imprisoned. (Only 6,300 Germans were actually interned compared with 45,000 of Great Britain's much smaller German-born community.) However, the CPI could and did launch a massive propaganda campaign that depicted German *Kultur* as intrinsically evil.

The CPI issued 60 million pamphlets, sent prewritten editorials to pliant (or merely lazy) newspaper editors, and subsidized the design and printing of posters conveying the impression that a network of German spies was ubiquitous in the United States. With money to be made in exploiting the theme, the infant film industry centered in Hollywood, California, rushed to oblige. A typical title of 1917 was *The Barbarous Hun*. In May 1917, a movie producer, Robert Goldstein, was arrested and convicted under the Espionage

Act for making a film about the American Revolution, *The Spirit of '76*. One scene showed a redcoat impaling an American baby on his bayonet. Goldstein's crime was to have aided the enemy by disparaging America's British ally.

At movie theaters during intermissions, some 75,000 "four-minute men," all volunteers, delivered patriotic speeches of that length, 7.5 million such messages in all. Film stars like action hero Douglas Fairbanks, comedian Charlie Chaplin, and "America's Sweetheart," Mary Pickford, appeared at liberty bond rallies and spoke anti-German lines written by the CPI.

Liberty Hounds and Boy Spies

The anti-German hysteria took laughable form as well (although laughing loudly might be risky). Restaurants revised their menus so that sauerkraut became "liberty cabbage,"

In Boston, where the Spanish flu first struck, doubtless carried there by returning soldiers, 202 people died on October 1, 1918. New York City reported 3,100 cases in one day; 300 died. Later in the month, 851 New Yorkers died in one day, the record for an American city. Philadelphia lost 289 people on October 6; within one week, 5,270 were dead. The city's death rate for the month was 700 times the usual. Similar figures came in from every large city in the country. Just as worrisome, the disease found its way to the most isolated corners of the United States. A winter logging camp in Michigan, cut off from the rest of humanity, was afflicted. Oregon officials reported finding lone sheepherders dead by their flocks.

Most public officials responded as well as could be expected during a catastrophe that no one understood. Congress, many of its members laid low, appropriated money to hire physicians and nurses to set up clinics. Many cities closed theaters, schools, and churches, and prohibited public gatherings such as parades and sporting events. Several cities required people to wear gauze masks and punished violators with fines of up to $100. Others, notably Kansas City, where the political boss frankly said that the economy was more important, carried on as usual. Kansas City was no harder hit than cities that took extreme precautions, which mystified moralists. (Nationwide and worldwide, about one-fifth of the population caught the Spanish flu; the death rate was 3 percent.)

Philadelphia gathered its dead in carts, as had been done during the bubonic plague epidemics of the Middle Ages. The city's A. F. Brill Company, a maker of trolley cars, turned over its wood shop to coffin makers. Authorities in Washington, D.C., seized a trainload of coffins headed for Pittsburgh.

Then, once again, the disease disappeared. There was a less lethal wave (perhaps another mutation) in the spring of 1919, with President Wilson one of the victims. But the worst was over about the time that the First World War ended, finally allowing physicians to reflect on the character of the disease and to wonder what they could do if it recurred.

There were some things to reflect upon. The first has already been noted: The Spanish flu struck very suddenly, giving individuals no way to fight it except to lie down and hope. Second, the disease went relatively easy on those people who are usually most vulnerable to respiratory diseases, the elderly, and it was hardest on those who usually shook off such afflictions, young people. In the United States, the death rate for white males between the ages of 25 and 34 was, during the 1910s, about 80 per 100,000. During the flu epidemic, it was 2,000 per 100,000. In a San Francisco maternity ward in October, 19 out of 42 women died of flu. In Washington, a college student telephoned a clinic to report that two of her three roommates were dead in bed and the third was seriously ill. The report of the police officer who was sent to investigate was, "Four girls dead in apartment." Old people died of the flu, of course, but the death rate among the elderly did not rise a single point during the epidemic!

Finally, people who had grown up in poor, big-city neighborhoods were less likely to get the disease and, if they got it, less likely to die of it than were people who had grown up in healthier rural environments.

These facts eventually led scientists to conclude that the Spanish flu was a mutation of a common virus that caused a flu that was nothing more than an inconvenience. It was postulated, although never proved, that the deadly germ was the issue of an unholy liaison between a virus that affected humans and another that affected hogs. Spanish flu became known as "swine flu."

If the theory was true, it explained why poor city people, who were more likely to suffer a plethora of minor diseases, had developed an immunity to the virus that farm people had not. Moreover, city people had no contact with swine, as farm folks did. Because old people were spared in 1918 and 1919, it may be that swine flu was related to the less fatal virus that had caused the epidemic of 1889 to 1890. Having been exposed to that "bug," the elderly were immune to its descendant during the Great War.

hamburgers became "Salisbury steak" (after a British lord), and frankfurters and wiener sausages, named after German and Austrian cities, became universally known as "hot dogs."

The real dog, the dachshund, had to be rebred into a "liberty hound." Towns with names of German origin voted to choose more patriotic designations. Berlin, Iowa, became Lincoln; Germantown, Nebraska, became Garland. German measles, a common childhood disease, was "patriotic measles." Hundreds of schools and some colleges dropped the German language from their curriculum. Dozens of symphony orchestras refused to play the works of German composers, leaving conspicuous holes in the repertoire. Prominent German Americans who wished to save their careers found it advisable to imitate opera singer Ernestine Schumann-Heink. She was a fixture at patriotic rallies, her ample figure draped with a large American flag and her magnificent voice singing "The Star-Spangled Banner" and "America the Beautiful."

But the firing of Germans from their jobs, discriminating against German farmers, burning of German books, and beating up German Americans were not so humorous. Nor was the treatment of other people designated as less than fully patriotic by organizations of self-appointed guardians of the national interest with names like "Sedition Slammers," "Terrible Threateners," and "Boy Spies of America." Members stopped young men on the streets and demanded to see their draft cards. It was not an atrocity, just an annoyance akin to the intrusiveness of the "thank you for not smoking" people of the 1990s. But the assumption that one citizen had the right to police another was indicative of an unhealthy social mood. The largest of the self-anointed enforcers of patriotism was the American Protective League. At one time, it numbered 250,000 members, although many people probably signed up merely to avoid being harassed themselves.

WILSON AND THE LEAGUE OF NATIONS

Why did Woodrow Wilson, a liberal before the war, tolerate and even encourage these activities? The answer lies in the fact that the president's dream of building a new world order became an obsession. Before the war, there was an easy-going quality to Wilson. He worked only three or four hours a day, and never on Saturday and Sunday. He was a regular at Washington Senators baseball games. When the war came, he hardly ever stopped toiling.

Like no president before him (but like several since), Wilson lost interest in domestic affairs except insofar as they affected his all-consuming foreign concerns. The onetime enemy of big government presided over its extraordinary expansion. Repression of dissenters, even unjust and illegal repression, appeared to hasten the defeat of the kaiser, so Wilson abandoned values that had guided his life.

The President's Obsession

In January 1918, Wilson presented Congress with his blueprint for the postwar world—his Fourteen Points. The Fourteen Points, Wilson said, were to be incorporated into the treaty that ended the war. Most of Wilson's points dealt with specific European territorial problems, but five general principles were woven through the plan.

First, defeated Germany must be treated fairly and generously in order to avoid the festering resentments that would lead to another war. Wilson was well aware that, for more than 40 years before World War I, French politicians demanded revenge for Germany's defeat of France in 1870. In practical terms, Wilson meant that Germany must not be stripped of territory populated by Germans and the nation must not be saddled with huge reparations payments such as French politicians were at that time telling their people they would be paid.

Second, Wilson said, the boundaries of all European countries must conform to nationality as defined by language. Wilson believed that the aspirations of people to gov-

ern themselves were a major cause of the war. No such concessions were to be made to the nonwhite peoples in Europe's colonies, of course, Britain and France being the world's two greatest empires. However, Wilson did call for Germany's colonies to be disposed of on some basis other than as spoils of war divided among the victors.

Third, Wilson demanded "absolute freedom upon the seas . . . alike in peace and in war." This was a reference to the German submarine campaign that Wilson blamed for American involvement, but it also harked back to Britain's historical inclination to use British primacy on the oceans to interfere with neutral shipping.

Fourth, Wilson demanded disarmament. It was obvious to all parties that the arms race of the two decades preceding the war had been a major cause of the tragedy.

Finally and most important in avoiding another Great War, Wilson called for the establishment of "a general assembly of nations," a congress of countries, to replace the alliances and secret treaties that contributed to the debacle of 1914. More than any other aspect of his program, the dream of a league of nations came to obsess the president.

A Self-Deluded Wilson

When an Allied breakthrough in the summer of 1918 put victory within view, Wilson turned nearly all his energies to planning for the peace conference to be held in Paris. He announced that he would personally head the American delegation.

The enormity of World War I justified his decision, but Wilson paid too little attention to a clear shift in the mood of the electorate. In the midterm election of 1918, just a week before the armistice, the voters returned Republican majorities of 240 to 190 to the House of Representatives and of 49 to 47 to the Senate. Not only was Congress Republican, but it had a decidedly unidealistic, unprogressive tinge. Old bosses and professional politicians who had resisted reform for a decade were coming back to Washington.

They were not all reactionaries or Wilson haters: They were the kind of men who were willing to deal. It was Wilson who was uncooperative. He did not recognize that the election of so many Republican regulars might reflect a weariness with the endless idealistic exhortations of his administration. The president did not even include a prominent Republican among the delegates he took with him to Europe on December 4, although any treaty had to be ratified by the Republican Senate.

Wilson also misinterpreted his reception in England, France, and Italy. Everywhere he went, he was cheered and buried in flowers by crowds of tens of thousands. It had to have been a heady experience for a man who, 10 years earlier, was content to be a university president hosting garden parties. Wilson believed that the people of Europe had risen to greatness along with him. They were voicing their support for a peace without victors and a postwar world organized on principles of justice.

Multiple-Choice Question

President Wilson regarded "national self-determination" as virtually a sacred element of his hopes for the postwar world. His secretary of state, Robert Lansing, thinking of the British and French empires, and the mixture of nationalities in southeastern Europe, where the "borders" between ethnic groups more likely defined villages and neighborhoods than countries, commented, "The phrase is simply loaded with dynamite. It will raise hopes which can never be realized. It will, I fear, cost thousands of lives."

Change *thousands* to *millions and counting*. Who was the better prophet?

(a) President Woodrow Wilson
(b) Secretary Robert Lansing

The Peace Conference

He was mistaken. The crowds were welcoming not the author of the Fourteen Points but Wilson the conqueror, the leader of the nation that had ended four years of stalemate. The leaders of the Allies, the men with whom Wilson sat down in Paris, understood this clearly. They knew that after four years of savagery and sacrifice on an unprecedented scale, the people of the victorious nations wanted to taste the fruits of victory. The other three members of the "Big Four"—Clemenceau of France, Lloyd George of Great Britain, and Orlando of Italy—paid lip service to Wilson's selfless ideals, but once behind the closed doors of the conference room, they put their national and political interests first.

Georges Clemenceau was candid. "God gave us the Ten Commandments and we broke them," he said. "Wilson gives us the Fourteen Points. We shall see." Clemenceau was a cagey, tough, and nasty infighter whom a lifetime in politics had turned into a cynic. He blamed Germany for the war and meant that Germany would pay for the death and destruction. Belgium and France had been the battlefields, not Germany. Germany was physically untouched. The Allies had crossed the German border at only one point at the time of the armistice. Wilson might speak of a peace without reparations; the entire northeast of France was a ruin. Germany had to pay for it.

British prime minister David Lloyd George was personally cordial to Wilson, and there was no ravaged earth in Britain. But Lloyd George was no idealist, and his constituents had suffered the loss of almost a million sons, husbands, and fathers, with a million more permanently maimed. There were billions in pensions to be paid to them and to the widows of the dead soldiers. But the British economy was shattered. Lloyd George too held Germany liable for the suffering and damage.

Vittorio Orlando of Italy went to Versailles (the old royal palace where the treaty talks were held) to ensure that Italy was rewarded with Austrian territory, particularly the South Tyrol and the Dalmatian port of Fiume. The Tyrol's

▲ *The "Big Four" at the Versailles Conference: Vittorio Orlando of Italy, David Lloyd George of Great Britain, Georges Clemenceau of France, and President Woodrow Wilson. None had the international popularity and prestige that Wilson enjoyed. All three of the others had national (and political) self-interests to serve that conflicted with Wilson's plan for a "peace without victory."*

200,000 people were German-speaking Austrians; Fiume's population was largely Croatian. That Italy should have them was a blatant violation of Wilson's principle of "national self-determination."

The Japanese delegate, Count Nobuaki Makino, meant to retain the German colonies in the Pacific that Japan had seized. So much for Point Five.

So Much for the Fourteen Points

One by one, the Versailles Conference redrew Wilson's blueprint until the president's chaste Greek temple looked like a farmhouse to which rooms, dormers, and lean-tos had been added over a century. Three of the Fourteen Points survived intact; six were completely scuttled; five were compromised almost beyond recognition.

Wilson had no choice but to give in. Clemenceau pointed out that Germany had extracted large reparations from France after the Franco-Prussian War, although France had been the aggressor only technically, and that war too had been fought in France, not in Germany. In creating the new nations of Poland and Czechoslovakia, regions populated by Germans had to be included within their borders. Otherwise, Poland would have no seaport (which Wilson himself had, in fact, promised), and Czechoslovakia, without the mountains of the Sudetenland, would be defenseless. Indeed, if all Germans living contiguously had been incorporated into Germany, the nation would have a larger German population than it had in 1914. Victors do not write treaties that enlarge the power of the vanquished.

In the Balkans, Wilson's national self-determination—ethnically homogeneous nations—was impossible. The region was a crazy quilt of Hungarian, Romanian, German, Croatian, Serbian, Slovenian, Bulgarian, and Albanian counties and towns. Romanian villages sat cheek by jowl with Hungarian villages. Every sizable city was home to several ethnic groups. The only alternative to Balkan nations with large ethnic minorities nursing ancient resentments was an unimaginable, forced relocation of millions of people. Italy's demand of the South Tyrol was utterly without justification. Even the Italian army said that the province was not essential to Italian defense. But Orlando wanted it to show Italian voters their sacrifices had been rewarded, and he got his prize (although not Fiume).

Cruel realities exposed the Fourteen Points as the ivory tower doodlings of an idealist who was still very much a college professor. Wilson faced up to this, although he never openly admitted it. Staking all on the League of Nations, believing that it would resolve the injustices in the Treaty of Versailles, Wilson gave in. He had no choice.

Article 10

Shelving the Fourteen Points did not much bother the senators who would ratify or reject the Treaty of Versailles, particularly the 12 of the 49 Republican senators, mostly

westerners, who announced that they were irreconcilable in their opposition to it. They were predominantly isolationists who had opposed going to war in 1917. To them, entering the war had been a mistake. They meant to isolate the United States from Europe's corruption and squabbles—not, in the League of Nations, involve Americans in every one of them.

In March 1919, the other 37 Republican senators signed a round-robin stating they would vote to ratify the treaty if Wilson agreed to certain reservations, which varied from senator to senator. The reservations that counted revolved around Article 10 of the Covenant of the League of Nations. It pledged all member states to "preserve against external aggression the territorial integrity and . . . political independence of all members." Article 10, the reservationists said, committed the United States to go to war if any other league member were attacked. Bulgaria? Uruguay? To the reservationists, that was a surrender of national sovereignty, of America's independence of action.

Wilson replied that Article 10 was nothing more than a moral obligation; the United States was not surrendering its independence of action. This was cant. If the obligation was merely moral, it was meaningless, which Wilson, who wrote it, did not believe. Nevertheless, although he had given in to the Allies on dozens of questions, he refused to change a word of Article 10 in order to win the backing of enough Republican senators—not many were needed—to get the Treaty of Versailles ratified. In this righteous recalcitrance, he created an opening for the chairman of the Senate Foreign Relations Committee, Henry Cabot Lodge of Massachusetts, who openly and explicitly admitted he "hated" Wilson, to destroy the president.

The Fight for the League

Lodge was an unlikely giant-killer. He was not especially popular with his colleagues in the Senate. As determined to have his way as Wilson was, he was devoid of the greatness to which Wilson could rise. In the battle over the League of Nations, however, Lodge proved to be an infinitely shrewder politician. Perceiving that Wilson was growing less flexible as the debate developed, Lodge became open and cooperative with even the "mild reservationists," Republicans who wanted to vote for the league. Understanding that the longer the debate dragged on, the less the American people would take an interest in it, Lodge played for time. He read the entire 264 pages of the treaty into the record of his committee's hearings, even though it had been published and placed on every senator's desk.

Lodge's calculations were dead right. Although a majority of Americans probably favored American participation in the league during the first months of 1919, their interest waned slowly but perceptibly in the summer.

The climax came in September. With the treaty about to come before the Senate, Wilson undertook an exhausting 8,000-mile speaking tour. He believed that by rallying the people behind him, he could bring pressure on the reservationist senators to vote for the treaty as it stood. By September 25, when he moved into Colorado, the crowds seemed to be with him. At Pueblo, however, his speech was slurred, and he openly wept. Wilson had suffered a mild stroke or was on the verge of a nervous breakdown due to exhaustion. His physician canceled the tour and rushed him back to Washington. A few days later, Wilson crumpled to the floor of his bedroom, felled by a cerebral thrombosis, a blood clot in the brain.

The Invisible President

No one knows just how seriously Wilson was disabled in 1919. For six weeks, his protective, strong-willed wife isolated him from everyone but physicians. She screened every document brought to him and returned them with shaky signatures at the bottom. When suspicious and concerned officials insisted on seeing the president, they discovered that his left side was paralyzed and his speech was halting. However, he appeared to be in complete control of his wits. To a senator who told him, "We've all been praying for you," he replied, "Which way, Senator?"

Wilson did not meet officially with his cabinet for six months, and photographs of that occasion show a haggard old man with an anxiety in his eyes that cannot be found in any earlier picture. Even if the clarity of his thinking was not affected, because Wilson in the pink of health had refused to consider compromising with Lodge, his removal from the scene probably had little effect on the outcome of the battle.

The outcome was defeat. In November, on Wilson's instructions, the Democratic senators voted with the irreconcilables to kill the treaty with the Lodge reservations by a vote of 55 to 39. When the treaty was introduced without the reservations, the reservationists and the irreconcilables defeated it against the Democrats. In March, over Wilson's protest, 21 Democrats worked out a compromise with the reservationist Republicans and again voted on the treaty. The 23 Democrats who went along with Wilson's insistence that he get the original treaty or no treaty at all made the difference. They and the irreconcilables defeated it.

The Election of 1920

Incredibly, Wilson believed that he could win the League of Nations in the presidential election of 1920. He wanted to

▲ *Senator Henry Cabot Lodge's ancestors were among the earliest Puritans in Massachusetts. He was a "Boston Brahmin," a member of the elite of ancestry and respectability. As late as 1890 in Congress, he fought for African American civil rights. Then he became fast friends with Theodore Roosevelt under the influence of the same theories of Anglo-Saxon racial superiority that guided Roosevelt. He was a brilliant political manipulator. Determined to kill Wilson's League of Nations, he turned Wilson's near majority in the Senate into a squabbling fragment.*

be the Democratic party's nominee. That was too much for even the most loyal Wilsonians. They ignored Wilson's hints and chose Governor James M. Cox of Ohio, a party regular who looked like a traveling salesman. For vice president, the Democrats nominated a staunch young Wilsonian with a magical name, the undersecretary of the navy, Franklin D. Roosevelt. The Democrats were pessimistic. But maybe the Roosevelt name on the Democratic ticket would win enough progressive votes to put the party across.

The Republicans had better reason to expect victory. The knew they were the majority party. Wilson's victory in 1912 was a fluke, made possible by the split of the Republican vote. He won reelection in 1916 by a hair because western voters believed, as Wilson did not, that he could keep the country out of the war. The Republican victory in the congressional elections of 1918, even with the war still raging, confirmed their majority standing.

As often happens when a party's candidate looks like a shoo-in, there was a cat fight for the nomination. General Leonard Wood, an old comrade of Theodore Roosevelt (but no progressive), battled Illinois Governor Frank O. Lowden, who had a reputation as an innovative scientific farmer. Both arrived in Chicago with large blocs of votes, but, thanks to a cadre of favorite-son candidates, neither had a majority.

Early in the proceedings, reporters cornered a wheeler-dealer from Ohio named Harry M. Daugherty and asked him who he thought would be nominated. Daugherty replied genially: "Well boys, I'll tell you what I think. The convention will be deadlocked. After the other candidates have failed, we'll get together in some hotel room, oh, about 2:11 in the morning, and some 15 men, bleary-eyed with lack of sleep, will sit down around a big table and when that time comes Senator Harding will be selected."

Brown Brothers

▲ *Republican candidate Warren G. Harding campaigned from the front porch of his middle-class home in Marion, Ohio, deliberately reminding voters of the "good old days" of William McKinley. He was a superb public speaker and strikingly handsome.*

MAP 38:1 Presidential Election, 1920 Harding's election restored the Republican party's "natural" supremacy in national elections. Indeed, he swept the entire nation in the electoral college except the South, and he even carried West Virginia and Tennessee.

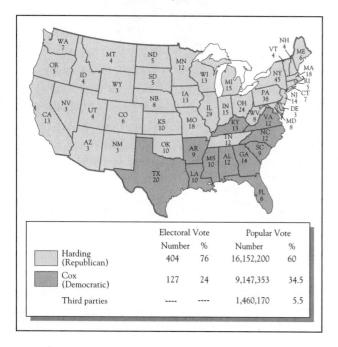

		Electoral Vote		Popular Vote	
		Number	%	Number	%
	Harding (Republican)	404	76	16,152,200	60
	Cox (Democratic)	127	24	9,147,353	34.5
	Third parties	----	----	1,460,170	5.5

Warren G. Harding of Ohio, a handsome, congenial man, was considered one of the least competent members of the Senate. Journalists and fellow senators joked about him. Perhaps because of that, he was acceptable to all Republicans but the now marginal progressives. Because Harding had been a mild reservationist on the League of Nations, Henry Cabot Lodge (in whose smoke-filled room at the Blackstone Hotel the nomination took place) probably assumed he could control him.

The Great Bloviator

Harding waffled on the Treaty of Versailles, sometimes appearing to favor it with reservations, other times hinting he would let the whole thing die. The theme of his campaign was the need for the country to cool off after two decades of experimental reform and wartime crusading. This strategy allowed Harding to make use of his technique of "bloviation." Bloviating, as Harding was happy to explain, was "the art of speaking for as long as the occasion warrants, and saying nothing." In Boston, Harding declared that "America's need is not heroism but healing, not nostrums but normalcy, not agitation but adjustment, not surgery but serenity, not the dramatic but the dispassionate, not experiment but equipoise, not submergence in internationality but sustainment in triumphant nationality."

The acerbic journalist H. L. Mencken said that Harding's speech reminded him of "stale bean soup, of college yells, of dogs barking idiotically through endless nights." But he added that "it is so bad that a sort of grandeur creeps through it." A Democratic politician remarked that the normalcy speech "left the impression of an army of pompous phrases moving over the landscape in search of an idea."

But Harding did have an idea. The great bloviator sensed that no issue, including the League of Nations, was as important to the American people in 1920 as getting back to "normalcy." He was right. He won 61 percent of the vote, more than any candidate who preceded him in the White House since popular votes were recorded.

Wilson lived quietly in Washington until 1924. His wit returning after his retirement, he said, "I am going to try to teach ex-presidents how to behave." He set a good example. A semi-invalid specter out of the past, he took drives almost daily in the elegant Pierce-Arrow automobile that was his pride and joy, attended vaudeville performances and baseball games, and watched movies, of which he was an avid fan, at home.

Unlike Harding (whose funeral he lived to attend), Wilson was a giant who loomed over an age. His intelligence, dignity, steadfastness, and sense of rectitude overshadowed even the boisterous Theodore Roosevelt, something Teddy himself must have sensed (he hated Wilson). Wilson's end was, therefore, more tragic than that of any other president, including those who were assassinated. For Wilson, like the tragic heroes of great drama, was murdered not by his enemies or by his weaknesses, but by his own virtues.

for FURTHER READING

The foremost study of the American home front during World War I is David Kennedy, *Over Here: The First World War and American Society,* 1980. See also Ellis W. Hawley, *The Great War and the Search for a Modern Order: A History of the American People and Their Institutions, 1914–1920,* 1979; the early chapters of William E. Leuchtenburg, *The Perils of Prosperity, 1914–1932,* 1958; Arthur S. Link, *Woodrow Wilson: War, Revolution, and Peace,* 1979; Preston Slosson, *The Great Crusade and After,* 1930; Daniel M. Smith, *The Great Departure: The United States and World War I, 1914–1920,* 1965; and the later chapters of Robert H. Wiebe, *The Search for Order, 1880–1920,* 1967.

Worthwhile studies of diplomacy include Thomas A. Bailey, *Woodrow Wilson and the Great Betrayal,* 1945; John M. Blum, *Woodrow Wilson and the Politics of Morality,* 1956; John A. Garraty, *Henry Cabot Lodge,* 1953; N. G. Levin Jr., *Woodrow Wilson and World Politics: America's Response to War and Revolution,* 1968; the classic Harold Nicholson, *Peacemaking: 1919,* 1939; and Ralph Stone, *The Irreconcilables: The Fight Against the League of Nations,* 1970.

On economic mobilization, see Robert Cuff, *The War-Industries Board: Business-Government Relations During World War I,* 1973. On social aspects of the wartime experience, see Maurine W. Greenwald, *Women, War, and Work: The Impact of World War I on Women Workers in the United States,* 1980; Frederick C. Luebke, *Bonds of Loyalty: German-Americans and World War I,* 1974; Frederick L. Paxson, *American Democracy and the World War,* 1948; and William Preston Jr., *Aliens and Dissenters: Federal Suppression of Radicals, 1903–1933,* 1953.

American JOURNEY ONLINE AND INFOTRAC *COLLEGE* EDITION

Visit the source collections at http://ajaccess.wadsworth.com and http://infotrac.thomsonlearning.com, and use the Search function with the following key terms to explore documents, images, audio and video clips, articles, and commentary related to the material in this chapter:

Carrie Chapman Catt	National American Woman Suffrage Association
Fourteen Points	Nineteenth Amendment
Herbert Hoover	Versailles Conference
Influenza epidemic of 1918	W. E. B. DuBois
League of Nations	Woodrow Wilson

Additional resources, exercises, and Internet links related to this chapter are available on *The American Past* Web site: http://history.wadsworth.com/americanpast7e.

HISTORY ONLINE

Wartime Posters
http://bigbird.lib.umn.edu/umimage/servlet/SearchImage
A selection of propaganda posters from World War I, when poster art was at its apex.

Influenza 1918
www.pbs.org/wgbh/amex/influenza/timeline/
A detailed timeline of the devastating pandemic; prepared by the Public Broadcasting System.

THE DAYS OF HARDING

Troubled Years 1919–1923

© UPI/Bettmann/Corbis

My candle burneth at both ends;
It will not last the night.
But, ah, my foes, and, oh, my friends—
It gives a lovely light.

Edna St. Vincent Millay

Grown up, and that is a terribly hard thing to do. It is much easier to skip it and go from one childhood to another.

F. Scott Fitzgerald

THE 1920S HAVE come down to us with a ready-made personality, the "Roaring Twenties": Worn out by the prolonged fervor of the progressive years and disillusioned by a righteous war that spectacularly failed to save humanity from itself, the American people shrugged, set out to have a little fun, and ended up having a lot of it.

Images of the Roaring Twenties readily flood the mind: speakeasies; college boys and flapper girls defying stodgy moralists during breaks from dancing to the exciting new jazz played by carefree black musicians; bootleggers and gangsters, somehow menacing and engaging at the same time. F. Scott Fitzgerald captured—created?—the age in his stories and novels.

The 1920s were the golden age of sport: Babe Ruth's Yankees were the superteam of baseball; Harold "Red" Grange was the hero of the midwestern religion of football; Jack Dempsey and Gene Tunney were mythic prizefighters; Robert T. "Bobby" Jones of Georgia made the rich man's game of golf popular with both participants and spectators; and William "Big Bill" Tilden did the same for the once aristocratic tennis.

Commercial radio made its debut: The first broadcast told of Warren G. Harding's landslide in the election of 1920. The movies were booming—with Charlie Chaplin, Rudolph Valentino, and unabashedly sexy Clara Bow, the "It" girl with the "bee-sting" lips, rumored (by her press agents) to entertain entire football teams. The automobile, the modern world's amulet of personal freedom, was everywhere, from the homely Model T Ford to the Stutz Bearcat and Dusenberg, still among the most glorious creations of the automaker's craft.

The list could go on, but at any length it is a distortion. Only a small proportion of the American population—the wealthy and the comfortably fixed middle classes of the cities, suburbs, and sizable towns—enjoyed even a vague semblance of the roaring good times. And the gravy years did not add up to a decade but were five or six in number, beginning only after the death of President Harding.

"THE WORST PRESIDENT"

Between 1919 and 1923, American life was characterized by contradictions, uncertainties, tensions, and fears. In fact, during the years immediately preceding, and the two following, the inauguration of President Harding in March 1921, American society was on edge, as was the man whom most presidential historians have called "the worst president."

Gamaliel

A newspaperman, Warren Gamaliel Harding worked his way up in Ohio politics with a smile, a firm handshake, reliable support of the Republican party line, and the discovery by Republican political bosses that whenever they asked him for a favor, Harding said yes. Harding himself said that if he had been born a woman, he would have been forever "in the family way." He was unable to say no.

For Harding, the Senate, to which Ohio sent him in 1914, was heaven. Being senator called for making speeches; the self-styled "bloviator" was a master orator. But, as just one senator among 96, he was not expected to take the lead in anything. However, with a surplus of prima donnas crowding the Senate floor, a passive, obliging fellow was more than welcome. The Senate was a club in which members watched out for one another. No one objected that Harding, still saying yes, helped old cronies find government jobs they were unfit to perform. And the Senate left the affable Ohioan with plenty of time to enjoy the all-night poker, bourbon, and cigars parties that were Harding's second most favorite recreation.

Newspaper reporters were more restrained in dealing with the private lives of persons in high public office than they are today. They criticized Harding as the least effective senator, but they steered clear of his adulteries with a series of mistresses. Only after Harding's death did one of his lady friends, Nan Britton, go public with the story that Harding had fathered her illegitimate daughter.

A Decent Man

It is not difficult to feel sympathy for Harding. He was a weak man, but he lacked hypocrisy—an extraordinary virtue in a politician—and he had no illusions about his intelligence and capacity for leadership. He freely admitted that he could not hope to be "the best president" and said he would try to be "the best liked." Harding was personally kind and decent. After the nation's experience with the brilliant but self-righteous Wilson, the American people did not regard an ordinary mind and a self-effacing personality as unattractive.

Harding displayed his humanity when, at Christmas 1921, he pardoned Eugene V. Debs and other socialists who had opposed the war. (Wilson commuted the sentences of a hundred small fish convicted under the dubious Espionage Act but remained vindictive toward Debs to the end.) Harding personally pressured the directors of United States Steel Corporation to reduce the workday in their mills to 8 hours, not because he challenged the owners' right to do with their property as they chose but because he was appalled at the idea of men working 12-hour days at such jobs.

Most striking was Harding's response when political enemies whispered that he had African blood. In an era when almost all white people thought in at least mildly racist terms, that kind of talk could ruin a career. Other politicians would have responded to the smear with a lawsuit or yet uglier counterattacks. Harding shrugged: How did he know whether or not one of his forebears "had jumped the fence"?

Bum Rap
Harding's critics made fun of his campaign slogan, "normalcy," as soon as he spoke it. All is fair in politics. However, Harding was not exhibiting his ignorance of the dictionary, which listed *normality,* but not *normalcy.* His speechwriter had written "normality." Harding changed it because "normality" was popularly associated with a person's mental health. He later explained what he meant by *normalcy:* "a regular, steady order of things."

Nevertheless, three generations of historians, to the present, have continued to mock the word. To do so today, after a generation-long ravaging of the English language by politicians, bureaucrats, journalists, single-issue pressure groups, intellectuals, and academics—in an age when a television reporter cannot speak for 30 seconds without calling something, ranging from a 14-year-old sex-pot rock singer to a breakfast cereal box, an "icon"—is not very gracious. As far as "normalcy" is concerned, Harding has gotten a bum rap.

Presidents and Baseball
In 1910, William Howard Taft instituted the custom of the president throwing out the first ball of the baseball season, in Washington, when there was a team there. The most avid presidential baseball fan was his successor, Woodrow Wilson, who often watched the Washington Senators play, from his limousine in foul territory beyond the right-field flagpole. (A spare player stood nearby to shield Wilson from foul balls.)

Harding, Herbert Hoover, Franklin D. Roosevelt, and Harry S. Truman were also fans, and Jimmy Carter was a pretty good softball player. Ronald Reagan had been a baseball announcer as a young man and portrayed the great pitcher Grover Cleveland Alexander in a film of 1952. As president, however, he rarely remained at a game longer than ceremony required. In April 1989, by contrast, President George Bush took Egyptian president Hosni Mubarak to a game, and both stayed to the end.

The National Pastime

Originally, baseball was a gentleman's game, played by wealthy amateurs for pleasure. By the turn of the twentieth century, baseball was a business, potentially lucrative but risky. The players were paid for their skills by teams organized into two major leagues, the National and the American. The profits to the owners, who called themselves "sportsmen" and their properties "clubs," lay in paid admissions to games. The better the team, the more people were willing to pay to attend; it stood to reason that club owners would seek to build winning teams. However, it did not always work that way. Although the players competed to win, the sportsmen did not compete with one another to get the best players.

In order to avoid bidding wars for the services of star pitchers and hitters, the club owners devised the "reserve clause," which was in every player's contract. The reserve clause was based on the proposition that a baseball player was a professional like a physician or lawyer and not an employee. Unlike a machinist or miner, who (as employers never tired of saying) were free to quit whenever they chose, the professional baseball player could not. He was under contract. In signing the reserve clause, he agreed that he would not play for another team without the club's consent. His services were reserved unless the club owner "sold" or "traded" him (his contract) to another owner for whom the player had no choice but to play—if he wanted to stay in baseball.

As in other businesses, policies varied from team to team. The owner who was, perhaps, most blatantly motivated by money was Cornelius "Connie Mack" McGillicuddy, who owned and managed the Philadelphia Athletics (the "A's"). The dominant team in the American League before World War I, the A's won six pennants and three World Series. Twice Mack sold off his star players for cash he could pocket, relegating Philadelphia's pride to the league cellar. He was to do it again after 1931, when the A's were better than the fabled Babe Ruth Yankees.

Charles A. Comiskey, owner of the Chicago White Sox, was another kind of businessman. Until the war, he was content with mediocre players to whom he paid the lowest salaries in the major leagues. Then, during the war, while attendance in other cities declined, the White Sox jelled behind hard-hitting outfielder Joseph "Shoeless Joe" Jackson and third baseman George "Buck" Weaver. After finishing high in the standings in 1917 and 1918, the White Sox won the American League pennant in 1919 and were regarded by the experts as unbeatable in the World Series. The National League champion was the upstart and unrespected Cincinnati Reds.

There was trouble for the White Sox, however. Although their sterling play had caused attendance and profits to soar, Comiskey had taken the lead in calling for a league-wide pay cut. At a time when wages in almost every job were rising, the two leading White Sox pitchers, who won 50 games between them, were paid a combined salary of only $8,600. Adding insult to exploitation, Comiskey allowed his champion players considerably lower expenses than any other owner when the team was on the road.

The White Sox lost the World Series to the Reds. An investigation during the winter and spring revealed that it was no mere upset. Eight White Sox players, including Jackson, had conspired with gamblers to throw the Series so that the gamblers could make a killing on their long-shot bets on the Reds.

Comiskey had been aware of the fix all along (there were plenty of rumors even before the Series), but he was willing to sacrifice the championship for the chance to intimidate future players. Indeed, although the eight accused "Black Sox" were acquitted in criminal court for lack of hard evidence, they were banned from playing professional ball for life by a newly installed commissioner with broad powers, Judge Kenesaw Mountain Landis. Like the head of a government commission, Landis showed no interest in disciplining owners whose actions threatened the game, but he backed the owners in disputes with players.

Not every club owner was as cash oriented as Mack or as exploitative as Comiskey. During the same years that Landis was burnishing baseball's reputation for honesty, an ugly, pot-bellied, spindly legged, and atrociously vulgar Baltimorean was revolutionizing the game and winning huge salaries from his ungrudging employers, the New York Yankees.

George Herman "Babe" Ruth started in baseball as a pitcher—he was excellent—for the Boston Red Sox. In 1919, the year of the Black Sox scandal, while playing the outfield on days he did not pitch, Ruth hit 29 home runs, double the number of any previous player. Baseball before Ruth was a game of tactics played by lithe, swift men who eked out runs one at a time with scratch hits off overpowering pitchers and gritty base running. Tyrus J. "Ty" Cobb of the Detroit Tigers, a genuinely mean-spirited man whose specialty was sliding into second with file-sharpened cleats slicing the air, was the best player of the 1910s.

Now, with a single swing, the "Sultan of Swat" could put up to four runs on the scoreboard, and the fans loved it. Purchased from the Red Sox by the Yankees for $100,000—itself an unprecedented windfall under the reserve clause—Ruth hit 59 home runs in 1921, the record until his own 60 in 1927. Rather than haggle endlessly with their golden goose, the Yankee ownership paid him annually higher salaries. By the end of the decade, when his pay was higher than that of the president of the United States, Ruth shrugged nonchalantly, "I had a better year than he did."

Not only did Ruth make the Yankees the best team in baseball; he made them the richest. In 1923, New York opened the largest baseball grounds of the era, Yankee Stadium, which was properly nicknamed "the house that Ruth built."

Other owners and Commissioner Landis took notice too. If home runs sold tickets, they would have more home runs. The baseball itself was redesigned into a livelier "rabbit ball," and the slugger became the mythic figure in the game. Hack Wilson of the Chicago Cubs hit 56 home runs in 1930, setting the National League's record; and Jimmy Foxx of the Philadelphia Athletics was eclipsing Ruth himself by 1932, when he hit 58 (and was promptly sold by Connie Mack). The New York Yankees remained the team that most totally staked its fortunes on men who swung the heavy bat, and it was the club that was the most liberal with a paycheck. It would not have much mattered to Connie Mack and Charles Comiskey, but the Yankees were also, of course, the most successful team in the history of the sport.

Smart Geeks

Harding made some excellent appointments to his cabinet. As secretary of commerce, he picked Herbert Hoover. Although Franklin D. Roosevelt had assumed that Hoover was a Wilsonian Democrat, he was, in fact, a Republican by inheritance and temperament. If Hoover was slightly appalled by the backslapping Harding, Harding was ill at ease with the all-business Hoover. He called Hoover (not to his face) "the smartest geek I know."

As he had during the war, Hoover worked without conspicuous self-promotion; he believed that his achievements would take care of his career. He mollified conservative Republicans by encouraging the formation of voluntary associations in industry and agriculture rather than, in the manner of the progressives, putting the government in the driver's seat. Hoover hoped that these organizations would eliminate waste, develop uniform standards of production, and end "destructive competition."

Harding named Charles Evans Hughes secretary of state. This was a gesture to the progressive wing of the party. A man of moderate temperament, an able Supreme Court justice between 1910 and 1916, Hughes had waffled on the League of Nations, as Harding had. By 1921, that issue was dead. However, because the Senate had not ratified the Treaty of Versailles, the United States was still officially at war with Germany. Hughes resolved the problem by prevailing on Congress to resolve that the war was over and by recognizing the new German republic.

The Treaty of Washington

Hughes's most important achievement, or so it seemed at the time, was to finagle the other major naval powers into reducing the size of their fleets. Ignoring the League of Nations, he gathered representatives of the naval powers in Washington. The delegates, expecting the usual round of receptions and platitudes about the pressing need for disarmament, were snookered when Hughes opened the conference with a detailed plan for reducing the size of the world's navies. All powers were to scrap some capital ships (battleships and battle cruisers) and to cancel plans for future naval construction.

Everyone agreed that the arms race was instrumental in causing the world war. The delegates at the Washington Conference had little choice but to listen. Hughes reminded them that by reducing the size of their navies, their governments would save millions: The construction of a single capital ship was a major line item in a national budget.

In the Treaty of Washington of 1921, the five major naval powers agreed to limit their fleets according to a ratio that reflected their interests and defensive needs. For each 5 tons that Great Britain and the United States kept afloat in capital ships, Japan would have 3, and France and Italy, somewhat smaller fleets.

Each nation gave up ships, but each benefited too. Great Britain maintained equality on the high seas with the United States, a primacy that American plans for ship construction would have destroyed. (The United States scrapped 30 battleships and cruisers that were under construction or on the drawing boards.) The American government slashed its expenditures, a high priority for the Harding administration. Japan, which needed only a Pacific navy (whereas Britain and the United States had worldwide interests), got parity—even superiority—in the Pacific. Italy and France were spared the strain of an arms race that would bankrupt them but remained dominant in the Mediterranean.

The Harding Scandals

The work of Hoover and Hughes just about sums up the accomplishments of the Harding administration. The president's other appointees were either servants of narrow special interests or outright crooks. Secretary of the Treasury Andrew Mellon pursued tax policies that extravagantly favored the rich. More dismaying in the short run were the cronies to whom Harding gave government jobs for old times' sake. No sooner were they settled in their Washington offices than they set about filling their pockets and ruining their generous friend in the White House.

Attorney General Harry Daugherty winked at violations of the law by political allies. Probably with Daugherty's connivance, Jesse L. Smith, a close friend of the president, sold favorable decisions and public offices for cold cash. Charles R. Forbes, the head of the Veterans Administration, pocketed money intended for hospital construction. The grandest thief of all, Secretary of the Interior Albert B. Fall, leased the navy's petroleum reserves at Teapot Dome, Wyoming, and Elk Hills, California, to two freewheeling oilmen, Harry Sinclair and Edward L. Doheny. In return, Fall accepted "loans" of about $300,000. Fall tarred Harding with his corruption because he had earlier persuaded the president to transfer these oil reserves from the authority of the navy to Fall's Department of the Interior.

By the summer of 1923, Harding knew that his administration was shot through with thievery. When he set out on a vacation to Alaska, he knew that it was only a matter of time before the scandals hit the newspapers. His health was suffering; the famous handsome face is haggard in the photographs. Nevertheless, he remained loyal to his treacherous pals. He allowed Forbes to flee abroad, and he took no action against the others.

Jesse Smith eventually killed himself. Mercifully, perhaps, for he was personally innocent of wrongdoing, Harding died shortly after disembarking from his vacation cruise

Father of the Backyard Barbecue
Among Henry Ford's inventions was the charcoal briquette. He developed the process for making the briquettes in order to make use of the mountains of wood scraps produced by the manufacture of dashboards and other wooden parts for the Model T. He and Thomas Edison built the first briquette factory and turned it over to a partner, Charles Kingsford, to operate.

at San Francisco. Only later did the nation learn of the crooks in his administration and the juicy irregularities in the president's personal life. So tangled were Harding's affairs that scandalmongers suggested that Harding's wife poisoned him to spare him the disgrace that was coming, and they were widely believed. Actually, the president suffered massive heart failure.

SOCIAL TENSIONS: LABOR, REDS, IMMIGRANTS

If Harding was tortured by the tensions in his heart, the nation was contending with social tensions that strained and snapped while he was in the White House. Had Harding been a pillar of moral strength and probity—had Woodrow Wilson or Calvin Coolidge been elected president in 1920—the years associated with unhappy Harding would have been no less troubled by labor unrest, the fear of Communism, immigration, race, and religion.

1919: A Year of Strikes

During the First World War, the American Federation of Labor seemed to be part of the federal power structure. In return for recognition of their respectability, most unions did not strike for the duration of hostilities. Unfortunately, although wages rose slowly during 1917 and 1918, the prices of consumer goods rose much more. Then they soared during a runaway postwar inflation. War's end also meant the cancellation of huge government contracts. Tens of thousands of people in war-related jobs were thrown out of work, leading to the inevitable: 3,600 strikes in 1919 involving 4 million workers.

The strikers' grievances were generally valid, but few Americans outside the labor movement were sympathetic. When employers described the strikes of 1919 as the work of revolutionaries aimed at destroying middle-class decency, much of America agreed. In Seattle, a dispute that began on the docks of the busy Pacific port turned into a general strike involving almost all the city's 60,000 working people. Most of the strikers were interested in nothing more than better pay. However, the concept of the general strike was associated with class war and revolution. Seattle mayor Ole Hansen depicted the dispute as an uprising sponsored and led by dangerous foreign Bolsheviks. With the help of the United States Marines, Hansen crushed the strike.

The Steelworkers' Walkout

The magnates of the steel industry employed similar methods to fight a walkout in September 1919 by 350,000 workers, mostly in the Great Lakes region. The men had good reason to strike. Many of them worked a 12-hour day and a seven-day week. It was not unusual for individuals to put in 36 hours at a stretch. That is, if a man's relief failed to show up, he might be told to stay on for another 12-hour shift or lose his job. When the extra shift ended, his own began again.

Library & Archives Division, Historical Society of Western Pennsylvania, Pittsburg, Pa.

▲ *A handbill announcing the failure of the steel strike of 1919—in eight different languages. Many steelworkers were immigrants, particularly from Slavic eastern Europe.*

For this kind of life, steelworkers took home subsistence wages. For some Slavic immigrants in the industry, that home was not even a bed to themselves. They contracted with a boardinghouse to rent a bed half the day. After their wearying shift and a quick meal, they rolled under blankets still warm and damp from the body of a fellow worker who had just trudged off to the mill.

These wretched conditions were well known. And yet, the heads of the industry, Elbert Gary of United States Steel and Charles Schwab of Bethlehem Steel, persuaded the public that the strike of 1919 was the work of revolutionary agitators like William Z. Foster. Although Foster's leadership was in the American Federation of Labor's bread-and-butter tradition, he had been a Wobbly in the past (and he would become the head of the American Communist party), so the company's line was plausible. Moreover, many steelworkers were immigrants from eastern Europe, the nursery of Bolshevism. The strike failed.

The Boston Police Strike

The Boston police strike of 1919 frightened Americans more than any other. Whereas the shutdown of even a basic industry like steel did not touch the daily lives of most people, the absence of police officers from the streets caused a jump in crime as professional hoodlums, lowlifes, and the desperately poor took advantage of the situation.

Boston's policemen, mostly of Irish background, were underpaid. They earned 1916 wages, not enough to support their families decently in a city where prices had tripled during the war. Nevertheless, they commanded little public support when they walked out. When Massachusetts governor Calvin Coolidge ordered the National Guard into Boston to take over police functions and break the strike, the public applauded. When Samuel Gompers asked Coolidge to restore the beaten workers to their jobs, the governor replied, "There is no right to strike against the public safety by anybody, anywhere, anytime." It made Coolidge a national hero and won him the Republican vice presidential nomination in 1920.

The Red Scare

Public reaction to the strikes of 1919 revealed a widespread hostility toward recent immigrants and second-generation Americans. This xenophobia took its most virulent form in the "red scare" of 1919. Even before the end of World War I, a new stereotype replaced the "Hun" as the villain Americans loved to hate: the seedy, lousy, bearded, and wild-eyed Bolshevik—the "red."

The atrocities during the civil war following the Russian Revolution of 1917 were real, lurid, and numerous. Nevertheless, American newspapers exaggerated them and even invented tales of mass executions, torture, children turned against their parents, and women proclaimed the common sexual property of all men. Americans were ready to believe the worst about a part of the world from which so many immigrants had recently come.

Many believed that foreign-born Communists were a major threat to the security of the United States. In March 1919, the Soviets organized the Third International, or Comintern, an organization explicitly dedicated to fomenting revolution worldwide. So it seemed to be no accident when, in April, the Post Office discovered 38 bombs in the mail addressed to prominent capitalists and government officials. In June, several bombs reached their targets. One bomber who was identified—he blew himself up—was a foreigner, an Italian. Then, in Chicago in September 1919, two American Communist parties were founded, with the press emphasizing the immigrant element in the membership.

In reality, a tiny minority of American immigrants and ethnics were radicals, and most prominent Communists boasted of white Anglo-Saxon Protestant ancestry as impeccable as Henry Cabot Lodge's. Max Eastman, the editor of the radical wartime magazine *The Masses,* was of old New England stock. John Reed, whose *Ten Days That Shook the World* remained for many years the classic account of the Russian Revolution, was a bright-eyed Harvard boy from Portland, Oregon. William Z. Foster had no ethnic ties. William D. Haywood, who fled to the Soviet Union rather than go to prison, said he could trace his ancestry "to the Puritan bigots." Moreover, neither they nor the foreign-born radicals posed a real threat to established institutions. Within a few years, the combined membership of the two Communist parties and the (nonrevolutionary) Socialist party numbered only in the thousands.

The Palmer Raids

But dread of a ghost can be as compelling as fear of a grizzly bear. Americans' fear of Communism was intense in 1919. The temptation to exploit the anxiety was too much for President Wilson's attorney general, A. Mitchell Palmer, who thought he might be able to ride the red scare into a presidential nomination by ordering a series of well-publicized raids on Communist offices.

Only 39 of the hundreds Palmer arrested could legally be deported, but the attorney general put 249 people on a steamship dubbed the "Soviet Ark" and sent them to Russia. On New Year's Day 1920, Palmer's agents again swooped down on hundreds of locations, arresting 6,000 people. Some of them, such as a Western Union delivery boy, merely had the bad luck to be in the wrong place at the wrong time. Others were arrested while peering into the windows of Communist storefronts. All were jailed at least briefly.

Palmer's celebrity fizzled when he predicted mass demonstrations on May Day, the international socialist and Communist holiday, and nothing happened. By midsummer, the great red scare was over, but antiforeign sentiment continued to shape both government policy and popular culture.

Sacco and Vanzetti

The most celebrated victims of the marriage of antiradicalism to xenophobia were Nicola Sacco and Bartolomeo

▲ *Bartolomeo Vanzetti and Nicola Sacco became the center of a worldwide protest in what began as an ordinary armed robbery and murder case. Ballistics tests done late in the twentieth century indicate that Sacco was probably involved, but the evidence against them in the 1920s was scanty and, in part, contrived.*

Vanzetti. In 1920, the two Italian immigrants were arrested for an armed robbery in South Braintree, Massachusetts, during which a guard and a paymaster were killed. They were promptly found guilty of murder and sentenced to die in the electric chair.

Before they could be executed, however, the recently founded American Civil Liberties Union, several Italian American groups, and some labor unions publicized the fact that the hard evidence against Sacco and Vanzetti was scanty, that some, in fact, appeared to have been invented by the prosecution. The presiding judge at the trial, Webster Thayer, had been openly prejudiced against the defendants; he was overheard speaking of them as "damned dagos."

Sacco and Vanzetti won admiration by acting with dignity in prison. They insisted on their innocence of the murders but refused to compromise their political beliefs. "I am suffering," Vanzetti said, "because I am a radical and indeed I am a radical; I have suffered because I was an Italian, and indeed I am an Italian. . . . but I am so convinced to be right that if you could execute me two times, and if I could be reborn two other times, I would live again to do what I have done already."

The movement to save Sacco and Vanzetti was international. Even the Italian dictator, Benito Mussolini, who was savaging anarchists at home without a semblance of the trial Sacco and Vanzetti enjoyed, protested the verdict. Nevertheless, the two were finally executed in 1927. By that time, the men's guilt or innocence of the murders was irrelevant to all: The majority were glad to see the two anarchists punished. Sacco and Vanzetti's defenders could see nothing in the case against them except ethnic and political prejudice.

The Passing of the Great Race

In 1883, Emma Lazarus had written, "Send these, the homeless, tempest-tost to me, I lift my lamp beside the golden door." As if they had heard her, European immigrants poured into the United States at high levels until 1915, when naval war made the Atlantic crossings risky. In 1918, immigration had declined to 110,000.

Even before the war, many Americans of white Anglo-Saxon Protestant and old-immigrant stock had been nervous about the flood of eastern and southern Europeans. Unlike earlier immigrants, including the once despised Irish, the new immigrants seemed determined not to become American. At first a cultural and social anxiety, concern about the new immigrants took on racist overtones when respected anthropologists described significant genetic distinctions among the peoples of Europe. The most influential of these writers was William Z. Ripley, whose *Races of Europe* was published in 1899. Ripley divided Caucasians into the Teutonic, Alpine, and Mediterranean races. Although all three had their redeeming traits (the Mediterranean Italians, for example, were credited with a finely developed artistic sense), there was no question that Teutons—Britons, Germans, northern Europeans generally—were the ones with a dependable commitment to liberty and to the American way of life. Slavic peoples got very bad reviews.

In 1916, a respected natural scientist, Madison Grant, took up where Ripley left off. In *The Passing of the Great Race,* Grant maintained that, through intermarriage with old-stock Americans, the new immigrants were literally destroying, through dilution, the nation's prized genetic heritage. The book was immensely successful, running through several editions. (During the war, Grant demoted the Germans out of the "great race.") After the war, when immigration soared again—to 805,000 in 1921, mostly from the "lesser" stock—the time for action had come.

Immigration Restriction

There was a precedent for restricting immigration on the basis of race. In 1882, Congress had excluded the Chinese from the United States. In the same year, Congress determined that criminals, idiots, lunatics, and those likely to become a public charge (people with glaucoma, tuberculosis, and venereal disease) would no longer be admitted. By 1900, the Immigration Restriction League began to call for a general immigration law that would discriminate against other "genetic inferiors"—southern and eastern Europeans.

Four times between 1897 and 1917, Congress tried to discriminate against the new immigrants by enacting a bill requiring all newcomers to pass a literacy test. (Few peasants from southern and eastern Europe could read and write.) Four times, three of them by Wilson, the bills were vetoed. The importance of ethnic voters to the Democratic party and the demand of industry for cheap labor stymied the restrictionists.

Then the election of 1920 brought the Republicans to power. In 1921, Congress enacted, and President Harding signed, a law limiting annual immigration to 350,000 people. Each year, each European nation was entitled to send to the United States a number equal to 3 percent of the number of its nationals who were residents of the United States in the base year of 1910. In 1924, an amendment reduced the number of immigrants from outside the Americas to 150,000, lowered the national quota to 2 percent, and changed the base year to 1890. Most southern and eastern Europeans had emigrated to the United States after 1890. So the quotas of poor countries, such as Poland, Czechoslovakia, Hungary, Romania, Yugoslavia, Bulgaria, Greece, and Italy, were very low. For example, the annual quota for Italy was a minuscule 5,802; for Poland, 6,524; for Russia, 2,784; and for Syria, 100. All were inevitably filled within the first few months of each year.

By contrast, the quotas for the comparatively prosperous countries of northern and western Europe, the nations of the old immigration, were generous and rarely filled. The annual quota for Great Britain under the 1924 law was 75,000, five times the number of British immigrants who actually came. During the 1930s, an average of only 2,500 Britons emigrated to the United States each year.

SOCIAL TENSIONS: RACE, MORALITY, RELIGION

The 1920s were also a time of tension in relations between whites and blacks; between Americans who found consolation in traditional moral codes and those who rejected them; and between country and city, between rural people and urbanites.

Race Riots and Lynchings

W. E. B. DuBois, the head of the National Association for the Advancement of Colored People (NAACP), had urged African Americans to enlist in the army, rather than waiting for the draft. He believed that if blacks demonstrated patriotism, black claims to social equality would, after the armistice, be irresistible. As a historian, he should have known better. His

The Granger Collection, New York

▲ *Lynch mobs had so little fear of punishment they often took photographs of their handiwork. This murder of five was the worst single instance of a phenomenon that increased in the aftermath of the First World War.*

reasoning was the same as Frederick Douglass's during the Civil War. The NAACP did grow during the war. Its periodical, *The Crisis,* had 100,000 subscribers in 1918.

But DuBois's hopes were quickly dashed. In 1919, there was a race riot in Elaine, Arkansas, in which several hundred blacks and whites were arrested. Twelve were sentenced to death. (The Supreme Court later freed them.) In Chicago, an African American teenager swimming in Lake Michigan drifted into "whites only" water. He was murdered, and, for five days, whites and blacks battled in the streets; 38 people were killed. The death toll in race riots for the summer was 120. In Tulsa in 1921, a race riot destroyed a thousand homes and shops in the African American business district. Probably a hundred people died.

In 1919, 76 blacks were lynched, more than in any year since 1904. Ten of them were veterans, several still in uniform. The annual number of lynchings exceeded 50 for several years, then, in 1924, suddenly dropped despite the federal government's failure to act. In 1922, the House of Representatives passed the Dyer Bill, which provided for federal prosecution of sheriffs and other police officials who cooperated with or ignored lynchings in their jurisdictions. The bill died in the Senate because southerners and some northern Democrats opposed it.

Lynchings declined because middle-class white southerners and the southern press became disgusted by the sectional folkway. They pressured law enforcement officials to act, instead of disappearing, when talk of a lynching began to circulate. The automobile also played a part, giving southern police a mobility they had not previously known. And African American resistance increased, heartened by an increasing

---

The More Things Change . . .

Showboat, a Broadway musical of 1927, introduced the classic "Ol' Man River" to America. The original lyrics began:

> Niggers all work on the Mississippi,
> Niggers all work while the white folks play

In a film of the musical a few years later, the line was changed to:

> Darkies all work on the Mississippi. . . .

African American singer Paul Robeson found this offensive too. When he sang the song, it began:

> There's an old man called the Mississippi. . . .

A Broadway revival of *Showboat* in 1946 rendered it:

> Colored folks work. . . .

In a 1951 movie, it had become:

> Here we all work. . . .

In a 1993 revival, it was back to:

> Niggers all work on the Mississippi. . . .

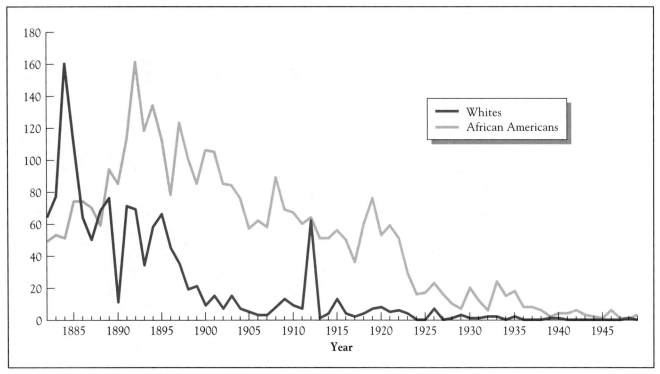

CHART 39:1 Until the 1890s, there was nothing specifically racial about the victims of lynch mobs. Beginning in the Populist era, it became very much a crime against African Americans. Lynching dropped precipitously only in the mid-1920s, when, ironically, the second Ku Klux Klan was at its peak.

self-confidence and militancy among the blacks who had emigrated to the North during the war.

Black Nationalism

Marcus Garvey, born in the British colony of Jamaica, had come to the United States in 1916. He quickly concluded that American whites would never accept blacks as equals. Proud of, rather than defensive about, his race, he rejected the social integration demanded by the NAACP. His alternative was for blacks to found a nation in Africa. Nationhood would win respect, Garvey said, pointing to the fact that protests from Japan had discouraged California from putting Asians into segregated schools.

Garvey's Universal Negro Improvement Association (UNIA) was based on pride in race. "When Europe was inhabited by a race of cannibals, a race of savages, naked men, heathens, and pagans," Garvey told cheering throngs in New York's Harlem, "Africa was peopled by a race of cultured black men who were masters in art, science, and literature."

Garvey made little headway in the South, but in the North, urban blacks joined UNIA in droves. Claims of a membership of 4 million were exaggerated, but UNIA probably had the ear of that many African Americans. At its peak, it had 700 branches in 38 states. Garvey's *Negro World* had 200,000 subscribers, more than *The Crisis*.

Garvey was a showman. He bedecked himself in extravagant uniforms and founded paramilitary orders with exotic names like the "Dukes of the Niger" and the "Black Eagle

▲ *Marcus Garvey, whose black nationalist UNIA was briefly very popular among African Americans, understood the need for theater, but not careful accounting. He was imprisoned for mail fraud.*

Flying Corps." Even W. E. B. DuBois, although still committed to integration of blacks into American society, wrote, "The spell of Africa is upon me. The ancient witchery of her medicine is burning in my drowsy, dreamy blood."

Black nationalism unnerved whites accustomed to a docile African American population. When Garvey ran afoul of the law with one of his business enterprises, the authorities moved against him with an ardor bearing little relationship to the seriousness of his offense. More because of mismanagement than fraud (Garvey, like so many people suddenly flooded with money, was sloppy with the accounts), the Black Star Line, a steamship company with three vessels, sold worthless stock through the mails at $5 a share. Some 35,000 African Americans lost $750,000, a minor take during the 1920s. Nevertheless, the government sent Garvey to prison for five years, and UNIA never recovered.

The Ku Klux Klan

Garvey's ritual, costume, and ceremony were paralleled in a white racist organization, the Ku Klux Klan (KKK). The twentieth-century KKK was founded in 1915 by William Simmons, a Methodist minister. After viewing *The Birth of a Nation,* a film that glorified the suppression of blacks after the Civil War, Simmons organized in the North as well as the South.

Under Hiram Wesley Evans, the KKK gave local units and officials exotic names such as Klavern, Kleagle, Grand Dragon, and Exalted Cyclops. Evans was a better businessman than Garvey (who had kind words for the Klan because it too preached separation of the races). Like the old Millerites, the Klan's central office had a monopoly on "official" bedsheet uniforms that all members were required to buy. Local organizers were provided a cash incentive by giving them a percentage of all money that they collected, a kind of franchised bigotry. By the mid-1920s, membership in the Klan may have risen to 4.5 million.

In the South, the KKK was an antiblack organization. Elsewhere, KKK leaders exploited whatever hatreds, fears, and resentments were most likely to keep the bedsheet orders rolling in. In the Northeast, where Catholics and Jews were numerous, Klan leaders inveighed against them. In the Owens Valley of California, a region of small farmers whose water was drained southward to feed the growth of Los Angeles, the big city was the enemy. In the Midwest, some Klaverns concentrated their attacks on saloon keepers who ignored Prohibition and on "lovers' lanes," where teenagers in automobiles flouted traditional morality the old-fashioned way. The Klan

▲ *Ku Kluxers gathered around a cross in the woods for prayer or the Klan's "jumbo-jumbo." The Klan's signal to blacks or Catholics or Jews to beware of its power was a burning cross.*

reflected the fear of generally poor, Protestant, small-town people that the America they knew was being destroyed by immigrants, cities, and modern immorality.

KKK power peaked in 1924, when the organization had as members or supporters numerous state legislators, congressmen, senators, and even the governors of Oregon, Ohio, Tennessee, and Texas. In Indiana, Klan leader David Stephenson was the state's political boss. At the Democratic national convention of 1924, the Klan was strong enough to prevent the party from adopting a plank critical of its bigotry and to veto the nomination of a Catholic, Governor Aldred E. Smith of New York.

The KKK declined as rapidly as UNIA. In 1925, Grand Dragon Stephenson was found guilty of second-degree murder in the death of a young woman whom he had taken to Chicago on a tryst. In an attempt to win a light sentence, he turned over evidence showing that virtually the whole administration was involved in thievery and that Indiana's Klan politicians were thoroughly corrupt. By 1930, the KKK dwindled to 10,000 members.

Wets and Drys

The social cleavage between cities and country and small towns was also evident in the split that developed after the Eighteenth Amendment went into effect in 1920. Violation of Prohibition law was widespread. While some bootleggers smuggled liquor into the country from Mexico, the West Indies, and Canada, distillers in isolated corners of rural America continued to practice their ancient craft.

Politically, however, there was a geographical and demographic dimension to the battle between "drys" (those who supported Prohibition) and "wets" (those who opposed it).

Drys were strongest in the South and in rural areas generally, where the population was largely composed of old-stock Americans who clung to fundamentalist Protestant religions. The wets had the support of big cities, where Roman Catholics and Jews, who had little sympathy for Prohibition, were numerous.

Many wet mayors and city councils refused to help federal officials enforce Prohibition. Democratic mayor James J. Walker of New York openly frequented fashionable speakeasies (illegal saloons). Republican "Big Bill" Thompson of Chicago ran for office on a "wide-open-town" platform and won. Illinois governor Len Small pardoned bootleggers as quickly as they were convicted, some violent gangsters included. Consequently, smuggling, illegal distilleries and even breweries, and theft of industrial and medicinal alcohol were commonplace. Supplying the nation's drinkers could be an extremely lucrative business. In Chicago, by 1927, Alphonse "Al" Capone's bootleg ring grossed $60 million supplying liquor and beer to the Windy City's speakeasies.

Gangsters as Symbols

As far as Al Capone was concerned, he was a businessman pure and simple. He supplied 10,000 speakeasies and em-

AP/Wide World Photos

▲ *Al Capone thought of himself as a businessman providing a product people obviously wanted: alcohol. After years of trying (and failing) to catch him in illegal activities, the federal government succeeded only in a conviction for income tax evasion.*

Bottoms Up

One argument wets marshaled against Prohibition was that forbidding drinking resulted in an actual *increase* in drinking. The statistics, although fragmentary, do not bear them out. Between 1906 and 1910, per capita alcohol consumption in the United States was 2.6 gallons per year. In 1934, the first year after the Prohibition amendment was repealed, consumption stood at 1.2 gallons. Not until 1971, a generation after Prohibition, did per capita consumption of alcohol reach pre–World War I levels. The death rate from chronic alcoholism peaked in the United States in 1907, at 7.3 per 100,000. By 1932, the last full year of Prohibition, the rate had declined to 2.5 per 100,000.

Prohibition did cause one alcohol-related problem: the 50,000 "jake walkers" who roamed America's streets. "Jake walking" was a nervous disorder caused by drinking poisonous methyl or wood alcohol ("jake"). Too much at a time was fatal; smaller quantities over time resulted in a loss of muscular control so that victims walked in jerky steps, their toes touching the ground before their heels. Jake walkers were unknown when potable ethyl alcohol was legal.

ployed 700 people. He and other gangsters needed the administrative acumen of a corporation executive to run their affairs and the same kind of political influence that conventional businessmen courted. "What's Al Capone done?" he told a reporter. "He's supplied a legitimate demand. . . . Some call it racketeering. I call it a business. They say I violate the Prohibition law. Who doesn't?" With a lot of money at stake, rival gangs engaged in open, bloody warfare for control of the trade. More than 400 gangland slayings made the name of Chicago synonymous with mob violence, although other cities had only slightly better records. Few innocent bystanders were killed in these frays. As conscious of public relations as other businessmen, Capone and his ilk kept their violence on a professional level.

Americans appalled by the gangsters did not overlook the fact that the most prominent of them were "foreigners" or ethnics. Capone and his predecessors in Chicago, Johnny Torrio and "Big Jim" Colosimo, were Italian. Dion O'Bannion (Capone's rival), "Bugsy" Moran, and Owney Madden were Irish. Arthur "Dutch Schultz" Flegensheimer of New York was of German background. "Polack Joe" Saltis came from Chicago's Polish West Side. Maxie Hoff of Philadelphia, Solly Weissman of Kansas City, and "Little Hymie" Weiss of Chicago were Jews.

Illegal business attracted members of groups on the bottom of the social ladder because success in it required no social status or family connections, no education, and, to get started, little money. With less to lose than the respectable and socially established people who patronized the speakeasies, ethnics with a crooked bent were less likely to be discouraged by the high risks involved. But the majority of Americans were not inclined to take a sociological view of the matter. To them, organized crime was violent, and "foreigners" were the source of it.

Anti-Semitism

The hatred of Jews that was to acquire nightmarish proportions in Germany had its counterpart in the United States, albeit never as vicious as it was under Adolf Hitler. For a time during the 1920s, Henry Ford financed a newspaper, the *Dearborn Independent,* that claimed, as Hitler did, that Jews in general were party to an "international conspiracy" to destroy Western Christian civilization. The most astonishing aspect of this kind of anti-Semitism was that it posited an alliance between wealthy Jewish bankers like the Rothschild family of Europe and their worst enemies, socialists and Communists who were Jews.

These allegations were not taken seriously by many people in the United States. However, anti-Semitism was acceptable and even respectable when it took the form of keeping Jews out of some businesses (banking, for example) and social clubs. A number of universities applied Jewish "quotas" when they admitted students. Jews were admitted, but only up to a certain percentage of each class.

Hooray for Hollywood

The first filmmakers set up shop wherever they happened to be. Most worked around New York City. By the 1920s, however, moviemaking was in Hollywood, one of the myriad communities that grew together to form Los Angeles. The usual explanation of the choice of location was the weather; southern California is one of the sunniest parts of the nation, and early filmmakers depended on natural light. But there was another reason for choosing Hollywood. Filmmakers took considerable liberties with copyright and contract law, and they had a long legal battle with Thomas Edison, who claimed royalties on every movie filmed by the camera he invented. Hollywood was only a hundred miles from the Mexican border. If a case got serious, filmmakers could make a quick dash out to Tijuana.

Hollywood as Symbol

Show business had also been a low-status enterprise that provided few competitive advantages to established social groups. The film industry, which was booming by 1919, turning out 700 films a year for the country's movie houses (half the world's total) and supplying more than 75 percent of the films shown elsewhere in the world, was founded and dominated by Jews, mostly foreign-born: former scrap dealer Louis B. Mayer (MGM), Adolph Zukor (Paramount), Carl Laemmle (Universal), William Fox (Fox), Joseph Schenck (Twentieth Century), Samuel Goldwyn, and the four Warner Brothers.

Consequently, when protest against nudity and loose moral standards in Hollywood films boiled over, it had an ethnic flavor. Preachers who demanded that controls be slapped on filmmakers attributed immorality on the silver screen to "non-Christian" influences designing to subvert Protestant America.

By 1922, Hollywood's moguls feared that city and state governments were on the verge of banning their films. They headed them off by joining together to censor themselves. Keenly sensitive to the anti-Semitism in the anti-Hollywood campaign, the studio bosses hired a man who was the epitome of the small-town midwestern Protestant to be chief censor and film-industry spokesman: Will Hays of Indiana, postmaster general under Harding. Hays drafted a code that forbade filmmakers to allow adultery to go unpunished or to show divorced people in a sympathetic light. The Hays Code's hostility toward showing a married couple in bed together actually contributed to an increase in the sale of twin beds.

Filmmakers sometimes defied the Hays Code, but not the Walt Disney studios. When Hays told Disney to remove the udders from his cartoon cows, he did.

The Evolution Controversy

The clash between traditional values and the worldliness of the twentieth century was most evident in the controversy that developed around the theory of the evolution of species

▲ *Celebrated defense attorney Clarence Darrow and three-time presidential candidate William Jennings Bryan were personally hostile to one another by the end of the Scopes "Monkey Trial" but were persuaded to pose together for a photograph.*

propounded half a century earlier by Charles Darwin. Many scientists and churchmen said there was no contradiction between the biblical account of the creation of the world (if seen as literary) and Darwin's contention that species emerged and changed character over the eons. The Catholic Church tacitly accepted this view in dodging the controversy. Fundamentalist Protestants, however, insisted on the literal truth of the Bible. Threatened by the fast-changing times and urged on by celebrities like evangelist Billy Sunday and William Jennings Bryan, who was still kicking, they tried to prohibit the teaching of evolution in public schools. Tennessee enacted a law to that effect.

In the little Appalachian town of Dayton, Tennessee, in the spring of 1925, a group of friends who were arguing about evolution decided to test the new state law in the courts. One of them, a high school biology teacher named John Scopes, agreed to violate the law in front of adult witnesses. Scopes would explain Darwin's theory, submit to arrest, and stand trial.

The motives of the men were mixed. The earnest young Scopes hoped that the law would be struck down by the courts as unconstitutional. Some of his friends wanted to see it confirmed. Others, Dayton businessmen, did not particularly care either way. They looked on a celebrated trial as a way to put their town "on the map" and as a way to make money when curiosity seekers, sensation mongers, cause pleaders, and reporters—the more the merrier—flocked to Dayton in search of lodgings, meals, and other services.

The "Monkey Trial"

Dayton's boosters succeeded beyond their dreams. The "Monkey Trial," so called because evolution was popularly interpreted as meaning that human beings were descended from apes, attracted broadcasters and reporters by the hundreds; among them was the nation's leading iconoclast, Henry L. Mencken, who came to poke fun at the "rubes" of the Bible belt.

Rube number one was William Jennings Bryan, aged now—he died shortly after the trial—who agreed to come to Dayton to advise the prosecution. Bryan wanted to fight the case on the strictly legal principle that, in a democracy, the people of a community had the right to dictate what might and what might not be taught in tax-supported schools. His advice was ignored. Their heads spinning from the carnival atmosphere of the town, even the prosecuting attorneys wanted to debate religion versus science.

The defense, funded by the American Civil Liberties Union, was game. Led by the distinguished libertarian lawyer Arthur Garfield Hays, the attorneys planned to argue that the biblical account of creation was a religious doctrine and therefore could not take precedence over science because of the constitutional separation of church and state. The defense also maintained that freedom of intellectual inquiry, including a teacher's right to speak his or her mind in the classroom, was essential to the health of a democracy.

Hays was assisted by the era's leading criminal lawyer, Clarence Darrow, who loved publicity and the drama of courtroom confrontation more than he loved legal niceties. Darrow regarded the trial as an opportunity to discredit fundamentalists by making their leader, Bryan, look like a superstitious old fool. Foolishly—he was angry—Bryan allowed Darrow to put him on the stand as an expert witness on the Bible. Under the trees—the judge feared that the tiny courthouse would collapse under the weight of the crowd—Darrow and Bryan talked religion and science. Was the world created in six days of 24 hours each? Was Jonah literally swallowed by a whale?

Darrow's supporters rested content that Bryan turned out looking like a monkey, but they lost the case. Scopes was found guilty and given a nominal penalty. But that was small consolation to the fundamentalists who were crestfallen when Bryan admitted that some parts of the Bible may have been meant figuratively. In fact, the only winners in the Monkey Trial were Dayton's businessmen, who raked in outside dollars for almost a month, and the decade's aficionados of ballyhoo, who got plenty. This was appropriate, for, by 1925, the second year of Calvin Coolidge's "New Era," raking in money and ballyhoo were what America was all about.

for FURTHER READING

Not the definitive history of the 1920s, but still the most enjoyable, is Frederick Lewis Allen, *Only Yesterday,* 1931. Also readable and less subjective are William E. Leuchtenburg, *The Perils of Prosperity, 1914–1932,* 1958; Robert K. Murray, *The Harding Era,* 1967; and George Soule, *Prosperity Decade: From War to Depression, 1917–1929,* 1947.

On the crisis of labor in 1919 and after, see Irving Bernstein, *The Lean Years,* 1960; David Brody, *Labor in Crisis: The Steel Strike of 1919,* 1965; Robert L. Friedheim, *The Seattle General Strike,* 1965; and Francis Russell, *A City in Terror: 1919, the Boston Police Strike,* 1975. On the xenophobia that was related closely to fears of a social uprising, see John Higham, *Strangers in the Land,* 1955; Robert K. Murray, *Red Scare,* 1955; and William Preston Jr., *Aliens and Dissenters: Federal Suppression of Radicals, 1903–1933,* 1963.

The history of African Americans during the 1920s has been the subject of several excellent books in recent decades. See Nathan J. Huggins, *Harlem Renaissance,* 1972; Gilbert Osofsky, *Harlem: The Making of a Ghetto, 1890–1930,* 1966; William Tuttle Jr., *Race Riot: Chicago and the Red Summer of 1919,* 1970; and Theodore G. Vincent, *Black Power and the Garvey Movement,* 1971.

The response of white America to rapidly changing times is the subject of D. M. Chalmers, *Hooded Americanism,* 1965; N. J. Clark, *Deliver Us from Evil,* 1976; Ray Ginger, *Six Days or Forever,* 1958; Kenneth T. Jackson, *The Ku Klux Klan in the Cities, 1915–1930,* 1967; Don S. Kirschner, *City and Country: Rural Responses to Urbanization in the 1920s,* 1970; and Lawrence Levine, *Defender of the Faith: William Jennings Bryan, The Last Decade,* 1965. See also George M. Marsden, *Fundamentalism and American Culture,* 1980.

Other social and cultural themes are treated in Loren Baritz, *The Culture of the Twenties,* 1969; Isabel Leighton, *The Aspirin Age,* 1949; Larry May, *Screening Out the Past,* 1980; Humbert S. Nelli, *The Business of Crime,* 1976; John Roe, *The Road and the Car in American Life,* 1971; Andrew Sinclair, *Prohibition: The Era of Excess,* 1962; and Robert Sklar, *Movie-Made America,* 1975.

On the politics of the Harding era, see Wesley Bagby, *The Road to Normalcy,* 1962; Stanley Cohen, *A. Mitchell Palmer: Politician,* 1963; Robert K. Murray, *The Politics of Normalcy,* 1973; Burt Noggle, *Teapot Dome: Oil and Politics in the 1920s,* 1962; J. W. Prothro, *Dollar Decade: Business Ideas in the 1920s,* 1954; Francis Russell, *The Shadow of Blooming Grove: Warren G. Harding in His Times,* 1968; and Andrew Sinclair, *The Available Man,* 1965.

AMERICAN JOURNEY ONLINE AND INFOTRAC COLLEGE EDITION

Visit the source collections at http://ajaccess.wadsworth.com and http://infotrac.thomsonlearning.com, and use the Search function with the following key terms to explore documents, images, audio and video clips, articles, and commentary related to the material in this chapter:

Black nationalism	Sacco and Vanzetti
Calvin Coolidge	Scopes trial
F. Scott Fitzgerald	Teapot Dome
Franklin D. Roosevelt	Warren G. Harding
Ku Klux Klan	William Tilden
Marcus Garvey	

Additional resources, exercises, and Internet links related to this chapter are available on *The American Past* Web site: http://history.wadsworth.com/americanpast7e.

HISTORY ONLINE

Red Scare

http://newman.baruch.cuny.edu/digital/redscare

Images of the days of the great "Red Scare" and American society between 1918 and 1921.

The Seattle General Strike

http://faculty.washington.edu/gregoryj/strike

Information, photographs, and resource guide to a strike that paralyzed a large city in 1919.

Tennnessee v. John Scopes

www.law.umkc/faculty/projects/ftrials/scopes/scopes.htm

Multi-format presentation of the "Monkey Trial."

Marcus Garvey

www.isop.ucla.edu/mgpp/

Biography, photographs, and recordings of the black nationalist leader of the 1920s.

CALVIN COOLIDGE AND THE NEW ERA

When America Was Business 1923–1929

Courtesy of Sears, Roebuck & Company

Civilization and profits go hand in hand. . . . The business of America is business.

Calvin Coolidge

Perhaps the most revolting character that the United States ever produced was the Christian businessman.

H. L. Mencken

VICE PRESIDENT COOLIDGE was visiting his father in tiny Plymouth Notch, Vermont, when he got the news of Harding's death. Instead of rushing to Washington, Coolidge walked downstairs to the farmhouse parlor, where his father, a justice of the peace, administered the presidential oath by the light of a kerosene lamp. To the very pinnacle of his political career, Coolidge was the epitome of unpretentious rectitude. Or, some have suggested, he had a knack for showmanship.

THE COOLIDGE YEARS

Calvin Coolidge was not a bit like his predecessor. Far from strapping and handsome, he had a pinched face that, even when he smiled, seemed to say he wished he were somewhere else. Alice Roosevelt Longworth, the acidulous daughter of Teddy Roosevelt, said that Coolidge looked as though he had been weaned on a pickle.

Harding's private life was tawdry; Coolidge was impeccably proper, even dreary, in his personal habits. His idea of a good time was a nap. He spent 12 to 14 hours out of 24 in bed, except on slow days, when he was able to sneak in a few extra winks. When, in 1933, writer Dorothy Parker heard the news Coolidge had died, she asked, "How could they tell?"

A Quiet, Clever Man

Coolidge might have cracked a smile at that. He was known as "Silent Cal," but when he spoke, he was witty. Attempting to break the ice at a banquet, a woman seated next to Coolidge told him that a friend had bet her that the president would not say three words to her all evening. "You lose," Coolidge replied, and returned to his plate. "I found out early in life," this successful politician noted, "that you don't have to explain something you haven't said."

And he was clever. At a meeting of American heads of state in the West Indies, Coolidge was sitting in a semicircle with his colleagues when a waiter began to walk down the

Brown Brothers

▲ *Calvin Coolidge actually did enjoy angling, but he probably wore a boater (a dressy summer hat) in the creek for the sake of the photographers.*

He was surely at one with the American people in abdicating political and cultural leadership to the business community. Coolidge worshiped financial success and believed that millionaires knew what was best for the country. "The man who builds a factory builds a temple," he said, an odd piety indeed for a man who devoted not a day of his life to business.

Keeping Cool with Coolidge

Coolidge quickly rid his cabinet of the racketeers and hacks he inherited from Harding. He retained Harding's appointees from the business world, most notably Herbert Hoover (with whom he was as uncomfortable as Harding had been) and Secretary of the Treasury Mellon. He then sat back to preside over the most business-minded administration to his time. In return, business's praise of his administration was higher than the skyscrapers they built in New York and Chicago. The Republicans crowed about "Coolidge prosperity," the recovery from the erratic postwar economy that began in 1923. Thanks to the president's unblemished record of honesty, the Republicans never suffered a voter backlash because of the Harding scandals.

In 1924, the Democrats tore themselves apart. The convention, held in New York, pitted the Empire State's favorite son, Alfred E. Smith, against William G. McAdoo, whose support came mostly from the South and the West. Smith was a Roman Catholic and had the backing of ethnics in the Northeast and urban Midwest. He was a symbol of their arrival in American politics. McAdoo, although no bigot himself, was supported by many southerners and westerners who regarded Catholicism with, at best, distaste and by virulently anti-Catholic Ku Klux Klansmen. So bitter was the split that neither candidate would yield for more than a hundred ballots, long after it was obvious neither could win the nomination.

Finally, the weary delegates settled on Wall Street lawyer John W. Davis. He did not have to neglect his lucrative practice for long. Davis won a mere 29 percent of the vote to Coolidge's 54 percent. Aged Robert La Follette, try-

line serving drinks. It was Prohibition; if Coolidge took a drink while out of the country, it would make juicy front-page news. Reporters and photographers (who were undoubtedly enjoying their daiquiris) waited on tenterhooks for the waiter to reach Coolidge. If Coolidge resolutely turned the waiter away, it would be a mild insult of his host. Coolidge knew how to handle the situation. The instant before the waiter tried to serve him, he bent down to tie his shoe and remained hunched over until the waiter moved on.

Coolidge was nowhere near as laconic as he was said to be. In 1917, the year the United States went to war, Woodrow Wilson gave 17 speeches. In 1925, when nothing much happened to command the attention of the president, Coolidge gave 28. It was small talk and chitchat, for which he had no patience, although he did like to clown around. He posed for photographers in costumes that were ludicrous on him: a 10-gallon hat or a Sioux war bonnet. He strapped himself into skis on the White House lawn and dressed as a hardworking farmer, haying in patent leather shoes with his Pierce Arrow in the background. The photos were Coolidge's way of saying that he was at one with the American people of the 1920s in enjoying novelties and pranks. On being asked about the costumes, he said that "the American public wants a solemn ass as president and I think I'll go along with them."

ing vainly to revive the Progressive party, captured 17 percent of the popular vote and won his native Wisconsin.

For four more years, Calvin Coolidge napped through good times. It was eight months after he left office, in October 1929, that what businessmen called the "New Era" came crashing to an end. Ironically, in view of the impending Great Depression, Coolidge retired from office with great reluctance. It was whispered that when the Republican convention of 1928 took his coy statement "I do not choose to run for president in 1928" as a refusal to run and nominated Herbert Hoover, Coolidge threw himself on his familiar bed and wept.

Mellon's Tax Policies

The keystone of New Era government was the tax policy of the secretary of the treasury, Andrew Mellon of Pittsburgh. Mellon looked less like the political cartoonist's big businessman—a bloated moneybags—than like a fit, sporting duke, but a moneybags he was. With chiseled aristocratic features, dressed in deftly tailored suits and tiny pointed shoes that shone like newly minted coins, Mellon was one of the three or four richest men in the world, a banker with close ties to the steel industry.

Believing that prosperity depended on the extent to which capitalists reinvested their profits in economic growth, Mellon favored the rich by slashing taxes that fell most heavily on them. He reduced the personal income tax for people who made more than $60,000 a year, and, by 1929, the treasury was actually shoveling taxes back to large corporations. United States Steel received a tidy refund of $15 million.

To make up the loss in the government's revenues, Mellon cut expenditures. The costs of government that he conceded were indispensable were paid for in two ways. First, Mellon raised the tariff on imports, a double benefit for industrial capitalists. In the Fordney-McCumber tariff of 1922, import duties reached levels unheard of for a generation.

Second, Mellon sponsored increases in regressive taxes, that is, taxes that fell disproportionately on the middle and lower classes. The costs of some kinds of postal services increased. The excise tax was raised, and a federal tax was imposed on automobiles. Both were paid by consumers. To those who complained that these measures penalized the middle classes and, to some extent, the poor, Mellon replied that the burden on each individual was small and that his overall scheme helped ordinary people as well as the rich.

Mellon contended that when businessmen reinvested their government-sponsored windfalls, they created jobs and, therefore, the means to a better standard of living for all. The share of the middle and lower classes in Coolidge prosperity would "trickle down" to them. Moreover, the inducement to get rich, encouraged by business culture, would reinvigorate the spirit of enterprise among all Americans.

For six years, from late 1923 to late 1929, it appeared as if Mellon were right. He was toasted as "the greatest secretary of the treasury since Alexander Hamilton." Just how much damage his financial policies did to the national economy would not be known until after the collapse of the New Era. As early as 1924, however, Mellon's dedication to the immediate interests of big business and banking drew criticism that he was helping to make a shambles of the international economy.

A Foreign Policy for Bankers

At the Versailles peace conference, economist John Maynard Keynes had argued against saddling Germany with huge reparations payments. The war had pushed all the European powers, Germany included, to the brink of bankruptcy (and Russia over the cliff). Germany spent more during four years of war than during the previous four decades of the nation's existence. To add $33 billion in reparations to Germany's problems was to court disaster.

Later, when the Nazis came to power in Germany, Keynes and others looked back and said that the flow of international payments, reparations from Germany to Britain and France and payments of debts from Britain and France to the United States, had made it possible for extremists, who blamed Britain and France for bleeding Germany, to win popular approval.

Recent research shows that Germany's financial difficulties were not the consequence of the reparations. Between 1918 and 1932, Germany's actual reparations payments were $4.5 billion. This was less than France, with its smaller economy, had paid Germany after the Franco-Prussian War, and France had not gone smash. In fact, because the United States underwrote German reparations by making loans to Germany, when the loans were not repaid, Germany actually came out ahead on the balance sheets.

Nevertheless, during the 1920s, many financiers believed that the flow of gold from Germany to France and Britain, then to the United States, and, in loans, back to Germany, had to be addressed.

One way out of the morass was for the United States to import more European products. But the Fordney-McCumber tariff, a vital part of Mellon's fiscal policy, shut the door on that idea. Alternatively, the United States could forgive Britain and France all or most of their debts, in return for which they would cancel reparations payments from Germany. The international economy would, so to speak, have a fresh start. Unfortunately, an administration that was closely allied with bankers would not do that. "They hired the money, didn't they?" Coolidge said of the French and British war debts. Indeed, the circular movement of money was (in the short run) putting big profits into American vaults. The United States agreed to a rescheduling of reparations and loan payments in 1924 and 1929, but not to a reduction of the total burden. The American economy was indirectly damaged because capital that could have been invested at home to "trickle down" in the form of jobs was devoted to an exchange of money benefiting no one but Wall Street.

Isolationism?

After the Treaty of Washington, the Harding and Coolidge administrations resisted making cooperative cause with other nations. There was no question of joining the League

Fads, Sensations, and Ballyhoo

Fads (fashions wildly popular for a short period), sensations (events or people of intense popular interest), and ballyhoo (a clamor promoting a fad, a sensation, or a new toilet disinfectant now available at your local grocery) were not new to the 1920s. And they are so much a part of twenty-first-century life that we are inured to them.

But they were virtually the theme of popular culture in the 1920s, and people had not yet developed the immunities that enable us to survive them without emotional scars.

Some fads were commercial, paying—briefly—bonanza profits for those who jumped in quickly enough to exploit them. A mania for crossword puzzles was launched by a new company's, Simon and Schuster's, first book. Yo-yos made money for their manufacturers. Mah-jongg, a Chinese gambling game with such complex rules it is possible no American ever played it correctly, was introduced in 1922. The next year, although the games were expensive, Chinese-made mah-jongg tiles outsold radios. It was an obsession of middle- and upper-class women, some of whom played all day, every day. Chinese manufacturers ran out of the shinbones of calves from which the tiles were made and had to be supplied by Chicago's slaughterhouses.

Roller skates made money for their makers and somewhat less for owners of rinks. Dance marathons, couples competing to see which pair could "dance" the longest (in fact, after a day or two, hanging on to one another and trying, during breaks, to slip laxatives into competitors' drinks), were small-time operations dependent on paid admissions by people who enjoyed pathos.

Other fads made little or no money for anyone: for example, contract bridge (a card game)—a mania rivaling mah-jongg—or college boys swallowing live goldfish. Exhibitionists (still at it, trying to get into the *Guinness Book of World Records*) had no reward beyond seeing their names in print: "Clarence Tillman, 17, local high school student, put 40 sticks of chewing gum in his mouth at one time, sang *Home, Sweet Home,* and between verses of the song, drank a gallon of milk."

Barnstormers, daredevils who walked on or dangled from a plane's wing, could not charge admission for an exhibition in plain sight for miles around. They counted on fees from county fairs, which were tiny. One barnstormer said that the greatest personal danger he faced during the short-lived fad was starvation. Flagpole sitting—balancing for days atop a flagpole—was less dangerous but equally unprofitable. For reasons the best historians have been unable to discover, Baltimore was the storm center of the fad, with as many as 20 flagpole sitters at one time. The mayor crowed with pride of his citizenry's achievement.

Newspapers ballyhooed innocuous events to increase sales: the visits of the Prince of Wales in 1924 and Queen Marie of Romania in 1926; the death of movie sex symbol Rudolph Valentino at age 31; the 655-mile trek across Alaska by a dog, Balto, to bring diphtheria serum to a sick Eskimo in Nome. The prince, the queen, and Valentino's funeral were mobbed by thousands of people who, mercifully, were not asked to reflect on why they were there. Statues of Balto were erected. Charles Lindbergh, who made the first nonstop flight across the Atlantic, created hysteria wherever he went. Gertrude Ederle was only marginally less lionized when she swam the English Channel. In 1927, Nan Britton's *The President's Daughter,* about the child she bore by Warren G. Harding, sold 50,000 copies.

---

of Nations belatedly, as more and more Americans became convinced that it had been a mistake to intervene in the war that produced the league. American efforts on behalf of maintaining the peace were restricted to proclamations of goodwill much like William Jennings Bryan's cooling-off treaties. In 1928, Secretary of State Frank B. Kellogg joined with French foreign minister Aristide Briand to write a treaty that outlawed war as an instrument of national policy. Eventually, 62 nations signed the Kellogg-Briand Pact, a clear indication that, as a statement of pious sentiment, the pact was meaningless.

The foreign policy of the 1920s is usually described as "isolationist." This is something of a misnomer. Toward Latin America, the Harding and Coolidge administrations were active and aggressive on behalf of the interests of American investors. American investments in Latin America climbed from about $800 million in 1914 to $5.4 billion in 1929. The United States replaced Great Britain as the chief economic power in Latin America, particularly in the Caribbean.

The poorer Latin American nations sorely needed capital, and to that extent, every dollar invested there was potentially a boon—if the population of the host countries had benefited from development. Unfortunately, American investors had little interest in how the Latin American countries were governed until their profits were threatened by political instability. They ignored the depredations of the predatory elites they funded until they were in trouble.

When dictators in the "banana republics" were unable to contain popular resentments, American investors turned to Washington for protection of their investments. By 1924, American officials directly or indirectly administered the finances of 10 Latin American nations. For at least parts of the decade, the marines occupied Nicaragua, Honduras, Cuba, Haiti, and the Dominican Republic.

PROSPERITY AND BUSINESS CULTURE

In the early twenty-first century, when the economy is shaky because of the government's irresponsibility in the 1980s and 1990s, it is easy to see the damage wreaked by the Coolidge administration. But the voters of the 1920s sup-

Publishing, not Baltimore, was the storm center of sensationalism. All newspapers covered in detail stories like the 18-day entrapment in a Kentucky cave of Floyd Collins, who was dying slowly of exposure. (His neighbors sold hamburgers to the crowds at the entrance to the cave.) When evangelist Aimee Semple McPherson disappeared for 37 days in 1926, then emerged from the Arizona desert, claiming she had been kidnapped, she re-created her abduction for photographers. Reporters prolonged the story by revealing that Aimee had actually been holed up in a "love nest."

Sex sold. The trial of movie comedian Roscoe "Fatty" Arbuckle for the death of a young woman at an orgiastic party was national news in 1922, along with the unsolved murder of movie bigwig William Desmond Taylor because he was said to have been "involved" with stars Mabel Normand and Mary Miles Minter. (In fact, Taylor was homosexual; Normand and Minter really were "just good friends.") Fortuitously, a sensational murder case came along annually, the greatest of them the trial of Chicago rich boys Nathan Leopold and Richard Loeb for the "thrill" killing of a 14-year-old neighbor boy.

The New York *Mirror* actually forced the police to reopen a murder case on which they had given up for lack of evidence. An Episcopal minister, Edward Hall, and his lover, Mrs. James Mills, had been found shot on an isolated farm. The *Mirror* produced an eccentric neighbor who raised hogs, immediately dubbed "the pig woman." She claimed that Reverend Hall's widow and several of her relatives had killed the paramours. (They were acquitted and successfully sued the *Mirror*.)

The *Mirror* was a tabloid. These new dailies (the first, in 1919, was the New York *Daily News*) were half the size of traditional newspapers and opened like a book. The format was a brilliant idea, appealing to people who rode crowded subways and trolley cars. But the tabloids were more than convenient: They virtually ignored traditional news and, lavishly plastering their pages with large photographs, reported sex scandals and violent crimes in breathless, suggestive prose. Their popularity was instantaneous. Within five years, the *Daily News* had the largest circulation in the nation. Its biggest scoop was a front-page photograph of the electrocution of Ruth Snyder, who had murdered her husband. The picture was taken illegally with a hidden camera.

Even tabloid aficionados were a bit put off by the *Evening Graphic,* which they called the *"Pornographic."* It was published by Bernarr MacFadden, the "father of physical culture," who had been having trouble with obscenity laws for decades, mostly for displaying his well-sculpted body wearing little clothing. MacFadden solved the problem of how to illustrate a story when there were no photographs by using the "composograph," which was put together by pasting photos of the celebrities of the moment on cartoons of titillating scenes. One showed Enrico Caruso welcoming Valentino to Italian heaven.

MacFadden also published the immensely popular women's magazine *True Story:* tear-jerking love stories as sexy as the law allowed and constantly testing the legal limits, supposedly "told" by ordinary women "just like" the readers. Founded in 1926, it was soon selling 2 million copies of each issue. MacFadden followed with *True Romances, True Detective,* and others, all written, cover to cover, by writers in cubicles in MacFadden's offices.

---

ported Silent Cal with the same enthusiasm with which voters elected Presidents Reagan and Clinton. Times were good when they were president: Who could foresee what would follow? The Republican party held comfortable majorities in every Congress between 1920 and 1930. Only in the South, some lightly populated western states, and a few big cities could the Democrats count on winning an election.

The Anticlimactic Election of 1928

In 1928, the 54 percent of the vote that Coolidge had won in 1924 rose to 58 percent. The victorious Republican candidate was Herbert Hoover, who was, in his energy and celebrations of business, an even better exemplar of the New Era than Silent Cal.

Hoover's opponent, Alfred E. Smith of New York, had spent four years mending fences with southerners and westerners. Smith was unable to win over the bigots. For the first time since Reconstruction, a number of prominent southern whites, including Methodist bishop James Cannon, urged voters to support the Republican party because a Catholic could not be trusted with presidential power. They also drummed on Smith's opposition to Prohibition. Indeed, Smith not only urged repeal, but he openly flouted the law. Herbert Hoover may have been personally dubious about Prohibition, but in 1928, playing his politics correctly, he called it "a great social and economic experiment, noble in motive and far-reaching in purpose."

Smith also invited the hostility of southern, western, and rural voters with his rasping, nasal New York accent. Heard over the radio—or "raddio" as Smith called it—his voice conjured up all the unsavory images associated with New York City.

Still, had Al Smith been a Kansas Baptist who drank nothing stronger than Dr. Pepper, he would have lost in 1928. Business and the Republican party reigned supreme because of the general prosperity of the New Era and because a great many Americans were convinced that businessmen were the new messiahs Woodrow Wilson had tried so hard to be.

The Shape of Prosperity

Industrial and agricultural productivity soared during the 1920s, even though there was not much increase in the size of

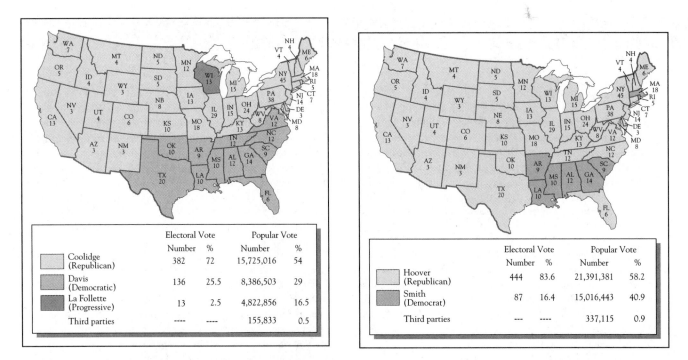

MAPS 40:1 AND 40:2 Presidential Elections, 1924 and 1928 The Democratic candidate, Wall Street lawyer John W. Davis, won only the Solid South in 1924. Because of his Catholicism, 1928 candidate Al Smith lost four southern states Davis had won, but Smith did carry heavily Catholic Rhode Island and Massachusetts.

the industrial workforce and the number of agricultural workers actually declined. Wages did not, however, keep up with the contribution that more efficient workers were making to the economy. Whereas dividends on stocks rose 65 percent between 1920 and 1929, wages increased only 24 percent.

Nevertheless—more shades of the 1990s—the increase in wages was enough to satisfy most of the working people who enjoyed them, particularly because consumer goods were relatively cheap and business promoted an alluring new way for a family to live beyond its means—consumer credit.

Buy Now, Pay Later

Before the 1920s, borrowing was something one did in order to build a business, get crops into the ground, or to buy a farm. Borrowed money was invested in productivity, thus providing the means with which to retire the debt. Or people borrowed in order to buy a home. There was no increase in productivity in home ownership; but the mortgage was secured by real property, and the family had "an estate." During the 1920s, Americans began to borrow simply in order to live more pleasantly. They went into debt not to produce or to provide their families a home, but to consume and enjoy.

The chief agency of consumer borrowing was the installment plan. A refrigerator that sold for $87.50 could be ensconced in a corner of the kitchen for a down payment of $5 and monthly payments of $10. Even a comparatively low-cost item like a vacuum cleaner ($28.95) could be had for $2 down and "E-Z payments" of $4 a month. During the New Era, 60 percent of all automobiles were bought on

time; 70 percent of furniture; 80 percent of refrigerators, radios, and vacuum cleaners; and 90 percent of pianos, sewing machines, and washing machines. With 13.8 million people

Let's Have a Look Under the Hood

Americans and Britons speak a different language when they talk about their cars. What Americans call the "hood," the British call the "bonnet." These are some other differences:

American English	British English
clunker or junker	banger
gas	petrol
generator	dynamo
headlight	headlamp
muffler	silencer
station wagon	estate wagon
trunk	boot
windshield	windscreen

The two vocabularies provide a little case study in how languages develop. The automobile roared into history long after the United States and Great Britain had gone their separate political and cultural ways, but before instantaneous electronic communication allowed words coined on one side of the Atlantic to become immediately familiar on the other.

Because the early automobile was largely a French development, many American automotive terms were taken from the French language: *automobile* itself, *cabriolet* (later shortened to *cab*), *chassis, chauffeur, coupe, garage, limousine,* and *sedan.*

▲ *The automobile was plenty democratized by the 1920s, and, thanks to installment buying, a middle-class family could drive in something better than a Model T Ford.*

owning radios by 1930 (up from next to none in 1920), the ordinary Americans who basked in the glow of Coolidge prosperity were also up to their necks in hock.

Moralists pointed out that borrowing to consume was a sharp break with American ideals of frugality, as expressed in the axioms of Benjamin Franklin. Others spoke more loudly and in sweeter tones. They were the advertisers, members of a new profession dedicated to creating desires in people—the advertising men called them "needs"—that people had never particularly felt before.

Buy, Buy, Buy

The earliest advertisements were announcements. In the nineteenth century, merchants placed tiny notices in newspapers—the size of "classifieds" today—describing what they had for sale. During the 1870s, Robert Bonner, the editor of a literary magazine, accidentally learned the curious effect of repetition on the human brain; it was much the same as the effect of repetition on a dog being trained to "sit." He placed his usual one-line ad in a daily newspaper—"Read Mrs. Southworth's New Story in the Ledger." The typesetter misread his specification of "one line" as "one page." The line ran over and over, down every column. To

Anxiety Ad

The text that follows is from a magazine advertisement of the 1920s for Listerine Antiseptic, a mouthwash. The illustration that accompanied it showed an elderly, attractive, poignantly sad woman sitting in a darkened parlor (with a photograph of Calvin Coolidge on the wall), poring over old letters and a photograph album:

Sometimes, when lights are low, they come back to comfort and at the same time sadden her—those memories of long ago, when she was a slip of a girl in love with a dark-eyed Nashville boy. They were the happiest moments of her life—those days of courtship. Though she had never married, no one could take from her the knowledge that she had been loved passionately, devotedly; those frayed and yellowed letters of his still told her so. How happy and ambitious they had been for their future together. And then, like a stab, came their parting . . . the broken engagement . . . the sorrow and the shock of it. She could find no explanation for it then, and now, in the soft twilight of life when she can think calmly, it is still a mystery to her.

The advertiser then went on so as to leave no doubt that "halitosis"—bad breath—was the source of the woman's personal tragedy.

Bonner's surprise, the blunder did not bankrupt him; his magazine sold out in an afternoon.

The lesson was unmistakable. During the 1890s, C. W. Post, without a cent to his name, borrowed enough money to plaster an entire city with the name of his new breakfast cereal, Post Toasties. He was a millionaire within a month. Bombarded by the name—printed in newspapers, painted on the sides of buildings, and slipped under doors on leaflets—people bought the stuff as if commanded to do so by an absolute monarch. By the 1920s, advertisers had moved on to making preposterous claims and telling outright lies in newspapers and magazines, on billboards along highways (a new medium, thanks to the automobile), and on the radio. They discovered the effectiveness of sexual titillation. Pictures of suggestive young ladies were the centerpieces of advertisements for such products as soda pop, tickets on railroads, razor blades, and luxury automobiles.

Advertising was now a "profession," and the pros styled themselves as practical psychologists. They sold goods by exploiting anxieties and, in the words of Thorstein Veblen, "administering shock effects" and "trading on the range of human infirmities which blossom in devout observances, and bear fruit in the psychopathic wards." In the age of Coolidge, the makers of Listerine Antiseptic, a mouthwash, invented the disease "halitosis," of which the symptoms included nothing more than a curter than usual greeting from a friend: "Even your best friend won't tell you" that you have "BAD BREATH." Listerine made millions. A picture of a wealthy fop on a yacht, conversing with a beautiful young woman, was captioned: "You'd like to be in this man's shoes . . . yet he has 'ATHLETE'S FOOT'!" Fleischmann's yeast, losing its market as people bought bread instead of baking it at home, advertised their product as just the thing to cure constipation and eradicate adolescent pimples. The success of "anxiety advertising" made underarm deodorants, without which humanity had functioned for millennia, a necessity.

Chain Stores

With manufacturers of small-ticket items like toothpaste and mouthwash spending millions to create a demand for their products, it became advantageous to retail advertised goods on a nationwide basis. Individual mom-and-pop grocery stores and locally owned haberdasheries and sundries shops sold comparatively few cans of Chef Boy-Ar-Dee spaghetti, Arrow shirts, and tubes of Ipana toothpaste. Therefore, they paid the wholesaler a premium price. A centrally managed chain, however, could buy the same goods by the ton at a cheaper unit price and reduce shipping charges through "vertical integration." The result was that they sharply undersold the mom-and-pop stores.

By 1928, 860 chain stores competed for the dollars of a population that was eating more expensively. Among the biggest success stories between 1920 and 1929 were the first supermarkets: Piggly Wiggly (which grew from 515 to 2,500 stores), Safeway (which grew from 766 to 2,660 stores), and A&P (Atlantic and Pacific Tea Company, which grew from 4,621 to 15,418 stores). During the same period, chains came to dominate the sundries and clothing trades (F. W. Woolworth grew from 1,111 outlets to 1,825; and J. C. Penney, from 312 to 1,395), auto parts (Western Auto

▲ *Radio was the boom consumer industry of the 1920s, and it was improved as rapidly as computers were in the 1990s. The farmer milking his cow in the early 1920s is listening to the radio. (Note the earphones.) In fact, he is tuning it with his left hand. That contraption is the crystal tuner and antenna. By the end of the decade, the household radio could be a piece of furniture that did the family proud.*

grew from 5 locations to 54), tobacco (United Cigar grew from 2,000 shops to 3,700), and the retailing of gasoline. Standard Oil of New Jersey owned 12 gas stations in 1920; in 1929, it owned a thousand.

The Limits of Prosperity

A few economists joined moralists to criticize the runaway consumption. They pointed out that the day would dawn when everyone who could afford a car, a washing machine, and other durable consumer goods would have them. They would no longer be buying, and the consumer industries would be in trouble.

THE familiar phrase "as good as Buick" suggests that you see and drive the car that others use as the Standard of Comparison before you spend your money.

"WHEN BETTER AUTOMOBILES ARE BUILT · · · BUICK WILL BUILD THEM"

The Better Buick

▲ *In 1920, women were arrested on beaches for not wearing stockings to cover their calves. A few years later, General Motors was selling Buicks by baring women's thighs.*

▲ *Sears, Roebuck, already the country's giant in mail-order sales, opened retail stores to compete with other great chains in even smallish towns.*

Another major weakness of the Coolidge economy was that significant numbers of Americans did not share in the good times and were, therefore, shut out from the buying spree. The 700,000 to 800,000 coal miners and 400,000 textile workers and their dependents suffered depressed conditions and wages throughout the decade; they did not buy their share of cars and vacuum cleaners. Staple farmers were once again struggling after the good old days of 1900–1920. Farmers who were doing well lived where there was no electricity; they bought no appliances that had to be plugged in. The southern states generally lagged far behind the rest of the country in income and standard of living. Rural blacks, Indians, and Hispanics tasted Coolidge prosperity only in odd bites.

Business Culture

But economically deprived groups are rarely politically articulate when mainstream society is at ease in its world. In the 1920s, mainstream America was quite at ease, and businessmen took the credit for their comfort.

Locally, small businessmen's clubs, like Rotary, Kiwanis, Lions, and Junior Chambers of Commerce, seized community leadership and preached boosterism: "If you can't boost, don't knock." Successful manufacturers like Henry

Ford were looked to for wisdom on every imaginable question. Any man who made $25,000 a day, as Ford did during most of the 1920s, must be an oracle. Even the man once the most hated in America, John D. Rockefeller, now in his 80s and retired in Florida, became a figure of respect and affection, thanks to Coolidge prosperity, the skillful image building of public relations expert Ivy Lee, and Rockefeller's extraordinary charity.

The career of an advertising man, Bruce Barton, showed just how thoroughly the business culture dominated the way Americans thought. In 1925, Barton published *The Man Nobody Knows*. It depicted Jesus not as a brooding fel-

low with a beard but as a businessman, a hail fellow-well-met, a sport, an entrepreneur, and an advertising genius whose religion was a successful company. Instead of finding Barton's hallucinations blasphemous, Americans bought *The Man Nobody Knows* by the hundreds of thousands. It was a best-seller for two years!

John Jacob Raskob of General Motors promoted the worship of business in popular magazines such as the *Saturday Evening Post*. Because the value of most kinds of property was rising throughout the 1920s under the stewardship of business, Raskob said, it was a simple matter for workingmen to save a little money and invest it, thus becoming capitalists themselves. Middle-class Americans with a small nest egg in the bank believed him. They plunged their savings into one get-rich-quick scheme after another, feeding, but at the same time dooming, the speculative economy.

GET-RICH-QUICK SCHEMES

The most colorful get-rich-quick craze centered on Florida, previously an isolated agricultural state. Train connections with eastern and midwestern cities, retirement to Florida by such celebrities as Rockefeller and Bryan, and the ballyhoo of ingenious promoters like Wilson Mizner and Rockefeller's onetime associate Samuel Flagler, who developed several Florida resorts, put people on notice of the Sunshine State's possibilities as a vacation and retirement paradise.

The Florida Land Boom

The development of places like Fort Lauderdale and Miami Beach would take time, of course. The way to make money from their futures was to buy orange groves and sandy wasteland at bargain prices, and hold the land for resale to the actual builders of vacation hotels and retirement homes. By traditional standards, the number of people rich enough to make such long-term commitments was small. In 1925, however, Florida's boosters persuaded people of modest means to send their money south by promoting a get-rich-quick speculative fever that fed on itself.

The price of Florida land rose not because new residents were pouring in by the hundreds of thousands but because speculator A bought from speculator B, expecting to sell to speculators C, D, and E as quickly as possible, at an even higher price. Some lots in Miami Beach on which no one was dreaming of building changed hands a dozen times within a few months, the price climbing with every sale. At the height of the craze, a Miami newspaper ran more than 500 pages of advertisements of land for sale. There were over 2,000 real estate offices in the little city.

Since the price of every acre in Florida seemed to be skyrocketing, many northerners were willing to buy sight unseen, and frauds were inevitable. More than a few snowbound dreamers in Chicago and Minneapolis purchased tracts of alligator-infested swamp from fast-talking salesmen who assured them that they were purchasing a site that

Piggly Wiggly was looking at covetously. Others bought beachfront lots that were closer to the ocean than they counted on—underneath 6 feet of salt water at high tide. But the fuel of the mania was not fraud. It was a foolishness inherent in the species, brought out by a culture that exalted moneymaking above all else.

As with all speculative crazes, the day arrived when there were no more buyers, no one willing to bet on higher future prices. After a few months of making mortgage payments on land that was not moving, would-be land barons decided, in as herdlike fashion as they had bought, to get out of Florida real estate. The market was flooded with offerings at ever declining prices. The speculators who were caught holding overpriced property saw paper fortunes evaporate; the banks that had loaned them money to speculate failed; people who trusted those banks with their savings lost their accounts.

The Florida crash was triggered by a hurricane that demonstrated, as Frederick Lewis Allen put it, what a soothing tropical wind could do when it got a running start from the West Indies. The price of Florida land plunged to dollars per acre. Citrus farmers who had cursed themselves a thousand times for selling their groves so cheaply at the beginning of the boom discovered that, thanks to a chain of defaults, they were back in possession of their orchards only a little worse for the wear of speculators tromping through them. Wilson Mizner, who lost more than $1 million in a month, was good humored about the debacle. "Always be pleasant to the people you meet on the way up," he said, "because they are always the very same people you meet on the way down."

Margin Mania

Even before Florida busted, middle-class Americans began to fuel another speculative mania, driving up the prices of shares on the New York Stock Exchange.

Speculation in stocks had always been a game for the rich. However, the prosperity of the 1920s created savings accounts for middle-class Americans. In order to tap their capital, stockbrokers opened offices nationwide and offered speculators an installment plan in which, so it seemed, there were no installments to pay.

That is, investors with just a few hundred or thousand dollars to risk in the market could buy stocks "on margin." They bought shares of RCA, the New York Central, or Illinois Widget by putting down as little as 10 percent of the price of those companies' shares. Thus, they were able to hold title to 10 times as many shares as they could afford to buy with cash. The broker loaned them the balance of the stocks' actual price, with the stocks serving as collateral. The money the speculator owed was the "margin." When the shares were sold, presumably at a big profit, the loan was paid off, and the far-seeing speculators pocketed 10 times what they would have made had they been stupid enough to buy with cash. At least that was how the 1.5 million Americans playing the market in 1926 understood buying on margin to work.

The Bull Market

Beginning in 1927, that was how it did work. Prices of shares soared as more and more people rushed "into the market" to buy. During the summer of 1929, values went crazy. American Telephone and Telegraph climbed from $209 a share to $303; General Motors went from $268 to $452 on September 3. Some obscure companies' stocks enjoyed even more dizzying rises. And with each tale of a fortune made overnight, related breathlessly or with smug self-congratulation at country club, lodge hall, community dance, or on Sunday after church, more people were hooked, carrying their savings to stockbrokers, whose offices were as easy to find as auto parts stores. In 1928 and 1929, 600 local offices were opened, an 80 percent increase in access to the market.

Ideally, the value of a share in a corporation represented the earning capacity of the company. Ideally, the money that a corporation realized by selling shares was expended to improve the company's plant, equipment, and marketing capacity, and in other productive ways. Thus, when the price of stock in General Motors or RCA rose, it represented—ideally—the expansion of the automobile and radio industries.

During the Coolidge bull market, however, the prices of shares represented little more than the willingness of people to pay those prices because, as in Florida, they expected someone else to buy from them at yet higher prices. It was immaterial to such speculators that the companies in which they had put their money did not pay dividends or use their capital to improve productive capacity. The rising prices of stocks fed on themselves. It became more profitable for companies to put their capital into speculation—making loans to margin buyers, for example—than into production. The face value of shares in the Coolidge bull market bore little relationship to the health of the American economy. In fact, by October 1929, $16 billion of the value of shares on the New York Stock Exchange, 18 percent of all capitalization, was in loans on margin.

Politicians, unable to understand what was happening or afraid to appear pessimistic in a time of buoyant optimism, reassured their constituents that there was nothing wrong. When a few concerned economists warned that the bull market was a bubble that had to burst with calamitous consequences, others scolded them. President Coolidge told people that he thought stock prices were cheap, effectively encouraging others to rush to the broker. The Federal Reserve Bank fueled the mania by lowering its interest rates to a record low in 1927.

▲ *Wall Street during the Crash of October 1929. No doubt many of the milling speculators and brokers were saying, "I knew I should have gotten out in September. I knew it."*

The Inevitable

Joseph P. Kennedy, a Boston millionaire (and father of President John F. Kennedy), said in later years that he sold all of his stocks during the summer of 1929 when the man who shined his shoes mentioned that he was "playing the market." Kennedy reasoned that if a man working for tips was buying stock, there was no one left out there to bid prices higher. The crash was coming soon. Movie star Charles Chaplin did not have a story about it, but he too sold all his stocks in 1929.

Kennedy and Chaplin were right. On September 3, 1929, the average price of shares on the New York Stock Exchange peaked and then dipped sharply. For a month, prices spurted up and down. Then, on "Black Thursday," October 24, a record 13 million shares changed hands, and values collapsed. General Electric fell more than 47 points on that one day; stocks of other major companies dropped almost as much.

On Tuesday, October 29, the wreckage was worse. In a panic now, speculators dumped 16 million shares. Clerical workers on Wall Street had to work through the night just to sort out the avalanche of paperwork. When the dust settled, more than $30 billion in paper value had been wiped out.

It was phony value, representing the irrational belief that prices could rise indefinitely. Nevertheless, it was value people believed was in their pockets. Its sudden eradication profoundly shook business confidence and popular faith in business culture. The Great Crash eventually contributed to the hardship of millions of people who could not have distinguished a share in Seaboard Air Lines from the label on a bottle of cognac.

Crash and Depression

The Great Crash of 1929 did not cause the Great Depression of the 1930s. That was the result of fundamental weaknesses in the economy that had little to do with the mania for speculation. But the crash did accelerate the decline in the American economy that was quietly under way by New Year's Day 1930.

Middle-class families that had played the market lost their savings. Banks that had loaned money to speculators went belly up. When they closed their doors, they wiped out the savings accounts of frugal people who looked on a bank as a vault protecting their money from thieves.

Corporations whose cash assets were decimated shut down operations or curtailed production, throwing people out of work or cutting their wages. Those who had taken out mortgages during the heady low-interest days of 1928 and 1929 were unable to meet payments and lost their homes; farmers lost the means by which they made a living. That contributed to additional bank failures.

Virtually everyone had to cut consumption, thus reducing the sales of manufacturers and farmers and stimulating yet another turn in the downward spiral. Curtailed production of everything from Baby Ruth bars to luxury automobiles meant increased unemployment and yet another reduction in consumption by those newly thrown out of work. And so it went, from buy, buy, buy, to down, down, down.

for FURTHER READING

See these several general histories of the 1920s: Frederick Lewis Allen, *Only Yesterday*, 1931; Loren Baritz, *The Culture of the Twenties*, 1969; Paul A. Carter, *The Twenties in America*, 1968; Ellis W. Hawley, *The Great War and the Search for a Modern Order: A History of the American People and Their Institutions, 1917–1933*, 1979; William E. Leuchtenburg, *The Perils of Prosperity, 1914–1932*, 1958; and George Soule, *Prosperity Decade: From War to Depression, 1917–1929*, 1947.

On politics, see Oscar Handlin, *Al Smith and His America*, 1958; John D. Hicks, *Republican Ascendancy, 1921–1933*, 1960; E. A. Moore, *A Catholic Runs for President*, 1956; Theodore D. Saloutos and John D. Hicks, *Twentieth-Century Populism: Agricultural Discontent in the Middle West, 1900–1939*, 1951; D. R. McCoy, *Calvin Coolidge: The Quiet President*, 1967; Arthur M. Schlesinger Jr., *The Crisis of the Old Order*, 1957; William Allen White, *A Puritan in Babylon*, 1938; and Joan Hoff Wilson, *Herbert Hoover: Forgotten Progressive*, 1975.

On economic and financial questions, see Irving Bernstein, *The Lean Years*, 1960; C. P. Kindleberger, *The World in Depression, 1929–1939*, 1973; J. W. Prothro, *Dollar Decade: Business Ideas in the 1920s*, 1954; and the incomparable John K. Galbraith, *The Great Crash*, 1955.

Visit the source collections at http://ajaccess.wadsworth.com and http://infotrac.thomsonlearning.com, and use the Search function with the following key terms to explore documents, images, audio and video clips, articles, and commentary related to the material in this chapter:

Alfred E. Smith
Calvin Coolidge
Charles Lindbergh
Dawes Act

Dorothy Parker
Progressive Party
Stock market crash of 1929
Teapot Dome scandal

Additional resources, exercises, and Internet links related to this chapter are available on *The American Past* Web site:
http://history.wadsworth.com/americanpast7e.

HISTORY ONLINE

The Coolidge Era and the Consumer Economy
http://memory/loc.gov/ammem/coolhtml/coolhome.html
Excellent multi-format portrait of the Roaring Twenties.

Ad Access
http://scriptorium.lib.duke..edu/adaccess/browse.html
Examples of consumer good advertising.

NATIONAL TRAUMA

The Great Depression 1930–1933

From the Collections of the Library of Congress

What our country needs is a good big laugh. If someone could get off a good joke every ten days, I think our troubles would be over.

Herbert Hoover

Prosperity is just around the corner.

Herbert Hoover

T HE STOCK MARKET crash made headlines. The depression began without fanfare, but, by the end of 1930, it had engulfed the nation in something far more serious than the collapse in the value of securities. And bad times did not fully dissipate until 1939, when the economy was jolted into prosperity by another world war.

The Great Depression was the most serious economic crisis in American history. It was, second to the Civil War, more jarring morally for the American people than any other experience. People who lived through the First World War and the Roaring Twenties found their recollections of those periods almost inconsequential after 1930. People who grew up during the 1930s would recall the deprivation, anxieties, and struggles of their childhood as vividly as they remembered the Second World War of which they were a part.

Not until the late 1960s did a generation come of age for which the Great Depression was "ancient history." Not until 1980, half a century after the depression began, did voters in a national election decisively repudiate the "liberals" whom the Great Depression brought to the fore.

THE FACE OF CATASTROPHE

Not every memory of the 1930s was a bad one. Many people took pride that when times were at their toughest, they carried on vital cultural, social, and personal lives. Whether the memories were negative or positive, however, the depression generation was the last American generation to date whose character and values were forged in an era of drastic economic decline and deprivation.

The Numbers

During the first year after the crash of the stock market, 4 million workers lost their jobs. By 1931, 100,000 people were fired each week. By 1932, 25 percent of the workforce was unemployed: 13 million people with about 30 million dependents. African American workers, "the last hired and

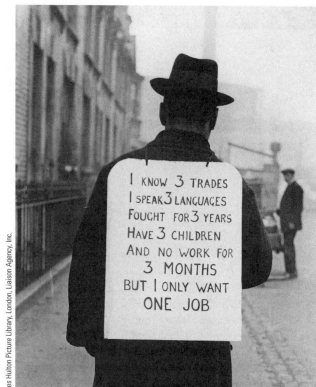

▲ *An unemployed workingman with style. His wit may or may not have been enough to find him employment.*

The sign reads:

I KNOW 3 TRADES
I SPEAK 3 LANGUAGES
FOUGHT FOR 3 YEARS
HAVE 3 CHILDREN
AND NO WORK FOR
3 MONTHS
BUT I ONLY WANT
ONE JOB

The Ongoing Crash

The stock market crash of 1929 was not a precipitous collapse followed by slow recovery. The prices of stocks continued to slide during the depression. In 1930, all stocks taken together had lost half their value. They declined in price another 30 percent by 1932. The stock market did not reach 1929 levels until World War II.

the first fired," suffered a higher unemployment rate than whites, 35 percent. In Chicago, 40 percent of those people who wanted work could not find it. In Toledo, 80 percent were unemployed. In some coal-mining towns like Donora, Pennsylvania, virtually no one had work.

Employees who held on to their jobs took pay cuts. Between 1929 and 1933, the average weekly earnings of manufacturing workers fell from $25 to less than $17. Farmers' income plummeted from a low starting point. By the winter of 1933, corn growers were burning their crop for heat—shades of the 1890s—because they could not sell it. Growers of wheat estimated that it took five bushels to earn the price of a cheap pair of shoes. The wholesale price of cotton dropped to five cents a pound.

Banks failed at a rate of 200 a month during 1932, wiping out $3.2 billion in savings accounts. When New York City's Bank of the United States went under in December 1930, 400,000 people lost their deposits. Much of the money was in small accounts that had been squirreled away by working people as a hedge against economic misfortune.

Hundreds of thousands of people lost their homes between 1929 and 1933 because they could not meet mortgage payments. One farm family in four was pushed off the land by 1933, mainly in the cotton, grain, and pork belts of the South and Midwest. With their customers unable to buy, more than 100,000 small businesses went bankrupt, 32,000 just in 1932 (88 per day). Doctors and lawyers reported huge

drops in income. Some schools closed for lack of money; in others, teachers took sharp cuts in pay or worked without pay as the only means of keeping schools open. Some teachers in Chicago were not compensated for 10 years.

What Depression Looked Like

People who did not personally suffer were reminded of the depression at every turn. More than 5,000 people lined up outside of a New York employment agency each week to apply for 500 menial jobs. When the city government of Birmingham, Alabama, called for about 800 workers to put in an 11-hour day for $2, 12,000 applicants showed up. In 1931, a Soviet agency, Amtorg, announced openings for 6,000 skilled technicians who were willing to move to Russia; 100,000 Americans said they would go. Once-prosperous workers and small businessmen sold apples or set up shoe-shine stands on street corners.

Charitable organizations were not up to the flood of newly impoverished people. Philadelphia's social workers managed to reach only one-fifth of the city's unemployed in order to provide $4.23 relief money to a family for a week, not enough to buy food, let alone pay for clothing, rent, and fuel. Soup kitchens set up by both religious and secular groups offered little more than a crust of bread and a bowl of thin stew, but for three years, they were regularly mobbed. A journalist described the crowd at the Municipal Lodging House in New York City in 1930: "There is a line of men, three or sometimes four abreast, a block long, and wedged tightly together—so tightly that no passer-by can break through. For this compactness there is a reason: those at the head of the grey-black human snake will eat tonight; those farther back probably won't."

On the outskirts of large cities (and right in the middle of New York's Central Park), homeless men and women built shantytowns out of scavenged lumber, scraps of sheet metal, packing crates, and cardboard boxes. The number of people who simply wandered the land—a new generation of tramps,

A Chicken in Every Pot

The Republican party slogan in the election campaign of 1928 had been "A Chicken in Every Pot and Two Cars in Every Garage." In 1932, the advertising man who had coined it was out of work and panhandling in order to feed his family.

▲ *Men line up for a free meal at a soup kitchen in New York City. Note that practically all are wearing hats or caps, an essential item of a man's wardrobe in the 1930s. A hatless man by definition wasn't "seriously" looking for work. Also note the orderliness of the queue. Only four relaxed policemen can be seen.*

this one including women—brought the face of catastrophe to rural America. Because it was impossible to stay the flood, railroads gave up trying to keep people off freight trains. Detectives for the Missouri Pacific railroad counted 14,000 people hopping its freights in 1928; in 1931, 186,000. Rough estimates indicate that 1.5 million people were moving around in search of casual work, and others were simply moving around; 6,500 illegal riders were killed or injured in 1931–1932.

Desertion of their families by unemployed men and the divorce rate both rose. Births declined from 3 million in 1921 to 2.4 million in 1932. Some moralists and sociologists believed that the depression was destroying the American family.

Others thought hardship caused families to pull together. This seemed true of the odyssey of the "Okies" and "Arkies." In the mid-1930s, the difficulties of depression were compounded by a natural disaster over much of Oklahoma, Texas, Kansas, and Arkansas: Dust storms literally stripped the topsoil from the land and blacked out the sun. In several counties of eastern Oklahoma, 90 percent of the population went on the dole. Some areas lost half their population as people fled across the desert to California, typically in decrepit Model T Fords piled with ragged possessions. John Stein-

beck captured their desperation, and their inner resourcefulness, in *The Grapes of Wrath,* a novel published in 1939.

THE FAILURE OF THE OLD ORDER

Will Rogers, himself an "Okie" and the nation's most popular humorist, quipped that the United States would be the first country to go to the poorhouse in an automobile. He was trying to restore a sense of proportion to the way people thought about the Great Depression. No one was starving, President Hoover added in one of his many ham-handed attempts to ease tension.

Pay Cut

In 1929, the last year of prosperity, Lefty O'Doul had a batting average of .398 for the Philadelphia Phillies. This achievement earned him a raise of only $500. In 1930, the first year of the depression, O'Doul hit .308, hardly a poor average. His salary was cut $1,000.

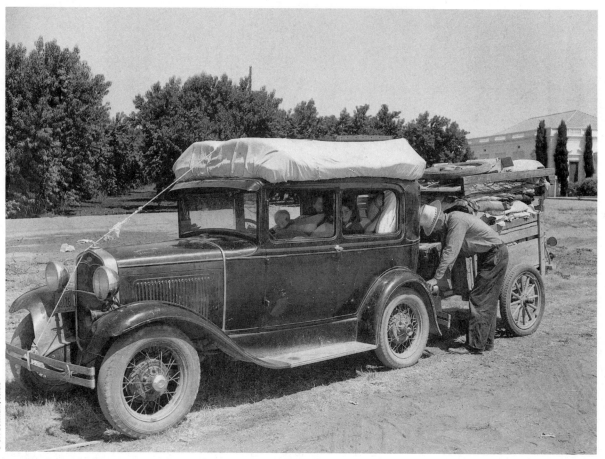

▲ *Okies, ruined by the dust bowl, emigrating to California. Virtually all made the trip on U.S. Route 66, making it the nation's best-known (and most romanticized) highway. Interstate 40 has superseded it today.*

Both men were right. There was no plague or famine. Indeed, to many people the troubling paradox of America's greatest depression was that deprivation was widespread in a country that was blessed with plenty. The potential of American factories to churn out goods was untouched, but they stood silent or working at a fraction of capacity because few could afford to buy their wares. Farms were pouring forth food in cornucopian abundance, but hungry people could not afford it. One of the most striking images of the early 1930s transformed a mild, white-haired California physician into an angry crusader. Early one Saturday morning, Dr. Francis E. Townsend looked out his window to see old women picking through the garbage pails of a store that was heaped high with foodstuffs. "Ten men in our country could buy the whole world," Will Rogers said, "and ten million can't buy enough to eat."

The Tragedy of Herbert Hoover

Business and the Republican party had reaped credit for the breezes of prosperity. Now they took the blame for the whirlwind of depression, and the recriminations were aimed particularly at the president, Herbert Clark Hoover. The shantytowns where the homeless dwelled were called "Hoovervilles"; newspapers used for warmth by men sleeping on park benches were "Hoover blankets"; a pocket turned inside out was a "Hoover flag"; a boxcar was a "Hoover pullman."

Still regarded as a great humanitarian when he entered the White House in 1929, Hoover was the callous tormentor of the people a year later. Celebrated for his energy and efficiency as secretary of commerce, Hoover as president was perceived as paralyzed by the economic crisis. When Hoover made one of his rare public appearances, a motorcade through the hard-hit industrial city of Detroit, crowds on the sidewalk greeted him with silence and sullen stares. The president could not even take a brief vacation without arousing scorn. "Look here, Mr. Hoover, see what you've done," an Appalachian song had it. "You went a-fishing, let the country go to ruin."

In truth, Hoover's self-confidence decayed rapidly during his presidency. If never a warm man, Hoover had always exuded confidence. Now he sat subdued, withdrawn, and embittered in the White House. Sitting down to talk with him, an adviser said, was like sitting in a bath of ink.

Hoover was maligned unjustly when critics called him uncaring, a do-nothing president, a stooge for the big businessmen. The president was moved by the suffering in the

▲ *One of dozens of "Hoovervilles," quickly erected in empty space (there was one in New York's Central Park) by families who lost their homes. Some survived for years, unmolested by authorities as long as they were orderly, which most were.*

country. He gave much of his income to charity. Far from paralyzed, he worked as hard at his job as James K. Polk had. Nor was he a Coolidge, letting business do as it pleased; Hoover led the federal government to greater intervention in the economy than had any preceding president except Wilson. It would soon be forgotten, but the man who replaced Hoover in the White House, Franklin D. Roosevelt, criticized Hoover for improperly *expanding* the powers of government.

No One Has Starved

At the worst of times early in the Great Depression, it was common to say that "no one has starved." But some came close, as these two excerpts from the *New York Times* indicate:

MIDDLETOWN, N.Y., December 24, 1931.–Attracted by smoke from the chimney of a supposedly abandoned summer cottage near Anwana Lake in Sullivan County, Constable Simon Glaser found a young couple starving. Three days without food, the wife, who is 23 years old, was hardly able to walk.

DANBURY, Connecticut, September 6, 1932.–Found starving under a rude canvas shelter in a patch of woods on Flatboard Ridge, where they had lived for five days on wild berries and apples, a woman and her 16-year-old daughter were fed and clothed today by the police and placed in the city almshouse.

Hoover's Program: Not Enough

Something had to be done. A good many Americans were old enough to recall that the somewhat less severe depression of the 1890s had led to a briefly terrifying social unrest. Some of the progressives had established the precedent that government was responsible for guiding the economy. Only in flush times like the Coolidge years could an administration abdicate its obligations and remain popular. Indeed, Hoover promptly broke with the immediate past by cutting Mellon's regressive consumer taxes in order to encourage purchasing and, therefore, he hoped, production.

Hoover spent $500 million a year on public works, government programs to build or improve government properties. These projects created some jobs that would otherwise not have existed. The most famous of them was the great Boulder Dam, now called Hoover Dam, on the Colorado River southeast of Las Vegas. The great wall of concrete was the single most massive example of government economic planning and construction to its time. It provided work for thousands. But the dam did nothing in the short run for those who were not building it or providing services to its construction workers.

In the Reconstruction Finance Corporation (RFC), established by Congress in 1932, Hoover created an agency to help banks, railroads, and other key economic institutions stay in business. The RFC loaned money to companies that were basically sound but were hamstrung by a lack of operating capital.

The trouble was that cutting consumer taxes did nothing for those who were unemployed; and those who still had jobs inclined not to spend what little windfalls came their way but to squirrel them away against the day when they might be out of work. Moreover, there was a glut in the middle class—it had been predicted—of "big-ticket" durable consumer goods like appliances and automobiles.

The RFC was not popular. Nothing Hoover did was popular. People in big personal trouble saw the RFC not as an agency for recovery but as relief for big business while they were told to fend for themselves.

The Blindness of the Rugged Individual

More was needed—massive relief to get the very poor, who were growing in numbers, over the crisis. This Hoover would not authorize. A self-made man, he had forgotten the role of talent and good luck in getting ahead. He believed that "rugged individuals"—he used the phrase—who looked to no one but themselves, were the secret of American cultural vitality. For the federal government to encourage that trait of the national character was one thing; for the government to sponsor handouts was quite another. Federal relief measures were not, in Hoover's opinion, the first step in defeating the depression but the first step in emasculating the American spirit. There was a difference between helping

▲ *Boulder Dam, also called Hoover Dam, the first great public works program of the Great Depression. It was a miracle of engineering that created another kind of miracle with the electricity it generated, the city of Las Vegas, Nevada.*

Belgians devastated by war and helping Americans deprived by an economic dislocation.

Hoover also clung to assumptions that prevented him from realizing just how much federal guidance was needed. Failing to recognize that state boundaries had no economic significance, he urged the states to take the lead in fighting the depression. Viewing government as much like a business, he was particularly inflexible when it came to the ideal of a balanced budget and the government's power to manipulate the value of the currency.

Government, Hoover insisted, must spend no more money than it collected; the books must balance. As for money questions, Hoover knew that during every depression since the Civil War, only Greenbackers, Populists, and others regarded as radicals proposed increasing the supply of money (deliberately inflating prices) in order to stimulate the economy. Each time, they had been defeated; and each time, the country had emerged from hard times more prosperous than before. Hoover was positive that this cycle would be repeated if the old faith was kept: if the budget was balanced and the dollar backed by gold.

An International Depression

For a few months in 1931, Hoover's prediction that "prosperity was just around the corner" seemed to be coming true. Most economic indicators made modest gains. Then, the entire industrialized world followed the United States into the pit. In May, a major European bank, the Kreditanstalt of Vienna, went bankrupt, shaking other European banks that had propped it up. In September, Great Britain abandoned the gold standard. That is, the Bank of England ceased to redeem its paper money in gold coin. Worried that all paper money would lose its value, international investors withdrew $1.5 billion in gold from American banks, further weakening the financial structure and launching a new wave of business failures.

In the United States, the worst consequence of the European financial collapse was what it did to Hoover's state of mind. It persuaded him that America's depression was not the fault of domestic problems that he might help remedy but of foreigners over whom he had no power. The most cosmopolitan president since John Quincy Adams had sunk to the ignorant provincial's easy inclination to blame others—foreigners—for his misfortune. The result was that, by 1932, the administration really was paralyzed.

AMERICA'S REACTION

If Hoover's failure represented the inability of New Era Republicans to cope with the depression, radicals were unable to offer a plausible alternative. Critics of capitalism believed that the crisis represented the death throes of the system and that they would soon be in power. To an extent, they, like Hoover, waited for inevitable forces beyond their control to summon them to the helm.

Weeknights at Eight

Commercial radio broadcasting began in 1920; the first radio network, the National Broadcasting Company (NBC), was founded in 1926. It was only during the depression, however, that the medium perfected the programming formula that hooked Americans. There was still plenty of music, news, and sporting events. But there were also, during the day, soap operas for housewives; in the afternoons—after school—mostly adventure programs for children; and, in the evening, comedy, dramatic, and mystery series "for the entire family."

Radio receivers were ensconced in about 12 million American households in 1930. By 1940, they were in 28 million. Fully 86 percent of the American people had easy daily access to radio sets. Radios were designed to disguise their electronics within a prized piece of furniture. Some were sleekly modern art deco; others, gothic with the pointed arches of a medieval cathedral.

Hard times were a big reason for the expansion of radio. It was free entertainment. During the 1920s, the average price of a receiver had been $75. During the 1930s, a serviceable set could be bought for $10 or $20, an amount that all but the destitute could scrape up.

The New Deal played a part in the radio boom. Although cities and towns were electrified before 1933, very little of the countryside was. Private power companies were not interested in the small return to be had from stringing wire miles into the middle of nowhere. By putting the advantages of electrification for country people above profits, Franklin D. Roosevelt's Rural Electrification Administration brought isolated farm families into the mainstream. More than 57 million people were defined as "rural" in 1940. Country folks depended more on the crackling broadcasts to brighten their lives than city dwellers did.

Makers of low-priced consumer goods rushed to advertise on the networks: NBC, the Columbia Broadcasting System, and Mutual. NBC had two networks, red and blue. When antitrust proceedings forced NBC to dispose of one of them, the American Broadcasting Company was born. In 1935, networks and local stations took in $113 million from advertisers. Operating expenses were estimated at $80 million. In 1940, expenses were up to $114 million, but advertising revenues had almost doubled to $216 million.

The manufacturers of Pepsodent toothpaste got the best bargain of all. In 1928, they contracted with two white minstrel-show performers in Chicago who did a program in southern black dialect *Sam 'n' Henry*. When the show went national, the performers picked two new names, and the series became *Amos 'n' Andy*. From the start, the show won a popularity that became the standard by which later "blockbuster" successes were measured.

Essentially, *Amos 'n' Andy* was minstrel humor with a plot set in Harlem, now the capital of black America. One of the performers, Freeman Gosden of Richmond, said that he based the character of Amos Jones on an African American boyhood friend. Amos was the honest, hardworking proprietor and sole driver of the Fresh Air Taxi Company (his cab had no windshield). Never during the program's 32 years on radio, nor after it had moved to television, was Amos an offensive character. However, he became a comparatively minor part of the program. The protagonist was George "Kingfish" Stevens, a fast-talking con man who dependably bungled his swindles, outsmarting himself.

The Kingfish's usual mark, Andrew "Andy" H. Brown, was infinitely gullible, a character whom even the Kingfish could bilk. Andy's survival depended on the con man's ineptitude or on Amos's intervention.

Everyone in America, it sometimes seemed, listened to the program, which ran on weeknights at eight o'clock. Few needed to be told what Amos, Andy, and the Kingfish, and even the minor characters, were like: Lightnin', who swept up the men's lodge, the Mystic Knights of the Sea; the shyster lawyer Algonquin J. Calhoun; and wives Ruby Jones and Sapphire Stevens. Ruby was as decent as Amos; Sapphire was a shrew who made life as miserable for George as he made it for Andy.

In November 1960, *Amos 'n' Andy* went from radio to television in a weekly half-hour format with African American actors who mimicked the voices created by Gosden and Charles Correll. However, the show had vociferous critics. During the 1950s, when the African American struggle for civil rights came to a head, the National Association for the Advancement of Colored People and numerous African American journalists denounced its stereotypes as "a gross libel on the Negro."

The show's sponsors pointed out that blacks enjoyed the program as much as whites did (which appears to have been so until the 1960s). And Gosden had a point when he insisted that the show "helped characterize Negroes as interesting and dignified human beings." But it is easier today to see his point than it was in 1960. Today, television is full of African American comedy shows playing on stereotypes. Amos, Andy, the Kingfish, and the others were, ultimately, stock theatrical characters (with a racial dimension) dating back at least as far as Shakespeare. In 1960, however, the civil rights movement was led by middle-class African Americans who were sensitive to any image of black people that was not respectable. After 100 episodes on TV, *Amos 'n' Andy* went off the air.

The Not-So-Red Decade

After polling only 267,000 votes in prosperous 1928, Socialist party presidential candidate Norman Thomas won 882,000 in 1932. Communist candidate William Z. Foster doubled his vote from 49,000 to 103,000. But the combined anticapitalist vote of less than a million was minuscule compared with the 23 million cast for the Democrats in that year and even the 16 million won by the discredited Hoover. Thomas's total in 1932 was less than the Socialist party had won 20 years before, when the electorate was much smaller and the economy in better health.

Later in the 1930s, Communism made some converts among intellectuals and in the leadership of some labor unions. Distinguished writers like Mary McCarthy, Edmund Wilson, and Granville Hicks joined the Communist party.

Even F. Scott Fitzgerald, the chronicler of the "flaming youth" of the 1920s, flirted with Marxist ideas that he did not understand. Theodore Dreiser, the dean of American novelists, wanted to join the Communist party but was told by party leaders that he could do more good for the cause outside the organization than if labeled a red.

The Communist love of conspiracy and manipulation drove intellectuals out of the party as quickly as they joined. It also prevented the Communists from establishing a base in the labor movement, despite making contributions to its growth that, in retrospect, can be seen to have been invaluable. Wyndham Mortimer of the United Automobile Workers, labor journalist Len De Caux, lawyer Lee Pressman, and other Communists and "fellow travelers" (sympathizers who were not party members) devoted their lives to building up the union movement. However, most Communist labor unionists either denied or thickly camouflaged their affiliation with the party and their anticapitalist ideology. The result was that few rank-and-file union members were exposed to, let alone converted to, Communism. When anti-Communist labor leaders took the offensive against the reds in the 1940s, they found it easy to oust party members from the unions that they had created.

A Curious Response

Americans simply did not interpret the Great Depression as evidence that capitalism had failed. During good times, Americans subscribed to the philosophy that individual success was the fruit of individual initiative, only secondarily the result of social conditions. So their initial response to the depression was to blame themselves for the hardships that beset them. Sociologists and journalists reported on homeless hitchhikers who apologized for their shabby clothing. A walk through any big-city park revealed unsuccessful job seekers slumped on benches, heads in hands, elbows on knees, collars drawn up, wondering where they, not the system, had failed.

The Gillette Company, a manufacturer of razor blades, exploited the feeling of personal failure by running an advertisement that showed a husband reporting shamefully to his wife that he still had not found a job. The message was that employers had turned him down not because there were no jobs for anybody but because he cut a poor appearance with his poorly shaved whiskers. A maker of underwear put the responsibility for the unemployment of a bedridden man squarely on his own shoulders. He was out of work not because 13 million others were but because he wore an inferior brand of undershirt and so caught a cold that he well deserved.

Long after the depression ended, it was the proud boast of many families that however bad things got, they never went "on the county," never took handouts from public welfare agencies. The unmistakable message was that coping with hard times was a personal responsibility. The implication for radicals who sought to direct anger and frustration against the system was not encouraging.

Episodes of Violence

There was violence. Hungry, angry people rioted in St. Paul and other cities, storming food markets and clearing the shelves. Wisconsin dairy farmers stopped milk trucks and dumped the milk into ditches, partly in rage at the low prices paid by processors, partly to dramatize their need for help. In Iowa, the National Farmers' Holiday Association told hog raisers to withhold their products from the market—to take a holiday—and attracted attention by blockading highways. Eat your own products, Holiday Association leader Milo Reno told the Iowans, and let the money men eat their gold.

▲ *The Bonus Boys' camp on Anacostia Flats, Washington, D.C., after the attack led by General Douglas MacArthur. The incident was the last nail in President Hoover's coffin.*

But such incidents were isolated and exceptional. For the most part, Americans coped with the depression peacefully and without a thought about revolution or riot. In fact, the most violent episode of the early depression was launched not by stricken people but by the authorities, the attack on the "Bonus Expeditionary Force" in Washington, D.C., in the summer of 1932.

The "Bonus Boys" were 20,000 First World War veterans and their wives who massed in Washington to demand that Congress, as a relief measure, vote them a $1,000 bonus for their wartime service that was scheduled to be paid in 1945. The economic crisis, they claimed, justified making the payment immediately. When Congress adjourned in July 1932 without doing so, all but about 2,000 of the demonstrators left the capital. Those who remained, squatted in empty government buildings or moved into a Hooverville on Anacostia Flats, on the outskirts of the city. They policed themselves, cooperated with authorities, and were generally peaceful.

Hoover, frustrated by the stubbornness of the depression and his unpopularity, persuaded himself that the Bonus Boys were led by Communist agitators. (Actually, the most influential organization among them was the militantly anti-Communist American Legion.) The president sent General Douglas MacArthur to clear out those who were living in government buildings. MacArthur, a talented soldier with a record of making up his own orders, called up armored vehicles and tear gas not only to clear out the buildings but to make short work of the Bonus Boys on Anacostia Flats, which Hoover had not authorized. Nevertheless, Hoover let MacArthur's insubordination pass, and the president's reputation sank lower as Americans mulled over the spectacle of young soldiers attacking old soldiers.

Midwestern Robin Hoods

Americans displayed their disenchantment with traditional values in indirect ways. Businessmen, universally lionized just a few years earlier, became objects of ridicule in films, on radio programs, and in the columns and comic strips of daily newspapers.

The most curious example of popular cynicism was the admiration lavished on a new kind of criminal, the midwestern bank robber who exploited automobiles and the wide-open highways of the Midwest to flee the scene of his dirty work. The press transformed John Dillinger, "Pretty Boy" Floyd, "Machine Gun" Kelly, Bonnie Parker and Clyde Barrow, and "Ma" Barker and her family-centered gang into Robin Hoods.

Unlike the businessmen-gangsters of Prohibition, the depression bank robbers were small-time hoodlums who botched as many holdups as they pulled off. They were reckless with their guns, killing bank guards and even innocent bystanders in their attempts to create an atmosphere of confusion to cover their escape. "Wanted" and their faces known, they could enjoy the money they stole only in dingy hideouts. However, because they robbed the banks that had

ruined many poor people and because they came from rural (and white Anglo-Saxon Protestant) backgrounds—no Italians in this business—the outlaws aroused a kind of admiration among midwesterners down on their luck.

Some of the gangsters cultivated the image of Robin Hood. John Dillinger (who killed 10 men) made it a point to be personally generous. "Pretty Boy" Floyd, who operated chiefly in Oklahoma, never had trouble finding people who would hide him from the authorities. When he was buried in Salisaw, Oklahoma, in 1934 (after being gunned down in Ohio), 20,000 people attended the ceremony. Bonnie Parker sent snapshots and doggerel epics to newspapers, celebrating the exploits of "Bonnie and Clyde."

Movies: The Depression-Proof Business

Hollywood, especially Warner Brothers studios, exploited the gangster craze by making movies that slyly glamorized lawbreakers. Still leery of censorship, the studios always wrote a moral end to their gangster films—the wrongdoer paid for his crimes in a hail of bullets or seated in the electric chair. But the message was clear: Criminals played by George Raft, Edward G. Robinson, and James Cagney had been pushed into their careers by poverty and social injustice and had redeeming qualities (which no film ever said of Al Capone).

The film industry did not suffer a depression. Movies flourished during the worst years, occupying the central position in American entertainment that they would hold until the coming of television. In the middle of the decade, 19 of the 25 highest salaries in the United States, and 40 of the highest 63, were paid to executives in motion pictures. Star actors and actresses raked it in as usual.

Admission to films was cheap. Each week, 85 million people paid an average of 25 cents (10 cents for children) to see Marie Dressler, Janet Gaynor, Shirley Temple, Mickey Rooney, Jean Harlow, and Clark Gable in a dizzying array of adventures and fantasies. The favorite themes were escapist. During the mid-1930s, Shirley Temple, an angelic little blond girl who sang and danced, led the list of moneymakers. Her annual salary was $300,000, and her films made $5 million a year for Fox Pictures. Royalties from Shirley Temple dolls and other paraphernalia made her a multimillionaire before she reached puberty (which ended her career). Director Cecil B. DeMille specialized in costume epics, especially those that transported viewers into biblical times.

Choreographer Busby Berkeley made millions for Warner Brothers by staging plotless dance tableaux featuring dozens of beautiful starlets (transformed by mirrors and trick photography into hundreds). People bought tickets to Berkeley films to escape the gray rigors of depression life. For the same reason, they supported the production of hundreds of low-budget westerns each year. The cowboy was still a figure of individual freedom in a world in which public events and private lives had become all too complexly interrelated.

Some directors specialized in didactic films on social themes that were often hard hitting. Frank Capra's specialty for Columbia Pictures was films that lovingly celebrated old American values and threats to them. Typically, they pitted decent ordinary men and women against indolent, parasitical, and usually crooked businessmen and politicians. Warner Brothers prided itself on being the studio with a social conscience.

Music, Music, Music

At first almost destroyed by the depression, the popular music business rebounded quickly to rank a close second behind the movies as Americans' entertainment outside the home. Sales of records, about $50 million a year during the 1920s, collapsed in 1932 to $2.5 million. The chief casualties were the hillbilly and African American blues singers and jazz musicians whose customers were among the hardest hit social groups in the country. Companies like Columbia, Decca, and RCA discontinued their "race record" lines—aimed at African Americans—and only a few black and Appalachian artists, like Bessie Smith, Louis Armstrong, Jimmie Rodgers, and the Carter Family continued to make money.

The 78-rpm record, which cost 35 cents, and the jukebox, which provided a play for a nickel, slowly revived the business. By 1939, there were 225,000 jukeboxes in the United States, scratching up 13 million records a year. Sales of records increased from 10 million in 1933 to 33 million

in 1938 (and then soared, with the return of prosperity, to 127 million in 1941).

The chief beneficiaries were the "big bands," which played swing, an intricately harmonized orchestral jazz music intended for dancing. For 50 cents (and sometimes less), young "jitterbuggers" could dance for three hours to the music of Benny Goodman, Harry James, or dozens of other groups. It was not an every-evening diversion. The 50 cents needed for admission was precious enough that the big bands had to rush from city to city on a series of one-night stands. Even the most popular orchestras might play in 30 different ballrooms in as many nights.

Nevertheless, they were lionized when they came to town. In the Palladium Ballroom in Hollywood, California, Harry James once drew 8,000 dancers in a single night, 35,000 in a week. At other capitals of swing music, like the Glen Island Casino in New Rochelle, New York, big bands earned extra revenue by playing on the radio too. Because a good radio could be ensconced in the parlor for $10 or $20 and operated for the cost of electricity, it was far and away depression-era America's favorite distraction.

THE ELECTION OF 1932

The fact that thinking back on a favorite radio program or visits to a ballroom or a movie theater decorated like a Turkish seraglio conjured up memories that glowed with nostalgia meant that many people would remember the Great Depression as quite a good time. In the summer of 1932, however, when the economy hit bottom, the country's mood was somber and anxious.

A Roosevelt for the Democrats

Senator Joseph I. France of Maryland challenged Hoover for the Republican presidential nomination and actually won primaries in New Jersey, Pennsylvania, Illinois, and Oregon. But American political parties do not abandon incumbent presidents, even when renomination means, as it did in 1932, a sure victory for the other party. Without joy, the Republicans named President Hoover to bear the brunt of the reaction against the New Era.

Democratic hopefuls fought a hair-pulling fight to win a ticket to the White House. The chief candidates at the Chicago convention were John Nance Garner of Texas, who had inherited the McAdoo Democrats of the South and West; Al Smith, the party's standard bearer in 1928, who believed he deserved a second go; and Governor Franklin D. Roosevelt of New York, once Smith's protégé but now a national figure in his own right.

When the beginnings of a convention deadlock brought back memories of 1924 and a bitterly divided party, some Garner supporters switched to Roosevelt and gave him the nomination. With a nose for the dramatic, Roosevelt broke with tradition, according to which a nominee waited at his home to be informed of the convention's decision. He flew

---

Straight Shooters

Radio flourished during the Great Depression, playing a major role in the lives of children as well as adults. The national networks dedicated late afternoons and early evenings to juvenile programs featuring young heroes like Little Orphan Annie and Jack Armstrong (the "All-American Boy"), aviators and space explorers, and cowboys like the Lone Ranger and Tom Mix (who was a real person and had been a real cowboy).

Most combined strident morality and patriotism with cliff-hanging adventure, encouraging habitual listening and consumption of the sponsor's product by offering premiums (secret decoder rings) and by forming clubs. Tom Mix's club was called the "Straight Shooters" and required members to swear a pledge:

I promise to shoot straight with my parents by obeying my father and mother.

I promise to shoot straight with my friends by telling the truth always, by being fair and square at work and at play.

I promise to shoot straight with myself by striving always to be my best, by keeping my mind alert and my body strong and healthy.

I promise to shoot straight with Tom Mix by regularly eating good old Hot Ralston, the official Straight Shooter cereal, because I know Hot Ralston is just the kind of cereal that will help build a stronger America.

---

to Chicago (thus conveying a sense of urgency) and told the cheering Democrats that he meant to provide a "new deal" for the American people. In so saying, Roosevelt simultaneously slapped at Republican policies during the 1920s (the New Era) and reminded people of both major parties that he was a distant cousin of the energetic president of the Square Deal, Theodore Roosevelt.

The Campaign

Hoover's campaign was dispirited. He was in the impossible position of having to defend policies that had clearly failed. Roosevelt, on the contrary, like any candidate who expects to win, avoided taking controversial stands. Any strong statement on any specific question could only cost him votes. At times, indeed, Roosevelt seemed to be calling for the same conservative approach to the economic crisis that Hoover already had tested; he warned against an unbalanced budget and reassured voters that he was no radical.

The most obvious difference between the president and his challenger was personality: Hoover's gloom versus Roosevelt's buoyant charm. Roosevelt smiled constantly. As he whisked around the country, he impressed everyone as a man who knew how to take charge, liked to take charge, and was

From the Collections of the Library of Congress

▲ *In his campaign, Franklin D. Roosevelt said nothing to lead voters to believe he would launch a massive reform program. In effect, he ran by contrasting his ebullient, confident personality to Hoover's glumness.*

perfectly confident in his ability to lead the country out of its crisis. The theme song of Roosevelt's campaign, blared by brass bands or played over loudspeakers at every whistle stop and rally, was the bouncy "Happy Days Are Here Again."

Only after his lopsided victory—472 electoral votes to Hoover's 59—did it become clear that Roosevelt had spelled out no program for recovery. Because inauguration day came a full four months after the election, there was one more long winter of depression under Herbert Hoover. The repudiated president, now a recluse in the White House, recognized that a void existed and tried to persuade Roosevelt to endorse his actions.

Roosevelt nimbly avoided making any commitments either in favor of or opposed to Hoover's policies. He took a quiet working vacation. He issued no statements of substance, but he was far from idle. Roosevelt met for long hours with experts on agriculture, industry, finance, and relief. Organized by Raymond Moley, a professor at Columbia University, this "brains trust," as reporters called it, marked a significant shift in the personnel who ran Washington. During the 1920s, the capital was a businessman's town. Now they were turning over their apartments and selling their homes to intellectuals, men (and a few women) from universities who hungered to have a go at running the country.

MAP 41:1 Presidential Election, 1932 Never had an electoral college map looked like Roosevelt's victory map in 1932. Only in New England, and Pennsylvania, where the old Republican machine still ran the show, did the Republicans carry any states.

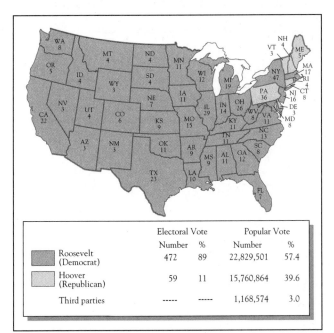

	Electoral Vote		Popular Vote	
	Number	%	Number	%
Roosevelt (Democrat)	472	89	22,829,501	57.4
Hoover (Republican)	59	11	15,760,864	39.6
Third parties	-----	-----	1,168,574	3.0

for FURTHER READING

Arthur M. Schlesinger Jr., *The Crisis of the Old Order,* 1957, and *The Coming of the New Deal,* 1959, provide a superb overview of the critical years of the early 1930s. See also Irving Bernstein, *The Lean Years,* 1960; the early chapters of Michael Bernstein, *The Great Depression: Delayed Recovery and Economic Change in America, 1929–1939,* 1987; Caroline Bird, *The Invisible Scar,* 1965; Milton Friedman, *The Great Contraction,* 1965; C. P. Kindleberger, *The World in Depression, 1929–1939,* 1973; Albert Romesco, *The Poverty of Abundance: Hoover, the Nation, and the Great Depression,* 1965; Jordan A. Schwarz, *The Interregnum of Despair: Hoover, Congress, and the Depression,* 1970; and Studs Terkel, *Hard Times,* 1970. Still worth reading is the sequel to *Only Yesterday,* Frederick Lewis Allen, *Since Yesterday,* 1940. A unique and rewarding portrait of Americans in the depression is Studs Terkel, *Hard Times,* 1970.

Valuable books on special subjects are Roger Daniels, *The Bonus March,* 1971; John A. Garraty, *Unemployment in History: Economic Thought and Public Policy,* 1979; James N. Gregory, *American Exodus: The Dust Bowl Migration and Okie Culture in California,* 1989; Susan Estabrook Kennedy, *The Banking Crisis of 1933,* 1973; Donald Lisio, *The President and Protest,* 1974; Van L. Perkins, *Crisis in Agriculture,* 1969; Robert Sklar, *Movie-Made America,* 1975; and Raymond Walters, *Negroes and the Great Depression,* 1970.

Franklin D. Roosevelt has been the subject of numerous biographies, both political and personal. Among the most rewarding are James MacGregor Burns, *Roosevelt: The Lion and the Fox,* 1956; Frank Freidel, *Franklin D. Roosevelt,* 1952–1973; and Joseph P. Lash, *Eleanor and Franklin,* 1971. Also see H. G. Warren, *Herbert Hoover and the Great Depression,* 1956.

AMERICAN JOURNEY ONLINE AND INFOTRAC COLLEGE EDITION

Visit the source collections at http://ajaccess.wadsworth.com and http://infotrac.thomsonlearning.com, and use the Search function with the following key terms to explore documents, images, audio and video clips, articles, and commentary related to the material in this chapter:

Franklin D. Roosevelt
Great Depression
Herbert Hoover
Hoovervilles

Shirley Temple
Swing music
The Grapes of Wrath

Additional resources, exercises, and Internet links related to this chapter are available on *The American Past* Web site: http://history.wadsworth.com/americanpast7e.

HISTORY ONLINE

America from the Great Depression to World War II
http://memory/loc.gov/ammem/fsohome.htm/
A treasury of photographs of depression era America.

Voices from the Dust Bowl
http://lcweb2.loc.gov/ammem/afctshtml/tshome.html
Text, video, and audio of the great drought of the 1930s.

Weedpatch Camp
www.weedpatchcamp.com/
A very good portrait of an "Okie" migrant camp in California, the camp on which John Steinbeck based his camp scenes in *Grapes of Wrath.*

REARRANGING AMERICA

FDR and the New Deal 1933–1938

© Bettmann/Corbis

This generation of Americans has a rendezvous with destiny.

Franklin D. Roosevelt

A FEW DAYS BEFORE his inauguration in 1933, Franklin D. Roosevelt (who would come to be known popularly as "FDR") visited Miami. From the crowd surging around him, a jobless worker named Joe Zangara, later found to be mentally unbalanced, emptied a revolver at Roosevelt's party. Anton Cermak, the mayor of Chicago, died from his wounds. The president-elect escaped without a scratch.

Americans learned from the episode that they had a leader who was cool in a crisis. Roosevelt barely flinched during the chaos. But what else did they know about him? Not much on March 4, 1933, and that little was not entirely encouraging.

THE PLEASANT MAN WHO CHANGED AMERICA

Henry Cabot Lodge had called Roosevelt "a well-meaning, nice young fellow, but light"; Edith Galt Wilson had dubbed him "more charming than able." In 1932, Walter Lippmann, dean of political columnists, called Roosevelt "a pleasant man who, without any important qualifications, would very much like to be president." Many wondered if a person who had enjoyed so pampered and sheltered a life as Roosevelt had was capable of appreciating the hardship that had befallen millions of Americans.

Silver Spoon

The new president was born into an old, rich, and idle New York family. Boyhood vacations were spent in Europe and at yachting resorts in Maine and Nova Scotia. He attended the most exclusive private schools and was adored and sheltered to the point of suffocation by his mother. When Roosevelt went to Harvard, Sara Roosevelt packed up, followed him, and rented a house near the university so that she could keep an eye on her boy. FDR's wife, Eleanor Roosevelt, was from the same tiny, exclusive social set. Indeed, she was the president's distant cousin.

Even the charm with which Roosevelt ran his campaign—the jaunty air, the toothy smile, the cheery small talk—was a quality of the socialite. Roosevelt seemed to be the real-life incarnation of a genial but fluffy character Cary Grant would play in several movies: "Tennis, anyone?"

And yet, from the moment FDR delivered his ringing inaugural address—the clouds over Washington parting on cue to let the sun through—it was obvious that he was a natural leader. From the first day, Roosevelt dominated center stage as cousin Theodore had done 30 years earlier, and without the bluster and bullying. He held 83 press conferences in 1933 and 96 in 1940. (Recent presidents have had 4 or 5 a year.)

Where Teddy had been liked and enjoyed, FDR was loved. Poor sharecroppers and African Americans living in big cities tacked his photograph to a wall of their homes next to prints of Christ in Gethsemane and named their children after him.

He was also hated. It was said that some of the nation's wealthiest people could not bear to pronounce his name. Much to the amusement of Roosevelt's supporters, they referred to him through clenched teeth as "that man in the White House" and as a "traitor to his class." Robert R. McCormick, publisher of the Chicago *Tribune,* headlined a story of the 1936 Democratic convention "Soviets Meet at Philadelphia."

Roosevelt's Contribution

Roosevelt's unbounded self-confidence was itself a contribution to the battle against the depression. His optimism was infectious. The change of mood he brought to Washington and the country was astonishing. Shortly after assuming office, he exploited his charisma by launching a series of "fireside chats" on the radio. In an informal living-room manner, he explained to the American people what he was trying to accomplish and what he expected of them. Millions listened respectfully, as if he were sitting with them.

But Roosevelt was more than a charmer. He was not afraid to make decisions or to accept responsibility (although he preferred it if others took the blame for blunders). He acted. A day after he was sworn in, he called Congress into special session for the purpose of enacting crisis legislation, and he declared a bank holiday. Calling on emergency presidential powers, he ordered all banks to close their doors temporarily in order to forestall additional failures. Although the immediate effect of the bank holiday was to tie up people's savings, the drama and decisiveness of his action won wide approval.

In 1933, Justice Oliver Wendell Holmes Jr. said that the president had "a second-class intellect." Roosevelt was, in fact, far from brilliant. He never fully understood the com-

plex economic and social processes with which his administration had to grapple, and he did not think it necessary that he should. If he was an indifferent student, he had the professors at his command. He sought the advice of his "brains trust" and was open to suggestions from all quarters. But because he never doubted his responsibilities as the nation's elected chief, he maintained his authority over his stable of headstrong intellectuals, many of them prima donnas. He stroked their vanities when it suited his purposes, played one brains-truster against another, and retained the personal loyalty of some whose advice he rejected. Faces in the White House anterooms changed. Friends became critics. But Roosevelt never lacked talented advisers because he did not fear talent and because advisers knew he listened.

In the end, Roosevelt's greatest strength was his flexibility. "The country needs bold, persistent experimentation," he said. "It is common sense to take a method and try it. If it fails, admit it frankly and try another." Roosevelt's pragmatism not only suited the American temperament, but it contrasted sharply with Hoover's insistence that policies conform to a tattered ideology.

A Real First Lady

Not the least of FDR's assets was his remarkable wife, Eleanor. Only much later, in the age of anything-goes journalism, did Americans learn that their marriage had been shattered years earlier by an affair between Franklin and Eleanor's personal secretary, Lucy Mercer. Eleanor offered

AP/Wide World Photos

▲ *FDR was charming with everyone. Eleanor Roosevelt was at home with everyone and felt a genuine compassion for those at the bottom of society.*

a divorce; Franklin begged off; Eleanor said that Lucy had to go, and she did, or so Eleanor thought.

A divorce would have ended Roosevelt's political career short of the presidency. Not until 1952 did a divorced man run for the presidency, unsuccessfully; not until 1980 was one elected. Divorce would also have denied FDR the services of his one aide who may be called indispensable. During the New Deal years, the homely, shrill-voiced Eleanor was thought of by friend and foe alike as the president's alter ego. She was his legs, for FDR was paralyzed from the waist down by polio, unable to walk more than a few steps in heavy, painful steel leg braces. Eleanor was a locomotive. With no taste for serving tea and chucking the chins of Boy Scouts visiting the White House, she raced around the country, picking through squalid tenements, wading in mud in Appalachian hollows, and descending into murky coal mines to see how the other half made do. Whereas FDR was cool, detached, calculating, and manipulative, Eleanor was compassionate, deeply moved by the misery and injustices suffered by the "forgotten" people at the bottom of society.

She interceded with her husband to appoint women to high government positions. She supported organized labor when FDR tried to straddle a politically difficult question. She made the grievances of African Americans her particular interest and persuaded her husband to name blacks, like educator Mary McLeod Bethune, to high government posts. Much of the affection that redounded to FDR in the form of votes was earned by "that woman in the White House." It was Eleanor, as much as the New Deal, who engineered the switch of 90 percent of the African American vote from the Republicans to the Democrats.

The Hundred Days

Never before or since has the United States experienced such an avalanche of legislation as Congress enacted during the spring of 1933. By nature deliberate, Congress was jolted by the crisis and by Roosevelt's demands to pass most of his proposals without serious debate, a few without reading the bills through. During what became known as the "Hundred Days," FDR and his brains-trusters were virtually unopposed. Conservative congressmen simply shut up, cowed by their own failure and the decisiveness of the New Deal majority.

Aid for Banks and Farms

The most pressing problems were the imminent collapse of the nation's financial system, the massive foreclosures on farm and home mortgages, and the distress of millions of unemployed workers.

The Emergency Banking Act eliminated weak banks merely by identifying them. Well-managed banks in danger of folding were saved when the Federal Reserve System issued loans to them. Just as important, when the government permitted banks to reopen, people concluded that they were safe. They ceased to withdraw their deposits and returned funds that they had taken home and out of circulation. Roosevelt also halted the drain on the nation's gold reserve by forbidding its export and, in April, by taking the nation off the gold standard. No longer could paper money be redeemed in gold coin that was hoarded. Instead, the value of money was based on the government's word, and the price of gold was frozen by law at $35 an ounce. ("Well, that's the end of western civilization," a Wall Street financier said.)

The New Deal attempted to halt the dispossession of farmers by establishing the Farm Credit Administration. The Farm Credit Administration refinanced mortgages for farmers who had missed payments. Another agency, the Home Owners' Loan Corporation, provided money for town and city dwellers who were in danger of losing their homes.

Help for the Helpless

Nothing better illustrated the contrast between Hoover's inaction and Roosevelt's flexibility than the establishment of the Federal Emergency Relief Administration (FERA). Whereas Hoover had resisted federal relief measures on ideological grounds, FERA quickly distributed $500 million to states so that they could save or revive their exhausted programs for helping the desperately poor. The agency was headed by Harry Hopkins, an Iowan-turned-New-York-social-worker with a cigarette dangling from his lip and a fedora pushed back on his head.

Hopkins disliked handouts. He believed that people who were able to work should be required to work in return for government assistance. It did not matter to him that the jobs they did were not particularly useful. His point was that government-paid jobs should not only get money into the hands of those who needed it but also give relief workers a sense of personal worth.

Keynes

New Deal economics is often described as "Keynesian," after the British economist John Maynard Keynes. When Keynes and FDR met, however, Roosevelt could not comprehend what Keynes was saying, and Keynes later called the president an economic illiterate.

The New Deal did, nevertheless, reflect some of Keynes's principles. For example, Keynes argued that consumption, not investment, was the key to prosperity in a modern economy. Therefore, in times of depression, massive deficit spending by the government (spending borrowed money) should be used in order to stimulate consumption. Private investment would go to where the profits were. Although far from consistently, and perhaps inadequately understood by the president, this is what the New Deal did.

Nevertheless, Hopkins recognized that the crisis of 1933 was so severe that money had to be gotten out into the country more quickly than jobs could be invented. Temporarily setting aside his belief in work for pay in administering FERA, he won FDR's confidence with his able and energetic direction of the program. There was waste and bureaucratic boondoggling, but FERA created hope where there had been despair.

▲ *The CCC was immensely popular. Only New Deal haters flirting with insanity disapproved. Run by the army with a quasi-military discipline, it gave young men jobs "in the woods," did badly needed conservation work in national forests, built trails in national parks, and—part of the deal—sent money home monthly to workers' families.*

© Bettmann/Corbis

Alphabet Soup: The CCC

New bureaucracies were the order of the day in 1933. With an initial appropriation of $500 million, the Civilian Conservation Corps (CCC) employed 274,375 young men between the ages of 17 and 25 in 1,300 camps. In 1935, CCC workers numbered 502,000 in 2,514 camps. Eventually, some 2.9 million people served in the corps, about 10 percent of them African American.

Signed on for six-month terms and organized into crews, they reforested land that had been raped by cut-and-run lumbermen and undertook other conservation projects in national parks and forests. The CCC built 46,854 bridges, 318,076 check dams, 3,116 fire lookouts, 87,500 miles of fence, and 33,087 miles of terracing to resist erosion. For this, each worker was paid $30 a month, of which $22–$25 was sent home; the CCC provided bed and board. The idea was to provide relief for the families of CCC workers and a tonic for the consumer economy.

The CCC was one of the New Deal's most popular programs both because of the kind of work it did and because it got city boys into the fresh air of the woods and mountains, always desirable in American eyes.

Alphabet Soup: CWA and WPA

Critics of the CCC fastened on the quasi-military discipline with which the army ran the program, but the idea of relief through jobs rather than through charity remained a mainstay of the New Deal. The Civil Works Administration (CWA), which Harry Hopkins headed after November 1933, put 4 million unemployed people to work within a few months. They built roads, constructed public buildings—post offices, city halls, and recreational facilities—and taught in bankrupt school systems.

When the CWA spent more than $1 billion in five months, FDR shuddered and called a halt to the program. But private investors would not or could not take up the slack, and unemployment threatened to rise once again. In May 1935, the president turned back to Hopkins and Congress to establish the Works Progress Administration (WPA).

The WPA broadened the CWA's work program. In addition to basic construction and repair, the agency hired artists to paint murals in public buildings and organized actors into troupes that brought theater to people who never had seen a play. Photographers created a treasury of Americana, taking 77,000 pictures. The Writer's Project, with John Cheever as editor, and other soon-to-be-distinguished contributors such as Saul Bellow, Ralph Ellison, and Richard Wright, as well as hundreds of writers of no fame, wrote guidebooks to each

The Granger Collection, New York

▲ *The WPA put artists to work in public buildings (not just federal buildings) all over the country painting murals that were masterpieces of the art. This mural in California depicts the state's mission era, when Franciscan friars gathered Indians into self-sufficient communities protected from Spanish ranchers and the army.*

of the 48 states, many of which are still seen as models of the genre. In the South, the WPA sent out workers to collect the reminiscences of old people who remembered having been slaves. By 1943, when the agency was liquidated, it had spent more than $11 billion and employed 8.5 million people. The National Youth Administration, part of the WPA, provided jobs for 2 million high school and college students.

Repeal

The repeal of the Twenty-First Amendment (which had established Prohibition) might be listed as one of the New Deal's relief measures. On March 13, 1933, FDR called for the legalization of weak beer, and when the amendment was ratified in December, most states legalized more potent drinks.

Certainly, many people looked on the privilege of buying drink legally as relief. An Appalachian song praising Roosevelt pointed to repeal of Prohibition as his most important act: "Since Roosevelt's been elected, moonshine liquor's been corrected. We've got legal wine, whiskey, beer, and gin." Breweries and distilleries were up and running as if they had been closed for no more than a week. Wine makers, most of whom had torn out their vines and planted orchards, needed several years to recover.

The NRA

The New Deal's relief programs were successful. Direct benefits reached only a fraction of the people who were hardship cases, but they were usually the worst off. The government's mere willingness to act was, if intangibly, a morale booster. To the New Dealers, however, relief was just a stopgap. They wanted to put the government to work stimulating economic recovery. In this, they were less effective.

The National Recovery Administration (NRA) was a bold and controversial attempt to bring order and prosperity to the shattered economy. The NRA was headed by General Hugh Johnson, something of a blowhard but also an inexhaustible organizer and cheerleader. A onetime Bull Mooser, he was a zealous believer in an ordered economy.

Johnson supervised the drafting of codes for each basic industry and, before long, some less-than-basic industries too. The codes set minimum standards of quality for products and services, fair prices at which they were to be sold, and the wages, hours, and conditions under which employees in the various industries would work. Section 7(a) of the National Industrial Recovery Act was pathbreaking in the area of labor relations: It required companies that agreed to the codes to bargain collectively with their workers through labor unions that a majority of the company's employees selected.

The NRA was designed to eliminate waste, inefficiency, and destructive competition—the goal of industrial consolidators since John D. Rockefeller. In making the federal government the referee among companies and between employers and employees, the NRA was the heir of Theodore Roosevelt's New Nationalism and of the mobilization of the economy during the First World War. The difference was that the NRA codes were compulsory and meant to be permanent. A business was bound to its industry's code not by the moral suasion on which Hoover based his trade associations but by the force of law. Noncompliance meant prosecution.

Blue Eagle Mania

Critics of the NRA, including some within the New Deal, likened it to the Fascist system that had been set up in Italy after 1922 by Benito Mussolini, and even to Hitler's Nazi economy in Germany. This was unfair. Mussolini and Hitler suppressed free labor unions; the NRA gave them a role in making industrial policy.

More to the point was the criticism that "Blue Eagle" functionaries (the NRA's symbol was a stylized blue eagle) sometimes went ridiculously far in their codes. Johnson was code crazy; he wanted to regiment peripheral and even trivial businesses. There was a code for the burlesque "industry" that specified how many strippers were to undress per performance, what vestments they were to discard, and the quality of tassels and G-strings. Had prostitution been legal in the United States, Johnson would have gone to even greater lengths.

Such extremes were made possible by the enthusiasm with which Americans initially took to the NRA. Rooted on by the bombastic Johnson, 200,000 people marched in an NRA parade in New York, carrying banners emblazoned with the NRA motto, "We Do Our Part." The blue eagle was painted on factory walls, pasted on shop windows, and adopted as a motif by university marching bands.

Briefly, Hugh Johnson seemed as popular as Roosevelt himself. He was certainly more conspicuous. Johnson stormed noisily around the country, publicly castigating as "chiselers" those businessmen who did not fall into line. He apparently inherited his personality from his mother, who, at an NRA rally in Tulsa, said, "People had better obey the NRA because my son will enforce it like lightning, and you can never tell when lightning will strike."

THE NEW DEAL THREATENED—AND SUSTAINED

The New Deal suffered its first setback in the Supreme Court. The Court was conservative in 1935: Seven of the nine justices had been appointed by Taft, Harding, Coolidge, and Hoover. Out of synchronization with the revolution taking place in government, the "nine old men" (as FDR was to denounce them) declared two major New Deal legislation reforms unconstitutional and threatened others.

Death of the Blue Eagle

The NRA was killed by a suit brought by a small company specializing in slaughtering chickens for use in the kosher kitchens of observant Jews. The Schechter brothers, owners of

▲ *During its brief history, the popular NRA was promoted with Hollywood-style hoopla. Here, "bathing beauties" are stenciled with the NRA's symbol, the blue eagle, the idea being that when they tanned in the sun, they would have a pale eagle to show off.*

the company, found the sanitary standards mandated by the NRA code incompatible with the ritual requirements of kosher slaughter. They claimed that NRA regulations represented unjustifiable federal interference in intrastate commerce. (Their business was almost entirely within New York State.) In 1935, the Supreme Court ruled unanimously that the Schechter brothers were right: The NRA was unconstitutional.

There was little fuss. Both Roosevelt's and the popular enthusiasm for the NRA, once red hot, had cooled since 1933. Many codes were so nit-picking as to be ridiculous, even impediments to recovery. Moreover, Congress moved promptly to salvage the one provision of the codes that still had widespread support, section 7(a). In the Wagner Labor Relations Act of 1935, the New Dealers reinstated the requirement that employers recognize and negotiate with labor unions that had the support of a majority of the company's employees. In fact, the Wagner Act went farther by setting up the National Labor Relations Board to investigate unfair labor practices and to issue cease and desist orders to employers found guilty of such practices.

Farm Policy

A similar salvage operation preserved parts of the Agricultural Adjustment Act, which the Supreme Court negated in 1936. Enacted during the Hundred Days, the Agricultural Adjustment Act established the Agricultural Adjustment Administration (AAA) to enforce the principle of parity, for which farmers' organizations had agitated throughout the 1920s.

Parity meant increasing farm income from the depths to which it had plummeted, to the ratio that farm income had borne to the prices of nonfarm products during the prosperous years of 1909 to 1914. The AAA accomplished this by restricting farm production. Farmers who raised wheat, corn, cotton, tobacco, rice, and hogs were paid subsidies to keep some of their land out of production. The costs of this expensive program ($100 million was paid to cotton farmers in one year) were borne by a tax on processors—millers, refiners, butchers, and packagers—which was then passed on to consumers in higher food, clothing, and tobacco prices.

Because the 1933 crop was already in the ground when the AAA was created, it was necessary to destroy some of the harvest. "Kill every third pig and plow every third row under," Secretary of Agriculture Henry A. Wallace said. The results were mixed. Many people were repelled by the slaughter of 6 million pigs and 220,000 pregnant sows. Others less sensitive wondered why food was being destroyed when millions were hungry. (In fact, 100 million pounds of the prematurely harvested pork was diverted to relief agencies, and inedible waste was used as fertilizer.) Nevertheless, the AAA worked; the income of hog farmers began to rise immediately.

Fully a quarter of the 1933 cotton crop was plowed under, and the fields left fallow. Unfortunately, because cotton farmers tended those fields still under cultivation more intensely, production actually rose in 1933. Within two years, however, cotton (and wheat and corn) prices rose by over 50 percent.

A less desirable effect of the AAA was to throw people off the land. Landlords dispossessed tenant farmers in order

Café Society

Many thousands of middle-class speculators were ruined in the collapse of 1929. Some were impoverished. The very rich, however, suffered only a loss in paper wealth, not in the way they lived. For the first year or so of the New Deal, the wealthy were not as conspicuous socially as they had been during the 1920s. By 1935, they were coming out again, albeit in a new kind of social whirl.

Unlike the high society of Mrs. Astor and Bradley Martin, with its regal ballrooms and private railroad cars, and unlike the "flaming youth" in Stutz Bearcats, flaunting their sexuality and slumming at speakeasies in African American neighborhoods where black jazz musicians were making their mark, the "café society" of the 1930s centered around former posh speakeasies that had come above ground as restaurants and nightclubs. There, one sat, chatted, and danced, seeing and being seen. In New York City, the capital of café society, the chic clubs were El Morocco, the Stork Club, and the 21 Club, still reveling in its supposedly cryptic speakeasy designation, its address.

The young had always been an important part of high society. Marrying daughters to European noblemen or socially acceptable rich Americans had been the avocation of the wealthy in the late nineteenth century. Youth had set fashions in the social whirl of the 1920s. In café society, the "rich, young, and beautiful" were the centerpiece.

Ordinary Americans were intrigued by the café set. Whom Alfred Gwynne Vanderbilt was dating was breathlessly reported in nationally syndicated "society columns" by hangers-on like Walter Winchell and "Cholly Knickerbocker," who were welcome in café society because they were its publicists. It was news if the heiress of a widget fortune dropped in at El Morocco several times a week in order to dance the rumba with her "agile husband." Naughtier items made reference to agile hubbies dancing the rumba with willowy debutantes who were not their wives.

Debutantes (or "debs"), young women who were said to be "coming out" (when, in fact, they had been lounging around nightclubs since they were 15 or 16), were the queens of café society. The leading deb of 1937 was Gloria "Mimi" Baker, whose mother replied to someone who called her a decadent aristocrat, "Why Mimi is the most democratic person, bar none, I've ever known." In fact, café society was "democratic" in ways that earlier high societies had not been. Because status was based on beauty, on what passed in the circles as wit, and simply on being well known, the café set admitted movie stars, athletes, and musicians. They, in turn, were delighted to rub shoulders and dance the rumba with the very rich.

International "playboys" jumped at the opportunity to do more than be photographed at nightclubs they could not afford, and therein lay the great morality play of the 1930s, a large part of the explanation for the fascination of ordinary Americans. Like people who attend automobile races, the readers of gossip columns were interested in the collisions as much as in the competition.

Barbara Hutton, who had to stick to painful diets in order to keep her weight down to glamour level, was sole heiress to $45 million made in very small increments in the five-and-dimes of F. W. Woolworth. In 1933, she married Alexis Mdivani, who claimed to be a dispossessed Russian prince. Almost immediately after the marriage, the debonair Mdivani began to make Barbara miserable, railing at her weight problem. Drawing on the $1 million that Barbara's father had given him as a wedding present, the prince spent much of his time with other women. In 1935, Barbara won Mdivani's consent to an unmessy divorce by paying him $2 million.

Almost immediately, she married a Danish count, Kurt von Haugwitz-Reventlow. Hutton showered the playboy with gifts, including a $4.5 million mansion in London. They were divorced in 1937. The same photographers who snapped pictures of laughing, dancing debutantes at the Stork Club rushed to get shots of tearful Barbara Hutton, the "poor little rich girl."

Some of the people who pored over the pathetic pictures pretended sympathy. "She's made mistakes," wrote columnist Adela Rogers St. Johns, "been a silly, wild, foolish girl, given in to temptations—but she's still our own. . . . an American girl fighting alone across the sea." Others openly took pleasure in her self-inflicted misery. "Why do they hate me?" Barbara asked. "There are other girls as rich, richer, almost as rich."

---

to collect the subsidies fallow land would earn. Between 1932 and 1935, 3 million American farmers lost their livelihood. Most of them were poor black and white tenants in the South.

Anxious Days

Despite its undesirable consequences, New Dealers were devoted to the AAA. Its rejection by the Supreme Court was a far more serious blow than the loss of the Blue Eagle. Again, they salvaged what they could. In the Soil Conservation and Domestic Allotment Act, parity and the limitation of production were restored under the guise of conserving soil.

Much more worrisome was the fear that, piece by piece, the Supreme Court would dismantle the entire New Deal. Roosevelt's supporters were particularly worried about the Rural Electrification Act and the Tennessee Valley Authority (TVA).

The Rural Electrification Administration (REA) brought electricity to isolated farm regions that were of no interest to private utility companies. It was vulnerable to court action because it put the government into the business of distributing power, indirectly competing with private enterprise. The TVA was farther-reaching yet. It was a massive government construction, flood control, and electrification project that shaped an entire region, a model of progressive government economic and social planning.

The TVA

The TVA was the brainchild and lifelong darling of Senator George Norris, a Republican progressive who advocated economic planning and regional development engineered by the government. Although he was from Nebraska, Norris had fastened on the valley of the Tennessee River, in the southern Appalachians, as the place to put his ideas to work.

Almost every year, the wild Tennessee River flooded its banks and brought additional hardship to southern Appalachia, already one of the nation's poorest regions. Norris's idea was to use the stricken region as a laboratory. The government would construct a system of dams both to control the floods and to generate electricity. In homes, the cheap power would bring the people of Appalachia into the twentieth century. The electricity would also make possible the construction of factories, especially for the manufacture of fertilizers, which would invigorate the economy of a chronically depressed region.

Norris also pointed out that by generating electricity itself, the government would be able to determine the fairness of the prices of power charged by private companies elsewhere in the country. Until the 1930s, the actual cost of generating electrical power was something of a mystery outside of the industry.

During the 1920s, Henry Ford tried to buy key sites on the Tennessee River from the government, notably Muscle Shoals, a tumultuous rapids, in order to build a privately owned power plant. Norris fought Ford off in Congress, arguing that the Tennessee Valley provided the best laboratory for testing theories of regional planning. Fortunately for Norris, scandalous government giveaways of valuable property, notably the oil reserves at Teapot Dome, were quite alive in the public memory. However, although he was able to keep Muscle Shoals and other sites in federal hands, Norris was unable to push through his plan for government development of the Tennessee Valley until Roosevelt's election.

Creeping Socialism

Fiscal conservatives attacked the astronomical costs of the New Deal. Herbert Hoover spoke of the decimal point in the government's debts "wandering around among the regimented ciphers trying to find some of the old places it used to know."

The TVA and REA were assailed as socialistic. Big business, which had approved FDR's banking reforms and, briefly, the NRA, launched a political offensive against programs that put the government into the production and distribution of electrical power. As early as 1934, some bankers and leaders of big business founded the American Liberty League, which accused Roosevelt of trying to destroy free enterprise and set up a socialist dictatorship.

Most Liberty Leaguers were Coolidge-Mellon Republicans, but they were joined by some prominent Democrats, including two of the party's presidential nominees, John W. Davis and Alfred E. Smith. Davis was a corporate lawyer, so he found Liberty League company familiar. Smith had abandoned his role as the lad from the "Sidewalks of New York" (his old political theme song) for much more comfortable seats on corporate boards of directors.

Combating the Liberty Leaguers was like swatting mosquitoes for Roosevelt. Americans were still wary of big business, even bitter toward it. FDR labeled the Liberty Leaguers "economic royalists." They never had much of a following.

The Supreme Court was another matter, a major threat to the New Deal. Making one of his rare political miscalculations, Roosevelt proposed to save the New Deal by packing the Court with additional justices who would endorse his reforms.

The reaction was universally hostile. The New Deal remained popular, but Roosevelt's court-packing scheme smelled of tampering with the Constitution. Roosevelt quickly retreated, and the crisis passed when the Court, perhaps alarmed, approved several key New Deal laws thought vulnerable. Then Father Time lent a hand; beginning in 1937, retirements and deaths on the Court enabled Roosevelt to appoint a New Deal majority to the bench without tampering with the size of the Court. When FDR died in 1945, eight of the nine justices were his appointees.

THE SPELLBINDERS

FDR made his court-packing proposal in 1937, at the beginning of his second term. For a while, however, it had appeared he might not win reelection. The threat came not from the Republican party but from three popular demagogues (the "spellbinders") whom Roosevelt and his chief political strategist, Postmaster General James A. Farley, genuinely feared.

Father Coughlin

With the coming of depression, Charles E. Coughlin, a Canadian-born Catholic priest, transformed his religious radio program into a platform for his political beliefs. At first, Coughlin enlisted his mellow, baritone voice and Irish genius with the spoken word to support Roosevelt. Not a man to shun extravagance, he said, in 1933, "The New Deal is Christ's deal."

Within a year, however, Coughlin became convinced that the key to solving the depression was an overhaul of the national monetary system, including the abolition of the Federal Reserve banks. Despite Roosevelt's reputation among the "economic royalists" as a radical, the president had no patience for such extreme proposals. But Coughlin had a huge and devoted following—perhaps 10 million listeners. His increasingly scathing attacks worried FDR, Farley, and other Democratic tacticians. Coughlin's audience was made up largely of Catholics in the big northeastern and midwestern states, traditionally Democratic voters.

Well Funded

In 1934, radical novelist Upton Sinclair won the Democratic party's nomination for governor of California by proposing a comprehensive social welfare program known as "End Poverty in California," or "EPIC." FDR was less than delighted by the emergence of another spellbinder in the party; he sat out the campaign. The Republicans spent $4 million in the successful effort to defeat Sinclair. In 1932, the Republicans had spent only $3 million nationally in the campaign to reelect President Hoover.

Dr. Townsend

Dr. Francis E. Townsend, a California physician, was rather different from the high-voltage Coughlin. Himself 66 years old in 1933, Townsend was the champion of the nation's aged. He proposed that the federal government pay a monthly pension of $200 to all people over 60 years of age, with two conditions attached.

First, the pensioners would be forbidden to work. Second, they would spend every cent of their pension within the month. Thus, Townsend said, the plan would not only provide security for the nation's elderly but would reinvigorate the economy, creating jobs for young men and women, as the old folks pumped every cent they made into consumption. By 1936, 7,000 Townsend Clubs claimed a membership of 1.5 million.

The principle of the Townsend plan is far more edifying than the principle of the pensions politicians, corporate executives, and university presidents pay themselves today— so much money that their pensions are, in effect, estates for their heirs. However, economists showed that the Townsend plan was not financially plausible, and Roosevelt rejected it. Townsend then went into the opposition and laid tentative plans to ally his followers to the disciples of Father Coughlin and of Roosevelt's most serious political rival, Senator Huey P. Long of Louisiana. A third party with such a base would indeed be a threat to FDR. Almost every vote the alliance won would be a vote subtracted not from the Republicans but from the Democrats, and Huey Long was a political campaigner as good as they get.

The Kingfish

Huey Long rose from among the poor white farm folk of northern Louisiana to educate himself as a lawyer. He never forgot the poor. He built a successful political career as a colorful populistic orator who baited the railroad and oil industry elites that ran the state. Unlike most southern demagogues, Long did not resort to race baiting. He supported segregation, a given in southern politics, but he won the support of many of those Louisiana blacks, mostly in New Orleans, who voted. Unlike racist southern demagogues, Long provided social services for African Americans too.

As governor of Louisiana between 1928 and 1932, Long built roads and hospitals, and provided free textbooks and lunches for schoolchildren—benefits almost unknown elsewhere in the South and far from universal in the North and West. Long was an egotistical and effective showman. He called himself the "Kingfish" after a clownish character on the popular radio program *Amos 'n' Andy*. He was certainly Louisiana's Kingfish, virtually a dictator. He made Louisiana State University (LSU) the best public university in the South and personally led the cheers when the LSU football team played its great rival, the University of Alabama. One year, when a circus was to open in Baton Rouge on the date of an important LSU game, Long stifled the competition by closing down the circus on the grounds that lion tamers were cruel to animals.

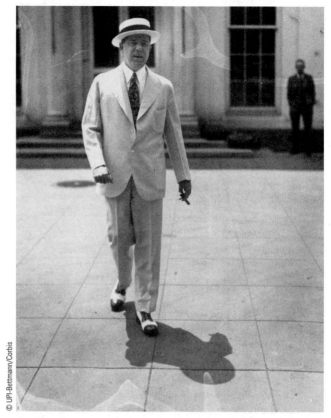

© UPI-Bettmann/Corbis

▲ *Huey Long, a puzzle to this day. He was a southern demagogue who baited the rich but refused to encourage hostility toward African Americans. He was virtually a dictator in Louisiana but provided the people of the state, blacks and whites, with better social services than anywhere else in the South.*

The New Deal Supreme

People loved Huey Long, not only in Louisiana (which he continued to run even after going to the Senate in 1933) but all over the South and Midwest. He based his presidential ambitions on a plan called "Share the Wealth" or "Every Man a King." He called for a tax confiscating every dollar over $1 million in annual salaries and a heavy tax on large incomes less than $1 million. To people struggling for ne-

As Maine Goes . . .

In the nineteenth century, the people of Maine elected their governor in September, almost two months before the presidential election. The saying "As Maine goes, so goes the nation" reflected the significance attributed to the results there. In the first 28 presidential elections in which Maine voters participated, the state's record in picking the winner was 22 to 6, good but not good enough to bet the farm on, as Herbert Hoover learned in 1932: He won Maine but few other states.

In 1936, Maine again looked to vote Republican. Democratic party campaign manager James Farley quipped, "As Maine goes, so goes Vermont." He was right on the button. FDR won every state that year except Maine and Vermont.

cessities and blaming the rich for the depression, it was an appealing program. Why did anyone need more than a million a year, anyway?

Long's following was larger than either Townsend's or Coughlin's, and, again, he attracted mostly Democratic voters. Roosevelt had good reason to fear what his candidacy would mean in 1936. Moreover, FDR believed Long a threat to democracy ("I'm the Constitution around here," Long liked to say.) But what to do?

Roosevelt's solution was co-optation. He undercut Coughlin's financial program by making moderate monetary reforms. To steal Townsend's thunder, he sponsored the Social Security Act of 1935. Its pensions were pennies compared with the $200 per month of which the Townsendites dreamed. Nevertheless, for the first time, the United States government assumed responsibility for funding and paying pensions for people too old to work. To co-opt Huey Long, in 1935, Roosevelt revised the income tax law. It did not abolish annual incomes over a million, but it taxed people in the upper brackets heavily—theoretically (but rarely in practice) up to 90 percent.

FDR's reforms were half a loaf compared to what the spellbinders wanted. But so great was Roosevelt's personal popularity that his rivals lost support and, eventually, lost heart. Townsend's clubs declined slowly, as did Coughlin's radio audience. (The "radio priest" was silenced, however, only when he preached a Nazi-like anti-Semitism, praising Adolf Hitler, and his bishop ordered him off the radio.) Long was removed from the scene by fate. In 1935, he was assassinated by a young man whose family Long had, in his arrogance, injured.

And so, in the election of 1936, Roosevelt had to face only the likable and moderate Republican governor of Kansas, Alfred M. Landon. Landon had such difficulty coming up with an issue on which he differed with FDR that he chose one that cost him votes: He called Social Security pensions "unjust, unworkable, and a cruel hoax." Landon carried Maine and Vermont; Roosevelt, the other 46 states.

THE LEGACY OF THE NEW DEAL

Even before the election, Roosevelt shifted the direction of his reforms. In 1933, he had thought of the New Deal as a new deal for everyone. He believed that the Hundred Days had saved American capitalism from the political extremism that, in Europe and Japan, was destroying democratic governments. He felt betrayed when big business, instead of recognizing his services, vilified him.

In 1935, threatened by the spellbinders and encouraged by Eleanor, who genuinely felt a kinship with the disadvantaged, the president became, to an extent, the president of the people at the bottom. Their response in 1936 was pretty good evidence that, politically, he had made the right choice. It was this break with "the classes" and FDR's association with "the masses" that made the New Deal a period of American history ranking in significance with the age of the War for Independence and the era of the Civil War.

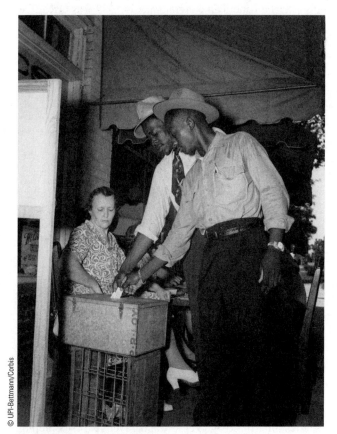

▲ *African Americans in the northern states found there were no legal obstacles (or violent reprisal) to exercising the right to vote. During the 1930s, blacks not only converted from the Republican to the Democratic party, but they voted in annually increasing numbers.*

© UPI-Bettmann/Corbis

Blacks: The New Democrats

After 1936, Roosevelt emphasized the economic problems of the disadvantaged. However, on the unique disadvantages faced by African Americans because of the color line, FDR was nearly silent. The Democratic party still depended heavily on its southern bloc, and southern politicians were still committed to white supremacy and Jim Crow segregation. Roosevelt refused even to speak in favor of a federal antilynching bill, and he accepted segregation by race in southern work gangs on federal building projects like the TVA. (Roosevelt did, however, resist southern white pressure to pay African American federal employees less than whites doing the same jobs.)

He was cordial to lobbyists from the National Association for the Advancement of Colored People, and Eleanor Roosevelt saw to it that he received and listened to individual black leaders, like Mary McLeod Bethune. Black people moved into more than a third of new housing units constructed by the federal government, and they shared proportionately in relief and public works projects. As a result, there was a revolution in African American voting patterns. In 1932, about 75 percent of black voters were loyal Republicans. They still thought of the Republican party as the party of Lincoln and emancipation, and of Republican congressmen as the chief supporters of antilynching bills. The only African American congressman in 1932 was Oscar De Priest of Chicago, a Republican.

By 1936, more than 75 percent of African American voters were Democratic. Even De Priest was defeated by a black New Dealer—and the trend continued for 40 years, until blacks were more than 90 percent Democratic.

The Growth of the Unions

Roosevelt wedded organized labor to the Democratic party. Left to his own prejudices, he would have stayed neutral in disputes between unions and employers. However, when militant unionists like John L. Lewis of the coal miners (a lifelong Republican) and Sidney Hillman and David Dubinsky of the large needle-trades unions made it clear they would throw their influence behind the president only in return for the administration's support, Roosevelt gave in. Lewis raised $1 million for the president's 1936 election campaign. In return, Roosevelt consented to be photographed accepting the check, smiling with approval on the burly, bushy-browed Lewis. Sidney Hillman became one of FDR's most important advisers. FDR's stock answer to requests of which he approved, but for which he wanted labor's approval too, was "Clear it with Sidney."

"The President wants you to join the union," the Committee on Industrial Organization told workers in basic industries after FDR signed the Wagner Act. At first a faction within the American Federation of Labor, the committee left the AFL in 1937 to form an entirely new association of unions, the Congress of Industrial Organizations (CIO). Massive organizational campaigns won recruits in unprecedented numbers.

Striking truck drivers in Minneapolis battle police. Such confrontations were common as the union movement grew to unprecedented size. There was more violence in the 1930s related to union organization than in any other arena of American life. It was caused, almost invariably, by employers or sympathetic police.

The parent organization of the United Steel Workers was founded in 1936. By May 1937, it had 325,000 members. The United States Steel Corporation, the nerve center of antiunionism in the industry, recognized the union as bargaining agent without a strike.

The United Automobile Workers enlisted 370,000 members in a little more than a year. The story was similar among workers in other basic industries: rubber, glass, lumber, aluminum, electrical products, coal mining, the needle trades, and even textiles. "The union" came to have a mystical significance in the lives of many workers. Workers fought for the right to wear union buttons on the job. The union card became a certificate of honor. Hymns were reworded to promote the cause. Professional singers like Woody Guthrie, Pete Seeger, and Burl Ives lent their talents to organizing campaigns. In 1933, fewer than 3 million American workers belonged to a union. In 1940, 8.5 million did; in 1941, 10.5 million.

Employer Violence

Not every employer responded as sensibly as United States Steel. Tom Girdler of Republic Steel called the CIO "irresponsible, racketeering, violent, communistic" and threatened to fight the union with armed force. In this heated atmosphere occurred the "Memorial Day Massacre" of 1937, so called because Chicago police attacked a crowd of union members, killing 10 and seriously injuring about a hundred.

Although he eventually came to terms with the United Automobile Workers, Henry Ford at first responded to the new union as Girdler did. He employed an army of toughs from the Detroit underworld and fortified his factories with tear gas, machine guns, and grenades. At the "Battle of the Overpass" in Detroit, Ford "goons" (as antiunion strong-arm forces were called) beat organizer Walter Reuther and other union officials until they were insensible. Violence was so common in the coalfields of Harlan County, Kentucky, that the area became known in the press as "Bloody Harlan."

The Bottom Line

The greatest achievement of the New Deal was to ease the economic hardships suffered by millions of Americans and, in doing so, to preserve their confidence in American institutions. In its relief measures, particularly those agencies that put jobless people to work, Roosevelt's administration was a resounding success.

As a formula for economic recovery, the New Deal failed. When unemployment dropped to 7.5 million early in 1937 and other economic indicators looked bright, Roosevelt began to dismantle many expensive government programs. The result was renewed collapse, a depression within a depression. Conditions in 1937 never sank to the levels of 1930–1933. But the recession of 1937 was painful evidence that for all their flexibility, experimentation, and spending, the New Dealers had not unlocked the secret of maintaining prosperity during peacetime. Only when preparations for another world war led to massive purchases of American goods from abroad (and to rearmament at home) did the Great Depression end. By 1939, the economy was on the upswing. By 1940, with Europe at war, the Great Depression was history.

Through such programs as support for agricultural prices, rural electrification, Social Security, insurance of bank deposits, protection of labor unions, and strict controls over the economy, the federal government came to play a part in people's daily lives such as had been inconceivable before 1933. In the TVA, the government became an actual producer of electrical power and commodities such as fertilizers. It was not socialism, as conservative critics of the New Deal cried, but in an American context, it was something of a revolution.

Although unavoidable, the most dubious side effect of the new system was the extraordinary growth in the size of government. Extensive government programs required huge bureaucracies to carry them out. The number of federal employees rose from 600,000 in 1930 to a million in 1940. In that bureaucracies are ultimately concerned with their own well-being above all else and inevitably divert funds meant for their mission to pay benefits to bureaucrats (not to mention the aggravations of dealing with bureaucracies), the New Deal contributed to American life, along with its many blessings, a phenomenon that has, at one time or another, driven every American to near distraction.

A Political Revolution

Between 1896 and 1933, the Republican party was the nation's majority party. The only Democratic president of the era, Woodrow Wilson, won only because of very special circumstances. During the 36 years before Roosevelt's first election, the Democrats had a majority in the House of Representatives only 10 years, and in the Senate only 6, all when Wilson was president.

The Great Depression and New Deal changed everything. FDR and Jim Farley forged a new majority consisting of southern whites, northern and western liberals, blue-collar workers (particularly union members and urban white ethnics), and African Americans, with substantial support from western farmers. The New Deal alliance was not without problems. Beginning in 1937, some southern Democrats who disapproved of even the New Deal's minimal concessions to blacks and the prominence in Washington of "Yankee liberals" often voted with Republicans against New Deal measures. By 1940, a coalition of Republicans and southern Democrats in Congress could be a majority.

Still, grassroots support for the New Deal among southern whites prevented the crack from becoming a split during FDR's presidency. The Democratic majority forged during the 1930s lasted for half a century. During the 50 years between 1930 and 1980, a Republican lived in the White House only 18 years. During the same 50 years, Republicans had a majority in the Senate only six years and in the House of Representatives only four. Between 1930 and 1997, two-thirds of a century, the Republican party simultaneously controlled presidency, Senate, and House just two years, 1953 to 1955. To date, there have never been more than 55 Republican senators out of 100.

for FURTHER READING

First of all, see the biographical studies and general works listed in the "For Further Reading" section of Chapter 41. Other basic studies of the New Deal are Paul Conkin, *The New Deal*, 1975; William E. Leuchtenburg, *Franklin D. Roosevelt and the New Deal, 1932–1940*, 1963; and Arthur M. Schlesinger Jr., *The Coming of the New Deal*, 1959, and *The Politics of Upheaval*, 1960.

One of the most insightful books about the New Deal yet written is Alan Brinkley, *The End of Reform: New Deal Liberalism in Recession and War*, 1995. On specific problems faced by the New Deal, see Susan Estabrook Kennedy, *The Banking Crisis of 1933*, 1973; C. P. Kindleberger, *The World in Depression, 1929–1939*, 1973; Roy Lubove, *The Struggle for Social Security, 1900–1935*, 1968; Thomas K. McCraw, *T.V.A. and the Power Fight, 1933–1939*, 1971; Michael Parrish, *Security Regulation and the New Deal*, 1970; and Elliott Rosen, *Hoover, Roosevelt, and the Brains Trust*, 1977.

On Roosevelt's critics, see Alan Brinkley, *Voices of Protest: Huey Long, Father Coughlin, and the Great Depression*, 1982; Abraham Holtzman, *The Townsend Movement*, 1963; Irving Howe and Lewis Coser, *The American Communist Party*, 1957; D. R. McCoy, *Angry Voices: Left of Center Politics in the New Deal Era*, 1958; C. J. Tull, *Father Coughlin and the New Deal*, 1965; and T. Harry Williams, *Huey Long*, 1969.

On labor, see Sidney Fine, *Sit-Down: The General Motors Strike of 1936–1937*, 1969. Other insightful monographs include Frank Freidel, *F.D.R. and the South*, 1965; Paul A. Kurzman, *Harry Hopkins and the New Deal*, 1974; Richard D. McKinzie, *The New Deal for Artists*, 1973; and Harvard Sitkoff, *A New Deal for Blacks*, 1978.

Visit the source collections at http://ajaccess.wadsworth.com and http://infotrac.thomsonlearning.com, and use the Search function with the following key terms to explore documents, images, audio and video clips, articles, and commentary related to the material in this chapter:

Civil Works Administration
Civilian Conservation Corps
Eleanor Roosevelt
Fireside chats
Franklin D. Roosevelt
Huey Long
John L. Lewis
Mary McLeod Bethune
National Recovery Administration
New Deal
Tennessee Valley Authority
Works Progress Administration

Additional resources, exercises, and Internet links related to this chapter are available on *The American Past* Web site: http://history.wadsworth.com/americanpast7e.

HISTORY ONLINE

New Deal Network
http://newdeal/feri.org/index.htm
Text and photographs illustrating the New Deal and the era.

Migrant Labor Camp Photographs
http://dynaweb.oac.odlib.org/dynaweb/ead/calher/drobish/
Photographs from the collection of Harry Drobish at the Bancroft Library.

ANOTHER GREAT WAR

*America and the World
1933–1942*

I ask that the Congress declare that since the unprovoked and dastardly attack by Japan on Sunday, December seventh, a state of war has existed between the United States and the Japanese Empire.

Franklin D. Roosevelt

IN 1933, THE year Franklin D. Roosevelt became president, Adolf Hitler, head of the extreme right-wing National Socialist, or Nazi, party, was named chancellor in Germany. The character and values of the two new national leaders could hardly have been more different. The patrician Roosevelt was a liberal, dedicated to democracy. The bourgeois Hitler was contemptuous of democracy and individual freedoms.

Nevertheless, comparisons between the two were inevitable. Pundits noted that both were virtuosos in using modern means of communication. Roosevelt was at his best as a voice on the radio; in his "fireside chats," he calmly reassured Americans that, through reform, they could preserve what was of value in their way of life. Hitler was at his best over loudspeakers, exhorting Germans to blame the Versailles Treaty for their troubles and to hate those whom he defined as enemies within, particularly Communists and Jews.

Roosevelt and Hitler would clash, but only after the United States experimented with a foreign policy designed to avoid entanglement in another great war.

NEW DEAL FOREIGN POLICY

When he took office, Roosevelt seemed to be as uninterested in foreign policy as Woodrow Wilson had been. Like Wilson, he passed over professional diplomats in naming his secretary of state. He made a political appointment, a courtly senator from Tennessee, Cordell Hull, whose elegant bearing belied his log-cabin origins.

Hull and Roosevelt were generally content to follow the guidelines charted by Hoover and his secretary of state, professional diplomat Henry L. Stimson. Where they departed from precedent, their purpose was to reinforce the New Deal's program for economic recovery at home.

The Good Neighbor

Roosevelt and Hull even adopted Hoover's phrase, "good neighbor," to describe the new role the United States would play in Latin America. Roosevelt withdrew the United States

Marines from Nicaragua, the Dominican Republic, and Haiti, where they had been keeping order. Like Hoover, he refused to intervene in Cuba despite the chronic civil conflict in the island and America's long-standing practice, citing the Platt Amendment, to send in troops in times of trouble.

In 1934, when peace returned to Cuba under a pro-American president who later became dictator, Fulgencio Batista, Hull formally renounced the Platt Amendment. No longer would the "Colossus of the North" use its power to force its way in the Caribbean. As a consequence of this about-face, no United States president was ever so well liked in Hispanic America as Roosevelt was. Even when, in 1938, Mexico seized the properties of American oil companies and offered little compensation, Roosevelt took a conciliatory stand. A few years later, American diplomats worked out a fair settlement with Mexico, acceptable to all but the greediest of the dispossessed oilmen.

By then, the Good Neighbor policy was reaping precious benefits for the United States. The Second World War had begun, but despite strenuous German efforts to secure a foothold in the Western Hemisphere, most Latin American nations backed the United States. The few neutrals that were cozy with Hitler were very cautious. Had even one South American country permitted Nazi Germany to establish bases on its soil, it would have inhibited the American contribution to the war in Europe and likely forced an intervention such as FDR had renounced.

The Stimson Doctrine

Toward Asia, New Deal diplomacy also moved along paths staked out during the Hoover administration. The problem in the East, as policy makers saw it, was to maintain Chinese independence and American access to China's trade—the Open Door policy—in the face of an aggressive and expansion-minded Japan. Complicating the problem, China's Nationalist party government, headed by Generalissimo Chiang Kai-shek, was inefficient, ignored in large parts of the country, and increasingly corrupt.

Late in 1931, taking advantage of the chaos, Japanese military officers detached the province of Manchuria from China and set up a puppet state called Manchukuo. Hoover considered but rejected Stimson's proposal that the United States retaliate by imposing severe economic sanctions on Japan, denying Japan raw materials, particularly oil and iron, vital to Japanese industry and its navy. Instead, Hoover announced that the United States would not recognize the legality of any territorial changes resulting from the use of force. Curiously, this policy became known as the Stimson Doctrine.

The Stimson Doctrine was little more than a rap on the knuckles. Japanese militarists, driven by a compelling sense of national destiny, shrugged the Stimson Doctrine off. In 1932, Japan launched an attack on Shanghai. In 1937, the Japanese bombed the city, one of the first massive aerial bombings of a civilian population. Nevertheless, Roosevelt went no further than Hoover had in 1932. He (and the tottering League of Nations) responded with words alone. With economic problems so serious at home, Roosevelt would not risk war with Japan for the sake of a China so dubiously governed and divided.

Recognition of the Soviet Union

When Roosevelt parted ways with Hoover, the impetus was that all-pervasive bugbear, the depression. Thus, in May 1933, Roosevelt scuttled an international conference in London for the purpose of stabilizing world currencies. Delegates of 64 nations had gathered with Hoover's approval and, so they assumed, with Roosevelt's. Before discussions actually began, however, Roosevelt announced that he would not agree to any decisions that ran contrary to his domestic recovery program, specifically his decision to take the United States off the gold standard. The conference collapsed.

In November 1933, Roosevelt formally recognized the Soviet government, which four presidents had refused to do. In part, this was a realistic decision that was long overdue. For good or ill, the Communist party dictatorship headed by Joseph Stalin was firmly in control of the Soviet Union. But Roosevelt was also swayed by the argument that the Soviet Union would provide a large market for ailing American manufacturers. This proved to be an illusion. Soviet Russia was too poor to buy much of anything from anyone.

New Directions, Old Strictures

Increasing trade was also the motive behind Secretary of State Hull's strategy of reducing tariff barriers through reciprocity. With a southern Democrat's distaste for high tariffs, Hull negotiated reciprocal trade agreements with 29 countries. The high Republican rates of the 1920s were slashed by as much as half in return for other nations' agreements to lower their barriers against American exports.

Roosevelt probably would have liked his administration to take a more active part in the affairs of nations than the United States did. He admired the forcefulness of his cousin Theodore Roosevelt, and both FDR and Hull were Wilson-

Better Public Relations Through Chemistry

As the nation's biggest munitions manufacturer, E. I. du Pont de Nemours and Company (or "DuPont") had a serious public relations problem during the 1930s. The Nye Committee investigations into American entrance into World War I often centered on DuPont as one of the "merchants of death." The coming of World War II and the nation's renewed need for munitions redeemed DuPont. Even earlier, however, DuPont's creation of nylon, the first completely synthetic textile and a miracle fabric in its versatility, created a new benign image for the company.

This was not dumb luck. Nylon was the fruit of DuPont's extremely expensive program of pure research, launched in 1928 in the hope that scientists pursuing their own interests would find new salable products.

ian internationalists. FDR had enthusiastically supported the League of Nations when it was first proposed, and, while recovering from polio during the early 1920s, he studied and wrote about foreign policy.

But FDR was first and foremost a politician who thought about voters at every turn. He knew that it was political suicide for a president to wander too far from popular prejudices, and, according to a public opinion poll in 1935, 95 percent of Americans were isolationists. They believed the United States had no vital interests to protect in either Europe or Asia.

Suspicion of Europe was reinforced by the theory that the economic collapse of the Old World was responsible for the American depression. This feeling intensified between 1934 and 1936, when Senator Gerald Nye of North Dakota began a series of investigations into the political machinations of the munitions industry. Nye claimed that the United States was maneuvered into the First World War by "merchants of death," such as the giant DuPont Corporation, which were only too willing to see young men slaughtered for the sake of sales. This belief was popularized in a bestselling book of 1935, *The Road to War* by Walter Millis, and many academic historians took a similarly jaundiced view of the reasons why, in 1917, Americans had gone "over there."

Neutrality

In a series of Neutrality Acts passed between 1935 and 1937, Congress said "never again" with an exclamation point. Taken together, the three laws warned American citizens against traveling on ships flying the flags of nations at war (no *Lusitania*s this time) and required nations at war to pay cash for all American goods they purchased and to carry them in their own ships. There would be no United States flagships sunk even by accident and no American property lost because of a war among Europeans. Finally, belligerent nations were forbidden to buy arms in the United States and to borrow money from American banks. This law was designed to prevent the emergence of a lobby of munitions makers and bankers with a vested interest in the victory of one side in any conflict that erupted.

Critics of the Neutrality Acts argued that they worked to the disadvantage of countries that were the victims of aggression. Those nations would be unprepared for war, whereas aggressor nations would equip themselves in advance. This was certainly the message of Fascist Italy's invasion of Ethiopia in 1935. But Americans were interested only in avoiding a repetition of the events that took them into war in 1917.

U.S. Army Photograph

▲ *Adolf Hitler entertains Spain's Francisco Franco. With massive aid, including combat troops, Germany and Italy enabled Franco's victory in his war against Spanish republicans.*

THE WORLD AT WAR AGAIN

Each year brought new evidence that the world was drifting into another bloodbath. In 1934, Hitler began rearming Germany. In 1935, he introduced universal military training, and Italy invaded Ethiopia, one of only two independent nations in Africa. In 1936, Francisco Franco, a reactionary general, launched a rebellion against the unstable democratic government of Spain and received massive support from both Italy and Germany, including combat troops who treated the Spanish Civil War as a rehearsal for a bigger show.

In July 1937, Japan sent land forces into China and quickly took the northern capital, then called Peiping, and most of the coastal provinces. In March 1938, Hitler forced the political union, or *Anschluss,* of Austria to Germany, increasing the resources of what Hitler called the "Third Reich," or third empire. In September, claiming that he wanted only to unite all Germans under one flag, Hitler demanded that Czechoslovakia surrender the Sudetenland to him.

The Sudetenland was largely populated by people of German language and culture. But it was also the mountainous natural defense line for Czechoslovakia, the only democratic state in central Europe. Nevertheless, in the hope that they could win peace by appeasing Hitler, Britain and France agreed to the takeover. Hitler mocked their mis-

placed goodwill within months. In March 1939, he seized the rest of Czechoslovakia, where the people were Slavic.

The Aggressor Nations

In some respects, the three aggressor nations of the 1930s were very different. Japan was primarily motivated to expand into China for economic reasons. A modern industrial nation, Japan was poor in basic natural resources like coal and iron. China was rich in both; Japanese leaders meant to displace the United States and Great Britain as the dominant economic powers on the Asian mainland.

Until the summer of 1941, Japanese policy makers were divided between militarists who believed they must have war with the United States and Britain (and looked forward to it), and moderates who believed they could best serve their country's purposes by coming to an understanding with the United States. American trade was important to Japan; indeed, Japan was America's third largest customer, importing vast quantities of cotton, copper, scrap iron, and oil.

Italy under the Fascists seemed locked into poverty. Dictator Benito Mussolini, a strutting buffoon in his public posing but ruthless in his use of power, made do with the appearance of wealth and might. Ethiopia was an easy touch, a backward country that sent soldiers with antiquated

▲ *Benito Mussolini,* Il Duce *("the leader"), was a comical figure to many Americans. But he ruled Italy ruthlessly and, in 1935, launched the aggression that was to lead to war in Europe by invading and conquering Ethiopia.*

muskets and even spears to combat Mussolini's tanks. Only so weak a nation could have fallen to Italy's poorly trained and ill-equipped army. Mussolini's tanks were designed more for parades than for war. Some were actually made of sheet metal that could be dented with a swift kick. By itself, Mussolini's Italy represented no threat to world peace. Some Americans applauded what progress the Italian economy had made under Fascist rule. Others laughed at newsreel films of Mussolini's slapstick antics.

Aside from his Charlie Chaplin moustache, there was nothing comical about Adolf Hitler. His strutting was all too serious because his theater was a populous nation, potentially the richest and most powerful in Europe. Moreover, Hitler was far more cunning than Mussolini. He knew what he wanted and had said it, explicitly, in an autobiography entitled *Mein Kampf,* or *My Struggle:* German domination of the European continent. While his strategy was not without risks, Hitler seemed brilliantly to grasp just how much he could get away with in dealing with the other European powers. Or, as some historians have suggested, he was very lucky.

Perverted Nationalism

In other ways, the three aggressor nations were similar. Japanese militarists, Italian Fascists, and German Nazis were all stridently antidemocratic. They sneered at the ideals of popular rule and individual liberties, regarding them as the sources of the world's economic and social problems. In the place of traditional principles of democratic humanism, they exalted the totalitarian state as mystically personified in a single person: Hirohito, the divine emperor of Japan; Mussolini, the Italian "duce" (Italian for "leader"); and Hitler, the German "Führer" (German for "leader").

The aggressor nations were, of course, militaristic. Their governments idolized armed force as the best means of serving their national purposes. If militarism could be less than ominous in a poor country like Italy, it was frightening when combined with fanatical Japanese nationalism or the Nazi gospel of German racial superiority. The Japanese considered East and South Asia to be their garden, off limits to westerners who had dominated the region for a century and more. Japanese soldiers were sworn to solemn oaths to die serving emperor and homeland.

Nazi racism was criminal from its inception. Drawing on ancient Germanic mythology, nineteenth-century pseudoscience, and populist anti-Semitism, it taught that "non-Aryans" were subhuman degenerates who had no claims on the "master race" except to serve it. After disposing of, exiling, or silencing Germany's Communists, Socialists, and democrats, Nazi paramilitary organizations began to routinely brutalize German Jews. Hitler stripped Jews of civil rights and, during the war, murdered those who remained in Germany, herding them into extermination camps along with millions of Jews from conquered lands, gypsies, congenitally disabled people, and homosexuals.

War

In September 1939, when Hitler invaded Poland, ostensibly to attach the German-speaking "Polish corridor" to the Third Reich, Britain and France finally drew the line and declared war. However, neither nation was prepared to help Poland, and Hitler had neutralized the Soviet Union by signing a nonaggression pact with the Communist dictator Joseph Stalin. Stalin knew that Russia was on Hitler's list, but he distrusted Britain and France and needed time to prepare. And he wanted territory for a buffer: While Hitler's legions invaded Poland from the west, Russian soldiers streamed into eastern Poland and the small Baltic states of Latvia, Lithuania, and Estonia.

An uneasy quiet fell over Europe during the winter of 1939–1940. Journalists spoke of a "phony war" in which neither side attacked the other. In fact, the French and British were committed to a defensive war. Remembering the terrible loss of life in World War I when the men went over the top, they huddled behind the Maginot line, a system of fortifications to which the French had dedicated vast resources.

The Germans had other plans. Appreciating what the motor vehicle meant to armed conflict, they were preparing for Blitzkrieg (literally, "lightning war"): massive land, sea, and air attacks with which, in the spring, crack German armed forces overran Denmark, Norway, Luxembourg, Belgium, and the Netherlands. In June 1940, France collapsed, and the British managed to evacuate their troops and some

▲ *German troops march on the Champs Elysées in Paris in 1940. In the summer of 1940, France fell with a suddenness that alarmed Americans.*

© Bettmann/Corbis

MAP 43:1 German and Italian Aggression, 1934–1939 Italy's invasion of Ethiopia in 1935 was the first episode in a series of territorial aggression by the Fascist and Nazi powers that culminated in World War II. Only with Germany's invasion of Poland in September 1939 did France and England respond with a declaration of war.

The Party Line

A week before Germany invaded the Soviet Union, the Almanac Singers, loosely associated with the Communist party, released a record, *Songs for John Doe,* that included the antiwar lyrics "I hate war, and so does Eleanor, and we won't be safe until everybody's dead."

After Russia was invaded, the American Communist party was instructed to work for American intervention in the war. *Songs for John Doe* was quickly withdrawn from the market, and people who had already purchased it were asked to return it. It is a very rare item today.

garded as his greatest blunder: He invaded the Soviet Union while Britain was undefeated.

Stalin, who would later depict himself as Russia's savior, was oddly unprepared for the onslaught. In May, the British told him the exact date the Germans planned to invade. German companies under contract to the Soviet Union ceased to make shipments. And yet, Soviet armies were stunned and disintegrated. Three million Soviet troops were put out of commission before the fall, when, finally, the Red Army held. The fighting was barbaric on both sides. Hitler lost 750,000 men in the first year in Russia, more than in the entire war to that point. Still, his *Wehrmacht* (as the German military was called) nearly surrounded Leningrad in the north and threatened Moscow. The next year, 1942, the Germans advanced in the south, to Stalingrad.

THE UNITED STATES AND THE WAR

The fall of France, the heroic resistance of Britain, and, to a lesser extent, the invasion of Russia changed American attitudes toward neutrality. With the exception of neutral Sweden, Switzerland, and Eire (Ireland), Britain and France were the last democracies in Europe. Moreover, ugly pro-Axis and racist rhetoric in the United States by small but noisy Nazi organizations, such as William Dudley Pelley's Silver Shirts and Fritz Kuhn's German-American Bund, as well as German machinations in Latin America, persuaded Americans that Hitler had no intention of stopping in Europe. In March 1940, during the "phony war," 43 percent of Americans thought that a German victory in Europe would threaten the United States. By July, almost 80 percent thought so.

Roosevelt's Influence on Public Opinion

Franklin D. Roosevelt played no small part in shaping this change of opinion. As early as 1938, when few Americans could conceive of getting involved in a foreign war and the French and British governments were appeasing Hitler, Roosevelt concluded that only a show of force—or the use of it—would stop the Führer. In this opinion, he was one with Winston Churchill.

French units from the port of Dunkirk only by mobilizing virtually every ship and boat capable of crossing the English Channel. The motley fleet returned nearly 340,000 men to England to await a German invasion. They were demoralized, but they were not in prisoner-of-war camps.

The Invasion of Russia

"We shall fight on the beaches, we shall fight on the landing grounds, we shall fight in the fields and in the streets, we shall fight in the hills; we shall never surrender," said the new British prime minister, Winston Churchill. His eloquence inspired Americans as well as Britons. But few were truly confident that the British alone could withstand a German onslaught.

Instead of invading Great Britain, Hitler ordered relentless aerial bombardment of the country while Germany expanded its power to the south. Mussolini's Italy had joined the war against France (forming with Germany the Rome-Berlin "Axis") and faced British and Anzac (Australian and New Zealand Army Corps) troops in Libya in North Africa. Then in June 1941, the Führer made what is generally re-

But whereas Churchill was in the opposition and could snipe at Britain's policy of appeasement, waiting for events to rally public opinion behind him, Roosevelt was president. He could not afford to get too far ahead of the country, least of all in preparing for war. (He deliberately avoided the word *preparedness*.) FDR's technique was to float trial balloons by delivering militant anti-Nazi speeches. If the popular reaction was hostile, he backed off; if friendly, he moved ahead.

In 1939, at FDR's behest, Congress amended neutrality policy so that war materials could be sold on a cash-and-carry basis. (American ships were still banned from the trade.) In 1940, with a large majority of Americans worried about how a Nazi victory would affect them, FDR announced that he was trading 50 old destroyers the British needed to counter German submarines for eight naval bases in Bermuda, Newfoundland, and British colonies in the Caribbean. Roosevelt described the deal as a defensive measure, which, strictly speaking, was the truth.

Defense was also the rationale for the Burke-Wadsworth Act of September 1940, which appropriated $37 billion to build up the navy and army air corps and instituted the first peacetime draft law in American history. The draft was a lottery. More than 16 million young men were registered, each given a number between 1 and 8,500. Henry L. Stimson (now FDR's secretary of war) picked the first number (which was 158), and the other 8,499 were drawn in order so that a man knew the likelihood he would be called soon or later. The first draftees were in uniform by November 1940; 900,000 would be called up under the law for one-year terms of service.

It was comparatively easy to win support for these measures. Even the draft had the approval of two-thirds of the population. Nevertheless, when Roosevelt decided to break with tradition in 1940 and run for a third term as president, he felt it necessary to reassure the American people regarding war. "Your boys," he said, "are not going to be sent into any foreign wars."

The Third Term

Despite the shift in public opinion in favor of fighting Hitler, Roosevelt feared that a Republican nominee cool toward aiding Britain might eke out a victory against any Democrat but himself. The leading Democratic candidates were, in fact, an uninspiring lot: the provincial, tobacco-chewing vice president, John Nance Garner; Jim Farley, a political manager without a vision in his history; and Joseph P. Kennedy, a rich businessman who thought his prejudices were principles.

So FDR blithely ignored the two-term tradition, and the Democrats were delighted with his decision, especially because the Republicans chose a surprisingly attractive nominee, Wendell Willkie. Willkie, a utilities magnate, had been a Democrat most of his life. Personable, eloquent, and moderate, Willkie made it clear that he differed not at all with the president's foreign policy and only in degree on domestic questions.

Thus, Willkie criticized the obvious waste of many New Deal programs without calling for their abolition. He assailed the increased presidential powers Roosevelt had assumed as reeking of dictatorship, but he did not propose dismantling the huge executive apparatus the New Deal had created. Willkie claimed that he was the better bet to keep the United States out of war, but he supported arming for defense and aiding Great Britain. In short, he offered the kind of choice that was better resolved by sticking to the known quantity.

Still, Willkie ran a strong race, winning more popular votes than any losing candidate before him. Roosevelt's popularity had declined, but it had peaked so high he still had a comfortable cushion. The president ran a confident incumbent's campaign. He did his job while the exuberant challenger barnstormed the country. Although Roosevelt's third-term victory was a landmark, it was an anticlimax.

Undeclared War on Germany

A few weeks after the election, Roosevelt responded to Winston Churchill's plea for additional aid by sending the Lend-Lease Bill to Congress. As enacted, the Lend-Lease Act provided that the United States would serve as the "arsenal of democracy," turning out arms of all sorts to be "loaned" to Britain. Eventually, with lend-lease extended to the Soviet Union, aid under the act totaled $54 billion.

To help the British defend their shipping against "wolf packs" of German submarines, Roosevelt proclaimed a neutral zone that extended from North American waters to Iceland. He sent troops to Greenland, a possession of conquered Denmark, and ordered American destroyers to patrol the sea lanes, warning British ships of enemies beneath the waves. This permitted the British to concentrate their navy in home waters.

This put the United States at war in everything but name. Indeed, in August 1941, Roosevelt met with Churchill on two ships, the British *Prince of Wales* and the American cruiser *Augusta,* off the coast of Newfoundland. There, they

Lend-Lease

Britain could not afford to pay for the American destroyers that Winston Churchill requested in 1940. Britain had spent $4.5 billion in the United States for arms, and, in December 1940, had only $2 billion in reserve. Roosevelt explained the "loan" of the ships to Britain with the following parable:

Suppose my neighbor's house catches fire, and I have a length of garden hose. If he can take my garden hose and connect it up with his hydrant, I may help him to put out the fire.

Now what do I do? I don't say to him before that operation, "Neighbor, my garden hose cost me $15; you have to pay me $15 for it." What is the transaction that goes on? I don't want $15—I want my garden hose back after the fire is over.

Rationing and Scrap Drives

German submarines set a pair of four-man sabotage teams ashore in Florida and on Long Island (they were captured immediately) and, in June 1942, sank two ships within view of vacationers at Virginia Beach, Virginia. Japanese subs ran a few torpedoes up on California beaches, and several paper bombs, explosives held aloft by balloons pushed by the wind, detonated over Oregon, causing a forest fire. The Japanese occupied two islands at the far end of the Aleutians. Otherwise, the continental United States was physically untouched by the war. People on the home front experienced the war only in the form of shortages in consumer goods and, even then, not to a degree that could be called sacrifice.

Reproduced from the Collections of the Library of Congress

Boys and girls showing off the results of their scrap iron drive. These were genuine contributions to the war effort. Scrap iron was recycled into both civilian goods and war materiel. Scrap metal yards were emptied as quickly as they were filled.

les tire dealer provided 5,000 tons of trade-ins. People cleared closets of old overshoes, and the secretary of the interior took to picking up rubber doormats in federal office buildings. Reclaimed rubber was not suitable to tire manufacture, but it was used to make other products.

It was fear of a rubber shortage, not of a gasoline shortage, that was behind the first controls on drivers. FDR proclaimed a nationwide speed limit of 35 miles per hour, and pleasure driving— difficult to define, of course— was banned. Zealous officials of the Office of Price Administration (OPA) jotted down license numbers at picnics, racetracks, concert halls, and athletic events. The total miles a car could be driven was lim-

Because the Japanese controlled 97 percent of the world's rubber-tree plantations in Malaya, automobile tires were the first consumer goods to be taken off the market. Washington froze the sale of new tires and forbade recapping early in 1942; the armed forces badly needed tires, and the national stockpile of rubber was only 660,000 tons, just about what civilians consumed in a year. Huge quantities of rubber were collected in scrap drives. A Seattle shoemaker contributed 6 tons of worn rubber heels that, for some reason, he had saved. A Los Ange-

ited by the category of the sticker issued to each car owner. Ordinary motorists received "A" stickers entitling them to 4 gallons of gasoline a week, later 3, and, for a short time, just 2. A "B" on the car added a few gallons; B stickers were issued to workers in defense plants for whom there was no public transportation. Physicians and others whose driving was essential got "C" cards, a few more gallons. Truckers ("T") got unlimited gas, as did some others, including political bigwigs who got "X" cards (a point of angry resentment). Counterfeiting of gas cards (usu-

adopted the Atlantic Charter, which amounted to mutual war aims reminiscent of Wilson's Fourteen Points. The charter called for self-determination of nations after the war; free trade and freedom of the seas; the disarmament of aggressor nations; and some new means of collective world security, a provision that would evolve into the United Nations.

It was only a matter of time before guns were fired. After a few ambivalent incidents involving German submarines and American destroyers, the USS *Reuben James* was sunk in October 1941, with a loss of 100 sailors.

A Nasty Debate

Roosevelt still did not ask Congress for a formal declaration of war. He hoped, without much confidence, that Britain and the Soviet Union could defeat Germany without the expenditure of American lives. More important, Roosevelt did not want to go to war without a unified people behind him. By

the fall of 1941, he had his majority. Most Americans had concluded, grimly rather than with enthusiasm, that Hitler had to be defeated. Even the Communist party, which had loudly opposed American aid to Britain until Hitler invaded the Soviet Union, had moved overnight to the prowar camp. Big business had concluded that Hitler represented a threat to American commercial primacy as well as to democracy.

But there was a vocal opposition. In addition to the pro-German Bund and Silver Shirts, the effectively pro-German Father Coughlin, and pacifists led by Socialist Norman Thomas, isolationists had organized the well-funded and active America First Committee. Former president Herbert Hoover, ex–New Dealer Hugh Johnson, and progressive intellectuals like Charles A. Beard despised Hitlerism. They were, however, equally antagonistic toward the Soviet Union and were somewhat anglophobic. Going to war, they thought, would entrench the Communists in Moscow and protect the British Empire, an unworthy goal. The America First Com-ally C category) was common, as was theft of stickers from government warehouses. The OPA discovered that 20 million gallons worth of cards were stolen in Washington alone.

Surplus gasoline could not be collected, but just about every other commodity vital to the war effort could be and was. Organizations like the Boy Scouts sponsored scrap drives through 1942 and 1943, collecting iron, steel, brass, bronze, tin, old nylon stockings (for powder bags), and bacon grease (for munitions manufacture). Many of these campaigns were more trouble than they were worth, but not those that collected iron, steel, tin, and paper. Scrap iron and steel made a significant contribution to the national output, and about half of the tin and paper products came not from mines and forests but from neighborhood drives. So assiduous were the Boy Scouts in their scrap-paper drive of 1942 that, in June, the government had to call a temporary halt to it; the nation's recycling mills simply could not keep up with the supply of "raw materials."

The tin shortage was responsible for the rationing of canned goods. In order to buy a can of corn or sardines, as well as coffee, butter, cheese, meat, and some other food items, a consumer had to hand the grocer ration stamps as well as money. The stamps were issued regularly in books and served as a second, parallel currency. In order to buy a pound of hamburger, a shopper needed stamps worth 7 "points" as well as the purchase price. A pound of butter cost 16 points; a pound of cheese, 8 points; and so on. The tiny stamps—which were color-coded red (meat, butter), blue (processed food), green, and brown—were a bother. More than 3.5 billion of them changed hands every month. In order to restock shelves, a grocer had to turn in the stamps he had collected from customers to a wholesaler, who, in turn, had to deposit them with a bank in order to make additional purchases.

Except for butter, rations were not stringent. The weekly sugar ration was 8 ounces a person, about as much as a dentist would wish on a patient in the best of times. In 1943, despite rationing, the American standard of living was 16 percent higher than it had been in 1939. By 1945, Americans were eating more food and spending more money on it than ever before. Only butter consumption dropped appreciably, from 17 to 11 pounds per capita per year.

The OPA noticed a curious fact about consumer habits in the cases of coffee and cigarettes. Coffee was rationed because of the shortage of ships available to carry it from South America. When rationing began in November 1942 (1 pound per person every five weeks), people began to hoard it. At restaurants, diners traded their dessert for an extra cup. When rationing of coffee was discontinued in July 1943, sales of coffee dropped! Then, in the fall, when a coffee stamp was mistakenly included in ration books, Americans stripped market shelves bare. When the OPA announced that there would be no coffee ration, sales dropped again.

Cigarettes were rationed because 30 percent of the industry's production was reserved for the armed forces, which comprised only 10 percent of the population. The government was, in effect, subsidizing the smoking habit among the men and women in the armed forces. At home, the operation of the principle that scarcity equals status may have caused an increase in smoking.

A more salutary consequence of wartime shortages was the popularity of gardening. There was no shortage of fresh vegetables, and they were never rationed. But canned vegetables were, and space on trucks and trains was at a premium. So the government encouraged "victory gardens." Some 20.5 million individuals and families planted them. By 1945, consumers were raising between 30 and 40 percent of all the vegetables grown in the United States. When the war was over, however, Americans quickly shed their good taste. By 1950, they had returned to canned vegetables and the frozen products of Clarence Birdseye.

mittee hammered on the theme that going to war in 1917 was a mistake. Let the British pull their own chestnuts out of the fire this time. The America Firsters had the celebrity backing that, 50 years later, would be a pillar of American electoral politics. Aviators Charles Lindbergh and Eddie Rickenbacker, film actress Lillian Gish, and Alice Roosevelt Longworth (Teddy's daughter and FDR's cousin) spoke at their rallies or just stood up and waved.

The America First Committee's case was weakened because most members agreed that the United States should arm for defense. Roosevelt and the rival Committee to Defend America by Aiding the Allies described every contribution to the British cause in just such terms, confounding their critics. Nevertheless, Roosevelt hesitated. He confided to Winston Churchill that he would not ask for a declaration of war until some dramatic incident—in other words, a direct attack on the United States—forced the America Firsters into silence.

As it turned out, both sides of the debate missed the point. Everyone's eyes were on Europe and the Atlantic. The incident that put the United States into the war was plenty dramatic, but it happened in the Pacific.

THE DECLARATION

When France fell to Germany, the Japanese moved into the French colonies of Indochina. The war in China with Chiang Kai-shek dragged on, but the "peace party" in the Japanese cabinet, headed by Prince Fumimaro Konoye, continued to negotiate with the United States, hoping for an American concession so as to neutralize the "war party" of General Hideki Tojo. When Tojo was named premier in October 1941, he gave the negotiators until early November to come up with a formula for peace that the United States would accept. It was impossible, as Tojo knew. Even the peace party's minimum demand was that Japan be recognized as the dominant economic power in China. That could not be reconciled with America's Open Door policy.

Pearl Harbor

Curiously, on the same day, unbeknownst to each other, the Japanese and American governments both concluded that they were unlikely to resolve their differences. Although talks continued, Secretary of State Hull handed Japanese-American relations over to the War Department. Within hours, halfway around the world, Admiral Isoroku Yamamoto was instructed to begin preparations for an attack on Pearl Harbor, the huge American naval base in Hawaii.

Yamamoto had consistently opposed war with the United States. He had told the cabinet, "If I am told to fight regardless of the consequences, I shall run wild for the first six months or a year, but I have utterly no confidence for the second or third year." His aerial attack on Pearl Harbor on December 7, 1941, was tactically brilliant. His planes sank or badly damaged eight battleships, seven other vessels, and 188 airplanes, killing or wounding 3,435 servicemen.

But Yamamoto's heart was not in the giddy celebrations of his fleet. The three American aircraft carriers he believed would be at Pearl Harbor were at sea when the assault force struck. Yamamoto understood that air power was the key to war in the broad Pacific: Pearl Harbor was the proof of it; no Japanese ship even approached Hawaii. And the United States had not lost a single carrier. "I fear we have only awakened a sleeping giant," he told his officers, "and his reaction will be terrible."

The Reaction

The giant awakened with a start. Pearl Harbor was attacked on Sunday. The next day, Roosevelt went before Congress and described December 7, 1941, as "a day that will live in infamy." He got his unanimous vote, or very nearly so. Between both houses of Congress, only Representative Jeannette Rankin of Montana, a pacifist who also had voted against entry into the First World War, refused to vote for the declaration of war.

In every city in the nation for weeks, the army's and navy's recruitment offices were jammed with young men.

▲ *The United States fleet and most American aircraft in Hawaii were devastated by the Japanese attack on Pearl Harbor on December 7, 1941. Fortuitously, the navy's aircraft carriers were at sea and were untouched.*

MAP 43:2 Japanese Empire, 1931–1942 As distant as it was from Japan, the outer defensive perimeter in August 1942 was not as far as Admiral Yamamoto believed necessary to force the United States to a negotiated peace. He had hoped to occupy Midway Island (for regular air strikes against Hawaii), all of New Guinea, the Solomon Islands, and northern Australia in order to deny the United States a land base from which to launch an effective counterattack.

Pearl Harbor was so traumatic an event in the lives of Americans that practically every individual would remember exactly what he or she was doing when news of the attack was announced.

Quietly at the time, more openly later, Roosevelt's critics accused him and other top officials of having plotted to keep Pearl Harbor and nearby Hickham Field, an airfield, unprepared for the attack. It was said that Washington knew the assault was coming but withheld vital intelligence from Hawaii, sacrificing American lives for the political purpose of getting the United States into the war.

In fact, the lack of preparation at Pearl Harbor was stupid and shameful. As early as 1924, airpower advocate General Billy Mitchell said that Pearl Harbor was vulnerable to air attack. In 1932, Admiral Harry Yarnell sneaked two aircraft carriers and four cruisers to within bombing range of Oahu before he was detected. Had his force been hostile, an attack like that of December 7, 1941, would have ensued. In early December 1941, numerous indications that something was brewing either were ignored or reached the appropriate commanders after unjustifiable delays. At Hickham Field, fighter planes were drawn up wing tip to wing tip so that they could be protected against sabotage on the ground. This made their destruction from the air all the simpler, and, when the attack began, few fighters were able to get into the air.

But to say that there was a conspiracy among the highest ranking officials in the government is without foundation. The blunders of the military in Hawaii were just another example of the incompetence chronic in all large organizations. The key to the stunning Japanese victory was the planning behind it.

Nevertheless, there is no doubt that Roosevelt was relieved to officially get into the war with a united people behind him. He was completely convinced by December 1941 that the survival of democracy, freedom, and American influence in the world depended on the defeat of the aggressor nations, which only American might could ensure.

Getting the Job Done

Of all the nations that went to war, only the Japanese, whose participation in the First World War was nominal, celebrated at the start of it. In Europe and the United States, there was very little of the exuberance with which Europeans greeted the first days of World War I and with which both northerners and southerners in America began the Civil War. In the United States, throughout World War II, the attitude was that there was a job to be done.

The popular songs of the era, such as "I'll Be Seeing You" and "I'll Never Smile Again," were melancholy in tenor, about separation and the longing to be together again—a far cry from the foot-stomping patriotism of George M. Cohan's anthem of World War I, "Over There." Seven times during the war, popular illustrator Norman Rockwell painted covers for the *Saturday Evening Post* showing an American soldier coming home.

Mobilization for Victory

The mobilization of the military had begun before Pearl Harbor. By December 1941, more than 1.5 million Americans were in uniform. By the end of the war, the total number of soldiers, sailors, and airmen, and women in auxiliary corps, climbed to 15 million.

The draft accounted for the majority of these GIs ("GI" is short for "government issue," the designation of military uniforms and other equipment). Boards made up of local civic leaders worked efficiently and with remarkably few irregularities to fill the armed forces. The "Friends and Neighbors," who informed young men of their fate with the salutation "Greetings," exempted only the physically disabled and those with jobs designated as essential to the war effort, including farmers and agricultural workers. (One draftee in three was rejected for physical reasons.) As time passed, another category of exemption was added, "sole surviving sons"—men of draft age all of whose brothers had been killed in action. In the windows of homes that lost a soldier were hung small red, white, and blue banners, with stars enumerating the house's losses. The lady of the house was called a "Gold Star Mother."

Money was mobilized too. When the war began, the government was spending $2 billion a month on the military. During the first half of 1942, the expenditure rose to $15 billion monthly. By the time Japan surrendered in August 1945, the costs of the war totaled more than $300 billion. In less than four years, the American government spent more money than it had spent during the previous 150 years of the nation's existence. The national debt, already high in 1941 at $48 billion, doubled and redoubled to $247 billion.

Big Business

A few businessmen resisted government policies, particularly the wartime labor laws. One of the least graceful was Sewell L. Avery, head of the retail chain Montgomery Ward. The New Deal had saved his company from bankruptcy, and, during the war, full employment meant bonanza profits for retailers like Montgomery Ward. But Avery had to be carried bodily to jail for refusing to obey a law that guaranteed his employees the right to join a union.

He was not typical. Most big businessmen, including former opponents of the administration, accepted unionization and rushed to Washington to assist the government. They were responding in part to the need for national unity. Corporate executives also recognized that wartime expenditures meant prosperity. General Motors, for example, received 8 percent of all federal expenditures between 1941 and 1945, $1 of every $12.50 that the government spent.

Few criticisms came from the General Motors boardroom. Indeed, General Motors president William S. Knudsen was one of the most prominent "dollar-a-year men," business executives who worked for Roosevelt without pay. He headed the War Resources Board, established in August 1939 to plan for the conversion of factories to military production. There was a bit of cynical talk about the patriotic sacrifice dollar-a-year men were making, but the country did need their organizational know-how.

New Alphabet Agencies

After the congressional elections of 1942, which brought many conservative Republicans to Washington, Roosevelt announced that "Dr. New Deal" had been dismissed from the country's case and "Dr. Win-the-War" was now engaged. He explained that since there was now full employment, social programs were no longer necessary.

The establishment of new government agencies continued apace, however. In addition to Knudsen's War Resources Board, the Supplies Priorities and Allocation Board, under Donald M. Nelson of Sears Roebuck and Company, was commissioned to ensure that raw materials, particularly the scarce and critical ones, were diverted to military industries. The Office of Price Administration had the task of controlling consumer prices so that the combination of high wages and scarce goods did not cause runaway inflation.

Kaiser Graphic Arts

▲ *Liberty ships under construction. By the end of the war, one was sent to sea every day.*

Liberty Ships

Mass production means making a commodity no better than it has to be in order to function. The idea is to turn the product out in vast numbers, quickly and cheaply. Mass production is, obviously, the basis of the high standard of living enjoyed by the masses of people in the United States and other wealthy nations.

However, one of the most amazing applications of the principles of mass production was not in the manufacture of consumer goods but in the production of the "Liberty ships," freighters built to carry the goods of war.

Liberty ships were no-frills boxcars of the seas: 441 feet long, 57 feet across the beam, with a rudimentary engine. Some 800 of them were lost during the war, most to enemy action but more than a few in storms. Because they were welded rather than riveted together, Liberty ships were not the sturdiest of vessels.

But welding was what made it possible for American shipyards employing men and women who had never before built ships to float a Liberty ship in as few as 40 days after the keel was laid. Some 2,700 were built between 1941 and 1944. At the end of the war, several rolled down the ways each day. Liberty ships were so cheap that when one completed a single voyage (carrying freight enough to fill 300 railroad cars), it had paid for itself. Their design was such a masterpiece of simplicity that, with just a few old salts aboard, inexperienced crews of 45 (plus 35 navy gunners) could sail one.

After Pearl Harbor, the National War Labor Board was set up to mediate industrial disputes. Its purpose was to guarantee that production was not interrupted and that wage increases were kept within government-defined limits. This irked many of Roosevelt's former supporters in the labor movement, none of them more important than John L. Lewis of the United Mine Workers, who returned to the Republican party. But the National War Labor Board also worked to ensure that employees were not gouged by avaricious employers. The board was reasonably successful. There were strikes, including a serious one led by Lewis in 1943; but labor relations were generally good, and union membership continued to rise.

The Office of War Mobilization was the most important of the new government agencies. Theoretically, it oversaw all aspects of the mobilized economy, as Bernard Baruch had done during the First World War. It was considered important enough that James F. Byrnes of South Carolina resigned from the Supreme Court to head it as a kind of assistant president.

Success

The size of the federal government swelled at a dizzying rate, from 1.1 million civilian employees in 1940 to 3.3 million in 1945. (State governments grew at almost the same rate.) Inevitably, there was waste (agencies doing the same thing), inefficiency (agencies at cross-purposes fighting with one another), and corruption (lots of people doing nothing).

But with national unity and military victory constantly touted as essential, the few critics of the problems, such as Republican senator Robert A. Taft of Ohio, were unable to have much effect. Taft liked to complain. The most effective check on waste, inefficiency, and corruption was the Senate War Investigating Committee, which was headed by a New Deal Democrat, Senator Harry S. Truman of Missouri.

The lessons learned during the First World War and the administrative skills of dollar-a-year men and New Deal–trained bureaucrats worked wonders on production. New factories and those formerly given to the manufacture of America's automobiles canceled civilian production and churned out trucks, tanks, the famous jeeps, and amphibious vehicles in incredible numbers. In 1944 alone, 96,000 airplanes (260 per day) rolled out of American factories. Industrialist Henry J. Kaiser perfected an assembly line for producing simple and cheap but serviceable freighters, the "Liberty ships." By 1943, his mammoth yards were christening a new one every day. American shipbuilders sent 10 million tons of shipping down the ways between 1941 and 1945. The Ford Motor Company alone produced more war materiel than all of Italy did.

The Workers

Unemployment vanished. Factories running at capacity had difficulty finding people to fill jobs. There was a significant shift of population to the West Coast as the demands of the Pacific war led to the growth of defense industries in Seattle,

Oakland, San Diego, and Long Beach. Among the new Californians (the population of the Golden State rose from 6.9 million in 1940 to 10.5 million in 1950) were hundreds of thousands of African Americans. Finding well-paid factory jobs previously closed to them, blacks also won a sense of security unknown to earlier generations, because of the color-blind policies of the Congress of Industrial Organizations–affiliated unions and FDR's executive order in 1941 that war contractors observe fair practices in employing blacks.

Women, including many of middle age who had never worked for wages, entered the labor force in large numbers.

▲ *Women in an aircraft factory. There was hardly an occupation in industry at which women did not work during World War II.*

A Jim Crow Military

African Americans served in every branch of the armed forces, but in racially segregated units. As in World War I, enlisted men were usually assigned the least desirable duty. A notable exception was the Ninety-Ninth Air Force Fighter Squadron, the "Tuskegee Airmen," who fought in the European theater.

Black nurses were subjected to an indignity they bitterly resented. When not caring for wounded African American soldiers, they were assigned to German prisoners of war rather than to hospitals for American whites.

A black soldier traveling in the South in April 1944 told of being unable to get coffee at any diner or restaurant. Finally, the men in his group were given cups at a railroad station lunchroom, but they had to stand outside. "About a dozen German prisoners of war, with two American guards, came to the station," the soldier explained. "They entered the lunchroom, sat at the tables, had their meals served, talked, smoked, in fact had quite a swell time. I stood on the outside looking in, and I could not help but ask myself why are they treated better than we are?"

The symbol of the woman performing "unwomanly" jobs was "Rosie the Riveter," who was pictured with biceps like a boxer's, assembling airplanes and tanks with heavy riveting guns. Women performed just about every kind of job in the industrial economy. Rosie dressed in slacks, tied up her hair in a bandanna, and left her children with her mother. But, off the job, she remained reassuringly feminine by the standards of the time. By the end of the war, 16.5 million women were working; they were more than a third of the civilian labor force.

Curiously, few of these independent women were feminists. Rosie after Rosie told newspaper reporters that she looked forward to the end of the war, when she could quit her job and return to the home as wife and mother. Women were the perfect wartime workforce: intelligent, educated, energetic, patriotic, and, most of them, uninterested in competing with the soldiers who eventually would come back and take their jobs.

Prosperity

The Office of Price Administration was remarkably successful in its difficult assignment. Coveted consumer goods—coffee, butter, sugar, some canned foods, meat, shoes, liquor, silk, rayon, and nylon—were scarce because of rationing, but high wages gave workers the money to spend on what was available. (Real wages rose 50 percent during the war.) The black market, illegal sale of rationed goods, never got out of control, and prices rose only moderately between 1942 and 1945. Instead of consuming wholesale, Americans pumped their wages into savings accounts, including $15 billion in loans to the government in the form of war bonds. It became a point of patriotic pride with some women to paint the seam of a nylon stocking on their calves (although a pair of stockings was still coveted).

There was an element of good-humored innocence in the way Americans fought the Second World War. If they did not believe that a problem-free world would follow victory, which few doubted lay ahead, Americans were confident that they and their allies were in the right. By the time the fighting was over, 290,000 Americans were dead. Shocking as that figure is, however, American losses were negligible compared to the losses of other belligerents. Winston Churchill had described the year 1940, when the British stood alone against Nazism, as "their finest hour." The years America was at war were our finest day.

for FURTHER READING

General studies of foreign policy during the 1930s include Selig Adler, *Uncertain Giant: American Foreign Policy Between the Wars,* 1966; Charles A. Beard, *American Foreign Policy in the Making, 1932–1940,* 1946; Robert Dallek, *Franklin D. Roosevelt and American Foreign Policy, 1932–1933,* 1957; and John E. Wiltz, *From Isolationism to War, 1931–1941,* 1968. A book that profoundly influenced the writing of diplomatic history in the United States during the last generation is William A. Williams, *The Tragedy of American Diplomacy,* 1962.

More specifically focused are Warren Cohen, *America's Response to China,* 1971; W. S. Cole, *America First: The Battle Against Intervention,* 1953; Roger Dingman, *Power in the Pacific,* 1976; Robert A. Divine, *The Illusion of Neutrality,* 1962; Lloyd C. Gardner, *Economic Aspects of New Deal Diplomacy,* 1964; Manfred Jonas, *Isolationism in America, 1935–1941,* 1966; Warren F. Kimball, *The Most Unsordid Act: Lend-Lease, 1939–1941,* 1969; Melvin P. Leffler, *The Elusive Question: America's Pursuit of European Stability,* 1979; Basil Rauch, *Roosevelt: From Munich to Pearl Harbor,* 1950; and Bryce Wood, *The Making of the Good Neighbor Policy,* 1961.

American-Japanese relations in the years leading up to Pearl Harbor remain a highly controversial subject. Just a few of the many books on the subject are Robert J. Burtow, *Tojo and the Coming of War,* 1961; Herbert Feis, *The Road to Pearl Harbor,* 1950; Akira Iriye, *After Imperialism: The Search for a New Order in the Far East, 1921–1933,* 1965; Gordon W. Prange, *At Dawn We Slept: The Untold Story of Pearl Harbor,* 1981; and Robert Wohlsetter, *Pearl Harbor: Warning and Decision,* 1962.

Biographical studies pertinent to this chapter are James MacGregor Burns, *Roosevelt: The Soldier of Freedom,* 1970; Wayne S. Cole, *Gerald P. Nye and American Foreign Relations,* 1962; Elting E. Morison, *Turmoil and Tradition: A Study of the Life and Times of Henry L. Stimson,* 1960; and J. W. Pratt, *Cordell Hull,* 1964.

Visit the source collections at http://ajaccess.wadsworth.com and http://infotrac.thomsonlearning.com, and use the Search function with the following key terms to explore documents, images, audio and video clips, articles, and commentary related to the material in this chapter:

Adolf Hitler
Benito Mussolini
Franklin D. Roosevelt
Lend-Lease Bill
Neutrality Acts
Open Door policy
Pearl Harbor
Stimson Doctrine
Winston Churchill
World War II

Additional resources, exercises, and Internet links related to this chapter are available on *The American Past* Web site: http://history.wadsworth.com/americanpast7e.

HISTORY ONLINE

After the Day of Infamy
http://memory.loc.gov/ammem/afophhtml.html
Recorded interviews "on the street" after the attack on Pearl Harbor.

What Did You Do in the War, Grandma?
www.stg.brown.edu/projects/WWII
Oral history of 26 "Rosie the Riveters" from Rhode Island.

FIGHTING WORLD WAR II

At the Pinnacle of Power 1942–1945

We are now in this war. We are all in it—all the way. Every single man, woman, and child is a partner in the most tremendous undertaking of our American history.

Franklin D. Roosevelt

U.S. Navy Photo in the National Archives

NAZI GERMANY WAS defeated by British pluck, Russian blood, and American industrial might. By holding out alone against Hitler in 1940 and 1941, Britain prevented the Nazis from establishing an impregnable "Fortress Europe." The British saved the base that made an invasion of continental Europe possible. In sustaining sickening casualties—26 million people dead—the Soviet Union sapped the might of the German military. The United States kept both Britain and Russia afloat with the Lend-Lease Act, and, beginning in 1942, America turned the tide of the war with the full force of the world's most powerful economy. The Pacific war against imperial Japan—a huge effort in itself—was largely an American show.

American strategists designed much of the formula that won World War II. The American military oversaw the huge and intricate apparatus of two simultaneous wars. Without the full participation of the United States, Germany and Japan might have been fought to a negotiated peace. The regimes that ruled them would have remained in power. The crushing defeat of Nazism and Japanese militarism was one of the greatest contributions of the United States to Western civilization.

THE WAR WITH JAPAN

Americans knew that they were in a fight between December 1941 and August 1945. Adults remembered the day Pearl Harbor was attacked; D Day, when the invasion of Europe began; the day Franklin D. Roosevelt died; VE Day, when Germany surrendered; and VJ Day, when Japan surrendered. The memories ended up sweet, sustaining a generation with the knowledge that their lives had meaning. But the war began with defeat.

Humiliation and Anger

The first months after Pearl Harbor brought nothing but bad news. Immediately after Admiral Yamamoto paralyzed the American Pacific fleet, the Japanese army advanced easily into Malaya, Hong Kong, the Philippines, Java, and Guam. Within a few weeks, the dramatic Japanese battle flag, rays emanating from the rising sun, snapped in the breezes of British Singapore and Burma, and the Dutch East Indies, present-day Indonesia.

There was heroism in the disaster. On Wake Island in the central Pacific, 450 marines held off a Japanese onslaught for two weeks, killing 3,000 before they surrendered. On Luzon in the Philippines, 20,000 GIs under General Douglas MacArthur, and a larger force of Filipinos, fought valiantly on the Bataan Peninsula and the rocky island of Corregidor in Manila Bay. At first, the men thought they would be relieved. Slowly, the sickening truth sank in: They were quite alone, isolated by an ocean from a crippled navy, the doomed "battling bastards of Bataan." Grimly, they accepted the hopeless task of delaying the Japanese.

General MacArthur did not stay. Once Roosevelt realized that the Philippines must fall, he ordered the nation's best-known general to flee to Australia. FDR must have been tempted to let MacArthur fall into Japanese hands. He disliked and distrusted the general. Indeed, aside from a coterie of devoted aides, MacArthur riled much of the American military establishment. He was an egomaniac and a posturer, carefully cultivating an image complete with props—sunglasses and corncob pipe. "I studied dramatics under MacArthur," General Dwight D. Eisenhower wryly remarked. He had repeatedly interpreted his orders to suit himself.

Nevertheless, FDR believed MacArthur essential to winning the war against Japan. The general's connection with the Philippines was lifelong, intimate, and mutually affectionate. When MacArthur left the islands, he promoted his mystique and inspired the Philippine resistance with a radio message that concluded, "I shall return."

On May 6, the last ragged defenders of Corregidor surrendered. Humiliation in a dismaying military defeat gave way to furious anger when reports trickled back to the United States of Japanese cruelty toward the prisoners on the infamous Bataan Death March. Of 10,000 men forced to walk to a prison camp in the interior, 1,000 died on the way. (Another 5,000 died in Japanese camps before the war was over.)

Japanese Strategy

During the siege of Corregidor, the Japanese piled up victories in South Asia and Oceania. Yamamoto's plan was to establish a defensive perimeter of heavily fortified islands far enough from Japan that the Americans, after recuperating

---

Prisoners of War

The Americans who surrendered on Wake Island and in the Philippines were prisoners of war for more than three years. About 35 percent died in the Japanese camps, but that was not the war's worst statistic. Two-thirds of the Russians taken prisoner by the Germans died in camps. As many as 80 percent of the Germans captured by the Russians died. Only 1 percent of Germans in American prisoner-of-war camps died, and the figure was lower for Americans in German stalags.

MacArthur and the Joint Chiefs

General MacArthur's campaign was of tertiary importance to the Joint Chiefs of Staff. Only 15 percent of American resources were assigned to his front. His army had only 5 tons of supplies per soldier, compared to 15 tons per soldier in North Africa.

This was because there was no urgency to MacArthur's advance on Japan; the European front was urgent. MacArthur blamed shortages (and much else) on Chief of Staff George Marshall, whom he despised. Marshall did not much like MacArthur either; but, in fact, he went out of his way to accommodate MacArthur's demands and argued that several incidents of insubordination (a MacArthur specialty) should be ignored.

Even paranoids have real enemies, however. Admiral Ernest J. King of the Joint Chiefs so hated MacArthur that his knee-jerk reaction to everything the general said or did was negative.

---

from Pearl Harbor, could not bomb the home islands or force the kind of battle in which the Japanese could be decisively defeated. Then, the Japanese believed, they could negotiate a treaty that left Japan in control of the resources of China and South Asia.

By early May 1942, the first phase of the plan—establishment of an outer perimeter—seemed near completion. Japanese soldiers occupied the Solomon Islands and most of New Guinea. At Port Moresby, however, Australian and American forces halted the advance, preventing a serious assault on Australia. Yamamoto moved his fleet, as yet unscathed, to the Coral Sea off Australia's northeastern coast. His object was to cut the supply line between Hawaii and Australia, thus choking off the resistance in New Guinea.

The Coral Sea and Midway

On May 6 and 7, 1942, the Japanese and American fleets fought a standoff battle. The Battle of the Coral Sea was a unique naval encounter in that the ships of the opposing forces never caught sight of one another. Carrier-based aircraft did the fighting, against one another and against enemy vessels. The Japanese lost fewer ships and planes than the Americans did, but the battle was no Japanese victory. Yamamoto was forced to abandon his plan to cut the southern shipping lanes.

Instead, he looked to the central Pacific, where Japanese supply lines were more secure. His object was the American naval and air base on the island of Midway, about a thousand miles northwest of Hawaii. There, between June 3 and June 6, 1942, the Japanese suffered a crucial defeat. The American fleet, under Admirals Raymond A. Spruance and Frank Fletcher, lost the carrier *Yorktown* to Japanese dive-bombers and torpedoes, but American planes destroyed four Japanese carriers.

It was worse than a one-for-four trade. Japan lacked the wealth and industrial capacity to replace fabulously expensive vessels, such as aircraft carriers, which the United

MAP 44:1 **The Pacific Theater** The Japanese Empire faced attacks on four fronts: British imperial troops attacked Burma from India; with American aid in materiel, Chinese Nationalists and Communists fought the Japanese in China on a static front; General MacArthur drove through New Guinea to the Philippines; and Admiral Chester Nimitz island-hopped through the central Pacific toward Iwo Jima and Okinawa, from which American planes could bomb Japan virtually without opposition. The latter two assaults were the ones that counted; Japan concentrated most troops against them.

States easily could and did. Japan's offensive capacity was smashed just seven months after Pearl Harbor. Moreover, by holding Midway, the Americans controlled the central Pacific. Much earlier than he had planned, Yamamoto had to shift to defending what the Japanese had won.

Yamamoto did not live to see the disastrous end of the war that he had tacitly predicted. In 1943, the Americans cracked the Japanese navy's code and learned that Yamamoto would be flying over Bougainville in the Solomon Islands. They shot down his plane, and Yamamoto was killed. Japan never produced another naval commander of his sagacity or, during the war, another statesman of his good sense.

Anti-Japanese Hysteria

Not even the megalomaniacs among Japan's military rulers entertained the possibility of invading the United States. Nevertheless, the stunning Japanese victories of early 1942 and the success of a few submarines in torpedoing ships off Oregon and California caused ripples of invasion hysteria to wash over the Pacific states. Newspaper magnate William Randolph Hearst, who had baited the Japanese with racial insults for 50 years, deluded himself into believing that he was a prime target. He hurriedly moved out of San Simeon, his fantastic castle on an isolated stretch of the central California coast,

▲ *Japanese internees. It was injustice, and support for the program is a blemish on the records of the era's otherwise most admirable public figures. But the camps were not prisons. Physical conditions varied from adequate to comfortable; and most of the people in charge of internment were sympathetic to the Japanese Americans and disapproved of the program.*

for safer haunts. Humbler but equally nervous citizens organized patrols to keep an eye on the surf from the Canadian border to San Diego. For a few days, parts of Los Angeles were near panic.

In California communities, anger over Pearl Harbor coalesced with long-standing racial hostility toward Japanese Americans to produce outbreaks of violence. Gangs of teenage toughs (and men) beat up Japanese and other Asian Americans; people of Chinese and Korean descent took to wearing buttons identifying their origins.

West Coast politicians demanded the internment of Japanese-born noncitizens, known as issei, and even their native-born children, the nisei. At first, the Justice Department resisted. Investigations had revealed that only a handful of Japanese Americans, most of whom were known to the Federal Bureau of Investigation, were disloyal and might represent a threat of sabotage. The Japanese consul in Los Angeles had advised Tokyo that no help would be forthcoming from the Japanese American community.

But when the attorney general, soon to be governor of California, Earl Warren, and the commanding general at San Francisco's Presidio, John W. DeWitt, joined the anti-Japanese clamor, Roosevelt gave in. DeWitt argued, in a tri-umph of logic, that "the very fact that no sabotage has taken place to date is a disturbing and confirming indication that such action will be taken." FDR's Executive Order 9066 forbade "Japanese," including American citizens, to reside in a broadly defined coastal zone. About 9,000 nisei tried to leave the zone but were thwarted by hostility, turned back at the Nevada line, or prevented from buying gasoline. In the first months of 1942, the federal government forcibly removed 110,000 Japanese Americans from their homes, interning them in camps in seven states, from inland California to Arkansas.

More than a few government officials were appalled by the idea of American concentration camps. Because the criteria for relocation were ancestry and race, the federal government seemed clearly to be violating the Fourteenth Amendment to the Constitution. But feelings were too high for constitutional niceties. "If the Japs are released," Earl Warren said in June 1943 when there was talk of closing the camps, "no one will be able to tell a saboteur from any other Jap." In *Korematsu v. the United States* in 1944, a Supreme Court dominated by New Deal liberals voted six to three to uphold an action that cost 110,000 people their freedom for several years and about $350 million in lost property.

A Better Record

In Hawaii, where about a third of the population was of Japanese ancestry, the nisei were treated brusquely but not grossly abused. A few thousand known sympathizers with Japan were arrested, but, as a vital part of the islands' workforce, Japanese Hawaiians had to cope only with prejudice and the inconvenience of martial law, which affected everyone. After repeated requests for a chance to prove their patriotism, 17,000 Japanese Hawaiians and some nisei from the mainland fought against the Germans in Italy, turning in one of the war's best unit records for bravery. Others acted as interpreters in the Pacific theater.

Treatment of conscientious objectors and the few individuals who opposed the war on political grounds was exemplary by comparison with the treatment of Japanese Americans. Never did government action approach the ugliness of the First World War period. Some 40,000 men were classified "4E," religious conscientious objectors; 13,000 of them were imprisoned because they refused to perform any service whatsoever. (Almost a third were Jehovah's Witnesses.)

Some 1,700 known Nazis and Fascists were arrested, and 10,000 German aliens were interned. (They were, in fact, the last internees to be released.) But German Americans and Italian Americans were not persecuted as a people. In retrospect, this might appear to be surprising since the war against Japan was at bottom a war about economic domination of Asia, whereas Nazi Germany was clearly a criminal state.

But the Japanese were of a different race from most Americans and had a vastly different cultural attitude toward war and the treatment of prisoners. Americans found it easier to hate the enemy in Asia and thus to shrug off injustices toward Japanese Americans.

THE FIRST OBJECTIVE: DEFEATING GERMANY

Even before the Battle of Midway, President Roosevelt and his advisers concluded, in Chief of Staff Marshall's words, "Germany is still the prime enemy and her defeat is the key to victory. Once Germany is defeated, the collapse of Italy and the defeat of Japan must follow." Their reasoning was sound. Japan did not threaten the Western Hemisphere, but Germany could. The Nazis had ideological bedmates in several South American republics, and there were large German populations in Brazil, Uruguay, and Argentina.

Most important, American strategists knew that, in time, Japan must inevitably buckle under the sheer weight of superior American power; there was no rush in the Pacific. However, if Hitler had too much time in which to entrench his regime on the continent of Europe, it might be impossible to defeat him.

Friction Among the Allies

Roosevelt and British prime minister Churchill sometimes disagreed, but the two men were bound together by mutual affection, admiration, and trust. Their relations with Soviet premier Stalin, however, were marred by suspicions, which, on Stalin's part, bordered on paranoia. Churchill was a staunch anti-Communist before the war and made no bones about the fact that the Russian alliance was a marriage of convenience. Roosevelt had a soft spot for Stalin personally and believed he could allay the Soviet leader's suspicions that he and Churchill wanted to sit out the ground war while Germany and the Soviet Union bled each other to exhaustion.

In order to weaken the German onslaught in Russia, the United States Army Air Corps (later the independent Air Force) joined the British in nearly constant day and night bombing raids over Germany. Eventually, 2.7 million tons of bombs would level German cities. Roosevelt also dispatched massive shipments of arms and other supplies to Russia, and, on an impulse, told Stalin that, before 1942 was out, the British and Americans would open a second front in the west, easing the pressure on the Soviets.

But a significant second front was out of the question in 1942. American industry was only in the process of converting to wartime production. The best the two western Allies could muster was an attack on German and Italian forces in North Africa.

The African Campaign and Stalingrad

The British and Anzac forces had fought a seesaw stalemate in Libya and Egypt with Italian troops and German field marshal Erwin Rommel's Afrika Korps since the beginning of the war. In mid-1942, the Germans and some Italian desert forces held a line not far from Alexandria, threatening the Suez Canal, Britain's link with India.

In October, under the command of British general Bernard Montgomery, their arsenal beefed up by Sherman tanks from the United States, the British launched a counterattack at El Alamein. Montgomery sent the Germans reeling, and, in November 1942, as he advanced from the east, Americans commanded by General Dwight D. Eisenhower landed far to the west in French North Africa.

Making a deal with French forces, who were under the thumb of the Germans, Eisenhower moved eastward and, at Kasserine Pass in February 1943, American tank forces fought the first major American battle in the European theater. It was a stinging but not decisive defeat for the United States. Soon thereafter, however, Hitler recalled Rommel, "the desert fox," to Germany. Without him at the helm, and overwhelmed by Allied material superiority, the Afrika Korps collapsed.

Almost simultaneously, deep within the Soviet Union, the Russians won one of the pivotal victories of the war when they surrounded and captured 250,000 seasoned German soldiers at Stalingrad. There seemed little doubt in any Allied capital that the course of the war had been turned against the Germans. Roosevelt told Churchill that "Uncle Joe," as he called Stalin, "is killing more Germans and destroying more equipment than you and I put together."

The Invasion of Italy

In July 1943, an American, British, and Anzac force opened what they hoped would be a second front by invading Sicily. They conquered the island in six weeks, and Americans got a colorful hero to crow about: the commander of the Third Army, General George Patton, who led the race across the island. Patton was spit-and-polish; he sometimes ordered men at the front to shave daily, wear neckties, and wash their jeeps. He rallied them in coarse "blood and guts" language and was a personally brave, even reckless, commander of tanks. (Patton believed in reincarnation and thought he had lived as any number of fabled soldiers in past lives.)

Allied troops moved into Italy proper and knocked the Italian army out of the war. Already harassed by anti-Fascist guerrillas behind the lines, *Il Duce* was ousted by Field Marshal Pietro Badoglio, who believed, quite correctly, that his country had become Hitler's pawn.

Nevertheless, the victories in Italy soon soured. Hitler rescued Mussolini and established him as the puppet head of the "Republic of Salo" in northern Italy. To take the place of the Italian troops who went over to the Allies, he withdrew German units to strongholds south of Rome. It was ruggedly

Preserving a Virile Race
General Patton could be loony. In the final months of the war, he ordered all winners of the Medal of Honor and Distinguished Service Cross to the rear. He feared they would try to outdo themselves and be killed: "In order to produce a virile race, such men should be kept alive."

GI Racketeers
In Naples, where supplies for American forces in Italy were landed, a third of the total materiel, from arms to cigarettes, was stolen by GI rings that sold the goods on the Italian black market. At one point, an entire train disappeared.

mountainous country, and only after eight months of bloody, almost constant battle, did the Allies reach the capital.

Then, once again, the Germans held. Despite massive bombardment that plunged Italian cities into famine, Hitler was able to establish a strong defensive line across the Italian boot. Germany itself would fall to the Allies before they made much headway against the German army's positions in Italy; Italy was not the second front that Stalin wanted.

Ike

That front would be an Allied assault, in 1944, across the English Channel: "Operation Overlord." It was to be the largest amphibious invasion in world history. To command it, Roosevelt and Chief of Staff George C. Marshall made a surprising choice, General Dwight D. Eisenhower, known universally as "Ike." Eisenhower had had a respectable career in the peacetime army. He had been an able enough field commander in North Africa but was by no means a Patton or MacArthur. Eisenhower was a desk general, an executive; but just such an organizer was what was called for by an enterprise on the scale of Overlord.

Eisenhower had another indispensable talent. He was a diplomat. He had a temper; close aides were terrified by his tirades in private. But when the doors opened and colleagues entered, he was supremely affable, smiling, conciliatory, willing to bend on nonessentials, pleasantly firm in pushing through plans on which he had his orders. Eisenhower had a genius for smoothing over differences among headstrong associates, with whom he was surrounded. Churchill was a great man and aware of it. Field Marshall Montgomery was not, but he thought he was. The leader of the Free French in Britain, Charles de Gaulle, would not accept the fact that he was a major ally more out of courtesy than because of the forces at his disposal. Eisenhower even had a friendly working relationship with Soviet marshal Georgy Zhukov.

Ike's Contingency Plan
Knowing that he would be busy on D Day, General Eisenhower scribbled out the following note to be dispatched to Washington in the event that the invasion was a failure: *Our landings in the Cherbourg-Havre area have failed to gain a satisfactory foothold and I have withdrawn the troops. My decision to attack at this time and place was based upon the best information available. The troops, the air corps and the navy did all that bravery and devotion to duty could do. If any blame or fault attaches to the attempt it is mine alone.*

▲ *D Day, the "Longest Day." The massive scale of the invasion is captured by this amazing photograph, taken shortly after the landing.*

D Day and Allied Blitzkrieg

Eisenhower was thorough. He knew that if Operation Overlord failed, another invasion of Europe could not be mounted for several years and by then might not be feasible. His task was immense beyond imagining. He had to mobilize 4,000 vessels, 11,000 aircraft, tens of thousands of motor vehicles, and weapons of various sorts, all the while billeting and training 2 million soldiers. So massive an operation was not unnoticed by the Germans, of course, but the British and Americans successfully kept secret the date of D Day and, rather more remarkable, the place of the invasion.

The date was June 6, 1944, and the place was Normandy in northwestern France. Eisenhower's caution and meticulous planning of detail paid off. In one day, 175,000 soldiers were put ashore. By the end of June, there were 450,000 troops in France and 71,000 vehicles. The army charged across France and into Paris on August 25. By September, they were in Belgium and across the German border, farther than the Allies had penetrated at the end of the First World War.

Politics and Strategy

The British and Americans disagreed about how to finish off Germany. Montgomery wanted to concentrate all Allied forces in a single thrust into the heart of Germany, a traditional strategy that had much to recommend it. Tactfully, Eisenhower overruled him. In part, his decision was military: He feared that with exposed flanks and a single extended supply line, the Germans might surround the exposed army. Ike preferred to exploit the Allied superiority in men and armament by advancing slowly on a broad front extending from the North Sea to the border of Switzerland.

There was a diplomatic consideration too. Still sustaining tremendous casualties as they pushed the Germans westward, the Russians remained suspicious of American and British motives. Stalin jumped at every rumor that his allies were considering a separate peace. Some American diplomats feared that too rapid an American and British thrust would arouse Stalin's suspicions that, when Germany was finished off, the Allies would turn on the Red Army. Eisenhower also worried about spontaneous trouble between his soldiers and the Soviets if an orderly rendezvous was not arranged. That recommended a slower advance. Finally, the single-thrust plan was Montgomery's idea; he would command it. Eisenhower did not share his British colleague's supreme confidence in Montgomery's abilities, and Ike's superiors would not allow the larger American army to be commanded by a foreigner.

"Replacement"

When British and German divisions were drastically reduced by casualties, they were withdrawn and replaced by fresh divisions. The American army kept decimated divisions on the front line and replaced the men they had lost. The divisions that fought from Normandy to Germany had a 100 percent replacement rate. Four divisions had a 200 percent replacement rate.

Amphibious Landing

"Tarawa was not a very big battle, as battles go, and it was all over in seventy-two hours," wrote G. D. Lillibridge, who was a second lieutenant there in November 1943. The casualties were only 3,300 marines, about the same number of elite Japanese, and 2,000 Japanese and Korean laborers who doubled as soldiers. A few months earlier, half a world away at Stalingrad, 250,000 Germans surrendered.

And yet, like Stalingrad, "Bloody Tarawa" was a pivotal battle. If the totals were minor, the incidence of casualties was high. Lillibridge's 39-man platoon lost 26; 323 of 500 drivers of landing craft died; overall, more than a third of the Americans involved were killed or wounded. The figures stunned the admirals who planned the battle.

It was their introduction to the fanaticism of the Japanese. Only 17 of 5,000 Japanese on the tiny atoll of Betio were captured, most of them because they were too seriously wounded to commit suicide.

This willingness to die for a code of honor incomprehensible to Americans was not something that could be taught in a training film. It was bred into Japan's young men from infancy. In his reflections on the battle, Lillibridge remembered a Japanese his platoon had trapped. Another Japanese marine was moaning in agony from his wounds. The defender would reassure his dying friend, then hurl challenges and insults at Lillibridge's platoon.

Betio was 2 miles long and 800 yards wide—half the size of New York's Central Park. The Japanese airstrip there was the chief objective of the American assault. Japanese planes based in Tarawa worried American supply lines between Hawaii and Australia. In a way, by November 1943, Tarawa was the final fragment of Japanese offensive capability.

Tarawa was also an experiment. Admirals Chester W. Nimitz and Raymond Spruance wanted to test their theories of amphibious assault before what they anticipated would be far more difficult fighting in the Marshall Islands. "There had to be a Tarawa, a first assault on a strongly defended coral atoll," an American officer explained.

Amphibious assault against an entrenched enemy was a new kind of war for the American military. Ironically, they thought that Tarawa would be easy. They had no illusions about the fierceness of Japanese soldiers, but the Japanese had been digging in there a comparatively short time. The American assault force was overwhelming, covering 8 square miles of the Pacific. The naval bombardment itself would "obliterate the defenses." Lieutenant Lillibridge told his platoon that "there was no need to worry, no necessity for anyone to get killed, although possibly someone might get slightly wounded."

The predawn bombardment did destroy Rear Admiral Keiji Shibasaki's communications with most of his troops. However, the network of concrete blockhouses, coconut-log pillboxes, and underwater barricades was substantially untouched by the big guns and bombs. Nature was a Japanese ally in the battle. The tide was lower than expected, so the larger American landing crafts could not clear the reef that fringed Betio. All but the first wave of marines had to wade, breast deep, 800 yards to shore.

This was the element of amphibious attack in the Pacific that was really tested at Tarawa: Could men with no more armor than "a khaki shirt" and no way to defend themselves even get to the beach, let alone establish enough of a base from which to displace an enemy that, during these same critical minutes, freely wreaked havoc?

Getting to the beach was the first horror that would haunt the survivors of Tarawa and subsequent Pacific landings for the rest of their lives. Men remembered it as a "nightmarish turtle race," run in slow motion. It was "like being completely suspended, like being under a strong anesthetic." "I could have sworn," said one marine, "that I could have reached out and touched a hundred bullets." "The water," said another, "never seemed clear of tiny men." They had to push through the floating corpses of their comrades, amid hundreds of thousands of fish killed by the bombardment, stepping on other dead marines. The lagoon was red with blood for hours.

The second nightmare waited on the beach. Shibasaki had constructed a seawall of coconut logs, 3 to 5 feet high. It looked like a shelter. In fact, Japanese mortars had been registered to batter the long, thin line, and to peek above it meant drawing the fire of 200 well-positioned Japanese machine guns. Marines remembered that they were capable of moving beyond the seawall only because to remain there meant certain death. About half the American casualties were suffered in the water; most of the rest, on the beach.

One by one, almost always at close quarters, the blockhouses and pillboxes were wiped out. Betio was taken in three days, only one more than called for by commanders who thought it would be a "walkover." The aftermath was almost as devastating as the battle. The vegetation that had covered the island was literally destroyed. Thousands of corpses floating in the surf and festering in the blockhouses bloated and rotted in the tropical heat. The triumphant marines looked like anything but victors. They sat staring, exhausted, just beginning to comprehend what they had been through. "I passed boys who . . . looked older than their fathers," General Holland Smith said. "It had chilled their souls. They found it hard to believe they were actually alive."

Smith and the other commanders learned from the "training exercise" at Tarawa, not least that one did not gamble on tides over coral reefs. Not until the last months of the Pacific war, when the close approach to the Japanese homeland made larger forces of Japanese defenders even fiercer in their resistance, would the extremity of Tarawa's terror be repeated.

The Pacific commanders also learned that although the vast American superiority of armament and firepower was essential and telling, taking the Pacific island was much more personal and human an effort than twentieth-century military men had come to assume. With a grace rare in a modern officer, General Julian Smith frankly asserted, "There was one thing that won this battle . . . and that was the supreme courage of the Marines. The prisoners tell us that what broke their morale was not the bombing, not the naval gunfire, but the sight of Marines who kept coming ashore."

MAP 44:2 Allied Advances in Europe and Africa The successful defense of Stalingrad and D Day, the Allied invasion of Normandy, were the key battles in the defeat of Nazi Germany. With the significant exception of the Battle of the Bulge, a German counteroffensive that shook the Allies late in 1944, it was a steady, terrible war of attrition and constant German retreat after Stalingrad and D Day.

The Battle of the Bulge and the End

For a while in 1944, it appeared that Eisenhower's strategy of advancing slowly was a mistake. Reports from the Dutch underground reported widespread hunger as the Germans looted the country. In the summer, V-2 rockets from sanctuaries inside Germany began to rain down on London, killing 8,000 people. The V-2s were not decisive weapons from a military point of view, but with the end of the war in sight, their psychological effect was disheartening. There was no advance warning from a V-2 except a whine high in the sky, a few seconds of silence, and an explosion.

Worse was a totally unexpected German counteroffensive in Belgium in the cold and snowy December of 1944. German troops pushed the Americans and British back, creating a bulge in the lines that threatened to split the Allied forces in two. Not since Corregidor had Americans fought so desperately on the defensive. A division under General Anthony McAuliffe was surrounded at Bastogne but refused to surrender. ("Nuts!" McAuliffe replied to the German commander when he demanded his capitulation, making McAuliffe famous. A cleverer remark was that of an unidentified medic: "They've got us surrounded, the poor bastards.") Then, a break in the weather allowed the Allies to exploit their superiority in the air. After two weeks, they advanced again. One by one, German defenses collapsed.

A Hitler close to breakdown withdrew to a bunker under the chancery in Berlin, where he presided over the disintegration of his "thousand-year empire." To the end, he thought in terms of the perverse romanticism of Nazi ideology. It was "Götterdämmerung," the final battle of the Norse gods. The German people deserved their fate for letting the Führer down. On April 30, 1945, Hitler committed suicide

after naming Admiral Karl Doenitz his successor as Führer. A few days later, Doenitz surrendered.

Wartime Diplomacy

Eisenhower's sensitivity to Russian suspicions reflected President Roosevelt's policy. He had insisted on "unconditional surrender," in part, at least, to assure Stalin that he and Churchill would not make a separate peace with Germany. At a meeting with Stalin at Teheran in Iran late in 1943, and again at Yalta in the Crimea in February 1945, FDR did his best to assuage the Russian dictator's fears by acquiescing in (or, at least, by not strenuously resisting) Stalin's proposals for the organization of postwar Europe.

In later years, when the Soviet Union was the Cold War enemy and Americans lamented Russian domination of eastern Europe, Yalta became a byword for diplomatic blunder—even for a treasonous sellout to Communism. It was at Yalta that Roosevelt (and Churchill) tacitly consented to Stalin's insistence that the Soviet Union had "special interests" in eastern Europe, that is, governments friendly to the Soviet Union.

Some right-wing extremists were later to say that FDR betrayed the Poles, Czechs, Hungarians, Romanians, and Bulgarians because he was himself sympathetic to Communism. Other less hysterical analysts suspected that the president's weariness and illness, obvious by 1945 in his haggard face and sagging jaw, affected his reasoning in dealing with the ever calculating Stalin.

Whatever effect Roosevelt's failing health had on his mental processes, there was nothing irrational about his concessions at Yalta. He did not give Stalin anything that Stalin did not already have. In February 1945, the Red Army was occupying the very countries that Stalin envisioned as friendly buffer states against future threats from the West. No doubt Churchill and FDR expected the states of eastern Europe to have greater independence than they were to have. Historians disagree as to whether Stalin intended to enforce an iron grip on the region in 1945 or came to that decision two years later, when the Cold War was under way.

THE TWILIGHT OF JAPAN, THE NUCLEAR DAWN

Also influencing Roosevelt at Yalta was his desire to enlist the Soviet Union in the war against Japan in order to save American lives in the final battles. Although agreeing that the Red Army would attack Japanese forces in China, Stalin insisted on delaying action until the Soviet Union felt secure in Europe.

Pacific Strategy

After Midway in June 1942, the United States aided the Chinese in their long war with the Japanese by flying supplies from British India "over the hump" of the Himalayas. The

▲ *Churchill, Roosevelt, and Stalin at the Yalta Conference. Ordinary Americans were startled by the age and weariness in the president's face. (Both Churchill and Stalin were older men.) Some people close to FDR suspected that he did not have long to live.*

Kuomintang troops under Chiang Kai-shek and Communist soldiers commanded by Mao Zedong tied down a huge Japanese army in China. But, hostile toward one another, they never forced the kind of battle the Americans wanted so as to force the Japanese to weaken their defenses in the Pacific.

American forces in the Pacific were under two commands virtually independent of one another. After the conquest of the Solomon Islands, necessary to ensure Australia's security, one force, under General Douglas MacArthur, pushed toward the Japanese via New Guinea and the Philippines. MacArthur, who sincerely believed he was America's man of destiny, acted as if he were also immortal. He exposed himself to Japanese fire until physically restrained by his aides. Although he ordered his men to take antimalaria drugs, he refused them himself. He was also a superb commander—

his troops made 87 amphibious landings, all successful— and no other commander in the war worked so hard to minimize his men's casualties.

The other American advance on Japan, through the central Pacific, was commanded by Admiral Chester W. Nimitz. MacArthur's goal, personal as well as strategic, was to reach the Philippines, where a benign American colonial regime had been rewarded by an active anti-Japanese resistance; Nimitz's was to conquer islands close enough to Japan that American planes could bomb the country.

Island Warfare

To soldiers slogging through the mud and cold of Europe, the troops in the Pacific were on a picnic, basking in a lovely

▲ *Soldiers who made it to the beach in an amphibious landing on a Pacific island. The worst was not necessarily behind them. Every Japanese position had to be taken in almost face-to-face combat.*

climate and only occasionally meeting the enemy in battle. Life behind the lines in the Pacific could be pleasant, but it could be miserable too. "Our war was waiting," novelist James Michener wrote. "You rotted on New Caledonia waiting for Guadalcanal. Then you sweated twenty pounds away in Guadal waiting for Bougainville. . . . And pretty soon you hated the man next to you, and you dreaded the look of a coconut tree."

But, in Nimitz's theater of operations, capturing islands that were specks on the map meant battles more vicious than any in Europe, "a blinding flash . . . a day of horror . . . an evening of terror." The Japanese soldier was a formidable enemy. He was indoctrinated with a fanatical sense of duty and taught that it was a betrayal of national and personal honor to surrender, no matter what the circumstances. Japanese soldiers were sworn to fight to the death, killing as many of the enemy as they could.

To an astonishing degree, they did. It took the Americans six months to win control of microscopic Guadalcanal in the Solomons, even though the defenders did not have time to complete their fortifications. In New Guinea and along the route through the Gilbert, Marshall, and Mariana Islands that Nimitz followed, the concrete bunkers and gun emplacements were stronger than in the Solomons, and the resistance of the Japanese, chilling. Marines discovered at places like Tarawa in the Gilberts in November 1943 that when a battle was over, they had few prisoners. They had to kill almost every Japanese on the island at high cost to themselves. (On the island of Attu in Alaska, which, meaninglessly, the Japanese occupied during much of the war, only 27 soldiers were captured; 2,700 committed suicide when they could fight no more.)

As MacArthur and Nimitz moved closer to Japan, the fighting grew tougher. Attacking the Marianas and the Philippines in 1944, both American forces were hit hard. But MacArthur's dramatic return to Luzon boosted morale, and Nimitz's capture of the Marianas enabled large land-based

Language Lessons

Much of the fighting in the Pacific was at close quarters. Japanese soldiers were taught a little English to shout at the Americans: "Surrender, all is resistless" and "FDR eat s___."

American planes to bomb the Japanese homeland at will. The wooden cities of Japan went up like tinder when hit by incendiary bombs. A single raid on Tokyo on March 9, 1945, killed 85,000 people and destroyed 250,000 buildings.

A Fight to the Last Man

By the spring of 1945, Japan's situation was hopeless. Germany was defeated, freeing hundreds of thousands of battle-hardened soldiers for combat in the Pacific. Japan's leaders correctly calculated that the Soviet Union was on the verge of declaring war on them. After the huge Battle of Leyte Gulf in October 1944 (it involved 282 warships, more than at the Battle of Jutland in World War I), the Japanese navy ceased to exist for practical purposes, while the Americans cruised the seas with 4,000 ships, shelling the Japanese coast at will. United States submarines destroyed half of Japan's merchant fleet within a few months.

Some Japanese leaders put out peace feelers via the Russians, but fanatics high in the government prevented an open appeal. They were themselves victims of the extreme nationalistic fervor they instilled in their men, and they still had 5 million soldiers in uniform: 2 million in Japan, 2 million in China. With so many soldiers fighting to the death, the taking of islands close to Japan resulted in high casualties for Americans too. Iwo Jima, a desolate, tiny volcano needed for a landing strip, cost 4,000 American lives. The invasion of Okinawa, part of the Japanese homeland, killed or wounded 80,000 Americans. In the same fighting, more than 100,000 Japanese died; only 8,000 surrendered. (Another 100,000 civilians may have committed suicide.)

Japanese determination to fight to destruction was demonstrated by kamikaze ("divine wind") suicide attacks—cheap planes packed with explosives and piloted into American ships by poorly trained but fanatical pilots. At Okinawa, they sunk 30 ships and damaged 300. The greatest (although ineffective) kamikaze weapon was the biggest battleship in the world, the *Yamato*. Knowing that carrier-based planes could sink it, the Japanese navy had kept the *Yamato* at home throughout the war. On April 6, 1945, with no reason to preserve it longer, the behemoth, with 2,300 sailors aboard and just enough fuel for a one-way trip, steamed for Okinawa.

Navajo Code Talkers

About 400 Navajo Indians served with the marines in the Pacific in a unique capacity: as "code talkers." In combat, the code talkers handled communications between different units by using a code in the Navajo language. It was an unwritten language with unique linguistic rules and subtle inflections essential to correct understanding. The code talkers completely confounded the Japanese who intercepted the messages; the code was never cracked. It was widely believed, but probably not true, that each Navajo was assigned a non-Navajo partner whose orders were to shoot him if they were in danger of being captured.

Glorious Victory

Just before the invasion of the Philippines, Japanese admiral Shigeru Fukudane, whose task force was in fact devastated, reported that he had sunk 11 American carriers, 2 battleships, and various other warships. Emperor Hirohito declared a national holiday.

In fact, the United States Navy lost no ships to Fukudane. Admiral Halsey released a comment: "The Third Fleet's sunken and damaged ships have been salvaged and are retiring at high speed toward the enemy."

The *Yamato* never fired a shot. A carrier task force sank it the next day.

The military estimated that the invasion of Japan, scheduled for November 1, 1945, would cost 1 million casualties, as many as the United States had suffered in more than three years in both Europe and the Pacific.

A Birth and a Death

This chilling prediction helped to make the atomic bomb appealing. The Manhattan Project, code name of the group that built the bomb, dated from 1939, when the physicist Albert Einstein, a refugee from Nazism, wrote to President

Was the Bomb Necessary?

At first, there was only wonder at a bomb that could destroy a whole city, and joy that the war was over. Within a few years, however, Americans began to debate the wisdom and morality of having used the atomic bomb. When novelist John Hersey's *Hiroshima* detailed the destruction of the city in vivid, human terms, some of Truman's critics stated that he was guilty of a war crime worse than any the Japanese had perpetrated, and exceeded only by the Nazi murder of 6 million European Jews. Truman's defenders replied that the nuclear assaults on Hiroshima and Nagasaki were more humane than an invasion would have been.

When others said that a Japanese surrender could have been forced by a demonstration of the bomb on an uninhabited island, as Secretary of War Stimson had suggested, Truman's defenders pointed out that no one knew for sure the device would work. An announced demonstration that fizzled would have further encouraged the Japanese diehards.

Much later, historians known as "revisionists" suggested that "Little Boy" and "Fat Man" were dropped not primarily to end the war with Japan but to inaugurate the Cold War with the Soviet Union. In bombing Japan, the revisionists claimed, Truman put the Russians on notice that the United States held the trump card in any postwar dispute. Because history is not a science, capable of absolute proof, the debate over the use of the bomb will continue indefinitely. Only two things are certain: The atomic bomb ended the Second World War decisively and ahead of schedule, and it ushered in a new and dangerous epoch in world affairs, the nuclear age.

▲ *A view of Hiroshima after it was flattened by an atomic bomb, August 6, 1945.*

Roosevelt that it was possible to unleash inconceivable amounts of energy by nuclear fission, the splitting of an atom. Einstein was a pacifist, but he knew that German scientists were capable of producing a nuclear bomb. Such a device in Hitler's hands first was an appalling prospect.

Einstein was too prestigious to ignore, and the government secretly allotted $2 billion to the Manhattan Project. Under the direction of J. Robert Oppenheimer, scientists worked on Long Island, underneath a football stadium in Chicago, and at isolated Los Alamos, New Mexico. In April 1945, they told Washington that they were four months away from testing a bomb.

The decision whether or not to use it did not fall to President Roosevelt. Reelected to a fourth term in 1944 over Thomas E. Dewey, the governor of New York, Roosevelt died of a stroke on April 12, 1945. He was at Warm Springs, Georgia, sitting for a portrait painter when he said, "I have a terrific headache," slumped in his chair, and died.

The outpouring of grief that swept the nation at the loss of the man who was in office longer than any other president was real and profound. Silent crowds lined the tracks to watch the train that brought FDR back to Washington for

World War II Casualties

	Total Mobilized	Killed or Died	Wounded
United States	16,113,000	407,000	672,000
China	17,251,000	1,325,000	1,762,000
Germany	20,000,000	3,250,000	7,250,000
Italy	3,100,000	136,000	225,000
Japan	9,700,000	1,270,000	140,000
USSR	–	6,115,000	14,012,000
United Kingdom	5,896,000	357,000	369,000
Total	72,060,000	12,860,000	24,430,000

The Costs of War

As these figures show, the Second World War was the most expensive war that the United States ever fought:

Revolutionary War	$149.0 million
War of 1812	124.0 million
Mexican War	107.0 million
Civil War (Union only)	8.0 billion
Spanish-American War	2.5 billion
First World War	66.0 billion
Second World War	560.0 billion
Korean War	70.0 billion
Vietnam War	121.5 billion

the last time. People wept in the streets. But in Washington, the sorrow was overshadowed by apprehensions that his successor, Harry S. Truman, was not up to his job.

Truman, "Little Boy," and "Fat Man"

Truman was an honest politico who rose as a dependable, hard worker in the Kansas City Democratic machine. He proved his abilities as chairman of an important Senate committee during the war but impressed few as the caliber of person to head a nation. Unprepossessing in appearance, bespectacled, a dandy (he once operated a haberdashery), and given to salty language, Truman was nominated as vice president in 1944 as a compromise candidate. Democratic conservatives wanted the left-liberal vice president elected in 1940, Henry A. Wallace, out of the number two spot, but they could not force southerner James J. Byrnes on the liberals. The two wings of the party settled on Truman.

Truman was just as shocked by his accession to the presidency. "I don't know whether you fellows ever had a load of hay or a bull fall on you," he told reporters on his first day in office, "but last night the moon, the stars, and all the planets fell on me." If he too was unsure of his abilities, Truman knew how to make difficult decisions and never doubted his responsibility to lead. A plaque on his desk read "The Buck Stops Here"; as president, he could not "pass the buck" to anyone else.

When advisers informed him that the alternative to using the atomic bomb was a million American casualties, he did not hesitate to give the order to use it. On August 6, a bomb nicknamed "Little Boy" was dropped on Hiroshima, killing 100,000 people in an instant and dooming another 100,000 to death from injury and radiation poisoning. Two days later, the bomb "Fat Man" was exploded over Nagasaki.

Incredibly, some in the Japanese high command still wanted to fight on. Had they known that the Americans had no more atomic bombs in their arsenal, they might have carried the debate. But Emperor Hirohito stepped in and agreed to surrender on August 14, 1945, if he was allowed to remain emperor. The United States agreed. The war ended officially on the decks of the battleship *Missouri* on September 2.

for FURTHER READING

The standard history of the American war is Albert R. Buchanan, *The United States and World War II,* 1962. More comprehensive studies include Martha Hoyle, *A World in Flames: A History of World War II,* 1970, and Fletcher Pratt, *War for the World,* 1950. Although hardly a study in objectivity, Winston Churchill, *The Second World War,* 1948–1953, will be rewarding to every student.

On diplomatic and political issues, see Robert Beitzell, *The Uneasy Alliance: America, Britain, and Russia, 1941–1943,* 1972; Gabriel Kolko, *The Politics of War: The World and United States Foreign Policy, 1943–1945,* 1968; Joseph P. Lash, *Roosevelt and Churchill,* 1976; and especially Thomas Fleming, *The New Dealers' War: FDR and the War Within World War II,* 2001.

Military history is a major topic of Stephen Ambrose, *The Supreme Commander: The War Years of General Dwight D. Eisenhower,* 1970; William Manchester, *American Caesar: Douglas MacArthur, 1880–1960,* 1978; Samuel Eliot Morison, *The Two-Ocean War: A Short History of the United States Navy in the Second World War,* 1963; Cornelius Ryan, *The Longest Day,* 1959; John Toland, *The Last Hundred Days,* 1966, and *The Rising Sun:*

The Decline and Fall of the Japanese Empire, 1970; and Russell F. Weigley, *The American Way of War: A History of United States Military Strategy and Policy,* 1973.

Books on the home front include John M. Blum, *V Was for Victory: Politics and American Culture During World War II,* 1976; Roger Daniels, *Concentration Camps USA,* 1971; some chapters of Carl M. Degler, *At Odds: Women and the Family in America from the Revolution to the Present,* 1980; Jack Goodman, *While You Were Gone: A Report on Wartime Life in the United States,* 1946; Richard Lingeman, *Don't You Know There's a War On?* 1970; and Michi Weglyn, *Years of Infamy: The Untold Story of America's Concentration Camps,* 1976.

The reasons for the dropping of the atomic bomb on Japan in 1945 are hotly argued in Gar Alperovitz, *Atomic Diplomacy: Hiroshima and Potsdam,* 1965; Herbert Feis, *The Atomic Bomb and World War II,* 1966; and Greg Herken, *The Winning Weapon,* 1980. See also John Hersey's classic, *Hiroshima,* 1946; Richard Rhodes, *The Making of the Atomic Bomb,* 1987; and Martin Sherwin, *A World Destroyed,* 1975.

American Journey ONLINE *and* InfoTrac College Edition

Visit the source collections at http://ajaccess.wadsworth.com and http://infotrac.thomsonlearning.com, and use the Search function with the following key terms to explore documents, images, audio and video clips, articles, and commentary related to the material in this chapter:

"Fat Man" and "Little Boy"	Harry S. Truman
Battle of the Bulge	Hiroshima
D-Day	Japanese internment
Douglas MacArthur	Nagasaki
Franklin D. Roosevelt	

Additional resources, exercises, and Internet links related to this chapter are available on *The American Past* Web site: http://history.wadsworth.com/americanpast7e.

HISTORY ONLINE

Suffering Under a Great Injustice

http://memory.loc.gov/ammem/aamhtml/aahome.html

Ansel Adams's photographs of life in Japanese American internment camps.

World War II

www.multied.com/wars.html

Information on major battles—photographs and maps.

45

COLD WAR

The U.S. and the Nuclear Age 1946–1952

© Bettmann/Corbis

The release of atomic energy constitutes a new force too revolutionary to consider in the framework of old ideas.

Harry S. Truman

Science has brought forth this danger, but the real problem is in the minds and hearts of men.

Albert Einstein

The world has achieved brilliance without wisdom, power without conscience. Ours is a world of nuclear giants and ethical infants.

Omar Bradley

FEW WARS HAVE ended as abruptly as the war with Japan. Planning to fight village to village, then stunned by the news of the atomic bomb, the Japanese government collapsed overnight. Never was a new historical era so unmistakably proclaimed as by the fireballs over Hiroshima and Nagasaki. In 1945, the world knew that it had undergone a major passage.

THE SHADOW OF COLD WAR

The world had not left the past behind. History is legacy. The consequences of actions past live on whether or not people choose to recognize them. Three legacies of the Second World War were so profound that they shaped the United States and the world for half a century and are still with us.

Legacies

The first legacy of the Second World War was the powerful weapon that ended it. Nuclear bombs meant that it was technologically possible for humanity to set back civilization by centuries and perhaps even to shatter the natural balance of the earth.

A second legacy of the war was the recognition that human beings were quite capable of "pushing the button." Not that President Truman's decision to use atomic bombs against Japan was reprehensible. Neither Truman nor his advisers understood the potential of nuclear fission and the more frightening science to which it would lead. The revelation was the Allied and Russian discovery in the spring of 1945 that reports of genocide in German-occupied Europe were not exaggerated. The Nazis had systematically exterminated

▲ *Concentration camp inmates awaiting release by Allied troops in 1945. These men were slave laborers. The photographs from the extermination camps were horrifying.*

6 million Jews and probably a million other people, many of them in camps specifically designed for killing people and disposing of bodies on a mass scale. The photographs of the walking skeletons of Dachau, Belsen, Auschwitz, and Buchenwald; the "shower baths" where the victims were gassed; the cremation ovens; the human garbage dumps, arms and legs protruding obscenely from heaps of corpses—these spectacles mocked pretensions to the essential decency of humanity such as even the slaughter of the First World War had not done. That, at least, had been mindless. The Holocaust was not.

The third legacy of the war was that only two nations emerged from it genuine victors—the United States and the Soviet Union—and that, once the Nazis were defeated, the two victors had little in common. For two years after the war, Russian and American leaders tried to preserve the wartime alliance or, at least, to maintain the pretense of cooperation. By 1947, however, the two great powers were in a "cold war," a state of belligerence without violent confrontation.

At first, Americans were more annoyed than frightened by what they saw as Soviet ingratitude and treachery. The Americans held the trump card, the bomb. Then, in September 1949, the Soviets successfully tested a nuclear device. The catastrophe of which the species had shown itself capable could be ignited at any time.

Roots of Animosity

The origins of the Cold War lay in the nature of Communist ideology. The American commitment to democratic government and individual liberties was incompatible with the conviction of the Bolsheviks of 1917 that they could create a classless, Communist society by means of a repressive dictatorial state in Russia, which would also foment revolution throughout the world.

Landscaping Opportunities

A pamphlet of 1950 about bomb shelters, *How to Survive an Atomic Bomb,* advised: "Things are probably going to look different when you get outside. If the bomb hit within a mile and a half of where you are, things are going to look very different."

By 1933, when the United States extended diplomatic recognition to the Soviet Union, it was obvious to both parties that neither the overthrow of Stalin's regime nor worldwide Communism was just around the corner. Practicality dictated that two of the most populous countries in the world had to communicate with one another.

The Nazi threat made military allies of the Soviets and the United States, and there was, inevitably, a warming of feelings toward Russians among ordinary Americans. FDR recognized, quite correctly, that Stalin was no more driven by ideological principle than he was. Both men were realists. FDR believed that, when Germany was defeated, the two could "make a deal"—the two of them, face to face—that would ensure, if not friendship, at least peace between them. Roosevelt had become that personal in his conception of constructing a new world order. And he was neither the first nor the last human being to ignore the fact that a day was coming when he would not see the sunset.

Exactly what Stalin had in mind in 1945 cannot be known. His public statements and diplomatic demands were often uncongenial to the United States but, taken at face value, not beyond negotiation.

An Insoluble Problem

Then Roosevelt was dead. Again, to what degree his death changed the way Stalin and his advisers thought is a matter of conjecture. At the very least, they became more suspicious of American intentions, particularly as to future use of nuclear weapons.

In the United States, policy makers who believed the Soviets were as committed as ever to the ideology of worldwide Communist revolution—or conquest—had a more receptive listener in President Truman. Nevertheless, the United States continued to act as if it had been agreed at Yalta that the liberated nations of eastern Europe would be liberal, democratic, and open to trade with the West while being "friendly" to the Soviet Union.

At best, this was naive. Democracy and freedom, as defined in the Atlantic Charter, were alien to eastern European history and culture. Moreover, some eastern European countries, most notably Poland, were historically hostile to Russia. It had been Russia, long before the Communists, that had ruled Poland, often brutally. The notion that the war against the Nazis had ushered in a new era in Russo-Polish relations was resoundingly discredited in 1943 when the Germans released evidence that the Red Army had massacred 5,000 captured Polish officers at Katyn in 1940.

Then, late in the war, with Russian troops advancing rapidly toward Warsaw, the Polish government in exile in London called for an uprising behind German lines. Stalin abruptly halted the Russian advance, and the Germans were able to butcher the poorly armed Polish partisans. A democratic Poland could not be "friendly" to Russia by any definition of the word. A Poland subordinate to the Russians could not be democratic.

Truman's Stance

Truman was no sly manipulator like Roosevelt. As a man and as president, in Dean Acheson's words, he was "straightforward, decisive, simple, entirely honest." He neither liked nor trusted the Soviets and did not hide it. Even before he first met Stalin at Potsdam, he summoned Soviet Ambassador V. M. Molotov to the White House and scolded him so harshly for Russian policy that Molotov exclaimed, "I have never been talked to like that in my life!" For a man who was so close to the brutal, bullying Stalin, this was surely not the truth, but that Molotov said it indicates how hardnosed Truman had been.

By 1946, it was obvious that the Russians were not going to permit free elections in Poland. Although Truman was restrained in official pronouncements, he applauded Winston Churchill's speech in Fulton, Missouri, in March 1946: An "iron curtain" had descended across Europe, the former prime minister said, and it was time for the Western democracies to call a halt to the expansion of atheistic Communism.

In September 1946, Truman again signaled the confrontational turn of his Soviet policy. He fired Secretary of Commerce (and former vice president) Henry A. Wallace, the one member of his cabinet who called openly for accommodating Soviet anxieties. *Appeasement* was a dirty word in postwar Washington.

Containment and the Truman Doctrine

By 1947, Truman's policy went beyond merely "getting tough with the Russians." In an article signed by "Mister X"

The GI Bill

The government was generous with the veterans of World War II. The "GI Bill of Rights" provided them unprecedented educational opportunities. Of 14 million men and women eligible to attend college free under the GI Bill, 2.2 million actually did. Colleges and universities swelled in size. The University of Wisconsin had 9,000 students in 1945 and 18,000 in 1946. Elite Stanford University went from 3,000 to 7,000 in the same year.

The GI Bill educated 22,000 dentists, 67,000 physicians, 91,000 scientists, 238,000 teachers, 240,000 accountants, and 450,000 engineers. Inevitably, some veterans abused the bill and became college professors.

The 52-20 Club

Members of the 52-20 Club of 1945 and 1946 were demobilized soldiers and sailors who were allowed $20 a week for 52 weeks or until they found a job. Although many were accused of avoiding work because of this payment, the average length of membership in the club was, in fact, only three months.

in the influential journal *Foreign Affairs,* a Soviet expert in the State Department, George F. Kennan, argued that because of the ancient Russian compulsion to expand to the west and the virtually pathological Soviet suspicion of the Western nations, it would be impossible to come to a quick, amicable settlement with the Russians. American policy must, therefore, be to contain Russian expansion by drawing clear limits as to where the United States would tolerate Russian domination—in effect, those parts of Europe that already were under Russian military control.

Kennan predicted (quite correctly, it turned out) that the Soviets would test American resolve, but cautiously. If the United States made it unmistakably clear that crossing the line of containment meant war, the Soviets would stop. Kennan envisioned a long period of tense, suspicious relations, a cold war. In time, when the Russians felt secure, it would be possible to deal with them diplomatically and establish a genuine peace. In the meantime, cold war was preferable to more bloodletting and destruction.

At the same time that the containment policy was being revealed to the public, Truman was presented with an opportunity to put it into practice. In early 1947, the Soviets stepped up their support of Communist guerrillas in Greece and Communist political parties in Italy and France. On March 12, Truman asked Congress to appropriate $400 million in military assistance to the pro-Western governments of Greece and Turkey. This principle of decisively supporting anti-Communist regimes with massive aid came to be known as the Truman Doctrine.

The Marshall Plan

On June 5, 1947, Secretary of State George C. Marshall proposed a more ambitious program, soon called the Marshall Plan. The United States would spend huge sums to reconstruct Europe economically. Not only were former allies invited to apply for assistance, but so were defeated Germany (then divided into British, French, American, and Soviet zones of occupation) and neutral nations, such as Sweden and Switzerland. Marshall even invited the Soviet Union and the nations behind the Iron Curtain to participate.

Marshall and Truman calculated that Russia and its satellite states would reject the offer. By late 1947, Stalin's troops were firmly in control of the countries of eastern and central Europe, including the one nation there with a democratic tradition, Czechoslovakia. Already in June 1946, Stalin had made it clear that he would tolerate no Western interference in these countries. He turned down a proposal by elder statesman Bernard Baruch to outlaw nuclear weapons because the plan involved enforcement on the scene by the United Nations, which had been formed in 1945.

The Soviets did condemn the Marshall Plan. Massive American aid went to 16 nations, in some of which a political purpose was served—overcoming the economic and social chaos in which Communism flourished. But aid was also sent to countries where there was no Communist threat, such as Switzerland, the Netherlands, Ireland, and Norway. Winston Churchill called the Marshall Plan "the most unsordid act in history."

Lines Drawn

Containment worked. Neither Greece and Turkey nor Italy and France fell to pro-Russian guerrillas or Communist political parties. The Russians most seriously tested American resolve in June 1948 when Stalin blockaded West Berlin, deep within Communist East Germany. Unable to provision the city of 2 million by train and truck, the United States seemed to have two options: give up Berlin or invade East Germany. Instead, a massive airlift was organized. For a year, huge C-47s and C-54s flew in the necessities and a few of the luxuries that the West Berliners needed in order to hold out. Day and night, planes flew into Berlin, unloaded, and returned for a new load. There were more than 250,000 flights, carrying 2 million tons of everything from candy bars to coal. The massiveness and immense scale of the operation made it clear that the United States did not want war but would not tolerate further Soviet expansion.

▲ *Berlin schoolchildren watch a C-54 landing the food they would eat and the clothes they would wear. The Berlin airlift was a massive and finely integrated operation. Air force mechanics changed 60,000 spark plugs on airlift planes every month.*

The Soviets responded as Kennan predicted. Instead of shooting down the planes, they watched. In May 1949, having determined that the United States would not give in, the Soviets lifted the blockade.

By that time, the Cold War had entered a new phase. In April 1949, with Canada and nine European nations, the United States established the North Atlantic Treaty Organization (NATO), the first peacetime military alliance in American history. The NATO countries promised to consider an attack against any of them as grounds for going to war. The Soviets then wrote the Warsaw Pact, an alliance of the nations of eastern Europe. In September 1949, the Soviet Union exploded its first atomic bomb, and soon thereafter, the United States perfected the hydrogen bomb, a much more destructive weapon. The nuclear arms race was under way.

DOMESTIC POLITICS UNDER TRUMAN

Although President Truman effected a decisive foreign policy, he struggled with postwar domestic problems. These were rapid inflation, a serious housing shortage, and a series of bitter industrial disputes. At first, Truman seemed to

founder. Professional politicians and ordinary voters alike began to question his competence. In his predecessor's regal shadow, Truman cut a second-rate figure. Compared with dynamic Eleanor Roosevelt, who was even more active in liberal causes after her husband's death, Bess Truman was a frumpy homebody. Postwar America seemed to have a leader who was not up to its challenges.

The Republican Comeback of 1946

Capitalizing on the anxieties, the Republicans ran their congressional election campaign of 1946 on the effective two-word slogan "Had Enough?" Apparently, the voters had. They elected Republican majorities in both houses of Congress for the first time since 1928. A freshman Democratic senator who survived the landslide, J. William Fulbright of Arkansas, suggested that Truman resign in favor of a Republican president. The Republicans did not take this seriously, but, positive they would elect their nominee in 1948, they set out to dismantle as much of the New Deal as they could.

Their most striking success was the Taft-Hartley Labor-Management Relations Act of 1947. Enacted over Truman's veto, it reversed the New Deal's active support of the union movement. Taft-Hartley emphasized the rights of workers to refuse to join unions, by abolishing the "closed shop." That is, under the Wagner Act of 1935, when a majority of a company's employees chose a union as their bargaining agent with the company, all the company's employees were required to belong to that union as a condition of employment. Taft-Hartley guaranteed the jobs of individuals who refused to join.

Taft-Hartley was not, as Truman called it, a "slave labor" law; nor did it cripple the union movement. Indeed, its chief effect was to arouse organized labor, now more than 10 million strong, to rally behind Truman. This unexpected support (for Truman had not been considered especially friendly to organized labor) showed the president a way to fight the Republican Congress. He vetoed 80 of its anti–New Deal enactments, thus converting himself into a crusading liberal. When Republican critics mocked his homey manners and common appearance, he turned the tables on them by denouncing his enemies in Congress as stooges of the rich and privileged. Coining his own slogan, the "Fair Deal," he sent to Capitol Hill proposal after proposal that expanded social services. Among his programs was a national health insurance plan such as most European nations had adopted.

Civil Rights

The Truman health plan failed, as did his proposal that Congress take action to end lynching of African Americans in the South, declare the poll tax illegal, and protect the employment of blacks who had gotten good jobs during the war. A coalition of southern Democrats and northern Republicans (for whom blacks were no longer voting) defeated the bill. Truman responded with an executive order banning racial

discrimination in the army and navy, in the civil service, and in companies that did business with the federal government.

Personally, Truman believed that "most whites are superior to most blacks." But he also believed in equal treatment under the law and was disturbed by an increase in lynchings in 1946. He did not attack "Jim Crow" segregation in the southern states. But he went much further than Roosevelt ever had in chipping away at the civil inequality of African Americans.

Four Candidates

By the spring of 1948, Truman's popularity was on the upswing. Americans were getting accustomed to, even fond of, the president's hard-hitting style. Nevertheless, no political expert gave Truman a chance to survive the presidential election in November. The Democrats had been in power 16 years, longer than any party since the Virginia dynasty of Jefferson, Madison, and Monroe. The inefficiency of many New Deal bureaucracies was undeniable, and rumors of corruption were persistent.

Then, to turn difficult into impossible, the party split three ways. Henry A. Wallace led left-wing liberals into the newly formed Progressive party. He claimed to be FDR's true heir and insisted that there was no reason to abandon the nation's wartime friendship with the Soviet Union. Democrats from the Deep South, angry at Truman's civil rights reforms and a condemnation of racial discrimination in the party platform written by the liberal mayor of Minneapolis, Hubert H. Humphrey, formed the States' Rights, or "Dixiecrat," party. They named Strom Thurmond of South Carolina as their candidate.

Thurmond had fewer illusions of winning the election than did Wallace, who had a mystical streak. Thurmond's purpose was to deny Truman the election, thus impressing on northern Democrats the necessity of sticking to their traditional acquiescence to southern segregation.

Presented with what looked like a gift victory, the Republicans passed over their leading conservative, Senator Robert A. Taft of Ohio. Taft had led the congressional assault on the New Deal, but he was a peevish, unattractive character, driven as much by personal resentment, it seemed, as by principle. Republican party bosses calculated that if any candidate would send swing voters back to the Democrats, it was Taft. They chose the safe Thomas E. Dewey, the party's candidate in 1944, to take on Truman.

Give-'Em-Hell Harry

Dewey's strategy was tried and true. Every poll showed him winning with ease. Therefore, as other sure victors had done, he ran a low-key, noncommittal campaign, avoiding any strong positions that might alienate groups of voters.

Truman, faced with defeat, had nothing to lose by pulling out all the stops. "Give 'em hell, Harry," a supporter shouted at a rally, and Truman did. In the spring, he traveled 9,500 miles by train, delivering 73 speeches in 18 states.

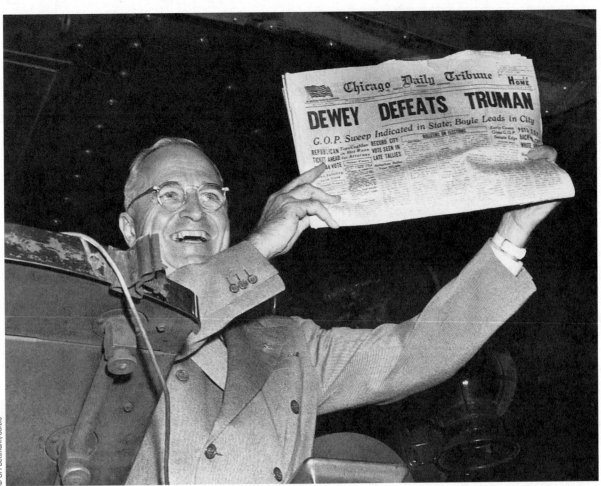

▲ *Harry S. Truman displays the premature edition of the Chicago* Tribune *that announced the election of a new president.*

During the summer of 1948, he called Congress into special session, and a corps of assistants led by Clark Clifford sent bill after bill to the Republican Congress. As the Republicans voted down his proposals, Truman went back on tour, totaling up 32,000 miles and 356 speeches, 16 in one day. He blamed the nation's problems on the "no-good, do-nothing Eightieth Congress." Did Americans want four years of negativism under Thomas E. Dewey?

On election night, the editors of the Republican Chicago *Tribune* glanced at the early returns, which favored Dewey, and decided to scoop the competition by publishing an edition declaring the New Yorker the new president. The next day, Harry Truman took great pleasure in posing for photographers while pointing to the *Tribune*'s headline, for Dewey had not won. Truman narrowly squeaked out victories in almost all the large industrial states and the majority of farm states. His popular vote was under 50 percent, and he lost several southern states to Thurmond. But he was president by a whopping 303 to 189 electoral vote margin.

CONTAINMENT AND CHINA

Truman's victory did not mean the "Fair Deal" he had promised. The president, like Wilson and FDR, soon found himself preoccupied with such serious problems abroad that domestic reform seemed insignificant by comparison.

In Asia, only the Philippines and Japan were firm American allies. Given independence in 1946, the Philippines remained beholden to American financial aid and responded with pliant friendship. In Japan, a capitalist democracy was slowly emerging as a consequence of massive Marshall Plan–type assistance and the enlightened military occupation of the country under Douglas MacArthur. Understanding Japanese traditions better than he understood American, MacArthur established himself as a shogun, or a military dictator who ruled while the emperor reigned. The shogun was a familiar figure in Japanese history, and the Japanese were comfortable with MacArthur.

Rejected Option

China was another story. As they had for decades, Chiang Kai-shek's Nationalists and Mao Zedong Communists remained at odds and sporadically at war. American policy makers were split as to what the United States should do. In the early years of the Second World War, General Joseph "Vinegar Joe" Stilwell had peppered Washington with warnings that Chiang's government was hopelessly corrupt and

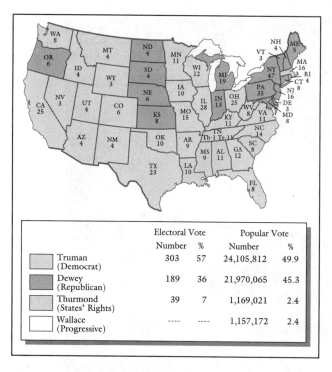

	Electoral Vote		Popular Vote	
	Number	%	Number	%
Truman (Democrat)	303	57	24,105,812	49.9
Dewey (Republican)	189	36	21,970,065	45.3
Thurmond (States' Rights)	39	7	1,169,021	2.4
Wallace (Progressive)	----	----	1,157,172	2.4

MAP 45:1 Presidential Election, 1948 Dewey's near sweep of the Northeast and his big lead in early returns from the Midwest sent Republicans to bed on election day thinking they had won. By the middle of the next day, however, Truman was on top in Ohio and Illinois, for a swing of a hundred electoral votes, and the late-reporting West was almost solidly Democratic. The election of 1948 was one of the greatest surprise upsets in the history of American presidential elections.

his army incapable of facing the Japanese. He urged improving contacts with Mao's forces, which, if they called themselves Communists, were really peasants exploited by Chiang's government.

After the war, acting as a special envoy to China, George C. Marshall suggested that the Chinese Communists were not tools of the Soviet Union but could be encouraged to chart an independent course through American cooperation. Mao was bent on revolutionary change at home, particularly in regard to land, which was in the hands of an elite allied to Chiang. Marshall, like many others familiar with the Nationalists, did not find Mao's program altogether unattractive.

The China Lobby

With the Cold War intensifying in Europe, the proposal to seek a rapprochement with the Chinese Communists found little support. Moreover, Chiang had his American friends—an active, articulate, and well-connected "China Lobby" organized by his brilliant wife, Madame Chiang, who spent much of her time in the United States. The China Lobby drew support from conservative congressmen; from influential religious leaders like the Catholic archbishop of New York, Francis Cardinal Spellman; and from much of the press, most importantly Henry L. Luce, the publisher of *Time* magazine, and his wife, Clare Boothe Luce, a Republican congresswoman and eloquent speaker.

Through 1949, the China Lobby bombarded Americans with information, some of it false: most Chinese supported Chiang; Chiang was defeating Mao's forces on the battlefield; and Mao was a Soviet stooge. So effective was the campaign that Americans were shocked at the end of the year when Chiang suddenly fled the mainland for the island province of Taiwan (then better known as Formosa). Americans thought that Chiang was winning the war. Rather than admitting its deceit, the China Lobby insisted that Chiang had not been repudiated by the Chinese people but betrayed by inadequate American support. They urged that aid be increased and that Chiang be "unleashed" for an assault on the mainland.

Truman and his new secretary of state, Dean Acheson, knew better than to unleash Chiang Kai-shek. To have done so would have meant either humiliation when he was defeated or American involvement in a war on the mainland of Asia, which every military strategist, from Douglas MacArthur on down, warned against. Whether Truman and Acheson ever rued the fact that they had ignored the advice of Stilwell, Marshall, and others to come to terms with Mao's Communists is not clear. Whether American friendship would have significantly changed the course of Chinese history under Mao is also beyond knowing. What is known is that China as a foe was dangerous and unpredictable precisely because China was not, as many Americans continued to believe, a Soviet satellite.

A Faltering Containment Policy

Truman and Acheson applied the principle of containment to China despite the fact that George Kennan's analysis had been based on Russia's history and culture, not China's. Moreover, unlike in Europe, where the line of containment was clear, no one, Truman and Acheson included, knew just where the United States could not afford to allow the Chinese to expand.

Japan was off limits, of course, and the China Lobby insisted that the Nationalists on Taiwan were sacrosanct. But what of Quemoy and Matsu, two tiny islands off the coast of China that were occupied by Chiang's Nationalists? And what of the Republic of Korea, set up by the United States in the southern half of the former Japanese colony of Chosen? Was it to be protected like the nations of western Europe?

These questions had not been resolved when, in June 1950, Communists in control of Korea north of the thirty-eighth parallel (38 degrees north latitude, which had marked the American and Russian occupation zones) crossed the border en masse and quickly drove the South Korean army and the American Eighth Army to the toe of the peninsula.

The Korean Conflict

Truman had an American fleet in Korean waters, and he responded immediately and forcibly. Thanks to the absence of the Soviet delegation to the United Nations (UN), he was able to win the vote necessary to make the UN the sponsor of a "police action" on the peninsula. With the United States providing almost all the "police," General MacArthur took command of the expedition.

MAP 45:2 The Korean War During the frantic last half of 1950 until 1953, newspapers regularly, sometimes daily, ran front-page maps of Korea to show the rapidly changing front line. Then the war bogged down in a stalemate.

In a daring maneuver that might have served as the capstone of a brilliant military career, MacArthur engineered an amphibious landing at Inchon, deep behind North Korean lines. American soldiers cut off and captured 100,000 North Korean troops. MacArthur took back all of South Korea in just two weeks.

The Americans and ROKs (soldiers of the Republic of Korea) then surged northward, crossing the thirty-eighth parallel in September 1950. By October 26, they had occupied virtually the whole country. One American unit stood on the banks of the Yalu River, the ancient border between Korea and Chinese Manchuria.

The victory was so quick that neither Truman nor the UN had time to reflect on MacArthur's assurances that the Chinese would not intervene in the war. MacArthur was dead wrong. Perhaps confusing China Lobby propaganda with

Jehovah's Witnesses

During the Truman years, millions of Americans were introduced to the Jehovah's Witnesses. Rather than preaching from street corners, the Witnesses knocked on the doors of grand homes, newly built middle-class tract houses, and urban apartments. Always neatly dressed, always in pairs, often racially mixed, they clutched handbags stuffed with copies of two monthly magazines, *The Watchtower* and *Awake!* The Witnesses were never jolly or backslapping in time-honored American evangelical tradition. They were solemn, even grim. Their ice-breaking question was cheerless: Did the householder think that all was well with the world?

In a world where the smell of the extermination camps and Hiroshima lingered, the Jehovah's Witnesses won many invitations to come in and talk. The sect that was 70 years old in 1949, but still tiny, began to grow, and the numbers of its fulltime ringers of doorbells became more conspicuous. In 1978, the Witnesses numbered more than 600,000 in the United States and 2 million worldwide. Their Watchtower Tract Society was one of the largest publishing houses in the world. *Awake!* alone had a circulation of 8 million in 34 languages.

The Witnesses took shape during the 1870s in Allegheny City, Pennsylvania. The founder, Charles Taze Russell, was a Presbyterian who, like many troubled believers before him, found grievous flaws in the traditional faiths and believed himself to be "God's mouthpiece."

At first, the Witnesses seemed like just another variant on the fundamentalist, millenarian, catastrophe-minded groups that spring up in times of trying social ferment. They taught that the Bible was "inspired and historically accurate," a single, reassuring absolute in a world of flux and instability. In the 1980s, American Witnesses were nimbler in finding the apt biblical citation for an occasion than were the deans of America's most prestigious divinity schools.

Like the Millerites of the 1840s, the Witnesses said that "the end of the world" was nigh. In 1876, Russell predicted that Armageddon—the final battle between good and evil—would occur in 1914. When the First World War, with its unprecedented horrors, erupted in that year, Witness membership jumped. Russell's successor named 1918, the end of the Great War, as *the date*. Others have set it at 1925, 1941, 1975, and 1984. In times of anxiety like the early nuclear age, the perception that the state of the world precludes an indefinite future is a common response, particularly by those whom society has re-

jected, despised, or merely left behind. Like other fundamentalist groups, the Witnesses were most successful among the poor and downtrodden.

However, the Witnesses were unique fundamentalists. They were not anti-Semitic or racist. The Witnesses rejected racial discrimination of any kind. As a consequence, they have been immensely successful among African Americans.

Hardly right-wing superpatriots, the Witnesses considered all governments evil—America's included. Their meeting-houses, called "Kingdom Halls," indicated that they considered themselves subjects of God (Jehovah). They merely submitted to those powers of the state that did not conflict with Jehovah's law. They did not participate in government or even vote.

Because they refused to serve in the armed forces, thousands of Witnesses were imprisoned during World War II. They puzzled authorities by their passivity and self-enforced order in prison, and also by their disdain for other conscientious objectors, except as possible converts. The Witnesses were not pacifists in any but the functional sense of the word. They looked forward with zest to Armageddon when they would themselves take up arms for Jehovah and exterminate those who had rejected their message.

The Jehovah's Witnesses are also unusual in that they do not believe in hell. When Jehovah's reign begins, the "instruments of Satan" will simply cease to exist. A material universe will be ruled by 144,000 Witnesses, who alone, with Jesus, will reside in heaven.

In their vision of the post-Armageddon earth, their emergence in the Truman and Eisenhower years can be seen in a curious way. Pictorial depictions of Jehovah's kingdom show lions lying down with lambs (an ancient biblical image), but the restored Eden is a broad, weedless lawn mowed as closely as a golf green, surrounding a sprawling ranch-type house such as was the ideal for Americans in the 1950s. Smiling, loving, neatly and conventionally dressed and barbered suburbanites, albeit of all races, populate this paradise. Often, guests are arriving for a backyard barbecue.

The Witnesses' paradise is the consumer paradise that advertisers of automobiles, television sets, furniture, and carpets touted during the postwar years. Such aspirations in a time of increasing affluence allowed most Americans to cope with the anxieties of the Truman era. To the Witnesses, they represented the world after Armageddon.

---

official American policy, the Chinese feared that the ease of the victory in Korea meant an attack on Manchuria. Twice before, Manchuria had been the avenue through which China had been invaded. Although the United States had drawn on history in framing containment policy in Europe, it failed to consider what history had to say about a conquest of Korea. Mao threw 200,000 Chinese "volunteers" at the Americans. By the end of 1950, these veterans, hardened by the long war with the nationalists, drove MacArthur back to a line that zigzagged across the thirty-eighth parallel.

There, whether because the Chinese were willing to settle for a draw—a containment policy of their own—or because American troops found their footing and dug in, a stalemate ensued. For two years, the Americans, ROKs, and token delegations of troops from other UN countries fought the North Koreans and Chinese over forlorn hills and ridges that did not even have names, only numbers given them by the military. Even after armistice talks began in a truce zone at Panmunjom, the war dragged on. The Chinese had protected their borders, and the Americans had ensured the independence of the Republic of Korea. But in the Cold War, with ideological principles taking on a religious significance on both sides, neither side knew quite what to do. Some days at Panmunjom, the negotiators simply sat at the table facing one another, saying nothing.

MacArthur's Debacle

With good reason, the American people were frustrated. Not five years after the Second World War, the Korean War put 5.7 million young men in uniform, killed 37,000 of them, and wounded 100,000. Defense expenditures soared from $40 billion in 1950 to $71 billion in 1952. Truman and Acheson said that the goal was containment, but having contained, they were unable to conclude hostilities. What was wrong?

In the early spring of 1951, General MacArthur offered an answer. Forgetting his own warning against a war with the Chinese on the Asian mainland, he complained to reporters that the only reason he had not won the war was that Truman would not permit him to bomb the enemy's supply depots in Manchuria. Later, MacArthur went further; he sent a letter to Republican Congressman Joseph W. Martin in which he wrote, "There is no substitute for victory," and directly assailed the commander in chief for accepting the stalemate. In April, Martin went public with the letter.

Not even George McClellan had so blatantly attacked the president's constitutional authority as commander in chief. Truman's military advisers were appalled, and on April 11, with their support, the president fired MacArthur. A clear majority of Americans were shocked. They remembered the general's brilliant war against Japan. They were ignorant of MacArthur's many acts of insubordination or, like the crowd at a baseball game when a batter instructed to bunt hits a home run, they cheered, reckoning that MacArthur knew better how to fight the war than Truman did. Returning home, the general was feted with ticker tape parades and cheered by Congress (a Democratic Congress) after a speech heard on the radio by more people than had tuned in to Truman's inaugural address in 1949.

MacArthur concluded his speech by quoting a line from an old barracks song, "old soldiers never die; they just fade away." But he had no intention of fading anywhere. Establishing his residence and a kind of command center at New York's Waldorf-Astoria Hotel, MacArthur issued a series of

▲ *New York City's traditional ticker tape parade for General MacArthur after his dismissal and retirement. He was a national hero of almost unprecedented magnitude—for a month.*

political proclamations. He wanted the Republican nomination for the presidency in 1952.

But the brilliant general was a poor politician. Half his life had been spent outside the country, and his vision of himself as a messiah included the assumption that the people would come to him. They did not. As the very good politician Harry S. Truman calculated when he dismissed the general, the enthusiasm for MacArthur dissipated within months. Meanwhile, the Korean conflict dragged on, chewing up lives.

YEARS OF TENSION

Periodically in American history, during times of great political or social stress, people have turned to conspiracy theories

Bureaucratic Misrepresentation
Before 2000, the official death count for the Korean War was 52,246. That number was carved on the Korean War Veterans Memorial.

In June 2000, it was revealed that the bureaucracy had included in the total deaths in the military during the years of the Korean conflict, from all causes and no matter where they occurred. Of 20,617 deaths of military personnel off the battlefield, only 3,275 occurred in Korea. The corrected total of Korean War deaths is 36,940.

Flying Saucers
In 1947, a commercial pilot over the state of Washington sighted a cluster of "saucerlike things" and reported them to the federal government. By 1950, 600 Americans a year were seeing flying saucers. No one ever proved if the sightings were frauds, the fruit of mass hysteria, evidence of visitors from outer space, or some new top-secret air force plane.

Hollywood, looking for a kind of film with which to combat television, had no trouble making a choice. The early 1950s saw dozens of movies about extraterrestrial creatures visiting earth, usually bent on destruction.

to account for their frustrations. The era of the Korean War was such a time. Large numbers of Americans came to believe that their failure to achieve a sense of security after the victory in the Second World War was the work of sinister forces working quietly within the United States.

"Twenty Years of Treason"

The view that, at Yalta, President Roosevelt sold out eastern Europe to Stalin was an early expression of this paranoia, the belief that betrayal explained the Communist menace. Then, in March 1947, President Truman inadvertently fueled anxieties by ordering government employees to sign loyalty oaths, statements that they did not belong to the Communist party or to other disloyal groups. Eventually, 30 states followed the federal example, requiring a loyalty oath even of employees who waxed the floors of the state university's basketball courts.

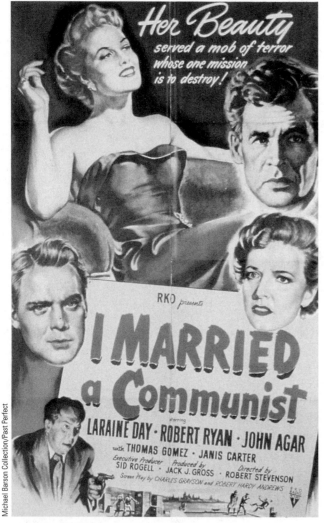

Michael Barson Collection/Past Perfect

▲ *Hollywood did not miss the Communist scare. Screenwriters accused of Communist sympathies were blacklisted, and the studios rushed into production films encouraging the belief in widespread subversion. Ads for* I Married a Communist *did not forget sex but complicated it with the horrors of cohabitation with a Communist.*

Truman contributed to the belief that there was treason in government by allowing his supporters to "red bait" Henry Wallace in the 1948 presidential campaign. Wallace was eccentric, even wacky, and his analysis of Soviet intentions in 1948 was mistaken. The tiny American Communist party supported him in 1948, but he was no Communist stooge. In calling him one, as many Democrats did, they created a political tactic that, in the end, could only work against them. If there were traitors in high places, the Democratic party was responsible for them because, as of 1952, they had been running the country for 20 years.

Before 1952, frustrated right-wing Republicans, like John Bricker of Ohio and William F. Knowland of California, raised the specter of "twenty years of treason." The two chief beneficiaries of the scare were Richard M. Nixon, a young first-term congressman from southern California, and Joseph McCarthy, the junior senator from Wisconsin.

Alger Hiss and Richard Nixon

Richard M. Nixon built the beginnings of his career on the ashes of the career of a former New Deal bureaucrat named Alger Hiss. A bright young Ivy Leaguer during the 1930s, when he went to Washington to work in the Agriculture Department, Hiss had risen to be a middle-level aide to Roosevelt at the Yalta Conference. He was aloof and fastidious in manner, rather a snob, and a militant liberal.

In 1948, journalist Whittaker Chambers, who admitted to having been a Communist during the 1930s, accused Hiss of having helped him funnel classified American documents to the Soviets. At first, Chambers aroused little fuss. He had a reputation for erratic behavior and wild claims. His accusations of Hiss seemed nothing but an irresponsible smear. Legally, because of the statute of limitations, none of the acts of which Hiss was accused could be prosecuted, and he was no longer working for the government. It was Hiss who forced the issue when, indignantly, he swore under oath that Chambers's claims were lies. He said he did not even know Chambers.

To liberals, the well-spoken Hiss, with his exemplary record of public service, was obviously telling the truth. The seedy Chambers was a liar. But many ordinary Americans, especially working-class ethnics and citizens of western farming states, were not so sure. With his nasal aristocratic accent and expensive tailored clothing, Hiss represented the eastern establishment, traditionally an object of suspicion, and the long-entrenched New Deal bureaucracy, of which they had grown weary.

Congressman Nixon shared these feelings. On little more than a hunch, he pursued the Hiss case when other Republicans had lost interest. Nixon persuaded Chambers to produce microfilms that seemed to show that Hiss had indeed retyped classified documents. Questioning Hiss at a congressional hearing, Nixon poked hole after hole in Hiss's testimony.

Largely because of Nixon, Hiss was convicted of perjury (that is, lying under oath). It was suddenly plausible to wonder how many other New Dealers had been spies. Re-

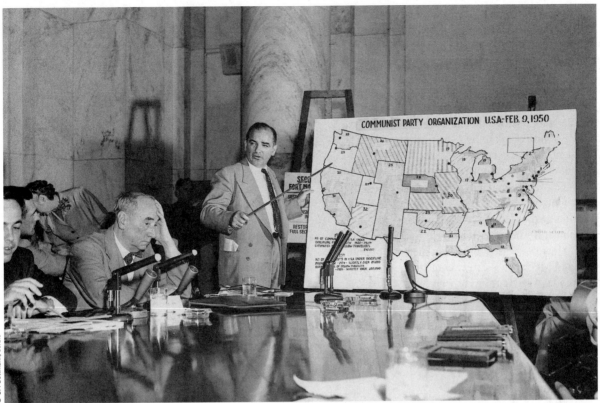

▲ *Senator Joe McCarthy during the hearings about his accusations that the United States Army harbored Communists. It was the end of his career. The only party member McCarthy could find in the army was a dentist.*

publicans pointed out that Hiss was a personal friend of Secretary of State Dean Acheson.

Senator Joe McCarthy

Senator Joseph McCarthy of Wisconsin was as unlikely a character as Nixon to play a major role in the government of a nation. Socially awkward and furtive, he was also a bully. McCarthy was facing an election in 1952 that he seemed likely to lose, his record in the Senate having been less than sparkling. Groping for an issue, he rejected suggestions that he focus on the advantages the proposed St. Lawrence Seaway would bestow on Wisconsin, a Great Lakes state. Too dull. Instead, almost by accident, McCarthy discovered that anxiety about Communist subversion was his ticket to political stardom.

In 1950, McCarthy told a Republican audience at Wheeling, West Virginia, that he had a list of 205 Communists who were working in the State Department with the full knowledge of Secretary Acheson. In other words, Acheson himself actively abetted Communist subversion.

McCarthy had no such list. Only two days later, he could not remember if he had said the names totaled 205 or 57. He never released a single name and never fingered a single Communist in government. Because he was so reckless, interested only in publicity, McCarthy had stumbled on the effectiveness of the "big lie"—making fabulous accusations so forcefully and repetitively that many people conclude they must be true.

When a few senators denounced his irresponsibility, McCarthy showed just how sensitive was the nerve he had touched. Senator Millard Tydings of Maryland was a conservative whose family name gave him practically a proprietary interest in a Senate seat in his state. In 1950, McCarthy threw his support behind Tydings's opponent. He fabricated a photograph—like a tabloid composograph without the jokes—showing Tydings shaking hands with American Communist leader Earl Browder. Tydings was defeated.

McCarthyism

Following Tydings's defeat, civil libertarians worried that other senators who opposed McCarthy would be afraid to speak up lest they suffer the same fate. By 1952, McCarthy was so powerful that Republican presidential candidate Dwight D. Eisenhower, whose military career had been sponsored by George C. Marshall, refrained from praising Marshall in Wisconsin because the former secretary of state was one of McCarthy's "traitors."

Political Cleansing

During World War II, about 100 federal employees were fired, and another 30 resigned because of investigations into their backgrounds. Between 1947 and 1956, there were 2,700 dismissals and 12,000 resignations described as "security related."

Liberal Democrats in Congress rushed to prove their own loyalty by voting for dubious laws, such as the McCarran Internal Security Act, which effectively outlawed the Communist party and defined dozens of liberal lobby groups as "Communist fronts." The McCarran Act even provided for the establishment of concentration camps for disloyal citizens in the event of a national emergency. The Supreme Court fell into line with its decision in *Dennis et al. v. United States* (1951). By a vote of six to two, the Court agreed that it was a crime to advocate the forcible overthrow of the government, a position that Communists were defined as holding by virtue of their membership in the party.

At the peak of McCarthy's power, only a very few universities (including the University of Wisconsin) and journalists like cartoonist Herbert Block and television commentator Edward R. Murrow refused to be intimidated. Not until 1954, however, did McCarthy's career come to an end. Failing to get preferential treatment for a friend of his chief aide, Roy Cohn, McCarthy accused the United States Army of being infiltrated by Communists. This recklessness emboldened the Senate to move against him. He was censured in December 1954 by a vote of 72 to 22. It was only the third time in American history that the nation's most exclusive club turned on one of its own members.

The Making of a Politician

Nixon and McCarthy built their careers on exploiting and aggravating anxieties. Less directly, the leader of the conservative Republicans, Senator Taft of Ohio, did the same. Taft encouraged his party's hell-raisers as a way of chipping away at the hated Democrats.

But the American people turned neither to Taft nor to a mover and shaker to guide them through the 1950s. Instead, they chose a man with no background in party politics, whose strength was a warm personality and whose talent was a knack for smoothing over conflict.

After World War II, General Dwight David Eisenhower wrote his memoirs of the war, *Crusade in Europe,* and, early in 1948, he accepted the presidency of Columbia University. Leaders of both parties approached him in his office with offers to nominate him as president. Truman himself told Eisenhower ("Ike") that if he would accept the Democratic nomination, Truman would gladly step aside.

Eisenhower was not interested. He was a career military man who, unlike MacArthur, believed that soldiers should stay out of politics. It is not certain that Eisenhower ever bothered to vote before 1948. But he did not like academic life. Ike's intellectual interests ran to pulp western novels. After a lifetime accustomed to military order and expecting his instructions to be carried out, he found the chaos of shepherding academics intolerable.

As one of New York City's most eminent citizens, however, Eisenhower drifted into close professional and personal association with the wealthy eastern businessmen who dominated the moderate wing of the Republican party.

They showered him with gifts such as had turned General Grant's head and investment advice that was inevitably sound. As an administrator himself, something of a businessman in uniform, Eisenhower found it easy to assimilate their politics.

In 1950, Ike took a leave of absence from Columbia to command NATO troops in Europe. There, because the Korean War dragged on to no conceivable end, because of MacArthur's insubordination (which shocked him), and because of the rise of demagogues like McCarthy, he grew receptive to the pleas of his Republican friends that he had a duty to run for president. Like them, Eisenhower did not wish to return the United States to the pre–New Deal free-enterprise idyll that Taft fantasized. Ike and his supporters were at peace with the basic reforms of the Roosevelt era. What disturbed Eisenhower was corruption in the Truman administration, excessive government expenditures, and bureaucratic waste. Gradually, Eisenhower realized he could defeat any Democrat by virtue of his personal popularity whereas, with the quietly fanatical Senator Taft as the Republican nominee, the party would very likely be defeated.

The Campaign of 1952

In fact, many conservative Republicans who admired Taft wanted Eisenhower to run. They were more interested in victory at the polls than in honoring their veteran leader. They agreed with the Eisenhower moderates that Taft's uncom-

MAP 45:3 Presidential Election, 1952 Eisenhower's victory in the election of 1952 was a true landslide. He even carried four southern states that, previously, had been almost sure wins for the Democrats.

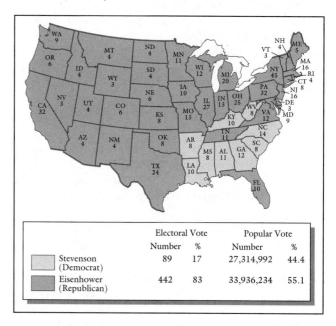

	Electoral Vote		Popular Vote	
	Number	%	Number	%
Stevenson (Democrat)	89	17	27,314,992	44.4
Eisenhower (Republican)	442	83	33,936,234	55.1

▲ *Eisenhower ("Ike") campaigning in Iowa in the fall of 1952. His smiling, fatherly image was what the country wanted.*

promising principles would alienate voters who had benefited from the New Deal and knew it but who were otherwise weary of the long Democratic era.

Eisenhower's opponent was the governor of Illinois, Adlai E. Stevenson. He was a liberal, but he had played no role in the increasingly unpopular Truman administration. Stevenson was also a superb campaigner, personable, witty, and as attractively modest in manner as Eisenhower. For a few weeks late in the summer of 1952, it appeared that Stevenson was catching up with Ike. Stevenson enchanted reporters covering the election with his eloquence, whereas Eisenhower, who functioned best in small groups, seemed to bumble on the podium.

But Stevenson labored under too many handicaps, and Eisenhower's shrewd campaign managers made the most of them. They actually turned Stevenson's intelligence and glibness against him, pointing out that "eggheads" (intellectuals) were precisely the people who were responsible for "the mess in Washington." In October, Eisenhower himself administered the deathblow. While Stevenson defended the policies on which the limited war in Korea was based, Eisenhower promised that, when he was elected, he would personally "go to Korea" and end the aimless war.

Landslide

Stevenson won nine southern states. Although he supported civil rights for African Americans, he brought the Dixiecrats back into the Democratic party by naming as his running mate a southern moderate, John Sparkman of Alabama. Otherwise, Eisenhower swept the nation, winning 55 percent of the popular vote and 442 electoral votes to Stevenson's 89.

In December, before he was inaugurated, Eisenhower kept his promise to go to Korea. He donned military gear and was filmed sipping coffee with soldiers on the front lines. He had long recognized that the stalemate was senseless and that an all-out conventional offensive was foolish. Now, without bluster, he threatened to use the atomic bomb to end the war. It was surely a bluff he had no intention of following through on; Eisenhower had disapproved of using the bomb against Japan. But it worked: The Chinese agreed to end to hostilities in July 1953.

It was an auspicious beginning. Then, in March 1953, the bugbear of American frustrations, the Soviet dictator Stalin, died. The first summer of the Eisenhower presidency was scarcely under way when Americans could feel they had embarked on a new age of normalcy.

for FURTHER READING

There are several good general histories of the postwar era: William L. O'Neill, *American High: The Years of Confidence, 1945–1960,* 1987; James Gilbert, *Another Chance,* 1984; and James T. Patterson, *Grand Expectations: The United States 1945–1974,* 1996.

On Truman and his administration, see David McCullough, *Truman,* 1992; Robert H. Ferrell, *Harry S Truman and the Modern American Presidency,* 1994; Alonzo L. Hamby, *Man of the People: A Life of Harry S Truman,* 1995; and the articulate president's own *Memoirs,* 1955–1956.

Good specialized studies include William C. Berman, *The Politics of Civil Rights in the Truman Administration,* 1970; Susan Hartmann, *Truman and the Eightieth Congress,* 1971; James T. Paterson, *Mr. Republican: A Biography of Robert A. Taft,* 1975; and Allen Yarnell, *Democrats and Progressives: The 1948 Election as a Test of Postwar Liberalism,* 1974.

Diplomatic problems of the times are treated in Herbert Feis, *From Trust to Terror: The Onset of the Cold War, 1945–1950,* 1970; John L. Gaddis, *The United States and the Origins of the Cold War, 1941–1947,* 1972; Ronald W. Powaksi, *The Cold War, 1917–1971,* 1998; Walter Le Feber, *America, Russia, and the Cold War, 1945–1980,* 1981; Thomas G. Paterson, *Cold War Critics: Alterna-*tives to American Foreign Policy in the Truman Years, 1972; and, for its provocations, William Appleman Williams, *The Tragedy of American Diplomacy,* 1962.

On Korea, see Carl Berger, *The Korea Knot: A Military-Political History,* 1957; R. F. Haynes, *The Awesome Power: Harry S. Truman as Commander in Chief,* 1973; William Manchester, *American Caesar: Douglas MacArthur,* 1978; G. D. Paige, *The Korean Decision,* 1968; David Rees, *Korea: The Limited War,* 1964; and John W. Spanier, *The Truman-MacArthur Controversy,* 1965.

McCarthyism and other manifestations of the red scare of the early 1950s are treated in David Caute, *The Great Fear: The Anti-Communist Purge Under Truman and Eisenhower,* 1978; Stanley Kutler, *The American Inquisition,* 1982; Norman D. Markowitz, *Rise and Fall of the People's Century: Henry A. Wallace and American Liberalism, 1941–1948,* 1974; Victor Navasky, *Naming Names,* 1980; William L. O'Neill, *A Better World,* 1982; Thomas C. Reeves, *The Life and Times of Joe McCarthy,* 1982; Allen Weinstein, *Perjury! The Hiss-Chambers Conflict,* 1978; M. J. Heale, *American Anti-Communism: Combatting the Enemy Within, 1880–1970,* 1990; and Richard G. Powers, *Not Without Honor: The History of American Anti-Communism,* 1995.

AMERICAN JOURNEY ONLINE AND INFOTRAC COLLEGE EDITION

Visit the source collections at http://ajaccess.wadsworth.com and http://infotrac.thomsonlearning.com, and use the Search function with the following key terms to explore documents, images, audio and video clips, articles, and commentary related to the material in this chapter:

Adlai Stevenson	Joseph McCarthy
Alger Hiss	Marshall Plan
Dwight D. Eisenhower	Thomas E. Dewey
Harry S. Truman	Truman Doctrine

Additional resources, exercises, and Internet links related to this chapter are available on *The American Past* Web site: http://history.wadsworth.com/americanpast7e.

HISTORY ONLINE

The Korean War
www.multied.com/wars.html
Information, photograph, and maps of battles of the Korean War.

U.S. Objectives and Programs for National Security
www.fas.org/irp/offdocs/nsc-hst/nsc-68.htm
Facsimile of a "Top Secret" document prepared for President Truman by the National Security Council.

The Rosenberg Trial
www.umkc.edu/faculty/projects/ftrials/rosenb/ROSENB.htm
Excellent in-depth insights into the celebrated and controversial spy trial.

CHAPTER

46

EISENHOWER COUNTRY

American Life in the 1950s

> *I Like Ike.*
>
> Eisenhower campaign slogan, 1952
>
> *I Still Like Ike.*
>
> Eisenhower campaign slogan, 1956

THE VOTERS OF 1952 wanted no upheaval. They wanted a change of pace. Most Americans accepted the fact that the Cold War would drag on indefinitely, but they wanted an end to the Korean War, which was killing soldiers while negotiators blathered on and on. Most Americans approved of the basic changes the New Deal had made in their lives. However, after 20 years of Democratic party government, they were ready for new faces.

Americans wanted to cool off. They were weary of the moral demands of reform and war. There was an air of 1920 about the election of 1952: The voters opted for a normalcy in which they could savor the rewards of living in the world's richest nation.

LEADERSHIP

Reassurance is what Dwight D. Eisenhower gave them. The grinning, amiable Ike was a perfect regent. He kept the peace through two full terms. He replaced the jaded political pros, do-gooder intellectuals, and bureaucratic liberal reformers of the Roosevelt-Truman era with administrators like himself and with the wealthy businessmen who had become his friends.

Ike's advisers were not colorful. "Eight millionaires and a plumber," a Democrat sniffed about Eisenhower's cabinet, and Secretary of Labor Martin Durkin, leader of the American Federation of Labor plumbers' union, resigned within a year to be replaced by another millionaire. When Congress created the Department of Health, Education, and Welfare, Eisenhower's pick to head it was not a social worker with a lifelong cause to serve, but Oveta Culp Hobby, the head of the Women's Army Corps during the war. She was a military bureaucrat like Ike himself.

Ike's Style and Its Critics

Eisenhower's style was calculated to soothe. Rather than leaping into political catfights with claws flashing—Truman's way—Ike sidled away from the caterwauling, leaving it to subordinates. His special assistant, Sherman Adams, screened everyone who applied to see the president. He turned back those who might aggravate Ike, involve him in a controversy, or trick him into making an embarrassing statement. Adams studied every document that was to cross the president's desk, weeding out those he thought trivial and summarizing the others. Eisenhower disliked study or even reading more than a page or so on any subject; he wanted to see "briefs" such as he had dealt with in the army.

Critics claimed that Adams was more powerful than an appointed official should be. They said he made many presidential-level decisions himself, and he probably did. But there was never any doubt that the flinty, abrupt New Englander had Eisenhower's confidence. In 1958, when it was revealed that Adams rigged some government decisions to favor a longtime friend, businessman Bernard Goldfine, and accepted an expensive gift from Goldfine, Adams was forced to resign. Eisenhower let him go, but he bitterly resented the loss of an aide who served him well.

The president delegated considerable authority to the members of his cabinet. *They* were to study the details of issues, report to him, and, if they disagreed among themselves, to debate the question—briefly. Ike, the commander with ultimate responsibility, listened and handed down his decision. Whenever possible, he preferred compromise to backing one adviser against another. That was how he had worked during the Second World War.

Liberal Democrats, especially intellectuals, outsiders now, poked fun at Eisenhower's losing battle with the English language. Not a reflective man and never happy before large audiences, Eisenhower often lapsed into gobbledygook at press conferences. He spoke in disjointed phrases, or his sentences meandered endlessly, finally trailing off in a scratch of the head without ever quite touching on the question he had been asked. Eisenhower's aides suggested that Ike knew exactly what he was doing when he appeared to be incoherent. When it did not suit him to answer a questioner, he deliberately confused them. They may well have been

right; Eisenhower was quite a good writer, and his prose was simple, direct, and clear.

Eisenhower's love of leisure aroused critics. The nation was drifting, they said, while Ike relaxed on his gentleman's farm on the battlefield at Gettysburg—he did study that historic battle—and took too many vacations in climes where the golf courses were always green, the clubhouses air conditioned, and the martinis dry.

An Age of Prosperity

But Ike's critics found listeners only in other critics. The majority of Americans did not object to a president who took it easy. In 1956, when Ike ran for reelection against Adlai Stevenson a year after suffering a serious heart attack and just a few months after undergoing major surgery, the voters reelected him by a larger margin than in 1952. Better easygoing Ike in questionable health than a healthy, eloquent Adlai Stevenson calling on them to roll up their sleeves and make America better.

For most Americans, the 1950s were good times, an age of a prosperity that extended to more people than the prosperity of the 1920s had. Despite the New Deal, there had been no shift in the distribution of wealth. The poor remained about as numerous as they had been. The lowest-paid 20 percent of the population earned the same 3 to 4 percent of national income that they had earned during the 1920s. The wealthiest 20 percent of the population continued to enjoy 44 to 45 percent of the national income. The remaining 60 percent of the population, therefore—the great American middle class—was proportionately no better off than before.

The difference in the 1950s was the size of the pie from which all were taking their slices. America was vastly richer as a result of the extraordinary economic growth of the 1940s. Americans in the middle found themselves with a great deal of discretionary income, money not needed for the immediate necessities. In 1950, discretionary income totaled $100 billion, compared with $40 billion in 1940. The sum increased steadily throughout the decade.

The old values—thrift and frugality—dictated that such extra money be saved. However, with a generation of daily denial behind them, the hard times of the Great Depression and the sacrifices of the war, the newly affluent middle class itched to spend its money on goods and services that made life more comfortable, varied, and stimulating. New consumer-oriented industries popped up like dandelions to urge them on.

Consumption

"Enjoy yourself," a popular song went. "It's later than you think." Americans did. They lavished their money on a cornucopia of goods and services—some trivial, some momentous in their cultural consequences, and most designed to amuse and entertain. The middle classes upgraded their diets, eating more meat and vegetables and fewer of the bulky, starchy bread and potatoes that had sustained their parents. Mass-produced convenience foods, like frozen vegetables, became staples of the middle-class diet. If July in January came with a loss of quality, frozen peas and carrots could be prepared in 5 or 10 minutes in boiling water, freeing people to enjoy additional leisure time.

Fashion, buying clothes in order to be in style, was now a diversion for tens of millions rather than a handful of very rich. Mass-producers of clothing copied the creations of Paris couturiers with affordable department store versions of the latest thing. They encouraged the impulse to be a step ahead of neighbors by changing styles annually. In 1953, more Americans could identify Christian Dior, the French clothing designer who was all the rage, than knew the name of the plumber in Eisenhower's cabinet.

Fads

Like the prosperous 1920s, the 1950s were a decade of fads (perhaps the beginning of an epoch of fads that will never end). Late in 1954, a Walt Disney television program about the frontiersman and politician Davy Crockett kicked off a mania for coonskin caps (usually made from rabbit, cat, or synthetic fur), lunch boxes decorated with pictures of Davy shooting bears, and plastic "long rifles" and bowie knives reasonably safe for use in backyard Alamos. The magic name of Crockett printed on virtually any homey object increased its sales. In less than a year, Americans bought 10 million coonskin caps, spending $100 million commemorating the Tennesseean who never quite made it big himself.

In 1958, a toy manufacturer brought out a plastic version of an Australian exercise device, a hoop that was twirled around the hips by means of hula-like gyrations. Almost overnight, 30 million "hula hoops" were sold for $1.98, 100 million within six months. Four Wham-O factories could not keep up with demand, and at least two instances of parents hijacking trucks carrying hula hoops were reported. Within a year, a hoop could be had for 50 cents.

A more durable mania was Mattel Corporation's "Barbie," an anatomically not-quite-correct doll of a voluptuous teenager. Ten inches high, Barbie was herself a voracious consumer, an inspiration to her preteen owners. Their parents purchased so much clothing and accessories for Barbie that Mattel was soon the nation's fourth largest manufacturer of "women's clothing."

A chemical compound, chlorophyll, became a rage when manufacturers of more than 90 products, ranging from chewing gum to dog food, said that the green stuff improved the odor of those who chewed it, shampooed or bathed with it, and rubbed it into their armpits. Americans spent $135 million on chlorophyll products. The boom may have busted when the American Medical Association pointed out that goats, notoriously hard on the nose, consumed chlorophyll all day, every day. Or, it just may have run its course, as fads do.

As in the 1920s, some fads profited no one but the newspapers and magazines that reported them. College students competed to see how many of them could squeeze into a telephone booth or a tiny Volkswagen. Some social critics warned that such inane behavior and the celerity with which Americans rushed to do what others were doing revealed a conformism in the culture that, if far from dangerous, was not healthy.

The Boob Tube

The most significant consumer bauble of the decade was the home television receiver. Workable as early as 1927, and introduced as a broadcast medium in 1939, "radio with a picture" remained a toy of electronics hobbyists until after the Second World War. In 1946, there were only 8,000 privately owned TV sets in the United States, 1 for every 18,000 people.

Then, gambling that middle-class Americans were ready to spend their money on yet another kind of entertainment, the radio networks plunged into television, making extensive programming available. Manufacturers of TV sets, like Dumont, peddled their product as a healthy social innovation: "There is great happiness in the home where the family is held together by this new common bond— Television!"

By 1950, almost 4 million sets had been sold, 1 for every 32 people in the country. By 1970, more households were equipped with a TV set than had refrigerators, bathtubs, or indoor toilets. Never had a whole society fallen so suddenly and hopelessly in love with a device.

At first, high-minded network executives hoped that television would be an agent of education and cultural uplift. Several corporations making consumer products sponsored programs bringing serious plays, both classics and

▲ *Children born after World War II were the first generation to grow up with television, and it made a difference. They were "hooked" to a degree their parents never were.*

© UPI-Bettmann/Corbis

dramas written for television, to the small screen. Playwrights like Paddy Chayefsky and Rod Serling got their start writing for *Playhouse Ninety* and *Studio One.*

But American television, like radio, was a private enterprise that depended on advertisers for its profits, and advertisers soon learned that a mass audience wanted light entertainment. Americans made a multimillionaire of "Mr. Television," Milton Berle, who had been a fair to middling burlesque comic and occasional Hollywood clown. A New York gossip columnist entirely lacking in stage personality, Ed Sullivan, became a national celebrity by hosting a variety show that surrounded a big-name singer or comedian with acts by trained dogs, trained birds, trained seals, and ventriloquists.

Cowboys and Quiz Shows

Beginning in 1955, the networks launched more than 40 different dramas set in an imaginary Wild West. By 1957, one-third of "prime time," the evening hours between supper and bedtime, were taken over by horses, sheriffs, bad men, and saloon girls with hearts of gold. In Los Angeles, it was possible to watch 64 hours of westerns each week.

One of the first, *Gunsmoke,* ran through 635 half-hour episodes. It was estimated that a quarter of the world's population saw at least one program in which Marshall Matt Dillon made Dodge City, Kansas, safe for decent, law-abiding citizens. Another popular show, *Death Valley Days,* revived the career of actor Ronald Reagan and set him off on a trail that led to the White House.

"Mad Man" Muntz

The early television industry was a competitive free-for-all, with dozens of manufacturers hoping to establish themselves as giants of the industry. One of the most intriguing contenders was Muntz TV, which hawked its inexpensive sets as if they were gadgets at a county fair. "Mad Man" Muntz told television viewers that he got his name because he wanted to give his sets away but his wife would not let him: "She says I'm crazy." There was, inevitably, a "shakeout," and Muntz was shaken out. The industry was dominated by a few, mostly established, electronics companies like RCA. In the 1970s, American TV manufacturers were largely displaced by Japanese imports.

Quiz shows offering large prizes—$64,000 and up—also caught the popular imagination. Millions watched entranced as intellectuals and idiot savants rattled off the names of opera characters and kings of Poland. Then, in 1959, it was revealed that Charles Van Doren, a Columbia University professor and scion of a distinguished academic family, had been fed the correct answers before broadcasts of *The $64,000 Question.* It would not have been so bad had Van Doren not agonized like a soap opera heroine as he pretended to retrieve some obscure morsel of knowledge from deep within his mind. Academics said they were shocked—absolutely shocked—by Van Doren's betrayal of their integrity. Ordinary folks just changed the channel. *Gunsmoke* was still going strong, although its writers admitted some stress coming up with plots. "We've used up De Maupassant," said one, "and we're halfway through Maugham."

Social and Cultural Consequences

The social and cultural consequences of America's marriage to the "boob tube" are still not fully appreciated. In the short run, television seemed near to killing off other popular entertainment, such as the movies, social dancing, and radio. Hollywood studios that specialized in churning out low-budget films, like Republic Studios, went bankrupt because the neighborhood theaters that showed them on weekdays could not compete and had to shut down. However, prestigious studios like Metro-Goldwyn-Mayer, Columbia, and Warner Brothers survived by producing epics so spectacular that the small black-and-white TV screen could not rival them. Some producers cautiously experimented with themes that TV home entertainment avoided with a shudder, mostly sex—what else? Only when Hollywood began producing shows for TV, however, did the industry prosper as it had before television.

TV and the Movies

In 1946, 82 million Americans went to the movies each week. Ten years later, only about half that many did. The other half was at home with the boob tube.

The big bands that had toured the country, playing for local dances since the 1930s, broke up when deserted dance halls closed. However, the recorded music industry was untouched. It merely shifted from dance bands to ballad singers like Perry Como, Jo Stafford, Patti Page, Tony Bennett, and Frankie Laine, who could promote sales of their recordings on television. Radio adapted to the big change by scrapping the dramatic and comedy shows that television could do with pictures, and offering instead a format of recorded music, news, sports, and weather aimed at people who were driving their cars or who, when they were working, could not watch TV.

Curiously, the "one-eyed monster" did not much change the reading habits of adult Americans. They were staring into the flickering blue light for three hours a day, but the time they devoted to magazines and newspapers declined very little. Purchases of books, particularly cheap paperback editions, rose 53 percent over what they had been during the 1940s.

What Americans cut out in order to watch TV was socializing with one another. Instead of chatting with neighbors or with relatives on the phone, instead of meeting at dances and clubs, Americans barricaded themselves in their homes, hushing up and resenting all interruptions. The frozen food industry invented the "TV dinner," a complete meal that could be put in and taken out of the oven during commercials and eaten in silence from a "TV table," a metal tray on folding legs, one for each member of the nuclear family, perhaps an extra pair for when grandparents paid a visit. Shhh!

Fears for the Future

Rather more worrying was the passive zeal with which children were enslaved to the tube. Networks and local stations filled late-afternoon hours and Saturday and Sunday mornings with programs aimed at children, gladly sponsored by toy makers and manufacturers of breakfast cereals and sweets. If adults who grew up before television continued to read, children did not. In 1955, a book by Rudolf Fleisch called *Why Johnny Can't Read* presented Americans with disturbing evidence that they were raising a generation of functional illiterates.

Nevertheless, and regardless of class, race, occupation, or region, Americans took television to their hearts. For good or ill, they were exposed at the same moment to the same entertainment, commercials, and even speech patterns. Because the networks preferred announcers who spoke "standard American English," regional variations in speech began to decline. City people and country people, sharply divided by different worldviews a generation earlier, came to look, speak, and think alike.

SUBURBIA AND ITS VALUES

Neither country folk nor urbanites set the cultural tone of the 1950s. The people who did were the pioneers of a brand-new kind of community, the middle-class automobile suburb.

▲ *Levittown, New York. Just about every house was identical to every other. When the Levitts perfected their mass-production techniques, they had a house ready for occupancy every 15 minutes.*

The essence of the good life, in the 1950s, was to set up house in a single-family dwelling in a "tract" or "subdivision" where everything was new.

Flight from the Cities

The massive shift in population from cities to suburbs had a racial component. It was "white flight," middle- and working-class white families fleeing the spread of African American neighborhoods that had begun during the war when southern blacks poured into northern cities to escape segregation and find factory jobs. Expanding African American neighborhoods intruded into white neighborhoods, and conflict, especially between teenagers, increased.

Aside from the increase in black population in the cities, the virtual suspension of residential construction during the war presented recently married white couples—four years worth of them at once in 1945—with a serious housing shortage. The few apartments and houses available in cities brought premium prices.

Demolishing old neighborhoods to build new housing—necessarily tall apartment buildings—temporarily worsened the shortage. The solution, first understood by the Levitt brothers, who had built barracks for the military during the war, was to develop entirely new communities far enough from the cities that land was cheap, close enough to them that breadwinners could get to work. Of the million housing starts in 1946 (2 million in 1950), compared with 142,000 in 1944, the vast majority were in the suburbs.

The Levitts mass-produced housing. In their first development, Levittown, New York, they used only two or three different blueprints. The houses of Levittown were identical, constructed all at once and very quickly. An army of excavating machines descended on a potato farm, grading hundreds of acres at a sweep and laying out miles of gently curving streets within a few days. Before they were done, battalions of men laid down water, gas, sewer, and electrical lines, while teams of carpenters began to erect hundreds of simple, identical shells at one time.

Then came waves of roofers, plumbers, electricians, painters, and others, each finishing its specialized task on a house within hours or even minutes. They trotted from one to the next. The Levitts had guessed right. Buyers were so anxious they bought from maps and offered to take care of cleaning up themselves rather than delay moving in for a few days. Overnight, Levittown was a city of 17,000 occupied homes. The Levitts and imitators worked similar miracles on the outskirts of every large city. By 1960, as many Americans lived in suburbs as in large cities.

Bland Conformists or Social Trailblazers?

Suburbia insisted its inhabitants conform to unwritten rules as rigorously as any peasant village ever had. The adult population of the new communities was homogeneous: 95 percent white, 20 to 30 years of age, with young children, lots of children, almost all the families living on roughly the same income from skilled occupations and white-collar jobs.

Except for those with strong attachments to unions, suburbanites were staunch supporters of the Eisenhower equilibrium. Orange County, a supersuburb of Los Angeles, was notorious for voting Republican. Critics of suburbanites called their culture superficial and bland. They swelled the membership lists of churches and synagogues but insisted religion not disturb them. Rabbi Joshua Liebman, Catholic Bishop Fulton J. Sheen, and the Reverend Norman Vincent Peale became wealthy by preaching that the purpose of religion was to make people feel good. The Reverend Billy Graham emerged as the country's leading revivalist by shelving the fire-and-brimstone side of the revival tradition.

A survey of Christians showed that although 80 percent believed that the Bible was the revealed word of God, only 35 percent could name the authors of the four gospels (50 percent could not name one). Jewish suburbanites founded Reform temples that rejected traditional practices that set them apart from their Christian neighbors, particularly dietary laws and strict observance of the Sabbath.

Suburban life was insular, in part because home ownership demanded time to keep the place up. In the age of McCarthyism, William Levitt imputed profound political portent to his mass-produced housing. "The man who owns his own home and lot," he said, "cannot be a communist. He has too much to do." The new communities had been built without the corner stores that provided city people with their needs and daily shoppers with a daily social life a short walk from the front door. Suburbanites bought their food, cleansers, and toilet paper at supermarkets along the highways where the tracts had been built. They drove to them, perhaps listening to the radio, but not socializing.

And yet, the very newness of their communities required the suburbanites to devise new ways of doing things and new institutions from scratch. Lacking established

Elevator Music

"Elevator music," deliberately bland music played at low volume in the background in restaurants, hotels, offices, shops—and elevators—is heard by more than 100 million Americans each day. It was called "furniture music" by its creator, a composer named Eric Satie, who said in 1920 that it would "fill the same role as light and heat—as *comfort*." Satie urged Americans, "Don't enter a house which does not have furniture music," but the concept caught on only after 1934, when the name "Muzak" was coined.

Muzak is played in the Pentagon and in the White House. President Lyndon Johnson pumped Muzak all over his ranch in Texas by mounting speakers on trees. After the advent of automated phone answering systems that put callers on hold until a customer service representative was available, practically everyone phoning a big business or government agency got to hum along for at least a few minutes.

▲ *This photographer caught several characteristics of suburbia: the idyll early residents found in their new life; the cars in the driveway (although most have gone to work with father); mother attractively dressed in the latest style even to water the lawn; and children everywhere.*

social services and governments, they formed an intricate network of voluntary associations entirely supported by private funds and energies. There were the new churches and synagogues, thousands of new chapters of political parties, garden clubs, literary societies, and bowling leagues. School districts and school boards had to be created. Most important of all were extrascholastic programs revolving around suburban children: dancing schools, Cub Scouts and Brownies, little leagues, community swimming pools.

With everyone a stranger in town, the informal cocktail party and backyard barbecue were effective ways for people to introduce themselves to one another. Unlike at a formal dinner, guests milled around the stand-up parties, finding compatible friends painlessly—and efficiently. Alcohol lubricated conversation among strangers, and statisticians noticed that suburbia effected a change in American drinking habits. Consumption of neutral spirits like gin and vodka, which could be disguised in sweet soda pop or fruit juices for people who did not particularly like the taste of booze, soared. Whiskey, the all-American liquor with a decidedly acquired taste, declined in popularity.

Insolent Chariots

Suburbia would not have been possible had not automobiles been readily available. Most of the postwar developments were built where public transportation did not exist or, at best, commuter train stations were miles away. In turn, the

growth of suburbia made the automobile king, a necessity of life and, in some ways, a tyrant. Every family needed a car. Even when father took the train to the city, he had to be driven to the station. And the suburban housewife clocked dozens, even a hundred, miles a day: buying groceries, shopping, and, most of all, chauffeuring children from school to doctor and dentist and from little league to dance lessons to, in the sea of children, an interminable series of birthday parties. The demand for the automobile was so great that the two-car family became a common phenomenon: One suburban family in five owned two vehicles.

Sales of new cars rose from none during the war to 6.7 million in 1950 and continued at that level. In 1945, there were 25.8 million automobiles registered in the United States. By 1960, with the population increased by 35 percent, car ownership more than doubled, to 61.7 million vehicles.

The automobile was the most important means by which people displayed their status. Unlike the size of paychecks and bank accounts, the family car showed; it sat in the driveway for all to see. Automobile manufacturers created finely honed images for their chariots. The family that was "moving up" could show it by "trading up" from a humble Ford, Plymouth, or Chevy to a Dodge, Pontiac, or Mercury, and

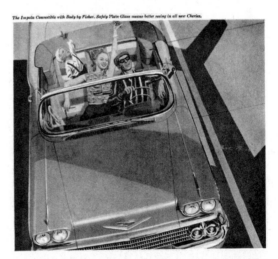

The Impala Convertible with Body by Fisher. Safety Plate Glass means better seeing in all new Chevies.

YOU'LL HAVE PLENTY TO SHOW OFF *in the high-spirited performance of your* **NEW CHEVROLET.** *With its radical new Turbo-Thrust V8* and new action in all engines, it's so quick, agile and eager that once you take the wheel, you'll never want to leave it. You've got your hands on something really special!*

Your pride can't help showing just a bit when you slide behind the wheel of this new Chevrolet. You couldn't be sitting prettier—and you know it.

You're in charge of one of the year's most looked at, most longed for cars. Chevy's crisply sculptured contours and downright luxurious interiors are enough to make anybody feel like a celebrity.

Move your foot a fraction on the gas pedal and you feel the instant, silken response of a unique new kind of V8. You ride smoothly and serenely—cushioned by deep coil springs at every wheel. You can even have a real air ride*, if you wish.

See your Chevrolet dealer. . . . Chevrolet Division of General Motors, Detroit 2, Mich. **Optional at extra cost.*

CHEVROLET

▲ *Chevrolet, Ford, and Plymouth were the lowest-priced American cars and the best-sellers. All three (all American cars!) were big, and advertisements made them look even bigger. With only one child, unusual in 1958, the date of this ad, this couple, Mom a Marilyn Monroe look-alike, could impress the neighbors with their sportiness.*

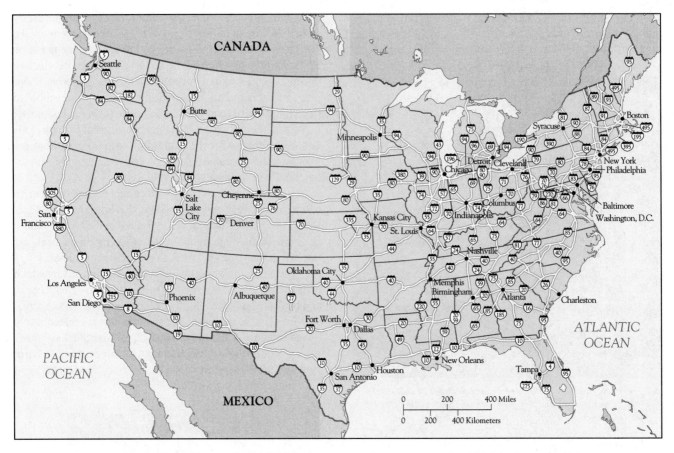

MAP 46:1 Interstate Highway System   The interstate highway system as originally conceived. The final digit of east-west highways was an even number; that of north-south highways, an odd number. Later, three-digit interstates, mostly ring roads around large cities, were added.

could talk about owning a Chrysler, Lincoln, or Cadillac. Easy credit made it possible for people to "keep up with the Joneses" by buying beyond their means, going deeply into debt for the sake of appearances. From 1946 through 1970, short-term loans—money borrowed to buy consumer goods—increased from $8 billion to $127 billion!

The Automobile Economy

Nearly universal car ownership in the suburbs promoted the growth of businesses devoted to cars or dependent on them. Service stations (gasoline consumption doubled during the 1950s), parts stores, car washes, drive-in restaurants, and drive-in movie theaters blossomed around residential suburbs. The suburban shopping "mall" or "plaza" replaced the city center in suburban lives. In 1945, there were 8 automobile-oriented shopping centers in the United States. In 1960, there were almost 4,000.

Automobiles demanded roads. In 1956, Washington responded with the Interstate Highway Act, under which the government began pumping $1 billion a year into road construction. (By 1960, this rose to $2.9 billion a year.) Over 41,000 miles of the new highways ran cross-country, but 5,000 miles of freeway were urban, connecting suburbs to big cities.

Not only did this road network encourage further suburban sprawl, but it made the cities even less livable for all but

the rich. Already sapped of their middle classes, once-lively urban neighborhoods were carved into isolated run-down residential islands walled off by the massive concrete abutments of the freeways. Suburbanite cars roared in on them daily, clogging the streets, raising noise levels, and fouling the air. Progressively poorer (and blacker) without a middle-class tax base, cities deteriorated physically and suffered from underfunded schools and hospitals and rising crime rates. During the 1960s, city-center department stores and light industries joined the movement to the suburbs, relocating in shopping centers or on empty tracts near the residential suburbs. When they left, they took not only the taxes they had paid but jobs previously available to city dwellers.

The Baby Boom

During the 1930s, about 2.5 million babies were born in the United States each year. In 1946, the total was 3.4 million. No one was surprised. The war had separated millions of couples for years. After a few years of catching up, demographers said, the lower birthrate typical of the first half of the century would reassert itself. They were wrong. Annual births continued to increase until 1961 (4.2 million) and did not drop to pre–baby boom levels until the 1970s.

Although all social groups participated in the baby boom, children were most noticeable in suburbia because

The World of Fashion

In 1840, the British consul in Boston noted that Americans did not observe social proprieties in dressing. Instead of wearing clothing appropriate to their social station, Americans dressed more or less alike, and democracy of dress did not mean a drabbest common denominator. On the contrary, servant girls were "strongly infected with the national bad taste for being over-dressed; they are, when walking the streets, scarcely to be distinguished from their employers." They were *fashionable.*

By the mid–twentieth century, the democratization of fashion was complete. The wealthy had a monopoly on the latest from Paris for only as long as it took the American garment industry to copy designs and mass-produce cheap versions of expensive "originals." Indeed, the insistence of American women of every social class on their right to dress as the arbiters of fashion pleased shortened the natural life cycle of a fashion. The only way the wealthy woman could display her immunity to spending restraints was to jump rapidly from one "look" to another, always, if frantically, ahead of the power shears and sewing machines of New York's garment district. In 1940, the American clothing industry was taking in $3 billion annually. By the end of the 1950s, it was, by some criteria, the third largest industry in the United States.

The fashions of the Second World War were a product of four forces: the effective shutdown of the design business in German-occupied Paris; the rationing of materials; the prominence of the military in daily life; and the entry of women into the professions and jobs previously held by men.

American designers had been so dependent on Paris for ideas. So, they were disoriented by the fall of France and able on their own to come up with only a variant on the 1930s styles. A factor forcing change was the government's restrictions on the amount of fabric that might go into clothing. Skirts could be no larger than 72 inches around. Belts more than 2 inches wide, more than one patch pocket on blouses, and generous hems were forbidden, as were frills, fringes, and flounces. The result was a severe look in women's dress, accentuated by the fact that with so many uniforms on the streets, civilian clothing took on a military look. It also took on a "masculine" look; the silhouette of women's clothing was straight and angular, with padded shoulders emulating the male physique.

In 1947, Christian Dior, a Paris designer, reestablished French primacy in the fashion world. His "New Look" cele-brated the end of wartime shortages with long, full, and flowing skirts. More interesting, Dior proclaimed a new femininity in fashion. "Your bosoms, your shoulders and hips are round, your waist is tiny, your skirt's bulk suggests fragile feminine legs," an American fashion editor wrote. Dior blouses were left unbuttoned at the top, and more formal bodices were cut in a deep V or cut low to expose shoulders.

The Frenchman was either very lucky or a very shrewd psychologist. In the United States, the chief market for fashion in the postwar years, women were opting in droves for the home over the office, factory, and public life. But the domesticity of the 1950s did not mean long hours of tedious, dirty housework. Thanks to labor-saving home appliances and the money to buy them, a yen for recreation and partying after the austere years of rationing, and the slow but steady relaxation of moral codes, the 1950s housewife was able to be "fashionable" and was, in the New Look created by Christian Dior.

Another postwar phenomenon affecting fashion was the baby boom. Just as the numerical dominance of young people led to juvenile themes in films and popular music, the two-thirds of the female population that was under 30 years of age affected the way all women dressed. "For the first time in fashion," wrote Jane Dormer, "clothes that had originally been intended for children climbed up the ladder into the adult wardrobe." Although Dior and the Parisian couturiers continued to decree what was worn on formal occasions, American teenagers set the standards for casual wear, not only for themselves but for women of all but the most advanced ages. The most conspicuous of these styles was that of the ingenue: "childlike circular skirts," crinolines, hoop skirts, and frilled petticoats that were seen not only at junior high school dances but at cocktail parties on mothers of five. Women began to wear their hair loose and flowing or in ponytails, both styles earlier associated with juveniles.

Hollywood both responded to and fed the fashion by coming up with actresses such as Audrey Hepburn, Debbie Reynolds, and Sandra Dee, who specialized in innocent, naive, little-girlish parts. Well into their 30s, they (and their emulators) clung to what clothing historian Anne Fogarty has called the "paper doll look." Not until the 1960s, when women adopted new values, would this fashion, like all fashions to a later age, look ridiculous.

---

almost all suburban adults were young. Proportionately, children were more numerous there than in city or country. Businesses catering to children, from toy stores to diaper services, were suburban fixtures.

Beginning about 1952, when the first boom babies started school, massive efforts were required to provide educational and recreational facilities for them. As the baby boomers matured, they attracted attention to the needs of each age group they swelled. By the end of the 1950s, economists observed that middle-class teenagers were a significant consumer group in their own right. They had $10 billion to spend each year, every cent of it discretionary! Their necessities were provided by their doting parents.

Young people's magazines appeared, *Seventeen* (clothing and cosmetics for girls) and *Hot Rod* (automobiles for boys). Film studios made movies about adolescents and their problems. In the 1950s, teenagers claimed a new kind of popular music—rock 'n' roll—as peculiarly their own. Rock 'n' roll was derived from African American rhythm and blues but sanitized for juveniles and usually performed by whites.

Rock 'n' roll could be seen as rebellious, always a come-on for adolescents. Elvis Presley, a truck driver from Memphis, might have been ignored had his career depended on his superb baritone. But he entranced teenagers and scandalized their parents with an act that included suggestive hip movements. Mostly, however, unlike rhythm and blues,

▲ Rebel Without a Cause *was aimed at teenagers. Its theme, the rebellion of well-to-do Los Angeles teenagers, could not attract adults, all of whom were depicted as boorish or insensitive, unlike, of course, young people.*

rock 'n' roll was juvenile. Whereas the older pop music dealt with themes more or less adult, the new music's subjects were senior proms, double-dating, and teenage lovers lost tragically to their friends while racing to beat the Twentieth Century Limited to the crossing. A new kind of record, the nearly unbreakable 45-rpm disk that sold for only 89 cents, competed very well for teenage dollars.

St. Paul recognized that children did childish things. But what of the adults of the 1950s who adopted adolescent fashions, ideals, and role models? By the end of the decade, one of television's most popular programs was *American Bandstand,* an afternoon show on which teenagers rock 'n' rolled to the latest records and expressed adolescent opinions. Teenagers watched it, of course, but so did housewives at their ironing boards. Adults discussed the relative merits of their favorite pubescent dancers. Never before had adult society taken so much notice of teenage culture. The baby boom generation seemed to take little notice of adults.

A New Role for Women

Middle-class America's twin obsessions with enjoying life and catering to its children caused a significant, if passing, shift in the status of women. Since the beginning of the century, women of all social classes had been moving into occupations and professions that had been masculine monopolies.

By the 1940s, women were still a minority of physicians and lawyers, although they were no longer oddities. During the war, Rosie the Riveter seemed to have hastened the blurring of the line between what men did and what women did.

When the war ended, however, women embraced the traditional roles of wife, homemaker, and mother. By the 1950s, middle America once more assumed that woman's place was in the home. The 1950s woman was not the shrinking violet of the nineteenth century. She was constantly out and about, the vortex of a lively social whirl. Wives, as sociable hostesses and companions, were considered partners in furthering their husbands' careers. Women's magazines like *Cosmopolitan* and *Redbook* (although not the *Ladies Home Journal*) first hinted, then shouted, that wives should be "sexy."

Sexiness got a sort of boost from two books by University of Indiana Professor Alfred Kinsey, *Sexual Behavior in the Human Male* (1948) and *Sexual Behavior in the Human Female* (1953). Although Kinsey phrased his conclusions from 18,000 interviews in dry-as-dust social sciences prose, his revelation that premarital and extramarital sexual intercourse, unorthodox sexual practices, and homosexual episodes were common made for sensational reading and intense discussion. Poor Kinsey was condemned as promoting immorality, unnatural practices, and unspeakable acts, and even of being a Communist.

AGAINST THE GRAIN

There would be no significant challenge to sexy domesticity until 1963, when Betty Friedan published *The Feminine Mystique.* In this best-seller, Friedan said that American women had lost ground in their fight for emancipation since 1945. She defined the home as a prison, woman as sex objects as demeaning, and said that women should move out into the world of jobs, politics, and other realms Friedan defined as productive. She was not the only critic of postwar popular culture.

Dissenters

As early as 1942, Philip Wylie's *Generation of Vipers* told the country that indulgence of children, particularly by their mothers ("Momism"), was creating tyrannical monsters. When juvenile delinquency rates soared during the 1950s, his book enjoyed a second, much larger sale. John Keats attacked the sterility of suburban life, especially the social irresponsibility of the developers who left new developments without vital social centers. Later, in *Insolent Chariots,* he turned his attention to the automobile as an economic tyrant and a socially destructive force.

In *The Organization Man* (1956), William H. Whyte Jr. fastened on the workplace, arguing that jobs in the huge corporations and government bureaucracies that dominated the American economy placed the highest premium on anonymity, lack of imagination and enterprise, and conformity.

Sociologist David Riesman suggested in *The Lonely Crowd* (1950) that Americans were becoming "other-directed." They no longer took their values from their heritage, from within themselves, but thought and acted according to what was acceptable to those around them.

Sloan Wilson fictionalized the conformism and cultural aridity of suburban life in *The Man in the Gray Flannel Suit* (1955), a novel about a suburban commuter who works in the advertising industry. In *The Hidden Persuaders* (1957), Vance Packard reinforced the assault on advertising by pointing out that all Americans were manipulated by advertisements that played not on the virtues of the product for sale but on feelings and insecurities.

Beatniks and Squares

The beat generation, or "beatniks," had a less articulate critique of Eisenhower tranquility. Originally a literary movement centered around novelist Jack Kerouac and poet Allen Ginsberg, "beat" evolved into a bohemian lifestyle in New York's Greenwich Village, San Francisco's North Beach, and Venice, California.

Beatniks rejected what they considered the intellectually and socially stultifying culture of the 1950s. They shunned mainstream employment and mocked consumerism and conformity by dressing in T-shirts and rumpled khaki trousers. Beatnik women used no cosmetics and did not "do" their hair. They made an issue of the lack of furniture in their cheap walk-up apartments, called "pads" after the mattress on the floor.

The beatniks were intellectual. They prided themselves on discovering and discussing obscure writers and philosophers, particularly exponents of an abstruse form of Buddhism called Zen. They rejected the ostensibly strict sexual morality of the "squares" and lived together without benefit of marriage. Their music was jazz as played by blacks, whom they regarded as free of the corruption of white America.

Beatniks simultaneously repelled, amused, and fascinated conventional Americans. Moralists demanded that police raid beatnik coffeehouses in search of marijuana (which beatniks introduced to white America) and amateur poets reading sexually explicit verse.

But sexual mores were changing in suburbia too. To be divorced was no longer to be shunned as a leper. The courts approved the publication of books formerly banned as obscene, with celebrated cases revolving around D. H. Lawrence's *Lady Chatterley's Lover* and Henry Miller's *Tropic of Cancer*. The furor over Ginsberg's long poem *Howl* (1955) made it a best-seller. Suburbanites, the favorite targets of the beatniks, flocked to Greenwich Village and North Beach on weekends to dabble in beatnik fashions. Like most cultural rebels, the beatniks did not really challenge society's basic assumptions. They merely provided another form of entertainment.

Black America's Fight for Civil Rights

Rather than sniping at trivialities like "lifestyle," African American protest set out to demonstrate to whites that the mansion America built in the 1950s included a cellar in

A beatnik coffeehouse. To moralists, it replaced the saloon as the American den of iniquity. No alcohol was served, but the patrons were scruffy and racially mixed, and they listened to poetry considered obscene (which was its only virtue—almost all beatnik poetry was terrible).

AP/Wide World Photos

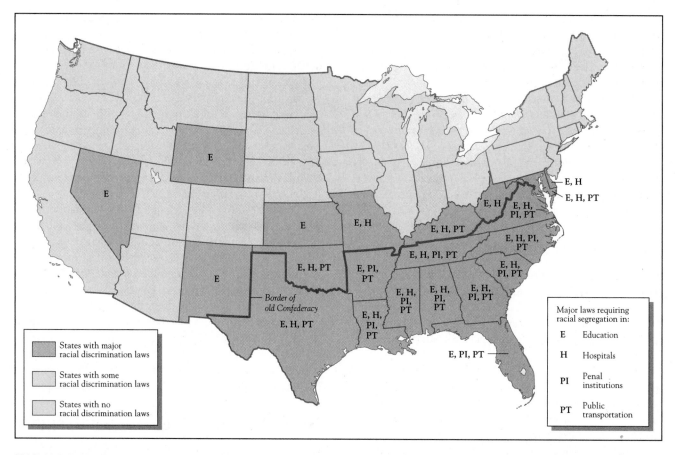

MAP 46:2 Racial Segregation, 1949 The legal "color line" was close to absolute in the former slave states, but a majority of states had some sort of law discriminating against African Americans in public accommodations. Pennsylvania, shown here as having no racial discrimination laws, had one state teacher's college for blacks only. In the New Jersey seashore resort of Wildwood, African Americans were, by custom, restricted to one small section of beach and to one night when they were allowed on the boardwalk.

which basic civil rights were systematically denied to 15 million people.

For more than half a century, black leaders such as DuBois, Mary McLeod Bethune, A. Philip Randolph, and Bayard Rustin had fought a frustrating battle against racial prejudice. Their most important organization, the National Association for the Advancement of Colored People, won some significant victories in the courts. Lynching almost disappeared in the 1950s. Under Truman, the armed forces were desegregated (black recruits were no longer placed in all-black units), and the Supreme Court ordered several southern states to admit blacks to state-supported professional schools because the segregated medical and legal training they offered blacks was not equal in quality to that provided for whites.

Nevertheless, when Eisenhower moved into the White House, the former slave states plus Oklahoma and Kansas retained laws that segregated parks, movie theaters, waiting rooms, trains, buses, and schools. A few other states permitted one form or another of racial segregation. (Fifteen states explicitly prohibited it.)

In the Deep South, public drinking fountains and toilets were labeled "white" and "colored," and some states provided different Bibles in court for swearing in witnesses. This color line had had federal sanction since 1896, when,

in the case of *Plessy v. Ferguson,* the Supreme Court declared that racially separate public facilities were constitutional as long as they were equal in quality.

The Brown Case

In 1954, Thurgood Marshall, the National Association for the Advancement of Colored People's legal strategist, argued before the Supreme Court that racially separate schools were intrinsically unequal because segregation burdened African Americans with a constant reminder of their inequality. In *Brown v. Board of Education of Topeka* (1954), the Court unanimously agreed.

In some parts of the South, school administrators complied quickly and without incident. Southern white distaste for Jim Crow segregation was quiet, but it did exist. However, in Little Rock, Arkansas, in September 1957, a mob of white adults greeted the first black pupils to enroll in Central High School with shouts, curses, and rocks. Claiming that he was protecting the peace, but actually currying the favor of white racists, Governor Orval Faubus called out the Arkansas National Guard to prevent the black children from enrolling.

Privately, Eisenhower blamed the turmoil on Earl Warren, the chief justice he had appointed, as well as Faubus.

Jackie Robinson

Not a single major-league city was truly southern, but big-league baseball remained strictly (although unofficially) white longer than any other sport. After World War II, Branch Rickey, owner of the Brooklyn Dodgers, decided it was time to end the color line. There were better African American players in the Negro League than Jackie Robinson. But he was the league's youngest star, an all-around athlete, and Rickey believed he had the character to survive the taunts of both fans and other players. He asked Robinson, for the sake of proving whites and blacks could play together, to put up with abuse in silence for two years. Robinson began major-league play in 1947. Although he was naturally feisty, he kept his promise to Rickey for an entire season and won the Rookie of the Year award. By the end of the season, Larry Doby had been hired by the Cleveland Indians. In 1948, more African Americans were playing in the big leagues, and Robinson figured he need no longer put up with the often vile abuse. He began to fight back and lost no fans because of his insistence on complete equality.

▲ *The "colored waiting room" at a train depot. Since 1896, separate public facilities were legal if they were "equal." They rarely were, by any measure. Thurgood Marshall, of the National Association for the Advancement of Colored People, persuaded the Supreme Court to declare segregated schools unconstitutional because, by their very separation, even well-funded African American schools taught their pupils they were not equal in rights.*

Sharing the belief of many Americans that no great harm was done by school segregation, Eisenhower regarded the Brown decision as a mistake. By arousing African Americans to protest, it disturbed the tranquility that Ike treasured. Nevertheless, the Court had spoken. To Ike, a Supreme Court ruling had the force of federal law, and Faubus was defying it. Eisenhower superseded the governor's command of the National Guard and ordered the troops to enforce the integration of Central High. Overnight, the mission of the Arkansas National Guard was reversed.

From the Courts to the Streets

The battle to integrate the schools dragged on for a decade. Beginning in 1955, however, the civil rights movement ceased to be a protest of lawyers and lawsuits and became a peaceful revolution by hundreds of thousands of blacks no longer willing to be second-class citizens.

The leader of the upheaval was Martin Luther King Jr., a young preacher in Montgomery, Alabama. In December 1955, Rosa Parks, a seamstress, refused to give up her seat on a bus to a white man, as city law required. King became the spokesman for a boycott of Montgomery's buses by African Americans. The dispute attracted journalists and television reporters from all over the country.

King's house was bombed, and he explained his strategy for ending racial discrimination from the wreckage of his front porch. Nonviolent civil disobedience, King said, meant refusing to obey morally reprehensible laws such as those that sustained segregation, but without violence. When arrested, protesters should not resist. Not only was this the moral course of action, but it was politically effective. When decent white people were confronted, on their television sets, with police officers brutalizing peaceful blacks and their white supporters simply because they demanded their

rights as citizens, they would, King believed, force the politicians to change the laws.

Although it led to considerable suffering by demonstrators and to several deaths, King's strategy worked. A few important labor leaders, such as Walter Reuther of the United Automobile Workers, marched with the young minister and helped finance the Southern Christian Leadership Conference, which King founded to spearhead the fight for equality. After 1960, when the conference's youth organization, the Student Nonviolent Coordinating Committee, peacefully violated laws that prohibited blacks from eating at lunch counters in the South, white university students in the North picketed branches of the offending chain stores in their hometowns. When white mobs burned a bus on which white and black "freedom riders" were defying segregation in public transportation, the federal government sent marshals south to prosecute violent racists.

Although King fell out of favor with some younger blacks in the late 1960s, he loomed over his era as only President Eisenhower did, and with greater historical consequence. After his assassination in 1968, under circumstances that remain somewhat mysterious, several states made his birthday a holiday; in 1986, it became an official federal holiday. But King and African Americans only began their fight for equality during the Eisenhower years. It was the next decade, the troubled 1960s, that saw the end of civil discrimination based on race.

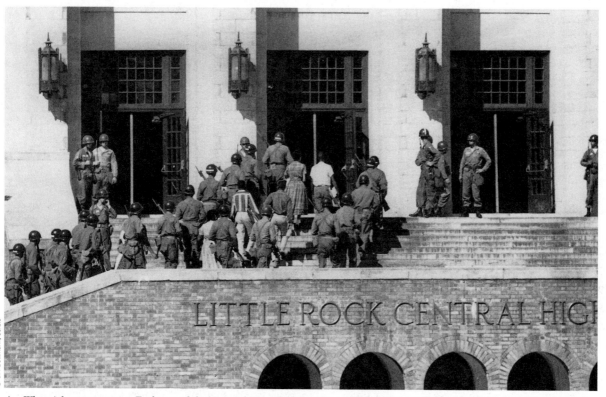

▲ *When Arkansas governor Faubus used the National Guard, a federal force, to prevent the integration of Little Rock's Central High School, President Eisenhower was enraged and commanded the Guard to enforce the Supreme Court's decision.*

for FURTHER READING

Solid general histories of the period include C. C. Alexander, *Holding the Line: The Eisenhower Era, 1952–1961,* 1975; James Gilbert, *Another Chance: America Since 1945,* 1984; Godfrey Hodgson, *America in Our Time: From World War II to Nixon,* 1976; William E. Leuchtenburg, *A Troubled Feast: American Society Since 1945,* 1979; and William L. O'Neill, *American High: The Years of Confidence, 1945–1960,* 1987.

On American society, in addition to O'Neill's *American High,* see Daniel Boorstin, *The Image,* 1962; John Kenneth Galbraith, *The Affluent Society,* 1958; William Chafe, *The American Woman: Her Changing Social, Economic, and Political Roles,* 1988; Eugenia Kaledin, *Mothers and More: American Women in the 1950s,* 1984; David Riesman, *The Lonely Crowd: A Study of the Changing American Character,* 1950; William H. Whyte, *The Organization Man,* 1956; and Robert C. Woods, *Suburbia,* 1959. The

bohemian dissenters of the era are treated in Bruce Cook, *The Beat Generation,* 1971.

Racial segregation and its crumbling have been studied extensively. See James Baldwin, *The Fire Next Time,* 1963, and Martin Luther King Jr., *Stride Toward Freedom,* 1958, for insights into black resentments and aspirations. Also see Archibald Cox, *The Warren Court: Constitutional Decision as an Instrument of Reform,* 1968; Richard Kluger, *Simple Justice: The History of* Brown v. Board of Education *and Black America's Struggle for Equality,* 1975; Philip B. Kurland, *Politics, the Constitution, and the Warren Court,* 1970; Louis E. Lomax, *The Negro Revolt,* 1963; Benjamin Muse, *Ten Years of Prelude: The Story of Integration Since the Supreme Court's 1954 Decision,* 1964; C. E. Silberman, *Crisis in Black and White,* 1964; and Stephen B. Oates, *Let the Trumpet Sound: The Life of Martin Luther King, Jr.,* 1982.

AMERICAN JOURNEY ONLINE AND INFOTRAC COLLEGE EDITION

Visit the source collections at http://ajaccess.wadsworth.com and http://infotrac.thomsonlearning.com, and use the Search function with the following key terms to explore documents, images, audio and video clips, articles, and commentary related to the material in this chapter:

Baby boom
Beatnik
Betty Friedan
Brown v. Board of Education
Dwight D. Eisenhower

Interstate Highway Act
Jackie Robinson
Quiz shows
Television
The Feminine Mystique

HISTORY ONLINE

Ad Access

http://scriptorium.lib.duke.edu/adaccess/browse.html

Advertisements for consumer goods from the 1910s to the 1950s, including ads for television sets.

Afro-American Almanac

http://w.toptags.com/aama/

Documents and photographs dealing with the Civil Rights Movement.

47

IKE AND CAMELOT

*Policies Under
Eisenhower and Kennedy
1953–1963*

© UPI-Bettmann/Corbis

*The middle of the road is all of the usable surface. The
extremes, right and left, are in the gutters.*

Dwight D. Eisenhower

*We stand today on the edge of a new frontier—the
frontier of the 1960s—a frontier of unknown opportunities and perils—a frontier of unfulfilled hopes and
threats.*

John F. Kennedy

DWIGHT D. EISENHOWER and John F. Kennedy were
very different presidents. They were of different generations and different political parties; they differed significantly in both their policies and personal styles. The decade
during which they lived in the White House, however, seems
in retrospect to have comprised a coherent era. Americans
were prosperous as never before and despite the anxieties of
the Cold War, they were confident of their society in ways
they have never been since. The conflicts, turmoil, and tur-
bulence that showed themselves soon after the assassination
of President Kennedy in 1963 created an America that may
not be a worse place than the America "before Dallas" (the
city in which Kennedy was killed) but that is a country less
at peace with itself.

MODERATION AT
HOME AND ABROAD

Dwight D. Eisenhower was an old-fashioned man. As a career soldier, he had been insulated just enough from political and social developments that he could still think about
government as people had in the small towns in Kansas and
Texas in which he had grown up at the turn of the century.
As president, he soon realized that the wealthy businessmen
who had befriended him after the war did not really believe
in the platitudes about free enterprise that he swapped with
them and that he gave voice to in his speeches. But he sincerely did.

The tremendous expansion of the federal government
during the New Deal and Second World War disturbed Eisenhower. Perhaps because the peacetime army in which he
served before 1940 had been so stingily funded, he shuddered at the size of the federal budget. As an officer, just a
major when the war began, he had worked within stringent

budgets. He had no choice. So he was appalled by the annual deficits that had piled up into a mountain of national debt by 1953. When he took office, and to a lesser extent throughout his presidency, he believed that businessmen in the private sector were better qualified to manage the economy than Washington's bureaucrats were. A lifetime in the military, however, had made him a pragmatist, not an ideologue. "Dynamic conservatism," the awkward name he gave his economic and social program, was a compromise between, on the one hand, traditional and right-wing Republican values and, on the other, the America the New Deal had made.

Dynamic Conservatism

Ike's secretary of agriculture, Ezra Taft Benson of Utah, was an unabashed reactionary in his hostility toward government regulation and social welfare programs. Given his way, Benson would have rampaged like an avenging angel through the federal bureaucracies that implemented them.

When Dr. Jonas Salk developed a vaccine that promised to wipe out polio, a scourge of children, Secretary of Health, Education, and Welfare Oveta Culp Hobby said the federal government would not fund an immunization program. That would be socialistic.

Secretary of Defense Charles Wilson (formerly the head of General Motors) sounded like a ghost from the Coolidge era when he told a Senate committee that "what is good for the country is good for General Motors and vice versa."

Many officials in the administration shared these views, but Eisenhower did not. Benson's Agriculture Department continued to subsidize agriculture. Indeed, when grain production outstripped demand and farm income dipped, farm subsidies were increased.

▲ *A scene most Americans saw in 1954 or 1955: mothers with preschool children lined up to be injected with the Salk polio vaccine. Schoolchildren were inoculated at school.*

The Soil Bank Act of 1956 authorized the payment of money to landowners for every acre they took out of cultivation. Within 10 years, one of every six dollars that farmers and agricultural corporations pocketed came not from sales of their produce but from the federal government—for crops that were never planted.

When Congress was flooded with angry protests of Hobby's statement from the parents of the baby boomers, Ike gave his blessing to a federal program to immunize children. His administration purchased surplus crops to be used in school lunch programs as well as in foreign aid.

And General Motors did not run the country. Early on, Eisenhower discovered the risks of trusting his businessmen friends too closely when he backed a private company, Dixon-Yates, in a dispute with the Tennessee Valley Authority as to which would construct and run a new generating facility for the Atomic Energy Commission. Rather than representing "free enterprise" against "creeping socialism," Dixon-Yates, Ike discovered, was mired deeply in collusion with Atomic Energy Commission officials in what amounted to a raid on the treasury—"socialism for the rich." He withdrew his support of Dixon-Yates and accepted a face-saving compromise in which the city of Memphis, in the public sector but not the "socialistic" Tennessee Valley Authority, built the plant. In his farewell address in 1960, Eisenhower warned of the power of the "military-industrial complex," high-ranking army and navy officers shoveling federal money to defense contractors in return for high-paying sinecures when they retired from the service.

In 1957 and 1958, a serious recession threw 7 percent of the workforce out of their jobs. Ike responded with several New Deal–like public works projects. More than 10 million names were added to the list of Social Security recipients during Eisenhower's presidency. "Dynamic conservatism" was not the conservatism of Robert Taft.

Continuation of the Cold War

The Cold War continued under Eisenhower. Indeed, every president between Harry S. Truman and William J. Clinton had to shape their foreign policies around the central fact that the United States was locked into an often tense confrontation with the Soviet Union that required well-thought-out and delicate maneuvers.

In 1953, the Soviet Union had been a nuclear power for four years. (Great Britain exploded its first atomic bomb in 1952.) The Soviets had planes capable of reaching the United States, but, with American air bases throughout western Europe, there was no question that America would suffer less in a nuclear exchange than the Soviets would. Moreover, the United States had begun construction of a hydrogen bomb potentially a thousand times more powerful than the fission bombs that were in both American and Russian arsenals.

Still, a nuclear attack on the Soviet Union would be a war against civilians in cities, not against soldiers. A secret study in 1953 revealed that dropping atomic bombs on the huge Soviet armies in eastern Europe would have negligible effect on their capacity to sweep across western Europe, where the cities, if not American cities, would have already been devastated by Russian bombs. Such a war was morally unacceptable to all but a few hysterical people in the military and government. Even if morality were set aside, the results of a Soviet-American war—the Warsaw Pact's conventional armies being far larger than those of the North Atlantic Treaty Organization—would run counter to the central purpose of American foreign policy since 1939: first the rescue, then the preservation, of freedom and democracy in Europe.

Containment policy was premised on the hope that, in time, a more comfortable Soviet Union would be amenable to a resolution of its confrontation with the United States that was satisfactory to both sides. Such hopes were raised in 1953 when the longtime Russian dictator, Joseph Stalin, suspicious to the point of mental imbalance in his final years, died and was succeeded by a consortium of Communist party leaders. Nonetheless, in part for reasons of economy, Eisenhower's defense policy accelerated the construction of nuclear weapons.

More Bang for a Buck

Secretary of the Treasury George Humphrey wanted to balance the federal budget, to spend no more money in a year than was collected in taxes. With Eisenhower committed to lowering taxes, this meant drastic reductions in government spending. By far the largest single item in the federal budget was the military. Secretary of State John Foster Dulles believed in managing the Soviet Union and China by threat-

ening "massive retaliation" (a code phrase for nuclear war) for any hostile actions toward the United States or its allies. Eisenhower had ended the Korean War by just such a threat. Both men's purposes could be served by a relatively inexpensive program of military spending that came to be called "more bang for a buck."

Eisenhower slashed spending on the conventional army and navy and concentrated on building up America's nuclear arsenal: atomic and hydrogen bombs and the sophisticated ships, planes, and missiles capable of delivering them to Soviet targets. The president assured Americans (and uneasy western Europeans) that his policy was strictly defensive. The United States would not start a nuclear war, he said, but the Soviet Union might very well do so or, if the Soviets were not deterred by the threat of massive retaliation, unleash their armies on western Europe.

Critics pointed out that "more bang for a buck" meant all or nothing. The United States could annihilate Soviet cities but, with a weakened conventional army and navy, might not be able to respond to localized Soviet or Chinese provocations, such as Truman had responded to in Greece, Turkey, and Korea. Secretary Humphrey was not impressed. With the frustrations of the "limited war" in Korea so recently put to rest, he growled that the United States had "no business getting into little wars." "Let's intervene decisively with all we have got," he said, "or stay out."

In fact, in 1958, when Eisenhower feared that Communists were close to striking at a government in Lebanon friendly to the United States, he was able to squelch the threat and stabilize the Lebanese government with a rapid deployment of marines.

Peaceful Coexistence

Eisenhower wanted to be remembered as a man of peace, and the United States was directly involved in no significant military action during his eight years in office. In part, he was lucky. Stalin's death was followed by several years of government by committee, a figurehead premier, and murky maneuvering for power among Russia's "collective leadership." The man who ended up on top was a rotund, homely, and very clever Ukrainian named Nikita Khrushchev, who was very different from Stalin.

Khrushchev bewildered American kremlinologists (as experts on the Soviet Union were called), and that may have been one of his intentions. At times, he was a coarse buffoon who drank too much vodka and showed it. Visiting the United Nations in New York, he stunned the assembly of dignitaries when he protested a disagreeable speech by taking off his shoe and banging it on the desk in front of him. At other times, Khrushchev was witty, charming, and ingratiating; he was slick.

In 1956, Khrushchev denounced Stalin, his totalitarian regime, and the crimes he had perpetrated. Statues of the old Bolshevik were removed almost everywhere in the Soviet Union; Stalin's corpse was removed from Lenin's tomb (Lenin stayed); Stalingrad, site of the great Soviet victory in World War II, became Volgograd. The new premier issued bellicose challenges to the United States, but then he called for "peaceful coexistence" with American capitalism. The Cold War would be resolved, Khrushchev said, by historical forces—he was decidedly a Marxist—not by armed conflict. When he said, "We will bury you," to American capitalists, he made it clear he was not their pal; but he meant, rather than war, that the world would peacefully choose the Soviet way of life.

Debate in the Kitchen

The contrast between American and Soviet ways of life in the 1950s and 1960s mocked Khrushchev's boast. If Stalin's government by terror was gone, Soviet citizens still remained under tight political controls. The secret police were more selective in their depredations than they had been but remained intact, well funded, and capable of ruthless action against dissenters. When, in 1958, Russian writer Boris Pasternak was awarded the Nobel Prize for a novel critical of the Bolshevik regime that he published abroad, *Dr. Zhivago,* Khrushchev did not jail or murder him, as Stalin would have done, but he did force Pasternak to decline the award and put him under virtual house arrest.

The Soviet economy remained sluggish, badly managed. In part because a country inestimably poorer than the

AP/Wide World Photos

▲ *Vice President Nixon's "kitchen debate" with Nikita Khrushchev, about American abundance and the drabness of Soviet daily life, was well planned—by Nixon. Photographers were positioned to catch just such shots as this: a stunned Khrushchev unable to respond.*

Suburban Landscape

Until the 1950s, most American cities were densely populated and compact. Crowded urban neighborhoods still abutted directly on open country. As late as 1940, there were 10,000 acres of farmland within the city limits of Philadelphia.

There were suburbs, but they did not resemble the classic American suburban community we know. Before the Second World War, suburbs radiated out from cities like buttons sewn on ribbons, along the commuter train lines that made them possible. Railroad suburbs were themselves compact: two- or three-story homes on small lots and apartment blocks of five and six stories. Prewar suburbanites had fled the dirt, noise, traffic, and crowding of big cities, but they had to live near the railway station that was the community's lifeline. All but the wealthiest commuters walked from their homes to the train. Shops, markets, banks, public buildings, movie theaters, and the like clustered around the railroad station.

After the war, an entirely new suburban landscape appeared. Postwar suburbs were attached to cities not by trains but by the automobile. Rather than radiating out from cities in ribbons, the new suburbs surrounded cities like a doughnut. Highways into the cities were soon inadequate for the burgeoning population, but suburban voters quickly saw to it that better roads were built (making the further growth of the doughnut possible).

To young couples moving to the suburbs from a small city apartment or a bedroom in the home of a parent, the grass lawns and sapling trees in even the least pretentious communities, like Levittown, New York, seemed like countryside. In the old railroad suburbs, only the homes of the wealthy were built on lots with large "front yards" and "backyards." Modest postwar tracts were built on quarter-acre lots, and some developers competed for buyers by advertising larger estates. To the first residents, their home was a ranch. Indeed, the domestic architecture favored by the new suburbanites was the "ranch house," the brainchild of Clifford May of San Diego. A designer of grand homes during the 1930s, May was inspired by the traditional single-story dwellings of the Hispanic Southwest, where the weather was mild (or hot), where acreage was plentiful, and where adobe construction discouraged building walls much more than 10 feet high. During the Depression, May designed about 50 homes in southern California that were, in his words, "about sunshine and informal outdoor living." His ranch houses featured courtyards and rooms with double doors that opened to the clement outdoors.

The outdoor lifestyle was not possible all year in the Northeast and Midwest. Winters were long, cold, and messy. Two-story construction made more sense by every criterion, from the cost of land to conservation of heat. But single-story homes had caught the suburban imagination and came to be a status symbol. May himself built tracts of "Yankee version" ranch houses with board-and-batten or clapboard siding instead of stucco, and shingle, rather than tile, roofs. Courtyards made no sense back East, but picture windows let a view of the outdoors in without the weather. Much of Levittown, Pennsylvania, was built in ranch houses costing between $9,900 and $15,500.

The new suburbs had no center, no railroad station surrounded by shops. However, the supermarket, a large self-service store providing just about everything needed to keep house, was ideal for the new suburbs. The supermarket dated from 1930,

when Michael Cullen opened a "warehouse grocery" on Long Island, New York. Cullen patented a shopping cart that held a week's worth of groceries, and he touted himself as "the world's greatest price wrecker." He kept costs down by locating his supermarkets in factories and warehouses that had been closed during the Depression. Landlords were delighted to sign long leases with him at minimal rents. Cullen lured shoppers to his stores by offering at cost about 300 of the 1,000 items he stocked.

In order to exploit the supermarket's bargains, however, a shopper needed a car. Until the end of World War II, supermarkets had little effect on the smaller and pricier but conveniently located mom-and-pop grocery stores and small chain neighborhood groceries, like Piggly Wiggly, A&P, and American Stores, which remained the norm of food retailing in railroad suburbs as well as cities. In 1940, there were only 6,000 supermarkets in the United States, about 1 for every 22,000 people.

By 1950, with automobile suburbs sprawling outside every large city, there were 14,000 supermarkets nationwide, 1 per 11,000 people. In 1951, new ones opened at a rate of 3 a day. By 1960, the supermarket was the chief source of the American family's daily bread. In 33,000 supermarkets (1 per 5,400 people, just about the saturation point), Americans purchased 70 percent of the food they consumed. Car-owning suburbanites had transformed the American means of food distribution as well as the landscape.

The first drive-in theater opened in 1933 in Camden, New Jersey, on a highway between Philadelphia and the seashore. Richard Hollingshead had the idea while showing home movies in his backyard during hot summer evenings. He laid out a tract of wasteland into 50-foot-wide aisles, built ramps so that viewers could see over the cars in front of them, sunk the projection pit, and charged 25 cents per person, a maximum of one dollar per car, to watch old movies, the only kind distributors would let him have. Hollingshead brought film soundtracks to his patrons with a few huge speakers, which meant he had to shut down during cold weather, when customers could not leave their car windows open. In the 1940s, drive-in operators solved the problem of seasonal closings by wiring individual in-car speakers to the projection booth.

The drive-in theater was perfect for the new suburbs. Almost all of the new suburbanites were young couples with small children. Taking the family to a traditional movie theater was not an attractive prospect. Small children would squirm, squall, and run around; other patrons would complain; Mom and Dad would have words. Operators of drive-ins touted their theaters as family centers where adults could chat, kids could frolic safely in playgrounds below the towering screens, and "inveterate smokers could smoke without offending others." There were 10 drive-in theaters in the United States in 1939. Between 1945 and 1950, 5,000 were built.

The drive-in soon had a second image. Indeed, a writer for *Motion Picture Daily* commented when Hollingshead opened the very first, "The Romeos who lost out in the back seats of picture houses [because of censorious ushers] are waking up in a new world." The suburban drive-in theater continued to prosper as a "passion pit" when the tots gamboling in the playground in the 1940s became the lusty teenagers of the 1950s and 1960s.

United States had to match American spending on armaments, daily life in Russia was drab. Long lines of people at shops waiting not only for the most modest of luxuries but for basic foodstuffs were hardly an appealing alternative to the American consumer cornucopia.

Vice President Nixon exploited the drama of the contrast when he visited Moscow in 1959. He snookered the rarely snookered Khrushchev into a debate on capitalism versus Communism in front of a mock-up of an appliance-filled American kitchen at a Russian exposition. American photographers were carefully placed to capture Nixon's commercial in what was called the "kitchen debate." Still, there was nothing contrived about the yawning gulf between material life in the two nuclear powers, and Khrushchev knew it. He wanted some sort of rapprochement with the United States so that he could divert some of Russia's arms race expenditures to improving Soviet agricultural production and creating consumer industries.

Nixon trumped Khrushchev in the kitchen, but in diplomatic savvy, Secretary of State John Foster Dulles was a disaster compared to the flexible and opportunistic Russian premier.

Dull, Duller, Dulles

On the basis of his credentials, Dulles should have been a masterful foreign minister. He was related to two previous secretaries of state, and his diplomatic career stretched back 50 years. When he was out of government, Dulles practiced international law with a firm considered the best in the business. But Dulles was handicapped by a personality impossible in the world of diplomacy ("Dull, Duller, Dulles," the Democrats gibed) and an unworkable worldview.

Dulles was a Calvinist of a type thought extinct by the end of the eighteenth century. Woodrow Wilson had been stern; Dulles believed that satanic evil dwelled in the breasts of Communists. He was unable to respond when Khrushchev hinted that he wanted to ease tensions. In 1955, the Soviets agreed with the United States, France, and Britain to withdraw all troops from Austria, which they had occupied for 10 years, allowing the creation of a non-Communist, neutral democracy there. That alone should have convinced Dulles that the Soviets were not monomaniacal in their determination to expand Communism, but it did not.

Dulles's narrowness made him unpopular not only in the Third World (countries aligned with neither the United States nor the Soviet Union) but also among America's allies. To make matters worse, Dulles insisted on representing the United States in person. He flew 500,000 miles on the job, demoralizing American ambassadors by making them ceremonial figures who greeted his plane at the airport and then disappeared. Two decades later, Henry Kissinger scored spectacular successes with personal diplomacy; Dulles should have been locked up in the basement of the State Department.

Dulles's moral categories and half a century of living with empires and pliant Latin American republics had left him incapable of adjusting to the realities of the 1950s. The European colonial empires were falling apart; new Asian and African countries were founded almost annually. Committed at least in word to social and economic reform, usually socialist in part, the leaders of these new nations were rarely pro-Soviet, and they needed American financial aid.

In Latin America, reformers opposed to corrupt and repressive dictatorships had by necessity to call for the reduction or regulation of American economic power in their countries. All but the infantile ideologues among them recognized the benefits of maintaining amicable relations with the nation that had created the Marshall Plan and possessed nearly half the world's wealth. By shunning them as enemies, Dulles was midwife to the birth of violent, anti-American revolutionaries in half a dozen Latin American republics.

The Wrong Friends

Instead of exploiting goodwill toward the United States and the cordiality of nations wanting money, Dulles divided the world into "us" and "them," with "us" defined as those nations that lined up behind the United States in every particular. He wrote off independent-minded national leaders, all revolutionary movements, and many reformers, as inspired by Communism. This meant that, too often (with the help of his brother, Allen Dulles, who headed the covert Central Intelligence Agency [CIA]), he threw American influence behind reactionary regimes, including sometimes brutal dictatorships in Portugal, Nicaragua, the Dominican Republic, and Cuba, simply because they were "with us."

In 1953, the United States helped the unpopular shah of Iran to oust a reform-minded prime minister, Mohammed Mossadegh, despite the fact that, since Iran shared a long border with the Soviet Union, no Iranian government could afford to cozy up to Russia. In 1954, the CIA played a major role in overthrowing the democratically selected prime minister of Guatemala, Jacobo Arbenz Guzmán, because he planned to expropriate banana plantations owned by an American company.

Also in 1954, Dulles refused to sign the Geneva Accords, an agreement ending a long war against the French (whom the United States had aided financially) in Vietnam. The victorious National Liberation Front in Vietnam was led by Communists friendly to Russia, but, because of an ancient enmity between Vietnam and China, the Vietnamese may have been open to cooperation with the United States. The Dulleses, however, intended to intervene in Vietnam covertly, a decision that was to grow into tragedy for both countries.

Brinkmanship: Theory and Practice

Eisenhower did not object when Dulles preached "brinkmanship," which Dulles defined as "the ability to get to the verge without getting into war," in effecting American policy. However, when Dulles said it was American policy not merely to hold the line against the Soviet Union but to encourage people living under Communism to overthrow their oppressors, brinkmanship became too hot a potato for Ike.

Over the United States' official radio network in Europe, the Voice of America, and the covertly funded Radio

Free Europe, broadcasters broadly implied to eastern Europeans that the United States would assist them if they rebelled against the Soviets. To what extent the message affected the Poles and Russians in June 1956 is difficult to say. However, when Poles rioted in favor of Wladyslaw Gomulka, a Communist but a cautious critic of total Russian domination of the country, the Soviets quickly relented and allowed Gomulka to take power.

Then, the Hungarians rose up in favor of a more strident critic of the Soviets, Imre Nagy. It appeared Russia would again compromise. But, within days, riot became widespread rebellion, and the rebels appealed to the United States to send troops or, at least, assistance. When Eisenhower was silent, fearing that intervention would mean leaping over the brink, the Soviets invaded Hungary and brutally suppressed the rebels. Hundreds of thousands of Hungarians had to flee the country. They hated the Soviet Union but were justly disillusioned with John Foster Dulles.

Dulles also hinted that the United States would support Chiang Kai-shek if the nationalist Chinese leader, in exile on Taiwan, invaded the Communist People's Republic of China. However, when the Communists began to shell two tiny islands controlled by Chiang, Quemoy and Matsu, Ike backed off. He said the United States would defend Taiwan, but not two insignificant rocks in the Formosa Strait. The artillery exchanges between the two Chinas developed into a ritual. At one point, the Communists insisted only on the right to shell Quemoy and Matsu on alternate days.

Also in 1956, when Egypt seized the Suez Canal, Eisenhower and Dulles first appeared to encourage Britain, France, and Israel to invade Egypt. However, after their troops had landed and Khrushchev threatened to send Russian "volunteers" to help Egypt, Eisenhower denounced the invasion, forcing a humiliating withdrawal. Brinkmanship made for roof-raising speeches in an auditorium. At the edge of the chasm, it was unnerving.

Summitry and the U-2

When Dulles resigned a month before he died of cancer in 1959, Eisenhower personally took charge of foreign policy. Curiously, given the fact he had allowed Dulles free rein, Ike was well equipped to handle diplomacy. Of all American presidents, only Hoover and John Quincy Adams had spent more of their lives abroad than Ike had. Eisenhower lived for long periods in France, England, the Philippines, Panama, and Algeria. His experience in dealing with American allies during World War II had demanded a diplomatic virtuoso.

For a time, Ike seemed to be easing Soviet-American tensions. He and Khrushchev outdid one another with statements of goodwill, and they agreed to exchange friendly visits. Khrushchev scored a public relations success on his United States tour in 1959. On his best behavior, he captivated many Americans with his unaffected interest in everyday things. Khrushchev even drew laughter when, having been refused admission to Disneyland, he explained that the reason was that the amusement park was a disguise for rocket installations.

Eisenhower's visit to Russia was scheduled for May 1960. Ike had been as close to a hero in the Soviet Union during the war as a foreigner could be. He had remained friendly with Marshall Georgy Zhukov, a general who had been unafraid to disagree with Stalin. There was reason to expect the good-natured Ike would be as great a personal success in Russia as Khrushchev had been in America.

Then, on May 5, Khrushchev announced that the Russians had shot down an American plane in their airspace. It was a U-2, a top-secret high-altitude craft designed for spying. Assuming that the pilot was killed in the crash (or had committed suicide, as U-2 pilots were provided the means to do), Eisenhower said that it was a weather-monitoring plane that had wandered off course.

Khrushchev pounced. He revealed that the pilot was alive and had confessed to being a spy. Possibly because he hoped to salvage Eisenhower's visit, Khrushchev hinted that Ike should lay the blame on subordinates. Ike refused to do so. Smarting under Democratic criticism that he had never been in charge of foreign policy, he acknowledged that he had personally approved the flight. Khrushchev assailed Eisenhower as a warmonger and canceled Ike's tour. The Cold War was quite chilly again.

1960: A Changing of the Guard

The chill perfectly suited the strategy of a contender for the 1960 Democratic presidential nomination, John Fitzgerald Kennedy. A 42-year-old senator from Massachusetts, Kennedy claimed that the Eisenhower administration had, with its stingy spending policies, allowed the Russians to open a dangerous "missile gap," a gross disparity between the number of rockets the Soviets had available to strike the United States and the number of missiles in the American arsenal. This was nonsense. Eisenhower had spent plenty on missiles and nuclear warheads. And the alarm Kennedy feigned blithely ignored the fact that any exchange of nuclear weapons was insane. But Eisenhower could not effectively respond; the number of American missiles and the American estimate of Russian striking power were classified information.

Changing Times

Personally, Eisenhower was still popular in 1960. Had he been able and willing to run again, the 70-year-old president would have defeated any Democrat. However, the Twenty-Second Amendment to the Constitution, pushed through by Republicans in 1951 as a posthumous slap at FDR, forbade a third term.

The Republican party's choice to succeed Ike was Vice President Richard M. Nixon. Nixon had transcended his reputation as a red baiter while maintaining his connections with Republicans obsessed with Communism.

The Democrats believed he was beatable. With some reason, they thought that Ike's presidency was an aberration, Eisenhower's personal triumph. The majority coalition of voters that Democrats had put together during the New Deal was largely intact. The Democrats had controlled both houses of Congress for six of Eisenhower's eight years as president. A second generation of Democratic liberals emphasized cultural issues more than the social and economic issues of the New Dealers, but the popularity of critics of 1950s conformity and blandness, such as William H. Whyte, Vance Packard, and John Keats, indicated that slogans on themes like "change," "newness," and "youthful" would have voter appeal.

The Democrats had in their pocket the votes of black northerners, labor unions, white ethnics, the big cities, and, a little less confidently, the South, where the electorate was still almost entirely white. Intellectuals, especially academics, were mostly liberal. Their numbers were small, but they were articulate and active in politics. Weekly opinion magazines such as the *Nation* and the *New Republic* relentlessly criticized the "lethargy" of the Eisenhower years. Although most daily newspapers were owned by Republicans, many reporters and columnists were liberals. They exhausted the cliché that it was "time to get the country moving again."

JFK: Ambitions, Handicaps, Appeal

John F. Kennedy had been thinking about the presidency since he was first elected to Congress in 1946. His father, a multimillionaire and himself a politician, had been patiently guiding JFK's career toward that goal. As a senator, Kennedy was innocuously middle-of-the-road, reticent even to criticize Joe McCarthy or to support the civil rights movement. He was following the advice of another Massachusetts politician, Calvin Coolidge, who had said that anything you do not say cannot be held against you.

Kennedy was less prudent in his personal life. He was a womanizer, constantly seeking sex and, like a teenager, boasting to friends of the number of his one-night conquests. He maintained longer relationships with several mistresses, including actress Marilyn Monroe and Judith Exner, who had personal connections with organized crime. Today, when reporters devote their lives to ferreting out sex scandals, Kennedy would have had to retire to the country clubs of Cape Cod. But shenanigans like his were almost always

▲ *John F. and Jacqueline Kennedy, young, attractive, and stylish, cut a figure that could hardly have differed more from the 70-year-old Eisenhowers or even the young but decidedly unglamorous Nixons. The "classy" atmosphere Kennedy brought to Washington appealed not only to university people but to upwardly mobile suburbanites too.*

kept out of the papers during the 1950s. And Kennedy had a splendid cover: In 1953, he had married an attractive and personable high-society girl, Jacqueline Bouvier. She enjoyed Kennedy's prominence and added to his "charisma," a word little used before 1960, but one that, since, has been attached to tens of thousands of 15-minute celebrities.

Kennedy had a handicap of which virtually no one knew, not even his coterie of devoted advisers. Although he looked in the pink of health, he was a physical mess. Wartime injuries to his back caused him constant, serious pain unless he popped narcotic painkillers like popcorn. He suffered from Addison's disease, requiring daily doses of cortisone, and chronic colitis, prostatitis, and sinusitis. He took as many as a dozen drugs a day.

But Kennedy even exploited a long stay in the hospital in 1955. He supervised the writing of a book of essays (published with him as author), *Profiles in Courage*. The essays were portraits of politicians who had put principle ahead of political expediency. The politically expedient message of the book was not obscure.

A very well known handicap was the fact that Kennedy was Roman Catholic. Democratic politicos believed that their party could not win the presidency with a Catholic nominee. Anti-Catholicism was still endemic in the South's Bible belt; a Democrat nominee needed the South's electoral votes. Even the father of Martin Luther King Jr., a Baptist minister, expressed the common prejudice.

When he won the Democratic primary in West Virginia, a basically southern Bible belt state where Catholic voters were few, Kennedy convinced northern party bosses (themselves Catholics) he could lick the problem. After he was nominated, he discredited anti-Catholic prejudice by forthrightly telling the Southern Baptist Convention (a hotbed of anti-Catholicism), "If this election is decided on the basis that 40,000,000 Americans lost their chance of being president on the day they were baptized, then it is the whole nation that will be the loser in the eyes of history."

An Exciting Campaign

Kennedy won the nomination, barely, on the first ballot. He then made a move that surprised everyone, including, as it turned out, JFK himself and his closest adviser, his brother Robert F. Kennedy. JFK's most important Democratic party rival was Lyndon B. Johnson of Texas, the majority leader of the Senate. Needing support in the South, Kennedy offered the vice presidential nomination to Johnson. Kennedy and his brother were sure Johnson would decline. He was powerful, and he ran the Senate by syrupy persuasion, horse trading,

and muscle. He was a master manipulator. And Johnson's ego and energy were immeasurable. The Kennedys were sure he would scoff at running for an office another Texan, John Nance Garner, had called "not worth a pitcher of warm piss." By inviting him, however, the Kennedys could hope Johnson would put his talents to work in the southern states.

Johnson shocked them by accepting. He saw a "no lose" decision. Texas law allowed him to run for both vice president and reelection to the Senate. If the Republicans won the presidential election, he would still be majority leader and the front-runner for the 1964 Democratic nomination. If Kennedy and he won, Johnson would be justly credited for the victory because of having ensured the party southern electoral votes that would, otherwise, have been lost on the religion issue. Even Texas, with the most electoral votes of any southern state, had voted Republican in 1952 and 1956.

Richard Nixon had a tough job. He had to defend Eisenhower's policies while appealing to the youth and change mania. (Nixon was only five years older than Kennedy.) He handled this juggling act remarkably well, but not without cost. Emphasizing his experience in the executive branch, he created an image of the responsible diplomat that did not mesh with his past reputation for free-swinging smears and dirty tricks. Pro-Kennedy reporters revived the nickname "Tricky Dicky" and the line "Would you buy a used car from this man?" Kennedy wisecracked that Nixon played so many

▲ *Knowing they were in a tight race and each confident he had the better case, both Nixon and Kennedy readily agreed to the first face-to-face debates in a presidential campaign. Only a few candidates since have dodged televised debates. However, with caution—the fear of blundering—drummed into the debaters by their handlers, memorable moments have been few.*

parts that no one knew who the real Nixon was, including the vice president himself.

The popular vote was closer than in any election since 1888. Kennedy won a wafer-thin margin of 118,574 votes out of almost 70 million, less than 50 percent. (A latter-day Dixiecrat won 500,000 votes and 15 electoral votes.) Kennedy's 303 to 219 electoral vote margin, decisive on the face of it, concealed very close scrapes in several large states. Kennedy may well have carried Illinois (27 electoral votes) because of extensive ballot box fraud in Chicago.

Some pundits said that Kennedy won because his wife was more glamorous than Pat Nixon, who abhorred public life, or because the Massachusetts senator looked better on camera in the first of four televised debates with Nixon. Nixon was, in fact, nervous. Beads of perspiration collected on his upper lip, and ineptly applied makeup failed to cover his five-o'clock shadow. But such explanations are ridiculous. Nixon looked fine and performed quite well in the other three debates. It was just a very close election; they happen.

Nevertheless, gradually but relentlessly, after 1960, candidates for elective office turned to professional media advisers who "packaged" and "sold" them like toothpaste, gin, or a week in the Bahamas. Image became as important as issues in elections and, in time, virtually banished issues from election campaigns. Today, of course, this phenomenon is in its resplendent glory.

CAMELOT

As president, Kennedy was a master at projecting an attractive image. Although no more an intellectual than Eisenhower (his favorite writer was Ian Fleming, creator of the British superspy James Bond), the new president won the hearts and talents of the intelligentsia by inviting venerable poet Robert Frost to read verse at his inauguration and cellist Pablo Casals to perform at the White House. Athletic and competitive, Kennedy appealed to young suburbanites by releasing photographs of his large family playing rough-and-tumble touch football at their Cape Cod vacation home.

There were plenty of Kennedy haters, but the vigor of his administration (*vigor* was a favorite Kennedy word) and his charm, wit, and self-deprecating humor captivated many Americans. Inspired by *Camelot,* a blockbuster musical of the early 1960s, they spoke of the Kennedy White House as if it were an idyll like King Arthur's mythical realm.

Adultery destroyed Arthur's Camelot, and Kennedy did not cease to have his women, even in the White House. However, the Kennedy Camelot was brought down not by sin but by a lone Mordred who struck at a kingdom, to all appearances, in splendid moral health.

The New Frontier

Kennedy's inaugural address was eloquent and moving. "The torch has been passed to a new generation of Americans," he said. And he challenged Americans, "Ask not what your country can do for you; ask what you can do for your

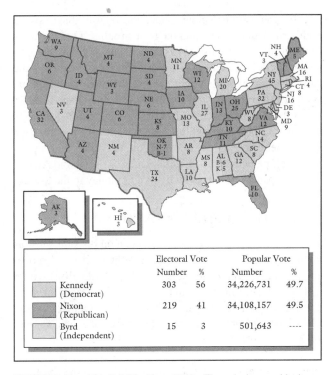

	Electoral Vote		Popular Vote	
	Number	%	Number	%
Kennedy (Democrat)	303	56	34,226,731	49.7
Nixon (Republican)	219	41	34,108,157	49.5
Byrd (Independent)	15	3	501,643	----

MAP 47:1 Presidential Election, 1960   The only geographical feature of the electoral vote in 1960 was the Republicans' near sweep of the West. Kennedy won the election by carrying five of the seven states with the biggest electoral counts.

country." He sent Congress a pile of legislation that was more innovative than any presidential program between the time of FDR's Hundred Days and Ronald Reagan's conservative agenda of 1981.

The "New Frontier," as Kennedy called his program, included federal aid to education (both to institutions and, in the form of low-interest loans, to students), assistance to chronically depressed Appalachia and the nation's decaying city centers, and help for the poor, the ill, and the aged. In 1962, Kennedy proposed a massive space research and development program to overtake the Soviet Union, which had sent an artificial satellite into orbit in 1957. Kennedy meant to put an American on the moon by 1970.

Despite Democratic majorities in Congress, JFK was frustrated. Not only did most Republicans oppose the New

The Kennedy Wit
These are some tidbits of JFK's famous wit:

When we got into office, the thing that surprised me most was to find that things were just as bad as we'd been saying they were.

Washington is a city of Southern efficiency and Northern charm.

It has recently been observed that whether I serve one or two terms in the presidency, I will find myself at the end of that period at what might be called an awkward age—too old to begin a new career and too young to write my memoirs.

Frontier, but neither Kennedy nor Johnson was able to swing southern Democrats behind the New Frontier. The southerners traditionally opposed big government spending on anything but defense and public works projects located in the South, and they were angered when the president and his brother, Attorney General Robert F. Kennedy, made friendly overtures to the growing civil rights movement. Kennedy was able to push through only a few of his proposals, such as the inexpensive Peace Corps (volunteers working in underdeveloped countries in Latin America, Asia, and Africa) and the space program (which brought money to the South).

The Civil Rights Movement

Kennedy wanted southern congressmen on his side. He was willing to go slow in accommodating the civil rights movement. But African Americans and their white allies would not be put off. Martin Luther King Jr.'s Southern Christian Leadership Conference, its offshoot, the Student Nonviolent Coordinating Committee, and older groups like the Congress of Racial Equality were energized by the change of administrations. They stepped up their fight against racial discrimination on several fronts, sponsoring demonstrations, protests, and nonviolent civil disobedience throughout the South.

White mobs pummeled black and white demonstrators, and law officers turned high-pressure fire hoses on them, unleashed attack dogs, and tortured demonstrators with electric cattle prods. Black churches, the typical meeting places of civil rights workers, were firebombed, and several children were killed. An interstate bus carrying Congress of Racial Equality "freedom riders" was burned to the ground. In April 1963, Medgar Evers, the moderate leader of the National Association for the Advancement of Colored People in Mississippi, was shot to death in the driveway of his home.

JFK and Robert F. Kennedy (now attorney general) could not ignore the violence. However, they were forced to act only when two southern governors, Ross Barnett of Mississippi and George Wallace of Alabama, said that they would personally prevent the integration of their state universities. The Kennedys tried to cut a deal with them by phone. When the governors would not budge, the Kennedys sent 400 marshals and 300 soldiers to the University of Mississippi. It cost $4 million to ensure James Meredith his right to attend a state university he paid taxes to support. In Alabama, Governor Wallace made a show of personal resis-

▲ *Already a hero to African Americans and their de facto spokesman—the first individual of whom that could be said since Booker T. Washington—Martin Luther King Jr. meant the March on Washington to be so persuasive a plea for civil equality for blacks that the Democrats would commit their party to it. He succeeded, largely because of the eloquence of his "I Have a Dream" speech, which ranks with Lincoln's second inaugural address as the greatest in the history of American oratory.*

tance for the benefit of photographers and his political future, then stepped aside for the marshals.

The March on Washington

The Kennedys were wedded to the civil rights movement, however, only by a massive rally, the March on Washington of August 1963, led by Martin Luther King Jr. Believing he could force decisive federal action through a dramatic demonstration, King led 200,000 marchers to the Lincoln Memorial, where he delivered his greatest sermon. "I have a dream today," he began, and continued with these inspiring words:

> I have a dream today that one day . . . little black boys and black girls will be able to join hands with little white boys and white girls and walk together as sisters and brothers. . . . When we let freedom ring, when we let it ring from every village and every hamlet, from every state and every city, we will be able to speed up that day when all of God's children, black men and

---

Prejudice

Referring to racial prejudice, African American contralto Marian Anderson observed, "Sometimes, it's like a hair across your cheek. You can't see it, you can't find it with your fingers, but you keep brushing at it because the feel of it is irritating."

On the same subject, author James Baldwin said, "It is a great shock at the age of five or six to find that in a world of Gary Coopers you are the Indian."

---

white men, Jews and Gentiles, Protestants and Catholics, will be able to join hands and sing, in the words of that old Negro spiritual, "Free at last! Free at last! Thank God Almighty, we are free at last!"

King (and segregationist white senators) left Kennedy no choice but to take sides with the civil rights movement. Southern segregationists were not supporting his program anyway, and to shun King meant putting the black Democratic vote in the North at risk. Kennedy announced his support for a sweeping civil rights bill to be debated in Congress in 1964. If understood only years later, it was a moment of portentous significance in American electoral politics.

KENNEDY'S FOREIGN POLICY

Kennedy was a Cold Warrior. He sounded like John Foster Dulles when he said, "Freedom and Communism are in deadly embrace; the world cannot exist half-slave and half-free." Although he soon learned that the "missile gap" was a myth, he lavished money on research programs designed to improve the rockets with which, in the case of war with Russia, nuclear weapons would be delivered.

Flexible Response and the Third World

However, Kennedy's foreign policy advisers, mostly from universities and "think tanks," like Walt W. Rostow and McGeorge Bundy, disdained both brinkmanship and threatening "massive retaliation" at every Soviet provocation. Instead, updating containment policy, they advocated a policy of "flexible response." The United States would respond to Soviet and Chinese actions in proportion to their seriousness.

If the Soviets or Chinese were suspected of actively aiding guerrilla movements fighting regimes friendly to the United States, the United States would fund the military forces of those regimes and send advisers to improve them. If the Soviets were suspected of subverting elections in the Third World, the United States would launch its own covert manipulative operations. Kennedy sponsored the development of elite antiguerrilla units in the army, most notably the Special Forces, or Green Berets. He increased funding of the spy network maintained by the CIA, which had 15,000 agents around the world.

Eisenhower had thought in traditional terms, that wealthy Europe and Japan were the areas that counted in the Cold War competition. Kennedy, by contrast, stated, "The great battleground for the defense and expansion of freedom today is the whole southern half of the globe—Asia, Latin America, Africa, and the Middle East—the lands of the rising peoples."

He preferred to back democratic reform movements in the developing countries. Kennedy took the lead in organizing the Alliance for Progress in the Western Hemisphere, a program that offered economic aid to Latin American nations in the hope that they would adopt free institutions. However, the choice in the volatile Third World was rarely between liberal reform movements and Communist dictatorship. Envy of American riches, the perception that the United States indiscriminately supported exploitative dictators, Soviet opportunism, and the romantic zaniness that is found in most revolutionary movements meant that Third World liberation movements were, at best, suspicious of American intentions and willing to overlook the Russian record because of the Soviets' revolutionary rhetoric. Consequently, Kennedy and his successors often found their only friends among reactionaries.

The Bay of Pigs

"Flexible response" was a disaster in Cuba. Since 1959, Cuba (once a pliant American dependency) had been under the control of a revolutionary regime headed by Fidel Castro. In 1960, baiting the United States in interminable but effective speeches, Castro began to expropriate American property before negotiating compensation. Eisenhower approved a secret CIA project to arm and train 2,000 anti-Castro Cubans in Florida and Central America.

They were not ready to move until after Kennedy took over. JFK had his misgivings—it was not his project, after all—but the CIA assured him that Castro was unpopular. At the sound of the first explosion, the CIA said, anti-Castro rebellions would break out all over the island.

On April 17, 1961, the anti-Castro forces waded ashore at the Bay of Pigs, on Cuba's southern coast. It went wrong from the start. There was no uprising. Castro's soldiers, seasoned by years of guerrilla warfare, made short work of the outnumbered and poorly trained invaders. Instead of ousting an anti-American but possibly still flexible regime, Kennedy pushed Castro, who feared another invasion, into the arms of the Soviets.

The Bay of Pigs fiasco heartened Nikita Khrushchev to take a harder line toward the United States than he had taken through most of the 1950s. At a summit meeting in Vienna in June, Kennedy found himself outwitted and upstaged. The Ukrainian tongue-tied him in private and, when they were before reporters, patronized him as a nice boy who only needed experience. A man of perhaps excessive self-confidence, Kennedy returned home seething with anger. Khrushchev was encouraged by Vienna to act more recklessly. The Soviets resumed nuclear testing in the atmosphere and ordered the sealing of the border between East and West Berlin.

The Berlin Wall

The Communist regime of East Germany was plagued by defections, particularly by trained technologists who could double and triple their incomes in West Germany's booming economy. This "brain drain" was crippling East German industry, and western propagandists made hay of the defections: East Germans were "voting with their feet." To put an end to it, Khrushchev built a wall around West Berlin that was as ugly in reality as it was symbolically.

Republicans urged Kennedy to bulldoze the wall immediately. Kennedy let it stand. The wall was, he reasoned, a propaganda catastrophe for the Soviets everywhere. Moreover, JFK concluded that the Berlin Wall, being within East Germany, was not a test of containment. Demolishing it would mean trespassing in—invading!—East Germany, which was specifically forbidden by containment policy. And Khrushchev might respond with force (Eisenhower's fear during the Hungarian uprising), leading to a spiraling into the unthinkable nuclear war. Kennedy did not engage in brinkmanship—until October 1962.

The Missile Crisis

In October 1962, a U-2 flight over Cuba revealed that the Soviets were constructing installations for launching nuclear missiles at the United States. Such a threat a mere hundred miles from the United States was intolerable. Before informing the public, however, Kennedy assembled his most trusted advisers. He quickly rejected a proposal by Dean Acheson that bombers be immediately dispatched to destroy the missile sites and the suggestion that American troops invade Cuba. Although the president did not know why at the time, he decided correctly. The CIA (incorrectly again) had told him that there were only a handful of Soviets on the island; in fact, there were 40,000 Russian troops in Cuba. The CIA also grossly underestimated the size of the Cuban army, which numbered 270,000 men and women.

After hours of agonizing discussion, Kennedy adopted his brother's moderate and flexible approach to the crisis. Announcing the discovery of the missile sites to the American people, he proclaimed a naval blockade of Cuba and demanded that the Soviets dismantle the installations and return all nuclear devices to the Soviet Union. Castro panicked. He fled to a bunker beneath the Soviet embassy and demanded a Russian nuclear strike on the United States. Because Kennedy had made it clear he wanted to talk, Castro's hysteria gave Khrushchev pause. He too believed in pragmatic, flexible response. He shuddered at the thought of the Soviet Union's cities as radioactive ruins. Now he wondered about his Cuban ally's reliability.

Still, for four days, work on the sites continued, and Soviet ships carrying 20 missiles continued on their way to Cuba. (Twenty missiles were already there; 40 would represent a third of the Russian arsenal.) Americans gathered solemnly around their television sets, apprehensive that the nuclear holocaust would begin any minute, with no more warning than a siren. Secretary of State Dean Rusk revealed that the White House was nervous too. "We're eyeball to eyeball," he said.

Rusk added, "I think the other fellow just blinked." The Cuba-bound freighters stopped in midocean. After several hours, shadowed by American planes, they turned around. On October 26, Khrushchev sent a long conciliatory letter to Kennedy in which he said he would remove the missiles if the United States solemnly pledged never to invade Cuba. The next day, he sent another letter. This one said that the Soviets would withdraw the nuclear weapons from Cuba if the United States removed its missiles from Turkey, which bordered the Soviet Union.

Before the missile crisis began, Kennedy had been considering dismantling the Turkish missile sites as a gesture of

▲ *The Cuban missile crisis did not rivet Americans to their television sets as Kennedy's assassination would do. The deliberations were top-secret and known to only a handful of people in Washington and the Soviet Union. But few people changed channels when President Kennedy explained how close to nuclear war the nation was.*

friendship. However, reasoning from the difference between the two Soviet notes that there was division and indecision in the Kremlin, as well as from the unease he and his advisers were experiencing, he saw a chance for a diplomatic victory. Kennedy ignored Khrushchev's second note, as if it had been lost in the mail, and accepted the terms of the first letter. On October 28, Khrushchev accepted.

Improved Relations

The president believed that the Cuban missile crisis was the turning point of his presidency. He made commemorative gifts to everyone who advised him during that tense October. In fact, both Kennedy and the Soviets were shaken by their flirtation with catastrophe. Both sides acted more responsibly after 1962. A "hot line" was installed between the White House and the Kremlin so that, in future crises, Russian and American leaders could communicate instantly. Then, following a Kennedy speech, the Soviet Union joined the United States and the United Kingdom in signing a treaty that banned nuclear testing in the atmosphere. France and China, the other nuclear powers, did not sign.

Assassination

By the fall of 1963, Kennedy had regained the confidence he exuded in 1960. Triumph in the Cuban missile crisis made him less uncomfortable about his alienation of southern white segregationists. He believed that the Civil Rights Act proposed for the election year of 1964 would ensure the electoral votes of the populous northeastern states, where the African American vote was critical. His triumph in the

Modern Communications

When George Washington died in Virginia in 1799, it took a week for the news to reach New York City, almost another week to reach Boston. Within half an hour of John F. Kennedy's assassination, 68 percent of the American people knew about it. Most of them remained glued to television sets for several days.

missile crisis might overcome the misgivings of all but the most rabid segregationists. Things looked good. He agreed to accompany Vice President Johnson on a political tour of Texas to shore up support there.

The tour began with cheering crowds. Kennedy was reassured. Then, as the motorcade passed through Dealey Plaza in downtown Dallas, the president's head was blown to bits by rifle fire. Within hours, Dallas police arrested Lee Harvey Oswald, a ne'er-do-well former marine and sometimes hanger-on of pro-Castro groups who worked in a textbook clearinghouse overlooking Dealey Plaza.

Kennedy's death unleashed a storm of anxieties and conspiracy theories. Because Dallas was home to several paranoiac right-wing political organizations, including the John Birch Society, which held that Dwight D. Eisenhower was "a conscious agent" of international Communism, many liberals were inclined to blame right-wing kooks for the assassination. They circulated stories of Dallas schoolchildren cheering when they heard Kennedy had been killed. No political group has a monopoly on moronism.

Oswald's own political associations were, however, entirely with organizations of the left. Indeed, he had lived for a time in the Soviet Union and tried to renounce his American

▲ *President and Mrs. Kennedy in their open limousine minutes before the president was murdered. He was in high spirits. A year from the election of 1964, his popularity was increasing; his apprehensions that his reception in Texas would be cool, if not hostile, had been allayed.*

citizenship. Right-wingers were confirmed in their belief that Communist agents were, indeed, everywhere.

Lee Harvey Oswald did not clear things up. Two days after his arrest, he was shot to death in the basement of the Dallas police headquarters by a nightclub operator named Jack Ruby. Ruby claimed he was distressed to the point of distraction by the death of a president he idolized. Ruby was a somewhat sleazy character with underworld associates. His appearance into the plot added the theory that the Mafia had killed Kennedy. (The Mafia conspiracy gained adherents in later years when Kennedy's sexual relationship with Judith Exner, who was also the mistress of gangster Sam Giancana, was revealed.)

A commission headed by Chief Justice Earl Warren found that Oswald was part of no conspiracy. He acted alone. He was a misfit like Charles Guiteau and Leon Czolgosz. He wanted to do "a great thing." Some sloppiness in gathering evidence and soft spots in several of the Warren Commission's conclusions only intensified belief in conspiracies and multiplied the number of theories. Although several independent investigations confirmed the commission's findings (although faulting much of its work), suspicions never died. In 1988, a large majority of Americans said that they did not accept the official account of the murder. In 1991, a Hollywood film implicating numerous government agencies in the killing, all coordinated by an aesthete from New Orleans, was a huge commercial success.

John F. Kennedy was not a major president, not even a "near great," an unfortunate term some historians have been forced to use. He accomplished little domestically, and, in foreign policy, his success in the missile crisis was to pale in significance beside his then barely noticed military intervention in Vietnam, an involvement that was to escalate out of control and poison American life.

Still, the assassination was truly a national tragedy. Kennedy had aroused an idealism and patriotic selflessness that, after his death, were to dissipate into disillusionment, cynicism, and mindless political and social mischief, the consequences of which are with us today. Daniel Moynihan, an official in the administration who was to become a prominent senator from New York, summed it up pretty well for a generation, telling of a conversation at Kennedy's funeral: "Journalist Mary McGrory said to me that we'll never laugh again. And I said, 'Heavens, Mary. We'll laugh again. It's just that we'll never be young again.'"

for FURTHER READING

Overviews of the 1950s and 1960s include John Brooks, *The Great Leap,* 1966; William Chafe, *The Unfinished Journey,* 1986; James Gilbert, *Another Chance: America Since 1945,* 1984; Godfrey Hodgson, *America in Our Time: From World War II to Nixon,* 1976; and William E. Leuchtenburg, *A Troubled Feast: American Society Since 1945,* 1979.

On the Eisenhower years, see C. C. Alexander, *Holding the Line: The Eisenhower Era, 1952–1961,* 1975; Stephen Ambrose, *Eisenhower the President,* 1984; Eisenhower's own *The White House Years,* 1965; P. A. Carter, *Another Part of the Fifties,* 1983; B. W. Cook, *The Declassified Eisenhower,* 1981; Robert A. Divine, *Eisenhower and the Cold War,* 1981; T. Hoopes, *The Devil and John Foster Dulles,* 1973; Peter Lyon, *Eisenhower: Portrait of a Hero,* 1974; Richard M. Nixon, *Six Crises,* 1962; William L. O'Neill, *American High: The Years of Confidence, 1945–1960,* 1987; Elmo Richardson, *The Presidency of Dwight D. Eisenhower,* 1979; and H. G. Vatter, *The U.S. Economy in the 1950s,* 1963.

The era of John F. Kennedy's brief presidency has been studied as intensively as Eisenhower's. See Ronald Berman, *America in the Sixties,* 1968; Bruce Miroff, *Pragmatic Illusions: The Presidential Politics of John F. Kennedy,* 1976; William L. O'Neill, *Coming Apart: An Informal History of the 1960s,* 1971; L. G. Paper, *The Promise and the Performance: The Leadership of John F. Kennedy,* 1975; Herbert Parrnet, *Jack: The Struggle of John Fitzgerald Kennedy,* 1980, and *JFK: The Presidency of John Fitzgerald Kennedy,* 1983; and Arthur M. Schlesinger Jr., *A Thousand Days,* 1965. On Kennedy's election, see the first in a series of studies by Theodore H. White, *The Making of the President1960,* 1961. Kennedy's assassination has been the subject of so many books—some crackbrained, some insightful—that it is impossible to make a representative list in fewer than half a dozen pages. Perhaps the one with which to begin a study of that tragic event is William Manchester's sensible and well researched *Death of a President,* 1967.

 AMERICAN JOURNEY ONLINE AND INFOTRAC COLLEGE EDITION

Visit the source collections at http://ajaccess.wadsworth.com and http://infotrac.thomsonlearning.com, and use the Search function with the following key terms to explore documents, images, audio and video clips, articles, and commentary related to the material in this chapter:

Bay of Pigs	Kennedy assassination
Cold War	Kitchen debates
Dwight D. Eisenhower	Martin Luther King Jr.
Jacqueline Bouvier Kennedy	Nikita Khrushchev
John F. Kennedy	Richard Nixon

Additional resources, exercises, and Internet links related to this chapter are available on *The American Past* Web site: http://history.wadsworth.com/americanpast7e.

HISTORY ONLINE

African American Odyssey

http://memory.loc.gov/ammem/aaohtml/aohome.html

Several multi-format collections concerning African American history from the Library of Congress.

The Kennedy Assassination

http://mcadams.posc.mu.edu/home.htm

Examination of the numerous theories as to who killed John F. Kennedy and why: an excellent resource; photos; links.

JOHNSON'S GREAT SOCIETY

Reform and Conflict 1961–1968

Gino Beghe

> We have a problem in making our power credible, and Vietnam is the place.
>
> *John F. Kennedy*

> The battle against Communism must be joined in Southeast Asia with strength and determination.
>
> *Lyndon B. Johnson*

IN CLASSICAL DRAMA, the tragic hero conquers great obstacles to rise to lofty heights, not always by fastidious means. Then, at the pinnacle of his glory, he is destroyed, not primarily by his enemies (although they are on hand to pick up the pieces) but by defects in the hero's character.

Presidents Lyndon Baines Johnson (known as "LBJ") and Richard M. Nixon were tragic figures. Both rose to win their nation's highest honor, the presidency. Both savored power as they savored nothing else on earth. Both were masters of the spheres in which they preferred to labor: Johnson as a domestic reformer in the footsteps of his idol, Franklin D. Roosevelt; Nixon as an arranger of affairs among nations, which he regarded as the president's principal job.

And both ended their careers in disgrace: Johnson because he clung stubbornly to a cause both lost and discredited; Nixon because of actions that not only were unworthy of a president but can be explained only as a reflection of his character. Johnson's undoing came about in foreign policy, which had never particularly interested him; Nixon's, on the domestic front, which he believed could take care of itself.

LYNDON BAINES JOHNSON

If Kennedy's Camelot contrasted dramatically with Eisenhower's Washington, Lyndon Johnson's style was a sharp break from Kennedy's. His ego was as big as Kennedy's. LBJ so liked his FDR-style initials that he named his two daughters, and renamed his wife, so that their initials would be *LBJ* too. Kennedy's life had been privileged: Harvard and northeastern upper class. Johnson was folksy. He came from a middling ranching family in the hill country of central Texas and attended a teacher's college. He taught school for a year, but Johnson was drawn to the tumult and machinations of Texas politics. In 1931, he went to Washington as a congressman's aide and became a devotee of the New Deal. His Democratic party faith in the power of government to do good never wavered.

Johnson was elected to Congress in 1936. Except for brief service in the navy, he remained there until, in 1948, he won a

Senate seat by so narrow a margin of questionable votes that Texans called him "Landslide Lyndon." Texas politicians had been called worse; Johnson shrugged and attached himself to House Speaker Sam Rayburn, one of the most powerful men in Washington. By 1955, he was majority leader of the Senate.

The "Johnson Treatment"

LBJ was as deft a manipulator of a legislative body as ever there was. In turns, he put together majorities by administering large doses of syrupy Texas charm, cutting deals with senators on pet projects to bring money to their districts, and, when necessary, twisting arms. The gossip was that Johnson "had something" on almost everyone in the Senate, that he tacitly blackmailed those who resisted him. If it was not true, Johnson did nothing to squelch the belief.

As vice president, Johnson was declawed. Out of the Senate, he was unable to swing southern congressmen behind the New Frontier. As president of a grief-stricken nation, however, he pushed through Kennedy's stalled proposals and much more: a comprehensive reform program Johnson called the "Great Society." His first presidential act was, however, a $10 billion tax cut, always a crowd pleaser with an election a year away.

A Southerner Ends Segregation

Also before the election of 1964, Johnson sponsored a veritable revolution in the civil status of African Americans, the Civil Rights Act of 1964, which put the Fourteenth Amendment to the Constitution, virtually in abeyance for almost a century, to work.

Between 1955 and 1964, when civil rights activists were fighting to end racial segregation in the South, a few voices suggested that when the Jim Crow laws were gone, white and black southerners would have healthier relationships than black and white northerners would. They reasoned that although legal segregation was a southern institution, interaction between southern blacks and whites was personal, "human." In the North, by contrast, although blacks suffered few legal disabilities, residential segregation isolated the two races as if they were two nations in a cold war.

As long as southern police forces were brutalizing civil rights workers, few took the prediction seriously. But it was Lyndon Johnson, formally a defender of segregation laws as late as 1960—a Texas politician had to be—who killed Jim Crow. In fact, Johnson had personally found segregation distasteful for many years. He had said privately, "I'll tell you what's at the bottom of [segregation]. If you can convince the lowest white man he's better than the best colored man, he won't notice you're picking his pocket. Hell, give him somebody to look down on, and he'll empty his pockets for you."

By 1964, like the Kennedys, Johnson believed that the future of the Democratic party in national elections depended on the African American vote in the large northern cities and, because die-hard white southern racists would bolt from the party, in the South too. The Civil Rights Act of 1964 decisively ended segregation in public schools and pulled down the "white" and "colored" signs on public accommodations that had been a part of everyday southern life for more than half a century. The act also created the Fair Employment Practices Commission to work toward ending a yawning employment gap between the white and black workforces.

The predictions of better race relations in the South than in the North proved correct. Whereas all the violence in the civil rights fight in the South was the work of whites, riots by blacks in northern cities marred Johnson's presidency: Harlem and Paterson, New Jersey, in 1964, in the wake of the Civil Rights Act's passage; Los Angeles ("the Watts riot") in 1965; a hundred other towns and cities the same year, after Martin Luther King Jr. was murdered; Newark and Detroit in 1967; a dozen others.

The Freedom Summer

Even before the Civil Rights Act, the Student Nonviolent Coordinating Committee (SNCC, pronounced "snick") had turned its attention to the right of African American southerners to vote. SNCC's numbers were limited, so the campaign was concentrated in the state of Mississippi. SNCC picked a tough fight. Rural Mississippi whites were as stubborn in their commitment to racism as any southern population. The symbol of the state's Democratic party was not a donkey but a white cock crowing, "White Supremacy." If Mississippi could be cracked, SNCC reasoned, the disenfranchisement of blacks would crumble all over the South.

Most SNCC workers, as many white as black, were college students, so the "Freedom Summer" began at the end of the spring semester 1964. It was a disillusioning experience. The mostly northern SNCC workers had romanticized the mostly poor, uneducated, and parochial African American population of Mississippi as a noble mass needing only SNCC enlightenment to rise up. (They were not the first young idealists in history to delude themselves about an underclass.)

Instead, they found African Americans as wary of outsiders as the "rednecks" among whom they lived and cautious to the bone after generations of lynchings that went unpunished and the daily humiliation of Jim Crow. The message SNCC workers brought was all very nice. Farmers brought ice water to the porches of their often dilapidated homes, listened politely, rocked in the evening heat, and thanked the young folks for stopping by. But they knew that, come September, their new friends would go back to college while they remained in Mississippi, vulnerable to economic manipulation and even violence if they tried to register as voters.

Not even the presence of hundreds of SNCC workers and dozens of newspaper reporters during the summer stayed racist retaliation. SNCC workers were routinely harassed, tailed at high speed on lonely Delta roads by cars full of men. Near tiny Philadelphia, Mississippi, an African American SNCC worker and two whites were kidnapped and murdered with the connivance of local police.

Despite the terror, Mississippi blacks and a few white allies, led by the forceful Fannie Lou Hamer, organized the Mississippi Freedom Democratic party and sent a delegation to the 1964 Democratic convention in Atlantic City, New

Jersey. The Freedom Democrats demanded that they, and not the segregationist regular Democrats, be recognized by the national party.

President Johnson did not want to write off the white South. Working through longtime civil rights advocate Hubert Humphrey, whom LBJ selected to be his vice presidential running mate, Johnson tried to fashion a compromise, dividing Mississippi's convention votes between the rival groups. The Freedom Democrats were not happy with "half a loaf," but the segregationists were furious. They walked out of the convention, announcing that they would vote Republican in November. The secession was inconsequential in 1964; it proved to be the harbinger of a revolution in southern party politics.

THE GREAT SOCIETY

Another apparently inconsequential, even comical, episode at the Atlantic City convention was an augury of the future with profound implications for the Democrats. On the boardwalk outside the convention hall (the site of the annual Miss America Pageant), a small group of women calling themselves the Women's Liberation Movement burned their brassieres in a small bonfire. If the meaning of the symbolism was unclear, the incident made for titillating photos in the newspapers. But it was a politically historic moment. It marked the beginning of the Democratic party's transformation from the party guarding the gains of working-class and poor rural whites into a party dominated by middle-class

liberals dedicated primarily not only to the civil rights of African Americans but, in time, just about any social or cultural group that could make a case that it was "victimized."

The Election of 1964

The November election seemed to prove that the Democrats had calculated well. Johnson won 61 percent of the popular vote and majorities in all but six states, five of them southern. The Democrats had a majority of 68 to 32 in the Senate and 295 to 140 in the House, the greatest imbalances since the New Deal.

But Johnson's landslide victory owed less to his promise of a "great society" than to the nation's enduring grief over the murder of President Kennedy and the fact that the Republican candidate, Senator Barry Goldwater of Arizona, willingly allied himself with right-wing extremists, including conspiracy cults and the wacky John Birch Society, then at the peak of its influence, with hundreds of "reading rooms" throughout the country. The "Birchers" were the link between the McCarthyites of the 1950s and the fundamentalist conservatives of the final decades of the century, and more extreme in their rhetoric than either. Joe McCarthy had said there were a couple hundred Communists in the government subverting it. The Birchers said that the federal and state governments were run by Communists, as were education, charities, African American organizations, and most churches.

Goldwater personally was a temperate, if not particularly thoughtful, man, and he was no racist. However, rather

"Ten, nine, eight, seven . . .

six, five, four, three . . .

two, one . . .

These are the stakes. To make a world in which all of God's children can live . . .

or to go into the dark. We must either love each other or we must die . . .

VOTE FOR PRESIDENT JOHNSON ON NOVEMBER 3.

The stakes are too high for you to stay home."

▲ *A controversial and effective Democratic party television commercial in 1964. Widespread fear that Republican candidate Goldwater would be trigger-happy with nuclear weapons accounts for Johnson's landslide victory.*

than repudiate the fanatics, he told the Republican convention of 1964, "Extremism in the pursuit of liberty is no vice." Worse, in an age of a nuclear balance of terror, the grandson of a gun-toting frontier merchant made it sound as if the Cold War with the Soviet Union would be decided on the basis of which country was "tougher." He spoke casually about the use of nuclear weapons. The Democrats depicted him as a man who would rush to push the red button in a crisis.

The Voting Rights Act of 1965

In the Voting Rights Act of 1965, the federal government put its powers behind the right of African Americans to vote. Protected in this right for the first time since the Reconstruction, southern blacks rushed to register. Only 10 years after Martin Luther King Jr.'s boycott against segregation on buses in Montgomery, the legal obstacles to racial equality were gone. Before long, southern white politicians who had built their careers on race baiting were showing up at black gatherings—beaming, shaking hands, kissing babies, and lamenting past misunderstandings.

A former SNCC worker, Julian Bond, was elected to the Georgia state assembly. He was amused that businessmen who had denounced him as a dangerous radical now took him out to lunch. By the early 1970s, all southern Democrats were courting African American voters. In Alabama's gubernatorial election of 1982, George Wallace, the southern symbol of resistance to integration in the 1960s, not only courted black votes but owed his election to them: Alabama's blacks found his Republican opponent by far the worse choice. When his political career ended, Wallace apologized and asked the forgiveness of African Americans for his racist past.

Even southern Republicans, who became the spokesmen for southern white racism (and the South's majority party), used code to communicate with their supporters. By 1982, the former Dixiecrat Strom Thurmond of South Carolina, now a Republican, was addressing black audiences.

More to Democratic liking, the Voting Rights Act of 1965 also prompted an increase in African American voting in the northern and western states. Not only Atlanta and New Orleans but Newark, Gary, Indiana, and Detroit elected black mayors during the 1970s. By 1984, the nation's second and third largest cities, Chicago and Los Angeles, plus Philadelphia, had black mayors. Tom Bradley of Los Angeles, a former policeman, just missed winning the governorship of California in 1982.

Johnson's Domestic Program

LBJ idolized FDR. He wanted history to remember him as the president who completed the social reforms the New Deal had started, for making possible an America "where no child will go unfed and no youngster will go unschooled; where every child has a good teacher and every teacher has good pay, and both have good classrooms; where every human being has dignity and every worker has a job; where

education is blind to color and employment is unaware of race; where decency appeals and courage abounds."

Johnson's "War on Poverty," directed by the Office of Economic Opportunity, funded the Job Corps, which retrained the unemployed for the new kinds of jobs available in high-technology industries. The Office of Economic Opportunity provided catch-up education in "Head Start" schools for boys and girls from impoverished families (white as well as black) and tutored inadequately prepared students so they could attend universities. Volunteers in Service to America was a domestic Peace Corps. It sent social workers into decaying inner cities and poor rural areas. Medicare provided government-funded health insurance for the elderly, chronically ill, and very poor.

For working-class and middle-class families, the Great Society generously funded schools, colleges, and universities, and provided cheap student loans that made higher education possible for hundreds of thousands of young people who, otherwise, could not have afforded it.

Some of Johnson's programs were enacted before the election of 1964. Most came after LBJ's great victory brought hordes of freshman Democratic congressmen from traditionally Republican districts; they were beholden to the president's landslide for their seats. With so many large social agencies created so quickly, some incompetence and corruption were inevitable. In colleges, professors who had lived on niggardly pay could now pocket big salaries by administering government-funded programs. Many simply did not know what they were doing. Even without waste and corruption, the Great Society would have been expensive. It was not, however, the domestic budget that destroyed Lyndon B. Johnson's administration.

VIETNAM! VIETNAM!

"Were there no outside world," journalist Theodore H. White wrote in 1969, "Lyndon Johnson might conceivably have gone down as the greatest of twentieth-century presidents." Obviously, White had written off that possibility just five years after LBJ's landslide victory. So had many of the president's devotees. By 1967, no one was saying, as LBJ's aide, Jack Valenti had said, "I sleep each night a little better . . . because Lyndon Johnson is my president." More typical was the remark of Senator Eugene McCarthy, a Democrat: "We've got a wild man in the White House, and we are going to have to treat him as such."

What happened? Vietnam happened. President Johnson mired the United States in a war in a Southeast Asian country that, before 1964, most Americans could not have found on a globe. American involvement in Vietnam began with covert action by the Central Intelligence Agency during the Eisenhower administration. Kennedy introduced American combat soldiers (11,000 when he was killed) to save the pro-American regime in South Vietnam from a Communist-led guerrilla insurrection. But it was Johnson who made the Vietnam War into a toxin that poisoned American society.

▲ *Ho Chi Minh was both a nationalist and a Communist. It remains an enigma which "ism" was more important to him—that is, to what extent and to what point in time a United States not fixated on fighting Communism everywhere could have bargained with him. Historically, it does not matter; as long as there was the Cold War, American policy makers were fixated on fighting Communism.*

A Long Way from the LBJ Ranch

Indochina (present-day Vietnam, Laos, and Cambodia) had been a French colony. As was French imperial policy, France fostered the development of a native elite that embraced French culture and, for the most part, Roman Catholicism. This elite prospered and shared in colonial government; Catholic peasants enjoyed small advantages over the mostly Buddhist majority.

Resentment of foreign masters is as old as empires are. In Vietnam in the twentieth century, resentment took the form of nationalism. Its leader was Ho Chi Minh, who, while educating himself in Paris in 1920, was a founding member of the French Communist Party. Ho lived in Russia and China until World War II, when he returned to Vietnam to organize a guerrilla movement, the Vietminh, to fight the Japanese who occupied the country.

Partly because he thought Ho more nationalist than Communist, partly because he detested French imperialism, President Roosevelt wanted Vietnam independent after the war. In 1945, Ho, with non-Communist support, proclaimed the Republic of Vietnam, patterning the proclamation on the American Declaration of Independence. When French forces returned, he agreed to keep Vietnam within the French imperial community as long as the nation was self-governing.

The French government refused and set up a puppet regime. The Vietminh returned to the jungles and rice paddies and launched a guerrilla war that lasted eight years. In 1950, defining Ho Chi Minh as a Soviet stooge, the United States began to funnel aid to the French. However, after a decisive defeat in the battle of Dien Bien Phu in 1954, the French went home. The Geneva Accords of 1954 divided independent Vietnam into two transitional zones at the seventeenth parallel. Ho's Vietminh would administer the northern half of the country from Hanoi; a non-Communist government, the south from Saigon. After two years, the bitterness and tumult presumably abated, nationwide democratic elections would elect Vietnam's permanent government.

American Involvement

There was plenty of bitterness in Vietnam. Between 1954 and 1956, about a million anti-Communist North Vietnamese, many of them Catholic, fled to south of the seventeenth parallel. The Eisenhower administration, pressured by the fiercely anti-Communist China lobby, covertly assisted a Vietnamese exile living in the United States, Ngo Dinh Diem, in returning to South Vietnam. Diem, touted in the United States as Vietnam's George Washington, received $320 million just in 1955. Still, it was clear to all he would lose to Ho Chi Minh in the elections scheduled for 1956. With Washington's support, Diem canceled the elections and proclaimed South Vietnam's independence of North Vietnam.

Another South Vietnamese leader might have succeeded. But Diem's vision was narrow, blinded by his privileged past. He was surrounded by corrupt relatives, whom he indulged. He levied high taxes, jailed even moderate dissenters, and favored Roman Catholics. In 1960, several opposition groups, including Communists, formed the National Liberation Front (NLF) and launched yet another guerrilla war in a country that nature seemed to have designed for such combat. The NLF attacked isolated patrols of Diem's soldiers, murdered village officials loyal to him, bullied and terrorized unfriendly peasants, and curried the favor of others. The NLF actually set up local governments in parts of the country, collecting taxes and enforcing the law.

Diem described the NLF as Vietcong—Vietnamese Communists—although there were many non-Communists in the NLF. He appealed to the United States for more aid, claiming that the guerrillas were aided by North Vietnam, which was true enough. Both the Eisenhower and Kennedy administrations pumped millions into his regime.

Kennedy's Uncertainty

Kennedy's advisers urged him to send troops as well as money. The president hesitated. He had been stung by the advice of the Central Intelligence Agency in the Bay of Pigs fiasco and justly wondered why Diem's 250,000-strong Army of the Republic of Vietnam (ARVN) could not handle 15,000 poorly equipped, mostly part-time peasant rebels. At first, he sent only 3,000 Green Berets, experts in counterinsurgency, to advise the ARVN. When the situation worsened, troops were sent to defend American bases; by late 1963, there were 16,000 American soldiers in South Vietnam.

Kennedy had, however, soured on Diem. When Buddhist monks led protests in Saigon and Hue, a few setting themselves aflame in intersections, high-ranking ARVN officers approached the American embassy proposing to oust the unpopular president. Kennedy approved and put an air force plane at the ready to take Diem and his family into exile in the United States. Instead, Diem, his relatives, and close associates were savagely murdered. A month later, Kennedy was dead. ("The chickens have come home to roost," Malcolm X said.) As Americans mourned Kennedy, South Vietnam descended into political chaos as one general toppled another. The NLF increased its sway over the countryside.

Not long before his death, Kennedy hinted that he wanted out of the misadventure. When told by the military that another increase in the number of American troops in Vietnam would turn the tide, he replied that to get involved more deeply was like "taking a drink": "The effect wears off, and you have to take another."

MR. JOHNSON'S WAR

President Johnson agreed to a modest increase in the American presence in early 1964, but he, like Kennedy, seemed to want out. Through intermediaries, he offered economic aid to North Vietnam in return for opening peace talks. With the NLF riding high, North Vietnam replied that it could not speak for the NLF, which was, in fact, still made up largely of southerners. The NLF, the Vietcong, refused to negotiate until American troops were withdrawn from the country.

Dominoes

Johnson refused to withdraw American troops. He shared with John Foster Dulles the conviction that Communism was a monolithic movement directed ultimately from the Kremlin. Just enough men and supplies reached the NLF from the north to convince him that the conflict in Vietnam was not a civil war but a war of subversion dependent on outsiders. Johnson also subscribed to the "domino theory" of Communist expansion awkwardly propounded by President Eisenhower: "You knock over the first one, and what will happen to the last one is the certainty that it will go over very quickly."

When Johnson looked at Southeast Asia, he saw a line of fallen dominoes stretching from Russia through China to North Korea and North Vietnam, and a line of standing dominoes in South Vietnam, Laos, Cambodia, Indonesia, Malaysia, the Philippines, and even Japan. As early as 1961, he had said, "We must decide whether to help these countries to the best of our ability or throw in the towel in the area and pull back our defenses to San Francisco." As president, he vowed that he was "not going to be the President who saw Southeast Asia go the way China went."

In August 1954, LBJ was told that North Vietnamese patrol boats had attacked American destroyers in the Gulf of Tonkin. He asked Congress for authority "to take all necessary measures to repel any armed attack against the forces of the United States and to prevent future aggression." Only two senators voted against the Gulf of Tonkin Resolution, Wayne Morse of Oregon, a lifelong maverick, and Ernest Gruening of Alaska. Gruening said that he would not vote for "a predated declaration of war." In fact, Johnson was to use the Gulf of Tonkin Resolution to turn the Vietnam conflict into a major war. By the end of 1964, the American military contingent in South Vietnam had increased to 23,000 men still described as "advisers."

Escalation

In February 1965, the Vietcong attacked an American base near Pleiku. Citing the Gulf of Tonkin Resolution, Johnson sent in 3,500 marines, the first official combat troops. In April, 20,000 more troops arrived. By the end of 1965, there were 200,000 American soldiers in South Vietnam. This number doubled by the end of 1966 and reached 500,000 by the end of 1967.

Between 1965 and 1968, the air force bombed North Vietnam. To deprive the Vietcong of cover in the jungle that spread across much of South Vietnam, planes sprayed defoliants over tens of thousands of acres, killing trees, underbrush, and many crops. American soldiers then moved in, on search-and-destroy missions.

Johnson's policy of step-by-step increases in the intensity of the war was known as "escalation." The object was to demonstrate to the enemy that fighting the technologically superior American military machine was hopeless. Briefly in 1965 and 1967, LBJ stopped bombing and offered peace talks.

Both proposals were rejected. Instead, North Vietnam met each American escalation with an escalation of its own. Beginning in 1964 and escalating in 1966, North Vietnam sent its own soldiers south to replace dead Vietcong. Within two years, 100,000 North Vietnamese were in the war. A civil war between South Vietnamese had become a war between Americans and North Vietnamese. China and the Soviet Union also escalated their contributions to the war. Both countries supplied North Vietnam with ground-to-air missiles and other sophisticated weapons.

The Tet Offensive

At the beginning of 1968, the American commander, General William Westmoreland, announced that victory was within reach. His timing could not have been worse. Within days, during celebrations of Tet, Vietnam's lunar new year, 70,000 Vietcong and North Vietnamese launched simultaneous attacks on 30 South Vietnamese cities. For several days, they controlled much of Hue. In Saigon, commandos attacked the American embassy. The Vietcong took back jungle areas the search-and-destroy missions had cleared.

The Americans regrouped, and, when the Tet Offensive was over, the Vietcong and North Vietnamese had suffered horrendous casualties. By any military definition, the battle was an American victory. In May, North Vietnam agreed to begin peace talks in Paris. However, the American people's confidence in the war was shaken. The number of American boys dead, reported each evening on television, had soared from an average of 26 a week in 1965, to 96 a week in 1966, and 180 a week in 1967. In 1968, more than 280 Americans were killed in Vietnam each week. The cost of the war had risen to $25 billion a year, nearly $70 million a day!

Despite this tremendous effort and loss of life, victory seemed as distant as ever. A few weeks after the Tet Offensive, public approval of Johnson's handling of the war dropped from 40 percent to 26 percent. LBJ was stunned. Years later, two top aides reported they were sufficiently worried about his judgment that they secretly consulted psychiatrists.

TROUBLED YEARS

Johnson craved "consensus," a word he used as often as Kennedy called for "vigor." In making his plea for civil

▲ *American soldiers tend a wounded comrade. The bonds of experiencing battle together were as powerful in Vietnam as in any American war, but the army's morale was poor, largely because the government never made a quite plausible case as to why it was worth fighting.*

rights legislation, he adopted the slogan "We Shall Overcome." He meant that all Americans would rise above the blight of racial hatred and discrimination. Another favorite presidential saying was a quotation from the Book of Isaiah, "Let us come together." The old manipulator wanted a unity of Americans behind him, his Great Society, and the war in Vietnam. The practical politician was also a dreamer, for what he got was a people more divided than at any time since the Civil War. Vietnam was the major cause of the division, but not the only one.

Hawks and Doves

Until 1965, the chief critics of Johnson's Vietnam policy were conservative Republicans like Barry Goldwater, retired generals, and right-wing extremists. They said that in moving so cautiously, Johnson was making the same mistake President Truman had made in Korea. He was fighting for a limited purpose—a negotiated peace—rather than for the total victory that was America's tradition. Known as "hawks," they wanted to use the whole of American military might to obliterate the Vietcong and North Vietnam. Former air force chief of staff Curtis LeMay called for bombing North Vietnam "back into the Stone Age." Former actor Ronald Reagan said, "We should declare war on North Vietnam. We could pave the whole place over by noon and be home by dinner."

Once LBJ escalated the war, however, his chief critics were "doves"—those who called for a unilateral end to the fighting or, at least, more earnest efforts to negotiate a peace. As the war dragged on and the casualty lists mounted, this antiwar movement grew in size and militancy.

Most doves were liberal Democrats: congressmen, university professors, schoolteachers, ministers, priests, nuns, some working people, many middle-class professionals, and even a few retired generals. College students, although immune to the draft, provided the numbers that made the protest conspicuous.

Mass demonstrations made for good television news features and put the antiwar movement at the center of public attention. In October 1965, 100,000 people attended demonstrations in 90 cities. In April 1967, about 300,000 Americans marched in opposition to the war in New York and San Francisco. Some young men burned their draft cards and went to jail rather than into the army. Some 40,000 went into exile to avoid the draft, most to Canada and Sweden, which refused to extradite them. More than 500,000 soldiers deserted, almost all briefly, during the Vietnam years, and there were some 250,000 "bad discharges." Draft dodgers with influential social and political connections joined the National Guard in order to avoid combat service.

The Arguments

The antiwar movement had no unifying ideology. A few protesters were members of radical groups like the Progressive Labor party, a tiny sect that admired Mao Zedong. They openly hoped that Ho Chi Minh would defeat the "imperialist capitalist" United States. Many youthful romantics, who knew little about Communism, were enchanted by the spectacle of the outnumbered, poorly equipped Vietcong resisting American power.

Other doves, like the famous pediatrician Dr. Benjamin Spock, were anti-Communists. However, they believed that the United States was fighting against the wishes of a majority of the Vietnamese people and, therefore, was in the wrong. They disapproved of the fact that their powerful nation was showering terrible destruction on a small country.

Religious pacifists like Quakers opposed the war because they opposed all wars. Other morally concerned people, who agreed that some wars were justified, felt that the war in Vietnam was not one of them. They objected to the fact that, with no clear battle lines, American troops unavoidably made war on civilians as well as on enemy soldiers. Bombs and defoliants took many innocent lives. And there were atrocities. The most publicized occurred at the village of My Lai in March 1968 when American troops killed 347 unarmed men, women, and children. The Vietcong were

▲ *A pacifistic poster of the Vietnam era. Pacifists, opposing all war, were important in the antiwar movement of the 1960s but were a minority of the protesters. Others regarded the Vietnam War as a particularly bad war; yet others were pro-Vietcong; still others said the war simply could not be won.*

guilty of similar crimes, but that, doves said, did not justify Americans stooping to the same level.

Some critics of the war emphasized politics and diplomacy. They pointed out that the United States was exhausting itself fighting in a small, unimportant country while the power of China and the Soviet Union was untouched. Diplomat George Kennan and Senator William Fulbright of Arkansas argued that the United States was neglecting its commitments elsewhere in the world. Senators Gaylord Nelson of Wisconsin and Wayne Morse of Oregon pointed out that the American war effort was alienating other Third World nations and even America's best allies.

Black Separatism

The antiwar movement was not the only expression of discontent in the Great Society. Ironically, the noisiest protesters came from groups that had benefited most from LBJ's domestic reforms. College and university students were exempted from the drafts and, both personally and indirectly, were subsidized by the Great Society. Professors' salaries had soared to upper-middle-class levels because of LBJ. Some of the fiercest anti-Johnson rhetoric came from young African Americans for whom the president, with justice, believed he had been a second Lincoln. Although the vast majority of blacks faithfully voted Democratic, many young militants in the North assailed racial reconciliation and integration, the goal not only of Johnson, but of Martin Luther King Jr.

Their talisman was not integration but "Black Power," which meant different things to different people. To civil rights campaigner Jesse Jackson, and to some intellectuals like sociologist Charles Hamilton, Black Power meant pressure politics in the time-honored tradition of American ethnic groups: African Americans demanding concessions for their race on the basis of the votes they could either deliver to, or withhold from, a political candidate. (Jackson coined the term *African American* in the 1990s, in part to define black people as an ethnic voting bloc.)

To a tiny group of black nationalists in the tradition of Marcus Garvey, Black Power meant demanding a part of the United States for the formation of a separate nation for blacks only (usually Georgia, Alabama, and Mississippi). Only some professors took them seriously.

To the great majority, Black Power amounted to little more than fad and fashion: dressing up in dashikis, wearing hairstyles called "Afros," and cutting off friendships and casual social relationships with whites.

Black Power was, at best, a cry of anguish and anger about the discrimination of the past and the discovery that civil equality did little in itself to remedy the social and psychological burdens of being black, a minority, in a white nation. The right to vote and ready welcome to whatever restaurant an individual could afford did not touch the problems of poverty and high unemployment among blacks, inferior educational opportunities, health problems of a severity few whites knew, high black-on-black crime rates in the cities, and a sense of inadequacy—the "mark of op-

pression"—bred into the African American community over three centuries. Only the proponents of Black Power who wanted to use a black voting bloc to win concessions had a political program. Black separatism was psychologically consoling and socially energizing but, ultimately, pointless for the masses of African Americans.

Malcolm X and Violence

The most formidable spokesman for black separatism was Malcolm Little, a onetime petty criminal who styled himself "Malcolm X," stating that a slave owner had stolen and destroyed his African name. An adherent of a religious sect known as the Nation of Islam, or Black Muslims (Christianity was the "white man's religion"), Malcolm was a spellbinding orator. He rejected Martin Luther King Jr.'s call to integrate into American society. Instead, Malcolm said, blacks should separate from whites and glory in their negritude. Many young people, mostly in the North, were captivated by this gospel of defiance. One convert was a West Indian, Stokely Carmichael of SNCC, who expelled whites from the organization in 1966. "If we are to proceed toward true liberation," Carmichael said, "we must cut ourselves off from white people." He took SNCC out of the civil rights movement and, soon, into extinction.

Malcolm X's admonition to meet white racist violence with black violence appealed to former civil rights workers who had been beaten by police and to teenagers in the urban ghettos. Carmichael's successor as the head of SNCC, Hubert Geroid "H. Rap" Brown, proclaimed as his motto "Burn, Baby, Burn." In Oakland, California, two students, Huey P. Newton and Bobby Seale, formed the Black Panther Party for Self-Defense. They were immediately involved in violent confrontations with police because of their insistence that they be allowed to patrol black neighborhoods with firearms. When Martin Luther King Jr. was shot

Marketing Malcolm

In America today, almost everything can be, and is, sold. In 1991 and 1992, marketers found a way to make money out of Malcolm X, who had almost faded from memory in the quarter century after his assassination. Sensing that a new generation of black (and white) young people would "get off on" Malcolm's defiance of convention, a movie director, Spike Lee, made a biographical film depicting Malcolm X as a hero, El-Hajj Malik El-Shabazz, "king of the African Americans."

Lee and others marketed Malcolm X baseball hats, X T-shirts, X coffee mugs, X brand potato chips ("We dedicate this product to the concept of X," that is, the suppressed heritage of African Americans), even X air fresheners for cars ("This is the lowest-priced item for Afro-Americans to show their support"). Warner Brothers, which had released Lee's film, responded piously to complaints, "The last thing we want is a poor product dragging down the image of Malcolm X."

Drugs and the Sixties

Two "mind-bending" drugs were at the core of the "counter-culture" of the 1960s: cannabis and LSD. Cannabis is hemp, a plant cultivated in America for its fiber since colonial times. George Washington grew it at Mount Vernon; in Kentucky, it became a commercial crop rivaling tobacco. Some Indian tribes smoked the dried leaves of the plant with tobacco to dull pain. Several southern planters noticed that their slaves smoked or chewed the leaves, but took little interest. Before the Civil War, few people observed that inhaling the smoke from burning hemp leaves was good for a "high," including physicians who prescribed cannabis in a tincture to treat pain, poor appetite, hysteria, and depression.

Its use as a "recreational drug" in the United States has two origins. In the midcentury vogue for things Turkish that also produced the "Zouave" regiments of the Civil War, , middle class swells in eastern cities organized hashish clubs where they enjoyed the euphoria they had read about in the books of French novelists Alexandre Dumas and Honoré de Balzac. More important, many Mexicans in the Texas and New Mexico borderlands used marijuana for its intoxicating effects. (El Paso enacted the first antimarijuana law in the United States.) The practice spread to New Orleans, where patrons of the city's high-class brothels noticed that the African American musicians who invented jazz there put themselves into a daze with marijuana, no doubt to survive the ungodly long hours worked.

During the 1920s, white musicians attracted to jazz when it spread to the North adopted "weed" (or "reefers" or "pot") from their black teachers. The beatniks of the 1950s picked up on marijuana in the jazz clubs they frequented. Hippies inherited marijuana use from the beat generation.

LSD—lysergic acid diethylamide—is a man-made drug with a much shorter pedigree. It was synthesized in 1938 by a Swiss researcher, Dr. Albert Hoffman, who was looking for a new headache medication. He set LSD aside as a dead end. But, in 1943, Hoffman ingested some of it and reported that he fell into "a kind of drunkenness which was not unpleasant and which was characterized by extreme activity of imagination . . . an uninterrupted stream of fantastic images of extraordinary plasticity and vividness and accompanied by an intense, kaleidoscope-like play of colors."

In the late 1950s, the cerebral British writer Aldous Huxley, who had already experimented with mescaline, a natural hallucinogenic drug, as a way to enhance his intellectual perceptions, "dropped acid" and wrote glowingly of its potential to inspire artistic creativity. LSD was not then an illegal substance (marijuana was, under federal laws of 1936, 1951, and 1956), and a young psychologist at Harvard, Timothy Leary, began experimenting with the drug. He soon abandoned science for the joy of his mystical experiences during "trips." When he began to preach the use of LSD like a priest with a prescription for spiritual salvation, Harvard fired him. In 1966, just in time for San Francisco's Summer of Love, when the country first learned about the flower children, Leary founded the League for Spiritual Discovery. He toured the country with sound and light shows to spread the gospel of LSD.

Jolyon West, a researcher who examined regular LSD users (and administered LSD to an elephant, which expired, and to Siamese fighting fish, which swam up and down instead of forward and backward), concluded that the drug was dangerous. He said of one young man he interviewed, "[He] reminds me of teenagers I've examined who've had frontal lobotomies. . . . This boy likes himself better. You have to realize that lobotomies make people happy. They attenuate those inner struggles and conflicts that are characteristics of the human condition."

Such warnings did not influence hippies. Their purpose, however poorly most articulated it, was, in Leary's words, to "tune in, turn on, and drop out," ostensibly from the materialistic mass culture of America but necessarily from the internal unhappiness that reality has been known to stimulate. LSD and marijuana did the trick in the short run; few adolescents and young adults of any era think about the long run.

The beatniks had looked on marijuana as recreational, fun, relaxing. Leary and the hippies saw pot and LSD as sacraments. Some New Leftists who wanted to span the gap between the political movement and the apolitical counterculture said that using drugs was itself revolutionary: "Drug consciousness is the key to it." Abbie Hoffman, a charter member of SNCC who had worked to register African American voters in Mississippi and was a prominent leader of the antiwar movement, told of a girl who approached him: "We got to talking about civil rights, the South, and so on. She asked about drugs. I asked if she had ever taken LSD. When she responded that she hadn't, I threw her a white capsule."

The New Left's revolution never occurred. But the personal revolutions of the 1960s and 1970s numbered in the tens of millions. LSD did not make the transition into the frankly materialistic and self-indulgent hedonism of the 1970s. The evidence piled up that Jolyon West had known the drug better than Timothy Leary had. Marijuana use, however, without its 1960s religious significance, spread rapidly the length and breadth of American society. In 1969, a country-and-western singer sold millions of copies of a record called "Okie from Muskogee." It was a superpatriotic, anti–longhaired hippie song about salt-of-the-earth Oklahomans that began, "We don't smoke marijuana in Muskogee." A newspaper reporter wondered. He drove to Muskogee and bought an ounce of "pot" within half an hour of parking his car.

and killed by a white racist, James Earl Ray, in 1968, the Black Muslims increased in numbers.

Malcolm X himself knew that to promote violence, except in self-defense, was suicide. Himself rehabilitated by the Muslims, he insisted that African Americans face up to the fact that they were responsible for some of their woes, notably the often violent crime in black neighborhoods of which blacks were the victims. His strict moral code led to his downfall. On learning that the head of the Nation of Islam was a racketeer and a womanizer, he left the organization

▲ *Malcolm X appealed to African Americans, mostly young, whose anger toward white America impelled them to be defiant rather than to demand acceptance by whites as equals in an integrated America. He was a superb orator, perhaps more popular with white college students than with African Americans generally.*

and became an orthodox Muslim, which meant rejecting all racism. He was gunned down by Black Muslim assassins in 1965.

The Student Movement

Just as troubling as the radical aspects of the Black Power movement was discontent among university students. Already by 1963, it was clear that the baby boomers were not apolitical, as the youth of the 1950s had been. Students demonstrated against capital punishment, protested against violations of civil liberties by the House Un-American Activities Committee, and worked in the civil rights movement. In 1963, Students for a Democratic Society (SDS) issued the Port Huron Statement, a comprehensive critique of American society largely written by a graduate of the University of Michigan, Tom Hayden. SDS called for young people to take the lead in drafting a program by which the United States could be made genuinely democratic and a force for peace and justice.

Like the Black Power organizations, the "New Left," as SDS and similar groups were collectively labeled, was not so much a political movement with a coherent program as an explosion of anger and frustration. Tom Hayden and others tried

to channel student energies into concrete concerns, like the problems of the poor and the power of large corporations. But most of the campus riots of the late 1960s were unfocused, aimed at local grievances such as student participation in setting university rules, or directed against the war in Vietnam, a matter beyond the power of university presidents and local merchants (the targets of student rebellion) to resolve.

The era of massive campus protests began at the University of California at Berkeley with the founding of the Free Speech movement in 1964. In 1968, the demonstrations took a violent turn when students at Columbia University seized several buildings and refused to budge until their ill-defined and ever shifting demands were met. (They were forcibly removed by police.)

The Counterculture

For many young people, the New Left was a way station, a place to spend the night on the way to a purely personal rebellion. In the Haight-Ashbury district of San Francisco and in New York's "East Village" in 1967, thousands of teenagers congregated to establish what they called a "counterculture," a new way of living based on "love," a word of many meanings. Love, to the "flower children" or "hippies," as they called themselves, amounted to promiscuous sex, drugs, and extravagant, colorful fashions that, like adolescent fashions since the 1920s, were designed to identify their wearers as a distinct group and to outrage those outside the group.

Conventional Americans were, in fact, alternately outraged and amused by the apparent laziness and immorality of the "longhaired kids." "Far more interesting than the hippies themselves," sociologist Bennett Berger observed, "is America's inability to leave them alone." In New York and

▲ *Hippies at a "Be-In"—a party: "stoned" on marijuana, the young men ponder the possibility of imminent "love" with the dancers.*

San Francisco, tour buses took curiosity seekers through hippie neighborhoods as if they were exotic foreign countries. Entrepreneurs, compelled to find a way to make money out of everything, found that commercializing the counterculture was easy. Advertisers used hippie themes to sell their clients' wares. (Advertisers exploited black separatism and the New Left too. Manufacturers of highly competitive consumer goods like soft drinks touted their own as the choice of African Americans. "Join the Dodge rebellion" was the theme of that automobile's television commercials for several years.) Musical groups devised "acid rock," and hippies embraced it as their music.

True-believer flower children retreated from the cities to communes that intellectuals compared to the utopian communities of nineteenth-century America. However, individual self-gratification was the central principle of hippiedom, and drugs played a large part in the counterculture. Few communal ventures lasted much beyond the visits of journalists and photographers recording the first moments of the brave new world. "Do your own thing" was a hippie mantra; taking out the garbage and disinfecting the commune commode were few hippies' "thing."

THE ELECTION OF 1968

Lyndon Johnson, able to shout gleefully while striding through an airplane in 1964, "I am the king! I am the king!" discovered in 1968 that not even a reigning monarch can survive a serious social, cultural, and moral crisis. He did not even try. Early in 1968, the Great Society in tatters, he announced that he would not run for reelection. The man who brought LBJ to this humiliating pass was a previously quiet senator from Minnesota, Eugene McCarthy.

Eugene McCarthy

Eugene McCarthy was a tall man with a gray solemnity about him. His record as a liberal workhorse was solid, but no one thought of him as a mover and shaker. When he was elected to the Senate, Minnesota already had its walking earthquake of energy and exuberance in Hubert Humphrey. But McCarthy was anguished by the issue that Humphrey, vice president after 1965, had no choice but to dodge, the war in Vietnam. Late in 1967, McCarthy announced that he would stand as a candidate for the Democratic presidential nomination, challenging President Johnson on that issue.

Pundits admired McCarthy's dignity, principle, and pluck. Some were enchanted by his diffidence: With plenty of mediocrities lusting after public office, McCarthy seemed genuinely to believe that a public servant should be called to serve. The experts gave him little chance to beat Johnson in the primaries. McCarthy's only power base was the antiwar movement. The labor unions, vital to Democratic success at the polls, begrudged him several votes he had cast against their legislative programs. He struck no chord among either blacks or white ethnics, bulwarks of the party. He had little support in the South, and he positively disdained big-city bosses like Chicago's Richard E. Daley (the feeling was mutual).

Johnson's Retirement

Time was to prove the experts right. In early 1968, however, antiwar activists were so aroused that, like Barry Goldwater's right-wing Republican shock troops in 1964, they were able to turn the Democratic party upside down. Thousands of university students dropped their studies and rushed to New Hampshire, scene of the first presidential primary. They got "clean for Gene," shearing their long hair, shaving their beards, and donning neckties, brassieres, and tidy jumpers so as not to distract the people of the conservative state from the issue at hand—the war. Sleeping on the floors of the McCarthy campaign's storefront headquarters, they rang door bells, handed out pamphlets at supermarkets, and stuffed envelopes.

President Johnson knew enough of the country's anxiety over the war to be concerned. He kept his name off the ballot; the governor of New Hampshire ran as his stand-in. The vote between him and McCarthy was evenly split, but that amounted to a rebuke of an incumbent president in a traditionally cautious state. McCarthy's supporters had good reason to look forward to primary victories elsewhere, and Johnson knew it. He announced he would retire when his term expired.

The Democrats: Who Will End the War?

The announcement caught everyone by surprise, including Vice President Humphrey, who was in Mexico on a goodwill tour. He rushed back to Washington to throw his hat in the ring. He had an edge on McCarthy because of his longstanding ties with labor, African Americans, big-city Democratic machines, the party's professionals, and contributors generous with a dollar.

McCarthy's people expected Humphrey to run and welcomed the contest. Humphrey was the administration candidate identified with the war. What they could not foresee was that in the wake of Johnson's withdrawal, Robert F. Kennedy, now senator from New York, also announced his candidacy.

Kennedy was a threat to both McCarthy and Humphrey. Johnson had eased him out of his cabinet, so he was not identified with the war. His connections with minorities were as strong as Humphrey's and much stronger than McCarthy's. He was a personal friend of Cesar Chavez, leader of the mostly Hispanic farmworkers' union in California and the Southwest. Even with blacks, on whose behalf Humphrey had labored since the 1940s, Kennedy was personally popular. When Martin Luther King Jr. was assassinated in April 1968, Bobby Kennedy's response seemed more sincere than the respects paid by any other Democrat. Kennedy had maintained his connections with the old-line party professionals and the labor movement. Indeed, within the Democratic party, his political realism and opportunism made him anathema only to the moralists who supported McCarthy. They attacked Kennedy as avidly as they attacked Johnson and Humphrey, as an exemplar of the "old politics."

Kennedy ran well in the primaries, although not without setbacks. McCarthy won the next-to-last primary in Oregon. Then, on the very night Kennedy won the final primary in California, he was assassinated, shot point-blank in the head by Sirhan B. Sirhan, a Jordanian who disliked Kennedy's support for the Jewish state of Israel.

The fourth murder of a prominent political leader in five years demoralized the antiwar Democrats and contributed to weeklong riots in Chicago during the Democratic national convention. Most of Kennedy's supporters found it impossible to swing behind McCarthy; instead, they backed Senator George McGovern of South Dakota. With a divided opposition, Humphrey won the Democratic nomination on the first ballot. Humphrey chose a Roman Catholic running mate, Senator Edmund B. Muskie of Maine. (Both McCarthy and Kennedy were Catholic.)

▲ *Robert F. Kennedy celebrating his victory in the Democratic primary in California. Moments after this picture was taken, he was dead. Had Kennedy survived, his contacts with party stalwarts who turned to Hubert Humphrey after Kennedy's death might well have made him the party's nominee in 1968.*

Nixon and Wallace

Richard M. Nixon easily won the Republican nomination at a placid convention in Miami. Although the former vice president had retired from politics in 1962 after failing in an attempt to become governor of California, he had doggedly rebuilt his position within the Republican party. He firmed up his support among eastern moderate Republicans and won over Republican conservatives by working hard for Goldwater in 1964. After 1964, Nixon attended every local Republican function to which he was invited, no matter how small the town, how insignificant the occasion, or how dubious the candidate he was to endorse. By making himself available to the party's grassroots workers, the far-from-charismatic Nixon built up active cadres of supporters.

The Democrats remained divided. Many in the antiwar wing of the party announced that they would vote for the pacifist pediatrician Benjamin Spock. Humphrey tried to woo them back by hinting that he would end the war, but, as Johnson's vice president, he could not repudiate LBJ's policy. Humphrey's ambiguity enabled Nixon to waffle on the war issue. He espoused a hawkish military policy at the same

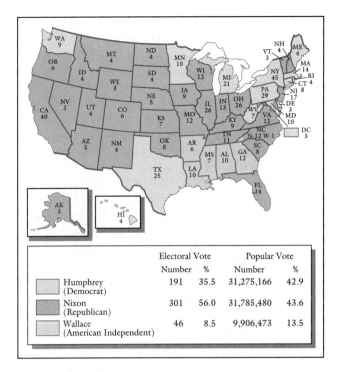

	Electoral Vote		Popular Vote	
	Number	%	Number	%
Humphrey (Democrat)	191	35.5	31,275,166	42.9
Nixon (Republican)	301	56.0	31,785,480	43.6
Wallace (American Independent)	46	8.5	9,906,473	13.5

MAP 48:1 Presidential Election, 1968 George Wallace's strategy was to deny both Nixon and Humphrey a majority in the electoral college. Had he carried three or four more southern states, he would have succeeded.

time that he reminded voters that a Republican president, Dwight D. Eisenhower, had ended the stalemate in Korea.

The chief threat to a Nixon victory was the American Independent party, founded by Governor George Wallace when he concluded he had no chance to win the Democratic nomination. A diminutive, combative man—reporters called him a bantam fighting cock—Wallace barnstormed the country and attempted to forge a coalition of southern segregationists, right-wing extremists, and blue-collar working people who felt that the Democratic party had forgotten them in its anxiety to appeal to blacks. The "white backlash" appeared to grow after Robert Kennedy was killed. Many blue-collar white ethnics who had liked Kennedy found Wallace more to their taste than civil rights pioneer Hubert Humphrey.

A Close Call

Wallace knew he could not win the election. His purpose was to win enough electoral votes that neither Humphrey nor Nixon had a majority. Then the House of Representatives would elect the next president. Because each state casts one vote when the House selects the president, anti-integration southern congressmen under Wallace's leadership could then make a deal with Nixon: a reversal of Democratic party civil rights policies in return for their votes.

Fearing this possibility, Humphrey called on Nixon to pledge jointly with him that neither would deal with Wallace and his thinly veiled appeal to racism. Humphrey proposed

▲ *Martin Luther King Jr.'s funeral in Atlanta. His casket was pulled on a farmer's wagon by mules to symbolize the esteem in which he was held by black southerners. Only Frederick Douglass and Booker T. Washington commanded such widespread support among African Americans. No one has since.*

that he and Nixon agree that in the case that neither won in the electoral college, the candidate with the fewer electoral votes would direct his supporters in the House to vote for the electoral vote leader. The Wallace campaign would then be irrelevant.

Believing that Wallace would take more votes from Humphrey than from him, Nixon evaded the challenge. In the end, it did not matter. Although Wallace did better than any third-party candidate since 1924, winning 13.5 percent of the popular vote and 46 electoral votes, Nixon eked out a plurality of 500,000 votes and a majority in the electoral college. It was close. A rush of blue-collar workers back to Humphrey during the final week of the campaign indicated to some pollsters that Humphrey might have won had the election been held a week or two later. Some Democratic strategists blamed the loss on Johnson, who, peevish now even toward his loyal vice president, did little to help Humphrey.

The Prophet of '68

No one better understood the meaning of the election of 1968—even before it was held—than Republican party strategist Kevin Phillips, who foresaw that his party would be the dominant party at the end of the twentieth century. "Sure, Hubert [Humphrey] will carry Riverside Drive in November," Phillips said, referring to a New York City neighborhood fashionable among intellectuals and well-to-do liberals. "La-de-dah. What will he do in Oklahoma?"—among frustrated working people. Even George Wallace's candidacy was helping the Republicans in the long run: "We'll get two-thirds to three-fourths of the Wallace vote in 1972. I'd hate to be the opponent in that race. When Hubie loses, [Eugene] McCarthy and [Congressman Allard] Lowenstein backers are going to take the party so far to the left they'll just become irrelevant. They'll do to it what our economic royalists did to us in 1936."

for FURTHER READING

See the "For Further Reading" section of Chapter 47 for overviews of the 1960s. In addition, see Ronald Berman, *America in the Sixties,* 1968; Robert Caro, *The Years of Lyndon Johnson,* 1982; Jim F. Heath, *Decade of Disillusion: The Kennedy-Johnson Years,* 1975; Doris Kearns, *Lyndon Johnson and the American Dream,* 1976; Merle Miller, *Lyndon: An Oral Biography,* 1980; William L. O'Neill, *Coming Apart: An Informal History of the 1960s,* 1971; Richard Walton, *The Foreign Policy of John F. Kennedy,* 1972; Theodore H. White, *The Making of the President, 1964,* 1965, and *The Making of the President, 1968,* 1969.

There are enough books dealing with the Vietnam War, its causes, and its consequences to fill a library. Among the most useful contemporary books are Frances Fitzgerald, *Fire in the Lake,* 1972, and David Halberstam, *The Making of a Quagmire,* 1966. See also G. M. Kahn, *Intervention: How America Became Involved in Vietnam,* 1986; Gabriel Kolko, *Anatomy of a War,* 1985; George Herring, *America's Longest War,* 1986; and Marilyn B. Young, *The Vietnam-American Wars,* 1991.

On the antiwar movement and related agitations of the 1960s, see David W. Levy, *The Debate over Vietnam,* 1995; Joseph R. Conlin, *The Troubles: A Jaundiced Glance back at the Movement of the 1960s,* 1982; Morris Dickstein, *Gates of Eden: American Culture in the Sixties,* 1977; Todd Gitlin, *The Whole World Is Watching,* 1981; Theodore Roszak, *The Making of a Counter-Culture,* 1969; Kirkpatrick Sale, *SDS,* 1973; and Irwin Unger, *The Movement,* 1974.

On the more significant civil rights movement, see D. Garrow, *Bearing of the Cross,* 1986; Alex Haley, *The Autobiography of Malcolm X,* 1965; Sam A. Levitan et al., *Still a Dream: The Changing Status of Blacks Since 1960,* 1975; Anthony Lewis, *Portrait of a Decade,* 1964; David Lewis, *King: A Critical Biography,* 1970; Stephen B. Oates, *Let the Trumpet Sound,* 1982; James T. Patterson, *America's Struggle Against Poverty, 1900–1980,* 1981; H. Sitkoff, *The Struggle for Black Equality,* 1981; and Harold Zinn, *SNCC,* 1965.

AMERICAN JOURNEY ONLINE AND INFOTRAC COLLEGE EDITION

Visit the source collections at http://ajaccess.wadsworth.com and http://infotrac.thomsonlearning.com, and use the Search function with the following key terms to explore documents, images, audio and video clips, articles, and commentary related to the material in this chapter:

Barry Goldwater	Lyndon B. Johnson
Black Power	Malcolm X
Cesar Chavez	Richard Nixon
Fannie Lou Hamer	Student Nonviolent Coordinating Committee (or SNCC)
Freedom Summer	Tet Offensive
Haight-Ashbury	Voting Rights Act of 1965
Ho Chi Minh	Women's Liberation Movement

Additional resources, exercises, and Internet links related to this chapter are available on *The American Past* Web site: http://history.wadsworth.com/americanpast7e.

HISTORY ONLINE

The Wars for Vietnam
http://vietnam.vassar.edu/
A collection of documents concerning the war assembled at Vassar College.

The Vietnam War
www.multied.com/wars.html
Information, photo, maps, key battles of the Vietnam War.

Psychedelic '60s
www.lib.virginia.edu/exhibits/sixties/index.html
Done in "hippie" style, this is a serious multi-media look at the counter culture and its historical roots.

49

PRESIDENCY IN CRISIS

The Nixon, Ford, and Carter Administrations 1968–1980

Official White House Photo

In a country where there is no hereditary throne nor hereditary aristocracy, an office raised far above all other offices offers too great a stimulus to ambition. This glittering prize, always dangling before the eyes of prominent statesmen, has a power stronger than any dignity under a European crown to lure them from the path of straightforward consistency.

James Lord Bryce

Americans expect their presidents to do what no monarch by Divine Right could ever do—resolve for them all the contradictions and complexities of life.

Robert T. Hartmann

THE HEROES OF Greek myth were constantly pursuing Proteus, the herdsman of the seas, for he could foresee the future and, if captured, had to reveal what he knew. Proteus was rarely caught. He also had the power to assume the shape of any creature, enabling him to wriggle out of his pursuers' grasp.

Richard Milhous Nixon, his enemies said, was never quite captured because he was always changing his shape. John Kennedy said that Nixon pretended to be so many different people that he had forgotten who he was. Liberals called him "Tricky Dicky." At several turns of his career, even his Republican boosters were constrained to assure Americans that the "Old Nixon" was no more; it was a "New Nixon" who was running for office.

The "Real Nixon," like the real Proteus, remained elusive and enigmatic to the end. Senator Barry Goldwater said that Richard Nixon was "the most complete loner I've ever known."

THE NIXON PRESIDENCY

Nixon is a compelling historical figure. He lacked the personal qualities thought essential to success in late-twentieth-century politics: He was not physically attractive; he lacked social grace, wit, and "charisma." No one ever said of him, "He's a nice guy." Nixon was shy; his manner was furtive. He disguised his discomfort in front of a crowd by willing it, by changing his shape.

Odd Duck

The liberals' dislike of Nixon had the intensity of a hatred, but those who hated the liberals did not love Nixon. President Eisenhower came within a hair of dumping him as his running mate in 1952 and considered replacing him in 1956. In 1960, when Nixon was running for president by emphasizing his experience, Ike humiliated him by saying he was unable to recall an instance in which Nixon contributed to an important decision.

The right-wing Republicans Nixon served well for two decades accepted his leadership without trusting him. When Nixon faced the premature end of his presidency, aides who owed their careers to him stumbled over one another in their haste to turn on him. All was forgiven at his funeral in 1994: Eulogists focused on his achievements, which were numerous, one momentous. Aside from his daughters, however, no one at the memorial ceremonies at Nixon's boyhood home in Whittier, California, spoke of him with affection.

Richard Nixon clawed his way from a middle-class background in southern California to the top of the heap through hard work and the tenacious bite of a pit bull. Although he overstated it in his autobiographical *Six Crises,* he overcame formidable obstacles. If the self-made Horatio Alger boy is an American hero, Nixon belongs in the pantheon, for he was all pluck and little luck. Whatever else historians may say of Richard Nixon, he earned everything he ever got.

Political Savvy

President Nixon had little interest in domestic matters. He believed that "the country could run itself domestically without a president." He left all but the most important decisions to two young White House aides, H. R. Haldeman and John Ehrlichman. With a studied arrogance that amused them, Haldeman and Ehrlichman insulated Nixon from Congress and sometimes from his cabinet. They were themselves unpopular. Like Nixon, they would have few friends when the roof collapsed on the administration.

Politicking, which Nixon never enjoyed, he left to Vice President Spiro T. Agnew, a former governor of Maryland whom Nixon named to the ticket to attract the blue-collar and ethnic voters whom third-party George Wallace was trying to seduce. Agnew was an energetic campaigner and relished his role as Nixon's hit man. He stormed around the country delighting Republican conservatives by flailing antiwar students and the weak-willed, overpaid educators who indulged them in their disruptive activities. He excoriated liberal Supreme Court justices and the news media. Agnew was fond of tongue-twisting alliteration. His masterpiece was "nattering nabobs of negativism," that is, journalists.

Agnew's liberal baiting provided Nixon with a superb smoke screen, for, despite his many denunciations of bigspending liberal government, the president had no interest in dismantling the bureaucracies the Great Society had created. His only major modification of Lyndon Johnson's welfare state was the "New Federalism": turning federal revenues over to the states so that they could run social programs. The New Federalism actually increased the overall size of the nation's government bureaucracies and the inefficiency and waste inevitable in large organizations.

On other fronts, Nixon might as well have been a Democrat. He sponsored a scheme for welfare reform, the Family Assistance Plan, that was to provide a flat annual payment to poor households if their breadwinners registered with employment agencies. (It failed in Congress.) When, in 1971, Nixon worried that a jump in inflation might threaten his reelection the following year, he slapped on wage and price controls, a Republican anathema since World War II.

And yet, Democrats could not gloat, and few Republicans yelped. Nixon understood that the people who ran his party cared only about power and business-friendly government. The grassroots "conservatives" he called the "silent majority" were largely indifferent, or even favorable, toward liberal economic policies. They were repelled by the social

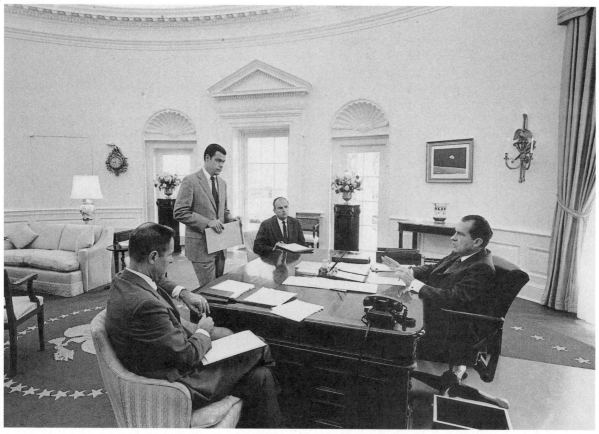

▲ *President Nixon in the Oval Office with his young aides, H. R. Haldeman (foreground) and John Ehrlichman (seated, rear). Nixon secretly recorded his conversations in his inner sanctum. His decision to do so was curious, if for no other reason than because the tapes revealed him to be foul mouthed. In the end, proof on the recordings of his implication in criminal activities destroyed him.*

and cultural causes that 1970s liberals embraced; by what they considered kid-gloves treatment of African Americans; by assaults on traditional moral codes by feminists and gay rights activists; by the anti-Americanism prominent in the antiwar movement and, increasingly, preached by liberal academics; and by Supreme Court decisions they said hobbled police in dealing with criminals.

The Warren Court

Fourteen associate justices served with Chief Justice Earl Warren between 1953 and 1969, many of them at odds with him. Nevertheless, the label "Warren Court" had some justification. Under Warren, the Supreme Court practiced "judicial activism" (reading new meanings into the Constitution in order to ensure justice and fairness by contemporary standards) as opposed to "judicial restraint" (adhering strictly to the meaning of those who wrote the Constitution and its amendments). Judicial activism, its critics said, turned the Court into a legislative body serving political ends. Judicial restraint required the justices to refuse to hear cases involving political issues and to apply the letter of the law to the cases they judged.

The first important decision of the Supreme Court under Warren, *Brown v. Board of Education of Topeka* (1954), faintly presaged the Warren Court's character. In ruling that

segregation of public schools by race was unconstitutional, *Brown* drew on contemporary sociological and psychological sources to interpret the equality clause of the Fourteenth Amendment. Putting African Americans in separate schools, the Court said, was unequal treatment because, no matter how well funded their schools were, segregation fixed in black pupils a sense of their inferior status in society.

Segregationists (and some legal experts who abhorred segregation) said that, in *Brown,* the Court was making law,

Griswold and Roe

A Warren Court decision that was to open a can of political worms only after Warren's retirement was *Griswold v. Connecticut* (1965). It asserted an individual's right to privacy, a very broad reading of the Constitution, on the grounds that the enumerated rights in the Bill of Rights had "penumbras" that provided constitutional standing to practices not mentioned in the Constitution.

In *Roe v. Wade* (1973), four years after Warren retired, the Court drew on *Griswold* (and other precedents) to rule that state legislatures could not deny a woman's right to an abortion. Ironically, the opinion was written by a justice Nixon had appointed to bring judicial restraint to the Supreme Court, with the concurrence of Warren Burger, whom Nixon named to replace Earl Warren.

infringing on powers the Constitution reserved to legislative bodies. The complaint was not new. In 1905, progressives had protested when a pro-employer Supreme Court struck down a New York law forbidding child labor. Liberals howled in 1935 when business-minded justices declared two New Deal programs unconstitutional. The new twist after 1954 was that progressives and liberals celebrated the Warren Court's judicial activism, whereas conservatives (soon mostly Republicans) wrung their hands in dismay.

A series of Warren Court decisions concerning the rights of people accused of crimes caused another uproar. Culminating in *Miranda v. Arizona* (1966), the Warren Court ruled that evidence of a crime seized in a search could not be used against a defendant unless it had been specifically described in the search warrant; that even an obviously guilty criminal had to be freed if police, while questioning him, denied him access to a lawyer; and that, when making an arrest, police were required to explain that the Fifth Amendment protection against self-incrimination permitted the accused criminal to refuse to answer any questions put to him. The Court's decisions were based more on the questions "Is it fair?" and "Does it protect the individual?" than "Does the Constitution explicitly forbid it?" *Miranda,* for example, discarded the principle taught schoolchildren for a generation that "ignorance of the law is no excuse."

When, in 1968, Chief Justice Warren feared that Nixon (whom he despised) would win the presidential election, he resigned so that President Johnson could name his successor. Johnson blundered. He promoted a Texas crony already on the Court, Abe Fortas, to the chief justiceship. Republicans almost immediately discredited Fortas by revealing that he had accepted fees for public appearances that were, at best, dubious. Warren remained to preside at Nixon's inauguration and was only then replaced by Warren Burger, a proponent of judicial restraint.

NIXON AND VIETNAM

Nixon had watched the Vietnam War prematurely terminate Lyndon Johnson's political career. "The damned fool" Johnson had, in the words of a protest song, mired the country "hip deep in the Big Muddy" and was helpless to do anything but to tell the nation to "push on." Nixon had bigger fish to fry. He wanted out of the war. But how? The North Vietnamese refused to negotiate.

Vietnamization

Nixon's objection to the war was political. By sending a huge army to Vietnam, which sustained high casualties without making discernible progress, Johnson had transformed an annoying but marginal antiwar movement into massive disillusionment with the adventure. In order to isolate the hard-core protesters from the majority of the population, he assigned Spiro Agnew the job of smearing the militants as anti-American, while he reduced American casualties by turning the war over to the South Vietnamese.

The United States would "participate in the defense and development of allies and friends," he said, but Americans would no longer "undertake all the defense of the free nations of the world." Nixon opted for "Vietnamization" of the war. "In the previous administration," he explained, "we Americanized the war in Vietnam. In this administration we are Vietnamizing the search for peace."

The large but unreliable Army of the Republic of Vietnam (ARVN) was retrained to replace Americans on the bloody front lines. As South Vietnamese units were deemed ready for combat, American troops came home. At about the same rate that LBJ had escalated the American presence, Nixon de-escalated it. From a high of 541,000 American soldiers in South Vietnam when Nixon took office, the American force declined to 335,000 in 1970 and 24,000 in 1972.

Nixon returned the American role in the war to where it had been in 1964. The trouble was that, in 1964, North Vietnamese troops in South Vietnam had been minimal; by 1970, they were the enemy. As Nixon hoped, the influence of the student antiwar movement declined. What he did not anticipate was that another less theatrical, but far more formidable, opposition emerged. Mainstream Democrats who had dutifully supported Johnson's war, including congressmen and senators, now demanded that the Republican Nixon make more serious efforts to negotiate an end to it.

Expansion of the War

Even Republican senator George Aiken suggested that the United States simply declare victory and pull out of Vietnam. Nixon could not go as far as that. He was beholden for his election to "hawks" who believed that Johnson failed in Vietnam because he had not been tough enough. Nixon reassured them: "We will not be humiliated. We will not be defeated." As much as he and his personal foreign policy guru, Henry A. Kissinger, wanted done with the war, they believed they had to salvage the independence of South Vietnam in order to save face.

So, while Nixon reduced the American presence in Vietnam, he tried to bludgeon North Vietnam into negotiations by expanding the scope of the war with low-casualty air attacks. In the spring of 1969, he sent bombers over neutral Cambodia to destroy sanctuaries where about 50,000 North Vietnamese troops rested between battles. For a year, the American people knew nothing of this new war. Then, in 1970, Nixon sent ground forces into Cambodia, an action that could not be concealed.

The result was renewed uproar. Critics condemned the president for attacking a neutral nation. Several hundred university presidents closed their campuses for fear of student violence. Events at two colleges proved their wisdom. At Kent State University in Ohio, the National Guard opened fire on demonstrators, killing four and wounding eleven. Ten days later, although the issue was not clearly the war, two students demonstrating at Jackson State College in Mississippi were killed by police.

Congress reacted to the widening of the war by repealing the Gulf of Tonkin Resolution. Nixon responded that repeal was immaterial. As commander in chief, he had the right to take whatever military action he believed necessary. Nonetheless, when the war was further expanded into Laos in February 1971, ARVN troops carried the burden of the fighting.

Falling Dominoes

Vietnamization did not work. Without American troops by their side, the ARVN was humiliated in Laos. The Communist organization in that country, the Pathet Lao, grew in strength until, in 1975, it seized control of the country. Tens of thousands of refugees fled.

In Cambodia, the consequences were worse. Many young Cambodians were so angered by the American bombing that they flocked to join the Khmer Rouge, which increased in size from 3,000 in 1970 to 30,000 in a few years. In 1976, the commander, Pol Pot, came to power with a regime as criminal as the Nazi government of Germany. In three years, Pol Pot's fanatical followers murdered 3 million people in a population of 7.2 million!

Eisenhower's Asian dominoes had fallen not because the United States was weak in the face of a military threat but because the United States had endlessly expanded a war that, in 1963, was little more than a brawl. In the process, Indochinese neutrals like Cambodia's Prince Sihanouk were undercut. By the mid-1970s, North Vietnam was dominated by militarists; Laos, by a small Communist organization; and Cambodia, by a monster.

In South Vietnam, the fighting dragged on until the fall of 1972, when, after suffering 12 days of earthshaking bombing, the North Vietnamese finally agreed to meet with Kissinger and arrange a cease-fire. They signed the Paris Accords, which went into effect in January 1973. The treaty required the United States to withdraw all troops from Vietnam within 60 days and the North Vietnamese to release the prisoners of war they held. Until free elections were held, North Vietnamese troops could remain in South Vietnam.

South Vietnamese president Nguyen Van Thieu believed he had been sold out. Nixon had left him facing a massive enemy force. For two years, the country simmered. In April 1975, the ARVN collapsed, and the North Vietnamese moved on a virtually undefended Saigon. North and South Vietnam were united, Saigon renamed Ho Chi Minh City. Ironically, Cambodia's nightmare ended only when the North Vietnamese invaded the country, overthrew Pol Pot, and installed a puppet regime.

The Bottom Line

America's longest war ravaged a prosperous country. Once an exporter of rice, Vietnam was short of food through the 1980s. About a million ARVN soldiers lost their lives, the Vietcong and North Vietnamese about the same number. Estimates of civilian dead ran as high as 3.5 million. About 5.2 million acres of jungle and farmland were ruined by defoliation. American bombing also devastated hundreds of cities, towns, bridges, and highways. The air force dropped more bombs on Vietnam than on Europe during World War II.

The vengeance of the victors (and Pol Pot) caused a massive flight of refugees. About 10 percent of the people of Southeast Asia fled after the war. Some spent everything they owned to bribe venal North Vietnamese officials to let them go. Others piled into leaky boats and cast off into open waters, unknown numbers to drown. To the credit of the United States, some 600,000 Vietnamese, Laotians, Cambodians, and ethnic minorities like the Hmong and Mien (whom every government in Southeast Asia mistreated) were admitted to the United States.

The war cost the United States $150 billion, more than any other American conflict except World War II. Some 2.7 million American men and women served in the conflict; 57,000 of them were killed, and 300,000 were wounded. Many men were disabled for life. Some lost limbs; others were poisoned by Agent Orange, the toxic defoliant the army used to clear jungle. Yet others were addicted to drugs or alcohol. Mental disturbances and violent crime were alarmingly common among Vietnam veterans.

And yet, for 10 years, Vietnam veterans were ignored and shunned. Politicians, not only liberals who opposed the war but also the superpatriotic hawks who wanted the troops to fight on indefinitely, neglected to vote money for government programs to help them. Only in 1982, almost a decade after the war ended, was a monument to the soldiers erected in Washington, D.C.

Principled Foreign Policy

So bitter was the American defeat in Vietnam that, as late as 1990, the United States officially insisted that Pol Pot was the legal ruler of Cambodia. In 1991, the United States engineered a settlement in which the murderous Khmer Rouge shared in the government of the nation.

NIXON-KISSINGER FOREIGN POLICY

Nixon called the Vietnam war a "sideshow." Henry A. Kissinger said that it was a mere "footnote to history." Both men wanted to bring the conflict to an end so that they could bring about a complete reordering of relations among the world's great powers.

▲ *Vietnamese refugees fleeing Hue during the final victory of the Vietcong and North Vietnamese in 1975. Ten percent of the population eventually fled the country. The United States admitted 600,000 refugees as immigrants.*

The Long Crusade

For more than 20 years before the Nixon presidency, virtually all American policy makers divided the world into two hostile camps and a "Third World" of unaligned, mostly undeveloped states. Nuclear weapons made all-out conflict between the United States and the Soviet Union unthinkable except if the only alternative was the annihilation of just one of them. Ideology made antagonism and mistrust inevitable. The only prospect for change was the peaceful internal collapse of one of the superpowers.

Before he was elected president, Nixon expressed nothing to indicate that he imagined another possibility, but when the opportunity for a revolution in American foreign policy presented itself, he seized it.

Premises of Détente

Nixon recognized that the world had changed significantly since the beginning of the Cold War and his political career. The bipolar view of geopolitics had become obsolete with Japan, once a docile American dependency, now the world's third largest economic power; the nations of western Europe groping their way toward unity and an independent economic, political, and military role; and the People's Republic of China, if it was ever subservient to the Soviet Union, no longer so. Reports had reached the West of Chinese-Soviet battles on their 2,000-mile border.

Nixon meant to win his niche in history by effecting a diplomatic reshuffling after which the *five* centers of power dealt with one another rationally and, therefore, with a modicum of confidence. In 1971, he said, "It will be a safer world and a better world, if we have a strong and healthy United States, Europe, Soviet Union, China, Japan—each balancing the other, not playing one against the other, an even balance."

There was no idealism in Nixon's goal of détente (relaxation of tensions). He prided himself on being a hardheaded realist and chose another, Henry Kissinger, as his in-house adviser on foreign policy, who probably introduced the president to the French word that he attached to his policy.

Kissinger on the Cold War
Commenting on relations between the United States and the Soviet Union, Henry Kissinger said:

The superpowers often behave like two heavily armed blind men feeling their way around a room, each believing himself in mortal peril from the other whom he assumes to have perfect vision. . . . Each tends to ascribe to the other side a consistency, foresight and coherence that its own experience belies. Of course, over time even two blind men can do enormous damage to each other, not to speak of the room.

▲ *Henry Kissinger, President Nixon's foreign policy advisor and then his Secretary of State, cultivated the image of a ladies' man on the Washington social scene. His escorts were inevitably glamorous like actress Shirley MacLaine.*

Kissinger was a witty, urbane, brilliant, and cheerfully conceited refugee from Nazism. Although he had lived in the United States for 30 years, his German accent was as thick as if he had just flown in from Frankfurt, which led some of his critics to see it as just another of his many affectations. There was nothing affected in his dedication to *Realpolitik*—the amoral, opportunistic approach to diplomacy associated with Kissinger's historical idol, Count Otto von Bismarck. Kissinger believed that the leaders of the Soviet Union and China were as little concerned with ideals and sentiments as he and Nixon were. They only needed encouragement to launch a new era. His calculation was dramatically confirmed in 1971, when the Vietnam War was still raging and the ripest of denunciations were still flying among Chinese, Russians, and Americans.

Rapprochement with China

Once the Korean War was concluded, the only contacts between China and the United States had been mutual imprecations. Then, in 1971, an American table-tennis team touring Japan received an invitation from the People's Republic to fly over and play a few games before returning home. Thus were diplomatic signals conveyed in the East.

Kissinger virtually commanded the Ping-Pong players to go (they were trounced—the Chinese could not have been expected to pick basketball) and opened talks with Chinese diplomats. He flew secretly to Beijing, where he arranged for a goodwill tour of China by Nixon himself. Only then was the astonishing news released: The lifelong scourge of Red China would tour the Forbidden City, view the Great

Wall, and sit down with chopsticks at a Mandarin banquet with Chairman Mao Zedong and Chou En-lai, drinking toasts to Chinese-American amity with fiery Chinese spirits.

In fact, Nixon's meeting with Mao was ceremonial; the chairman was senile. However, Chou (who, it turned out, had long advocated better relations with the United States) was still alert and active. His protégés, Hua Kuo-feng (who succeeded Mao in 1976) and Deng Xiaoping (who had done time for advocating quasi-capitalist economic reforms) reassured Nixon that he had calculated correctly in coming to China.

Chinese students were invited to study at American universities, and China opened its doors to American tourists, who came by the tens of thousands, clambering up the Great Wall and buying red-ribboned trinkets by the ton. American businessmen involved in everything from oil exploration to the bottling of soft drinks flew to China, anxious to sell American technology and consumer goods in the market that had long symbolized the traveling salesman's ultimate territory. The United States dropped its veto of Communist China's claim to a seat in the United Nations (an absurd position from the start) and established a legation in Beijing. In 1979, the two countries established full diplomatic relations.

Soviet Policy

China did not prove much of a customer. Japan grabbed the market in electronic consumer baubles; Japan already owned the American market! Before long, the Chinese were cutting into America's sales elsewhere of films, recordings, and other popular entertainments by making unauthorized "bootleg" copies. The impelling motive of the Chinese in courting the United States was not economic exchange but China's chilly relations with the Soviet Union. They were "playing the America card."

That was all right with Nixon and Kissinger. They were "playing the China card," putting the fear of a cozy Chinese-American relationship into the Soviets. The gambit worked. In June 1972, just months after his China trip, Nixon flew to Moscow and signed an agreement to open what came to be called the Strategic Arms Limitation Talks (usually known as "SALT"), the first significant step toward slowing down the arms race since the Kennedy administration.

At home, the photos of Nixon clinking champagne glasses with Mao and hugging Brezhnev bewildered right-wing Republicans and flummoxed Nixon's liberal critics. In fact, as Nixon understood, only a Republican like himself with impeccable Cold Warrior credentials could have accomplished what he did.

Shuttle Diplomacy

Nixon was grateful to Kissinger and, in 1973, named him secretary of state. For a year, Kissinger's diplomatic successes piled up. His greatest triumph came in the Middle East after the Yom Kippur War of 1973, in which Egypt and Syria attacked Israel and, for the first time in the long Arab-Israeli conflict, fought the Israelis to a draw.

▲ *President and Mrs. Nixon at the Great Wall of China. All Americans were astonished by such photographs. Hard-line Republican Cold Warriors were flabbergasted. For more than a quarter century, Americans had been told that Communist China was an outlaw nation.*

Knowing that the Israelis were not inclined to accept less than victory and fearing what a prolonged war in the oil-rich Middle East would mean for the United States, Kissinger shuttled, seemingly without sleep, between Syria, Egypt, and Israel, carrying proposal and counterproposal for a settlement. Unlike Dulles, who had also represented American interests on the fly, Kissinger was an ingratiating diplomat. He ended the war, winning the gratitude of Egyptian president Anwar Sadat while not alienating Israel.

After 1974, Kissinger lost his magic touch, in part because of revived world tensions that were not his doing. Soviet premier Leonid Brezhnev may have wanted to reduce the chance of a direct conflict between Russia and the United States. However, he was enough of an old Bolshevik to continue aiding guerrilla movements in Africa and Latin America. Cuba's Fidel Castro, with a large army to keep in trim, loaned combat troops to several countries, notably Angola in southwestern Africa.

Nixon and Kissinger were also willing to fight the Cold War by proxy in the Third World, competing with the Soviets for spheres of influence. Although right-wing Republicans opposed to détente stepped up their attacks on Kissinger, he was actually pursuing their kind of confrontational policies in strife-torn countries like Angola.

The most damaging mark on Kissinger's record as the diplomat in chief of a democratic country was revealed in 1974. The previous year, he had covertly aided, and may have instigated, a coup by the military in Chile that overthrew and murdered the president, Salvador Allende. Allende was a championship-caliber bungler; but he was also Chile's democratically elected leader, and his American-backed successor, Augusto Pinochet, instituted a barbaric and brutal regime marked by torture and murder of opponents.

WATERGATE AND GERALD FORD

By 1974, when news of the Pinochet connection broke in the United States, Kissinger was no longer serving Richard Nixon. The crisis of the presidency that began when Lyndon Johnson was repudiated became graver when Nixon was forced to resign in disgrace. The debacle had its beginnings in the election campaign of 1972, in which, thanks to the transformation of the Democratic party, victory was in Nixon's pocket from the start.

A New Definition of Liberalism

Between 1968 and 1972, privileged "New Age" liberals, dedicated to the antiwar movement, sympathetic to minorities, and enthusiastic about women's liberation, gay rights, and other lifestyle issues, rather than New Deal concerns for working people, won control of several key Democratic party

PRESIDENCY IN CRISIS **729**

Sex: From No-No to Obsession

The traditional American code of sexual morality—a middle-class code—was Christian sexual morality plus the prohibition, in polite society, of talking about sex in any way but with euphemisms. Nineteenth-century bowdlerizers deleted the earthiness from Shakespeare and published Bibles heavily edited for the abstemious.

Total ignorance of sexual mechanics was not uncommon among the daughters of the hyperrespectable "Victorian" middle and upper classes. Diaries and memoirs reveal that many a bride was shocked on her wedding night. Some brides-to-be who were taken aside by an older sister before the nuptials and informed of what the honeymoon held in store thought that they were the victims of a crude joke. The "double standard" allowed young men to be better educated. Thought to be slaves of irresistible urges, men were not "ruined" by "sowing wild oats."

The traditional sexual code forbade masturbation, fornication, adultery, and, within marriage, oral and anal sex. Homosexuality was "the sin that dare not speak its name." By 1900, most states had laws making these acts and pornography criminal as well as immoral. Anthony Comstock, head of the New York Society for the Suppression of Vice, was pathologically obsessed with sex. In 1873, he succeeded in promoting a federal law that, on the face of it, forbade mailing information about contraception but that was employed against anything sexual of which "Comstockery" disapproved.

The code was no more a reflection of actual practice than laws forbidding theft meant there was no embezzlement, robbery, or burglary in America. Some daughters of the middle class had illegitimate babies, although they were kept secret if the family could afford to send the mother to be on an extended visit with "an aunt." It is impossible to know how widespread adultery was. It made the newspapers only when an irate husband killed the man who had cuckolded him, the lovers did away with the superfluous husband, or adultery was cited as grounds in a celebrated divorce.

The code began to totter at the turn of the twentieth century, when jobs and bright lights attracted respectable young women to the big city. Freed from family supervision, they "dated" young men without chaperones, and some, the sexual urge being what it is, experimented. American women born after 1900, maturing during the Roaring '20s, indulged in premarital sex far more often than their mothers had. If traditional sexual morals did not restrain a woman, the only powerful deterrent to enjoying a "liberated" sex life was the fear of pregnancy. Margaret Sanger, who devoted her life to disseminating information about birth control and contraceptive devices, was harassed not so much because she wanted to spare married women the constant pregnancies that impoverished them and ruined their health—which was Sanger's goal—but because of the (justified) belief that knowledge of contraception encouraged unmarried women and girls to tread where they should not.

The "sexual revolution"—anything goes—began in 1960, when an oral contraceptive was marketed by G. D. Searle Pharmaceuticals. Efforts to keep "the pill" out of the hands of unmarried girls and young women were, of course, doomed from the start. The flower children, in their determination to defy their parents in every way, defined the "love" on which the counterculture was based primarily as promiscuous sex: sex on a whim with anyone because it was pleasurable and natural, which was what counted. The hippies shocked people by talk-

---

committees through which they retooled the party machinery. The new procedures and standards for selecting convention delegates penalized longtime party stalwarts: labor unions, big-city machines, those southern "good old boys" who had not already gone Republican, and other political professionals. The McGovern reforms (named for the liberal, antiwar senator from South Dakota, George McGovern) guaranteed representation to party conventions on the basis of gender and race.

The Election of 1972

Consequently, the Democratic convention that met in Miami in the summer of 1972 was the youngest convention ever. There were far more women, blacks, Hispanics, and Indians on the floor than ever before, and most were militantly antiwar. They nominated Senator McGovern and adopted a platform calling for a negotiated end to the Southeast Asian war (then Vietnamized but expanded) and supporting the demands of feminist organizations that abortions be available to women who wanted them.

A decent man profoundly grieved by the war, McGovern tried to distance himself from the most extreme proposals his supporters put before the convention, notably the demand that homosexuality be accepted as an alternative lifestyle. McGovern understood that such a plank was unlikely to win the favor of blue-collar workers who traditionally voted Democratic. The gay rights debate was scheduled for late at night, when few were watching the convention on television, and quietly shelved. McGovern emphasized his pledge to bring peace in Vietnam, tax reforms to benefit middle- and lower-income people, and his record of integrity as compared with Nixon's reputation for deviousness.

But Vietnamization had reduced the arguments of the antiwar movement to pleas for morality. Virtually no labor unions supported McGovern, and most of the old Democratic pros sat on their hands. McGovern had moderated the demands of the lifestyle liberals, but he could not repudiate them any more than Goldwater could have repudiated the John Birch Society in 1964. But the cold fact was, the Miami convention did not represent the views of the electorate.

Nixon won 60.8 percent of the popular vote, a swing of 20 million votes in eight years. He carried every state but Massachusetts (and the District of Columbia). The fact that he was a shoo-in from the beginning of the campaign makes ing about sex too—endlessly—but that taboo had already been felled. A series of court decisions put books that had long been banned into the bookshops. In 1959, D. H. Lawrence's *Lady Chatterley's Lover,* long suppressed because of its explicitly sexual passages, was cleared for sale in the United States. In 1966, the Supreme Court approved publication of an eighteenth-century pornographic classic, *Fanny Hill.* In 1969, the Court said that, because of the "right of privacy," it was not illegal merely to possess obscene or pornographic material.

During the 1970s, casual sex and pornography went bigtime. Languishing cinemas ran nothing but pornographic films and tried, with some success, to attract women as dates or in groups. "Singles bars," explicitly advertised as places where one could meet a sexual partner for a "one-night stand," were fixtures in every city and many towns. "Adult motels" suspended mirrors on ceilings and pumped pornographic movies to TV sets in perfumed rooms. Apartment complexes were retooled with party rooms, saunas, and hot tubs to accommodate "swinging singles." Marriage practices could hardly remain unaffected. The divorce rate soared from 2.5 divorces per 1,000 marriages in 1965 to 5.3 per 1,000 in 1979. The rate of illegitimate births tripled during the 1960s and 1970s, and the number of abortions increased at an equal rate.

Homosexuals benefited from the new openness and relaxation of sexual attitudes. They began "coming out of the closet," proclaiming that their sexuality was an important part of their individual identity and nothing of which to be ashamed. Hundreds of gay and lesbian groups took to the streets in colorful parades. They formed lobbies, soon supported by the "politically correct," to push for laws preventing discrimination against homosexuals in housing and employment. The din was such that someone remarked, "The sin that dare not speak its name cannot sit down and shut up."

"Swinging" on a mass scale proved to be a fad among heterosexuals. Singles bars and singles apartments lost their panache. Pornographic movie theaters closed by the hundreds, in part because, except to aficionados of the genre, the films were dreary and boring—when you've seen one, you've seen them all—but mostly because the Internet brought porn into homes.

Venereal disease caused a decline in casual sex from the frenzy of the 1970s. A penicillin-resistant strain of gonorrhea made the rounds among "swingers"; chlamydia and herpes, relatively innocuous venereal infections, reached epidemic proportions. Rather more serious was a new affliction, Acquired Immune Deficiency Syndrome—AIDS—which slowly and agonizingly killed most of its victims. In developed countries like the United States (although not in the Third World), AIDS was largely a disease of homosexuals and intravenous drug users (it is transmitted only by contact with blood). But, into the 1990s, it was not described as threatening only gays and junkies, in part because it was not politically correct to do so, in part because researchers would have had great difficulty getting funds to research a disease thought to be the exclusive problem of groups on which conventional Americans looked with distaste.

It is difficult to imagine a reversal of the sexual revolution short of a totalitarian government that would make the Taliban's Afghanistan look like a permissive regime. The human sex drive is overwhelming, something that traditional moralists obviously understood, judging by the zeal with which they attempted to repress it.

the surreptitious activities of his Committee to Reelect the President (an unwisely selected name—it abbreviated as "CREEP"), and Nixon's approval of them, impossible to explain except as a reflection of an abnormal psychology.

The Watergate Cover-Up

On June 17, 1972, early in the presidential campaign, Washington police arrested five men who were trying to plant electronic eavesdropping devices in Democratic party headquarters in an upscale apartment and office complex called the Watergate. Three of the suspects were on CREEP's payroll. McGovern tried to exploit the incident as part of his integrity campaign but got nowhere when Nixon and his campaign manager, Attorney General John Mitchell, denied any knowledge of the incident and denounced the burglars as common criminals.

Nixon may have known nothing about the break-in in advance. However, he learned shortly thereafter that the burglars acted on orders from aides close to him. He never considered reporting or disciplining his men. Instead, he instructed his staff to find money to hush up the men in jail. Two of them, however, James E. McCord and Howard Hunt, refused to take the fall. They informed Judge John Sirica that they had taken orders from highly placed administration officials.

Rumors flew. Two reporters for the *Washington Post,* Robert Woodward and Carl Bernstein, made contact with an anonymous informant, still identified only as "Deep Throat" (the title of a pornographic movie), who fed them inside information. A special Senate investigating committee headed by Sam Ervin of North Carolina picked away at the tangle from yet another direction, slowly tracing not only the Watergate break-in and cover-up but other illegal acts and "dirty tricks" to the White House.

The Imperial Presidency

Each month brought new, dismaying insights into the inner workings of the Nixon presidency. On Nixon's personal command, an "enemies list" had been compiled. On it were journalists, politicians, intellectuals, and even movie stars who criticized Nixon. One Donald Segretti was put in charge of spreading half-truths and lies to discredit critics of the administration. G. Gordon Liddy, who was involved in the

Watergate break-in, proposed fantastic schemes involving yachts and prostitutes to entrap political enemies in career-ending scandals. The dirty-tricks campaign grew so foul that not even J. Edgar Hoover, the never squeamish head of the FBI, would touch it.

Watergate was just one of several illegal break-ins sponsored by the administration. Nixon's aides engineered the burglary of a Los Angeles psychiatrist's office to secure information about his patient, Daniel Ellsberg, a Defense Department employee who published confidential information about the prosecution of the war in Vietnam.

Observers spoke of an "imperial presidency." Nixon and his coterie had become so arrogant in the possession of power that they believed they were above the law. Indeed, several years later, Nixon was to tell an interviewer on television, "When the president does it, that means it is not illegal."

If imperial in their pretensions, however, "all the president's men" were singularly lacking in a sense of nobility. One by one, Nixon's aides abandoned ship, each convinced that he was being set up as the fall guy for his colleagues. The deserters described their roles in the Watergate cover-up and dirty-tricks campaign, and named others higher up who told them what to do. In the midst of the scandal, Vice President Spiro Agnew pleaded no-contest to income tax evasion and charges that he accepted bribes when he was governor of Maryland. Agnew was forced to resign in October 1973. He was replaced under the Twenty-Fifth Amendment by Congressman Gerald Ford of Michigan.

Resignation

Then came Nixon's turn, and he was, as the old saw has it, hoisted on his own petard. He had recorded conversations in the Oval Office that clearly implicated him in the Watergate cover-up. (These recordings also revealed him to use the language of a sailor: The public transcripts of the tapes were peppered with "expletive deleted.") After long wrangles in

---

Persistence

When Nixon ran for reelection in 1972, he became the seventh person to run for president three times as the nominee of a major party. These were the seven and the dates of their nominations (the years they won are in boldface):

Thomas Jefferson: 1796, **1800, 1804**
Andrew Jackson: 1824, **1828, 1832**
Henry Clay: 1824, 1832, 1844
Grover Cleveland: **1884,** 1888, **1892**
William Jennings Bryan: 1896, 1900, 1908
Franklin D. Roosevelt: **1932, 1936, 1940, 1944**
Richard M. Nixon: 1960, **1968, 1972**

Technically, John Adams, like FDR, ran for president four times. That is, although it was intended he be elected as George Washington's vice president in 1788 and 1792, constitutionally, he was, like Washington, a candidate for president. Before 1804, there were no vice presidential candidates; the presidential candidate who finished second in the electoral college became vice president.

Eugene V. Debs was the Socialist party presidential candidate five times: 1900, 1904, 1908, 1912, and 1920. Norman Thomas was the Socialist party candidate six times: 1928, 1932, 1936, 1940, 1944, and 1948.

---

the courts, the president was ordered to surrender the tapes to the courts.

That Nixon did not destroy the tapes early in the crisis, before destruction was itself a criminal offense, is difficult to understand. Some insiders said he intended to make money by selling them after he retired. Others said that, like Lyndon Johnson, his mind cracked during the crisis. Nixon had, for some years, been medicating himself with illegally acquired Dilantin, a drug that alleviates anxiety. Secretary of State Kissinger was startled when Nixon asked him to kneel with him and pray. (Neither was a religious man.) Secretary of Defense Schlesinger quietly informed the Joint Chiefs of Staff not to carry out any orders from the White House until they were cleared with him or Kissinger.

After the House of Representatives Judiciary Committee recommended impeaching Nixon, he threw in the towel. On August 9, 1974, on national television, he resigned the presidency and flew to his home in San Clemente, California.

A Ford, Not a Lincoln

Gerald Ford had held a safe seat in the House from Michigan. He rose to be minority leader on the basis of seniority and party loyalty. His ambition was to be Speaker of the House before he retired; events made him vice president and, quickly, president.

Ford was an object of some ridicule. Lyndon Johnson told reporters that Ford's problem dated from the days when he played center on the University of Michigan football team without a helmet. Others quipped that he could not walk and chew gum at the same time. Newspaper photographers laid in

---

Constitutional Contradiction?

Gerald Ford was appointed to the vice presidency under the provisions of the Twenty-Fifth Amendment, which was ratified in 1967. It stipulates that "whenever there is a vacancy in the office of the Vice President, the President shall nominate a Vice President." When Ford succeeded to the presidency, he appointed Nelson A. Rockefeller to the vice presidency. Neither the president nor the vice president held office by virtue of election. However, as some constitutional experts were quick to point out, Article 2, Section 1 of the Constitution provides that the president and vice president are to "be elected."

In fact, the contradiction was always there, if never put to the test. The Constitution and laws hold that the secretary of state and the Speaker of the House are next in line to the presidency after the vice president. A case could be made that the Speaker is elected, but not the secretary of state.

Nixon's (now Ford's) refusal to launch a frontal attack on government regulation and the liberal welfare state.

A Tank Half Empty

The most serious of the woes facing Ford struck at one of the basic assumptions of twentieth-century American life: that cheap energy was available in unlimited quantities to fuel the economy and support the freewheeling lifestyle of the middle class.

By the mid-1970s, 90 percent of the American economy was generated by the burning of fossil fuels: coal, natural gas, and especially petroleum. Fossil fuels are nonrenewable sources of energy. Unlike food crops, lumber, and water—or, for that matter, a horse and a pair of sturdy legs—they cannot be called on again once they have been used. The supply of them is finite. Although experts disagreed about the extent of the world's reserves of coal, gas, and oil, no one challenged the obvious fact that one day they would be no more.

The United States was by far the world's biggest user of nonrenewable sources of energy. In 1975, while comprising about 6 percent of the world's population, Americans consumed a third of the world's annual production of oil. Much of it was burned to less-than-basic ends. Americans overheated and overcooled their offices and houses. They pumped gasoline into a dizzying variety of purely recreational vehicles, some of which brought the roar of the freeway to the wilderness and devastated fragile land. Their worship of the private automobile meant that little tax money was spent on public mass transit. They packaged their consumer goods in throwaway containers of glass, metal, paper, and petroleum-based plastics; supermarkets wrapped lemons individually in transparent plastic and fast-food cheeseburgers were cradled in Styrofoam caskets to be discarded within seconds of being handed over the counter. The bill of indictment, drawn up by conservationists, went on, but, resisting criticism and satire alike, American consumption increased.

OPEC and the Energy Crisis

About 61 percent of the oil that Americans consumed in the 1970s was produced at home, and large reserves remained under native ground. But the nation also imported huge quantities of crude oil. In October 1973, Americans discovered just how little control they had over the 39 percent of their oil that came from abroad.

In that month, the Organization of Petroleum Exporting Countries (OPEC) temporarily halted oil shipments and announced the first of a series of big jumps in the price of their product. One of their justifications was that the irresponsible consumption habits of the advanced Western nations, particularly the United States, jeopardized their future. That is, if countries like Saudi Arabia and Nigeria continued to supply oil cheaply, consuming nations would continue burn it profligately, thus hastening the day when the ran dry. On that day, if the oil-exporting nations had

▲ Gerald Ford, the "accidental president" who won widespread affection by not pretending to be anything but the forthright and hardworking public servant he had been in Congress. Despite serious economic problems, he was defeated only narrowly in 1976, when he ran in his only national election.

Official White House Photo

wait to snap shots of him bumping his head on door frames, tumbling down the slopes of the Rockies on everything but his skis, and slicing golf balls into crowds of spectators.

And yet, Ford's simplicity and forthrightness were a relief after Nixon's squirming and deceptions. He told the American people that fate had given them "a Ford, not a Lincoln." Democrats howled "deal" when Ford pardoned Nixon of all crimes he may have committed, but Ford's explanation—that the American people needed to put Watergate behind them—was plausible and in character. Two attempts to shoot him by deranged women in California helped to win sympathy for the first president who had not been elected to any national office.

Despite his unusual route to the White House, Gerald Ford had no more intention of being a caretaker president than John Tyler had when he became the first president to succeed to the office by reason of death. But it was Ford's misfortune, as it had been Tyler's, to face serious problems without the support of an important segment of his party. The Republican party's right wing, now led by former California governor Ronald Reagan, did not like détente or

▲ *Several times during the 1970s, gasoline was in such short supply Americans had to wait in lines, often for hours, to fill up. Some cities had no gasoline for sale for days at a time. The entire state of Hawaii was brought nearly to a halt awaiting tankers from California.*

the basis for another kind of economy, they would be destitute. Particularly in the Middle East, there were few alternative resources to support fast-growing populations. By raising prices, OPEC said, the oil producing nations would earn capital with which to build for a future without petroleum, while encouraging the consuming nations to conserve, thus lengthening the era when oil would be available.

From a geopolitical perspective, there was much to be said for the argument, but few ordinary Americans (and few greedy dissolutes in the OPEC countries) thought geopolitically. Arab sheiks and Nigerian generals grew rich, and American motorists were stunned when they had to wait in long lines in order to pay unprecedented prices for gasoline. In some big cities and Hawaii, gasoline for private cars was hardly to be had for weeks.

The price of gasoline never climbed to Japanese or European levels, but it was shock enough for people who were accustomed to buying "two dollars' worth" to discover that two dollars bought a little more than enough to drive home. Moreover, the prices of goods that required oil in their production climbed too. Inflation, already 9 percent during Nixon's last ... 12 percent a year when Ford was president.

ow!

ice controls such as Nixon em-
campaign called WIN! (short for

"Whip Inflation Now!"). He urged Americans to deter inflation by refusing to buy exorbitantly priced goods and by ceasing to demand higher wages. The campaign was ridiculed from the start, and, within a few weeks, Ford quietly retired the WIN! button that he was wearing on his lapel. He had seen few others in his travels around the country and began to feel like a man in a funny hat.

Instead, Ford tightened the money supply in order to slow down the economy, which resulted in the most serious recession since 1937, with unemployment climbing to 9 percent. Ford was stymied by a vicious circle: Slowing inflation meant throwing people out of work; fighting unemployment meant inflation; trying to steer a middle course meant "stagflation"—mild recession plus inflation.

Early in 1976, polls showed Ford losing to most of the likely Democratic candidates. Capitalizing on this news, Ronald Reagan, the sweetheart of right-wing Republicans, launched a well-financed campaign to replace him as the party's candidate. Using his control of the party organization, Ford beat Reagan at the convention, but the travails of his two years in office took their toll. He could not overcome the image that he was the most accidental of presidents, never elected to national office. His full pardon of Nixon came back to haunt him. In November 1976, he lost narrowly to a most unlikely Democratic candidate, James Earl Carter of Georgia, who called himself "Jimmy." The Democrats were back, but the decline in the prestige of the presidency continued.

QUIET CRISIS

Since Eisenhower, every president had been identified closely with Congress. Kennedy, Johnson, Nixon, and their defeated opponents had all been senators. The day of the governor candidate seemed to have ended with FDR. Governors did not get the national publicity that senators did. Then, Jimmy Carter came out of nowhere to win the Democratic nomination in 1976. His political career consisted of one term in the Georgia assembly and one term as governor.

Indeed, it was Carter's lack of association with the federal government that helped him win the nomination and, by a slim margin, the presidency. Without a real animus for Gerald Ford, many Americans were attracted to the idea of an "outsider," which is how Carter presented himself. "Hello, my name is Jimmy Carter, and I'm running for president," he told thousands of people face to face in his softly musical Georgia accent. Once he started winning primaries, the media did the rest. When television commentators said that there was a bandwagon rolling, voters dutifully responded by jumping on it.

Inauguration day, when Carter and his shrewd but uningratiating wife, Rosalynn, walked the length of Pennsylvania Avenue, was very nearly the last entirely satisfactory day of the Carter presidency. Whether the perspective of time will attribute his failure as chief executive to his unsuitability to the office or to the massiveness of the problems he faced, it is difficult to imagine historians of the future looking at the Carter era other than as it is now remembered, dolefully.

Peacemaking

Carter had his successes. He defused an explosive situation in Central America, where Panamanians were protesting American sovereignty over the Panama Canal Zone. The narrow strip of United States territory bisected the small republic and seemed to be an insult in an age when nationalist sensibilities in small countries were as touchy as boils.

Most policy makers saw no need to hold on to the Canal Zone in the face of the protests. The United States would be able to occupy the canal within hours in the case of an international crisis. In 1978, the Senate narrowly ratified an agreement with Panama to guarantee the permanent neutrality of the canal itself while gradually transferring sovereignty over it to Panama, culminating on December 31, 1999. Ronald Reagan, who began to campaign for the presidency as soon as Carter was inaugurated, denounced the treaty, but widespread protest dissipated quickly.

Carter's greatest achievement was to save the rapprochement between Israel and Egypt that began to take shape in November 1977 when Egyptian president Anwar

▲ *Jimmy Carter's finest day as president. In 1978, he managed to persuade (or threaten) Israeli prime minister Menachem Begin (right) to sign the Camp David Accords with Egyptian president Anwar Sadat. Carter should have been awarded the Nobel Peace Prize. He was awarded the prize in 2002, but for his humanitarian work after leaving the presidency.*

Sadat risked the enmity of the Arab world by calling for a permanent peace in the Middle East before the Israeli Knesset, or parliament. Rather than cooperate with Sadat, Israeli prime minister Menachem Begin, himself a former terrorist, refused to make concessions commensurate with the Egyptian president's high-stakes gamble.

In 1978, Carter brought Sadat and Begin to meet with him at Camp David, the presidential retreat in the Maryland woods outside Washington. There, Sadat grew so angry with Begin's refusal to compromise that he actually packed his suitcases. Although Carter was unable to persuade Begin to agree that the west bank of the Jordan River, which Israel had occupied in 1967, must eventually be returned to Arab rule, he did bring the two men together. In March 1979, Israel and Egypt signed a treaty.

The End of Détente

Whereas Carter advanced the cause of peace in the Middle East, he shattered the détente that Nixon, Kissinger, and Ford had nurtured. Like Nixon, Carter virtually ignored his first secretary of state, a professional diplomat, Cyrus Vance, and depended on a White House adviser, Zbigniew Brzezinski, for advice.

Unlike the flexible and opportunistic Kissinger, Brzezinski, a Polish refugee from Communism, was an anti-Soviet ideologue. Brzezinski's hatred of the Soviet Union blinded him to opportunities to improve relations between the nuclear superpowers. Moreover, whereas Kissinger had been a charmer, Brzezinski was tactless and crude in a world in which protocol and manners could be as important as substance. The foreign ministers of several of America's allies discreetly informed the State Department that they would not deal with him under any circumstances.

Carter's hostility toward the Soviet Union had different origins. A deeply religious man, moralistic to the point of sanctimony, he denounced the Soviet Union for trampling on human rights. In March 1977, Carter interrupted and set back the Strategic Arms Limitation Talks with completely new proposals. Eventually, a new SALT-II treaty was negotiated and signed, but Carter withdrew it from Senate consideration in December 1979 when the Soviet Union invaded Afghanistan to prop up a client government there. Détente was dead.

The Economy Under Carter: More of the Same

Inflation reached new heights under Carter, almost 20 percent ~~~ng 1980. By the end of the year, one dollar was worth only ~~~ values. That is, on average, it took one dollar ~~~ 1940 cost 15 cents. The dollar ~~~s loss during the 1970s.

~~~ulted for the energy crisis. After ~~~ricans became more energy con-~~~ "gas guzzlers" with more efficient ~~~ sensible turn contributed to the

nation's economic malaise, however. American automobile manufacturers had repeatedly refused to develop small, energy-efficient cars. For a time during the 1960s, after the success of the Germans' Volkswagen Beetle, Ford, General Motors, and Chrysler made compact cars. But within a few years, compacts had miraculously grown to be nearly as large as the road monsters of the 1950s. In the energy crunch of the 1970s, American automakers had nothing to compete with a flood of Japanese imports: Toyotas, Datsuns, and Hondas. The automobile buyer's dollars sailed across the Pacific.

Even then, by 1979, oil consumption was higher than ever, and an even higher proportion of it was imported than in 1976. American oil refiners actually cut back on domestic production, which led many people to wonder if the crisis was genuine or just a cover while the refiners reaped windfall profits—which they did. As prices soared, the oil companies paid dividends such as the always healthy industry had never known.

The price of electricity rose by 200 percent. Utility companies called for the construction of more nuclear power plants in anticipation of even higher rate increases. But Americans had become apprehensive about nuclear energy as an alternative to fossil fuels, following an accident and near catastrophe at the Three Mile Island nuclear plant near Harrisburg, Pennsylvania; the release, at about the same time, of *The China Syndrome,* a film that portrayed a disconcertingly similar accident; and the revelation that a big California reactor about to go online was crisscrossed with construction flaws and built over a major earthquake fault. Was anything in America going right?

Malaise

Carter was repeatedly embarrassed by his aides and family, and himself had a talent for blunders. Genuinely suspicious of the Washington establishment, he surrounded himself with cronies from Georgia who did not, or would not, understand the etiquette and rituals of the capital. Banker Bert Lance, whom Carter wanted as budget director, was tainted by petty, unacceptable loan scams; Ambassador to the United Nations Andrew Young met secretly with leaders of the terrorist Palestine Liberation Organization, which the United States did not recognize as a legitimate representative of the Palestinians. Carter had to fire Young.

The national press, stimulated by the role of journalists in exposing the Watergate scandal, leaped on every trivial incident—a Carter aide tipsy in a cocktail lounge or the president's "down-home" brother Billy's ridiculous opinions—to embarrass the president. Carter honestly but foolishly told an interviewer for *Playboy* magazine, "I've looked on a lot of women with lust. I've committed adultery in my heart many times." In 1980, when Carter's presidency was on the line, his mother told a reporter, "Sometimes when I look at all my children, I say to myself, 'Lillian, you should have stayed a virgin.'"

The Carter administration lacked direction. "Carter believes fifty things," one of his advisers said, "but no one thing. He holds explicit, thorough positions on every issue under the sun, but he has no large view of relations between them." Carter was not unlike most Americans in his engineer mentality. He believed it best to face each specific problem as it arose, working out a specific solution for each.

Such pragmatism had worked for Franklin D. Roosevelt. It did not work for Jimmy Carter. With him at the helm, government resembled a ship without a rudder, drifting aimlessly. Carter was sensitive to what journalists called a national "malaise," but he only embarrassed himself when he tried to address the amorphous problem. He called 130 prominent men and women from every sector of American life to Washington; having listened to them, he was able to announce only that there was "a crisis of the American spirit"—right back where he started from.

for FURTHER READING

James Gilbert, *Another Chance: America Since 1945,* 1984, provides a general overview of this period; Godfrey Hodgson, *America in Our Time,* 1976, deals with the first part of it. However, we are too close to the 1970s to expect too dependable a narrative history of the decade. Many contemporary historians were themselves participants and partisans during these years. Many of the major players are still around, trying to shape their posterity.

Some have written memoirs, perhaps as much for monstrous advances from publishers as for self-justification. These accounts can, nevertheless, be useful and are valuable sources. See Richard M. Nixon, *RN: The Memoirs of Richard Nixon,* 1978; George McGovern, *Grassroots,* 1977; Gerald R. Ford, *A Time to Heal: The Autobiography of Gerald R. Ford,* 1979; Henry A. Kissinger, *White House Years,* 1979, and *Years of Upheaval,* 1982; Jimmy Carter, *Keeping Faith,* 1982; and Rosalynn Carter, *First Lady from Plains,* 1984. A fascinating study of Nixon written before his fall is Garry Wills, *Nixon Agonistes,* 1970. On Kissinger, see Robert Morris, *Uncertain Greatness: Henry Kissinger and American Foreign Policy,* 1977.

Carl Bernstein and Robert Woodward, *All the President's Men,* 1974, is by the two reporters for the *Washington Post* who doggedly investigated the Watergate affair and helped bring about Nixon's fall. Perhaps the most insightful analysis of what happened is Arthur M. Schlesinger Jr., *The Imperial Presidency,* 1973. See also T. H. White, *Breach of Faith,* 1975; Leon Jaworski, *The Right and the Power,* 1976; and Sam Ervin, *The Whole Truth: The Watergate Conspiracy,* 1980.

On national politics and policy during the 1970s, see David Broder, *The Party's Over,* 1972; Samuel Lubell, *The Hidden Crisis in American Politics,* 1970; A. J. Reichley, *Conservatives in an Age of Change: The Nixon and Ford Administrations,* 1981; and Theodore H. White, *The Making of a President, 1972,* 1973. For foreign policy, see Henry Kissinger's memoirs listed above. On specific issues, see R. L. Garthoff, *Détente and Confrontation,* 1985; A. E. Goodman, *The Lost Peace: America's Search for a Negotiated Settlement of the Vietnam War,* 1978; R. A. Pastor, *Condemned to Repetition,* 1987 (on Central America); W. B. Quandt, *Decade of Decision: American Foreign Policy Toward the Arab-Israeli Conflict,* 1978; and G. Sick, *All Fall Down: America's Tragic Encounter with Iran,* 1985.

AMERICAN JOURNEY ONLINE AND INFOTRAC COLLEGE EDITION

Visit the source collections at http://ajaccess.wadsworth.com and http://infotrac.thomsonlearning.com, and use the Search function with the following key terms to explore documents, images, audio and video clips, articles, and commentary related to the material in this chapter:

Détente
Earl Warren
H. R. Haldeman
Henry Kissinger
John Ehrlichman

Kent State
Richard Nixon
Vietnamization
Watergate

HISTORY ONLINE

Nixon White House Phone Calls
www.c-span.org/executive/presidential/nixon.asp
Audio extracts from the tape recordings that brought President Nixon down.

Iranian Hostage Crisis
www.louisville.edu/library/ekstrom/govpubs/subjects/hist/iranhostage.html
Documents of the Iranian hostage crisis of 1979-1981, including excerpts from a hostage's diary.

MORNING IN AMERICA

The Age of Reagan 1980–1993

The White House/David Hume Kennerly

I have long believed there was a divine plan that placed this land here to be found by people of a special kind, that we have a rendezvous with destiny. Yes, there is a spirit moving in this land and a hunger in the people for a spiritual revival. If the task I seek should be given to me, I would pray only that I could perform it in a way that would serve God.

Ronald Reagan

REPUBLICANS LOOKED FORWARD to 1980. Carter had won the White House by a slim margin only because as a southerner, he had carried southern states that had, before 1976, been inexorably drifting into the Republican column. All over the country, his popularity had been eroded by "stagflation" and the perception that he was, simply, ineffective. Then came the disaster.

THE AYATOLLAH AND THE ACTOR

Americans, Jimmy Carter included, believed that Reza Pahlavi, the pro-American shah of Iran, was a popular ruler. With the wealthy and the westernized Iranian middle class, he was. The shah had worked to modernize Iran, promoting industry and finance with the country's huge revenues from oil.

Impoverished Iranians, however, industrial workers as well as the masses of farmers, hated the shah. Pious Muslims were appalled that he emphasized Iran's pre-Muslim past, paying only lip service to Islam. Leftists and liberals among the westernized middle class were alienated by the ruthlessness of SAVAK, the secret police, in suppressing even moderate criticism of the shah's policies. Few in America knew it—Carter described Iran as an "island of stability" in the chaotic Middle East—but the country had been simmering for years when, in January 1979, as unexpectedly as the Communist victory in China 30 years earlier, the shah fled the country.

The Iranian Tragedy

Muslim clerics led by Ayatollah Ruholla Khomeini seized power. In October, when Carter reluctantly admitted the shah to the United States for medical treatment, Iranian students seized the United States embassy in Teheran, taking 50 Americans hostage. For more than a year, they languished in

▲ *American diplomats taken hostage in Teheran. They were separated, moved from place to place, sometimes lived in filth, and were mistreated for a year. Americans grew frustrated by President Carter's inability to free them.*

confinement as President Carter tried to apply reason and diplomacy in a conflict with people motivated by religious and anti-American fanaticism. Then, a poorly conceived attempt to rescue the hostages ended abruptly in a fiasco as American helicopters collided while landing outside the capital of Teheran. Carter's reputation for ineffectiveness grew even worse. Not until January 20, 1981, the day he handed the presidency over to Ronald Reagan, were the imprisoned diplomats released.

Sympathy for the ayatollah in the United States, even among knee-jerk critics, was short-lived. His regime executed not only political opponents but "moral offenders," including people who owned videotapes of Hollywood films. Next to him, the shah looked like Good King Wenceslas.

The Election of 1980

Carter easily beat back a challenge for the Democratic presidential nomination by Massachusetts senator Edward Kennedy. Ronald Reagan, the darling of the Republican conservatives, defeated middle-of-the-road Republicans George Bush and Congressman John Anderson. When Anderson announced he would run as an independent, Reagan placated Republican moderates by naming Bush his running mate.

Rather than frontally attack Carter's handling of the hostage crisis, Reagan blasted his foreign policy in generalities. He pointed to America's low prestige abroad, attributing it to Carter's "softness." A massive military buildup and the will to use force, Reagan said, were needed to end the slide of American influence, prestige, and pride. Domestically, Reagan focused on the weak economy. He promised to reduce regulation of business, which, he said, destroyed initiative. He would bring a stop to inflation, increase employment, cut government spending (except on the military), and balance the federal budget by 1984.

The Ayatollah

Khomeini's fanaticism helped prolong an eight-year war with Iraq that killed 200,000 Iranians, including boys, barely teenagers, dispatched on suicide missions. In 1989, he issued a fatwa—a proclamation—promising salvation (and money) to the Muslim who killed a British author, Salman Rushdie, for writing an offensive book. Khomeini embarrassed many pious Muslims, but his power in Iran was unquestioned.

The Year of Silver

In 1980, Nelson Bunker Hunt and William Herbert Hunt, sons of a right-wing extremist billionaire, launched an audacious scheme to corner the nation's silver supply. They planned to buy so much silver that the threat of scarcity would drive the price of the metal up, allowing them to cash in at what would have been incredible profits. They actually cornered 200 million ounces of silver, half the world's deliverable supply. The price of silver climbed from less than $5 an ounce to more than $50. Americans (and others) rushed their silver wedding gifts to buyers to be melted down—so much for Aunt Lulu's thoughtfulness, good taste, and expenditure.

The scheme failed. The Federal Reserve Bank and other major owners of silver flooded the market, and the price collapsed to less than $10 within weeks. The Hunts had failed but did not have to go on welfare.

Fundamentalist preacher-politicians, like the Reverend Jerry Falwell, organized independent political action committees to promote the belief that liberal social and cultural policies were responsible for a decline in American morality. Falwell's Moral Majority blamed the Democrats for everything from the high divorce rate to the increase in violent crime in big cities.

The Mandate

The experts predicted a close election. Several said the winner would be decided by California, the last big state to report returns. In fact, the election of 1980 was over two hours before the polls closed on the West Coast. Reagan won an electoral college landslide, 489 votes to just 49 for Carter. He won 43.9 million popular votes to Carter's 35.5 million, with 5.7 million going to John Anderson. Apparently, many voters had lied to the pollsters, perhaps embarrassed to say they were going to vote for a former movie star.

The half-century-old Democratic party coalition was dead. The Irish American and Italian American vote, always dependably Democratic, went to Reagan. In all but three states, Slavic Americans voted Republican. Jews, once 80 percent Democratic, split evenly, as did labor union members. Reagan won 60 percent of the vote among the elderly, who—conventional wisdom had it—voted to protect their Social Security, which meant voting Democratic. Young people, lionized by liberal intellectuals for the virtue of their innocence since the 1960s, cast 60 percent of their votes for the aged Republican candidate.

The Moral Majority's political action committees defeated half a dozen liberal Democratic senators they had targeted, including 1972 presidential nominee George McGovern. For the first time in nearly 30 years, the Republicans had a majority in the Senate. The Democrats still held the House. However, several conservative Democrats, startled by the results, announced that they would support the president. A new era had begun.

THE REAGAN REVOLUTION

Reagan turned 78 before he left the White House in 1989, making him the oldest person ever to hold the post; a few years after retiring, he was struck down by Alzheimer's disease. And yet, this elderly actor stamped his personality and values on the 1980s as indelibly as Franklin D. Roosevelt had impressed his on the 1930s.

Man of the Decade

"He has no dark side," an aide said of Reagan. "What you see is what you get." Americans had seen a good deal of Ronald Reagan for more than 40 years. He appeared in 54 films in the 1930s and 1940s, in many as the lead. During the 1950s, he hosted a popular television show. Always political—a New Deal liberal as a young man!—Reagan became

Bonzo

Liberals made fun of Ronald Reagan's movie career, particularly his role in a low-budget film, *Bedtime for Bonzo,* in which he costarred with a chimpanzee. They got nowhere. The president loved Hollywood, never apologized for being in the movies, and even had the last laugh about Bonzo. When a reporter asked him to autograph a publicity photo of him and the chimp, he wrote underneath his signature, "I'm the one with the watch."

a tireless and eloquent campaigner for conservative causes. He was governor of California between 1967 and 1975.

Few people disliked Reagan personally. He may have been a zealot—his mind was not complex—but his manner was avuncular and good natured. He was a master of the homey, morale-building sound bite ("The difference between an American and any other person is that the American lives in anticipation of the future because he knows what a great place it will be"). A cheerful storyteller, Reagan was a walking *People* magazine with a treasury of show-business anecdotes. He conveyed his good humor to both large audiences and small groups gathered in a parlor. He won the affection of even some political critics shortly after his inauguration when, after being shot in the chest by a unbalanced young man, he cracked a joke on the operating table. Reagan was called the "Great Communicator" for his ability to sell himself and his policies. He was also called the "Teflon president": He was so well liked that nothing messy stuck to him, neither his own poor decisions, nor an administration that brimmed with scandal, nor the ridicule of soured former aides.

The criticisms that did not stick to Reagan were legion. After a lifetime at home in the Babylon of Hollywood, evincing no interest in religion, he presented himself as a born-again Christian to accommodate fundamentalist voters. More than a hundred officials in his administration were accused of misconduct; most resigned, and some went to jail. Reagan's popularity rating remained steady. Liberal Garry Wills threw up his hands: Reagan had "bedazzled" the nation.

Social Policies

Reagan believed that, under the domination of liberals, the Supreme Court had become results oriented, tacitly legislating a political agenda in their judicial decisions. The consequences were the social ills Reagan saw around him, such as the "coddling" of lawbreakers.

During his eight years in office, a series of vacancies allowed him to continue the transformation of the Court that Richard Nixon had begun. (Carter appointed no justices.) Reagan's first appointee was Sandra Day O'Connor of Arizona, a protégé of Nixon's most conservative appointee, William Rehnquist. By naming her—the first woman on the Court—Reagan snookered feminists, virtually all of them Democrats, for they had no choice but to applaud; at the same time, he was adding a dependably conservative vote to

▲ *Sandra Day O'Connor, the first woman to sit on the Supreme Court, with President Reagan and Chief Justice Warren Burger.*

the Court. In 1986, Reagan made the forceful Rehnquist chief justice and added Antonin Scalia, a brilliant arch-conservative with a biting writing style, to the Court. Only in 1988, at the end of his term, did Reagan have trouble getting his nominees confirmed. The Senate found Robert Bork, a genuinely talented jurist, too political; a second nominee, a mediocre candidate, was dumped when "old friends" revealed he had smoked marijuana while in law school.

The episode was embarrassing to Reagan because he had made political hay out of his "War on Drugs." His devoted wife, Nancy Reagan, stung by jibes that she cared for little but expensive evening gowns, headed a campaign against the use of illicit drugs among American teenagers called, with Reagan simplicity, "Just Say No!"

Reaganomics

Reagan's popularity owed in part to good luck. Some of the problems that had hobbled Ford and Carter resolved themselves after 1980. A vicious eight-year war between Iran and Iraq prevented the ayatollah from further vexing the United States. The senility of Soviet leader Leonid Brezhnev and, after his death in 1982, three years of geriatric caretaker leadership, left the Cold War adversary virtually without direction until 1985. The Organization of Petroleum Exporting Countries, which had dictated world energy prices during the 1970s, fell apart, and the retail cost of gasoline collapsed.

But the keystone of Reagan's popularity was the fact that, after two economically difficult years, his presidency was a time of steadily increasing prosperity. The good times, Reagan believed, were due to his economic policy, which critics called "Reaganomics."

Reaganomics was based on the "supply-side" theories of economist Arthur Laffer, who emphasized increasing the nation's supply of goods and services while allowing the distribution of wealth—each person's share—to take care of itself. In essence, this meant cutting the taxes in the upper-income brackets. Whereas modestly fixed people would spend tax savings on consumer goods, supply-siders argued, the affluent already had all the extras. They would invest their tax savings, thus providing the economy with capital. The economic growth that resulted would mean jobs for people on the bottom. The formerly unemployed would no longer need public

Urban Decay

In New York City every day between 1977 and 1980, 600 to 2,100 subway cars were out of service because of age, mistreatment, or vandalism. Between 80 and 300 trains had to be canceled each day. There were 2,200 to 5,000 fires in the New York subway system each year. In 1980, it took 40 minutes to take a trip on the subway that took 10 minutes in 1910.

assistance (enabling government to reduce spending on social programs), and they would begin to pay taxes. Greater revenues would allow Reagan to balance the budget, as he had promised he would do.

Prosperity in Practice

Democrats with a sense of history pointed out that Reaganomics closely resembled Calvin Coolidge's "trickle-down" economics, which had contributed to the Great Depression. Reagan was not impressed. At his behest, Congress reduced taxes by 25 percent over three years. The drop, for those with good incomes, was considerable. An upper-middle-class family making $75,000 a year paid federal income taxes of 52.9 percent during the 1950s and 39.3 percent during the 1970s. By 1985, after the Reagan tax cut, such a family was taxed only 29.6 percent on its income. The rich did even better. The average tax bill for an annual income of $500,000 to $1 million in 1981 was $301,072. By the time Reagan left office, it was $166,066—proportionately less than a western European waiter paid.

Government revenues dropped by $131 billion, which Reagan said he would make up by slashing expenditures on bureaucracy and social programs. He cut 37,000 jobs from the federal payroll and reduced spending on education, medical research, food stamps, and other programs instituted during the 1960s to aid the poor. Federal spending on low-income housing dropped from $32 billion in 1980 to $7 billion in 1988.

The Mushrooming Deficit

But Reaganomics did not work as the president and Arthur Laffer had predicted it would. Much of the middle-class tax break went not into investment but into consumption of ever more expensive luxury goods. By 1986, investment in manufacturing was only 1 percent higher than it had been in the recession year of 1982. However, sales of high-priced homes had boomed. Expensive imports, like Jaguar and Mercedes-Benz automobiles, soared. Americans imported better wines and, for a few years, even their drinking water: Perrier, a bottled French mineral water, became a mania.

Money to feed the consumption binge also came from abroad. West German, Japanese, and Arab investors pumped money into the United States, buying real estate, corpora-tions, banks, stocks, and United States Treasury bonds in huge blocks. From being the world's leading creditor nation when Reagan took office, the United States became the world's biggest debtor. In 1981, foreigners owed America $2,500 for each American family of four. By 1989, the United States owed foreigners $7,000 for each family of four.

The federal deficit—the government's annual debt—grew worse each year Reagan was in office. The costs of Social Security, pensions, and especially Reagan's military buildup were immense. The president did not miss a step. He regularly called for a constitutional amendment mandating a balanced budget while his administration spent and borrowed at levels that smashed all records. In 1981, the federal government owed $738 billion, about 26 cents on each dollar produced and earned in the United States that year. In 1989, the debt was $2.1 trillion, about 43 cents on each dollar produced and earned. The president who criticized Jimmy Carter's borrowing borrowed more money in eight years than 39 previous presidents had borrowed in two centuries! That he continued to charm the majority of Americans hints at aspects of human nature that, in a history textbook, can, happily, be passed by.

Deregulation

Since the New Deal, the federal government had regulated most important aspects of national economic life. This regulation, Reagan said, discouraged the spirit of enterprise. As president, he weakened the regulatory apparatus by abolishing some agencies and cutting the budgets of others. To head some offices, Reagan appointed officials who deliberately neglected to do their jobs. Airlines, trucking companies, banks, and stockbrokers found there were fewer federal watchdogs apt to drop in, and those who did were quite friendly.

Profits increased. Airlines closed down routes where profits were slim and raised fares on the well-traveled air lanes. In 1981, a person could fly from San Francisco to Los Angeles for $36. In 1989, the same ticket cost $148. Getting from big cities to small ones by air, however, became very expensive, when it was possible. By the hundreds, small towns that had boasted regularly scheduled flights lost them. Consumer advocates claimed that the deregulated airlines sent unsafe planes and unqualified pilots aloft. Similar criticisms were made of the condition of trucks and the qualifications required of truck drivers. In fact, serious accidents involving big "semi" trucks increased during the decade.

Who's Got What?

In 1929, the year of the Great Crash, the richest 1 percent of Americans owned 44 percent of the nation's net household wealth. This lopsided distribution of wealth was widely believed to have been a major cause of the economic crisis of the 1930s.

By 1976, the richest 1 percent's share of the nation's wealth was reduced to 20 percent. By 1989, the year Ronald Reagan left office, the top 1 percent owned 48 percent of the nation's net wealth, more than in 1929.

Priorities in the 1980s

In 1983, the United States spent 57 cents per capita on public broadcasting, as compared to $10 per capita in Japan, $18 in Great Britain, and $22 in Canada. In the private sector, the cost of making one episode of the television program *Miami Vice* was $1.5 million. The annual budget of the vice squad in the city of Miami, Florida, a major clearinghouse for imported drugs, was just $1.1 million.

Several of Reagan's appointees to environmental agencies despised the people they called "tree huggers"—conservationists and environmentalists. The head of the Environmental Protection Agency, Anne Burford, was forced to resign in 1983 when it was revealed she had actively interfered with the enforcement of the agency's regulations. Reagan's secretary of the interior, James Watt of Colorado, tried to open protected scenic coastline to offshore oil drillers.

Watt was a leader of the "sagebrush rebels," western businessmen who wanted the federal government to turn public lands over to the states, which would then open them to exploitation by mining, logging, and grazing companies. So arrogant and tactless was Watt, however, that "tree hugger" environmental groups grew rapidly. The Wilderness Society had 48,000 members in 1981 and 240,000 in 1989. The Natural Resources Defense Council increased its membership from 85,000 to 170,000. The World Wildlife Fund had 60,000 members in 1982 and 1 million in 1990. The Sierra Club and Audubon Society made similar gains.

Reagan was nonplused. He even vetoed a clean water act aimed at stopping the dumping of toxic industrial wastes.

Financial Fraud

Deregulation of financial institutions led to irresponsible and sometimes corrupt practices in banks and savings and loan associations. In 1988 alone, 135 savings and loans had to be bailed out or closed by the Federal Savings and Loan Insurance Corporation. This agency, like the Federal Deposit Insurance Corporation for banks, insured savings accounts. Before the Reagan deregulation, however, the two agencies also enforced strict management standards on the people who ran the financial institutions. During the Reagan years, supervision was virtually nil, and shoddy practices multiplied. Even George W. Bush, son of the vice president, was involved in dubious transactions. An energy company paid him $120,000 during a year the company was losing $12 million. The company also loaned him $180,000 at low interest to buy stock in the company. Then, one week before huge losses were announced and the price of the company's stock dropped by 60 percent, Bush sold his shares for $850,000.

The champion wheeler-dealer of the 1980s was Michael Milken, who sold deregulated savings and loans billions of dollars in "junk bonds," loans that promised to pay high interest precisely because no prudent (or supervised) investor would touch them. Milken, who in one year collected $550 million in commissions, eventually went to jail. So did several prominent figures on Wall Street. Freed of close supervision by the Securities and Exchange Commission, respected stockbrokers turned to fraud. By paying bribes to executives in large corporations, they learned, before the general public did, of important decisions that affected the price of stocks. Using this insider information, they bought and sold shares at immense profits.

Through it all, the Reagan administration continued to approve corporate mergers and takeovers that did little but enrich a few individuals. In 1970, there were 10 corporate reshufflings paying fees of $1 million or more to those who arranged them. In 1980, there were 94; in 1986, 346. In 1988, the government approved a deal between tobacco giant R. J. Reynolds and the Nabisco Company despite the fact that, as even the principals admitted, the only consequences would be higher prices for consumers, fewer jobs in the two companies, and personal profits of $10 million for a handful of top shareholders.

The Election of 1984

In 1984, Walter Mondale of Minnesota, vice president under Jimmy Carter, won the Democratic party presidential nomination by beating back challenges from Senator Gary Hart of Colorado and the Reverend Jesse Jackson, a civil rights activist who, a few years later, was to coin the term *African American.* Jackson was a first-rate orator in the tradition of the black churches from which he had emerged an ordained minister. Hart was the New Age candidate, popular among fashionable, generally affluent people in their 20s and 30s who, although little interested in the social and economic policies of old-line Democrats, defined themselves as liberal.

Mondale, who was an old-style New Dealer, hoped that labor union support and what he called the "sleaze factor," the widespread corruption in the Reagan administration, would be enough to help him overcome the president's personal popularity. But he was unable to bring back the traditionally Democratic voters who had gone for Reagan in 1980. Mondale was perceived as a pork-barrel candidate,

▲ *Michael Milken, whose income exceeded $1.2 billion between 1985 and 1987, was jailed for violating federal regulations in selling high-risk and sometimes fraudulent junk bonds to savings and loans, many of which went under. Milken was in it for the adventure; he neither flaunted his wealth nor showed much interest in enjoying it.*

The Statistical American, 1980

The statistical American of 1980 was a Caucasian female, a little more than 30 years old. She was married to her first husband; she had one child and was about to have another. She was about 5 feet, 4 inches tall and weighed 134 pounds. Statisticians said that she had tried marijuana when she was younger but no longer used it, although she had friends who did. She did not smoke cigarettes; she did drink, but moderately, on "special occasions."

A study by a scientific management firm revealed she would spend 7 of the 75 years she would live in the bathroom, 6 years eating, 5 years waiting in lines, 4 years cleaning house, 3 years in meetings, 1 year "looking for things," eight months opening junk mail, and six months waiting at red lights.

The statistical American adult female considered herself middle-class. She had attended college and was likely to work outside the home; but shaky economic conditions during the first half of the decade made her job opportunities uncertain. Her household income was about $20,000 a year. She and her husband were watching their budget closely. By a tiny margin, she was more likely to be registered as a Democrat than as a Republican, but, if she voted in 1984 (also a statistical toss-up), she was more likely than not to have voted for Ronald Reagan. She had had a fling with the new feminism—"consciousness-raising" meetings with friends for a few months—but had lost interest after getting her husband to do a bigger share of the household chores. She had supported the Equal Rights Amendment, but its failure did not disturb her.

More than half of the statistical American's women friends were married. Most of those who had been divorced married again within three years. She attached no stigma to divorce and experienced only a slight sense of unease with people who lived with members of the opposite sex without benefit of marriage.

She did not think that homosexuality was nothing more than an "alternative lifestyle" on a moral parity with heterosexuality. She was both amused and repelled by the culture of the gay communities about which she read; but, by 1985, she was disturbed by the quantum leap in the spread of AIDS, which she regarded as a homosexual disease.

She almost certainly had sexual relations with her husband before they married and, almost as likely, with at least one other man. There was a fair chance that she had a brief affair after marrying.

The statistical American was more likely to be Protestant than Catholic but more likely to be Catholic than a member of any specific Protestant denomination. If she was a Catholic, she practiced birth control, most likely the pill, despite the church's prohibition of it. Catholic or Protestant, she attended church services far less frequently than her mother did.

The statistical American was in excellent health; she saw a dentist and a doctor more than once a year, and paid a little less than half the cost of her health care. Her life expectancy was almost 78 years; she would outlive her husband by 8 years, and, with few children, chances were that her old age would be economically trying.

The statistical American lived in a state with a population of about 3 million people—Colorado, Iowa, Oklahoma, Connecticut—and in a city of about 100,000—Roanoke, Virginia; Reno, Nevada; Durham, North Carolina.

As the question about her state and city of residence indicates, the statistical American of the 1980s is a somewhat absurd contrivance, distilled out of the majorities, means, and medians published by the United States Census Bureau, the responses to surveys taken by measurers of public opinion, and the probabilities of the educated guess.

---

promising something to every constituent group. Moreover, he proved politically clumsy for someone supposed to be a cynical old pro. He named a woman, Geraldine Ferraro, as his running mate despite the fact that feminists were not apt to vote Republican under any circumstances and Republican women were not moved by appeals to sisterhood. Mondale gained no votes by picking Ferraro and threw away a chance to use the vice presidential slot to appeal to former Democrats who had been seduced by the Great Communicator.

Reagan's popularity was at flood tide in 1984. He won by a landslide, carrying 59 percent of the vote and every state except Mondale's Minnesota and the District of Columbia. He announced that the theme of his second term was "Morning in America."

FOREIGN POLICY IN THE '80s

Reagan was a Cold Warrior. In 1982, he called Russia an "evil empire . . . the focus of evil in the world." In 1985, he promulgated the Reagan Doctrine—pretty much warmed-over John Foster Dulles—that the United States would sup-

port anti-Communist struggles everywhere in the world. By the time he left office in 1989, however, Reagan had scored a major breakthrough in nuclear arms reduction and set the stage for a historic rapprochement between the United States and the Soviet Union. His policies toward other parts of the world were also sometimes surprising.

South Africa and the Middle East

Reagan criticized South Africa's policy of apartheid (strict segregation of races), but he resisted calls for economic sanctions some said would force the South African regime to change. He continued to support rebels in Angola who were fighting a government backed by the Soviet Union and by troops from Cuba.

Reagan continued Jimmy Carter's policy of aiding anti-Russian rebels in Afghanistan despite the fact that they were Muslim fundamentalists like those who had swept Khomeini to power in Iran. In 1983, he sent marines to Lebanon, which was torn by a multisided war involving both religion and foreign intervention. When a suicide bomber driving an explosive-laden truck killed 241 sleeping marines, he withdrew the force. His Teflon worked as ever. Reagan was not widely criticized either for sending the marines in or for withdrawing them in failure.

In 1986, Reagan won applause by bombing Libya. The Libyan leader, Muammar Gadhafi, had long been suspected of financing terrorists. When American intelligence claimed to have evidence of a direct link between Gadhafi and terrorists in West Germany, American bombers raided several Libyan cities. Public opinion approved the expedition.

Central America

The president applied the Reagan Doctrine in the Caribbean and Central America. In October 1983, he ordered a surprise occupation of Grenada, a tiny island nation of 110,000 people. The island was in chaos after the assassination of a Marxist leader. Although critics feared that one such invasion would lead to others, the president's action was popular and successful.

His policy in Central America was more controversial. Many liberals opposed United States support of a repressive government in El Salvador and the administration's opposition to the revolutionary Sandinista government of Nicaragua. When, in 1983, El Salvador elected a moderate over an extreme rightist as president, criticism of Reagan's policy in that country faded too.

However, many in Congress continued to oppose American support of the Nicaraguan contras, guerrillas fighting the Sandinista government. Some said that the United States was causing turmoil and misery in an already wretched and long misgoverned country by keeping it at war. Others said that the contras were reactionary and antidemocratic. Still others feared that the United States would become involved in another quagmire like Vietnam. Beginning in October 1984, a worried Congress attached the Boland Amendments to several bills providing money for foreign aid. These prohibited the government from directly aiding military actions in Nicaragua.

The Iran-Contra Affair

Rather than accept the law, in February 1985, Reagan told top aides to "figure out a way to take action." They embarked on a bizarre adventure that mocked the president's depiction of world politics as a competition between good and evil. Two national security advisers, Robert McFarlane and John Poindexter, and a marine colonel, Oliver North, secretly sold 18 Hawk missiles to the Ayatollah Khomeini's Iran! Some of the huge profits from the deal simply disappeared into someone's pocket. The balance was given to the contras.

The roles of Defense Secretary Weinberger and the president in the affair were never clearly defined. Weinberger was indicted for withholding information, and Reagan changed his story several times. It was clear, however, that the president had either sanctioned violation of the Boland law or did not know what was going on in his administration.

Liberals screamed bloody murder. But Ronald Reagan was no ordinary political target. Times were good; stocks and real estate values were rising; football players were better than ever; and television entertainers brought tears and laughter nightly into American living rooms. The public seemed not to notice or to care. Colonel North, convicted in 1989 on three criminal charges, went on in 1994 to miss election to the Senate from Virginia by a narrow margin.

Changing Policies

Even before the Iran-Contra affair made the news, Reagan's foreign policy underwent significant changes. Rather than defend an anti-Communist dictator in Haiti in 1986, American agents played an important role in persuading him to go into exile. The United States also played a central role in the ouster of the pro-American but abysmally corrupt president of the Philippines, Ferdinand Marcos. When Marcos declared himself the victor in a disputed election, riots broke out throughout the country. Fearing a civil war, the United States supported his opponent, Corazon Aquino. Marcos was given asylum in Hawaii to get him out of the Philippines.

Reagan was unsuccessful in his attempt to ease out Manuel Noriega, the military dictator of Panama. Evidence indicated that Noriega was involved in smuggling cocaine and other drugs to the United States. He was indicted in the United States, and Reagan cut off the flow of American dollars to Panama. However, Noriega's hold on the Panamanian army was strong, and he rallied public support by baiting the United States, always a crowd pleaser in Latin America.

Weapons Buildup

The most important of Reagan's foreign policy shifts was in his view of the Soviet Union. Calling the second Strategic Arms Limitation Talks (SALT-II) treaty a "one-way street," with Americans making all the concessions to the Soviets, he refused to submit it to the Senate for ratification. In 1986, Reagan announced that the United States would no longer be bound by SALT-I.

In the meantime, the president had sponsored the greatest peacetime military buildup in the nation's history, spending $2 trillion on both old and new weapons systems. Battleships were taken out of mothballs and put to sea despite the fact that one could be sunk by one cheap missile in the armories of a dozen nations. Reagan revived the MX missile, which he renamed the Peacekeeper. When it was announced that the Peacekeepers were to be installed in old Minuteman missile silos, critics said if Reagan was not just pumping money into the treasuries of defense contractors, he was planning a first strike against the Soviets. It was well known that the Russians had the Minuteman sites targeted. The Peacekeepers were useless unless they were fired in a surprise attack.

In 1983, Pershing II missiles were installed in West Germany, from which they could hit Soviet targets in five minutes. The Russians responded by increasing their striking capability. A new arms race seemed to be under way. By 1985, the two superpowers had more than 50,000 nuclear warheads between them.

The most controversial of Reagan's weapons proposals was the Strategic Defense Initiative (SDI), known as "Star Wars" after a popular movie. In theory, SDI was a system by which satellites orbiting the earth would be equipped with computer-controlled lasers that could fire at missiles. Reagan claimed that the system would create an umbrella preventing a successful missile attack on the United States.

Criticism of Star Wars took several forms. Some scientists said that SDI simply would not work, pointing out that low-flying missiles and planes would be unaffected by lasers from space. Bankers worried that the astronomical costs of the project would bankrupt the United States. Antiwar groups said that SDI was an offensive, not defensive, weapon; by making the United States safer from nuclear attack, it would encourage a first-strike attack on the Soviet Union. Others said that the Soviets would simply develop countermeasures, which had always been the case in military technology, and the insanity would go on and on.

A Turn Toward Disarmament

Still, it was not criticism that led President Reagan to reverse direction in defense policies. During his second term, the hawkish Caspar Weinberger resigned as secretary of defense, and the more statesmanlike secretary of state, George Schultz, the dove of the Reagan administration, increased his influence over the president.

White House insiders said that Nancy Reagan played a major part in persuading the president to turn toward disar-

▲ *Nancy Reagan was enamored of the trappings of wealth, but obviously and most of all, she was devoted to her husband and his posterity. Some of President Reagan's aides said that her influence was key to the president's moves toward disarmament late in his administration.*

mament. Deeply devoted to her husband, she was concerned about his place in history, and she knew that presidents who worked for peace had higher historical reputations than those who seemed to be warmongers.

The concerns of allies in Europe also influenced the president. Chancellor Helmut Kohl of West Germany, President François Mitterrand of France, and Prime Minister Margaret Thatcher of Great Britain remained loyal to the North Atlantic Treaty Organization alliance. However, all made it clear that they were unnerved by some of Reagan's

Weapons

Ronald Reagan roundly criticized his predecessor, Jimmy Carter, for neglecting the American military and, in fact, increased Carter's defense budget by 28 percent. However, the weapons systems developed during the Carter administration, such as the Tomahawk Cruise Missile, the F-117 Stealth Fighter, and the HARM antiradar missile, proved to be keys to victory in the Gulf War against Iraq, whereas Reagan-era innovations had dubious outcomes. Star Wars died. The battleships Reagan recommissioned were put back into mothballs within a few years. And the B-1 bomber was a $30 billion flop. Just 97 planes were built; they were cursed by engine failure and ice accumulation on their wings.

more reckless speeches. Most important, the Soviet Union underwent profound changes during the 1980s.

Mikhail Gorbachev

In 1985, Mikhail Gorbachev emerged as head of both the Soviet government and Communist party. At home, Gorbachev tried to institute far-reaching economic and political reforms. His policy of perestroika ("restructuring") was designed to revive the Soviet economy, which had been moribund under strict government controls. He also instituted a policy of glasnost ("openness") that promised political and intellectual freedoms unheard of in the Soviet Union.

If his reforms were to succeed, Gorbachev needed to divert Soviet resources from the military to the domestic economy. Doing that depended on American cooperation. At first, Reagan resisted Gorbachev's proposals to end the arms race. Then, in Washington in December 1987, the two men, all smiles and handshakes, signed a treaty eliminating many short-range and medium-range missiles. The Soviets destroyed 1,752 missiles, and the Americans, 867. These represented only 4 percent of the nuclear missiles in existence. Nevertheless, nuclear power 32,000 times the force of the Hiroshima bomb was wiped out.

THE BUSH PRESIDENCY

The Democrats approached the presidential campaign of 1988 with high hopes. They believed that the Reagan presidency was an aberration, the personal triumph of a fabulously popular individual. A majority of governors were Democrats. The Democratic party enjoyed a comfortable majority in the House and had regained control of the Senate in 1986. Why should not the Democrats regain the presidency too?

The Seven Dwarfs

As always when election victory seems likely, the Democrats were swamped with would-be nominees. The front-runner in the early going was Gary Hart, the former senator from Colorado who had opposed Mondale in the 1984 primaries. But, in a bizarre sequence of events, including publication of a photo showing the married Hart with a beautiful young model on his lap aboard a yacht called the *Monkey Business,* political analysts suggested that the candidate's judgment was, perhaps, a little less than what was called for by the presidency.

When Hart withdrew from the race, the remaining candidates were ridiculed as the "seven dwarfs" for their deficiency of presidential stature. In fact, several of the dwarfs were able men, and Jesse Jackson remained, as he had been in 1984, one of the nation's most exciting speakers. Because he was black, however, Jackson was considered unelectable by most party professionals.

The professionals hoped that Senator Sam Nunn of Georgia, a thoughtful and respected expert on national defense, would jump into the 35 primary election races or that Governor Mario Cuomo of New York, another inspiring orator whose thoughtful humanism was tempered by hard-headed political realism, would run.

But neither did, and the nomination went to Governor Michael Dukakis of Massachusetts. The son of Greek immigrants, Dukakis was a successful governor, balancing budgets while the Reagan administration spent and borrowed. During his administration, a state with serious economic difficulties

▲ *Five presidents gather to dedicate the Ronald Reagan Presidential Library in 1993. From left to right: Bush, Reagan, Carter, Ford, and Nixon. Carter remarked, "At least all of you have met a Democratic president. I haven't had that honor."*

became a prosperous center of finance and high-tech industry. For vice president, Dukakis chose the courtly Senator Lloyd Bentsen of Texas, reminding voters of the Massachusetts-Texas combination that had won the election of 1960.

Bush for the Republicans

The Republican nominee was Vice President George Bush, who handily defeated Senator Robert Dole of Kansas in the primaries. Bush was a wealthy oilman who had held a number of appointed positions in government before becoming vice president under Reagan. He became the administration's chief cheerleader and attracted ridicule for his conversion to right-wing politics; but Bush's change of heart enabled him to establish ties with Republican conservatives who, earlier, had looked on him as a liberal.

As his running mate, Bush chose Senator Dan Quayle of Indiana, all of whose achievements since first tying his shoes seemed to owe to his father's wealth and influence. Quayle admitted he had "majored in golf" at university. There was also evidence that he had dodged military service during the Vietnam War when his father's friends created a place for him in the National Guard. Quayle's political career was built on his movie-star good looks and careful programming by political handlers. During the campaign of 1988, they made sure that he spoke mostly to screened groups of the party faithful or to high school and elementary school pupils.

The Campaign

Dukakis attacked Bush's judgment in picking Quayle, but Dukakis's public persona was mechanical and dull. Pundits joked of "Zorba the Clerk." By contrast, winning the Republican nomination seemed to liberate Bush. As Dukakis grew drabber and grayer, Bush exuded confidence and authority, promising both to continue the policies of the Reagan-Bush administration and to usher in "a kinder, gentler America."

While Bush took the high road, Republican strategists smeared Dukakis because a murderer paroled in Massachusetts during his governorship killed again. They hammered on the fact that Dukakis was a member of the American Civil Liberties Union, which had become a citadel of New Age liberalism, defending pupils wearing T-shirts bearing obscene messages to school. Dukakis was put on the defensive, forced to point out that he was not responsible for Massachusetts parole policies and that he disagreed with many of the American Civil Liberties Union's preachments. But he never gained the initiative. Bush led throughout the campaign and won 54 percent of the vote.

Dubious Legacy

A few months before Bush's election, Ronald Reagan told a joke to an audience of Republicans. Two fellows, he said, were out hiking in the woods when they saw a grizzly bear coming over the hill toward them. One of them immediately reached into his pack, pulled out a pair of sneakers, and started removing his boots and putting on the sneakers. The other said, "You don't think you can outrun that grizzly, do you?" And the first one said, "I don't have to. I just have to be able to outrun you."

Reagan outran George Bush. When he retired to his California ranch in January 1989, it still appeared to be morning in America. In fact, George Bush inherited a host of problems that were to make him a one-term president.

The Collapse of Communism

In May of 1989, thousands of student demonstrators gathered in Tiananmen Square, the huge plaza at the center of the Chinese capital, and demanded glasnost-like reforms in China. Within two days, there were a million people in the square. The drama was played out live on American television, for two news bureaus were in Beijing to cover a visit by Soviet premier Gorbachev. Americans even caught some glimpses of the brutal suppression of the rebellion, which resulted in at least 500, and according to some sources 7,000, deaths.

Communist hard-liners succeeded in holding on to power in China. In eastern Europe, however, the countries that had been satellites of the Soviet Union since World War II exploited Gorbachev's relaxation of controls to oust their Communist rulers. Poland elected a non-Communist government in mid-1989. By the end of the year, Czechoslovakia followed suit. In October, Erich Honecker, the Communist chief of East Germany, resigned; the next month, a festive crowd breached the Berlin Wall. In December, the much hated dictator of Romania, Nicolae Ceausescu, was murdered by revolutionaries. In April 1990, Hungary elected an anti-Communist government. In a few astonishing months, a European order almost half a century old was liquidated.

Communist party control of the Soviet Union also dissipated. Glasnost had successfully opened up Soviet society, but perestroika had not succeeded in bringing vitality to the Soviet economy. Food shortages in cities led to increasing protests. On May Day 1990, Communism's holiday, Gorbachev and his colleagues were roundly jeered as they reviewed the traditional parade. A few days later, Boris Yeltsin, a critic of Gorbachev, was elected president of the Russian Republic, the largest constituent republic of the Soviet Union. For the next year and a half, Yeltsin increased his following at Gorbachev's expense by calling for a free-market economy and supporting claims to independence in many of the other 14 republics. At the end of 1991, the Soviet Union was formally dissolved.

Successes in Latin America

George Bush could crow that Republican policies had won the Cold War, and he did. The get-tough policy and the fabulously expensive arms race laid bare the fatal weaknesses of the Communist states. Rather more important, with the leaders of the Soviet Union preoccupied by the specter of

THE SOVIET BLOC, 1947–1989

Legend:
- Soviet Bloc
- Non-Bloc Communist Nations
- NATO Countries
- Neutral nations

0   250   500 Miles
0   250   500 Kilometers

SWEDEN
DENMARK
BALTIC SEA
EAST GERMANY
POLAND
WEST GERMANY
CZECHOSLOVAKIA
SWITZ.
AUSTRIA
HUNGARY
ITALY
YUGOSLAVIA
ROMANIA
BULGARIA
ALBANIA
GREECE
TURKEY
SOVIET UNION
BLACK SEA
CASPIAN SEA
ARAL SEA

EASTERN EUROPE, 2003

Legend:
- Russia
- Independent, Formerly Soviet Republics
- Independent, Formerly Soviet Satellites
- Independent, Albania and Formerly Yugoslavia
- NATO Countries
- Neutral nations

SWEDEN
DENMARK
BALTIC SEA
ESTONIA
LATVIA
LITHUANIA
RUS.
BELARUS
GERMANY
POLAND
CZECH REPUBLIC
SLOVAKIA
UKRAINE
RUSSIA
SWITZ.
AUSTRIA
HUNGARY
SLOVENIA
CROATIA
BOS.& HERZ.
SERBIA
ROMANIA
MOLDOVA
ITALY
BULGARIA
MACEDONIA
ALBANIA
GREECE
TURKEY
GEORGIA
ARMENIA
AZER.
AZERBAIJAN
BLACK SEA
CASPIAN SEA
ARAL SEA
KAZAKSTAN
UZBEKISTAN
TURKMENISTAN

MAP 50:1 The Soviet Bloc, 1947–1989 (*top*); Eastern Europe, 2003 (*bottom*) The map of central and eastern Europe was changed more radically in the early 1990s than it had been even by the Treaty of Versailles following World War I. The *Times* of London had the bad luck to publish a new edition of its definitive world atlas just as the lines were being redrawn. In a desperate effort to sell the obsolete book, the *Times* advertised it as an atlas of the "old world order."

chaos at home, Bush and his secretary of state, James Baker, were able to win a series of victories in both the corridors of diplomacy and on the battlefield.

In December 1989, Bush succeeded in toppling Manuel Noriega from power in Panama. After an American military officer was shot in Panama City, Bush unleashed 24,000 troops. Within a few days, with little loss in American lives, Noriega was out of power and a client government installed.

In February 1990, as Soviet and Cuban aid to Nicaragua dried up, the Sandinistas were voted out of power by a political alliance backed by the United States. A less desirable right-wing party took control of El Salvador but, thanks to

▲ *The demolition of the Berlin Wall, the central symbol of the collapse of the Soviet bloc and the end of the Cold War, was giddily celebrated in the undivided city.*

American prodding, moderated its policies and signed an armistice and agreement with leftist rebels, ending the long war in that country. World affairs were going well for the president.

Crisis in the Middle East

Bush's greatest success abroad was in the Middle East. It was precipitated in August 1990 by Iraq's occupation of Kuwait, a small sheikdom floating on oil. Fearing that Iraqi president Saddam Hussein would next invade Saudi Arabia, the Bush administration secured a unanimous vote in the United Nations Security Council calling for a boycott of all foreign trade with Iraq. Although rich in oil, Iraq needed to import many of the materials needed to support a modern economy.

But Bush and Secretary of State Baker did not believe economic sanctions would resolve the problem. They feared, with plenty of precedents to back them up, that as time went on, the boycott would disintegrate. That fear, and apprehensions for the security of Saudi Arabia, prompted Bush to send a token American military force to Saudi Arabia on August 7. Far from buckling, Hussein grew more defiant, annexing Kuwait. Bush then sent more than 400,000 troops to Arabia. Other nations, particularly Britain and France, sent contingents.

The Hundred Hours' War

In January, after Saddam Hussein ignored a United Nations ultimatum that he must evacuate Kuwait, the American-led force launched a withering air attack that, in little more than a week, totaled 12,000 sorties. With an American television reporter in Baghdad, the world was presented with the phenomenon of watching a war from both sides.

In the face of this onslaught, Hussein sent most of his air force to neighboring Iran, leaving the skies to American planes. Probably, like some Americans, he believed that his huge army, dug in behind formidable defenses, could turn back any ground assault. He was wrong. His army was large,

MAP 50:2 The Gulf War, 1991 After weeks of bombardment that destroyed Iraqi communications and completely demoralized the poorly trained Iraqi army, American and allied troops advanced through Kuwait and Iraq virtually without opposition. Confident that the Iraqis would depose Saddam Hussein, President Bush, with an eye on containing Iran, allowed the best Iraqi divisions, in frantic retreat, to escape unscathed.

but most Iraqi soldiers were poorly trained and mistreated by their officers. The air war was chillingly effective, not only devastating Iraqi communications and the transportation system but terrifying frontline Iraqi troops. When the ground attack came on February 23, 1991, most surrendered without resistance. In just a few days, the Iraqi army was routed by a daring flanking action designed by commanding general Norman Schwarzkopf. Believing that Saddam could not survive the humiliating defeat, that his generals would oust him, Bush ordered a halt to the ground war when it was 100 hours old, leaving the Iraqi army's best units intact.

Mixed Results

It was a portentous blunder. Hussein was not ousted in disgrace. He remained in power and rebuilt his military force. Kuwait's reactionary ruling family made few changes in that country. Even the apparently salutary fact that the United Nations had moved decisively against an errant member proved to be meaningless. Briefly, it appeared that dictators of small countries were put on warning that mischief would not be tolerated. Hostages held for years by antiwestern Islamic organizations were released in 1991.

▲ *Virtually the entire Iraqi army collapsed within days during George H. Bush's "Hundred Hours' War." Unfortunately, the president halted the advance and permitted a fragment of the army to escape, assuming it would be needed to ensure stability under a new Iraqi government. Instead, what was left of the army remained under the control of Saddam Hussein.*

Then, however, when a vicious multisided ethnic war broke out in Yugoslavia, neither the United Nations, the North Atlantic Treaty Organization, nor the European Community took decisive action to end it. For three years, while the United States and the nations of western Europe issued empty threat after empty threat, Bosnian Serbs, Croatians, and Muslims battled one another with a tribal savagery.

Nor did the Gulf War preserve George Bush, as he believed it would. He proclaimed that, under his leadership, Americans had put the "Vietnam syndrome," a demoralized army and defeatism at home, behind them. The president's ratings in public opinion polls soared in early 1991. In the excitement of watching a miraculously successful war on television, Americans seemed to forget their serious economic problems at home. But it was only for a season. By 1992, a presidential election year, a recession that would not abate virtually relegated the Hundred Hours' War to the realm of ancient history.

Primary Elections of 1992

Bush was challenged in the Republican primaries by a right-wing television commentator, Patrick Buchanan, who had vociferously opposed the Gulf War. Buchanan won no early primaries, but by taking almost 40 percent of the Republican votes in some states, he signaled that Bush was in trouble in his own party.

The Democratic party's primary campaign proved to be unlike any other in recent history. Instead of one candidate in the field pulling ahead early and coasting to the nomination, several of the would-be nominees won the convention delegates of at least one state. Senator Thomas Harkin of Iowa, a liberal with a populist tinge, won his own state. Paul Tsongas of Massachusetts won New Hampshire and Maryland. Senator Robert Kerrey of Nebraska won South Dakota. Most surprising of all, former California governor Jerry Brown, despite a nagging reputation for bizarre beliefs—he was sometimes called "Governor Moonbeam"—won most of the delegates from Colorado.

Then, however, Governor William Clinton of Arkansas rushed to the head of what humorist Russell Baker called "the march of the Millard Fillmores." He rode out a past as a Vietnam War draft evader, accusations of adultery, and claims that he was too slick to be trusted. He sewed up the convention before it met. Clinton's strategy was to woo the New Age liberals who had supported Gary Hart by speaking for liberal lifestyle issues (he was proabortion, pro–affirmative action, and called for an end to discrimination against homosexuals) while appealing to moderates with an economic policy that emphasized growth.

Election Oddities

Clinton's 44.9 million votes were the most ever won by a Democratic party candidate. He won an absolute majority of the votes only in Arkansas and the District of Columbia. Bush's 39.1 million votes were 15.4 million fewer than Ronald Reagan had won in 1984. He did not win a majority in any state. Perot's 19.7 million votes were twice the total won by any previous third-party candidate. He won a plurality in no state.

The Election of 1992

Some populist conservatives who had never liked the aristocratic Bush swarmed to the independent candidacy of H. Ross Perot, a self-made Texas billionaire. Although he offered little in the way of a program, hundreds of thousands of uneasy Americans formed local "Perot for President" organizations. The candidate himself pledged to spend millions of his own money in the cause. By July, polls showed him leading both Bush and Clinton.

On the day Clinton was to accept the Democratic nomination, Perot was on the ballot in 24 states. Then, suddenly, he quit the race, claiming that he and his daughter had been threatened by assassins. Many of Perot's supporters condemned him, but others continued to gather signatures on petitions. Perot jumped back into the contest and outclassed both Bush and Clinton in the first of the candidates' televised debates. His 19 percent in the general election was more than any third-party presidential candidate had won since Theodore Roosevelt in 1912.

Perot's candidacy helped Bill Clinton carry several mountain states that had not gone Democratic since 1964. Clinton also won California, a Republican stronghold for decades. In electoral votes, the entire Northeast and several southern states also went Democratic. Although Clinton won only 43 percent of the popular vote—the fourth lowest total for a winning president—he had 370 electoral votes to Bush's 168.

for FURTHER READING

Books about an era as recent as the Age of Ronald Reagan are, in one sense, not books of history. Although the 1980s are in the past, they are within the living memories of so many Americans—and so many contemporary issues and phenomena were vital during the 1980s too—that a disinterested perspective, easy when the subject is in the distant past, is not possible for even historians determined to be objective.

One of the shrewdest commentators on the age was Garry Wills, whose *Reagan's America: Innocent at Home,* 1987, is as provocative as his contemporary study of Nixon. Also useful in understanding the symbol of the 1980s is Reagan's own *Where's the Rest of Me?* 1965, an account of his conversion from youthful liberalism to the conservative politics for which he will be remembered. Also on this subject, see A. Edwards, *Early Reagan: The Rise to Power,* 1987. Two of the many books by principals in the Reagan administration are Donald Regan, *For the Record,* 1988, and Larry Speakes, *Speaking Out,* 1988. See also P. Steinfels, *The Neoconservatives,* 1979, and S. Blumenthal, *The Rise of the Counter-Establishment,* 1986.

On foreign policy during the 1980s, see R. L. Garthoff, *Détente and Confrontation: American-Soviet Relations from Nixon to Reagan,* 1985, which does not, however, deal with Reagan's turn toward accommodation with the Soviets late in his last term. On covert operations, see G. F. Treverton, *Covert Action,* 1987, and B. Woodward, *Veil: The Secret Wars of the C.I.A., 1981–1987,* 1987. P. Kennedy, in *The Rise and Fall of the Great Powers,* 1987, may offer an explanation of why contemporary Americans find their nation's place in the world so perplexing.

American JOURNEY ONLINE AND INFOTRAC COLLEGE EDITION

Visit the source collections at http://ajaccess.wadsworth.com and http://infotrac.thomsonlearning.com, and use the Search function with the following key terms to explore documents, images, audio and video clips, articles, and commentary related to the material in this chapter:

Deficit spending
George H. W. Bush
Mikhail Gorbachev
Ronald Reagan

Sandra Day O'Connor
Supply-side economics
Tiananmen Square

Additional resources, exercises, and Internet links related to this chapter are available on *The American Past* Web site: http://history.wadsworth.com/americanpast7e.

HISTORY ONLINE

Pictorial History of Ronald Reagan
http://victorian.fortunecity.com/manet/404/
A good (although uncritical) multimedia biography of Ronald Reagan.

Desert Storm
www.desert-storm.com/
A student-created compendium of information and images about the Gulf War of 1991.

THE MILLENNIUM YEARS

Decadence? Renewal?
1993–2003

© Reuters NewMedia Inc./Corbis

History never looks like history when you are living through it. It always looks confusing and messy, and it always feels uncomfortable.

John W. Gardner

When people accept futility and the absurd as normal, the culture is decadent.

Jacques Barzun

IN 1930, TWO recent university graduates published *1066 and All That.* The book was a satire of what they remembered as students from their course in the history of England. Written on the level of an answer on an essay exam that would deserve a C, the book is a series of hilarious snap judgments based on fuzzy recollections of lectures and textbook reading: This king was "a good king," a British setback in battle was "a bad thing," and so on. *1066* concludes with World War I, which, in truth, marked the end of Britain's reign as the world's greatest power. The final sentence is, "America was thus clearly top nation, and History came to a."

America has been "top nation" ever since, and history has not come to a stop. The twentieth century was, however, as much a time of trial as of glory for Americans: the Great Depression; World War II; the long, unnerving nuclear standoff with the Soviet Union; Vietnam. Three of the century's last seven presidents blatantly broke the law. The era culminated in a decade of greed and corruption in business.

CULTURAL DISSONANCE

Americans celebrated January 1, 2000, as the beginning of a new millennium. The party was festive, but not everyone donned a paper hat. Nagging at some of the country's most thoughtful men and women was the apprehension that the United States was rotting culturally, socially, morally, and politically. In 2000, a respected scholar in his 90s, Jacques Barzun, wrote that our civilization was "decadent." Curiously, Barzun employed the same image with which *1066 and All That* concluded. Decadence, he wrote, is not history coming to a stop. Decadence is "a very active time, full of deep concerns, but peculiarly restless, for it sees no clear lines of advance. . . . Institutions function painfully. Repetition and frustration are the intolerable result. Boredom and fatigue are great historical forces."

Barzun pointed to "the open confessions of malaise" in America, "the search in all directions for a new faith or faiths, dozens of cults . . . the impulse to PRIMITIVISM," and endless bickering. "Most of what government sets out to do for the public good is resisted as soon as it is proposed," he wrote. "Not two, but three or four groups, organized or impromptu, are ready with contrary reasons as sensible as those behind the project. The upshot is a floating hostility to things as they are."

Cults

Most of the cults of the later twentieth century were rackets. Some targeted adults who had good jobs or owned small businesses. Gurus promised them, in return for large fees (sometimes everything the suckers owned), to reveal the mystical secret to greater financial success. Others promised lots of sex. In rural Oregon in 1981, the Bhagwan Shree Rajneesh collected several thousand followers in his well-guarded ashram by promising orgies. Other cults attracted emotionally discombobulated teenagers and young adults with little experience of life and less appreciation for their inherited culture. The most successful were transcendental meditation (TM) and the Moon Unification Church.

Emerging during the 1960s, the brainchild of the Maharishi Mahesh Yogi, TM promised inner peace reflected in extraordinary personal powers. The maharishi sold training courses in meditation, awarding graduates with unique mantras—syllables on which they were to concentrate when transcending. When some movie stars and rock 'n' roll idols endorsed TM, the maharishi was swamped by seekers clutching wads of dollars. For a few years, TM was big business. When the baby boom generation turned from enhancing their consciousness to consumerism in the 1970s, the maharishi advertised that TM was also the way to increase one's income and collection of consumer goods.

Sun Myung Moon, a Korean, headed the Unification Church and preached a theology that boiled down to the doctrine that he, Moon, was God. Thousands of young Americans (many more worldwide) placed their lives in his hands. The "Moonies" (as mockers dubbed the faithful) cut off all contact with family and friends. Moon made all their personal decisions, even selecting each Moonie's spouse. He simultaneously married thousands of just-introduced couples at massive ceremonies.

The Unification Church built up capital in dimes and quarters. At airports and other busy public places, Moonies, smiling robotically as if they were drugged, cornered hurrying travelers and shoppers and asked for donations. They offered a flower, thrust into the target's face, as a premium. The impatient were rude; the intimidated and the kindly contributed. Few accepted the flower, helpfully cutting Moonie operating expenses.

With the take, Moon purchased farms, food-processing plants, and even a newspaper. Menial jobs at these enterprises were filled by Moonies whose pay was bed, board, close supervision, and continuing indoctrination. Distraught parents called it "brainwashing." Some hired professional "deprogrammers" to seize their Moonie children physically and shock them out of their trances.

New Age

True cultists like the Moonies were few compared to the hordes of Americans who embraced one or another manifestation of "New Age," which did not require converts to withdraw into a fortified cloister. New Age was a "New Global Movement Toward Spiritual Development, Health and Healing, Higher Consciousness, and Related Subjects." With roots in the hippie counterculture of the 1960s, its influence peaked in the 1980s and 1990s. New Age books were published by the hundreds of titles annually; New Age art (sunsets, misty mountains) adorned calendars and teacups; New Age music (twanging sitars, not much melody) replaced Muzak in small, independently owned shops selling the books and recordings along with 1960s drug paraphernalia, tarot cards, distilled scents, divination bones, and crystals possessing who knew what powers.

The market was huge: Mainstream bookshops and record stores added New Age departments next to the westerns and romances. Sedona, a wealthy community in the red-rock country of Arizona, became a New Age pilgrimage destination because of the concentration there, beyond the golf courses, of spiritually energizing "vortexes." Marfa, Texas, offered mysterious dancing lights in the nocturnal sky, and motels much cheaper than Sedona's.

▲ *More than a thousand "Moonies" are simultaneously joined in matrimony by God (the Rev. Sun Myung Moon). The brides and grooms had, according to Moonie custom, only just made one another's acquaintances.*

Alternative Lifestyle

Like the cults, New Age promised a "transformative experience." This was emphatically "spiritual," not religious. Western religion—Christianity and Judaism—were "traditional," "conventional," "old." New Age rejected tradition, convention, and as much of mainstream American lifestyle as New Agers found it convenient to leave behind. New Age embraced the novel, the non-American, the non-Western, the primitive—whatever was "alternative."

Rather than take a throbbing toe to a physician, New Agers sought out holistic practitioners, Vedantic healers, vegetarian grocers, a dozen schools of massage, acupuncturists, aromatherapists, and herbalists. They pored over fantasies that had been written for children and books such as J. R. R. Tolkien's *Lord of the Rings,* and discussed the wisdom therein with the gravity of Talmudists. They were fascinated by (nonbiblical) prophets like the sixteenth-century Michel de Nostradamus and the twentieth-century American Edgar Cayce. They subscribed to supernatural or extraterrestrial explanations of plane crashes, puzzling noises in the cellar, and dreams of being tucked into bed with Marie Antoinette. New Age needed no publicity department. With the spread of cable television, armies of television reporters assigned to fill the endless hours of cable airtime with cheaply produced stories sought out New Agers for interviews. In the late 1990s, the Internet provided a fishery vaster than Newfoundland's Grand Banks.

New Age was not political. However, because it could be dabbled in by people who had jobs, lived within society, mated (in "new equalitarian relationships"), and raised children (with a "new openness"), the mentality it encouraged shaped American culture as the cults did not. The "political correctness" that rattled American education in the final decades of the century had other origins—a "postmodernist" intellectual movement that rejected absolute truths—but it also reflected New Age in its scorn for Western culture, patronization of groups the mainstream had marginalized, enamoration with causes that discomfited conventional Americans, contempt for ordinary workaday white people, and intolerance of dissent.

Party-Line Universities

When intolerance took the form of a vegetarian disdaining eaters of cheeseburgers, it was harmless. When college students and professors were bullied for opposing the dictates of political correctness (PC), insistence on intellectual conformity challenged the principle of freedom of inquiry on which American higher education had been based for a century.

The Occult Right

PC was only rarely violent against persons. Such was not the case with its mirror image on the far right of the political spectrum. Bewildered by cultural and moral upheavals, some Christian fundamentalists hatched visions of a great conspiracy of New Agers, intellectuals, liberals, feminists, gay rights lobbies—and eventually all Democratic politicians who supported their causes, including, after 1993, the Clinton administration. These "conspirators," it was believed, were working together to destroy Christianity and American values, and had to be stopped.

The occult right's medium was "talk radio," a phenomenon that appeared in the 1980s when AM radio stations lost the music broadcasting business to FM stations and looked around frantically for a cheap-to-produce format that would keep them in business. Their salvation was pioneered in 1983 by a former disc jockey, Rush Limbaugh. Limbaugh harangued against affirmative action, abortion on demand, illegal immigrants, homosexuals, gun control, New Age looniness, and other reflections of the era's cultural dissonance.

Limbaugh himself was well prepared, witty, and good humored. Most of his hundreds of imitators were uninformed boors. They survived, even prospered, by shouting and encouraging listeners who phoned in to call for violence against the enemy such as their hosts, by law, had to avoid. Talk radio's audience was huge. By 2000, Limbaugh's daily three-hour program was broadcast on 660 stations. Nor was the audience exclusively the "angry white working-class males" on whom liberals found it easy to look down. A fifth of talk radio listeners were African American (almost double the proportion of blacks in the population), almost half were women, a third were middle-class, and about 20 percent said they were Democrats.

Ugly consequences were inevitable. In Idaho, a group of "survivalists" preparing for Armageddon fired on federal officials who were investigating them. Return fire killed the wife and child of the group's leader. In Waco, Texas, in 1993, federal agents besieged the compound of the Branch Davidians, a Christian conspiracy cult, for 51 days, then stormed it. Eighty people were killed, including 20 children. Exactly two years later, retaliating against the "Zionist occupation government" in Washington that he held responsible for Waco, one Timothy McVeigh parked a truck packed with explosives next to the Murrah Federal Building in Oklahoma City. The blast killed 168.

Feminists and proponents of racial and ethnic (but not intellectual) diversity in colleges, and censors of language that was "insensitive," demanded that universities require students and faculty to participate in "sensitivity-training" programs administered by the politically correct.

True believers in PC were, probably, never numerous. However, they were able to set the tone in many universities because to be labeled a racist, sexist, homophobe, etc., which PC militants labeled those who questioned them, was like being labeled a "red" by the McCarthyites of the 1950s—enough to ruin a career. Silence—conformity—won toleration. Students learned which instructors would lower their grades if they voiced an unacceptable opinion. Junior faculty knew what shibboleths to approve in order to win favorable reports from the committees that handed out tenure and promotions. For academic administrators, PC was a bonanza: The apparatus that was needed to enforce it meant more high-paying nonteaching university jobs.

Examples of PC's power to intimidate provided conservative journalists with plenty of copy. Thus, in 1998, when 3,000 copies of an anti-PC publication at Georgetown University were destroyed, one campus newspaper ignored the incident; a second applauded the theft; and the university president said nothing. When feminists at Ohio State destroyed a student newspaper because it had published an "offensive" cartoon, the university stated, "The big thing was the cartoon, not the missing papers." In 2000, an anthropology professor at Bowling Green University in Ohio was forbidden to teach a course called "Political Correctness" because, in the words of the curriculum committee, "We forbid any course that says we restrict free speech."

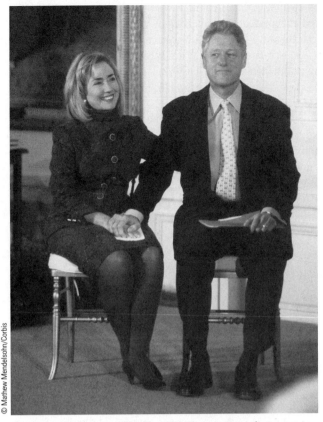

© Mathew Mendelsohn/Corbis

▲ *Hillary Rodham and President Bill Clinton convey the impression of a harmonious and happy married couple. Mrs. Clinton blundered during one of their first joint interviews but behaved with flawless dignity during the exposure of the president's sordid sexual adventures.*

CLINTON AND THE WORLD

The president whom Timothy McVeigh regarded as a traitor, William Jefferson Clinton, was, in fact, no ideologue. Clinton was a political opportunist whose sights had been set on the presidency since he was a teenager in Hot Springs, Arkansas. He devoted his quick intelligence and considerable charm to advancing himself in politics, and he thought in the long term. He attended the Catholic elite's Georgetown University, a shrewd choice for a Southern Baptist boy with national ambitions. He won admission to the prestigious law school at Yale University, no big deal for sons of Yale alumni like Clinton's predecessor and successor, George H. Bush and George W. Bush, but ingress into a national elite such as few men of Clinton's background could imagine.

A Masterful Politician

At Yale, Clinton met his future wife, the equally intelligent and politically ambitious Hillary Rodham. She had been a Republican. Bill Clinton was a liberal Democrat from the start. He idolized John F. Kennedy, supported the Great Society and—well modulated—opposed the Vietnam War. He dodged the draft but knew better than to jeopardize his political career by burning his draft card. He quietly hedged his bets by seeking a noncombat place in the Arkansas National Guard, an expedient identified with well-to-do, pro-war Republicans like Dan Quayle and George W. Bush.

In 1978, just 32, Clinton was elected governor of Arkansas. He sponsored a traditional liberal social and economic program, and state taxes climbed. He was defeated when he ran for reelection in 1980. Clinton got the message: Regulating big business and advancing the interests of the less privileged were no ticket to political advancement during the Age of Reagan.

Clinton dropped the label "liberal," styling himself a "New Democrat," that is, a fiscally responsible centrist friendly to business. Beginning in 1982, he won four successive gubernatorial elections. His energy was boundless; he loved to campaign; he savored the 1980s equivalent of kissing babies—schmoozing at fund-raising parties. His success at the polls and his golden touch as a fund-raiser made him a national figure. By 1992, Clinton had everything going for him but his goatish sex drive, which exposed him to a career-ending scandal. Clinton's sexual escapades were common gossip in Little Rock political circles, but the governor was lucky or, as his frustrated Republican opponents said, "slick."

Foreign Policy: Somalia and Haiti

Clinton entered the White House lacking a foreign policy. This was inevitable with the Cold War ended. During the era of bipolar nuclear standoff, the essence of every president's foreign policy was given to him: He had one big problem—the Soviet Union. Clinton was immediately beset by a series of little problems. Although he had his failures, the pragmatist proved to be generally effective in resolving them.

Resource-poor Somalia had been a minor plaything during the Cold War, first a Soviet client, then an American one. After 1989, the country was no longer geopolitically important to either country and Somalia's bonanza financial aid evaporated. Clans headed by venal warlords plunged the country into vicious civil war, reducing the capital of Mogadishu to a shambles. Water supply, power, telephones, police—all virtually vanished. Teenage thugs with sophisticated leftover weapons terrorized the streets. The arid countryside starved.

With United Nations approval, American troops intervened. As a relief mission, they were successful. Somalia's famine was ended. However, when American troops tried to capture the most destructive of the Somali warlords, the civil war resumed, this time with American troops in the middle. One patrol of peacekeepers was literally torn to pieces by a Mogadishu mob. Clinton had to negotiate just to get American soldiers out of the country without further casualties.

Haiti, long the poorest state in the Western Hemisphere, was, by the 1990s, on the verge of a Somalia-type chaos, and the country's proximity to the United States gave its agony an urgency beyond unpleasant videotape on the evening news. Thousands of refugees fled the country in boats incapable of making a landfall. Their desperate hope was to be picked up by the United States Coast Guard, whence they could petition for political asylum in the United States.

Americans were already uneasy about the massive immigration of uneducated, impoverished people from other Caribbean and Central American nations. Many were persuaded to urge intervention, by a "Haitian lobby" headed by the deposed president of Haiti in exile in the United States, Jean-Bertrand Aristide, and by American liberals who, since Vietnam, had flatly opposed foreign military adventures.

Clinton's military intervention was a debacle. In October 1993, a few hundred Haitian rowdies humiliated the president when they turned an American warship back from the docks of the capital, Port-au-Prince. Clinton nimbly changed direction. He assembled a blue-ribbon diplomatic team headed by former president Jimmy Carter and popular general Colin Powell. They persuaded Haiti's military dictators to go into exile. In September 1994, 3,000 American troops landed, returning Aristide to the presidency. They trained the police and army the country needed in order to function minimally (and stem the flight of refugees to America).

Clinton may have dangled a cash incentive in front of Haiti's generals in order to score his success. He "bought" other diplomatic victories, most notably, securing the agreement of North Korea's militarist regime to suspend development of nuclear weapons.

Bosnia: Ethnic Hatred

Somalia and Haiti were nations: countries with clear-cut borders and populations sharing common languages, religions, and ways of life. Bosnia-Herzegovina in the Balkans was multicultural. Three hostile ethnic populations had lived in peace with one another there only when forced to do so by authoritarian regimes: the Turks, the Austrians, and, after 1945, the Yugoslavian Communists.

After the disintegration of Yugoslavia, Bosnian Serbs attacked Bosnian Croatians and Bosnian Muslims, who also battled one another. The Croatians and Serbs were well armed by independent Croatia and Serbia (still officially called Yugoslavia). The Muslims, ignored even by the richest Islamic countries, suffered atrocities.

Some Americans called for intervention. Others said the western European nations should stabilize what was, after all, a European country. A third group opposed any action, arguing that nothing that happened in Bosnia affected American interests and that intense ethnic hatreds were as intrinsic to Balkan life as lamb stew. Indeed, every truce Clinton, Russia, the United Nations, and the North Atlantic Treaty Organization engineered fell apart in weeks, even days. Finally, by the end of 1995, a combination of American air strikes and economic pressure on Serbia to rein in the Bosnian Serbs established enough stability to permit American and European soldiers to move in as peacekeepers.

During Clinton's second term, Kosovo, a province of Serbia but with a majority population of Albanian Muslims, reprised the Bosnian crisis. The Serbian president, Slobodan Milosevic, responded to Muslim agitation for independence by sending in troops to carry out a program of "ethnic cleansing," killing or driving out Kosovo's Albanians. Fearing the entire Balkans would be drawn into a war, the North Atlantic Treaty Organization, led by the United States, pacified the province.

Mexico and NAFTA

Clinton pushed the North American Free Trade Agreement (NAFTA) through Congress against a potent, if oddly assorted, opposition: the declining labor movement to which Democrats had traditionally deferred; the flaky billionaire-politician Ross Perot and his Reform party; and isolationists like television commentator Pat Buchanan.

NAFTA provided for the elimination, over 15 years, of trade barriers among Canada, the United States, and Mexico. It was an emulation of the European Community, which had been an economic boon for western Europe.

Mexico quickly became, after Canada, the nation's second biggest trading partner. Each day during the 1990s, a million barrels of crude oil, 432 tons of peppers, 250,000 lightbulbs, 100 to 200 Volkswagens, and $51 million in au-

What's Imported?

Even without NAFTA and the General Agreement on Tariffs and Trade (also signed by Clinton), it was difficult in the 1990s to say what was a domestic product and what was imported. The Ford Crown Victoria was assembled in Canada; the Mercury Grand Marquis included parts made in six different countries. Forty percent of all "Japanese" cars sold in America were manufactured in the United States. Television sets bearing the American trademark Zenith were, in fact, Mexican products. Mitsubishi TVs were manufactured in Santa Ana, California.

tomobile parts crossed the border into the United States. On both sides of the Rio Grande in Texas and northeastern Mexico, a bilingual culture, neither American nor Mexican but bound together by mutual economic interests, emerged almost overnight.

Clinton hoped that greater prosperity in Mexico would stem the massive illegal Mexican emigration into the United States. However, NAFTA significantly helped only the Mexican states of Nuevo León and Coahuila. Impoverished Mexicans from farther south continued to sneak across the border in stupefying numbers.

Newcomers

Between 1924 and 1965, immigration had been a minor facet of American life. The southern and eastern Europeans who were the mainstay of the "new immigration" of 1880–1924 were effectively excluded because of their national origins. Until 1943, Chinese could not legally enter the United States.

Ethnic discrimination was eliminated from immigration law in 1965. The change meant little to eastern Europeans and Chinese living under Communist regimes. However, the gigantic refugee problem created by the Vietnam War, and a law of 1980 making admission easier for political refugees, opened the gates to Vietnamese, Laotians, Indochinese tribal peoples like the Hmong, and Chinese from Southeast Asia. During the century's final decades, the Asian American population doubled to 11 million. About 800,000 Cubans emigrated during the same period. Most settled in Florida, especially Miami, where they were so numerous that half the city was called "Little Havana."

There were Russian Jewish, Haitian, Dominican, Arab and other Muslim, and Nigerian immigrants. But by far the greatest influx was from Mexico, augmented by Central Americans with similar cultures. Almost 4 million Mexicans entered the United States, and many more illegally.

Like the "new immigrants" at the beginning of the century, they had been impoverished by a modernization at home that rendered them economically superfluous.

The reception accorded the immigrants was much like that the "new immigrants" experienced 80 years earlier: anxiety that they could not be assimilated. In fact, although the newcomers also gathered in ethnic enclaves, they may have been more amenable to "Americanization" than most of the "new immigrants" had been. Asian Americans, particularly, embraced America's "get ahead" culture. The frequency with which first-generation Asian immigrant children won national spelling bees and science fairs became a national joke. Most Asian American organizations opposed affirmative action because Asians won admission to colleges and professional schools on their merits in larger proportions than Caucasian applicants did.

The greatest stress of the late-century immigration was language. By 2003, Spanish was the first language of 18 million Americans. Because 90 percent of Mexican Americans lived in the southwestern corner of the country—adjacent to Spanish-speaking Mexico—many Americans worried about the future of the culturally and politically unifying role of the English language. During the 1970s and 1980s, French linguistic nationalism in Quebec had come close to destroying the Dominion of Canada.

A lobby called "U.S. English" worked to make English the official national language by constitutional amendment and the exclusive language of state governments by law. Most liberal Democrats fought these proposals. The education lobby insisted that Spanish-speaking children be schooled at least partly in their native tongue (more jobs). The state of California published its official documents in Spanish (and a dozen other languages). U.S. English publicized polls showing that a majority of Spanish-speaking and Asian immigrants wanted their children educated exclusively in English, but scored few legislative victories.

John Ledgard/The Economist

▲ *Election day in southern California. The large numbers of Mexicans in the southwest worried some Americans (José displaced Michael as the most common name given baby boys in both Texas and California). Would the borderlands be Mexicanized? These all-American "Vote for . . ." posters, however, implied an Americanization of Hispanic Americans, as did the insistence of most Mexican immigrants that their children be educated in the English language.*

CLINTONIAN AMERICA

Clinton's domestic policies reprised the formula that had been so successful in Arkansas. Fiscally, he was conservative, as, in practice, conservative Republicans were not. From Reagan to George W. Bush, they jabbered incessantly about balancing the budget, whereas, when in power, they spent and borrowed as no liberal Democrat dared. Clinton was the most frugal president since Calvin Coolidge. He systematically reduced the number of federal employees and the federal deficit. Several years of his presidency, his budgets turned in a surplus (the government collected more in taxes than it spent), and the national debt declined.

Clinton was a liberal in his active promotion of the incorporation of African Americans into the political and social mainstream. It may have been his only heartfelt principle, but Clinton's goodwill toward African Americans and personal identification with blacks was real. The president also tried to enact a reform of the nation's health care that had been on the liberal agenda since the 1940s. Partly because of his own mistakes, however, he failed.

Health Care

During the 1990s, Americans with medical insurance enjoyed excellent health care, but at a greater cost than in any other nation. The annual per capita expenditure on medical care was $3,700. (In Switzerland, the second most expensive country, costs were $2,644.) Americans paid several times what the people of other nations paid for prescription drugs, including drugs manufactured in the United States. Moreover, in 1993, 39 million Americans had no insurance. Consequently, by virtually every index of public health (infant mortality, death of women in childbirth, and so on), the United States ranked lower than every other developed nation and some countries less than wealthy—thirty-seventh in the world overall. Only Haiti and Bolivia had lower immunization rates than the United States.

A large part of the explanation was unalloyed greed. Pharmaceutical companies took profits of 1,000 percent and more. In the aggregate, medical students seemed more interested in money and leisure than in health care. Most aspired to be specialists who worked far fewer hours than general practitioners and had several times their income. About 70 percent of physicians in Britain and Germany, and 51 percent in Canada, were primary care doctors. In the United States, just 13 percent of physicians were. The health care bureaucracy, like administration in government, education, and corporations, was grotesquely bloated. The number of American physicians increased by 50 percent between 1983 and 1998. The number of "health care managers" increased 683 percent.

Hillary Clinton's Project

Harry S Truman and Lyndon Johnson failed to enact comprehensive health care programs because the American Medical Association (the doctors' lobby), the drug and medical insurance companies, and their Republican allies tarred their programs as "socialist." Clinton faced the same opposition (although, by the 1990s, doctors and insurance companies were bitterly at odds). So he rejected a health care reform proposal patterned on culturally similar Canada's successful "single-payer" health insurance: Everyone paid premiums, and a consortium of insurance companies paid medical bills according to a scale of fees set by the government.

Instead, Clinton tried to appease American insurance companies by leaving them (and their profitability) intact. In return for accepting regulation and subsidies, insurers would extend coverage to those who could not afford to pay premiums.

Clinton's scheme was actually much more complicated. No one, including the voluble president, ever explained clearly how it would work. This played into the hands of the antireform forces in Congress. They saddled a semicoherent bill with amendments that turned the Clinton proposal into gibberish.

▲ *President Clinton addresses Congress in 1995. Albert Gore (left) was a loyal and industrious vice president who would win a plurality of popular votes in his run for the presidency in 2000 but lose in the electoral college. Speaker of the House Newt Gingrich (right) tried to topple Clinton with his congressional muscle and destroyed his own career in the process.*

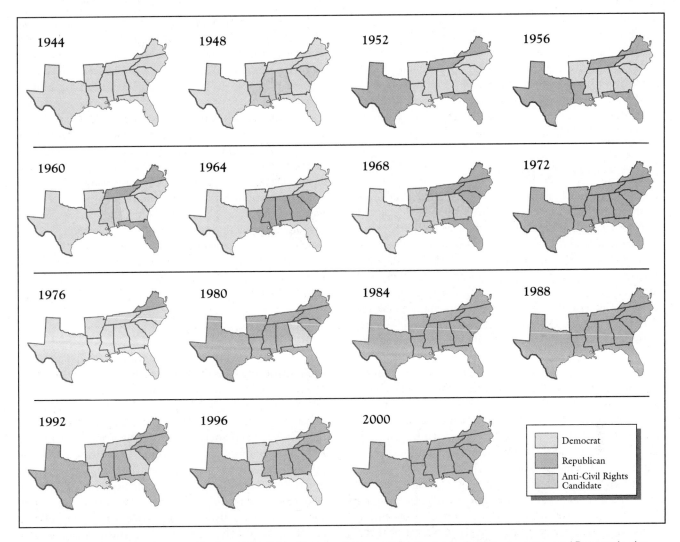

MAP 51:1 The Solid South Changes Parties, 1944-2000 Between 1880 and 1944, the former Confederate states voted Democratic—thus the name "Solid South." All but a handful of black southerners, who were Republican, were disenfranchised. Except in Tennessee, a large majority of white southerners voted Democratic because the national party supported white supremacy in the South. Almost all electoral college maps for elections between 1880 and 1940 would be identical to the 1944 map shown here. Race was the reason the South was solidly Democratic.

Race was also the reason why, in fits and starts beginning in 1948, the former Confederate states moved from the Democratic to the Republican column—a political revolution.

By 1948, most African American voters in the North had become Democrats. In that year, Democratic liberals included a call for civil rights for blacks in the party platform. In protest, four southern states voted "Dixiecrat." Between 1952 and 1968, the South was no more solid in its voting patterns than the rest of the country. Race played a role in the third-party successes in 1960 and 1968, but the Republican victories in the South in 1952 and 1956 were largely due to Dwight D. Eisenhower's personal popularity. Unease in the Bible belt about John F. Kennedy's Catholicism explains the Republican victories in the South in 1960.

After the Democratic party's Voting Rights Act of 1965, black southerners voted—Democratic—in increasing numbers. However, offended white southerners now voted Republican because the national Republican party was, albeit not openly, indifferent to African American causes. (Fewer than 10 percent of blacks nationally voted Republican.) After 1968, the Democrats were able to win enough white votes in the South to combine with their black political base and carry southern states only when the party nominated a southerner to run for president: Jimmy Carter of Georgia in 1976 (but not in 1980), and Bill Clinton in 1992 and 1996.

In 2000, when both presidential candidates were southerners, the former Confederate states voted solidly Republican. The electoral votes of the "Solid South" put George W. Bush in the White House; he lost the popular vote. The political revolution was complete.

Clinton also blundered when he appointed his wife to head the campaign to win political support for health care reform. Hillary Clinton was able, but she was out of her depth contending with Republican politicos and powerful, entrenched lobbies. Moreover, she had gotten off to a bad start as first lady. During the 1992 campaign, Clinton had hinted at a kind of "copresidency" with Mrs. Clinton: "You get two for the price of one." But the "copresident" almost immediately depicted herself as a snobbish rich girl when she told a TV interviewer that she was not the kind of woman who stayed home and baked chocolate chip cookies and when she sneered at a country-and-western lyric that called on women to "stand by your man." That sort of thing went over swimmingly at feminist luncheons but was profoundly insulting to women who baked cookies and believed in spousal loyalty.

Mrs. Clinton good-humoredly did penance for her gaffes by whipping up batches of cookies for groups visiting the White House, but the damage was done. The opponents of health care reform outflanked her at every turn. In the summer of 1994, Clinton abandoned his proposal.

The Midterm Election

In the congressional election of 1994, the Republicans won control of both the Senate and House. The new Speaker of the House, a pugnacious right-winger, Newt Gingrich, called it a "revolution." Within a year, 137 Democratic officeholders, including several congressmen, switched to the Republican party. Among them was the Democrats' Native American trophy senator from Colorado, Ben Nighthorse Campbell.

The election of 1994 was less a personal setback for Clinton (as he would soon demonstrate) than it was another milestone in the drift of the electorate from the Democratic majority of 1932–1968 to a Republican ascendancy that continued into the twenty-first century. The generation of Americans whose lives had been enhanced by the New Deal was gone or going. Beginning in 1968, working- and middle-class white voters, in ever increasing numbers, came to see the Democratic party as the party of minorities and what some saw as outlandish causes: feminism, abortion on demand, gay rights, and similar "lifestyle" issues.

A Republican strategist, Kevin Phillips, was the first to recognize the growing disenchantment with the changing Democratic party. He urged the Republicans to tap the unease by abandoning their lapdog subservience to big business and becoming instead a populist party that was fiscally responsible. Richard M. Nixon's victory in the election of 1968 owed in part to Phillips's insights. In the 1980s, however, Ronald Reagan showed that Republicans could exploit conventional Americans' cultural and moral discomfort while continuing to serve the rich. (A bitter Phillips denounced the Reagan Republicans for remaining the "party of the plutocrats.")

None of this was lost on Clinton. Indeed, his policies indulged big business and the wealthy as lavishly as Reagan's had. His Securities and Exchange Commission brought not a single action for fraudulent manipulation of stock prices during a decade when American business practices plumbed unexplored depths of corruption. During his presidency, while the earnings of the poorest fifth of the population rose by 1 percent, the income of the richest fifth climbed by 15 percent. On his last day in office, Clinton issued 170 pardons, absolving, among others, billionaire Marc Rich, who had been a fugitive in Switzerland for 17 years because of a $50 million tax swindle, and four men who had bilked federal education and housing agencies out of $40 million. (Many more of Reagan's aides were in prison when he retired, but he pardoned only 10 people.)

It was not the elite but ordinary Americans of conventional moral views who rebuked the Democrats in 1994. Just as Reagan had been obligated to pay lip service to the views of the fundamentalist right, Clinton, with no more conviction in the matter than Reagan, had to appease the politically correct wing of the Democratic party. Unlike Reagan, Clinton repeatedly burned his fingers. When he ordered the military to enlist and commission open homosexuals, the uproar was so great that he had to retreat to a policy of "don't ask, don't tell," which had been unspoken army and navy policy since George Washington was a colonel. Clinton was also embarrassed when a woman he appointed to a high position in the Justice Department was exposed to have espoused multiple votes in elections for members of minority groups as compensation for injustices suffered by their ancestors, and by his surgeon general, who said in a speech that public schools should teach children how to masturbate.

These were Clinton's contributions to the Republican victory in 1994. Fortunately for Clinton, however, when it came to blundering, he was not in Newt Gingrich's league.

1996: A Personal Victory

Gingrich was a Reagan Republican without a scintilla of Reagan's personality. The victory he engineered in the election of 1994 went to his head. As Speaker, believing his own press releases, he thought his power equaled Clinton's. Ignoring the fact that Clinton had erased the deficit, Gingrich spoke of cutting Medicare and Social Security costs. That was a mistake Reagan never made. It was one thing to cut expenditures on programs helping the impoverished. Poor people did not vote in large numbers. It was quite another to arouse the elderly who, mobilized by the American Association of Retired Persons, were politically active. Gingrich handed the political center, which had given the Republicans their victory in 1994, back to a president who knew how to woo it.

Then, late in 1995, the Gingrich Congress refused to vote the administration operating expenses, an act unprecedented in irresponsibility. Clinton had no choice but to lay off thousands of federal workers, shut down federal offices, and close popular facilities like the national parks. Gingrich capitulated. Clinton greeted 1996, his reelection year, with his popularity rising.

The Republican candidate was a witty and quintessential midwesterner, Senator Robert Dole of Kansas. A sturdy party regular for almost half a century and majority leader of the Senate, Dole was up to the job. His handicaps were his age (he was 72), a loathing for the humiliations of po-

Investigating Whitewater

The Republicans were maniacal in their investigations of Whitewater. Although it was clear by the summer of 1996 that they could not implicate the Clintons in a crime, they dragged the inquiry out until 2000. After five years and an expenditure of $50 million, all they had was the likelihood that Hillary Clinton had cut a few corners, such as half the lawyers in the nation are paid to cut weekly.

litical campaigning that he would not suppress, and a self-deprecating honesty in responding to questions.

Dole revived the Whitewater scandal that had played a minor role in the campaign of 1992. In 1978, the Clintons had invested borrowed money in a vacation home development in Arkansas called Whitewater. The project flopped, and (according to Clinton's accusers) the governor steered state money to Hillary Clinton's law firm that was used to help bankers recoup their Whitewater losses. Under their guidance, Mrs. Clinton turned a small personal investment in commodities into a huge profit.

In the spring of 1996, two of the Clintons' Whitewater associates were convicted of fraud. But Republicans thirsting for Clinton blood could not turn their suspicions of the Clintons into allegations that would stick. The Whitewater issue fizzled. Neither did Republican revelations that the Democratic party had sold "sleepovers" in the White House to big campaign contributors catch on. In November, Clinton again failed to win half the popular vote (Ross Perot was in the race again), but he easily carried the electoral college, 379 to 159. It was a personal victory. The Democrats failed to gain control of Congress.

Cyber-America

By 1996, the stock market was beginning a 1920s-style boom. "Clinton prosperity" was based on computers, just as Coolidge prosperity had been built on the "high-tech" industries of the New Era: automobiles and radio. Computers changed Americans' daily routines as profoundly as automobiles had and more than radio had. During the 1960s, government, educational bureaucracies, and big business computerized their operations. At first, many people were troubled by the new experience: In order to apply for jobs, collect government checks, and enroll in courses at school, they had to fill in boxes on "IBM cards," then carry machine-punched cards of which they could make no sense from one clerk who could make no sense of them to yet another clerk. Were the machines that alone could read the cards running the world? Science fiction writers churned out tales of societies tyrannized by computers. The masterpiece of the genre was a film of 1968, *2001: A Space Odyssey,* in which the villain was HAL, a computer that spoke in a voice both soothing and sinister.

Despite *2001* (and the declaration in 1977 of the president of Digital Equipment Corporation that "there is no reason anyone would want a computer in their home"), Americans began to adopt little HALs during the 1970s. By 1977, IBM had sold 25,000 "personal computers." By 1981, there were 2 million of them in American homes and offices, and the mania was just starting.

The Internet Bubble

The Internet, instantaneous linkage of computers over telephone lines, was, like the computer, developed for the military. However, it was turned over to the National Science Foundation for civilian use in 1990: fortuitous timing for Bill Clinton. With the growth of the World Wide Web, anyone who was online could, by typing a search word, gain access to a world of research tools. The Web also opened up what seemed to be infinite commercial possibilities.

One could book airline tickets and hotel rooms or buy just about anything sold anywhere in the world from home. Internet companies, called "dot-coms" after the ".com" suffix on most Web sites, popped up like daffodils, their owners sanguine they would take over retailing from shops and mail-order companies. More than 300 dot-coms issued stock in 1998 and 1999. Web sites that provided services or information free told investors they would reap huge dividends from the advertising the sites plastered on computer screens.

Nine percent of American households were on the Internet in 1996, 20 percent in 1998, and 50 percent by 2001. How could an investor lose? Capital swarmed to any enterprise connected with the Web. "Breathe the word 'Internet' around a stock, and anything can happen." In 1996, the value of stock in Yahoo, a search engine, rose 153 percent in one day. Other start-up companies had similarly giddy experiences. In fact, all stocks, including shares in "old-economy" companies, followed the uphill trek at slower but steady rates.

A Day in the Life . . .

On a given day in 1996:

6,000 Americans died

11,000 babies were born (31 percent of the mothers were not married)

7,000 people got married

3,000 people got divorced

170,000 people were injured

495 million pieces of mail were handled by the post office

27 million ATM transactions were processed

Land of Convenience

"Convenience," no matter how wasteful or absurd, sold during the 1990s. Each year, Americans discarded 170 million tons of trash, half a ton per person. Much of it was made up of products designed to be discarded after one use. Every day, on average, each American discarded almost 5 pounds of "disposables": 123 million paper and plastic cups, 44 million paper and plastic diapers, 5.5 million razor blades and disposable razors, 4.4 million disposable pens, and nearly 1 million disposable cigarette lighters.

Convenience was time-saving—sort of. On average, the ubiquitous microwave oven cut four minutes a day from the time a household devoted to food preparation. The automatic dishwasher saved one minute a day in cleanup time. When New York City's telephone company's information service offered to dial a phone number just provided a caller for a charge of 35 cents, more than 20 percent of the callers opted for it. It saved them two seconds.

In so heady an atmosphere, it was no more acceptable to mention 1929 than it was to bring up venereal disease at a college beer party. Bill Gates, whom computer software made the world's richest person, wrote in 1995: "Gold rushes . . . encourage impetuous investments. A few will pay off, but when the frenzy is behind us, we will look back incredulously at the wreckage of failed ventures and wonder, 'Who founded these companies? What was going on in their minds?' "

There was, for example, www.doodoo.com, which delivered a box of horse manure to any house in America for $19.95. Others less ridiculous would, nevertheless, seem to have been doomed to anyone who thought about them for five minutes: dot-coms making restaurant reservations (why not use the phone?) and taking orders for the week's milk, eggs, and Cheez-Its (easier than 10 minutes at the supermarket?). And, as in the 1920s, there were too many heavily financed dot-coms competing in markets that were obviously limited: travel agencies, medical advisers, wine and cigar dealers, chinaware discounters—all retail sales.

As is inevitable in a soaring stock market, there was fraud. But the Clinton luck held, just as, in the boom of the 1920s, Calvin Coolidge's luck had. From 2,365 in 1990, the stock market peaked at more than 11,000 (a rise of 400 percent) in 2000, Clinton's final year as president.

Pretty Woman

Clinton was also lucky, but barely, when he perjured himself during a sex scandal of his own making. The Republicans first turned to the president's libido in 1996 when Whitewater fizzled as a campaign issue. A right-wing foundation promoted a lawsuit by Paula Jones, who had been an Arkansas state employee when Clinton was governor. Jones said that Clinton had invited her to his hotel room, exposed himself, and asked her to perform fellatio. Another Arkansas woman said then-governor Clinton had physically accosted her, leaving her with a visible injury on her lip. There was corroboration: The testimony of the women's friends to whom they had fled immediately after their unsettling experiences.

A commission investigating Whitewater, headed by Republican lawyer Kenneth Starr, found Monica Lewinsky, who, at age 22, had been an unpaid intern at the White House in 1995. She had told friends of an ongoing affair with Clinton. When White House aides became aware of the hanky-panky, they fired Lewinsky. Clinton sent her to his friend, Vernon Jordan, who found her a job in New York City. Her salary looked very much like hush money.

When Lewinsky first testified before the Starr commission, she denied having an affair. However, one of her confi-

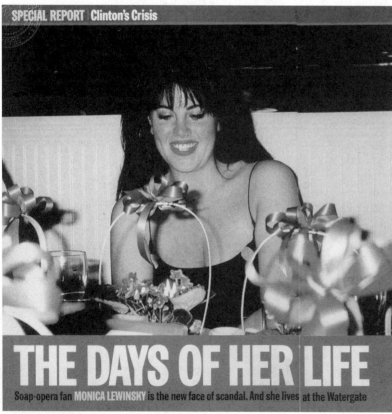

SPECIAL REPORT **Clinton's Crisis**

THE DAYS OF HER LIFE
Soap-opera fan **MONICA LEWINSKY** is the new face of scandal. And she lives at the Watergate

▲ *Monica Lewinsky first lied under oath about her sexual liaison with President Clinton, then told the Starr commission he had asked her to do so. She described their encounters in detail and provided Starr with physical evidence she had saved. It was this evidence that exposed the president as a perjurer.*

dantes had recorded their phone conversations. Starr advised Lewinsky that she would be prosecuted for perjury unless she cooperated. She did. Clinton stonewalled and waxed indignant, swearing under oath that he had had no sexual relationship with "that woman." Starr sprung his trap: He had physical evidence, one of Lewinsky's dresses stained with the president's semen. Clinton admitted to "inappropriate sexual contact" with Ms. Lewinsky.

Impeachment

The Starr report, released in September 1998, described the Clinton-Lewinsky encounters in exquisite detail. Clinton's supporters denounced it as pornography. Starr, they said, should have listed the dates and circumstances of the encounters—period. They had a point. But the pro-Clinton forces were equally tawdry. Feminists who had run a Republican senator from Oregon out of office in 1994 for kissing women called Paula Jones "trailer park trash" and Lewinsky a conniving slut. Intellectuals wrote long essays in prestigious journals explaining that the president had not perjured himself because fellatio was not sex, such as intercourse was.

On December 19, 1998, the House of Representatives impeached the president on several counts of perjury and obstruction of justice (Lewinsky's claim that Clinton had instructed her to lie to Starr). The debate in the Senate (the jury in federal impeachment trials) centered on the value of Lewinsky's uncorroborated evidence and whether or not Clinton's lies amounted to the "high crimes and misdemeanors" the Constitution states as warranting conviction. The debate

was immaterial. It was a Republican versus Democrat contest, and, in the evenly divided Senate, the prosecution had nowhere near the two-thirds majority needed to convict. Clinton was acquitted.

The Election of 2000

The only reputation to emerge enhanced from the mess was Hillary Rodham Clinton's. Never widely liked, she won admiration by weathering the humiliating scandal with quiet dignity. Ironically, she became a sympathetic figure when she "stood by her man." In 2000, she was elected senator from New York.

Vice President Albert Gore, who lay low during the scandal, was the Democratic nominee. Republicans contending for the nomination included businessman Steve Forbes; polemicist Pat Buchanan; Elizabeth Dole (the wife of Robert Dole); and Alan Keyes, an African American so eloquent he won every televised debate hands down but, of course,

AP/Wide World Photos

▲ *George W. ("Dubya") Bush was considered the family clown as a young man. He pulled himself together, exploited his father's connections to succeed in business, and was popular as governor of Texas.*

Feminism After Lewinsky

When virtually all prominent feminists backed President Clinton in the Monica Lewinsky scandal, the women's movement lost moral credibility in its most effective issue over the preceding decade: sexual harassment in the workplace. Friends of the movement like Clinton were, in effect, exempt from the charge.

By 2000, as far as preferential treatment for women was concerned, affirmative action was a dead letter. Women outnumbered men as undergraduates, as entering students at the Yale, Stanford, and Johns Hopkins medical schools, and in pharmacy and veterinary schools. Women were 44 percent of law school students. Anti–affirmative action organizations took to using white women as plaintiffs in suits aimed at destroying racial preferences in education.

By 2002, sorely in need of a new issue to keep the dues rolling in, the National Organization for Women was reduced to proclaiming outrage because the prestigious Augusta National Golf Club (site of the Master's Tournament) accepted multimillionaire males as members but not multimillionaire females. One member of the National Organization for Women wrote that if Augusta National was the best issue feminism could come up with, "then stick a fork in the movement. It's done. We've achieved our goals and should disband."

had no chance for the nomination because of his race. The front-runners were Senator John McCain of Arizona and Governor George W. Bush of Texas, the son of ex-president George H. Bush. McCain won primaries in New England, but Bush—called "Dubya" to distinguish him from his father, George H.—was the candidate of the Republican establishment. His campaign raised an unprecedented $60 million.

Gore's personal morality was as clean as Clinton's was squalid. His public presence, however, was wooden. He espoused traditional liberal proposals to appeal to working people; paid lip service to some politically correct causes as Clinton had done; and, also emulating Clinton, tried to occupy the political center, depicting Bush as big business's stooge. He picked a respected middle-of-the-road senator, Joseph Lieberman of Connecticut, to run for vice president.

George W. Bush played the Texas good old boy and pointed to his success as a governor. The Democrats tried to exploit Bush's prodigal youth but, with their sitting president a prodigal middle-aged man, made little headway. "Dubya" made gestures to retain the loyalty of fundamentalists and the Republican right wing, but not much was required. With the Reform party in a shambles, they had nowhere else to go.

Bush's vulnerability was the fact he appeared to be "not very bright." In fact, Bush's SAT scores had been higher than Clinton's, but "Dubya" was undeniably an ignoramus. An interviewer sandbagged him by administering an easy quiz of general knowledge that Bush failed miserably. He thought Nigeria was a continent and Africa a country. The list of his public gaffes ran on for pages: "One of the great things about books is sometimes there are some fantastic pictures." "It isn't pollution that's harming the environment. It's the impurities in our air and water."

Republicans responded by implying that a committee of experienced advisers would "advise" Bush. They came close to saying that the vice presidential nominee, Richard "Dick" Cheney, a former secretary of defense who was clearly no dummy, would be something of a copresident.

The election was more than close. Gore had a 500,000 popular vote plurality, but neither candidate won a majority in the electoral college. Florida's returns were contested, and the situation was much more knotty than it had been in the disputed election of 1876. It involved irregularly counted absentee ballots, unreliable voting machines, punch-out ballots to which the "chads" (the paper punch-outs) were still clinging, and sloppy erasures on pencil-marked ballots. The dispute took a month to resolve. On December 9, by a vote of five to four, the Supreme Court effectively gave the election to Bush, with the four dissenters assailing the majority decision in blistering language.

Did Bush really win Florida? No one can say. From the day after the election to the day after the Supreme Court's decision, everyone involved, Supreme Court justices included, looked not for facts, but for the formula that would put their man in the White House. Both sides' arguments shifted radically several times to accommodate their goals. A political scientist discovered that had the Republicans'

initial brief been adopted to decide the election, Gore would have won Florida by 3 votes. Had the Democratic party's first formula been implemented, Bush would have won the state by 1,665 votes.

CATASTROPHE, RENEWAL, WAR

The new president's situation was unenviable. More Americans had preferred his opponent. He himself had not stolen Florida's electoral votes, but neither had he won them on election day. Like Rutherford B. Hayes in 1877, who was dubbed "Rutherfraud," Bush's legitimacy was shaky. The Republican majority in the House was slender, and the Democrats gained control of the Senate when a Republican senator quit the party to become an independent. During the administration's first months, Vice President Cheney made as many presidential-level announcements as "Dubya" did.

9/11

Then, on September 11, 2001, suicide terrorists hijacked four airliners, crashing one into the Pentagon and two into the twin towers of New York's World Trade Center. When (by cellular phone) the news reached passengers on a fourth hijacked plane, men knowing they were as good as dead heroically stormed the cockpit, sacrificing their lives so that another building, probably the White House, would be spared. The plane crashed in rural Pennsylvania.

The total destruction of the World Trade Center was videotaped start to finish. The world witnessed a horror such as had been associated with special effects in Hollywood disaster films. In New York, 2,801 people died, including 343 firefighters and 75 police officers who were in the buildings within minutes of the first attack.

In a country hardly touched by foreign enemies since the War for Independence, the national anguish was unprecedented. For months, dazed Americans watched telecasts of crumbling skyscrapers, the search for bodies, and burials, day after day, of dead office workers, plane passengers, and firefighters.

The perpetrators were immediately identified as agents of al Qaeda, a fanatical Muslim terrorist organization headed by a Saudi millionaire, Osama bin Laden. Bin Laden operated from Afghanistan, then controlled by the fanatical Taliban, which the United States had helped bring to power by supporting fundamentalist Muslims against the Soviet Union in the 1970s. The Taliban had transformed a functional coun-

No, Virginia, There Is Nothing Sacred
In August 2002, the Hallmark company released a line of greeting cards to be sent during the week before September 11; "9/11" T-shirts and baseball caps had been on the market for months.

team was arrested weeks before September 11; authorities had refused to examine information in his personal computer out of respect for his "right to privacy."

A People United

Predictably, a few professors climbed on soapboxes to say that the point was not the atrocities but Americans' lack of respect for Muslims. Remarkably, none was harmed. A few Arab Americans were manhandled, but, otherwise, popular retaliation against American Muslims did not extend beyond insults and graffiti. Rarely has a people responded to an event such as 9/11 with the decency and restraint of Americans after the catastrophe.

Publishers rushed dozens of books about Islam into print. Virtually all emphasized the point that acts like 9/11 were no more intrinsic to the Muslim religion than murdering abortionists was a Christian act. Few of the books focused on the fact that many of the resentments in the Muslim world that produced fanatics like al Qaeda (and widespread approval of them) were due to nothing the United States had done but were the fruit of their own social systems and tensions between the religion of the zealous and the ignorant and the realities of the twenty-first-century world—of "history."

President Bush made a point of honoring Islam in every statement in which he condemned the terrorists and promised prompt retribution. Indeed, he rose to the occasion as few people, supporters as well as critics, would have predicted him capable. Overnight, the dubious "Dubya" was dignified, compassionate, temperate, eloquent, forceful, and decisive. Americans united behind him.

The minority president's "approval rating" reached unprecedented levels. Bush quickly secured the cooperation of Afghanistan's neighbors and rushed military aid to the country's "Northern Alliance," which was already fighting the Taliban. A well-planned attack was launched. Virtually all large Taliban and al Qaeda forces were destroyed immediately or surrendered without a fight. Taliban and al Qaeda soldiers who, weeks earlier, had been beating up immodest women on the streets of Kabul scattered to the mountains. Osama bin Laden himself escaped; his whereabouts remained unknown into 2003.

War on Terror—and Iraq

Bush exploited his popularity at home and sympathy abroad to announce a "war on terror." Al Qaeda leaders captured in Afghanistan were imprisoned at Guantanamo Bay in Cuba so they could be questioned without the interminable legal snarls their lawyers would engineer in American courts. The highest-level captives were in undisclosed locations. Hundreds of suspected Muslim terrorists in the United States were rounded up. Every European country also exploited the mood of outrage to arrest Muslim extremists they had been watching. American airport security, exposed as slapdash (the terrorists all carried razor knives), became as stringent

▲ *The horror that brought Americans together as a people. New York's World Trade Center was completely destroyed. In Washington, the Pentagon was badly damaged. A fourth hijacked plane was heading toward Washington, probably to attack the White House or Capitol, when heroic passengers rushed the suicide terrorists. The plane crashed in the Pennsylvania countryside.*

© Reuters NewMedia Inc./Corbis

try into a hellhole. They had ended all education for girls, required women in public to cover themselves head to toe, destroyed pre-Muslim antiquities regarded as world treasures, and preached hatred of non-Muslims.

At first, 9/11 looked like the masterstroke of a diabolically efficient organization. Within a few months, however, it was learned that the conspirators had been rather sloppy, dropping clues to their intentions sometimes to save a few hundred dollars. Pilot-training schools reported to American intelligence agencies surly Arab "students" paying cash to learn how to fly an airliner but waving off instructors' suggestions that they must also know how to take off and land—pretty obvious stuff. One of the suicide bombers virtually spelled the plot out to an Agriculture Department employee in Florida when he applied for government aid to learn how to fly crop duster planes, long known as the means by which terrorists in the United States would disseminate chemical or biological toxins in populated areas. A suspected terrorist who was probably a member of the suicide as Israel's. Attorney General John Ashcroft proposed far-reaching suspensions of civil liberties but retreated to his most modest innovations in the face of protest. The Homeland Security Act gave the federal government broader powers in dealing with perceived terrorist threats.

Even before Afghanistan was adequately stabilized, Bush and Secretary of Defense Donald Rumsfeld turned the war on terror toward Saddam Hussein's regime in Iraq. Many people were puzzled. For 10 years, Saddam's only provocations had been blowhard threats to kill George H. Bush, and the like. There was no evidence of an Iraq–al Qaeda connection. Nevertheless, Bush proclaimed that if future World Trade Center disasters were to be averted, Saddam's regime and his "weapons of mass destruction" (chemical and biological weapons and missiles to deliver them) had to be destroyed.

Bush's characterization of Saddam as a monster was unanswerable: Saddam's regime had murdered hundreds of political opponents, tortured thousands and killed tens of thousands of Kurds and Shiite Muslims. Twice he had invaded neighboring countries. A huge secret police ensured that the common people were terrified into submission. It was plausible that Saddam Hussein had stockpiled chemical and biological weapons. But there was no hard evidence. After a year, Bush and Secretary of State Colin Powell were able to provide only shards of circumstantial evidence that Saddam possessed an arsenal that would justify a preemptive attack.

Painted into a Corner

Germany opposed invasion. More important (because they held veto power in the United Nations Security Council), so did France, Russia, and China. The United States, Great Britain, and Australia built up their assault force in Kuwait, Saudi Arabia, and the Persian Gulf; Bush delayed the attack (some experts said to the military disadvantage of what Bush called "the coalition") while American diplomats tried to find a formula for a United Nations resolution that would placate the powers that opposed the war.

If Bush had painted himself into a corner by massing troops south of Iraq, the French and German governments did the same by their obstructionism. The worldwide post-9/11 sympathy for the United States dissipated everywhere. By the end of 2002, European public opinion, even in Great Britain, denounced Bush as a "warmonger," as did the people and governments in most Muslim countries. There were massive protests in every large world city, including in the United States. The French and German governments were hamstrung.

Pacifists opposed the war, of course. Most Arab countries were pro-Iraq, although rarely pro-Saddam. Some opponents of the war, at home and abroad, protested Bush's plans because, as always in human history, they opposed everything the world's greatest power espoused. Some people called for bridling Saddam Hussein by means short of war. Some geopolitical analysts cautioned that the destruction of Saddam's regime would plunge the entire Middle East, volatile at the best of times, into chaos. Albert Gore

and others pointed out that by fixating on Iraq, the United States was forgetting the fact that al Qaeda, an enemy that had actually struck a blow, was not yet destroyed. North Korea, a militarist dictatorship armed with missiles capable of hitting South Korean and Japanese cities, exposed the risks of the Iraq fixation by announcing that it was resuming its program to construct nuclear warheads. Early in 2003, always reliable Turkey voted against allowing the coalition to invade Iraq from the north.

The Second Iraq War

Nevertheless, on March 19, 2003, following a final rebuff by the United Nations, the "coalition of the willing" invaded. The major part of the war was astonishingly swift and, for the coalition, low in casualties. During two weeks of withering air and missile assaults, British marines surrounded Basra, Iraq's second largest city while American soldiers and marines sped in three columns to the outskirts of Baghdad. On their 300 mile charge, they by-passed several major Iraqi cities from which "fedayeen" (irregular militia dressed as civilians) sallied and briefly disrupted supply lines. Suicide bombers dressed as civilians killed soldiers manning checkpoints. Experts warned daily in newspapers and on television that the invaders faced a block-by-block bloodbath in Baghdad.

But it was not to be. The defenders of Baghdad (and Basra) collapsed or, rather, evaporated. On April 9, American tanks rolled unopposed into the heart of the city. Crowds of Iraqi men celebrated hysterically, destroying statues of Saddam Hussein. Mobs looted government buildings in both major cities. One videotape showed a man running off with a vase of plastic flowers. The antiwar protesters, hundreds of thousands strong three weeks earlier, evaporated too. (Like armies, antiwar protests thrive on victory.) France, Germany, and the United Nations stated that they should have important roles in the reconstruction of Iraq without explicitly mentioning the oil that would pay for it.

The media, both American and foreign, had emphasized the deaths of civilians in a manner that can be described as lovingly. ("Balanced coverage" is a term useful only to students preparing for exams in journalism courses.) In fact, the Second Iraq War was historically singular, perhaps unique, in the military's fastidious avoidance of residential areas in their massive bombardments, even after it was known that Iraqi soldiers hid in hospitals, schools, and mosques. The vaunted might of the Iraqi military was a chimera. Snipers and suicide terrorists continued to take lives, but the army and Saddam Hussein's "elite" Republican Guard crumbled before battles were fairly joined.

On the Home Front

Little noticed in a nation obsessed by Iraq, the Bush administration quietly expanded the pro–big business, pro-wealthy domestic policies of the "Reagan Revolution." The Clinton surpluses disappeared; the national debt soared again. Bush raised farm subsidies that Clinton had reduced. He increased logging in national forests that had not yet recovered from Reagan's "cut and run" permissiveness. He withdrew the United States from the Kyoto global warming treaty and eased pollution controls on industry. He scrapped limits on dumping coal-mining wastes in streams and rejected automobile fuel efficiency standards presented him after a long study. The fines the Environmental Protection Agency was authorized to impose were reduced by 60 percent. With an expensive war a month away, Bush's proposed budget for 2003 actually reduced revenues by sharply cutting taxes on rich Americans who were already paying less in taxes than they had between the 1930s and the 1980s.

The High-Tech Bubble

The stock market peaked in March 2000. A rapid collapse in values was triggered by the bursting of the high-tech bubble. Dot-coms folded by the hundreds, some because they were absurd enterprises from their inception, some because their directors squandered capital on advertising and their own bloated salaries. The Internet advertising bonanza never materialized. Web surfers, who had been going to the bathroom during television commercials for 50 years, ignored the ads on their computer monitors. Capitalized at $135 million, AllAdvantage.com had assured advertisers their spiels would be seen because AllAdvantage would *pay* Internet users 50 cents an hour to allow ads to stream across their screens. Two million people signed up. In three months, advertisers paid AllAdvantage $10 million; AllAdvantage paid its members $40 million.

The predicted revolution in retailing proved illusory. In 2000, less than 1 percent of American retail sales were made online. In early 2001, the shares of a third of dot-coms devoted to huckstering were valued at less than $10. An Internet wine merchant capitalized at $200 million dismissed 235 of 310 employees in January 2001 and was foreclosed in April. Internet use continued to increase. But, perhaps dismaying to those who had envisioned a nobler new cyber-America, the category of Web site getting the most hits was pornography.

A ballyhooed telecommunications boom also busted. Executives overbuilt and bled their capital reserves to enrich themselves personally, destroying billions in investment and throwing tens of thousands of employees out of work. The century-old Montana Power Company had monopolized electricity sales in the state in return for close regulation by the Montana legislature. Its power was as cheap as anywhere in the nation, and the company paid annual dividends of 7 percent.

Rather than taking pride in running a model corporation providing an essential public service, in 1997, Montana Power and the Wall Street brokerage house Goldman Sachs convinced the Montana legislature to deregulate the electrical power industry in the state. This enabled Montana Power to sell its mines, dams, and power lines for $2.7 billion. The company got out of the power business entirely, renamed itself Touch America, and pumped its capital into telecommunications, burying fiber optic cables all over the thinly populated West. There were, of course, few customers. Hundreds of workers lost their jobs and pension savings; the price of electricity in Montana soared (briefly by 800 percent); shares in Touch America dropped from $30 to 33 cents. There was a bright side: Goldman Sachs pocketed a fee of $20 million, and Touch America's top executives divided up a tenth of the company's capital.

Country Club Crooks

The collapse of several corporations exposed fraud and outright thievery among the big-business elite. The directors and executives of Enron (an energy broker), abetted by their auditor, the gigantic accounting firm Arthur Andersen, stole or destroyed $67 billion of their stockholders' investments. WorldCom (a telecommunications company) lost $9 billion

DOONESBURY

▲ *In his comic strip* Doonesbury, *Garry Trudeau brilliantly mocked just about every American social, cultural, and political foible for three decades. He was able to extract a wry laugh from the bursting of the Internet bubble, which launched the stock market collapse that began in 2000. The cartoonist poked fun at the fact that, in the 1990s, there was no penalty for those in the upper echelons of business for being no good at their jobs.*

to theft and $140 billion in stock value, all covered up by accountants for five years so that the company could woo more suckers to invest. Webvan squandered $1.2 billion in start-up capital, much of it going into the pockets of the company's organizers. Two weeks before Webvan declared bankruptcy, its founder sold his shares at a personal profit of $2.7 million.

In the corporate world of the era of Bill Clinton and George W. Bush, there was no penalty in big business for being a failure. In April 2001, hours before filing for bankruptcy, the Pacific Gas and Electric Company paid its top executives bonuses! Coca-Cola's CEO, after supervising the loss of $4 billion in capital, was given a severance check for $18 million. AT&T fired CEO John Walter after nine months because he "lacked intellectual leadership." Nevertheless, AT&T wrote him a check for $26 million. Under Jill Barad, at the height of Clinton prosperity, the toy manufacturer Mattel lost $2.5 billion. Barad went back on the job market with $40 million in her purse.

Jacques Barzun did not include cynical, conscienceless greed as a sign of a society's decadence. Edward Gibbon, whose *Decline and Fall of the Roman Empire* appeared in 1776, the year the United States declared its independence, did.

for FURTHER READING

Recent history is, as John Gardner wrote, confusing and messy. This is because both writer and reader are part of what has gone on around them. If it is difficult to be objective when trying to understand European-Indian conflict in the seventeenth century, it is dishonest and self-delusory to claim detachment when writing of a president about whom one reads in the newspapers. "People," novelist James Baldwin wrote, "are trapped in history and history is trapped in them."

If objectivity is out of the question, thoughtfulness and honesty are not. A few such examinations of recent political history are Thomas Byrne and Mary D. Edsall, *Chain Reaction*, 1992; Jack

W. Germond and Jules Witcover, *Mad as Hell: Revolt at the Ballot Box*, 1993; Stephan Gillon, *The Democrats' Dilemma*, 1992; William Greider, *Who Will Tell the People?* 1992; Kathleen Hall Jamieson, *Packaging the Presidency*, 1992; and Kevin Phillips, *Boiling Point: Democrats, Republicans, and the Decline of Middle Class Prosperity*, 1993.

Also see David Maraniss, *First in His Class: A Biography of Bill Clinton*, 1995; Bob Woodward, *The Agenda: Inside the Clinton White House*, 1994; Kenneth Baer, *Reinventing Democrats*, 2000; and John Hohenberg, *Reelecting Bill Clinton: Why America Chose a "New" Democrat*, 1997.

 AMERICAN JOURNEY ONLINE AND INFOTRAC COLLEGE EDITION

Visit the source collections at http://ajaccess.wadsworth.com and infotrac.thomsonlearning.com and use the Search function with the following key terms to explore documents, images, audio and video clips, articles, and commentary related to the material in this chapter.

Affirmative Action	Newt Gingrich
AIDS	North American Free Trade Agreement (NAFTA)
Bill Clinton	Oklahoma City bombing
Branch Davidians	Ronald Reagan
Clinton impeachment	Ross Perot
George W. Bush	September 11, 2001
Kenneth Starr	Terrorism
Monica Lewinsky	Whitewater Investigation

HISTORY ONLINE

The War in Afghanistan
www.multied/com/enduring freedom/index.html
Maps and text concerning the United States intervention in Afghanistan.

Political Humor
http://politicalhumor.about.com/cs/georgewbush/
Selection of humor mocking President George W. Bush.

APPENDIX

The Declaration of Independence

*The Constitution of the
United States of America*

Admission of States

Population of the United States

Presidential Elections

*Presidents, Vice Presidents,
and Major Cabinet Officers*

Cabinet Level Departments

Justices of the U.S. Supreme Court

*Political Party Affiliations
in Congress and the Presidency*

The Declaration of Independence

The Unanimous Declaration of the Thirteen United States of America,

When in the Course of human events it becomes necessary for one people to dissolve the political bands which have connected them with another, and to assume among the Powers of the earth, the separate and equal station to which the Laws of Nature and of Nature's God entitle them, a decent respect to the opinions of mankind requires that they should declare the causes which impel them to the separation.

We hold these truths to be self-evident, that all men are created equal, that they are endowed by their Creator with certain unalienable Rights, that among these are Life, Liberty and the pursuit of Happiness. That to secure these rights, Governments are instituted among Men, deriving their just Powers from the consent of the governed. That whenever any Form of Government becomes destructive of these ends, it is the Right of the People to alter or to abolish it, and to institute new Government, laying its foundation on such principles and organizing its Powers in such form, as to them shall seem most likely to effect their Safety and Happiness. Prudence, indeed, will dictate that Governments long established should not be changed for light and transient causes; and accordingly all experience hath shewn, that mankind are more disposed to suffer, while evils are sufferable, than to right themselves by abolishing the forms to which they are accustomed. But when a long train of abuses and usurpations, pursuing invariably the same Object evinces a design to reduce them under absolute Despotism, it is their right, it is their duty, to throw off such Government, and to provide new Guards for their future security. Such has been the patient sufferance of these Colonies; and such is now the necessity which constrains them to alter their former Systems of Government. The history of the present King of Great Britain is a history of repeated injuries and usurpations, all having in direct object the establishment of an absolute Tyranny over these States. To prove this, let Facts be submitted to a candid world.

He has refused his Assent to Laws, the most wholesome and necessary for the public good.

He has forbidden his Governors to pass Laws of immediate and pressing importance, unless suspended in their operation till his Assent should be obtained; and when so suspended, he has utterly neglected to attend to them.

He has refused to pass other Laws for the accommodation of large districts of people, unless those people would relinquish the right of Representation in the Legislature, a right inestimable to them and formidable to tyrants only.

He has called together legislative bodies at places unusual, uncomfortable, and distant from the depository of their Public Records, for the sole Purpose of fatiguing them into compliance with his measures.

He has dissolved Representative Houses repeatedly, for opposing with manly firmness his invasions on the rights of the People.

He has refused for a long time, after such dissolutions, to cause others to be elected; whereby the Legislative Powers, incapable of Annihilation, have returned to the People at large for their exercise; the State remaining in the mean time exposed to all the dangers of invasion from without, and convulsions within.

He has endeavoured to prevent the Population of these States; for that purpose obstructing the Laws for Naturalization of Foreigners; refusing to pass others to encourage their migrations hither, and raising the conditions of new Appropriations of Lands.

He has obstructed the Administration of Justice, by refusing his Assent to Laws for establishing Judiciary Powers.

He has made Judges dependent on his Will alone, for the tenure of their offices, and the amount and payment of their salaries.

He has erected a multitude of New Offices, and sent hither swarms of Officers to harass our People, and eat out their substance.

He has kept among us, in times of peace, Standing Armies without the Consent of our legislatures.

He has affected to render the Military independent of and superior to the Civil Power.

He has combined with others to subject us to a jurisdiction foreign to our constitution, and unacknowledged by our laws; giving his Assent to their Acts of pretended Legislation:

For Quartering large bodies of armed troops among us:

For protecting them, by a mock Trial, from Punishment for any Murders which they should commit on the Inhabitants of these States:

For cutting off our Trade with all parts of the world:

For imposing Taxes on us without our Consent:

For depriving us in many cases, of the benefits of Trial by Jury:

For transporting us beyond Seas to be tried for pretended offences:

For abolishing the free System of English Laws in a neighbouring Province, establishing therein an Arbitrary government, and enlarging its Boundaries so as to render it at once an example and fit instrument for introducing the same absolute rule into these Colonies:

Text is reprinted from the facsimile of the engrossed copy in the National Archives. The original spelling, capitalization, and punctuation have been retained. Paragraphing has been added.

For taking away our Charters, abolishing our most valuable Laws, and altering fundamentally the Forms of our Governments:

For suspending our own Legislatures, and declaring themselves invested with Power to legislate for us in all cases whatsoever.

He has abdicated Government here, by declaring us out of his Protection, and waging War against us.

He has plundered our seas, ravaged our Coasts, burnt our towns, and destroyed the lives of our people.

He is at this time transporting large Armies of foreign Mercenaries to compleat the works of death, desolation and tyranny, already begun with circumstances of Cruelty and perfidy scarcely paralleled in the most barbarous ages, and totally unworthy the Head of a civilized nation.

He has constrained our fellow Citizens taken Captive on the high Seas to bear Arms against their Country, to become the executioners of their friends and Brethren, or to fall themselves by their Hands.

He has excited domestic insurrections amongst us, and has endeavoured to bring on the inhabitants of our frontiers, the merciless Indian Savages, whose known rule of warfare, is an undistinguished destruction of all ages, sexes and conditions.

In every stage of these Oppressions We have Petitioned for Redress in the most humble terms: Our repeated Petitions have been answered only by repeated injury. A Prince, whose character is thus marked by every act which may define a Tyrant, is unfit to be the ruler of a free People.

Nor have We been wanting in attentions to our British brethren. We have warned them from time to time of attempts by their legislature to extend an unwarrantable jurisdiction over us. We have reminded them of the circumstances of our emigration and settlement here. We have appealed to their native justice and magnanimity, and we have conjured them by the ties of our common kindred to disavow thee usurpations, which, would inevitably interrupt our connections and correspondence. They too have been deaf to the voice of justice and of consanguinity. We must, therefore, acquiesce in the necessity, which denounces our Separation, and hold them, as we hold the rest of mankind, Enemies in War, in Peace Friends.

WE, THEREFORE, the Representatives of the UNITED STATES OF AMERICA, in General Congress, Assembled, appealing to the Supreme Judge of the world for the rectitude of our intentions, do, in the Name, and by Authority of the good People of these Colonies, solemnly publish and declare, That these United Colonies are, and of Right ought to be FREE AND INDEPENDENT STATES; that they are Absolved from all Allegiance to the British Crown, and that all political connection between them and the State of Great Britain, is and ought to be totally dissolved; and that, as Free and Independent States, they have full Power to levy War, conclude Peace, contract Alliances, establish Commerce, and to do all other Acts and Things which Independent States may of right do. And for the support of this Declaration, with a firm reliance on the protection of divine Providence, we mutually pledge to each other our Lives, our Fortunes and our sacred Honor.

The Constitution of the United States of America

We the People of the United States, in Order to form a more perfect Union, establish Justice, insure domestic Tranquility, provide for the common defence, promote the general Welfare, and secure the Blessings of Liberty to ourselves and our Posterity, do ordain and establish this Constitution for the United States of America.

Article. I.

SECTION. 1. All legislative Powers herein granted shall be vested in a Congress of the United States, which shall consist of a Senate and House of Representatives.

SECTION. 2. The House of Representatives shall be composed of Members chosen every second Year by the People of the several States, and the Electors in each State shall have the Qualifications requisite for Electors of the most numerous Branch of the State Legislature.

No Person shall be a Representative who shall not have attained to the Age of twenty five Years, and been seven Years a Citizen of the United States, and who shall not, when elected, be an Inhabitant of that State in which he shall be chosen.

Representatives and direct Taxes[1] shall be apportioned among the several States which may be included within this Union, according to their respective Numbers, which shall be determined by adding to the whole Number of free Persons, including those bound to Service for a Term of Years, and excluding Indians not taxed, three fifths of all other Persons.[2] The actual Enumeration shall be made within three Years after the first Meeting of the Congress of the United States, and within every subsequent Term of ten Years, in such Manner as they shall by Law direct. The Number of Representatives shall not exceed one for every thirty Thousand, but each State shall have at Least one Representative; and until such enumeration shall be made, the State of New Hampshire shall be entitled to chuse three; Massachusetts eight; Rhode Island and Providence Plantations one; Connecticut five; New York six; New Jersey four; Pennsylvania eight; Delaware one; Maryland six; Virginia ten; North Carolina five; South Carolina five; and Georgia three.

When vacancies happen in the Representation from any State, the Executive Authority thereof shall issue Writs of Election to fill such Vacancies.

The House of Representatives shall chuse their Speaker and other Officers; and shall have the sole Power of Impeachment.

SECTION. 3. The Senate of the United States shall be composed of two Senators from each State, chosen by the Legislature thereof, for six Years; and each Senator shall have one Vote.[3]

Immediately after they shall be assembled in Consequence of the first Election, they shall be divided as equally as may be into three Classes. The Seats of the Senators of the first Class shall be vacated at the Expiration of the second Year, of the second Class at the Expiration of the fourth Year, and of the third Class at the Expiration of the sixth Year, so that one third may be chosen every second Year; and if Vacancies happen by Resignation, or otherwise, during the Recess of the Legislature of any State, the Executive thereof may make temporary Appointments until the next Meeting of the Legislature, which shall then fill such Vacancies.[4]

No Person shall be a Senator who shall not have attained to the Age of thirty Years, and been nine Years a Citizen of the United States, and who shall not, when elected, be an Inhabitant of that State for which he shall be chosen.

The Vice President of the United States shall be President of the Senate, but shall have no Vote, unless they be equally divided.

The Senate shall chuse their other Officers, and also a President pro tempore, in the Absence of the Vice President, or when he shall exercise the Office of President of the United States.

The Senate shall have the sole Power to try all Impeachments. When sitting for that Purpose, they shall be on Oath or Affirmation. When the President of the United States is tried, the Chief Justice shall preside: And no Person shall be convicted without the Concurrence of two thirds of the Members present.

Judgment in Cases of Impeachment shall not extend further than to removal from Office, and disqualification to hold and enjoy any Office of honor, Trust or Profit under the United States: but the Party convicted shall nevertheless be liable and subject to Indictment, Trial, Judgment and Punishment, according to Law.

SECTION. 4. The Times, Places and Manner of holding Elections for Senators and Representatives, shall be prescribed in each State by the Legislature thereof, but the Congress may at any time by Law make or alter such Regulation, except as to the Places of chusing Senators.

The Congress shall assemble at least once in every Year, and such Meeting shall be on the first Monday in December, unless they shall by Law appoint a different Day.[5]

Text is from the engrossed copy in the National Archives. Original spelling, capitalization, and punctuation have been retained.

[1]Modified by the Sixteenth Amendment.

[2]Replaced by the Fourteenth Amendment.

---

[3]Superseded by the Seventeenth Amendment.

[4]Modified by the Seventeenth Amendment.

[5]Superseded by the Twentieth Amendment.

SECTION. 5. Each House shall be the Judge of the Elections, Returns and Qualifications of its own Members, and a Majority of each shall constitute a Quorum to do Business; but a smaller Number may adjourn from day to day, and may be authorized to compel the Attendance of absent Members, in such Manner, and under such Penalties as each House may provide.

Each House may determine the Rules of its Proceedings, punish its Members for disorderly Behaviour, and, with the Concurrence of two thirds, expel a Member.

Each House shall keep a Journal of its Proceedings, and from time to time publish the same, excepting such Parts as may in their Judgment require Secrecy; and the Yeas and Nays of the Members of either House on any question shall, at the Desire of one fifth of those Present, be entered on the Journal.

Neither House, during the Session of Congress, shall, without the Consent of the other, adjourn for more than three days, nor to any other Place than that in which the two Houses shall be sitting.

SECTION. 6. The Senators and Representatives shall receive a Compensation for their Services, to be ascertained by Law, and paid out of the Treasury of the United States. They shall in all Cases, except Treason, Felony and Breach of the Peace, be privileged from Arrest during their Attendance at the Session of their respective Houses, and in going to and returning from the same; and for any Speech or Debate in either House, they shall not be questioned in any other Place.

No Senator or Representative shall, during the Time for which he was elected, be appointed to any civil Office under the Authority of the United States, which shall have been created, or the Emoluments whereof shall have been encreased during such time; and no Person holding any Office under the United States, shall be a Member of either House during his Continuance in Office.

SECTION. 7. All Bills for raising Revenue shall originate in the House of Representatives; but the Senate may propose or concur with Amendments as on other Bills.

Every Bill which shall have passed the House of Representatives and the Senate shall, before it become a Law, be presented to the President of the United States; If he approve he shall sign it, but if not he shall return it, with his Objections to that House in which it shall have originated, who shall enter the Objections at large on their Journal, and proceed to reconsider it. If after such Reconsideration two thirds of that House shall agree to pass the Bill, it shall be sent, together with the Objections, to the other House, by which it shall likewise be reconsidered, and if approved by two thirds of that House, it shall become a Law. But in all such Cases the Votes of both Houses shall be determined by yeas and Nays, and the Names of the Persons voting for and against the Bill shall be entered on the Journal of each House respectively. If any Bill shall not be returned by the President within ten Days (Sundays excepted) after it shall have been presented to him, the Same shall be a Law, in like Manner as if he had signed it, unless the Congress by their Adjournment prevent its Return, in which Case it shall not be a Law.

Every Order, Resolution, or Vote to which the Concurrence of the Senate and House of Representatives may be necessary (except on a question of Adjournment) shall be presented to the President of the United States; and before the Same shall take Effect, shall be approved by him, or being disapproved by him shall be repassed by two thirds of the Senate and House of Representatives, according to the Rules and Limitations prescribed in the Case of a Bill.

SECTION. 8. The Congress shall have power To lay and collect Taxes, Duties, Imposts and Excises, to pay the Debts and provide for the common Defence and general Welfare of the United States; but all Duties, Imposts and Excises shall be uniform throughout the United States;

To borrow Money on the credit of the United States;

To regulate Commerce with foreign Nations, and among the several States, and with the Indian Tribes;

To establish an uniform Rule of Naturalization, and uniform Laws on the subject of Bankruptcies throughout the United States;

To coin Money, regulate the Value thereof, and of foreign Coin, and fix the Standard of Weights and Measures;

To provide for the Punishment of counterfeiting the Securities and current Coin of the United States;

To establish Post Offices and post Roads;

To promote the Progress of Science and useful Arts, by securing for limited Times to Authors and Inventors the exclusive Right to their respective Writings and Discoveries;

To constitute Tribunals inferior to the Supreme Court;

To define and punish Piracies and Felonies committed on the high Seas, and Offences against the Law of Nations;

To declare War, grant Letters of Marque and Reprisal, and make Rules concerning Captures on Land and Water;

To raise and support Armies, but no Appropriation of Money to that Use shall be for a longer Term than two Years;

To provide and maintain a Navy;

To make Rules for the Government and Regulation of the land and naval Forces;

To provide for calling forth the Militia to execute the Laws of the Union, suppress Insurrections and repel Invasions;

To provide for organizing, arming, and disciplining, the Militia, and for governing such Part of them as may be employed in the Service of the United States, reserving to the States respectively, the Appointment of the Officers, and the Authority of training the Militia according to the discipline prescribed by Congress;

To exercise exclusive Legislation in all Cases whatsoever, over such District (not exceeding ten Miles square) as may, by Cession of particular States, and the Acceptance of Congress, become the Seat of the Government of the United States, and to exercise like Authority over all Places purchased by the Consent of the Legislature of the State in which the Same shall be, for the Erection of Forts, Magazines, Arsenals, dock-Yards, and other needful Buildings;—And

To make all Laws which shall be necessary and proper for carrying into Execution the foregoing Powers, and all other Powers vested by this Constitution in the Government of the United States, or in any Department or Officer thereof.

SECTION. 9. The Migration or Importation of such Persons as any of the States now existing shall think proper to admit, shall not be prohibited by the Congress prior to the Year one thousand eight hundred and eight, but a Tax or duty may be imposed on such Importation, not exceeding ten dollars for each Person.

The Privilege of the Writ of Habeas Corpus shall not be suspended, unless when in Cases of Rebellion or Invasion the public Safety may require it.

No Bill of Attainder or ex post facto Law shall be passed.

No Capitation, or other direct, Tax shall be laid, unless in Proportion to the Census or Enumeration herein before directed to be taken.

No Tax or Duty shall be laid on Articles exported from any State.

No Preference shall be given by any Regulation of Commerce or Revenue to the Ports of one State over those of another: nor shall Vessels bound to, or from, one State, be obliged to enter, clear, or pay Duties in another.

No Money shall be drawn from the Treasury, but in Consequence of Appropriations made by Law, and a regular Statement and Account of the Receipts and Expenditures of all public Money shall be published from time to time.

No Title of Nobility shall be granted by the United States: And no Person holding any Office of Profit or Trust under them, shall, without the Consent of the Congress, accept of any present, Emolument, Office, or Title, of any kind whatever, from any King, Prince, or foreign State.

SECTION. 10. No State shall enter into any Treaty, Alliance, or Confederation; grant Letters of Marque and Reprisal; coin Money; emit Bills of Credit; make any Thing but gold and silver Coin a Tender in Payment of Debts; pass any Bill of Attainder, ex post facto Law, or Law impairing the Obligation of Contracts, or grant any Title of Nobility.

No State shall, without the Consent of the Congress, lay any Imposts or Duties on Imports or Exports, except what may be absolutely necessary for executing its inspection Laws: and the net Produce of all Duties and Imposts, laid by any State on Imports or Exports, shall be for the Use of the Treasury of the United States; and all such Laws shall be subject to the Revision and Controul of the Congress.

No State shall, without the Consent of Congress, lay any Duty of Tonnage, keep Troops, or Ships of War in time of Peace, enter into any Agreement or Compact with another State, or with a foreign Power, or engage in War, unless actually invaded, or in such imminent Danger as will not admit of delay.

Article. II.

SECTION. 1. The executive Power shall be vested in a President of the United States of America. He shall hold his Office during the Term of four Years, and, together with the Vice President, chosen for the same Term, be elected, as follows:

Each State shall appoint, in such Manner as the Legislature thereof may direct, a Number of Electors, equal to the whole Number of Senators and Representatives to which the State may be entitled in the Congress: but no Senator or Representative, or Person holding an Office of Trust or Profit under the United States, shall be appointed an Elector.

The Electors shall meet in their respective States, and vote by Ballot for two Persons, of whom one at least shall not be an Inhabitant of the same State with themselves. And they shall make a List of all the Persons voted for, and of the Number of Votes for each; which List they shall sign and certify, and transmit sealed to the Seat of the Government of the United States, directed to the President of the Senate. The President of the Senate shall, in the Presence of the Senate and House of Representatives, open all the Certificates, and the Votes shall then be counted. The Person having the greatest Number of Votes shall be the President, if such Number be a Majority of the whole Number of Electors appointed; and if there be more than one who have such Majority, and have an equal Number of Votes, then the House of Representatives shall immediately chuse by Ballot one of them for President; and if no Person have a Majority, then from the five highest on the List the said House shall in like Manner chuse the President. But in chusing the President, the Votes shall be taken by States, the Representation from each State having one Vote; A quorum for this Purpose shall consist of a Member or Members from two thirds of the States, and a Majority of all the States shall be necessary to a Choice. In every Case, after the Choice of the President, the Person having the greatest Number of Votes of the Electors shall be the Vice President. But if there should remain two or more who have equal Votes, the Senate shall chuse from them by Ballot the Vice President.[6]

The Congress may determine the Time of chusing the Electors, and the Day on which they shall give their Votes; which Day shall be the same throughout the United States.

No Person except a natural born Citizen, or a Citizen of the United States, at the time of the Adoption of this Constitution, shall be eligible to the Office of President, neither shall any Person be eligible to that Office who shall not have attained to the Age of thirty five Years, and been fourteen Years a Resident within the United States.

In Case of the Removal of the President from Office, or of his Death, Resignation, or Inability to discharge the Powers and Duties of the said Office, the Same shall devolve on the Vice President, and the Congress may by Law provide for the Case of Removal, Death, Resignation or Inability, both of the President and Vice President, declaring what Officer shall then act as President, and such Officer shall act accordingly, until the Disability be removed, or a President shall be elected.[7]

The President shall, at stated Times, receive for his Services, a Compensation, which shall neither be encreased nor diminished during the Period for which he shall have been elected, and he shall not receive within that Period any other Emolument from the United States, or any of them.

---

[6]Superseded by the Twelfth Amendment.

[7]Modified by the Twenty-fifth Amendment.

Before he enter on the Execution of his Office, he shall take the following Oath or Affirmation:—"I do solemnly swear (or affirm) that I will faithfully execute the Office of President of the United States, and will to the best of my Ability, preserve, protect and defend the Constitution of the United States."

SECTION. 2. The President shall be Commander in Chief of the Army and Navy of the United States, and of the Militia of the several States, when called into the actual Service of the United States; he may require the Opinion, in writing, of the principal Officer in each of the executive Departments, upon any Subject relating to the Duties of their respective Offices, and he shall have Power to grant Reprieves and Pardons for Offences against the United States, except in Cases of Impeachment.

He shall have Power, by and with the Advice and Consent of the Senate, to make Treaties, provided two thirds of the Senators present concur; and he shall nominate, and by and with the Advice and Consent of the Senate, shall appoint Ambassadors, other public Ministers and Consuls, Judges of the supreme Court, and all other Officers of the United States, whose Appointments are not herein otherwise provided for, and which shall be established by Law; but the Congress may by Law vest the Appointment of such inferior Officers, as they think proper, in the President alone, in the Courts of Law, or in the Heads of Departments.

The President shall have Power to fill up all Vacancies that may happen during the Recess of the Senate, by granting Commissions which shall expire at the End of their next Session.

SECTION. 3. He shall from time to time give the Congress Information of the State of the Union, and recommend to their Consideration such Measures as he shall judge necessary and expedient; he may, on extraordinary Occasions, convene both Houses, or either of them, and in Case of Disagreement between them, with Respect to the Time of Adjournment, he may adjourn them to such Time as he shall think proper; he shall receive Ambassadors and other public Ministers; he shall take Care that the Laws be faithfully executed, and shall Commission all the Officers of the United States.

SECTION. 4. The President, Vice President and all civil Officers of the United States, shall be removed from Office on Impeachment for, and Conviction of, Treason, Bribery, or other high Crimes and Misdemeanors.

Article. III.

SECTION. 1. The judicial Power of the United States, shall be vested in one supreme Court, and in such inferior Courts as the Congress may from time to time ordain and establish. The Judges, both of the supreme and inferior Courts, shall hold their Offices during good Behaviour, and shall, at stated Times, receive for their Services, a Compensation, which shall not be diminished during their Continuance in Office.

SECTION. 2. The judicial Power shall extend to all Cases, in Law and Equity, arising under this Constitution, the Laws of the United States, and Treaties made, or which shall be made, under their Authority;-to all Cases affecting Ambassadors, other public Ministers and Consuls;—to all Cases of admiralty and maritime Jurisdiction;—to Controversies to which the United States shall be a Party;—to Controversies between two or more States;—between a State and Citizens of another State;[8]—between Citizens of different States,—between Citizens of the same State claiming Lands under Grants of different States, and between a State, or the Citizens thereof, and foreign States, Citizens or Subjects.

In all Cases affecting Ambassadors, other public Ministers and Consuls, and those in which a State shall be Party, the supreme Court shall have original Jurisdiction. In all the other Cases before mentioned, the supreme Court shall have appellate Jurisdiction, both as to Law and Fact, with such Exceptions, and under such Regulations as the Congress shall make.

The Trial of all Crimes, except in Cases of Impeachment, shall be by Jury; and such Trial shall be held in the State where the said Crimes shall have been committed; but when not committed within any State, the Trial shall be at such Place or Places as the Congress may by Law have directed.

SECTION. 3. Treason against the United States, shall consist only in levying War against them, or in adhering to their Enemies, giving them Aid and Comfort. No Person shall be convicted of Treason unless on the Testimony of two Witnesses to the same overt Act, or on Confession in open Court.

The Congress shall have Power to declare the Punishment of Treason, but no Attainder of Treason shall work Corruption of Blood, or Forfeiture except during the Life of the Person attainted.

Article. IV.

SECTION. 1. Full Faith and Credit shall be given in each State to the public Acts, Records, and judicial Proceedings of every other State. And the Congress may by general Laws prescribe the Manner in which such Acts, Records and Proceedings shall be proved, and the Effect thereof.

SECTION. 2. The Citizens of each State shall be entitled to all Privileges and Immunities of Citizens in the several States.

A Person charged in any State with Treason, Felony, or other Crime, who shall flee from Justice, and be found in another State, shall on Demand of the executive Authority of the State from which he fled, be delivered up, to be removed to the State having Jurisdiction of the Crime.

No Person held to Service or Labour in one State, under the Laws thereof, escaping into another, shall, in Consequence of any Law or Regulation therein, be discharged from such Service or Labour, but shall be delivered up on Claim of the Party to whom such Service or Labour may be due.

SECTION. 3. New States may be admitted by the Congress into this Union; but no new State shall be formed or erected within the Jurisdiction of any other State, nor any State be

[8]Modified by the Eleventh Amendment.

formed by the Junction of two or more States, or Parts of States, without the Consent of the Legislatures of the States concerned as well as of the Congress.

The Congress shall have Power to dispose of and make all needful Rules and Regulations respecting the Territory or other Property belonging to the United States; and nothing in this Constitution shall be so construed as to Prejudice any Claims of the United States, or of any particular State.

SECTION. 4. The United States shall guarantee to every State in this Union a Republican Form of Government, and shall protect each of them against Invasion; and on Application of the Legislature, or of the Executive (when the Legislature cannot be convened) against domestic Violence.

Article. V.

The Congress, whenever two thirds of both Houses shall deem it necessary, shall propose Amendments to this Constitution, or, on the Application of the Legislatures of two thirds of the several States, shall call a Convention for proposing Amendments, which, in either Case, shall be valid to all Intents and Purposes, as Part of this Constitution, when ratified by the Legislatures of three fourths of the several States, or by Conventions in three fourths thereof, as the one or the other Mode of Ratification may be proposed by the Congress; Provided that no Amendment which may be made prior to the Year One thousand eight hundred and eight shall in any Manner affect the first and fourth Clauses in the Ninth Section of the first Article; and that no State, without its Consent, shall be deprived of its equal Suffrage in the Senate.

Article. VI.

All Debts contracted and Engagements entered into, before the Adoption of this Constitution, shall be as valid against the United States under this Constitution, as under the Confederation.

This Constitution, and the Laws of the United States which shall be made in Pursuance thereof; and all Treaties made, or which shall be made, under the Authority of the United States, shall be the supreme Law of the Land; and the Judges in every State shall be bound thereby, any Thing in the Constitution or Laws of any State to the Contrary notwithstanding.

The Senators and Representatives before mentioned, and the Members of the several State Legislatures, and all executive and judicial Officers, both of the United States and of the several States, shall be bound by Oath or Affirmation, to support this Constitution; but no religious Test shall ever be required as a Qualification to any Office or public Trust under the United States.

Article. VII.

The Ratification of the Conventions of nine States, shall be sufficient for the Establishment of this Constitution between the States so ratifying the Same.

Done in Convention by the Unanimous Consent of the States present the Seventeenth Day of September in the Year of our Lord one thousand seven hundred and Eighty seven and of the Independence of the United States of America the Twelfth. **In witness** whereof We have hereunto subscribed our Names,

Articles in Addition to, and Amendment of, the Constitution of the United States of America, Proposed by Congress, and Ratified by the Legislatures of the Several States, Pursuant to the Fifth Article of the Original Constitution.

Amendment I[9]

Congress shall make no law respecting an establishment of religion, or prohibiting the free exercise thereof; or abridging the freedom of speech, or of the press; or the right of the people peaceably to assemble, and to petition the Government for a redress of grievances.

Amendment II

A well regulated Militia, being necessary to the security of a free State, the right of the people to keep and bear Arms shall not be infringed.

Amendment III

No Soldier shall, in time of peace, be quartered in any house, without the consent of the Owner, nor in time of war, but in a manner to be prescribed by law.

Amendment IV

The right of the people to be secure in their persons, houses, papers, and effects, against unreasonable searches and seizures, shall not be violated, and no Warrants shall issue, but upon probable cause, supported by Oath or affirmation, and particularly describing the place to be searched, and the persons or things to be seized.

Amendment V

No person shall be held to answer for a capital or otherwise infamous crime, unless on a presentment or indictment of a Grand Jury, except in cases arising in the land or naval forces, or in the Militia, when in actual service in time of War or public danger; nor shall any person be subject for the same offence to be twice put in jeopardy of life or limb; nor shall be compelled in any criminal case to be a witness against himself, nor be deprived of life, liberty, or property, without due process of law; nor shall private property be taken for public use, without just compensation.

---

[9]The first ten amendments were passed by Congress September 25, 1789. They were ratified by three-fourths of the states December 15, 1791.

Amendment VI

In all criminal prosecutions, the accused shall enjoy the right to a speedy and public trial, by an impartial jury of the State and district wherein the crime shall have been committed, which district shall have been previously ascertained by law, and to be informed of the nature and cause of the accusation; to be confronted with the witnesses against him; to have compulsory process for obtaining witnesses in his favor, and to have the Assistance of Counsel for his defence.

Amendment VII

In suits at common law, where the value in controversy shall exceed twenty dollars, the right of trial by jury shall be preserved, and no fact tried by a jury, shall be otherwise re-examined in any Court of the United States, than according to the rules of the common law.

Amendment VIII

Excessive bail shall not be required, nor excessive fines imposed, nor cruel and unusual punishments inflicted.

Amendment IX

The enumeration in the Constitution, of certain rights, shall not be construed to deny or disparage others retained by the people.

Amendment X

The powers not delegated to the United States by the Constitution; nor prohibited by it to the States, are reserved to the States respectively, or to the people.

Amendment XI[10]

The Judicial power of the United States shall not be construed to extend to any suit in law or equity, commenced or prosecuted against one of the United States by Citizens of another State, or by Citizens or Subjects of any Foreign State.

Amendment XII[11]

The Electors shall meet in their respective States and vote by ballot for President and Vice-President, one of whom, at least, shall not be an inhabitant of the same State with themselves; they shall name in their ballots the person voted for as President, and in distinct ballots the person voted for as Vice-President, and they shall make distinct lists of all persons voted for as President, and of all persons voted for as Vice-President, and of the number of votes for each, which

lists they shall sign and certify, and transmit sealed to the seat of the government of the United States, directed to the President of the Senate;—The President of the Senate shall, in the presence of the Senate and House of Representatives, open all the certificates and the votes shall then be counted;—The person having the greatest number of votes for President, shall be the President, if such number be a majority of the whole number of Electors appointed; and if no person have such majority, then from the persons having the highest numbers not exceeding three on the list of those voted for as President, the House of Representatives shall choose immediately, by ballot, the President. But in choosing the President, the votes shall be taken by states, the representation from each state having one vote; a quorum for this purpose shall consist of a member or members from two-thirds of the states, and a majority of all the states shall be necessary to a choice. And if the House of Representatives shall not choose a President whenever the right of choice shall devolve upon them, before the fourth day of March next following, then the Vice-President shall act as President, as in the case of the death or other constitutional disability of the President.—The person having the greatest number of votes as Vice-President, shall be the Vice-President, if such number be a majority of the whole number of Electors appointed, and if no person have a majority, then from the two highest numbers on the list, the Senate shall choose the Vice-President; a quorum for the purpose shall consist of two-thirds of the whole number of Senators, and a majority of the whole number shall be necessary to a choice. But no person constitutionally ineligible to the office of President shall be eligible to that of Vice-President of the United States.

Amendment XIII[12]

SECTION 1. Neither slavery nor involuntary servitude, except as a punishment for crime whereof the party shall have been duly convicted, shall exist within the United States, or any place subject to their jurisdiction.

SECTION 2. Congress shall have power to enforce this article by appropriate legislation.

Amendment XIV[13]

SECTION 1. All persons born or naturalized in the United States, and subject to the jurisdiction thereof, are citizens of the United States and of the State wherein they reside. No State shall make or enforce any law which shall abridge the privileges or immunities of citizens of the United States; nor shall any State deprive any person of life, liberty, or property, without due process of law; nor deny to any person within its jurisdiction the equal protection of the laws.

SECTION 2. Representatives shall be apportioned among the several States according to their respective numbers, counting

---

[10]Passed March 4, 1794. Ratified January 23, 1795.

[11]Passed December 9, 1803. Ratified June 15, 1804.

[12]Passed January 31, 1865. Ratified December 6, 1865.

[13]Passed June 13, 1866. Ratified July 9, 1868.

the whole number of persons in each State, excluding Indians not taxed. But when the right to vote at any election for the choice of electors for President and Vice-President of the United States, Representatives in Congress, the Executive and Judicial officers of a State, or the members of the Legislature thereof, is denied to any of the male inhabitants of such State, being twenty-one years of age, and citizens of the United States, or in any way abridged, except for participation in rebellion, or other crime, the basis of representation therein shall be reduced in the proportion which the number of such male citizens shall bear to the whole number of male citizens twenty-one years of age in such State.

SECTION 3. No person shall be a Senator or Representative in Congress, or elector of President and Vice-President, or hold any office, civil or military, under the United States, or under any State, who, having previously taken an oath, as a member of Congress, or as an officer of the United States, or as a member of any State legislature, or as an executive or judicial officer of any State, to support the Constitution of the United States, shall have engaged in insurrection or rebellion against the same, or given aid or comfort to the enemies thereof. But Congress may by a vote of two-thirds of each House, remove such disability.

SECTION 4. The validity of the public debt of the United States, authorized by law, including debts incurred for payment of pensions and bounties for services in suppressing insurrection or rebellion, shall not be questioned. But neither the United States nor any State shall assume or pay any debt or obligation incurred in aid of insurrection or rebellion against the United States, or any claim for the loss or emancipation of any slave; but all such debts, obligations, and claims shall be held illegal and void.

SECTION 5. The Congress shall have the power to enforce, by appropriate legislation, the provisions of this article.

Amendment XV[14]

SECTION 1. The right of citizens of the United States to vote shall not be denied or abridged by the United States or by any State on account of race, color, or previous conditions of servitude—

SECTION 2. The Congress shall have power to enforce this article by appropriate legislation.

Amendment XVI

The Congress shall have power to lay and collect taxes on incomes, from whatever source derived, without apportionment among the several States, and without regard to any census or enumeration.

Amendment XVII[15]

The Senate of the United States shall be composed of two Senators from each State, elected by the people thereof, for six years; and each Senator shall have one vote. The electors in each State shall have the qualifications requisite for electors of the most numerous branch of the State legislatures.

When vacancies happen in the representation of any State in the Senate, the executive authority of such State shall issue writs of election to fill such vacancies: Provided, That the legislature of any State may empower the executive thereof to make temporary appointments until the people fill the vacancies by election as the legislature may direct.

This amendment shall not be so construed as to affect the election or term of any Senator chosen before it becomes valid as part of the Constitution.

Amendment XVIII[16]

SECTION 1. After one year from the ratification of this article the manufacture, sale, or transportation of intoxicating liquors within, the importation thereof into, or the exportation thereof from the United States and all territory subject to the jurisdiction thereof for beverage purposes is hereby prohibited.

SECTION 2. The Congress and the several States shall have concurrent power to enforce this article by appropriate legislation.

SECTION 3. This article shall be inoperative unless it shall have been ratified as an amendment to the Constitution by the legislatures of the several States, as provided in the Constitution, within seven years from the date of the submission hereof to the States by the Congress.

Amendment XIX[17]

The right of citizens of the United States to vote shall not be denied or abridged by the United States or by any State on account of sex.

Congress shall have power to enforce this article by appropriate legislation.

Amendment XX[18]

SECTION 1. The terms of the President and Vice-President shall end at noon on the 20th day of January, and the terms of Senators and Representatives at noon on the 3d day of January, of the years in which such terms would have ended if this article had not been ratified; and the terms of their successors shall then begin.

SECTION 2. The Congress shall assemble at least once in every year, and such meeting shall begin at noon on the 3d day of January, unless they shall by law appoint a different day.

SECTION 3. If, at the time fixed for the beginning of the term of the President, the President elect shall have died the Vice-

---

[14]Passed February 26, 1869. Ratified February 2, 1870.

[15]Passed May 13, 1912. Ratified April 8, 1913.

[16]Passed December 18, 1917. Ratified January 16, 1919.

[17]Passed June 4, 1919. Ratified August 18, 1920.

[18]Passed March 2, 1932. Ratified January 23, 1933.

President elect shall become President. If a President shall not have been chosen before the time fixed for the beginning of his term, or if the President elect shall have failed to qualify, then the Vice-President elect shall act as President until a President shall have qualified; and the Congress may by law provide for the case wherein neither a President elect nor a Vice-President elect shall have qualified, declaring who shall then act as President, or the manner in which one who is to act shall be selected, and such person shall act accordingly until a President or Vice-President shall have qualified.

SECTION 4. The Congress may by law provide for the case of the death of any of the persons from whom the House of Representatives may choose a President whenever the right of choice shall have devolved upon them, and for the case of the death of any of the persons from whom the Senate may choose a Vice-President whenever the right of choice shall have devolved upon them.

SECTION 5. Sections 1 and 2 shall take effect on the 15th day of October following the ratification of this article.

SECTION 6. This article shall be inoperative unless it shall have been ratified as an amendment to the Constitution by the legislatures of three-fourths of the several States within seven years from the date of its submission.

Amendment XXI[19]

SECTION 1. The eighteenth article of amendment to the Constitution of the United States is hereby repealed.

SECTION 2. The transportation or importation into any State, Territory, or possession of the United States for delivery or use therein of intoxicating liquors, in violation of the laws thereof, is hereby prohibited.

SECTION 3. This article shall be inoperative unless it shall have been ratified as an amendment to the Constitution by conventions in the several States, as provided in the Constitution, within seven years from the date of the submission hereof to the States by the Congress.

Amendment XXII[20]

No person shall be elected to the office of the President more than twice, and no person who has held the office of President, or acted as President, for more than two years of a term to which some other person was elected President shall be elected to the office of the President more than once.

But this Article shall not apply to any person holding the office of President when this Article was proposed by the Congress, and shall not prevent any person who may be holding the office of President, or acting as President, during the term within which this Article becomes operative from holding the office of President or acting as President during the remainder of such term.

Amendment XXIII[21]

SECTION 1. The District constituting the seat of Government of the United States shall appoint in such manner as the Congress may direct:

A number of electors of President and Vice President equal to the whole number of Senators and Representatives in Congress to which the District would be entitled if it were a State, but in no event more than the least populous State; they shall be in addition to those appointed by the States, but they shall be considered, for the purposes of the election of President and Vice President, to be electors appointed by the State; and they shall meet in the District and perform such duties as provided by the twelfth article of amendment.

SECTION 2. The Congress shall have power to enforce this article by appropriate legislation.

Amendment XXIV[22]

SECTION 1. The right of citizens of the United States to vote in any primary or other election for President or Vice President, or for Senator or Representative in Congress, shall not be denied or abridged by the United States or any State by reason of failure to pay any poll tax or other tax.

SECTION 2. The Congress shall have power to enforce this article by appropriate legislation.

Amendment XXV[23]

SECTION 1. In case of the removal of the President from office or of his death or resignation, the Vice President shall become President.

SECTION 2. Whenever there is a vacancy in the office of the Vice President, the President shall nominate a Vice President who shall take office upon confirmation by a majority vote of both Houses of Congress.

SECTION 3. Whenever the President transmits to the President pro tempore of the Senate and the Speaker of the House of Representatives his written declaration that he is unable to discharge the powers and duties of his office, and until he transmits them a written declaration to the contrary, such powers and duties shall be discharged by the Vice President as Acting President.

SECTION 4. Whenever the Vice President and a majority of either the principal officers of the executive department or of such other body as Congress may by law provide, transmit to the President pro tempore of the Senate and the Speaker of the House of Representatives their written declaration that the President is unable to discharge the powers and duties of his office, the Vice President shall immediately assume the powers and duties of the office of Acting President.

---

[19]Passed February 20, 1933. Ratified December 5, 1933.

[20]Passed March 12, 1947. Ratified March 1, 1951.

[21]Passed June 16, 1960. Ratified April 3, 1961.

[22]Passed August 27, 1962. Ratified January 23, 1964.

[23]Passed July 6, 1965. Ratified February 11, 1967.

Thereafter, when the President transmits to the President pro tempore of the Senate and the Speaker of the House of Representatives his written declaration that no inability exists, he shall resume the powers and duties of his office unless the Vice President and a majority of either the principal officers of the executive department or of such other body as Congress may by law provide, transmit within four days to the President pro tempore of the Senate and the Speaker of the House of Representatives their written declaration that the President is unable to discharge the powers and duties of his office. Thereupon Congress shall decide the issue, assembling within forty-eight hours for that purpose if not in session. If the Congress, within twenty-one days after receipt of the latter written declaration, or, if Congress is not in session, within twenty-one days after Congress is required to assemble, determines by two-thirds vote of both Houses that the President is unable to discharge the powers and duties of his office, the Vice President shall continue to discharge the same as Acting President; otherwise, the President shall resume the powers and duties of his office.

Amendment XXVI[24]

SECTION 1. The right of citizens of the United States, who are eighteen years of age or older, to vote shall not be denied or abridged by the United States or by any State on account of age.
SECTION 2. The Congress shall have power to enforce this article by appropriate legislation.

Amendment XXVII[25]

No law, varying the compensation for the service of the Senators and Representatives, shall take effect, until an election of Representatives shall have intervened.

---

[24]Passed March 23, 1971. Ratified July 5, 1971.

[25]Passed September 25, 1989. Ratified May 7, 1992.

Admission of States

Order of admission	State	Date of admission	Order of admission	State	Date of admission
1	Delaware	December 7, 1787	26	Michigan	January 26, 1837
2	Pennsylvania	December 12, 1787	27	Florida	March 3, 1845
3	New Jersey	December 18, 1787	28	Texas	December 29, 1845
4	Georgia	January 2, 1788	29	Iowa	December 28, 1846
5	Connecticut	January 9, 1788	30	Wisconsin	May 29, 1848
6	Massachusetts	February 6, 1788	31	California	September 9, 1850
7	Maryland	April 28, 1788	32	Minnesota	May 11, 1858
8	South Carolina	May 23, 1788	33	Oregon	February 14, 1859
9	New Hampshire	June 21, 1788	34	Kansas	January 29, 1861
10	Virginia	June 25, 1788	35	West Virginia	June 20, 1863
11	New York	July 26, 1788	36	Nevada	October 31, 1864
12	North Carolina	November 21, 1789	37	Nebraska	March 1, 1867
13	Rhode Island	May 29, 1790	38	Colorado	August 1, 1876
14	Vermont	March 4, 1791	39	North Dakota	November 2, 1889
15	Kentucky	June 1, 1792	40	South Dakota	November 2, 1889
16	Tennessee	June 1, 1796	41	Montana	November 8, 1889
17	Ohio	March 1, 1803	42	Washington	November 11, 1889
18	Louisiana	April 30, 1812	43	Idaho	July 3, 1890
19	Indiana	December 11, 1816	44	Wyoming	July 10, 1890
20	Mississippi	December 10, 1817	45	Utah	January 4, 1896
21	Illinois	December 3, 1818	46	Oklahoma	November 16, 1907
22	Alabama	December 14, 1819	47	New Mexico	January 6, 1912
23	Maine	March 15, 1820	48	Arizona	February 14, 1912
24	Missouri	August 10, 1821	49	Alaska	January 3, 1959
25	Arkansas	June 15, 1836	50	Hawaii	August 21, 1959

Population of the United States
(1790–1999)

Year	Total population (in thousands)	Number per square mile of land area (continental United States)	Year	Total population (in thousands)	Number per square mile of land area (continental United States)
1790	3,929	4.5	1829	12,565	
1791	4,056		1830	12,901	7.4
1792	4,194		1831	13,321	
1793	4,332		1832	13,742	
1794	4,469		1833	14,162	
1795	4,607		1834	14,582	
1796	4,745		1835	15,003	
1797	4,883		1836	15,423	
1798	5,021		1837	15,843	
1799	5,159		1838	16,264	
1800	5,297	6.1	1839	16,684	
1801	5,486		1840	17,120	9.8
1802	5,679		1841	17,733	
1803	5,872		1842	18,345	
1804	5,065		1843	18,957	
1805	6,258		1844	19,569	
1806	6,451		1845	20,182	
1807	6,644		1846	20,794	
1808	6,838		1847	21,406	
1809	7,031		1848	22,018	
1810	7,224	4.3	1849	22,631	
1811	7,460		1850	23,261	7.9
1812	7,700		1851	24,086	
1813	7,939		1852	24,911	
1814	8,179		1853	25,736	
1815	8,419		1854	26,561	
1816	8,659		1855	27,386	
1817	8,899		1856	28,212	
1818	9,139		1857	29,037	
1819	9,379		1858	29,862	
1820	9,618	5.6	1859	30,687	
1821	9,939		1860	31,513	10.6
1822	10,268		1861	32,351	
1823	10,596		1862	33,188	
1824	10,924		1863	34,026	
1825	11,252		1864	34,863	
1826	11,580		1865	35,701	
1827	11,909		1866	36,538	
1828	12,237		1867	37,376	

Figures are from *Historical Statistics of the United States, Colonial Times to 1957* (1961), pp. 7, 8; *Statistical Abstract of the United States: 1974*, p. 5, Census Bureau for 1974 and 1975; and *Statistical Abstract of the United States: 1988*, p. 7.

(continued)

Population of the United States *(continued)*
(1790–1999)

Year	Total population (in thousands)	Number per square mile of land area (continental United States)	Year	Total population (in thousands)[1]	Number per square mile of land area (continental United States)
1868	38,213		1907	87,000	
1869	39,051		1908	88,709	
1870	39,905	13.4	1909	90,492	
1871	40,938		1910	92,407	31.0
1872	41,972		1911	93,868	
1873	43,006		1912	95,331	
1874	44,040		1913	97,227	
1875	45,073		1914	99,118	
1876	46,107		1915	100,549	
1877	47,141		1916	101,966	
1878	48,174		1917	103,414	
1879	49,208		1918	104,550	
1880	50,262	16.9	1919	105,063	
1881	51,542		1920	106,466	35.6
1882	52,821		1921	108,541	
1883	54,100		1922	110,055	
1884	55,379		1923	111,950	
1885	56,658		1924	114,113	
1886	57,938		1925	115,832	
1887	59,217		1926	117,399	
1888	60,496		1927	119,038	
1889	61,775		1928	120,501	
1890	63,056	21.2	1929	121,700	
1891	64,361		1930	122,775	41.2
1892	65,666		1931	124,040	
1893	66,970		1932	124,840	
1894	68,275		1933	125,579	
1895	69,580		1934	126,374	
1896	70,885		1935	127,250	
1897	72,189		1936	128,053	
1898	73,494		1937	128,825	
1899	74,799		1938	129,825	
1900	76,094	25.6	1939	130,880	
1901	77,585		1940	131,669	44.2
1902	79,160		1941	133,894	
1903	80,632		1942	135,361	
1904	82,165		1943	137,250	
1905	83,820		1944	138,916	
1906	85,437		1945	140,468	

[1]Figures after 1940 represent total population including armed forces abroad, except in official census years.

(continued)

Population of the United States *(continued)*
(1790–1999)

Year	Total population (in thousands)	Number per square mile of land area (continental United States)	Year	Total population (in thousands)[1]	Number per square mile of land area (continental United States)
1946	141,936		1973	211,909	
1947	144,698		1974	213,854	
1948	147,208		1975	215,973	
1949	149,767		1976	218,035	
1950	150,697	50.7	1977	220,239	
1951	154,878		1978	222,585	
1952	157,553		1979	225,055	
1953	160,184		1980	227,225	64.0
1954	163,026		1981	229,466	
1955	165,931		1982	232,520	
1956	168,903		1983	234,799	
1957	171,984		1984	237,001	
1958	174,882		1985	239,283	
1959	177,830[2]		1986	241,596	
1960	180,671	60.1	1987	234,773	
1961	186,538		1988	245,051	
1962	189,242		1989	247,350	
1963	189,197		1990	250,122	
1964	191,889		1991	254,521	
1965	194,303		1992	245,908	
1966	196,560		1993	257,908	
1967	198,712		1994	261,875	
1968	200,706		1995	263,434	
1969	202,677		1996	266,096	
1970	205,052	57.52	1997	267,744	
1971	207,661		1998	270,299	
1972	209,896		1999	274,114	

[1]Figures after 1940 represent total population including armed forces abroad, except in official census years.

[2]Figures after 1959 include Alaska and Hawaii.

Presidential Elections
(1789–1832)

Year	Number of states	Candidates[1]	Parties	Popular vote	Electoral vote	Percentage of popular vote[2]
1789	**11**	**George Washington***	**No party designations**		**69**	
		John Adams			34	
		Minor Candidates			35	
1792	**15**	**George Washington**	**No party designations**		**132**	
		John Adams			77	
		George Clinton			50	
		Minor Candidates			5	
1796	**16**	**John Adams**	**Federalist**		**71**	
		Thomas Jefferson	Democratic-Republican		68	
		Thomas Pinckney	Federalist		59	
		Aaron Burr	Democratic-Republican		30	
		Minor Candidates			48	
1800	**16**	**Thomas Jefferson**	**Democratic-Republican**		**73**	
		Aaron Burr	Democratic-Republican		73	
		John Adams	Federalist		65	
		Charles C. Pinckney	Federalist		64	
		John Jay	Federalist		1	
1804	**17**	**Thomas Jefferson**	**Democratic-Republican**		**162**	
		Charles C. Pinckney	Federalist		14	
1808	**17**	**James Madison**	**Democratic-Republican**		**122**	
		Charles C. Pinckney	Federalist		47	
		George Clinton	Democratic-Republican		6	
1812	**18**	**James Madison**	**Democratic-Republican**		**128**	
		DeWitt Clinton	Federalist		89	
1816	**19**	**James Monroe**	**Democratic-Republican**		**183**	
		Rufus King	Federalist		34	
1820	**24**	**James Monroe**	**Democratic-Republican**		**231**	
		John Quincy Adams	Independent Republican		1	
1824	**24**	**John Quincy Adams**	**Democratic-Republican**	108,740	84	30.5
		Andrew Jackson	Democratic-Republican	153,544	99	43.1
		William H. Crawford	Democratic-Republican	46,618	41	13.1
		Henry Clay	Democratic-Republican	47,136	37	13.2
1828	**24**	**Andrew Jackson**	**Democratic**	**647,286**	**178**	**56.0**
		John Quincy Adams	National Republican	508,064	83	44.0
1832	**24**	**Andrew Jackson**	**Democratic**	**687,502**	**219**	**55.0**
		Henry Clay	National Republican	530,189	49	42.4
		William Wirt	Anti-Masonic	}	7	
		John Floyd	National Republican	} 33,108	11	2.6

[1]Before the passage of the Twelfth Amendment in 1804, the Electoral College voted for two presidential candidates; the runner-up became vice president. Figures are from *Historical Statistics of the United States, Colonial Times to 1957* (1961), pp. 682–83; and the U.S. Department of Justice.

[2]Candidates receiving less than 1 percent of the popular vote have been omitted. For that reason the percentage of popular vote given for any election year may not total 100 percent.

*Note: Boldface indicates the winner of each election.

Presidential Elections
(1836–1888)

Year	Number of states	Candidates	Parties	Popular vote	Electoral vote	Percentage of popular vote[1]
1836	26	**Martin Van Buren**	**Democratic**	**765,483**	**170**	**50.9**
		William H. Harrison	Whig		73	
		Hugh L. White	Whig		26	
		Daniel Webster	Whig	739,795	14	
		W. P. Mangum	Independent		11	
1840	26	**William H. Harrison**	**Whig**	**1,274,624**	**234**	**53.1**
		Martin Van Buren	Democratic	1,127,781	60	46.9
1844	26	**James K. Polk**	**Democratic**	**1,338,464**	**170**	**49.6**
		Henry Clay	Whig	1,300,097	105	48.1
		James G. Birney	Liberty	62,300		2.3
1848	30	**Zachary Taylor**	**Whig**	**1,360,967**	**163**	**47.4**
		Lewis Cass	Democratic	1,222,342	127	42.5
		Martin Van Buren	Free Soil	291,263		10.1
1852	31	**Franklin Pierce**	**Democratic**	**1,601,117**	**254**	**50.9**
		Winfield Scott	Whig	1,385,453	42	44.1
		John P. Hale	Free Soil	155,825		5.0
1856	31	**James Buchanan**	**Democratic**	**1,832,955**	**174**	**45.3**
		John C. Frémont	Republican	1,339,932	114	33.1
		Millard Fillmore	American	871,731	8	21.6
1860	33	**Abraham Lincoln**	**Republican**	**1,865,593**	**180**	**39.8**
		Stephen A. Douglas	Democratic	1,382,713	12	29.5
		John C. Breckinridge	Democratic	848,356	72	18.1
		John Bell	Constitutional Union	592,906	39	12.6
1864	36	**Abraham Lincoln**	**Republican**	**2,206,938**	**212**	**55.0**
		George B. McClellan	Democratic	1,803,787	21	45.0
1868	37	**Ulysses S. Grant**	**Republican**	**3,013,421**	**214**	**52.7**
		Horatio Seymour	Democratic	2,706,829	80	47.3
1872	37	**Ulysses S. Grant**	**Republican**	**3,596,745**	**286**	**55.6**
		Horace Greeley	Democratic	2,843,446	2	43.9
1876	38	**Rutherford B. Hayes**	**Republican**	**4,036,572**	**185**	**48.0**
		Samuel J. Tilden	Democratic	4,284,020	184	51.0
1880	38	**James A. Garfield**	**Republican**	**4,453,295**	**214**	**48.5**
		Winfield S. Hancock	Democratic	4,414,082	155	48.1
		James B. Weaver	Greenback-Labor	308,578		3.4
1884	38	**Grover Cleveland**	**Democratic**	**4,879,507**	**219**	**48.5**
		James G. Blaine	Republican	4,850,293	182	48.2
		Benjamin F. Butler	Greenback-Labor	175,370		1.8
		John P. St. John	Prohibition	150,369		1.5
1888	38	**Benjamin Harrison**	**Republican**	**5,477,129**	**233**	**47.9**
		Grover Cleveland	Democratic	5,537,857	168	48.6
		Clinton B. Fisk	Prohibition	249,506		2.2
		Anson J. Streeter	Union Labor	146,935		1.3

[1]Candidates receiving less than 1 percent of the popular vote have been omitted. For that reason the percentage of popular vote given for any election year may not total 100 percent.

[2]Greeley died shortly after the election; the electors supporting him then divided their votes among minor candidates.

Presidential Elections
(1892–1932)

Year	Number of states	Candidates	Parties	Popular vote	Electoral vote	Percentage of popular vote[1]
1892	**44**	**Grover Cleveland**	**Democratic**	**5,555,426**	**277**	**46.1**
		Benjamin Harrison	Republican	5,182,690	145	43.0
		James B. Weaver	People's	1,029,846	22	8.5
		John Bidwell	Prohibition	264,133		2.2
1896	**45**	**William McKinley**	**Republican**	**7,102,246**	**271**	**51.1**
		William J. Bryan	Democratic	6,492,559	176	47.7
1900	**45**	**William McKinley**	**Republican**	**7,218,491**	**292**	**51.7**
		William J. Bryan	Democratic; Populist	6,356,734	155	45.5
		John C. Wooley	Prohibition	208,914		1.5
1904	**45**	**Theodore Roosevelt**	**Republican**	**7,628,461**	**336**	**57.4**
		Alton B. Parker	Democratic	5,084,223	140	37.6
		Eugene V. Debs	Socialist	402,283		3.0
		Silas C. Swallow	Prohibition	258,536		1.9
1908	**46**	**William H. Taft**	**Republican**	**7,675,320**	**321**	**51.6**
		William J. Bryan	Democratic	6,412,294	162	43.1
		Eugene V. Debs	Socialist	420,793		2.8
		Eugene W. Chafin	Prohibition	253,840		1.7
1912	**48**	**Woodrow Wilson**	**Democratic**	**6,296,547**	**435**	**41.9**
		Theodore Roosevelt	Progressive	4,118,571	88	27.4
		William H. Taft	Republican	3,486,720	8	23.2
		Eugene V. Debs	Socialist	900,672		6.0
		Eugene W. Chafin	Prohibition	206,275		1.4
1916	**48**	**Woodrow Wilson**	**Democratic**	**9,127,695**	**277**	**49.4**
		Charles E. Hughes	Republican	8,533,507	254	46.2
		A. L. Benson	Socialist	585,113		3.2
		J. Frank Hanly	Prohibition	220,506		1.2
1920	**48**	**Warren G. Harding**	**Republican**	**16,143,407**	**404**	**60.4**
		James N. Cox	Democratic	9,130,328	127	34.2
		Eugene V. Debs	Socialist	919,799		3.4
		P. P. Christensen	Farmer-Labor	265,411		1.0
1924	**48**	**Calvin Coolidge**	**Republican**	**15,718,211**	**382**	**54.0**
		John W. Davis	Democratic	8,385,283	136	28.8
		Robert M. La Follette	Progressive	4,831,289	13	16.6
1928	**48**	**Herbert C. Hoover**	**Republican**	**21,391,993**	**444**	**58.2**
		Alfred E. Smith	Democratic	15,016,169	87	40.9
1932	**48**	**Franklin D. Roosevelt**	**Democratic**	**22,809,638**	**472**	**57.4**
		Herbert C. Hoover	Republican	15,758,901	59	39.7
		Norman Thomas	Socialist	881,951		2.2

[1]Candidates receiving less than 1 percent of the popular vote have been omitted. For that reason the percentage of popular vote given for any election year may not total 100 percent.

Presidential Elections
(1936–2000)

Year	Number of states	Candidates	Parties	Popular vote	Electoral vote	Percentage of popular vote[1]
1936	48	**Franklin D. Roosevelt**	**Democratic**	**27,752,869**	**523**	**60.8**
		Alfred M. Landon	Republican	16,674,665	8	36.5
		William Lemke	Union	882,479		1.9
1940	48	**Franklin D. Roosevelt**	**Democratic**	**27,307,819**	**449**	**54.8**
		Wendell L. Willkie	Republican	22,321,018	82	44.8
1944	48	**Franklin D. Roosevelt**	**Democratic**	**25,606,585**	**432**	**53.5**
		Thomas E. Dewey	Republican	22,014,745	99	46.0
1948	48	**Harry S Truman**	**Democratic**	**24,105,812**	**303**	**49.5**
		Thomas E. Dewey	Republican	21,970,065	189	45.1
		J. Strom Thurmond	States' Rights	1,169,063	39	2.4
		Henry A. Wallace	Progressive	1,157,172		2.4
1952	48	**Dwight D. Eisenhower**	**Republican**	**33,936,234**	**442**	**55.1**
		Adlai E. Stevenson	Democratic	27,314,992	89	44.4
1956	48	**Dwight D. Eisenhower**	**Republican**	**35,590,472**	**457**	**57.6**
		Adlai E. Stevenson	Democratic	26,022,752	73	42.1
1960	50	**John F. Kennedy**	**Democratic**	**34,227,096**	**303**	**49.9**
		Richard M. Nixon	Republican	34,108,546	219	49.6
1964	50	**Lyndon B. Johnson**	**Democratic**	**43,126,506**	**486**	**61.1**
		Barry M. Goldwater	Republican	27,176,799	52	38.5
1968	50	**Richard M. Nixon**	**Republican**	**31,785,480**	**301**	**43.4**
		Hubert H. Humphrey	Democratic	31,275,165	191	42.7
		George C. Wallace	American Independent	9,906,473	46	13.5
1972	50	**Richard M. Nixon**	**Republican**	**47,169,911**	**520**	**60.7**
		George S. McGovern	Democratic	29,170,383	17	37.5
1976	50	**Jimmy Carter**	**Democratic**	**40,827,394**	**297**	**50.0**
		Gerald R. Ford	Republican	39,145,977	240	47.9
1980	50	**Ronald W. Reagan**	**Republican**	**43,899,248**	**489**	**50.8**
		Jimmy Carter	Democratic	35,481,435	49	41.0
		John B. Anderson	Independent	5,719,437		6.6
		Ed Clark	Libertarian	920,859		1.0
1984	50	**Ronald W. Reagan**	**Republican**	**54,281,858**	**525**	**59.2**
		Walter F. Mondale	Democratic	37,457,215	13	40.8
1988	50	**George H. Bush**	**Republican**	**47,917,341**	**426**	**54**
		Michael Dukakis	Democratic	41,013,030	112	46
1992	50	**William Clinton**	**Democratic**	**44,908,254**	**370**	**43.0**
		George H. Bush	Republican	39,102,343	168	37.4
		Ross Perot	Independent	19,741,065		18.9
1996	50	**William Clinton**	**Democratic**	**47,402,357**	**379**	**49**
		Robert J. Dole	Republican	39,198,755	159	41
		H. Ross Perot	Reform	8,085,402		8
2000	50	**George W. Bush**	**Republican**	**50,456,062**	**271**	**47.9**
		Albert Gore	Democratic	50,996,582	266	48.4
		Ralph Nader	Green	2,858,843		2.7

[1]Candidates receiving less than 1 percent of the popular vote have been omitted. For that reason the percentage of popular vote given for any election year may not total 100 percent.

Presidents, Vice Presidents, and Major Cabinet Officers

President	Vice President	State	Treasury	War	Justice (Attorney General)
George Washington 1789–1797	John Adams 1789–1797	Thomas Jefferson 1789–1794	Alexander Hamilton 1789–1795	Henry Knox 1789–1795	Edmund Randolph 1789–1794
		Edmund Randolph 1794–1795 Timothy Pickering 1795–1797	Oliver Wolcott 1795–1797	Timothy Pickering 1795–1796 James McHenry 1796–1797	William Bradford 1794–1795 Charles Lee 1795–1797
John Adams 1797–1801	Thomas Jefferson 1797–1801	Timothy Pickering 1797–1800 John Marshall 1800–1801	Oliver Wolcott 1797–1801 Samuel Dexter 1801	James McHenry 1797–1800 Samuel Dexter 1800–1801	Charles Lee 1797–1801
Thomas Jefferson 1801–1809	Aaron Burr 1801–1805 George Clinton 1805–1809	James Madison 1801–1809	Samuel Dexter 1801 Albert Gallatin 1801–1809	Henry Dearborn 1801–1809	Levi Lincoln 1801–1805 John Breckinridge 1805–1807 Caesar Rodney 1807–1809
James Madison 1809–1817	George Clinton 1809–1813 Elbridge Gerry 1813–1817	Robert Smith 1809–1811 James Monroe 1811–1817	Albert Gallatin 1809–1814 George Campbell 1814 Alexander Dallas 1814–1816 William Crawford 1816–1817	William Eustis 1809–1813 John Armstrong 1813–1814 James Monroe 1814–1815 William Crawford 1815–1817	Caesar Rodney 1809–1811 William Pinkney 1811–1814 Richard Rush 1814–1817
James Monroe 1817–1825	Daniel D. Tompkins 1817–1825	John Quincy Adams 1817–1825	William Crawford 1817–1825	George Graham 1817 John C. Calhoun 1817–1825	Richard Rush 1817 William Wirt 1817–1825
John Quincy Adams	John C. Calhoun 1825–1829	Henry Clay 1825–1829	Richard Rush 1825–1829	James Barbour 1825–1829 Peter B. Porter 1828–1829	William Wirt 1825–1829

(continued)

Presidents, Vice Presidents, and Major Cabinet Officers *(continued)*

President	Vice President	State	Treasury	War	Justice (Attorney General)
Andrew Jackson 1829–1837	John C. Calhoun 1829–1833 Martin Van Buren 1833–1837	Martin Van Buren 1829–1831 Edward Livingston 1831–1833 Louis McLane 1833–1834 John Forsyth 1834–1837	Samuel Ingham 1829–1831 Louis McLane 1831–1833 William Duane 1833 Roger B. Taney 1833–1834 Levi Woodbury 1834–1837	John H. Eaton 1829–1831 Lewis Cass 1831–1837 Benjamin Butler 1837	John M. Berrien 1829–1831 Roger B. Taney 1831–1833 Benjamin Butler 1833–1837
Martin Van Buren 1837–1841	Richard M. Johnson 1837–1841	John Forsyth 1837–1841	Levi Woodbury 1837–1841	Joel R. Poinsett 1837–1841	Benjamin Butler 1837–1838 Felix Grundy 1838–1840 Henry D. Gilpin 1840–1841
William H. Harrison 1841	John Tyler 1841	Daniel Webster 1841	Thomas Ewing 1841	John Bell 1841	John J. Crittenden 1841
John Tyler 1841–1845		Daniel Webster 1841–1843 Hugh S. Legaré 1843 Abel P. Upshur 1843–1844 John C. Calhoun 1844–1845	Thomas Ewing 1841 Walter Forward 1841–1843 John C. Spencer 1843–1844 George M. Bibb 1844–1845	John Bell 1841 John C. Spencer 1841–1843 James M. Porter 1843–1844 William Wilkins 1844–1845	John J. Crittenden 1841 Hugh S. Legaré 1841–1843 John Nelson 1843–1845
James K. Polk 1845–1849	George M. Dallas 1845–1849	James Buchanan 1845–1849	Robert J. Walker 1845–1849	William L. Marcy 1845–1849	John Y. Mason 1845–1846 Nathan Clifford 1846–1848 Isaac Toucey 1848–1849
Zachary Taylor 1849–1850	Millard Fillmore 1849–1850	John M. Clayton 1849–1850	William M. Meredith 1849–1850	George W. Crawford 1849–1850	Reverdy Johnson 1849–1850
Millard Fillmore 1850–1853		Daniel Webster 1850–1852 Edward Everett 1852–1853	Thomas Corwin 1850–1853	Charles M. Conrad 1850–1853	John J. Crittenden 1850–1853
Franklin Pierce 1853–1857	William R. King 1853–1857	William L. Marcy 1853–1857	James Guthrie 1853–1857	Jefferson Davis 1853–1857	Caleb Cushing 1853–1857

(continued)

Presidents, Vice Presidents, and Major Cabinet Officers *(continued)*

President	Vice President	State	Treasury	War	Justice (Attorney General)
James Buchanan 1857–1861	John C. Breckinridge 1857–1861	Lewis Cass 1857–1860 Jeremiah S. Black 1860–1861	Howell Cobb 1857–1860 Philip F. Thomas 1860–1861 John A. Dix 1861	John B. Floyd 1857–1861 Joseph Holt 1861	Jeremiah S. Black 1857–1860 Edwin M. Stanton 1860–1861
Abraham Lincoln 1861–1865	Hannibal Hamlin 1861–1865 Andrew Johnson 1865	William H. Seward 1861–1865	Salmon P. Chase 1861–1864 William P. Fessenden 1864–1865 Hugh McCulloch 1865	Simon Cameron 1861–1862 Edwin M. Stanton 1862–1865	Edward Bates 1861–1864 James Speed 1864–1865
Andrew Johnson 1865–1869		William H. Seward 1865–1869	Hugh McCulloch 1865–1869	Edwin M. Stanton 1865–1867 Ulysses S. Grant 1867–1868 John M. Schofield 1868–1869	James Speed 1865–1866 1865 Henry Stanbery 1866–1868 O. H. Browning 1866–1869
Ulysses S. Grant 1869–1877	Schuyler Colfax 1869–1873 Henry Wilson 1873–1877	Elihu B. Washburne 1869 Hamilton Fish 1869–1877	George S. Boutwell 1869–1873 William A. Richardson 1873–1874 Benjamin H. Bristow 1874–1876 Lot M. Morrill 1876–1877	John A. Rawlins 1869 William T. Sherman 1869 William W. Belknap 1869–1876 Alphonso Taft 1876 James D. Cameron 1876–1877	Ebenezer R. Hoar 1869–1870 Amos T. Akerman 1870–1871 G. H. Williams 1871–1875 Edwards Pierrepont 1875–1876 Alphonso Taft 1876–1877
Rutherford B. Hayes 1877–1881	William A. Wheeler 1877–1881	William M. Evarts 1877–1881	John Sherman 1877–1881	George W. McCrary 1877–1879 Alexander Ramsey 1879–1881	Charles Devens 1877–1881
James A. Garfield 1881	Chester A. Arthur 1881	James G. Blaine 1881	William Windom 1881	Robert T. Lincoln 1881	Wayne MacVeagh 1881
Chester A. Arthur 1881–1885		F. T. Frelinghuysen 1881–1885	Charles J. Folger 1881–1884 Walter Q. Gresham 1884 Hugh McCulloch 1884–1885	Robert T. Lincoln 1881–1885	B. H. Brewster 1881–1885

(continued)

Presidents, Vice Presidents, and Major Cabinet Officers *(continued)*

President	Vice President	State	Treasury	War	Justice (Attorney General)
Grover Cleveland 1885–1889	T. A. Hendricks 1885	Thomas F. Bayard 1885–1889	Daniel Manning 1885–1887 Charles S. Fairchild 1887–1889	William C. Endicott 1885–1889	A. H. Garland 1885–1889
Benjamin Harrison 1889–1893	Levi P. Morton 1889–1893	James G. Blaine 1889–1892 John W. Foster 1892–1893	William Windom 1889–1891 Charles Foster 1892–1893	Redfield Procter 1889–1891 Stephen B. Elkins 1891–1893	W. H. H. Miller 1889–1893
Grover Cleveland 1893–1897	Adlai E. Stevenson 1893–1897	Walter Q. Gresham 1893–1895 Richard Olney 1895–1897	John G. Carlisle 1893–1897	Daniel S. Lamont 1893–1897	Richard Olney 1893–1897 Judson Harmon 1895–1897
William McKinley 1897–1901	Garret A. Hobart 1897–1899 Theodore Roosevelt 1901	John Sherman 1897–1898 William R. Day 1898 John Hay 1898–1901	Lyman J. Gage 1897–1901	Russell A. Alger 1897–1899 Elihu Root 1899–1901	Joseph McKenna 1897–1898 John W. Griggs 1898–1901 Philander C. Knox 1901
Theodore Roosevelt 1901–1909	Charles Fairbanks 1905–1909	John Hay 1901–1905 Elihu Root 1905–1909 Robert Bacon 1909	Lyman J. Gage 1901–1902 Leslie M. Shaw 1902–1907 George B. Cortelyou 1907–1909	Elihu Root 1901–1904 William H. Taft 1904–1908 Luke E. Wright 1908–1909	Philander C. Knox 1901–1904 William H. Moody Charles J. Bonaparte 1906–1909
William H. Taft 1909–1913	James S. Sherman 1909–1913	Philander C. Knox 1909–1913	Franklin MacVeagh 1909–1913	Jacob M. Dickinson 1909–1911 Henry L. Stimson 1911–1913	G. W. Wickersham 1909–1913
Woodrow Wilson 1913–1921	Thomas R. Marshall 1913–1921	William J. Bryan 1913–1915 Robert Lansing 1915–1920 Bainbridge Colby 1920–1921	William G. McAdoo 1913–1918 Carter Glass 1918–1920 David F. Houston 1920–1921	Lindley M. Garrison 1913–1916 Newton D. Baker 1916–1921	J. C. McReynolds 1913–1914 T. W. Gregory A. Mitchell Palmer 1919–1921

(continued)

Presidents, Vice Presidents, and Major Cabinet Officers *(continued)*

President	Vice President	State	Treasury	War	Justice (Attorney General)
Warren G. Harding 1921–1923	Calvin Coolidge 1921–1923	Charles E. Hughes 1921–1923	Andrew W. Mellon 1921–1923	John W. Weeks 1921–1923	H. M. Daugherty 1921–1923
Calvin Coolidge 1923–1929	Charles G. Dawes 1925–1929	Charles E. Hughes 1923–1925 Frank B. Kellogg 1925–1929	Andrew W. Mellon 1923–1929	John W. Weeks 1923–1925 Dwight F. Davis 1925–1929	H. M. Daugherty 1923–1924 Harlan F. Stone 1924–1925 John G. Sargent 1925–1929
Herbert C. Hoover 1929–1933	Charles Curtis 1929–1933	Henry L. Stimson 1929–1933	Andrew W. Mellon 1929–1932 Ogden L. Mills 1932–1933	James W. Good 1929 Patrick J. Hurley 1929–1933	J. D. Mitchell 1929–1933
Franklin Delano Roosevelt 1933–1945	John Nance Garner 1933–1941 Henry A. Wallace 1941–1945 Harry S Truman 1945	Cordell Hull 1933–1944 E. R. Stettinius, Jr. 1944–1945	William H. Woodin 1933–1934 Henry Morgenthau, Jr. 1934–1945	George H. Dern 1933–1936 Harry H. Woodring 1936–1940 Henry L. Stimson 1940–1945	H. S. Cummings 1933–1939 Frank Murphy 1939–1940 Robert Jackson 1940–1941 Francis Biddel 1944–1945
Harry S Truman 1945–1953	Alben W. Barkley 1949–1953	James F. Byrnes 1945–1947 George C. Marshall 1947–1949 Dean G. Acheson 1949–1953	Fred M. Vinson 1945–1946 John W. Snyder 1946–1953	Robert P. Patterson 1945–1947 Kenneth C. Royall 1947 *Secretary of Defense* James V. Forrestal 1947–1949 Louis A. Johnson 1949–1950 George C. Marshall 1950–1951 Robert A. Lovett 1951–1953	Tom C. Clark 1945–1949 J. H. McGrath 1949–1952 James P. McGranery 1952–1953
Dwight D. Eisenhower 1953–1961	Richard M. Nixon 1953–1961	John Foster Dulles 1953–1959 Christian A. Herter 1957–1961	George M. Humphrey 1953–1957 Robert B. Anderson 1957–1961	Charles E. Wilson 1953–1957 Neil H. McElroy 1957–1961 Thomas S. Gates 1959–1961	H. Brownell, Jr. 1953–1957 William P. Rogers 1957–1961

(continued)

Presidents, Vice Presidents, and Major Cabinet Officers *(continued)*

President	Vice President	State	Treasury	Defense	Justice (Attorney General)
John F. Kennedy 1961–1963	Lyndon B. Johnson 1961–1963	Dean Rusk 1961–1963	C. Douglas Dillon 1961–1963	Robert S. McNamara 1961–1963	Robert F. Kennedy 1961–1963
Lyndon B. Johnson 1963–1969	Hubert H. Humphrey 1965–1969	Dean Rusk 1963–1969	C. Douglas Dillon 1963–1965 Henry H. Fowler 1965–1968 Joseph W. Barr 1968–1969	Robert S. McNamara 1963–1968 Clark M. Clifford 1968–1969	Robert F. Kennedy 1963–1965 N. deB. Katzenbach 1965–1967 Ramsey Clark 1967–1969
Richard M. Nixon 1969–1974	Spiro T. Agnew 1969–1973 Gerald R. Ford 1973–1974	William P. Rogers 1969–1973 Henry A. Kissinger 1973–1974	David M. Kennedy 1969–1970 John B. Connally 1970–1972 George P. Schultz 1972–1974 William E. Simon 1974	Melvin R. Laird 1969–1973 Elliot L. Richardson 1973 James R. Schlesinger 1973–1974	John M. Mitchell 1969–1972 Richard G. Kleindienst 1972–1973 Elliot L. Richardson 1973 William B. Saxbe 1974
Gerald R. Ford 1974–1977	Nelson A. Rockefeller 1974–1977	Henry A. Kissinger 1974–1977	William E. Simon 1974–1977	James R. Schlesinger 1974–1975 Donald H. Rumsfeld 1975–1977	William B. Saxbe 1974–1975 Edward H. Levi 1975–1977

(continued)

Presidents, Vice Presidents, and
Major Cabinet Officers *(continued)*

President	Vice President	State	Treasury	Defense	Justice (Attorney General)
Jimmy Carter 1977–1981	Walter F. Mondale 1977–1981	Cyrus R. Vance 1977–1980 Edmund S. Muskie 1980–1981	W. Michael Blumenthal 1977–1979 G. William Miller 1979–1981	Harold Brown 1977–1981	Griffin Bell 1977–1979 Benjamin R. Civiletti 1979–1981
Ronald W. Reagan 1981–1989	George H. Bush 1981–1989	Alexander M. Haig, Jr. 1981–1982 George P. Shultz 1982–1989	Donald T. Regan 1981–1985 James A. Baker 1985–1988 Nicholas F. Brady 1988–1989	Caspar W. Weinberger 1981–1987 Frank C. Carlucci 1987–1989	William French Smith 1981–1985 Edwin Meese 1985–1988 Richard Thornburgh 1988–1989
George H. Bush 1989–1992	J. Danforth Quayle 1989–1992	James A. Baker 1989–1992 Lawrence S. Eagleburger 1992	Nicholas F. Brady 1989–1992	Richard Cheney 1989–1992	Richard Thornburgh 1989–1990 William Barr 1990–1992
William Clinton 1993–2001	Albert Gore 1993–2001	Warren M. Christopher 1993–1996 Madeleine K. Albright 1997–2001	Lloyd Bentsen 1993–1994 Robert E. Rubin 1994–1999 Lawrence H. Summers 1999–2001	Les Aspin 1993–1994 William J. Perry 1994–1997 William S. Cohen 1997–2001	Janet Reno 1993–2001
George W. Bush 2001–	Richard Cheney 2001–	Colin L. Powell 2001–	Paul H. O'Neill 2001–2003 John W. Snow 2003–	Donald H. Rumsfeld 2001–	John Ashcroft 2001–

Cabinet Level Departments

(The heads of cabinet level departments are known as the Secretary of the Department except for the head of the Justice Department, the Attorney General, and until 1971, the head of the Post Office, the Postmaster General.)

Department	Year Established	Modifications
State	1789	
Treasury	1789	
War	1789	In 1947, the War Department became a sub-cabinet level division of the Department of Defense.
Justice	1789	
Post Office	1789	In 1971, the Post Office became the United States Postal Service, an independent agency; the head of the USPS did not sit in the president's cabinet.
Navy	1798	In 1947, the Navy Department became a sub-cabinet level division of the Department of Defense.
Interior	1849	
Agriculture	1889	
Commerce and Labor	1903	In 1913, the Department was divided into two cabinet-level departments—Commerce and Labor.
Commerce	1913	
Labor	1913	
Defense	1947	
Health, Education, and Welfare	1953	In 1980, the Department was divided into two cabinet-level departments—Health and Human Services, and Education.
Housing and Urban Development	1966	
Transportation	1966	
Energy	1977	
Health and Human Services	1980	
Education	1980	
Veterans' Affairs	1989	
Homeland Security	2003	

Justices of the U.S. Supreme Court

Chief Justices appear in bold type

	Term of Service	Years of Service	Appointed by
John Jay	1789–1795	5	Washington
John Rutledge	1789–1791	1	Washington
William Cushing	1789–1810	20	Washington
James Wilson	1789–1798	8	Washington
John Blair	1789–1796	6	Washington
Robert H. Harrison	1789–1790	—	Washington
James Iredell	1790–1799	9	Washington
Thomas Johnson	1791–1793	1	Washington
William Paterson	1793–1806	13	Washington
John Rutledge[1]	1795	—	Washington
Samuel Chase	1796–1811	15	Washington
Oliver Ellsworth	1796–1800	4	Washington
Bushrod Washington	1798–1829	31	J. Adams
Alfred Moore	1799–1804	4	J. Adams
John Marshall	1801–1835	34	J. Adams
William Johnson	1804–1834	30	Jefferson
H. Brockholst Livingston	1806–1823	16	Jefferson
Thomas Todd	1807–1826	18	Jefferson
Joseph Story	1811–1845	33	Madison
Gabriel Duval	1811–1835	24	Madison
Smith Thompson	1823–1843	20	Monroe
Robert Trimble	1826–1828	2	J. Q. Adams
John McLean	1829–1861	32	Jackson
Henry Baldwin	1830–1844	14	Jackson
James M. Wayne	1835–1867	32	Jackson
Roger B. Taney	1836–1864	28	Jackson
Philip P. Barbour	1836–1841	4	Jackson
John Catron	1837–1865	28	Van Buren
John McKinley	1837–1852	15	Van Buren
Peter V. Daniel	1841–1860	19	Van Buren
Samuel Nelson	1845–1872	27	Tyler
Levi Woodbury	1845–1851	5	Polk
Robert C. Grier	1846–1870	23	Polk
Benjamin R. Curtis	1851–1857	6	Fillmore
John A. Campbell	1853–1861	8	Pierce
Nathan Clifford	1858–1881	23	Buchanan
Noah H. Swayne	1862–1881	18	Lincoln
Samuel F. Miller	1862–1890	28	Lincoln
David Davis	1862–1877	14	Lincoln
Stephen J. Field	1863–1897	34	Lincoln
Salmon P. Chase	1864–1873	8	Grant
William Strong	1870–1880	10	Grant
Joseph P. Bradley	1870–1892	22	Grant
Ward Hunt	1873–1882	9	Grant

[1]Acting Chief Justice; Senate refused to confirm appointment.

(continued)

Justices of the U.S. Supreme Court *(continued)*

Chief Justices appear in bold type

	Term of Service	Years of Service	Appointed by
Morrison R. Waite	1874–1888	14	Grant
John M. Harlan	1877–1911	34	Hayes
William B. Woods	1880–1887	7	Hayes
Stanley Matthews	1881–1889	7	Garfield
Horace Gray	1882–1902	20	Arthur
Samuel Blatchford	1882–1893	11	Arthur
Lucius Q. C. Lamar	1888–1893	5	Cleveland
Melville W. Fuller	1888–1910	21	Cleveland
David J. Brewer	1890–1910	20	B. Harrison
Henry B. Brown	1890–1906	16	B. Harrison
George Shiras, Jr.	1892–1903	10	B. Harrison
Howell E. Jackson	1893–1895	2	B. Harrison
Edward D. White	1894–1910	16	Cleveland
Rufus W. Peckham	1895–1909	14	Cleveland
Joseph McKenna	1898–1925	26	McKinley
Oliver W. Holmes, Jr.	1902–1932	30	T. Roosevelt
William R. Day	1903–1922	19	T. Roosevelt
William H. Moody	1906–1910	3	T. Roosevelt
Horace H. Lurton	1910–1914	4	Taft
Charles E. Hughes	1910–1916	5	Taft
Willis Van Devanter	1911–1937	26	Taft
Joseph R. Lamar	1911–1916	5	Taft
Edward D. White	1910–1921	11	Taft
Mahlon Pitney	1912–1922	10	Taft
James C. McReynolds	1914–1941	26	Wilson
Louis D. Brandeis	1916–1939	22	Wilson
John H. Clarke	1916–1922	6	Wilson
William H. Taft	1921–1930	8	Harding
George Sutherland	1922–1938	15	Harding
Pierce Butler	1922–1939	16	Harding
Edward T. Sanford	1923–1930	7	Harding
Harlan F. Stone	1925–1941	16	Coolidge
Charles E. Hughes	1930–1941	11	Hoover
Owen J. Roberts	1930–1945	15	Hoover
Benjamin N. Cardozo	1932–1938	6	Hoover
Hugo L. Black	1937–1971	34	F. Roosevelt
Stanley F. Reed	1938–1957	19	F. Roosevelt
Felix Frankfurter	1939–1962	23	F. Roosevelt
William O. Douglas	1939–1975	36	F. Roosevelt
Frank Murphy	1940–1949	9	F. Roosevelt
Harlan F. Stone	1941–1946	5	F. Roosevelt
James F. Byrnes	1941–1942	1	F. Roosevelt
Robert H. Jackson	1941–1954	13	F. Roosevelt
Wiley B. Rutledge	1943–1949	6	F. Roosevelt

(continued)

Justices of the U.S. Supreme Court *(continued)*

Chief Justices appear in bold type

	Term of Service	Years of Service	Appointed by
Harold H. Burton	1945–1958	13	Truman
Fred M. Vinson	1946–1953	7	Truman
Tom C. Clark	1949–1967	18	Truman
Sherman Minton	1949–1956	7	Truman
Earl Warren	1953–1969	16	Eisenhower
John Marshall Harlan	1955–1971	16	Eisenhower
William J. Brennan, Jr.	1956–1990	34	Eisenhower
Charles E. Whittaker	1957–1962	5	Eisenhower
Potter Stewart	1958–1981	23	Eisenhower
Byron R. White	1962–1993	31	Kennedy
Arthur J. Goldberg	1962–1965	3	Kennedy
Abe Fortas	1965–1969	4	Johnson
Thurgood Marshall	1967–1994	24	Johnson
Warren E. Burger	1969–1986	18	Nixon
Harry A. Blackmun	1970–1994	24	Nixon
Lewis F. Powell, Jr.	1971–1987	15	Nixon
William H. Rehnquist[2]	1971–	—	Nixon
John P. Stevens III	1975–	—	Ford
Sandra Day O'Connor	1981–	—	Reagan
Antonin Scalia	1986–	—	Reagan
Anthony M. Kennedy	1988–	—	Reagan
David Souter	1990–	—	Bush
Clarence Thomas	1991–	—	Bush
Ruth Bader Ginsburg	1993–	—	Clinton
Stephen G. Breyer	1994–	—	Clinton

[2]Chief Justice from 1986 (Reagan administration).

Political Party Affiliations in Congress and the Presidency, 1789–2003*

Congress	Year	House* Majority Party	House* Principal Minority Party	House* Other (except Vacancies)	Senate* Majority Party	Senate* Principal Minority Party	Senate* Other (except Vacancies)	President and Party
1st	1789–1791	Ad-38	Op-26	—	Ad-17	Op-9	—	F (Washington)
2nd	1791–1793	F-37	DR-33	—	F-16	DR-13	—	F (Washington)
3rd	1793–1795	DR-57	F-48	—	F-17	DR-13	—	F (Washington)
4th	1795–1797	F-54	DR-52	—	F-19	DR-13	—	F (Washington)
5th	1797–1799	F-58	DR-48	—	F-20	DR-12	—	F (John Adams)
6th	1799–1801	F-64	DR-42	—	F-19	DR-13	—	F (John Adams)
7th	1801–1803	DR-69	F-36	—	DR-18	F-13	—	DR (Jefferson)
8th	1803–1805	DR-102	F-39	—	DR-25	F-9	—	DR (Jefferson)
9th	1805–1807	DR-116	F-25	—	DR-27	F-7	—	DR (Jefferson)
10th	1807–1809	DR-118	F-24	—	DR-28	F-6	—	DR (Jefferson)
11th	1809–1811	DR-94	F-48	—	DR-28	F-6	—	DR (Madison)
12th	1811–1813	DR-108	F-36	—	DR-30	F-6	—	DR (Madison)
13th	1813–1815	DR-112	F-68	—	DR-27	F-9	—	DR (Madison)
14th	1815–1817	DR-117	F-65	—	DR-25	F-11	—	DR (Madison)
15th	1817–1819	DR-141	F-42	—	DR-34	F-10	—	DR (Monroe)
16th	1819–1821	DR-156	F-27	—	DR-35	F-7	—	DR (Monroe)
17th	1821–1823	DR-158	F-25	—	DR-44	F-4	—	DR (Monroe)
18th	1823–1825	DR-187	F-26	—	DR-44	F-4	—	DR (Monroe)
19th	1825–1827	Ad-105	J-97	—	Ad-26	J-20	—	C (J. Q. Adams)
20th	1827–1829	J-119	Ad-94	—	J-28	Ad-20	—	C (J. Q. Adams)
21st	1829–1831	D-139	NR-74	—	D-26	NR-22	—	D (Jackson)
22nd	1831–1833	D-141	NR-58	14	D-25	NR-21	2	D (Jackson)
23rd	1833–1835	D-147	AM-53	60	D-20	NR-20	8	D (Jackson)
24th	1835–1837	D-145	W-98	—	D-27	W-25	—	D (Jackson)
25th	1837–1839	D-108	W-107	24	D-30	W-18	4	D (Van Buren)
26th	1839–1841	D-124	W-118	—	D-28	W-22	—	D (Van Buren)
27th	1841–1843	W-133	D-102	6	W-28	D-22	2	W (Harrison) W (Tyler)
28th	1843–1845	D-142	W-79	1	W-28	D-25	1	W (Tyler)
29th	1845–1847	D-143	W-77	6	D-31	W-25	—	D (Polk)
30th	1847–1849	W-115	D-108	4	D-36	W-21	1	D (Polk)
31st	1849–1851	D-112	W-109	9	D-35	W-25	2	W (Taylor) W (Fillmore)
32nd	1851–1853	D-140	W-88	5	D-35	W-24	3	W (Fillmore)
33rd	1853–1855	D-159	W-71	4	D-38	W-22	2	D (Pierce)
34th	1855–1857	R-108	D-83	43	D-40	R-15	5	D (Pierce)
35th	1857–1859	D-118	R-92	26	D-36	R-20	8	D (Buchanan)
36th	1859–1861	R-114	D-92	31	D-36	R-26	4	D (Buchanan)
37th	1861–1863	R-105	D-43	30	R-31	D-10	8	R (Lincoln)
38th	1863–1865	R-102	D-75	9	R-36	D-9	5	R (Lincoln)
39th	1865–1867	U-149	D-42	—	U-42	D-10	—	R (Lincoln) R (Johnson)
40th	1867–1869	R-143	D-49	—	R-42	D-11	—	R (Johnson)
41st	1869–1871	R-149	D-63	—	R-56	D-11	—	R (Grant)
42nd	1871–1873	R-134	D-104	5	R-52	D-17	5	R (Grant)
43rd	1873–1875	R-194	D-92	14	R-49	D-19	5	R (Grant)
44th	1875–1877	D-169	R-109	14	R-45	D-29	2	R (Grant)
45th	1877–1879	D-153	R-140	—	R-39	D-36	1	R (Hayes)
46th	1879–1881	D-149	R-130	14	D-42	R-33	1	R (Hayes)
47th	1881–1883	R-147	D-135	11	R-37	D-37	1	R (Garfield) R (Arthur)
48th	1883–1885	D-197	R-118	10	R-38	D-36	2	R (Arthur)

*Letter symbols for political parties. Ad—Administration; AM—Anti-Masonic; C—Coalition; D—Democratic; DR—Democratic-Republican; F—Federalist; J—Jacksonian; NR—National—Republican; Op—Opposition; R—Republican; U—Unionist; W—Whig.

Source: *Historical Statistics of the United States: Colonial Times to the Present,* Various eds. Washington, D.C.: GOP.

(continued)

Political Party Affiliations in Congress and the Presidency, 1789–2003 *(continued)*

Congress	Year	House Majority Party	House Principal Minority Party	House Other (except Vacancies)	Senate Majority Party	Senate Principal Minority Party	Senate Other (except Vacancies)	President and Party
49th	1885–1887	D-183	R-140	2	R-43	D-34	—	D (Cleveland)
50th	1887–1889	D-169	R-152	4	R-39	D-37	—	D (Cleveland)
51st	1889–1891	R-166	D-159	—	R-39	D-37	—	R (B. Harrison)
52nd	1891–1893	D-235	R-88	9	R-47	D-39	2	R (B. Harrison)
53rd	1893–1895	D-218	R-127	11	D-44	R-38	3	D (Cleveland)
54th	1895–1897	R-244	D-105	7	R-43	D-39	6	D (Cleveland)
55th	1897–1899	R-204	D-113	40	R-47	D-34	7	R (McKinley)
56th	1899–1901	R-185	D-163	9	R-53	D-26	8	R (McKinley)
57th	1901–1903	R-197	D-151	9	R-55	D-31	4	R (McKinley) R (T. Roosevelt)
58th	1903–1905	R-208	D-178	—	R-57	D-33	—	R (T. Roosevelt)
59th	1905–1907	R-250	D-136	—	R-57	D-33	—	R (T. Roosevelt)
60th	1907–1909	R-222	D-164	—	R-61	D-31	—	R (T. Roosevelt)
61st	1909–1911	R-219	D-172	—	R-61	D-32	—	R (Taft)
62nd	1911–1913	D-228	R-161	1	R-51	D-41	—	R (Taft)
63rd	1913–1915	D-291	R-127	17	D-51	R-44	1	D (Wilson)
64th	1915–1917	D-230	R-196	9	D-56	R-40	—	D (Wilson)
65th	1917–1919	D-216	R-210	6	D-53	R-42	—	D (Wilson)
66th	1919–1921	R-240	D-190	3	R-49	D-47	—	D (Wilson)
67th	1921–1923	R-301	D-131	1	R-59	D-37	—	R (Harding)
68th	1923–1925	R-225	D-205	5	R-51	D-43	2	R (Coolidge)
69th	1925–1927	R-247	D-183	4	R-56	D-39	1	R (Coolidge)
70th	1927–1929	R-237	D-195	3	R-49	D-46	1	R (Coolidge)
71st	1929–1931	R-267	D-167	1	R-56	D-39	1	R (Hoover)
72nd	1931–1933	D-220	R-214	1	R-48	D-47	1	R (Hoover)
73rd	1933–1935	D-310	R-117	5	D-60	R-35	1	D (F. Roosevelt)
74th	1935–1937	D-319	R-103	10	D-69	R-25	2	D (F. Roosevelt)
75th	1937–1939	D-331	R-89	13	D-76	R-16	4	D (F. Roosevelt)
76th	1939–1941	D-261	R-164	4	D-69	R-23	4	D (F. Roosevelt)
77th	1941–1943	D-268	R-162	5	D-66	R-28	2	D (F. Roosevelt)
78th	1943–1945	D-218	R-208	4	D-58	R-37	1	D (F. Roosevelt)
79th	1945–1947	D-242	R-190	2	D-56	R-38	1	D (Truman)
80th	1947–1949	R-245	D-188	1	R-51	D-45	—	D (Truman)
81st	1949–1951	D-263	R-171	1	D-54	R-42	—	D (Truman)
82nd	1951–1953	D-243	R-199	1	D-49	R-47	—	D (Truman)
83rd	1953–1955	R-221	D-211	1	R-48	D-47	1	R (Eisenhower)
84th	1955–1957	D-232	R-203	—	D-48	R-47	1	R (Eisenhower)
85th	1957–1959	D-233	R-200	—	D-49	R-47	—	R (Eisenhower)
86th	1959–1961	D-283	R-153	—	D-64	R-34	—	R (Eisenhower)
87th	1961–1963	D-263	R-174	—	D-65	R-35	—	D (Kennedy)
88th	1963–1965	D-258	R-177	—	D-67	R-33	—	D (Kennedy) D (Johnson)
89th	1965–1967	D-295	R-140	—	D-68	R-32	—	D (Johnson)
90th	1967–1969	D-247	R-187	1	D-64	R-36	—	D (Johnson)
91st	1969–1971	D-243	R-192	—	D-58	R-42	—	R (Nixon)
92nd	1971–1973	D-255	R-180	—	D-54	R-44	2	R (Nixon)
93rd	1973–1975	D-242	R-192	1	D-56	R-42	2	R (Nixon, Ford)
94th	1975–1977	D-291	R-144	—	D-61	R-37	2	R (Ford)
95th	1977–1979	D-292	R-143	—	D-61	R-38	1	D (Carter)
96th	1979–1981	D-277	R-158	—	D-58	R-41	1	D (Carter)
97th	1981–1983	D-242	R-192	—	R-54	D-45	1	R (Reagan)
98th	1983–1985	D-266	R-167	2	R-55	D-45	—	R (Reagan)
99th	1985–1987	D-252	R-183	—	R-53	D-47	—	R (Reagan)
100th	1987–1989	D-258	R-177	—	D-55	R-45	—	R (Reagan)
101st	1989–1991	D-262	R-173	—	D-57	R-43	—	R (Bush)
102nd	1991–1993	D-267	R-167	1	D-57	R-43	—	R (Bush)
103rd	1993–1995	D-256	R-178	1	D-56	R-44	—	D (Clinton)

(continued)

Political Party Affiliations in Congress and the Presidency, 1789–2003 *(continued)*

| Congress | Year | House | | | Senate | | | President and Party |
		Majority Party	Principal Minority Party	Other (except Vacancies)	Majority Party	Principal Minority Party	Other (except Vacancies)	
104th	1995–1997	R-230	D-204	1	R-52	D-48	—	D (Clinton)
105th	1997–1999	R-228	D-206	1	R-55	D-45	—	D (Clinton)
106th	1999–2001	R-223	D-211	1	R-55	D-45	—	D (Clinton)
107th	2001–2003	R-221	D-212	2	D-50	R-49*	1	R (Bush)
108th	2003–2005	R-229	D-205	1	R-51	D-48	1	R (Bush)

*Senator James M. Jeffords of Vermont, a Republican when the 107th Congress convened, changed his party identification to Independent and voted with the Democrats in organizing the Senate.

CREDITS

Chapter 1

Reproduced from the Collections of the Library of Congress, 254.

Chapter 18
Reproduced from the Collections of the Library of Congress, 257; Culver Pictures, 259; Reproduced from the Collections of the Library of Congress, 261; The Granger Collection, 262; Reproduced from the Collections of the Library of Congress, 265; Southern Historical Collection, The University of North Carolina at Chapel Hill, NC. Penn. School Papers: Slave Houses, 266.

Chapter 19
Record of the War Dept. General & Special Staffs, National Archives, 268; The Granger Collection, New York, 269; Old Sturbridge Village, photo by Henry E. Peach, 270; Record of the War Dept. General & Special Staffs, National Archives, 271; © UPI-Bettmann/Corbis, 273; Missouri Historical Society, 275; Abby Aldrich Rockefeller Folk Center, Williamsburg, VA, 276; Sophia Smith Collection, Smith College, Northhampton, Mass., 279.

Chapter 20
Reproduced from the Collections of the Library of Congress, 281; Culver Pictures, 282; © Bettmann/Corbis, 285; #1940, Association of American Railroads, 289; Denver Public Library, Western History Collection, 290; From the Collections of the Library of Congress, 291 and (top) 292; Yale Collection of Western Americana, Beinecke Rare Book and Manuscript Library, (bottom) 292.

Chapter 21
North Wind Picture Archives, 295; California State Library, 298; The Granger Collection, New York, 302; © Corbis, 303; Culver Pictures, Inc. (top) 304 and © Corbis, (bottom) 304; North Wind Picture Archives, 305.

Chapter 22
Reproduced from the Collections of the Library of Congress, 308; The Granger Collection, New York, 309, 310, and 311; © Bettmann/Corbis, 319; Reproduced from the Collections of the Library of Congress, 320 and 321.

Chapter 23
The Cooper Union Museum, New York, 324; Photo by Timothy O'Sullivan, Chicago Historical Society, 325; The Cooper Union Museum, New York, 327; Albert Bierstadt, Guerrilla Warfare (Picket Duty in Virginia) 1862. The Century Association, 328; The Granger Collection, New York, 331; Williamson Art Gallery &Museum, Birkenhead, England, 335; The Granger Collection, New York, 336; National Park Services, Antietam National Battlefield, 338.

Chapter 24
National Park Service, Harpers Ferry Center, 341; Reproduced from the Collections of the Library of Congress, 342 and 343; National Park Service, Harpers Ferry Center, 346; © Bettmann/Corbis, 347; Brown Brothers, 348; © Bettmann/Corbis, 350 and 354.

Chapter 25
National Archives, 356 and 357; Reproduced from the Collections of the Library of Congress, 358; The Valentine Museum, 360; North Wind Picture Archives, 362; Reproduced from the Collections of the Library of Congress, 365; The Granger Collection, New York, 366; Culver Pictures, Inc., 368.

Chapter 26
University of Hartford Collection, 371; Harcourt Picture Collection, 372; Keystone-mast Collection, UCR/California Museum of Photography. UC, Riverside, (top) 375; The Smithsonian Institution, (bottom) 375; Culver Pictures, Inc., 378; University of Hartford Collection, 379; The Granger Collection, New York, 383; Culver Pictures, Inc., 385.

Chapter 27
Southern Pacific Transportation Company, 387; From the Collections of the Library of Congress, 388; University of Oregon Library, 389; U.S. Dept. of Interior, National Park Services, Edison National Historic Site. Photo taken by Matthew Brady, 1878, 390; The Granger Collection, New York, 393; Southern Pacific Transportation Company, 397; The Granger Collection, New York, 401.

Chapter 28
Reproduced from the Collections of the Library of Congress, 404; Courtesy of The New York Historical Society, New York City, 405; Reproduced from the Collections of the Library of Congress, 407; North Wind Picture Archives, 408; © Bettmann/Corbis, 410; The Granger Collection, New York, 412; Keystone-Mast Collection UCR/ California Museum of Photography, UC Riverside, 413; Photograph by Byron. The Byron Collection, Museum of the City of New York, 416; The Granger Collection, New York, 417.

Chapter 29
Reproduced from the Collections of the Library of Congress, 419; Culver Pictures, Inc., 420; Museum of the City of New York, #RiisEE, photography by Lewis Hine. The Jaco A. Riis Collection, 421; Culver Pictures, Inc., 423; Reproduced from the Collections of the Library of Congress, 424; © Bettmann/Corbis, 426; AP/Wide World Photos, 428; The Granger Collection, New York, 431.

Chapter 30
Reproduced from the Collections of the Library of Congress, 434; Museum of the City of New York, 435; W. Louis Sonntag, Jr., The Bowery at Night, 1895. Museum of the City of New York, 438; Keystone-Mast Collection, UCR/California Museum of Photography. UC Riverside, 440; Reproduced from the Collections of the Library of Congress, 441 and 443; Chicago Historical Society, 444; © Bettmann/Corbis, 445.

Chapter 31
Reproduced from the Collections of the Library of Congress, 447; Courtesy of the American Museum of Natural History, New York, 449; National Museum of American Art, Washington DC/Art Resources, NY, 450; Smithsonian Institution, Bureau of American Ethnology, 453; Reproduced from the Collections of the Library of Congress, 455; Erwin E. Smith Collection of the Library of Congress, 456; © Bettmann/Corbis, 461.

Chapter 32
Reproduced from the Collections of the Library of Congress, 463; National Archives, 466; Nebraska State Historical Society Photograph Collections, 467; Reproduced from the Collections of the Library of Congress, 469; The Granger Collection, New York, 471; © Bettmann/Corbis, 473; The Kansas State Historical Society, Topeka, Kansas, 475.

Chapter 33
Reproduced from the Collections of the Library of Congress, 478, 479, and 485; The Granger Collection, New York, 486; Adapted from *Liberty, Equality, Power: A History of the American People,* by John M. Murrin, et al. Copyright © 2002, 1999, 1996 by Thomson Learning, 487; Hawaii State Archives, 489; UPI-Bettmann/Corbis, 490 and 494; Adapted from *American Passages: A History of the United States,* by Ayers, et al. Copyright © 2000 by Harcourt, Inc., 491; Adapted from *Liberty, Equality, Power: A History of the American People,* by John M. Murrin, et al. Copyright © 2002, 1999, 1996 by Thomson Learning, 493.

Chapter 34
Reproduced from the Collections of the Library of Congress, 496 and 497; Culver Pictures, 499; Reproduced from the Collections of the Library of Congress, 500; Museum of the City of New York, 504; © Collection of The New York Historical Society, 506; © Bettmann/Corbis, 507; Boston Public Library, 508.

INDEX

Cultural diffusion, 2–3
Cultural diversity: among Indians, 60
Culture(s): business, 595–596; European view of
American, 250–251; of immigrants, 432, 434; of
Mexico, 281; middle class, 497; Paleo-Indian, 2;
patriotic, 196–197; of Plains Indians, 448–449; of
slaves, 279–280; Spanish-Indian, 282; urban, 446;
Wild West in American, 457–459
Cumberland Gap, 131
Cumberland River: in Civil War, 334, *334*
Cumberland Road, 205
Cuomo, Mario, 747
Currency: controversy over circulation of, 383
Currier, Nathaniel, 237
Currier and Ives prints, 237, *265*
Curse of Capistrano, The (McCulley), 286
Curtis, Cyrus H. K., 502
Custer, George Armstrong, 158, 452
Custer's Last Stand, 452, *453*
Custis, Martha. *See* Washington, Martha
Czechoslovakia, 568, 630, 652, 662
Czolgosz, Leon, 492

Dachau, 660
"Daisy Ad," *708*
Daisy Miller (James), 502
Dakota Sioux Indians, 454–455
Dale, Thomas, 26
Daley, Richard J., 717
Dallas, 703
Danbury, Connecticut, 605
Dance: African American, 269
Danckhaerts, Jasper, 63
Daniels, Josephus, 561
Dark horse: use of term, 289
Darrow, Charles, 608
Darrow, Clarence, 528, *584, 585*
Darwin, Charles, 411
Daugherty, Harry M., 570, 575
Davenport, John, 38
Davis, Angela, 756
Davis, David, 368
Davis, Jeff (Arkansas governor), 513
Davis, Jefferson, 276, 333; in Civil War, 331, 348;
filibusters and, 305; flight from Richmond, 350; as
president of Confederacy, 319–320, *320*; as
secretary of war, 303–304; transcontinental
railroad and, 304
Davis, John W., 588, 621
Davis, Joseph, 276–277, 303
Davis, Nathaniel, 234
Dawes, William, 113
Dawes Severalty Act (1887), 452, 453
D Day, *649*
Deadwood, South Dakota, 459, *461*
Deaf people: reforms for, 249–250
Dealey Plaza, Dallas, 703
Dean, James, *684*
Dearborn, Fort, 178
Dearborn Independent (newspaper), 583
Death rate: in cities, 443; of slaves, 71
Deaths: from flu epidemic of 1918-1919, 564; job-related,
421
Debates: Kennedy-Nixon, *698, 699*; Lincoln-Douglas,
312–314; over Omnibus Bill, 300–301, *302*;
Webster-Hayne, 236, *236*
De Bow, J. D. B.: on U.S. expansion, 294
Debs, Eugene V., 423, 517–518, 535, 732; election of
1904 and, 527; Harding and, 573; imprisonment
of, 562
Debt: assumption of, 152; British debt to U.S., 543;
farming and, 466–467; repayment after
Revolution, 151–152; in South, 51
Debtors: in Georgia, 43
Decadence, 753
Decatur, Stephen, 171, *171,* 196, 220
De Caux, Len, 608
Declaration of Independence, 105, 117, 119; abolitionists
and, 265; Franklin and, 77; Gothic type and, 116;
Jefferson and, 164; signing of, *116*
"Declaration of Rights and Grievances," 99
"Declaration of Sentiments and Resolutions," 255
"Declaration of the Cause and Necessity of Taking Up
Arms," 115
Declaratory Act (1766), 103
Decline and Fall of the Roman Empire (Gibbon), 770
Dedrick, Florence, 530
Deep South: secession of, 317. *See also* South
Deep Throat, 731
Deere, John, 466
Deerfield, Massachusetts, 83, *84*

Defeatism: during Civil War, 333
Defense budget, 746
Defense Department: spending at, 746
Defense industries: "arsenal of democracy" and, 633;
conversion to wartime production and, 647;
DuPont and, 628; growth of, 640; as "merchants of
death," 628
Defense of the Seven Sacraments (Henry VIII), 19
Defense spending, 638; England and, 633; U.S. wars and,
656; in World War II, 638
Deficit spending, 616
Deflation, 472; retirement of greenbacks and, 382
De Forest, Lee, 390
De Gaulle, Charles, 648
Delaware: as proprietary colony, 42
Delaware Indians, 60, 95, 125, 175
Delaware River: Washington's crossing of, 124
De La Warr, Baron. *See* West, Thomas
Delegates: to Constitutional Convention, 143–144
DeMille, Cecil B., 609
Democracy: Hamilton on, 144; Loyalist attitude toward,
121; state constitutions and, 134
Democracy in America (Tocqueville), 250, 404
Democratic National Convention (1968), 718
Democratic party: Compromise of 1850 and, 302;
corruption in South, 364; Coughlin, Charles, and,
623; creation of, 216; election of 1844 and,
288–289; election of 1860 and, 316–317; election
of 1896 and, 479–480, 480–481, *481*; fusion with
Populists, 480, 481–482; in late 19th century,
372–373; legacy of Civil War and, 374; Long,
Huey, and, 623; McAdoo Democrats, 610; party
realignment and, 625; progressivism and, 534–535;
Redeemers in, 365, 367; split in 1948, 664; tariffs
and, 382; in Thirty-First Congress, 303; two-thirds
rule and, 534; white supremacy and, 624; World
War I and, 557. *See also* Elections
Democratic Republicans (Democrats), 213
Democratic socialists, 512
Democratization: in politics, 216–217; in voting, 217
Demonetization Act (1873), 473
Demonstrations. *See* Protest(s)
Dempsey, Jack, 572
Deng Xiaoping, 728
Denmark, 631, 633
Dennis et al. v. United States (1951), 672
Departments of government. *See* specific departments
Dependent Pensions Act (1889), 375
Depew, Chauncey, 525
Depression, 399; of 1819, 233; of 1838, 237; of 1870s,
431; of 1890s, 382, 407, 414, 476. *See also* Great
Depression
De Priest, Oscar, 624
Deregulation: financial frauds and, 743; in 1980s,
742–743
Descent: Iroquoian maternal, 94
Deseret, 246
Desert: in West, 448
"Desert fox," 648
Desertion: in Civil War, 314, 327
De Smet, Pierre-Jean, 287
Détente, 727–728, 736
Detroit: African American mayor in, 709; Battle of the
Overpass in, 624–625; in Great Depression, 604,
624; rioting in, 707; in War of 1812, 178
Detroit, Fort: Indians at, 158
Dew, Thomas Roderick, 264
Dewees, William, 151
Dewey, George, 486
Dewey, Thomas E., 664–665
DeWitt, John W., 646
Dias, Bartholomeu, 9
Díaz, Porfirio, 281, 540
Dickens, Charles, 250, 251
Dickinson, Charles, 220
Dickinson, Emily, 404, 501
Dickinson, John, 98, 116, 136
Diem, Ngo Dinh, 711
Dien Bien Phu, 710
Diet: pork and beef in, 264, 265
Dillinger, John, 609
Dingley Tariff, 532
Dior, Christian, 677, 683
Diplomacy: under Articles of Confederation, 139; Carter,
Haiti, and, 758; dollar, 494; gunboat, 494; Iranian
hostage crisis and, 739; southern cotton diplomacy,
332; *Trent* incident and, 332–333; of Wilson,
539–540; XYZ Affair and, 161; Zimmerman
telegram and, 546. *See also* Foreign policy
Direct current, 391

Direct election of senators, 475, 513
Disabled people: Nazis and, 631
Disarmament, 746–747; after World War I, 566
Discrimination: against German Americans, 565; against
immigrants, 578; against Jews, 583; progressives
and, 513
Disease: among African slaves, 71; AIDS and, 731;
brought to Hawaii, 255; Columbian Exchange and,
15–16; in crowded cities, 443–444; drinking and,
158; between 1890-1910, 496; flu epidemic of
1918-1919 and, 564, *564*; immigration and, 428; in
Jamestown, 26; in Mexican War, 292;
occupational, 421; pellagra as, 468; in rice lands,
52; smallpox as, *15*; in Spanish-American war,
486, 488. *See also* Malaria; specific diseases
Disestablishment: of Anglican Church, 134
Disney, Walt: Hays Code and, 583
Disneyland, 676, 696
Disraeli, Benjamin, 289
Dissenters, 36–38
Distilleries, 561
Distinguished Service Cross, 648
Distribution bill (1836): for internal improvements, 233
District of Columbia, 261, 296
Diversity: in Middle Colonies, 57; in New York colony,
40; of Paleo-Indians, 2–3
Divorce, 80
Dix, Dorothea, 250–251, 328
"Dixie" (song), 344
Dixiecrats, 664, 673, 699, *761*
Dixon-Yates, 691
DNA: of earliest Americans, 2
Doby, Larry, 687
Dr. Zhivago (Pasternak), 693
Doctors. *See* Physicians
Dodd, Samuel C. T., 402
Doenitz, Karl, 652
Doheny, Edward L., 575
Dole, Elizabeth, 765
Dole, Robert, 748, 762–763
Dollar: adoption of, 134; under Articles of Confederation,
139; naming of, 152
Dollar diplomacy, 494
Domesticated animals: Columbian Exchange and, 15–16
Domestic Manners of the Americans, The (Trollope), 174,
250–251
Domestic service: slaves in, 272; women in, 422
Domestic sphere, 520
Dominican Republic, 10, 628, 695; immigrants from,
759; intervention in, 492; marines in, 540
Dominion of New England, 55
Domino theory, 711, 726
Donelson, Fort: battle of, 334, 342
Dongan, Thomas, 57
Donnelly, Ignatius P., 471, 474, 475
Donora, Pennsylvania: during Great Depression, 602
Doonesbury, *769*
Dorchester Heights, 122
Dorgan, Tad, 503
Dorival, John, 175
Dormer, Jane, 683
Dorr's Rebellion, 217
Dot-coms, 763–764, 769
Doubleday, Abner, 507
Doublespeak: in Gulf War, 745
"Doughboys": in World War I, 551, 554
Doughface, 306, 316
Douglas, Stephen A., 288, *304*; Compromise of 1850 and,
301; debates with Lincoln, 312–314; election of
1856 and, 311; election of 1860 and, 316; Freeport
Doctrine and, 314, 316; Kansas-Nebraska Act and,
305–306, 308; transcontinental railroad and,
304–305
Douglass, Frederick, 255, 270–271, 273–274, 579
Dowd, Charles F., 392
"Down the river" flow: of slave trade, 274, *276*
Dowries, 79
Draft (military): African Americans in World War I and,
559; antidraft riots in Civil War, 326; during Civil
War, 326–327; resistance to, 713; World War I and,
556–557, 558; World War II and, 632, 638
Draft dodgers: during Civil War, 314, 327
Draft laws: exemptions to, 326
Drake, Edwin, 401
Drake, Francis, 20, *21,* 29, 68
Drawbacks: in oil industry, 402
Dreamland, 504
Dred Scott decision, 315; legal status of slavery and, *313*
Dred Scott v. Sandford, 311–312
Dreiser, Theodore, 502; Communist party and, 608
Dressler, Marie, 609

Kitchin, Claude, 548
Klondike, 459
Knights of Labor, *424,* 424–425
Knights of the White Camellia, 364
Knowland, William F., 670
Know-Nothings, 254, 255, 311, 315
Knox, Henry, 122, 150, *150*
Knox, Philander C., 526
Knudsen, William S., 639
Kodak cameras, 499
Kohl, Helmut, 746
Konoye, Fumimaro, 635
Korea, 650, 692. *See also* Korean War
Korean Americans: World War II and, 646
Korean War, 666–669, *667;* cost of, 656; Eisenhower and, 673; election of 1952 and, 673; end of, 673; as "limited war," 692; nuclear threat and, 692
Korean War Veterans Memorial, 669
Korematsu v. the United States, 646
Kosciuszko, Thaddeus, 127
Kosovo: ethnic cleansing in, 758
Kreditanstalt (Vienna), 606
Kremlin, 703
Krygier, Annetja, 79
Kuhn, Fritz, 632
Kuhn, Loeb, and Company, 406, 407–408
Ku Klux Klan, *580, 581,* 581–582; founding of, 364; legend of Reconstruction and, 364; violence against blacks by, 364–365, *366*
Kulturkampf, 432
Kuwait: Iraqi invasion of, 750
Kyoto global warming treaty: Bush, George W., and, 769

Labor: apprentice programs and, 68–70; industrialization and, 206, 388; Lowell girls and, 206–207; machines and, 203; in New England, 36; organization of, 422–426; servants as, 69–70; slaves as, 27, 272; steelworkers' strike and, 576; for sugar plantations, 92; violence and, 422–423; westward movement and, 186; in World War I, 558. *See also* Labor unions; Servants; Slaves and slavery; Strikes
Labor contractors: immigrants and, 429
Labor contracts: for freedmen, 361
Labor Day, 425
Labor unions: civil rights and, 687; "closed shop" and, 664; Communist party (American) and, 608; development of, 424; employer violence and, *624,* 624–625; during Great Depression, 624; Industrial Workers of the World (IWW), 518, 519–520; Knights of Labor and, *424,* 424–425; McGovern and, 731; music and, 624; National Association of Manufacturers and, 426; National Labor Union and, 424; National Recovery Administration and, 618; in Progressive Era, 512, 518; Roosevelt, Franklin, and, 624; Taft-Hartley Act and, 663–664; Wagner Act and, 619; during World War II, 638, 639. *See also* Strikes; specific unions
Ladies' Home Journal (magazine), 502, 684
Lady Chatterley's Lover (Lawrence), 685, 731
Laemmle, Carl, 557
Lafayette, Marie-Joseph, marquis de, 126, 128; French Revolution and, 154; at Valley Forge, *128*
Laffer, Arthur, 741
Laffite, Jean, 179
LaFlesche, Susette, 64
La Follette, Robert ("Fighting Bob"), 511, *516,* 516–517; election of 1912 and, 533; election of 1924 and, 588–589; Wisconsin idea of, 516; World War I and, 556
Lake Erie, 178
Lake Texcoco, 6
Lancaster Turnpike, 187, 205
Lance, Bert, 736
Land: Benton's programs for, 186; boom in Florida, 596–597; conservation and, 529–531; constitutional provision for acquiring, 167; English acquisition of, 63; of Great American Desert, 282–283; Homestead Act and, 353; Indian assimilation, Dawes Act, and, 453; justifying seizures of, 63; Mexican cessions of, 292, *293;* Mexican grants in Alta California, 286; Morrill Act and, 354; in New England, *53;* policy toward, 184; railroads and, 353, 395, *397,* 398; sectionalism and, 186–187; speculation in, 131, 184–185, 233; for state universities, 499; survey system for, 138, *138;* in Virginia, 27; western, under Articles of Confederation, 136. *See also* West; Westward movement
Land Act (1804), 184
Land bridge: across Bering Strait, 1

Landis, Kenesaw Mountain, 574
Landlord's Game, 608
Land Office, 185, 186
Landon, Alfred, 623
Landowners: in proprietary colonies, 39
Lane, Joseph, 316
Language(s): English vs. Spanish, 759; Indian, 61; Native American, 61–62; Paleo-Indian, 2; renaming of German-based terms, 564–565
L'Anse aux Meadows, Newfoundland, 7
Laos, 710, 711, 726
Laotian immigrants, 759
Laramie, Fort, 287
La raza, 281
Larned, Samuel, 247
La Salle, Sieur de (René-Robert Cavelier), 67
Las Casas, Bartolomé de, 13–14
Las Vegas, Nevada: Hoover Dam and, 606
Lateen sails, 9
Latham, Mary, 36
Latin America: Alliance for Progress and, 701; Dulles, John Foster, and, 695; Germany and, 632; Good Neighbor Policy and, 627–628; interventions in, 492–494; reactionaries in, 701; revolutionaries in, 695; Roosevelt, Theodore, and, 492; U.S. investments in, 590; Wilson and, 540; and World War II, 628
Latvia and Latvians, 427, 631
Law(s): antiprostitution, 522; against cigarettes, 470; employer liability, 421; on manumission, 266; rider and, 296; on teaching slaves to read, 266. *See also* specific laws
Lawrence, D. H., 685, 731
Lawrence, Kansas: sack of, 310
Lawyers: women as, 501
Laying-by time, 272
Lazarus, Emma, 578
Leadville, Colorado, 459
League for Spiritual Discovery, 715
League of American Wheelmen, 505
League of Nations, 568, 575, 589–590; Harding on, 571; Sino-Japanese War and, 628; United Nations and, 662; Wilson and, 566–571
Leary, Timothy, 715
Lease, Mary Elizabeth ("Mother"), 471, *473,* 475, 501
Leatherstocking Tales (Cooper), 250
Lebanon, 692; marines in, 744–745
Lecompton Constitution, 312
Lee, Ann (Mother), 247
Lee, Fitzhugh, 488
Lee, Fort, 123
Lee, Henry, 148
Lee, Jason, 287
Lee, Richard Henry, 98, 116
Lee, Robert E., *342;* in Civil War, 331, 333, 336, 337, *337,* 339, 341–342, 343–344, *345,* 347, 348; at Harpers Ferry, 316; state loyalty of, 322; surrender at Appomattox Courthouse, 350
Legal suasionists: as division of teetotalers, 253
"Legend of Sleepy Hollow, The" (Irving), 250
Legends. *See* Folklore
Legislature: House of Burgesses as, 29. *See also* Assembly; specific bodies
Lehr, Harry, 414
Lehrer, Tom, 756
Leiden Pilgrims, 31–32
Leisler, Jacob, 55
Leisler's Rebellion, 85
Leisure: bicycling and, 505–506; exercise and, 505; health resorts and, 503; sports and, 507–509; working class and, 503–505
LeMay, Curtis, 713
Lending: for land speculation, 185
Lend-Lease Act (1941), 633, 643
Leni-Lenape: use of name, 60. *See also* Delaware Indians
Lenin, Vladimir Ilyich, 553
Leningrad, 632
Leo X (Pope), 19
Leopard (ship), 172
Lèse-majesté: crime of, 100
Leslie, Frank, *311*
Letter of Prester John, 7
Letters to Ladies, Detailing Important Information Concerning Themselves and Infants (Ewell), 151
Levant: trade and, 8
Lever Act, 561
Leviathan (ship), 551
Levitt, William, 680
Levitt brothers, 680
Levittowns: in New York, *679,* 680, 694; in Pennsylvania, 694

Lewinsky, Monica, *764,* 764–765
Lewis, John L., 624, 639
Lewis, Meriwether, 168–169
Lewis, Oliver, 509
Lewis and Clark expedition (1804-1805), *168,* 168–169
Lexington, Battle of, *113,* 113–114
Liberal Republicans, 368, 369
Liberals and liberalism: in World War I, 563
Liberator, The, 261, *261,* 263, 268
Liberia, 258, 259, *260*
"Liberty and union speech" (Daniel Webster), 237
Liberty party, 270, 290
Liberty ships, 639, *639,* 640
Libraries: public, 503
Libya, 632, 647, 745
Liddy, G. Gordon, 731–732
Lieber, Francis, 234
Lieberman, Joseph, 766
Liebman, Joshua, 680
Life and Memorable Actions of George Washington, The (Weems), 197
Life expectancy: in colonies, 77; 1890-1910, 496; in New England, 52–53
Lifestyle: birthing in Federalist period and, 151; of Civil War soldiers, 327; of Eastern Woodlands Indians, 62; French and Indian, 67; along frontier, 174; of late 19th century rich, 413–416; in Merrymount, 32; middle class and, 497; of New Agers, 755; in Northwest Territory, 140; Paleo-Indian, 2; of sailors, 24; of slaves, 266; in South, 50–51; in Twenties, 572; in Virginia, 26
Light bulb, 390, 391
Liliuokalani (Hawaii), 489, *489,* 490
Lillibridge, G. D., 650
Limbaugh, Rush, 756
Limited liability corporation, 400
Limited war, 692
Lincoln, Abraham, 292, 306, 308, *319,* 389; during Civil War, 328, 334, 336, 341, 345; election of 1860 and, 316–317; election of 1864 and, 352; Emancipation Proclamation and, 337–339; Gettysburg Address of, 352, 353; Johnson, Andrew, and, 358; leadership of, 320; meeting with Confederate delegation, 350; pre-Civil War compromises and, 319; Stowe, Harriet Beecher, and, 271; writ of habeas corpus and, 333
Lincoln, Benjamin, 128
Lincoln, Tom, 182, 183
Lincoln-Douglas debates, 312–314
Lincoln Memorial: March on Washington and, 700
Lincoln University, 501
Lindbergh, Charles A., 590, 597, 635
Lindsay, Vachel, 510
Lingg, Louis, 410
Lippmann, Walter, 613
Liquor. *See* Alcohol
Literacy: in New England, 36; as test for immigrants, 578
Literature: comic books, 647; early American, 250; European on American culture, 250; of James, Henry, 501–502; naturalism in, 502; patriotic, 197; realism in, 502; of Twain, Mark, 501; *Uncle Tom's Cabin,* 271
Lithuania and Lithuanians, 427, 631
Little, Frank: lynching of, 563
Little Big Horn: battle at, 158, 452
Little Blue Books, 589
"Little Boy," 657
Little Giant. *See* Douglas, Stephen A.
Little Italy, 434
Little Orphan Annie, 610
Little Rock, Arkansas, 686–687, *688*
Little Sarah (ship), 155
Little Turtle (chief), 158
"Little War" *(petite guerre),* 82–83, 88
Living conditions: urban, 443
Livingston, Robert R., 167; Declaration of Independence and, 117
Lloyd, Henry Demarest, 480
Lloyd George, David, 551, 567, *567*
Lobby groups: Grand Army of the Republic (GAR) as, 375
Locke, John, 42
Locofocos, 232
Locomotives, 194. *See also* Railroads
Lodge, Henry Cabot, 483, 488–489, 494, *569;* on Roosevelt, Franklin, 613; Treaty of Versailles, League of Nations, and, 568–569; World War I and, 548
Logan, James, 78
Log cabin, *37,* 140, *140*

of, 209; romantic image of, 268–270; runaways and, 278–279; slave-owner relationships, 275–276; in South Carolina, 81; task system and, 273, 276; territories and, 296; in Texas, 284; thievery and, 278; Thirteenth Amendment and, 268, 355; in Virginia, 27; vulnerability of, 73–74; West African roots of, 72–73, *73*; in West Indies, 92; westward expansion and, 288–290; whippings and, *271,* 271, 275; white southern perspective on, 271–270; written passes for movement of, 267; on yeoman farms, 272. *See also* Abolition and abolitionism; Enslavement

Slave trade, 68, 72–73, 145, 208, 271, 274, *276*; abolition of, 277; within Africa, 72; Ashanti, *260*; illegal, 277; in Rhode Island, 54; termination of, 258; in Washington, D. C., 300

Slavic world: World War I and, 542

Slavocratic conspiracy, *311,* 312

"Slavocrats," 297, 310

Slide, Kelly, Slide, 508

Slidell, John, 332–333

Slocum, Henry, 342

Slovenes, 427

Slums, 443, *445*

Small, Len, 582

Small businessmen's clubs, 595

Smallpox, *15,* 89; epidemic during Revolutionary War, 120

Smellie, William, 151

Smith, Alfred E., 511, 523, 588, 621; Catholicism of, 588, 591; election of 1928 and, 591; election of 1932 and, 610; Klan and, 582

Smith, Bessie, 610

Smith, Hamilton S., 501

Smith, Holland, 650

Smith, Jedediah, 287

Smith, Jesse L., 575

Smith, John, 25, 26, 28; Squanto and, 32

Smith, Joseph, 245–246, *246*

Smith, Julian, 650

Smith, Sidney, 250

Smith College, 499

"Smoke-filled room": at 1920 Republican convention, 570

Smoking. *See* Tobacco and tobacco industry

Smuggling, 47; of molasses, 84; of slaves, 277

Smyth, Richard, 70

SNCC. *See* Student Nonviolent Coordinating Committee (SNCC)

Social class. *See* Classes

Social Darwinism, 411–412; Sumner, William Graham, and, 412; survival of the fittest and, 483

Social Democratic Herald, 562

Social feminists, 520

Social gospel, 411

Socialism: during Great Depression, 621

Socialist party of America, 517, 562, 577; Debs and, 732; election of 1908 and, 532; election of 1912 and, 535; election of 1928 and, 607; election of 1932 and, 607

Socialists, 634; hatred for Russia by, 543; Roosevelt, Theodore, 527–528; World War I campaign against, 562

Social mobility, 79–80, 394

Social programs: Reagan and, 742; of Wilson, 537–538

Social reform: World War I and, 557

Social Security: contributions and pensions, 623; recession and, 691; Townsend, Francis, and, 622, 623

Social Security Act (1935), 623

Social services: during Great Depression, 602, *603,* 616; Long, Huey, and, 622; political machines and, 384–385

Society: alcohol and, 582; biracial, 260; evolution and, 583–585; along frontier, 174; gangsters in, 582–583; Hollywood and, 583; in Jamestown, 26; labor unrest in, 576–577; in New England, 36; Puritan, 36; race and, 570–582; in South Carolina, 51; Spanish, 12–13; in World War I, 558–561

Society of Freemasons. *See* Masons

Society of Friends. *See* Quakers

Sociology for the South, A (Fitzhugh), 265

Sod houses, 464, 467, *467*

Soil: in Middle Colonies, 57; in New England, *53*

Soil Bank Act (1956), 691

Soil Conservation and Domestic Allotment Act, 620

Soldiers: black soldiers in World War I, *544,* 559, *559,* 560; Boston Massacre and, 106; in Civil War, 326, 327, *327,* 330; colonial, 112–113; patriot, 120; professional, 81; in Somalia, 758; in Spanish-

American War, 488; women in Civil War, 327; in World War I, 551. *See also* Redcoats

Solid South: party changes in (1944-2000), *761. See also* South

Solomon Islands, 637, 644, 645, 653, 654

Somalia: intervention in, 757–758

Somme, Battle of the, 545–546, 550

Songs. *See* Music; specific songs

Songs for John Doe (recording), 632

Sonntag, Louis, *438*

Sonoma, 282

Sonorans: gold mining and, 299

Soto, Hernando de, 13

South, 47; agriculture in, 468–469; antislavery movement in, 257–258, 259–260; blacks in government of, 364; blacks in population of, 258; Bourbons in, 367, 373; California as free state and, 298; after Civil War, *357;* Clay's American System of manufacturing and, 189; colonization movement and, 259; corruption in Reconstruction governments, 364; cotton industry in, 204, *209;* crops of (1860), *274;* decline of slavery in, 207–208; Democratic party in, 372; exclusion of blacks from politics in, 481–482; fears of slave rebellion in, 261–262; free blacks in, 267; gender balance in, 62; higher education for blacks in, 501; Ku Klux Klan in, 364–365; legend of Reconstruction about, 363–364; life expectancy in, 77; lifestyle in, 50–51; mercantilism in, 47–49; military occupation of, 361, 369; Muskogean speakers in, 62; North and, 257; public school systems in, 364; Radical Reconstruction in, 361–362, *362;* Redeemers in, 365, 367; Republican party in, 368; revival of slavery in, 209; secession of, 317, *318;* slave rebellions in, 262–263; slavery in, 135, 263–267; Solid South and (1944-2000), *761;* suppression of abolitionism in, 263–264; tariffs and, 186–187; tenants and sharecroppers in, 468; Tidewater-Piedmont conflict in, 47–49; tobacco industry in, 470. *See also* Civil War (U.S.); Confederacy; Reconstruction

South Africa, 744

South America: Columbian Exchange and, 14–16; Magellan and, 11; Spanish exploration of, 13

Southampton, Virginia: Turner's Rebellion in, 263

South Carolina, 42, 51–52, 83; French in, 29; indigo in, 81; Regulators in, 108; secession of, 317; slavery in, 62, 72, 81; tariffs, nullification, and, 225–226

South Carolina Exposition and Protest, The (Calhoun), 225–226, 229

Southeast: Spanish exploration of, 13

South End House, 437

Southern Agriculturalist, 266

Southern Alliance, 470

Southern Baptist Convention, 698

Southern Christian Leadership Conference (SCLC), 687, 700

Southern Farmers Alliance, 476

Southern Pacific Railroad, *396,* 398, 517; power of, 405–406

South Pass, Wyoming, 287

South Tyrol, 567–568

Southwest: Indians of, *60;* Spanish in, 13, 29

Soviet Bloc (1947-1989), *749*

Soviet Union, 741; Afghanistan and, 736; Allies and, 649; Austria and, 695; blockade of West Berlin and, 662–663; Carter and, 736; Clinton and, 757; Cold War origins and, 655, 660; collapse of, 748; containment and, 662; Cuban missile crisis and, 702–703; daily life in, 695; diplomatic recognition of, 628, 661; economy of, 693, 695; German invasion of, 632; Goldwater on, 709; Gorbachev in, 747; "hot line" and, 703; and Japan in World War II, 652; jobs during Great Depression in, 602; Lend-Lease and, 633, 643; Marshall Plan and, 662; nonaggression pact with Hitler and, 631; nuclear weapons program of, 660, 691, 701; "peaceful coexistence" and, 693; Poland and, 661, 696; prisoners of war and, 644, 648; Reagan and, 745, 746; United Nations boycott and, 666; U.S. military aid to, 647; U.S. spy plane and, 696; Vietnam War and, 712; Warsaw Pact and, 663; World War II and, 643, 648, 656. *See also* Russia

Space exploration: under Kennedy, 699

Spain: Catholicism in, 19; Columbus and, 6–7; dollar and, 134, 139, *139,* 152; England and, 20; exploration by, 8–9, 10, 13; Florida and, 29, 42; Franco and, 629, 630; Indian contacts with, 62; Louisiana and, 90, 122; Louisiana Purchase and, 167; Mississippi

River commerce and, 139; North American colonies of, 29; Oregon Country and, 285; Pinckney's Treaty and, 156; Revolution and, 126; war for throne of, 83–84; War of Jenkins' Ear and, 87–88. *See also* Spanish-American War; Spanish Empire

Spalding, Albert G., 507–508

Spanish-American War, 484–487, *487;* armed forces in, 486–487; cost of, 656; yellow press and, 484

Spanish Armada, 22

Spanish Civil War, 630

Spanish Empire, 11–14, 23; Indians in, 13–14; New Spain of, 281; sale of Florida by, 199; wealth from, 18

Spanish Flat, California, *298*

Spanish flu. *See* Flu

Spargo, John, 421, 514

Sparkman, John, 673

Speakeasies, 582

Special Forces: during Kennedy administration, 701

Specie Circular (1836), 233, 237

Spectator sports. *See* Sports

Speculation: Bank War and, 233; boom/bust cycles and, 184–185; in land, 131, 596–597; Panic of 1819 and, 185; squatters and, 186; in stock market, 597–599; westward movement and, 183–184

Speedwell (ship), 32

Spellbinders, 621–623

Spelling: Webster, Noah, and, 197

Spellman, Francis, 666

Spelman College, *413*

Spencer, Herbert, 411–412

Spending: government, 166

Spice Islands, 7. *See also* Indonesia

Spies, August, 410

Spies and spying: female spies in Civil War, 327

Spinning machines, 203, *203*

Spirit of '76, The (Goldstein), 564

Spirit of Saint Louis (plane), 597

Spirituals, 279

Spock, Benjamin, 713, 719

Spoils system, 373; Jackson and, 223

Sports: baseball as, 506–507, 574; basketball as, 507; boxing as, 508–509; football as, 507; horse racing as, 508; in Twenties, 572

Spotsylvania: Battle of, 347

Sprague, Frank J., 439

Spruance, Raymond A., 644, 650

Squanto, 32

Squatters: Preemption Act and, 239; westward movement and, 186

Staffordshire potteries, *102*

Stalin, Joseph: Allies and, 649; Churchill and, 647; death of, 673, 692; Khrushchev and, 693; Marshall Plan and, 662; mental imbalance of, 692; nonaggression pact with Hitler and, 631; at Potsdam, 661; Roosevelt, Franklin, and, 647, 652, 661; at Teheran, 652; Truman and, 661; war strategy of, 652; at Yalta, 652, *653*

Stalingrad, 632, 648, 693

Stalwarts, 376, 378

Stamp(s): use of term, 98

Stamp Act (1765), 98; protests against, 98–99, *100;* repeal of, *102,* 102–103

Stamp Act Congress (1765), 99, 100

Standardization: of geographic names, 393; of time zones, 392

Standard of living: of Indians, 64; world economy and, 428

Standard Oil Company, 402, 459

Standard Oil Trust, 402; breakup of, 533

Standing armies, 95

Standish, Miles, 32, 33, *33*

Stanford, Leland, 405, 413, 419, 499

Stanford University, 413, 499

Stanton, Edwin, 362

Stanton, Elizabeth Cady, 255, 256, 498, 520

Stanwix, Fort, *124*

Starr, Kenneth, 764

"Stars and Bars" (Confederate flag), 333

"Star-Spangled Banner, The" (Key), 176

"Star Wars." *See* Strategic Defense Initiative (SDI, "Star Wars")

State(s): church separation from, 134; constitutions in, 133–135; Fourteenth Amendment and former Confederate states, 361; from Northwest Territory, 138; powers reserved to, 147; relationship with federal government, 145; western land claims of, 136, *137*

State governments: Confederate veterans' pensions and, 375; of former Confederate states, 357; Radical Reconstruction and, 361

Cape
Flattery

Puget
Sound

130°W

120°W

110°W

100°W

R   O   C   K   Y

Missouri

River

CASCADE   RANGE

COAST   RANGES

Columbia

River

COLUMBIA   PLATEAU

GREAT   PLAINS

Cape Blanco

BLACK
HILLS

40°N
Cape
Mendocino

River

Snake

River

M   O   U   N   T   A   I   N   S

North
Platte

River

San Francisco Bay

SIERRA   NEVADA

CENTRAL   VALLEY

Sacramento   River

Lake
Tahoe

GREAT
BASIN

Great
Salt Lake

Green   River

Platte   River

South
Platte

River

Platte

San Joaquin

River

Arkansas

COAST   RANGES

Death
Valley

Colorado   River

COLORADO
PLATEAU

Point
Conception

MOJAVE   DESERT

PACIFIC
OCEAN

Salton
Sea

Gila   River

30°N

Red

LLANO
ESTACADO

Kauai

Niihau
Kaula

Oahu

Molokai

PACIFIC
OCEAN

Lanai

Maui

Kahoolawe

20°N

Hawaii

160°W

155°W

75 Miles

0

75 Kilometers

0

ARCTIC OCEAN

70°N

BROOKS RANGE

RUSSIA

Arctic Circle

Bering Strait

River

Yukon

ALASKA RANGE

CANADA

170°E

60°N

100 Miles

0

BERING
SEA

100 Kilometers

0

Kenai
Peninsula

PACIFIC OCEAN

Kodiak
Island

GULF OF
ALASKA

60°N

180°

Aleutian Islands

160°W

150°W

140°W

Rio   Grande

M   E   X   I   C   O